J. C. McReynolds

SOCIOLOGY
IN A CHANGING WORLD

FOURTH EDITION

SOCIOLOGY

IN A CHANGING WORLD

WILLIAM KORNBLUM

City University of New York, Graduate School and University Center

In collaboration with

CAROLYN D. SMITH

HARCOURT BRACE
COLLEGE PUBLISHERS

Fort Worth   Philadelphia   San Diego   New York   Orlando   Austin   San Antonio
Toronto   Montreal   London   Sydney   Tokyo

Publisher	Christopher P. Klein
Senior Acquisitions Editor	Stephen T. Jordan
Developmental Editor	Amy Hester
Senior Project Editor	Angela Williams Urquhart
Production Manager	Cynthia Young
Art Director	Garry Harman
Photo Researcher	Elsa Peterson Ltd.
Permissions Editor	Aimé Merizon
Copy Editor	Michele Gitlin

Requests for permission to make copies of any part of the work should be mailed to:
Permissions Department, Harcourt Brace & Company, 6277 Sea Harbor Drive, Orlando, FL 32887-6777.

Address for Editorial Correspondence
Harcourt Brace College Publishers, 301 Commerce Street, Suite 3700, Fort Worth, TX 76102

Address for Orders
Harcourt Brace & Company, 6277 Sea Harbor Drive, Orlando, FL 32887
1-800-782-4479, or 1-800-433-0001 (in Florida)

ISBN: 0-15-503290-9

Library of Congress Catalogue Number: 96-76567

Printed in the United States of America

6 7 8 9 0 1 2 3 4 5 032 10 9 8 7 6 5 4 3 2 1

USING *SOCIOLOGY IN A CHANGING WORLD:* A GUIDE TO LEARNING FROM YOUR TEXTBOOK

Sociology in a Changing World, **Fourth Edition,** is designed to give you a thorough introduction to the principles of sociology and to illuminate and illustrate the many concepts, terms, and examples that will be presented in the sociology course.

Sociology in a Changing World, Fourth Edition, is a complete educational program devoted to helping you learn and to helping instructors teach. The program is based on six essential principles:

- *Exercising a Global Perspective:* Because we live in an increasingly global society, a global perspective is incorporated throughout the textbook.

- *Observing Social Change:* A key to studying sociology is observing social change among individuals, groups, and societies around the world.

- *Applying Sociology:* By applying sociology to everyday life, your comprehension is made more complete.

- *Learning Through Visual Presentation:* An extensive visual presentation maximizes learning by reflecting contemporary cultural assumptions and tastes.

- *Incorporating Diversity in Theory and Research:* The research of women and minorities is contextually presented and well-balanced.

- *Presenting Accessible Scholarship:* The scholarship is presented in an accessible style, promoting comprehension of the material.

The following pages will introduce you to the many features of *Sociology in a Changing World,* Fourth Edition, and show you how to use the learning aids provided to enhance your study of sociology.

Beginning-of-Chapter Elements: Each chapter is introduced with a preview of the chapter material in an organized and consistent format.

Chapter Outlines: As advance organizers, the outlines preview the topics that will be discussed in the chapter.

Opening Vignettes: These stories of high interest capture your attention and introduce the subject matter of the chapter.

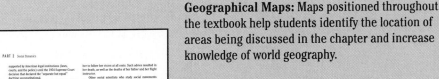

Geographical Maps: Maps positioned throughout the textbook help students identify the location of areas being discussed in the chapter and increase knowledge of world geography.

Then and Now: Visual comparisons present historical perspectives on social change and encourage you to utilize sociological concepts. Images that contrast past with present accompany a discussion of how social change has affected a particular social condition.

Using the Sociological Imagination: This popular feature presents examples of how sociologists apply their imaginations to understanding the changes in society.

Global Social Change: Extensive examples of important worldwide changes reinforce the textbook's theme of social change and its enhanced commitment to advancing a global perspective.

552 **PART 4** Social Institutions

BOX 18.2 SOCIOLOGICAL METHODS

Tracing the Influence of a Remarkable Teacher

In an unusual study of teacher–student interaction, Eigil Pedersen and Therese Annette Faucher (1978) demonstrated the persisting value of an outstanding primary school teacher. The study is unusual because the social scientists were actually looking for a general pattern of low teacher expectations. Instead, they found an exception that demonstrated the powerful effects an exceptional teacher can have on students. In scientific research, an unexpected result that leads to a new insight is known as *serendipity*.

Pedersen and Faucher began their study of IQ and achievement patterns among disadvantaged children at a school that was marked by high rates of failure. A high percentage of the school's graduates failed in their first year of high school and dropped out. The researchers attempted to explain these failure rates in terms of the concept of the "self-fulfilling prophecy," the idea that if teachers expect students to do poorly, the students are likely to perform accordingly. But if the negative prophecy seems to work in many instances, can we find evidence that a *positive* self-fulfilling prophecy—the belief that students can perform well—will also work? This is what makes Pederson and Faucher's study so interesting.

As they examined the IQ scores of pupils in the school's first grade classes, the researchers found a clear association between changes in a pupil's IQ and the pupil's family background, first grade teacher, and self-concept. Further examination of the school's records revealed a startling fact: The IQs of pupils in one particular teacher's first grade class were significantly more likely to increase in subsequent years than the IQs of pupils in first grade classes taught by other teachers. And pupils who had been members of that class were more than twice as likely to achieve high status as adults as pupils who had been members of other first grade classes (see table).

What was so special about Miss A, as the outstanding teacher was labeled? First, she was still remembered by her students when they were interviewed 25 years after they had been in her class. More than three quarters of those students rated her as very good or excellent as a teacher. "It did not matter what background or abilities the beginning pupil had; there was no way that the pupil was not going to read by the end of grade one." Miss A left her pupils with a "profound impression of the importance of schooling, and how one should stick to it" and "gave extra hours to the children who were slow learners." In nonacademic matters, too, Miss A was unusual:

When children forgot their lunches, she would give them some of her own, and she invariably stayed after hours to help children. Not only did her pupils

remember her, but she apparently could remember each former pupil by name even after an interval of 20 years. She adjusted to new math and reading methods, but her success was summarized by a former colleague this way: "How did she teach? With a lot of love!" (pp. 19–30)

In summing up their findings, Pedersen and Faucher stated that their data "suggest that an effective first-grade teacher can influence social mobility" (p. 29). Their findings differ from those of Coleman (1976) and Jencks (1972), who believe that there is little correlation between school experiences and adult status. Pedersen and Faucher agree that further research on the relationship between teacher effects and adult status is needed. However, "In the meantime, teachers . . . should not accept too readily the frequent assertion that their efforts make no long-term difference to the future success of their pupils" (p. 30). As debates continue over how much difference good teaching can make and as governments and school systems wonder whether they should do more to reward good teaching, the results of this study bear careful review.

Adult Status, by First Grade Teacher				
	FIRST GRADE TEACHER			
ADULT STATUS	**MISS A**	**MISS B**	**MISS C**	**OTHERS**
High	64%	31%	10%	39%
Medium	36	38	45	22
Low	0	31	45	39
Total	100%	100%	100%	100%
(*N*)	(14)	(16)	(11)	(18)
Mean adult status	7.0	4.8	4.3	4.6

Note: (*N*) = Number of students who could be located and interviewed 25 years later.

"Adult status" was determined from interviews that included questions on occupational status and work history, highest grade completed, rent paid and number of rooms, and related indicators of social position.

Source:
Effects
Educa
Fellow

teachers can make a big difference in children's lives, a fact that gives increased urgency to the need to improve the quality of primary school teaching. The reforms carried out by ed-

ucationa
teaching
ment the

Sociological Methods: Throughout the textbook, Dr. Kornblum applies research to every area of sociology. By integrating methodology, rather than confining it to a single chapter, he reinforces the importance of research.

THE

PERSONAL CHALLENGE

Social Change and Sociological Careers

It is reasonable to wonder, as you work your way through this course, what the study of sociology can do for you. All introductory college courses are designed to acquaint students with fields that they may want to delve into further in the future. But perhaps more than other introductory courses, sociology can help you understand how society and social change are affecting your own life and the lives of people around you. Sociology is not unique in that sense, but it offers some powerful concepts and methods for understanding how the world is changing and with what consequences, personal and otherwise.

President Bill Clinton reads sociology. So does Speaker of the House Newt Gingrich. And so do thousands of leaders in business and government who want to get a handle on how current social changes may be altering the way they go about their professional and personal lives. Sociology is a growing field throughout the world. As the pace of global social change quickens—with new cities, new technologies, and new forms of cooperation and conflict appearing all the time—the contributions of sociological theory and practice become increasingly important.

If you should decide to major in sociology and

the book.) Of course, you need not become a professional sociologist to find that knowledge of the field gives you great advantages in understanding society and social change.

Sociology is an excellent background for careers in law, business, public administration, health, and law enforcement, to name just some of the major professional areas that are voracious consumers of sociological information. Market research, which seeks to predict and shape consumer behavior, is a form of applied sociology. The allied field of opinion research, which charts changes in beliefs and attitudes, is also based almost entirely on sociological principles and methods. Professionals in the health care industry need to know about changes in diet and other consumptive behavior (smoking, exercise, and so on) among different population groups, and people with backgrounds in sociology are often asked to fill these information needs. Indeed, wherever major changes are occurring you will find sociologists at work along with other professionals, charting the changes and attempting to predict their consequences.

The study of sociology beyond the introductory level can lead to advanced skills in computation, data analysis, and statistics. Research experience in the field can greatly increase your ability to understand social situations and get along with people from different backgrounds. As the world continues to shrink and people from different cultures and societies come into greater contact with one another, sociological skills become increasingly valuable.

The Personal Challenge: Social change affects every student's life. This new feature illustrates how social change is altering the lives of students and encourages you to take an active part in changing your world.

CHAPTER 12 Inequalities of Social Class **363**

FIGURE 12.8

MAPPING SOCIAL CHANGE

Source: 1990 Census.

Median Household Income for U.S. Counties
- $30,057 or more
- $18,100–22,736
- $22,737–30,056
- $18,099 or less

U.S. median: $30,056

Poor Counties in the United States
This map shows all of the counties of the United States, grouped by average income. The extremes of wealth and poverty in U.S. society are apparent. Or are they?

Actually, such a map is more useful in revealing areas of poverty outside central cities than within them. This is because impoverished inner-city communities usually are only a portion of a densely urban county that may also include affluent and middle-class communities. Their incomes raise the average so that the pockets of inner-city poverty do not appear on the map.

This map still reveals a great deal about the places where poor people live. For example, along the Mississippi river, especially in Arkansas and Mississippi, we see groups of counties whose residents' average income is in the lowest range. The same is true in parts of the arid Southwest. Why are there such high concentrations of poor residents in these counties?

and agricultural corporations. The land is farmed by African American and poor white workers who earn extremely little. Thus, the delta region has a pattern of agrarian stratification that results in high rates of poverty. In the impoverished counties of the Southwest, the land often contains mineral and water resources that are controlled by a small number of wealthy individuals and corporations; Chicanos, Native Americans, and poor whites do not share in the wealth created by these resources, and the counties in which they live have low average incomes.

The isolated poor counties of the mountain states in the West often suffer from a newer form of poverty. In these areas economic growth is due to tourism, second-home developments, skiing, and other pursuits of the affluent upper and upper-middle classes. Farms, small-town businesses, and the trailer parks where the resort workers live may be located in a nearby valley, which

Mapping Social Change: Significant demographic and ecological data are included through the coordinated use of maps, data, and photos. Chapter 2 introduces this new feature by discussing the growing use of areal data as well as computer technology in analyzing the social environment. Subsequent chapters use similar groupings to enhance comprehension of complex subjects.

Study Charts: These new summary charts organize the flow of ideas pertaining to a particular topic for ease of studying and to increase comprehension of the text material.

Research Frontiers: The last section of each chapter applies current research and policy issues to the subject matter in the chapter. It shows how research is conducted, then applies the findings to real-world situations, providing a deeper understanding of the role research plays in the field of sociology.

Visual Sociology: A photo essay in each chapter illustrates how sociologists interpret and analyze the data in photographs as part of their research, thus demonstrating how integral the visual aspect is to sociology. Special Visual Sociology sections in Chapters 1 and 10 incorporate fine art into the discussions.

End-of-Chapter Elements: Each chapter concludes with material that offers opportunities for review and further study.

Chapter Summaries: For quick review, these sections condense the main points of the contents in the chapters and provide key terms in italics.

Think About It Critically: This is the introductory paragraph of the Summary section, posing an issue to think about critically as you read through the body of the Summary.

Critical Response: The final paragraph of the Summary section is a response to the issue discussed in Think About It Critically and the material covered in the body of the Summary.

Glossary: At the end of the chapter, a listing of the boldfaced key terms appears with definitions and page references.

Where To Find It: To encourage and enhance further research on topics covered in the chapter, Dr. Kornblum provides a collection of suggested readings with a brief synopsis of each book and journal.

Appendix: Careers in Sociology: In this special section following the last chapter in the textbook, Dr. Kornblum gives some insights into the career opportunities for students majoring in sociology. He provides answers to commonly asked questions.

Alphabetical End-of-Book Glossary: Arranged in alphabetical order, the glossary provides a definition for each of the boldfaced key terms that appear throughout the book.

FEATURES

Global Social Change

Using the Sociological Imagination

The Personal Challenge

PREFACE

The more I study, teach, and do research in sociology, the more I love the subject. No other area of intellectual work overlaps with so many other fields of knowledge; none straddles the sciences and the humanities so squarely or offers such varied insights into the vexing questions of our own time. It is out of this conviction that I undertook the demanding task of creating and revising this book. My greatest hope is that it will convey the excitement of sociological discovery and move its readers to take more advanced courses in the field.

Sociology and sociological research are in ever-increasing demand throughout the world. Major, often tumultuous, changes are creating a growing demand for scientific description and analysis of human behavior. With such immensely important societal changes as the end of the Cold War and the fall of the Soviet empire, sociological concepts and methods are being applied with increasing frequency throughout the world. And the study of sociology is attracting a far more diverse student population than was true when the field was little more than an academic specialty. *Sociology in a Changing World* thus is designed not only to meet the requirements of the standard introductory course, but also to address recent changes in the discipline, the students, and the work of sociologists.

This textbook is designed for the basic introductory course, but I hope its emphasis on the frontiers of sociological research and its combination of classic and new research will make it a useful reference source for students to carry with them through more advanced social-science courses. One major way in which *Sociology in a Changing World* differs from other sociology textbooks is in its consistent focus on issues of social change. Moreover, it is not slanted toward one or another perspective, ideological or methodological; rather, it presents ample evidence of the strengths and weaknesses of the interactionist, functionalist, and conflict approaches to the explanation and prediction of social change. In addition, it has a stronger grounding in demographic, ecological, and historical methods than is found in existing comprehensive texts. And, throughout the text, an effort is made to strike a balance between the use of global comparisons and historical material and research about American culture and the social changes occurring today in the United States.

I hope that both instructors and students will be able to benefit from the strengths of this book. With each new edition I have had the benefit of much collegial criticism from my graduate students (who often use the book in their own classes) and from my professional colleagues at the City University and elsewhere. I have tried to use their comments and suggestions wherever possible and appropriate. I know, also, that any book can be improved. Like my students and colleagues, you will undoubtedly have ideas about improvements that might be made in future editions. Please feel free to send your ideas or comments to me at the CUNY Graduate School, 33 West 42nd Street, New York, NY 10036.

HIGHLIGHTS OF THE FOURTH EDITION

Sociology in a Changing World has gone through its most extensive revision yet to reflect continuing changes in our own and other societies. Throughout this revision process, numerous colleagues were consulted for their ideas, suggestions, and overall input regarding sociology, teaching sociology, and sociology textbooks in general. Certain criteria appeared numerous times and quickly became the six primary principles behind the revision that resulted in this fourth edition. These six essential principles are:

- *Exercising a Global Perspective:* Because we live in an increasingly global society, a global perspective is incorporated throughout the textbook.
- *Observing Social Change:* A key to studying sociology is observing social change among individuals, groups, and societies around the world.
- *Applying Sociology:* By applying sociology to everyday life, students' comprehension is made more complete.
- *Learning Through Visual Presentation:* An extensive visual presentation maximizes learning by reflecting contemporary cultural assumptions and tastes.
- *Incorporating Diversity in Theory and Research:* The research of women and minorities is contextually presented and well-balanced.
- *Presenting Accessible Scholarship:* The scholarship is presented in an accessible style, promoting comprehension of the material.

Many of the fourth edition's features are in response to these principles. For example, Visual Sociology, Mapping Social Change, and Then and Now are visually oriented presentations of sociological concepts and changing societal conditions. The Personal Challenge, which illustrates how social change is altering students' lives and encourages students to take an active part in changing their worlds, inspires students to observe social change, apply sociology, and exercise a global perspective. Likewise, the new Research Frontiers sections, which apply current research and policy issues to the chapter subject matter, involve diversity in theory and research.

Major content revisions have been made throughout the book in response to feedback from my colleagues. I have transposed the chapters on culture and social structure so that culture now appears first. The chapter on inequalities of gender and age has been replaced by two largely new chapters, allowing for greater depth of coverage of both topics. In addition, the chapters on socialization, social change, social class, and the family have been extensively revised. I have also added the following new discussions on important topics:

- *Chapter 2:* mapping of social data
- *Chapter 4:* the theory of post-industrial society
- *Chapter 5:* the Bell Curve controversy, role playing, and "face work"
- *Chapter 8:* protest cycles and action frames
- *Chapter 10:* dilemmas of social change, and the postmodernist critique
- *Chapter 12:* classes in post-industrial society
- *Chapter 16:* stepparenting, conflict in families, "family values," and class conflict
- *Chapter 19:* the changing social contract

DISTINCTIVE FEATURES

Sociology in a Changing World differs from its competitors primarily in its emphasis on social change. Throughout, the book highlights the tension between attempts to modify social institutions and efforts to maintain traditional modes of behavior. The text also tries to point out the unanswered questions on the frontiers of social-scientific research. The following are the special features that incorporate this teaching philosophy:

- *Beginning-of-chapter elements* preview the chapter material in an organized and consistent format.
- *Chapter outlines* serve as advance organizers, previewing the topics that will be discussed in the chapter.
- *Opening vignettes*—some fictional, some based on classic sociological writings, some from recent literature, but all illustrating the questions to be addressed in the chapter— begin each chapter to capture the students' attention and introduce them to the subject matter.
- *Geographical maps* help the reader pinpoint the locations of countries and cities discussed in the text.
- *Then and Now* is a new visual feature that contrasts photos of a particular social condition in the past and today.
- *Feature boxes,* including *Sociological Methods, Global Social Change,* and *Using the Sociological Imagination,* are found within the chapters.
- *The Personal Challenge* is a new box discussing the impact of social change on aspects of students' everyday lives.
- *Mapping Social Change,* a new feature, uses maps and photos to show the distribution of a condition or characteristic throughout the United States or the world.
- *Study charts* summarize material for ease of studying.
- *Research Frontiers,* the final section of each chapter, discusses current research in subject areas covered in the chapter, relating it to applied research and policy issues.
- *Visual Sociology,* a photo essay in each chapter, shows how sociologists analyze photographs or other visual material as part of their research.
- *End-of-chapter elements* offer opportunities for review and further study.
- *Chapter summaries* are presented at the end of each chapter. Each summary is a thorough but concise rendering of the key

concepts and relationships presented in the chapter and is framed by a critical thinking question and a possible response.

- *End-of-chapter glossaries* are convenient; students will not have to flip to the end of the book to review important terms and their definitions.
- *Where to Find It,* at the end of each chapter, lists a set of suggested readings that includes not only books and journal articles but also basic references and data sources.

NEW TO THIS EDITION

Among the features listed above, three new features deserve special mention:

Mapping Social Change. Increasingly, sociology textbooks devote valuable space to maps because instructors realize that students need more opportunities to develop their knowledge of the world's regions and environments. Often, however, maps showing areal distributions of important social phenomena like poverty are presented with little explanation or enticement to the student to study relationships within the map. The Mapping Social Change features in *Sociology in a Changing World* invite the student to study and think about regional and national phenomena. By juxtaposing a general map with a detailed inset map and a photo, I hope to engage the student in thinking about the social conditions or changes highlighted in the feature.

Then and Now. Previous editions of this textbook used woodcuts and other illustrations to remind the student of social conditions prevailing in earlier eras, thereby focusing attention on cultural and structural change. This edition makes this comparative visual focus more explicit by highlighting a social phenomenon or situation as it occurs today and comparing it with the same condition as it occurred in an earlier historical period.

The Personal Challenge. This new boxed feature will help students connect major social changes with actual conditions and forces in their own lives. The focus is on how changes in norms, economic conditions, and other important aspects of the social world are affecting people with whom the student can easily identify.

ORGANIZATION OF THE TEXTBOOK

In organizing the book, I resisted the temptation to radically rearrange the standard introductory sociology course. There are traditional approaches to the subject that deserve respect, such as presenting an overview of sociology and its history, introducing the basic research methods, examining the dimensions of social inequality, and including a series of chapters on major social institutions. But I have added to this solid, time-tested framework, and in some cases, have moved a chapter from its traditional position in an introductory textbook.

The first 10 chapters of the book set forth most of the concepts that any student needs to know and be able to use. This makes the book easy to adapt to courses of different length. In addition, the first three parts of the book introduce many of the basic sociological explanations of social stability and change. This means that topics like urbanization and social movements are presented in the first half of the book rather than in later sections. Other fundamental concepts are presented in these early chapters as well. I refer repeatedly to these concepts in the second half of the book, rather than introducing them and then going on to entirely new material.

The book is divided into four parts:

Part 1, Social Foundations, introduces the "human science" of sociology: Chapter 1 traces the history of sociology and introduces the major perspectives used by sociologists, and Chapter 2 describes the methods used by sociologists in conducting their research. The next two chapters focus on some of sociology's most fundamental concepts: culture (Chapter 3) and the elements of social structure (Chapter 4).

Part 2, Social Dynamics, covers many of the processes that seem to account for social stability and change: Chapter 5 discusses socialization, and Chapter 6 examines the structure of groups and how people behave in groups of different kinds. Chapters 7, 8, and 9 move from the structure and function of groups within a society to the processes that change societies. Chapter 7 deals with deviance; Chapter 8 looks at collective behavior and social movements; and Chapter 9 explores the relationships among population growth, urbanization, and community. Chapter 10 summarizes the ways in which sociologists think about and conduct research on the causes and consequences of social change.

The five chapters in **Part 3, Social Divisions,** examine social inequality, particularly in American society. Chapter 11 introduces the concept of social stratification. Chapter 12 deals with inequalities of social class, and Chapters 13, 14, and 15 focus on social inequalities due to race, ethnicity, gender, and age.

Part 4, Social Institutions, applies the concepts and perspectives discussed earlier in the book to an analysis of several major institutions: Chapter 16 explores the changing nature of the family, Chapter 17 introduces religion, and Chapter 18 covers education and communications media. Chapter 19 deals with economic institutions, and Chapter 20 discusses political institutions. Finally, Chapter 21 analyzes the institutions of science, technology, and medicine.

ANCILLARY PACKAGE*

Harcourt Brace College Publishers may provide complimentary instructional aids and supplements or supplement packages to those adopters qualified under our adoption policy. Please contact your sales representative for more information. If, as an adopter or potential user, you receive textbooks or supplements you do not need, please return them to your sales representative or send them to:

ATTN: Returns Department
Troy Warehouse
465 South Lincoln Drive
Troy, MO 63379

For the Instructor

Instructor's Manual
Written by William Kornblum and Carolyn Smith, the Instructor's Manual includes lecture outlines, instructional goals, teaching suggestions that explain the distinctive features and central con-

*Note: IBM is a registered trademark of International Business Machines Corporation. Macintosh is a registered trademark of Apple Computer, Inc. *EasyTest, FullTest,* and *RequesTest* are trademarks of Engineering Software, Inc. *EXAMaster+* is a trademark of Harcourt Brace College Publishers. *SimCity* is a trademark of Maxis Software.

cepts of each chapter, topics for discussion, and suggestions for using the charts, tables, and visual features.

Test Bank
Prepared by Carol Boggs of the University of North Carolina, Charlotte, the Test Bank includes multiple-choice, true/false, and short-answer questions. The Test Bank contains more than 3100 questions, approximately 150 per chapter.

Computerized Test Bank
Available in IBM, Macintosh, and Windows formats, *EXAMaster+* software allows you to create tests using fewer keystrokes. Easy-to-follow screen prompts guide you step-by-step through test construction. *EXAMaster+* gives you three ways to create tests:

- *EasyTest* lets you create a test from a single screen. It compiles a test using questions you've chosen from the database, or randomly selects questions based on the parameters you specify.
- *FullTest* gives you a whole range of options for test creation. With *FullTest,* you may:
  - select questions as you preview them on screen
  - edit existing questions, or add your own questions
  - add or edit graphics (in MS-DOS version)
  - link related questions, instructions, and graphics
  - have questions randomly selected from a wider range of criteria
  - create your own criteria on two open keys
  - block specific questions from random selection
  - print up to 99 different versions of the same test and answer sheet
- *RequesTest* is for the instructor without access to a computer. You may call our Software Support Line and order tests that conform to your criteria. Harcourt Brace will compile the test and either mail or fax it to you within 48 hours.

The Sociological Imagination Video Segments
Instructors may select from 12 video segments developed from the Dallas County Community College District telecourse in introductory sociology. All programs are 26-minute clips from the actual telecourse and highlight relevant subject matter. The television course is coordinated with the fourth edition of *Sociology in a Changing World.*

Harcourt Brace Video Library
A variety of video programs are available to enrich classroom presentations. Selections from Films for the Humanities and Sciences include *The Sandwich Generation: Caring for Both Children and Parents, The Good Society,* and *Attorney General Janet Reno* among others. Also available are video programs from the Public Broadcasting System and the Annenberg/CPB Video Series.

Overhead Teaching Transparencies
Classroom lectures will be enhanced with this collection of full-color transparencies that illustrate sociological concepts. All contain information to supplement (not duplicate) material in the textbook.

Sociological Insights for a Changing World
This innovative videodisc offers still images, charts, graphs, and captivating video footage in a series of 10 modules. Topics cover such fascinating and controversial issues as the 1960s drug culture, patterns of deviance in the expanding population, racism,

and religion. Each module presents an outline of topics, a historical perspective, and a discussion of contemporary trends and predictions for the future. A Viewer's Guide and LectureActive presentation software are available.

For the Student

Study Guide

Written by William Kornblum and Carolyn Smith, the Study Guide provides students with a self-paced review of the text. Each chapter begins with an outline and learning objectives, followed by a fill-in-the-blank review, a matching exercise in which key terms are matched with their definitions, a self-test consisting of 15 multiple-choice and 5 true/false questions, and a short-answer section that requires the student to apply concepts presented in the textbook. Answers to the matching exercises and self-tests are provided. The Study Guide also includes a section that encourages students to think and write critically about what they have learned in each chapter of the textbook.

The Sociological Imagination
Telecourse Study Guide

Extensively revised, this Study Guide is written as a companion to the telecourse, *The Sociological Imagination.* Each lesson introduces overviews of the text and video program. Lesson guidelines provide a list of goals at the beginning of every lesson, and suggested readings supplement the textbook. The Study Guide is written by Jane Penny of Eastfield College and Glenn Currier, project sociologist for *The Sociological Imagination* telecourse.

SimCity Software

This educational version of *SimCity* software is geared to sociology using environmental, economic, or geographical variables to teach the volatile nature of sociology. It allows the user to create his or her own society, an experience instructors and students will find invaluable. User's guide included.

SocialStat Software

Although *SocialStat* is extremely simple to learn and use, it is a powerful interactive data analysis program which makes extensive use of graphics. Students can run frequency distributions or two- or three-way cross-tabulations or calculate chi-square values—and have the results in a few seconds. *SocialStat* software and its accompanying User's Guide are written by Dean Savage, City University of New York, Queens College.

CD-ROM

The CD-ROM is an interactive student learning tool that corresponds with the fourth edition of *Sociology in a Changing World.* It provides dynamic multimedia presentations of the most complex and important concepts in sociology. Students using the CD-ROM will have personal access to resources that will enhance their learning of key concepts in sociology through contemporary multimedia articles, video footage, slide shows, illustrations, review and testing material, audio scripts, software exercises, demonstrations, internet access, and more. An order card is enclosed with this textbook. If the card is missing, you may order by calling 1-800-225-5425.

ACKNOWLEDGMENTS

The new edition of *Sociology in a Changing World* is the culmination of two years of steady work—weekly writing and editing for a year, plus another year of production-related tasks. The values in a book like this are the work of many minds and hands. From the contributions of the social scientists who have reviewed the manuscript and the sociology students who have commented on previous editions, to the final touches of detail before the book is printed, there are scores of people whose contributions are essential at every step in the process. It is exciting to launch a new edition of the text, just as it is gratifying to thank those who made it possible. I have had the benefit of continuity in editors and professional friends who have advised me since the first edition. But each edition also brings in new publishing professionals whose influences help keep the book fresh and up-to-date.

First among the many people who continue to influence this project is my editor and collaborator Carolyn Smith. Carolyn first encouraged me to take on this project, and when my resolve wavered, her faith in our ability to complete it sustained me. Carolyn has untangled my prose, agonized with me over reviewers' comments, and kept track of the endless details that go into creating a scholarly text. There is not one word in this book that she has not thought about; every page bears the stamp of her expertise. Guy Smith also has my gratitude for his supportiveness during the long and demanding revision process.

The visual identity of this book, its creative use of photographic material for sociological example and method, have always been extremely important to me and to everyone involved in the making of this textbook. Our aim has been to create a textbook that would integrate sociological ideas with the design and layout of the book. In this edition the design, created by Garry Harman of Harcourt Brace, and the art and photo programs continue to emphasize creative treatments of data presentation and visual sociology.

My colleagues at the City University of New York have been unstinting with their suggestions and advice. My dear friend and colleague, Vernon Boggs, was always my greatest personal ally in the making of this book. His untimely death deprives me of someone whose deep commitment to teaching and research in sociology were a sustaining example. My longtime collaborator and friend, Terry Williams, continues to influence my thinking on key issues in sociology and life. Rolf Meyersohn has been heroic in his generosity with books and articles and words of encouragement. My colleague Charles Kadushin's intimate knowledge of the publishing world has been invaluable on many occasions, as have Paul Attewell's mastery of trends in sociological research and methods, and the profound knowledge of social movements and class theory shared by Stanley Aronowitz, William DiFazio, and Bogdan Denitch. If I have managed to avoid a natural predisposition toward male bias, much of the credit must go to Susan Kornblum, Cynthia Epstein, Judith Lorber, June Nash, Barbara Katz Rothman, and many other colleagues who have shared their insights and knowledge. My colleagues Lily Hoffman, John Mollenkopf, and Charles Winick are unstinting in sharing their sociological insights and knowledge of new literatures. Renata Reimann, while deeply engaged in her own dissertation research, provided essential commentary and scholarly services for the creation of the new chapters on gender and age.

The thoughtful comments we receive about the book and the encouragement of many students and colleagues are immensely rewarding. Their corrections and constructive suggestions too are most welcome. Many colleagues throughout the United States offer me wise counsel and scholarly advice, for which I continue to be deeply grateful. But I owe a special debt to my colleague and friend, Carol Chenault of Calhoun Community College, Decatur, Alabama, for her abiding interest in the textbook and her generosity. Professor Chenault's comparative visual sociology is featured in Chapter 14.

No single author can hope to adequately represent a field as large and complex as sociology. Over several years of textbook writing, I have learned that the comments and suggestions offered by reviewers and users of the book are essential to its suc-

cess. Many dedicated Harcourt Brace sales representatives have taken the time to introduce me to instructors who use the book. In addition, the comments of numerous reviewers have helped me to correct mistakes of fact, interpretation, and emphasis. I might disagree with some of them, but I always find them helpful.

Each edition of the book has benefited from the insights of reviewers. I gratefully acknowledge the following instructors who contributed to the fourth edition of *Sociology in a Changing World:*

Barry Adams
University of Windsor

Rita Argiros
St. Cloud State University

Ed Armstrong
University of Wisconsin—Stout

Matilda Barker
Cerritos College

Scott A. Beck
East Tennessee State University

Cliff Broman
Michigan State University

Brent Bruton
Iowa State University

Marvin A. Camfield
Walters State Community College

Carole M. Carroll
Middle Tennessee State University

Carol Deming Chenault
Calhoun College

Donna K. Crossman
Greenville Technical College

Glenn Currier
El Centro College

Mita Dhariwal
Bakersfield College

Dennis R. Dubs
Harrisburg Area Community College

Douglas Farley
Niagara County Community College

Frank Forwood
Northeast Louisiana University

Michael J. Fraleigh
Bryant College

Kirsten Gronbjerg
Loyola University (Chicago)

Larry J. Halford
Washburn University

Rudy Harris
Des Moines Area Community College

Lily M. Hoffman
City College in New York

Drew Hurley
Santa Fe Community College

Mike Hurtado
Citrus College

Mark Kassop
Bergen Community College

Ruby C. Lewis
Dekalb College—Central Campus

Mits Maeda
Cypress College

Allan McCutcheon
University of Delaware

Anthony J. Mendonca
Community College of Allegheny County—
Allegheny Campus

Karen Mundy
Lee College

Ann S. Oakes
Idaho State University

Novella Perrin
Central Missouri State University

Dick Phillips
Kalamazoo Valley Community College

Judy Porta
Las Positas College

Leroy Reed
Central Florida Community College

Joseph Ribal
El Camino College

Ellen Rosengarten
Sinclair Community College

Joel C. Snell
Kirkwood Community College

Larry D. Stokes
University of Tennessee—Chattanooga

Lorene Taylor
Valencia Community College

Doren Thompson
Washtenaw Community College

Marcella Thompson
University of Arkansas—Fayetteville

Jacquelyn A. Troup
Cerritos College

William Trush
Kalamazoo Valley Community College

Tim Tuinstra
Kalamazoo Valley Community College

David Van Merlo
St. Charles County Community College

Steven L. Vasser
Mankato State University

Jack Weller
University of Kansas

Leslie E. Wooten
Cleveland State Community College

Stacey G. H. Yap
Plymouth State College

Richard Yinger
Palm Beach Community College

Wayne Zatapek
Tarrant County Junior College—Northeast

Herbert Zeigler
Chesapeake College

The textbook continues to benefit from the helpful comments of the following instructors who reviewed for previous editions:

Elizabeth Almquist
University of North Texas

Michele Aronica
Saint Joseph's College

Augustine Aryee
Fitchburg State College

Dorothy Balancio
Mercy College

Richard Bales
Illinois Central College

Bernard Beck
Northwestern University

Phillip Bosserman
Salisbury State College

R. E. Canjar
University of Maryland

Chuck Carselowey
Oklahoma City Community College

Robert E. Clark
Midwestern State University

Mary Beth Collins
Central Piedmont Community College

Vasilikie Demos
University of Minnesota

Jack Dison
Arkansas State University

Ken Elder
Southeastern Oklahoma State University

Martin Epstein
Middlesex Community College

Charles E. Faupel
Auburn University

Joseph Galaskiewicz
University of Minnesota

Eric P. Godfrey
Ripon College

John Hall
University of California

Scarlett Hardesty
University of Arizona

Denny Hill
Georgia Southern College

Benton Johnson
University of Oregon

Laura Kramer
Montclair State College

Kathryn Kuhn
University of Texas

Martin L. Levin
Emory University

Theodore Long
Merrimack College

Joseph Marolla
Virginia Commonwealth University

George Martin
Montclair State College

Virginia McKeefery-Reynolds
Northern Illinois University

Jerry L. L. Miller
University of Arizona

Ephraim Mizruchi
Syracuse University

James D. Orcutt
The Florida State University

Larry M. Perkins
Oklahoma State University

David L. Preston
San Diego State University

J. D. Robson
University of Arkansas

John Roman
University of Maine

Jeffrey P. Rosenfeld
Nassau Community College

Wesley Shrum
Louisiana State University

Richard L. Simpson
The University of North Carolina

Gary Spencer
Syracuse University

Paul Stowell
Wenatchee Valley College

Kathleen Tiemann
Mercer University

C. Edwin Vaughan
University of Missouri

Theodore C. Wagenaar
Miami University

Eric A. Wagner
Ohio University

Joe Walsh
Bucks County Community College

Chaim I. Waxman
Rutgers, The State University of New Jersey

Timothy Wickham-Crowley
Georgetown University

Kenneth Wilson
East Carolina University

Steven R. Wilson
Temple University

Thomas J. Yacovone
Los Angeles Valley College

William W. Zellner
Doane College

In preparing this edition of the textbook, I needed the help of a team of professional editors and publishers who would recognize the strengths of the book and work with me to make improvements while keeping the basic elements of the original content and design. I found such people in Stephen T. Jordan, Amy Hester, Julie McBurney, Chris Klein, and Ted Buchholz of Harcourt Brace. They all encouraged me whenever I had good ideas and were sensitive in their criticism. My thanks also go to Garry Harman for his text design and supervision of the art program, to Elsa Peterson for the development of the photo program, to Cindy Young for her supervision of the production process, and to Angela Williams for her skillful and thorough editorial coordination.

Thanks also go to Guy Smith for his research assistance; to Margo Smith for her professional camera work; to Eve Kornblum for contributing many ideas, especially for the photo program; and to my students at the City University of New York, both graduates and undergraduates, for keeping me "turned on" to sociology.

William Kornblum

ABOUT THE AUTHOR

William Kornblum is a professor of sociology at the Graduate School of the City University of New York, where he helps train future instructors and researchers in the social sciences. He also teaches undergraduates at various campuses of the City University, including Queens College, Hunter College, and City College.

A specialist in urban and community studies, Kornblum began his teaching career with the Peace Corps in the early 1960s, when he taught physics and chemistry in French-speaking West Africa (see the introduction to Chapter 10). He received his doctorate in sociology from the University of Chicago in 1971. He has also taught at the University of Washington at Seattle and worked as a research sociologist for the U.S. Department of the Interior. At the CUNY Graduate School, he directs research on

youth and employment and on urban policy. With his longtime research partner, Terry Williams, he recently coauthored *The Uptown Kids,* a sociological portrait of teenagers and young adults growing up in high-rise public housing projects. He is also the principal investigator of Project TELL, a longitudinal study of the ways in which home computers can improve the life chances of young people at risk of dropping out of school.

The author's other publications include *Blue Collar Community,* a study of the steel-making community of South Chicago; *Growing Up Poor* (with Terry Williams), a study of teenagers growing up in different low-income communities in the United States; and *Social Problems,* a comprehensive textbook about social problems and social policies in the United States.

To Susan, my partner in the Great Adventure, and Morris Janowitz, my mentor

BRIEF CONTENTS

CONTENTS

CHAPTER 9

Population, Urbanization, and Community   238

CHAPTER 10

Global Social Change   272

PART 3   Social Divisions

CHAPTER 11

Stratification and Social Mobility   308

CHAPTER 12

Inequalities of Social Class   340

CHAPTER 17

Religion   502

CHAPTER 18

Education and Communications Media   534

CHAPTER 19

Economic Institutions   568

CHAPTER 20

Politics and Political Institutions   602

CHAPTER 21

Science, Technology, and Medicine   632

PART 1

Social
Foundations

Social change is occurring around us all the time. Neighborhoods change as newcomers move in or more housing is built; factories close or open in response to changes in the economies of other continents; wars and natural disasters push people out of their homelands; new technologies alter old lifestyles and stimulate people to find new ways of living. Sociology is the science that attempts to make sense of these changes. It is devoted to studying why social change occurs and how it affects people in different societies or within a single society.

The first part of this book introduces some basic sociological concepts. Chapter 1 shows how sociology developed into a science that can help us understand the world around us and how it changes. Chapter 2 describes the methods sociologists use in conducting their research. When we talk about culture in Chapter 3, we are referring to the making of human consciousness—how we think and communicate and how these processes make society itself possible. Chapter 4 introduces the elements of social structure and explains how various kinds of societies have developed over time.

CHAPTER 1

Sociology: An Introduction

Twenty-three-year-old Kenya James is working to help residents of the Barry Farms housing development in West Capital, a poor community in Washington, D.C. He and other volunteers on his crew are part of the Corps for National Service. The crew is working with neighborhood leaders to find ways of ridding the buildings of lead-based paint. Chips of fallen paint eaten by a hungry child can cause lead poisoning, which can result in permanent damage to the brain and other vital organs. Lead-based paint is no longer used in more affluent neighborhoods, but it is still used occasionally in low-income urban neighborhoods. Worse still, in many cases the older lead-based paint has never been removed or adequately covered over.

"The people in this neighborhood have so much to worry about," Kenya sighs, "like where their next check is coming from, how to feed themselves and their kids. . . . Lead paint is not usually something they have given that much thought to. We need to help them understand why it's such a danger to the kids."

Kenya is proud to be a member of the Corps for National Service. Although he has not yet finished college, he is the leader of his crew because he has the most direct experience with communities like West Capital. He comes from the same kind of urban neighborhood and has natural skills as a public speaker and community organizer. "The others on my crew," he points out, "they had, like, more of the usual opportunities, help from parents to go to college and all. Me, well, you know how it was, I had to struggle just to get out of the 'hood, just to survive and not get killed. . . . We get paid a stipend of $7,640 for about 11 months and if we finish the term we get an educational grant of $4,725 which I am desperate for. That's the only way I'm going to be able to finish college."

Kenya is disturbed by the widespread opposition to the national service program. "I read what they say in Congress, that all this federal aid to poor people and poor communities should be cut, and like that." He and the other volunteers wonder whether they will be able to continue. "It's true," he adds, "that in a sense we are not volunteers because we are paid a stipend, but many of us could be working for much more pay." Kenya feels that were it not for national service, he might never have had a chance to gain the leadership experience he is getting in the lead paint program. And he knows that without the funds set aside by the program, he might never have a chance to go back to college.

THE SOCIOLOGICAL IMAGINATION

When Kenya James talks about the implications of national service for himself and other young volunteers, he is using his sociological imagination. When he argues with the program's opponents, he is thinking sociologically. He may not always be aware of this, and sometimes he is thinking about his own personal problems rather than those of the crew or the community, but it is his sociological imagination that got him out of his own neighborhood and into a new life. Like Kenya and others who debate the merits of national service, you too have a sociological imagination. In this book we hope to help you develop this special insight, which will equip you to use sociological knowledge in your daily life. Most of all, we hope to enable you to use your sociological imagination to gain wisdom about the society in which we all participate and for whose future we are all responsible.

Most people need some help in applying their sociological imagination. Often they fail to distinguish between social forces and personal troubles. If they become unemployed, they blame themselves for failing to do better; if they divorce, they blame each other. When they see crime, they blame "human nature"; when they see success, they praise individual achievement. But this tendency to think of life as a series of individual mistakes or successes blinds them to the fact that social conditions also shape individual lives, often in ways for which individuals can hardly be held accountable. And the habit of seeing events mainly in terms of how they affect individuals blinds people to the possibility of improving the way their society is organized.

Sociologists are concerned with how **social conditions** influence our lives as individuals. Social conditions are the realities of the life we create together as social be-

Kenya James is shown looking for work in his hometown, New York City, before he joined Americorps and was assigned to work on community projects in Washington, D.C.

ings. Conditions such as poverty or wealth or crime and drug use, for example, differ from biological facts (facts concerning our behavior and needs as animals) and psychological facts (facts about our patterns of behavior as individuals). Sociologists do not deny that psychological facts are important. Differences among individuals help some people cope with stress better than others, seize opportunities that others allow to slip by, or fail where others succeed. But before saying that the success or failure of an individual or group is due to psychological causes, the sociologist tries to look at how social conditions such as poverty or wealth, war, or changes in the availability of jobs affect the individual's chances of success.

According to sociologist C. Wright Mills, who made famous the term **sociological imagination,** people often believe that their private lives can be explained mainly in terms of their personal successes and failures. They fail to see the links between their own individual biographies and the course of human history. Often they blame themselves for their troubles without grasping the effects of social change on their lives. "The facts of contemporary history," Mills cautions, "are also facts about the success and the failure of individual men and women."

> When a society is industrialized, a peasant becomes a worker; a feudal lord is liquidated or becomes a businessman. When classes rise or fall, a man is employed or unemployed; when the rate of investment goes up or down, a man takes new heart or goes broke. When wars happen, an insurance salesman becomes a rocket launcher; a store clerk, a radar man; a wife lives alone; a child grows up without a father. (1959, p. 3)

According to Mills, neither a person's biography nor the history of a society can be understood unless one takes into account the influence of each on the other. The social forces of history—war, depression or recession, increases in population, changes in production and consumption, and many other social conditions—become the forces that influence individuals to behave in new ways. But those new ways of behavior themselves become social forces and, in turn, shape history.

To take just one example, the not-so-distant ancestors of many African Americans were brought to the Western Hemisphere in slave ships. African Americans have experienced slavery, war, emancipation, segregation, and rural and urban poverty. In reaction to the historical forces that deprived them of full citizenship in the United States, African Americans developed a variety of behaviors, from the spirituals that expressed their deep feelings of religious faith and protest, to boycotts and demonstrations against segregation. These protests and demonstrations themselves became powerful social forces that continue to shape the history of the American people. The kind of volunteer program that Kenya works in, and the neighborhoods to which he and the other recruits are assigned, are in part the product of protests against persistent poverty and segregation.

In the neighborhoods where Kenya works, people seem to be trapped in an endless cycle of poor jobs, government aid, more poor jobs, and so on. Massive changes in the U.S. economy, which have replaced higher-paying manufacturing jobs with lower-paying service jobs, seem to have further narrowed the future for children in the communities where national service crews are assigned. Kenya often wonders whether volunteer programs make a difference in the lives of people in those communities. Are their problems due to their own sense of hopelessness or to larger economic and social changes, or to both? As Kenya ponders these questions he is using his sociological imagination to sort out the individual and social influences on people's lives. We will be doing the same kind of thinking throughout this book.

By applying the sociological imagination to events in Haiti, where desperate people risked their lives to flee a dangerous dictatorship, or in Bosnia, where rapes of defenseless women and girls have been commonplace events in times of civil war, one can begin to "grasp history and biography and the relations between the two within society" (Mills, 1959, p. 6). One of the main objectives of this book is to help you apply your sociological imagination to an understanding of the social forces that are shaping your own biography and those of the people you care about. The sociological imagination can help us avoid needlessly blaming ourselves for the troubles we encounter in life. It can help us understand, for example, why some people are rich and powerful but many others are not; why the benefits of good health care or enriching education are available to some but not to others; or why women may find themselves resenting the men in their lives. The sociological imagination helps us sort out which facts about ourselves are explained by our place in society and which ones are a result of our own actions. Above all, the sociological imagination can suggest ways in which we can realistically bring about change in our lives and in society itself.

SOCIOLOGY, THE HUMAN SCIENCE

The questions Kenya James asks about the community where he works and the role of government programs like national service are a good example of what sociology attempts to explain. To answer them, one would need to ex-

plore the effects of major social changes like the decline of manufacturing and the rise of information and service industries, or the vast changes that have taken place in Congress in recent years. We would need to know more about how people in communities like West Capital are adapting to these changes. We would need to know what steps they are taking, both together and separately, to cope with changes in their community and in their individual lives. Sociology gives us the concepts and methods to find answers to these questions.

Sociology is the scientific study of human societies and human behavior in the many groups that make up a society. Sociologists must ask difficult, sometimes embarrassing, questions about human life in order to explore the consequences of cataclysmic events like those that shut down factories or enslave an entire people. To understand the possible futures of people who confront such drastic changes, sociologists are continually seeking knowledge about what holds societies together and what makes them bend under the impact of major forces such as war and migration.

THE SOCIAL ENVIRONMENT
The knowledge sociologists gather covers a vast range. Sociologists study religious behavior; conduct in the military; the behavior of workers and managers in industry; the activities of voluntary associations like parent-teacher groups and political parties; the changing relationships between men and women or between elderly individuals and their parents; the behavior of groups in cities and neighborhoods; the activities of gangs, criminals, and judges; differences in the behaviors of entire social classes—the rich, the middle classes, the poor, the down-and-out; the way cities grow and change; the fate of entire societies during and after revolutions; and a host of other subjects. But how to make sure the information gathered is reliable and precise, how to use it to build theories of social cohesion and social change—that is the challenge faced by the young science of sociology.

As in any science, there are many debates in sociology about the appropriate ways to study social life and about which theories or types of theories best explain social phenomena. Most sociologists, however, would agree with the following position:

> Human actions are limited or determined by "environment." Human beings become what they are at any given moment not by their own free decisions, taken rationally and in full knowledge of the conditions, but under the pressure of circumstances which delimit their range of choice and which also fix their objectives and the standards by which they make choices. (Shils, 1985, p. 805)

This statement expresses a core idea of sociology: Individual choice is never entirely free but is always determined to some extent by a person's environment. In sociology, *environment* refers to all the expectations and incentives established by other people in a person's social world. For the sociologist, therefore, the environment within which an individual's biography unfolds is a set of people and groups and organizations, all with their own ways of thinking and acting. Certainly each individual has unique choices to make in life, but the social world into which that person was born—be it an Indian reservation, an urban ghetto, a comfortable suburb, or an immigrant enclave in a strange city—determines to varying degrees what those choices will be.

LEVELS OF SOCIAL REALITY

In their studies of social environments, sociologists look at behaviors ranging from the intimate glances of lovers to the complex coordination of a space shuttle launch. Thus, for purposes of analysis we often speak of social behavior as occurring at three different levels of complexity: micro, middle, and macro.

The **micro level** of sociological observation is concerned with the behaviors of the individual and his or her immediate others—that is, with patterns of interaction among a few people. One example is Erving Goffman's studies of the routine behaviors of everyday life. Goffman's research showed how seemingly insignificant ways of acting in public actually carry significant meanings. Thus, in a study titled "Territories of the Self" (1972), Goffman categorized some of the ways in which we use objects as "markers" to claim a personal space:

Markers are of various kinds. There are "central markers," being objects that announce a territorial claim, the territory radiating outward from it, as when sunglasses and lotion claim a beach chair, or a purse a seat in an airliner, or a drink on a bar the stool in front of it. . . . There are "boundary markers," objects that mark the line between two adjacent territories. The bar used in supermarket checkout counters to separate one customer's batch of articles from the next is an example. (pp. 41–42)

The last time you placed your sweater or book on the empty seat next to you on a bus, you told yourself that when someone came for the seat you would take up your things. But you hoped that the stranger who was coming along the aisle would get your message and choose another seat; you would claim your extra space as long as possible. You communicated all this by the manner in which you placed your marker and the persistence with which, by your body language, you defended "your" space.

Some sociologists deal almost exclusively with a much larger-scale, or **macro,** level of analysis. The macro level of social life refers to whole societies and the ways in which they are changing—that is, to revolutions, wars, major changes in the production of goods and services, and similar social phenomena that involve very large numbers of people. One example of macrosociological analysis is the study of how the shift from heavy manufacturing to high-tech industries has affected the way workers earn their livings. Another is the study of how the invasion and settlement of the American West in the nineteenth and

Each of these passengers in a railroad station waiting room has claimed a personal territory. Each has taken a separate bench and has chosen to sit at one end of the bench. If another person came to that bench, he or she would probably choose to sit as far away as possible.

early twentieth centuries gave rise to the beliefs and actions that drove Native Americans onto reservations.

Middle-level social phenomena are those that occur in communities or in organizations such as businesses and voluntary associations. Middle-level social forms are smaller than entire societies but larger than the micro-level social forms in which everyone involved knows everyone else or is in close proximity to the others (as on a bus or in a classroom). When Kenya James thinks about how new laws passed by Congress will affect the lives of children and parents in his community, he is thinking about how change at the macro level of society will affect life at the middle and micro levels—that is, in the community and in the homes of its residents.

These three levels of sociological analysis can be helpful in understanding the experience of the immigrants from Asia, Africa, or Latin America who may be appearing in your town or community, or one nearby. Macro-level social forces like war or overpopulation may account for the influx of immigrants. Middle-level social forces such as the availability of work at low wage and skill levels, or the presence of earlier arrivals from other nations, may help explain why certain immigrant groups become concentrated in particular communities within the United States. And at the micro level of analysis there will be, especially at first, important differences in the way immigrant and native-born people interact on a daily basis.

The study chart below presents the three basic levels of sociological analysis, as well as some examples of the types of studies conducted at each level. Throughout this book we show how the sociological imagination can be applied at different levels of society. In this chapter we set the stage by describing the basic perspectives from which mod-

ern sociologists approach the study of social conditions. In the next chapter we outline the procedures and methods used by sociologists in conducting their research. We begin here with a brief description of the origins and development of the science of sociology.

FROM SOCIAL THOUGHT TO SOCIAL SCIENCE

Like all the sciences, sociology developed out of prescientific longings to understand and predict. The central questions of sociology have been pondered by the world's great thinkers since the earliest periods of recorded history. The ancient Greek philosophers believed that human societies inevitably arose, flourished, and declined. They tended to perceive the past as better than the present, looking back to a "golden age" in which social conditions were presumed to have been better than those of the degraded present. Before the scientific revolution of the seventeenth century, the theologians and philosophers of medieval Europe and the Islamic world also believed that human misery and strife were inevitable. As the Bible put it, "the poor always ye have with you." Mere mortals could do little to correct social conditions, which were viewed as the work of divine Providence.

THE AGE OF ENLIGHTENMENT
The roots of modern sociology can be found in the work of the philosophers and scientists of the Great Enlightenment, which had its origins in the scientific discoveries of

STUDY CHART **Levels of Sociological Analysis**			
ANALYTICAL LEVEL		**SOCIAL BEHAVIORS STUDIED**	**TYPICAL QUESTIONS**
	Macro	Revolutions; intercontinental migrations; emergence of new institutions.	How are entire societies or institutions changing?
	Middle	Relations in bureaucracies; social movements; participation in communities, organizations, tribes.	How does bureaucracy affect personality? Do all social movements go through similar stages?
	Micro	Interaction in small groups; self-image; enactment of roles.	How do people create and take roles in groups? How are group structures created?

the seventeenth century. That pivotal century began with Galileo's "heretical" proof that the earth was not the center of the universe and ended with the publication of Isaac Newton's *Principia Mathematica.* Newton is often credited with the founding of modern science. He not only discovered the laws of gravity and motion but, in developing the calculus, also provided later generations with the mathematical tools whereby further discoveries in all the sciences could be made.

Hard on the heels of this unprecedented progress in science and mathematics came a theory of human progress that paved the way for a "science of humanity." Francis Bacon in England, René Descartes and Blaise Pascal in France, and Gottfried Wilhelm Leibniz in Germany were among the philosophers who recognized the social importance of scientific discoveries. Their writings emphasized the idea of progress guided by human reason and opposed the dominant notion that the human condition was ordained by God and could not be improved through human actions (Bury, 1932; Nisbet, 1969).

Today we are used to inventions crowding one upon another. Between the childhood of our grandparents and our own adulthood, society has undergone some major transformations: from agrarian to industrial production; from rural settlements and small towns to large cities and expanding metropolitan regions; from reliance on wood and coal as energy sources to dependence on electricity and nuclear power; from typewriters to computers. But in the seventeenth century people were used to far more stability. Ways of life that had existed since the Middle Ages were not expected to change in a generation.

The rise of science transformed the social order. As was often said at the time, science "broke the cake of custom." New methods of navigation made it possible to explore and chart the world's oceans and continents. Applied to warfare, scientific knowledge enabled Europeans to conquer the peoples of Africa, Asia, and the Western Hemisphere. In Europe, those conquests opened up new markets and stimulated new patterns of trade that hastened the growth of some regions and cities and the decline of others. The entire human world had entered a period of rapid social change that continues today and shows no signs of ending.

THE AGE OF REVOLUTION
The vehicle of social change was not science itself, since relatively few people at any level of society were practicing scientists. Rather, the modern era of rapid social change is a product of the many new social ideas that captured people's imagination during the eighteenth century. The series of revolutions that took place in the American colonies, in France, and in England all resulted in part from social movements unleashed by the triumphs of science and reason. The ideas of human rights (that is, the rights of all humans, not just the elite), of democracy versus rule by an

absolute monarch, of self-government for colonial peoples, and of applying reason and science to human affairs in general—all are currents of thought that arose during this period.

The revolutions of the eighteenth century loosed a torrent of questions that could not even have been imagined before. The old order of society was breaking down as secular (i.e., nonreligious) knowledge replaced sacred traditions. The study of laws and lawmaking and debates about justice in society began to replace the idea that kings and other leaders had a "divine right" to rule. Communities were breaking apart; courts and palaces and great estates were crumbling as people struggled to be free. What would replace them? Would the rule of the mob replace the rule of the monarch? Would greed and envy replace piety and faith? Would there be enough opportunities in the New World for all the people who were being driven off the land in the Old World? Would the factory system become the new order of society, and if so, what did that imply for the future of society?

No longer could the Scriptures or the classics of ancient Greece and Rome be consulted for easy answers to such questions. Rather, it was becoming evident that new answers could be discovered through the **scientific method:** repeated observation, careful description, the formulation of theories based on possible explanations, and the gathering of additional data about the questions that followed from those theories. Why not use the same methods to create a science of human society? This ambitious idea led to the birth of sociology. It is little wonder that the French philosopher Auguste Comte thought of sociology, even in its infancy, as the "queen of sciences," one that would soon take its rightful place beside the reigning science of physics. It was he who coined the term *sociology* to designate the scientific study of society. Comte believed that the study of social stability and social change was the most important subject for sociology to tackle. He made some of the earliest attempts to apply scientific methods to the study of social life.

THE GREAT EUROPEAN SOCIOLOGISTS
In the nineteenth century an increasing number of philosophers and historians began to see themselves as specializing in the study of social conditions and social change. They attempted to develop global theories of social change based on the essential qualities of societies at different stages of human history, and they devoted much of their attention to comparing existing societies and civilizations, both past and present. As Comte put it, the age of discovery had revealed such an array of societies that "from the wretched inhabitants of Tierra del Fuego to the most advanced nations of Western Europe," there is such a great diversity of societies that comparisons among them will yield much insight into why they differ and how they change (1971/1854, p. 48).

THEN AND NOW

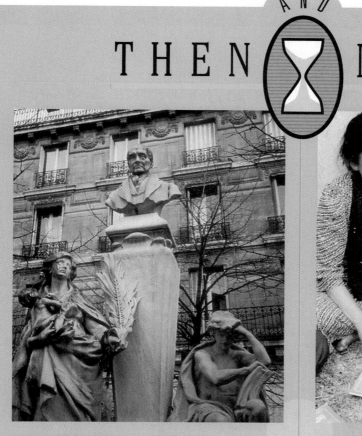

SOCIOLOGY: A GLOBAL SCIENCE

As it originated in the work of Auguste Comte, represented here by his statue in the Place de La Sorbonne in Paris, sociology was based on the study of history and philosophy. In the nineteenth century it was dominated by university scholars with a deep understanding of Western social thought. There were a few exceptions, such as W. E. B. Du Bois and the brilliant Muslim social thinker Ibn Khaldun, but for the most part the founders of sociology were European men.

Today sociology is far more diverse in every aspect. The photo of Manjula Giri shows a modern sociologist from a developing nation, Nepal, who is both a university-trained scholar and a dedicated social activist. Giri has written about the failure of revolution in Nepal to improve the conditions of rural women. In her own village she is using her sociological skills to help local women to develop a women's farming cooperative. She has also started literacy classes and is planning to expand her work to other villages in the region. Giri is an example of the scholar-activist, a dual role that is increasingly common throughout the poorer regions of the world.

The early sociologists tended to think in macrosociological terms. Their writing dealt with whole societies and how their special characteristics influence human behavior and social change. Karl Marx, for example, was both highly appreciative and extremely critical of the societies of his day. His analysis of those societies led him to predict major upheavals arising from conflicts between the owners of wealth and the impoverished workers. The French sociologist Émile Durkheim did not agree with Marx's prediction that violent revolutions would transform society. Durkheim's theories explain social change as resulting from population growth and from changes in the ways in which work and community life are organized. Still another pioneering European theorist, Max Weber, was the first to understand the overwhelming importance of bureaucratic forms of social organization in modern societies and to point out their increasing dominance in the lives of individuals. (See Box 1.1 for more about these founders of sociology.)

BOX 1.1   USING THE SOCIOLOGICAL IMAGINATION

Sociological Pioneers of the Nineteenth Century

Most sociologists would agree that the nineteenth-century social theorists who had the greatest and most lasting influence on the field were Karl Marx, Émile Durkheim, and Max Weber. All three applied the new concepts of sociology to gain an understanding of the immense changes occurring around them.

German-born Karl Marx (1818–1883) became a radical philosopher as a young man and was embroiled in numerous insurrections and attempts at revolution in Germany and France. Forced to flee Germany after the abortive European revolution of 1848, he lived and worked in England for the rest of his life. Often penniless, Marx worked for hours on end in the library of the British Museum, where he developed the social and economic theories that would have a major influence on sociological

Karl Marx

thought. His famous treatise *Capital* is a detailed study of the rise of capitalism as a dominant system of production. In this work and elsewhere, Marx set forth an extremely powerful theory to explain the transformations taking place as societies became more industrialized and urbanized. He believed that those transformations would inevitably end in a revolution in which the workers would overthrow capitalism, but he also felt that revolution could be hastened through political action.

Émile Durkheim (1858–1917) was the founder of scientific sociology in France. His books, among which the best known are *The Division of Labor in Society, Rules of the Sociological Method,* and *Suicide,* were pioneering examples of the use of comparative data to assess the directions and consequences of social change. The first university professor with a chair in the "social sciences," Durkheim was soon surrounded by a brilliant group of academic disciples who were deeply interested in understanding the vast changes that occurred in societies as they became more populous, more urbanized, and more technologically complex. In 1898 Durkheim and his colleagues established the first scientific journal in sociology, *L'Année sociologique* (*The Sociological Year*). This journal and much of Durkheim's own writing were among the first examples of the application of statistics to social issues. (See the discussion of suicide in Chapter 2.)

Max Weber (1864–1920) was a German historian, economist, and sociologist. Weber's life, like Durkheim's, spanned much of the second half of the nineteenth century and the early decades of the twentieth. Like the other early sociologists, therefore, Weber witnessed the tumultuous changes that were bringing down the old order. He saw monarchies tottering in the face of demands for democratic rule. He observed new industries and markets spanning the globe and linking formerly isolated peoples. He saw and described the rise of modern science and jurisprudence and modern ways of doing business. The growing tendency to apply rational decision-making procedures, rather than

Each of these three sociological pioneers based his theories on detailed reviews of the history of entire societies. Marx wrote about the origins of free enterprise and capitalism in the Western nations. Durkheim wrote about the transformations that occur as societies evolve from hunting and gathering to industrial production. Weber produced volumes about the organizations found in precapitalist and capitalist societies. But to become a science rather than merely a branch of philosophy, sociology had to build on the research of its founders. The twentieth century brought changes of such magnitude at every level of society that sociologists were in increasing demand. Their mission was to gain new information about the scope and meaning of social change.

THE RISE OF MODERN SOCIOLOGY

We credit the European social thinkers and philosophers with creating sociology, but nowhere did the new science find more fertile ground for development than in North America. By the beginning of the twentieth century, sociology was rapidly acquiring new adherents in the United States and Canada, partly owing to the influence of European sociologists like Marx and Durkheim, but even more because of the rapid social changes occurring in North America at the time. Waves of immigrants to cities and towns, the explosive growth of population and industry in the cities, race riots, strikes and labor strife, moral crusades against crime and vice and alcohol, the demand for women's suffrage—these and many other changes caused

Émile Durkheim

Max Weber

All three of these pioneers in sociology were scholars of great genius. They were also political activists. Marx, of course, was the most revolutionary of the three and devoted much of his energy to the international socialist movement. Durkheim was a lifelong socialist but was more moderate than Marx. While he took stands on many political issues, he did not devote himself to political activities. As a young man Weber had been involved in the movement to create a unified German nation, but as a mature scholar he developed a belief in "value-free" social science. A social scientist might draw research questions from personal political beliefs, but the research itself must apply scientific methods. This view, which Durkheim also shared, did much to advance sociology to the level of a social science rather than just a branch of philosophy.

merely relying on tradition, was for Weber a dramatic departure from the older ways of feudal societies and mercantile aristocracies. Weber compared many different societies to show how new forms of government and administration were evolving.

American sociology to take a new turn. There was increasing demand for knowledge about exactly what changes were occurring and who was affected by them. In North America, therefore, sociologists began to emphasize the quest for facts about changing social conditions—that is, the empirical investigation of social issues.

Empirical information refers to carefully gathered, unbiased data regarding social conditions and behavior. In general, modern sociology is distinguished by its relentless and systematic search for empirical data to answer questions about society. Journalists, for example, also seek the facts about social conditions, but they must cover many different events and situations and present them as "stories" that will attract their readers' interest. Because they usu-

ally cannot dwell on one subject very long, journalists frequently must content themselves with citing examples and quoting experts whose opinions may or may not be based on empirical evidence. In contrast, sociologists study a situation or phenomenon in more depth, and when they do not have enough facts they are likely to say, "That is an empirical question. Let's see what the research tells us, and if the answers are inconclusive we will do more research." Evidence based on measurable effects and outcomes is required before one can make an informed decision about an issue.

To use the sociological imagination to ask relevant questions and to seek answers to those questions backed by evidence that can be verified by others are among the

THE
PERSONAL CHALLENGE
Social Change and Sociological Careers

It is reasonable to wonder, as you work your way through this course, what the study of sociology can do for you. All introductory college courses are designed to acquaint students with fields that they may want to delve into further in the future. But perhaps more than other introductory courses, sociology can help you understand how society and social change are affecting your own life and the lives of people around you. Sociology is not unique in that sense, but it offers some powerful concepts and methods for understanding how the world is changing and with what consequences, personal and otherwise.

President Bill Clinton reads sociology. So does Speaker of the House Newt Gingrich. And so do thousands of leaders in business and government who want to get a handle on how current social changes may be altering the way they go about their professional and personal lives. Sociology is a growing field throughout the world. As the pace of global social change quickens—with new cities, new technologies, and new forms of cooperation and conflict appearing all the time—the contributions of sociological theory and practice become increasingly important.

If you should decide to major in sociology and pursue a career in this exciting field, you will join approximately 25,000 professional sociologists currently at work in North America. Of this number, the majority are employed in college teaching. Approximately one third work in careers in applied fields outside colleges and universities (Donow, 1990; Lyson & Squires, 1993). (For more information on careers in sociology, see the Appendix at the end of

the book.) Of course, you need not become a professional sociologist to find that knowledge of the field gives you great advantages in understanding society and social change.

Sociology is an excellent background for careers in law, business, public administration, health, and law enforcement, to name just some of the major professional areas that are voracious consumers of sociological information. Market research, which seeks to predict and shape consumer behavior, is a form of applied sociology. The allied field of opinion research, which charts changes in beliefs and attitudes, is also based almost entirely on sociological principles and methods. Professionals in the health care industry need to know about changes in diet and other consumptive behavior (smoking, exercise, and so on) among different population groups, and people with backgrounds in sociology are often asked to fill these information needs. Indeed, wherever major changes are occurring you will find sociologists at work along with other professionals, charting the changes and attempting to predict their consequences.

The study of sociology beyond the introductory level can lead to advanced skills in computation, data analysis, and statistics. Research experience in the field can greatly increase your ability to understand social situations and get along with people from different backgrounds. As the world continues to shrink and people from different cultures and societies come into greater contact with one another, sociological skills become increasingly valuable.

chief goals of modern sociology. Anyone can make assertions about society or about why people behave the way they do. "I think it's human nature to act selfishly, no matter what kind of education people have" is a common assertion that is not backed up by any solid evidence. As you read this book you will learn that to strengthen your sociological imagination you must learn how to apply evidence to your views and admit that your opinions can be modified by that evidence.

The Social Surveys. The empirical focus of American sociology began largely as an outgrowth of the reform movements of the late nineteenth and early twentieth centuries. During this period the nation had not yet recovered from the havoc created by the Civil War. Southern blacks were migrating to the more industrialized North in ever-increasing numbers, and at the same time millions of European immigrants were finding ill-paid jobs in the larger cities, where cheap labor was in great demand. By the turn of the century, therefore, the nation's cities were crowded with poor families for whom the promise of "gold in America" had become a tarnished dream. In this time of rapid social change, Americans continually debated the merits of social reform and proposed new solutions for pressing social issues. Some called for socialism, others for a return to the free market, or a ban on labor organizations, or an end to immigration, or the removal of black Americans to Africa. But where would the facts to be used in judging those ideas come from?

In order to gain empirical information about social conditions, dedicated individuals undertook numerous "social surveys." Jacob Riis's (1890) account of life on New York's Lower East Side; W. E. B. Du Bois's (1967/1899) survey of Philadelphia blacks; Emily Balch's depiction of living conditions among Slavic miners and steelworkers in the Pittsburgh area (1910); and Jane Addams's famous *Hull House Maps and Papers* (1895), which described the lives of her neighbors in Chicago's West Side slum area—these and other carefully documented surveys of the living conditions of people experiencing the effects of rapid industrialization and urbanization left an enduring mark on American sociology. Box 1.2 presents an excerpt from the landmark survey conducted by Du Bois, the first black sociologist to gain worldwide recognition. Du Bois helped direct sociological research to racial and social issues in minority communities, using empirical data to provide an objective account of the dismal social conditions of northern blacks at the turn of the century.

The Chicago School and Human Ecology. By the late 1920s the United States had become the world leader in sociology. The two great centers of American sociological research were the University of Chicago and Columbia University. At these universities and others influenced by them, two distinct approaches to the study of society evolved. The *Chicago school* emphasized the relationship between the individual and society, whereas the

major East Coast universities, which were more strongly influenced by European sociology, tended toward macro-level analyses of social structure and change.

The sociology department at the University of Chicago (the oldest in the nation) extended its influence to many other universities, especially in the Midwest, South, and West. At that time the department was under the leadership of Robert Park and his younger colleague Ernest Burgess. Park in particular is associated with the Chicago school. His main contribution was to develop an agenda for sociological research that used the city as a "social laboratory." Park favored an approach in which facts concerning what was actually occurring among people in their local communities (the micro and middle levels) would be collected within a broader theoretical framework. That framework attempted to link macro-level changes in society, such as industrialization and the growth of urban populations, to patterns of settlement in cities and to how people actually lived in cities.

In one of his essays on this subject, Park began with the idea that industrialization causes the breakdown of traditional "primary-group" attachments (those of family members, age-mates, or clans). After stating the probable relationship between the effects of industrialization and high rates of crime, Park asked several specific questions:

> What is the effect of ownership of property . . . on truancy, on divorce, and on crime?
>
> In what regions and classes are certain kinds of crime endemic?
>
> In what classes does divorce occur most frequently? What is the difference in this respect between farmers and, say, actors?
>
> To what extent in any given [ethnic] group . . . do parents and children live in the same world, speak the same language, and share the same ideas, and how far do the conditions found account for juvenile delinquency in that particular group? (1967/1925a, p. 22)

This set of research questions, of which those quoted here are a small sample, inspired and shaped the work of hundreds of sociologists who were influenced by the Chicago school. To this day Chicago remains the most systematically studied city in the United States, although similar research has been carried out in other large cities throughout the nation.

As you can see from the types of questions Park asked, the distinctive orientation of the Chicago school was its emphasis on the relationships among social order, social disorganization, and the distribution of populations in space and time. Park and Burgess called this approach **human ecology.** With many modifications, it remains an important, though not dominant, perspective in contemporary sociology.

Human ecology, as Park and others defined it, is the branch of sociology that is concerned with population

BOX 1.2 SOCIOLOGICAL METHODS

The Social Survey

W. E. B. Du Bois was one of the first American sociologists to publish highly factual and objective descriptions of life in American cities. An African American, Du Bois earned his doctorate in philosophy at Harvard before the turn of the century, when sociology was still regarded as a subfield of that discipline. But, as can be seen in this excerpt from his account of black life in Philadelphia about a century ago, Du Bois was able to sharpen his arguments about the effects of racial discrimination with simple but telling statistics.

> For a group of freedmen the question of economic survival is the most pressing of all questions; the problem as to how, under the circumstances of modern life, any group of people can earn a decent living, so as to maintain their standard of life, is not always easy to answer. But when the question is complicated by the fact that the group has a low degree of efficiency on account of previous training; is in competition with well-trained, eager and often ruthless competitors; is more or less handicapped by . . . discrimination; and finally, is seeking not merely to maintain a standard of living but steadily to raise it to a higher plane—such a situation presents baffling problems to the sociologist. . . .

W. E. B. Du Bois

> And yet this is the situation of the Negro in Philadelphia; he is trying to better his condition; is seeking to rise; for this end his first need is work of a character to engage his best talents, and remunerative enough for him to support a home and train up his children well. The competition in a large city is fierce,

A scene from the Philadelphia neighborhoods described by Du Bois around the turn of the century.

growth and change. In particular, it seeks to discover how populations organize themselves to survive and prosper. Human ecologists are interested in how groups that are organized in different ways compete and cooperate. They also look for forms of social organization that may emerge as a group adjusts to life in new surroundings.

A key concept for human ecologists is *community*. There are many ways of defining this term, just as there are many ways of defining most of the central concepts of sociology. From the ecological perspective, however, the term *community* usually refers to a population that carries out major life functions (e.g., birth, marriage, death) within a and it is difficult for any poor people to succeed. The Negro, however, has two especial difficulties: his training as a slave and freedman has not been such as make the average of the race as efficient and reliable workmen as the average native American or as many foreign immigrants. The Negro is, as a rule, willing, honest and good-natured; but he is also, as a rule, careless, unreliable and unsteady. This is without doubt to be expected in a people who for generations have been trained to shirk work; but an historical excuse counts for little in the whirl and battle of breadwinning. Of course, there are large exceptions to this average rule; there are many Negroes who are as bright, talented and reliable as any class of workmen, and who in untrammeled competition would soon rise high in the economic scale, and thus by the law of the survival of the fittest we should soon have left at the bottom those inefficient and lazy drones who did not deserve a better fate. However, in the realm of social phenomena the law of survival is greatly modified by human choice, wish, whim and prejudice. And consequently one never knows when one sees a social outcast how far this failure to survive is due to the deficiencies of the individual, and how far to the accidents or injustice of his environment. This is especially the case with the Negro. Every one knows that in a city like Philadelphia a Negro does not have the same chance to exercise his ability or secure work according to his talents as a white man. Just how far this is so we shall discuss later; now it is sufficient to say in general that the sorts of work open to Negroes are not only restricted by their own lack of training but also by discrimination against them on account of their race; that their economic rise is not only hindered by their present poverty, but also by a widespread inclination to shut against them many doors of advancement. . . .

What has thus far been the result of this complicated situation? What do the mass of the Negroes of the city at present do for a living, and how successful are they in those lines? And in so far as they are successful, what have they accomplished, and where they are inefficient in their present sphere of work, what is the cause and remedy? These are the questions before us, and we proceed to answer the first

in this chapter, taking the occupations of the Negroes of the Seventh Ward first. . . .

Of the 257 boys between the ages of ten and twenty, who were regularly at work in 1896, 39 per cent were porters and errand boys; 25.5 per cent were servants; 16 per cent were common laborers, and 19.5 per cent had miscellaneous employment. The occupations in detail are as follows:

Total population, males 10 to 20	651	
Engaged in gainful occupations	257	
Porters and errand boys	100	39.0%
Servants	66	25.5
Common laborers	40	16.0
Miscellaneous employment		
Teamsters	7	
Apprentices	6	
Bootblacks	6	
Drivers	5	
Newsboys	5	
Peddlers	4	
Typesetters	3	
Actors	2	
Bricklayers	2	
Hostlers	2	51 19.5
Typists	2	
Barber	1	
Bartender	1	
Bookbinder	1	
Factory hand	1	
Rubber worker	1	
Sailor	1	
Shoemaker	1	
	257	100%

Source: Du Bois, 1967/1899, pp. 97–99.

Note: This simple table includes much useful information, but modern tables present data more efficiently. See Chapter 2 for a detailed discussion of the presentation of data in tables.

particular territory. Human ecology does not assume that there will ever be a "steady state" or an end to the process of change in human communities. Instead, it attempts to trace the change and document its consequences for the social environment. What happens when newcomers "invade" a community? In what way are local gangs a response

to recent changes in population or in the ability of members of a community to compete for jobs? Not only do populations change, but people's preferences and behaviors also continually change. So do the technologies for producing the goods and services we want. As a result, our ways of getting a living, our modes of transportation, and our choices of leisure activities create constant change, not just in communities but in entire societies.

The Chicago school became known for this "ecological" approach, the idea that the study of human society should begin with empirical questions about population size, the distribution of populations over territories, and the like. The human ecologists recognized that there are many other processes by which society is shaped, but their most important contribution to the discipline of sociology was to include the processes by which populations change and communities are formed.

Modern ecological theories also consider the relations between humans and their natural environment. We will see that the way people earn their livelihood, the resources they use, the energy they consume, and their efforts to control pollution all have far-reaching consequences not only for their own lives but also for the society in which they live. These patterns of use and consumption also have an increasing impact on the entire planet—so much so that ecological problems are becoming an ever more important area of sociological research. (See Figure 1.1.)

MAJOR SOCIOLOGICAL PERSPECTIVES

Sociological *perspectives* are based on different problems of human society, such as the problem of population size, the problem of conflict between populations, the problem of how people become part of a society, and other issues that we will encounter throughout this book. Although human ecology remains an important sociological perspective, it is by no means the only one employed by modern sociologists. Other perspectives, to which we now turn, guide empirical description and help explain social stability and social change.

INTERACTIONISM

Interactionism is the sociological perspective that views social order and social change as resulting from all the immense variety of repeated interactions among individuals and groups. Families, committees, corporations, armies, entire societies—indeed, all the social forms we can think of—are a result of interpersonal behavior in which people communicate, give and take, share, compete, and so on. If there were no exchange of goods, information, love, and all the rest—that is, if there were no interaction among people—obviously there could be no social life at all.

The interactionist perspective usually generates analyses of social life at the micro level of interpersonal relationships, but it does not limit itself to the micro level of social reality. It also looks at how middle- and macro-level phenomena result from micro-level behaviors or, conversely, how middle- and macro-level influences shape the interactions among individuals. From the interactionist perspective, for example, a family is a product of interactions among a set of individuals who define themselves as family members. But each person's understanding of how a family ought to behave is a product of middle- and macro-level forces: religious teachings about family life, laws dealing with education or child support, and so on. And these are always changing. You may have experienced the consequences of changing values that cause older and younger family members to feel differently about such issues as whether a couple should live together before marrying. In sum, the interactionist perspective insists that we look carefully at how individuals interact, how they interpret their own and other people's actions, and the consequences of those actions for the larger social group (Blumer, 1969b; Frank, 1988).

The general framework of interactionism contains at least two major and quite different sets of issues. One set has to do with the problems of exchange and choice: How can social order exist and groups or societies maintain stability when people have selfish motives for being in groups—that is, when they are seeking to gain as much personal advantage as they can? The second set of issues involves how people actually manage to communicate their values and how they arrive at mutual understandings. Research and explanations of the first problem fall under the heading of "rational choice" (or exchange theory), while the second issue is addressed by the study of "symbolic interaction." In recent years these two areas of inquiry have emerged as quite different yet increasingly related aspects of the study of interaction.

Rational Choice—The Sociological View. Adam Smith, whose famous work *The Wealth of Nations* (1910/1776) became the basis for most subsequent economic thought, believed that individuals always seek to maximize their pleasure and minimize their pain. If over time they are allowed to make the best possible choices for themselves, they will also produce an affluent and just society. They will serve others, even when they are unaware that they are doing so, in order to increase their own benefit. They will choose a constitution and a government that protects their property and their right to engage in trade. They will seek the government's protection against those who would infringe on their rights or attempt to dominate them, but the government need do little more than protect them and allow them to make choices based on their own reasoning.

You may have already encountered this theory, known as *utilitarianism,* in an economics or political science course. In sociology it is applied to a variety of issues. Often this rational-choice view of interaction is referred to as *exchange theory* because it focuses on what people seem to be getting out of their interactions and what they in turn are contributing to the relationship or to the larger group. In every interaction something is being exchanged. It may be

FIGURE 1.1

MAPPING SOCIAL CHANGE

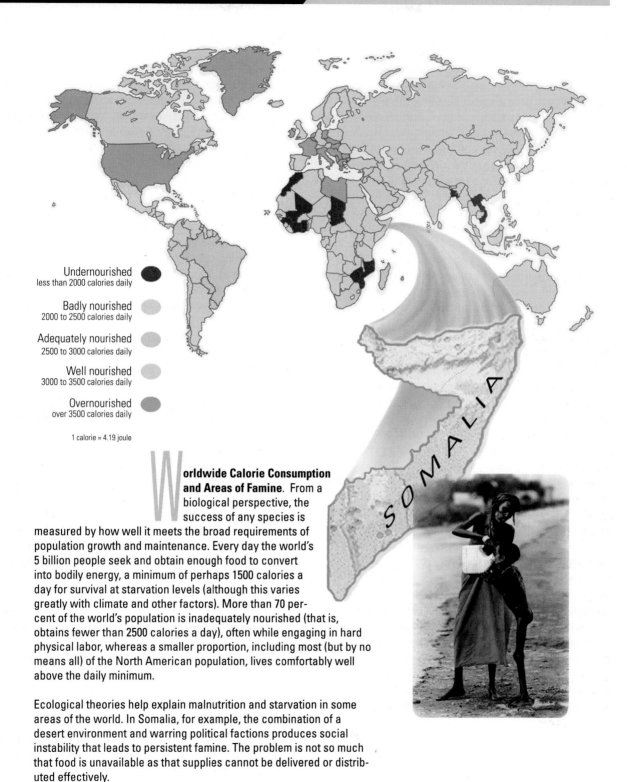

Undernourished
less than 2000 calories daily

Badly nourished
2000 to 2500 calories daily

Adequately nourished
2500 to 3000 calories daily

Well nourished
3000 to 3500 calories daily

Overnourished
over 3500 calories daily

1 calorie = 4.19 joule

Worldwide Calorie Consumption and Areas of Famine. From a biological perspective, the success of any species is measured by how well it meets the broad requirements of population growth and maintenance. Every day the world's 5 billion people seek and obtain enough food to convert into bodily energy, a minimum of perhaps 1500 calories a day for survival at starvation levels (although this varies greatly with climate and other factors). More than 70 percent of the world's population is inadequately nourished (that is, obtains fewer than 2500 calories a day), often while engaging in hard physical labor, whereas a smaller proportion, including most (but by no means all) of the North American population, lives comfortably well above the daily minimum.

Ecological theories help explain malnutrition and starvation in some areas of the world. In Somalia, for example, the combination of a desert environment and warring political factions produces social instability that leads to persistent famine. The problem is not so much that food is unavailable as that supplies cannot be delivered or distributed effectively.

time or attention, friendship, material values (e.g., wages or possessions), or less easily calculated values like esteem or allegiance. The larger the number of interacting members, the more complex the types of exchanges that occur among them. When people perceive an interaction as being one-way, they begin to feel that they are being exploited or treated unfairly and will usually leave the relationship or quit the group (Homans, 1961). In industry, for example, if workers feel that they are not being paid enough for their work they may form a union, bargain collectively with the bosses, or even go on strike. But in doing so each worker will weigh potential benefits against potential losses—losses in pay, in esteem, in friendship, and so forth. The choices are not always easy, nor are the motivations always obvious. When many values are involved, the rational calculation of benefits and costs becomes even more difficult.

Rational-choice models of behavior prompt us to look at *patterns* of behavior to see how they conform to and depart from normal expectations of personal profit and loss. But those models do not always identify the underlying values. How we learn what to value in the first place, how we communicate our choices and intentions, how we learn new values through interaction—all are subjects that require other concepts besides those found in rational-choice theories of behavior. Such questions lead us toward research on how human interaction is actually carried out and understood by people in their daily lives.

Symbolic Interactionism. When we make choices about our interactions with other people, we may be said to be acting rationally. But there are likely to be other forces shaping our behavior as well. For example, you may select a particular course because the instructor is rumored to be good. But what does "good" mean—clear and well organized? an easy grader? friendly? humorous? The dimensions of a choice can be complicated, and we may not be aware of everything that goes into our decisions. For example, you may, without realizing it, choose a course as much to be with certain other people as to be in that particular course. Our choices tell other people about us: what we like, what we want to become, and so on. Indeed, the way people dress, the way they carry themselves (body language), the way they speak to each other, and the gestures they make convey a great deal of information that is not always intentional or expressed in speech. There are levels of communication that give information without speaking it, or speak one thing and mean another. But words are of great importance too, and the content of communication is made explicit in words and sentences. Sociologists refer to all these aspects of behavior as *symbolic interaction.* From the symbolic-interactionist perspective, "society itself tends to be seen as a mosaic of little scenes and dramas in which people make indications to themselves and others, respond to those indications, align their actions, and so build identities and social structures" (Rock, 1985, p. 844; see also Hughes, 1958; Goffman, 1959).

Symbolic interactionists call attention to how social life is "constructed" through the mundane acts of social communication. For example, in all the choices students make—their joining of friendship groups, their learning of the informal rules of the school, their challenging and breaking of those rules—the social order of student society, or "college culture," is actually "constructed." Erving Goffman, whose work was mentioned earlier, is known for his research on these processes. Goffman applied the symbolic-interactionist perspective to the study of everyday interactions like rituals of greeting and departure, to daily life in asylums and gambling houses, and to behavior in streets and public places. His work examines how people behave in social situations and how their "performances" are rated by others.

The power of symbolic interactionism lies in its ability to generate theories about how people learn to play certain roles and how those roles are used in the social construction of groups and organizations. However, if we want to think sociologically about more complex phenomena, such as the rise of bureaucratic organizations or the reasons that some societies experience revolutions, we also need the concepts developed by two other perspectives: functionalism and conflict theory.

FUNCTIONALISM

Is society simply the sum total of countless micro-level exchanges and communicative interactions, or do the organizations within a society have properties independent of the actions of individuals? When we speak of the family, the army, the corporation, or the laboratory, we generally have in mind an entity marked by certain specific functions, tasks, and types of behavior. The army requires that its members learn to engage in armed combat, even if that is not what they will be doing most of the time. The family requires that its members behave in nurturant ways toward one another. The farm requires that those who run it know how to plant and harvest. Individual interactions may determine how well a given person performs these various tasks, but it is the larger organization—the army, the family, the farm—that establishes specific ways of behaving, of doing the work of that organization, which the individual must master. In this sense the organization, which exists longer than any of its members, has its own existence.

The **functionalist** perspective in sociology asks how society manages to carry out the functions it must perform in order to maintain social order, feed large masses of people each day, defend itself against attackers, produce the next generation, and so on. From this perspective the many groups and organizations that make up a society form the structure of human society. This social structure is a complex system designed to carry out the essential functions of human life. The function of the family, for example, is to raise and train a new generation to replace the old; the function of the military is to defend the society; the function of schools is to teach the next generation the beliefs and skills they will need to maintain the society in the future; and a major function of religion is to develop shared ideas of morality.

When a society is functioning well, all its major parts are said to be "well integrated" and in equilibrium. But periods of rapid social change can throw social structures out of equilibrium. Entire ways of life can lose their purpose or function. When that happens, the various structures of society can become poorly integrated, and what were formerly useful functions can become "dysfunctional."

Consider an example. In agrarian societies, in which most people work the land, families typically include three generations, with many members in each generation all living close to one another. Labor is in great demand; many hands are needed where there are no machines to perform work in fields and barnyards and granaries. The emphasis on early marriage and large numbers of children found in the agrarian family is highly functional for such a society. But when the society industrializes and its agriculture becomes mechanized, families may continue to produce large numbers of children even though the demand for farmhands has decreased. When they grow up, those children may migrate to towns and cities. The migrants are

likely to continue to value large families and to have numerous children, but if there are a limited number of jobs in the cities they may join the ranks of the unemployed and their children may grow up in poverty. In this situation the family can be said to be poorly integrated with the needs of the society; the value of large family size has become dysfunctional: It no longer contributes to the well-being of groups or individuals.

CONFLICT THEORY

A major flaw in the functionalist perspective is the fact that we have rarely seen anything approaching equilibrium in human societies. Conflict and strife appear to be as basic to society as harmony, integration, and smooth functioning. In our century alone, two world wars and many civil wars have disrupted the lives of millions of people. Almost as devastating was the Great Depression of the 1930s, the most severe economic slump in modern history. Worst of all were the nightmares of the Nazi Holocaust and the purges of Stalinist Russia, in which more than 20 million people were exterminated.

The world wars, the Depression, and the Holocaust shocked and demoralized the entire world. They also called into question the optimism of the nineteenth- and early

In Sarajevo, the physical and emotional scars of war will last long after the cessation of hostilities. As wars become more destructive, the study of social conflict and its solutions takes on even greater urgency.

twentieth-century social philosophers, many of whom believed in the promise of progress through modern science and technology. Between 1914 and the end of World War II, modern ideas and technologies were used for horrible purposes often enough to disillusion all but the most ardent optimists. Bewildered intellectuals and political leaders turned to sociology to find some explanation for those horrors.

One explanation was provided by Marxian theory. According to Marx, the cause of conflict in modern times could be found in the rise of capitalism. Under capitalism, forms of exploitation and domination spread. For example, in the early period of industrial capitalism workers were forced to work twelve hours a day, six days a week; in less developed areas of the world large populations were virtually enslaved by the new colonial powers.

At the heart of capitalism, for Marx, is conflict among people in different economic classes, especially between those who control wealth and power and those who do not. Marx argued that the division of people in a society into different classes, defined by how they make a living, always produces conflict. Under capitalism this conflict occurs between the owners of factories and the workers. Marx believed that class conflict would eventually destroy or at least vastly modify capitalism. His theory is at the heart of what has come to be known as the **conflict perspective.**

In the 1960s, when protests against racism and segregation, the Vietnam War, pollution of the environment, and discrimination against women each became the focus of a major social movement, the conflict perspective became more prominent. It clearly was not possible to explain the rapid appearance of major social movements with theories that emphasized how the social system would function if it were in a state of equilibrium. Even Marxian theory did not do a very good job of predicting the protest movements of the 1960s or their effects on American society. The environ-

mental movement and the women's movement, for example, were not based on economic inequalities alone, nor were the people who joined them necessarily exploited workers. Sociologists studying the role of conflict in social change therefore had to go beyond the Marxian view. Many turned to the writings of the German sociologist Georg Simmel (1904), who argued that conflict is necessary as a basis for the formation of alliances. According to Simmel, conflict is one means whereby a "web of group affiliations" is constructed. The continual shifting of alliances within this web of social groups can help explain who becomes involved in social movements and how much power those movements are able to acquire.

The concept of *power* holds a central place in conflict theory. From the functionalist perspective, society holds together because its members share the same basic beliefs about how people should behave. Conflict theorists point out that the role of power is just as important as the influence of shared beliefs in explaining why society does not disintegrate into chaos. Power is the ability of an individual or group to change the behavior of others. A nation's government, as we will see in Chapter 4, usually controls the use of force (a form of power) to maintain social order. For sociologists who study conflict and power, the important questions are who benefits from the exercise of power and who loses. For example, when the government intervenes in a strike and obliges workers to return to their jobs, does the public at large benefit or does the corporation against which the workers were striking? And what about the workers themselves? What do they gain or lose? Such questions are central to conflict theory today (Gramsci, 1971).

THE MULTIDIMENSIONAL VIEW OF SOCIETY
Each of the sociological perspectives leads to different questions and different kinds of observations about social

STUDY CHART Major Sociological Perspectives

	DESCRIPTION	GENERATES QUESTIONS ABOUT...	APPLICATIONS
Interactionism	Studies how social structures are created in the course of human interaction.	How people behave in intimate groups; how symbols and communication shape perceptions; how social roles are learned and society is "constructed" through interaction.	Educational practice, courtroom procedure, therapy.
Functionalism	Asks how societies carry out the functions they must perform; views the structures of society as a system designed to carry out those functions.	How society is structured and how social structures work together as a system to perform the major functions of society.	Study of formal organizations, development of social policies, management science.
Conflict Theory	Holds that power is just as important as shared values in holding society together; conflict is also responsible for social change.	How power affects the distribution of scarce resources and how conflict changes society.	Study of politics, social movements, corporate power structures.

(PERSPECTIVE)

BOX 1.3 USING THE SOCIOLOGICAL IMAGINATION

Perspectives on Pledging

It's a spring ritual on many campuses. At colleges and universities where the fraternity-sorority, or "Greek," system is not strong, it may affect only a few people. At colleges with strong fraternities and sororities, hundreds of freshman or sophomore pledges may be required to do outrageous things like shine their fraternity brothers' shoes in the student union or chauffeur their sorority sisters wherever they wish to be taken. Although pledging rituals become controversial when pledges are killed or injured in cruel hazing incidents, usually the only damage is to the pledge's pride. Most people take the annual rituals of pledging and hazing for granted. For the sociologist, however, pledging has meanings that are revealed through application of the basic sociological perspectives.

From a functionalist perspective, pledging accomplishes the goal of building high levels of group

solidarity and cohesion. The function of pledging, in this view, is to produce loyal "brothers" and "sisters" who know their roles in the organization—the fraternity or sorority to which they have pledged. The abuse heaped on pledges by upperclassmen brings them closer together. Adversity forges tight bonds among the members of the entering class. In the final rituals of the pledge season, the animosities between the pledge class and the older members will be smoothed over. All will share the secret knowledge of the group and will have sworn allegiance to one another and to the organization.

The interactionist perspective would focus on the actual behavior of the pledges and their tormentors. An interactionist would question whether all pledges behave the same way under pressure. What about those who try to maintain their individuality? What about the upperclassmen who don't believe in the rituals as strongly as others do? Such differences come out in subtle (and sometimes not so subtle) exchanges among the people involved as they seek to maintain their own identities and negotiate their way through the pledging rituals. These interactions point to the way the group actually behaves, rather than to the way it might ideally function if everyone had the same experience.

From a conflict perspective, pledging is a way in which the Greek organizations build solidarity in their members. This resembles the functionalist view, but a conflict theorist might go further and seek evidence of conflict between the fraternity or sorority population and other segments of the college community. Such evidence would indicate that the solidarity of the Greek groups detracts from the solidarity of the university community by introducing competing allegiances and attachments. Moreover, a conflict theorist would predict that allegiances to Greek organizations might reinforce other forms of cleavage on campus, such as those based on wealth or on racial and religious characteristics.

Each of these sociological perspectives could produce much more analysis of pledging and similar rituals. Behind the commonplace activities of daily life there are often many layers of social meaning. No single perspective is adequate to explain those meanings fully. We hope to show throughout this book that while there is often much overlap among the three major perspectives, the ability to apply all three can greatly enhance our understanding of social phenomena.

life. From the ecological perspective come questions about how populations can exist and flourish in various natural and social environments. From the interactionist perspective come questions about how people get along and behave in groups and organizations of all kinds. Functionalism asks questions about how society is structured and how it works as a social system. And the conflict perspective asks how power is used to maintain order and how conflict changes society. These different perspectives developed as

sociologists asked different questions about society. In contemporary sociology each continues to stimulate relatively distinct research based on the types of questions being asked. Yet a great deal of research combines the insights of different perspectives in ways that vastly increase the power of the resulting analysis. The study chart on page 9 summarizes the major sociological perspectives and the kinds of questions they ask. Box 1.3 presents an example of the multidimensional view of society.

ART AND THE SOCIOLOGICAL EYE

Drawing and painting give us our earliest evidence of human beings' desire to understand social life and to communicate that understanding to others. For instance, although we cannot know in much detail how the preliterate cave dwellers of southern Europe and northern Africa lived during the late Ice Age more than 10,000 years ago, cave paintings like the hunting scene shown here can give us glimpses into the way prehistoric humans felt about their lives. Note how carefully the artist rendered this typical hunting scene, with special attention to the placement of the hunters before the onrushing antelope. In the very choice of the hunting subject, the ancient artist is communicating a message about what was uppermost in the minds of our early ancestors.

The art of any of the world's peoples, past or present, can likewise be "read" for evidence of how people organize their society, for the nature of interpersonal relationships, for what they value as sacred or simply enjoyable, and for what they despise. Thus, in the painted limestone carving of the Egyptian prince Rahotep and his wife Nofret, probably executed by an official artist of the pharaoh in about 2610 B.C., we see striking evidence that the rulers of one of the world's first civilizations could have either dark or light skin. Outward features such as skin color or hair must not have had the meaning they do in many societies today. And look at how the couple's dress reveals differences in what must have been considered proper appearance for men and

Amphora *by Exekias, about 530 B.C. Black figure amphora with Achilles and Ajax playing dice.*

Cave painting from Los Caballos, Spain.

Prince Rahotep and His Wife Nofret, *artist unknown, about 2610 B.C. Painted limestone, height 47".*

women of their social standing. Her breasts are covered, but his chest is bare; his only ornaments are a thin necklace and an equally thin mustache, whereas her hair and jewelry are far more elaborate.

In the same manner, the art of people with histories and ways of life that we may think of as far different from our own can show how much experience we actually share. The figures painted on a vase more than 2,500 years ago demonstrate that soldiers in ancient Greece often had time on their hands just as modern soldiers do. Like their modern counterparts, they also enjoyed passing the time by gambling. Similarly, we can "read" the meaning of the soapstone carving by an Eskimo artist as a statement about the universal quality of parental love and nurturing, just as the scene from an eighteenth-century Japanese woodcut can be read as evidence of long-standing traditions of male dominance and female subordination in Japanese society.

One of the goals of this book is to help you train your sociological eye, to help you learn to interpret the events around you and discover what they convey about social organization and social interaction. As in any introductory course, you will be learning to apply many concepts. And because the concepts and theories of sociology pertain almost exclusively to the study of societies and how they change, the visual material in each chapter is used as a way of applying sociological ideas and highlighting major areas of social change.

Consider three more examples. The famous wedding portrait painted by Jan van Eyck in 1434 can be interpreted at a number of levels. On the surface it is simply a painting of a newly married bride and groom, people of obvious wealth and social standing, in their bedroom. But at a deeper level of meaning, the painting is a study in the symbols associated with marriage in Europe during the fifteenth century. The wedding bed was understood as a symbol of marital fidelity, the dog as a symbol of trust; and the couple have removed their shoes to show that they stand on the holy ground of matrimony. These and other symbols in the painting could not be understood, however, without some study of the way people of that time thought about marriage and its relationship to religious belief.

Portrait of the Actor Sawamura Sojuro, *by Katsukawa Shunsho, 1781. Woodcut on paper, 14' x 10".*

Mother and Child, *by Ennutsiak of Frobisher Bay, date unknown. Green stone and red paint or ink, 6.4 x 4.4 x 8.3 cm.*

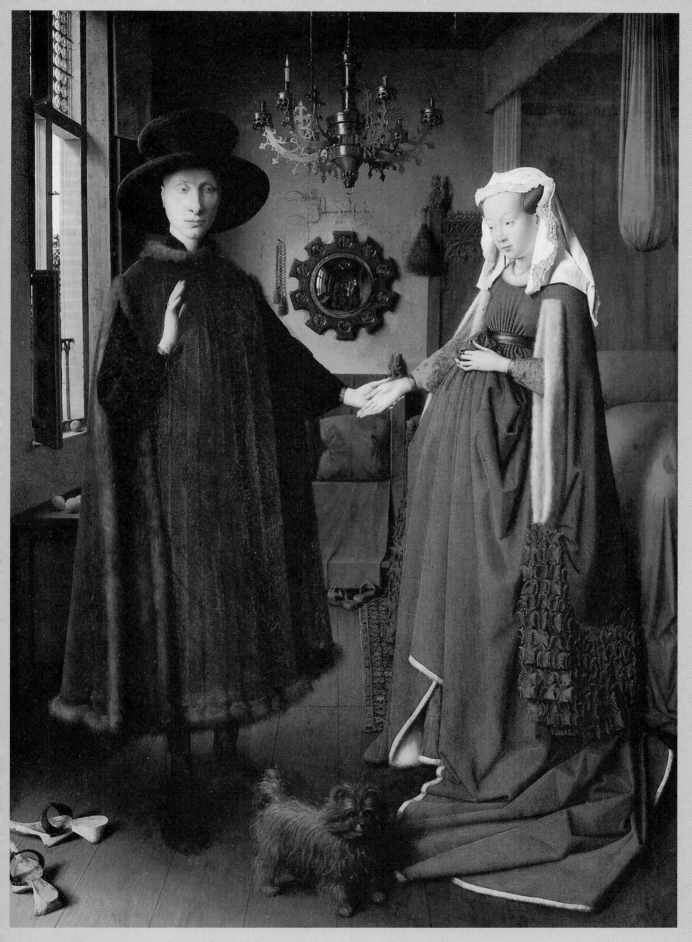

The Marriage of Giovanni and Giovanna Canami, *by Jan van Eyck, 1434. Panel, 33" x 22½".*

Peasant Wedding, *by Pieter Bruegel the Elder, about 1565. Panel 45" x 64".*

The Gleaners, *by François Millet, 1848. Oil on canvas, 21" x 26".*

Similarly, if we seek visual evidence about the lives of the peasants who till the soil throughout much of the world, we can find it in works like Pieter Bruegel's 1565 painting of the rough pleasures at a peasant wedding and François Millet's moving depiction, nearly three centuries later, of women gleaning bits of fallen grain after the harvest. It would be difficult to empathize with the experience of peasants or of people from any social world other than our own without the ability to recognize the sociological implications of paintings, photographs, and the actual scenes we witness firsthand in daily life.

But let us not confuse sociology and fine art. These artists were not sociologists, nor were they necessarily seeking to make points about society and social change. Their goals were to use the forms of everyday life to create something that would please them and their patrons, to capture the nuances of shape and form, to convey the emotional quality of a scene. The task of the sociologist is to read their art for its social meaning, without detracting from the magic that makes art beautiful and timeless.

It is important to be aware that there is no single, unifying set of theories explaining how societies are formed or why they change. The major perspectives and the social scientists who develop them often seek to explain different aspects of social phenomena. Throughout this book we will show how current sociological research uses one or more of these perspectives to address major controversies over social theory. For example, functionalists often argue that too much equality in wages or salaries deprives people of the incentive to work hard to get ahead. Conflict theory suggests, conversely, that too much inequality causes civil strife (Davis & Moore, 1945). In later chapters we will show how current research addresses this and other controversies generated by the different sociological perspectives.

Social life encompasses such a vast array of phenomena that it is doubtful whether a single set of theories will ever explain everything we seek to know about social order and change. As sociologist Joseph Gusfield warns, anyone waiting for a social-scientific Einstein is not merely waiting for a train that will not arrive but is in the wrong station (Bernstein, 1988, p. A14). Nevertheless, the student who can grasp and apply the major sociological perspectives will be armed with a powerful set of tools with which to deepen his or her understanding of how and why the social world is changing. Together, the sociological imagination and the basic sociological perspectives can help you see beyond the headlines and gain greater insight into events occurring in the world today (see Box 1.4). You will also be better equipped to understand their relevance to your own life, both now and in the future. Perhaps you will be motivated to choose a career in sociology.

BOX 1.4 GLOBAL SOCIAL CHANGE

Sociologists in Global Focus

The International Sociological Association meets in world session every 4 years, usually in a major regional capital. Its last world conference was held in Delhi, India, in 1991. Hundreds of professional sociologists from all over the world convened to discuss their common research interests and the key trends producing change in their societies. Two of the most important subjects discussed in research papers presented at the conference were the dramatic changes occurring in the former Soviet-dominated nations of Europe and Asia, and the increasingly urgent problems of world population growth. Almost every subject covered in this book, however, was represented in papers presented at the conference.

The sociologists who attend the world conferences are among the most prominent social scientists in their nations. But they represent hundreds of other people with sociological training. Sociologists who conduct academic research are the most visible segment of the field. Throughout the world, however, even more sociologists work for government agencies, planning and evaluation firms, market research companies, public opinion research corporations, and many other organizations.

I. Ibrahiem is a sociologist who uses his training to help new nations develop their political institutions. A native of Egypt and a United Nations staff professional, he has been assigned to help conduct an election in the Spanish Sahara, a territory in Africa the size of California located to the south of Morocco and north of Mauritania. Some members of this desert region's sparse population (approximately 48,000 at the last census) wish to be independent of Morocco while others wish to see their territory annexed to that kingdom. Ibrahiem and his UN colleagues are monitoring the registration of voters (most of whom arrive at their field stations by camel), a task that requires delicate negotiations with all the factions of this vast war-weary region of sandstorms and intense heat.

Ibrahiem uses his sociological training in Egypt and the United States to better understand the cultures of the nomadic desert bands he works with. As a Muslim he knows that the very traditional and orthodox desert Muslims must be addressed with particular care when matters of gender and age are involved. And because women may register and vote, this is a political as well as a social issue.

Ibrahiem specializes in translating the many varieties of desert Arabic. His work uses sociology every day. Although he will probably not become a college or university sociologist, he is writing a doctoral thesis because he loves the subject and because the advanced degree will enhance his professional stature in the international community. In every nation of the world today there are people like him who apply their sociological imaginations and training to solving the problems of a changing world.

SUMMARY

THINK ABOUT IT CRITICALLY

If asked about their problems by social researchers, many people will blame themselves for such problems as divorce, lack of money, lack of education, unemployment, or lack of direction in life. Most often they will conclude that their failures result from faults in their character. Maybe they are right. Are people not responsible for their fate? When sociologists point to the role of environmental conditions, do they excuse individual failings?

Sociology is the scientific study of human societies and of human behavior in the groups that make up a society. It is concerned with how *social conditions* influence our lives as individuals. The ability to see the world from this point of view has been described as the *sociological imagination.*

Sociologists study social behavior at three levels of complexity. *Micro-level* sociology deals with behaviors that occur at the level of the individual and immediate others. The *middle level* of sociological observation is concerned with how the social structures in which people participate actually shape their lives. *Macro-level* studies attempt to explain the social processes that influence populations, social classes, and entire societies.

The scientific discoveries of the seventeenth century led to the rise of the idea of progress, as opposed to the notion of human helplessness in the face of divine Providence. In the eighteenth century, revolutions in Europe and North America completely changed the social order and gave rise to new perspectives on human social life. Out of this period of social and intellectual ferment came the idea of creating a science of human society. Sociology, as the new science was called, developed in Europe in the nineteenth century. During that formative period a number of outstanding sociologists shaped and refined the new discipline. Among them were Karl Marx, Émile Durkheim, and Max Weber.

In the twentieth century sociology developed most rapidly in North America, spurred by the need for empirical information concerning social conditions. Numerous "social surveys" were conducted around the turn of the century, and by the late 1920s two distinct approaches to the study of society had evolved at American universities. The "Chicago school" focused on the relationship between the individual and society, whereas the major East Coast universities leaned toward macro-level analysis.

Under the leadership of Robert Park and Ernest Burgess, the Chicago school developed the approach known as *human ecology.* This perspective emphasizes the relationships among social order, social disorganization, and the distribution of populations in space and time. Fundamental to this approach is the concept of community, meaning a population that carries out major functions within a particular territory.

Modern sociologists employ other basic perspectives besides human ecology. *Interactionism* is a perspective that views social order and social change as resulting from all the repeated interactions among individuals and groups. One version of this approach is rational-choice or exchange theory, which focuses on what people seem to be getting out of their interactions and what they contribute to them. Another is the symbolic-interactionist perspective, which studies how social structures are actually created in the course of human interaction.

Functionalism, in contrast, is concerned primarily with the large-scale structures of society; it asks how those structures enable society to carry out its basic functions. In the decades since World War II this perspective has been strongly challenged by *conflict theory,* which emphasizes the role of conflict and power in explaining not only why societies change but also why they hold together.

None of the major sociological perspectives is fully independent of the others. Each emphasizes different questions and different observations about social life. Used in combination, they greatly increase our ability to understand and explain almost any aspect of human society.

CRITICAL RESPONSE

Sociology does not excuse individual failure. It does, however, focus on the larger social forces that shape people's fates. People are indeed responsible for their own lives, but often they do not realize how much the odds are stacked against them or, conversely, the extent to which their social position creates advantages for them and their offspring. The sociological imagination helps one understand the complex interrelationships between individual actions and social forces.

GLOSSARY

social conditions: the realities of the life we create together as social beings. (p. 6)

sociological imagination: according to C. Wright Mills, the ability to see how social conditions affect our lives. (p. 6)

sociology: the scientific study of human societies and human behavior in the groups that make up a society. (p. 7)

micro-level sociology: an approach to the study of society that focuses on patterns of social interaction at the individual level. (p. 8)

macro-level sociology: an approach to the study of society that focuses on the major structures and institutions of society. (p. 8)

middle-level sociology: an approach to the study of society that focuses on relationships between social structures and the individual. (p. 9)

scientific method: the process by which theories and explanations are constructed through repeated observation and careful description. (p. 10)

human ecology: a sociological perspective that emphasizes the relationships among social order, social disorganization, and the distribution of populations in time and space. (p. 15)

interactionism: a sociological perspective that views social order and social change as resulting from all the repeated interactions among individuals and groups. (p. 18)

functionalism: a sociological perspective that focuses on the ways in which a complex pattern of social structures and arrangements contributes to social order. (p. 20)

conflict theory: a sociological perspective that emphasizes the role of conflict and power in society. (p. 22)

WHERE TO FIND IT

BOOKS

The Sociological Imagination (C. Wright Mills; Oxford University Press, 1959). Still the best and most passionate statement of what the sociological imagination is, by the person who coined the phrase.

Invitation to Sociology: A Humanist Perspective (Peter Berger; Doubleday Anchor, 1963). A lively look at the science and craft of sociology by an author with a predominantly interactionist perspective.

Classic Disputes in Sociology (J. A. Anderson et al., eds.; Allen & Unwin, 1987). A valuable introduction to the basic questions and debates in sociology.

Sociology for Pleasure (Marcello Truzzi; Prentice-Hall, 1974). A collection of studies of offbeat social groups and situations—gypsies, cults, nudist-camp visitors, and many others—that reminds the reader that sociology can illuminate little-known social worlds.

Masters of Sociological Thought (Lewis Coser; Harcourt Brace Jovanovich, 1977). An indispensable source for anyone interested in in-depth treatments of the contributions made by the founders of sociology.

The Handbook of Sociology (Neil J. Smelser; Sage Publications, 1988). A collection of reviews of the literature in major sociological fields.

JOURNALS

Contemporary Sociology. The official journal of book reviews in sociology.

American Sociological Review. The journal of the American Sociological Association. Articles in this journal are often quite technical and may be somewhat advanced for the beginning student, but they offer a good perspective on current research.

American Journal of Sociology. The oldest journal in sociology; a treasure trove of articles going back to the early decades of the century. Consult the index for earlier papers, and recent issues for excellent new research.

OTHER SOURCES

Encyclopedia of Sociology (Edgar F. Borgatta, ed.; Macmillan, 1992). A comprehensive collection of essays that define and discuss the concepts and methods of sociology and social science.

Sociological Abstracts. A set of reviews of existing literature on a variety of social-scientific subjects. The abstracts are organized by topic and offer brief overviews of original research papers and other articles.

CHAPTER 2

The Tools of Sociology

The debate became so heated that the shredded Styrofoam cups littering the table were blown first one way, then another. College-cafeteria debates are often loud and energetic, especially when the subject is welfare. On this occasion one of the contestants, a member of the Young Conservatives Club, claimed that the nation's welfare policies encourage dependency. His liberal opponent, though an old friend, tended to get hot under the collar and mix personal attacks with logic. "You stingy bastard," he shouted. "Don't you know that if they are given a chance to work, people who are on welfare try to get off it as soon as possible?" The debate raged on, just as it does in society as a whole. But what were the contestants really asking, and what data were they using to back up their arguments?

"You're letting your bleeding heart cloud your vision," the young conservative countered. "Haven't you ever noticed how many fancy cars, Cadillacs and Lincolns, there are in _____ [a poor part of town]? Those

people collect welfare and watch the soaps until their boyfriends come by to take them for a ride. Would you go out looking for work when you could spend your time watching TV and cruising for fried chicken?" The liberal answered by asserting that "people on welfare are forever trying to get off it. Every week my uncle has welfare mothers coming into his office asking for work. If they watch television, it's because they can't work and have nothing else to do."

Both of these "commonsense" sociologists were making inferences from their own observations, which were not necessarily accurate or relevant to the question being asked. Moreover, although they were arguing about "welfare," they had not adequately defined the terms of the debate. At its broadest level, their question was whether welfare—wealth transferred from the society as a whole to certain categories of people—results in increased social and psychological dependency and reduced motivation. In this question, "people on welfare" could include

those who receive low-cost student loans, tax breaks for depleting oil wells, low-cost federal flood insurance, disability payments, or any of hundreds of other direct and indirect subsidies available to certain categories of people. Clearly, our cafeteria debate did not refer to all of these categories. It centered on poor people who receive welfare in the form of payments from the government.

A researcher must make the question as specific as possible before deciding what methods to use to gather data that will provide an answer. In our debate, the contestants were probably referring to households receiving Aid to Families with Dependent Children (AFDC), the main form of welfare assistance to poor parents who are not in the labor force or receiving unemployment benefits.

Given these qualifications of the term *welfare,* the question a researcher might ask would probably be something like: Does the current system of AFDC payments create dependency, which prevents the recipients from seeking employment or other ways of getting off welfare? Thinking about this more specific question leads to other questions such as, What categories of people are most likely to be included on the welfare rolls? and, How long do they stay on welfare? With questions that specify the populations to be studied and the key variables to consider (time on the welfare rolls, education, available jobs, reasons for terminating or continuing welfare, and the like), the social scientist can begin to design research that will go beyond the impressionistic, unscientific data (such as the presence of Cadillacs and Lincolns in poor neighborhoods) that so often enter into discussions of social issues.

APPLYING THE SOCIOLOGICAL IMAGINATION

As citizens of a great democracy, we are encouraged to form opinions about the social issues of our time. We hear endless arguments about crime, poverty, the success or failure of education, the relative pay of men and women, and many other important questions. Candidates seeking our votes are eager to tell us what to believe about social issues and what society should do about them. But often the claims and recommendations we hear are contradictory. The explanations given for such problems as poverty and "welfare dependency," for example, may suggest very different solutions. How is an informed citizen to make decisions about the causes of social conditions or what should be done to remedy them? This is where sociology comes in. Sociology brings scientific methods to bear on these debates.

Most people associate social-scientific research with questionnaires, opinion surveys, and statistical reports. This is unfortunate. True, sociologists throughout the world use these research techniques, but they also use many other methods to explore social conditions. In this chapter we review many of the most common research tools used by sociologists. We will show how sociological research conforms to the rules of the scientific method and how the findings lead to changes in theories and to new research.

Anyone who embarks on scientific research, no matter what the subject or the method used, will go through many intellectual and emotional ups and downs before the work is done. Very often it will appear that the research is easy to define and conduct; soon, however, it will seem far more complicated, and the research questions themselves may appear less well defined than they did at the outset. This can be just as true in biology or chemistry as it is in sociology or another social science. Nevertheless, in all research projects certain basic steps must be completed, although not always in the order listed here:

1. *Deciding on the problem.* At first this may be simply a subject or topic of interest. Eventually, however, it must be worded in the form of a specific research question or questions in order to provide a focus for the rest of the work.

2. *Reviewing the literature.* Usually others have conducted research on the same topic. Find their reports and use them to determine what you can accomplish through your own research.

3. *Formulating research questions.* The work of others points to questions that have not been answered. Your own interest, time, resources, and available methods help determine what specific questions within your broad topic you can actually tackle.

4. *Selecting a method.* Different questions require different types of data—which in turn suggest different methods of data collection and analysis. Some of those methods are described in detail in this chapter.

5. *Analyzing the data.* Data are analyzed at each stage of the research, not just when preparing the final report.

In this chapter we act as if this step-by-step procedure is always followed by researchers in the social sciences. But do not assume that this procedure can be applied to every research question. One does not always progress easily from one step to another, and often one must go back and repeat earlier steps. In addition, some research questions require that we devise new ways of conducting research or new combinations of existing research methods.

FORMULATING RESEARCH QUESTIONS

A good deal of information is required even to know what situations or events one should study in conducting research on a particular social issue. General questions about societies or social behavior have to be translated into specific questions that can be studied using observations and measures of all kinds. Émile Durkheim's study of suicide (1951/1897) provides a good example of the process by which a sociologist converts a broad question about social change into the specific questions to be addressed in an empirical study—one that gathers evidence to describe behavior and to prove or disprove explanations of why that behavior occurs. These explanations are often, but not always, stated in the form of a **hypothesis,** a statement that expresses an informed (or "educated") guess regarding the possible relationship between two or more phenomena.

In his study of suicide Durkheim challenged the intellectuals and scientists of his day. Through the presentation of verifiable statistical evidence on suicide rates in different societies he demonstrated that he could predict where and when suicides would be more numerous. Psychological reasons might account for why a particular individual committed suicide, but Durkheim showed that "social variables" such as religion or fluctuations in economic

THEN AND NOW

SUICIDE IN THE PUBLIC SPOTLIGHT

The stock market crash of 1929 led to the suicides of people who had lost fortunes and faced immediate bankruptcy. More recently, the popular rock star Kurt Cobain killed himself. Both examples illustrate the key findings of Durkheim's pioneering studies of suicide. The suicide of an individual stockbroker or celebrity can be explained by the individual's state of mind at the time. However, the tendency for people to kill themselves when their fortunes change suddenly, or for celebrities to live out-of-control lives that often end in suicide, can be explained by social influences that cause people to feel lost or adrift. Durkheim labeled this feeling *anomie* and traced it to a lack of integration of the individual into social groups and communities.

conditions could explain differences in the number of suicides from one society or region to another.

The question that eventually led Durkheim to his empirical study of suicide actually had nothing to do with suicide. He began by thinking about the consequences of large-scale social change in Western nations. In particular, he believed that industrialization and the rapid growth of cities weakened people's attachment to their local communities. As they became increasingly anonymous and isolated, they were more likely to engage in a variety of self-destructive acts, the most extreme being suicide. In Durkheim's view, the act of suicide could be explained as much by social variables like rates of marriage and divorce as by individual psychological variables like depression or despair. Thus for Durkheim the study of suicide was a way of exploring the larger concept of integration or lack of integration into society: He sought to discover whether people who were less well integrated into society (i.e., more isolated from other people) were more likely to commit suicide.

If this view was correct, Durkheim reasoned, the rates of suicide among various populations should vary along with measures of social integration. He therefore formulated these hypotheses, among others:

- Suicide rates should be higher for unmarried people than for married people.
- Suicide rates should be higher for people without children than for people with children.
- Suicide rates should be higher for people with higher levels of education (education emphasizes individual achievement, which weakens group ties).
- Suicide rates should be higher in Protestant than in Catholic communities (Protestantism places more stress on individual achievement than Catholicism does, and this in turn weakens group ties).

Each of these hypotheses specifies a relationship between two variables that can be tested—that is, proved true or false—through empirical observation. In sociology, **variables** are characteristics of individuals, groups, or entire societies that can vary from one case to another. In the hypotheses just presented, the suicide rate is a social variable. Religion, education, marital status, and number of children are other variables in these hypotheses.

The techniques Durkheim used to establish a set of hypotheses became a model for modern social-scientific research. We would use the same techniques in designing a study of the welfare question. For example, we could state at least the following hypotheses about welfare and dependency:

- Welfare dependency, as measured by length of time on the welfare rolls, varies directly with (i.e., in the same direction as) rates of unemployment in the recipient's community. In other words, the higher the rate of unemployment in the welfare recipient's community, the longer the recipient's stay on welfare will be.
- Welfare dependency varies inversely with (i.e., in the opposite direction as) the recipient's education. That is, the higher a welfare recipient's level of education, the shorter the recipient's stay on welfare will be.
- Welfare dependency varies inversely with the age of the first child.[1] Because welfare payments are made to mothers with children under age 18, we can expect that stays on welfare will be longer for women with young children. The older the children, then, the less likely the mother is to remain on welfare.

Each of these hypotheses states a relationship between two variables. The **dependent variable** is the one we want to

explain (in this case, welfare dependency), and the **independent variable** is a factor the researcher believes causes changes in the dependent variable. It is necessary to be extremely careful in making statements about causality, however. All social phenomena are caused by a number of variables rather than by only one or two. We can say that lack of education is a cause of welfare dependency, for example, but we must immediately qualify that statement because many mothers who lack education are not on welfare. Thus we say that lack of education is one cause of welfare dependency, since women with more education have an easier time finding alternatives to welfare payments. (We discuss the issue of causality more fully later in the chapter.)

But, clearly, the story is more complicated than that. For some, welfare becomes a way of life; for others, it is merely a transition to another job or family or both. How can we find out why some mothers become dependent on welfare payments while others soon leave the welfare rolls? Many sociologists have argued that before anyone can develop a set of testable hypotheses about the causes of welfare dependency (or any other complex social situation) it is necessary to know a great deal about the actual experiences of the people involved. Thus even a sociologist who has never been on welfare can attempt to see the world from the viewpoint of welfare recipients and to find out what their daily lives are like. If they exist, such studies are usually the first ones consulted when the sociologist begins research on a particular problem.

REVIEWING THE LITERATURE

Perhaps the insights one would need to understand the issues surrounding welfare dependency are already available in the "literature"—in existing books or journal articles, published statistics, photos, and other materials. There is no need to conduct new research if the answers sought are already available. Most sociological research therefore begins in the library with a "review of the literature."

To stimulate our sociological imagination about welfare dependency, we need to look at a variety of studies that deal with this issue. But it takes some imagination just to think of the kinds of studies to look for. The various sociological perspectives described in Chapter 1 can help organize the search, especially when the perspectives are framed as questions.

Who? How Many? Where?   Who are we talking about and where are they found? This is a way of phrasing the ecological perspective, which suggests why that perspective is helpful in beginning research on an issue. In researching almost any subject involving human behavior, it is helpful to ask who is involved and in what numbers, and where the behavior in question occurs. The ecological perspective gives rise to two types of studies: community studies and demographic studies.

---

[1] All of these hypotheses have been shown to be correct (Bane & Ellwood, 1983; Ellwood, 1988).

Community studies are one of the richest research traditions in sociology. They portray the typical day-to-day life of a particular population. An example of a community study of a welfare population is Carol Stack's *All Our Kin* (1974). Stack spent 2 years in close company with a group of women, most of whom were on welfare. She visited with them in their kitchens and living rooms. She accompanied them to clinics and welfare offices, day care centers, churches, and local markets. Stack's study shows that the typical welfare budget is inadequate to provide a "decent" life for an American family. Yet welfare becomes a way of life for some women because it takes so much time to deal with the various social-service agencies and to cope with the problems of poverty that they are unable to accumulate the money or skills they need to escape from their situation.

Stack's study is only one of many studies of poor communities. There are community studies of the rural poor, the aged poor, poor teenagers, and many other populations that have high rates of welfare dependency. *Demographic studies* are also useful in studying poverty and welfare, as they provide counts of people in various relevant population categories—in this case, people on welfare, going on welfare, or getting off welfare. For example, the welfare population referred to in the argument at the beginning of the chapter consists of black single mothers living in central-city slums. But demographic studies have shown that there are at least twice as many white women as black women on welfare and that in some rural areas high proportions of people of all races are on the welfare rolls. Another common assumption is that when women go on welfare they remain on it forever. But demographic studies (which, among other things, measure the ways in which people earn their income) show that 66 percent of women who go on welfare remain on the welfare rolls for periods of 2 years or less, and most never do so again (Bane, 1992; Bane & Ellwood, 1983; O'Neill et al., 1984).

How Is the Situation Defined? Studies that take an interactionist approach to welfare and poverty tend to look at how people on welfare interact with one another and with people in the welfare system. In her book *Hustling and Hard Work,* for example, Betty Lou Valentine (1978) shows that people at the lowest levels of the economic order often speak with one another about their condition. They discuss their problems in making ends meet and in coping with the temptation to supplement low welfare payments through illegal activities, or "hustling." Those who do resort to hustling justify it as simply "trying to survive." The great value of interactionist studies like Valentine's is that they allow one to see a social world, such as that of chronic welfare recipients, from the inside.

What Groups or Organizations Are Involved? This question stems from the functionalist perspective. It asks how society is organized to deal with a social issue or problem. Functionalist sociologists are concerned with how social policies actually function, as opposed to how they are supposed to function. Kirsten A. Grønbjerg (1977), for example, showed that welfare as a system evolved as a result of Americans' demand that the federal government "do something" about poverty. But she found that certain policies demanded by the public (e.g., requiring that there be no adult male in the welfare recipient's household) do little to reduce welfare dependency. We will see later in the chapter that experimental studies have attempted to trace the consequences of changes in the organization and operation of welfare programs (Auletta, 1982; Katz, 1990).

Who Has the Power? This is a key question arising from the conflict perspective. Studies that take a conflict approach to poverty frequently criticize the operation of the welfare system. They find that the existing organization of welfare grants is a means by which those with power attempt to control the behavior of the poor, rather than a system designed to offer support to less fortunate members of society. Thus, in their book *Regulating the Poor* (1971), Frances Fox Piven and Richard Cloward showed that welfare rolls expand in times of high unemployment and contract when low-paying jobs are more plentiful. They interpreted this finding as indicating that the welfare system is used by policymakers to maintain a "reserve" of unemployed, less skilled workers who will be forced to take the worst jobs when they become available. When social-welfare programs have been improved, the authors found, it was usually because the poor themselves forced policymakers to pay attention to their needs (Piven & Cloward, 1971, 1982).

The foregoing are only a few of the studies one would find in a review of the literature on welfare and poverty. They are not cataloged according to the basic sociological perspectives. Rather, one needs to know what questions each of these perspectives raises about an issue. For any research subject, if you ask questions about who and where and how people interact, what organizations and policies guide their actions, and who has the power, you will be well on your way toward a thorough review of what is known about the issue.

THE BASIC METHODS

Once the researcher has specified a question, developed hypotheses, and reviewed the literature, the next step is to decide on the method or methods to be used in conducting the actual research. Sociological research methods are the techniques an investigator uses to systematically gather information, or data, to help answer a question about some aspect of society. The variety of methods that may be used is vast, with the choice of a method depending largely on the type of question being asked. The most frequently used methods are observation, experiments, and surveys. These are summarized in the study chart below.

OBSERVATION

Participant Observation. Much sociological research requires direct observation of the people being studied. Community studies like Stack's study of women on welfare are based on lengthy periods spent observing a particular group. This research method is rarely successful unless the sociologist also participates in the daily life of the people he or she is observing—that is, becomes their friend and a member of their social groups. Therefore, the central method of community studies is known as **participant observation.** The sociologist attempts to be both an objective observer of events and an actual participant in the social milieu under study—not an easy task for even the most experienced researcher. In such situations the observer faithfully records his or her observations and interactions in *field notes,* which supply the descriptive data that will be used in the analysis and writing phases of the study.

An excellent example of a study based on participant observation is Douglas A. Harper's book *Good Company* (1982). (Photographs from this book appear in the Visual Sociology section of Chapter 7.) Harper spent many months riding on freight trains and living in "jungles" with hoboes.

His goal was to describe how hoboes, or tramps or bums as they are often called, actually live and how they learn to trust or distrust one another in a world considered deviant by members of "respectable" society. Here is how Harper describes the experience of getting into the world of the hobo:

> I'd been in the yards a couple of days, peeking around, asking questions and making plans. Every time I've gone back to the freights I've had to cross an emotional hurdle—they seem too big, too fast, too dangerous, and too illegal—and I get used to the idea by spending a few days in the yards, testing the waters. . . . I was shifting back into a tramp world for the fourth or fifth time. I'd made cross-country trips on freights and I'd spent some weeks the winter before living on Boston's skid row. These experiences were trips into a life I ordinarily did not lead. (1982, p. 3)

This kind of research describes the quality of life of the people involved, and for that reason it is often called *qualitative* research in order to distinguish it from the *quantitative* research methods we will consider shortly. James Coleman observes that in qualitative research "we report a stream of action in which the interlinking of events suggests how the [social] system functions" (1964, p. 222). He supplies an example of this kind of research

STUDY CHART The Basic Methods

METHOD	DESCRIPTION	EXAMPLE
Participant Observation	A form of field observation in which the observer participates to some degree in the lives of the people being observed.	Martin Sanchez-Jankowski spends many months with youth gangs, gaining their trust and learning gang norms regarding violence.
Unobtrusive Measures	Observational techniques that measure behavior but intrude as little as possible into actual social settings.	Media researchers find out what radio stations different types of cars are tuned to in order to learn about the listening tastes of different segments of the public.
Controlled Experiment	An experimental situation in which the researcher manipulates an independent variable in order to observe and measure changes in a dependent variable.	Judith Gerone of the Manpower Research and Development Corporation conducts controlled experiments to find out what types of training and job programs are most effective in reducing state welfare rolls.
Field Experiment	An experimental situation in which the researcher observes and studies subjects in their natural setting.	Milton Rokeach meets three delusional mental patients, each of whom believes he is Jesus Christ. He introduces them to each other to learn how they incorporate conflicting information into their self-presentations.
Survey	Research in which a sample of respondents drawn from a specific population respond to questions either in an interview or on a questionnaire.	A team of National Opinion Research Corporation sociologists survey the public about their sexual behavior and attitudes.

Sociologist Terry Williams and photographer Margaret Morton have been observing the way of life of the homeless people who live in the maze of tunnels underneath the city of New York. Once he came to know and trust them, the man depicted here explained himself to them in these words: "I was living very good. I had good apartment. Now I don't got nothing. Now look what I got. I ain't got no other place to go. I ain't going to sleep in the street. I ain't going to shelter, that's for sure. . . . They steal your money, they steal your clothes, you have to fight . . . I'd rather be over here. Got my privacy. Got my water. I got my food, my TV, my heater, my blanket. Ain't no way in the world I'm going to go" (quoted in Morton, 1995, p. 137).

from his study *The Adolescent Society* (1961), in which he links the social groups that form in American high schools to different kinds of achievement in school. In the following passage a student describes to Coleman the process whereby he became a member of the school's "top" clique:

> Well, I'll tell you, like when I came over here, I had played football over at _____. I was pretty well known by all the kids before I came over. And when I came there was _____ always picking on kids. He hit this little kid one day, and I told him that if I ever saw him do anything to another little kid that I'd bust him. So one day down in the locker room he slammed this kid against the locker, so I went over and hit him a couple of times, knocked him down. And a lot of the kids liked me for doing that, and I got on the good side of two or three teachers. (1964, p. 222)

Qualitative research carried out "in the field" where behavior is actually occurring is the best method for analyzing the processes of human interaction. If Coleman had not actually spoken with the high school football player, he would not have obtained such a clear description of how a newcomer becomes accepted in the most prestigious group in the school. A shortcoming of this approach, however, is that it is usually based on a single community or social system, which makes it difficult to generalize the findings to other social settings. Thus community studies and other types of qualitative studies are most often used for exploratory research, and the findings serve as a basis for generating hypotheses for further research.

Unobtrusive Measures. Observation can employ numerous other techniques besides direct participa-

tion. Among these are **unobtrusive measures**—that is, observational techniques that measure the effects of behavior but intrude as little as possible into actual social settings. Here are some examples:

> The floor tiles around the hatching-chick exhibit at Chicago's Museum of Science and Industry must be replaced every six weeks. Tiles in other parts of the museum need not be replaced for years. The selective erosion of tiles, indexed by the replacement rate, is a measure of the relative popularity of exhibits.

> Chinese jade dealers have used the pupil dilation of their customers as a measure of the client's interest in particular stones. (Webb et al., 1966, p. 2)

> To study changes in the diet of Americans, investigators sifted through more than 2,000 household trash collections to measure the amount of fat being trimmed from meat packages. (Rathje, 1993)

Observations like these can be transformed into useful measures of the variables under study. Their nature is limited only by the researcher's creativity, and they intrude far less into people's lives than do interviews or participant observation.

Visual Sociology. An increasingly popular set of observational techniques involves the use of photography and videotape, or visual sociology. These techniques can be just as obtrusive as interviewing, if not more so, but they can also be used in unobtrusive ways, depending on the questions being asked. An example of the use of photographic data is the research on nonverbal communication conducted by Edward Hall (1959) and Ray Birdwhistell (1970). These studies demonstrated how people in various cultures use different nonverbal signs and align themselves spatially in different ways during their interactions. The photos show, for example, that in Mediterranean cultures people approach one another much more closely than they do in northern European or Asian cultures. These small differences in behavior can become very important in interpersonal relations.

Another example of visual sociology is the use of photographic materials in studies of urban life. In recent years the use of systematic observation coupled with photography has become widespread in studies of how people use public places. Probably the most influential sociologist in this field is William H. Whyte, author of *The Social Life of Small Urban Spaces* (1980). Whyte relies on time-lapse photography to describe the nuances of social interaction in public places. The use of photography in the study of urban spaces is illustrated in the photo essay at the end of this chapter. Similar essays appear in the Visual Sociology sections of subsequent chapters.

EXPERIMENTS

Although for both moral and practical reasons sociologists do not have many opportunities to perform experiments, there is a large literature in the social sciences, especially social psychology (an interdisciplinary science that draws ideas and researchers from both sociology and psychology), that is based on experiments. There are two experimental models that social scientists use frequently. The first and most rigorous is the controlled experiment conducted in a laboratory. The second is the field experiment, which is often used to test public policies that are applied to some groups and not to others.

Controlled Experiments. The **controlled experiment** allows the researcher to manipulate an independent variable to observe and measure changes in a dependent variable. The experimenter forms an **experimental group** that will experience a change in the independent variable (the "treatment") and a **control group** that will not experience the treatment but whose behavior will be compared with that of the experimental group. (The control group is similar to the experimental group in every other way.) This type of experiment is especially characteristic of studies at the micro level of sociological research.

Consider an example. Which line in Figure 2.1(b) appears to match the line in Figure 2.1(a) most closely? Could anything persuade you that a line other than the one you have selected is the correct choice? This simple diagram formed the basis of a famous series of experiments conducted by Solomon Asch in the early 1950s. They showed that the opinion of the majority can have an extremely powerful influence on that of an individual.

Asch's control group consisted of subjects[2] who were seated together in a room but were allowed to make their judgments independently. When they looked at sets of lines like those in Figure 2.1, the subjects in this group invariably matched the correct lines, just as you no doubt have. But in the experimental group a different result was produced by the introduction of an independent variable: group pressure.

Asch's experimental group consisted of subjects who were asked to announce their decisions aloud in the group setting. Each subject was brought into a room with eight people who posed as other subjects but were actually confederates of the experimenter. When the lines were flashed on a screen, those "subjects" all chose a line that was not the matching one. When it was the real subject's turn to choose, he or she was faced with the unanimous opinion of a majority of "subjects" who had picked the wrong line. Thirty-two percent of the real subjects went along with the majority and chose the wrong line as well. And even among the subjects Asch called "independent" (the 68 percent of the real subjects who gave the correct response despite the pressure of the majority) there was a great deal of variation. Some gave the correct response at all times, whereas others gave it only part of the time. This conforming response was less likely when there was at least one other

| FIGURE 2.1 | Lines Used in the Asch Experiment on Conformity |

(a)

(b)

A   B   C

Cards like these were used in the Asch experiment. Subjects were asked to judge the lengths of various lines by comparing them with the three lines on the bottom card. The line on the top card quite obviously matches line B on the bottom card; all of the judgments were this simple.

[2]The term *subject* refers to a person who participates in a controlled experiment.

person in the group who also went against the majority. By varying the number of people who said that the shorter line was longer, Asch was varying the degree of group pressure experienced by the subject. Higher levels of the independent variable (group pressure) thus produced more "errors," or choices of the wrong line (Asch, 1966).

Field Experiments. Field experiments are used extensively in evaluating public programs that address specific social problems. In these experiments there is usually a "treatment group" of people who participate in the program and a control group of people who do not. In one example of this type of experiment, Angelo Atondo, Mauro Chavez, and Richard Regua of California's Evergreen Valley College attempted to test the theory that if students at risk of failure are linked up with adult mentors from their own communities their chances of success will improve. This popular theory stems in part from an influential article in the *Harvard Business Review* titled "Everyone Who Makes It Has a Mentor" (Collins & Scott, 1978). Many successful people from all walks of life, especially people who have escaped from impoverished backgrounds, say that they benefited greatly from the guidance of a mentor who steered them toward constructive goals. Most mentors do not actually tutor the individuals they spend time with; instead, they teach through conversation and example.

Researchers have found little evidence to prove that mentors actually make a difference. Unless one can compare students who had mentors with similar students who did not, it is impossible to say with any scientific certainty—that is, beyond individual stories of success or failure—whether the mentors made a difference. The Evergreen Valley College researchers therefore assigned 115 entering Latino students with low English proficiency to Latino mentors with excellent English skills. Their control group was composed of a comparable number of Latino students with similar characteristics; these students were not assigned to mentors. Both groups attended the same classes and took the same exams. At the end of the semester 89 percent of the students with mentors passed the freshman English course, but only 46 percent of the students in the control group passed the same course. Later, more of the students with mentors went on to four-year colleges. While much more controlled research of this nature needs to be done before we can fully understand how mentors help students overcome their educational problems, this example shows how a field experiment can advance our understanding of a social issue like success and failure in school (Bashi, 1991).

Sociologists can conduct "natural experiments" when two similar groups receive differing treatments and the results can be measured. An example of such an experiment that is relevant to debates about welfare dependency concerns teenage pregnancy. Some scholars argue that welfare payments to women with dependent children create an incentive for teenagers to have babies and live on welfare. But in the United States welfare payments are determined by state governments. Some states pay relatively high benefits, while in others the benefits are very low. This situation presents an opportunity to test the hypothesis that rates of teenage pregnancy increase as welfare benefits increase. In fact, when we compare states like California and Pennsylvania (which pay the highest welfare benefits to young mothers) with states like Mississippi and Alabama (which pay the lowest) we find no difference in the rates of pregnancy among poor teenagers. This suggests that welfare benefits alone cannot be used to explain why young unmarried women from low-income households become pregnant (Ellwood & Summers, 1986). These issues are discussed more fully in Chapter 12.

The Hawthorne Effect. A common problem of experimental studies is that just by paying attention to people in an experimental group the researcher may be introducing additional variables. This problem was recognized for the first time in the late 1930s, when a team of researchers led by Elton Mayo conducted a famous series of experiments at Western Electric's Hawthorne plant. The purpose of the study was to determine the effects of various environmental and social conditions on the workers' productivity. One hypothesis was that improvements in the physical features of the workplace (such as better lighting) and improved social conditions (coffee breaks, different methods of payment, and so on) would result in greater productivity (the dependent variable). But it appeared that *no matter what* the experimenters did, the workers' productivity increased. When the experimenters improved the lighting, the workers' productivity increased over that of the control group. When they dimmed the lights, productivity went up again. This was true even when the workers were subjected to somewhat worse conditions or were returned to their original conditions.

At first this series of experiments was considered a failure, and the researchers concluded that the variables they were introducing had little to do with the changes in productivity that resulted. But on further reflection they realized that the real independent variable was not better working conditions but, simply, *attention*. The workers liked the attention they were getting; it made them feel special, so they worked harder. This realization led the researchers to design experiments dealing with the effects of attention from supervisors and better communication between workers and managers; those experiments led to a new philosophy of worker-management relations, described in Chapter 18. Today the term *Hawthorne effect* is used to refer to any unintended effect that results from the attention given to subjects in an experiment.

The Hawthorne effect occurs in a variety of experimental situations. For example, in the Evergreen Valley College experiment described earlier it is possible that the students with mentors were more successful than the students in the control group because they were getting extra attention from adults. Over time the effects of that attention may disappear and the experimenters may conclude that once the novelty of the extra attention wears off, students with mentors do not do appreciably better than others. Sophisticated evaluations of educational change try to anticipate the Hawthorne effect by making sure that the experimental group does not get more attention than the control group.

SURVEY RESEARCH

A sociological survey asks people to give precise information about their behavior, their attitudes, and at times the behavior and attitudes of others (e.g., other members of their households). There is a world of difference between the modern sociological survey and the "social surveys" conducted around the turn of the century (see Chapter 1). Those surveys attempted to present an unbiased, factual account of the social conditions of a specific community; their findings could not be applied to other groups. In contrast, today's survey techniques make it possible to generalize from a small sample of respondents to an entire population. An example is election polls, in which a small sample of 1,000 or 2,000 respondents can be used to predict how the entire electorate will vote in a presidential election. Done properly, the modern survey is one of the most powerful tools available to social scientists.

Surveys are the central method used in election polling, market research, opinion polling, television ratings, and a host of other applications. The most ambitious and most heavily used sociological surveys are national censuses. A *national census* is a full enumeration of every member of the society—a regular system for counting its

---

The Current Population Survey

The Current Population Survey (CPS) is a sample survey conducted each month by the Bureau of the Census. Its purpose is to update the decennial national census with monthly data. Each month census enumerators conduct interviews at 58,000 randomly selected American households. These interviews are the nation's only source of information on total employment and unemployment. The CPS is also the most comprehensive source of information on the personal characteristics of the total population, such as age, sex, race, marital and family status, veteran status, educational background, and ethnic origin.

Rena Tieser

The difficulty of obtaining this kind of information is illustrated by some of the occupational hazards faced by Rena Tieser, a field interviewer for the Census Bureau. In conducting interviews for the Current Population Survey, Tieser has walked in on seances, marijuana, and "extracurricular activity" in addition to facing the usual difficulties presented by dogs, crime, vacationers, unlisted telephone numbers, and non-English speakers.

Tieser and her colleagues are each assigned about 50 households, which are interviewed in four consecutive months and again in the same months a year later. The first and fifth interviews are conducted face-to-face and referred to as "personals"; the rest are done by telephone. The most difficult people to interview, according to Tieser, are aspiring individuals who have encountered hard times: "They don't want to talk about it" (quoted in Hershey, 1988, p. D1).

In addition to questions about their employment status, respondents to the CPS are asked questions about other characteristics, such as their marital status, living arrangements, money income, educational attainment, and fertility. The data collected in this way are used to create reports that are published annually. These annual series include Series P-20, *Population Characteristics;* Series P-25, *Population Estimates and Projections;* Series P-27, *Farm Population;* and Series P-60, *Consumer Income.*

The Current Population Survey is quite costly (the monthly total is over $2 million), and there are some limitations on the usefulness of the data obtained by this means. For one thing, the data are not useful for describing local and regional populations, since the number of households in any given locality interviewed by the CPS is too small to provide meaningful data. Nevertheless, the survey does provide major social indicators, such as unemployment, on a regular basis, and for this reason it is an extremely valuable tool of macro-level sociological analysis.

FIGURE 2.2   Public Support for Environmental Action, 1973–1994

Source: National Opinion Research Center, 1994.

people and determining where and under what conditions they live, how they work and gain income, their patterns of family composition, their age distribution, their levels of educational attainment, and related data. Without these measures, a nation cannot plan intelligently for the needs of its people. The United States conducts a national census every ten years. The 1990 census, the twenty-first in the nation's history, was the largest and most complex ever undertaken; it enumerated about 250 million people in 106 million housing units.

Once a national census has gathered the basic demographic and ecological facts about a nation's people, it is possible to add more information through the use of smaller and far less costly **sample surveys.** In the United States, this is done regularly through the Census Bureau's Current Population Survey (CPS). From the CPS we get monthly estimates of employment and unemployment, poverty, births, deaths, marriages, divorces, social insurance and welfare, and many other indicators of the social well-being and problems of the American people. Box 2.1 describes the CPS in more detail.

Opinion Polls.   Another type of survey research pioneered by sociologists earlier in this century is the opinion poll. Today opinion polling is a $2.5 billion industry (Rothenberg, 1990). Opinion polls are used by marketing firms to help corporations make decisions about their products. Political candidates and their staffs use polls to measure the progress of their campaigns. And elected officials use polls to monitor public opinion on key political and economic issues.

A good example of an opinion survey is the General Social Survey (GSS) conducted by the National Opinion Re-

search Center (NORC). This poll uses a relatively small sample of respondents, selected at random, whose opinions about a wide variety of issues can be generalized to the entire population of American adults.

To get a better idea of how opinion surveys are carried out, let us look at a series of results from the GSS on environmental issues. Figure 2.2 shows how Americans responded to questions about how they feel about levels of government spending for environmental preservation and environmental regulations. Since the questions were asked almost every year during the last two decades, the series of responses gives us a strong indication of trends in public opinion on this important issue. Clearly, a majority of people in the United States favor environmental preservation (and spending for such programs). In recent years that support, while still strong, has decreased. Similar data for other social issues, such as health care and crime, would show that the public is increasingly wary of government spending in these areas. One can also see, by looking at the "Don't know" response, that most of the Americans polled had an opinion on the issue, and that the proportion who lack an opinion has decreased somewhat over time.

Since poll takers often wish to confront respondents with the possible consequences of their opinions, questions about spending of tax money on a social issue like the environment are quite helpful. In essence, people are being asked not only about their support of a policy but also about their willingness to see their tax dollars spent for that purpose. The results in Figure 2.2 show that an increasing majority of Americans feel that spending for the environment should be increased. This sentiment became less prevalent during the energy crisis of the late 1970s but has increased dramatically in recent years as concern about such problems as acid rain and global warming has outstripped spending on these problems by the federal government.

The NORC General Social Survey is conducted each year, if possible, among a nationwide random sample of at least 1,500 adults. The term **sample** refers to a set of respondents selected from a specific population. The first step in selecting a sample is to define the population to be sampled; in our example the population consists of adult American citizens. The next step is to establish rules for the *random* selection of respondents. The goal of this procedure is to ensure that within the specified population everyone has an equal chance, or probability, of being selected to answer the survey questions. A sample in which potential respondents do not all have the same probability of being included is called a *biased sample.* To avoid bias, respondents must be selected by some process of random sampling.[3] In other words, any form of "volunteering" to be interviewed must be eliminated. (For example, the researcher cannot intentionally select his or her friends to be part of the sample.) Only a random sample can be considered truly representative of the target population.

Surveys that are not based on random samples can be very misleading. In a famous example from the early days of surveys, researchers predicted that candidate Alf Landon would defeat the incumbent President, Franklin D. Roosevelt. They based their prediction on data from a telephone survey, but at the time many low-income households did not have telephones. The survey therefore overrepresented the opinions of those with higher incomes, who were less likely to vote for Roosevelt. Roosevelt won the election, and since then political pollsters have been much more alert to the problem of sample bias. But many contemporary surveys also produce biased results. Most mail surveys and many telephone surveys that claim to be conducting research are actually marketing surveys designed to tap the opinions of particular subgroups rather than a representative sample of the entire population.

Before leaving the subject of opinion polling, we should mention one additional point. Polls are subject to *sampling error.* A sampling error of plus or minus three percentage points, for example, would be normal in a national sample of 1,500 to 2,000 respondents. This is important information for anyone who reads and interprets poll data. It means that a difference of 3 percent or less between the percentages of American adults expressing certain opinions could be due to chance rather than to a real difference in the distribution of opinions. In other words, it is possible that just by chance a higher percentage of people with a certain opinion was included in the sample than is actually the case in the total population. The possibility of sampling

error is more critical when there is a very small difference between two sets of responses—for example, when 51 percent of the sample favors one presidential candidate and 49 percent favors another. In this example the survey analysts would have to conclude that the election is "too close to call."

Questionnaire Design.   Just as important as careful selection of the sample to be interviewed is the design of the *instrument,* or questionnaire, to be used in the survey. Questionnaire design is both a science and an art. Questions must be worded precisely yet be easily understood. Above all, the questions must be worded so as to avoid biasing the answers. For example, the General Social Survey asked whether the United States was spending too much, too little, or about the right amount on "assistance to the poor." About 66 percent of the respondents answered "too little." But when the word "welfare" was substituted for "assistance to the poor," the findings were almost reversed, with slightly less than 50 percent responding that too much was being spent on welfare (Kagay & Elder, 1992). (See Box 2.2.)

One of the first decisions to make in designing survey questions is whether they should be open or closed. **Closed questions** require respondents to select from a set of answers, whereas **open questions** allow them to say whatever comes to mind. The items in Box 2.2 are examples of closed questions. An example of an open question would be "Please tell me how you feel about your neighborhood." In answering this type of question the respondent can say that he or she does not like the neighborhood at all or give one or more reasons for liking it. The interviewer attempts to write down the answers in the respondent's own words.

When researchers wish to include both forced-choice categories and freely given opinions in a single survey, the questionnaire usually begins with open questions and then shifts to closed questions on the same subject. Survey instruments that rely on open questions are often called *interview guides.* They guide the researcher's questions in certain directions and emphasize certain categories of information, but they also allow the interviewer to follow up respondents' comments with further questions.

RESEARCH ETHICS AND THE RIGHTS OF RESPONDENTS

In asking any type of question in a survey or other type of sociological study, the researcher must be aware of the rights of respondents. Much sociological research deals with the personal lives and inner thoughts of real human beings. Although most of that research seems relatively innocent, there are many times when the questions asked or the behaviors witnessed may be embarrassing or even more damaging. In one famous example, Laud Humphreys (1970, 1975) studied interactions between men seeking casual sexual encounters in public restrooms. Many of his colleagues attacked him for invading the men's privacy.

---

[3] Random sampling is accomplished by a variety of statistical techniques that are discussed in more advanced courses.

Avoiding Bias in Survey Questions

In *Asking Questions: A Practical Guide to Questionnaire Design* (1982), survey researchers Seymour Sudman and Norman Bradburn of the National Opinion Research Center describe a common abuse of survey methods: the use of biased questions. In a questionnaire mailed to them by a lobbying group the authors noticed questions like these:

1. Do you feel there is too much power concentrated in the hands of labor union officials?

    yes _____   no _____

2. Are you in favor of forcing state, county, and municipal employees to pay union dues to hold their government jobs?

    yes _____   no _____

3. Are you in favor of allowing construction union czars the power to shut down an entire construction site because of a dispute with a single contractor, thus forcing even more workers to knuckle under to union agencies?

    yes _____   no _____

These questions violate even the simplest rules of objectivity in questionnaire design. As the authors point out, they are "loaded with nonneutral words: 'forcing,' 'union czars,' 'knuckle under.' " Such questions are "deceptive and unethical, but they are not illegal" (p. 3).

To eliminate bias, one would have to begin by rephrasing the questions. For example, the first question could read something like this:

1. Which answer best sums up your feeling about the amount of power held by labor union officials today?
    a. too much power
    b. about the right amount of power
    c. too little power
    d. don't know

Fair questions avoid nonneutral words and give the respondent an opportunity to answer on either side of the issue or to say that he or she does not know. Whenever you read the results of a survey, ask yourself if the questions are free of obvious bias, if they are specific or general, and if they are threatening or nonthreatening to the respondent. Such an evaluation can make a great difference in how you view the answers.

Others defended him for daring to investigate what had until then been a taboo subject (homosexuality and bisexuality). After all, they reasoned, Humphreys was careful to keep the men's identities secret. But he also followed some of the men home and conducted interviews with them there. They were not aware that he knew about their homosexual activities, and upon reflection Humphreys admitted that he had deceived his subjects.

Sociologists continue to debate the ethical dilemmas raised by Humphreys's research and by studies like the Asch experiment (in which the subject is duped and may feel embarrassed). As a result of such controversies, the federal government now requires that research involving human subjects be monitored by "human subjects review panels" at all research institutions that receive federal funding. A research review must be undertaken before a study can be funded or approved for degree credit. To pass the review, the researcher must provide proof that he or she has taken precautions to protect the fundamental rights of human subjects. Those rights include privacy, informed consent, and confidentiality.

The right of **privacy** can be defined as "the right of the individual to define for himself, with only extraordinary exceptions in the interest of society, when and on what terms

his acts should be revealed to the general public" (Westin, 1967, p. 373). **Confidentiality** is closely related to privacy. When a respondent is told that information will remain confidential, the researcher may not pass it on to anyone else in a form that can be traced to that respondent. The information can be pooled with information provided by other respondents, but extreme care must be taken to ensure that none of the responses can be traced to a particular individual.

Informed consent refers to statements made to respondents (usually before any questions are asked) about what they are being asked and how the information they supply will be used. It includes the assurance that their participation is voluntary—that is, that there is no compulsion to answer questions or give information. The respondent should be allowed to judge the degree of personal risk involved in answering questions even when an assurance of confidentiality has been given.

The ethics of social research require careful attention. Before undertaking research in which you plan to ask people questions of any kind, be sure you have thought out the ethical issues and checked with your instructor about the ethics of your methods of collecting data and presenting them to the public.

ANALYZING THE DATA

Survey research normally is designed to generate numerical data regarding how certain variables are distributed in the population under study. To understand how such data are presented and analyzed, refer to Tables 2.1, 2.2, and 2.3. We will use these tables as a framework for a discussion of some of the basic techniques of quantitative data presentation and analysis. Other types of sociological data and analytical techniques are explained at appropriate points in later chapters.

In approaching a statistical table, the first step is to read the title carefully. The title should state exactly what information is presented in the table, including the *units of analysis*—that is, the entity (e.g., individual, family, group) to which a measure applies. In Tables 2.1 and 2.2, the units of analysis are households; in Table 2.3, they are married-couple households.

Also check the source of the information presented in the table. This is usually given in a source note at the end of the table. The source indicates the quality of the data (census data are considered to be of very high quality) and tells the reader where those data can be verified or further information can be obtained.

FREQUENCY DISTRIBUTIONS

As you begin to study the table, make sure you understand what kind of information is being presented. The numbers in Table 2.1 are **frequency distributions.** For each year (1970 and 1994), they show how various types of households were distributed in the U.S. population. Frequency distributions indicate how many observations fall within each category of a variable. Thus, within the category "Married-Couple Family" of the variable "Type of Household," Table 2.1 indicates that there were 63,401,000 households in the United States in 1970 and that the total increased to 97,107,000 by 1994.

Table 2.1 can tell us a great deal about social change in the United States. For example, social scientists use the term *household* to designate all the people residing at a given address, provided that the address is not a hospital, school, jail, army barracks, or other "residential institution." A household is not necessarily a married-couple family, as is evident from the categories listed in Table 2.1. There are also many households in which a male, with or without his own children, or a female, with or without her own children, is the primary reporting adult. There are also millions of nonfamily households, in which the adults reporting to the census takers are not related (over 28 million in 1994). These include people who are roommates, people who are cohabiting, people who are sharing a house or apartment but do not consider themselves roommates, and many other possibilities.

In earlier times it was considered unfortunate and a bit odd for a woman who was not a widow to head a household with children. It was assumed that a true family was composed of a male head, his wife, their children, and anyone related to them by blood who lived on their premises. The numbers in Table 2.1 show, however, that the number of female-headed households more than doubled between 1970 and 1994. The data also show that there was an increase in the number of family households (from 51.4 million in 1970 to 68.5 million in 1994), and almost as great a jump in the number of nonfamily households (from 11.9 million in 1970 to 28.6 million in 1994).

PERCENT ANALYSIS

Comparing the numbers for 1970 and 1994 in Table 2.1 can be misleading. Remember that these are absolute numbers. They show that the number of nonfamily households has increased and that the number of female-headed and male-headed households has also increased. However, so has the number of married-couple families. And so has the total number of households. How, then, can we evaluate the importance of these various changes?

To compare categories from one period to another, we need a way of taking into account changes in the overall size of the population. This can be done through **percent analysis.** Here is an example:

Table 2.1 shows that between 1970 and 1994 the number of male-headed households with one or more children rose from 341,000 to 1,314,000—an almost fourfold increase. But how important is this increase in view of the increase in the total population between 1970 and 1994? By using the total number of households in each year as the base and calculating the percentage of each household type for that year, we can "hold constant" the effect of the increase in the total number of households. In the case of male-headed households with one or more children, we find that the increase as a percentage of all households (from 0.54 percent in 1970 to 1.35 percent in 1994) is not as important as the increase in absolute numbers would suggest. The calculation is as follows:

$$341{,}000/63{,}401{,}000 \times 100 = 0.54$$
$$1{,}314{,}000/97{,}107{,}000 \times 100 = 1.35$$

Table 2.2 presents each household type as a percentage of total households in that year. In this way it eliminates the effect of the increase in overall population size between 1970 and 1994. The percentages in Table 2.2 reveal some significant changes that would not be evident from a comparison of absolute numbers. For example, although Table 2.1 seems to indicate that there has been an increase in married-couple families, Table 2.2 shows that when we control for the overall increase in households, married couples actually declined as a proportion of the total, from 70.5 percent in 1970 to 54.8 percent in 1994. The proportion of female-headed families, especially those with children, increased during the period. So did the proportion of nonfamily households.

TABLE 2.1	Types of Households in the United States, 1970 and 1994 (in thousands)		
TYPE OF HOUSEHOLD		**1970**	**1994**
All households		63,401	97,107
Family households		51,406	68,490
No own children under 18		22,725	34,471
With own children under 18		28,732	34,018
Married-couple family		44,728	53,171
No own children under 18		19,196	28,113
With own children under 18		25,532	25,058
Male householder		1,128	2,913
No own children under 18		887	1,599
With own children under 18		341	1,314
Female householder		5,500	12,406
No own children under 18		2,642	4,759
With own children under 18		2,858	7,647
Nonfamily households		11,945	28,617

Source: *Statistical Abstract,* 1995.

TABLE 2.2	Types of Households in the United States, 1970 and 1994 (percentage of total households)		
TYPE OF HOUSEHOLD		**1970**	**1994**
All households		100.0	100.0
Family households		81.2	70.5
No own children under 18		35.8	35.5
With own children under 18		45.3	35.0
Married-couple family		70.5	54.8
No own children under 18		30.3	29.0
With own children under 18		40.3	25.8
Male householder		1.9	3.0
No own children under 18		1.4	1.6
With own children under 18		0.5	1.4
Female householder		8.7	12.8
No own children under 18		4.2	4.9
With own children under 18		4.5	7.9
Nonfamily households		18.8	29.5

Source: *Statistical Abstract,* 1995.

TABLE 2.3	Married-Couple Families, by Number of Own Children Under 18, 1970 and 1994 (percentage of total households)	
	1970	**1994**
Married-couple families	100.0	100.0
No own children under 18	42.9	52.9
With own children under 18	57.1	47.1

But we cannot yet view these findings as definite. We must examine them carefully to be sure we are making the right kinds of comparisons. Look again at Table 2.2. In the category of married-couple families, those with no children of their own decreased as a proportion of total households—from 30.3 percent in 1970 to 29.0 percent in 1994. But this apparent decrease is due to the overall increase in other types of households. It is still not clear whether, among married-couple families, those without children decreased in relation to those with children. Indeed, if we take only the married-couple households and compare categories within it, as shown in Table 2.3, we see that *as a proportion of married-couple households,* those without children actually increased from 42.9 percent to 52.9 percent.

This example should convince you to pay close attention to the comparisons made in numerical tables. In this example we see that married couples with children accounted for a smaller percentage of all married-couple households in 1994 than in 1970, but we would not have seen this without making the additional comparison presented in Table 2.3.

CORRELATIONS

The term **correlation** refers to a specific relationship between two variables: As one varies in some way, so does the other. Although the calculation of correlation is covered in statistics courses, for our purposes it will be helpful to know that the measure of correlation between two variables, termed the *correlation coefficient,* can vary between +1.0 and −1.0, with 0.0 representing no measured correla-

tion at all. A correlation coefficient of +1 would indicate that the variables are positively and perfectly related—a change in one variable produces an equivalent change in the same direction (increase or decrease) in the other variable. A correlation coefficient of −1 would mean that the variables are perfectly inversely related—a change in one produces an equivalent change *in the opposite direction* in the other. In reality most variables are not perfectly correlated, and correlation coefficients usually fall somewhere between these two extremes.

The search for correlations is a common strategy in many kinds of research. In market research, for example, the investigator seeks correlations between the use of certain products and other social variables. (Thus the consumption of beer correlates with the proportion of male consumers in a target population such as baseball fans; the consumption of light beer correlates with the proportion of older, more weight-conscious male consumers; and so on.)

Social scientists who conduct research on the American family have supplied correlations between length of time on welfare (to return to our earlier example) and independent variables like education, income, and race. They have found, for example, that among female single parents time on welfare is highly correlated with lack of education and income. If you were to take other courses in sociology and statistics, you would learn techniques for calculating the strength of correlations among variables and for sorting out the effects of different variables on the dependent variable you are studying. You would, for example, be able to determine the separate effects of education, income, race, age, and the like on welfare dependency.

Correlation and Causation. Although correlation can be very useful in the analysis of relationships among variables, it must not be confused with causation. Often a strong correlation that seems to indicate causality is in fact a spurious or misleading relationship. Take the example of storks and babies. The fable that storks bring babies seemed to be based on a statistical reality: In rural Holland until recent decades there was a correlation between storks nesting in chimneys and the presence of babies in those households. The more storks, the more babies. In fact, however, the presence of babies in the home meant more fires in the fireplace and more heat going up the chimney to attract storks to nest there. Storks do not bring babies; babies, in effect, bring storks. But the real causal variable is heat, something that was not suggested in the original commonsense correlation.

The fact that two variables are correlated proves only that they are associated in such a way that variations in one are accompanied by regular variations in another. We can say, for example, that lack of household income and receipt of AFDC are correlated; as the number of households in poverty increases, so does the number of households receiving AFDC. But this does not mean that lack of household income *causes* receipt of AFDC. In fact, many people who are poor are not eligible for AFDC because they are men or because they do not have children below the age of 18. In a sense, then, the laws establishing the AFDC program, not poverty itself, cause welfare recipiency. Correlations may suggest the possibility of causality, but one must be extremely careful in making the leap from correlation (association) to causation.

MAPPING SOCIAL DATA

Data about individuals or households can be mapped in precise ways, providing a powerful tool for analyzing sociological data (Monnier, 1993). In a sense, the mapping of data is a form of correlation. The variable under study—it could be poverty, crime, educational achievement, an illness like AIDS, or any other variable—is mapped over a given territory, thereby correlating the variable with location.

Figure 2.3 shows an early example of the mapping of social data. Walter Reckless, a sociologist working in Chicago during the early decades of this century, was interested in finding out where vice crimes like prostitution were occurring. First he counted and noted the locations of all the brothels known from police records. Then he created a map that showed each location as a dot. The map revealed that many brothels were located in poor neighborhoods inhabited mainly by recent immigrants from European nations and African Americans who had migrated from the South. The map led Reckless to ask some additional questions. Were brothels located in the immigrant and African American communities because the residents used the services of prostitutes? Or was there another explanation? To answer this question, Reckless had to find out about the clientele served by the brothels. His observations revealed that relatively few immigrants or African Americans patronized them. The majority of the clients were well-off white males. Once he had gained the trust of the madams and the gangsters who sponsored them, he learned that "respectable" men preferred to visit brothels in neighborhoods far away from their own and that the police were far more willing to "look the other way" when prostitution and other vices were concentrated in immigrant and racial ghettos than when the same kinds of businesses were located in more affluent neighborhoods (Reckless, 1933).

Contemporary sociologists are making increasing use of sophisticated mapping techniques. An example is presented in Figure 2.4, which maps the spatial distribution of white-collar workers in San Antonio, Texas. This is an example of research by sociologist Michael White (1987), who studies the characteristics of neighborhoods in U.S. cities and towns. It shows that households with white-collar workers tend to be concentrated on the northern edges of the central city, extending outward into the northern suburbs. Of course, different cities will show different patterns of concentration. Such maps provide a useful way of showing how people's choices about where to live can shape an entire metropolitan region.

In the San Antonio map, the units of area categorized by percentage of white-collar workers living there are examples of *census tracts*. A census tract is a small geographic area within a metropolitan region defined by the U.S. Bureau of the Census. All maps of sociological data use some kind of areal unit, such as counties or census tracts. In later chapters we will present additional examples of mapping of sociological data.

THEORIES AND PERSPECTIVES

The material presented in Tables 2.1, 2.2, and 2.3 is valuable because it shows how the nation's most important survey, the census, reveals fundamental changes in the structure of the population. But how do these facts about household composition relate to larger trends and issues?

FIGURE 2.3   **Vice Areas in Local Communities of Chicago, 1930**

Legend

No. Key	No. Key
1. Rogers Park	23. Humboldt Park
2. West Ridge	24. West Town
3. Uptown	25. Austin
4. Lincoln Square	26. West Garfield Pk.
5. North Center	27. East Garfield Pk.
6. Lake View	28. Near West Side
7. Lincoln Park	29. North Lawndale
8. Near North Side	30. South Lawndale
9. Edison Park	31. Lower West Side
10. Norwood Park	32. Loop
11. Jefferson Park	33. Near South Side
12. Forest Glen	34. Armour Square
13. North Park	35. Douglas
14. Albany Park	36. Oakland
15. Portage Park	37. Fuller Park
16. Irving Park	38. Grand Blvd.
17. Dunning	39. Kenwood
18. Montclare	40. Washington Pk.
19. Belmont Cragin	41. Hyde Park
20. Hermosa	42. Woodlawn
21. Avondale	43. South Shore
22. Logan Square	44. Chatham

45. Avalon Park	53. West Pullman	61. New City	69. Greater Grand Cr.
46. South Chicago	54. Riverdale	62. West Elsdon	70. Ashburn
47. Burnside	55. Hegewisch	63. Gage Park	71. Ashburn Gresham
48. Calumet Heights	56. Garfield Ridge	64. Clearing	72. Beverly
49. Roseland	57. Archer Heights	65. West Lawn	73. Washington Hgts.
50. Pullman	58. Brighton Park	66. Chicago Lawn	74. Mount Greenwood
51. South Deering	59. McKinley Park	67. West Englewood	75. Morgan Park
52. East Side	60. Bridgeport	68. Englewood	

Source: Reckless, 1933.

Note: This is a reworking of the original map in Walter Reckless' study of vice areas in Chicago. Each dot on the map represents a house of prostitution known to the Chicago police at the time of the study.

The census reveals trends, but it does not explain those trends unless an investigator armed with a set of hypotheses goes to work on the facts to make them prove or disprove a theoretical point.

A **theory** is a set of interrelated concepts that seeks to explain the causes of an observable phenomenon. Some theories attempt to explain an extremely wide range of phenomena, while others limit their explanations to a narrower range. In physics, for example, Newton's theory of gravitation related the force of gravity to the mass and distance between objects, but it did not try to explain why the force of gravity existed in the first place or how it was related to other forces, such as electromagnetism, that could be observed in nature. Einstein's theory of relativity, on the other hand, attempted to explain the relationships among all natural forces, and it predicted forces that had not yet been observed, such as those that are released by nuclear fission.

It is often said that sociology lacks highly predictive theories like those of the physical sciences, but this is a debatable point. If theories are judged by their ability to explain observable phenomena and predict future events, then sociology has some powerful theories. At the beginning of this century Émile Durkheim used his theory of social integration to predict the social conditions that would

FIGURE 2.4   **Percentage of White-Collar Workers in San Antonio, by Census Tract**

Less than 30%

30% to 40%

40% to 50%

Greater than 50%

Source: White, 1987.

VISUAL SOCIOLOGY

All photography in this book is "visual sociology" in the sense that we have chosen pictures that highlight social situations, social relationships, and social institutions. But in assembling a group of photos we can communicate more subtle cues about what it feels like to be in a particular situation or relationship. Through photographs we can convey a great deal about the culture, social structure, and patterns of interaction that characterize a particular social setting, at the same time that we leave the reader free to make his or her own judgments. Sociologists routinely use photography to focus on types of behavior, on the way people sort themselves out in space and time, on patterns of inequality, and much more. These are all aspects of visual sociology that appear in this volume.

TIMES SQUARE: THE CITY AS SOCIAL LABORATORY

The founders of American sociology were fascinated by the city. It was ever-changing, always challenging, always attracting newcomers, new talent, new ideas, new energies (Matthews, 1977). The same can be said of cities today. For the urban sociologist, therefore, the city is an ideal social laboratory. For those of us who conduct much of our research in New York City, there is no more fascinating place to watch social changes occur than the famous Times Square and 42nd Street entertainment district (Boggs & Kornblum, 1985).

Although it is widely known as one of the nation's most famous entertainment districts, Times Square and West 42nd Street in Manhattan is actually, as you can readily see from these photos, many different places to people from different social worlds.

To the police, to social reformers, and to members of the movement against pornography, Times Square is a "combat zone," meaning that it is a place where the norms of conventional society do not hold, where commercial sex and street hustling are tolerated, and where almost "anything goes."

To the streetwise sophisticate, Times Square, especially 42nd Street (or The Deuce, as it is known), is a place where thousands of people pass by in a short period and one can sell almost anything because there will always be a buyer or a "mark" to be fleeced. It's a street of porn hawkers, food and jewelry vendors, chess hustlers, drug peddlers, and on and on.

To theater producers, Times Square is the center of the nation's largest and most famous rialto. The Shubert theaters and other well-known theater buildings form the Broadway stage, which offers entertainment for millions of theatergoers each year and provides employment for hundreds of actors and musicians, stagehands, writers, producers, and many others. The area still has its specialized neighborhoods, such as Tin Pan Alley, where songs are sold and musical instruments purchased. Along Broadway, movie houses compete with live theater for audiences. Major film producers use Times Square to open their new productions. The area has an international appeal as well, with Japanese and other foreign firms competing with U.S. corporations to advertise on the billboards above the theaters and other buildings.

The sociologist who wishes to study trends in popular culture could find few better natural locations in which to watch the trendsetters appear, enjoy their fleeting fame, and soon be replaced with the newest fad or overnight sensation. The Times Square entertainment district is also a wonderful place for sociologists like Vernon Boggs (shown here on one of his frequent observation walks in the area) to watch for changes in the way street hustlers compete for tourist dollars and in how police officers deploy their forces to control the area's public space.

increase rates of suicide. The same theory of social integration predicted the conditions that would lead to the rise of totalitarian regimes like that of the Nazis in Germany. Max Weber's theory of bureaucracy is valuable in explaining the experiences we are likely to have in organizations of all kinds. And Karl Marx's theory of class conflict is still the dominant explanation of the revolutions that occurred in feudal and early capitalist societies. No single sociological theory can explain all the complexities of human social life and social change, but in this respect sociology is not very different from other social and physical sciences. Different economic theories compete for the attention of policymakers, and the theory of relativity has not fully explained the physical forces that produced the universe.

To cope with the many levels of social explanation, sociologists come to their work armed with **theoretical perspectives:** sets of interrelated theories that offer explanations for important aspects of social behavior. Like the methods of observation and analysis discussed in this chapter, theoretical perspectives are tools of sociological research. They provide a framework of ideas and explanations that helps us make sense of the data we gather. The basic theoretical perspectives are the ones discussed in Chapter 1: interactionism, functionalism, and conflict theory. We also rely on the ecological perspective for descriptive data regarding communities and populations. At times these perspectives offer competing explanations of social life; at other times they seek to explain different aspects of society; and at still other times they are combined in various ways.

Toward the end of each chapter of this book we will show how practicing sociologists use questions and hypotheses derived from these perspectives in their research. Our knowledge about societies and how they change is advanced through scientific competition among sociologists who approach their subjects from different theoretical perspectives.

SUMMARY

THINK ABOUT IT CRITICALLY

Abbott Pierce, a student in an introductory sociology course, is interested in doing research on human sexuality. He believes that men think of sex as a form of sport while women think of it as an emotional bond. He decides to do a survey on the subject. He writes down some questions and starts asking them of people he meets on campus. What would his instructor and his classmates say about the way he is conducting his research? As you read this summary, keep this question in mind.

In all scientific research certain basic steps must be completed: deciding on the problem, reviewing the literature, formulating research questions, selecting a method, and analyzing the data. Not all researchers follow these steps in the order given, and often one or more steps must be repeated.

The first step in designing social research is formulating the question—that is, asking a question about a social situation that can be answered through the systematic collection and analysis of data. Often the research question is expressed in the form of a hypothesis. A *hypothesis* states a relationship between two *variables* that can be tested through empirical observation. The variable that is to be explained is the *dependent variable.* The other variable, a factor that the researcher believes causes changes in the dependent variable, is the *independent variable.*

Before collecting new data, a professional researcher reviews as much existing research and other data sources as possible. This "review of the literature" sometimes supplies all the data necessary for a particular study.

The most frequently used research methods in sociology are observation, experiments, and surveys. Observation may take the form of *participant observation,* in which the researcher participates to some degree in the life of the people being observed. It may also take the form of *unobtrusive measures,* or observational techniques that measure behavior but intrude as little as possible into actual social settings. Visual sociology involves the use of photography and videotape to observe people in a variety of settings.

Sociological experiments can take one of two basic forms: the controlled experiment and the field experiment. In a *controlled experiment* the researcher establishes an *experimental group,* which will experience the "treatment" (a change in the independent variable), and a *control group,* which will not experience the treatment. The effect of the treatment on the dependent variable can be measured by comparing the two groups. *Field experiments* take place outside the laboratory and are often used in evaluating public programs designed to remedy specific social problems. The treatment group consists of people who experience a particular social program, and the control group consists of comparable people who do not experience the program. A common problem of experimental studies is the *Hawthorne effect,* which refers to any unintended effect resulting from the attention given to subjects in an experiment.

The third basic method of sociological research, the survey, asks people to give precise information about their behavior and attitudes. The most ambitious surveys are national censuses; the data obtained in a census can be supplemented by smaller, less costly *sample surveys.* A *sample* is a selection of respondents drawn from a specific population. To ensure that everyone in the specified population has an equal chance of being selected, the respondents must be selected by some process of random sampling.

Questionnaire design is an important aspect of survey research. Questions must be precisely worded, easy to understand, and free of bias. *Closed questions* require the respondent to select from a set of answers, whereas *open questions* allow respondents to say whatever comes to mind.

Sociological researchers must always consider the rights of human subjects. *Privacy* is the right to decide the terms on which one's acts may be revealed to the public. *Confidentiality* means that the researcher cannot use responses in such a way that they can be traced to a particular respondent. *Informed consent* means that respondents must be told how the information they supply will be used and that they must be allowed to judge the degree of personal risk involved in answering questions.

The data gathered in a survey are usually presented in the form of statistical tables. In reading a table it is important to know what the units of analysis are and what kinds of data are being presented. *Frequency distributions,* given in absolute numbers, reveal the actual size of each category of a variable, but to compare the numbers for different years it is necessary to use *percent analysis.* Analyzing data often leads to the discovery of *correlations,* or specific relationships between two variables. Correlation should not be confused with causation. Mapping of data about individuals or households also provides a powerful tool for analyzing sociological data.

Once data have been presented and analyzed, they can be used to generate new hypotheses. The types of hypotheses that might be developed depend on the researcher's *theoretical perspective*—a set of interrelated theories that offer explanations for important aspects of social behavior. The functionalist, interactionist, and conflict perspectives give rise to quite different hypotheses.

CRITICAL RESPONSE

Abbott is trying to apply a sociological approach to an important issue: how men and women think about sex. But did he first consult other people's research? Did he actually formulate a set of hypotheses based on what he had read and his own research goals? Did he carefully consider the *ethics of his research plan? Clearly he did not. He needs to think more critically about his research plan. And he needs to master the rules of scientific method before he undertakes any empirical research, especially research with human subjects.*

GLOSSARY

hypothesis: a statement that specifies a relationship between two or more variables that can be tested through empirical observation. (p. 36)

variable: a characteristic of an individual, group, or society that can vary from one case to another. (p. 38)

dependent variable: the variable a hypothesis seeks to explain. (p. 38)

independent variable: a variable the researcher believes causes a change in another variable (i.e., the dependent variable). (p. 38)

participant observation: a form of observation in which the researcher participates to some degree in the lives of the people being observed. (p. 40)

unobtrusive measures: observational techniques that measure behavior but intrude as little as possible into actual social settings. (p. 41)

controlled experiment: an experimental situation in which the researcher manipulates an independent variable in order to observe and measure changes in a dependent variable. (p. 42)

experimental group: in an experiment, the subjects who are exposed to a change in the independent variable. (p. 42)

control group: in an experiment, the subjects who do not experience a change in the independent variable. (p. 42)

field experiment: an experimental situation in which the researcher observes and studies subjects in their natural setting. (p. 43)

Hawthorne effect: the unintended effect that results from the attention given to subjects in an experimental situation. (p. 43)

sample survey: a survey administered to a selection of respondents drawn from a specific population. (p. 45)

sample: a set of respondents selected from a specific population. (p. 46)

closed question: a question that requires the respondent to choose among a predetermined set of answers. (p. 46)

open question: a question that does not require the respondent to choose from a predetermined set of answers. Instead, the respondent may answer in his or her own words. (p. 46)

privacy: the right of a respondent to define when and on what terms his or her actions may be revealed to the general public. (p. 47)

confidentiality: the promise that the information provided to a researcher by a respondent will not appear in any way that can be traced to that respondent. (p. 47)

informed consent: the right of respondents to be informed of the purpose for which the information they supply will be used and to judge the degree of personal risk involved in answering questions, even when an assurance of confidentiality has been given. (p. 47)

frequency distribution: a classification of data that describes how many observations fall within each category of a variable. (p. 48)

percent analysis: a mathematical operation that transforms an absolute number into a proportion as a part of 100. (p. 48)

correlation: a specific relationship between two variables. (p. 49)

theory: a set of interrelated concepts that seeks to explain the causes of an observable phenomenon. (p. 51)

theoretical perspective: a set of interrelated theories that offer explanations for important aspects of social behavior. (p. 54)

WHERE TO FIND IT

BOOKS

Handbook of Survey Research (Peter Rossi et al.; Basic Books, 1983). The latest in comprehensive, though rather technical, coverage of issues in the design, administration, and analysis of sociological survey research.

The Practice of Social Research (Earl Bobbie; Wadsworth, 1992). A practical text that introduces the ways in which sociologists actually formulate their research questions and conduct their research.

Unobtrusive Measures: Nonreactive Research in the Social Sciences (Eugene J. Webb et al.; Rand McNally, 1966). A pathbreaking treatise on how to develop scientific techniques for observing social life in nondisruptive ways.

In the Field: Readings on the Field Research Experience, 2nd ed. (Carolyn D. Smith & William Kornblum, eds.; Praeger, 1996). A selection of personal accounts by a group of noted ethnographic researchers, designed to give students a sense of what it is actually like to conduct ethnographic research, especially participant observation.

How to Lie with Statistics (Darrell Huff; Norton, 1954). A charming and valuable book about the uses and misuses of quantitative data. To know how to lie with statistics is also to know how to unmask those who would lie and to credit those who use numbers and statistics properly.

Participatory Action Research (William F. Whyte, ed.; Sage Publications, 1991). A collection of essays by social scientists who are engaged in action projects in the United States and Third World nations. The projects are designed to create social changes that will improve food supplies, agricultural practices, or industrial production. The book highlights ways in which the researcher can be an active participant in social change without losing scientific credibility.

OTHER SOURCES

Statistical Abstract of the United States (U.S. Bureau of the Census). The first source consulted for quantitative facts about the population of the United States. Published annually.

Census of the United States. An invaluable tool for all the social sciences, but one that requires a patient user. There are volumes for all states and cities in the United States. The tables show population totals and subtotals by sex, age, race, and occupation. Published every 10 years on the basis of analysis of the data gathered in the national census.

The American Statistics Index (Congressional Information Service Inc.). The best single source for statistics collected by agencies of the U.S. government. Published monthly and collected into an annual volume, this index offers the most complete list of public statistics available in the United States.

American Demographics. A magazine devoted to applications of census and opinion survey data to marketing and other studies of consumer behavior.

CHAPTER 3

Culture

For Native Americans, the coming of the Europeans to the New World marked the beginning of a long-drawn-out disaster. This is how sociologist Russell Thornton, himself a Native American, describes it:

> In the centuries after Columbus these "Indians" suffered a demographic collapse. Numbers declined sharply; entire tribes, often quickly, were "wiped from the face of the earth." This is certainly true of the American Indians on the land that was to become the United States of America. For them the arrival of the Europeans marked the beginning of a long holocaust, although it came not in ovens, as it did for the Jews. The fires that consumed North American Indians were the fevers brought on by newly encountered diseases, the flashes of settlers' and soldiers' guns, the ravages of "firewater," the flames of villages and fields burned by the scorched-earth policy of vengeful Euro-Americans. The effects of this holocaust of North American Indians, like that of the Jews, was millions of deaths. In fact, the holocaust of the North American tribes was, in a way, even more destructive than that of the Jews, since many American Indian peoples became extinct. (Thornton, 1987, pp. xv–xvi)

Recent scholarship has shown that even when Indians and settlers tried to live as neighbors it was very difficult for them to do so (Cronon, 1983). Seemingly simple differences could result in major conflicts. One major source of conflict was the different ways in which Indians and settlers related to the land. The settlers tended to think of the bounty offered by their new environment as inexhaustible. They were not nearly as aware of the rhythms of nature as the Indians were, nor did they know how to live in harmony with nature without destroying its resources. So when they saw the Indians moving from one hunting or fishing ground to another as the seasons changed, they concluded that the Indians were not "improving the land" as proper farmers did. Over and over again, Europeans justified the taking of the Indians' forests and meadows by claiming that the Indians had no sense of ownership of the land because they did not clear it and farm it.

It would be difficult to overestimate the shock and confusion the Indians must have felt as they were continually driven from their traditional hunting and fishing grounds by the encroaching Europeans. The resulting conflicts were often bloody, with injuries and deaths on both sides, but the effects of the Europeans' technological superiority were especially devastating. The Europeans' cannon and rifles gave them the ultimate power to inflict their will on the Indians. No wonder that wherever they encountered the Europeans, the Indians began to covet the powerful new killing tools made of iron and steel. No wonder that the Europeans never doubted, even as they learned from the Indians how to survive in their new environment, that their own way of life was the only "true" civilization. Indeed, so powerful did the notion of European superiority become that even today we celebrate the "discovery" of the New World by European explorers. Too often we forget that what happened in 1492 was not the discovery of a new world but the establishment of contact between two worlds, both already old (Jennings, 1975; Parry, 1963).

THE MEANING OF CULTURE

Was the European way of life really superior? Were the Europeans really doing the Indians a service? In fact, the arrival of the "civilized" Europeans spelled the doom of many Native American societies. But even when cultural contact occurs on a more equal basis, as it does when people from different modern cultures meet, it is difficult to achieve understanding and arrive at mutually beneficial forms of cooperation. Why is this so? Many of the answers may be found in the study of human culture.

In everyday speech the word *culture* refers to pursuits like literature and music. But these forms of expression are only part of the definition of culture. To the social scientist, "a humble cooking pot is as much a cultural product as is a Beethoven sonata" (Kluckhohn, 1949, quoted in Ross, 1963, p. 96). Culture is a basic concept in sociology because it is what makes humans unique in the animal kingdom. All the familiar forms of social organization, from the simplest family to the most complex corporation, depend on culture for their existence. But although societies cannot exist without cultures, the two are not the same thing. *Societies* are populations that are organized to carry out the major functions of life. A society's *culture* consists of all the ways in which its members think about their society and communicate about it among themselves.

We can define **culture** as all the modes of thought, behavior, and production that are handed down from one generation to the next by means of communicative interaction—speech, gestures, writing, building, and all other communication among humans—rather than by genetic transmission, or heredity. This definition encompasses a vast array of behaviors, technologies, religions, and so on—in other words, just about everything made or thought by humans. Among all the elements of culture that could be studied, social scientists are interested primarily in aspects that explain social organization and behavior. Thus, although they may analyze trends in movies and popular music (which significantly affect behavior in the modern world), they are even more likely to study aspects of culture that account for phenomena like the behavior of people in corporations or the conduct of scientific research.

Quilt making is a highly social folk art form. This quilt, created by University of Mississippi graduate student Patti B. Melton, is actually a sociology paper about quilt making reproduced on an original quilt. It blends ideas with material culture.

DIMENSIONS OF CULTURE

The culture of any people on earth, no matter how simple it may seem to us, is a complex set of behaviors and artifacts. A useful framework for thinking about culture was suggested by Robert Bierstedt (1963). Bierstedt views culture as having three major dimensions: **ideas,** or ways of thinking that organize human consciousness; **norms,** or accepted ways of doing or carrying out ideas; and **material culture,** or patterns of possessing and using the products of culture. Figure 3.1 presents some examples of these three dimensions, along with two aspects of culture—*ideologies* and *technologies*—that combine elements from more than one dimension.

Ideas. As indicated in Figure 3.1, theories about how the physical world operates (scientific ideas), strongly held notions about what is right and wrong (values), and traditional beliefs, legends, and customs (folklore) are among the most important types of ideas found in any given culture. Of these, values are especially important because people feel so strongly about them and because they often undergo changes that result in social conflict (as we can see in contemporary debates about "a woman's right to control her reproductive destiny" versus "a fetus's right to life").

FIGURE 3.1 Dimensions of Culture

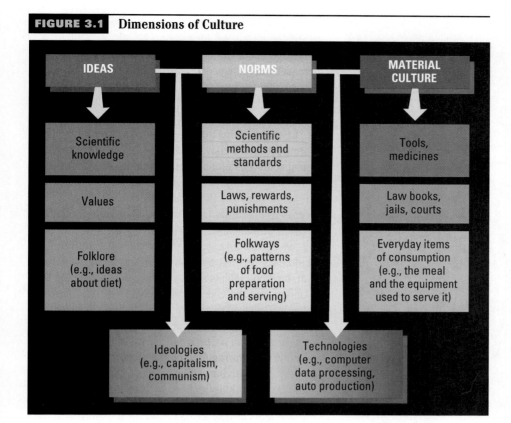

Values are socially shared ideas about what is right. Thus for most people in North America education is a value; that is, they conceive of it as a proper and good way to achieve social standing. Loyalty to friends and loved ones, patriotism, the importance of religion, the significance of material possessions—these and other values are commonly found in our culture and many others, but of course there are wide differences in how people interpret these values and in the extent to which they adhere to them. In small tribal and peasant societies there tends to be far greater consensus on values than in large, complex industrial societies. In a large and diverse society like ours, there is bound to be a good deal of conflict over values. Some people are satisfied with the way wealth and power are distributed, for example, while others are less satisfied with the status quo. Some people feel that it is desirable to attempt to improve one's own well-being and that society as a whole gains when everyone strives to be well-off. Others assert that the value of individual gain conflicts with the values of community and social cohesion; too great a gap between the well-off and the not-well-off creates suffering, envy, crime, and other problems.

In societies undergoing rapid and far-reaching social change, such as the United States, there is bound to be conflict over values. Controversies over "family values," the sanctity of marriage, obligations to children, and similar issues tend to be particularly intense because people's individual experiences differ greatly. The more diversity there is among the people who share a basic culture, the more conflict there is likely to be over certain aspects of that culture. Such disputes often turn on ideas about how to behave—that is, on the norms governing behavior in a society.

Norms. From people's beliefs in what is right and good—that is, from their values—are derived the norms of a society. Values are more abstract than norms; they are the ideas that support or justify norms. Norms are specific rules of behavior or, as Robert Nisbet (1970) wrote, "the adjustments which human beings make to the surrounding environment. We may think of them as solutions to recurring problems or situations" (p. 225). But norms involve more than behavior. Any given norm is supported by the idea that a particular behavior is correct and proper or incorrect and improper. "The moral order of society is a kind of tissue of 'oughts': negative ones which forbid certain actions and positive ones which [require certain] actions" (Nisbet, 1970, p. 226).

If we think about a complex aspect of everyday life like driving a car, it is evident that without norms life would be far more chaotic and dangerous than it already is. When we drive we keep to the right, obey traffic lights and speed limits, and avoid reckless behavior that could cause accidents. These are among the many norms that allow the automobile to be such an essential article of North American culture.

The tendency for people to decorate themselves is found in practically all human cultures. These women of the Akha tribe in Thailand display their wealth in the form of elaborate headdresses.

Examples of norms are easy to find. Take the college or high school classroom. The classroom is organized according to norms of educational practice: There should be a textbook or books; there should be class discussion; there should be assignments, exams, grades. Note that these "shoulds" correspond to actual behavior. Norms usually refer to behavior that we either approve or disapprove of. However, members of a culture often disagree about how a particular norm operates. Thus in the case of classroom organization there is considerable debate about what educational practices are most effective. In Israel, for example, there is debate among orthodox and liberal Jews over whether boys and girls should be separated in classrooms, and similar debates divide fundamentalist and more secular Muslims in other Middle Eastern societies.

In societies where values are in conflict or where changes are occurring rapidly, norms are also subject to change. This can readily be seen in the case of smoking. The norms governing smoking are changing rapidly as a result of changing values regarding health. Until recent years the norms governing smoking in the United States were very liberal. One could light up almost anywhere, and non-

smokers were expected not to complain. Recently, however, greater emphasis on fitness and health, as well as new knowledge about the dangers of secondhand smoke, have increased the value people place on clean air and tipped the balance against the earlier norms. But the change has not occurred without conflict between smokers and nonsmokers and their representatives in courts and legislatures.

Laws are norms that are included in a society's official written codes of behavior. Laws are often developed by a specialized occupational group, such as priests in the ancient world and legislators, judges, and lawyers in the modern world. Some of the oldest examples of laws are the Code of Hammurabi, the ancient Babylonian code that specified punishments equal to the gravity of the crime (e.g., an eye for an eye, a tooth for a tooth); the Ten Commandments, written by God, according to the Old Testament, on stone tablets at least 1,600 years before the birth of Christ; and the codes of Confucius, written and interpreted by the royal scribes of the ancient Chinese empire. In our time, laws are the special province of professional lawmakers, but all citizens participate in a network of laws and other written regulations that govern daily life. Basic behaviors like driving, going to school, marrying, and investing are greatly influenced by laws governing the conduct of these activities.

At times we may grumble or protest against laws that we find overly restrictive. And there is always some group planning to protest a law that is under consideration in a legislative body like Congress. But when we regard the world beyond our own society we see that the rule of law could save millions of lives if only it could be achieved in places like the former Yugoslavia, or Rwanda, or many of the nations of the former Soviet Union. On the other hand, even in nations where the rule of law is generally accepted, social scientists often find that new laws have unintended consequences. For example, when extremely strict laws against adult drug-dealing were passed, the dealers began recruiting teenagers to sell drugs. The lawmakers never intended the new laws to encourage teenagers to become dealers, but in many states that is what happened (Bayer, 1991). Quite often laws have unintended consequences because they were created in response to vigorous efforts by people who espouse particular ideologies.

Ideologies. As indicated in Figure 3.1, **ideologies** combine two dimensions of culture; they are sets or systems of ideas and norms. Ideologies combine the values and norms that all the members of a society are expected to believe in and act upon without question. A classic study of the emergence of an ideology was Max Weber's (1974/1904) analysis of the link between Protestantism and capitalism *(The Protestant Ethic and the Spirit of Capitalism).* Weber noticed that the rise of Protestantism in Europe coincided with the rise of private enterprise, banking, and other aspects of capitalism. He also noticed that a majority of the most successful early capitalists were

THEN AND NOW

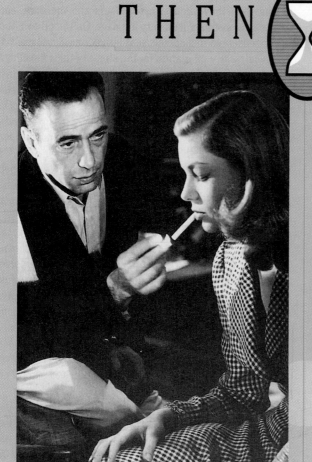

THE ONCE GLAMOROUS HABIT

How quickly norms can change, and how much confusion those changes can bring. Smoking is a fine example. In less than 4 decades this behavior changed from a glamorous activity to an act that many people consider deviant.

For most of this century smoking was extremely popular. The majority of Americans smoked, and smoking was even more popular in England and on the European continent. Humphrey Bogart and Lauren Bacall smoked, as did most other movie stars, as well as many athletes and famous journalists. Smoking reached its peak of popularity during and just after World War II. Children often began smoking steadily by age 14, encouraged to do so by ubiquitous advertising that associated smoking with success, sensuality, and, in the case of the famous Marlboro cowboys, masculinity.

Today much has changed. Smoking has been shown to be extremely dangerous to health, not only the health of the smoker but also the health of people exposed to tobacco smoke. In consequence, the norms and values associated with smoking are being challenged throughout most Western nations. New norms restricting smoking in public places and in most offices are creating a deviant group of smokers who must linger outside their offices to satisfy their craving and enjoy a cigarette.

Protestants. Weber hypothesized that their religious values taught them that salvation depended not on good deeds or piety but on how they lived their entire lives and particularly on how well they adhered to the norms of their "callings" (occupations). As a result, the Protestants placed a high value on frugality and abstinence. To prove that they were worthy of salvation, they devoted themselves tirelessly to commerce and plowed their profits back into their firms. But Catholics, who did not share these values, were less single-mindedly dedicated to their business ventures. They often spent their profits on good deeds rather than investing them in their businesses. Weber attempted to show how a set of religious values and norms combined with economic norms to create the ideology of capitalism.

A contemporary example of an ideology may be found among religious fundamentalists. Christian fundamentalists in the United States generally share a set of ideas and norms of behavior that include the value of prayer, the value of family and children, the negative value of abortion and secular humanism (an ethical system based on scientific knowledge rather than on religious teachings), the belief in salvation and redemption for one's sins, and other values.

Material Culture. The third dimension of culture identified by Bierstedt is material culture. Material culture consists of all the things that a society produces. Mundane things like pots and pans or the wooden eating bowls of nonindustrial societies; immensely complex systems of things, such as the space shuttle; cherished items of religious worship like rosary beads or Indian fetish necklaces—all take their shape and purpose from the ideas of the culture that produces them. Members of societies that place a high value on science and efficiency are used to seeing these values expressed in material objects. For example, we design our houses to conserve energy and create desirable combinations of view and privacy. We may take older forms like the ranch house or the Cape Cod bungalow and modify them to suit modern purposes; in this way our houses combine tradition with usefulness. The particular form that appeals to us is usually a result of many different ideas, including what we know from our own upbringing, what we can afford, how much space we require, and the environmental conditions we anticipate.

The same is true throughout the world. If one travels in Africa, for example, one will find large areas in which people build square houses with thatched roofs or roofs of corrugated metal. Suddenly one will pass into a region where the people build round houses with steeply pitched roofs. In another region people may live in sprawling apartmentlike complexes built of sand and mortar. When asked why they prefer a particular kind of dwelling, people usually say "Because we have always built our houses this way." In other words, their answers are based on ideas of what is right for them. But on further discussion a traveler with a sociological imagination will discover that the different building forms also express functional ideas. The mud-walled "apartments" of the desert village seem cramped and dark to Western eyes, but the people of the village will explain that they often sleep outdoors and the dark, cool rooms are most useful on very hot days. On the other hand, the tribespeople in a society that builds round houses may give a spiritual explanation for the shape of their dwellings; they may believe that corners are places where evil spirits can lurk. In sum, different cultures may give different reasons for the form and function of an element of material culture such as a house, but in all cultures one will find a material culture that stems from that culture's most important ideas (Kidder, 1985; Rybczynski, 1987).

Technologies. Technologies are another aspect of culture that spans two of Bierstedt's major dimensions. (See Figure 3.1.) **Technologies** are the things (material culture) and the norms for using them that are found in a given culture (Bierstedt, 1963; Ellul, 1964). Without the norms that govern their use, things are at best confusing and at worst useless or dangerous. In the United States, for example, new telecommunications technologies based on computers, modems, and networks like the Internet are a powerful means of communicating information over long distances. But norms for using these new technologies—such as norms about privacy, freedom of speech, and personal accountability—are only now developing, often out of serious conflicts about what content should and should not be tolerated on the networks.

Guns are another case in which norms governing use of the things themselves are very much in dispute. Most Americans agree that people should be free to own and use hunting weapons—but what about handguns, assault rifles, machine guns, and rocket launchers? What, if any, restrictions should there be on the distribution and use of such weapons? As we will see in later chapters, the debate about appropriate norms for controlling the distribution and possession of deadly firearms that are clearly not designed for hunting is an indication of a deeper cultural conflict over the right to bear arms versus the state's monopoly over the use of force.

NORMS AND SOCIAL CONTROL

Norms are what permit life in society to proceed in an orderly fashion without violence and chaos. Shared norms contribute enormously to a society's ability to regulate itself without constantly resorting to the coercive force of armies and police. The term **social control** refers to the set of rules and understandings that control the behavior of individuals and groups in a culture. Park and Burgess (1921) noted that throughout the world there are certain basic norms that contribute to social control. "All groups have such 'commandments' as 'Honor thy father and mother,' 'Thou shalt not kill,' 'Thou shalt not steal'" (p. 787).

The wide array of norms that permit a society to achieve relatively peaceful social control is called its

normative order. It is the normative order that creates what Morris Janowitz has termed "the capacity of a social group, including a whole society, to regulate itself" (1978, p. 3). This self-regulation requires a set of "higher moral principles" and the norms that express those principles. The norms define what makes a person a "good" member of the culture and society.

The most important norms in a culture are often taught as absolutes. The Ten Commandments, for example, are absolutes: "Thou shalt not kill," "Thou shalt not steal," and so on. Unfortunately, people do not always extend those norms to members of another culture. For example, the same explorers who swore to bring the values of Western civilization (including the Ten Commandments) to the "savage" Indians of the New World thought nothing of taking the Indians' land by force. Queen Elizabeth I of England could authorize agents like Sir Walter Raleigh to seize remote "heathen and barbarous" lands without viewing this act as a violation of the strongest norms of her own society (Jennings, 1975; Snipp, 1991). Protests by the Indians often resulted in violent death, but the murder of Indians and the theft of their land was rationalized by the notion that the Indians were an inferior people who would ultimately benefit from European influence. In the ideology of conquest and colonial rule, the Ten Commandments did not apply.

In the social sciences, punishments and rewards for adhering to or violating norms are known as **sanctions.** Cultural norms vary according to the degree of sanction associated with them. Rewards can range from a smile to the Nobel Prize; punishments may vary in strength from a raised eyebrow to the electric chair. During the period of European colonial expansion, the murder of a native was far less strongly sanctioned than was the murder of another European.

The most strongly sanctioned norms are called **mores.**[1] They are norms that people consider vital to the continuation of human groups and societies, and therefore they figure prominently in a culture's sense of morality. **Folkways,** on the other hand, are far less strongly sanctioned. People often cannot explain why these norms exist, nor do they feel that they are essential to the continuation of the group or the society. Both terms were first used by William Graham Sumner in his study *Folkways* (1940/1907). Sumner also pointed out that laws are norms that have been enacted through the formal procedures of government. Laws often formalize the mores of a society by putting them into written form and interpreting them. But

[1] This term, pronounced "morays," is the plural of the Latin word *mos*, "custom."

Young people who engage in radical piercing are implicitly challenging conventional notions about personal adornment. Their behavior does not violate the mores of their culture, but the new folkways they are choosing may be disapproved of in some parts of society.

laws can also formalize folkways, as can be seen, for example, in laws governing the wearing of clothing in public places.

Sumner also pointed out that a person who violates mores is subject to severe moral indignation whereas one who violates folkways is not. People who violate folkways such as table manners or dress codes may be thought of as idiosyncratic or "flaky," but those who violate mores are branded as morally reprehensible. Thus among prisoners there are norms for the treatment of other prisoners, based on the types of crimes they committed "outside." Rapists and child molesters are moral outcasts; their offenses are the most reprehensible. Such offenders are often beaten and tormented by other prisoners.

Box 3.1 presents a typology of norms according to their degree of sanction and their mode of development—that is, whether they are formal or informal. Laws and other norms, such as company regulations or the rules of games and sports, are known as *formal norms.* They differ from *informal norms,* which grow out of everyday behavior and do not usually take the form of written rules, even though they too regulate our behavior. For example, when waiting to enter a movie theater, it is usually permissible to have one member of a small group save a place in line for the others, who may return later. And in a "pickup" basketball game a player can call a foul and the opposing player usually cannot contest the call. Of course, there are times when such norms are disputed, depending on how the people involved define the situation. In the case of the basketball game, when the player on whom the foul is called disagrees with the call—and the score is extremely close—different definitions of the situation can lead to conflict.

CULTURE AND SOCIAL CHANGE

Cultures in all societies change, and much of social science is devoted to trying to understand and predict those changes. Norms and values that once were thought to be odd or criminal may come to be shared by the majority of the society's members, and the opposite can occur as well. In the 1996 Olympic Games, for example, American women dominated many events in which they had previously been weak performers. In the past, American women were often reluctant to lift weights and improve their strength for fear of being considered unfeminine. As the level of world competition increased, Americans found ways to overcome the older values that said women had to be soft in order to be feminine. Star female athletes continue to demonstrate to the American public that a woman can be muscular and athletic and still project a "feminine" identity.

Figure 3.1 and Box 3.1 present some key aspects of human culture, but they leave out all the social processes whereby elements of culture are produced and changed and diffused from one society to another. An unsuspecting reader might even conclude that a society's norms and values are shared equally by all of its members, which is hardly an accurate view of culture. Any given norm is likely to be obeyed to varying degrees by different people within a culture. Consider the norms about marriage, fertility, and parenthood in the United States. All may agree that young couples should not have children out of wedlock. They may also agree that abortion is not a desirable means of birth control. Unmarried couples who are expecting a child resolve the conflict between these norms in different ways: Some obtain an abortion; others get married; still others decide to have the baby out of wedlock, perhaps giving it up for adoption. Some unmarried mothers decide to raise their children alone. One way or another, such events in people's intimate family lives require difficult choices among often contradictory norms.

When large numbers of people reject the normative order for private gain, as appears to be occurring in some regions of the former Soviet Union, the result may be higher rates of crime and civil strife. Similarly, as populations grow and societies become larger and more complex through immigration and urban growth, conflicts over values and norms are likely to become more severe. In times of great social change and conflict, cultures tend to become more punitive and coercive in attempting to maintain order, often without success. Even where there is much consensus about norms, however, new ideas, styles, and

This nineteenth-century painting shows a woman depositing her newborn infant in a "receptacle for foundlings" probably associated with a church or cathedral. Women who violated the norms of legitimate fertility by bearing children out of wedlock were often forced to give up their infants.

BOX 3.1 SOCIOLOGICAL METHODS

Constructing a Typology of Norms

Typologies are ways of grouping observable phenomena into categories in order to identify regularities in what may appear to be a great variety of observations. For example, there are so many social norms that the average person has no hope of ever sorting them out without some kind of system for organizing them. In the chart presented here, the subject is norms of various types. The sociologist constructs the types by comparing various dimensions along which norms may differ. The norms listed in the Ten Commandments, for example, differ in many ways. The norm "Thou shalt not kill" not only is generally believed and passed along from one generation to the next but also is codified in laws. So is the commandment "Thou shalt not steal," which is an important part of the written laws of our society. But the commandment "Remember the Sabbath day, to keep it holy" is not a written law in the United States, at least not in the federal statutes.

In some states and communities there are laws that specify that businesses must close on Sunday, but not all religious groups recognize Sunday as the Sabbath. In addition, ideas about what behaviors are appropriate on the Sabbath are changing, and laws governing those behaviors are being challenged. These differences indicate that norms may differ according to whether they are informally taught to new generations or whether they are formal, written "laws of the land."

Another dimension along which norms may differ is the degree to which they are sanctioned—that is, the degree to which adherence is rewarded and violation is punished. The norm that men do not wear hats indoors is relatively weak. On the other hand, the norm that men and women do not casually display (or "flash") their genitals is strongly sanctioned.

Using these two comparative dimensions—mode of development (formal vs. informal) and degree of sanction

(weak vs. strong)—we can create four categories: (1) norms that are informal and are weakly sanctioned (e.g., table manners, dress fashions), (2) norms that are informal but are strongly sanctioned (e.g., adultery), (3) norms that are part of the formal legal code but are weakly sanctioned (parking regulations, antismoking laws, etc.), and (4) norms that are formal laws and are strongly sanctioned (e.g., capital offenses like murder of a police officer or treason in wartime).

By juxtaposing the two dimensions, each with its two categories, we arrive at a fourfold classification of norms (see chart). But as Max Weber (1949) observed, such a classification is an "ideal-typical" arrangement of observations in a form that accentuates some aspects and neglects others. These ideal types (folkways, mores and taboos, misdemeanor laws, and felonies or capital offenses) are useful because they establish standards against which to compare the norms of other cultures. For example, not all cultures treat the norm about the Sabbath the way Americans do. In parts of Israel or the Islamic lands one could be arrested for violating the Sabbath laws. Typologies like this one also help identify areas of social change, as when one compares the way the Sabbath was treated in American laws earlier in this century, when stores were obliged to close on Sunday, with the way it is treated today, when Sunday is often viewed as another shopping day.

But the aspects of society described by ideal types are rarely so uncomplicated in real life. Even the norms that seem most formal and unambiguous, such as the prohibition against murder, become murky under some conditions, as in cases of self-defense or in war, or in arguments about the death penalty and abortion. Studies of how actual behavior departs from the ideal-typical version invariably offer insights into how cultures and social structures are changing in the course of daily life.

	DEGREE OF SANCTION	
MODE OF DEVELOPMENT	RELATIVELY WEAK	RELATIVELY STRONG
Informal	Folkways, fashions	Taboos, mores
Formal	Misdemeanor laws, some rules, guidelines, civil rights laws	Capital-offense laws, felony laws

BOX 3.2 GLOBAL SOCIAL CHANGE

Norms of Tobacco Use

What happens in a culture when a widespread norm turns out to encourage behavior that is destructive? What does it take to change such norms and behavior? How long does the change take? What will occur in other societies to which the norm is spreading, and what are the moral responsibilities of the culture that is spreading the norm? Norms of tobacco use in the United States and throughout the world raise these questions with great urgency. The answers are swirling in the tobacco smoke that fewer Americans, but an increasing number of people in other nations, are consuming.

Tobacco was used by Native Americans for its intoxicating effects, as a medicinal substance, and for religious ceremonies (Ravenholt, 1990). Early European explorers and conquerors spread its use to Europe and other ocean trading societies (e.g., Turkey and Japan) during the sixteenth and seventeenth centuries. In England pipe smoking was extremely popular in Queen Elizabeth's court in the late 1500s, but when James I assumed the throne after Elizabeth's death in 1603, the world witnessed its first great narcotics debate. The new king believed tobacco to be "a custome lothesome to the eye, hateful to the nose, harmfull to the braine, dangerous to the lungs" (quoted in Austin, 1978, p. 6). The king soon realized, however, that his efforts to ban tobacco use would not stem its spread among people who could afford it. He therefore decided to make

Number of Cigarettes Consumed Annually per Adult (Age 18 and Older, United States), 1900–1990

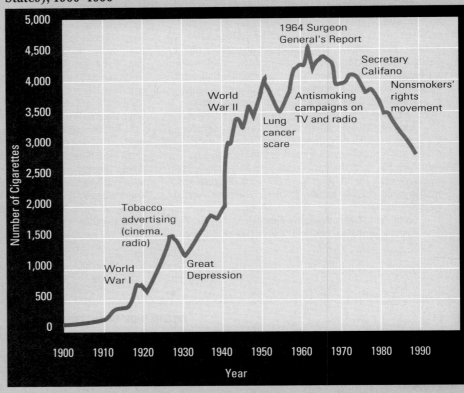

Source: Economic Research Service, U.S. Department of Agriculture.

technologies contribute to changes in norms and behaviors (see Box 3.2).

Another important issue in understanding culture and social change is the question of the extent to which human culture is determined by biological factors, if at all. Are there any features that all human cultures share—any norms, for example, that are found in all known societies? And what happens when two cultures exist within the same society or nation? The remainder of this chapter explores these questions, beginning with one that has long been a subject of lively debate: the connection between culture and biology.

tobacco a source of royal revenue by granting land in the Virginia colony to settlers who promised to grow tobacco as a cash crop whose importation he could control and tax.

Despite its high cost, the use of tobacco spread rapidly, especially in the form of snuff (powdered tobacco), which was popular among the European upper classes in the 1700s. Cigars and cigarettes were introduced to Europe and the United States in the early 1800s by soldiers returning from wars in the Middle East. During the American Civil War smoking became popular among soldiers, who enjoyed a particularly American style of tobacco consumption, the chewing of a mixture of tobacco leaves and molasses. The invention of cigarette rolling machines in the late nineteenth century and their use in tobacco factories in Virginia and North Carolina made the supply of cigarettes almost unlimited and guaranteed that the economies of those states would be dominated by tobacco cultivation for many generations.

During the twentieth century, spurred by modern advertising techniques and the development of mass media, the rate of cigarette consumption in the United States increased a hundredfold, from 2.5 billion cigarettes smoked in 1900 to a peak of 640 billion in 1988. The influence of American civilization throughout the world during this period also caused huge increases in worldwide cigarette consumption even as evidence of the health hazards of regular smoking mounted.

Although the accompanying chart shows that cigarette smoking is declining in the United States, smoking is on the rise elsewhere in the world. Cigarette smoking is now the most serious and widespread form of addiction in the world. It accounts for almost 5 million deaths annually in the United States, and the death toll from tobacco use is rising in other nations. In China, for example, cultivation, export, and consumption of tobacco are on the rise; given the size of the Chinese population, this represents an ominous trend for world health.

There is evidence in the declining curve of cigarette consumption in the United States that campaigns against smoking and concern about the hazards of tobacco use are rapidly changing the norms of smoking. Once considered chic and sexy, smoking is now increasingly seen as dangerous to the smoker and to others nearby. But levels of smoking in the United States remain extremely high (see table), suggesting that the norms established over a century of tobacco use are extremely difficult to reverse. And given the popularity of smoking elsewhere in the world, the prospects for turning smoking into a negatively rather than a positively sanctioned norm are dim.

Annual Adult per Capita Consumption of Manufactured Cigarettes, Selected Countries

Cuba	3,920	Italy	2,460	Costa Rica	1,340	Laos	490
Greece	3,640	France	2,400	Mexico	1,190	Ghana	380
Poland	3,300	Germany	2,360	Morocco	1,070	Nigeria	370
United States	3,270	Turkey	1,970	Indonesia	1,050	Bolivia	330
Japan	3,270	Colombia	1,920	Iraq	980	Bangladesh	270
Canada	3,180	Malaysia	1,840	Thailand	900	India	160
Switzerland	2,960	Portugal	1,730	Pakistan	660	Nepal	150
Libya	2,850	Brazil	1,700	Iran	620	Ethiopia	60
Australia	2,720	Netherlands	1,690	Senegal	610		
Korea, Republic of	2,660	China	1,590	Kenya	550		

Source: Ravenholt, 1990.

CULTURE, EVOLUTION, AND HUMAN BEHAVIOR

Of all the species of living creatures on this planet, human beings are the most widely distributed. The early European explorers—Columbus, Magellan, Cook, da Gama, and many others—marveled at the discovery of human life thriving, more or less, in some of the earth's most inhospitable environments. Nevertheless, they were convinced that the "savages" they encountered were inferior to the more powerful Europeans; in fact, they had difficulty accepting the idea that the native peoples were fully human. In other words, they considered them biologically as well as culturally inferior.

Groups that are in conflict often accuse their enemies of being biologically inferior. The Nazis claimed that the Jews were a biologically inferior people. Serbian Orthodox Christians think of the Muslim Bosnians as innately inferior, just as some people in the United States believe that African Americans and other groups, such as Puerto Ricans, are inferior. These and other examples of racial and ethnic prejudice will be discussed more fully in later chapters. Here we need to emphasize that differences in culture are frequently viewed as innate biological differences between distinct peoples.

Students of sociology must see beyond this tendency to confuse cultural and biological differences. To do so, it is first necessary to understand how the famous naturalist Charles Darwin revolutionized modern thinking on these issues. Darwin's theory of evolution and, in particular, of natural selection is a starting point for scientific explanations of the differences among the animal species, including the human species (Eisley, 1961).

DARWIN'S THEORY OF NATURAL SELECTION

Darwin's theory of **natural selection** is the central explanation of how living species evolve to adapt to their changing environments. It is based on the observation that unexpected physical changes, or *mutations,* in organisms occur more or less randomly from one generation to the next. When those mutations improve an individual organism's ability to survive in its environment, the new traits are "selected for"; that is, an individual that possesses those traits is more likely to survive, and hence more likely to reproduce and pass on its traits to the next generation, than individuals that lack the new traits. Over a few generations such mutations can become so extensive that two species are created where formerly there was only one. This process of natural selection accounts for the great diversity of animal and plant life on the earth and for the ability of animals and plants to adapt to new environments.

Darwin's theory was based on his empirical observations of the natural world, especially those he had made as a scientist aboard the HMS *Beagle* during an extensive voyage of exploration in the early 1830s. On that voyage Darwin had observed, in both fossils and living specimens, that some species of birds, turtles, and other animals had modified their physical form in ways that seemed to "fit" or "adapt" them to their environment. It took him almost two decades of study and reflection to make sense of his observations. After all, much of what he had observed directly challenged the fundamental beliefs of most of the religious and scientific leaders of his day. For when Darwin considered all the information, and especially his observations of similar species on different islands, it became clear to him that God had not created all the living things on earth at

once—instead, they had been evolving through natural selection over many millions of years. And this theory could be applied to all other species, including humans.

THE SOCIAL DARWINISTS

The theory of natural selection had a dramatic impact on biological science but an even greater effect on the prevailing views of human society. Among the social thinkers who were most profoundly influenced by Darwin was Herbert Spencer of England, whose writings in sociology and philosophy were to dominate intellectual life in much of the Western world from 1870 to 1890.

According to Spencer, the fact that humans, unlike other species, have remained similar even on different continents must be explained by the fact that we adapt to changes in our environment through the use of culture rather than through biological adaptation. This process, which can be termed **cultural evolution,** parallels biological evolution in that the most successful adaptations are handed down to the next generation (Geertz, 1973). Spencer had this process in mind when he coined the phrase "survival of the fittest." He meant that the people who are most successful at adapting to the environment in which they find themselves—that is, the better-educated, wealthier, more powerful people—are most likely to survive and to have children who will also be successful.

Spencer concluded that it is impossible, by means of intentional action, to improve on the course of cultural evolution. The task of sociology, as he saw it, is to discover that course through empirical observation and analysis. Sociologists should not engage in efforts to reform society—to aid the poor, for example. To do so would be futile, and it could have the damaging effect of violating the principle of survival of the fittest in favor of the "artificial preservation of those least able to take care of themselves" (Spencer, 1874, p. 343).

Spencer's view, which came to be known as **social Darwinism,** claimed to explain why some people prospered during the industrial revolution while others barely scraped by. The people who were being pushed off the land and into the factories and slums of the cities were less well equipped culturally to succeed in an urban environment than people who could innovate and invent. There was not much for government to do, according to Spencer's theory, besides keep the peace and let the most competitive groups in society flourish. In so doing, those groups would give less competitive groups a chance to survive, if not to thrive.

Darwin's theory of evolution thus spawned a revolution in social thought. It also produced North America's first prominent sociologist and social philosopher, William Graham Sumner. Sumner (1963/1911) developed a theory of society based on humans' need to adapt to an environment of scarcity. According to his theory, when resources, especially land, were plentiful, there would be peace, and institutions based on democratic forms of government could thrive. But eventually, when population growth made it necessary to distribute the same amounts of resources among more people, societies would lean toward oligarchy (rule by the most powerful) and greater use of coercion and force.

By the end of the nineteenth century, efforts to apply the theory of natural selection to human societies had reached their logical extreme. Largely as a result of the work of Spencer, Sumner, and their followers, early sociologists in the United States and other Western societies favored the view that Western culture, with its emphasis on competition within the capitalist system, was clearly superior to all others and that the people who were most successful at competing within that system were to be considered superior human beings.

The next generation of social scientists, who came to prominence around the turn of the century, rejected this theory. In Chicago and other U.S. cities where the industrial revolution was still occurring, they saw mounting evidence that wealth itself brings privilege to the children of the wealthy, regardless of whatever innate or learned traits they may possess. Cultural evolution, they argued, is a result of the development of more effective institutions and is not related to the innate qualities of individuals. Successful business firms, for example, are able to prosper in a highly competitive environment because of their superior organization. That is, their success can be explained without recourse to arguments about the genetic fitness of their leaders.

SOCIOBIOLOGY

The tendency to explain social phenomena in terms of biological causes such as physiology or genes is known as *biological reductionism.* For example, explanations of crime proposing that there are genes that produce criminal behavior reduce the explanation of crime to biological causes. Some form of biological reductionism has emerged in every generation since Darwin's time.

The most recent version of biological reductionism is **sociobiology.** This term, coined by the Harvard biologist Edward O. Wilson (1975), refers to efforts to link genetic factors with the social behavior of animals. When applied to human societies, sociobiology has drawn severe criticism from both social scientists and biologists. Nevertheless, some sociologists support the sociobiological hypothesis that genes can explain certain aspects of human society and behavior (Caplan, 1978; Quadagno, 1979; Sahlins, 1976; van den Berghe, 1979; Fox, 1989; Mascie-Taylor, 1990; Maxwell, 1991). Because this hypothesis is so controversial it deserves a closer look.

Let us take as an example the incest taboo, one of the strongest and most widespread norms in human life. The social scientist tends to explain the incest taboo as a cultural norm that is necessary for the existence of the family as a social institution. The family is an organized group with a need for well-defined statuses and roles. Should the different statuses within the family become confused, as would undoubtedly happen if sexual intimacy were permitted between children and their parents or between brothers and sisters, it would be difficult to maintain the family as a stable institution (Malinowski, 1927; Davis, 1939).

Sociobiology takes a different view. For the sociobiologist, the incest taboo develops from

> a deeper, more urgent cause, the heavy physiological penalty imposed by inbreeding. Several studies by human geneticists have demonstrated that even a moderate amount of inbreeding results in children who are diminished in overall body size, muscular coordination, and academic performance. More than 100 recessive genes have been discovered that cause hereditary disease . . . a condition vastly enhanced by inbreeding. (Wilson, 1979, p. 38)

Throughout most of the history of human evolution, sociobiologists point out, humans did not have any knowledge of genetics. Thus "the 'gut feeling' that promotes . . . sanctions against incest is largely unconscious" (Wilson, 1979, p. 40). Individuals with a strong predisposition to avoid incest passed on more of their genes to the next generation because their children were less likely to suffer from the illnesses that result from inbreeding. And over many centuries of natural selection of individuals who did not inbreed, humans developed "an instinct [to avoid inbreeding] which is based on genes" (Wilson, 1979, p. 40).

This leap, from the observation of a strong and persistent norm like the incest taboo to the belief that certain human behaviors are genetically programmed, is an example of the sociobiological hypothesis regarding human nature. Sociobiologists have proposed a hypothesis in which not only the incest taboo but also aggression, homosexuality, and religious feelings are genetically programmed, and they believe that future discoveries by geneticists will prove their hypothesis correct.

Although it is true that genes set limits on human abilities and can be shown to influence many aspects of brain functioning, the hypothesis that genetic programming establishes complex forms of normative behavior is not supported by direct evidence: There is as yet no proof that such genes or sets of genes actually exist (Lewontin, 1977, 1982). Nevertheless, the rules of science require that we not reject the sociobiological hypothesis and that it remain an open area of investigation.

The counterargument to sociobiology is that the human brain and other physical attributes are products of interaction between cultural and biological evolution and that in the past hundred thousand years of human evolution there has been relatively little organic change in our species. Instead, the important developments in human life have occurred as a result of social and cultural change. This widely accepted view of culture denies that humans have innate instincts such as an instinct to avoid incest. It argues instead that the great advantage of culture in human evolution is its creation of a basis for natural selection that would not be dependent on genes but would allow humans to adapt relatively quickly to any physical or social environment (Geertz, 1973).

Archaeological evidence shows that humans were using tools for primitive agriculture and making jewelry and personal adornments more than 30,000 years ago (Stevens, 1988). No doubt they began using fire even earlier. Once humans could use fire and hand tools and simple weapons, the ability to make and use these items increased the survival chances of those who possessed these skills. This would create conditions for natural selection in which the traits being "selected for" were those that had to do with the manipulation of cultural and social aspects of life. These abilities (dexterity, linguistic ability, leadership, social skills, and so on) would in turn influence the further development of the human brain, again through the process of natural selection.

This view is supported by research on primate behavior showing that the higher primates use simple tools and that they teach this cultural technique to their young (Goodall, 1968; Schaller, 1964). Jane Goodall (1968), for example, described how chimpanzees use sticks to probe for termites and chew leaves to produce a pulp to be used as a sponge to draw water out of tree stumps. These and many other instances of rudimentary culture among animal species demonstrate that culture is not unique to humans; that is, we are not alone in using culture to aid in adaptation. What happened in the case of humans that did not happen (or at least has not happened yet) in any other species is that at a certain stage in human prehistory our ability to alter our cultures in response to changing conditions developed so quickly that the human species entered a new realm of social life. In other words, culture became self-generating. And once it had been freed from genetic constraints, culture had no limits.

LANGUAGE AND CULTURE

Perhaps the most significant of the inventions made possible by culture is language. In fact, the learning of culture takes place through language. From our enormous capacity to use language is derived our collective memory (myths, fables, sayings, ballads, and the like), as well as writing, art, and all the other media that shape human consciousness and store and transmit knowledge. Note that although the capacity to learn language appears to be innate (Chomsky, 1965), language does not occur outside a cultural setting and indeed is the most universal dimension of human cultures.

To return to the example at the beginning of this chapter, as savage as they may have appeared to Columbus and his crew, the Native Americans had language. They could learn Spanish, just as the explorers could have learned their language if they had made an effort to do so. But without a language in which they could communicate with each other, the "Indians" and the explorers misunderstood each other far more than they would have if they had possessed this powerful communication tool. Without language, neither side could explain to the other its strange behaviors and different ways of dealing with the physical world.

What is unique about human language? Primatologists have shown that our closest evolutionary kin, the great apes (especially chimpanzees and pygmy chimpanzees), can learn language to some extent. Although their throats are not capable of producing the sounds that humans mold into language, apes do have the capacity to use language; that is, they can grasp the meanings of words as symbols for things and relationships. Through the use of sign language, or special languages using typewriters and other devices, apes can be taught a limited vocabulary.

To the surprise of many skeptics, Francine Patterson taught Koko, a female gorilla, American Sign Language. Koko learned more than 300 words. She also disproved the theory that apes can learn words but cannot invent new concepts. Koko invented sign words for *ring* ("finger bracelet") and *mask* ("eye hat") and was even able to talk in sign language about her feelings of fear, happiness, and shame (Hill, 1978). More recent research using a pygmy chimpanzee named Kanzi has revealed that apes may actually be able to learn language through observation and imitation, the way a child does, rather than through long and difficult training (Eckholm, 1985). Sue Savage-Rumbaugh has demonstrated that Kanzi recognizes English syntax, the patterns in the ordering of signs or words that give sentences different meanings. For example, Kanzi can distinguish between "Throw the potato at the ball" and "Throw the ball at the potato." Savage-Rumbaugh has also shown that Kanzi can acquire new words simply by listening and watching as other chimps learn (Savage-Rumbaugh & Lewin, 1995). This kind of imitative language learning was formerly thought to be beyond the ape's mental capacities.

Fascinating as these experiments are, they only confirm the immense difference in communicative ability between humans and the apes. After months of training, an adult ape can use language with no more skill than an average 2½-year-old human infant (Harris, 1983; Terrace, 1979). On the basis of the research conducted so far, primate researchers conclude that the apes' innate ability to learn language is severely restricted. No amount of training can produce in apes the more advanced uses of language, including complex sentences containing abstract concepts, that are found in all normal humans regardless of their culture (Eibl-Eibesfeldt, 1989). For example, every human language allows its speakers to express an infinite number of thoughts and ideas that can persist even after their originators are gone. This property of human language, which is not shared by any other known species (Eisley, 1970; Rymer, 1992 a,b), allows human groups to transmit elements of their culture from one generation to the next.

So complete is the human reliance on language that it often seems as if language actually determines the possibilities for thought and action in any given culture. Perhaps we are actually unable to perceive phenomena for which we have no nouns or to engage in actions for which we have no verbs. This idea is expressed in the **linguistic-relativity hypothesis.** As developed by the American linguists Edward Sapir and Benjamin Whorf in the 1930s, this hypothesis asserts that "a person's thoughts are controlled by inexorable laws or patterns of which he is unconscious. . . . His thinking itself is in a language—in English, in Sanskrit, in Chinese. And every language is a vast pattern-system, different from others" (Whorf, 1961, p. 135).

This observation was based on evidence from the social sciences, especially anthropology. For example, Margaret Mead's field research among the Arapesh of New Guinea had revealed that the Arapesh had no developed system of numbers. Theirs was a technologically simple society, and therefore complex numbering systems were not much use to them. They counted only "one, two, and one and two, and dog" (dog being the equivalent of four and probably based on the dog's four legs). To count seven objects, the Arapesh would say "dog and one and two." Eight would be "two dog," and twenty-four would come out as "two dog, two dog, two dog." It is easy to see that in this small society one would quickly become tired of attempting to count much beyond twenty-four and would simply say "many" (Mead, 1971).

Other cultures have been found to have only a limited number of words for colors, and as a result they do not make some of the fine distinctions between colors that we do. And in a famous example Whorf argued that many languages have ways of referring to time that are very different from those found in English and other Indo-European languages. In English we have verb tenses, which lead us to make sharp distinctions among past, present, and future time. In Vietnamese, in contrast, there are no separate forms of verbs to indicate different times; the phrase tôi đi về, for example, could mean "I'm going home" or "I went home" or "I will go home." The language of the Hopi Indians also lacks clear tenses, and it seemed to Whorf that this made it unlikely that the Hopi culture could develop the systems of timekeeping that are essential to modern science and technology.

Thus in its most radical form the linguistic-relativity hypothesis asserts that language actually determines the possibilities for a culture's norms, beliefs, and values. But there is little justification for this extreme version of the hypothesis. The Arapesh did not have a developed number system, but they could easily learn to count using the Western base-10 system. Once they were exposed to the money economy of the modern world, most isolated cultures formed words for the base-10 number system or else incorporated foreign words into their own vocabularies. They had no difficulty understanding the use of money, and this too became incorporated into so-called primitive cultures.

A more acceptable version of the linguistic-relativity hypothesis recognizes the mutual influences of culture and language. One does not determine the other. For example, someone living in Canada or the northern parts of the United States is likely to have a much larger vocabulary for talking about snow (loose powder, packed powder, corn snow, slush, and so on) than a person from an area where snow is rare. A person who loves to watch birds will have a much larger vocabulary about bird habitats and bird names than one who cares little about bird life. In each case we realize that in order to share the world of bird-watchers or of winter sports fans, we will need to learn new ways of seeing and of talking about what we see. So, although the extreme version of the linguistic-relativity hypothesis is incorrect, it has been a valuable stimulus toward the development of a less biased view of other cultures. We now understand that a culture's language expresses how the people of that culture perceive and understand the world and, at the same time, influences their perceptions and understandings.

CROSSING CULTURAL LINES

ETHNOCENTRISM AND CULTURAL RELATIVITY
As our discussion of language has shown, until we study other cultures it is extremely difficult to view our own with detachment and objectivity. Unless we can see ourselves as others see us, we take for granted that our own cultural traits are natural and proper and that traits that differ from ours are unnatural and somehow wrong. Our ways of behaving in public, our food and dress and sports—all of our cultural traits have become "internalized," so they seem almost instinctive. But once we understand another culture and how its members think and feel, we can look at our own traits from the perspective of that culture. This cross-cultural perspective has become an integral part of sociological analysis.

The ability to think in cross-cultural terms allows people to avoid the common tendency to disparage other cultures simply because they are different. However, most people live out their lives in a single culture. Indeed, they may go so far as to consider that culture superior to any other, anywhere in the world. Social scientists term this attitude **ethnocentrism.** Ethnocentrism refers to the tendency to judge other cultures as inferior in terms of one's own norms and values. The other culture is weighed against standards derived from the culture with which one

THE
PERSONAL CHALLENGE
Social Change and Intercultural Relations

It can take some courage to cross cultural boundaries. People who travel for any length of time in a new culture, espcially one whose language and norms are quite different from their own, often experience a sense of disorientation and confusion known as "culture shock." Sophisticated travelers learn how to cope with the feeling of being foreign. Businesspeople who work in global markets, for example, learn to feel at ease in strange cultures and not assume that they will be able to find a corner of home wherever they are. However, students who wish to become more culturally sophisticated may not need to travel very far. The resources for a cross-cultural experience could be available close to home.

More than 500,000 people from different cultures and societies settle in the United States each year. While most of them are concentrated in a few "gateway" cities like Miami, Los Angeles, and New York, increasing numbers are moving throughout the United States. It is likely that people from Asia, Latin America, Africa, or the Caribbean are moving into your own community. If so, it is also likely that their children are encountering various forms of social conflict and prejudice brought on by their foreignness. Adolescents and young adults are especially likely to express prejudice against those who are different. And the differences may not always be due to language or foreign forms of dress and diet. Minority or gay students may also feel like outsiders.

Reaching out to newcomers or those who are different can bring immense rewards. Cross-cultural friendships can change one's life in very positive ways. Mundane aspects of one's own life that are taken for granted can become subjects of animated discussion. By crossing cultural boundaries one can learn new ways of cooking, new ways of thinking about beauty, and much more. Often it takes some determination and a sense of security to resist the pressure to conform to the dominant group. But there is a wide and changing world of people who are different from us and from each other. By reaching out to those who are different, you can begin to develop the ability to move among them in a global environment.

is most familiar. The explorers' assumption that the Native Americans could benefit from the adoption of European cultural traits is an example of ethnocentric behavior. But such obvious ethnocentrism is not limited to historical examples. We encounter it every day—for example, in our use of the term *American* to refer to citizens of the United States and not to those of Canada and the South American nations. Another example is our tendency to judge other cultures by how well they supply their people with consumer goods rather than by how well they adhere to their own values.

To get along well in other parts of the world, a businessperson or politician or scientist must be able to suspend judgment about other cultures, an approach that is termed **cultural relativity.** Cultural relativity entails the recognition that all cultures develop their own ways of dealing with the specific demands of their environments. This kind of understanding does not come automatically through the experience of living among members of other cultures. It is an acquired skill.

There are limits, however, to the value of cultural relativity. It is an essential attitude to adopt in understanding another culture, but it does not require that one avoid moral judgment entirely. We can, for example, attempt to understand the values and ideologies of the citizens who supported the Nazi regime, even though we abhor what that regime stood for. And we can suspend our outrage at racism in our own society long enough to understand the culture that produced racial hatred and fear. But as social scientists it is also our task to evaluate the moral implications of a culture's norms and values and to condemn them when we see that they produce cruelty and suffering. To a large extent, worldwide outrage at South Africa's policies of apartheid (racial separation and enforced inferiority for black citizens) helped bring about the demise of those policies in the early 1990s.

CULTURAL UNIVERSALS

The cross-cultural approach to social research grew in part out of efforts to identify "cultural universals." If we could know, for example, whether the family as a social institution is found in all cultures, and how norms governing family behavior differ from one culture to another, we would be better equipped to understand how families adapt to various kinds of social change. In the United States the family is said to be characterized by the nuclear family unit (mother, father, and children) and by monogamy. But given our high rates of divorce and remarriage, it might be more accurate to describe the American family as tending toward what has been termed *serial monogamy*—that is, more than one spouse but only one at a time (Harris, 1983). Sociologists who study the family seek to discover whether this pattern exists in all industrial societies and whether it is also found in other types of cultures, in which case it could not be viewed as an adaptation to industrial society (Goode, 1971).

When we examine cultures for patterns of family organization that are like ours, we find that the nuclear family unit is the dominant family structure in many hunter-gatherer societies. In fact, the Eskimos have a kinship system so much like ours that the American system of measuring descent through the father's line, organizing families into small nuclear units, and encouraging remarriage after the death or departure of a spouse is sometimes referred to as the "Eskimo kinship system" (Harris, 1983; Murdock, 1967). Thus the nuclear family and serial monogamy are by no means unique to cultures that are adapting to an industrial social order.

In recent years the search for cultural universals has given way to other uses of cross-cultural comparisons. Every subfield of sociology has a literature on such comparisons. In cross-cultural studies of social stratification, for example, we generally try to find out whether the values attached to certain occupational statuses are shared all over the modern world.

Why do cross-cultural similarities exist? In some cases it is because elements of a culture have diffused across national boundaries and become part of a larger culture called a *civilization*. Because much cultural change occurs within the context of major civilizations, we devote the rest of this chapter to a discussion of civilizations and cultural change.

CIVILIZATIONS AND CULTURAL CHANGE

Civilizations are advanced cultures. They usually have forms of expression in writing and the arts, powerful economic and political institutions, and innovative technologies, all of which strongly influence other cultures with which they come into contact. Some civilizations, like those of ancient Egypt and Rome, declined thousands of years ago and exist today mainly in museums and in the consciousness of scholars, artists, and scientists. Others are living civilizations with long histories, like those of China and India, that were conquered by other civilizations and are rising again in forms that combine the old with the new. Islamic civilization is an example of such a civilization; much of the unrest in the Islamic world is due to conflicts that pit orthodox leaders like the late Ayatollah Khomeini against Western-influenced leaders like Jordan's King Hussein. Then there are the dominant civilizations of North America, Europe, the former Soviet Union, and Japan. They are dominant because they compete on a world scale to "export" their ideas and their technology—in fact, their entire culture or "blueprint for living."

Like most of the principal concepts in the social sciences, the concept of civilization can be elusive. It is used in many different contexts, in popular language as well as in social-scientific usage. In popular speech the word *civilization* is often used to make negative comparisons between people who adhere to the norms of polite conduct, and are therefore said to be "civilized," and those who are "uncouth" and act like "barbarians" or "savages." This is how the word was understood by the explorers of Columbus's time, and colonial conquest was justified in part as an effort to civilize the barbarians.

In his effort to trace the origins of Western notions of what is civilized and what is barbaric behavior, the German sociologist Norbert Elias (1978/1939) showed that much of what we call "civilized" behavior is derived from the norms of the courts of medieval Europe. Elias based his study on accounts by medieval writers of the spread of "courtesy" (the manners of the court) to other levels of society. The following are some examples from a thirteenth-century poem on courtly table manners:

> A man of refinement should not slurp his spoon when in company; that is the way people at court behave who often indulge in unrefined conduct.

> It is not polite to drink from the dish, although some who approve of this rude habit insolently pick up the dish and pour it down as if they were mad.

> A number of people gnaw a bone and then put it back in the dish—this is a serious offense. (p. 85)

Through his analysis of writings on manners Elias demonstrated that Western norms concerning the control of bodily functions, from eating and sleeping to blowing one's nose, arose in the Middle Ages as the courts consolidated their power over feudal societies and exported the standards of courtly behavior to the countryside. Such behavior became a sign that a person was a member of the upper classes and not a serf or a savage.

In the social sciences, the most common use of the term *civilization* stems from the study of changes in human society at the macro level, which often requires comparisons among major cultures. In this context, a **civilization** is "a cultural complex formed by the identical major cultural features of a number of particular societies. We might, for example, describe Western capitalism as a civilization, in which specific forms of science, technology, religion, art, and so on, are to be found in a number of distinct societies" (Bottomore, 1973, p. 130). Thus Italy, France, Germany, the United States, Sweden, and many other nations that have made great contributions to Western civilization all have private corporations, and their normative orders, laws, and judicial systems are quite similar. Even though each may have a different language and each differs in the way it organizes some aspects of social life

(European and North American universities define academic degrees differently, for example), they share similar norms and values and can all be said to represent Western civilization.

EFFECTS OF CULTURAL CONTACT

Although sociologists do not distinguish among cultures in terms of how "civilized" they are, this standard is often applied by members of different cultures when they come into contact with one another. The contact between Columbus and his crew and the natives of the West Indies is typical of such episodes. The explorers represented the relatively advanced civilization of Europe, while the "Indians" Columbus first encountered represented a much simpler culture, one that seemed totally "uncivilized" to the explorers. Throughout the period of world exploration, from the late fifteenth to the early nineteenth centuries, explorers and traders brought back reports of "savages" living in every part of the globe. These episodes of cultural contact (and often conflict as well) shaped the history of the next two centuries and continue to influence human existence.

Through such processes as exploration and conquest, civilizations invariably spread beyond their original boundaries. Figure 3.2 shows how through much of the nine-

FIGURE 3.2 **The British Empire in 1901**

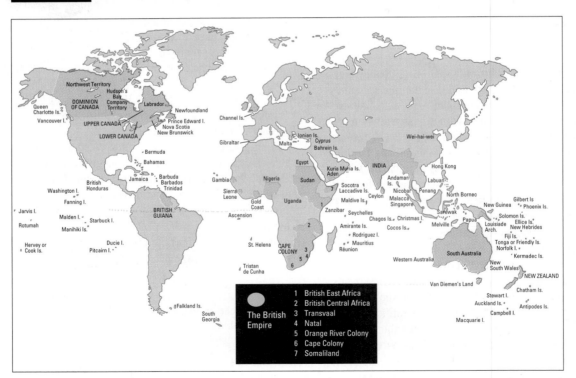

This map shows the extent of the British Empire in 1901. At the peak of its power, at the turn of the century, the empire had spread English civilization throughout the world. But its influence was strongest in peripheral, less industrialized lands. In a mere half-century most of the empire would crumble, but the effects of English civilization on language and social institutions throughout the world would endure.

Source: Eldridge, 1978.

STUDY CHART Effects of Cultural Contact

FORM OF CONTACT	DESCRIPTION	EXAMPLE
Acculturation	The process by which the members of a civilization incorporate norms and values from other cultures into their own.	Americans develop a taste for Italian, Chinese, and Mexican food, as well as other cuisines representing the cultures of the people who have joined their civilization.
Assimilation	The process by which culturally distinct groups within a civilization adopt the norms, values, and language of that civilization and gain equal statuses in its groups and institutions.	Spanish-speaking immigrants to the United States learn English and begin to move up the status hierarchy in education and jobs.
Accommodation	The process by which a smaller, less powerful society is able to preserve the major features of its culture even after prolonged contact with a larger, stronger culture.	Although conquered and forced onto reservations, Native Americans adapt by taking on many of the norms and values of the larger society while preserving aspects of their own culture.

teenth century England spread its version of Western civilization throughout the world as it conquered tribal peoples and established colonies in Africa and Asia. Colonial rule brought *cultural imperialism,* the imposition of a new culture on the conquered peoples. This meant that colonial peoples had to learn the languages of their conquerors, especially English, Spanish, French, Portuguese, and Dutch (or Afrikaans). Along with language came the imposition of ideologies like Christianity in place of older beliefs and religions.

According to the historian Fernand Braudel, "The mark of a living civilization is that it is capable of exporting itself, of spreading its culture to distant places. It is impossible to imagine a true civilization which does not export its people, its ways of thinking and living" (1976/1949, p. 763). In his research on the contacts and clashes between the great civilizations surrounding the Mediterranean Sea during the 1500s, Braudel uses three important sociological concepts to explain the spread of civilizations around the world: acculturation, assimilation, and accommodation. (See the study chart above.)

Acculturation. People from one civilization incorporate norms and values from other cultures into their own through a process called **acculturation.** Most acculturation occurs through intercultural contact and the borrowing or imitation of cultural norms. But there have been many instances of acculturation through cultural imperialism, in which one culture has been forced to adopt the language or other traits of a more dominant one. Thus people in societies that were colonized in the nineteenth century were forced to learn the language of the conquering nation.

Aspects of our culture that we take for granted usually can be shown to have traveled a complicated route through other cultures to become part of our way of life. Braudel's study of the Mediterranean civilizations shows that many of the plants and foods that became part of life around the Mediterranean Sea, and later were imported to the New World, were themselves borrowed from other cultures and incorporated into those of the Mediterranean societies. The process of acculturation can be traced in many other aspects of everyday life. As Ralph Linton has written:

> Our solid American citizen awakens in a bed built on a pattern which originated in the Near East. . . . He throws back covers made from cotton, domesticated in India. . . . He slips into his moccasins, invented by the Indians of the Eastern woodlands. . . . He takes off his pajamas, a garment invented in India, and washes with soap invented by the ancient Gauls. . . . He puts on garments whose form originally derived from the skin clothing of the nomads of the Asiatic steppes . . . and ties around his neck a strip of bright-colored cloth which is a vestigial survival of the shoulder shawls worn by the seventeenth-century Croatians. Before going out for breakfast he glances through the window, made of glass invented in Egypt, and if it is raining puts on overshoes made of rubber discovered by the Central American Indians and takes an umbrella, invented in southeastern Asia. (1936, p. 326)

The concept of acculturation can also be applied to how a newcomer people adopts the cultural ways of the host society. But acculturation is rarely a one-way process: At the same time that they are becoming more like their hosts in values and behavior, newcomers teach members of the host society to use and appreciate aspects of their own culture. Because of the cultural diversity of its population, examples of acculturation are especially prevalent in the

United States. For example, even small towns in the interior of the country have at least one Chinese restaurant, but often the food served in those restaurants is a highly acculturated form of the cuisine of China. Indeed, most of the things we think of as part of the American way of life, from hamburgers, pizza, and baseball to democracy and free enterprise, originally were aspects of other cultures. That they have become incorporated into American culture through acculturation, and in the process have become changed from their original forms, does not deny the fact of their "foreign" origin (see Box 3.3).

Assimilation and Subcultures. When culturally distinct groups within a larger civilization adopt the language, values, and norms of the host civilization and their acculturation enables them to assume equal statuses in the social groups and institutions of that civilization, we refer to that process as **assimilation.** When groups become assimilated into American society, for example, people often say that they have been "Americanized." Assimilation has been a major issue for immigrant groups in North America, as it still is for immigrants all over the world. It is no surprise, then, that we continually see articles in the press that ask such questions as: Will the various Hispanic peoples in America give up their language over time? Will American Jews marry members of other groups and lose their distinct identity? Will Italian Americans gradually forget their cultural heritage and come to think of themselves as "100 percent Americans" (Brimelow, 1995)? These are the kinds of questions that form the subject matter of racial and ethnic relations in pluralistic societies like those of the United States and the commonwealth of former Soviet republics. Both of these societies (which are also civilizations) are composed of a multitude of peoples, each of which once had its own culture but is under pressure to become assimilated into the dominant civilization.

When a culturally distinct people within a larger culture fails to assimilate fully or has not yet become fully assimilated, we say that it is a **subculture** within the larger culture. (The term is also applied to groups that have had significantly different experiences from those of most members of the society.) People who maintain their own subculture generally share many of the values and norms of the larger culture, but they retain certain rituals, values, traditions, and norms—and in some cases their own language—that set them apart. Thus we speak of African American, Latino, Native American, and a host of other subcultures in the United States. As explained in Chapter 13, these are also known as *ethnic groups,* since their members have a sense of shared descent, a feeling of being "a people" with a history and a way of life that exists within a larger and more culturally diverse society. The Visual Sociology section of this chapter illustrates how Native Americans may be viewed as an ethnic subculture in North American cities and how their historical experience as a

conquered people continues to shape their ways of thinking about life even in an urban milieu.

Ethnic subcultures are created out of the experience of migration or invasion and subsequent adaptation to a host culture. But subcultures are also created out of the experience of people in complex societies who actively seek to create and maintain a way of life distinct from that of other members of their society (Fischer, 1987; Gans, 1976). For example, there are subcultures in large cities composed of artists and other people whose livelihood depends on the arts: theater people, rock musicians and record producers, visual artists, gallery owners, art critics, curators. The list could be expanded to include avant-garde artists who band together to find new forms of expression and perhaps to poke fun at conventional norms. When a subculture that challenges the accepted norms and values of the larger society establishes an alternative lifestyle, we call it a **counterculture.** The hippies of the 1960s, along with members of New Left political groups, activists in the women's movement, and environmental activists, formed a counterculture that had a significant influence on American politics and foreign policy during the Vietnam War years (Roszak, 1969).

Frequently subcultures are under intense pressure to conform to the society's most widely accepted norms and values or to adapt to new ways, new technologies, or the like. Social scientists often investigate the changing norms and values of such subcultures—the gay subcultures, the subculture of rock musicians and other celebrities, or the subcultures of occupational groups like Appalachian miners, Wall Street lawyers, and doctors, among others (Backer, 1982; Bosk, 1979; Caudill, 1976; Erikson, 1976; Millman, 1976; Smigel, 1964). Frequently this research is valuable in predicting trends in such areas as drug use, popular music, or patterns of labor-management conflict and cooperation (Boggs & Meyersohn, 1988; Flores, 1988; Nyden, 1984).

Accommodation and Resistance. Throughout history many societies have withstood tremendous pressure to become assimilated into larger civilizations. But even greater numbers have been either wiped out or fully assimilated. Only a century ago, for example, one could still find many hundreds of hunter-gatherer societies throughout the world. Today there are probably fewer than a hundred, and these live in the most isolated regions of the earth.

Larger and smaller societies do not usually develop ways of living together without the smaller one becoming extinct or totally assimilated into the larger one. But when the smaller, less powerful society is able to preserve the major features of its culture even after prolonged contact, **accommodation** is said to have occurred. For example, in the Islamic civilization of the Middle East before the creation of Israel in 1948, Jews and other non-Muslims usually found it rather easy to maintain their cultures within the

North America's African Heritage

All the important streams of migration to North America have combined to produce the culture of the United States and Canada. Pizza (Italy), hamburgers (Germany), French fries—examples of the influence of immigrant groups on American material culture abound. Of all these cultural influences, perhaps the least well understood is the legacy of the people who were brought to North America from Africa as slaves, especially during the last three decades of the eighteenth century and the first half of the nineteenth.

One of the largest groups of slaves, who were captured in what is now the Congo and Angola, was made up of people from many tribes who shared a common language system, Bantu. Many of these Bantu-speaking slaves were landed in the Carolinas. By the end of the Civil War, the Carolinas had the largest concentration of people of African descent of any of the new states. In consequence, many of the names of towns and villages, rivers, streams, and other geographic features in those states are derived from Bantu words, often mixed with local Indian terms and transformed through long usage. Thus, Pinder Town in South Carolina is derived from the Bantu word for peanut, *mpinda*. George R. Stewart, an expert on place names, concludes that hundreds of small streams, swamps, and villages in the Carolinas, Mississippi, and Georgia received their names from the African slaves (Stewart, 1968; Vass, 1979).

The strongest evidence of African influence on contemporary American culture can be found in the Sea Islands along the Atlantic coast between Charlestown, South Carolina, and Savannah, Georgia. On the islands of Port Royal, Parris (famous for its Marine training base), Ladies, Hilton Head, and St. Helena reside the Gullah people. Also known as Geechi, they are descendants of slaves whose original tribes are believed to have lived in Angola (from which the term *Gullah* may be derived) and in the areas that are now Liberia and Sierra Leone. On the plantations the Gullah slaves grew indigo and the long-fiber cotton that made the region famous in the period before the Civil War. Some of them escaped to become leaders of slave rebellions. Others were arrested during the Civil War for singing spirituals like "Roll, Jordan, Roll" to which they had added verses about their dreams of freedom. To this day the religious practices, language, and place names of the Sea Island people bear witness to their African heritage (Creel, 1988).

A Gullah woman of the Sea Islands in a photograph taken early in this century.

larger Arab societies. Compare this pattern of accommodation with the experience of the Jews in Spain, who were forced to leave in 1492 in one of the largest mass expulsions in history.

Accommodation requires that each side tolerate the existence of the other and even share territory and social institutions. The history of relations between Native Americans and European settlers in the Western Hemisphere is a complex story of resistance and accommodation. Throughout the period of conquest, expansion, and settlement by the Europeans there was continual resistance by the native peoples. This resistance took many forms, including refusal to adopt Christianity, to speak English or Spanish, to sell goods and services to the settlers, and to fight in the Europeans' wars. Resistance did not save Native Americans from death by disease, military conquest, or famine, but it did allow them to maintain their cultures and to borrow from the settlers the cultural customs that were most advantageous to them. For example, the Plains Indians adopted horses from the Spanish explorers, which completely changed their culture, and much later they borrowed trucks from American culture, which helped them adapt to modern ranching.

RESEARCH FRONTIERS: CULTURAL CONFLICTS

Most cultures in the world today have had to confront the influence of at least one expanding civilization. In some instances the result has been prolonged conflict and the eventual annihilation of the smaller society. However, throughout the world it is as easy to find examples of failures in accommodation as it is to find examples of sharing and cooperation among cultures. Many of the conflicts that lead to severe social unrest, such as the conflict between Islamic and Eastern Orthodox Bosnians, or among warring tribal peoples in Rwanda, are based on cultural differences. Such conflicts may also occur *within* a culture. In the United States, for example, cultural differences are becoming more visible, and so are cultural conflicts. In no area of contemporary life is this more true than in the realm of intimacy and sexual behavior.

DIVORCE RATES AS A BAROMETER OF CULTURAL CHANGE

Many critics of contemporary American society blame the rising divorce rate and the increase in single-parent fami-

---

FIGURE 3.3 Divorce Rate, United States, 1860–1980

Source: Cherlin, 1981.

Note: Figures for 1860–1920 represent the number of marriages per 1,000 existing marriages; figures for 1921–1980 represent the number of marriages per 1,000 married women age 15 and over.

lies on changes in the norms of intimacy in couples that occurred during the social movements and counterculture of the 1960s. They seek a return to "traditional" norms of intimacy, including premarital celibacy, monogamy, and heterosexuality. These and other critics of diversity in sexual norms view the 1950s as a "golden age" of traditional norms regarding the conduct of intimate relations.

Sociologists who study trends in American culture point out that the 1950s were by no means a golden age of traditional behavior. Changes in American culture brought on by mass advertising, television, the growing equality of men and women, and the increasingly widespread desire for individual happiness had been developing throughout the century. These longer-term changes, they reason, should be reflected in statistics on divorce rates. On the other hand, if changes in sexual norms were a result of the social movements of the 1960s, there should be evidence of such a connection in statistics on divorce rates over time.

Figure 3.3 shows that there is some justification for each of these positions, but far more empirical support for the view that rising divorce rates are not a product of the tumultuous 1960s. Clearly, divorces have been increasing in frequency over a period going well back into the nine-teenth century. These data call into question any "golden age" theory of stability in American couples.

CHANGING SEXUAL NORMS

A survey by the National Opinion Research Center explored Americans' sexual attitudes and behaviors in great detail, using extremely careful interviewing methods (Laumann, 1994). This study shows that there have been vast changes, as well as a good deal of continuity, in the norms of American culture regarding sexual behavior. Figure 3.4 shows a major shift in norms regarding premarital sex with the person one eventually marries. About a third of the cohort of people born between 1933 and 1942, who came of age sexually during the 1950s, admit that they had sex with their spouse before marriage. For the cohort born between 1963 and 1974, who reached the age of sexual activity during the 1980s, the situation was almost completely reversed: The vast majority of men and a lesser majority of women report having had sex with their spouse before marriage.

These findings support the theory that there have been major changes in the norms of sexual intimacy since the 1950s. They do not, however, shed light on the relationship between what people *think* the norms are and how

---

FIGURE 3.4 Premarital Sex With Eventual Spouse, by Birth Cohort, United States

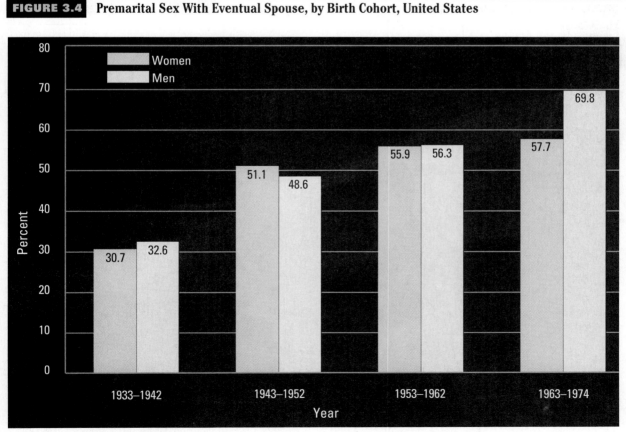

Source: Adapted from Laumann et al., 1994.

URBAN INDIANS

In the 1950s the federal government undertook a massive program to relocate Native Americans to Chicago, Denver, Los Angeles, and San Francisco. The Bureau of Indian Affairs supplied free one-way tickets to Indians seeking jobs in these urban centers. It also made a token effort to provide job training. But once it found a job for a relocated person, the government's responsibility ended.

In 1965 San Francisco State University studied the acculturation and adjustment of the relocated Indians. Part of the study was a photographic survey of 24 Indian homes by photographer John Collier. As this selection of Collier's photos shows, there was a direct relationship between adjustment to relocation and the "look" of an Indian home; that is, a family's ability to achieve cultural order in the home reflected its ability to cope with urban life.

The federal government defined successful relocation as "terminating" an Indian in the urban industrial wilderness. For the Native Americans, however, successful relocation was a more complex matter. For many, it meant a free

For the Pomo, relocation means isolation from a supportive ecology and extended family relationships.

A Navajo married to a Walipi living in Palo Alto. Indians must find renewal in the unfamiliar surroundings of urban living.

An Eskimo family from Alaska. Relocation dropped Arctic hunters into Oakland, California, where they have no friends. They go to movies or sit at home.

Like many successful relocatees, this affluent Sioux has retained his Indian allegiances: to Red Power groups in the Bay Area and back home in North Dakota. The flute is a symbol of his identity.

Pomos from Clear Lake, California, resettled in Oakland. For the younger generation, quality of education is a major variable in the success or failure of Indian relocation.

A Sioux family head living in a housing project in Alameda. Alcoholism is the chief threat of relocation.

When I visited this Eskimo family, the wife urged me to photograph her in her Arctic parka, with a wolf-tail ruff and squirrel-skin decorations. Proudly she posed in this Arctic wealth, a symbol of a world left behind.

trip and some valuable education before returning to settle in their original homelands. For many others, the relocation that was meant to result in assimilation instead created aggressive Red Power activists.

Unpredictably, urban survival required strengthening the "Indianness" of personalities. Without that, people tended toward neurosis or alcoholism. So relocation, a scheme designed to lose Indians in the nation's cities, instead caused a revival of Native American vitality. Their culture did not effectively follow Native Americans into the cities. But their music and writing, created for survival in the city, circulated back to the reservations.

The significant result of the policy of relocation, one that still remains, is a resurgence of Native American culture, not only richly costumed dances and songs, but also an aggressive and sophisticated Red Power movement, the last thing the Bureau of Indian Affairs wanted (Collier, 1981).

they actually *behave*. Many Americans still believe in the norm of premarital celibacy but find that it conflicts with a newer norm, the idea that couples should find compatibility and pleasure in their sexual relationship. The changes in behavior shown in Figure 3.4 indicate that sanctions against premarital sexual experimentation have weakened while the norm that couples should be happy in their sex lives has become stronger.

But there is never a complete substitution of new norms for old ones in a large and diverse population like that of North America. In consequence, we will always see differences in how norms are understood and in how they guide actual behavior. And these differences, especially when they concern major areas of moral conduct, will continue to produce conflict over norms and values.

These contrasting images of America in the 1950s demonstrate that even as society maintained its idealized view of itself, as represented in Norman Rockwell's paintings, it was also beginning to confront the rise of social problems such as juvenile delinquency, a theme of the film *Blackboard Jungle*.

SUMMARY

THINK ABOUT IT CRITICALLY

Sociologists say that in all societies there is a normative order that creates patterns of orderly behavior. But is there a normative order in the United States? When Vice President J. Danforth Quayle attacked the television show Murphy Brown *for condoning fatherless families, was he not showing that some of the society's most central norms are being ignored? And if they are so easily ignored that they can be the subject of a popular television series, how can we assert that there is a normative order?*

In the social sciences, *culture* refers to all the modes of thought, behavior, and production that are handed down from one generation to the next by means of communicative interaction. Sociologists are concerned primarily with aspects of culture that help explain social organization and behavior.

Culture can be viewed as consisting of three major dimensions: ideas, norms, and material culture. *Ideas* are the ways of thinking that organize human consciousness. Among the most important ideas are *values,* socially shared ideas about what is right. *Norms* are specific rules of behavior that are supported or justified by values; *laws* are norms that are included in a society's official written codes of behavior. *Ideologies* combine ideas and norms; they are systems of values and norms that the members of a society are expected to believe in and act on without question. A society's *material culture* consists of all the things it produces. *Technologies* combine norms and material culture; they are the things and the norms for using them that are found in a given culture.

Social control refers to the set of rules and understandings that control the behavior of individuals and groups in a culture. The wide array of norms that permit a society to achieve relatively peaceful social control is called its *normative order. Sanctions* are rewards and punishments for adhering to or violating norms. Strongly sanctioned norms are called *mores;* more weakly sanctioned norms are known as *folkways.*

One of the most hotly debated questions in the social sciences is how much, if at all, human culture is determined by biological factors. According to Darwin's theory of *natural selection,* mutations in organisms occur more or less randomly. Mutations that enable an individual organism to survive and reproduce are passed on to the next generation. It is this process that permits animals and plants to adapt to new environments.

Herbert Spencer and other social thinkers, who came to be known as *social Darwinists,* attempted to apply Darwin's theory to humans' ability to adapt to social environments. Spencer used the phrase "survival of the fittest" to describe this ability. People who were able to survive in the urban environment created by the industrial revolution were viewed as superior human beings.

A more recent attempt to attribute social phenomena to biological processes is *sociobiology,* which refers to efforts to link genetic factors with the social behavior of animals. According to the sociobiologists, such behaviors as incest avoidance, aggression, and homosexuality may be genetically programmed in human beings. As yet there is no evidence that such genes or sets of genes actually exist.

A more widely accepted view of culture denies that humans have innate instincts and states that at a certain stage in prehistoric times human culture became self-generating. Thus human evolution is not dependent on genes; instead, cultural techniques allow humans to adapt to any physical or social environment.

The learning of culture is made possible by language. Although apes have been taught to use language to some extent, human language is unique in that it allows its speakers to express an infinite number of thoughts and ideas that can persist even after their originators are gone. According to the *linguistic-relativity hypothesis,* language also determines the possibilities for a culture's norms, beliefs, and values. A less extreme form of that hypothesis recognizes the mutual influences of culture and language.

The notion that one's own culture is superior to any other is called *ethnocentrism.* To understand other cultures it is necessary to suspend judgment about those cultures, an approach termed *cultural relativity.* Cross-cultural research has been used in efforts to find "cultural universals," or cultural traits that are found among humans everywhere, but in recent years the search for cultural universals has given way to cross-cultural comparisons in specific areas of study.

Similarities among cultures have resulted from the processes by which cultures spread across national boundaries and become part of a larger, more advanced culture called a civilization. A *civilization* may be defined as a cultural complex formed by the identical major cultural features of a number of particular societies.

A key feature of civilizations is that they invariably expand beyond their original boundaries. The spread of civilizations can be explained by three processes: acculturation, assimilation, and accommodation. When people from one civilization incorporate norms and values from other cultures into their own, *acculturation* is said to occur. The process by which culturally distinct groups within a larger civilization adopt the language, values, and norms of the host civilization and gain equal statuses in its institutions is termed *assimilation.* (If a distinct people fails to assimilate fully, it is referred to as a *subculture*, but if it challenges the accepted norms and values of the larger society it may become a *counterculture*.) And when a smaller, less powerful society is able to preserve its culture even after prolonged contact with a major civilization, *accommodation* has taken place.

CRITICAL RESPONSE
When sociologists study the normative order of a society, they recognize that this order is always being challenged. In a society beset by rapid social change, norms are always being contested and redefined. Women who have achieved the ability to support children, for example, may reject the norm that insists on a two-parent family. The more both men and women challenge the norms of family life, the more conflict there will be over those norms and, at the same time, the more diversity there will be in both norms and behavior, as can be seen in the example of Murphy Brown.

GLOSSARY

culture: all the modes of thought, behavior, and production that are handed down from one generation to the next by means of communicative interaction rather than by genetic transmission. (p. 60)

ideas: ways of thinking that organize human consciousness. (p. 60)

norms: specific rules of behavior. (p. 60)

material culture: patterns of possessing and using the products of culture. (p. 60)

values: the ideas that support or justify norms. (p. 61)

laws: norms that are written by specialists, collected in codes or manuals of behavior, and interpreted and applied by other specialists. (p. 62)

ideologies: systems of values and norms that the members of a society are expected to believe in and act on without question. (p. 62)

technologies: the products and the norms for using them that are found in a given culture. (p. 64)

social control: the set of rules and understandings that control the behavior of individuals and groups in a particular culture. (p. 64)

normative order: the array of norms that permit a society to achieve relatively peaceful social control. (p. 65)

sanctions: rewards and punishments for abiding by or violating norms. (p. 65)

mores: strongly sanctioned norms. (p. 65)

folkways: weakly sanctioned norms. (p. 65)

natural selection: the relative success of organisms with specific genetic mutations in reproducing new generations with the new trait. (p. 70)

cultural evolution: the process by which successful cultural adaptations are passed down from one generation to the next. (p. 70)

social Darwinism: the notion that people who are more successful at adapting to the environment in which they find themselves are more likely to survive and to have children who will also be successful. (p. 70)

sociobiology: the hypothesis that all human behavior is determined by genetic factors. (p. 71)

linguistic-relativity hypothesis: the belief that language determines the possibilities for thought and action in any given culture. (p. 73)

ethnocentrism: the tendency to judge other cultures as inferior to one's own. (p. 73)

cultural relativity: the recognition that all cultures develop their own ways of dealing with the specific demands of their environments. (p. 74)

civilization: a cultural complex formed by the identical major cultural features of a number of societies. (p. 76)

acculturation: the process by which the members of a civilization incorporate norms and values from other cultures into their own. (p. 77)

assimilation: the process by which culturally distinct groups in a larger civilization adopt the norms, values, and language of the host civilization and are able to gain equal statuses in its groups and institutions. (p. 78)

subculture: a group of people who hold many of the values and norms of the larger culture but also hold certain beliefs, values, or norms that set them apart from that culture. (p. 78)

counterculture: a subculture that challenges the accepted norms and values of the larger society and establishes an alternative lifestyle. (p. 78)

accommodation: the process by which a smaller, less powerful society is able to preserve the major features of its culture even after prolonged contact with a larger, stronger culture. (p. 78)

WHERE TO FIND IT

BOOKS

Cultivating Differences: Symbolic Boundaries and the Making of Inequality (Michele Lamont & Marcel Fournier, eds.; University of Chicago Press, 1992). A collection of essays about how human cultures create and destroy boundaries among groups and societies.

The Interpretation of Cultures (Clifford Geertz; Basic Books, 1973). A set of essays that explore the many meanings of human culture, including a fine essay on the relationship between culture and human social and physical evolution.

Sex and Temperament in Three Primitive Societies (Margaret Mead; Morrow, 1935). A classic study that, on the basis of detailed observations, argues against the theory that the differing behavior of males and females is determined by genetic factors. Instead, Mead provides evidence for the theory that those differences are due to cultural training.

Cultural Anthropology, 4th ed. (Marvin Harris; HarperCollins, 1995). A basic textbook that covers in detail the cultures of nonindustrial peoples.

JOURNALS

Technology and Culture. A quarterly journal devoted to studies of the interrelationships between cultural and technological change.

Signs. A quarterly journal that supplies valuable data on women in various societies and cultures.

Daedalus. The journal of the American Academy of Arts and Sciences. It devotes entire issues to subjects of great importance in the world—such as AIDS, computers, violence, and nationalism—and contains some of the best writing on social and cultural change.

CHAPTER 4

Societies and Nations

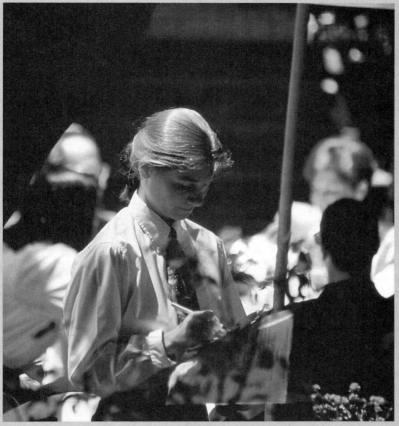

At the beginning of Sherri's second month on the job things were supposed to be getting easier, but they weren't. If anything, they were getting worse, especially the pressure during the lunch-hour madness. Lunch never seemed to go well. There were always more customers than she could handle. Too many tables to serve, busboys too slow, cooks yelling at her to pick up orders or write more clearly—things were so bad that she dreaded coming in to work. She was falling behind in her studies, too. This part-time waitressing job was turning out to be a disaster. And now that chubby guy at table 14 was leering at her.

"Oh, Miss," he called out as Sherri shot by under a huge tray of burger plates. "Oh, Miss, why are you ignoring me? I haven't even gotten a menu." "Be right there, Sir," she muttered.

She dealt out the burger plates as fast as she could and dashed back into the kitchen to get the soups for another table. "Where've you been hiding?" the cook shouted at her from behind his stainless steel counter. "You better get that soup outta here before I have to heat it up again. Let's go. Move!"

Sherri flew through the swinging doors with the tepid soups. Out of the corner of her eye she saw the chubby guy complaining to Karen, her supervisor, about the slow service. Karen shot her an angry glance. A party of six was waiting to be seated at one of her big tables, which needed to be cleaned off. It was too much. She felt the tears welling up in her eyes. Her makeup would be streaked. She headed for the restroom.

On the way Sherri felt a gentle touch on her shoulder. Betty, the veteran waitress who had broken her in when she started 5 weeks ago, smiled at her. "Take it easy, kid! It's not all that bad. My station is under control, so let me help you with the little fat guy and the others."

With her assured efficiency, Betty had Sherri's station under control in a matter of minutes. Later, after the rush was over, she took Sherri aside and showed her some tricks that would make the work easier, like warning the busboys when a table was almost ready to be cleaned up and working out a system for letting others know when she was having trouble. "You'll see," Betty assured her. "When you learn to assert yourself somewhat, and take care of emergencies first, and when you learn who you can ask for help, this job will be much easier."

In his extensive research on human relations in the restaurant industry, sociologist William F. Whyte (1984) found that high-pressure situations like the one Sherri faced often lead less determined, more thin-skinned waitresses to quit. The ones who stay are emotionally tougher, better able to cope with the pressure. But he also showed that the intervention of tough yet sensitive pros like Betty often helps newcomers learn how to deal with the pressure, especially by learning the "tricks of the trade." However, not all newcomers are fortunate enough to have caring mentors to help them over the rough spots, and many quit before they can learn how to perform their roles well.

THE SOCIAL ORDER

When our social relations don't seem to be going well—when we experience stress, pressure, or conflict with coworkers or friends—we often jump to the conclusion that we are to blame. We don't stop to look at the powerful influence of social organizations on our lives. Sherri began to think that the cook, the customers, and her supervisor were reacting to her as a person rather than as a waitress. The pressure of her own work made it difficult for her to see that the pressures the cook was experiencing caused him to lash out at her. Their conflict had much more to do with their roles in the social organization of the restaurant than with their individual personalities. One of the main goals of this chapter is to indicate the great diversity of human social structures and show how they influence individual behavior.

Of course, humans are not the only animals capable of social organization. We can learn a lot about life in human societies by comparing ourselves with other social animals. If you look closely at an ant colony or a beehive, for example, you can see a remarkable amount of organization. The nest or hive is a complete social world with workers, warriors, queen, drones, and so on. Each individual ant or bee has something to do and seems to do it quite well. But the differences between human societies and those of social animals like bees are even more important than the similarities. Unlike a human actor, an individual social animal is able to perform only a certain number of innate (inborn) tasks. The human can learn an infinite number of tasks. The individual bee is born a worker or a queen. Sherri, in contrast, can be a waitress, a college student, a lawyer, a mother, a voter, a taxpayer, and on and on.

We often assume that we know how society works and how to steer our way through it. But there will be times, especially when, like Sherri, we are learning to adapt to new social environments, when we will be unsure of what is expected of us and how we should perform. Worse still, there may be times when it seems that society itself is threatened, that its continued existence as we know it is endangered. We catch glimpses of the breakdown of society during riots or wars or severe economic recessions.

At earlier times in human history, plagues and famines were frequent reminders that people had little control over their own destinies. Today plagues and famines still occur, but we are more often faced with real or potential crises of our own making: war, genocide, environmental disasters, drug addiction, criminal violence. Thus, if we are to continue to exist and thrive as a species, it is vital

that we study societies and social structures—how they hold together, how they change, and why they sometimes seem to fall apart.

As in any science, we begin with some basic terms and definitions. The next few pages introduce the principal elements of social structure. (See the study chart on the following page.) Later sections of the chapter apply these and related concepts to an analysis of how societies have developed since the beginning of human history and how differences among societies affect the lives of individuals. We also discuss the important distinction between societies and nation-states.

SOCIETY AND SOCIAL STRUCTURE

The term society refers to a population of people (or other social animals) that is organized in a cooperative manner to carry out the major functions of life, including reproduction, sustenance, shelter, and defense. This definition distinguishes between societies and populations. The notion of a population implies nothing about social organization, but the idea of a society stresses the *interrelationships* among the members of the population. In other words, a population can be any set of individuals that we decide to count or otherwise consider, such as the total number of people living between the Rio Grande and the Arctic Circle, whereas a society is a population that is organized in some way, such as the population of the United States or Canada or the Amish people of Pennsylvania. In the modern world most societies are also (but not always) nation-states.

Social structure refers to the recurring patterns of behavior people create through their interactions and relationships. We say, for example, that the family has a structure in which there are parents and children and other relatives who interact in specific ways on a regular basis. The larger society usually requires that family members assume certain obligations toward each other. Parents are required to educate their children or send them to schools; children are required to obey their parents until they have reached an age at which they are no longer considered dependent. These requirements contribute to the structure of relationships that is characteristic of the family. (The social scientist's method of diagramming family relationships, shown in Box 4.1, creates a graphic depiction of family social structure.)

Throughout life individuals maintain relationships in an enormous range of social structures, of which families are just one. There are many others. People may be members of relatively small groups like the friendship or peer group and the work group. They may also be members of

STUDY CHART Elements of Social Structure

STRUCTURAL ELEMENT	DESCRIPTION	EXAMPLE
Group	Any collection of people who interact on the basis of shared expectations regarding one another's behavior.	A discussion group; a Bible study class; a local union.
Status	A socially defined position in a group.	Orderly, practical nurse, registered nurse, resident, chief resident (all statuses in a hospital ward).
Role	The way a society defines how an individual is to behave in a particular status.	The doctor diagnoses and treats illnesses; the nurse provides care to patients under the doctor's supervision.
Role Expectations	A society's expectations about how a role should be performed, together with the individual's perceptions of what is required in performing that role.	A major league center fielder is expected to have a batting average over .300, drive in more than 75 runs, and cover the field with a minimum of errors.
Institution	A more or less stable structure of statuses and roles devoted to meeting the basic needs of people in a society.	The military is the primary institution devoted to providing national defense.

larger structures like churches, business organizations, or public agencies. And they may participate in even more broadly based structures, such as political groups and party organizations, or interest groups like the National Rifle Association or Planned Parenthood. All of these social structures are composed of groups with different degrees of complexity and quite different patterns of interaction. A military brigade, for example, is far more complicated than a barbershop quartet, and people behave quite differently in each. But both are social structures. In such structures our time, our activities, and even our thoughts may be "structured" according to the needs and activities of the group.

ELEMENTS OF SOCIAL STRUCTURE

Groups. The "building blocks" of societies are social groups. A **group** is any collection of people who interact on the basis of shared expectations regarding one another's behavior. One's immediate family is a group; so are a softball team, a seminar, a caucus, and so on. But a collection of people on a busy street—a crowd—is not a group unless for some reason its members begin to interact in a regular fashion. Usually a crowd is composed of many different kinds of groups—couples, families, groups of friends, and so on. They may be molded into a single group in response to an event that affects them all, such as a fire that creates the need for the orderly evacuation of a building.

Statuses. In every group there are socially defined positions known as **statuses.** Father, mother, son,

daughter, teacher, student, and principal are examples of familiar statuses in the family and the school. There are an infinite number of statuses in human societies. In a corporation, for example, the statuses range from president and chief executive officer to elevator operator and janitor. Between these two extremes there could be thousands of other statuses.[1] Moreover, the corporation can always create new statuses if the need arises. Thus, in the 1970s, when American society agreed to combat racism and sexism in business and government, many corporations invented the status of affirmative action director to provide equal opportunities for workers of both sexes and all racial and ethnic groups. In the 1990s, as the larger society became more deeply concerned about environmental pollution and drug abuse, corporations began to create new statuses like pollution control manager or drug counselor. Each of these statuses then became part of the "corporate structure."

Human societies rely heavily on the creation of statuses to adapt to new conditions like environmental pollution and drug use, and one can often observe this adaptation occurring in daily life. In the family, for example, it is increasingly common (though not universally condoned) for young adults to cohabit before marriage or after divorce. As a large-scale phenomenon, this is a relatively

---

[1]Like many other sociological terms, *status* has more than one meaning. It can refer to a person's rank in a social system and also to a person's prestige—that is, the esteem with which others regard him or her. The fundamental meaning is the one we use here.

Using Kinship Diagrams to Portray Social Structure

Kinship diagrams like the one shown here provide a visual model of one type of social structure, that associated with family statuses extending over more than one generation. Such diagrams are used in both anthropology and sociology to denote lines of descent among people who are related by blood (children and their parents and siblings) and by marriage. To understand the chart one must know the meanings of the symbols used; these are explained in the key to the chart. The chart applies these symbols to show how cross-cousin marriages between members of different bands link the bands together into a larger structure of kinship networks.

The chart illustrates the social structure of a hunter-gatherer group. One individual, Ego, is used as a point of reference, and kinship links are traced from Ego's offspring, parents, grandparents, and more distant relatives.

In most hunter-gatherer societies it is not possible for the entire society to travel and hunt within the same territory because of scarcities of game and edible vegetation. Instead, the society is divided into natal bands—in this example, those formed by the male line of descent (grandfather, father, Ego, Ego's son).

The striped coloring within the kinship symbols refers to another characteristic of hunter-gatherer societies: Marriages within the band cannot occur because of the incest taboo, and there are specific rules governing marriage outside the band. Note that Ego has married his father's sister's daughter, or his first cousin on his father's side. Ego's wife's brother has married a woman from outside their band. This couple has come to live in the husband's natal band. Their daughter has married Ego's son, another cross-cousin marriage. Ego's daughter, on the other hand, will eventually marry someone from another band and live outside her natal band. By means of this custom the balance of women coming into and going out of the band is preserved.

Cross-cousin marriages, which are taboo in most Western societies, permit the hunter-gatherer band to develop a strong network of interfamily and interband kinship ties. This network widens over the generations and extends the ties of kinship throughout these small mobile societies.

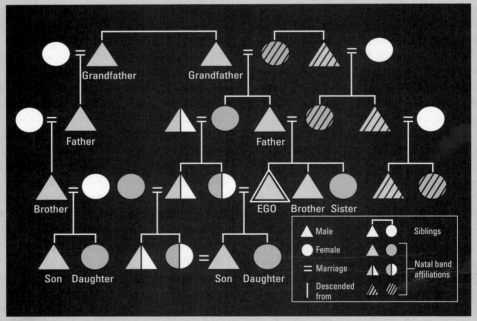

Source: Adapted from "The Origin of Society," by Marshall D. Sahlins. Copyright © September 1960 by Scientific American, Inc. All rights reserved.

new trend in American society, so new that we have not defined very well the new status of the person who participates in such a relationship. Do we say *boyfriend* or *girlfriend, lover, mate, significant other,* or what? The awkwardness of these terms is due to the fact that this is an emerging status that our society has not yet fully accepted or defined.

This example highlights an essential point about human social structure: It is never fixed or perfectly formed but instead is always changing and adapting to new conditions. Often the process of change involves much conflict and uncertainty, and often there is little consensus about how one should perform in a given status. Should the president of a corporation be an aloof, aggressive leader who directs subordinates with little regard for their feelings? Or should the president show concern for employees' feelings and personal needs and perhaps thereby gain greater loyalty and motivation? This is just one of thousands of dilemmas arising from questions about how we should act in a given social status. To clarify our thinking about statuses in groups and the behaviors associated with those statuses, sociologists make a distinction between a *status* and a *role.*

Roles and Role Expectations. The way a society defines how an individual is to behave in a particular status is referred to as a **role.** Sherri was not performing her role as waitress very well, according to the cook and the supervisor (who occupy other statuses within the social structure of the restaurant). Things improved when she got help from someone with more experience at performing the same role. Clearly, the ways in which people actually perform a role may vary widely. They are the product of **role expectations,** the society's expectations about how a role should be performed, together with the individual's perceptions of what is required in performing that role.

To appreciate the importance of role expectations you need only think of the mothers and fathers of your close friends: All hold the same statuses, but how different their behavior is! Part of that difference is due to personality—to psychological variables—but another part is due to how the individual mothers and fathers perceive what is expected of them in the statuses they hold. One mother and father may have been raised to believe that children should work to support the family. They will insist that their children get early job experience. Another couple may have been taught that childhood is too short and should be prolonged if possible. Other things being equal (e.g., adequate family income), that couple will not encourage their children to find jobs before they are more or less the same age the parents were when they went to work.

Social change makes for even more debate and anxiety about role expectations, a subject we discuss in more detail later in the chapter. For now, consider the example of a mother who is also an attorney (something that was rather rare before women gained greater access to professional training). Because of the demands of her profession, she may be unable to take on a leadership position in the school PTA. However, being active in the PTA may have been one of her role expectations for motherhood before the opportunity for a professional career (and the income it provides) became attractive. Now she may feel harried by the pressure of her conflicting statuses of mother and attorney—to say nothing of her other possible statuses, such as daughter, citizen, consumer, committee member, and so on. She may demand that her spouse perform tasks not traditionally associated with the status of husband, and he

may or may not modify his original role expectations about that status; in either case, there is likely to be some conflict in the family as it adjusts to these changes.

Another family, in which the mother is also in the labor force but there is no father in the home, has even more adjusting to do. The older children may take on parental roles far sooner than they might have in a two-parent family, but they may also resent this added responsibility and take out their anger on themselves and their siblings. In still another family, one that conforms to the tradition in which the mother is a homemaker and the father works outside the home, the pressures and conflict created by multiple role expectations may not occur in the early years. But what happens when the father retires and gives up his lifelong status of breadwinner? This is a time when traditional families frequently experience strain.

In sum, sociologists are interested in the way roles and statuses affect individual behavior. They also study how the lack of roles—for example, in the form of jobs—can affect people's lives. They do not deny the importance of personality, but they place greater emphasis on the influence of social structure as an explanation of individual behavior.

Organization in Groups. Groups vary greatly in the extent to which the statuses of their members are well or poorly defined. The family is an example of a group in which statuses are well defined. Although parents carry out their roles in different ways, the laws of their society define many of the obligations of parenthood, placing certain limits on what they can and cannot do. Other groups are much more informal. We may form groups for brief periods in buses, hallways, or doctors' offices. There are roles and statuses in these groups also, but they are variable and ill defined. All of the people riding on a bus are passengers, but they do not interact the way the members of a family do. At most, we expect civility and "small talk" from other passengers on a bus, but we demand affection and support from other members of our family. Social change is constantly making the structure of groups more varied and complex. To continue with our earlier example, the family may seem to have well-defined statuses, but high rates of divorce and remarriage have increased the proportion of families in which one parent is a stepparent (see Chapter 16). Consider the difference in role expectations for "mother" or "father" in a situation in which each spouse must interact with a new spouse, a new set of children, and a new set of in-laws as well as an ex-spouse and children in the first family, plus the old in-laws, plus his or her own parents. Balancing role expectations among the often competing demands of these groups can be a daunting task, one that was far less common when the norms of society made it difficult to divorce.

Groups also vary greatly in the ways in which they are connected with other groups into a larger structure known as an organization. An army platoon, for example, includes

FIGURE 4.1 Structure of a Typical Combat Brigade

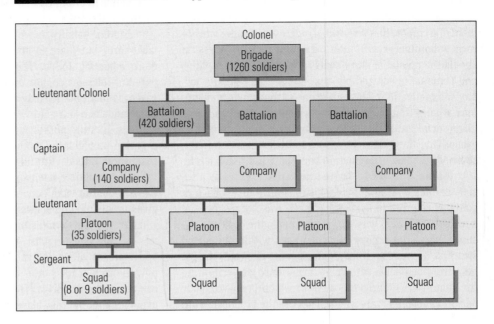

the well-defined statuses of private, corporal, sergeant, and lieutenant, each with specific roles to play in training and combat. Platoons are grouped together under the leadership of higher officers to form companies; this pattern is repeated at higher levels to create the battalion and the brigade, as shown in Figure 4.1.

Figure 4.1 shows the formal structure of a typical army combat brigade. It does not show the brigade's informal organization, which consists of the ways in which its members actually relate to one another on the basis of friendships or animosities or mutual obligations of various kinds. (The importance of informal organization within larger groups, such as bureaucracies, is discussed more fully in Chapter 6.)

SOCIAL INSTITUTIONS

The structure of most of the important groups in society is determined by shared definitions of the statuses and roles of their members. When such statuses and roles are designed to perform major social functions, they are termed **institutions.** In popular usage the word *institution* generally refers to a large bureaucratic organization like a university or hospital or prison (usually with cafeterias that serve "institutional food"). But although the word has this meaning in everyday language, the sociological use of the term should not be confused with this meaning.

In sociology, an institution is a more or less stable structure of statuses and roles devoted to meeting the basic needs of people in a society. The family is an institution that controls reproduction and the training of new generations. The market is an institution that regulates the production and exchange of goods and services. The military is an institution that defends a society or expands its territory

through conquest. Any particular family, corporation, or military unit is a group or organization within one of these institutions.

Within any given institution there are norms that specify how people in various statuses are to perform their roles. Thus to be a general or a new recruit or a supplier of military hardware is to have a definite status in a military institution. But to carry out one's role in that status is to behave in accordance with a normative system—a set of mores and folkways that distinguish a particular institution from others. For example, in a well-known paper on becoming a military recruit, Sanford Dornbusch (1955) described how all the signs of a person's status in civilian life, from fashions in dress to the use of free time, are erased in boot camp. The new status of recruit must be earned by adhering to all the norms of military life. So it is with every social institution: Each has a specific set of norms to govern the behavior of people within that institution.

Institutions of religion, education, politics, and economics tend to become more complex over time as the society changes. It is helpful, therefore, to think of large-scale societies like the United States as having a number of institutional *sectors* (sets of closely related institutions). For example, the economy is an institutional sector that includes markets, corporations, and other economic institutions. Politics is an institutional sector containing legal, executive, legislative, and other political institutions. Each of these institutions, in turn, is composed of numerous groups and organizations. The Chicago Mercantile Exchange is a market organization; the House of Representatives is a legislative organization. In this book, as in much social-scientific writing, the term *institution* is used to refer to institutional sectors (e.g., religion) as well as to the institutions included within a sector (e.g., Buddhism or Christianity).

The history of human societies is marked by the emergence of new institutions like the university or the laboratory. In fact, a dominant feature of human societies is the continual creation of new social institutions, a feature that the social theorist Talcott Parsons (1951, 1966) labeled **differentiation.** By this term, Parsons meant the processes whereby sets of social activities performed by one social institution are divided among different institutions. In small-scale agrarian societies, for example, the family not only performs reproductive and training functions but is also the primary economic institution. As societies become larger and more complex, the processes of differentiation result in the emergence of new institutions designed to manage economic production (corporations), train new generations (schools), develop new technologies (science), or perform other important social activities. (Many of those institutions are discussed in detail in Part 4.)

POPULATIONS AND SOCIETIES

The remarkable growth of the world's human population is the great biological success story of the last million years. Throughout most of the evolution of the human species, the world's population remained relatively small and con-

stant. At the end of the Neolithic period, about 8000 B.C., there were an estimated 5 million to 10 million humans, concentrated mainly in the Middle East, East Africa, southern Europe, and a few fertile river basins in India, China, Latin America, and Central America. The overall range of human existence was much wider—populations were moving north as the last Ice Age receded about 12,000 years ago—but the human population was nowhere near as widely distributed as it is today. By the time of Jesus there were an estimated 200 million people on the earth, and by the start of the industrial age, about the year 1650, there were an estimated 500 million. By 1945, however, the population had reached about 2.3 billion, and according to most reliable estimates it will reach about 6 billion by the year 2000. This trend is illustrated in Figure 4.2.

What explains the shape of this population curve, the gradual rise in the world's population during the late Stone Age, the increasing rate of growth in the early millennia of recorded history, the explosive growth after 1650? The answers have to do with the changing production technologies of societies and their ever-increasing ability to sustain their populations, not only those directly involved in acquiring food but the ever-larger numbers of non-food-producers as well. In other words, human population growth is related to the shift from hunting and gathering to agriculture and, later, to industrial production as the chief means of supplying people with the necessities of life.

FIGURE 4.2 World Population Growth From 8000 B.C. to A.D. 2000

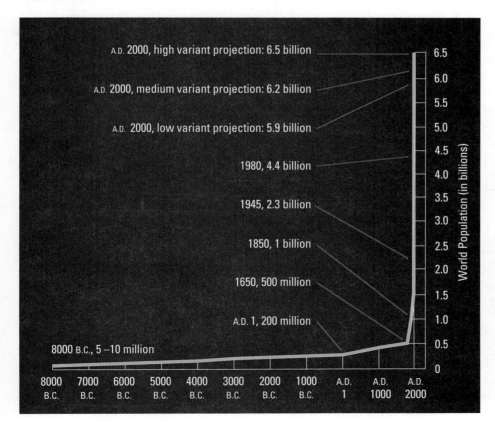

This chart shows world population growth since 8000 B.C. Note that the first, more gradual increase in world population is associated with the shift to agriculture, but that its effects are dwarfed by the impact of the industrial revolution, which began in the eighteenth century.

Source: Data from Office of Technology Assessment.

THEN AND NOW

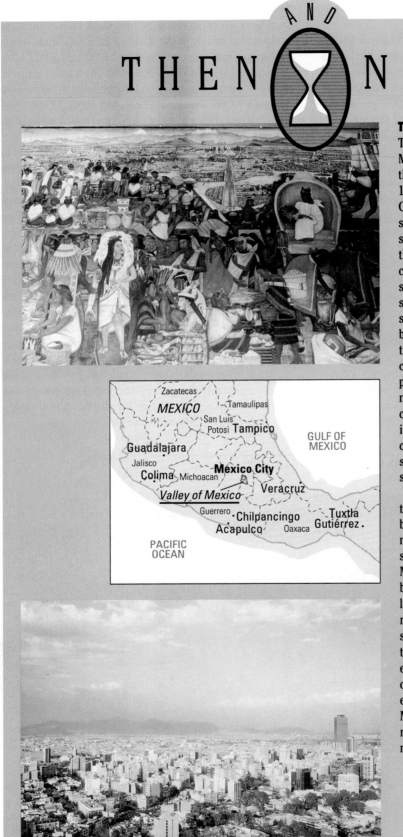

THE VALLEY OF MEXICO

This detail from a famous mural in Mexico's Palacio Nacional shows what the Valley of Mexico looked like in 1519, when conquistador Hernán Cortés and a small band of Spanish soldiers began their conquest of the strife-weakened Aztec empire. Under the emperor Montezuma, the Aztec capital, Tenochtitlan, was a marvel of social structure. The temples and settlements shown here, and the system of canals and green boulevards surrounding them, were the products of a highly developed and complex social system governed primarily by a priestly caste. As the mural suggests, Tenochtitlan was carefully planned to allow its inhabitants to enjoy the temperate climate of the high valley and was served by a sophisticated irrigation system (Iglesia, 1990).

Today, less than 500 years after the conquest, the Valley of Mexico is blanketed by Mexico City and the many urban comunities surrounding it. The social structure of Mexico City is extremely complex, because the city is both Mexico's largest commercial center and its national capital. The city is surrounded by ancient volcanos, and the valley floor is prone to earthquakes. Despite the problems created by rapid growth in an environmentally sensitive area, Mexico City continues to grow and is now one of the two or three largest metropolitan centers in the world.

THE FIRST MILLION YEARS: HUNTING AND GATHERING

A human lifetime is no more than a twinkling in time. What are 70 or 80 years compared with the billions of years of the earth's existence? What is one generation compared with the millions of years of human social evolution? Yet many of us hope to leave some mark on society, perhaps to change it for the better, to ease some suffering, to increase productivity, to fight racism and ignorance . . . what vaulting ambitions! And what a radical change from the world view of our ancestors! The idea that people can shape their society—or even enjoy adequate shelter and ample meals—is widely accepted today. But for most of human history mere survival was the primary motivator of human action, and thus a fatalistic acceptance of human frailty in the face of overwhelming natural forces was the dominant world view.

For most of the first million years of human evolution, human societies were developing from those of primates. Populations were small because humans, like other primates, lived on wild animals and plants. These sources of food are easily used up and their supply fluctuates greatly, and as a result periods of starvation or gnawing hunger might alternate with bouts of gorging on sudden windfalls of game or berries. Thus the hunting-and-gathering life that characterized the earliest human populations could support only extremely small societies; most human societies therefore had no more than about 60 members.

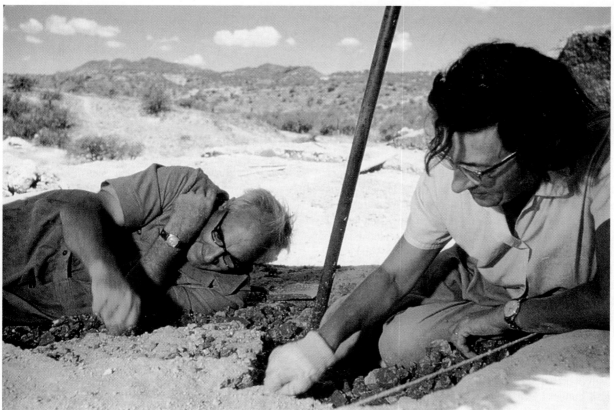

This photo shows Dr. Louis Leakey and his wife, Mary, painstakingly excavating bits of bone and tools at Olduvai Gorge in Tanzania. The Leakeys are among the world's most famous physical anthropologists and are responsible for much of what is now known about early human origins.

Social Structure And Settlement Before Agriculture

Archeological evidence now suggests hunter-gatherers had complex societies and elaborate settlements long before they began farming.

35,000-27,000 YEARS AGO
Western European foragers made beads and other ornaments using a system like an assembly line. The ivory beads shown here are 32,000 years old. The larger pendant, a schematic human form, is 27,000 years old. Use of such standardized objects for body ornaments points to the emergence of ideas of social status and hierarchy.

Source: Dr. Randall White

Source: Dr. Olga Soffer

26,000-12,000 YEARS AGO In the central Russian plain, people stayed in one place for most of the year, living in increasingly permanent communities. They used mammoth bones to build large structures for shelter and storage for food and materials. There is also evidence of trade in materials from near the Black Sea, 500 miles away.

12,500-10,500 YEARS AGO
The Natufians, living in and around what is now Israel, were the first hunter-gatherers to make the transition to permanent settlements, though they continued to live off the land rather than cultivating crops. Their elaborate stone houses with supporting pillars, like those at left, are the earliest evidence of such complex architecture. They had food preparation areas, with mortars and pestles, and storage areas for the wild grains that proliferated as the glaciers retreated. Spaces around the houses were paved.

Source: Dr. Donald O. Henry, "From Foraging to Agriculture," University of Pennsylvania Press

Illustrations by Patricia J. Wynne

Recent archaeological evidence indicates that some hunting-and-gathering societies began to develop permanent settlements long before the advent of agriculture. The emergence of farming was one of the changes that accelerated human social evolution, but the new evidence shows that in parts of what is now Europe and the Middle East there were stable settlements of hunter-gatherers as early as 30,000 to 20,000 years ago. These rather large and complex societies were most firmly established in the area that is now Israel at the end of the last Ice Age, some 13,000 to 12,000 years ago (Henry, 1989; Stevens, 1988).

Despite the slow pace of human evolution until about 35,000 years ago, some astonishing physical and social changes occurred during that long period, changes that enabled human life to take the forms it does today. Among them were the following:

- The development of an upright posture (which freed the hands for eventual use of tools) and an enlarged cerebral cortex, making possible vastly increased cognitive abilities and the development of language.

- Social control of sexuality through the development of the family and other kinship structures and the enforcement of the incest taboo.

- The establishment of the band of hunter-gatherers as the basic territorial unit of human society, coupled with the development of kinship structures that linked bands together into tribes. Within the band, the family became the primary economic unit, organizing the production and distribution of food and other necessities.

The chart in Box 4.1 illustrates how kinship ties link hunting-and-gathering bands together into a larger society. Anthropologists and sociologists often represent social structures with diagrams of this type. They show how people are related to one another and what their status is in relation to any other person in the social structure.

By the end of the last Ice Age, many aspects of this evolutionary process were more or less complete. Human societies had fully developed languages and a social structure based on the family and the band. To be cast out of the band for some wrongdoing—that is, to be considered a deviant person (see Chapter 7)—usually meant total banishment from the society and eventual death, either by starvation or as a result of aggression by members of another society (Salisbury, 1962). But warfare and violence were not typical of early human societies, as the social anthropologist Marshall Sahlins has pointed out:

> Warfare is limited among hunters and gatherers. Indeed, many are reported to find the idea of war incomprehensible. A massive military effort would be difficult to sustain for technical and logistic reasons. But war is even further inhibited by the spread of a social relation—kinship— which in primitive society is often a synonym for "peace." Thomas Hobbes' famous fantasy of a war of "all against all" in the natural state could not be further from the truth. War increases in intensity, bloodiness, duration, and significance for social survival through the evolution of culture, reaching its culmination in modern civilization. (1960, p. 82)

On the other hand, one must not romanticize the hunter-gatherers. Their lives were far more subject to the pressures of adaptation to the natural environment than has been true in any subsequent form of society. Individual survival was usually subordinated to that of the group. If there were too many children to feed, some were killed or left to die; when the old became infirm or weak, they often chose death so as not to diminish the chances of the others. Thus the frail Eskimo grandfather or grandmother

wandered off into the snowy night to "meet the polar bear and the Great Spirit." Additional thousands of years of social evolution would pass before the idea that every person could and should survive, prosper, and die with dignity would even occur to our ancestors.

THE TRANSITION TO AGRICULTURE

For some time before the advent of plow-and-harvest agriculture in the Middle East and the Far East, hunting-and-gathering societies were supplementing their diets with foods acquired through the domestication of plants and animals. In this way they were able to avoid the alternation of periods of feast and famine caused by reliance on animal prey. Karl Marx was the first social theorist to observe that social revolutions like the shift to agriculture or industrial production are never merely the result of technological innovations such as the plow or the steam engine. The origins of new forms of society are to be found within the old ones. New social orders do not simply burst upon the scene but are created out of the problems faced by the old order. Thus, as they experimented with domestication of animals and planting of crops, some hunting-and-gathering societies were evolving into nomadic shepherding, or **pastoral,** societies in which bands followed flocks of animals. Others were developing into **horticultural** societies in which the women raised seed crops and the men combed the territory for game and fish.

Regarding this momentous change in the material basis of human survival, the historian William McNeill made the following observation:

> The seed-bearing grasses ancestral to modern cultivated grains probably grew wild eight or nine thousand years ago

The "Ice Man," discovered in 1991 by hikers in the Italian Alps, is shown here with his hatchet and other items he was carrying when he died. These remains, the oldest sample of human flesh and organs ever discovered, are providing a wealth of knowledge about daily life in hunting-and-gathering societies 5,000 years ago.

FIGURE 4.3   **Agricultural Origins**

Source: McNeill, 1963.

in the hill country between Anatolia and the Zagros Mountains, as varieties of wheat and barley continue to do today. If so, we can imagine that from time immemorial the women of those regions searched out patches of wheat and barley grasses when the seeds were ripe and gathered the wild harvest by hand or with the help of simple cutting tools. Such women may gradually have discovered methods for assisting the growth of grain, e.g., by pulling out competing plants; and it is likely that primitive sickles were invented to speed the harvest long before agriculture in the stricter sense came to be practiced. (1963, p. 12)

As a result of these and other innovations, agriculture became the productive basis of human societies. Pastoral societies spread quickly throughout the uplands and grasslands of Africa, northern Asia, Europe, and the Western Hemisphere, and grain-producing societies arose in the fertile river valleys of Mesopotamia, India, China, and—somewhat later—Central and South America. (See Figure 4.3.) Mixed societies of shepherds and marginal farmers wandered over the lands between the upland pastures and the lowland farms.

The First Large-Scale Societies.   We have reached the beginning of recorded history (around 4000 B.C.), which was marked by the rise of the ancient civilizations of Sumer, Babylonia, China and Japan, Benin, and the Maya, Incas, and Aztecs. The detailed study of these societies is the province of archaeology, history, and classics.

But sociologists need to know as much as possible about the earliest large-scale societies because many contemporary social institutions (e.g., government and religion) and most areas of severe social conflict (e.g., class and ethnic conflict) developed sometime in the agrarian epoch—between 3000 B.C. and A.D. 1600.

From the standpoint of social evolution, the following dimensions of agrarian societies are the most salient (Braidwood, 1967):

- Agriculture allows humans to escape from dependence on food sources over which they have no control. Agrarian societies produce surpluses that do not merely *permit* but *require* new classes of non-food-producers to exist. An example is the class of warriors, who defend the surplus or add to it through plunder.

- Agriculture requires an ever-larger supply of land, resulting in conflicts over territory and in wars with other agricultural or pastoral societies.

- The need to store and defend food surpluses and to house the nonagrarian classes results in new territorial units: villages and small cities.

New Social Structures.   Freed from direct dependence on undomesticated species of plants and animals, agrarian societies developed far more complex social structures than were possible in simpler societies. Hunting-and-gathering societies divided labor primarily according to age and sex, but in agricultural societies labor was divided in new ways to perform more specialized tasks. Peoples who had been conquered in war might be enslaved and assigned the most difficult or least desirable work. Priests controlled the society's religious life, and from the priestly class there emerged a class of hereditary rulers who, as the society became larger and more complex, assumed the status of pharaoh or emperor. Artisans with special skills—in the making of armaments or buildings, for example—usually formed another class. And far more numerous than any of these classes were the tillers of the soil, the "common" agricultural workers and their dependents.

The process whereby the members of a society are sorted into different statuses and classes based on differences in wealth, power, and prestige is called **social stratification** and is described in detail in Chapter 11. In general, societies may be **open,** so that a person who was not born into a particular status may gain entry to that status, or **closed,** with each status accessible only by birth. A key characteristic of agrarian societies is that their stratification systems became extremely rigid. Because the majority of the people were needed in the fields, there were few opportunities for people to move from one level of society to another. These therefore were closed societies.

The emergence of agrarian societies was based largely on the development of new, more efficient production technologies. Of these, the plow and irrigation were among the most important. The ancient agrarian empires of Egypt, Rome, and China are examples of societies in which irrigation made possible the production of large food surpluses, which in turn permitted the emergence of central governments led by pharaohs and emperors, priests and soldiers. Indeed, some sociologists have argued that because large-scale irrigation systems required a great deal of coordination, their development led to the evolution of imperial courts and such institutions as slavery, which coerced large numbers of agrarian workers into forced labor (Wittfogel, 1957).

By the fifteenth century the world's population was organized into a wide variety of societies with many different types of cultures and civilizations. Figure 4.4 depicts the spread of human life over more than 150 million square kilometers of land in the year 1500, before the age of exploration and the industrial revolution. The 76 cultures and civilizations shown include hundreds of different societies, ranging from simple hunting-and-gathering societies to more advanced agrarian ones to civilizations that were already expanding and exporting their culture through conquest and trade. The areas numbered 1 to 27 on the map were inhabited by simple societies of hunters, gatherers, and fishers; those numbered 28 to 44 were inhabited by nomads and stockbreeders; areas 45 to 60 were inhabited by agricultural peoples, primarily peasants using hoes rather

than plows; and the remaining areas were more advanced civilizations. With the exception of the Mayan and Incan civilizations, all of the latter were found in Asia, the Middle East, and parts of Europe.

The areas where the earliest civilizations emerged are to this day the most densely inhabited parts of the world. In 1500 these civilizations were marked by their ability to produce food surpluses through the use of the plow, domesticated animals, wheels, and carts. Above all, they are marked by the importance of towns and cities as centers of administration and religious practice. Although the Mayan and Incan civilizations did not have the wheel or the plow, their advanced systems of astronomy, art, and writing make a strong argument for their inclusion as world civilizations.

The explorations led by Portugal, Spain, and England in the sixteenth and seventeenth centuries resulted in conquest and European settlement in many parts of the Western Hemisphere and Africa. Conquest caused radical disruptions in the internal development of the world's cultures and civilizations. But even more drastic would be the changes caused by the industrial revolution of the eighteenth and nineteenth centuries.

THE INDUSTRIAL REVOLUTION

In 1650, when Holland, Spain, and England were the world's principal trading nations (Block, 1990), the population of England was approximately 10 million, of which about 90 percent earned a livelihood through farming of one kind or another. Just 200 years later, in 1850, the English population had soared to more than 30 million, with less than 20 percent at work in fields, barns, and granaries. England had become the world's first industrial society and the center of an empire that spanned the world.

A similar transformation occurred in the United States. In 1860, on the eve of the Civil War, there were about 30 million people in the United States. Ninety percent of that population, a people considered quite backward by the rapidly industrializing English, were farmers or people who worked in occupations directly related to farming. A mere 100 years later, in 1960, only about 8 percent of Americans were farmers or agricultural workers, yet they were able to produce enough to feed a population exceeding 200 million. Today less than 3 percent of Americans work on farms and ranches. These dramatic changes in England and America—and in other nations as well—occurred as a result of the industrial revolution.

The industrial revolution is often associated with innovations in energy production, especially the steam engine. But the shift from an agrarian to an industrial society did not happen simply as a result of technological advances. Rather, the industrial revolution was made possible by the rise of a new social order known as **capitalism.** This new way of organizing production originated in nation-states, which engaged in international trade, exploration, and warfare. Above all, the industrial revolution depended on

FIGURE 4.4 **Civilizations, "Cultures," and Primitive Peoples, ca. 1500**

Hunting, fishing, food gathering

Nomadic and pastoral

Less developed cultures – using hoes

Advanced cultures

Densely populated civilizations – using plows

1. Tasmanians
2. Congo Pygmies
3. The Vedda (Ceylon)
4. Andamanese
5. Sakai and Semang
6. Kubu
7. Punan (Borneo)
8. Negritos of the Philippines
9. Ciboneys (Antilles)
10. Gê-Botocudos
11. Gran Chaco Indians
12. Bushmen
13. Australians
14. Great Basin
15. Lower California
16. Texas and northeastern Mexico

17. Patagonia
18. Indians of the southern coast of Chile
19. Athabascans and Algonkin (northern Canada)
20. Yukaghir
21. Eastern and central Eskimos
22. Western Eskimos
23. Kamchadal, Koryak, Chukchi
24. Ainu, Gilyak, Gol'dy
25. Northwest coast Indians (United States and Canada)
26. Columbia Plateau
27. Central California
28. Reindeer-herding peoples
29. Canary Islands

30. Sahara nomads
31. Arabian nomads
32. Pastoral mountain peoples in the Near East
33. Pastoral peoples of the Pamir region and Hindu Kush
34. Kazakh-Kirghiz
35. Mongols
36. Pastoral Tibetans
37. Settled Tibetans
38. Western Sudanese
39. Eastern Sudanese
40. Somali and Galla of northeastern Africa
41. Nilotic tribes
42. East African stock-rearing peoples

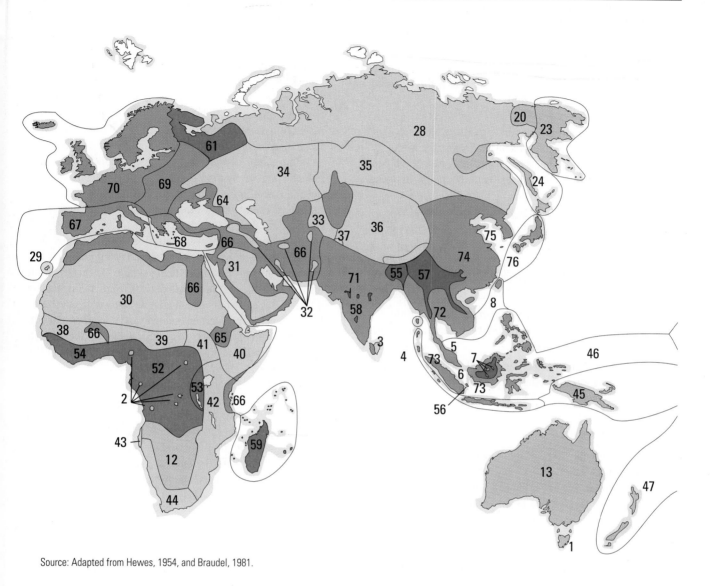

Source: Adapted from Hewes, 1954, and Braudel, 1981.

43. Western Bantu
44. Hottentots
45. Melanesian Papuans
46. Micronesians
47. Polynesians
48. American Indians (eastern United States)
49. American Indians (western United States)
50. Brazilian Indians
51. Chilean Indians
52. Congolese peoples
53. Lake-dwellers of East Africa
54. Guinea coasts
55. Tribes of the Assam and the Burmese highlands

56. Tribes of the Indonesian highlands
57. Highland peoples of Indochina
58. Mountain and forest tribes of central India
59. Malagasay
60. Caribbean peoples
61. Finns
62. Mexicans, Maya
63. Peru and the Andes
64. Caucasians
65. Ethiopia
66. Settled Muslims
67. Southwestern Europe
68. Eastern Mediterranean
69. Eastern Europe
70. Northwestern Europe

71. India (this map does not differentiate between Muslims and Hindus)
72. Lowlands of Southeast Asia
73. Indonesian lowlands
74. Chinese
75. Koreans
76. Japanese

the development of *markets,* social structures that would function to regulate the supply of and demand for goods and services throughout the world (Polanyi, 1944).

The transition from an agrarian to an industrial society affects every aspect of social life. It changes the structure of society in several ways, of which the following are among the most significant:

- The industrialization of agriculture allows many more people to be supported by each agrarian worker than ever before. Only a relatively small number of people live on the land; increasing numbers live in towns, cities, and suburbs.

- Industrial societies are generally far more receptive to social change than agrarian societies. One result is the emergence of new classes like industrial workers and scientific professionals (engineers, technicians) and new social movements like the women's movement and the movement for racial equality.

- Scientific, technical, and productive institutions produce both unparalleled wealth and unparalleled destructive capacities.

- The world "shrinks" as a result of innovations in transportation and communication. A "global society" develops, but at the same time the unevenness of industrialization leads to conflicts that threaten world peace.

These are only some of the important features of industrial societies. There are many others, which we analyze throughout this book. We will present research that shows how the types of jobs people find and the ways in which they spend their leisure time change as technology advances and their expectations change. We will also look into the ways in which other major institutions—especially the family—adapt to the changes created by the industrial revolution. In fact, we will continually return to the industrial revolution as a major force in our times.

The Theory of Post-Industrial Society. At present there is an important theoretical debate in the social sciences about whether the United States and other societies that experienced industrialization in earlier periods should now be considered "post-industrial societies." Sociologist Fred Block (1990) observes that ours is

> a strange period in the history of the United States because people lack a shared understanding of the kind of society in which they live. For generations, the United States was considered as an industrial society, but that definition is no longer compelling. Yet no convincing alternative has emerged in its absence. (p. 1)

In this book we continue to group the United States and the European nations among the world's industrial societies because they are major producers of manufactured goods. However, it should be noted that the businesses that produce those goods are dwindling in number owing to the effects of the industrial revolution in other areas of the world. Also, for the first time in U.S. history the number of jobs in services exceeds that of jobs in goods-producing industries. Far more jobs are created in restaurants and hotels each year than in steel mills and other kinds of factories (Kasarda, 1989). In addition, there is an ever-increasing demand for highly educated and trained workers in new industries that deal with high-speed transmission of information. Computers and telecommunications technologies are surely produced by "industries," but they are not the type of mass-employment "smokestack" industries that were the hallmark of earlier stages of the industrial revolution.

The theory of post-industrial society explores why these fundamental changes have come about and their impact, not only on post-industrial societies themselves but also on the cultures of other societies. There are also many questions about what will happen as the world's societies become ever more interdependent—and decisions made in metropolitan centers like Tokyo, Los Angeles, and London affect the lives of villagers in the most remote parts of the world (Giddens, 1984; Sassen, 1994). We will return to the issues raised by theories of industrialization and the emergence of post-industrial society throughout this book. For it is clear that while the most advanced and powerful nations are undergoing an economic transformation, in many other parts of the world the industrial revolution is in full swing, and in still other, more remote areas older forms of agrarianism and tribalism continue to thrive.

SOCIETY AND THE INDIVIDUAL

FROM GEMEINSCHAFT TO GESELLSCHAFT

Imagine that you grew up in an agrarian village or a town in a slowly industrializing society and then came to live in the United States, as millions of people do each decade. A difficult part of that experience would be getting used to the impersonality of modern American society when compared with the close relationships you had with people you had known all your life in your native society. American society would seem to be composed of masses of strangers organized into highly impersonal categories. You would have to get used to being a shopper, an applicant, a depositor, a fan, a commuter, and so on, and it would be necessary to shift from one to another of these roles several times in a day or even within a half hour.

Sociologists often describe this experience as a change from **gemeinschaft** (the close, personal relationships of small groups and communities) to **gesellschaft** (the well-organized but impersonal relationships of modern societies). These are German terms taken from the writings of the social theorist Ferdinand Tönnies (1957/1887). Complex industrial societies, Tönnies argued, have developed gesellschaft social structures like factories and office bureaucracies to such a degree that they tend to dominate day-to-day life in the modern world.

The American sociologist Charles H. Cooley applied this distinction to the micro level of society in his discussion of primary versus secondary groups. "By **primary groups,**" Cooley wrote,

> I mean those characterized by intimate face-to-face association and cooperation. They are primary in several senses, but chiefly in that they are fundamental in forming the social nature and ideals of the individual. [Such a group] involves the sort of sympathy and mutual identification for which "we" is the natural expression. (1909, p. 23)

Secondary groups, in contrast, are groups in which we participate for instrumental reasons—that is, in order to accomplish some task or set of tasks. Examples are school classrooms, town committees, and political party organizations. We do not have intimate relationships with other members of secondary groups; at least, we do not normally expect to do so and are not concerned about the fact that our relationships in such groups involve only a limited range of emotions. (See Box 4.2.)

Of course, when we speak of intimacy in primary groups we do not always refer to love and warm feelings. The intimacy of the members of a family refers to a highly charged set of emotions that can range from love to hate but rarely includes indifference. But in a secondary group indifference, or lack of personal involvement, is the norm. We therefore do not usually develop strong feelings toward all the other members of the organizations for which we work or the associations to which we belong, even though we may have one or more close friends among our workmates. The idea that people do not have to form primary attachments in work organizations also protects people with less power from those with more. Women in subordinate positions, for example, often need protection from men in more powerful positions who make sexual advances. Modern laws on sexual conduct in the workplace classify such behavior as illegal harassment. But the fact that we need such laws points up the degree of conflict we often experience in performing our roles.

ROLE AND STATUS IN MODERN SOCIETIES

Roles in Conflict.   Gesellschaft forms of social organization are more complex than gemeinschaft forms in terms of the number of statuses people hold and, thus, the number of roles they must perform. One result of this greater complexity is that roles in secondary groups or associations often conflict with roles in primary groups like the family. Much of the stress of life in modern societies is due to the anxiety we experience as we attempt to balance the demands of our various roles. This anxiety is captured in the terms *role conflict* and *role strain.*

Role conflict occurs when, in order to perform one role well, a person must violate another important role. Parents who are also employees may experience this kind of conflict when their supervisors ask them to put in extra time, which cuts into the time they are able to spend with their children. An article in the *Harvard Business Review* (Schwartz, 1989) supporting the idea that corporations should develop a two-track system, one for executives who sacrifice family concerns for the company and another for those who take time off for family needs, stimulated intense controversy in both business and social-scientific circles. The so-called mommy track was attacked as discriminating against women who wish to succeed in business careers while raising their children.

Research on how people behave in disasters also illustrates some of the effects of role conflict. For example, a police officer or firefighter who is on duty during a disaster that affects his or her own family may leave an assigned post to see to the safety of loved ones, thereby violating one role in order to fulfill another (Killian, 1952).

Role strain occurs when people experience conflicting demands in an existing role or cannot meet the expectations of a new one. For example, law enforcement agents face role strain as they attempt to enforce laws that the majority desires while protecting the rights of minorities. Thus federal rangers in the national forests and parks often experience role strain when they seek to balance the enforcement and community relations aspects of their role. Environmental laws may restrict the use of a wilderness area to hikers, but local residents may wish to drive their vehicles over old logging roads to reach isolated fishing or hunting grounds. When the rangers enforce the rules against local people (who are also their neighbors), they may experience severe role strain (Helvarg, 1994; Shanks, 1991).

Role strain in the form of anxiety over poor performance is at least as common as role strain caused by conflicting expectations. For example, the unemployed head of a family feels severe stress as a result of inability to provide for the family's needs (Bakke, 1933; Jahoda, 1982; Jahoda, Lazarsfeld, & Zeisel, 1971). The mother of a newborn baby often feels intense anxiety over how well she can care for a helpless infant, a feeling that is heightened if she herself is young and dependent on others (Mayfield, 1984).

Ascribed Versus Achieved Statuses.   Role conflicts may occur in simpler societies, but they are far more common in societies undergoing rapid change. One reason for the relative lack of role conflict in simpler, more stable societies is that in such societies a person's statuses are likely to be determined by birth or tradition rather than by anything the person achieves through his or her own efforts. These **ascribed statuses** (peasant, aristocrat, slave, and so forth) usually cannot be changed and hence are less

BOX 4.2 USING THE SOCIOLOGICAL IMAGINATION

Individual and Group in Three Societies

The accompanying photos can be used to compare typical groups in three types of societies: hunting-and-gathering, feudal, and modern. The pictures underline the contrasts among the three types of societies. They also offer some insight into what life in groups is like for the individual in those societies.

Hunting-and-gathering societies are represented by the hunter himself, in this case a !Kung bushman with his hunting bow. Among the bushmen of the Kalahari Desert in southwestern Africa, the typical primary group is the extended family, which includes hunters, younger and older family members, mothers, and babies—all living in close proximity and usually traveling long distances together as they follow the game to its seasonal feeding and watering grounds. The hunter shown here teaches the young his

skills, leads the family in its spiritual life, and performs a multitude of other roles that in modern societies are performed by specialists such as teachers and ministers.

The carefully coiffed woman with the ornate necklace is Marguerite of York, a fifteenth-century English noblewoman. In the style of late feudal times, she has created a high forehead by plucking or shaving her hair; her goals are to look well at court and to be accepted in the

likely to be subject to different role expectations. Such statuses are found in industrial societies too (statuses based on race or sex are examples), but they tend to become less important in modern institutions than **achieved statuses** like editor, professor, or Nobel Prize winner. (See Box 4.3.)

We expect to be able to achieve our occupational status, our marital and family statuses, and other statuses in the community and the larger society. Nevertheless, there is some tension in modern societies between the persis-

tence of ascribed statuses and the ideal of achieved statuses. The empirical study of that tension and of efforts to replace ascribed with achieved statuses (e.g., through equality of educational opportunity) is another major area of sociological research. We will show in later chapters that many of the social movements studied by sociologists arose as different groups in a society (e.g., African Americans, wage workers, immigrants, and the poor) organized to press for greater access to economic and social institutions like corporations and universities.

primary group of courtiers who attend the king and queen, as shown in the group engraving. The circle of courtiers was a typical group among the aristocracy of feudal England. Those who worked on the farms and in the towns never experienced the gay life of the courtiers, but neither could they imagine the rivalries and tensions of a highly competitive court life that were the daily experience of women like Marguerite of York.

The worker in a modern society uses technologies that were not even dreamed of in an earlier epoch. Those technologies involve workers in a network of large organizations like the firm, the labor union, and the factory—and separate their place of work from their life in the nuclear family, shown here enjoying a day at the beach. Note that the children and the parents are engaging in an activity that all can share equally, something that would have been most unusual in families of the feudal era or in those of hunting-and-gathering societies, in which the roles of children and adults and of men and women usually differ greatly.

Master Statuses. One reason so many groups have had to organize to obtain social justice is related to the way statuses operate in many societies. Although any person may fill a variety of statuses, many people find that one of their statuses is more important than all the others. Such a status, which is termed a **master status,** can have very damaging effects (Hughes, 1945). A black man, for example, may be a doctor, a father, and a leader in his church, but he may find that his status as a black American takes precedence over all of those other statuses. The same is often true for women. A woman may be a brilliant scientist and a leader in her community, and fill other statuses as well, but she may find that when she deals with men her status as a woman is more important than any of the others.

The effects of a master status are also felt by people who have been in prison, by members of various racial and ethnic groups, by Americans overseas (Smith, 1994), and by members of many other types of groups. For example, recent studies have shown that people who are noticeably overweight or obese often find that their status as a "fat

BOX 4.3 GLOBAL SOCIAL CHANGE

Social Structures in a Changing World

Social change modifies the social structures we experience in ways that are sometimes subtle and sometimes quite dramatic. This is true not only in our own society but throughout the world. Very often these changes are extremely disturbing for the people who experience them. If we think for a moment about how changes in the structure of a family confuse the lives of children who experience the breakup of one family and the formation of a more complex family (especially if both the mother and father remarry), we begin to get a sense of how powerful the experience of change in social structures can be. For entire societies as well as for individuals, changing social structures can be of immense importance and carry a high emotional charge. The shift from manufacturing to services in modern economies, the end of the cold war, and the declining fortunes of the British monarchy are examples of such changes.

The Shift from Manufacturing to Services. From the 1970s to the present, hundreds of thousands of workers in Europe and North America have lost their jobs as the older industrialized nations have rapidly automated their industries and sold production facilities to industrializing nations like Brazil, Argentina, and South Korea. Social scientists refer to these trends as structural changes because new ways of organizing work and new forms of production are replacing older industries and firms. Structural change in this instance means far fewer statuses (jobs) in companies that produce goods and more in organizations that produce services (banking, computer services, health care, etc.). At the same time, structural change is occurring rapidly in areas of the world whose economies are shifting from agricultural production to manufacturing. In Mexico, Brazil, and parts of Africa, and throughout Asia, the factory is replacing the farm as the dominant social structure.

The End of the Cold War. The fall of the Berlin Wall in 1989 symbolized the end of the cold war between the Soviet Union and the United States. This dramatic event ushered in a new and highly uncertain era of international relations, as can be seen in the increase in conflicts within nations like the former Yugoslavia. But the end of the cold war is also bringing about vast structural change in nations where military production and military employment had been important sources of jobs. In the

United States and the former Soviet Union more than 2 million men and women served in the military during the 1970s and much of the 1980s. Entry into the military was a common path to future employment for young people from modest and poor families in both parts of the world. And entire industrial regions were devoted to military production. Now that the threat of war between the superpowers has diminished, there is less need to employ large numbers of people in the military, and areas that once produced guns, submarines, jet fighters, and bombs are experiencing the wrenching effects of structural change.

The British Royal Family. The problems of the royal family in Great Britain are another example of how changes in social structures can capture worldwide attention. In the era of absolute monarchies kings and princes conducted their marital and extramarital relationships as they pleased, but after the overthrow of many monarchies in the eighteenth and nineteenth centuries, those that remained—most notably the British royal family—were expected to provide moral leadership, albeit without holding the reins of political power. Separation and divorce among royal couples like Prince Charles and Princess Diana were virtually unheard of. Because the royal family symbolized the central values of British society, a quarreling royal couple was expected to keep marital problems private and to maintain their marriage, even if it meant merely going through the motions. To separate was essentially to give up all claim to moral leadership, as well as to the right of succession to the throne. In return for being forever in the public eye, the royals were granted privileges and wealth that no commoner could hope to attain. But when the royals began to behave like ordinary couples, citizens began questioning why they should subsidize such an expensive social structure in the first place.

As these three examples indicate, changes in social structure affect everyone, from members of royal families to members of very average families and households. Around the world structural changes are experienced differently, depending on whose lives they touch and how, but such changes are occurring everywhere, and their effects are a subject of ongoing sociological research.

person" is a master status that denies them opportunities to be appreciated for their performance in other statuses, such as student or worker.

Patterns of discrimination and prejudice stemming from the problem of master statuses are not easily corrected. We will see at many points in this book that a major source of social change is the efforts of some groups to eliminate those patterns. But when changes actually occur in a society they often take the form of new national laws, such as laws against racial segregation or gender discrimi-

nation. This raises the question of the distinction between societies and nations.

SOCIETIES AND NATION-STATES

For most people in the world today, the social entity that represents society itself is the nation-state. The assumed correspondence between society and nation can be seen in the fact that expressions like "the United States" and

"American society" are often used interchangeably. Moreover, most people think of their society in terms of national boundaries; thus, if you were asked to name the society of which you are a member, you would be more likely to say "the United States" than "California" or "Chicago" or "the University of Texas." Yet as we will see shortly, societies and nations are by no means the same thing.

THE STATE

To understand the distinction between society and nation, we need to begin with the concept of the state. In a lecture at Munich University Max Weber described a state as:

> a human community that (successfully) claims *the monopoly of the legitimate use of physical force* within a given territory. . . . The right to use physical force is ascribed to other institutions or to individuals only to the extent to which the state permits it. The state is considered the sole source of the "right" to use violence. (quoted in Gerth & Mills, 1958, p. 78; emphasis in original)

The **state** thus may be defined as a society's set of political institutions—that is, the groups and organizations that deal with questions of "who gets what, when, and how" (Lasswell, 1936). The **nation-state** is the largest territory within which those institutions can operate without having to face challenges to their sovereignty (their right to govern). Weber was careful to note that the state has a monopoly over the use of force, which under certain circumstances it grants to other agencies (e.g., state and municipal governments). But the state gains this right—the source of its power to influence the behavior of citizens—from the people themselves, from their belief that it is *legitimate* for the state to have this power. As we will see in later chapters, the concepts of power and legitimacy are essential to understanding the workings of the modern state; indeed, power is a basic concept at all levels of human social behavior. Here, however, we must examine the idea of a state as it operates in the concept of nation-state or, simply, nation.

THE NATION-STATE

"One nation, under God, indivisible, with liberty and justice for all." We can say the words in our sleep. We do not usually give much thought to the significance of what we are doing when we repeat the Pledge of Allegiance. Yet repeating the pledge is a highly significant action: It enhances the legitimacy of the state and thus helps create the nation—in this case, the nation known as the United States of America.

But do all the inhabitants of the United States of America think of themselves as members of one nation? To a large extent they do, and this is one of the greatest strengths of that nation. Yet at various times in American history certain groups—African Americans, Native Americans, and the Amish, for example—have thought of themselves as separate peoples. And the idea of an "indivisible"

nation was fought out in one of the bloodiest wars the world has ever known, the American Civil War of 1861–1865.

In the century since the Civil War the United States has not experienced any real tests of its national solidarity. Countries like Canada, Lebanon, Zimbabwe, South Africa, Iran, Northern Ireland, and the nations that were formerly part of Yugoslavia—to name only a few—have been far less fortunate. For them, the issue of creating a national identity that can unite peoples who think of themselves as members of different societies remains a burning question.

Between 1945 and 1970, as peoples all over the world adjusted to the breakup of the European colonial empires, more than a hundred new states were created, many of them in the poorer regions of Africa and Asia. In these new nations, as in many of the nation-states that existed before the 1950s, the correspondence between national identity and society is often problematic, a situation that frequently produces social upheavals. In Nigeria, for example, the stability—indeed, the very existence—of the nation-state is endangered by animosities among the various societies included within its boundaries. Although the nation has rich oil resources and is the largest of the sub-Saharan nations, its per capita income fell to $250 in 1993 from $1,000 in 1980. This decline is due largely to conflicts among the major tribal groups and the failure of the nation-state's leaders to overcome those conflicts. Although there are scores of tribal and ethnic groups in the nation's population, the largest are the Hausa (21 percent), the Yoruba (20 percent), the Ibo (17 percent), and the Fulani (9 percent), each of which is afraid that the others might gain power at their expense (Olojede, 1995) (see Figure 4.5).

South Africa provides another example of differing levels of national and social identity. In 1994 the minority white government ended its policy of apartheid (racial separation) and yielded political power to the black majority under the leadership of Nelson Mandela and the formerly banned African National Congress. But black South Africans themselves often experience conflicts derived from differing tribal identities. The larger tribal populations, such as the Zulus, have their own kings and political leaders. Some are afraid that the incorporation of their people into a modern nation-state will cause them to lose their identity and rights as Zulus. As a result, there have been numerous episodes of conflict and violence between Zulu separatists and the members of the African National Congress.

The lack of a clear match between society and nation can be seen in the case of entire groups who think of themselves as "a people" (e.g., the Ibo, the Jews, Native Americans, the Chechens in Russia) as well as in smaller groups. You and your friends are part of "American society," by which we mean the populations and social structures found within the territory claimed by the nation-state known as the United States of America. But you are also part of a local community with smaller structures and more

FIGURE 4.5

MAPPING SOCIAL CHANGE

Source:
Adapted from
Kwamena-Poh,
Tosh, Waller, & Tidy, 1982, and Crowder, 1966.

Tribal Societies Within the Modern State of Nigeria.
Nigeria is the largest nation of Africa south of the Sahara desert. As the detailed map shows, it is composed of many societies with their own cultures and languages. Some, like the Hausa, are spread out over vast territories in the northern savannas; others, like the Tiv and Ibo, are clustered in the more densely populated coastal plains and on the delta of the mighty Niger River. Nigeria was once considered a leader in the development of democratic political institutions. It had a lively cultural and intellectual life and produced some of Africa's best novelists and playwrights. Today, after many years of civil war and military coups, Nigeria is a military dictatorship. Conflict between its many societies, often over the disposal of oil revenues from the Niger delta region, and rampant political and economic corruption

continually threaten the viability of this nation–state's democratic institutions.

Ken Saro-Wiwa, shown in the inset photo, is considered to be a martyr of Nigeria's democratic hopes. Despite protests throughout the world, this celebrated writer, environmental activist, and political dissident was executed by the Nigerian dictatorship late in 1995. Saro-Wiwa was the founder and leader of the Movement for the Survival of the Ogoni People in Nigeria's oil-rich Niger delta region. Although the government and the Dutch Shell Corporation had taken billions of dollars' worth of oil from their lands, the Ogoni, a small tribal society in the Cross River region, still live in mud huts and dig for yams with bamboo sticks. Acid rain and oil pollution have destroyed many productive farms. Saro-Wiwa was attempting to organize a peaceful social movement to protest these conditions. His arrest and execution is an example of how environmental issues increasingly become confounded with intergroup politics in this land of tribal conflict.

gemeinschaft or primary relationships. Indeed, this community level of society may have greater meaning for you in your daily life than society at the national level.

RESEARCH FRONTIERS: IMMIGRATION TO THE UNITED STATES

Throughout the world, one of the most difficult problems people face in their communities and societies is that of accommodating cultural diversity. The outbreaks of racism and ethnic hatred that occur in communities in the United States are similar in their origins, if not in their intensity, to those occurring in Bosnia and Chechnya and India. In each case religious, racial, or ethnic divisions in the population of the nation-state create animosities that sometimes escalate into acts of cruelty and outbreaks of violence. In the United States, the origins of cultural diversity lie in the fact that throughout its history the nation has attracted immigrants from many other countries, making it a "nation of immigrants." The waves of new immigrants often had difficulty adjusting to U.S. society, and their more established neighbors tended to resent the newcomers and to react with hostility.

Given its global importance, it is no wonder that ever since the founding of sociology the study of immigration and its consequences has held a central place in sociological research. This has been particularly true in the United States. Many of the research questions explored by the

Chicago school sociologists had to do with the fate of different immigrant and migrant groups in the cities. Would the newcomers get decent jobs? Would they be able to retain their native languages while they learned English? Were they more prone to criminal behavior and mental illness than more established, native-born populations? Would they compete for jobs with other less advantaged groups, such as African Americans and native-born Hispanics? Would they form segregated ethnic enclaves with others from the same background? Would they eventually vote as an ethnic bloc? These and many other questions about the newcomers were at the core of empirical research in sociology during the early decades of this century. Today, because of the rapid pace of new immigration, these issues are once again on the frontier of sociological research.

One of the foremost students of immigration and its impact on American society is Alejandro Portes of Johns Hopkins University. In his book *Immigrant America* (1990) Portes shows that, for the first time since before World War I, the United States "has become anew a nation of immigrants." Each year during the 1980s an average of about 600,000 immigrants and refugees were legally admitted into this country, and "a sizable if uncertain number of others enter and remain without legal status, clandestinely crossing the borders or overstaying their visas" (p. xvii). Unlike earlier flows of immigrants, the vast majority of today's newcomers are from Asia and Latin America.

About 40 percent of the 6 million newcomers who came to the United States during the 1980s settled in the six cities shown in Figure 4.6. This figure shows data for a

---

FIGURE 4.6 **Composition of Immigrant Flows to Six Major Metropolitan Destinations in a Typical Year**

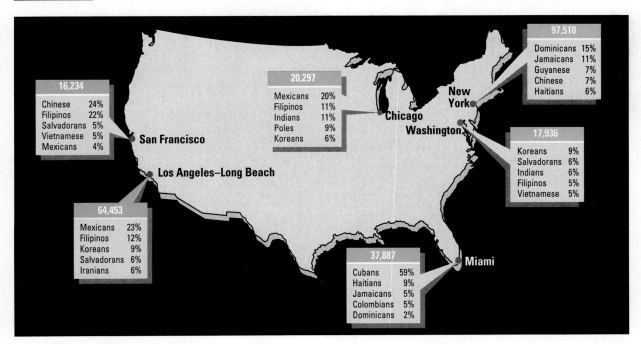

Source: Adapted from Portes & Rumbaut, 1990.

Note: Chinese include immigrants from mainland China only.

VISUAL SOCIOLOGY

THE SOCIAL STRUCTURE OF THE EMERGENCY ROOM

The emergency room (ER) of a big-city hospital is not a place for the squeamish observer. The deadening calm of the night shift may suddenly be broken by the crackle of the paramedics' radio, announcing that they are bringing in a severely wounded gunshot victim or a baby with a deadly high fever or three bleeding gang fighters. Immediately the routine work of the ER is suspended in a rush of activity. Even the less seriously ill or injured patients in the waiting room intuitively realize that their needs must be set aside for the life-threatening emergency.

Documentary photographer Eugene Richards (1989) spent many months conducting participant observation research in the emergency room of Denver General Hospital, known by local residents as the "knife and gun club." His

112

A man and a woman are the only people in the waiting room. Their child, I was told, has spinal meningitis. I sit close to them, but I can't think of anything to say. The silence is deadening. I feel frozen in place. I hide my camera and sit there for a half hour, until I see an ambulance pull up the ramp.

It's early in the day, I'm told, for a suicide attempt. The woman is 35 years old, still alive. There really is something fishlike about her, naked on the table with all those lines attached to her skin. And her skin is pale as ice. And her mouth is gaping open. . . .

5:00 P.M. The patient is a big-bellied guy with an American eagle on his left arm and a tongue hanging out tattooed to his chest. Insensible and bloody now, he had crashed his car at 80 miles per hour.

5:30 P.M. A teenage boy, claiming to be a member of a gang, shows the doctors the scars on his belly. He brags that he had refused medical treatment when he was stabbed, though he now looks terribly frightened. When a doctor reaches for his arm, he grimaces and tries to slide off the table. As the IV needle is slid in, he bites down on a rubber bottle cap, imitating something he must have seen in a John Wayne movie.

The chief surgeon leans forward and begins the cut. He cuts through the skin, looks, touches, cuts again. The other doctors join in. I'm conscious of the clicking of scissors, and that I'm breathing way too fast. Then, my God, they split the breastbone and position a spreader to push the ribs apart. It's done. They get to her heart, a punctured, failing heart.

At 1:00 A.M. the surgeons straighten up and turn all together towards the clock. They agree as to the time of death and pronounce her. After shooting some Polaroid pictures, they hurry out the door, probably to another patient. The nurses left behind turn off the machines, cut loose the lines and drainage tubes, and toss the surgical instruments into a pile; the interns close the dead woman's chest.

Lori Jones, clinical specialist: Actually, I've never done anything really great here, never saved anyone's life. The paramedics have. Yet patients have been lucky to have me as a nurse. No, I've never done things that are dramatic. I mean, I was happy because patients took their medicine as directed for 10 days. That's a feat in itself. . . .

This is a city hospital on the edge, losing money on indigent patients, and all around us is a massive system that has to raise more and more money, while politicians are threatening to close us down. So we are stretched incredibly thin, torn in so many different directions. It can be overwhelming.

photos capture the physically and emotionally draining work of the ER staff and the stark drama of the emergencies they deal with. In the text accompanying the photos, he often refers to the social structure of the ER. The roles of the ER staff are well defined, so that even if the work stretches them to the limits of endurance they know what they must do and how they must assist each other. Indeed, underneath its drama and emotion the ER is a marvel of human social organization, without which it could not be effective.

FIGURE 4.7　Principal Destinations of the Eight Largest Immigrant Groups in a Typical Year

Chinese 25,841
San Francisco (15%)　New York (27%)　Los Angeles (11%)

Cubans 28,916
New York (6%)　Tampa–St. Petersburg (3%)　Miami (77%)

Dominicans 24,858
New York (60%)　Bergen-Passaic (4%)

Filipinos 50,060
San Francisco (7%)　Los Angeles (16%)　San Diego (7%)

Indians 27,803
Chicago (8%)　New York (10%)　Los Angeles (4%)

Koreans 35,849
New York (8%)　Washington (4%)　Los Angeles (16%)

Mexicans 72,351
Los Angeles (21%)　San Diego (6%)　El Paso (6%)

Vietnamese 24,231
San Jose (7%)　Los Angeles (9%)　Anaheim (9%)

Source: Adapted from Portes & Rumbaut, 1990.

Note: Chinese include immigrants from mainland China only.

single year, 1987, but if one multiplies by 10 each of the numbers given, the result is a rough estimate of the number of people from the major recent immigrant groups who came to these cities during the decade. In fact, as Portes and his coauthor Rubén Rumbaut observe, people from more than 100 different nations arrived in the United States during this period—although the largest groups are those shown in the figure, and the preferred places for first settlement by these immigrants are the cities shown. Figure 4.7 shows the principal destinations of the eight largest immigrant groups.

Research by Portes and his colleagues shows that in Miami and other major U.S. cities the new immigrants are revitalizing old urban neighborhoods. Although concern over their growing numbers and economic influence has caused anti-immigration sentiment and demands for lower

immigration quotas, sociological research shows that once they achieve legal status and stable living conditions, the vast majority of immigrants become highly productive citizens.

Throughout the world, between the beginning of World War I in 1914 and the end of the 1970s, an estimated 120 million people were forced to move from one nation to another because of either political violence or severe economic disruption (Beijer, 1969; Zolberg, 1981). Being uprooted in this way means leaving behind old statuses and roles, giving up a way of life, and attempting to re-create these statuses and roles in a new society. It is little wonder, then, that patterns of migration and immigration, and their social consequences, have figured so centrally in the history of sociology.

SUMMARY

THINK ABOUT IT CRITICALLY
We often yearn for the "simpler" life of the village or the small town, where life seems less hectic and stressful. What is it about the contemporary world that makes our lives so often feel too busy and conflicted? And what would it actually be like for those of us who grew up in a metropolitan area of a modern society to make the transition to life in a small-scale society?

A *society* is a population of people or other social animals that is organized in a cooperative manner to carry out the major functions of life. *Social structure* refers to the recurring patterns of behavior that create relationships among individuals and groups within a society. The building blocks of human societies are *groups*—collections of people who interact on the basis of shared expectations regarding one another's behavior. In every group there are socially defined positions known as *statuses.* The way a society defines how an individual is to behave in a particular status is called a *role.*

A social *institution* is a more or less stable structure of statuses and roles devoted to meeting the basic needs of people in a society. Within any given institution there are norms that specify how people in various statuses are to perform their roles. New institutions continually emerge through the process of *differentiation.*

The growth of the world's population is directly related to the evolution of human social structures, which in turn is related to changes in production technologies. The first million years of human social evolution were characterized by a hunting-and-gathering way of life. During that time the family and other kinship structures evolved, and the band became the basic territorial unit of human society. The shift to agriculture is commonly linked with the invention of the plow, but for centuries human societies had been acquiring food through the domestication of plants and animals. Some became *pastoral societies* based on the herding of animals, while others evolved into *horticultural societies* based on the raising of seed crops. However, the first large-scale agrarian societies evolved after the development of plow-and-harvest agriculture.

Agrarian societies allow people to escape from dependence on food sources over which they have no control. In such societies, people produce surpluses that can be used to feed new classes of non-food-producers such as warriors. At the same time, these societies require increasing amounts of land, and this may lead to conflicts over territory. The need to store and defend food supplies and to house non-food-producers results in the growth of villages and small cities.

The next major change in human production technologies was the industrial revolution, the shift from agriculture to trade and industry. This began in England around 1650 and spread to the United States and other nations in the next two centuries. Its impetus came not only from technological advances but also from the rise of a new social order: *capitalism.*

The shift to industrial production affects social structure in several major ways. As a consequence of the industrialization of agriculture, relatively few people live on the land, whereas increasing numbers live in cities and suburbs. Greater openness to change results in the emergence of new classes and social movements. Scientific and technical advances produce tremendous wealth, and the world "shrinks" as a result of innovations in transportation and communication.

For the individual member of a human society, adaptation to a more modern society involves a shift from *gemeinschaft* (close, personal relationships) to *gesellschaft* (well-organized but impersonal relationships). *Primary groups* like the family are supplemented, if not replaced, by *secondary groups* (organizations or associations) whose members do not have strong feelings for one another. Roles in secondary groups often conflict with roles in primary groups, a situation known as *role conflict. Role strain* occurs when a person experiences conflicting demands within a single role.

Another difference between simpler and more advanced societies is that in the former almost all statuses are *ascribed* (determined by birth or tradition), whereas in the latter there is a tendency to replace ascribed statuses with ones that are *achieved* (determined by a person's own efforts). Sometimes a particular status takes precedence over all of an individual's other statuses; such a status is referred to as a *master status.*

When they think of a society, most people in the world today think in terms of the nation-state, or nation, of which they are members. (A *state* is a society's set of political structures, and a *nation-state* is the territory within which those structures operate.) But although the members of a society often think of themselves as members of a particular nation, this is not always so, and in extreme cases the lack of a clear match between society and nation can result in a civil war.

CRITICAL RESPONSE
Much of the stress of daily life is a result of role conflict and role strain. We play so many different roles that we may feel torn by conflicting demands and by the pressures of belonging to so many different groups. No doubt life in a village or town would be easier in some ways because we would belong to a smaller network of groups and would feel

less pressure to play different roles. On the other hand, used to a wider array of social groups, we might feel constrained and limited. We might begin to resent the extent to which everything about our lives was known to other people in the village, especially other members of the few groups to which we belonged. Indeed, it is often very difficult for someone who is used to life in a complex metropolitan society to get used to a smaller social world.

GLOSSARY

society: a population that is organized in a cooperative manner to carry out the major functions of life. (p. 90)

social structure: the recurring patterns of behavior that create relationships among individuals and groups within a society. (p. 90)

group: any collection of people who interact with one another on the basis of shared expectations regarding one another's behavior. (p. 91)

status: a socially defined position in a group. (p. 91)

role: the way a society defines how an individual is to behave in a particular status. (p. 93)

role expectations: a society's expectations about how a role should be performed, together with the individual's perceptions of what is required in performing that role. (p. 93)

institution: a more or less stable structure of statuses and roles devoted to meeting the basic needs of people in a society. (p. 94)

differentiation: the processes whereby sets of social activities performed by one social institution are divided among different institutions. (p. 95)

pastoral society: a society whose primary means of subsistence is herding animals and moving with them over a wide expanse of grazing land. (p. 99)

horticultural society: a society whose primary means of subsistence is raising crops, which it plants and cultivates, often developing an extensive system for watering the crops. (p. 99)

social stratification: the process whereby the members of a society are sorted into different statuses. (p. 101)

open society: a society in which social mobility is possible for everyone. (p. 101)

closed society: a society in which social mobility does not exist. (p. 101)

capitalism: a system for organizing the production of goods and services that is based on markets, private property, and the business firm or company. (p. 101)

gemeinschaft: a term used to refer to the close, personal relationships of small groups and communities. (p. 104)

gesellschaft: a term used to refer to the well-organized but impersonal relationships among the members of modern societies. (p. 104)

primary group: a small group characterized by intimate, face-to-face associations. (p. 105)

secondary group: a social group whose members have a shared goal or purpose but are not bound together by strong emotional ties. (p. 105)

role conflict: conflict that occurs when in order to perform one role well a person must violate the expectations associated with another role. (p. 105)

role strain: conflict that occurs when the expectations associated with a single role are contradictory. (p. 105)

ascribed status: a position or rank that is assigned to an individual at birth and cannot be changed. (p. 105)

achieved status: a position or rank that is earned through the efforts of the individual. (p. 106)

master status: a status that takes precedence over all of an individual's other statuses. (p. 107)

state: a society's set of political structures. (p. 109)

nation-state: the largest territory within which a society's political institutions can operate without having to face challenges to their sovereignty. (p. 109)

WHERE TO FIND IT

BOOKS

The Consequences of Modernity (Anthony Giddens; Stanford University Press, 1990). A thorough treatment of the elusive but centrally important concept of social structure.

Ecoscience: Populations, Resources, Environment (Paul R. Ehrlich, Anne H. Ehrlich, & John P. Holdren; Freeman, 1977). An authoritative text in human ecology with excellent background on population, societies, and the natural environment.

The Rise of the West (William K. McNeill; University of Chicago Press, 1970). Not as slanted toward Western civilizations as its title may suggest, this masterful history of the world's major civilizations is a valuable source of material on the social structures and ideas that shaped the modern world.

The Great Transformation: The Political and Economic Origins of Our Time (Karl Polanyi; Beacon, 1944). Essential reading on the sociological implications of the shift to a market economy during the eighteenth and nineteenth centuries.

An Embarrassment of Riches (Simon Schama; University of California Press, 1988). A brilliant cultural history of Dutch civilization with many implications for present-day sociology. Schama deals with the problem of how a society that achieved wealth rather early in its history also sought to share that wealth and to prevent its people from becoming profligate.

The Division of Labor in Society (Émile Durkheim; Free Press, 1964). Durkheim's classic treatment of the impact of the rise of industrial urban societies. The famous preface to the second edition presents a succinct statement of how social change forever alters older forms of community.

OTHER SOURCES

Historical Statistics of the U.S. from Colonial Times to 1970 (U.S. Bureau of the Census). An invaluable source of tables and charts showing changes in population, national origins, work, place of residence, and many other vital indicators of social change in the United States.

Statistical Yearbook (United Nations Educational, Scientific, and Cultural Organization [UNESCO]). Published annually, this is one of the best sources of comparative information about the world's nations and the trends occurring in them.

PART 2

Social Dynamics

From a helpless, entirely self-centered being, the human infant develops into a person capable of performing roles in a wide variety of social groups. Those groups, in turn, often develop and change—a small business founded by a few close friends, for example, may expand into a complex corporation with a structure far different from that of the original group. Likewise, the structure of an entire society may change as people find new ways of making a living and new ways of organizing to protect their interests. In response to such changes, some people may turn to crime or other socially disvalued behaviors, and others may form protest movements that seek to change the social order.

In Part 2 of this book we cover many of the processes that seem to account for social stability and change. In Chapter 5 we discuss socialization, the process by which individuals become fully participating members of their society. One major outcome of socialization is the ability to function in groups, the subject of Chapter 6. Chapter 7 discusses how and why people deviate from the norms of their culture, and Chapter 8 looks at collective behavior and social movements, phenomena that involve large numbers of people in a society and often bring about major social change. Chapter 9 examines the changes in the nature of human settlements that have accompanied the growth of the world's population. Finally, Chapter 10 summarizes the ways in which sociologists think about and conduct research on the changes that affect the daily lives of people in societies throughout the world.

CHAPTER 5

Socialization

"All this stuff about abstinence and virginity is getting me down," 16-year-old Carla sighed as she and her mother loaded the dishwasher. "Jack [her 18-year-old brother] can go out and fool around with different girls—but me, I'm supposed to act like a goody-two-shoes. It stinks. What happened to the sexual revolution anyway?"

Carla's mom listened patiently but without much agreement. Carla's complaint took her back to her own years in high school and college. When she was in school things were even worse. If a girl got even a hint of a reputation for being willing to have a sexual relationship, she could be labeled as "fast" or "loose." If the boys who had sex with her began to talk, she could be classified as one of the "town whores," while the boys would be viewed as simply acting out their "nature" as males. If she became pregnant, she would have little hope of ever attaining dignity in the community. And there was so much secrecy and anguish about sex. She had wanted things to be easier for her kids. Now, with the fear of AIDS and all the talk about "family values" and morality, the old double standard in sexual relations seemed to have come back into style.

In church, in school, and at home, Carla's brother Jack was constantly hearing about teenage celibacy. But he and his friends paid little attention. They wanted to go out and have fun with any girls who might be willing, and there still seemed to be plenty of them around. And Jack's father really seemed kind of proud to hear gossip about Jack's exploits. Of course, he often reminded Jack of the need for contraceptives, but why was it OK for Jack to be having sex and not for Carla?

"Things are changing so fast," mused Carla's mom. "It makes you wonder how our kids will know how to prepare their own children for the society they will be living in. Then again, if the old-fashioned double standard is coming back, maybe the changes aren't as drastic as they seem." Her grandparents, with their traditional ways, might be shocked by the rapidity of the changes taking place in the world around them.

BECOMING A SOCIAL BEING

The scene just described is representative of millions that occur each day throughout the world: children dealing with their parents' interpretations of norms, learning the rules of behavior in their cultures, rehearsing the roles they hope to attain in their societies, and at times questioning their parents' norms and values. This process, in which the culture of a society is passed on from one generation to the next, is the subject of this chapter.

Socialization is the term sociologists use to describe the ways in which people learn to conform to their society's norms, values, and roles. People develop their own unique personalities as a result of the learning they gain from parents, siblings, relatives, peers, teachers, mentors, and all the other people who influence them throughout their lives (Elkin & Handel, 1989). From the viewpoint of society as a whole, however, what is important about the process of socialization is that people learn to behave according to the norms of their culture. How people learn to behave according to cultural norms—that is, the way they learn their culture—makes possible the transmission of culture from one

generation to the next. In this way the culture is "reproduced" in the next generation (Danziger, 1971; Parsons & Bales, 1955).

Socialization occurs throughout life as the individual learns new norms in new groups and situations. However, for purposes of analysis socialization can be divided into three major phases. The first is *primary socialization*. It refers to all the ways in which the newborn individual is molded into a social being—that is, into a growing person who can interact with others according to the expectations of society. Primary socialization occurs within the family and other intimate groups in the child's social environment. *Secondary socialization* occurs in later childhood and adolescence, when the child enters school and comes under the influence of adults and peers outside the household and immediate family. *Adult socialization* is a third stage, when the person learns the norms associated with new statuses such as wife, husband, journalist, programmer, grandparent, or nursing home patient (Danziger, 1971).

There are a number of unresolved and highly controversial issues in the study of socialization, and we will explore several of them in this chapter.

Nature and nurture. What is the relative strength of biological (i.e., genetic) versus social influences on the individual? This issue, often referred to as the nature-nurture problem, is raised most strikingly in Carla's complaints about the double standard, which is based on the idea that men are by nature sexual predators whereas women need to deny their sexuality in order to protect their social standing. The nature-nurture issue suggests that biological influences can play an extremely important part in forming each individual's personality.

The social construction of the self. A second controversy in the study of socialization is the question of how a person's sense of self becomes established. We all learn to play many different roles—but how do the influences of others in our social world affect our role playing, and how do those experiences help form our sense of ourselves? How do people learn to conform to society's norms and to take the roles that society makes available to them?

Influences on socialization. How do different social environments, such as the affluent suburban school or the slum neighborhood or the military boot camp, influence socialization? In other words, how do different social environments produce different kinds of people? What are the influences throughout life of different agencies of socialization and different experiences with other people?

This baby is having a wonderful time being "socialized" by his siblings—but just wait until a parent comes into the room.

Gender socialization and sexual identity. Gender socialization refers to the ways in which we become the girls and boys and, gradually, the men and women of our society and culture. All the controversies over whether behavior is innate or learned are intensified when we consider the differences and similarities in the socialization of males and females. This is especially true in reference to the ways in which we are socialized to acquire a sexual identity.

In this chapter we explore each of these questions in detail. We will be concerned primarily with the socialization of "normal" members of society—people who are able to perform roles, to feel empathy for others, to express emotions and yet control feelings that are antisocial, to nurture others and raise children who will also be able to nurture, and to take on new roles as they grow older. But the failures of socialization can also tell us a great deal about what is involved in creating the social being. For instance, consider the case of Charles Manson, who was convicted for his part in the 1969 Tate–La Bianca murders. Not long before the murders, Manson had been released after serving a 10-year prison term. In fact, Manson, who was born in a state penitentiary, spent 17 of his first 35 years in more than a dozen penal institutions. His history is one of complete neglect. He was beaten with a heavy paddle, and he beat others. He was sodomized, and he sodomized others at knifepoint. In fact, he was so undersocialized for life outside prison that before his last release he pleaded to be allowed to stay there.

The issue in cases like Manson's is not whether we should excuse what such individuals have done but whether we can learn from their tragedies so as to prevent others. And scientists, biological and social, still have a good deal to learn. Socialization is an extremely complex process for each individual. Some people who were abused and neglected can nonetheless become good parents, despite the odds. Others who seem to have experienced all the right influences can end up doing evil things, again despite the odds (Wrong, 1961). Even if we could trace all the social influences on a person's development, there would remain many unanswered questions about the combined influences of the person's genetic potential and his or her social experiences—that is, the relative importance of nature and nurture.

NATURE AND NURTURE

Throughout recorded history there have been intense debates over what aspects of behavior are "human nature" and what aspects can be intentionally shaped through nurture or socialization. During all the centuries of prescientific thought, the human body was thought to be influenced by the planets, the moon, and the sun, or by various forces originating within the body, especially in the brain, heart, and liver. In the ancient world and continuing into the Mid-

dle Ages, blood, bile, phlegm, and other bodily fluids were thought to control people's moods and affect their personalities. Human behavior and health could also be affected by evil spirits or witches. While they are no longer dominant explanations of human behavior, none of these ideas has ever entirely disappeared.

In the eighteenth century a new and quite radical idea of the "natural man" emerged. The idea that humans inherently possess qualities such as wisdom and rationality, which are damaged in the process of socialization, took hold in the imaginations of many educated people. Social philosophers like Jean-Jacques Rousseau believed that if only human society could be improved, people raised in it would emerge with fewer emotional scars and limitations of spirit. This belief was based on the enthusiasm created by scientific discoveries, which would free humans from ignorance and superstition, and new forms of social organization like democracy and capitalism, which would unleash new social forces that would produce wealth and destroy obsolete social forms like aristocracy.

In the United States, Thomas Jefferson applied these ideas in developing the educational and governmental institutions of the new nation. Much later, in the nineteenth century, Karl Marx and other social theorists applied the same basic idea of human perfectibility in their criticisms of capitalism. A revolutionary new society, they predicted, would overturn the worst effects of capitalism and finally realize Rousseau's promise that a superior society could produce superior people. As these examples indicate, many of the most renowned thinkers of the last two centuries have rejected the belief that nature places strict limits on what humans can achieve.

THE FREUDIAN REVOLUTION

Sigmund Freud was the first social scientist to develop a theory that addressed both the "nature" and "nurture" aspects of human existence (Nagel, 1994; Robinson, 1994). For Freud, the social self develops primarily in the family, wherein the infant is gradually forced to control its biological functions and needs: sucking, eating, defecation, genital stimulation, warmth, sleep, and so on. Freud shocked the straitlaced intellectuals of his day by arguing that infants have sexual urges and by showing that these aspects of the self are the primary targets of early socialization— that the infant is taught in many ways to delay physical gratification and to channel its biological urges into socially accepted forms of behavior.

Freud's model of the personality is derived from his view of the socialization process. Freud divided the personality into three functional areas, or interrelated parts, that permit the self to function well in society.[1] The part from

---

[1]Freud never expected that actual physical parts of the brain that correspond to the id, ego, and superego would be discovered. Instead, he was referring to aspects of the functioning personality that are observed in the individual.

which the infant's unsocialized drives arise is termed the **id.** The moral codes of adults, especially parents, become incorporated into the part of the personality that Freud called the **superego.** Freud thought of this part of the personality as consisting of all the internalized norms, values, and feelings that are taught in the socialization process.

In addition to the id and the superego, the personality as Freud described it has a third vital element, the **ego.** The ego is our conception of ourself in relation to others, in contrast with the id, which represents self-centeredness in its purest form. To have a "strong ego" is to be self-confident in dealing with others and to be able to accept criticism. To have a "weak ego" is to need continual approval from others. The popular expression that someone "has a big ego" and demands constant attention actually signals a lack of ego strength in the Freudian sense.

In the growth of the personality, according to Freud, the formation of the ego or social self is critical, but it does not occur without a great deal of conflict. The conflict between the infant's basic biological urges and society's need for a socialized person becomes evident very early. Freud believed that the individual's major personality traits (security or insecurity, fears and longings, ways of interacting with others) are formed in the conflict that occurs as the parents insist that the infant control its biological urges. This conflict, Freud believed, is most severe between the child and the same-sex parent. The infant wishes to receive pleasure, especially sexual stimulation, from the opposite-sex parent and therefore is competing with the same-sex parent. To become more attractive to the opposite-sex parent, the infant attempts to imitate the same-sex parent. Thus for Freud the same-sex parent is the most powerful socializing influence on the growing child, for reasons related to the biological differences and attractions between the child and the opposite-sex parent.

Contemporary sociologists who are influenced by Freud's biologically and socially based theories have used his concepts of same-sex attraction and modeling of the same-sex parent's behavior to explain differences between men and women. Alice Rossi (1977), for instance, argues that women's shared experience of menstruation and childbearing creates a strong bond between mothers and daughters. Nancy Chodorow (1978) claims that women's earliest experiences with their mothers tend to convince them that a woman is fulfilled by becoming a mother in her turn; thus women are socialized from a very early age to "reproduce motherhood." Research on socialization has shown that men also are strongly influenced by the same-sex parent. Fathers often serve as models of behavior whom boys will emulate throughout their lives.

Freud's theory includes the idea that the conflicts of childhood reappear throughout life in ways that the individual cannot predict. The demands of the superego ("conscience") and the "childish" desires of the id are always threatening to disrupt the functioning of the ego, especially

in families in which normal levels of conflict are either exaggerated or suppressed. Note, however, that Freud focused on the traditional family, consisting of mother, father, and children. The more families depart from this conventional form, the more we need to question the adequacy of Freudian socialization theory.

BEHAVIORISM

In the early decades of this century Freud's theory was challenged by another branch of social-scientific thought, known as **behaviorism.** In contrast to Freud and others who saw many human qualities as innate or biologically determined (nature), behaviorists saw the individual as a *tabula rasa,* or blank slate, that could be written upon through socialization. In other words, individual behavior could be determined entirely through social processes (nurture). Behaviorism asserts that individual behavior is not determined by instincts or any other "hardware" in the individual's brain or glands. Rather, all behavior is learned.

Behaviorism traces its origins to the work of the Russian psychologist Ivan Pavlov (1927). Pavlov's experiments with dogs and humans revealed that behavior that had been thought to be entirely instinctual could in fact be shaped or **conditioned** by learning situations. Pavlov's dog, one of the most famous subjects in the history of psychology, was conditioned to salivate at the sound of a bell. The dog would normally salivate whenever food was presented to him. In his experiment, Pavlov rang a bell whenever the dog was fed. Soon the dog would salivate at the sound of the bell alone, thereby showing that salivation, which had always seemed to be a purely biological reflex, could be a conditioned, or learned, response as well.

The American psychologist John B. Watson carried on Pavlov's work with an equally famous series of experiments on "Little Albert," an 11-month-old boy. Watson conditioned Albert to fear baby toys that were thought to be inherently cute and cuddly, such as stuffed white rabbits. By presenting these objects to Albert at the same time that he frightened him with a loud noise (i.e., presented a negative stimulus), Watson showed that the baby could be conditioned to fear any fuzzy white object, including Santa Claus's beard. He also showed that through the systematic presentation of white objects accompanied by positive stimuli he could extinguish Albert's fear and cause him to like white objects again.

On the basis of his findings, Watson wrote,

"Give me a dozen healthy infants, well-formed, and my own specified world to bring them up in and I'll guarantee to take any one at random and train him to become any type of specialist I might select—doctor, lawyer, artist, merchant-chief and, yes, even beggar-man and thief, regardless of his talents, penchants, tendencies, abilities, vocations, and race of his ancestors." (1930, p. 104)

For the behaviorist, in other words, nature is irrelevant and nurture all-important.

Behaviorists who followed Watson—the most famous being B. F. Skinner—developed even more effective ways of shaping individual behavior. Skinner and his followers reasoned that in order to avoid failures in socialization it is necessary to completely control all the learning that goes on in the child's social environment (Skinner, 1976). Sociologists are critical of the notion that it is possible to control the world of the developing person. They argue that while the behaviorists may show us how some types of social learning take place, psychological research often does not deal with real social environments. It has very little to say about what is actually learned in different social contexts, how it is learned (or not learned), and the influences of different social situations on the individual throughout life (Elkin & Handel, 1989). One type of situation that has been of interest to sociologists studying socialization processes is that of the child reared in extreme isolation.

ISOLATED CHILDREN

The idea that children might be raised apart from society, or that they could be reared by wolves or chimpanzees or some other social animal, has fascinated people since ancient times. Romulus and Remus, the legendary founders of Rome, were said to have been raised by a wolf. The story of Tarzan, a boy of noble birth who was abandoned in Africa and raised by apes, became a worldwide best-seller early in this century and has intrigued readers and movie audiences ever since. However, modern studies of children who have experienced extreme isolation cast doubt on the possibility that a truly unsocialized person can exist.

The discovery of a **feral** ("untamed") **child** always seems to promise new insights into the relationship between biological capabilities and socialization, or nature and nurture (Davis, 1947). Each case of a child raised in extreme isolation is looked upon as a natural experiment that might reveal the effects of lack of socialization on child development. Once the child has been brought under proper care, studies are undertaken to determine how well he or she functions. Invariably those studies show that victims of severe isolation are able to learn, but that they do so far more slowly than children who have not been isolated (Malson, 1972).

In the late 1930s a noted sociologist, Kingsley Davis, was called to investigate the case of Anna, an 8-year-old girl who had been born out of wedlock to an impoverished and mentally impaired mother. For years Anna's mother had kept her locked up in an attic room to avoid her own father's anger. Aside from brief visits to deliver her food, Anna had almost no human contact. When Davis examined her she was unable to speak or walk, yet in her smile and obvious pleasure at human contact she seemed to show the potential to learn language and become socialized in other ways.

a

b

c

d

e

f

Few human behaviors seem more "natural" than the expression of emotion. People everywhere smile, laugh, cry, grit their teeth, wrinkle their noses in distaste—the gestures may differ from one culture to another, but the similarities are far more striking than the differences. Shown here are examples of the "eyebrow flash": (a) French woman, (b) Yanomami man, (c) Yanomami young woman, (d) !Kung woman (central Kalahari), (e) Huli man (Papua-New Guinea), (f) Balinese man.

Anna did respond to Davis and others who tried to toilet train her and teach her to speak. But her progress was slow, and unfortunately she died at the age of 10 from a disease that may have been caused by her previous isolation. The researchers were unable to determine whether her learning deficiencies were due to innate mental retardation or whether her retardation was a result of her cruel isolation in infancy.

A more recent case of social isolation in childhood is that of Genie, a girl born to a psychotic father and a blind and highly dependent mother. For the first 11 years of her life Genie was strapped to a potty chair in an isolated room of the couple's suburban Los Angeles home. From birth she had almost no contact with other people. She was not toilet-trained, and food was pushed toward her through a slit in the door of her room. When she was discovered by child welfare authorities after the mother told neighbors about the child's existence, the father committed suicide. Genie was placed in the custody of a team of medical personnel and child development researchers.

In the first few weeks after she was discovered, everyone who observed Genie was shocked. At first glance she

Genie drew this picture in 1977. At first she drew the picture of her mother and labeled it "I miss Mama." Then she drew more. The moment she finished, she took the researcher's hand and placed it next to what she had just drawn. She motioned for the researcher to write and said, "Baby Genie." Then she pointed under her drawing and said, "Mama hand." The researcher wrote the corresponding letters. Satisfied, Genie sat back and stared at the picture. There she was, a baby in her mother's arms.

looked like a normal child, with dark hair and pink cheeks and a placid demeanor. Very quickly, however, it became clear that she was severely impaired. She walked awkwardly and was unable to dress herself. She had virtually no language ability—at most, she knew a few words, which she pronounced in an incomprehensible babble. She spit continuously and masturbated with no sense of social propriety. In short, she was a clear case of a child who had been deprived of social learning and in consequence was severely retarded in her individual and social development. She was alive, but she was not a social being in any real sense of the term. She had not developed a sense of self, nor had she the basic ability to communicate that comes with language learning.

For years researcher Susan Curtiss (1977) studied Genie's slow progress toward language learning. Curtiss showed that Genie could learn many more words than a retarded person would be expected to learn, but that she had great difficulty with the more complex rules of grammar that come naturally to a child who learns language in a social world. Genie's language remained in the shortened form characteristic of people who learn a language late in life. Most significant, Genie never mastered the language of social interaction. She had great difficulty with words such as *hello* and *thank you,* although she could make her wants and feelings known with nonverbal cues.

Extensive tests showed that in many ways Genie was highly intelligent. But her language abilities never advanced beyond those of a third-grader. Genie gradually learned to adhere to social norms (e.g., she stopped spitting), but she never became a truly social being. Eventually the scientists who worked with her came to the conclusion that the most severe deprivation, the one that was the primary cause of her inability to become fully social and to master language, was her lack of emotional learning and especially her feelings of loss and lack of love. Genie herself expressed her inner longings in the picture shown here, which she drew at the age of about 16 (Rymer, 1992a, b).

THE NEED FOR LOVE

All studies of isolated children point to the undeniable need for nurturance in early childhood. They all show that extreme isolation is associated with profound retardation in the acquisition of language and social skills. However, they cannot establish causality, since it is always possible that the child may have been retarded at birth. Despite their lack of firm conclusions, studies of children reared in extreme isolation have pointed researchers in an important direction: They suggest that lack of parental attention can result in retardation and early death. This conclusion receives further support from studies of children reared in orphanages and other residential care facilities, which have shown that such children are more likely to develop emotional problems and to be retarded in their language development than comparable children reared by their parents (Goldfarb, 1945; Rutter, 1974; Spitz, 1945).

THEN AND NOW

THE INDOMITABLE HUMAN SPIRIT

Blind and deaf as a result of a serious illness when she was only 19 months old, Helen Keller appeared incapable of learning. In the late nineteenth and early twentieth centuries people like Helen were relegated to back wards of custodial care institutions or to back bedrooms in affluent homes. However, through the patient instruction of a gifted teacher, Helen learned to understand the connection between objects and the words for them. Suddenly this profoundly handicapped girl had a future in the social world. Helen Keller became a world-famous symbol of the unconquerable human spirit, blazing a trail that other people with disabilities and special needs have followed ever since.

In the early 1980s Terry Fox, a young runner who had lost a leg to cancer, became another hero of the human spirit by courageously attempting to run across his native Canada. Although he died before completing his grueling marathon run, he succeeded in covering half the distance. In a more recent example of the triumph of will over biological destiny, 19-year-old Craig Ludin is shown at his high school graduation. Craig was the first student with Down syndrome to graduate from a regular high school in his school district.

In a series of studies that have become classics in the field of socialization and child development, the primate psychologist Harry Harlow showed that infant monkeys reared apart from other monkeys never learned how to interact with other monkeys (Harlow & Harlow, 1962); that is, they could not refrain from aggressive behavior when they were brought into group situations. When females who had been reared apart from their mothers became mothers themselves, they tended to act in what Harlow could only describe as a "ghastly fashion" toward their young. In some cases they even crushed their babies' heads in their teeth before handlers could intervene. Although it is risky to generalize from primate behavior to that of humans, these studies of the effects of lack of nurturance bear a striking resemblance to studies of child abuse in humans. This research generally shows that one of the best predictors of abuse is whether the parent was also abused as a child (Kempe & Helfer, 1980; Kempe & Kempe, 1978; Keniston, 1977; Polansky et al., 1981).

These findings confirm our intuitive knowledge that nurturance and parental love play a profound, though still incompletely understood, role in the development of the individual as a social being. These and related findings offer support for social policies that seek to enrich the socialization process with nurturance from other caring adults—for example, in early-education programs. Yet many researchers and policy makers remain convinced that biological traits place limits on what individuals can achieve, regardless of the kind of nurturance they receive. In recent years proponents of this view have focused on the controversial question of how intelligence affects achievement (see Box 5.1).

A SOCIOLOGICAL SUMMARY

Neither extreme of the nature-nurture debate presents a complete picture of socialization. Nature may endow individuals with greater or lesser innate abilities, yet despite those differences most people learn to function as social beings. And while humans have an infinite capacity to learn behaviors of all kinds, through socialization they learn the particular behaviors required to function within their own culture and society. Nevertheless, the nature-nurture debate will endure and will continue to stimulate new research on the biological and psychological bases of behavior. In the meantime, most sociological research will focus on the following hypotheses:

1. *The social environment can unleash or stifle human potential.* Genetic and other biological traits establish broad boundaries for individual achievement, but the environment in which a person is raised can cause his or her potential to be realized more or less fully within those boundaries. (This insight is found in numerous folktales and jokes. "Who was the greatest artist who ever lived?" a newly defunct art critic asked Saint Peter on his way into heaven. "Why, it was Lucius Cadmore," answered Saint

Peter without a moment's hesitation. "But I never heard of him," said the sorely perplexed critic. "That's because he never had a chance to paint anything," Saint Peter explained.)

2. *The social environment presents an ever-changing array of roles and expectations.* Through socialization people learn to perform roles as members of a particular culture and society. As the society and its culture change, so do definitions of what makes a person well socialized. These changing definitions create endless possibilities for misunderstandings and conflict within the groups and institutions in which socialization takes place.

THE SOCIAL CONSTRUCTION OF THE SELF

The *self* is the outcome of socialization; it may be defined as "the capacity to represent to oneself what one wishes to communicate to others" (Elkin & Handel, 1989, p. 47). Genie, an isolated, unsocialized child, did not develop a self in early childhood. She did not learn to formulate in her own mind the words that would express her feelings to others. Through socialization, most children learn to convert cries of discomfort, hunger, or fear into socially understandable symbols like "Want bottle" or "Go out now." These utterances show that the young child has learned to recognize his or her inner states and communicate them to others. "The child who can do this is on his or her way to becoming human, that is, to being simultaneously self-regulating and socially responsive" (Elkin & Handel, 1989, p. 47).

In sociology the self is viewed as a social construct: It is produced or "constructed" through interaction with other people over a lifetime. Studies of how the self emerges therefore usually take an interactionist perspective.

INTERACTIONIST MODELS OF THE SELF

The American sociologist Charles Horton Cooley was a major contributor to the interactionist view of the development of the self. In *Human Nature and the Social Order* (1956/1902), he introduced the concept of the "looking glass self." The looking glass self is the reflection of our self that we think we see in the behaviors of others toward us. We continually pay attention to the behavioral cues of others; we wonder whether they think we look good, are expressing ourselves well, are working hard enough, and so on. As we mature, the overall pattern of these reflections of other people's opinions becomes a dominant aspect of our own identities—that is, of how we conceive of ourselves. Cooley believed that through these processes we actually *become* the kind of person we believe others think we are.

Language, Culture, and the Self. Cooley's insight into the role of others in defining the self was the foundation for the view of the self proposed by George Her-

BOX 5.1 USING THE SOCIOLOGICAL IMAGINATION

Is IQ Destiny?

In a recent study titled *The Bell Curve,* Richard Herrnstein and Charles Murray (1994) argue that inequality is increasing in the United States and other industrialized nations because of biological differences among various population groups in these societies. They claim that the growth in occupations requiring advanced education and technical skills is creating a demanding new economic environment in which many people are doomed to failure. They do not believe that efforts to address inequalities through preschool programs, improvements in public education, and the like will make a difference. The real obstacle, they argue, is intelligence, or rather the lack of it in vast numbers of people. Since by their reasoning intelligence is an innate trait that is distributed unequally among various subgroups of the population, social intervention cannot do much to equalize the economic effects of differences in intelligence.

Like many traits that vary from one person to another, such as height and weight, scores on intelligence tests are distributed in the shape of a "normal" or bell curve. Most people's IQ scores fall near the center of the distribution, while some are at either extreme. About these facts there is no argument. Murray and Herrnstein further assert, however, that scores on the bell curve of intelligence are creating what they call "cognitive classes"—that is, categories of people whom they label "very bright," "bright," "normal," "dull," and "very dull" (see chart). They note that 5 percent of the U.S. population falls within the left and right extremes of the curve, and another 20 percent are in Class II and Class IV. By this reasoning, approximately 50 million residents of the United States are classified in the lower cognitive classes.

Herrnstein and Murray also discuss the implications of the fact that the mean scores of some black and Hispanic population groups fall below those of whites and Asians. The authors attribute these differences to genetic factors rather than to the long-term effects of economic and social deprivation. We will return to some of the controversies and misunderstandings created by this research in Chapter 13. Here it will suffice to note that Herrnstein and Murray demonstrate a correlation between what they term *cognitive classes* (based on IQ scores) and poverty due to inability to succeed in a demanding economic environment (see table).

Most social scientists who have commented on Herrnstein and Murray's research are strongly opposed to the conclusions they reach, for several reasons. First, there has been much criticism of IQ as a single measure of intelligence. Many experts believe that intelligence is far too complex to be represented by a single measure like IQ (Gardner, 1983). Second, there is evidence of cultural and middle-class biases in the questions used to test IQ; examination of the test items reveals that they would be far

Defining the Cognitive Classes

Source: Herrnstein & Murray, 1994.

Caution: The labels imposed on this IQ curve and the scores used as boundaries between "cognitive classes" are those of Herrnstein and Murray and do not represent the thinking of many other social scientists.

more familiar to middle-class test takers than to those from a disadvantaged background. Third, the authors of *The Bell Curve* have been criticized for asserting that correlation is the same as causality. Just because IQ and poverty are correlated does not mean that IQ *causes* poverty. In Northern Ireland, for example, Catholic Irish individuals score lower on IQ tests than do Protestant Irish, but these differences in IQ are not found in the United States, where there are no differences in wealth or advantage between the two groups as there are in Northern Ireland. In other words, socialization in an impoverished environment could cause low IQ scores, rather than the other way around.

White Poverty by Cognitive Class

COGNITIVE CLASS	PERCENTAGE IN POVERTY
I Very Bright	2
II Bright	3
III Normal	6
IV Dull	16
V Very Dull	30
Overall average	7

Source: Herrnstein & Murray, 1994.

bert Mead. With Cooley, Mead believed strongly that the self is a social product. We are not born with selves that are "brought out" by socialization. Instead, we acquire a self by

observing and assimilating the identities of others (Nisbet, 1970). The vehicle for this identification and assimilation is language. As Mead wrote, "There neither can be nor could have been any mind or thought without language; and the early stages of the development of language must have been prior to the development of mind or thought" (quoted in Truzzi, 1971, p. 272).

This view of the emergence of the self places culture at the center of the formation of the self. The kind of person we become is in large part a result of the cultural influences that surround us during socialization. Through interaction with people who are Catholic, for example, one takes on the language, the jokes, the style of a person of that religion. If the father is a firefighter and the mother a nurse, certain attitudes about service to society and about illness and danger will carry over to the child. If the same child plays on sports teams with children in the neighborhood, the norms and values of those children and their parents will become part of the child's experience and will be incorporated into his or her personality. Another child, growing up on a Sioux Indian reservation, would learn some of the same values—such as fair play, reward for achievement, and good citizenship—but would also learn the norms and values of the Sioux (e.g., reverence for one's ancestors and for the natural environment).

As each person learns the norms of his or her culture and its various ways of communicating—whether through language, dress, or gestures—and as each experiences the influences of a particular family and peer group, a unique self is formed. The self, thus, is a product of many influences and experiences; every person emerges with a personality of his or her own, and each has incorporated to varying degrees the values of the larger society and of a particular subculture.

Role Taking: The Significant Other and the Generalized Other. For Mead (1971/1934), two of the most important activities of childhood are play and games. In play, the child practices taking the roles of others. If you watch preadolescent children play, you will see them continually "trying on" roles: "You be the mommy and I'll be the teacher, and you'll come to school to find out why . . ." or "Pretend I'm Michael Jordan and you're Reggie Miller and the score is tied in the fourth quarter. . . ." They are reenacting the dramas of winning and losing, or calling into question the behaviors of the schoolroom, or trying to understand sickness and death.

This idea of **role taking** is central to the interactionist view of socialization. It refers to the way we try to look at social situations from the standpoint of another person from whom we seek a response. Mead believed that children develop this ability in three stages, during which they gain their sense of self and learn to act as persons in society. He labeled them the *preparatory, play,* and *game* stages. (See the study chart below.)

In the *preparatory stage* the child attempts to mimic the behavior of people who are significant in his or her life. **Significant others** are people who loom large in our lives, people who appear to be directly involved in winning and losing, achieving and failing. They tend to be people after whom we model our behavior—or whose behavior we seek to avoid. In the preparatory stage the child's significant others are those who respond to calls for help and shape social behavior like language.

In Mead's second stage, the *play stage,* children play at being others who are significant in their lives:

> They play at being the others who are significant to them. They want to push the broom, carry the umbrella, put on the hat, and do all the other things they see their parents do, including saying what their parents say. The story is told of the four-year-old playing "daddy" who put on his hat and his coat, said "good bye," and walked out the front door, only to return a few minutes later because he didn't know what to do next. He had taken as much of his father's work role as he could see and hear—the ritualized morning departure. (Elkin & Handel, 1989, p. 49)

STUDY CHART Stages in the Development of Role Taking

STAGE	DESCRIPTION	EXAMPLE
Preparatory	The child attempts to mimic the behavior of people who are significant in his or her life.	A toddler tries to walk in her mother's shoes.
Play	Children play at being people who are significant in their lives, such as parents.	Three children play house: "You be the mommy, I'll be the daddy, and Joey can be the baby."
Game	Each child is able to become, in a symbolic sense, all the other participants in the game.	A group of neighborhood kids gather at a playground to play baseball.

BOX 5.2   USING THE SOCIOLOGICAL IMAGINATION

Beehive Soccer

Thousands of parents and coaches of Little League teams will want to argue with the following sociological assertion:

> Eugene, Ore., July 23—Children under the ages of 8 or 10 should not participate in organized, competitive sports programs, according to a panel of sports medicine experts at the Olympic Scientific Congress here....
>
> In the discussion on children, Dr. Vern Seefeldt, a specialist in motor development at the Youth Sports Institute at Michigan State University, said, "Beginning competition before a child is competent in the skills necessary for the sport can be damaging."
>
> He said "the most obvious reason for children to play sports" was to improve motor skills. But he said inability to develop skills "that promote the success of the team" is the reason most often cited by children for dropping out of sports....
>
> A sociologist, Jay Coakley of the University of Colorado in Colorado Springs, said, "Kids under 10 are incapable of the concept of a team with differing responsibilities shifting to different players depending upon the location and movement of a ball."
>
> "Anyone who has watched a youth soccer game is familiar with what I call 'beehive soccer,'" he said. "Shortly after play starts, all of the players are concentrated around the ball, despite the cries of the adults on the sidelines to stay in position."
>
> He said it would be "better to accept some chaos than to try to impose adult concepts of team play on children."

How much "chaos" should adults accept? The sociology of Little League coaching remains a wide-open field, but it would seem that some youngsters are able to take the role of the generalized other earlier than other children and that some coaches are better able than their less stoic colleagues to accept normal chaos. As sociologists often say, more research is needed before we can be sure.

Source: New York Times, July 24, 1984, p. C2. Copyright © 1984 by The New York Times Company. Reprinted by permission.

As children grow in age and experience, they enter what Mead called the *game stage.* To take part in a game a child must have already learned to become, in a symbolic sense, all the other participants in the game. Mead called this the ability to "take the role of the generalized other." Thus, in a baseball game,

> [The child] must know what everyone else is going to do in order to carry out his own play. He has to take all of these roles. They do not have to be present in consciousness at the same time, but at some moments he has to have three or four individuals present in his own attitude, such as the one who is going to throw the ball, the one who is going to catch it, and so on. (Mead, 1934, p. 151)

When we are able to take the role of the generalized other, we know that rules apply to us no matter who we are. We know, for example, that rules about not smoking in the school building apply equally to students, parents, and teachers and that those who violate the rules will not be excused because of their status (Mead, 1934).

The **generalized other** is a composite of all the roles of all the participants in the game. A person who participates in a game like baseball, for example, has developed the capacity for role taking and now (again using Mead's phrase) "takes the role of the generalized other." When little children play team games, they often have a hard time taking specific roles, as can be seen in the example of "beehive soccer" presented in Box 5.2. As children mature, they become increasingly competent at games and team sports.

The generalized other represents the voice of society, which is internalized as "conscience." For some people, the generalized other demands perfection and strict adherence to every rule. For others, the generalized other may be extremely demanding where sports and other games are concerned but much more relaxed about achievement in school or adherence to the norms of property. For still others, the generalized other may insist on amassing large amounts of money as the primary indicator of success, or it may require community service and not value financial success at all. Within any given culture, such variations will be wide but will tend to follow certain easily recognized patterns.

ROLE PLAYING AND "FACE WORK"

Why do Americans and Asians often have so much difficulty understanding each other even when they are playing the same role (e.g., student) and speaking the same language? Why are adolescents so "hung up" about their dealings with other kids? And why is it that in some communities seemingly small insults are treated as major signs of disrespect? These are all examples of the kinds of problems that arise when people actually play the roles for which they have been socialized. They can be analyzed according to the rules of interaction known as *face work.*

As Erving Goffman (1965) defines it, *face* is the positive social value a person claims for herself or himself by acting out a specific set of socially approved attributes (politeness, humor, strength, cuteness, sensitivity, etc.). Through his close observations of seemingly routine greetings, formulas of politeness, and the give-and-take of small talk, Goffman identified the rules of interaction whereby people seek to present a positive image of themselves, their "face." Once they have established a specific image, they seek to defend it against any possible threat that might cause them to "lose face." The concept of saving or losing face is found in cultures throughout the world. Indeed, in most Asian cultures the rules of face work are even more elaborate than in the West. (The importance of such unwritten rules of interaction is explored more fully in Chapter 6.)

Most of us take it for granted that we want to maintain our self-respect and not lose face or be embarrassed in social situations. But we do not give much thought to the actual interactions that serve to maintain face.

> Just as the member of any group is expected to have self-respect, so also he is expected to sustain a standard of considerateness; he is expected to go to certain lengths to save the feelings and the face of others present, and he is expected to do this willingly and spontaneously because of emotional identification with the others and with their feelings. . . . The person who can witness another's humiliation and unfeelingly retain a cool countenance himself is said in our society to be "heartless," just as he who can unfeelingly participate in his own defacement is thought to be "shameless." (Goffman, 1965, p. 10)

The way we apply these rules of face work in performing our roles differs according to the prestige of the people involved. When firing a junior clerk, for example, the boss does not go to nearly the same lengths to take into account the employee's feelings as he does when firing a vice presi-

dent. Recent studies of role playing among adolescents in inner-city communities draw on these insights. Where there is very little prestige of any kind for people to share, "fronting," or pretending to play roles that one cannot really perform (e.g., great ball player, ladies' man) is extremely common. So, therefore, are potential threats to one's face. Face work in such communities—among gang members, for example—can become a deadly business, especially in situations where one senses disrespect (i.e., feels that one is being "dissed") (MacLeod, 1995; Williams & Kornblum, 1994). Emotions play a strong part in these interactions. When people believe that they have seriously lost face, their feelings can run extremely high, especially if their peers do not hurry in to defend them.

Rapid social change tends to heighten the difficulties people have in playing the roles they have been socialized to perform. As Goffman points out,

> A person's performance of face-work, extended by his tacit agreement to help others perform theirs, represents his willingness to abide by the ground rules of social interaction. Here is the hallmark of his socialization as an interactant. If he and the others were not socialized in this way, interaction in most societies and most situations would be a much more hazardous thing for feelings and faces. (1965, p. 31)

As populations become more diverse through the processes of social change (e.g., immigration and migration), the possibilities for cultural confusion over the rules of successful role playing in school or on the street can multiply dramatically.

This interactionist perspective on socialization emphasizes how people become social actors and how they intuitively adopt the rules and rituals of interaction, such as face work, that exist in their cultures. But it does not address how people acquire their notions of morality. We know that people generally learn their values and ideas of morality as young children in the family, but research on child development shows that the acquisition of morality is not a simple matter.

THEORIES OF MORAL DEVELOPMENT

Throughout life people face a variety of moral dilemmas, and these have a significant effect on their personalities. Social scientists have devoted considerable study to the processes through which people develop concepts of morality. Among the best-known students of moral development are the Swiss child psychologist Jean Piaget and the American social psychologists Lawrence Kohlberg and Carol Gilligan.

Piaget stands with Freud as one of the most important and original researchers and writers on child development. In the 1920s he became concerned with how children understand their environment, how they view their world, and how they develop their own personal philosophies. To discover the mental processes unique to children he used what was then an equally unique method: He spent long hours with a small number of children simply having conversations with them. These open-ended discussions were devoted to getting at how children actually think. In this way Piaget discovered evidence for the existence of ideas that are quite foreign to the adult mind (Elkind, 1970). For example, the child gives inanimate objects human motives and tends to see everything as existing for human purposes. In this phase of his research Piaget also described the egocentric aspect of the child's mental world, which is illustrated by the tendency to invent words and expect others to understand them.

In the later phases of his research and writing, Piaget devoted his efforts to questions about children's moral reasoning—the way children interpret the rules of games and judge the consequences of their actions. He observed that children form absolute notions of right and wrong very early in life, but that they often cannot understand the ambiguities of adult roles until they approach adolescence. This line of investigation was continued by the American social psychologist Lawrence Kohlberg, whose theory incorporates Piaget's views on the development of children's notions of morality.

Kohlberg's theory of moral development emphasizes the cognitive aspects of moral behavior. (By *cognitive* we mean aspects of behavior that one thinks about and makes conscious choices about, rather than those one engages in as a result of feelings or purely intuitive reactions.) In a study of 57 Chicago children that began in 1957 and continued until the children were young adults, Kohlberg presented the children with moral dilemmas like the following:

> A husband is told that his wife needs a special kind of medicine if she is to survive a severe form of cancer. The medication is extremely expensive, and the husband can raise only half the needed funds. When he begs the inventor of the drug for a reduced price, he is rebuffed because the inventor wants to make a lot of money on his invention. The husband then considers stealing the medicine, and the child is asked whether the man should steal in order to save his wife. (Kohlberg & Gilligan, 1971)

On the basis of children's answers to such dilemmas at different ages, Kohlberg proposed a theory of moral development consisting of three stages: (1) *preconventional,* in which the child acts out of the desire for reward and the fear of punishment; (2) *conventional,* in which the child's decisions are based on an understanding of right and wrong as embodied in social rules or laws; and (3) *postconventional,* in which the individual develops a sense of relativity and can distinguish between social laws and moral principles. Very often subjects in the preconventional and conventional stages will immediately assume that stealing is wrong in the situation Kohlberg has posed, but postconventional thinking in older children will cause them to debate the fairness of rules against stealing, in view of the larger moral dilemma involved.

It should be noted that Kohlberg's studies involved children from secure American families. In those studies the children were brought up in fairly similar circumstances, so the results could not reflect the impact of differences in such factors as poverty versus affluence or nurturance versus neglect. Sociologists recognize, however, that throughout the world children are socialized in extremely diverse social environments and that a full understanding of moral development or any other aspect of socialization may require research comparing children reared in many different environments.

SOCIAL ENVIRONMENTS AND EARLY SOCIALIZATION

None of the theories of development we have reviewed touches on the many social and natural environments in which human beings are socialized. Suppose, for example, that Carla, whom we met at the beginning of the chapter, was being raised in a group home for adolescents whose parents were in prison or had been killed. Would she have received the same messages about virginity from other women around her? In an environment in which adult attention and love were limited, she might well have learned to use sex as a way of obtaining material and emotional rewards. Although this example is hypothetical, such situations are not uncommon. The number of children in the United States who are living in group homes, with relatives, or in other "zero parent" settings increased from about 7 percent in 1970 to nearly 10 percent in 1990 (Gross, 1992). This means that we must think of socialization as occurring in many different settings, some of which are more desirable than others.

Children are born into relatively affluent homes in American suburbs, into the squalid slums of Calcutta, the icy wastes of Siberia, the extreme poverty of the Somalian desert, and myriad other environments—yet in every case those who survive infancy are socialized to live and perhaps flourish in these diverse settings (see Box 5.3). Cross-cultural studies attempt to show how socialization processes vary in different societies and how they are affected by demographic trends (trends in population size and composition) within societies. This comparative view of socialization attempts to bring together the often competing viewpoints of biological, psychological, and sociological explanations of developmental patterns.

Let us take teenage fertility as an example. Most social scientists believe that a child born to a teenage mother is likely to face more difficulties throughout life than a child born to a mother who has matured into a young adult. But before considering the social consequences of teenage parenthood we need some evidence about how the United

BOX 5.3 GLOBAL SOCIAL CHANGE

Growing Up on the Street: A Worldwide Trend

Throughout the urbanizing areas of the world there has been an alarming increase in the number of children living without adult supervision, usually in the slums and back alleys of major regional and national capitals. Social-scientific knowledge helps us understand the causes of this dangerous trend and documents the negative consequences of the socialization of homeless children on the streets. Although the chances of reversing this trend are not good, sociologists and other professionals with social-scientific training are addressing the problem by attempting to create alternative institutions that can fill the socialization needs of these children.

Children without supervision spend much of their time out of school and on the streets. Typically they are orphans, children of homeless families, runaways with parents or guardians elsewhere, or children who have been lost during natural or social catastrophes such as earthquakes and civil wars.

The causes of homelessness among children vary from one continent to another. In Africa and Indonesia, where rates of maternal death in childbirth may exceed 1,000 per 100,000 live births, large numbers of children are orphaned at birth. After several years in a public orphanage, these children often find their way to the streets, where they are socialized to street life by older, more experienced children. The AIDS epidemic in large parts of Africa plus famine and civil strife in the Sahel region (extending from Mauritania to Chad) also contribute to the growing number of wandering children finding their way into urban centers.

In Central and South America, the population of street children is growing as a consequence of poverty and

abandonment as well as civil strife and political violence. In Guatemala, Nicaragua, Colombia, Brazil, and Peru—where civil strife in some rural areas has left thousands of children without parents—young, destitute migrants are flowing into regional urban centers. In Europe, similar problems are arising in Bosnia, Romania, and parts of the former Soviet Union, owing to civil wars and sudden shifts in family fortunes.

In more economically developed areas of the world, children born as orphans tend to be placed in public orphanages, but in these more affluent nations homelessness among children is also on the upswing. In the United States, for example, high rates of crack abuse and incarceration of parents from high-poverty neighborhoods have caused a large share of the increase in homeless street children. As the accompanying chart shows, by 1990 almost 10 percent of U.S. children were living in households not headed by a parent. Of these, many thousands will leave orphanages and group homes to live on the streets.

Throughout the world the socialization of street children is carried out by other children and adolescents. In order to survive, the homeless child needs protection from predatory adults. Most often the child finds the help of older children vital, but that help often comes at a high price in the form of sexual services, criminal activities, drug use, avoidance of school, and many other behaviors that will socialize the homeless young person for a life on the extreme margins of "respectable" society. To survive on the street, children must be members of an organized band or gang. Since legitimate employment is rarely available until they are older, they usually become adept at the hustles and

In the early decades of this century, when children routinely worked in textile mills and coal mines, the environment in which they were socialized forced them to take on adult roles at an early age. For some children growing up in America this is still true for different reasons.

scams of street life. They beg at busy intersections, scavenge garbage for food and fuel, find shelter where they can, and seek health care in the emergency rooms of hospitals. Their death rate, especially from violence and homicide, is extremely high.

Because street children tend to be most numerous in major urban centers, it is here that most nations have focused their efforts to address the problem. In Mexico, for example, authorities have developed communities of children that provide successful alternatives to street life. Their success is measured in the fact that the communities are not coercive; children can go and come as they wish, but many choose to stay in the communities, where they have decent shelter, safety, opportunities for education, and steady meals. Unlike orphanages, where children are frequently subjected to prisonlike rules and the arbitrary dictates of harassed adults, these communities give the children themselves the responsibility for governing the community and making decisions about their welfare.

In the United States, where there are more than 400,000 orphans and incarcerated young people living in institutions, the socialization that children experience in detention centers and juvenile correction centers often has the effect of preparing them to be more effective street hustlers and petty criminals when they are released. To date, the establishment of more successful socializing environments for homeless children has (with a few exceptions) been a matter of low priority. Left to survive by their wits, homeless street children scavenge, prostitute themselves, and beg, and as they grow older many turn to more violent and ambitious forms of crime.

Children Living in Households Not Headed by a Parent, United States

6.7 % 1970
8.3% 1980
9.7% 1990

Source: Annie E. Casey Foundation, Center for the Study of Social Policy.

States rates on this issue compared with other societies with similar levels of economic and social development. Figures 5.1 and 5.2 reveal that the United States has significantly higher rates of teenage pregnancy and abortion than other nations with comparable or more permissive laws and medical services. In Canada, for example, there are about 80 pregnancies per 1,000 women age 19, compared to more than 150 per 1,000 in the United States.

These comparative data suggest that U.S. teenagers are less socialized to control the consequences of their sexual behavior than teenagers from the other countries represented in the charts; they also have less information about reproduction and contraception. Additional data on the use of contraceptives in England and the United States offer some empirical support for this hypothesis. Cultural contradictions in American patterns of socialization also play a role in explaining these differences. In the United States we place a high value on sexuality, judging from our consumption of magazines and television programs that

focus on sex and sexual attraction. But we are also a society in which the frank discussion of sexual behavior in the home and school and even among friends is fraught with conflict. It seems that we socialize children to desire sex but not to know much about how to control it. Comparative studies show that one consequence is a higher number of children born to teenage mothers in the United States than in other nations (Jones et al., 1986).

Since teenage mothers are also more likely than nonteenagers to be single mothers and to be living in poverty, a major consequence of the high rate of teenage fertility in the United States is that proportionately more babies are born into homes in which they will not receive the attention and material benefits that will help them realize their full genetic potential (Furstenberg, 1976). In other words, these children start off at a disadvantage in that their mothers have not yet reached maturity themselves and are likely to be single parents who may be unable to provide their children with economic security, love, and discipline.

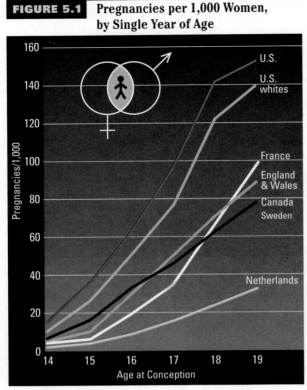

FIGURE 5.1 Pregnancies per 1,000 Women, by Single Year of Age

Source: Jones et al., 1986.

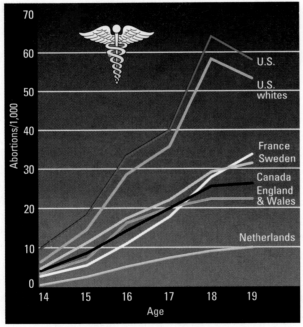

FIGURE 5.2 Abortions per 1,000 Women, by Single Year of Age

Source: Jones et al., 1986.

In seeking to update these figures, we learned that this is still the most recent comparative information available. These charts, therefore, should be read for the comparative information they provide, not as indicators of current rates of teenage pregnancy and abortion.

Urie Bronfenbrenner, one of the nation's most respected and original researchers in the field of childhood socialization, summarizes the conclusions of numerous studies with these two propositions:

> Proposition 1. In order to develop normally, a child needs the enduring . . . involvement of one or more adults in care of and joint activity withǏ the child.

> Proposition 2. The involvement of one or more adults in care of and joint activity with the child requires public policies that provide opportunity, status, resources, encouragement, example, and, above all, *time* for parenthood, primarily by parents, but also by other adults in the child's environment, both within and outside the home. (1981, p. 39)

No society can pass legislation requiring that a growing child experience love in the family or household. It can, however, formulate public policies that support the efforts of families to raise healthy children and socialize them well. It can do this, in part, by helping to provide children with the attention of caring adults outside the family, especially in agencies of socialization such as schools.

AGENCIES OF SOCIALIZATION

Agencies of socialization are the groups of people, along with the interactions that occur within those groups, that influence a person's social development throughout his or her lifetime (Elkin & Handel, 1989); **agents of socialization** are individuals, such as parents and teachers, who socialize others. The most familiar agencies of socialization are the family, schools, socializing agencies in the community, the peer group, and the mass media. Later in life adults may experience further socialization in the workplace, in universities, or in the military, to cite a few common examples. And people who wish to change self-destructive behaviors like drug addiction or alcoholism may be resocialized in "12-step" programs such as Alcoholics Anonymous. (Resocialization is discussed further in the next section.)

Within all agencies of socialization a number of processes are continually occurring that shape the individual's development. Among these are direct instruction, imitation or modeling of behavior, and reinforcement of particular behaviors (e.g., through rewards or punishments). Many of these processes appear in what sociologists call anticipatory socialization. Whenever an individual plays at a role he or she is likely to assume later in life, **anticipatory socialization** is taking place. By dressing up in adult clothing, for example, or by playing house, a child imitates the behavior of adults. The adolescent who attends a senior prom is being socialized in anticipation of a time when she or he will be expected to participate in formal social events. And a worker in a corporate setting may rehearse before coworkers a presentation she or he will later make to a potential client.

Another important aspect of agencies of socialization is that they must continually deal with social change. For example, as guns have become more readily available in large cities, peer groups have had to cope with the ever-present danger of violent death. As divorce and remarriage rates have risen, many families have had to deal with new structures that add much more complexity to family socialization patterns. As a result, the influence of social change on socialization patterns has become an important area of sociological research.

In the following pages we briefly consider several agencies of socialization: the family, the schools, the community, the peer group, and the mass media. We will encounter many of these agencies in later chapters as well.

The Family. The family is the primary agency of socialization. It is the environment into which the child is born and in which his or her earliest experiences with other people occur—experiences that have a lasting influence on the personality. Family environments vary greatly, not only in terms of such key variables as parents' income and education but also in terms of living arrangements, urban versus rural residence, number of children, relations with kin, and so on. Much contemporary research centers on the effects of different family environments on the child's development. For example, Michael Lewis and Candice Feiring's intriguing study of 117 families, "Some American Families at Dinner" (1982), shows that a typical 3-year-old child interacts regularly with a network of kin, friends, and other adults who may play a significant role in the child's early socialization. (See Box 5.4.)

One of the most significant changes occurring in American society today is the increase in the proportion of children growing up in poor families (almost 40 percent of all children under age 18) or in no family at all. In the early 1990s, nearly 10 percent of all children in the United States were growing up in households with no parent present. Most of these children (76 percent) were being socialized in the homes of grandparents and relatives; the remainder were living in group homes and with nonrelatives (Gross, 1992). There has also been a steady increase in the number of single-parent families, of which the vast majority are headed by women.

But changes in the way families are organized or how they cope with changing social conditions are not a new phenomenon. The values and ways of parents are never entirely valid for their children, although the degree to which this is true depends on how much social change is experienced from one generation to the next. Socialization creates the personalities and channels the behaviors of the members of a society, but that socialization is never entirely finished. Thus, in *Manchild in the Promised Land,* his masterpiece about growing up in Harlem during the period of rapid migration of blacks from the South, Claude Brown (1966) wrote that his rural-born parents did not "seem to be ready for urban life." Their values and norms of behavior made no sense to their son, who had to survive on Harlem's mean streets:

> When I was a little boy, Mama and Dad would beat me and tell me, "You better be good," but I didn't know what being good was. To me it meant that they just wanted me to sit down and fold my hands or something crazy like that. Stay in front of the house, don't go anyplace, don't get into trouble. I didn't know what it meant, and I don't think they knew what it meant, because they couldn't ever tell me what they really wanted. The way I saw it, everything I was doing was good. If I stole something and didn't get caught, I was good. If I got into a fight with somebody, I tried to be good enough to beat him. If I broke into a place, I tried to be quiet and steal as much as I could. I was always trying to be good. They kept on beating me and talking about being good. And I just kept on doing what I was doing and kept on trying to do it good. (p. 279)

Brown's story is the biography of a young man whose parents' experience with social change created a severe disjunction in their lives. This left them ill equipped to socialize their son for the demands of a new environment. And so he learned to survive on the streets. He became a thief and a gang fighter. But by his own account, later in his life he was greatly influenced by people who had studied the social sciences and created well-functioning institutions, special schools in particular, that could bring out his talents and socialize him for a more satisfying and constructive life than he had led as a child.

The Schools. For most of us, regardless of what our home life is like, teachers are generally the first agents of socialization we encounter who are not kin. In some cases children are also influenced by agents of socialization in the church (e.g., priests or rabbis), but for most children the school is the most important agency of socialization after the family. Children experience many opportunities to perform new roles in school (e.g., as student, teammate, etc.). No wonder, then, that in these first "public" appearances they tend to be highly sensitive to taunts or teasing by other children. Even very young children can become distraught when they feel that they are not wearing the "right" clothes.

Schools are institutions where differences between the values of the family and those of the larger society come into sharp focus. In some families, for example, there may be great concern about any form of sex education in school. Indeed, much of the conflict over educational norms—what ought to be taught, whether there should be prayer in school, and the like—stems from differences between the values of some families and the values that many educators wish to teach. Such conflicts point to the exceedingly difficult situation of schools in American society. Research on school–family and school–community relations has shown that the schools are expected to conserve the society's values (by teaching ideals of citizenship, morality,

BOX 5.4 **SOCIOLOGICAL METHODS**

Measures of Central Tendency

The following table, taken from Lewis and Feiring's study of American families, presents information about the social network of the typical 3-year-old:

The 3-Year-Old Child's Social Network ($N = 117$)*

	X	RANGE
Number of relatives other than parents seen at least once a week	3.20	0–15
Number of child's friends seen at least once a week	4.43	0–13
Number of adults seen at least once a week	4.38	0–24

*N refers to the number of subjects in a study.

Source: Lewis & Feiring, 1982, p. 116.

To understand this table you must know something about the common measures of central tendency. The one used in the table is the *mean*, represented by X. To arrive at this number each child's total number of friends, relatives, and other adults seen at least once a week is added to the totals for the other children in the sample. The grand total is then divided by the number of children in the sample. The resulting number can be used to represent the entire sample.

The other common measures of central tendency are the *median* and the *mode*. The median is the number that divides a sample into two equal halves when all the numbers in the sample are arranged from lowest to highest. The mode is simply the score that occurs most frequently in the sample. Sociologists make a point of specifying which of these measures they are using. They try to avoid the term *average* in statistical tables, as it can refer to any one of these measures.

To illustrate all three measures of central tendency, let us use the following data from 10 of the children in Lewis and Feiring's sample:

CHILD	NUMBER OF FRIENDS SEEN AT LEAST ONCE A WEEK
1	2
2	3
3	3
4	7
5	12
6	2
7	3
8	1
9	0
10	5
	38

In this example the mode would be 3 and the median would also be 3, but the mean would be 3.8.

family values, and the like) and, at the same time, to play a major role in dealing with innovation and change (by expanding the curriculum to include new knowledge, coping with children's perceptions of current events, addressing past patterns of discrimination, and the like) (Goslin, 1965; Meier, 1995).

In Chapter 18 we will return to questions of whether the schools help reproduce the status quo and maintain inequalities in society and whether they can actually affect the lives of disadvantaged students. Although many individuals credit schools (and even particular teachers) with bringing about important improvements in their lives, there is much debate on these questions in the social sciences.

The Community. Schools may be the most important agency of socialization outside the family, but there are a number of other significant agencies of socialization in most communities—including day care centers, scout troops, churches, recreation centers, and leagues of all kinds. These agencies engage in many and varied forms of socialization. Parades on Memorial Day and the Fourth of July, for example, reinforce values of citizenship and patriotism. Participation in team sports instills values of fair play, teamwork, and competitive spirit. The uniforms and equipment required for these activities stimulate shopping trips to suburban malls and downtown department stores, and those trips prepare children and adolescents for the time when they will be consumers (McKendrick, Brewer, & Plump, 1982; Newman, 1988).

Of all these agencies of socialization, the day care center is perhaps the most controversial. Polls often show that Americans have doubts about the effects of day care on very young children, and scandals involving charges of child abuse by day care workers intensify those fears. But when both parents work outside the home, or when single parents must work to support their children, day care centers may play a critical role in socialization. Many studies have shown that good quality centers are not harmful to children and in some cases may be beneficial, but the norm requiring that mothers stay home to care for young children remains strong in many communities (Kammerman, 1986).

The Peer Group. In the United States the peer group tends to be the dominant agency of socialization in middle and late childhood. **Peer groups** are interacting groups of people of about the same age. Among adolescents, peer groups exert a strong influence on their members' attitudes and values. Studies confirm the high degree of importance adolescents and adults alike attach to their friendship groups. Adolescents typically acquire much of their identity from their peers and consequently find it difficult to deviate from the norms of behavior that their peer group establishes (Gans, 1962, 1984; Homans, 1950; McAndrew, 1985; W. F. Whyte, 1943). In fact, the peer group may become even more important than the family in the development of the individual's identity.

There is often a rather high level of conflict within families over the extent to which the peer group influences the adolescent to behave in ways that are not approved of by the family. Even where conflict is limited, the peer group usually provides the child's first experience with close friendships outside the family. The peer group becomes the child's age-specific subculture—that is, a circle of close friends of roughly the same age, often with shifting loyalties.

The peer group usually engages in a set of activities that are not related to adult society. The peer subculture may, for example, include games that adults no longer play and may have forgotten. British researchers Iona and Peter Opie (1969) conducted a classic study of the games children play. They identified hundreds of games that were known by children between the ages of 6 and 10 all over England. They also identified the common elements in those games, such as chasing, pretending, and seeking, and found that in many of the games the central problem is to choose an "It," a seeker or chaser. The children's efforts to avoid being "It" seemed to express their desire to avoid roles that make them different from the others.

When children's peer groups are faced with conflict and social change—for example, in communities where there are high levels of poverty and demographic change, with groups of culturally distinct people moving in and out—the group often organizes itself in gangs for self-defense and aggression. There are many such gangs in large American cities characterized by rapid immigration, widespread drug use, and the ready availability of cheap handguns. Under these conditions both male and female peer groups may become extremely dangerous environments for socialization, yet they exert a strong attraction on adolescents who seek protection and companionship in what is perceived as a hostile world (Sanchez-Jankowski, 1991; Williams, 1989).

The Mass Media. The most controversial agency of socialization in American society is the mass media. In debates about the effects of the media on socialization, television comes under the greatest scrutiny because of the number of hours children spend in front of the "electronic baby-sitter." Estimates of how much television children watch differ, depending on the methodology used to conduct the study (especially since simply having the set turned on does not mean that the children are actually watching). Many studies have shown that the amount of television viewed varies, depending on whether the child comes from a poor home with few alternatives or a more affluent one where other activities are available. Children from poor homes in urban communities often have the set on for seven or more hours a day, as opposed to children from more affluent homes, where the set is turned on for three or four hours daily (Elkin & Handel, 1989; Wellins, 1990).

The effects of all this television viewing on children and adolescents are a subject of intensive research. In particular, the effects of seeing violent acts on television or listening to violent music like gangsta rap are hotly debated. There is no doubt that the amount of violence shown on TV is immense. George Gerbner, one of the nation's foremost researchers on TV violence, has been monitoring the number of violent acts shown on TV. His data indicate that the average child will have seen about 100,000 acts of violence on TV before graduating from elementary school—and the number is far higher for children from poor neighborhoods (Gerbner, 1990).

We will return to the subject of the media and their effects in Chapter 18. It should be noted here, however, that the effects of television on socialization are by no means all negative. Television, radio, and the movies provide windows onto social worlds that most people cannot otherwise enter. Children, adolescents, and adults in modern American society learn far more about current events, social issues, and the arts than people did before the advent of television.

SOCIALIZATION THROUGH THE LIFE COURSE

Childhood socialization is the primary influence on the individual. Whatever happens to a person later in life, the early childhood experiences that shaped the social self will continue to influence that person's attitudes and behavior. But people are also affected by their *life course:* the set of roles they play over a lifetime and the way those roles change as a consequence of social change. The life course of a person born before World War II, for example, would typically have involved service in the armed forces for men (perhaps including combat duty) and work in a factory (or noncombatant military service) for women. The life course of children born in the 1960s or 1970s is far less likely to include a long or intense experience of warfare. Natural disasters, major changes in the educational system or in the political stability of their society—these and other possible changes can influence the roles people play during their life course.

Changes in the culture of a society can also significantly alter the roles people play during their lives. In the first half of this century, for example, the role of wife was less likely to include periods of single parenthood than it is now. Fifty years ago the role of an elderly person was far more likely to involve relative poverty and dependence on younger family members than it does now. The need to adjust to changes in society and culture, and the fact that so many people are able to make such adjustments (though often with great difficulty) are evidence that socialization is not finished in childhood but continues throughout the life course (Riley, Foner, & Waring, 1988; Sorenson, Weinert, & Sherrod, 1986).

ADULT SOCIALIZATION

Two of the influences that produce socialization after childhood are significant others (especially new friends) and occupational mobility (especially new jobs). When one moves into a new neighborhood, for example, one often makes new friends, and their influence may lead to new activities. A person who has always been uninvolved in politics may, through the influence of new friends, become committed to a social movement such as the women's movement. New friends can also introduce a person to dangerous or unlawful activities such as drug use. One's *core identity*—the part of the self formed in early childhood that does not change easily—may prevent one from being overly influenced by a given peer group later in life, or it may actually cause that influence to be stronger (Elkin & Handel, 1989).

Such factors as stress and changing physical health may also have an influence. In a study of how people change their patterns of behavior later in life, Marjorie Fiske and David A. Chiriboga (1990) found that everyday hassles and the boredom of a routine, predictable existence have a greater impact on the changes adults seek in their lives than was indicated by earlier research.

In any new activity the newcomer or recruit must learn a new set of norms associated with the roles of the organization. Socialization associated with a new job, for example, often requires that a person learn new words and technical terms. The individual also needs to interact with a new peer group, usually composed of people whose work brings them together for long hours. And in most jobs the person will eventually be faced with choices between loyalty to peers and loyalty to those higher in the organizational

hierarchy who can confer benefits like raises and promotions. In these and most other adult socialization experiences, the choices people make will be highly influenced by the individual's core identity, which continually shapes his or her responses to new situations and challenges (Rosow, 1965).

RESOCIALIZATION

Many adults and even adolescents experience the need to correct certain patterns of prior social learning that they and others find detrimental. This need usually cannot be met through the normal processes of lifelong socialization, especially since the individual's negative behaviors may be leading toward a personal crisis and causing immense pain for family members and friends. Such a condition often responds to specific efforts at resocialization.

Resocialization is a process whereby individuals undergo intense, deliberate socialization designed to change major beliefs and behaviors. It is often aimed at changing behaviors like excessive drinking, drug use, and overeating—particularly common in affluent societies, where individuals are exposed to a great deal of choice and many pleasurable stimuli. Perhaps most widespread and pernicious among the addictions, alcoholism affects millions of people in North America and is involved in much of the marital strife that leads to family breakup. Alcoholics Anonymous is a voluntary group program that uses techniques of resocialization and peer example to help alcoholics reject old behaviors and learn new, more positive ones that do not involve drinking.

Much successful resocialization takes place in what are often called **total institutions** (Goffman, 1961). These are settings where people undergoing resocialization are isolated from the larger society under the control of a specialized staff whose members themselves may have experienced the same process of resocialization. All aspects of the inmates' daily lives are controlled, and supervision is constant. Drug treatment centers, for example, are often set up as total institutions for the resocialization of addicts. Even the smallest rewards, like extra time alone or more freedom to walk around the grounds, are controlled by the staff and bestowed only on inmates who have made progress toward the resocialization goals.

In the resocialization process the staff first attempts to tear down the individual's former sense of self. This stage may include various forms of degradation and abasement in which the individual is forced to reject the undesired thoughts and behaviors. In the next stage the staff rewards the individual's attempts to build a new sense of self that conforms to the goals of the resocialization process (e.g., a sober person who accepts responsibility for previous wrongs and achieves new interests and new awareness of personal strengths). However, while total institutions can be extremely powerful environments for resocialization, they sometimes run the risk of creating people who need to remain in their controlling environment—that is, people who have developed a need to be "institutionalized."

ERIKSON ON LIFELONG SOCIALIZATION

The theories of social psychologist Erik Erikson are especially relevant to the study of adult socialization and resocialization. Erikson agreed with Freud that a person's sense of identity is shaped by early childhood experiences. But Erikson also focused on the many changes occurring throughout life that can shape a person's sense of self and ability to perform social roles successfully. He demonstrated, for example, that combat experiences can produce damaged identities because soldiers often feel guilty about not having done enough for their fallen comrades (this is sometimes called "survivor guilt"). For Freud, in contrast, war-produced mental illness was always related to problems that the soldier had experienced in early childhood.

In *Childhood and Society* (1963), Erikson's central work on the formation of the self, the concept of identification takes center stage. Identification is the social process whereby the individual chooses other people as models and attempts to imitate their behavior in particular roles. Erikson noted that identification with these *role models* occurs throughout the life course. He pointed out that even older people seek role models who can help them through difficult life transitions.

For Erikson, every phase of life requires additional socialization to resolve the new conflicts that inevitably present themselves. Table 5.1 presents the basic conflicts that each person must resolve throughout life and indicates how a positive role model can help in resolving those conflicts. (The major theories of socialization are summarized in the study chart on page 144.)

Resocialization at any age usually requires a strong relationship between the individual and the role model. In the military or in a law enforcement agency, for example, the new recruit is usually paired with a more experienced person who offers advice and can show the recruit the essential "tricks" of the new role—"how it's really done." Thus, in Alcoholics Anonymous, once the self-confessed "drunk" faces up to that negative identity, he or she is taught new ways of thinking, feeling, and acting that do not involve drinking. An important step in this process is the development of a relationship with a *sponsor,* a person who has been through the same experiences and has made a successful recovery. In fact, one of AA's aims is to enable the resocialized alcoholic to eventually perform as a sponsor—that is, as a role model—for someone else who is going through the same process.

GENDER SOCIALIZATION

No discussion of socialization would be complete without some mention of gender socialization. Gender socialization refers to the ways in which we learn our gender identity and develop according to cultural norms of

TABLE 5.1	Erikson's View of Lifelong Socialization	
STAGE OF LIFE	**CONFLICT**	**SUCCESSFUL RESOLUTION IN OLD AGE***
Old Age	Integrity vs. despair	Wisdom and a sense of integrity strong enough to withstand physical disintegration.
Adulthood	Generativity vs. stagnation in interpersonal relationships	*Caritas* (caring for others) and *agape* (empathy and concern).
Early Adulthood	Intimacy vs. isolation in the quest for love	A sense of the complexity of relationships; value of tenderness and loving freely.
Adolescence	Identity vs. confusion; struggles over fidelity to parents or friends	A sense of the complexity of life; merger of sensory, logical, and aesthetic perception.
School Age	Industry vs. inferiority in the quest for competence	Humility; acceptance of the course of one's life and unfulfilled hopes.
Play Age	Initiative vs. guilt in the development of a sense of purpose	Humor; empathy; resilience.
Early Childhood	Autonomy vs. shame in the development of the will to be a social actor	Acceptance of the cycle of life, from integration to disintegration.
Infancy	Trust vs. mistrust	Appreciation of interdependence and relatedness.

*Erikson did not believe that elderly people necessarily resolve these conflicts entirely, but when they do, the results are as shown here.

SHOOTING BACK

The noted social scientist Robert Coles tells the story of a 10-year-old homeless girl he encountered in a shelter in Boston. The girl had drawn a picture of herself, but suddenly she picked up a black crayon and drew an X over the piece of paper she had been using. Saddened, Coles asked her why she had destroyed the picture. "That," she said, "is what people think of us, but they are wrong, and I know they are, and if I could, I'd tell them!"

In a project undertaken by UPI photographer Jim Hubbard and other news photographers, homeless children were given an opportunity to "tell them" through the medium of photography. The photographers lent the children cameras and accompanied them as they learned how to use the equipment and began taking pictures of their friends and the environment in which they lived.

Charlene's comment—My favorite picture that I took: that's me and my brother and my sister with a pigeon. My brother had found a pigeon, and the pigeon had been shot in the wing. My brother was trying to fix it, so I just told my brother to look at it, and I just put the timer on, focused it, and I ran over there to get in the picture. I want to be a photographer.

Comment to Charlene from schoolchild—I saw your picture, Birds, in the exhibit in New York. I saw it from way across the room and I felt drawn to it. . . . The girl on the left, her teeth show, like she understood pain and in that instant, experienced it for the bird.

Chris's comment—This is the kids on the train tracks, jumping. They are at the shelter. The best part of the shelter is the train track.

That environment was grim indeed. In Hubbard's words:

Shelter life is a journey into despair. It is life on the edge. Many of the shelters I visited were the scenes of round-the-clock violence, drug dealing, abuse and cases of parental neglect, and widespread chaos. They were places not fit for a child. . . . Between 1987 and 1989, five children died [at one of the shelters]. Two were stabbed to death by their overburdened father. One was hit by a train behind the shelter while playing the children's favorite game of tag with the train. There wasn't even a playground for these children except on worn-out mattresses that they pulled from the trash. (Hubbard, 1991, p. 4)

Shawn talking with Jim—A lot of the pictures that I had—I had sold them. Those pictures you all had blown up for me last time. *You sold them?* Yeah—to the people I took the pictures of. *The pictures you took of people here you sold to the people?* Yeah. *You are becoming a major businessman. I mean, I never heard of such a great thing. You were formerly selling crack. Now you are selling photographs. You may not make quite as much money, you probably won't get shot, you probably won't go to prison for selling photographs, plus it's a creative thing, follow? I'm going to help you on this, if you let me.*

The children's photographs, some of which are shown here, provide an eloquent statement about their world. In the midst of despair, they found occasional moments of enjoyment and hope. They played, fought, and took care of younger siblings. Their pictures contain ample evidence of agents of socialization at work—parents, peers, older brothers and sisters, and the news photographers who taught them the basics of photography. When Hubbard asked the young photographers to comment on their pictures (a technique of visual sociology known as *photo elicitation*), they responded with warmth and intelligence. Some of their comments are reproduced here.

In 1989 Hubbard and his colleagues established a nonprofit center in Washington, D.C., to teach photography and darkroom skills, painting, drawing, and creative writing. In 1990 a selection of the children's photographs were exhibited at a gallery in Washington, and in 1991 many of them were published in a book titled *Shooting Back.* As Coles explains in his preface to the book, the children "shot back" with their eyes, mind, and spirit; their pictures are visual statements about the world in which they are growing up and a moral statement about the society that allows such a world to exist.

Patricia Williams, with daughter Charlene, and Vanessa Johnson, with son Dion (another Shooting Back *photographer), before they were interviewed on the CBS Morning Show in 1990.*

Comment from Calvin—When I go back into the shelters, you know, I understand what they're feeling. I don't talk to them a lot about the environment because I know it's a low-life situation. They become your friends, so they open up to you more if you talk to them with the sense, like, I've been there before.

STUDY CHART Theories of Socialization

THEORIST	DESCRIPTION OF THEORY
Sigmund Freud	Through socialization the infant is gradually forced to channel its biological urges into socially accepted forms of behavior. Major personality traits are formed in the conflict between the child and its parents, especially the same-sex parent.
George Herbert Mead	Socialization is a process in which the self emerges out of interaction with others, not only in early infancy but throughout life. Role taking is central to socialization; role-taking ability develops through interaction during childhood in the preparatory, play, and game stages.
Jean Piaget	Children develop definite awareness of moral issues at an early age but cannot deal with moral ambiguities until they mature further. This insight is incorporated in Kohlberg's preconventional, conventional, and postconventional stages of moral development.
Erik Erikson	Throughout the life course the individual must resolve a series of conflicts that shape the person's sense of self and ability to perform social roles successfully. Central to this process is identification, in which the individual chooses other people as role models.

"masculinity" or "femininity." Gender is not synonymous with biological sex; rather, "scholars use the word *sex* to refer to attributes of men and women created by their biological characteristics and *gender* to refer to the distinctive qualities of men and women (or masculinity and femininity) that are culturally created" (Epstein, 1988, p. 6). By *gender identity* we mean "an individual's own feeling of whether she or he is a woman or a man, or a girl or a boy" (Kessler & McKenna, 1978, p. 10). Our ideas about what it means to be a man or a woman are different from our ideas about the anatomical definitions of males and females. These ideas are shaped by the values and socialization practices of our culture, but once they have become part of the self, they are usually extremely strong.

The strength and pervasiveness of gender socialization are illustrated by the case of Ron Kovic, the author of *Born on the Fourth of July.* Kovic saw himself as a red-blooded American male, a typical product of socialization for boys raised in his community. He was taught to be patriotic, to want to defend his country, to want to prove his manhood in combat and sexual conquest. When he became paralyzed in Vietnam and lost his manhood (in the narrow, conventional sense of that term), he began to doubt everything—including himself, his country, and his friends. His story raises some important issues, not least of which is how we form our ideas of manliness and womanliness and whether those ideas are helpful in meeting the demands of a changing world.

The story of Ron Kovic is a striking example of how powerful gender socialization is and the effects it can have on a person's life. Elsewhere in this book (especially in Chapter 14) we present other examples of the importance of gender in explaining life chances. But here let us take a more mundane example of the results of gender socialization: the way men and women view their own bodies. Men tend to think of their own bodies as "just about perfect," but women tend to think of themselves as overweight, at least when they compare themselves with a mental image of an attractive woman. These are the findings of a survey of 500 college-age men and women conducted by April Fallon and Paul Rozin (cited in Goleman, 1985a).

A striking indication of the role of agencies of socialization in the social construction of gender identity is the influence of the mass media in promoting ideal body types for men and women. These influences have a lot to do with why men tend to be happy with their bodies while many girls and women are extremely unhappy with theirs. Men dominate the media—radio, television, newspapers, and magazines—that communicate American culture to mass audiences. Girls and women are continually exposed to images of women created by men, and those images more often than not portray women as sex objects, to be judged by the shape and size of their breasts, the length of their legs, and the tightness of their skin (Chernin, 1981; Lurie, 1981). It is little wonder, then, that women feel worse about themselves than do men—about whom it has been said that it is sexy to be a sagging warrior or a somewhat wrinkled philosopher.

Among the many momentous changes that are occurring in the world today, those affecting gender socialization are among the most profound. Research on socialization in Asia and Africa, for example, shows how norms that favor boys over girls act to the detriment of female development. Studies from Bangladesh, India, Nepal, and Pakistan reveal that boys receive more and higher-quality food than girls, even though girls are often required to expend more calories on field and household work. In many poor nations it is common for boys to be fed before girls and for the higher-quality nutrients, especially proteins, to be consumed before the girls are allowed to eat. So strong are gender norms in those countries that most mothers are convinced that this practice is necessary when food is scarce (Jacobson, 1992). As a result of this and other socialization practices that place females at a disadvantage, the health and learning capacities of women are imperiled from an early age in many parts of the world.

RESEARCH FRONTIERS: SOCIALIZATION AND EMOTIONS

An active area of sociological research addresses an aspect of the nature-nurture debate: the question of whether differences in the way men and women express themselves and the way they think about interpersonal relations are innate or a product of gender socialization. Some observers of human behavior argue that emotions and emotional expression are innate. Women cry more easily than men, they assert, because over many millennia of human evolution women have tended to specialize in the emotional realm of life while men have tended to specialize in the rational and cognitive aspects, and these differences have been incorporated into the genetic makeup of the sexes. Most sociologists, on the other hand, would argue that much more evidence supports the claim that emotions, like many other aspects of human behavior, are learned through socialization and that differences in emotional behavior between the sexes are due to gender socialization (Fox, 1971; Wilson, 1978).

In recent years sociologists have made significant progress in studying how social structures such as organizational hierarchies bring out and may even require different types of emotional expression. Among the leaders in this field of study is Arlie Hochschild (1979, 1983). In her pathbreaking study of the work of airline flight attendants, she found that the only way women could gain positions on flight crews after World War II was by specializing in making people feel better about flying and helping them feel comfortable while in the air. Hochschild showed that flight attendants (who until recently were almost all female) are trained to follow certain norms of emotional expression or "feeling rules." To be "nice" or "sweet" is defined as a feminine trait in the airline industry, just as the assertiveness and confidence expressed by the male flight officers are thought to be masculine traits. Hochschild noted that women who feel comfortable with these norms tend to self-select themselves for entry into the occupation, al-

though they may eventually come to resent the stereotyping of their status.

Sociologist Cynthia Epstein points out that in many occupations the way women think about themselves has changed. She observes that in the 1960s, when she began interviewing women lawyers, they often denied that they were working as hard as their male colleagues in order to earn equally high salaries and have the same chances of gaining powerful positions in the firm. "In the 1960s it was unwomanly to concede such attitudes," she notes (1988, p. 88). Ten years later, when she reinterviewed the same women, she found that many felt free to express the desire for wealth and power and had developed strategies that would permit them to compete with men for available judgeships. Changing norms of acceptable aspiration and emotional expression among women have allowed some to shed the stereotype of women as lacking the ability to compete with men in performing rational, technical tasks. We will see additional evidence of these changes in later chapters.

SUMMARY

THINK ABOUT IT CRITICALLY
The radical behaviorist John B. Watson believed that he could shape any individual into a particular type of person if only he could begin early enough in the person's life. He could make someone selfish or generous, thoughtful or dull—at least this is what he believed. At the other extreme, many people who are not trained as behavioral scientists still believe in the "bad seed" theory of human behavior, the idea that some people are born bad or with evil tendencies and nothing can be done about this condition. How does the scientific study of socialization help us understand the limits of both these beliefs about how a person develops in society?

Socialization refers to the ways in which people learn to conform to their society's norms, values, and roles. Primary socialization consists of the ways in which the newborn individual is molded into a person who can interact with others according to the expectations of society. Secondary socialization occurs in childhood and adolescence, primarily through schooling; and adult socialization refers to the ways in which a person learns the norms associated with new statuses.

Among the most basic questions in the study of human socialization is that of "nature" versus "nurture": To what extent does the development of the person depend on genetic factors, and to what extent does it depend on learning? The first social scientist to develop a theory that addressed this issue was Sigmund Freud. Freud believed that the personality develops out of the processes of socialization through which the infant is gradually forced to control its biological urges. He divided the personality into three functional areas: the *id,* from which unsocialized drives arise; the *superego,* which incorporates the moral codes of elders; and the *ego,* or one's conception of oneself in relation to others.

In the growth of the personality, the formation of the ego or social self is critical. According to Freud, this takes place in a series of stages in which conflict between the demands of the superego and those of the id is always threatening to disrupt the functioning of the ego.

Behaviorism asserts that all behavior is learned. It originated in the work of Ivan Pavlov, who showed that behavior thought to be instinctual could in fact be shaped or conditioned by learning situations. This line of research was continued by John B. Watson, whose experiments revealed the ability of *conditioning* to shape behavior in almost any direction.

Studies of *feral children,* who have experienced extreme isolation or have been reared outside human society, show that such children are able to learn—but do so far more slowly than children who have not been isolated in early childhood. Other studies have found that normal development requires not only the presence of other humans but also the attention and love of adults. Children raised in orphanages and other nonfamily settings are more likely to develop emotional problems and to be retarded in their language development than comparable children reared by their parents.

Interactionist models of socialization stress the development of the social self through interaction with others. One of the earliest interactionist theories was Charles Horton Cooley's concept of the "looking glass self," the reflection of our self that we think we see in the behaviors of other people toward us. This concept was carried further by George Herbert Mead, who emphasized the importance of culture in the formation of the self. Mead believed that when children play, they practice *role taking,* or trying to look at social situations from the standpoint of another person. This ability develops through three stages. During the preparatory stage children mimic the behavior of the *significant others* in their social environment. During the play stage they play at being others who are significant in their lives. During the third stage, the game stage, they develop the ability to take the role of the *generalized other*—that is, to shape their participation according to the roles of the other participants.

In playing the roles for which they have been socialized, people adhere to rules of interaction known as "face work." They seek to present a positive image of themselves, their "face," and to avoid being embarrassed or "losing face."

Lawrence Kohlberg proposed a three-stage sequence of moral development in which the child's moral reasoning evolves from emphasis on reward and punishment to the ability to distinguish between social laws and moral principles.

Studies of the environments in which socialization occurs have found that normal development requires the involvement of one or more adults in the care of the child, as well as public policies that promote such involvement.

Agencies of socialization are the groups of people, along with the interactions that occur within those groups, that influence a person's social development. Within all agencies of socialization one finds a great deal of *anticipatory socialization,* in which the individual plays at a role that he or she is likely to assume later in life. After the family, the most important agencies of socialization are the schools. Other socializing agencies include day care centers, churches, leagues, and other associations. The dominant agency of socialization outside the family is the *peer group,* an interacting group of people of about the same age. Peer groups exert a significant influence on the individual from adolescence on. The mass media, especially television, are another significant agency of socialization in American society.

The roles a person plays over a lifetime are influenced by social change and by changes in the culture of his or her society. Socialization after childhood often occurs as a result of the influence of significant others and occupational mobility. A person's core identity shapes that individual's responses to new situations and challenges. *Resocialization* may occur at any time during adulthood. Sometimes people undergo resocialization to correct patterns of social learning that they and others find detrimental. Erik Erikson focused on *identification,* the social process whereby the individual chooses adults as role models and attempts to imitate their behavior.

An important aspect of socialization is *gender socialization,* or the ways we learn our gender identity and develop according to cultural norms of masculinity and femininity. Gender identity is an individual's own feeling of whether he or she is a male or a female.

CRITICAL RESPONSE

As sociologists study the diverse influences on a person's social self over a lifetime, they find little evidence to support either the radical behaviorist theory of the fully shapable self or the folk idea that a person's behavior is "God-given" or genetically programmed. Instead, their research indicates that the genetic endowments of the individual set limits on what he or she can achieve. In some special cases one's genes may provide immense opportunities to develop in a certain direction, but without the appropriate socialization experiences that potential may never be fully realized. In people with less outstanding genetic endowments, socialization experiences determine to what extent those endowments will be realized.

GLOSSARY

socialization: the processes whereby we learn to behave according to the norms of our culture. (p. 122)

id: according to Freud, the part of the human personality from which all innate drives arise. (p. 124)

superego: according to Freud, the part of the human personality that internalizes the moral codes of adults. (p. 124)

ego: according to Freud, the part of the human personality that is the individual's conception of himself or herself in relation to others. (p. 124)

behaviorism: a theory stating that all behavior is learned and that this learning occurs through the process known as conditioning. (p. 124)

conditioning: the shaping of behavior through reward and punishment. (p. 124)

feral child: a child reared outside human society. (p. 125)

role taking: trying to look at social situations from the standpoint of another person from whom one seeks a response. (p. 130)

significant other: any person who is important to an individual. (p. 130)

generalized other: a person's internalized conception of the expectations and attitudes held by society. (p. 131)

agencies of socialization: the groups of people, along with the interactions that occur within those groups, that influence a person's social development. (p. 136)

agents of socialization: individuals who socialize others. (p. 136)

anticipatory socialization: socialization that prepares an individual for a role that he or she is likely to assume later in life. (p. 136)

peer group: an interacting group of people of about the same age that has a significant influence on the norms and values of its members. (p. 139)

resocialization: intense, deliberate socialization designed to change major beliefs and behaviors. (p. 140)

total institution: a setting in which people undergoing resocialization are isolated from the larger society under the control of a specialized staff. (p. 140)

identification: the social process whereby an individual chooses role models and attempts to imitate their behavior. (p. 141)

gender socialization: the ways in which we learn our gender identity and develop according to cultural norms of masculinity and femininity. (p. 141)

WHERE TO FIND IT

BOOKS

Child, Family, Community: Socialization and Support, 3rd ed. (Roberta Berns; Harcourt Brace, 1993). A basic text in the field of socialization, with a good review of relevant sociological research.

The Child and Society, 5th ed. (Frederick Elkin & Gerald Handel; Random House, 1989). A basic text that offers in-depth coverage of most aspects of childhood socialization.

Not in Our Genes (R. C. Lewontin, Steven Rose, & Leon Kamin; Pantheon, 1984). A strong but fair critique of biological thinking in the field of human development.

In a Different Voice (Carol Gilligan; Harvard University Press, 1982). Argues that classic theories of human development are biased toward male development and hence neglect important aspects of socialization and personality development.

JOURNALS

Social Psychology Quarterly. A journal of the American Sociological Association that is devoted to recent research on "the processes and products of social interaction."

Sociological Studies of Child Development. An annual review of sociological research on socialization and child development begun in 1986. Represents many of the newest trends in this active area of sociological research.

Journal of Health and Social Behavior. A journal of the American Sociological Association that specializes in "sociological approaches to the definition and analysis of problems bearing on human health and illness" and often contains important articles on child welfare, socialization, and problems of health and development through the life cycle.

OTHER SOURCES

Basic Handbook of Child Psychiatry (Joseph D. Noshpitz, ed.; Basic Books, 1979). A two-volume work that contains many excellent articles about human development. The focus is interdisciplinary, although there is also an emphasis on abnormal socialization and treatment.

Statistical Yearbook. Published annually by the United Nations. This is a valuable source of comparative data on infant mortality and other indicators of the health of children, as well as statistical material on education, literacy, and other measures of socialization.

Interaction in Groups

"I used to fight a lot when I was young. Every afternoon I think I was the main event. Every afternoon. There was times when I was scared to fight, but I used to fight, because if I didn't fight and I didn't win my sister would beat the shit out of me when I got home, or my cousins they would hit me, you know" (Moore, 1991, p. 62).

The speaker is a member of a Los Angeles gang; she is being interviewed by sociologist Joan Moore. An expert on gangs, Moore has spoken with generations of gang members about changes in gang activity and behavior. She is especially interested in finding out why the level of violence in gangs has been increasing in recent years. In this interview a young Mexican American woman describes the intense pressure she felt from her peers in the gang, and from members of her family as well, to be tough and to fight. When Moore asks her about losing fights, she reacts with great emotion: "No, I couldn't lose. They didn't care how punched up I came home. I had to be a winner. That was the motto we had, you know, and if they beat you up you don't cry, you don't say nothing, you don't snivel" (Moore, 1991, p. 62).

The gang members Moore interviews—many of whom she has known for more than 20 years—always mention the need not to back down, not to "be a punk." This emphasis on gaining and maintaining the respect of fellow gang members is an often-recurring theme in the study of gangs. But Moore's research shows that as it has become increasingly difficult to find secure jobs and legitimate careers in poor minority neighborhoods, the level of violence attached to maintaining respect has risen. And as more gang members have served time in prison, their options for life outside the confined world of the neighborhood and its gang have diminished. In consequence, the gang peer group may have a stronger and more lasting influence on this young woman than would have been true in the past.

THE IMPORTANCE OF GROUPS

Moore's study of Los Angeles gangs is rich in examples of how people interact in groups. It also shows how frequently the strong norms or values of a peer group lead gang members to behave violently in particular situations. Other sociologists confirm Moore's findings about the importance of "respect" or honor among gang members (Horowitz, 1985; Sanchez-Jankowski, 1991). Martin Sanchez-Jankowski, who has conducted extensive comparative research on gangs throughout the United States, concludes that, contrary to what people often believe, most gang members do not enjoy fighting. Indeed, those who are not among the gang's leaders fear violence. "Fear of physical harm, however, is not sufficient to completely deter gang violence, because most gang members . . . believe that if you do not attack, you will be attacked" (1991, p. 177).

The social fabric of modern societies is composed of millions of groups. Gangs are only one example. Some groups are as intimate as a pair of lovers. Others, like the modern corporation or university, are extremely large and are composed of many interrelated subgroups. We need to perform well in all of these groups, and to have this ability is to be considered successful by others. But the knowledge needed for success in a group with a formal structure of roles and statuses is quite different from the "smarts" needed for success in intimate groups.

In this chapter we analyze some important aspects of the way people behave in groups. We begin by describing the most common types of groups and showing how they can be linked together by overlapping memberships. This first portion of the chapter illustrates the functionalist view of group interaction. It looks at the structure of groups and the way they function in society. It also provides typologies of groups and insights into how they are organized. However, simply describing categories of groups and their structure does not explain how groups maintain the commitment of their members or why they change. In the middle portions of the chapter we examine these questions, focusing on the give-and-take that occurs in groups of different types and on how these interactions produce group norms. This section illustrates interactionist research on behavior in groups. In the final section of the chapter we show how formal organization and bureaucracy operate to control conflict and cope with change in groups. The concepts introduced here will be used over and over again in other chapters, for, as we saw in Chapter 4, groups of all kinds are the building blocks of society.

CHARACTERISTICS OF SOCIAL GROUPS

We sometimes group people together artificially in the process of analyzing society (e.g., all the teenagers in a particular community). This results in a **social category,** a collection of individuals who are grouped together because they share a trait deemed by the observer to be socially relevant (e.g., sex, race, or age). But there are also groups in which we actually participate and in which we have distinct roles and statuses. These are **social groups.** A social group is a set of two or more individuals who share a sense of common identity and belonging and who interact on a regular basis. Group members are recruited according to specific criteria of membership and are bound together by a set of membership rights and mutual obligations. Throughout this chapter, unless indicated otherwise, when we refer to groups we mean social groups.

Group identity, the sense of belonging to a group, means that members are aware of their participation in the group and know the identities of other members of the group. This also implies that group members have a sense of the boundaries of their group—that is, of who belongs and who does not belong. Groups themselves have a social structure that arises from repeated interaction among their members. In those interactions the members form ideas about the status of each and the role each can play in the group (Holy, 1985; Homans, 1950; Hare et al., 1994). A skilled member of a work group, for example, may become the leader while an unskilled member may become recognized as the person others instruct and send on errands.

Through their interactions, group members develop feelings of attachment to each other. Groups whose members have strong positive attachments to each other are said to be highly cohesive, while those whose members are not very strongly attached to each other are said to lack cohesion. Groups also develop norms governing behavior in the group, and they generally have goals such as performing a task, playing a game, or making public policy. Finally, because groups are composed of interacting human beings we must also recognize that all groups have the potential for conflict among their members; the resolution of such conflicts may be vital to continued group cohesion.

Membership criteria, awareness and boundaries, a clear social structure, cohesion, norms and goals, and the possibility of conflict are among the dimensions that define different groups. If we briefly compare two types of groups—say, a computer bulletin board and a married couple—the importance of these dimensions becomes apparent. Membership in the couple is exclusive and cohesion is based on intimacy and trust. If he comes home and says, "Honey, I brought a new woman into our relationship—I think you'll like her," she is likely to throw him out—unless they happen to come from a culture that practices polygyny, and even then the sudden introduction of a new woman into the household will disrupt the cohesion of the original marital group. Among members of the computer bulletin board, in contrast, the only criterion for membership may be ownership of the proper equipment and payment of dues. Not all the members will know each other, and new members can be added without any sense of reduced cohesion as would occur in the case of the married couple.

GROUP SIZE AND STRUCTURE

If one walks along a beach on a nice summer day, the variety of groups one sees is representative of the range of social groups in the larger society. Many of the groups on the beach are composed of family members. Others are friendship groups, usually consisting of young men and women of about the same age. Some of these are same-sex groups; others include both males and females. Then there are groups that form around activities like volleyball. Still other groups may be based on occupational ties; the lifeguards and their supervisors or the food service workers are examples of such groups.

Primary and Secondary Groups. The distinction we made in Chapter 4 between primary and secondary groups helps clarify some of the differences among the groups one encounters on a sunny beach or anywhere else in society. Charles Horton Cooley defined **primary groups** as "those characterized by intimate face-to-face association and cooperation. They are primary in several senses, but chiefly in that they are fundamental in forming the social nature and ideals of the individual" (1909, p. 25). Out on the beach, the family groups are, of course, examples of primary groups. So are the groups of friends one observes lying near each other on the sand. And among the food service workers or the lifeguards there are probably some smaller friendship groups or cliques within the larger occupational group.

The occupational groups serving the beachgoers are examples of **secondary groups** (a concept we also introduced in Chapter 4 but need to use again here). The concept of a secondary group follows from Cooley's definition of primary groups, although he did not actually use the term (Dewey, 1948). Secondary groups are characterized by relationships that involve few aspects of their members' personalities. In such groups the members' reasons for participation are usually limited to a small number of goals. The bonds of association in secondary groups are usually based on some form of contract, a written or unwritten agreement that specifies the scope of interaction within the group. All organizations and associations, including companies with employers and employees, are secondary groups.

Within most secondary groups one can usually find a number of primary groups based on regular interaction and friendship. Scottish clans and Native American tribes, for example, are secondary associations that link individuals together through a network of kin relations. But within the clan or tribe there are many primary groups, often composed of men or women of roughly the same age.

Group Size and Relationships. As the number of people in a group increases, the number of possible relationships among the group's members increases at a greater rate. When there are two people in the group, there is just one relationship. But when a third person is added there are three possible relationships (A–B, B–C, A–C). When a fourth person joins the group there are six possible relationships; a group of only six people includes fourteen possible relationships. Box 6.1 describes this phenomenon in more detail.

When a group has more than six members, the relationships among the members become so complex that the group is likely to break up into smaller groups, at least temporarily. One sees this quite frequently at parties or other

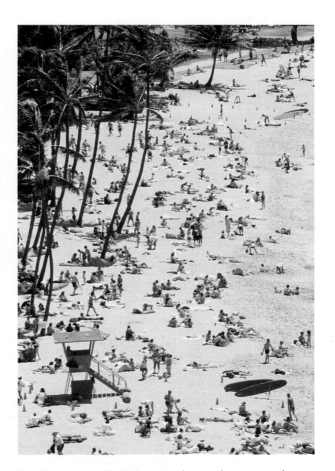

Beaches are excellent places to observe the way people group themselves in public. In this photo, note the way people cluster in primary groups and tend to leave as much space as possible between themselves and other groups.

BOX 6.1 SOCIOLOGICAL METHODS

Diagramming Group Structure

A variety of techniques, collectively known as *sociometry*, are used to study the structure of groups. The three most frequently used sociometric methods are basic group diagrams, diagrams that indicate the valence of group bonds, and sociograms, which chart individuals' preferences in groups.

At their simplest, group diagrams show the number of members in a group. Each member is represented by the same symbol, and the presence of a relationship between two members is shown by a line. The group diagrams in the figure labeled A show how the number of possible relationships increases geometrically as the number of members in the group increases arithmetically.

In a slightly more sophisticated type of diagram, a bond between group members is shown only if it actually exists in the group's interactions. Where there is no relationship between two members, no line is drawn between them. In a peer group it is usual for all the members to have a relationship, even if they do not all share the same strong feelings of friendship. But in work groups it is not uncommon for people to have relationships that are based on cooperation in carrying out specific tasks. If their work does not bring them together, they may not have any relationship at all.

Diagram B represents a group in a school where the third-grade (3G) and fourth-grade (4G) teachers who teach language arts are members of a committee convened by an assistant principal (AP). The diagram shows that three of

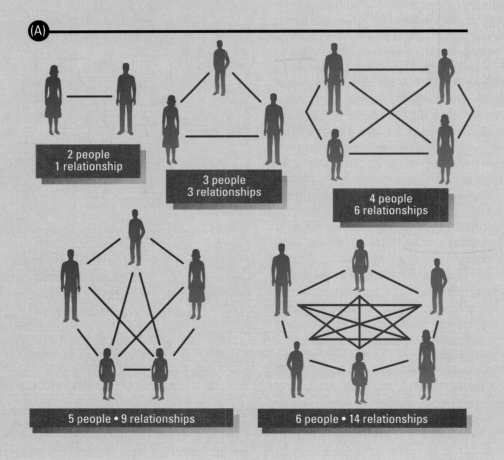

the teachers share relationships (either through cooperation in projects at work or through friendship), while the other teachers are linked to one another only through their work with the assistant principal.

Valence is the feeling that exists between any two people in a group. It refers to the value they place on their relationship. The most basic valence in a relationship is positive or negative—that is, like or dislike. In most friendship groups there is a balance of valences; otherwise the group will very likely break up. In diagram C, for example, Joe likes Dave and Marty and they reciprocate that liking, but Dave and Marty do not like each other. Joe must either convince the other two to like each other or choose between them.

the pressure is all on Marty. If Joe can show him that Dave likes him and if Dave continues to try to get along with him, the group is very likely to form a balanced triad, as shown in diagram E.

A difference in valence between two people can be indicated with a double line and two different signs. In diagram D, we see that Dave now likes Marty but Marty does not reciprocate. Perhaps he would like to have an exclusive relationship with Joe and views Marty as a threat. But now

In a larger group, such as a school classroom or a club, the members express their preferences for each other in many ways. They call each other to talk about the events of the day or week; they gossip about each other; they give each other advice or criticism. These preferences result in a structure of cliques that exists within the larger group. When social scientists wish to chart such a structure, they simply ask all the members of the group to list the three or four individuals in the group with whom they would most like to spend time. By indicating each choice with a line, the researchers create a diagram known as a sociogram. Diagram F is a simple sociogram showing preferences among nine boys and girls. It reveals, among other things, that there is a clique centering on Dave and another centering on Latasha.

social gatherings. Five or six people can carry on a conversation in which all participate. But as more people arrive the group tends to break up into several smaller groups of two, three, or four people. The difficulty of maintaining relationships as group size increases becomes greater when there are limited resources, such as seats in cars or at restaurants, and the group is forced to define the smaller groups that will interact more intimately. Intimacy and feelings of closeness to others decrease with group size.

The more possible relationships there are, the more likely it is that some of those relationships will be troubled by conflict and jealousy. In consequence, the larger the group, the more unstable it tends to be and the more likely it is to break up into smaller groups in which there are fewer possible relationships and a greater likelihood of positive bonds among all members. If a larger group devoted to specific goals is to maintain its cohesion in the face of the pressures created by primary attachments among its members, it will need a formal, agreed-upon structure of leaders and rules. Thus a group of friends who decide to meet regularly to play a favorite game (it could be golf, basketball, or any other activity) will find that as their numbers grow they need a formal structure—an elected or appointed leader, a calendar of events, a membership list, and written rules of conduct. In short, it will be transformed from a primary group into a secondary group or, more specifically, a formal organization.

Dyads and Triads. The basic principles of group structure and size were first described by the pioneering German sociologist Georg Simmel (1858–1918). Simmel perceived the need to study behavior in small and larger groups because groups are the basic units of life in all societies. Among his other contributions, he pointed out the significance of what he termed **dyads,** groups composed of only two people, and **triads,** groups composed of three people. He recognized that the strongest social bonds are formed between two people, be they best friends, lovers, or married couples. But he saw that dyads are also quite vulnerable to breakup, since if the single relationship on which it is based ends, the dyad ends as well.

When the dyadic bond is strong (and the two who share it often jealously guard their intimacy), the introduction of a new person into the group frequently causes problems. Conventional wisdom has much to say about this matter ("Two's a couple, three's a crowd"), and if one observes children's play groups it soon becomes clear that much of the conflict they experience has to do with the desire to have an exclusive relationship with a best friend. In families, too, the shift from a dyad to a triad often creates problems. A couple who are experiencing a high level of conflict may believe that a baby will offer them a challenge they can meet together, thereby renewing their love for each other. At first this may seem to be the case, but as the infant makes more demands on the couple's energy and time, the father may feel that the baby is depriving him of

attention from his wife, and he may become jealous of the newcomer. For some couples, the addition of a child can actually increase the chance of divorce—resulting in a stable mother–child dyad and a single male.

The instability of triads can also be seen among siblings. The third child often has a rough time of it. Not only is the third child "the baby" who imagines it impossible ever to perform as well as the older siblings, but he or she has committed the unintentional sin of breaking the bond between the two older children. Whenever one of the latter becomes intimate and loving toward "the baby," the other will demand attention and remind the third child that he or she is the newcomer. This point should not be exaggerated; sibling triads can be stable and happy. In general, however, the addition of a third child increases the possibility of conflict and coalitions within the family (Caplow, 1969; Deaux & Wrightsman, 1988).

COMMUNITIES

At a level of social organization between the primary group and the larger institutions of the nation-state are communities of all descriptions. **Communities** are sets of primary and secondary groups in which the individual carries out important life functions such as raising a family, earning a living, finding shelter, and the like. Communities may be either **territorial or nonterritorial.** Both include primary and secondary groups. In general, territorial communities are contained within geographic boundaries, whereas nonterritorial communities are networks of associations that form around shared goals. When people speak of a "professional community," such as the medical or legal community, they are referring to a nonterritorial community.

Territorial communities are populations that function within a particular geographic area, and this is by far the more common meaning of the term as it is used both in everyday speech and in social-scientific writing (Lowey, 1993; Suttles, 1972). Territorial communities are usually composed of one or more *neighborhoods*. The neighborhood level of group contact includes primary groups (particularly families and peer groups) that form attachments on the basis of proximity—that is, as a result of living near one another.

In studies of how people form friendship groups in suburban neighborhoods, both Herbert Gans (1976) and Bennett Berger (1968) found that proximity tended to explain patterns of primary-group formation better than any other variable except social class. Thus families that move into new suburban communities tend to find friends among others of the same social class who live near enough to allow ease of interaction and casual visiting; the same is true of students living in dorms on college campuses. On the international level, observers of the ethnic violence in Rwanda report that where members of the Hutu and Tutsi tribes live close to each other and cooperate in bringing in the harvest, they are far less likely to bear grudges and resort to violence than members of the same tribes who do not interact in their daily lives (Bonner, 1994).

That physical propinquity and social-class similarities explain how friendships form may seem self-evident to us. Moving into new neighborhoods or into dorms is a constant feature of life in a large urban society. But the idea that mere propinquity, rather than kinship or tribal membership, can explain patterns of association would shock many people in simpler agrarian societies, where mobility is not a fact of everyday life. As Robert Park noted, it is only under conditions of rapid and persistent social change that proximity helps explain why people form groups (Park, 1967/1926).

NETWORKS

In modern societies people form their deepest friendships in face-to-face groups, but these groups are, in turn, integrated into larger and more impersonal secondary-group structures that may extend well beyond the bounds of territorial communities. William F. Whyte opened *Street Corner Society* (1943), his study of street-corner peer groups, with this observation:

> The Nortons were Doc's gang. The group was brought together primarily by Doc, and it was built around Doc. When Doc was growing up, there was a kid's gang on Norton Street for every significant difference in age. There was a gang that averaged about three years older than Doc; there was Doc's gang, which included Nutsy, Danny, and a number of others; there was a group about three years younger, which included Joe Dodge and Frank Bonilli; and there was still a younger group, to which Carl and Tommy belonged. (p. 3)

Like the gangs Joan Moore studies in contemporary Los Angeles, the Nortons were active in a network of neighborhood-level peer groups. They would compete against other groups of boys of roughly the same age in a yearly round of baseball, bowling, and occasional interneighborhood fights (the latter occurring mainly in their younger teenage years). But the Nortons were also integrated into the community through some of its secondary associations. For example, at election time they were recruited by the local political party organization, and some were recruited by the racketeers who controlled their low-income neighborhood. Party organizations and organized-crime groups are examples of secondary associations that extend outside territorial communities.

In-Groups and Out-Groups. The "corner boys" studied by Whyte tended to be hostile toward similar groups from other street corners and even toward certain boys from their own territory. These distinctions between groups are common and are referred to as *in-group–out-group* distinctions. The **in-group** consists of one's own peers, whereas **out-groups** are those whom one considers to be outside the bounds of intimacy. Simmel observed that

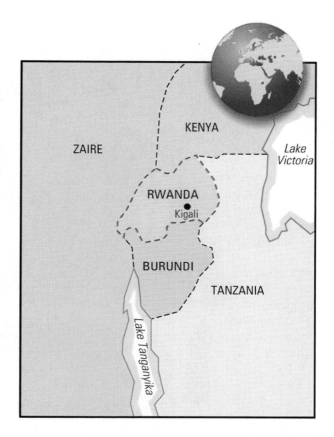

in-group–out-group distinctions can form around almost any quality, even one that many people would not consider meaningful at all. Thus, in a study of juvenile groups in a Chicago housing project, Gerald Suttles (1972) found that distinctions were made between boys who lived in lighter or darker brick buildings. Similarly, American children who have lived in foreign countries for several years may find themselves relegated to out-groups when they return to school in the United States (Smith, 1994).

In-group–out-group distinctions are usually based on such qualities as income, race, and religion. In "Cornerville," the community Whyte studied, group boundaries were based on educational background, particularly college versus noncollege education. One of Whyte's informants explained this distinction:

> In Cornerville the noncollege man has an inferiority complex. He hasn't had much education, and he has that feeling of inferiority. . . . Now the college man felt that way before he went to college, but when he is in college, he tries to throw it off. . . . Naturally, the noncollege man resents that. (Whyte, 1943, p. 79)

In-group–out-group distinctions often make it difficult for secondary associations to attract members from both groups. For example, when two ethnic or racial groups in a community make in-group–out-group distinctions, they

THEN AND NOW

CHANGING STYLES IN YOUTH GANGS

When Frederick Thrasher wrote his classic study of 1,313 Chicago gangs (1926), the city was undergoing explosive growth, especially due to immigration and migration from the rural midwest and south. Many of the street gangs evolved in poor immigrant neighborhoods as informal ethnic "turf defense" groups and athletic clubs. Thrasher described the boys in this "gang" photo, some of the Jersey Midgets, this way: "The gang is composed of about 30 boys, 11 to 14 years old, mostly Irish in nationality. It calls itself an athletic club." Later in the gang's development, the Midgets would probably become involved in some criminal activity and delinquency; still later, as the boys became young men, they would probably take some part in local politics.

Unlike the more strictly sex-segregated gangs of earlier periods, contemporary gangs are more likely to include young women, if not as members, then as "close associates." Modern gangs are less likely to begin as athletic clubs and more likely to form as ethnically homogeneous groups that graduate from turf defense to criminal activity, often in the violent milieu of the narcotics trade.

often find themselves drifting toward different political parties or forming distinct factions within the same party rather than uniting to find solutions to common problems.

Reference Groups.   An important area of sociological research is the study of how the decisions we make are influenced by significant or relevant others—that is, by people we admire and whose behavior we try to imitate. The ways in which other people influence our attitudes and behavior are often discussed in terms of the **reference group,** a group that the individual uses as a frame of reference for self-evaluation and attitude formation (Deaux & Wrightsman, 1988; Merton, 1968). Some reference groups set and enforce certain values and norms, while others serve as a standard for comparison (Hare, 1992).

An example of the influence of reference groups can be seen in a study of students at Bennington College conducted by Theodore Newcomb (1958). Newcomb found that conservative students often sought out groups of like-minded peers who would affirm the values they had brought with them from home. They also tended to go home for visits more often than liberal students did. By their senior year, however, they were likely to have shifted their attitudes to match those of a more liberal reference group, since the majority of the students and faculty at Bennington were liberal or radical.

The concept of reference groups has many practical applications. In market research, for example, it is common practice to determine where potential customers tend to seek help in forming their attitudes—which magazines, writers, or television commentators they turn to for guidance. These *opinion leaders,* as they are sometimes called, are the customer's reference group in a particular area of consumption (Katz, 1957).

Note that a reference group is not the same thing as a primary group. The friends with whom you spend much of your time are a primary group and are likely to act as a reference group as well. But we can have numerous reference groups, each of which influences us in different areas. As you choose a profession or career, you will be influenced by the values and norms of reference groups in that field. As you gain new statuses, such as that of parent, voter, or supervisor, you will look to other reference groups: child care experts, political commentators, and the like. A reference group thus can be quite limited in its relationship to you as an individual: Its influence may act on what you are to become rather than on what you are now.

Social Network Analysis.   The study of who people associate with, how those choices are made, and the effects of those choices on social structure and individual personality is known as *social network analysis.* The British social scientist Elizabeth Bott, one of the founders of this branch of sociology, describes a social network as follows:

> Each person is, as it were, in touch with a number of people, some of whom are directly in touch with each other and

some of whom are not. . . . I find it convenient to talk of a social field of this kind as a network. The image I have is of a set of points, some of which are joined by lines. The points of the image are people, or sometimes groups, and the lines indicate which people interact with each other. (1977, p. 256)

The diagrams in Box 6.1 illustrate social networks.

Social network analysis grew out of studies of the choices people make in becoming members of various social groups. Today network analysis extends beyond this rather narrow subject to studies illustrating how the interconnectedness of certain members of a society can produce interaction patterns that may have a lasting influence on the lives of people both within and outside the network (Cochran et al., 1990). Sociologist Aubrey Bonnett (1981), for example, studied *susus,* the rotating credit associations formed by West Indian ethnic groups in New York and other American cities. These associations are actually networks composed of numerous small groups of neighbors and kin who join with other similar groups, pay an entrance fee, and take turns borrowing funds from the association at far lower interest rates than a bank would charge. Bonnett showed that these associations bring together members of immigrant groups with different histories and values. As one *susu* organizer told him, "In my *susu* I have had members from all the islands. . . . You would be amazed to know how it has helped to get ourselves together, yes, this is really a West Indian thing" (p. 67).

Sociologists who study the rich and powerful have described the networks that provide the social contacts essential for success in entering and climbing upward in the corporate hierarchy. In their book *Preparing for Power,* for example, Peter Cookson and Caroline Persell (1985) describe how young men from elite social backgrounds develop strong attachments with others like them at prestigious prep schools such as those listed in Table 6.1. Through attendance at these schools, the children of the wealthy acquire a great deal of "cultural capital." All students gain some forms of cultural capital by mastering a range of academic and social skills, but prep school students acquire a special form of cultural capital that prepares them for life among the elite. They learn how to speak; how to behave at formal social gatherings; how to behave as a guest at a country home; what colleges, clubs, companies, and communities one should seek to enter; and what kind of spouse one should marry. In short, prep schools "integrate new brains with old wealth to revitalize the upper classes" (Cookson & Persell, 1985, p. 187).

Prep school students' social networks come into play when they apply to elite colleges, particularly Ivy League institutions like Harvard, Yale, and Princeton. Many of the administrators and admissions officers at the most prestigious colleges were former prep school students themselves and tend to show preference for applicants from those schools. Figure 6.1 shows that when graduates of

---

TABLE 6.1 The Most Socially Prestigious American Boarding Schools

SCHOOL	LOCATION	DATE OF FOUNDING
1. Phillips Academy	Andover, Mass.	1778
2. Phillips Exeter Academy	Exeter, N.H.	1783
3. Episcopal High School	Alexandria, Va.	1839
4. Hill School	Pottstown, Pa.	1851
5. St. Paul's School	Concord, N.H.	1856
6. St. Mark's School	Southborough, Mass.	1865
7. Lawrenceville School	Lawrenceville, N.J.	1883
8. Groton School	Groton, Mass.	1884
9. Woodbury Forest School	Woodberry Forest, Va.	1889
10. Taft School	Watertown, Conn.	1890
11. Hotchkiss School	Lakeville, Conn.	1892
12. Choate School	Wallingford, Conn.	1896
13. St. George's School	Newport, R.I.	1896
14. Middlesex School	Concord, Mass.	1901
15. Deerfield Academy	Deerfield, Mass.	1903
16. Kent School	Kent, Conn.	1906

Source: Baltzell, 1958.

FIGURE 6.1 Acceptance at Highly Selective Colleges, by Prep School Status and SAT Scores

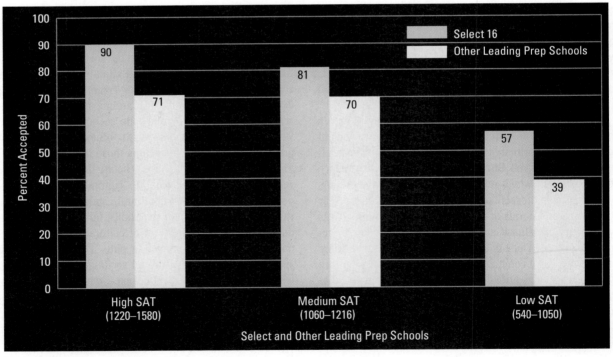

Source: Adapted from Cookson & Persell, 1985.

elite prep schools apply to the most competitive colleges, even those with low SAT scores are highly likely to gain admission. Later in life they will continue to benefit from the social bonds formed at prep school. As can be seen in Figure 6.2, business managers from upper-class backgrounds (those who are most likely to have attended elite prep schools) are more likely to become chief executive officers or to hold seats on the boards of major corporations than those from other social-class backgrounds.

In other research on social networks, sociologists have demonstrated how the networks of individuals and groups within which people interact provide social support in

FIGURE 6.2   **Achievement of High Corporate Position, by Manager's Class Background** [a]

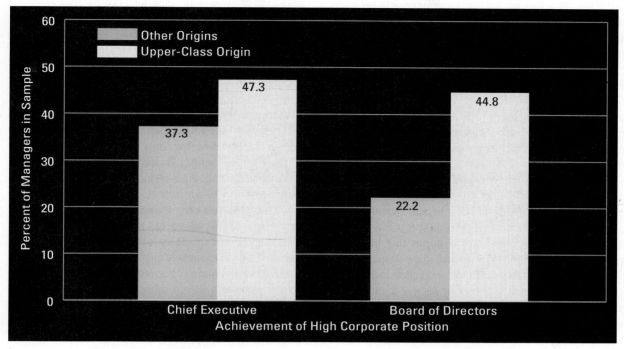

Source: Adapted from Cookson & Persell, 1985.

[a]Includes all college backgrounds.

times of stress or illness. Interestingly, this research often finds that people's social-support networks shrink as they become elderly and infirm and lose the ability to offer support or other resources in exchange (Fischer, 1982).

INTERACTION IN GROUPS

In the preceding section we discussed the basic building blocks of social structure, the primary group and the secondary group. We saw that these groups are embedded in more complex structures of groups, such as communities and social networks. We also saw how reference groups act to confirm an individual's values and behavior, and how the distinctions we make between in- and out-groups help us maintain the boundaries of the groups in which we participate. But these descriptions do not tell us what principles of interaction operate to produce cohesion or instability in groups. In this section, therefore, we take a closer look at interaction in groups.

Simply to observe that a society is a fabric of groups is to neglect two important questions: How can groups stay together in the first place, and how can a fabric of groups produce a cohesive society? Indeed, all around us we see evidence that groups constantly fall apart. Romantic ardor cools; marriages fail; friends argue and seek new friends; successful rock bands split up; businesses go bankrupt; entire nations are fragmented by social and economic up-

heavals. Certainly new groups are forming all the time, but others are continually breaking up.

When a group disintegrates we often hear explanations like "I felt that I was only giving and not getting"; "We started to grow in separate directions"; "I no longer shared their values"; or "He [she, they] wanted too much of the [credit, money, power]." In short, when one listens to explanations of why groups fail to stay together, it sounds as if people are continually seeking more rewards for themselves or blaming others for taking too much of whatever rewards are available—too much attention, affection, approval, prestige, money, power, or whatever. If this is the case, it does not seem likely that groups could have much cohesiveness or stability.

One can imagine even more serious effects of human greed and self-serving behavior. The seventeenth-century English philosopher Thomas Hobbes was deeply concerned about the relationship between the individual and society. How is society, or any group within it, possible if every individual puts his or her own interests above those of everyone else? Hobbes warned that the sum total of everyone's selfish acts would be a "war of all against all." In *Leviathan,* his monumental treatise on this problem, he concluded that humanity needs an all-powerful but benevolent dictator to prevent social chaos.

Today people throughout the world reject this notion. We strive to create a social order based on individual freedom, democracy, and the rule of law. Nevertheless, wherever we look we see major threats to such a social order.

Often such threats emerge when people feel that the groups they count on, such as political parties and legislatures, are not acting fairly. This brings us back to the question of how, given individual selfishness, humans can achieve order, cooperation, and trust in their associations rather than coercion, terror, and chaos.

PRINCIPLES OF INTERACTION

Social scientists have identified certain principles of interaction that help explain both stability and change in human groups. Among them are the pleasure principle, the rationality principle, the reciprocity principle, and the fairness principle.

The Pleasure Principle. People seek pleasure and avoid pain—although this basic principle implies nothing about what any particular person considers pleasurable or painful. As we will see shortly, this is a very personal matter that depends on the norms that have been internalized by the individual. In fact, many people seem to find pain or discomfort desirable; examples include athletes and dieters, who seek pain or deprive themselves of pleasure in order to experience the thrill of athletic victory or the satisfaction of wearing a smaller size.

The pleasure principle does not address the question of what people value; all it states is that once one knows what kind of pleasure one wants, one will seek more of it and less of other values that yield less personal pleasure (Bentham, 1789; Homans, 1961). When applied to behavior in groups, the pleasure principle simply means that over time people will continue to interact in a group in which they experience the pleasure of reward but will withdraw from groups in which the pain they experience outweighs their pleasure.

The Rationality Principle. In social life, a gain in pleasure may require some pain as well. For example, when two members of a group of friends become very close and find pleasure in their intimacy, the others may feel left out, and this causes some pain both to the two intimate friends and to those who feel left out. In larger groups, when a rule such as a ban on smoking is made, some members will derive more pleasure than others from the cleaner air. Those whose smoking pleasure is denied will experience an increase in pain. Whether consciously or not, people in groups calculate whether they think they will benefit personally from continued interactions with others in the group. Thus the smokers may decide that their loss of pleasure outweighs the gains they get by being in the group, and they may decide to withdraw. In the small friendship group, the other friends may feel that the pain of their jealousy outweighs the pleasure of their friendship with the intimate pair, and they may exclude them from the group.

The rationality principle means that people change their behavior according to whether they think they will be worse or better off as a consequence. In other words, in making decisions about their interactions with others, people tend to make rough calculations of costs and benefits.

Does the idea that people seek a net gain from their interactions mean that they are greedy or self-centered or lacking in motives other than materialism? Not at all. Of course, there are extremes: Hedonists are people who can enjoy only the pleasures of the body. Egotists are people who especially enjoy praise and have little capacity for giving to others. Altruists are people who enjoy giving to others, often at the expense of other pleasures. But most people strive to behave in ways that give them physical pleasure and ego gratification ("boosts" or "strokes") and also give them the satisfaction of helping others. How far they go in either direction depends on what other members of the group are doing (how giving others are, how selfish, how self-sacrificing, etc.)—which brings us to the principle of reciprocity in interaction.

The Reciprocity Principle. In group interactions people usually adhere to a norm stating that what others do for you, you should try to do for others. This is one of the world's most commonly followed rules of interaction; it is known as the norm of reciprocity (Homans, 1950). The Roman statesman Cicero recognized this principle when he wrote, "There is no duty more indispensable than that of returning a kindness. All men distrust one forgetful of a benefit." But it is not necessary to go back to ancient Rome for evidence that reciprocity is vital to continuing group interaction. Suppose that you and two classmates meet at a local pub. You pick up the check, and the other two agree to do so on future occasions. The next time, one of them pays the check. The third time, the third friend pleads a lack of cash and you each end up paying your own share. You and your second friend will feel that this is an embarrassing lapse on the part of your third friend. If such behavior continues, you will feel that the third friend takes more than he or she gives or thinks his or her company is worth the extra money paid by you. It is unlikely that this threesome will stay together very long if such imbalances continue.

Under what conditions could such a group continue in spite of the third friend's violation of the norm of reciprocity? One condition involves a loss of prestige for the third friend. You might ask him or her to make up the debt by doing something else for you. In that case the third friend takes a subordinate position in the group, doing your bidding to make up for the inability to reciprocate on an equal basis (Homans, 1961; Mauss, 1966/1925). On the other hand, suppose that the nonreciprocator is a movie star or a powerful politician. Then the other two members of the threesome might continue to pay in the hope that the third member would continue to spend his or her valuable time with them and that there would be an even greater reward for them in the future. This kind of relationship is quite common in social life. Social climbers seek ways to flatter and please someone who can confer prestige on them. Power seekers do the same in order to gain positions in which they will have power over others. A suitor may forgo reciprocity for quite a while in the hope of eventual conquest. In these situations and others like them, the participants in the interaction have an intuitive sense of what they are giving and what they are receiving or hope to receive in the future.

In the Bible the norm of reciprocity is stated in the form of the Golden Rule. "Do unto others as you would have others do unto you" in effect urges individuals to go beyond expectations of immediate reciprocity and set examples of higher moral behavior in the hope that others will follow them. In real life, however, people tend to prefer that their gains be as immediate as possible.

The Fairness Principle. We see ample evidence that people tend to expect certain kinds of treatment from others and that they tend to become angry when they do not receive it, especially when they themselves feel that they have done what is expected of them in the situation. We want the rules to apply equally to everyone in the game, be it a friendly game of pool or the more complex game of corporate strategy. When we are not rewarded in the same ways as others, we say that we are being treated unfairly.

The unfair condition in which a person or group has come to expect certain rewards for certain efforts, yet does not get them while others do, is called *relative deprivation.* In times of economic depression, for example, all groups in society must make do with less, and all feel deprived in comparison to their previous condition. If the economy begins to improve and some groups begin to get higher wages or more profits while others experience only limited improvement, members of the less successful group will feel deprived relative to others and will very likely become angry even though their own plight has actually improved somewhat (Merton & Kitt, 1950). The concept of relative deprivation is useful in explaining some aspects of group behavior and appears again in Chapter 8 when we discuss how major social changes like revolutions occur.

People's ideas about what is fair in their interactions with others often conflict with simple calculations of gain and loss. The fact that they might come out ahead in an interaction does not guarantee that they will feel good about it and continue the interaction. This was demonstrated in a series of studies by Daniel Kahneman and his associates (1986). A large number of respondents were asked to judge the fairness of this situation:

> A landlord rents out a small house. When the lease is due for renewal, the landlord learns that the tenant has taken a job very close to the house and is therefore unlikely to move. The landlord raises the rent $40 more than he was planning to.

An economist might argue that the tenant should think of the situation in terms of whether the rent increase is offset by the savings in the cost of travel to work (in terms of money, time, convenience, etc.). If the tenant still comes out ahead, it will make sense to sign the new lease (the rationality principle). But more than 90 percent of the respondents in Kahneman's survey said that the landlord was

being unfair. In real life, when people feel that a transaction like this is unfair they often end the interaction, even at some cost to themselves. In this case people intuitively felt that the landlord was unfairly taking advantage of a gain made by the tenant (the new job) without adding anything to the property to earn the right to raise the rent.

The pure-rationality model of behavior predicts that people will act in their own interests so as to maximize their profit. If we were simple profit takers, however, our feelings about fairness would not play such a strong part in explaining group interaction (Frank, 1988). But in fact these feelings are very powerful. Kahneman and his associates examined the strength of these feelings in an experiment in which they asked subjects to divide $20 with another player whom they could not see but were told was in the room. Only two choices were given: to give $10 to each player or to keep $18 and give the other player $2. Out of 161 subjects, 122—76 percent—offered the even split. From this the experimenters concluded that most people are motivated by their own ideas of fairness, presumably as a result of socialization over many years.

In real life, there are many examples of situations in which notions of fairness outweigh the principle of rationality. Barbers and beauticians do not charge more for haircuts on Saturday, nor do ski resorts usually charge more for lift tickets on holidays. Although they might like to profit from the higher demand at those times, they are afraid that people would regard the higher prices as unfair (Frank, 1988). On the other hand, there are many instances in which services are offered at higher rates during peak seasons or bargain offers such as early-bird specials or off-peak fares are used to encourage people to accept services at times other than those they might prefer.

Applications of the fairness principle can be seen in a great many group situations. In the famous study conducted by Elton Mayo and his associates at Western Electric's Hawthorne plant (see Chapter 2), the observers often noticed that workers used various forms of joking and sarcastic teasing to enforce the group's norms. They had a strong sense of what amount of work they should turn out, both individually and as a group, in order to merit their pay: a fair day's work for a fair day's pay. In the Bank Wiring Room, where workers hand-wired electrical circuits, it was common to see the members of a work group gang up and in a joking way hit a fellow worker on the shoulder when he produced more than the other members of the group. This practice was called "binging." A worker was binged by his coworkers if he produced too much in a day or if he did not produce enough, according to their definition of a fair day's work.

The Hawthorne researchers quickly realized that binging was part of the work group's culture. That culture—the group's norms of conduct and the ways in which its members interpreted those norms—was unique to that group and applied only when the group was at work. The culture of this work group had evolved over many years, its norms functioning to control the workers' responses to the demands of the company's managers. Thus, in a later analysis of the Bank Wiring Room observations, George Homans (1951) made the following comments:

> [The workers] shared a common body of sentiments. A person should not turn out too much work. If he did, he was a "rate-buster." The theory was that if an excessive amount of work was turned out, the management would lower the piecework rate so that the employees would be in the position of doing more work for approximately the same pay. On the other hand, a person should not turn out too little work. If he did he was a "chiseler"; that is, he was getting paid for work he did not do. (p. 235)

THE ECONOMIC PERSON VERSUS THE SOCIAL PERSON

The four basic principles of interaction in groups—pleasure, rationality, reciprocity, and fairness—contain some obvious (and fortunate) contradictions. People calculate their individual gain and loss in interactions; they act according to their own interests in many situations. Does this mean that people will always act selfishly? Not always, for we have seen that people also have deeply ingrained notions of reciprocity and fairness, which often prompt them to act in favor of the needs of the group or of society as a whole. Indeed, many situations that arise in the social world demonstrate the Hobbesian nightmare that would be created in a society whose members always acted in what they perceive as their self-interest.

Consider this example. It's the Friday evening rush hour. The streets downtown are crowded with cars, their drivers eager to get home. Although the light is about to turn red, some drivers move their cars into the intersection. They expect the traffic ahead of them to move forward so that they will be clear of oncoming traffic from the cross street. But alas, the traffic ahead does not move and the intersection is blocked. Now the cars on the cross street have a green light, but they cannot move. Fearing that they will miss their first opportunity to move, and amid much horn blowing and gnashing of teeth, some of these drivers also squeeze into the intersection. This chaotic and frustrating situation is known as gridlock. It is the result of a number of drivers acting in what they perceive as their own interests and not thinking about the needs of all the drivers as a group. The gridlock example is one among a great many that could be cited in which it is actually advantageous for individuals to behave in a prosocial manner rather than to maximize what they perceive as their immediate advantage (Shotland, 1985).

In many situations, however, there is serious conflict over what the best use of resources might be. Questions about who should have access to good medical care, quality education, or a safe and healthy environment involve considerations of individual gain versus the public good. It is not only because of the human tendency toward selfishness

that such conflict arises. Often there are disagreements about what different groups or classes of individuals *deserve*. We will come back often to this issue—when we discuss social inequalities, for example, and when we look at the problems involved in increasing equality of opportunity in modern societies.

COMMUNICATION AND BEHAVIOR IN GROUPS

"Human interaction," Herbert Blumer observed, "is mediated by the use of symbols, by interpretations, or by ascertaining the meaning of one another's actions" (1969b, pp. 179–180). By "mediated" Blumer meant that we do not normally respond directly to the actions of another person. Instead, we react to our own interpretations of those actions. When we see other drivers moving into an intersection against the light, for example, we begin to feel that everyone is out for themselves and we would be fools to hold back. These interpretations are made in the interval between the stimulus (the other person's action) and the response (our own action). Thus, in the account at the beginning of the chapter, the gang member must decide whether her honor is being attacked or, perhaps more important, whether her gang sisters and family members will demand that she defend her honor. Her decision to fight or not to fight will be guided by her interpretation and by her need to gain standing in the eyes of her peers.

What factors explain how people decide how to act and whether they should act for their own benefit or according to some notion of what is good for society? This question has been the subject of much research in the social sciences. Let us therefore take a brief look at some research on how people define their needs in social situations.

Definitions of the Situation. "Situations we define as real, are real in their consequences" stated W. I. Thomas (1971/1921), a pioneer in the study of social interaction. By this he meant that our understandings or definitions of what is occurring around us—whether they are correct or not—guide our subsequent actions. Thus, in a study of how dying patients are treated by medical groups in hospital emergency rooms, David Sudnow (1967) found that when a patient was brought in with no heartbeat, the person's age had a great deal to do with what happened next. The arrival of a younger patient who seemed to be dying would produce a frenzy of attempts to restart the heart. At times the entire group of medical personnel would become involved. But an old person with no heartbeat was far more likely to be pronounced dead on arrival, with little or no mobilization of the medical group. The patient's aged appearance caused the members of the group to define the situation as one in which urgent and heroic efforts were not required.

In another study of medical groups, Charles Bosk (1979) found that surgeons developed subtle techniques for covering up the mistakes of residents in training, depending on how a particular situation was defined. They

Lines, like this one at a movie location where people are waiting to be hired as extras, are governed by the norm "first come, first served." However, people in a line may allow this norm to be violated in some instances. Conflicts arise when people disagree over what kinds of violations are permissible.

would invoke those techniques when they believed a mistake was due to lack of knowledge. But mistakes they believed to be caused by carelessness would often be exposed. The guilty resident would be held up to public scorn, often at a high cost to the new surgeon's status among other doctors.

Both of the foregoing studies began by questioning how definitions of the situation account for the ways in which people interact. The emergency room teams that Sudnow observed were performing an unofficial cost–benefit analysis in deciding when to apply heroic measures to heart attack victims. The surgeons in Bosk's study were resolving a conflict between their teaching and medical functions: Young surgeons need to learn and practice, but patients need to receive the best possible care. The surgeon in training needs to maintain a good reputation among other doctors and nurses, even if he or she makes mistakes. Such conflicts are resolved by norms that define the legitimacy of mistakes in different situations. The subtle cues that define each situation are communicated through phrases, gestures, and other symbolic behavior, as well as through explicit evaluations of what was good and bad about a particular operation.

Ethnomethodology.   Studies based on this interactionist perspective use a variety of techniques. One of these is **ethnomethodology, the study of the underlying rules of behavior that guide group interaction.** This approach was used by Harold Garfinkel (1967) in studying how we use verbal formulas to create a flow of communication that we feel is normal and that we can understand. Garfinkel asked his students to engage in conversations with friends and family members in which they violated

some of the simple norms that most people follow in carrying on a conversation. Here is an example:

> VICTIM [*waving cheerily*]: How are you?
>
> STUDENT: How am I in regard to what? My health, my finances, my schoolwork, my peace of mind, my . . . ?
>
> VICTIM [*red in the face and suddenly out of control*]: Look! I was just trying to be polite. Frankly, I don't give a damn how you are. (Garfinkel, 1967, p. 44)

As this brief example shows, when the norms of spoken interaction that "entitle" us to continue or maintain a conversation are violated, the conversation often cannot continue because there is no longer a mutual area of interaction within which both parties tacitly agree to make sense.

The Dramaturgical Approach.   Another technique used in research on interaction in groups is the **dramaturgical approach.** This approach is based on the recognition that much social interaction depends on how we wish to impress those who may be watching us. For example, Erving Goffman (1965) observed that people change their facial expressions just before entering a room in which they expect to find others who will greet them. Couples who are fighting when they are "backstage" often present themselves as models of friendship when they are "frontstage"—that is, when they are in the presence of other people. And many social environments, such as hotels, restaurants, and funeral parlors, are explicitly set up with a front and a back "stage" so that the public is spared the noisy and sometimes conflicted interaction occurring "behind the scenes." Using these and other strategies to "set a stage" for our own purposes is known as **impression management.**

In a well-known study that applied this "dramaturgical" view of group interaction, James Henslin and Mae Briggs (1971) drew upon Briggs's extensive experience as a gynecological nurse. Their research showed how doctors and nurses play roles that define the situation of a pelvic examination as unembarrassing and attempt to save each participant's "face" or self-image. According to Henslin and Briggs, the pelvic examination is carried out in a series of scenes. First the doctor and the patient discuss the patient's condition. If the doctor decides that the patient needs a pelvic examination, the doctor will leave the room; this is the end of Scene 1. In Scene 2 the nurse enters. Her role is to work with the patient to create a situation in which the body of the patient is hidden behind sheets and her depersonalized pelvic area is exposed for clinical inspection. Through these preparations the patient becomes symbolically distanced from the doctor, allowing the next scene, the pelvic examination itself, to be desexualized. The props, the stage setting (the examining room), and the language used help define the situation as a nonsexual encounter, thereby saving everyone involved from embarrassment.

Altruism and the Bystander Effect.   Intentional efforts to set a stage for purposes of impression management are common in hospitals, restaurants, and many other social settings where patterns of behavior are predictable and regular. But in other public settings, especially streets, parks, and public transportation, people often try to hide behind their anonymity. They shy away from behavior that will be noticed, as illustrated in the following example of the *bystander effect.*

Late one night in 1964, Kitty Genovese was returning home from a social gathering when she was attacked by a man who had been following her. He caught up with her in front of a bookstore in the shadow of her apartment building. As she screamed for help, he stabbed her in the chest. Lights went on in some of the apartments, but no one intervened or called the police. One neighbor shouted from a window: "Let that girl alone." The stalker retreated and waited, and when the neighbor no longer seemed to be watching he resumed his attack. He stabbed and raped the young woman in a stairwell of her apartment house, but the police did not receive a call for help from any of her neighbors until thirty minutes after she had first cried out. Interviewed later, the neighbors said things like "I was tired" or "I assumed others were helping" or "Frankly, we were afraid."

This incident is often cited to illustrate the callousness and indifference of urban dwellers (Frank, 1988). It might seem from this and similar incidents that when faced with danger and other costs of helping (e.g., time in court, dealing with the police, loss of time from work) people make fairly selfish calculations of gain and loss. But what about all the unselfish acts of heroism one reads

about? Victims are dragged from fires and submerged cars and broken ice by self-sacrificing civilians, many of whom die in their efforts to help others. Did Kitty Genovese simply have a bad group of neighbors? Empirical evidence suggests that the situation is more complicated than that.

Studies by Bibb Latané and John Darley (1970) have shown under many experimental conditions that bystanders are likely to offer help to victims. But their research also shows that the presence of other people who do not help increases the chances that no one will help. In one simple experiment, a graduate student begins interviewing the subject. The interviewer excuses himself or herself for a moment and enters an adjacent room. Suddenly the waiting subject hears cries for help: "Oh my God, my foot . . . I . . . I can't get this thing off!" In about 70 percent of the trials, the subject rushes into the room and offers help. But when there is another person in the first room who just sits there and seems to be associated with the experimenter in some way, only 7 percent of the subjects intervene to help the "victim."

In the experiment just described, the helper can see that no one else has offered help. In the Kitty Genovese case, on the other hand, people could conveniently assume that others must be helping. The point is that when responsibility seems to be diffused rather than falling on a particular individual, people are more likely to avoid helping others. But when people cannot avoid defining the situation as involving them, they are likely to throw the rationality principle to the winds and intervene altruistically despite the potential costs to themselves (Deaux & Wrightsman, 1988; Rushton, 1980).

INTERACTION AND GROUP STRUCTURE

The examples just discussed involve decisions and strategies that individuals use in deciding whether to behave more selfishly or more altruistically in a given situation. But as members of groups we often explain our actions on the basis of our status in the group rather than on the basis of our individual expectations. "I must do this because I'm expected to lead," we might say, or "I can't decide that without talking to the others and especially to [the group's leader]." These explanations suggest that the structure of groups is a major factor in explaining behavior. But the basic principles of interaction—pleasure seeking, rationality, reciprocity, and fairness—can be used to explain the emergence of group structure in the first place.

Six college students of the same sex are hired to participate in a small-group experiment. All are unknown to one another before the experiment. The specific task they are asked to perform is of little importance except that it must involve all the members of the group in a cooperative effort and must not be so difficult that they become frustrated or so easy that they become bored.

Initially the group has no structure. All the subjects are peers, and all have come for the same reason: to earn some money for participating in the experiment. There are no

TABLE 6.2   Aggregate Matrix for 18 Sessions of Six-Man Groups

		INITIATED TO INDIVIDUALS						TOTAL TO INDIVIDUALS	TO GROUP AS WHOLE	TOTAL INITIATED
		1	2	3	4	5	6			
FROM INDIVIDUALS	1		1,238	961	545	445	317	3,506	5,661	9,167
	2	1,748		443	310	175	102	2,778	1,211	3,989
	3	1,371	415		305	125	69	2,285	742	3,027
	4	952	310	282		83	49	1,676	676	2,352
	5	662	224	144	83		28	1,141	443	1,584
	6	470	126	114	65	44		819	373	1,192
	Total Received	5,203	2,313	1,944	1,306	872	565	12,205	9,106	21,311

Source: *Social Behavior,* by George Caspar Homans. Copyright © 1961 by Harcourt Brace Jovanovich, Inc. Reprinted by permission of the publisher.

Note: Differences between the total number of interactions initiated and the number received are due to the fact that some utterances are answered indirectly by means of utterances directed at the entire group. The diagonal cells are empty because the experiments did not count utterances by a subject to himself.

predetermined statuses or roles. The students listen to a description of what they are to do and then are left alone to get the work under way. Actually they are being observed through a one-way mirror, and all their interactions are being recorded and counted.

Table 6.2 summarizes (or *aggregates*) the data obtained by counting all the interactions—including small utterances like "Oh" and "I see"—occurring in a group of six male subjects meeting for 18 one-hour sessions. This table shows who initiated each interaction and to whom it was directed, including interactions directed toward the group as a whole. The participants are ranked from high to low on this variable (i.e., initiating an interaction). Thus subject 1 spoke 1,238 times to subject 2, spoke 961 times to subject 3, and so on (Homans, 1961). Subject 1 initiated 3,506 utterances to specific individuals (e.g., "Why don't you . . . ?") and 5,661 utterances to the group as a whole (e.g., "Why don't we . . . ?"), for a total of 9,167 utterances over all the sessions—more than any of the other participants. You can see that subject 6 spoke only about one ninth as often as subject 1 and that most of what he said was directed to subject 1 (470 utterances). In fact, subject 1 received the most interaction from all the other participants, illustrating that people who initiate interactions are more likely to receive them. In later interviews the experimenters also found that subject 1 was the most respected member of the group.

What makes the person who initiates and receives the most communications the most respected member of the group? The reasons vary with the specific tasks the group is performing, but if we assume competence at those tasks, usually the person at the center of the communication is spending a lot of time helping others as well as helping the group accomplish its goals. That person not only is concerned with his or her own performance (the rationality

principle) but also takes pleasure in helping the others— giving approval, voicing criticism, making suggestions, and so on (the pleasure principle). In exchange for this help, the other members of the group give approval, respect, and allegiance to the central individual (the reciprocity principle).

Is the person who initiates the most interactions respected simply because he or she talks a lot? Common sense tells us that this is far from true. People who talk a lot but have little to contribute soon find that no one is paying attention to them. Their rate of interaction then drops sharply. Table 6-2 cannot show such changes in interaction patterns, but they are frequently observed in small-group studies. Other patterns have also been identified. Robert F. Bales and Philip Slater (1955), for example, observed that the person who initiated the most interactions—both in getting tasks done and in supporting the suggestions of others—often came to be thought of as a leader. The group began to orient itself toward that person and to expect leadership from him or her. A second member of the group, usually the one who initiated the second-highest number of interactions, was often the best-liked person in the group.

Bales and his colleagues concluded that groups often develop both a "task leader" (or instrumental leader) and another leader, whom they called a "socioemotional leader" (or expressive leader). The former tends to adhere quite strictly to group norms and to take the lead in urging everyone to get the work done. But this often leaves other members with ruffled feelings. The socioemotional leader is the person who eases the group over rough spots with jokes, encouragement, and attention to the group's emotional climate. Thus most classes have a class clown whose antics help release the tension of test situations, and most teams have a respected member who can also joke around and get people to relax under pressure. At times these roles are performed by the same person, but generally as the group settles into a given task there is an informal division of labor between the two kinds of leaders.

Recall the Bank Wiring Room observations mentioned earlier. The workers at the equipment wiring tables are an example of small-group structure. Their leader was the person who could turn out the most work in the shortest time and could also help the others do their work. The workers with higher status in the group were those who showed greater competence at their jobs and stronger allegiance to the norms of the group. Newer workers with lesser skills and less shared experience with the others were spoken to less and were less central to the group's interactions. Over time, as these workers were "binged" for producing too little or too much, the other workers would see how they handled the criticism and would form opinions of them accordingly.

One of the most striking aspects of the Hawthorne studies is that they revealed how norms about fairness in the work group are enforced through a particular kind of joking ritual (binging). But why are workers binged when they produce too much? That behavior points to the conflict between the norms of the small work group (which are based on fairness) and those of the larger corporation in which the group is embedded (which are based on rationality). The company would like to obtain greater productivity from the workers, but the workers have their own ideas about what is fair and their own ways of enforcing the group norm.

This example brings us to the principle that as group size increases, or as the number of groups in an organization increases, the leaders of the larger organization must invest in ways of controlling the behavior of groups within it (Hechter, 1987). Frequently this investment takes the form of agents of control such as foremen, accountants, inspectors, and the like. These roles become part of the formal structure known as bureaucracy.

FORMAL ORGANIZATIONS AND BUREAUCRACY

Informal organizations are groups whose norms and statuses are generally agreed upon but are not set down in writing. The Bank Wiring Room observations are a classic example of the dynamics of informal organizations. The members of the work groups in the wiring room followed group norms that limited their output. Usually such groups have leaders who help create and enforce the group's norms but have no formal leadership position in the company.

Formal organizations have explicit (often written) sets of norms, statuses, and roles that specify each member's relationships to the others and the conditions under which those relationships hold. Organization charts and job descriptions are typical of such organizations. Formal organizations take a wide variety of forms. For example, the New England town meeting is composed of residents of a town who gather to debate and discuss any issues the members wish to raise. The tenants' association of an urban apartment building is also composed of people who reside in a specific place, but its scope of action is usually limited to housing issues. Both of these are formal organizations, since there are rules defining who may participate and the scope and manner of that participation. As is true in many formal organizations, the members of town meetings and tenants' associations try to arrive at decisions through some form of democratic process—that is, by adhering to norms that allow the majority to run the organization but not to infringe on the rights of the minority.

A familiar type of formal organization is the **voluntary association.** People join groups like the PTA or the Rotary Club to pursue interests that they share with other members of the group. Voluntary associations are usually democratically run, at least in principle, and have rules and regulations and an administrative staff. Churches, fraternal organizations, political clubs, and neighborhood improvement groups are examples of voluntary associations often found in American communities. Sociologists study these associations in order to understand how well or poorly people are integrated into their society.

The rate of participation in voluntary associations has increased during the past few decades. In his review of research on association membership, Morris Janowitz (1978) concluded that "the long-term trend appears to be one of increasing levels of such participation" (p. 314). In 1946 Mirra Komarovsky found that more than half of her sample of 2,200 urban residents did not belong to any associations. In the 1960s, surveys showed a dramatic increase in association membership, and by the 1970s research results indicated that the majority of household members belonged to at least one voluntary association. And contrary to the hypothesis that inner-city residents are less likely to be active in organizations, Claude Fischer's (1982) studies of organization membership showed that city dwellers belong to an average of two groups while people living on the semirural fringe are, on the average, members of fewer than two groups.

Bureaucracies are another common type of formal organization. A **bureaucracy** is a specific structure of statuses and roles in which the power to influence the actions of others increases as one nears the top of the organization; this is in marked contrast to the democratic procedures used in other kinds of organizations. Voluntary associations, for example, usually have some of the elements of bureaucracies, but they are run as democratic structures in which power is based on majority rule rather than on executive orders as is the case in pure bureaucracies like General Motors or the U.S. Army.

We owe much of our understanding of bureaucracies to the work of Max Weber, who identified the following typical aspects of most bureaucratic organizations:

1. *Positions with clearly defined responsibilities:* "The regular activities required for the purposes of the organization are distributed in a fixed way as official duties."

2. *Positions ordered in a hierarchy:* The organization of offices "follows the principle of hierarchy; that is, each lower office is under the control and supervision of a higher one."

3. *Rules and precedents:* The functioning of the bureaucracy is governed "by a consistent system of abstract rules" and the "application of these rules to specific cases."

4. *Impersonality and impartiality:* "The ideal official conducts his office . . . in a spirit of formalistic impersonality . . . without hatred or passion, and hence without affection or enthusiasm."

5. *A career ladder:* Work in a bureaucracy "constitutes a career. There is a system of 'promotions' according to seniority, or to achievement, or both."

6. *The norm of efficiency:* "The purely bureaucratic type of administrative organization . . . is from a purely technical point of view, capable of attaining the highest degree of efficiency" (Weber, 1958/1922). (See the study chart below.)

Weber believed that bureaucracy made human social life more "rational" than it had ever been in the past. Rules, impersonality, and the norm of efficiency are some of the ways in which bureaucracies "rationalize" human societies. By this Weber meant that society becomes dominated by groups organized so that the interactions of their members will maximize the group's efficiency. Once the group's goals have been set, the officials in a bureaucracy can seek the most efficient means of reaching those goals. All the less rational behaviors of human groups, such as magic and ritual, are avoided by groups organized as bureaucracies. But the people in a bureaucracy may not take full responsibility for their actions. For this and other reasons, therefore, Weber had some misgivings about the consequences of the increasing dominance of bureaucratic groups in modern societies.

STUDY CHART Characteristics of Bureaucracy

CHARACTERISTIC	EXAMPLE
Positions Clearly Defined	Job or position descriptions detail the responsibilities of each job, avoiding confusion about the duties of each jobholder.
Positions Ordered in a Hierarchy	Positions in the company or agency are ranked from top to bottom so that each position reports to another and supervisory responsibilities are clear.
Rules and Precedents	"The way we do things" in an organization is often written down, becoming "the book" of rules to be followed by its members.
Impersonality and Impartiality	At least in principle, actual performance on the job, rather than personal likes or favors, determines each individual's performance rating.
Career Ladder	New jobs are posted so that employees have a chance to move up in the organization on the basis of achievement, seniority, or both.
Norm of Efficiency	The company continually seeks to increase its efficiency by increasing productivity per employee; this can lead to layoffs or downsizing.

TABLE 6.3	Maximum Shocks Administered in Four Variants of Milgram's Experiment				
SHOCK LEVEL	**VERBAL DESIGNATION AND VOLTAGE LEVEL**	**1 REMOTE** ($n = 40$)	**2 VOICE FEEDBACK** ($n = 40$)	**3 PROXIMITY** ($n = 40$)	**4 TOUCH PROXIMITY** ($n = 40$)
	Slight Shock				
1	15				
2	30				
3	45				
4	60				
	Moderate Shock				
5	75				
6	90				
7	105			1	
8	120				
	Strong Shock				
9	135		1		1
10	150		5	10	16
11	165		1		
12	180		1	2	3
	Very Strong Shock				
13	195				
14	210				1
15	225			1	1
16	240				
	Intense Shock				
17	255				1
18	270			1	
19	285	5*	1		1
20	300		1	5	1
	Extreme Intensity Shock				
21	315	4	3	3	2
22	330	2			
23	345	1	1		1
24	360	1	1		
	Danger: Severe Shock				
25	375	1		1	
26	390				
27	405				
28	420				
	XXX				
29	435				
30	450	26	25	16	12
	Mean maximum shock level	27.0	24.53	20.80	17.88
	Obedient subjects (%)	65.0	62.5	40.0	30.0

*Indicates that in Experiment 1, five subjects administered shock of 300 volts.

Source: *Obedience to Authority*, by Stanley Milgram. Copyright © 1974 by Stanley Milgram. Reprinted by permission of Harper & Row Publishers, Inc.

The four variants of Milgram's experiment differed in terms of the degree of proximity between the "teacher" and the "learner." The variants were: (1) remote (different rooms, in which the learner could be seen but not heard); (2) voice feedback (different rooms, in which the learner could be seen and heard); (3) proximity (both in the same room); and (4) touch proximity (both in the same room, in which the teacher was told to force the learner's hand onto the electrode).

BUREAUCRACY AND OBEDIENCE TO AUTHORITY

In Chapter 2 we discussed the experiments on conformity conducted by Solomon Asch. Asch's demonstration of the power of group pressure raised serious questions about most people's ability to resist such pressure. It also led to many other studies of conformity. None of those studies is more powerful in its implications and disturbing in its methods than the series of experiments on obedience to authority conducted by Stanley Milgram.

Milgram's study was designed to "take a close look at the act of obeying." As Milgram described it:

> Two people come to a psychology laboratory to take part in a study of memory and learning. One of them is designated as a "teacher" and the other as a "learner."
>
> The experimenter explains that the study is concerned with the effects of punishment on learning. The learner is conducted into a room, seated in a chair, his arms strapped to prevent excessive movement, and an electrode is attached to his wrist. He is told that he is to learn a list of word pairs; whenever he makes an error, he will receive electric shocks of increasing intensity.
>
> The real focus of the experiment is the teacher. After watching the learner being strapped into place, he is taken into the main experimental room and seated before an impressive shock generator. Its main feature is a horizontal line of thirty switches, ranging from 15 volts to 450 volts, in 15-volt increments. There are also verbal designations which range from SLIGHT SHOCK to DANGER—SEVERE SHOCK. The teacher is told that he is to administer the learning test to the man in the other room. When the learner responds correctly, the teacher moves on to the next item; when the other man gives an incorrect answer, the teacher is to give him an electric shock. He is to start at the lowest shock level (15 volts) and to increase the level each time the man makes an error, going through 30 volts, 45 volts, and so on. (1974, pp. 3–4)

The "learner" is an actor who pretends to suffer pain but receives no actual shock. The subject ("teacher") is a businessperson or an industrial worker or a student, someone who has been recruited by a classified ad offering payment for spare-time work in a university laboratory.

Milgram was dismayed to discover that very large proportions of his subjects were willing to obey any order given by the experimenter. In the basic version of the experiment, in which the "learner" is in one room and the "teacher" in another from which the "learner" is visible but cannot be heard, 65 percent of the subjects administered the highest levels of shock, while the other 35 percent were obedient well into the "intense shock" levels.

Milgram used a functionalist argument to explain the high levels of obedience revealed in his experiment: In bureaucratic organizations people seek approval by adhering to the rules, which often absolve them of moral responsibility for their actions. But he also explored the conditions under which conflict will take place—that is, the conditions under which the subject will rebel against the experi-

menter. As can be seen in Table 6.3, in situations in which subjects are forced to confront the consequences of their behavior their ability to rely on "duty" to justify that behavior seems to be diminished. This effect is presented in graphic form in Figure 6.3.

When Milgram published the results of these experiments, he was criticized for deceiving his subjects and, in some cases, causing them undue stress. The controversy created by this study was one of the factors leading to the establishment of rules for the protection of human subjects in social-scientific research (see Chapter 2).

COMMITMENT TO BUREAUCRATIC GROUPS

Another question related to the impact of bureaucracy on individuals is how bureaucratic groups—which are based on unemotional and "rational" systems of recruitment, decision making, and reward—can sometimes attract strong commitment from their members. One possible answer is ideology: People believe in the goals and methods of the bureaucracy. Another explanation is that people within a bureaucracy form primary groups that function to maintain their commitment to the larger organization. There is considerable research evidence showing that both explanations are valid—both ideology and primary-group ties may operate to reinforce people's commitment to the organization. A number of studies have addressed this question.

Primary Groups in Bureaucracies. In one of those studies, Morris Janowitz and Edward Shils were assigned by the U.S. Army to study the attitudes of German

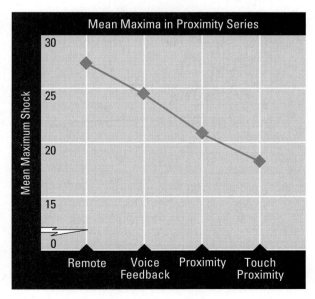

FIGURE 6.3 Mean Maximum Shocks in Four Variants of Milgram's Experiment

This graph illustrates the relation between the maximum shocks administered and the four variants of proximity between the "teacher" and the "learner" in Milgram's experiment.

Source: *Obedience to Authority,* by Stanley Milgram. Copyright © 1974 by Stanley Milgram. Reprinted by permission of Harper & Row Publishers, Inc.

THE PERSONAL CHALLENGE
Social Change and Business Scams

As corporations and smaller companies seek the efficiency and profits that are vital to their continued existence, they tend to eliminate jobs. People who had come to expect a secure income and familiar workmates are often faced with the challenge of forging a new way of life. Increasingly they are turning to self-employment (Siwolop, 1995).

Millions of people dream of owning their own business. But the rise in the number of individuals who want to build their own business organizations has also spawned an increase in the number of unscrupulous or shady characters hoping to profit from the mistakes of the unsuspecting or naive entrepreneur. Some insights into the way scam groups operate and a good measure of sociological skepticism can go a long way toward avoiding being taken in.

The National Consumers League, a nonprofit organization devoted to helping people avoid being swindled, receives more than 25 complaints a day from people all over the United States who have been defrauded in their efforts to start businesses. Viki Blum of Seattle, Washington, is one example. After losing a job with a major corporation, she invested $30,000 of her savings, including severance pay, in electronic game machines that she hoped to place in stores in her community. Her "territory" would yield a steady income. But to her dismay she discovered that the out-of-state company from which she bought the machines had sold her defective equipment. It had also sold similar machines to other entrepreneurs in the area, so that even if she got the equipment fixed she would have nothing like an exclusive territory to work in. When she sought to get her money back, she found that the company had moved and could not be located.

A sociologist in Viki's network of friends could probably have helped her avoid losing her hard-earned savings by asking these questions:

- *What commitments does the vendor have to the investor's community?* If the vendor is located elsewhere, especially if it is an out-of-state company, it may not need to worry about its reputation in the investor's community.

- *What do specialists in the investor's social network have to say about the offering?* We live in a world of divided labor and increasing specialization. This means that there are people in our own social networks, and in the various groups we belong to, who have expertise that they may be willing to share. Had Viki Blum sought the advice of a lawyer friend, she might have decided to be more cautious before investing.

- *Whom can the potential investor trust?* Scam groups often offer enticements like "profits with only part-time work," or "exclusive territory," or "no experience necessary." These are very attractive but should arouse suspicion. To counter suspicion, the scam outfit may use "singers," people who serve as references to sing the praises of the business scheme. The singers may be receiving special rewards for promoting the venture to new investors. We tend to want to trust others, especially when they are saying what we want to hear. But trust must be earned. The potential investor should meet with the vendor face-to-face and have an opportunity to ask questions and examine financial statements covering at least 3 years.

soldiers captured during World War II. They were attempting to discover what had made the German army so effective and committed that isolated units continued to fight even in the face of certain defeat. As Shils explained it, he and Janowitz "discovered the influence of small, closely knit groups on the conduct of their members in the performance of tasks set them from the outside" (1948, p. 48).

The soldiers of the German army behaved in this way not because of their ideological commitment to the Nazi cause but because of their loyalty to small combat units whose members had become so devoted to one another that to continue to fight even in the face of defeat, so as not to be dishonored as a group, seemed the only possible course of action. The close primary-group structure of the German army was one of the secrets of its success. The other was an extremely efficient organization. Ideology figured very little in its effectiveness.

Ideological Primary Groups.   Primary groups would seem to have no place in a "pure" bureaucracy, yet the study just cited, together with the Hawthorne experiments and other empirical studies, shows that there is no bureaucracy that completely eliminates primary groups. In the case of the German army, it appears that the development of primary groups among combat troops increased the effectiveness of the organization as a whole. Another important study of this subject was Philip Selznick's (1952) analysis of what made the Bolsheviks so effective that they won out in the fierce competition for political dominance in Russia. Selznick's data show that the ideologically based primary group was the key element in the Bolsheviks' orga-

nization. Small, secret "cells" of devoted communists were organized in neighborhoods, factories, army units, farms, and universities. Through years of tense and often dangerous political activity, the members became extremely devoted to one another and to their revolutionary cause. According to Selznick, this doubling of ideological and primary-group cohesion made the Bolsheviks themselves an "organizational weapon."

GROUPS IN COMPLEX SOCIETIES

As we saw in Chapter 4, in simpler tribal or peasant societies all social structures are primary groups. The tribal village is usually so small that everyone knows everyone else. The family, the extended family, the age- and sex-segregated peer groups, and even the village itself all allow for everyone to know everyone else and to interact on an almost daily basis. Typically these societies lack a secondary-group level of life. In traditional peasant societies, for example, there often were no associations that brought together soldiers or farmers or artisans in groups that extended beyond the limited bounds of the village. And yet that level of social life is what makes contemporary societies so efficient.

The differences between simpler and more complex societies can also make interactions among members of those societies confusing and frustrating (see Box 6.2). For

Many people join groups whose members are deeply committed to a particular leader or set of beliefs. Often they are seeking absolute answers and wish to avoid the choices that confuse so many others. The Waco tragedy, in which many followers of David Koresh were killed in a confrontation with federal authorities, is an example of the extremes such groups can resort to.

Communication and Interaction

Global social change continually produces waves of refugees and immigrants. For example, the new freedom to travel in the former Soviet satellite nations has produced thousands of ambitious immigrants. Civil strife in Central and Latin America, repression in some Asian societies (e.g., China and North and South Korea), growing poverty in the Philippines and Albania, and continuing turmoil in Cambodia and the Middle East have pushed families and individuals out of their homes and into the growing tide of worldwide migration. All of these changes are having profound effects on the linguistic diversity of North America and on how people in the Americas communicate and interact.

The United States continues to hold a global reputation as a place where immigrants can work to achieve success—and since it remains the nation with the most liberal immigration policies, it is no surprise that well over 500,000 legal immigrants and refugees (and an untold number of illegal entrants) seek to establish themselves in the "golden land" each year. In California alone, during the last decade about 3.6 million immigrants brought their languages and cultural norms to the nation's most diverse state. But no part of the nation missed the increases in cultural and linguistic diversity that result from immigration. Between 1980 and 1990, for example, the number of foreign-language speakers in the state of Georgia (not known as a primary destination of immigrants) increased from 134,000 to 285,000. All told, by the beginning of the 1990s more than 32 million residents of the United States did not speak English in their homes (Census Bureau, 1990).

The need for English as a Second Language (ESL) courses in schools and community centers throughout the nation is only one indication of the kinds of demands increased linguistic diversity is placing on communities where immigration rates are high. In time most Americans come to appreciate the diversity of languages spoken in the United States as a great cultural resource. But the welter of different languages spoken in some communities can also be a source of conflict. The extreme rapidity of the change has given rise to numerous controversies over how, and more specifically in what language, people should be expected to interact. For example, in 1989 a federal judge ruled that the Los Angeles suburb of Pomona had violated the civil rights of Korean and Chinese businesspeople by requiring them to place English signs on their shops. On the other hand, in the same community Filipino nurses lost a suit against a hospital that would not allow them to speak their native language, Tagalog, among themselves at work.

Elsewhere in the nation there is an active movement to make English the "official" language of the United States. This is accompanied by a crusade against the offering of bilingual education for children from other language groups. The problems of interaction across lingusitic divides are greatest in states with large proportions of foreign-language speakers, such as New Mexico (33.5 percent), California (31.5 percent), Texas (25.4 percent), Hawaii (24.8 percent), and New York (23.3 percent). Conversely, these states benefit the most from the wealth of new phrases and styles of communication stemming from their growing lingusitic diversity.

---

example, when they were first assigned to peasant villages in Africa and Asia, American Peace Corps volunteers were unprepared to cope with situations in which villagers came to them with requests for money or help with marital and family problems. For the young Americans, such requests were appropriate only among members of primary groups—and the villagers did not know how to engage in interactions that are typical of secondary groups (Luce, 1964).

In his most famous theoretical work, *The Division of Labor in Society* (1964/1893), Émile Durkheim reasoned that as a society becomes larger and more complex there is a vast increase in interdependence among its members as the labor needed to feed, house, educate, communicate with, transport, care for, and defend them becomes more complex. Faced with more choices regarding what work to prepare for, whom to interact with, and how to live life, the individual gains much more freedom than is available to a member of a simpler society, who (for better or worse) is

confined to a narrow set of village primary groups. But Durkheim also saw that the modern person could be overwhelmed by the choices open to him or her and might find it difficult to decide what groups to join and what norms to conform to.

Max Weber shared Durkheim's concern about the prospects for human happiness in the modern world. According to Weber (1958/1922), the fundamental paradox of modern society was the rise of bureaucracies, which greatly expanded the efficiency and rationality of society but "disenchanted the world." He meant that the modern formal organization, which is so effective in science, the military, the state (government), economic production, and almost every other aspect of modern life, at the same time deprives human life of a sense of magic and spirituality. The rise of fundamentalist movements in the Islamic world, for example, is in part a reaction against the influence of bureaucratic rationality in the institutions of secular states such as Egypt and Algeria.

Even in Western societies, where the process of bureaucratization is extremely advanced, people may feel overwhelmed by bureaucracy. The individual often feels like a tiny cog in a huge set of interlocking organizations. He or she fills specific statuses and enacts clearly defined roles yet feels more and more oppressed. Weber deplored the type of person that he felt was produced by the organizations of modern society: "a petty routine creature, lacking in heroism, human spontaneity, and inventiveness" (Weber, 1922, in Gerth & Mills, 1958, p. 50).

In his efforts to understand the behavior of individuals in the groups that are typical of modern societies, Weber distinguished between *rational* and *traditional* motives. Rational motives are easy to understand and predict because ends and means can be calculated and behavior changed on the basis of experience. Thus Weber proposed that business firms are rationally motivated. The producer uses the measures of costs and benefits to minimize production costs and maximize the market price for a given volume of goods. If buyers begin substituting another type of product, the producer must take immediate action, such as improving its product or producing a new one, to avoid losing money. All the members of the firm will be affected by these decisions. The producer cannot allow other sentiments to affect its actions, for to do so will in the long run only make matters worse for the firm.

At the opposite extreme from rationality is tradition. Traditional norms motivate our actions because we believe them to be right: We have always done things that way. The traditional norms of family life say that parents must care for their children, not because they will reward them later in life or because they will love them for doing so, but because they are parents and child care is what parents do. Religious groups may also require the unquestioning performance of certain rituals, not because they will necessarily help people enter heaven or make them better people, but simply because that is the way those rituals have always been performed.

Weber recognized that there are many possible combinations of motives between these two extremes. We can pursue profit but allow attachments to family members or people in our community to affect the extent to which we pursue economic goals. We can strive for success in the form of a promotion to a better job, but the effort will never entail purely rational behavior. To win a promotion we may need to show that we uphold the less formal traditions of the corporation—its styles of dress, for example—while at the same time demonstrating our ability to act rationally, to bring in more profits or save on costs or enhance the firm's power or prestige. In sum, life in complex organizations requires skill at performing roles in various types of groups within those organizations. It requires that we balance traditional and rational motives and that we understand the interactions between groups and among individuals within those groups.

RESEARCH FRONTIERS: WHY AMERICANS STILL JOIN GROUPS

Early in the nineteenth century the French aristocrat and social theorist Alexis de Tocqueville visited the United States. Like other European intellectuals, he considered the new nation a bold and controversial social experiment. He had doubts about the capacity of common people to govern themselves without the guiding hand of a strong aristocracy. But as he traveled through the former colonies he was pleasantly surprised by what he observed. He was particularly impressed by the number of associations and small groups to which people belonged. Americans, he wrote, are "a nation of joiners" (1956/1840).

Tocqueville's phrase is often quoted in descriptions of democratic societies. Democratic theory states that when people are given the freedom to associate with whomever they choose, they will form a complex civil society—that is, a society characterized by a never-ending and always changing array of freely formed nongovernmental groups. (See Chapter 8.) In fact, as we will see in later chapters, dictators who wish to curtail individual freedom invariably attempt to control the groups people can belong to.

The number of voluntary associations in the United States and other democratic nations has increased steadily since Tocqueville's day. But what kinds of groups are people forming? What needs are they seeking to satisfy through their group interactions? And how does social change affect the types of groups they form?

A recent study by sociologist Robert Wuthnow directly addresses these questions. Wuthnow's findings, described in his book *Sharing the Journey* (1994), are based on a large survey carried out by the Gallup Poll in which respondents were asked about their group affiliations and the benefits they derived from them. Table 6.4 presents Wuthnow's estimates of the major types of groups to which people in the United States belong. Religious groups engaging

TABLE 6.4	**Groups in the United States**	
	ESTIMATED NUMBERS	
	MEMBERS	**GROUPS**
Sunday school classes	18–22 million	800,000
Bible study groups	15–20 million	900,000
Self-help groups	8–10 million	500,000
Special interest groups		
Political/current events	5–10 million	250,000
Book/discussion groups	5–10 million	250,000
Sports/hobby groups	5–10 million	250,000

Source: Wuthnow, 1994.

FRIENDSHIP GROUPS

These photos capture some aspects of the universal experience known as friendship. They show friendship groups in societies throughout the world—from a group of wealthy English boarding school students to scenes from African villages. They convey the emotional quality of interaction among friends, but to the sociological observer they also reveal some characteristic features of friendship groups.

First, note the size of the groups. None numbers more than six or seven members. As Georg Simmel first pointed out in his writing on friendship and intimacy, the larger the group is, the more opportunities there will be for conflict and schism. Increasing size brings with it a greater likelihood of jealousy, competition for attention, and conflicting values, and these tensions tend to break larger friendship groups into smaller, more intimate ones like those shown here.

A second observation that we can draw from these photos has to do with gender differences in friendship groups. Children's friendship groups are involved in anticipatory socialization, in taking roles that will later be incorporated into adult statuses. Thus the girls are seen holding dolls and practicing the interactions that occupy so much of their mothers' time. And unlike the typical male friendship group, female groups often have the responsibility of caring for younger siblings, as we see in at least one of these photos. Males more typically engage in activities that involve physical prowess and changes in the environment, such as turning on a hydrant to create an instant street shower. We also see in these photos that gender segregation is normally the rule in friendship groups, although there may be many exceptions, such as when games are played in school.

Finally, these photos remind us of the emotional complexity of friendship. Friends can fight and make up, but people who are less than friends often cannot fight without ending the relationship. And consider the photo of the men hugging each other. Is this scene likely to occur in American culture? Perhaps today it is, but until quite recently such a show of emotion between men, even between a father and his son, was discouraged in our culture. Today this norm is changing, al-though in many other cultures it is still far more acceptable for men to hug and kiss each other than it is in North America.

in Bible study and Sunday school classes are by far the largest category; self-help groups in which people attempt to resocialize themselves, to replace old and often destructive patterns of behavior with new and more desirable ones, are the second largest category.

Sociologist Frank Reissman (1984) has been tracking the enormous growth of self-help groups over the past 30 years. His inventory of such groups continues to grow rapidly. Part of the reason for this growth, he believes, lies in the increasing need people feel to overcome compulsive behaviors or behavior that is harming their social attachments. There are groups for people recovering from addictions to gambling, smoking, marijuana use, and shoplifting; there are support groups for parents, grandparents, widows, and divorcees; there are groups for homosexuals, former fundamentalists, people with eating disorders, and families of sex offenders (Wuthnow, 1994).

As Table 6.5 indicates, the appeal of these "people changing" groups is quite wide. The table also shows that there are some differences in who joins small groups—more women than men, more middle-aged people than young ones, more people in the West than in the South or the Midwest, more members among the college educated. But the differences may be less important than the similarities in terms of race, urban or rural residence, and income.

Wuthnow's study revealed that people who join small groups are owning up to a deeply felt need to be part of a face-to-face primary group in which they attain a sense of community with others. Table 6.6 shows that there are often wide gaps between people's needs and the ability of group interactions to actually satisfy those needs. But these gaps do not seem to produce widespread disillusionment. In their search for a feeling of belonging and community, people continue to join groups of all kinds.

TABLE 6.5 Small-Group Membership in the United States (percentage of each category that is currently in a small group that meets regularly and provides caring and support for its members)	
National	40
Women	44
Men	36
Age 18–34	35
Age 35–49	42
Age 50 and over	45
High school or less	37
Some college	43
College graduates	48
Income less than $20,000 per year	39
Income $20,000–$39,000 per year	42
Income $40,000 or more per year	43
White Anglo	40
Black	41
Hispanic	46
South	39
Midwest	39
Northeast	41
West	45
In large cities	41
In medium cities	42
In towns or rural area	40

Source: Wuthnow, 1994.

TABLE 6.6 Meeting the Need for Community (percentage of group members who have (A) felt each need and (B) met each need fully)	A	B
Having neighbors with whom you can interact freely and comfortably	93	43
Being able to share deepest feelings with someone	94	57
Having friends who value the same things in life you do	98	58
Having people in your life who give you deep emotional support	98	66
Being in a group where you can discuss your most basic beliefs and values	90	50
Having friends you can always count on when you're in a jam	97	64
Having people in your life who are never critical of you	83	29
Being part of a group that helps you grow spiritually	90	53
Having cooperation rather than competition with people at work	85	31
Having people you can turn to when you feel depressed or lonely	96	62
Knowing more people in your community	95	32

Source: Wuthnow, 1994.

SUMMARY

THINK ABOUT IT CRITICALLY

"Imagine, in this day and age," a critic of the Catholic church recently complained, "when it is so difficult to find dedicated priests and nuns, that the church still insists on celibacy in its clerical staff." Although it is difficult to find men and women who are willing to take the vow of celibacy, the church has its reasons for maintaining the rule of celibacy for priests and nuns. A sociologist armed with knowledge of primary groups and bureaucratic organizations might also offer some insight into the issue. As you read the following summary, try to imagine how the sociologist would explain the church's position.

The social fabric of modern societies is composed of millions of groups of many types and sizes. Unlike a *social category,* a collection of individuals who are grouped together because they share a particular trait, a *social group* is a set of two or more individuals who share a sense of common identity and belonging and who interact on a regular basis. Those interactions create a social structure composed of specific statuses and roles.

A *primary group* is characterized by intimate, often face-to-face, association and cooperation. *Secondary groups* are characterized by relationships that involve few aspects of the personality; the members' reasons for participation are usually limited to a small number of goals. As the number of people in a group increases, the number of possible relationships among the group's members increases at a faster rate. A group composed of only two people is known as a *dyad.* The addition of a third person to form a *triad* reduces the stability of the group.

At the level of social organization between the primary group and the institutions of the nation-state are *communities. Territorial communities* are contained within geographic boundaries; *nonterritorial communities* are networks of associations formed around shared goals. Territorial communities are usually composed of one or more neighborhoods in which people form attachments based on proximity.

Groups formed at the neighborhood level are integrated into networks that may extend beyond geographic boundaries. Key factors in the formation of networks are *in-group–out-group* distinctions. Such distinctions can form around almost any quality but are usually based on such qualities as income, race, or religion. Another type of group is the *reference group,* a group the individual uses as a frame of reference for self-evaluation and attitude formation. The study of who people associate with, how those choices are made, and the effects of those choices is known as social network analysis.

Social scientists have identified certain principles of interaction that help explain both stability and change in human groups. Among them are the pleasure principle, the rationality principle, the reciprocity principle, and the fairness principle. The balance among these principles varies from one situation to another, with economic motives dominating in some instances and social needs winning out in others. From an interactionist perspective, an important factor determining how people behave in a given instance is their definition of the situation.

Studies of interaction in groups use a variety of techniques. *Ethnomethodology* is the study of the underlying rules of behavior that guide group interaction. The *dramaturgical approach* regards interaction as though it were taking place on a stage and unfolding in scenes. The strategies that people use to set a stage for their own purposes are known as *impression management.* Research on the bystander effect has shown that when responsibility seems to be diffused, people are more likely to avoid helping others. But when people define the situation as involving them, they will intervene despite the potential costs to themselves.

Research on small groups has shown that they tend to develop two kinds of leaders, a "task leader" who keeps the group focused on its goals and a "socioemotional leader" who creates a positive emotional climate.

Informal organizations are groups with generally agreed-upon but unwritten norms and statuses, whereas *formal organizations* have explicit, often written, sets of norms, statuses, and roles that specify each member's relationships to the others and the conditions under which those relationships hold. A *voluntary association* is a formal organization whose members pursue shared interests and arrive at decisions through some sort of democratic process. A *bureaucracy* is a formal organization characterized by positions with clearly defined responsibilities, the ordering of positions in a hierarchy, governance by rules and precedents, impersonality and impartiality, a career ladder, and efficiency as a basic norm.

One effect of the increasing dominance of bureaucracies in modern societies is the possibility that individuals will not take full responsibility for their actions. A study of obedience to authority conducted by Stanley Milgram raised serious questions about people's ability to resist pressure to carry out orders for which they are not personally responsible. Milgram also found, however, that rebellion against authority is more likely when individuals who rebel have the support of others. Other studies have found that commitment to bureaucratic organizations is greatest when it is supported by ideology or by strong primary-group attachments.

As a society becomes larger and more complex, it tends increasingly to be characterized by secondary groups and organizations. These make the society more efficient, but they can also cause confusion and unhappiness. Durkheim pointed out that members of complex societies have greater freedom to choose what groups to join and what norms to conform to but that they can be overwhelmed by the choices open to them. Weber examined the effects of the rise of bureaucracies in modern societies. In doing so he distinguished between rational motives, which are based on calculations of ends and means, and traditional motives, which are based on the belief that certain actions are inherently right.

CRITICAL RESPONSE

From the perspective of the church, the primary relationship that a priest or nun would have with a lover or spouse would detract from his or her spiritual bonds with God and the church. The sociologist might point out that this is a classic example of a norm that attempts to deal with the conflicts that often arise when members of closely bonded dyads are also members of a larger organization. The Catholic church solves the problem of conflicting loyalties by banning the marital dyad.

GLOSSARY

social category: a collection of individuals who are grouped together because they share a trait deemed by the observer to be socially relevant. (p. 150)

social group: a set of two or more individuals who share a sense of common identity and belonging and who interact on a regular basis. (p. 150)

primary group: a social group characterized by intimate, face-to-face associations. (p. 151)

secondary group: a social group whose members have a shared goal or purpose but are not bound together by strong emotional ties. (p. 151)

dyad: a group consisting of two people. (p. 154)

triad: a group consisting of three people. (p. 154)

community: a set of primary and secondary groups in which the individual carries out important life functions. (p. 154)

territorial community: a population that functions within a particular geographic area. (p. 154)

nonterritorial community: a network of relationships formed around shared goals. (p. 154)

in-group: a social group to which an individual has a feeling of allegiance; usually, but not always, a primary group. (p. 155)

out-group: any social group to which an individual does not have a feeling of allegiance; may be in competition or conflict with the in-group. (p. 155)

reference group: a group that an individual uses as a frame of reference for self-evaluation and attitude formation. (p. 157)

ethnomethodology: the study of the underlying rules of behavior that guide group interaction. (p. 163)

dramaturgical approach: an approach to research on interaction in groups that is based on the recognition that much social interaction depends on the desire to impress those who may be watching. (p. 163)

impression management: the strategies one uses to "set a stage" for one's own purposes. (p. 164)

informal organization: a group whose norms and statuses are generally agreed upon but are not set down in writing. (p. 166)

formal organization: a group that has an explicit, often written, set of norms, statuses, and roles that specify each member's relationships to the others and the conditions under which those relationships hold. (p. 166)

voluntary association: a formal organization whose members pursue shared interests and arrive at decisions through some sort of democratic process. (p. 166)

bureaucracy: a formal organization characterized by a clearly defined hierarchy with a commitment to rules, efficiency, and impersonality. (p. 166)

W H E R E   T O   F I N D   I T

BOOKS

Small Group Research: A Handbook (A. Paul Hare, Herbert H. Blumberg, Martin F. Davis, & Valerie Kent; Ablex, 1994). A recent and comprehensive survey of classic and contemporary research on human behavior in small groups.

Complex Organizations: A Critical Essay, 2nd ed. (Charles Perrow; Scott, Foresman, 1979). A comprehensive text on the sociology and politics of formal organizations.

The Presentation of Self in Everyday Life (Erving Goffman; Doubleday, 1959). One of the classics in the sociology of interaction at the micro level. A must-read for anyone wanting to gain greater insight into the dramaturgical approach to the analysis of social life.

Studies in Ethnomethodology (Harold Garfinkel; Prentice-Hall, 1967). A brilliant and controversial collection of original papers that illustrates what scientific concern for the most micro and subjective aspects of interaction can yield in the way of fresh insights into how people act in society.

Passions Within Reason: The Strategic Role of the Emotions (R. H. Frank; Norton, 1988). A highly readable treatment of a complex and often difficult subject, the relationships between emotion and social behavior. The emphasis is on rational behavior and its limits in the real world.

Extraordinary Groups: An Examination of Unconventional Life-Styles, 4th ed. (William M. Kephart; St. Martin's Press, 1991). A valuable collection of essays about unconventional groups that manage to maintain their solidarity despite their deviance from the mainstream. Includes material on ethnic groups, self-help groups like Alcoholics Anonymous, and unusual occupations.

JOURNALS

Administrative Science Quarterly. One of the principal journals in the field of organizations and behavior. A valuable source for theoretical and empirical studies of bureaucratic organizations like corporations, government agencies, and universities.

Human Organization. Another good source of research on the problems and possibilities of efforts to improve human organizations. More diverse in its scope than *Administrative Science Quarterly* but also oriented toward economic organizations like firms, labor unions, and regulatory agencies.

Urban Life and Culture. A journal specializing in articles about human interaction in urban settings. A source of new empirical studies from the interactionist perspective.

CHAPTER 7

Deviance and Social Control

Who among us will ever be able to forget the bombing of the federal office building in Oklahoma City in the spring of 1995? Perhaps the single worst crime in American history, it forever changed the lives of thousands of people in Oklahoma and elsewhere. The bombing also brought issues of violence and criminality in the United States to the attention of a world audience. The bombing and the debates that followed in its wake are a vivid example of how crime and violence can bring about drastic change in people's lives.

Shortly before the bombing, Julie Welch entered the building to be interviewed for a job with a federal agency. A vivacious, bright 24-year-old, Julie was just beginning her career when her life was cut short by a hideous act of terrorism. A few days later, in a television interview at the Welch home, Julie's father and two of her college friends bravely squelched their tears while they tried to make sense of a senseless event. "People may not agree on the laws or how to enforce them," one of Julie's friends said, "but that is why we have elections and legislators. This kind of violence destroys everything our country stands for."

The violence in Oklahoma City also served to remind us once again that crime and violence of all kinds are widespread and have an enormous effect on our lives. Drug-related crime is a major social problem as the crack epidemic continues to affect communities throughout the nation. White-collar crime among bankers and stockbrokers and politicians periodically robs thousands of people of their savings. Rates of domestic violence and child abuse are on the rise. The incidence of gang violence remains high in nearly all areas of the country. Crash programs are under way throughout the United States to build more prisons; the dockets of criminal courts are jammed with cases; law enforcement ranks among the top issues in political campaigns everywhere.

Does all this mean that the United States is becoming a nation of deviants and lawbreakers? What actually are the current trends in deviance and crime? And what can be done to alleviate the worst effects of crime and restore public faith in the courts and the laws? Research on these and related issues is a major field within sociology. No one can offer definitive answers, but sociologists are frequently looked to for research on trends in deviance and criminal behavior as well as explanations of those trends. As with any social condition, before a society can address its crime problems it must be able to distinguish symptoms from causes and to compare recent events with longer-term trends.

181

WHAT IS DEVIANCE?

Deviance, broadly defined, is behavior that violates the norms of a particular society. But because all of us violate norms to some degree at some time or other, we must distinguish between *deviance* and *deviants*. Deviance can be something as simple as dyeing one's hair purple or wearing outrageous clothing or becoming tipsy at a stuffy party. Or it may be behavior over which the individual has little control, such as being homeless and living on the street, or it may consist of more strongly sanctioned departures from the society's norms—such acts as rape, mugging, and murder. Not all deviance is considered socially wrong, yet it can have negative effects for the individual. For example, "whistle blowers" who publicize illegal or harmful actions by their employers deviate from the norms of bureaucratic organizations and are often threatened with the loss of their jobs. Yet at the same time they benefit the public by calling attention to dangerous or illegal activities. In recent years, therefore, Congress and the courts have tried to encourage whistle blowers and prevent reprisals against them. In 1992, for example, a federal judge awarded $7.5 million to Christopher Urda as a share of the $55.6 million the U.S. government saved as a result of his testimony against his employer (Stevenson, 1992b).

A deviant person, by contrast, is someone who violates or opposes a society's most valued norms, especially those that are valued by elite groups. Through such behavior deviant individuals become disvalued people, and their disvalued behavior provokes hostile reactions (Davis, 1975; Goffman, 1963; Sagarin, 1975; Schur, 1984). *Deviant* may be a label attached to a person or group. Or the word may refer to behavior that brings punishment to a person under certain conditions.

Cases of fraudulent business dealings by private individuals or influence peddling by government officials raise an important question: What are the conditions under which violations of norms are punished? Here is an area of conduct in which there is often some uncertainty about what is legal and what is merely sleazy. Such questions reveal that deviance is not absolute. As sociologist Kai Erikson explains it, deviance "is not a property inherent in certain forms of behavior; it is a property conferred upon these forms by the audience which directly or indirectly witnesses them" (1962, p. 307). Some of us may believe that influence peddling is deviant, while others may believe that it is acceptable. Which of our views become the norm—and which are to be enforced through rewards and punishments—is just as important as the behavior itself. This point is illustrated in Erikson's study of deviance among the New England Puritans, discussed in Box 7.1.

The study of deviance is central to the science of sociology, not only because deviance results in major social problems like crime, but also because it can bring about social change. Indeed, the Puritans were a deviant group in England at the time of their emigration to the New World. They challenged the authority of the king and many of the central norms that upheld the stratification system of feudal England. In the Massachusetts Bay Colony they created their own society, one in which they were no longer deviant. But, as Erikson showed, they also created their own forms of deviance, which reflected their unique problems as a society on a rapidly changing social frontier.

The ways in which a society prevents deviance and punishes deviants are known as **social control.** As we saw in Chapter 3, the norms of a culture, the means by which they are instilled in us through socialization, and the ways in which they are enforced in social institutions—the family, the schools, government agencies—establish a society's system of social control. In fact, social control can be thought of as all the ways in which a society establishes and enforces its cultural norms. It is "the capacity of a social group, including a whole society, to regulate itself" (Janowitz, 1978, p. 3).

The means used to prevent deviance and punish deviants are one dimension of social control. They include the police, prisons, mental hospitals, and other institutions responsible for applying social control, keeping order, and enforcing major norms. But if we had to rely entirely on official institutions to enforce norms, social order would probably be impossible to achieve (Chwast, 1965). In fact, the official institutions of social control deal mainly with the deviant individuals and groups that a society fears most. Less threatening forms of deviance are controlled through the everyday interactions of individuals, as when parents attempt to prevent their children from wearing their hair in the style of heavy metal or reggae musicians.

In this chapter we look first at the various meanings of deviance and at how those meanings emerge and change as a society's values change. Then we explore the major sociological perspectives on deviance and social control. The final section deals with the ecology of deviance—its distribution among people in different subcultures and income categories—and ends with an introduction to the organization and functioning of institutions of social control such as prisons.

BOX 7.1 USING THE SOCIOLOGICAL IMAGINATION

The Salem Witch Hunt

No one knows how the witchcraft hysteria began, but it originated in the home of the Reverend Samuel Parris, minister of the local church. In early 1692, several girls from the neighborhood began to spend their afternoons in the Parris kitchen with a slave named Tituba, and it was not long before a mysterious sorority of girls, aged between nine and twenty, became regular visitors to the parsonage. We can only speculate about what went on behind the kitchen door, but we know that Tituba had been brought to Massachusetts from Barbados and enjoyed a reputation in the neighborhood for her skills in the magic arts. As the girls grew closer together, a remarkable change seemed to come over them: perhaps it is not true, as someone later reported, that they went out into the forest to celebrate their own version of a black mass, but it is apparent that they began to live in a state of high tension and shared secrets with one another which were hardly becoming to quiet Puritan maidens. (Erikson, 1966, p. 141)

"The Trial of George Jacobs, August 5, 1692." Oil on canvas by T. H. Matteson, 1855. Jacobs was accused of witchcraft.

The girls quickly drew the concerned attention of Salem's ministers and its doctor. Unable to understand much about their hysterical state or to deny their claim that they were possessed by the devil, the doctor pronounced the girls bewitched. This gave them the freedom to make accusations regarding the cause of their unfortunate condition.

Tituba was the first to be accused and jailed. She was followed by scores of others as the fear of witches swept through the community. Soon women with too many warts or annoying tics were accused, tried, and jailed for their sins. Then the executions began. In the first and worst of the waves of executions, in August and September of 1692, at least 20 people were killed, including one man who was pressed to death under piled rocks for "standing mute at his trial."

For the sociologist, the Salem witch hunt of 300 years ago has meaning for today's world. In an award-winning study, Kai T. Erikson (1966) showed that the crime of witchcraft can be understood as a sign of "social disruption and change." In Europe only a half-century earlier, thousands of accused witches had been burned and hanged during the turbulent period when the European states were emerging from feudalism. The witch craze in backwoods New England also came during a time of great change. In 1692 the orthodox Puritan way of life was ending: Puritanism was being watered down by rough wilderness ways and urbane city values. The settlements were no longer hemmed in by the wilderness, and the Indians had been pushed away.

In his study of the Salem witch craze, Erikson showed that the punishment of suspected witches served as a defense against the weakening of Puritan society. By casting out the "witches," the Puritans were reaffirming their community values: strict adherence to religious devotion, fear of God, abstinence from the pleasures of secular society (drink, sex, music, dance), and the like. The trial and punishment of the so-called witches illustrates Émile Durkheim's earlier discovery that every society creates its own forms of deviance and in fact needs those deviant acts. The punishment of deviant acts reaffirms the commitment of a society's members to its norms and values and thereby reinforces social solidarity. On the surface, Durkheim argued, deviant acts may seem to be harmful to group life, but in fact the punishment of those who commit such acts makes it clear to all exactly what deviations are most intolerable. By Durkheim's reasoning, the stark images of punishment—the guillotine, the electric chair, the syringe, the wretched life behind bars—become opportunities to let the population know that those who threaten the social order will be severely judged.

DIMENSIONS OF DEVIANCE

Deviance is an especially controversial topic: There is usually much disagreement not only about which behaviors are deviant and which are not but also about which behaviors should be strongly punished and which should be condoned or punished only mildly. The debate over whether abortion should be legal is a good example of such disagreement. As Kai Erikson noted, "Behavior which qualifies one man for prison may qualify another for sainthood since the quality of the act itself depends so much on the circumstances under which it was performed and the temper of the audience which witnessed it" (1966, pp. 5–6).

Consider South African president Nelson Mandela. Mandela was released from a maximum-security prison in 1990 after serving almost 30 years of a life sentence for his leadership of the movement to end *apartheid,* South Africa's racial caste system. The dominant white minority in South Africa regarded Mandela and other opponents of apartheid as criminals. But the black majority viewed him as a hero and a martyr; indeed, black South Africans revere Mandela the way people in the United States revere George Washington. Until the black majority began to mobilize world opinion and other nations began to enforce negative sanctions against South Africa, the white minority was able to define Mandela's opposition to apartheid as a criminal activity.

The power to define which acts are legal and which are illegal is an important dimension of deviance. In the case of black protest in South Africa, it is the single most important dimension. In the United States, the power of some groups to define certain acts as deviant helps explain why influence peddling is not a crime but cultivating marijuana is. In this connection it is interesting to note that during the 1960s, when the children of powerful members of society began smoking marijuana, legislators found themselves under pressure to relax the enforcement of marijuana laws.

The fact that people in power can define what behavior is deviant and determine who is punished fails to explain differences in definitions of deviance in societies with different cultures. Behavior regarded as normal in one society may be considered highly deviant in another. For example, in the United States the drinking of alcoholic beverages is considered normal, but in orthodox Islamic culture it is forbidden. Even within a society, members of certain social groups may behave in ways that are considered deviant by others. Thus the official norms of the Catholic church do not permit the use of artificial methods of birth control, yet large numbers of Catholics use condoms, birth control pills, and other contraceptives. Similarly, the norms of Judaism require that the Sabbath be set aside for religious observance, yet many Jews work on the Sabbath and do not attend synagogue; in parts of Jerusalem they have occasionally been attacked by orthodox Jews for violating that norm. Clearly, differences in values are another important source of definitions of deviance and of disagreements about those definitions.

Another dimension of deviance has to do with attributes gained at birth (e.g., race or physical appearance) or other attributes that a person cannot control (e.g., having a convict as a parent), in contrast to actual behavior, which is usually voluntary. A criminal is deviant in ways that a mentally ill person is not, and it is criminal behavior that is most costly to society. Yet in many situations a mentally ill person is labeled as deviant, and this label may actually drive him or her toward criminality. A related issue is how people who deviate from generally accepted norms manage to survive in societies where they are considered outsiders. In fact, deviant people often form their own communities with their own norms and values, and these deviant subcultures sustain them in their conflicted relations with "normal" members of society.

An important point is that deviant subcultures, which engage in prostitution, gambling, drug use, and other "deviant" behaviors, could not exist were they not performing services and supplying products that people in the larger society secretly demand. It would be wise, therefore, not to draw the distinction between deviant and normal people too sharply. Many people deviate from the norm, and their deviations create opportunities for others whose identities and occupations are deviant.

In sum, three dimensions of social life—power, culture, and voluntary versus involuntary behavior—give rise to the major forces operating in any society to produce the forms of deviance that are typical of that society.

DEVIANCE AND STIGMA

To narrow the range of phenomena we must deal with in discussing deviance, let us keep in mind Erving Goffman's (1963) distinction between stigma and deviance. "The term **stigma**," Goffman stated, "refers to an attribute that is deeply discrediting" and that reduces the person "from a whole and usual person to a tainted and discounted one" (p. 3). People may be stigmatized because of mental illness, eccentricity, membership in a disvalued racial or nationality group, and the like. In some instances their stigma is visible to a stranger, as in the case of a disfigured person like the Elephant Man. Suffering from a disease that grossly distorted his face, the Elephant Man was rejected by society even though he was a highly intelligent person who was treated badly because of the groundless fear that he aroused in others. In other cases stigma is revealed only with growing acquaintance, as in the stigma attached to the children of convicts. For the stigmatized person, the disqualifying trait defines the person's master status (Becker, 1963; Scull, 1988). (See Chapter 4.) A blind person, for example, may be an excellent musician and a caring parent, but the fact that he or she is blind will outweigh these achieved statuses except in unusual cases like that of Stevie Wonder.

John Hurt, starring as the pathetically disfigured sideshow attraction in the film *The Elephant Man,* manages to escape his sadistic master through the help of the other freaks in the circus.

Stigmatized people deviate from some norm of "respectable" society, but they are not necessarily social deviants. The term *deviant,* Goffman argued, should be reserved for people "who are seen as declining voluntarily and openly to accept the social place accorded them, and who act irregularly and somewhat rebelliously in connection with our basic institutions" (1963, p. 143). Among the people Goffman classified as social deviants are "prostitutes, drug addicts, delinquents, criminals, jazz musicians, bohemians, gypsies, carnival workers, hoboes, winos, show people, full time gamblers, beach dwellers, homosexuals, and the urban unrepentant poor." Some people will find Goffman's list controversial; his point, however, is that these are examples of social groups that "are considered to be engaged in some kind of collective denial of the social order. They are perceived as failing to use available opportunity for advancement in the various approved runways of society" (1963, p. 144).

According to the definition of stigma, the population of social deviants is smaller than that of stigmatized individuals; only some stigmatized behaviors are socially deviant. Deviant behaviors are characterized by denial of the social order through violation of the norms of permissible conduct. This point should be kept in mind as we continue our discussion of criminals and other people who are considered social deviants.

DEVIANCE AND CRIME

Much of the study of social deviance focuses on crime. **Crime** is usually defined as an act, or the omission of an act, for which the state can apply sanctions. Those sanctions are part of the criminal law, a set of written rules that prohibit certain acts and prescribe punishments to be meted out to violators (Kornblum & Julian, 1995). But the questions of which specific behaviors constitute crime and how the state should deal with them are often controversial.

In every society there are some behaviors that almost everyone will agree are criminal and should be punished, and other behaviors that some consider criminal but others do not. All societies punish murder and theft, for example, but there is far more variation in the treatment of adultery, prostitution, and pornography. Indeed, the largest number of "crimes" committed in the United States each year are so-called public order crimes such as public drunkenness, vagrancy, disorderly conduct, prostitution, gambling, drug addiction, and certain homosexual interactions. Many sociologists claim that these are victimless crimes because they generally cause no physical harm to anyone but the offenders themselves (Schur, 1973; Silberman, 1980). Not all social scientists agree with this view, however. Some point out that crimes like prostitution actually inflict damage on society because they are usually linked with an underworld that engages in far more serious and costly criminal activities (Wilson, 1977).

In the United States, crime is considered one of the nation's most serious social problems. In 1994 the Federal Bureau of Investigation (FBI) reported that one violent crime occurred every 17 seconds and one property crime every 3 seconds. The most serious, most frequently occurring, and most likely to be reported crimes are called *index*

TABLE 7.1	The Crime Rate,* 1972, 1982, 1994		
	1972	**1982**	**1994**
Crime Index, total	3,961.4	5,603.6	5,637.0
Violent crime	401.0	571.1	772.6
Property crime	3,560.0	5,032.5	4,864.4
Murder	9.0	9.1	9.7
Forcible rape	22.5	34.0	41.1
Robbery	180.7	238.9	263.2
Aggravated assault	188.8	289.2	458.7
Burglary	1,140.8	1,488.8	1,089.0
Larceny-theft	1,993.6	3,084.8	3,133.2
Motor vehicle theft	426.1	458.8	642.1

*Rate per 100,000 inhabitants, calculated on number of offenses before rounding.

Source: FBI, 1995.

crimes by the FBI because they are included in its crime index, a commonly used measure of crime rates. These categories of crime, along with crime rates, are shown in Table 7.1.

For many decades criminologists and other social scientists have criticized the FBI's crime statistics on the ground that they do not reflect differences in effectiveness among crime-reporting agencies. For example, a more professional law enforcement agency in one community could show higher crime rates than an agency in another community that has done a haphazard job of collecting the statistics. Another serious problem is that there is no way of knowing the crime rates for the total population (rather than just for those who actually reported crimes). Since 1973, therefore, the Census Bureau and the Law Enforcement Assistance Administration have conducted semi-

annual surveys in which respondents are asked whether they or their businesses have been victims of robbery, rape, assault, burglary, or other forms of theft. In general, these *victimization surveys* show that the overall rate of serious crime is actually between two and three times higher than the reported crime index.

DEVIANCE AND CHANGING VALUES

One of the factors that make it especially difficult to gather and interpret statistics on crime is that definitions of crime and deviance are constantly changing as the society's values change. Almost every week, for example, there are reports in the media of men who have battered and even killed their wives, often after serving brief prison sentences for previous attacks on their spouses. Why, many ask, are law enforcement agencies unable to prevent and punish spouse abuse? Advocates of new laws and greater investment in prevention point out that until fairly recently a married woman was viewed as the husband's household possession. Although both husband and wife had sworn to "love, honor, and cherish" their partner, these norms were applied far more forcefully to women than to men. This double standard is changing as men and women become more equal before the law, but in the minds of many judges and juries this change is not yet complete, and men who abuse their spouses often receive relatively light sentences.

In any society, agreement on particular aspects of crime and deviance can range from weak (in cases in which there is much controversy) to strong (in cases in which there is little disagreement). Negative sanctions, or punishments, can also range from very weak to very strong. Capital punishment is the strongest sanction in the United States, with life imprisonment following close behind. Minor fines or the suggestion that a person undergo treatment for a behavior that is viewed as deviant are relatively weak sanctions. Nor are all sanctions formal punishments meted out according to law. Some deviance can be pun-

FIGURE 7.1	A Typology of Deviance in the United States

		STRENGTH OF SANCTION	
		Weak	Strong
DEGREE OF CONSENSUS	**Weak**	• Recreational drugs • Homosexuality • Abortion	• Sale of whiskey during Prohibition • Prostitution • Abortion before 1973 Supreme Court ruling
	Strong	• Schizophrenia • Driving while intoxicated • Public drunkenness • Corporate crime • Wife or child beating	• Major crimes (felonies) • Treason

FIGURE 7.2 **Deviance in the United States Before the Civil War**

STRENGTH OF SANCTION		
	Weak	Strong
DEGREE OF CONSENSUS — Weak	• Killing Native Americans • Lynching of African Americans • Prostitution • Wife or child beating	• Abortion • Indebtedness • Illegitimacy • Divorce • Adultery
DEGREE OF CONSENSUS — Strong	• Political corruption • Corporate crime	• Major felonies against whites • Treason • Homosexuality

ished by means of shunning or the "silent treatment," and milder infractions can be controlled by simply poking fun at the person in an attempt to change his or her behavior.

Figure 7.1 uses these distinctions to construct a typology of deviance as it is generally viewed in the United States in the late twentieth century. Figure 7.2 suggests what such a typology would have looked like before the Civil War. Together they highlight some of the continuities and changes in patterns of deviance in the United States over the last century. You will probably find points in them to argue with, which is further evidence of the difficulty of classifying deviant behaviors in a rapidly changing society.

Should driving while intoxicated (DWI) be classified as a deviant behavior? We all fear the drunk driver and agree that DWI is dangerous, but because so many of us are social drinkers we have found it difficult not to violate this norm, and consequently we have placed relatively mild sanctions on DWI except when the outcome is a fatal accident. In the late 1980s and early 1990s, however, organized groups opposed to drunk driving helped to change public

Come to where the Cancer is.

Smoking kills more Americans each year than alcohol, cocaine, crack, heroin, homicide, suicide, car accidents, fires, and AIDS combined.

Changing Americans' views of smoking from an accepted to a deviant activity requires changes in the image of smoking. This public service advertisement uses a child's prize-winning entry to turn the imagery used by tobacco companies to link smoking with outdoor activities into a negative representation.

attitudes, and the sanctions against DWI became stronger. In his study of this issue, Joseph Gusfield (1981) found that the highway death rate has been decreasing since 1945 but that the public's perception of the relationship between highway deaths and drunk driving has sharpened as a result of media coverage and lobbying by citizens' groups.

Our perception and treatment of homosexuality is another example of significant change in Americans' attitudes toward a deviant behavior and the strength of the sanctions invoked. A century ago homosexuality was widely regarded as a serious form of deviance. Homosexuals were persecuted whenever they were exposed. Today there is far less agreement on this subject. To be sure, homosexuality continues to be viewed as deviant by the majority of non-homosexuals, but it is tolerated to the extent that gay men and women are able to create their own communities and openly fight against such sanctions as discrimination in the labor market. Homosexuals have had some success in gaining passage of laws that would grant homosexual couples the legal standing of de facto married couples.

At the same time, however, the perception of AIDS as a "gay disease" has added to the stigma attached to the homosexual identity (Altman, 1987; Bayer, 1988). This can be

Taslima Nasrin, a world-renowned feminist author and poet from Bangladesh, is in hiding to avoid arrest or mob violence because of her criticism of Islamic gender norms. She is considered a courageous intellectual by many in the West but a deviant criminal by key political and religious authorities in her own country.

seen in the strenuous attack by Senator Jesse Helms of South Carolina on federal funding for AIDS research. The senator argues that because AIDS is a consequence of "disgusting and immoral behavior," it should not be singled out for special federal funding. Public health officials point out that AIDS is the leading cause of death among men and women aged 25 to 45 and that it is inaccurate to view it as a "gay disease," since it is spreading most rapidly among heterosexuals. Nevertheless, attacks on AIDS funding by Helms and other conservatives are an indication of the extent of the conflict over what constitutes deviance in sexual behavior.

Elsewhere in the world, the growing emphasis on religious orthodoxy in Islamic nations has led to attacks on writers and intellectuals who question Muslim norms. The Egyptian Nobel Prize winner Naguib Mahfouz, the Iranian novelist Salman Rushdie, and Bangladeshi poet and essayist Taslima Nasrin are among those who have experienced such attacks (Weaver, 1994). In the case of Nasrin, because she speaks and writes against the traditional norms that require women to remain in the home, to be bought as brides, and otherwise to be treated as male possessions, fundamentalist religious leaders have offered a reward (about $2,500) to anyone who succeeds in killing her. Nasrin is now in hiding in Europe. "I know if I ever go back I'll have to keep silent, stay inside my house," she says. "I'll never lead a normal life in my country, until my death" (quoted in Weaver, 1994, p. 60).

DEVIANT SUBCULTURES

Even when the majority of the population can be said to support a particular set of values, it will contain many subcultures whose lifestyles are labeled deviant by the larger population. A deviant subculture includes a system of values, attitudes, behaviors, and lifestyles that are opposed to the dominant culture of the society in which it is found (Brake, 1980). The members of the subculture are also members of the larger society; they have families and friends outside the subculture with whom they share many values and norms. But within the subculture they pursue values that are opposed to those of the larger or "mainstream" culture. Subcultures evolve their own rather insulated social worlds or communities, with local myths ("X is a slick dealer who once beat the tables in Vegas and was asked to leave the casino"), ways of measuring people's reputations ("he's a punk," "he's cool"), rituals and social routines, particular language or slang, formal and informal uniforms (e.g., the attire worn by bikers), and symbols of belonging such as tattoos (Simmons, 1985).

Subcultures of drug users and dealers provide many illustrations of the ways in which people who engage in deviant activities often develop their own vocabulary and norms. In his fascinating accounts of the subculture of crack dealers and crack-cocaine addicts, urban sociologist Terry Williams (1989, 1992) shows how everyone in the

THEN AND NOW

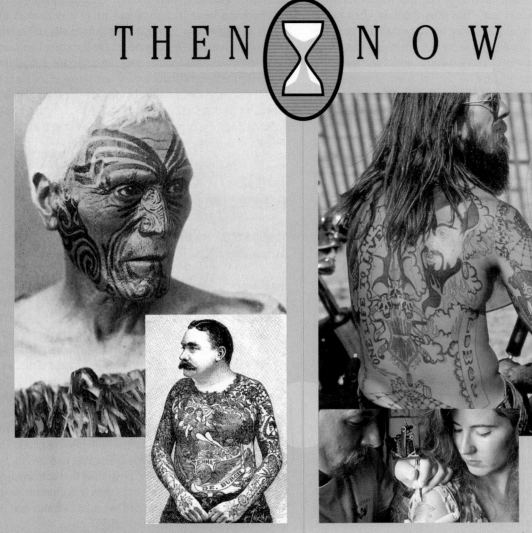

TATTOOS IN RITUAL AND FASHION

Throughout history, as people from different cultures have come into contact with each other, norms that are part of the core culture of one society have been adopted by deviant subcultures in other societies. In time these deviant symbols tend to become less deviant, mildly acceptable, and even fashionable. A fascinating example of this process is the spread of tattooing into the cultures of Europe and the United States.

European and American sailors who traveled through the fabled Pacific isles and Oceania in the eighteenth century were impressed by the *tattaw,* or tattoos, proudly worn by people of high status like the Maori chief shown here. The sailors adopted tattoos as a subcultural symbol of their "exotic" experience.

Later, criminals and prostitutes in European cities took to tattoos as a way of signifying their allegiance to their trades. With almost endless time to kill, prisoners made amateur tattoos (requiring hours of painful jabs with an inked pen) into symbols of their opposition to the "screws" and "pigs"—their jailors and tormentors. Soldiers of the colonial powers, such as the French legionnaire shown here, also adopted tattoos as a way of boasting of their various campaigns.

In the United States in recent decades the tattoo has become a sign of membership in certain subcultures, such as those of skinheads and bikers. But in the world of fashion, what was once thought of as deviant becomes daring and may eventually be fashionable, as seen in the contemporary use of the tattoo as a "fashion statement."

crack subculture—addicts, dealers, and hangers-on—uses the language of the famous TV series *Star Trek* in referring to the drug and its use. The drug itself is often called "Scotty," and smoking the drug is referred to as "beaming up." As addicts and dealers become more deeply enmeshed in the frantic world of crack-cocaine use, they spend increasing amounts of time in the company of people who speak their language and see the world as they do.

Similar examples of the power of the deviant subculture abound in the work of another sociologist, Janet Foster. Foster (1990) observed the lives of young criminal men in an English slum. In the following account of the feelings of a criminal's wife toward the police, Foster shows how the norms and attitudes of the criminals become assimilated into the thinking of women who have relationships with the men but are not themselves criminals:

> The two coppers came up that had nicked [arrested] him, and they said, "You all right, mate?" I thought how can you stand there and be so friendly? One of them looked at me and said, "Why don't you take a seat with the baby, love," and all this. I thought what are you being so nice for, you could be depriving my kid of a father here.... I know it's not their fault and they're for doing what they're paid to do, and it was more fool Jim for doin' it, you know. It was just bad luck that he got caught. That must be the first time I felt any real resentment against the police. (quoted in Foster, 1990, p. 104)

Professional criminals—including major drug dealers, bookmakers and gamblers, hired killers, and loan sharks—who think of their illegal activities as occupations, often become part of secret crime organizations. The best known of these (but hardly the only one) is the Mafia. Originally a Sicilian crime organization, the Mafia spread to the United States via Sicilian immigration in the late nineteenth century. Today families associated with the Mafia are active in most large cities in North America and elsewhere and often extract millions of dollars from legitimate businesses in exchange for "protection." In recent years there have been some successful crusades against the Mafia, but competing crime organizations are always ready to engage in lucrative criminal activities if the Mafia is weakened.

The subculture of organized crime is not unique to North America. In Japan, rates of homicide and mugging are small fractions of those in U.S. cities (Buruma, 1984), yet organized crime thrives there. The Yakuza, as the crime gangs are called, control many illegal businesses, just as they do in other countries, and they often resort to violence to discipline their members. As in the United States, organized crime in Japan is most directly associated with behaviors that are considered deviant, such as prostitution, gambling, and drug use, and a distinct subculture has emerged among those who engage in such behaviors.

In sum, many deviant subcultures flourish because they provide opportunities to engage in behavior that is pleasurable to some people but is considered deviant in "respectable" (conventional) society. Clearly, therefore, the line between what is normal and what is deviant is not nearly as distinct as one might believe from official descriptions of the norms of good conduct. On the other hand, one must recognize that membership in a deviant subculture, especially for those without money and power, often leads to exploitation and early death. In view of these problematic aspects of deviant subcultures, sociological and other explanations of deviant behavior take on special importance.

THEORETICAL PERSPECTIVES ON SOCIAL DEVIANCE

BIOLOGICAL EXPLANATIONS OF CRIME

Early in this century the Italian criminologist Cesare Lombroso (1911) claimed to have proved that criminals were throwbacks to primitive, aggressive human types who could be recognized by physical features like prominent foreheads, shifty eyes, and red hair. Although Lombroso's theory has been thoroughly refuted by modern researchers, efforts to link body type with crime seem destined to reappear from time to time. In the 1940s, for example, the psychologist and physician William Sheldon announced that body type was correlated with crime. He believed that human beings could be classified into three types: *ectomorphs,* or thin people; *endomorphs,* or soft, fat people; and *mesomorphs,* or people with firm, well-defined muscles. The latter were most prone to crime, according to Sheldon, but he neglected to account for the possibility that mesomorphs simply might have led harder lives than less muscular individuals and were better equipped to commit crimes that require strength (Glueck & Glueck, 1950).

The more modern biological view is represented in the influential work of social scientists Richard J. Herrnstein and James Q. Wilson. Their research has led them to conclude that both biology and social environment play important roles in producing criminals. In commenting on a recent study by researchers at the U.S. Department of Justice reporting that more than one third of adult criminals in U.S. jails have at least one parent who is or was a criminal, Herrnstein argues that whatever determines criminality "is transmitted both genetically and environmentally. So kids brought up in criminal families get a double exposure" (quoted in Butterfield, 1992b, p. A16).

A study by Deborah W. Denno offers support for this view. In her research on 1,000 African American boys from poor neighborhoods of Philadelphia, Denno (1990) found that a disproportionate number of individuals who had become criminals had histories of childhood hyperactivity. This genetically transmitted condition makes it difficult for children to concentrate and succeed in school. It also can make it hard for them to hold jobs. Thus Denno sees the causal chain as one of biological hyperactivity leading to social failure and then to crime.

But to many social scientists such studies are not convincing. Marvin E. Wolfgang, one of the nation's leading experts on criminality, points out that all the studies deal with people from poor neighborhoods, where a high proportion of people will be sent to jail whether they are related or not and whether they were hyperactive as children or not. Hyperactivity is also found in children from wealthier families but is not so often associated with criminal careers because the families can afford special schools and programs to deal with the condition (Butterfield, 1992b).

SOCIAL-SCIENTIFIC EXPLANATIONS OF DEVIANCE AND CRIME

Early sociological explanations of social deviance were also influenced by the biological concept of disease. The earliest of these explanations viewed crime as a form of social pathology, or social disease, that could be attributed to the evils of city life. Corruption, criminality, and depravity were thought to be bred in slums and to infect innocent residents of those grim communities, just as typhoid spread in

unclean surroundings and was passed by contact from one victim to another (Queen & Debler, 1940/1925). Thus many early juvenile training schools were built in rural areas where they would be isolated from the "corrupting" influence of cities (Platt, 1977).

The early sociological view of deviance and crime as resulting from "social pathologies" tended to rely on subjective terms and circular reasoning. To refer to crime or other forms of deviance as pathologies, for example, does not provide a theory of causality. It merely attaches a scientific-sounding term to behavior that the larger society finds wrong or offensive. It does not offer any insight into why the behavior occurs, what benefits it might provide for those who engage in it, and how it evolves from other behaviors or social conditions. In consequence, the view of deviance as a kind of disease was replaced by more objective and verifiable theories derived from the functionalist, interactionist, and conflict perspectives of modern sociology.

THE FUNCTIONALIST PERSPECTIVE

The functionalist theorist Robert K. Merton (1938) developed a typology of deviance based on how people adapt to

STUDY CHART   Theoretical Perspectives on Deviance

PERSPECTIVE	DESCRIPTION	CRITIQUE
BIOLOGICAL THEORIES	Crime and other forms of deviance are genetically determined.	There is evidence of effects of socialization.
SOCIOLOGICAL THEORIES **Social Pathology**	The deviant or criminal person is a product of a "social sickness" or social disintegration.	A popular notion, but discredited among professionals because it suggests no real theory of causality.
Functionalism	Deviance and crime result from the failure of social structures to function properly. Every society produces its own forms of deviance.	Does not explain why some people drift into deviant subcultures.
Conflict Theories *Cultural conflict*	Cultural conflict creates opportunities for deviance and criminal gain in deviant subcultures (e.g., prohibitions create opportunities for organized crime).	Explains a narrow range of phenomena.
Marxian theory	Capitalism produces poor and powerless masses who may resort to crime to survive. The rich employ their own agents to break laws and enhance their power and wealth.	Crime exists in societies that have sought to eliminate capitalism.
Interactionist Theories *Differential association*	Criminal careers result from recruitment into crime groups based on association and interaction with criminals.	Excellent explanation of recruitment but not as effective in explaining deviant careers.
Labeling	Deviance is created by groups that have the power to attach labels to others, marking particular people as outsiders. It is extremely difficult to shed a label once it has been acquired, and the labeled person tends to behave in the expected manner.	Not always supported by empirical evidence. People can also use labels (e.g., *drunk*) to change their behavior.

the demands of their society. Merton's aim was to discover "how some social structures *exert a definite pressure upon certain persons in society to engage in nonconformist rather than conformist conduct*" (p. 672). "Among the elements of social and cultural structure," Merton continued, "two are important for our purposes. . . . The first consists of culturally defined goals, purposes, and interests. . . . The second . . . defines, regulates, and controls the acceptable modes of achieving these goals" (pp. 672–673).

Merton's explanation of deviance is based on the concept of anomie, or normlessness. In his view, anomie results from the frustration and confusion people feel when what they have been taught to desire cannot be achieved by the legitimate means available to them. Merton believes that people in North America and other modern societies exhibit high levels of anomie because they are socialized to desire success in the form of material well-being and social prestige. For many, however, the means of attaining these culturally defined ends, such as hard work and saving, seem to be out of reach. This is especially true for people who experience rapid social changes, such as the closing of factories, and find themselves deprived of opportunities to attain what they have come to expect from life.

Consider some examples. Possession of money is a culturally defined goal. Work is a socially acceptable mode of achieving that goal; theft is not. Mating is also a culturally defined goal. Courtship and seduction are acceptable means of achieving it; kidnap and rape are not. But if theft and rape are unacceptable means of achieving culturally defined goals, why do they exist? According to Merton, the gap between culturally defined goals and acceptable means of achieving them causes feelings of anomie, which in turn make some people more likely to choose deviant strategies of various kinds.

Through socialization we learn the goals and acceptable means of our society. Most of us would love to be rich or powerful or famous. We accept these goals of our culture. We also accept the legitimate means of achieving them: education, work, the electoral process, plastic surgery, acting

school, and so on. We are conformists. But not everyone accepts either the cultural goals or the accepted means of achieving them. Some become "innovators" in that they explore (and often step over) the frontiers of acceptable goal-seeking behavior; others (e.g., hoboes) retreat into a life that rejects both the goals and the accepted means; some rebel and seek to change the goals and the institutions that support them; and still others reject the quest for these precious values while carrying out the rituals of social institutions. (In many bureaucracies, for example, one can find ritualists who have given up the quest for promotion yet insist on receiving deference from people below them in the hierarchy.) Merton's typology thus is based on whether people accept either the cultural goals of their society, the acceptable means of achieving them, or neither. Figure 7.3 presents this typology and Figure 7.4 gives examples of all the deviant types in Merton's framework.

You may be wondering what there is in Merton's theory that explains why some poor people resort to crime while so many others do not. The answer lies in the way people who experience anomie gravitate toward criminal subcultures. For example, adolescents who choose to steal to obtain things that their parents cannot afford must learn new norms—they must learn how to steal successfully and must receive some approval from peers for their conduct (Cloward & Ohlin, 1960). As a result, they drift toward deviant peer groups. But this explanation presents a problem for the functionalist perspective: If there are deviant subcultures, the idea that there is a single culture whose goals and means are shared by all members of society is called into question. The presence of different subcultures within a society suggests another possible cause of deviant behaviors: conflict between groups.

CONFLICT PERSPECTIVES

Cultural Conflict. In an influential essay, "Crime as an American Way of Life," Daniel Bell (1962a) observed that at the turn of the twentieth century cultural conflict developed between the "Big City and the small-town

Merton explained that (+) signifies "acceptance," (–) signifies "elimination," and (+/–) signifies "rejection and substitution of new goals and standards." The line separating rebellion from the other roles signifies that the individual no longer accepts the society's culture and structure; other individuals, although they may deviate, continue to accept the society's culture and structure.

FIGURE 7.3 **The Merton Typology—Modes of Adaptation by Individuals Within the Society or Group**

MODE OF ADAPTATION		CULTURAL GOALS	INSTITUTIONAL MEANS
	Conformity	+	+
	Innovation	+	–
	Ritualism	–	+
	Retreatism	–	–
	Rebellion	+/–	+/–

conscience. Crime as a growing business was fed by the revenues from prostitution, liquor, and gambling that a wide-open urban society encouraged and that a middle-class Protestant ethos tried to suppress with a ferocity unmatched in any other civilized society" (p. 128). This example of conflict between the official morality of the dominant American culture and the norms of subcultures that do not include strictures against gambling, drinking, prostitution, and the like encouraged the growth of criminal organizations. In the United States as in many other societies, such organizations thrive by supplying the needs of millions of people in cities, towns, and rural areas who appear to be law-abiding citizens yet engage in certain deviant behaviors.

The prohibition of alcoholic beverages in the United States from 1919 to 1933 is an example of how cultural conflict can lead to situations that encourage criminal activity. Prohibition has been interpreted as an effort by the nation's largely Protestant lawmakers to impose their version of morality on immigrant groups for whom consumption of alcohol was an important part of social life. Once they were passed, however, laws against the production and sale of alcoholic beverages created opportunities for illegal production, bootlegging (smuggling), and illegal drinking establishments (speakeasies). These in turn supported the rise of organized crime syndicates. The current laws against drugs like marijuana and cocaine have similar effects in that they lead to the clandestine production and supply of these illegal but widely used substances. Similar opportunities to make illegal profits arise when states pass laws raising the drinking age (Gusfield, 1966; Kornblum & Julian, 1995).

To recognize these effects of cultural conflict is not to condone the sale and use of illegal drugs. Rather, it is to be aware that whenever laws promoted by the powerful impose a set of moral standards on a minority, illegal markets are created that tend to be supplied by criminal organizations. Such organizations often act ruthlessly to control their markets, as can be seen in the murder of Mexican border guards who surprise drug smugglers, the killing of cocaine traffick-

ers by rival dealers in Miami or Los Angeles, or the periodic "wars" that break out between organized-crime families in many large cities.

Marxian Conflict Theory. For Marxian students of social deviance, the cultural-conflict explanation is inadequate because it does not take into account the effects of power and class conflict. Marxian sociologists believe that situations like Prohibition do not occur just because of cultural conflict. They happen because the powerful classes in society (i.e., those who own and control the means of production) wish to control the working class and the poor so that they will produce more. From the Marxian perspective, as criminologist Richard Quinney (1980) points out, "crime is to be understood in terms of the development of capitalism" (p. 41), as it was in Marx's original analysis. From this perspective, most crime is essentially a form of class conflict—either the have-nots taking what they can from the ruling class, or the rich and their agents somehow taking what they can from the poor. Box 7.2 shows that precapitalist societies can also be viewed as producing specific forms of crime, such as banditry.

The economic "robber barons"—John Jacob Astor, John D. Rockefeller, J. P. Morgan, Leland Stanford, Andrew Carnegie, and many others—amassed huge fortunes in the period of booming industrial growth following the Civil War. But they often resorted to illegal means in pursuing the culturally approved goal of great wealth. Among other tactics, they used violence to drive settlers off land they had purchased or to break strikes by workers, and they were not above manipulating prices in order to drive out competitors and monopolize the markets for steel, oil, coal, precious metals, food products, and numerous other goods. In Merton's typology of deviance, their actions would classify them as "innovators" (see Figure 7.4), but from a Marxian viewpoint they were merely carrying out "the logic of capitalism," which was based on the exploitation of the poor by the rich and powerful.

Marxian students of deviance point out that legal definitions of deviant behavior usually depend on the ability of the more powerful members of society to impose their will

FIGURE 7.4 **Examples of Social Roles Based on the Merton Typology**

MODE OF ADAPTATION		THE POOR	THE MIDDLE CLASS	THE RICH
	Conformity	The working poor	The suburban family	The wealthy civic leader
	Innovation	The mugger	The embezzler	The stock manipulator
	Ritualism	The chronic welfare recipient	The resigned bureaucrat	The hedonist
	Retreatism	The wino or junkie	The skidding alcoholic	The bohemian
	Rebellion	The bandit	The anarchist	The fascist

These examples are meant to illustrate possible outcomes, not stereotypes. Perceptions of approved goals and means may vary. In some cases, for example, the very rich, who feel that they could be even richer were it not for legal obstacles in their path, may choose to bend the rules. Also, a number of cultural values besides wealth shape the likelihood that a member of a given class will behave as he or she does.

BOX 7.2   USING THE SOCIOLOGICAL IMAGINATION

Poverty and Bandits

Bandits, brigands, train robbers, Robin Hoods—bad men and women of the frontiers appear throughout human history. Every society has its myths about great bandits, most of which are loosely based on the actual life histories of criminals who broke away from a life of rural poverty to terrorize the countryside and later became cultural heroes. According to the social historian Eric Hobsbawm (1981),

> The crucial fact about the bandit's social situation is its ambiguity. He [or, sometimes, she] is an outsider and a rebel, a poor man who refuses to accept the normal roles of poverty, and establishes his freedom by means of the only resources within reach of the poor: strength, bravery, cunning, and determination. This draws him close to the poor; he is one of them. It sets him in opposition to the hierarchy of power, wealth, and influence; he is not one of them. (p. 88)

The more successful the bandit is, however, the more he will be "inevitably drawn into the web of wealth and power, because, unlike other peasants, he acquires wealth and exerts power" (Hobsbawm, 1981, p. 88). Thus under some conditions the bandits of a society may actually form capitalist corporations of sorts, as was the case in the evolution of the Mafia out of the traditions of banditry in Sicily and southern Italy. Under conditions in which there is open class struggle, the bandit can become a revolutionary hero, as in the example of the legendary Mexican bandit Pancho Villa, who became a leader of the Mexican revolution in the early decades of this century.

In societies with well-developed mass media and movies, bandits like Bonnie Parker and Jesse James often become almost mythical figures. As their story is told and retold on the screen and on television, they become celebrities and the violence of their criminal careers receives less attention.

Bonnie Parker

Pancho Villa

Jesse James

on the government and to protect their actions from legal sanctions. Thus the crimes of the robber barons almost always went unpunished. Definitions of what is criminal and who should be punished are generally applied more forcefully to the poor and the working class (Balbus, 1978; Quinney, 1978; Turk, 1978).

Marx and his collaborator Friedrich Engels recognized that the working class (or *proletariat,* as they called it) would resort to individual crimes like robbery when driven to do so by unemployment and poverty, but they believed that the workers would be more likely to form associations aimed at destroying capitalism. The chronic poor, on the other hand, would form a class that Marx called the *lumpenproletariat,* people who were unable to get jobs in the capitalist system or were cast off for not working hard enough or for being injured or sick. Marx did not believe that members of this class would join forces with the proletariat. Instead, they would act as spies, informers, and thugs whose services could be purchased by the rich to be used against the workers. Marx agreed with other thinkers of his time who called the lumpenproletariat the "dangerous class" created by capitalism; from its ranks came thieves, prostitutes, gamblers, pickpockets, con artists, and contract murderers.

It can be helpful to think of crime and deviance as symptoms of the class struggles that occur in any society and to show that laws that define and punish criminal behaviors are often imposed by the powerful on those with less power. But to attribute crime as we know it to the workings of capitalism is to suggest that if capitalism were abolished, crime would vanish. This clearly is not the case. In China, for example, there are thousands of prisoners in a vast chain of prison camps. Many of those prisoners were convicted of the deviant act of opposing the dominant regime (Ning, 1995; Wu & Wakeman, 1995). And in Cuba homosexuality is considered a serious crime. It is severely punished because the society's leaders think of it as an offense against masculinity and a symbol of a "decadent" subculture. As these examples indicate, societies with Marxian ideologies are hardly free from their own forms of deviance and crime.

THE INTERACTIONIST PERSPECTIVE

Functionalist theories explain deviance as a reaction to social dysfunctions; conflict theories explain it as a product of deviant subcultures or of the type of class struggle that occurs in a society in a particular historical period. Neither of these approaches accounts very well for the issues of recruitment and production. *Recruitment,* in this context, refers to the question of why some people become deviants while others in the same social situation do not. *Production* refers to the creation of new categories of deviance in a society.

Recruitment Through Differential Association.   In 1940 the sociologist and criminologist Edwin H.

Sutherland published a paper, "White Collar Criminality," in which he argued that official crime statistics do not measure the many forms of crime that are not correlated with poverty. Outstanding among these are *white-collar crimes*—that is, the criminal behavior of people in business and professional positions. In Sutherland's words:

> White-collar criminality in business is expressed most frequently in the form of misrepresentation in financial statements of corporations, manipulation in stock exchange, commercial bribery, bribery of public officials directly or indirectly in order to secure favorable contracts and legislation, misrepresentation in advertising and salesmanship, embezzlement and misapplication of funds, short weights and measures and misgrading of commodities, tax frauds, misapplication of funds in receiverships and bankruptcies. These are what Al Capone called "the legitimate rackets." These and many others are found in abundance in the business world. (1940, pp. 2–3)

Sutherland was pointing out that an accurate statistical comparison of the crimes committed by the rich and the poor was not available. But his paper on white-collar crime also set forth an interactionist theory of crime and deviance:

> White collar criminality, just as other systematic criminality . . . is learned in direct or indirect association with those who already practice the behavior; and . . . those who learn this criminal behavior are segregated from frequent and intimate contacts with law-abiding behavior. Whether a person becomes a criminal or not is determined largely by the comparative frequency and intimacy of his contacts with the two types of behavior. This may be called the process of **differential association.** (pp. 10–11; emphasis added)

The concept of differential association offered an answer to some of the weaknesses of functionalist and conflict theories. Not only did it account for the prevalence of deviance in all social classes but it also provided clues to how crime is learned in groups that are culturally distinct from the dominant society. For example, in the 1920s sociologist Clifford Shaw (1929) observed that some Chicago neighborhoods had consistently higher rates of juvenile delinquency than others. These were immigrant neighborhoods, but their high rates of delinquency persisted regardless of which immigrant groups lived there at any given time. Sutherland's theory explained this pattern by calling attention to the culture of deviance that had become part of the way of life of teenagers in those neighborhoods. According to Sutherland, the teenagers became delinquent because they interacted in groups whose culture legitimated crime. It was not a matter of teenage delinquents deviating from conventional norms because the approved means of achieving approved goals were closed to them. Rather, they acted as they did because the culture of their peer group made crime an acceptable means of achieving desired goals.

In an empirical study that tested Sutherland's theory, Walter Miller (1958) found that delinquency in areas with high rates of juvenile crime was in fact supported by the norms of lower-class teenage peer groups. In 3 years of careful observation Miller found that delinquent groups had a set of well-defined values: trouble, toughness, smartness, excitement, fate, and autonomy. Whereas other groups felt that it was important to stay out of trouble, the delinquent groups viewed trouble—meaning fighting, drinking, and sexual adventures—as something to brag about, as long as they didn't get caught. Toughness as shown by physical prowess or fearlessness; smartness as evidenced by the ability to con or outsmart gullible "marks"; the excitement to be found in risking danger successfully; one's fate as demonstrated by luck or good fortune in avoiding capture; and the autonomy that crime seemed to provide in the form of independence from authorities—all were values of delinquent groups that distinguished them from nondelinquent groups in the same neighborhoods.

A study by criminologist Donald R. Cressey (1971/1953) supported the theory of differential association with the finding that embezzlers generally had to learn how to commit their crime by associating with people who could teach them how to commit it with the greatest likelihood of avoiding suspicion. Furthermore, Cressey also found that people who became embezzlers often had serious personal problems (marital difficulties, gambling, and the like) that directed them toward people who would influence them to commit this form of white-collar crime. When bank officials had problems of this sort, they were vulnerable to suggestions of deviant means of gaining money and solving personal problems while maintaining the outward signs of respectability.

Not all deviants are people whose means of achieving success have been blocked or who are acting out some form of class struggle or have associated with a deviant group. For example, many alcoholics and drug users are not thought of as deviant, either because their behavior is not considered serious or because it is not witnessed by other people. From an interactionist perspective, the key question about such people is how their behavior is understood by others. The central concepts that attempt to answer this question are *labeling* and the idea of the *deviant career.*

Labeling. According to symbolic-interactionist theory, deviance is produced by a process known as *labeling,* meaning a societal reaction to certain behaviors that labels the offender as a deviant. Most often, labeling is done by official agents of social control like the police, the courts, mental institutions, and schools, which distribute labels like "troublemaker," "hustler," "kook," or "blockhead" that stick, often for life (Becker, 1963; Erikson, 1962; Gusfield, 1981; Kitsuse, 1962; Lemert, 1967; Schur, 1984). Here is what occurs in the labeling process, according to Howard Becker:

Social groups create deviance by making the rules whose infraction constitutes deviance and by applying those rules to particular people and labeling them as outsiders. From this point of view, deviance is not a quality of the act the person commits, but rather a consequence of the application by others of rules and sanctions to an "offender." The deviant is one to whom that label has been successfully applied; deviant behavior is behavior that people so label. (1963, p. 9)

In a famous experiment that tested the effects of labeling, David Rosenhan (1973) and eight other researchers were admitted to a mental hospital after pretending to "hear voices." Each of these pseudopatients was diagnosed as schizophrenic. Before long many of the patients with whom the pseudopatients associated recognized them as normal, but the doctors who had made the diagnosis continued to think of them as schizophrenic. As the pseudopatients waited in the lunch line, for example, they were said to be exhibiting "oral-acquisitive behavior." Gradually the pseudopatients were released with the diagnosis of schizophrenia in remission, but none was ever thought to be cured.

Rosenhan and his researchers also observed that not only did the diagnosis of schizophrenia label the patient for life but the label itself became a justification for other forms of mistreatment. The doctors and hospital staff disregarded the patients' opinions, treated them as incompetent, and often punished them for infractions of minor rules. The hospital's social atmosphere was based on the powerlessness of the people who were labeled mentally ill.

Rosenhan's study accelerated the movement to reform mental institutions and to deinstitutionalize as many mental patients as possible. But studies of deinstitutionalized mental patients (many of whom are homeless), together with research on the problems of released convicts, have shown that the labels attached to people who have deviated become incorporated into their definitions of themselves as deviant. In this way labeling at some stage of a person's development tends to steer that person into a community of other deviants, where he or she may become trapped in a *deviant career* (Bassuk, 1984).

Deviant Careers. "There is no reason to assume," Becker (1963) points out, "that only those who finally commit a deviant act actually have the impulse to do so. It is much more likely that most people experience deviant impulses frequently. At least in fantasy, people are much more deviant than they appear" (p. 26). Becker suggests that the proper sociological question is not why some people do things that are disapproved of but, rather, why "conventional people do not follow through on the deviant impulses they have" (p. 26). According to Becker and other interactionists, the answers are to be found in the individual's commitment to conventional institutions and behaviors.

Commitment means adherence to and dependence on the norms of a given social institution. The middle-class youth's commitment to school, which has developed over many years of socialization in the family and the community, often prevents him or her from giving in to the impulse to play hooky. "In fact," Becker asserts, "the normal development of people in our society (and probably in any society) can be seen as a series of progressively increasing commitments to conventional norms and institutions" (p. 27).

Travis Hirschi studied how people become committed to conventional norms. Such commitment, he found, emerges out of the interactions that create our social bonds to others. When we are closely tied to people who adhere to conventional norms, we have little chance to deviate. And as we grow older, our investment in upholding conventional norms increases because we feel that we have more to protect. This process of lifetime socialization in groups produces a system of social control that is internalized in most members of the society (Hirschi & Gottfredson, 1980). (See Chapter 5 for more on socialization over the life course.)

By the same token, a person who once gives in to the impulse to commit a deviant act and is caught, or who becomes a member of a deviant group because it has recruited him or her, gradually develops a commitment to that group and its deviant culture. The reasons for taking the first step toward deviance may be many and varied, but from the interactionist perspective "one of the most crucial steps in the process of building a stable pattern of deviant behavior is likely to be the experience of being caught and publicly labeled as deviant" (Becker, 1963, p. 31).

In a well-known empirical study of youth gangs, William J. Chambliss (1973) applied both the conflict and interactionist perspectives. For 2 years Chambliss observed the Saints, a gang of boys from rather wealthy families, and the Roughnecks, a gang of poor boys from the same community. Both gangs engaged in car theft and joyriding, vandalism, dangerous practical jokes, and fighting—and in fact the Saints were involved in a larger overall number of incidents. But the Roughnecks were more frequently caught by authorities, described as "tough young criminals headed for trouble," and sent to reform school. The wealthier youths were rarely caught and were never labeled delinquent.

Chambliss observed that the Saints had access to cars and could commit their misdeeds in other communities, where they were not known. The Roughnecks hung out in their own community and performed many of their antisocial acts there. A far more important explanation, according to Chambliss, pertained to the relative influence of the boys' parents. The parents of the Saints argued that the boys' activities were normal youthful behavior; the boys were just "sowing their wild oats." Their social position enabled them to influence the way their children's behavior was perceived, an influence the parents of the Roughnecks did not have. Thus the Roughnecks were caught and labeled and became increasingly committed to deviant careers, but the Saints escaped without serious sanction.

In commenting on Chambliss's study, sociologists often note that members of both gangs engaged in deviant acts, referred to as **primary deviance,** but that only the Roughnecks were labeled delinquent by the police and the juvenile courts. As a result of that labeling, many of the Roughnecks went on to commit acts that sociologists call **secondary deviance**—that is, behaviors appropriate to someone who has already been labeled delinquent. (For example, in juvenile detention centers teenage offenders often learn deviant skills such as how to deal in drugs.) The distinction between primary and secondary deviance is useful because it emphasizes that most of us deviate from cultural norms in many ways; but once we are *labeled* deviant we tend to commit additional deviant acts in order to fulfill the negative definitions society has attached to us (Goode, 1994; Schur, 1971).

Reasonable as the labeling perspective appears, it has not always been borne out by empirical research. Some studies have found that people who have been labeled delinquent after being caught and convicted of serious offenses go on to commit other deviant acts, but other studies have found that labeling can lead to decreased deviance and a lower probability of further offenses (Rubington & Weinberg, 1987). (The various theoretical approaches to crime that we have discussed are summarized in the study chart on page 191.)

CRIME AND SOCIAL CONTROL

We have seen that crime as defined by a society's laws is only one aspect of the range of behaviors included in the study of deviance. But the general public and policy makers in government are most concerned with crime and its control. In this section, therefore, we touch on some of the most hotly debated issues in the control of crime and the treatment of criminals.

At the beginning of the chapter we defined social control in broad terms as all the ways in which a society establishes and enforces its cultural norms. Certainly it is true that without socialization and the controlling actions of social groups like the family, schools, the military, and corporations there would be much more anomie, crime, and violence. But in considering a society's means of controlling crime, sociologists most often study what might be called "government social control"—that is, the society's legal codes; the operation of its judicial, police, penal, and rehabilitative institutions; and the ways in which its most powerful members promote their views of crime, deviance, and social control (Black, 1984; Scull, 1988). The rates of crime and the ways in which crime affects communities in different parts of the society establish the need for these institutions of social control, as we will see in the following analysis of the ecology of crime in American society.

TABLE 7.2	The Crime Rate,* by Region of the United States, 1994			
	NORTHEAST	**MIDWEST**	**SOUTH**	**WEST**
Crime Index, total	4,344.5	4,816.1	5,848.4	6,151.9
Violent crime, total	662.1	600.7	768.6	805.4
Murder	7.1	7.5	10.7	9.4
Forcible rape	26.5	42.9	43.4	40.0
Robbery	291.3	200.2	221.0	256.3
Aggravated assault	337.3	350.1	493.5	499.7
Property crime, total	3,682.4	4,215.4	5,079.8	5,346.5
Burglary	803.8	886.2	1,206.1	1,162.7
Larceny-theft	2,279.6	2,869.0	3,329.0	3,384.0
Motor vehicle theft	598.9	460.1	544.7	799.8

*Offenses known to the police, per 100,000 population.

Source: FBI, 1995.

ECOLOGICAL DIMENSIONS OF CRIME

Table 7.2 shows that the incidence of different types of crime varies from one region of the country to another, with homicides highest in the southern states, and rape and assault lowest in the northeastern states. Ecological data like these are an essential starting point in research on the incidence of crime and provide some insights into why such regional differences exist. In the South, for example, high rates of gun ownership contribute to higher homicide rates. The higher average age of the population in the Northeast contributes to lower rates of rape and assault in that region, while greater disparities between rich and poor lead to a higher rate of robbery.

Another contribution of ecological analysis can be seen in data on the relationship between crime and the age composition of a population. Some political leaders and social scientists favor larger police forces and tougher law enforcement, and they argue that these policies are responsible for the decrease in the U.S. crime rate over the past few years. However, it must not be forgotten that the age composition of the U.S. population is changing rather quickly. Among other things, the baby boom generation has moved out of the young-adult years, those in which people are most likely to commit crimes. (About half of all reported violent crimes are committed by males between the ages of 15 and 24.) Thus, before taking credit for reducing crime rates, law enforcement agencies and advocates of tough anticrime measures must make certain that lower crime rates are not simply a result of a reduction in the most crime-prone portion of the population.

Still another variable that lends itself to ecological analysis is the effect of possession of firearms on homicide rates. As Figure 7.5 shows, the United States far outpaces other industrialized nations in number of homicides. No

other nation even comes close. This fact is often thought to reflect a greater overall level of violence in the United States than in other comparable nations. However, in a study comparing rates of violent crime in Denmark and northeastern Ohio, investigators found that rates of assault did not differ in the two areas. What did differ were rates of homicide using firearms; such crimes were much more frequent in Ohio. In Denmark the possession of handguns is banned, whereas in the United States "50 percent of all households have guns and one in five has a handgun" (Mawson, 1989, p. 239). (See Box 7.3.)

As mentioned earlier in the chapter, studies of criminal victimization, which ask people about their actual experiences with crime, have provided a major breakthrough in our understanding of crime in complex societies. For every 1,000 crimes reported in victimization surveys, only 540—slightly more than half—are reported to the police. Of those, only 65 result in arrests. Of all those arrested, 36 are convicted; of all those convicted, 17 are sentenced to custody. Of those, only 3 are sentenced to prison for more than 1 year (Zeisel, 1982). Thus, the probability that a criminal who is arrested will be sentenced to prison is minuscule. However, while the probability of arrest for an individual crime against property is low, criminals who commit many crimes do tend to get arrested eventually.

Most sociological studies of recidivism (the probability that a person who has served a jail term will commit additional crimes and be jailed again) indicate that there is an overall probability of 50 percent that recidivism will occur. Recidivism is most frequent among young minority males from poor backgrounds who are drug and/or alcohol addicts and have been imprisoned on numerous previous occasions for crimes against property (Land, 1989). Given both high crime rates and high rates of recidivism, it is little wonder that the search for solutions to the problem of

FIGURE 7.5

M A P P I N G   S O C I A L   C H A N G E

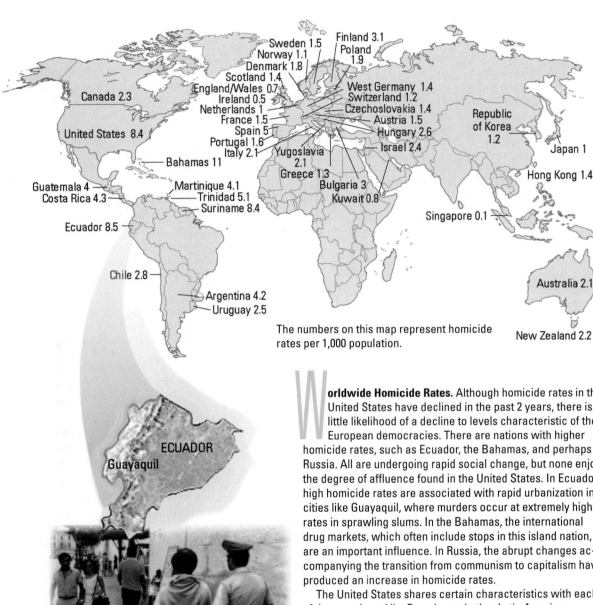

The numbers on this map represent homicide rates per 1,000 population.

Sweden 1.5
Norway 1.1
Denmark 1.8
Scotland 1.4
England/Wales 0.7
Ireland 0.5
Netherlands 1
France 1.5
Spain 5
Portugal 1.6
Italy 2.1
Finland 3.1
Poland 1.9
West Germany 1.4
Switzerland 1.2
Czechoslovakia 1.4
Austria 1.5
Hungary 2.6
Israel 2.4
Yugoslavia 2.1
Greece 1.3
Bulgaria 3
Kuwait 0.8
Republic of Korea 1.2
Japan 1
Hong Kong 1.4
Singapore 0.1
Canada 2.3
United States 8.4
Bahamas 11
Guatemala 4
Costa Rica 4.3
Martinique 4.1
Trinidad 5.1
Suriname 8.4
Ecuador 8.5
Chile 2.8
Argentina 4.2
Uruguay 2.5
Australia 2.1
New Zealand 2.2

Worldwide Homicide Rates. Although homicide rates in the United States have declined in the past 2 years, there is little likelihood of a decline to levels characteristic of the European democracies. There are nations with higher homicide rates, such as Ecuador, the Bahamas, and perhaps Russia. All are undergoing rapid social change, but none enjoy the degree of affluence found in the United States. In Ecuador, high homicide rates are associated with rapid urbanization in cities like Guayaquil, where murders occur at extremely high rates in sprawling slums. In the Bahamas, the international drug markets, which often include stops in this island nation, are an important influence. In Russia, the abrupt changes accompanying the transition from communism to capitalism have produced an increase in homicide rates.

The United States shares certain characteristics with each of these nations. Like Ecuador and other Latin American nations, it has a frontier tradition that fosters and still maintains norms of rugged individualism, including the use of guns. It also has a widening gap between rich and poor, with the poor often concentrated in ghetto slums. Drug activity contributes significantly to homicide rates, as in the Bahamas. And as in Russia, much of the deadly violence occurring in the United States stems from the activities of criminals in organized gangs.

BOX 7.3   GLOBAL SOCIAL CHANGE

Changing Patterns of Interpersonal Violence

If one were to ask the average Japanese citizen to name the most violent nation on earth, he or she would no doubt say that it is the United States. In 1993 a Japanese exchange student was shot to death in Louisiana when he wandered up to the wrong house looking for a party to which he had been invited. Believing him to be an intruder, the resident shot him in a moment of terror and confusion. In Japan this story was front-page news for many weeks.

We often hear that the United States is one of the most violent nations on earth, but the reasoning behind that claim as well as its possible causes demand careful consideration. After all, there is far more violence and mass bloodshed in Bosnia, Armenia, Somalia, or Lebanon than there is in the United States. But although war-torn regions of the world may experience more violence overall, the accompanying chart shows how high the United States ranks in rates of homicide, the most extreme form of interpersonal violence. By this measure, the United States is indeed among the global leaders (Reiss & Roth, 1993).

Interpersonal violence occurs between individuals, usually for personal reasons or selfish motives. In all societies people resort to violence when they become especially angered or feel that they must act in self-defense. One difference between nations with high homicide rates and those with lower rates is in the availability of lethal weapons, especially handguns. The nations that lead the world in homicide rates are characterized by widespread availability of handguns and limited success in controlling their distribution. But there is an even broader cultural explanation for why people in a given society arm themselves and are quicker to act violently toward each other.

Why do nations like England, Ireland, Japan, and Germany have murder rates that are less than one quarter of the U.S. rate? Is it because people in the United States are much more violently deviant than people in those nations? Social scientists do not believe that Americans are inherently more violent than other people. There are forms of violence in the British Isles, such as brutal fights after soccer games, that do not routinely occur in the United

States. But lethal violence is associated with a number of aspects of American history and contemporary social problems that are less prevalent in nations with less violence.

First, societies that go through a "frontier stage" of rapid social change during which social control is problematic for many decades tend to develop traditions of vigilantism, possession of personal weapons, and justification for their use under extreme circumstances. Ecuador and other Latin American nations that rank high in homicide rates share such traditions with the United States.

Second, nations that are experiencing large-scale drug epidemics tend to have high rates of violence. Again, the United States is in this category, along with nations like the Bahamas and Colombia (not shown in the chart). Where there are extensive illegal markets protected by armed agents, as is true of the cocaine trade and other underground markets, there is also a great deal of violence.

The nations of Great Britain traditionally have not armed their police forces and have made a point of applying strict sanctions against civilian possession of handguns. These norms show up in lower murder rates. In the United States, which until recently has not applied strong sanctions against gun possession, angry confrontations and domestic quarrels are much more likely to escalate into homicide— including bystander deaths associated with drug-related violence and conflicts among gangs. Efforts to pass gun control legislation are having greater success as a result of outrage over the deaths of children and bystanders, but such legislation is still opposed by powerful gun lobbies and the counternorm that suggests that the right to bear arms is an element of individual freedom.

In sum, the reasons why the United States has such high rates of interpersonal violence, as measured by its homicide rate, are related to its history of rapid social change, the current drug epidemic, and long-standing cultural conflict between norms against violence and norms that encourage the possession of personal weapons.

overcrowded prisons, as well as alternatives to imprisonment, occupies many researchers.

INSTITUTIONS OF COERCIVE CONTROL: COURTS AND PRISONS

When the United States consisted mainly of small agrarian communities, social control of deviance and crime was carried out by the local institutions of the family or the church. Parents, for example, were expected to control their children; if they did not, they would lose the respect of other members of the community. But as the size, complexity,

and diversity of societies increase, the ability of local institutions to control all of the society's members is diminished (Wirth, 1968/1938). Societies therefore develop specialized, more or less coercive institutions to deal with deviants. Courts, prisons, police forces, and social-welfare agencies grow as the influence of the community on the behavior of its members declines.

Capital Punishment—Cruel and Unusual?

Capital punishment provides an illustration of the issues raised by the use of coercive forms of social control. Only recently (during this century in some nations) has the

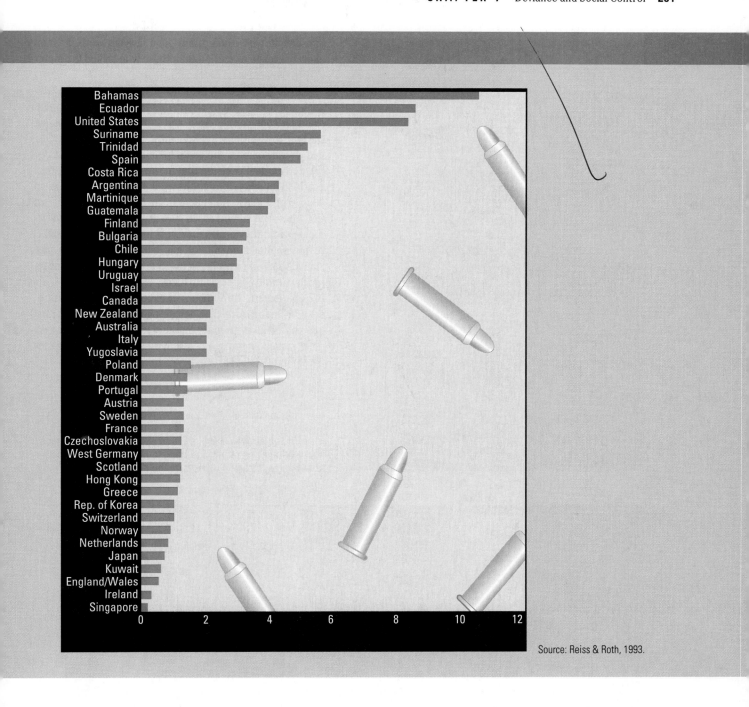

Bahamas						
Ecuador						
United States						
Suriname						
Trinidad						
Spain						
Costa Rica						
Argentina						
Martinique						
Guatemala						
Finland						
Bulgaria						
Chile						
Hungary						
Uruguay						
Israel						
Canada						
New Zealand						
Australia						
Italy						
Yugoslavia						
Poland						
Denmark						
Portugal						
Austria						
Sweden						
France						
Czechoslovakia						
West Germany						
Scotland						
Hong Kong						
Greece						
Rep. of Korea						
Switzerland						
Norway						
Netherlands						
Japan						
Kuwait						
England/Wales						
Ireland						
Singapore						

0   2   4   6   8   10   12

Source: Reiss & Roth, 1993.

death sentence come to be widely thought of as barbaric. In simpler societies and earlier civilizations, execution was more than a penalty carried out on an individual; it was also an occasion for a public ceremony. People attended beheadings and hangings, and hawkers sold them food and favors as they waited for the bloody pageant. The villain's death reaffirmed their common values, their solidarity as a people who could purge evil elements from their midst.

Today, by contrast, the value of capital punishment is a matter of heated debate. Although many people believe that the death sentence is necessary as a means of discourag-

ing some individuals from committing terrible crimes, others are convinced that there is no justification for putting another person to death, the more so because there is always the possibility that the person did not commit the crime for which he or she was executed. A recent study of this grim possibility provides evidence of as many as 18 wrongful executions in the United States since 1900 (Radelet & Bedau, 1992). In one of a series of studies of the equity of capital punishment, criminologists Marvin Wolfgang and Marc Riedel (1973) found that blacks were more likely than whites to be executed for the same crimes and that people who could afford good lawyers were far more likely to escape execution than those who lacked the means to hire the best legal defenders.

In 1972, swayed by evidence like that gathered by Wolfgang and Riedel and by arguments that capital punishment could be considered "cruel and unusual punishment" according to the Constitution (most other Western nations had already banned the death penalty), the Supreme Court ruled in a 5-to-4 decision that in the absence of clear specifications for when it might be used, the death sentence violated the Eighth Amendment to the Constitution. But Congress has since passed new legislation that legalized the death sentence, and the Court has not overruled it. As a result, capital punishment has been reinstated in many states; there are now between 15 and 30 executions a year in the United States, with Texas, Florida, Mississippi, and Arizona leading in numbers of executions carried out. Indeed, in many states the debate about capital punishment has shifted away from its morality to questions about technology, such as the use of lethal injections versus the electric chair.

In earlier periods of history, executions were public spectacles and often considered a form of entertainment. In modern societies that still practice execution, there is much less emphasis on public spectacle and much more on the technology employed to perform the execution.

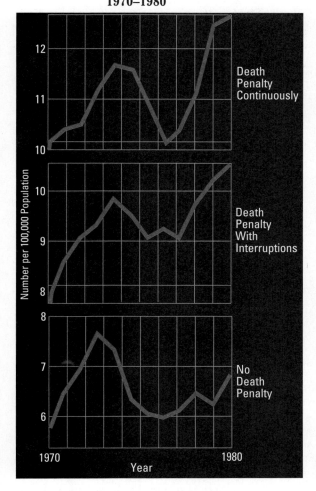

FIGURE 7.6   Homicide Rates in States With and Without the Death Penalty, 1970–1980

States that had the death penalty continuously: Arizona, Arkansas, Connecticut, Florida, Georgia, Montana, Nebraska, Nevada, Oklahoma, Texas, Utah, Virginia. States without the death penalty: Alaska, Hawaii, Iowa, Maine, Michigan, Minnesota, New Jersey, North Dakota, West Virginia, Wisconsin, Washington, D.C. All other states had the death penalty with interruptions.

Source: Zeisel, 1982.

But does capital punishment have the effect of deterring people from committing murder, as its advocates claim? Much of the evidence on this subject is negative. As Figure 7.6 shows quite clearly, little encouragement is found in comparisons among states that have the death penalty, states that have had it with interruptions, and states that have never had it. Yet in interviews with criminals charged with robbery James Q. Wilson (1977) found evidence that fear of the death penalty discouraged them from carrying guns. There is still considerable opposition to the death penalty among people who feel that it represents cruel and unusual punishment, but surveys indicate that the tide of public opinion has turned toward support for it. They also show, for better or worse, that the public's increased concern about crime has led to greater emphasis on use of the death sentence as retribution for murders

that have already been committed and less emphasis on the possible deterrent effect of capital punishment.

Plea Bargaining—A Revolving Door?   Capital punishment addresses a small but sensational part of the crime problem. Many more criminals will commit other types of crimes, and for them too the issue of punishment and rehabilitation is controversial. At present, judges and police officers feel hampered by the relatively limited array of treatments for criminal offenders, as well as the backlogs in the courts and the overcrowding of prisons. One means of reducing the pressure on the judicial system is **plea bargaining,** in which a person who is charged with a crime agrees to plead guilty to a lesser charge and thereby free the courts from having to conduct a lengthy and costly jury trial. The shorter sentences that result from this system diminish somewhat the size of prison populations. Plea bargaining has been criticized as "revolving-door justice"; however, criminologists estimate that an increase of only 20 percent in the number of offenders who are tried and imprisoned would place an intolerable burden on the correctional system (Reid, 1993; Rosett & Cressey, 1976).

Prisons—Schools for Crime?   Despite the small proportion of crimes resulting in arrest and imprisonment, prisons remain the social institution with the primary responsibility for dealing with criminals. From 1980 to 1995 the total number of Americans in prisons of all kinds tripled (see Figure 7.7). In addition to the prison population, there are about 3.5 million people on probation or

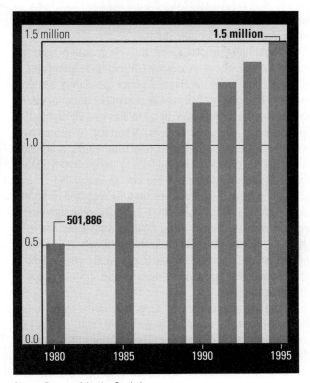

FIGURE 7.7   Inmates in Federal, State, and Local Prisons

Source: Bureau of Justice Statistics.

In the United States there is a trend toward more retribution and less investment in rehabilitation of prison inmates. In some states, the sight of prisoners working in chain gangs is increasingly common.

parole. It is estimated that within a decade more than 7.5 million people will be under some form of law enforcement surveillance in the United States.

The largest proportion of the new prisoners were arrested for the sale or possession of felonious quantities of narcotics and were imprisoned under mandatory sentencing laws that had been passed as part of the national war on drugs. But the arrests were by no means equally distributed among drug users and dealers. According to researchers with the Federal Sentencing Project, for young Americans from ghetto communities and many other impoverished areas "going to prison has become as inevitable . . . as going to college is for middle-class kids" (quoted in Butterfield, 1992a, p. E4). While there is widespread agreement on the need to punish drug dealers and users, there is growing debate over the desirability of sending them to prison, since it is highly likely that a young person who is imprisoned will learn more diverse and devious ways of breaking the law.

The arguments used to support reliance on prison as the central institution of punishment and reform are mainly functionalist in nature. The functions of prisons are said to be deterrence, rehabilitation, and retribution (i.e., punishment) (Goode, 1994; Hawkins, 1976). As Bruce Jack-son, a well-known student of prison life, explains it, a prison is supposed to deter criminals from committing crimes ("its presence is supposed to keep those among us of weak moral strength from actions we might otherwise commit"); it is supposed to rehabilitate those who do commit crimes ("within its walls those who have, for whatever reason, transgressed society's norms are presumably shown the error of their ways and retooled so they can live outside in a more acceptable and satisfactory fashion"); and it is supposed to punish criminals—the only function that it clearly fulfills (1972, p. 248).

Sociologists who study prisons and other kinds of total institutions have found that new members of such organizations usually undergo a period of resocialization during which they are deprived of their former statuses through haircuts, uniforms, and the like (Goffman, 1961). (See Chapter 5.) The goal of this process is to socialize the inmates to behave in ways that suit the organization's needs. But in most such organizations there is also a strong inmate subculture consisting of norms that specify ways of resisting the officials in favor of such values as mutual aid and loyalty among the inmates. Thus, in Bruce Jackson's (1972) collection of case histories of criminals and prison inmates, a seasoned convict summed up the world of the total institution as follows: "A penitentiary is like a prisoner of war camp. The officials are the enemy and the inmates are captured. They're on one side and we're on the other" (p. 253). But the same prisoner also described another aspect of life in total institutions. Often, as the following passage reveals, the inmates develop "institutional personalities." As they try to conform to the norms of the organization, they become dependent on the routines and constraints of minimal freedom and, hence, minimal responsibility:

> I like things to be orderly. You might say I'm a conservative, I like the status quo. If something's going smooth I like that. . . . Some people . . . kind of like it. Get institutionalized. You know, there's a lot of security in a place like this for a person. . . . They'll tell you when to get up, they'll tell you when to go to bed, when to eat, when to work. They'll do your laundry for you. You don't have to worry about anything else. (p. 253)

Only relatively recently, mainly in the second half of this century, has the goal of rehabilitation—the effort to return the criminal to society as a law-abiding citizen—been taken seriously as a function of prisons. Critics of the prison system, many of whom argue from a conflict perspective, often claim that far from rehabilitating their inmates, prisons in fact function as "schools for crime." As early as 1789 the great English philosopher and economist Jeremy Bentham wrote that "prisons, with the exception of a small number, include every imaginable means of infecting both body and mind. . . . An ordinary prison is a school in which wickedness is taught by surer means than can ever be employed for the inculcation of virtue" (pp. 351–352). In the intervening years many studies have attempted to show under what conditions this is true or not and what can be done to increase the deterrent effects of prison and prevent it from becoming a community that socializes criminals.

Yet there is much sociological research that defends prisons as a means of deterrence and a necessary form of retribution. James Q. Wilson (1977) holds to the functionalist position: Societies need the firm moral authority they gain from stigmatizing and punishing crime. He believes that prisoners should receive better forms of rehabilitation in prison and be guaranteed their rights as citizens once they are outside again. But, he states, "to destigmatize crime would be to lift from it the weight of moral judgment and to make crime simply a particular occupation or avocation which society has chosen to reward less (or perhaps more) than other pursuits" (p. 230). Some states, notably Louisiana, Alabama, and Florida, have taken the desire to get tough on crime to the extreme of reinstating chain gangs.

Whatever their sociological perspective, all students of the American prison system agree that by far the least successful aspect of prison life is rehabilitation. Research conducted in the 1970s consistently found that the only effective rehabilitation programs in prisons, measured by lower rates of recidivism, involve job training and education (Martinson, 1972). Indeed, during the 1980s, as prison populations more than doubled, sociologists and criminologists found that men from very poor and minority backgrounds were beginning to regard prison as the only way they could obtain job training, health care, and other social services. Prisons, after all, provide more adequate housing than the large urban shelters for the homeless, and in prison one gets three meals a day and, in some cases, a chance to improve one's skills and self-confidence.

The conservative mood of the United States in the 1990s is having a profound impact on rehabilitation programs in federal and state prisons. At this writing there are bills in Congress that would deny prisoners any opportunity to take courses for high school or college credit. Some legislators, showing far more interest in punishment than in rehabilitation, support a proposal that would void all court-ordered efforts to correct inhumane conditions in prisons (Kunen, 1995). As one of the nation's leading researchers on crime and prisons has observed, in our society "we have an exaggerated belief in the efficacy of imprisonment. The real problem is that we make life really terrible for some people and then blame them when they become dangerous" (Norval Morris, quoted in Butterfield, 1992a).

RESEARCH FRONTIERS: LIVING WITH DEVIANT LABELS

In 1994 sociologist James W. Trent, Jr., won a prestigious award from the American Association on Mental Retardation for his research on the effects of labeling people with mental limitations. Trent's research directly challenges theories such as those of Robert Herrnstein and Charles Murray (1994), which defend labels like "normal" and "below normal" and claim that there are strict biological limits on what people with low intelligence can achieve. (See Box 5-1 for a discussion of this issue.) One of the people described in James Trent's research is Emma Jane Nixon, a white woman from a well-to-do family in North Carolina who had given birth to a "Negro" child almost 60 years earlier, during the heyday of segregation. In the community where she lived, and in the eyes of her prominent family, the illegitimate birth was an intolerable embarrassment. Although Nixon, then in her twenties, had done reasonably well in school, her family and local social-welfare officials concluded that her behavior proved that she was mentally retarded. She was placed in a state home for the "feebleminded" and lived in such institutions for the rest of her life. Intelligence tests given to her in 1975 showed that her IQ was 85, about average for people of her age.

THE HOBO

Sociologist Douglas Harper has spent years studying the lives of people on urban skid rows and in hobo jungles. These are deviant populations according to the dominant norms of society. In Merton's typology (see Figure 7.3), the "bums," "hoboes," and "tramps" whom Harper describes would be classified as retreatists. But this term itself can become a superficial label, and unless social scientists attempt to discover what the worlds of such people are like, they are all simply lumped together as "deviant" when in fact there are norms and statuses and processes of socialization in these worlds also.

In his book *Good Company* (1982), from which the photos included here are taken, Harper discusses his experiences as a participant observer in the hobo's world. He contrasts the life of hoboes who still ride freight trains and find casual labor in the cities and western fruit farms, with the more sedentary life of skid row "bums." On his trip West, Harper met Carl, an experienced hobo who became the sociologist's mentor. In the following excerpt Harper describes how what he learned was related to his friendship with Carl:

Carl accepted my food because he was down and out, but he knew I was not a regular and he was suspicious of what he'd have to pay. During our first days together he realized I did not really know what to expect from him and he warned: "Some people on this road are helpless. When you start helpin' it's just like having a son. . . . They don't know where it stops! You got to support them—take care of them—you got to provide the hand and I won't do that. If a fella is on this road and he can't learn—then to hell with him." . . .

But even though Carl tried to make our relationship typical, it never was. At first he taught me how to make it on the road and ignored most of my questions. Something changed the chemistry between us and he stepped out of his normal role to tell me about his childhood, his parents, and his life before hitting the road. . . .

Just before I left he said: "I've noticed you change. You've learned that you can make it on the road—now if something overloads it'll always be in the back of your mind. . . . You watch yourself—you'll be reverting back." (pp. 141, 142)

Harper's photos are an important part of the material he collected. They became "a visual inventory of typical behavior in typical spaces—for this group." But the photos could not intrude on his participation in the tramp life, as he relates in the following passage:

As I involved myself more I had to reassess my purpose and methods. I could have continued as I had begun and produced a photographic study from the viewpoint of an outsider, but as I felt myself pulled into the life, my photographic activity changed very much. . . . I made few photographs during my time with Carl. I introduced myself as a writer and photographer and he did not seem to mind my taking pictures until we encountered people he'd known for a long time; then he made it clear that to carry on would be out of the question. . . . The relationship between the photographer and subject in a fieldwork experience is very complicated, but for me the rights and desires of the individuals we choose as subjects are more important than a final purpose that would justify making images when they would not be welcomed. The camera must sometimes be left behind. (pp. 146, 147)

Before her death in her mid-eighties, Nixon experienced all the theories and deviant labels that could be applied to people with limited intelligence or mental retardation. As Trent (1995) explains it, from the time she was first institutionalized as "feebleminded" until her death,

> The only official changes in Nixon's circumstances involved the labels used to describe her: "Moron" (a subset of "feebleminded") gave way to "mental defective," then to "mentally retarded" (still the most commonly used term) and, finally, "developmentally disabled." Every few decades, it seemed, her condition earned a few new syllables." (p. 18)

Just as the labels changed, so did theories about how to deal with people of supposed very low intelligence.

The 1840s may have been the best time for people who were then referred to as "idiots." The best treatment centers were run like small families in which everyone shared responsibilities and all assumed that the patients could make progress toward becoming independent and productive. Often they were trained to work on farms, which always needed more workers. Later in the nineteenth century, dramatic social changes such as rapid urbanization, immigration, and "boom and bust" economic cycles led to new labels and new theories about people of low intelligence. The more neutral-sounding term "feebleminded" began to replace the term "idiot," but more important, the professionals assigning the labels began to believe that urban vice, crime, vagrancy, illegitimacy, prostitution, and the decline of neighborhood cohesion made such people easy prey for shrewd and criminal characters. It would be best, they asserted, to institutionalize these people for their own protection.

During good economic times, the institutions tended to have enough resources to provide pleasant and positive environments, but each successive economic downturn produced reductions in public funding. In time, thousands of people labeled as feebleminded, or more recently as mentally retarded, learning disabled, profoundly retarded, or developmentally disabled, were living in squalid conditions in prisonlike state institutions.

In the 1970s an alliance of civil liberties advocates concerned about inhumane conditions, along with state officials who wanted to shift the cost of care to the federal government, succeeded in influencing Congress to include "mental retardation" under Medicare and the Supplemental Social Security program. This allowed states to deinstitutionalize persons labeled as mentally retarded and move them into federally subsidized community nursing homes and group homes. But this "community mental health" approach had limited success in addressing the problems of labeling.

The recent film *Forrest Gump* presented the idea that "a person ceases to be mentally retarded . . . the moment people quit defining him as such" (Trent, 1995, p. 18). Because his mother and other people in his life refused to accept the limiting label, Gump could go on to become a star football player, a war hero, a ping-pong champion, a millionaire, and a spiritual leader. In 1992, acting on the same theory, the American Association on Mental Retardation introduced a new policy stating that people are never mentally retarded in absolute terms; instead, they have differing "intensities of functional needs." By restructuring themselves to meet those needs, communities can essentially "cure" mental retardation by providing environments in which everyone can function to the best of his or her ability.

As Trent points out, this position converges in ironic ways with the ideas of those who see mental retardation as an immutable biological condition. Herrnstein and Murray (1994) argue for a return to old-fashioned caring neighborhoods that can offer mentally retarded citizens "a valued niche in society where they can live valued lives and help out in doing the mundane chores of daily life"—a position very close to that of the community mental health approach but without any suggestion of public funding.

According to Trent, this idea is wishful thinking. "Ridding people of labels is certainly better than declaring them permanently disabled," he argues, "but in America today neither approach is adequate" (1995, p. 22). Proposed massive cuts in social spending make it highly unlikely that neighborhoods will have the resources to provide caring environments in which labels need not apply. Trent continues:

> When the economy is unstable, as the past 150 years have shown, mentally retarded people land in institutions or jail or on the streets more often than they land in caring communities. . . . Without jobs and humane social programs, the most open-minded society offers its mentally retarded citizens little more than the illusion of integration and equality. (1995, p. 22)

The same reasoning could be applied to many other deviant populations in need of attention. In an era of shrinking public budgets, sociologists like James Trent will be carefully monitoring the actual experiences of people who must struggle to live with deviant labels.

THINK ABOUT IT CRITICALLY

*"We should just lock them all up and throw away the keys."
One often hears this view expressed by people who are
frustrated by crime in their communities. But would you
agree that social-scientific studies of deviance and crime
suggest that prison, while important as an institution of
social control, is limited in its effectiveness?*

Deviance, broadly defined, is behavior that violates
the norms of a particular society. The deviant label is
attached to a person who violates or opposes a society's
most valued norms. The ways in which a society
encourages conformity to its norms and prevents deviance
are known as *social control.*

There is usually much disagreement not only about
which behaviors are deviant but also about which ones
should be condoned or punished only mildly. An important
dimension of deviance is the power of some groups in
society to define which acts are legal and which are illegal.
Another dimension has to do with attributes that a person
cannot control, in contrast to actual behavior. In addition,
some people are thought of as deviant because of their
membership in a group that deviates from the norms of
the larger society. To the rest of society they are deviants,
but within the group they are not deviant but are
conforming to the group's norms.

Deviance should be distinguished from *stigma.* A
stigmatized person has some attribute that is deeply
discrediting, such as a disfiguring disease, but is not
necessarily a social deviant. The study of deviance is
concerned with social deviants—that is, people who
voluntarily violate the norms of their society. In particular,
the study of deviance focuses on criminal deviance: acts or
omissions of acts for which the state can apply sanctions.

As a culture's values and norms change, so do its
notions of what kinds of behavior are deviant and how they
should be sanctioned. The extent to which the members of
a society agree on whether or not a particular behavior is
deviant can range from weak (in cases in which there is
much controversy) to strong (in cases in which there is
little disagreement). Negative sanctions, or punishments,
can also range from very weak to very strong.

A deviant subculture includes a system of values,
attitudes, behaviors, and lifestyles that are opposed to the
dominant culture of the society in which it is found. Many
deviant subcultures are harmful to society because they
sustain criminal occupations. Others provide opportunities
to engage in behavior that is pleasurable to many people
but is considered deviant in "respectable" society. The
boundaries between what is normal and what is deviant
are not distinct.

Biological explanations of deviance relate criminality
to physical features or body type. These explanations
influenced the earliest sociological theories of deviance,
which viewed crime and other forms of social deviance as
varieties of "social pathology" that could be attributed to
the evils of city life. This view has been replaced by more
objective and verifiable theories drawn from the basic
perspectives of modern sociology.

Functionalist theories of deviance include Robert
Merton's typology based on how people adapt to the
demands of their society. In this view, through
socialization people learn what goals are approved of in
their society and the approved means of achieving those
goals. Individuals who do not accept the approved goals
and/or the legitimate means of achieving them are likely to
engage in deviant behaviors.

Functionalist theories have been criticized for
assuming that there is a single set of values shared by all
the members of a society. Conflict theorists stress the
relationship between cultural diversity and deviance. The
two main types of conflict theories are cultural conflict
theories and Marxian theories. Cultural conflict theories
concentrate on the ways in which conflicting sets of norms
result in situations that encourage criminal activity.
Marxian theories place more emphasis on class conflict,
explaining various types of crime in terms of the
social-class position of those who commit them.

Interactionist theories of deviance focus on the issues
of recruitment (the question of why some people become
deviant whereas others do not) and production (the
creation of new categories of deviance in a society). Edwin
H. Sutherland's theory of *differential association* holds that
whether or not a person becomes deviant is determined by
the extent of his or her association with criminal
subcultures. Interactionists believe that deviance is
produced by the process of *labeling,* in which the society's
reaction to certain behaviors is to brand or label the
offender as a deviant. Once acquired, such a label is likely
to become incorporated into the person's self-image and to
increase the likelihood that he or she will become
committed to a "deviant career."

Studies of the incidence of crime often start with
ecological data on crime rates. Studies of criminal
victimization, which ask people about their actual
experiences with crime, have made a major contribution to
the understanding of crime in complex societies.

The methods used to control crime change as
societies grow and become more complex. In larger, more
diverse societies the ability of local institutions to control
all of the society's members is diminished. Such societies

tend to develop standardized, more or less coercive institutions to deal with deviants. Among the most prominent institutions of social control in modern societies are courts and prisons.

The primary functions of prisons are said to be deterrence, rehabilitation, and punishment. However, prisons do not seem to deter crime, and only recently has the goal of rehabilitation been taken seriously. Numerous studies have found that prisons are not successful in rehabilitating their inmates and in fact often serve as "schools for crime." The only rehabilitation programs that appear to be effective are those that give inmates job training and work experience.

CRITICAL RESPONSE

Prisons and other law enforcement institutions, such as courts and police, cannot replace the more basic forms of social control, which are based on values and norms about morality and appropriate behavior. When there are a growing number of people in a society who no longer adhere to these values and norms, institutions of social control like prisons and the police will be overwhelmed. A citizen who applies the sociological imagination knows that prisons have an important place in the system of social control but that they cannot substitute for shared norms and values and willingness to adhere to them in daily life.

GLOSSARY

deviance: behavior that violates the norms of a particular society. (p. 182)

social control: the ways in which a society encourages conformity to its norms and prevents deviance. (p. 182)

stigma: an attribute or quality of an individual that is deeply discrediting. (p. 184)

crime: an act or omission of an act that is prohibited by law. (p. 185)

anomie: a state of normlessness. (p. 192)

differential association: a theory that explains deviance as a learned behavior determined by the extent of a person's association with individuals who engage in such behavior. (p. 195)

labeling: a theory that explains deviance as a societal reaction that brands or labels as deviant people who engage in certain behaviors. (p. 196)

primary deviance: an act that results in the labeling of the offender as deviant. (p. 197)

secondary deviance: behavior that is engaged in as a reaction to the experience of being labeled as deviant. (p. 197)

recidivist: a criminal who is returned to prison after having served at least one term there. (p. 198)

plea bargaining: a process in which a person charged with a crime agrees to plead guilty to a lesser charge. (p. 203)

In the spring of 1992 a riot erupted in Los Angeles after an all-white jury acquitted four police officers of brutally beating a black motorist who they claimed was resisting arrest. The riot put the plight of the nation's ghettos and impoverished urban communities squarely in the spotlight of public opinion. The terrible days of fire and destruction also called into question the policies of the national government. But this was by no means the first time that violence precipitated by racial issues had altered the course of American history.

On Max Weber's only trip to the United States, in 1904, he made an astute observation. "The Americans are a wonderful people," he wrote. "Only the Negro question and the terrible immigration form a big, black cloud" (Marianne Weber, 1975/1926, p. 315). The German sociologist's comments were prophetic. Fifteen

years after his visit, the smoldering tensions between blacks and whites (many of whom were immigrants) erupted in the massive Chicago race riot of 1919.

This tragic riot began at a public beach when black bathers, who believed that a young black boy who had drowned had been stoned by whites, began stoning the white bathers. The truth or falsehood of the rumors that raged through the city during the ensuing week made little difference to the rioters; blacks and whites fought pitched battles for 6 days and nights. The riot signaled the arrival of a new spirit of protest and new demands for equality among African Americans. At the time, the inferior condition of African American people in the United States was often enforced by brutal public beatings, lynchings, and vigilante raids by the Ku Klux Klan and other extremist groups. For black leaders like W. E. B.

Du Bois, the riot showed that blacks must organize to combat discrimination and racism.

The Chicago riot also shaped the future of the young field of sociology. As a member of the commission that investigated the riot, Robert Park became convinced that riots and other seemingly spontaneous behaviors of large numbers of people should become a major subject of sociological study. In the first textbook on sociology, Park and his collaborators made sure that the effects of riots and other forms of "social unrest" received intense attention. "The significance of social unrest," he wrote, "is that it represents at once a breaking up of the established routine and a preparation for new collective action" (quoted in Turner, 1967, p. 226). He argued that social unrest and collective behavior are particularly significant features of modern life:

"Not only in Europe but in Asia and in Africa new cultural contacts have undermined and broken down the old cultures. . . . The energies thus freed have produced a worldwide ferment" (p. 228).

These words could just as well have been written today, perhaps about unrest in Bosnia or India or East Africa. Throughout the world there are outbreaks of protest, demonstrations, and movements that are producing significant social change. In the United States, the 1992 Los Angeles riots, which were said to have affected the outcome of the presidential election in that year, were a reminder both of the power of spontaneous collective behavior and of the difficulty of closing the gap between the races in a multiethnic and multiracial society (Jaynes & Williams, 1989; Lemann, 1992; National Advisory Commission on Civil Disorders, 1968).

THE MEANINGS OF DISORDER

Imagine what it must have been like on that Chicago beach when the riot broke out. Suddenly a peaceful beach scene is transformed into chaos and extreme violence. Most people are panic-stricken. They round up their children, grab their belongings, and run for safety. Others remain behind and join in the fray. It seems as if the world has been turned upside down. Order is replaced by uncertainty, disorder, danger, rage.

How often such events occur in the modern world! Before you complete this course other angry riots may occur in Eastern Europe or Latin America, or perhaps in this country. But these terrifying episodes are not isolated events. As we saw in the case of the Chicago and Los Angeles riots, they are symptoms of deeper social conflicts and may engender social movements that bring about major changes in society.

In this chapter we look closely at outbreaks of civil disorder of all kinds, and especially at the uprisings associated with revolutions and the birth of new social institutions. Such momentous episodes, in which masses of people rage through the streets, are the most severe form of collective behavior. The race riots that occurred during the civil rights movement in the United States, the huge rallies and demonstrations that ushered in the Nazi regime in pre–World War II Germany, the strikes and picketing that spurred the labor movement, the demonstrations that enlivened the women's movement in the 1970s, the riots and demonstrations in Romania and other Eastern European dictatorships in 1989, and the rioting by young blacks in South Africa against apartheid—these are examples of the mass events that have shaped history in our own time.

But there are less extensive and less dangerous incidents of mass behavior in modern societies that are nonetheless important. Think of the panic that occurs when a local bank is rumored to be short of funds, or the joyful anticipation of the crowds that form outside ticket offices when a popular rock star announces a concert. These events also have economic and social significance: Banks fail when panicked depositors suddenly withdraw their savings; rock promoters wait in gleeful anticipation of full houses as the lines of ticket buyers form.

Many sectors of the American economy profit from the behavior of large numbers of people. The fast-food industry, for example, depends on the behavior of the millions of Americans who stop for burgers and fries as they stream home from beaches or concerts or movies. Every year the toy industry produces gimmicks like Teenage Mutant Ninja Turtles or toys that can be transformed from cars and trucks into killer robots—and fortunes are made and lost on the accuracy of predictions about whether the public will embrace such notions. The computer industry also has profited from fads and crazes: In the early 1990s people rushed to buy more powerful personal computers with CD drives and modems in order to join the "information society," only to realize that this new information channel was fraught with problems of its own, such as the possibility that children using the computer would be exposed to pornography and hate speech.

The study of mass or collective behavior encompasses a wide range of phenomena and presents many problems of classification and explanation. Yet this subject deserves our attention because of its influence on social change. The student occupation of Beijing's Tiananmen Square; the strikes and protests in Poland, Czechoslovakia, Hungary, and Romania that toppled Communist dictatorships; the antitax movements occurring throughout the United States—all attest to the immense power of people who are moved to engage in collective action for social change.

In our attempt to understand the nature and importance of these behaviors we turn first to the concepts that define their similarities and differences. Then we turn to theories regarding why these episodes occur, how social movements mobilize, and with what consequences. Finally, we discuss the concept of mass publics, especially the leisure and consumption behavior of large populations.

THE NATURE OF COLLECTIVE BEHAVIOR

The term **collective behavior** refers to a continuum of unusual or nonroutine behaviors that are engaged in by large numbers of people. At one extreme of this continuum is the spontaneous behavior of people who react to situations they perceive as uncertain, threatening, or extremely attractive. The violent fighting between blacks and whites during the Chicago race riot of 1919 is one example of spontaneous collective behavior. Another is the sudden action of coalminers who decide that conditions in the mines are unsafe and walk off their jobs in a sudden and unplanned wildcat strike. Such behaviors are not governed by the routine norms that control behavior at the beach or on the job (Smelser, 1962).

At the other extreme of the continuum of collective behaviors are rallies, demonstrations, marches, protest meetings, festivals, and similar events. These involve large numbers of people in nonroutine behaviors, but they are organized by leaders and have specific goals. When workers in a union plan a strike, for example, their picketing and rallies are forms of organized collective behavior whose purpose is to demonstrate their solidarity and their determination to obtain their demands. When blacks marched in commemoration of those who died in the 1919 race riot, the event was organized to build solidarity and publicize a new determination to resist racism. In such cases the organization that plans the event and uses collective behavior to

make its feelings or demands known is a **social movement.** Social movements are intentional efforts by groups in a society to create new institutions or reform existing ones. Such movements often grow out of more spontaneous episodes of collective behavior; once they are organized, they continue to plan collective events to promote their cause (Blumer, 1978; Genevie, 1978). Some movements, like the antiabortion movement, resist change; others, like the labor movement, have brought about far-reaching changes in social institutions. Still others, like the gay and lesbian movement, seek to gain the rights other groups have won. In this sense they are movements for full inclusion in society by people who feel that they are discriminated against. We will see in later chapters that many social movements in a multiethnic and culturally diverse society challenge discrimination and deviant labels (Tarrow, 1994).

The American labor movement provides many examples of the ways in which spontaneous episodes of collective behavior and the social movements associated with them can change the course of a society's development. During the nation's stormy transition from an agrarian to an industrial society, workers fought against the traditional right of employers to establish individual wage rates and to hire and fire workers as they pleased. They demanded instead the right to organize unions that could negotiate a collective wage rate (collective bargaining) for each category of workers. They also demanded better working conditions and benefits. Mass picketing, sit-down strikes, and pitched battles between workers and company agents or the police were everyday events in the 1890s.

Often the workers joined in walkouts, rioting, or other spontaneous collective actions when faced with mine disasters or intolerable working conditions. From these episodes of bitter conflict emerged the modern labor movement. In the ensuing decades, culminating in the period of New Deal legislation in the 1930s, the workers' demand for collective bargaining was *institutionalized.* By this we mean that the right to join unions and to bargain collectively was incorporated into the nation's laws. Labor unions thereby became recognized organizations and collective bargaining the recognized means of settling labor disputes. The unions, in turn, had to discipline their workers by specifying when collective behavior such as strikes and other actions could be used.

By the end of World War II labor unions and collective bargaining had become legitimate social institutions. In recent decades, however, drastic declines in industrial employment in North America and Europe, combined with renewed attacks on labor unions by employers, have led to a decrease in the ranks of organized labor. But major social movements that affect the lives of millions of people often go through cycles of growth and decline followed by a rebirth of activity. It remains to be seen whether this will be true of the labor movement (Geoghegan, 1991).

THEN AND NOW

CONTINUITY AND CHANGE IN RACIAL VIOLENCE

Racial rioting and violence has erupted periodically in American history. These two photos, separated by more than 70 years, have a chilling similarity. In the first, white men caught up in the frenzy of violence that accompanied the infamous Chicago riot of 1919 are stoning a black man. The second photo shows the beating of a white man during the Los Angeles riots in 1992. Both events are widely credited with having brought problems of American race relations to the center of public attention.

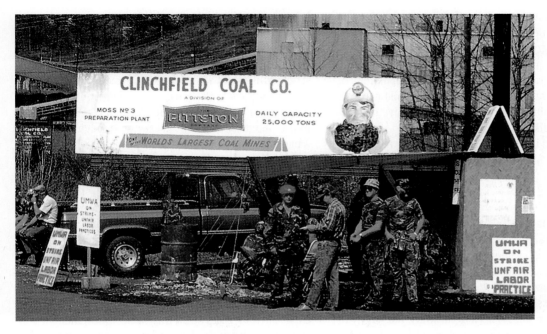

Although widely regarded as a declining social movement, the labor movement in the United States is still very much alive and accounts for much of the social change that affects working-class families in regions where coal-mining and other basic industries are predominant.

Spontaneous collective behavior, from which social movements often arise, can take many forms. Such behaviors range from the demonstrations and riots that mark major revolutions to the fads, fashions, crazes, and rumors that sweep through modern societies with such rapidity that what is new and shocking one day will be a subject of nostalgia the next. Some of these types of collective behavior become associated with social movements, but many do not. For example, in the early 1970s the craze known as streaking (in which one or more people ran nude in front of a large gathering) called attention to other forms of public nudity. Suddenly the number of beaches, parks, and recreation areas where people were going nude increased dramatically (Douglas & Rasmussen, 1977; Fortin & Ecker, 1978), and people who believed in the goodness of nude living joined forces with the older naturist movement to sponsor "nude-ins" and other collective events that publicized their beliefs. In the early 1990s groups of women in the Northeast protested bans on topless sunbathing at beaches and won some concessions from local authorities. Despite these sporadic protests, the naturist movement has not given rise to organizations dedicated to expressing nudist values; there is no nudist movement comparable to the civil rights movement or the women's movement.

A TYPOLOGY OF SPONTANEOUS COLLECTIVE BEHAVIORS

Sociologists who study collective behavior try to discover the conditions under which different types of spontaneous collective behavior occur and why these events do or do not become linked to social movements. Typologies that classify these phenomena are an important first step toward understanding why collective behavior assumes particular forms and develops through recognizable stages.

Crowds and Masses. Students of spontaneous forms of collective behavior often begin by examining the structure of such behavior—that is, by discovering whether the people who engage in a particular kind of behavior are in close proximity to one another or whether they are connected in a more indirect way. In this regard it is useful to distinguish between crowds and masses. A **crowd** is a large number of people who are gathered together in close proximity to one another (e.g., at a demonstration or a football game). A **mass** is more diffuse; it does not occur in a physical setting. A mass is a large number of people who are all oriented toward a set of shared symbols or social objects (Lofland, 1981); an example is the audience for a particular television program. Collective behavior can occur in crowds, in masses, or in both at once.

Motivating Emotions. The actual behavior a crowd or mass generates depends largely on the emotions the people involved feel are appropriate to express in a particular situation. They may be motivated by many desires—for excitement, for a change, for material gain, and so on—but outwardly most will express an emotion that the norms of the event suggest is appropriate. In the witch hunt described in Chapter 7, the people involved expressed fear and hysteria (although, as is true of all such events, some were "just going along with the crowd"). Hostility aroused by anger, desire for revenge, or enraged hatred is another common motivating emotion in episodes of collective behavior. Lynch mobs are one kind of hostile crowd. The crowd of angry strikers that violently opposes "scabs" trying to cross a picket line is another. At the mass level, the outbreak of animosity toward Islamic people immediately after the bombing of the federal office building in Oklahoma City in 1995 is an example of collective behavior provoked by hostility.

Joy is a third important emotion that motivates crowds and masses. The Mardi Gras celebrations in Latin America and New Orleans involve large, joyful crowds that create a "moral holiday" in which behaviors are tolerated that would not be acceptable in public at other times. At the mass level, the display of yellow ribbons and other signs of support for the troops and the joy that swept through the American population in 1991 when the Persian Gulf War ended quickly with minimal allied casualties are examples of joyful collective behavior.

By cross-classifying the most significant emotions that motivate collective behavior (fear, hostility, and joy) with the structural dimensions of crowd and mass, sociologist John Lofland created a typology that includes a wide range of spontaneous collective behaviors. This typology is presented in Figure 8.1. Can you think of examples of your own for the various types? Where, for example, would you place the Boston Tea Party, the riots that often occur during spring break in Florida, or the crowds of fans who came out to pay last respects to singer Jerry Garcia in 1995?

The Lofland typology is useful as a means of classifying some types of collective behavior, but remember that often there are interactions among these categories: Mass behavior may turn into crowd behavior; spontaneous collective behavior may generate a social movement. For example, when the stock market crashed in 1929 at the beginning of the Great Depression, crowds of panic-stricken investors spilled onto the streets of the financial districts of New York, Chicago, and San Francisco. There, within sight of one another, people found their fears magnified. And those fears quickly spread through the mass of Americans. The panic started among people who had made investments on credit, but it spread to people who merely had savings in local banks. Crowds of terrified savers descended on the banks, which were unable to handle the sudden demand for withdrawals because they themselves had been investing in stocks that were suddenly worthless. As a result, millions of Americans lost all their savings.

In the aftermath of the stock market crash and the resulting mass panic, social movements arose to seek reforms that would protect investors against similar episodes in the future. During the depression that followed the crash, citizens' fears about their lack of retirement or pension savings led to the development of new institutions like Social Security and deposit insurance. Today the American Association of Retired Persons, an organization that represents the interests of older people who once protested as an unorganized mass, is the largest single lobbying group in American politics.

DIMENSIONS OF SOCIAL MOVEMENTS

There are as many types of social movements as there are varieties of spontaneous collective behavior. Just think of how many "causes" can motivate people to take organized

FIGURE 8.1 Lofland's Typology of Spontaneous Collective Behaviors

BASIC EMOTION	SETTING	
	Crowd	Mass
Fear	• Panic exodus from burning theater • Hostages taken by terrorist groups aboard an airline	• Natural calamities • Red scares • Crime waves • Three Mile Island • Salem witch hunts
Hostility	• Political rallies, marches • Lynch mobs • Race riots	• Scapegoating of public figures • Waves of cross burnings
Joy	• Revival meetings • Rallies in Nazi Nuremberg • Mardi Gras carnival • Rock concerts • Sports events	• Gold rushes • Punk fashion • Jogging • Disco • *Star Wars, Star Trek* • Pet rocks

Source: *Social Psychology: Sociological Perspectives,* edited by Morris Rosenberg and Ralph H. Turner. Copyright © 1981 by The American Sociological Association. Reprinted by permission of Basic Books, Inc., Publishers.

STUDY CHART   Types of Social Movements

TYPE	DESCRIPTION	EXAMPLE
Revolutionary	Seeks to overthrow and replace existing stratification systems and institutions.	Bolsheviks
Reformist	Seeks partial changes in some institutions and values, usually on behalf of some segments of society rather than all.	Labor movement
Conservative	Seeks to uphold the values and institutions of society and resists attempts to change them.	Conservative movements
Reactionary	Seeks to return to the institutions and values of the past and do away with existing institutions and values.	Ku Klux Klan
Expressive	Devoted to the expression of personal beliefs and feelings.	Punk movement
Millenarian	Combines elements of revolutionary and expressive movements.	People's Temple

---

action. We have a social-welfare movement, an antitax movement, a civil rights movement, a women's movement, an environmental protection movement, a consumer movement, an animal rights movement, and on and on. Within each of these movements numerous organizations attempt to speak for everyone who supports the movement's goals. Actually, within any large social movement there are likely to be a number of different social movement organizations (sometimes referred to as SMOs) that may have different, and at times competing, ideas about how to achieve the movement's goals (Goode, 1992). As we will see shortly, the way such organizations operate and the goals they seek depend to a large extent on the characteristics of the social movement itself.

Classifying Social Movements.   Social movements can be classified into four categories based on the goals they seek to achieve, as follows:

1. *Revolutionary movements* seek to overthrow existing stratification systems and institutions and replace them with new ones (Hopper, 1950). The Russian Bolsheviks who founded the Communist party were a revolutionary social movement that sought to eliminate the class structure of Russian society. They also believed that the institutions of capitalism—the market and private property—must be replaced with democratic worker groups or *soviets* whose efforts would be directed by a central committee. Meanwhile certain other existing institutions, especially religion

and the family, had to be either eliminated or drastically altered.

2. *Reformist movements* seek partial changes in some institutions and values, usually on behalf of some segments of society rather than all. The labor movement is basically reformist. It seeks to alter the institutions of private property by requiring the owners of businesses to bargain collectively with workers concerning wages and working conditions and to reach an agreement that will apply to all the workers in the firm. Collective bargaining replaces the old system of individual contracts between workers and employers, but it does not totally destroy the institution of private property.

3. *Conservative movements* seek to uphold the values and institutions of society and generally resist attempts to change them, unless their goal is to undo undesired changes that have already occurred. The conservative movement in the United States seeks to reinforce the values and functions of capitalist institutions and to support the traditional values of such institutions as the family and the church.

4. *Reactionary movements* seek to return to the institutions and values of the past and, therefore, to do away with some or all existing social institutions and cultural values (Cameron, 1966). The Ku Klux Klan is part of a reactionary social movement that seeks a return to the racial caste system that was

supported by American legal institutions (laws, courts, and the police) until the 1954 Supreme Court decision that declared the "separate but equal" doctrine unconstitutional.

Other Types of Movements. Although they cover some of the movements that have had the greatest impact on modern societies, the preceding four categories do not include all the possible types of movements. Herbert Blumer (1969a), for example, identified a fifth category: *expressive social movements,* or movements devoted to the expression of personal beliefs and feelings. Those beliefs and feelings may be religious or ethical or may involve an entire lifestyle, as in the case of the punk movement of the 1980s. An important aspect of expressive social movements is that their members typically reject the idea that their efforts ought to be directed at changing society or the behavior of people who do not belong to their movement. Their quest is for personal expression, and if others choose to "see the light," that is welcome.

Some of the various New Age groups and organizations now popular in the United States fit quite well into the expressive social movement category. Non-native Americans who appropriate some aspects of Native American spirituality (including the use of sweat lodges or the practice of vision quests) but do not proselytize are examples of people involved in an expressive social movement. So are men who follow the teachings of poet Robert Bly, practicing collective drumming to bond together and express suppressed emotions. But, like the followers of any social movement, there can be those in expressive social movements whose extreme beliefs lead to tragedy, as in the 1996 case of the 7-year-old pilot whose parents encouraged her to follow her vision at all costs. Such advice resulted in her death, as well as the deaths of her father and her flight instructor.

Other social scientists who study social movements identify still more categories or develop subcategories that combine elements of those just presented. (See the study chart on page 219.) For example, in *The Pursuit of the Millennium* (1961), Norman Cohen analyzed what are known as *messianic* or *millenarian movements,* which are both revolutionary and expressive. A millenarian movement promises its followers total social change by miraculous means. These movements envision a perfect society of the future, "a new Paradise on earth, a world purged of suffering and sin, a Kingdom of the Saints" (p. xiii). Most millenarian movements are secular, but the term is derived from the Christian concept of the millennium, the return of Christ as the messiah who would save the world after a thousand years. Often millenarian movements begin as small movements with a charismatic leader (someone who seems to possess special powers) and a few devoted followers.

An example of a millenarian movement is the People's Temple, whose 900 members committed suicide by drinking cyanide-laced Kool-Aid in Jonestown, Guyana, on November 18, 1978. In his insightful study of the events leading up to the tragedy, sociologist John Hall (1987) demonstrates that popular interpretations of this shocking story are inadequate. The conclusion reached in most previous accounts is that the movement's leader, Jim Jones, was a deranged personality who acted as the Antichrist and led his misguided followers to their death. Such accounts, according to Hall, may be comforting expressions of moral outrage, but by exaggerating the influence of an individual personality they lead to wrong ideas about how such tragedies can occur.

In his analysis of the Jonestown tragedy, Hall shows that the members of the People's Temple were part of a cohesive social movement. Many were of modest means, some quite poor; in addition, most were black. They felt alienated from the larger society and saw the Temple as their community and often as their family. It is only by understanding the strength of their attachments to one another and to their belief in Jones's vision of a better world to come that one can make sense of what appears to be a senseless, insane episode of collective behavior. Faced with what they perceived as imminent attacks on the religious community they were building in the jungle, some Temple members worked themselves into a frenzy in which they became convinced that by drinking the poison they were "stepping over" into a better world. Others may or may not have felt these emotions; we cannot ever know. Probably some people thought the occasion was a practice suicide. In any case, Hall's study shows that Jones planned the act of "collective martyrdom" but that the vast majority of the Temple members followed to the end because of their unshaken belief in the goals of their social movement.

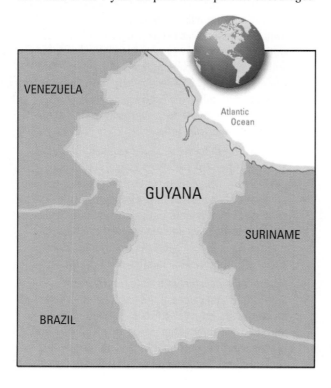

SOCIAL MOVEMENT THEORY

Early theories of collective behavior were derived from the notion that hysteria or contagious feelings like hatred or fear could spread through masses of people. One of the first social thinkers to develop a theory of collective behavior was Gustave LeBon. An aristocratic critic of the emerging industrial democracies, LeBon believed that those societies were producing "an era of crowds" in which agitators and despots are heroes, "the populace is sovereign, and the tide of barbarism mounts" (1947/1896, pp. 14, 207). LeBon thus developed the first modern theory of crowd behavior. In its usual definition, he pointed out, "the word 'crowd' means a gathering of individuals of whatever nationality, profession, or sex, and whatever be the chances that have brought them together." But from a psychological viewpoint a crowd can create conditions in which "the sentiments and ideas of all the persons in the gathering take one and the same direction, and their conscious personality vanishes" (quoted in Genevie, 1978, p. 9).

LeBon attributed the strikes and riots that are common in rapidly urbanizing societies to the fact that people are cut off from traditional village social institutions and jammed into cities, creating a mass of strangers. This view of early industrial societies was clearly exaggerated; research has shown that urban newcomers seek to form new social attachments, often drawing upon networks of people who came to the city from the same rural area or small town. But more important, research on crowds and riots has shown that despite the appearance of a "mob mentality" and psychological "contagion," people who participate in riots, demonstrations, and other forms of collective behavior actually have many different motivating emotions and may only *appear* to be following along blindly as if they were part of a herd. Also, the contagion theories of LeBon and others are not useful in understanding the full range of collective behaviors and social movements that arise from the strains and conflicts characteristic of rapidly changing industrial societies.

A CONTINUUM OF COLLECTIVE BEHAVIOR

Collective behaviors and social movements can be placed along a continuum according to how much they change the societies in which they occur. At one end of the continuum are revolutions; at the other are fads or crazes. In this century there have been three revolutions that have had a major impact on world history: the communist revolutions in Russia and China and the fascist revolution that brought Hitler to power in 1933. These can be placed at the high end of the continuum. At the low end are fads and crazes that may excite us for a while but usually do not bring about lasting change in the major structures of society (Turner, 1974). Some people become so completely involved in a fad or craze (as occurred, for example, among collectors of pogs) that they devote all their energies to the new activity.

Between the two extremes of revolutions and fads are social movements that capture the attention of masses of people and have varying effects on the societies in which they occur. The women's movement, the civil rights movement, and the environmental protection movement are examples of movements with broad membership in many nations and the continuing power to bring about social change. The gay liberation movement, the antiabortion movement, the evangelical movement, and the hospice movement (see Chapter 15) are examples of more narrowly focused movements that are concerned with a single issue or set of issues but also exert powerful pressure for change in the United States and other societies. Then there are movements that may involve large numbers of people for a brief time but have limited effects on society. An example is the movement to aid famine victims in Africa. In the United States, concern about hunger in Ethiopia originated among a small number of people, but when rock music promoters enlisted the help of major artists and the music industry to produce the benefit record "We Are the World" and the Live Aid Concert, millions of Americans took notice of the situation, and by buying records and attending concerts they contributed to famine relief. These more transient social movements serve to raise consciousness about a particular social condition, but they do not usually bring about lasting change.

Theories of collective behavior and social movements often seek to explain the origins and effects of revolutionary and reform movements (Kimmel, 1990; McAdam, McCarthy, & Zald, 1988). In the remainder of this section we discuss several such theories. We begin by examining the nature of revolutions and revolutionary movements. Then we consider theories that attempt to explain why major revolutions and revolutionary social movements have arisen and what factors have enabled them to succeed. Note that these are macro-level theories: They explain revolutions and the associated social movements as symptoms of even larger-scale social change.

THEORIES OF REVOLUTION

Sociologists often distinguish between "long revolutions," or large-scale changes in the ecological relationships of humans to the earth and to one another (e.g., the rise of capitalism and the industrial revolution), and revolutions that are primarily social or political in nature (Braudel, 1984; Wolf, 1984a, b). The course of world history is shaped by long revolutions, whereas individual societies are transformed by social revolutions like those that occurred in the United States, France, and Russia.

Political and Social Revolutions. Sociologist Theda Skocpol (1979) makes a further distinction between political and social revolutions. **Political revolutions**

are transformations in the political structures and leadership of a society that are not accompanied by a full-scale rearrangement of the society's productive capacities, culture, and stratification system. **Social revolutions,** on the other hand, sweep away the old order. They not only change the institutions of government but also bring about basic changes in social stratification. Both political and socialrevolutions are brought about by revolutionary social movements as well as by external forces like colonialism.

The American Revolution, according to Skocpol's theory, was a political revolution. The minutemen who fought against British troops in the Battle of Concord were a political revolutionary group that did not at first seek to change American society in radical ways. On the other hand, the revolutions that destroyed the existing social order in Russia and China in this century were social revolutions. Their goal was to transform the class structure and institutions of their societies.

Skocpol's analysis further shows that the actual outcomes of social revolutions depend on the kinds of coalitions formed among revolutionary parties and larger social classes. The communist revolutionaries in Russia, for example, did not join forces with the peasants as the Chinese communist revolutionaries did. One consequence was that in the former Soviet Union the peasants were persecuted during the revolution; their land was taken from them and many were forced to live on collective farms. These disruptions of the society's agrarian base severely weakened the economy. In China, however, while there were many disruptions of rural life after the communists took power, food production continued to to be carried out in villages and small landholdings. Peasant communist leaders replaced feudal landowners, but agricultural production did not suffer as it did in the former Soviet Union.

Why do revolutionary social movements arise, and what makes some of them content mainly with seizing power while others call for a complete reorganization of society? For most of this century the answer has been some version of Marxian conflict theory. This theory uses detailed knowledge of existing societies to predict the shape of future ones. According to Marx, the world would become capitalist; then capitalist markets would come under the control of monopolies; impoverished workers and colonial peoples would rebel in a generation of mass social movements and revolutions; and a new, classless society would be created in which the workers would own the means of production. (Marx's theory of class conflict leading to revolution is discussed in Chapters 7 and 11.)

Relative Deprivation. The idea that the increasing misery of the working class would lead workers to join revolutionary social movements was not Marx's only explanation of the causes of revolution. He also believed that under some conditions, "although the enjoyments of the workers have risen," their level of dissatisfaction could

rise even faster owing to the much greater increase in the "enjoyments of the capitalists, which are inaccessible to the worker" (Marx & Engels, 1955, Vol. 1, p. 94). This is a version of the theory known as **relative deprivation** (Stouffer et al., 1949). According to this theory, the presence of deprivation (i.e., poverty or misery) does not by itself explain why people join revolutionary social movements. Instead, it is the feeling of deprivation *relative to others*. We tend to measure our own well-being against that of others, and even if we are doing fairly well, if they are doing better we are likely to feel a sense of injustice and, sometimes, extreme anger. It is this feeling of deprivation relative to others that gives rise to revolutionary social movements.

Alexis de Tocqueville came to the same conclusion in his study of the causes and results of the French Revolution. He was struck by the fact that the revolution did not occur in the seventeenth century, when the economic conditions of the French people were in severe decline. Instead, it occurred in the eighteenth century, a period of rapid economic growth. Tocqueville concluded that "revolutions are not always brought about by a gradual decline from bad to worse. Nations that have endured patiently and almost unconsciously the most overwhelming oppression often burst into rebellion against the yoke the moment it begins to grow lighter" (1955/1856, p. 214). The Zapatista rebellion in the Mexican state of Chiapas is an example of a revolutionary movement that began among very poor Indian peasants but became a broader movement during a time of relative economic prosperity (Vilas, 1993).

Valuable as they are as broad theories of revolution, neither Marxian theory nor Tocqueville's analysis can fully explain the rise of revolutionary movements throughout the contemporary world, nor do they help much in understanding the changes major social movements go through as their goals and organizations change over time. These and related questions are analyzed more directly in recent theories of protest cycles and changes within social movements, to which we now turn.

PROTEST CYCLES, ACTION FRAMES, AND CHARISMA

In analyzing the revolutions that have occurred during the past 500 years, sociologist Charles Tilly concludes that there are no "neat formulations of standard, recurrent conditions for forcible transfers of state power" (1993, p. 237). However, he agrees with other social scientists who have pointed out that revolutionary social movements and other forms of protest often occur in cycles or waves of unrest. He cites the waves of protest that swept through Europe and North America in the late 1960s and the current wave of fundamentalist movements in much of the contemporary world. During such waves, he observes:

> One set of demands seems to incite another, social movement organizations compete with each other for support, demands

become more extreme for a while before subsiding. As this happens, activists often experiment with new ways of organizing, framing their demands, combating their enemies and holding on to what they have. (1993, p. 13)

Waves of Protest.   No theory adequately explains why particular waves of protest sweep through societies. But Sidney Tarrow (1994), another astute student of protest cycles, argues that waves of protest often result from major social shocks such as an international economic recession, the end of a period of warfare, or hasty actions by one or more governments. Such an episode occurred in Poland in the early 1980s when the communist regime announced large increases in the price of bread. The movement that ensued, known as Solidarity, demonstrated the weakness of that regime.

During cycles of protest there is a dramatic increase in social conflicts of all kinds, often resulting in violent episodes of collective behavior—riots, demonstrations, and counterdemonstrations. The heightened sense that change is in the air, often brought on by the activities of a few "early risers" among protest leaders (e.g., Lech Walesa and Mahatma Gandhi), triggers a variety of processes, including imitations of the protest elsewhere (e.g., Martin Luther King, Jr., and Nelson Mandela, who followed the example set by Gandhi). The wave of protest may also build momentum through diffusion, often spreading from larger cities to smaller towns and rural areas. New ideologies arise to justify collective action and help the movement mobilize a following (Tarrow, 1994).

Collective Action Frames.   The old saying that "the pen is mightier than the sword" refers to the power of ideas to shape our view of society and why it needs to be changed. In this century we have seen the revolutionary power of ideas embodied in *The Communist Manifesto* of Karl Marx and Friedrich Engels, Hitler's *Mein Kampf* ("My Struggle"), and the "Little Red Book" containing the sayings of Chairman Mao Zedong. In our own time such books as Newt Gingrich's *To Renew America* and William Bennett's *Book of Virtues* have presented ideas that motivate various conservative movements in the United States. Millions of people latch on to these ideas, not because they are incapable of forming their own ideas but because all of us are continually trying out ideas that seem to explain our times and help us make sense of our experiences in society. When faced with quandaries about what to do, what actions we should take or support, we often seek out ideas that are phrased as "collective action frames," sets of beliefs and interpretations of events that inspire and justify social movements (Snow & Benford, 1992). Collective action frames are described in more detail in Box 8.1.

Charisma.   Leadership plays an extremely important part in the success or failure of revolutionary social movements. The leaders of such movements are often said to have almost supernatural powers to inspire and motivate masses of followers. Max Weber (1968) called this ability **charisma.** A charismatic leader appears to possess extraordinary "gifts of the body and spirit" that mark him or her as specially chosen to lead. The voices that Joan of Arc heard, which convinced her to take up arms to save France, gave her the inspired commitment to her cause that is a central feature of charisma. Mahatma Gandhi, probably this century's greatest example of a charismatic leader, swayed the Indian masses with his almost supernatural spirituality and courage. Similarly, the extraordinary gifts of oratory, faith, and energy displayed by Martin Luther King, Jr., allowed him to emerge as the most influential leader of the American civil rights movement.

Often the movement's followers themselves attribute special powers to their leader. This process may produce additional myths about the leader's powers and add to whatever personal magnetism the leader originally possessed. For example, Hitler was no doubt a fiery orator, but his followers' frenzied reception of many of his ideas contributed to the perception that he possessed exceptional charisma.

Mahatma Gandhi, probably the most revered and charismatic political figure of the twentieth century, is shown here during a light moment with his granddaughters. Gandhi's techniques of nonviolence and passive resistance inspired Martin Luther King, Jr., and other leaders of political protest movements. But his followers often endured great personal sacrifice and physical danger, for his political strategies called for nonviolent civil disobedience in the name of higher moral values.

Collective Action Frames

Sociologist William A. Gamson (1992) is one of the leading students of political activism in the United States. His recent research on social movements focuses on the mental frameworks people develop in their thinking about social issues. He notes that social movements strive to offer one or more *collective action frames.* These are ways of thinking that justify the need for and desirability of a particular course of action. After studying the writings and speeches of activists in many different social movements, Gamson concluded that collective action frames have three important components:

1. *An injustice component,* a sense of moral indignation or outrage against a perceived injustice and the people who are said to be responsible for the condition.

2. *An agency component,* which embodies the idea that not only is there injustice, but together "we" can do something about the condition.

3. *An identity component,* which defines who "we" are, usually in opposition to a "they" with different tastes and values.

Gamson studies collective action frames by recording conversations in which people discuss social issues. In exploring the injustice component, for example, he listened carefully for statements like "That is just wrong," "That's unfair," "That really burns me up," or "That pisses me off." Such statements are marked by "explicit moral condemnation, unqualified by offsetting arguments and unchallenged by other group members," as in this example:

CHARACTERS:

Marjorie, a waitress, in her forties.
Judy, a data entry clerk, in her thirties.
Several others who don't speak in this scene.

(The group is near the end of a discussion of nuclear power):

MARJORIE: They should have taken all that money to nuclear power and everything—and you've got kids starving in America.

JUDY: Yeah.

MARJORIE: You've got homeless people. Where's your values? [*pause*] They suck. They really do suck.

JUDY: You're on tape.

[*laughter*]

MARJORIE: I don't care what I'm on. Still—it's obvious—when you pay millions and millions of dollars in nuclear plants when people in America are starving—

JUDY: Right.

MARJORIE: And you've got homeless people, no matter what they are—whether they're drunks or they're—whatever they are. Mentally ill people and you've got them living on a street. And you've got a family of five people—I worked for Legal Services of Greater Boston and I had people in the Milner Hotel, mothers with five kids in one room. Living. And we don't have places for them, but we have places to build nuclear plants. That's garbage. That's garbage! (Gamson, 1992, pp. 48–49)

Sociologists listen carefully to the way people like Marjorie frame issues. In this case the frame is injustice and the point being made is that too much money is being spent on nuclear plants while other, more pressing human needs go unmet. In this dialogue Marjorie is outspoken and not afraid of having her opinions recorded, whereas Judy is far more passive and concerned about voicing her opinions. The sociologist would probably conclude that within her circle of friends and coworkers Marjorie is a leader who often frames issues for others. As you listen to conversations like this one, observe how the leaders frame issues for the other participants.

The charisma of the leader may eventually pose problems for the movement. Every social movement must incorporate the goals and gifts of its leaders into the structure of the movement and eventually into the institutions of society. But how can this be done without losing track of the movement's original purpose and values? Scholars who follow Weber's lead in this area of research have termed this problem the *institutionalization of charisma* (Shils, 1970).

Weber recognized that the more successful a movement becomes in taking power and assuming authority, the more difficult it is to retain the zeal and motivation of its charismatic founders. Once the leaders have power and can obtain special privileges for themselves, they tend to resist continued efforts to do away with inequalities of wealth and power. Perhaps the most instructive example of this problem is the institutionalization of the ideals of Marx and

Lenin in the organization of the Bolshevik party in Russia after the revolution of 1917.

"Workers of the world, unite," Marx urged in *The Communist Manifesto;* "you have nothing to lose but your chains" (Marx & Engels, 1969/1848). The vision of a society in which poverty, social injustice, repression, war, and all the evils of capitalism would be eliminated formed the core of Marxian socialism. The founders of the Bolshevik party realized, however, that revolutions are not made with slogans and visions alone (Schumpeter, 1950). The unification of the workers required an organization that not only would carry forward the revolution but also would take the lead in mobilizing the Russian masses to work for the ideals of socialism. The charismatic leader who built this organization was Vladimir Ilyich Lenin.

Under the leadership of Lenin (and far more ruthlessly under his successor Josef Stalin), any Bolshevik who challenged party discipline was exiled or killed. Because the goals of the Bolsheviks were so radical and the need for reform so pressing, Lenin and Stalin argued that the party had to exert total control over its members in order to prevent spontaneous protests that might threaten the party's goals. By the same logic, other parties had to be eliminated and dissenters imprisoned. Such efforts by an elite to exert control over all forms of organizational life in a society are known as *totalitarianism.* All social movements that believe the ends they seek justify the means used to achieve them risk becoming totalitarian because they sacrifice the rule of law and the ideal of democratic process to gain power (Harrington, 1987; Howe, 1983).

Co-optation. Weberian theory predicts that social movements will institutionalize their ideals in a bureaucratic structure. And the more successful they are in gaining the power to change society, the more they will be forced to control the activities of their members. In fact, once a movement is institutionalized, with an administration and bureaucratic rules, its leaders tend to influence new charismatic leaders to become part of their bureaucracy, a process known as *co-optation.* In the labor movement, for example, maverick leaders who demand reform and instigate protests in their plants are often given inducements such as jobs in the union administration to keep them under control (Geschwender, 1977; Kornhauser, 1952). In politics, local party leaders may identify and co-opt a local leader who they think might pose a threat in the future, offering inducements such as support in an election campaign in return for loyalty to the party. In this way an outspoken environmentalist and history professor named Newt Gingrich was co-opted by the Republican leaders of Carrollton, Georgia, early in his political career.

SOCIAL MOVEMENTS AND CIVIL SOCIETY

Most of us will probably never belong to a revolutionary social movement, at least not one devoted to the violent overthrow of a government or society. Nor will many of us experience the deadening force of totalitarian rule. Most of us therefore will not find ourselves helping to rebuild the voluntary associations and communities, the leagues, the hobby groups, the unions and auxiliaries of our societies, as the people of many Eastern European nations are doing today. But many readers of this book will become members of organizations and groups of all kinds, which in turn may become affiliated with broader social movements.

This famous photo from the Holocaust shows Jewish families being rounded up for transport to concentration camps. Under Hitler, the National Socialists (Nazis) often resorted to public acts of terror to establish their absolute rule over German society. Such totalitarian regimes often use terror to destroy mutual trust among citizens.

THE PERSONAL CHALLENGE

Social Change and Social Movements

Wherever it occurs, social change results in an explosive growth of social movements. As societies around the world become enmeshed in global interrelationships, as old ways of making a living decline and new ones appear, as worldwide currents of thought such as nationalism, fundamentalism, or movements for equality sweep through their societies, people try to join forces and create social movements to cope with those changes. Every social movement has active members who seek to attract new recruits and will appeal to you for your attention and allegiance. The choices you make can help shape the future of your community and society. They can also change your life in both positive and, sometimes, negative ways.

As this chapter shows, millions of Americans are part of one or more social movements. However, there may be important differences between a social movement and a particular organization seeking to advance that movement's goals. For example, you may oppose abortion and consider yourself part of the pro-life movement, but you may not actually be a member of a pro-life organization within that movement. Similarly, you may favor better working conditions for workers and consider yourself an ally of the labor movement, but you may not actually be a member of a specific labor union within that broader social movement. If you continue to support the movement, attend information meetings, take part in demonstrations, and so on, before long you will be recruited for actual membership in an organization.

What questions can one ask about a social movement organization in deciding whether or not to join it? Here are a few especially important ones:

1. *Does the organization demand total allegiance to its leaders and goals?* How much will you have to give up in order to become active in the organization? Many organizations require total commitment. Some

demand that their members cut themselves off from previous friends and even from family members. This is especially true of cultlike political and religious organizations, which often make extreme demands on their members. New recruits are often brought along slowly so that at first the demands are not too severe. So look closely at what is expected of those who are in the organization's higher ranks and how much personal autonomy they must sacrifice. Beware of any organization that requires you to break other social ties so that you can devote yourself fully to its aims and activities.

2. *How does the organization arrive at strategies for achieving its goals?* All social movements must deal with the problem of how to make their demands and aims known to the public. Does the organization you are thinking of joining use democratic processes in deciding on its strategies? Do the members actually have a say in those decisions, or do they merely put a rubber stamp on policies that come "from above"? If the organization claims to be run democratically, you should be able to come up with real evidence that this is so. For example, does it give a full accounting of its finances to members? Does it have a history of corruption? If so, is it open about what it has done to replace corrupt leaders?

3. *What is the organization's stance on civil disobedience and the rule of law?* Many social movement organizations are formed to protest laws that are believed to be unjust. Their members challenge those laws by publicly violating them. Those who do so risk fines and even imprisonment. Civil disobedience has a long and honorable history in democratic societies. The abolition of slavery in the United States and of apartheid in South Africa, for example, probably would never have happened without civil disobedience. But how far should one go in challenging laws, even when they are believed to be

Political extremist Lyndon LaRouche (right) was sentenced to 15 years in prison for conspiring to defraud federal tax collectors and refusing to repay more than $30 million in loans from political supporters. Many of those supporters had neglected to inquire about LaRouche's authoritarian "ends justify means" beliefs before surrendering themselves to his powerful but corrupt leadership.

unjust? There are many forms of civil disobedience, from sitting down and blocking normal traffic to engaging in acts of violence. Beware of any organization that prides itself on its ability to resort to violence. Be extremely wary of any group that makes quick and undemocratic decisions that lead to civil disobedience.

Many organizations that espouse goals you agree with will argue that the ends justify the means, that the social crisis is so grave or the movement's goals so important that the rights and safety of group members and the public must be sacrificed. Think long and hard about the implications of this stance—consider, for example, the tragic history of the Soviet communists or the harm done by the Oklahoma City bombers—before you decide to join this kind of organization. Never hesitate to be an active citizen and a member of social movement organizations, but make sure you ask critical questions about any organization that seeks your allegiance.

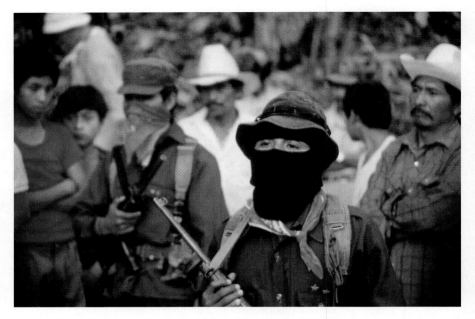

The Zapatistas, shown here in a demonstration in Chiapas, Mexico, are a recent example of a social movement that uses guerrilla tactics and the organization of unarmed peasants to seek land reform as a narrowing of the gap between the rich and the poor.

In contemporary societies an ever growing and changing array of groups and organizations are formed in the public sphere of social activity. Known as **civil society,** this sphere of nongovernmental, nonbusiness social activity is composed of millions of church congregations, sports leagues, amateur arts groups, charitable associations, ethnic associations, and much more. The Mexican sociologist Carlos M. Vilas explains it as follows:

> Civil society refers to a sphere of collective actions distinct from both the market and "political society"—parties, legislatures, courts, state agencies. Civil society is not independent of politics, but clearly, when people identify themselves as "civil society," they are seeking to carve out a relatively autonomous sphere for organization and action. (1993, p. 38)

In parts of the world where the gap between rich and poor is widening, people who participate in civil society are often recruited into movements calling for social and economic justice. Vilas observes, for example, that in Latin America activity in social movements "creates a confluence of the poor and middle classes . . . to confront the traditional alliance of the rich and powerful with the state" (1993, p. 41).

In more affluent regions of the world, civil society also flourishes and provides a rich source of recruits for social movements. As noted in Chapter 6, increasing membership in voluntary associations appears to be a long-term trend in the United States. National surveys conducted in the 1950s found that about one third of adult citizens were members of voluntary associations; today more than two thirds of American adults say that they belong to a voluntary association (Caplow et al., 1991). Since 1970 the number of registered nonprofit associations of all kinds has increased from somewhat over 10,000 to more than 22,000 (*Statistical Abstract,* 1994). While a significant minority of Americans are not members of any voluntary organizations or congregations, the majority are active members. From the standpoint of social movements, the importance of these facts is that many of the activists in social movements are recruited from the ranks of voluntary associations (e.g., through mailing lists or membership meetings).

Even people who never join social movements will surely find that their lives are changed by them. The social critic H. L. Mencken once said that if three Americans are in a room together for more than an instant, two of them will try to change the morals of the third. Campaigns against smoking, drinking, rock lyrics, violence on television, wearing of furs, abortion, and many other behaviors would seem to confirm this notion. So too would patterns in the growth of different types of voluntary associations. Since 1980 the number of nonprofit voluntary associations devoted to educational and cultural issues has increased by about 35 percent while the number devoted to public affairs has more than doubled (*Statistical Abstract,* 1995).

RESOURCE MOBILIZATION AND FREE RIDERS

What is the relationship between civil society and social movements? In sociology this is known as the *resource mobilization* question, referring to the fact that social movements need to mobilize existing leaders and organizations rather than simply relying on the participation of people who happen to be moved to action (Oberschall, 1973; Tilly, 1978; Walsh, 1981; Zurcher & Snow, 1981). A second, related issue is known as the *free rider problem.* This refers to the tendency of many people not to lend their support and resources—time, money, and leadership—to social movements but to reap the benefits anyway (Marwell & Ames, 1985; Olson, 1965).

Are these issues important? One need only think of all - the American workers who have benefited from the gains won by the labor movement without themselves making the effort to form unions. Or consider the rapid growth of the environmental protection movement in the late 1960s and early 1970s. What explains the speed with which that movement captured a central place in public-policy debates? In studying the growth of the movement for environmental quality, sociologist Carol Kronus (1977) found that out of a sample of 209 existing organizations in a midwestern city, more than half gave material and moral support to the new movement. And she found that the groups that did link up with the movement were ones whose goals were in agreement with those of the movement and whose members believed in taking action to improve the quality of life in their community. Free rider groups, on the other hand, agreed that "something should be done about pollution" but felt that other groups should take action before they were able to do so.

The free rider hypothesis predicts that some proportion of the potential members of a social movement will not lend their energies to the movement but will nonetheless hope that the movement will provide them with the benefits they desire. But how extensive will the free rider problem be? How many people will act out of self-interest and try to reap the rewards of the movement's activities without making any personal sacrifices? These are empirical questions on which there is a growing body of research findings.

One study of the free rider problem is Edward J. Walsh and Rex H. Warland's (1983) study of the social movement that emerged after the near-meltdown of a nuclear reactor on Three Mile Island (TMI) near Middletown, Pennsylvania, in 1979. After the accident antinuclear organizations grew in strength throughout the TMI area. Many opposed efforts to start up a reactor at the facility that had not been damaged. Walsh and Warland found that of those who opposed the start-up of the undamaged reactor, 87 percent were free riders in that they had not contributed in any way to the organizations opposing the start-up. And of those in favor of the start-up, 98 percent were free riders. Only a very small percentage—6 percent of those in opposition and 1 percent of those in favor—actually participated. Although this is a small proportion, it does show that there are people who are ready to be mobilized as activists on an important social issue. Not everyone is an apathetic or alienated free rider.

The TMI research suggests that a large majority of people will be free riders and will not join a social movement even when they strongly desire it to succeed and to win victories that will benefit them directly. Other research, however, indicates that the tendency to be a free rider is far less prevalent than the TMI study suggests. Data show that more than 85 percent of American households make chari-

table contributions of some kind. And public television and radio stations do succeed, after much persuasion, in raising the funds they need to continue operating, even though many people who enjoy listening or viewing would just as soon be free riders. Findings from thousands of laboratory experiments conducted since the early 1970s also contradict the free rider hypothesis, showing instead that many people make commitments and sacrifice individual gain in order to advance a cause. Still, the relatively low proportion of people who join a cause, vote in elections, or voluntarily support institutions like National Public Radio promises to make the free rider problem a subject of continuing social-scientific research (Frank, 1988; Hechter, 1987).

In predicting the success of any given social movement, resource mobilization theory points to the need to consider how well a movement enlists or mobilizes the resources available to it—for example, how well it deals with gender differences in recruiting members or how well it keeps recruits actively committed. Research by Doug McAdam (1992) on the experience of men and women in the civil rights movement during the early 1960s shows that organizations in the movement were constantly struggling with the problem of gender. White women who volunteered as civil rights workers often had more experience in organizations and civil rights activities than white male applicants but were less likely to be selected to participate. Those who were selected were often assigned jobs that were considered "women's work" unless they protested against such treatment. Indeed, McAdam found that many of the women who participated in the civil rights movement later became very active in the women's movement, in part because of their experiences in trying to assert their rights in the civil rights movement. Studies of participation in other social movements during the 1960s have yielded similar findings: Women are available to be mobilized by social movements, but once they became involved they often find themselves faced with issues of gender inequality.

Mobilization of the law is another aspect of resource mobilization theory that has been studied extensively in recent years (Hoffman, 1989). For example, in his research on how activists attempt to use laws and the courts to advance their cause, sociologist Robert Burstein (1991) shows that activists seeking to end discrimination against minorities in the labor force are increasingly petitioning the courts under the Equal Employment Opportunity (EEO) laws. Burstein and other researchers have found that social movements are more likely to use the tactics of protest and demonstration when they are outside the framework of the law, but when laws have been passed in response to their demands, they become more likely to initiate lawsuits to achieve their goals. Burstein shows that the more a group has mobilized its resources as a protest movement, the more it will be able to mobilize the law in its favor as well. Thus racial minorities and women's groups, two well-mobilized civil rights groups, do much better at winning enforcement of EEO laws than religious or ethnic minorities, which have less experience organizing and mobilizing members and money for their causes.

MASS PUBLICS AND PUBLIC OPINION

Most of the examples of social movements discussed in this chapter have had a lasting impact on the societies in which they occurred. In this section we apply the insights gained from earlier sections to some of the less world-shaking, yet still exciting, aspects of collective behavior in American life.

Over the past century North America has been transformed from a continent of wide-open spaces and agrarian settlements to the earth's technologically most advanced and socially most mobile region. Indeed, for the rest of the world North America is synonymous with both the best and the worst aspects of what has come to be known as "modern" society.

According to Reinhard Bendix (1969), **modernization** consists of all the political and economic changes that accompanied industrialization. Among the indicators of modernity are urbanization, the shift from agricultural to industrial occupations, and increasing literacy as well as the demand for greater political participation by the masses. Bendix is quick to point out that his definition does not necessarily apply everywhere in the world. Modernization may not always mean what it has meant in Western societies. But it is probable that, despite setbacks in some nations, modernization will always involve the extension of rights, values, and opportunities from the elites to the masses in a society.

None of these changes in the organization of societies came about without collective protests and social movements. For every radical movement there was a reactionary one, for every revolution a counterrevolution or at least an attempt at one. And social movements continue to exert pressure for change in our norms and institutions. The extension of voting rights to women and blacks had to be won through political struggle. Nor did the benefits of new technologies come automatically to American workers; they had to be won by the labor movement. Likewise, the rapidly expanding cities of North America became scenes of collective protest as new populations of immigrants and new occupational groups fought for "a piece of the pie" (Lieberson, 1980). It is hardly surprising, therefore, that so much sociological research is devoted to studying how modern society came about, discovering how much further some groups have to go to gain their share of the benefits of modernity, and analyzing the role of collective behavior in these major social changes.

Consider just one important consequence of the labor movement of the late nineteenth and early twentieth cen-

turies: the change in the length of the workweek. "Our lives shall not be sweated, from day until night closes," went the famous refrain of the Industrial Workers of the World (known as the Wobblies). "Hearts starve as well as bodies; give us bread but give us roses." Figure 8.2 shows how the demand for enough leisure to enjoy the finer things of life produced dramatic changes in the hours of work. Today we take the eight-hour day and the five-day week as the standard for full-time employment, but in 1919 American steelworkers shut down the entire industry in protest against the twelve-hour day and the six-day week (Brody, 1960). The concessions won by them and other workers were an essential part of the extension of the benefits of modernity to working people. The increase in leisure created by these changes in hours and days of work, along with greater social mobility owing to increased affluence, contributed to the development of mass publics (see Box 8.2).

MASS PUBLICS

Mass publics are large populations (regional or national) of potential spectators or participants who engage in collective behavior of all kinds. Typically this behavior consists of the formation of crowds, audiences, or streams of buyers and voters, but it can also include crazes, panics, and the spreading of rumors. Thus a massive traffic jam can turn into a dangerous panic; a joyful victory celebration can become a violent riot like the one that occurred after the Chicago Bulls won the National Basketball Association championship in 1992. The panic selling that occurred on Wall Street in October 1987 and resulted in a massive loss of investors' capital is a reminder that mass publics continue to exert important effects even when supposed safeguards are in place. For this reason alone, social scientists, urban planners, and governmental leaders increasingly recognize the need to cooperate in anticipating the behaviors of mass publics.

This recognition has come after some painful experiences. A famous case of failure to anticipate the possible reaction of mass publics occurred with the 1938 radio dramatization of H. G. Wells's novel *The War of the Worlds.* This broadcast, which vividly described an invasion of the earth by Martians, was presented to the radio audience in documentary fashion, beginning with a fictitious news flash and continuing with reports of a spacecraft landing in a New Jersey field and descriptions of the invading Martian army. Not realizing that the broadcast was only a dramatic presentation, hundreds of thousands of Americans began gathering in panicky crowds, while thousands of others jammed telephone lines in efforts to reach loved ones.

A few years later, when the dramatization was broadcast by Radio Quito using Ecuadorian place names, "the initial reaction was the same as in the United States. Multitudes poured out of the city in all directions, running and driving as far and as fast as they could" (Klass, 1988, p. 48). When listeners found out that the program had been a

FIGURE 8.2   Average Weekly Work Hours, 1850–1963

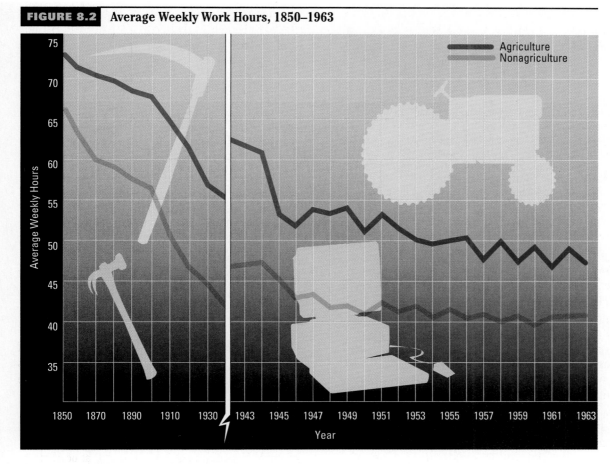

The brief increase in average hours of work between 1940 and 1943 (not shown on the chart) is due to the labor shortages that occurred during World War II.

Source: Data from Bureau of Labor Statistics; adapted from Dankert, Mann, & Northrup, 1965.

dramatization, they were so angry at the radio station that they burned it to the ground. As a result of experiences like these, broadcasters became far more careful in presenting fictitious accounts on the radio (Cantril, 1982/1940).

The availability of more time for leisure pursuits, the development of a mass market for automobiles, and the technological revolution in communications and the mass media have all exerted an immense influence on the lifestyles of mass publics, which in turn shape the society in which they live. For example, through their demands for roads, leisure facilities, and services that cater to a highly mobile lifestyle, Americans have transformed the physical landscape. Rural scenes of farms and small towns still exist, but throughout the nation they are being enveloped by networks of suburbs and shopping malls and pleasure grounds (stadiums, amusement parks, etc.) linked together by a labyrinth of highways (Carter, 1975; Flink, 1975; Thomas, 1956).

Mass publics have also created the conditions that make possible whole new industries. The hot dog, for example, was an innovation that allowed large numbers of people to eat while strolling along the boardwalk at Coney Island. But fast-food soon became an industry and even, as

McDonald's founder Ray Kroc (1977) described it, an art form:

> Consider, for example, the hamburger bun. It requires a certain kind of mind to see beauty in a hamburger bun. Yet, is it any more unusual to find grace in the texture and softly curved silhouette of a bun than to reflect lovingly on the hackles of a favorite fishing fly? Or the arrangement of textures and colors in a butterfly wing? . . . Not if you regard the bun as an essential material in the art of serving a great many meals fast. [p. 99]

The thousands of teenagers and young adults who work in the fast-food industry may not sing rhapsodies to buns and burgers; nevertheless, their industry owes its existence to the behavior of hungry, mobile multitudes—that is, mass publics.

PUBLIC OPINION

The presence of mass publics sets the stage for the emergence of public opinion as a powerful force in modern societies. **Public opinion** refers to the values and attitudes of mass publics. The kinds of behavior that develop out of

BOX 8.2 USING THE SOCIOLOGICAL IMAGINATION

The Charles Dickens Show

Do you ever glance at the popular magazines on supermarket racks while waiting in the checkout line? Many of the stories are about celebrities or "stars." What do you suppose it takes for those individuals to become stars?

When people lived in village societies, without roads, railroads, radio, television, or magazines, there was a need for roving entertainers who brought news of the distant royal courts to the people in the villages. Bards recited historical tales and related them to current events; minstrels sang ballads about the lives of the great and the legendary; actors often performed in open-air theaters. Few of these entertainers commanded great prestige, however. For example, Shakespeare's Globe Theatre was simply one of many rowdy places to which local people came for entertainment.

For entertainers like Diana Ross or the Beatles or Michael Jackson or Madonna to become celebrities, there first must be a mass public. Such entertainers must draw audiences from one end of the society to the other, which means that those audiences must share roughly the same values. And if people are going to travel to see a performer, they must be able to hear about the act; there must be media like the press and television that can promote it. There must also be people who concern themselves with scheduling, booking space, selling tickets, advertising, transporting, and otherwise making sure that the event meets people's expectations.

Who was the first celebrity in the modern sense? The English author Charles Dickens is a strong candidate. *A Christmas Carol, David Copperfield, Oliver Twist,* and others of his novels that were serialized in magazines during the 1840s and 1850s won him a devoted audience throughout the English-speaking world. Dickens had a brilliant sociological imagination, expressed not only in his social commentary but also in his understanding of the public. His books were more widely read than those of any other living author, and he gave immensely popular public readings from his works. Here is how Raymund FitzSimons (1970) describes Dickens and his audience:

> The public readings of Charles Dickens were the greatest one-man show of the nineteenth century. "Dickens is coming!" was the ecstatic shout in towns where he was announced to read. In London the cheers that greeted his appearance on the platform could be heard a block away. In Edinburgh he had to calm a rioting audience. In Glasgow the audience tried to storm the platform and carry him away. In Boston, New York, and Philadelphia people queued for tickets all night in temperatures well below freezing point.

Charles Dickens

The excesses of his public would today be more associated with a pop star than a writer reading extracts from his own works. Yet, in the true sense of the term, Dickens was a pop star, one of the greatest of all time. . . . The readings appealed, as did the books, to all ages and to all tastes, cultivated and simple. It was this universal appeal that put the readings into a different category from all other entertainments. . . .

For the readings were an entertainment . . . Dickens was a magnificent actor, with a wonderful talent for mimicry. He seemed able to alter not only his voice, his features, and his carriage but also his stature. He disappeared and the audience saw, as the case may be, Fagin, Scrooge, Pickwick, Mrs. Gamp, Squeers, Mrs. Gummidge, Micawber, Bill Sikes, or a host of others. (p. 15)

Other producers and entertainers in the past century, like P. T. Barnum and Jenny Lind, helped open people's eyes to the fact that mass audiences were available for the right entertainers. Under these conditions new talent could be discovered and promoted to stardom, and fortunes could be made in the process.

public opinion include fads, fashions, demands for particular goods and services, voting behavior, and much more.

Public opinion is shaped in part by collective behavior, especially social movements. An example is the rise of the conservative movement in the United States in the 1980s. The impact of this movement can be seen in the contrast between the results of the 1964 and 1984 presidential elections. In 1964 Barry Goldwater, who espoused many of the ideals of the current conservative movement, was overwhelmingly defeated by Lyndon Johnson, an outspoken proponent of liberal social-welfare policies. Twenty years later the pendulum of public opinion had swung to the other extreme, and the staunchly conservative Ronald Reagan beat a liberal candidate, Walter Mondale, by an even greater percentage of the electoral vote than Johnson had won in 1964.

During the 1992 presidential election campaign there seemed to be a voter backlash against extreme conservatism, reflected in the voters' rejection of Republican emphasis on "family values" as code words for disapproval of homosexuals, single parents, and other people with unconventional lifestyles. But the Republican victories in the 1994 congressional elections show that conservative values are at least temporarily in the ascendance once again. Supported by active social movements, particularly the antiabortion movement and those promoting Christian conservative causes, the Republicans now face the problem of satisfying the demands of those movements while persuading others that the party can accommodate their often conflicting needs.

Public opinion is also shaped by more fleeting shifts in the national mood as citizens respond to experiences that are shared by all, especially through the mass media. For example, no one knows for sure whether the severe droughts that burned crops in the United States and Canada in 1987 and 1988 were a symptom of global warming, but scientists' warnings about this possibility, and their explanations of the "greenhouse effect" caused by high levels of carbon dioxide and other gases in the atmosphere, were made far more vivid by media coverage of the drought. Public support for environmental protection was stimulated still further by media coverage of the oil spill by the *Exxon Valdez* in Alaska in 1989.

RESEARCH FRONTIERS: AMUSING THE MILLIONS

The idea that the United States is becoming "a nation of spectators" was a popular sociological notion in the 1950s. A contemporary version of this "spectatoritis" thesis is the claim that greater affluence and increased access to television and other media have transformed Americans into a nation of overweight "couch potatoes." A more sophisticated analysis of these issues is provided by the study of leisure in the United States and other advanced industrial nations. Indeed, the study of leisure is an important frontier of sociological research.

Since the 1940s the pursuit of leisure activities of all kinds has become a passion for those who can afford the time. This is true throughout most of the industrial world, not just in the United States and Canada (Machlis & Tichnell, 1985). People are spending more money on leisure pursuits and engaging in more diverse pleasures than ever before. In ancient Rome and feudal Europe only the nobility had leisure; everyone else toiled ceaselessly in the fields or at their crafts. The limited leisure available to the masses took the form of religious festivals and games. The notion that common people could enjoy leisure in specified blocks of time—weekends, holidays, vacations, retirement— would have been viewed as revolutionary.

The rise of modern social movements changed the expectations of "common folk" about many values, including leisure. For example, at the turn of the century the labor movement called for an end to the 12-hour workday. At around the same time, the conservation movement was pressing for preservation of the nation's virgin forests and the creation of national parks. The woman suffrage movement marched for women's right to vote, which would eventually lead to demands by women for more leisure time.

One consequence of the increase in leisure time in North America has been the steady growth of institutions devoted to leisure and recreation. It is estimated that more than 350 million visits are paid to national parks in the United States each year and that approximately 700 million visits are made to state parks. More than 45 million tickets to major league baseball games are sold each year, and about 15 million people attend NFL football games. About 415 million rounds of golf are played each year, more than 60 million people go bowling, and at least 9 million people own an outboard motor. There are some 1,100 opera companies in the nation; they perform for at least 14 million people a year. Try maneuvering through the traffic jam caused by a college football game when 60,000 fans are trying to get home for dinner. Imagine the same scene repeated simultaneously at thousands of other locations, some smaller and some larger, and you can begin to grasp the impact of leisure pursuits.

Data like those just presented tell only part of the story of leisure's impact on a modern society. In the United States, people's leisure preferences increasingly shape the landscape itself. Highways extend to beaches and mountain recreation sites. Large portions of states like Florida, Montana, Wyoming, Arizona, and California are managed as leisure and recreation areas by powerful state and national land-management agencies. Private vendors of recreation services (motels, tennis courts, restaurants, shops, etc.) crowd the tourist gateways to major attractions like Yellowstone Park or the Great Smokies. In major cities, leisure institutions like theaters, symphony orchestras, museums, sports complexes, and parks are vital to the local economy and culture. Without them, cities would become dark ghost towns after business hours. Urban planners and city leaders therefore compete to attract talent and develop such institutions into tourist and cultural centers. Leisure for the millions translates into jobs for hundreds of thousands of people in every region of the country.

THE NAMES PROJECT QUILT

The NAMES Project, and the famous quilt it has produced, is an example of a social movement, one that uses visual sociology in the most creative way one can imagine. As AIDS activist Elizabeth Taylor writes,

> The quilt is a moving depiction of stories of the loved ones of human beings who have died of AIDS. It reflects the true spirit of America. In their tragedy and grief over loss immeasurable, contributors to the quilt have used art and love to keep the spirit of their loved ones alive. [quoted in Ruskin, 1988, p. 7]

The NAMES Project and the quilt are the inspirition of Cleve Jones. When the actor Marvin Feldman, his dear friend of 14 years, died of AIDS at the age of 33, Jones went to his backyard with paint, stencils, and a sheet to create a memorial. He remembers spending the entire day thinking about Marvin. "I thought about why we were best friends and why I loved him so much. By the time I finished the piece, my grief had been replaced by a sense of resolution and completion." Jones realized that if people got together to make quilts as memorials to lost loved ones, the activity could be a redeeming and mobilizing way of confronting the AIDS epidemic.

A Quaker with years of political activism in his background, Jones became a gay activist when he was 18. In 1986, he appeared on *60 Minutes* and discussed his reactions to the discovery that he was HIV positive. Shortly thereafter, in Sacramento, he was attacked by two men who stalked him, calling him "faggot," and stabbed him in the back. During his convalescence, he thought more about the idea of the NAMES Project and the quilt, and after his recovery he joined with AIDS activists throughout the world to advertise the project. Before long, hundreds of groups of friends and family members were producing quilt panels to commemorate the loss of their loved ones.

On October 11, 1987, the quilt was displayed on the Mall in Washington, D.C.; it covered an area larger than two football fields. It was subsequently exhibited throughout the United States, focusing attention on the need for increased funding for research and the allocation of additional medical resources to the AIDS epidemic.

"There is nothing beautiful about AIDS. It is a hideous disease. . . . With the Quilt, we're able to touch people in a new way and open their hearts so that they no longer turn away from it but rather understand the value of all those lost lives."

"The saddest thing, I believe, for Roger Lyon," says his devoted friend, Cindy McMullin, "w how unfair it was to have to die without knowing how it— AIDS—is going to end."

WASH. D.C.
AUG. 2,1983

'I CAME HERE TODAY TO ASK THAT THIS NATION WITH ALL ITS RESOURCES AND COMPASSION NOT LET MY EPITAPH READ HE DIED OF RED TAPE.'

Neil Kent Augustine
NOV. 13, 1956 – DEC. 2, 1985

THE MEMORY OF EACH OF YOU LIVES IN OUR HEARTS.

WITH LOVE, FROM THE NURSES WHO SERVED YOU.

POSTON

Neil Patchek

Sixty-year-old homemaker Marian Mosner of Lincoln, Nebraska, made this panel for a man who worked with her son in Denver. She did not know her son's friend well but says, "I thought that there would be no recognition from his family. I felt bad about that. I feel bad about all the people who die of AIDS that nobody knows."

235

SUMMARY

THINK ABOUT IT CRITICALLY

It isn't nice to block the doorway.
It isn't nice to go to jail.
There are nicer ways to protest
But the nice ways always fail. . . .

Do you agree with this refrain from Malvina Reynolds's protest song? Is civil disobedience always necessary for a social movement to succeed?

The term *collective behavior* is used to refer to a continuum of unusual or nonroutine behaviors that are engaged in by large numbers of people. At one end of the continuum is the spontaneous behavior of people reacting to situations they perceive as uncertain, threatening, or extremely attractive. At the other end are events that involve large numbers of people in nonroutine behaviors but are organized by leaders and have specific goals. The set of organizations that plan such events is a *social movement.*

The study of spontaneous forms of collective behavior often begins by distinguishing between crowds and masses. A *crowd* is a large number of people who are gathered together in close proximity to one another. A *mass* is a large number of people who are all oriented toward a set of shared symbols or social objects. Collective behavior can occur in crowds, in masses, or in both at once. The actual behavior that a crowd or mass generates depends largely on the emotions people involved in the events feel are appropriate to express in those situations. The most significant categories of emotions that motivate collective behavior are fear, hostility, and joy.

Social movements have been classified into four types based on the goals they seek to achieve. Revolutionary movements aim to overthrow existing stratification systems and social institutions; reformist movements seek partial changes in some institutions and values; conservative movements attempt to uphold the existing values and institutions of society; and reactionary movements seek to return to the institutions and values of the past. In addition, there are expressive social movements, or movements devoted to the expression of personal beliefs and feelings, and millenarian movements, which are both revolutionary and expressive. Within any large social movement there are likely to be a number of different social movement organizations or SMOs.

Early theories of collective behavior were based on the notion that hysteria or contagious feelings like hatred or fear could spread through masses of people. Gustave LeBon attributed the strikes and riots common in rapidly urbanizing societies to a mob mentality created by the presence of large numbers of strangers in crowded cities.

Sociologists often distinguish between "long revolutions," or large-scale changes in the ecological relationships of humans to the earth and to one another, and revolutions that are primarily social or political. *Political revolutions* are transformations in the political structures and leadership of a society that are not accompanied by a full-scale rearrangement of the society's productive capacities, culture, and stratification system. *Social revolutions* not only change the institutions of government but also bring about basic changes in social stratification.

According to Marx, revolutions would occur as a result of the spread of capitalism: Impoverished workers and colonial peoples would rebel against the capitalists and create a new classless society. Also, Marx and Tocqueville pointed to the role of *relative deprivation,* noting that the feeling of deprivation relative to others—not the presence of deprivation itself—may give rise to revolutionary social movements.

More recent analyses have shown that revolutionary social movements often occur in cycles or waves. Waves of protest may result from major social shocks. During such periods there is a dramatic increase in social conflicts, often motivated by collective action frames, or sets of beliefs and interpretations of events.

Successful leaders of social movements are often said to have almost supernatural powers to inspire and motivate their followers. Max Weber called this ability *charisma.* Over time, however, those leaders' goals must be incorporated into the structure of the movement, a process that is referred to as the institutionalization of charisma. However, the more successful the movement, the more difficult it is to maintain the zeal of its founders. In extreme cases the process can end in totalitarianism, or efforts by an elite to control all forms of organizational life in a society.

The sphere of public nongovernmental, nonbusiness social activity is termed *civil society.* People who participate in civil society are often recruited into social movements. The resource mobilization question refers to the need to mobilize existing leaders and organizations to achieve a movement's goals. A related issue is the free rider problem, the tendency of many people not to lend their support and resources to social movements but to reap the benefits anyway.

In recent years activist groups have made increasing use of laws and the courts. Social movements are more likely to use the tactics of protest when they are outside the framework of the law, but when laws have been passed in response to their demands, they become more likely to initiate lawsuits to achieve their goals.

Mass publics are large populations of potential spectators or participants who engage in collective behavior. Such factors as increased leisure time, the almost universal use of automobiles, and the technological revolution in communications and the mass media have had an immense influence on the lifestyles of mass publics, which in turn shape the society in which they live.

The presence of mass publics makes possible the emergence of *public opinion,* or the values and attitudes of mass publics. The behavior that develops out of public opinion can take a variety of forms, including fads, fashions, and demands for particular goods and services. Public opinion is shaped in part by collective behavior, especially social movements. It is also affected by experiences that are shared by all the members of society through the mass media.

CRITICAL RESPONSE

Civil disobedience, violent protest, and other, more extreme activist tactics are often necessary in building a movement that will lead to social change. They call attention to a cause and move others to join. But necessary as they may be, these tactics alone are not sufficient to ensure a movement's success. Violence is especially risky, for it can impede the progress of a movement by making it appear extremist and irresponsible.

GLOSSARY

collective behavior: nonroutine behavior that is engaged in by large numbers of people responding to a common stimulus. (p. 215)

social movement: organized collective behavior aimed at changing or reforming social institutions or the social order itself. (p. 215)

crowd: a large number of people who are gathered together in close proximity to one another. (p. 217)

mass: a large number of people who are all oriented toward a set of shared symbols or social objects. (p. 217)

political revolution: a set of changes in the political structures and leadership of a society. (p. 221)

social revolution: a complete transformation of the social order, including the institutions of government and the system of stratification. (p. 222)

relative deprivation: deprivation as determined by comparison with others rather than by some objective measure. (p. 222)

charisma: a special quality or "gift" that motivates people to follow a particular leader. (p. 223)

civil society: the sphere of nongovernmental, nonbusiness social activity carried out by voluntary associations, congregations, and the like. (p. 228)

modernization: a term used to describe the changes that societies and individuals experience as a result of industrialization, urbanization, and the development of nation-states. (p. 230)

mass public: a large population of potential spectators or participants who engage in collective behavior. (p. 230)

public opinion: the values and attitudes held by mass publics. (p. 231)

WHERE TO FIND IT

BOOKS

Frontiers in Social Movement Theory (Aldon Morris & Carol McClurg Mueller, eds.; Yale, 1992). A collection of recent studies of social movements that includes examples from most new areas of research in this rapidly changing field.

The Crowd in History (George Rudé; Wiley, 1964). A fascinating account of the influence of riots, demonstrations, and protests on the history of the industrializing Western world.

Social Movements in an Organizational Society (Meyer N. Zald & John McCarthy, eds.; Transaction, 1987). A thorough analysis of competing explanations of the evolution of social movements.

A History of Recreation: America Learns to Play, 2nd ed. (Foster Rea Dulles; Appleton, 1965). A history of recreation in America that covers the transformation of the nation from one in which religion dominated all leisure to one characterized by differentiated leisure institutions such as theater, popular music, and sports of all kinds.

Collective Behavior (Ralph H. Turner & Lewis M. Killian; Prentice-Hall, 1987). Widely regarded as the best text on collective behavior and social movements; includes excellent discussions of the major concepts.

The Logic of Collective Action (Mancur Olson; Harvard University Press, 1965). A classic treatise on the costs and benefits of individual choices to engage in collective action; includes a good analysis of free riders.

Women's Movements in America: Their Successes, Disappointments, and Aspirations (Rita J. Simon & Gloria Danziger, eds.; Praeger, 1991). Assesses the relative success of a major social movement in securing positive change for women in the United States; contains excellent bibliographical material and references to other works.

OTHER SOURCES

The Gallup Poll. An annual compilation of polls taken throughout the year by Gallup, Inc.; available in the reference section of most college and university libraries.

The Utne Reader. A compilation of articles, many written by sociologically informed journalists, about current American trends, with much material on major social movements.

General Social Survey: Cumulative Codebook. Published by the National Opinion Research Center (NORC), University of Chicago. An annual survey that provides measures of the demographic characteristics and behaviors of a large sample of Americans. It is available through the data archives of most colleges and universities, along with other research reports published by the NORC.

CHAPTER 9

Population, Urbanization, and Community

Rob Wirtz, a 38-year-old Los Angeles fire captain, remembers that he awoke with a start in his bed at the station house when the emergency phone fell on his head. It was 4:31 A.M. on January 17, 1994, and the earth was shaking as he had never felt it shake before. In fact, he recalls, "Things were shaking so hard I could hardly get my pants up." Captain Wirtz was 15 miles from the earthquake's center, but when he rushed into the garage to check on the equipment, he saw the station's 38,000-pound fire engine bounding around like a giant toy.

At about the same time Carlos Guzman, age 6, watched in amazement as his room shook and sparks crackled from two transformers on poles outside his bedroom window. He remembers thinking that monsters were flying into his room.

The quake, centered on Northridge, California, measured 6.7 on the Richter scale. Aside from Hurricane Andrew, which struck Florida in 1992 and caused more than $30 billion in property damage, the Northridge quake was the costliest natural disaster in U.S. history. Miraculously, because people were still in their beds rather than crowded on the Los Angeles freeways, the death toll was limited to 60. Thousands of people were left homeless, however, and millions experienced agonizing weeks of delay as crews removed wreckage and hurried to repair the region's vital freeway system.

Almost exactly one year later, the major seaport of Kobe, Japan, was hit by an even larger earthquake. Again, the worst fatalities were avoided because the quake occurred before thousands of people entered the high-rise office buildings in the central business district. But elevated freeways crumpled like dry leaves, killing hundreds of people. In all, about 5,500 people were killed and more than 300,000 were homeless for months after the quake.

Some of the most desirable sites for cities—seacoasts, river flood plains, mountain slopes—are also the most risky places for human settlement because they are prone to natural disasters like earthquakes. But since cities are the ecological and cultural centers of modern societies, the growth of urban populations can be expected to continue indefinitely. And, as will become clear in this chapter, population growth means that cities and towns will continue to expand, creating still greater potential for disasters like the Kobe and Los Angeles quakes.

PEOPLE, CITIES, AND URBAN GROWTH

The human population continues to spread throughout the world. Although the vast majority of the world's people live in rural villages, in modern societies they typically live in cities or metropolitan areas rather than on farms or in small towns. In fact, 90 percent of Americans live within 25 miles of a city center (Berry, 1978; United Nations, 1987). This means that they live in the human-built environment of cities and suburbs; relatively few live in the "country" environment of rural areas. It also means, among many other things, that settlement occurs in unstable places that invite disaster.

The study of population growth and the growth of cities as centers of demographic and social change has long been a central field in sociology. In this chapter, therefore, we will see how increasing population size and other important changes in populations are connected with the rise of cities and metropolitan areas throughout the world. At the end of the chapter we will return to the study of natural and social disasters, which are an increasingly frequent consequence of life on an urbanizing planet.

THE POPULATION EXPLOSION

Before we can study the phenomenon of urbanization, we must understand the impact of population growth on the formation and expansion of cities. In Chapter 4 we described the extremely rapid growth of the world's population in the past three centuries. If you refer back to Figure 4.2, you can readily see that the *rate* of population growth has increased dramatically in this century alone, giving rise to the often-used term *population explosion*. The world's population is currently estimated at 5.6 billion, and according to recent United Nations forecasts it will increase by another 3.1 billion, to 8.7 billion, by the year 2025. This would represent growth over a 30-year period that is roughly equal to the entire world population in 1965.

At present about 90 million new people are added to the world's population each year. Most forecasts predict that this rapid growth will begin to decline by midcentury, but by then there could well be more than 14 billion people on a very crowded planet (American Assembly, 1990). Demographers point out, however, that crop production, famine and war, contraception, economic development, and many other variables affect population. The potential effects of these variables make it extremely difficult to predict trends in population growth. It is certain, though, that rapid population growth, especially in the poorer regions of the world, will continue in coming decades and will pose severe challenges to human survival and well-being (Davis, 1991; Lee, 1991). The pressures of population growth on resources of food, space, and water have produced changes in economic and social arrangements throughout history, but never before have those changes occurred as rapidly or on as great a scale as they are occurring today.

Malthusian Population Theory. Is there a danger that the earth will become overpopulated? The debate over population growth is not new. For almost two centuries social scientists have been seeking to determine whether human populations will grow beyond the earth's capacity to support them. The earliest and most forceful theory of overpopulation appeared in Thomas Malthus's *An Essay on Population* (1927–1928/1798). Malthus attempted to show that population size normally increases far more rapidly than the food and energy resources needed to keep people alive. Couples will have as many children as they can afford to feed, and their children will do the same. This will cause populations to grow *geometrically* (2, 4, 8, 16, 32, . . .). Meanwhile, available food supplies will increase *arithmetically* (2, 3, 4, 5, 6, . . .) as farms are expanded and crop yields increased. As a result, population growth will always threaten to outstrip food supplies. The resulting poverty, famine, disease, war, and mass migrations will act as natural checks on rapid population growth.

History has proved Malthus wrong on at least two counts. To begin with, we are not biologically driven to multiply beyond the capacity of the environment to support our offspring; Malthus himself recognized that people could limit their reproduction through delay of marriage or celibacy. The second fault of Malthusian theory is its failure to recognize that technological and institutional change could expand available resources rapidly enough to keep up with population growth. This has occurred in the more affluent regions of the world, where improvements in the quality of life have tended to outstrip population growth. Improvements in agricultural technology have also increased the yield of crops in some of the less developed parts of the world, such as India. But rates of population growth and exhaustion of environmental resources (firewood, water, grazing land) are highest in the poorest nations. Will reductions in population growth rates and increases in available resources also occur there? Or will the Malthusian theory prove correct in the long run? The theory known as the *demographic transition* provides a framework for studying this question, but before we explore this theory we need to know more about measuring population change.

Rates of Population Change. Populations change as a consequence of births, deaths, out-migration,

TABLE 9.1	Population Doubling Time, Selected Countries		
COUNTRY	POPULATION (MILLIONS)	ANNUAL GROWTH RATE* (PERCENT)	DOUBLING TIME** (YEARS)
India	930.6	1.9	36
China	1,218.8	1.1	62
Brazil	157.8	1.7	41
Bangladesh	119.2	2.4	29
Nigeria	101.2	3.1	22
Pakistan	129.7	2.9	24
Indonesia	198.4	1.6	43
Russia	147.5	−0.6	—
Mexico	93.7	2.2	34
United States	263.2	0.7	105

*Annual rate of natural increase.
**Number of years in which the population will double at current rate of increase.

Source: Population Reference Bureau, 1995.

and in-migration. The relationships of these variables to a society's total population are expressed in the *basic demographic equation:*

$$P_t = P_0 + (B - D) + (M_i - M_0)$$

where

P_0 = the census count for an earlier period
P_t = the census count for the later period
B = total births between P_0 and P_t
D = total deaths between P_0 and P_t
M_0 = out-migration between P_0 and P_t
M_i = in-migration between P_0 and P_t

Once they know the absolute values of the terms in this equation, demographers usually convert them into percentages in order to compare populations of different sizes. (We discussed the usefulness of such conversions in the discussion of percent analysis in Chapter 2.)

The most basic measures of population change are *crude rates,* or the number of events of a given type (e.g., births or deaths) that occur in a year divided by the midyear population (Bogue, 1969). Thus, the **crude birthrate** (CBR) is the number of births occurring during a year in a given population divided by the midyear population, and the **crude death rate** (CDR) is the number of deaths occurring during a year divided by the midyear population. These fractions are usually expressed as a rate per thousand persons. They are "crude" because they compare the total number of births or deaths with the total midyear population, when in fact not all members of the population are equally likely to give birth or to die.

The **rate of reproductive change** is the difference between the CBR and the CDR for a given population. It is a measure of the *natural increase* of the population; that is, it measures increases due to the excess of births over deaths and disregards in- and out-migration. At present there are several nations in which the rate of reproductive change is zero or less, meaning that there is no natural population growth. Germany, for example, had a CBR of 10 and a CDR of 11 in 1995, for an annual rate of increase of −0.1 percent. In Austria, the CBR was 12 and the CDR 10, for an annual rate of increase of 0.1 percent. In the United States, the rate of population growth is about 0.7 percent, representing an increase of about 2 million people per year. These rates are in dramatic contrast with the annual growth rates of countries like Syria and Guatemala, which are above 3 percent. Rates of population growth in selected countries are listed in Table 9.1.

We can easily see from Table 9.2 that an annual rate of population growth of only 1 percent will lead to an increase

TABLE 9.2	Relationship of Population Growth per Year and per Century	
POPULATION GROWTH PER YEAR (PERCENT)		POPULATION GROWTH PER CENTURY (PERCENT)
1		270
2		724
3		1,922

Source: Data from Worldwatch Institute.

of almost 270 percent in a century. Since World War II the world's population has been increasing at a rate of more than 1.5 percent—which means that by the year 2000 we can expect it to have passed the projected figure of 6 billion. The processes of population growth and the effects of its control are summarized in the phenomenon known as the demographic transition.

The Demographic Transition. The demographic transition is a set of major changes in birth and death rates that has occurred most completely in urban industrial nations in the last 200 years. We saw in Chapter 4 that the rapid increase in the world population in the past century and a half was due in large part to rapid declines in death rates. Beginning in the second half of the eighteenth century and continuing until the first half of the twentieth, there was a marked decline in death rates in the countries of northern and western Europe. Improvements in public health practices were one factor in that decline. Even more important were higher agricultural yields owing to technological changes in farming methods, as well as improvements in the distribution of food as a result of better transportation, which made cheaper food available to more people (Matras, 1973; Vining, 1985). At the same time, however, birthrates in those countries remained high. The resulting gap between birth and death rates produced huge increases in population. It appeared that the gloomy predictions of Malthus and others would be borne out.

In the second half of the nineteenth century, birthrates began to decline as couples delayed marriage and childbearing. As a result of lower birthrates, the gap between birth and death rates narrowed and population

growth slowed (see Figure 9.1). This occurred at different times in different countries, but the general pattern was the same in each case: a stage of high birthrates and death rates (the *high growth potential* stage) followed by a stage of declining death rates (the *transitional growth* stage) and, eventually, by a stage of declining birthrates (called the stage of *incipient decline* because it is possible for population growth rates to decrease at this point). These three stages are summarized in the study chart on page 243.

In the second, or transitional growth, stage of the demographic transition, the population not only grows rapidly but undergoes changes in its age composition. Because people now live longer, there is a slight increase in the proportion of elderly people in the population. There is also a marked increase in the proportion of people under age 20 as a result of significant decreases in infant and child mortality. This is the stage in which many less developed countries find themselves today: Death rates have dropped in the twentieth century because of improved medical care and public health measures, as well as increased agricultural production. Yet in these societies birthrates have remained high, causing phenomenal increases in population, especially in the younger, more dependent age groups.

No population has entered the third stage of the demographic transition without limiting its birthrate. This can be achieved by encouraging couples to marry later and postpone childbearing or by preventing pregnancies or births through various birth control techniques. In advanced industrial societies, many couples use both approaches, making their own decisions about whether and when to have children. In other societies, such as China and India, the state has attempted to limit population growth by promoting birth control through educational programs or, in the case of China, by imposing penalties on couples who have more than a prescribed number of children. Such measures have had some success, but often at a high political cost to national leaders, causing demographers to question whether the less developed countries will be able to complete the demographic transition. (See Box 9.1.)

Note that economic and social development is essential if the demographic transition is to occur. Death rates cannot decrease, or food supplies increase, without progress in social institutions like public health, medicine, and transportation. People in more developed societies tend to limit their family size because they seek economic advancement and wish to delay marriage and childbearing until they can support a family.

In many highly industrialized nations, on the other hand, population growth rates have fallen below the rate necessary to maintain the population at the existing level. If a fertility rate of two children or less per couple became the norm for an entire population, the growth rate would slow to zero or even a negative rate. The United States, New Zealand, Japan, Australia, and Canada all have total fertility rates of 2.0 or less (Population Reference Bureau, 1995). Similar low rates are appearing in many European

FIGURE 9.1 **The Demographic Transition: Sweden, 1691–1963**

The peaks in birth and death rates in the early 1800s are due to social unrest and war. The drop in deaths and simultaneous rise in births in the early 1700s was a result of peace, good crops, and the absence of plagues.

Source: Judah Matras, *Population and Societies*, Englewood Cliffs, N.J., © Prentice Hall, 1973. Permission of Armand Colin Éditeur.

STUDY CHART   The Demographic Transition

STAGE OF POPULATION GROWTH	TYPE OF SOCIETY	MAIN DEMOGRAPHIC FEATURES
High Growth Potential	Most types of preindustrial societies.	High death rates due to infant mortality and low life expectancy; high rates of fertility, relatively low rates of increase.
Transitional Growth Stage	Most societies in early stages of urban and industrial development where basic public health measures are being introduced (e.g., safe drinking water systems).	Decreasing mortality rates; continuing high rates of fertility.
Incipient Decline	Societies in more advanced stages of urban and economic development where people are delaying marriage and are more likely to use birth control.	Decreasing rates of mortality and fertility, with low or even negative rates of increase.

BOX 9.1   GLOBAL SOCIAL CHANGE

The Missing Girls and Lonely Bachelors of China

Among the greatest sociological mysteries in the world today is the fate of large numbers of girls born in China in recent years. Population experts believe that each year between 500,000 and 600,000 female births do not show up in official statistics. This large number of "missing" baby girls is believed to be an unintended consequence of China's drastic population control policies.

Under regulations imposed by the Chinese communist regime, couples are limited to one child (or, in some cases, two children). The goals of this policy—which is enforced through a system of heavy fines and other penalties—are "(1) to promote late marriage and later, fewer but healthier births with prevention of genetic and birth defects; (2) to advocate the practice of 'one couple, one child'; (3) to persuade rural couples with difficulties who wish for a second child to have proper spacing" (Yu, 1994, p. 489).

China's rulers justify their strict population policies by pointing out that "China's arable land is only 7 percent of the world's total, . . . but it has to support 22 percent of the world's population"—more than 1 billion people (Yu, 1994, p. 488). Already the amount of farm land per person is far lower in China than the world average.

According to official statistics, total fertility in China fell from 4.17 births per woman in 1973 to about 2 per woman in 1993, resulting in a drop in the natural population growth rate from 1.7 percent to 1.15 percent in the same period. If these figures are accurate (and population experts believe that they are), this would mean that the rate of growth of China's population has been brought under control. On the other hand, there is ample evidence that the population is not voluntarily controlling its fertility. The entire policy rests on the power of the communist

dictatorship, a fact that is illustrated by the mysterious shortage of baby girls in the annual birth statistics.

In China, as in many other cultures, ancient customs dictate that the family name is handed down only through males. Moreover, since young women generally live with the husband's family after marriage, it is male children who usually assume the responsibility of caring for their older parents. These norms produce a strong preference for male children, especially in rural areas.

Boys typically outnumber girls at birth. Normal sex ratios at birth in most societies vary between 104 and 105 boys for every 100 girls. In China this was the case before the 1970s, when the one-child policy went into effect. After that, male-to-female birth ratios became extremely skewed in favor of males. Population experts believe that girls are still being born in roughly the same numbers as before (amniocentesis and selective abortion are illegal), but that they are being sent away for adoption or raised secretly—or in some cases left to die, the victims of infanticide (Johansson & Nygren, 1991). No one can account for the missing thousands of girl babies.

Another consequence of the one-child policy is a large number of only children, who may receive a great deal of parental attention but do not have the benefit of growing up with brothers and sisters. Still another consequence is a shortage of marriageable women in some parts of China. Because men tend to marry somewhat younger women, the rising sex ratio works against their chances of finding a wife. The result is a growing number of lonely Chinese bachelors. Clearly the use of dictatorial methods to coerce fertility control has had some unintended, and very detrimental, consequences.

nations. This is a highly significant development; if it continues over a generation or more, it could result in negative rates of natural increase and, possibly, other consequences such as slower economic development and labor shortages. Continued low fertility could also result in increased immigration from countries with high birthrates to countries with lower birthrates.

A full exposition of the processes and politics of population control is not possible here. Suffice it to say that most sociologists would agree with the demographer Philip Hauser (1957) that low population growth rates are due primarily to a combination of delay of marriage, celibacy, and use of modern birth control techniques. This trend is beginning to occur in many less developed nations.

Figure 9.2 illustrates the demographic transition in Singapore, a nation in Southeast Asia that has undergone this important population change more recently. Note that the decline in deaths, which took almost a century and a half in Western industrial nations, took less than half a century in Singapore. The decline in births began in the late 1950s, spurred by rapid economic development, the new desire for smaller families, and widespread availability of contraceptives. Whereas in Western nations like Sweden this phase of declining births unfolded over more than a century, in Singapore this phase occurred in only about twenty years (between about 1955 and 1975). Although world population growth remains a serious problem, the demographic transition in formerly poor nations like this one

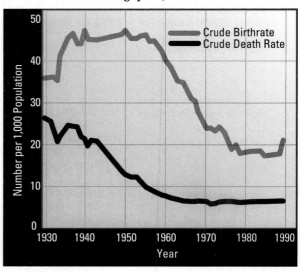

FIGURE 9.2 Crude Birth and Death Rates: Singapore, 1930–1988

Source: Davis, 1991.

shows that population control efforts along with economic development can have dramatic effects (Davis, 1991).

Population Growth and Urbanization. Studies of the demographic transition in Europe (Friedlander, 1969; Laslett, 1972, 1983) have concluded that its specific course in any given society depended on a complex combination of factors: higher age at marriage and fewer couples marrying, use of birth control techniques, increased education, migration to other countries, and rural–urban migration. Some of these factors are discussed in Box 9-2. In each case, however, the bulk of the population growth was absorbed by the cities. Rapid urbanization thus to some extent is an outgrowth of the demographic transition.

Urbanization refers to the proportion of the total population that is concentrated in urban settlements. Although urbanization and the growth of cities have occurred together, it is important to distinguish between the two. Cities can continue to grow even after the majority of the population is urbanized and the society's dominant institutions (e.g., government agencies, major markets, newspapers, television networks) are located in its urban centers.

Urbanization contributes to the lower birthrates that are characteristic of the third stage of the demographic transition. As Louis Wirth pointed out, "The decline in the birthrate generally may be regarded as one of the most significant signs of the urbanization of the Western world" (1968/1938, p. 59). In the city a variety of factors lead to the postponement of marriage and childbearing. For one thing, living space is limited. For another, newcomers to the city must find jobs before they can even think about marrying, and often they lack the ties to family and kin groups that might encourage them to marry and have children.

Studies of declining birthrates in non-Western countries find that—contrary to the experience of cities in

BOX 9.2 USING THE SOCIOLOGICAL IMAGINATION

The Power of Rural–Urban Migration

Immigration and migration are social forces that continually bring about change of all kinds. In Eastern Europe, for example, the animosities among nationality groups that threaten to cause war and violence can often be traced to earlier periods of immigration and resettlement of populations due to war and conquest. In the United States as well, immigration continually produces social change—especially in the major cities that serve as the gateways for newcomers.

Migration, which includes both immigration from a foreign nation and movement within national boundaries, is, along with birth and death rates, a key factor affecting population size. People have migrated from one region or country to another throughout history, compelled to seek new homes because they have exhausted their food supplies or been driven out by invaders or because they believe they will find a better life in the new land. Although people have migrated from rural areas to the city throughout history, rural-urban migration has become especially pronounced in the last two centuries.

The forces that impel residents of rural areas to migrate to cities are not fully understood. There is continual debate over whether rural people are "pushed" into cities by conditions beyond their control or "pulled" to cities by the attractions of city life. Of course, both push and pull factors affect rural–urban migration, but it is not clear exactly how they interact. It appears, however, that "it is the push of existing rural circumstances which suggests to the rural resident that things might be better in the urban area" (Breese, 1966, p. 80).

Several factors may be responsible for pushing people out of rural areas. Chief among these is overpopulation, which reduces the amount of food and work available per rural resident. Others include lack of opportunities to obtain farm land (e.g., as a result of *primogeniture,* in which only

the oldest son inherits land) and the seasonal nature of employment in agriculture. When rural people who are experiencing these conditions become aware of higher living standards in urban places, they may develop a sense of relative deprivation (see Chapter 8). "They view with great interest the reported higher income, access to education, and other rumored facilities of the urban area" (Breese, 1966, pp. 80–81). The feeling of relative deprivation is intensified by improvements in communication and transportation that provide rural people with more feedback about the advantages of life in the city.

A significant pull factor is the presence of relatives and friends in the city. These individuals can be called on for help when the rural migrant arrives in search of a new home and a job. This factor produces what is known as *chain migration,* a pattern in which a network of friends and relatives is transferred from the village to the city over time. The result is the formation of a small, homogeneous community within the city.

Chain migration operates across national boundaries as well as between rural and urban areas in the same country. For example, a large proportion of the immigrants to American cities in the twentieth century have been rural people from European and Asian countries. Once a few hardy souls have established a foothold, their families and friends can join them. In this way small ethnic communities are formed within the city—like the Chinatowns of New York and San Francisco, the Slovenian community in Cleveland, or the Mexican community in Chicago. Recently this pattern has been established in suburban portions of metropolitan areas as well as in central cities. Thus the suburbs of metropolitan areas in the South and West have become home to large numbers of immigrants from Vietnam (Portes & Rumbaut, 1990).

These Mexican immigrants are crossing the Rio Grande in hope of finding work in the United States.

the West, where urbanization has brought declining birthrates—the populations of some cities in Asia and Africa are increasing faster than those of rural areas. The reason seems to be that rapid change in rural areas, espe-

cially the mechanization of agriculture, pushes rural people to the cities, where they often live in shantytowns and villagelike settlements. In those settlements the rural tradition of large families is not quickly altered. In addition, because they have greater access to health care during pregnancy and childbirth, the infant death rate may be lower among the migrants than in rural villages. However, when these populations become part of the urban economy, they too begin to limit their family size (Lowry, 1990; Robinson, 1963).

In sum, urbanization is closely linked with rapid increases in population, yet the nature of life in cities tends to limit the size of urban families. Cities grow primarily as a result of migration, but new migrants do not find it easy to form families. Thus, in his research on the changing populations of Western industrial cities, Hauser (1957) showed that birthrates were lowest in the areas of the city that had the highest proportions of new migrants. There is also mounting evidence from archaeology that child sacrifice in ancient cities may have helped control urban populations (Browne, 1987). The eventual result of large-scale migration to cities may be a slowdown in population growth: As an increasing proportion of a society's population lives in cities, the rate of growth of the population as a whole tends to drop.

THE GROWTH OF CITIES

In Chapter 4 we noted that cities became possible when agricultural populations began to produce enough extra food to support people who were not directly engaged in agriculture, such as priests, warriors, and artisans. Changes in the technology of food production made it possible for increasingly larger populations to be supported by the same number of agricultural workers. This has been a central factor in the evolution of cities, but as we will see shortly, the most dramatic increases in urban populations have occurred only in the past 150 years.

The Urban Revolution. The increasing tendency of people throughout the world to live in cities has been referred to as the *urban revolution*. The extent of this "revolution" can be grasped by comparing a few figures. In 1800, only 3 percent of the world's people lived in cities with populations above 5,000, and of this proportion, a mere 2.4 percent lived in cities with populations above 20,000. Between 1800 and 1970, a period during which the world's population increased fourfold, the percentage of people living in cities with 5,000 or more inhabitants increased elevenfold, whereas that of people living in cities with 100,000 or more inhabitants increased almost fourteenfold. By 1970, fully one third of the world's population lived in cities (Matras, 1973; Vining, 1985).

These data indicate not only that increasing percentages of the world's population are living in cities but also that the cities themselves are larger than ever before. The growth of cities in this century has given rise to the concept of the **metropolitan area**, in which a central city is surrounded by a number of smaller cities and suburbs that are closely related to it both socially and economically. Most people in the United States live in large metropolitan areas, as Box 9.3 demonstrates.

Large-scale urbanization is a relatively recent development in human history. As Kingsley Davis (1955) pointed out:

> Compared to most other aspects of society—such as language, religion, stratification, or the family—cities appeared only yesterday, and urbanization, meaning that a sizable proportion of the population lives in cities, has developed only in the last few moments of man's existence. (p. 429)

Although there were a few cities as early as 4000 B.C., they were very small and were supported by large rural populations. The famous cities of ancient times were minuscule by modern standards: Babylon covered roughly 3.2 square miles, Ur some 220 acres (Davis, 1955).

Preindustrial cities like Ur and Nineveh, early Athens and Rome, and the ancient Mayan cities were vastly different from the cities we know today. They did not grow

A classic preindustrial city, Palenque was a vital civil and religious center of Mayan civilization over half a millennium before the arrival of Europeans.

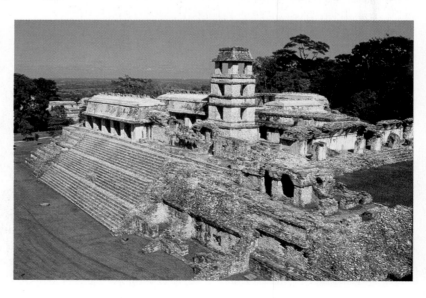

BOX 9.3 **SOCIOLOGICAL METHODS**

Defining Metropolitan Areas

Formal definitions of urban places have changed considerably in the twentieth century. Traditionally, an urban place was defined as any incorporated area with 2,500 or more inhabitants. But this definition became highly unsatisfactory as cities expanded and their surrounding areas became increasingly urbanized, especially after World War II. As early as 1910 the U.S. Bureau of the Census introduced the concept of the *metropolitan district,* or metropolitan area. This concept has been refined quite often as urban growth has engulfed the rural areas adjacent to cities. Moreover, as cities and their suburbs have begun to run into each other, it has become necessary to distinguish between central cities and the surrounding metropolitan areas.

In 1984 the Census Bureau established new definitions of urban areas that remain in effect today. The basic types of urban areas are the metropolitan statistical area, the primary metropolitan statistical area, and the consolidated metropolitan statistical area. A *metropolitan area* is a geographic area with a population of at least 100,000 consisting of a nucleus with a population of at least 50,000 together with adjacent communities that have a high degree of economic and social integration with that nucleus. The term *statistical areas* refers to the fact that these definitions are used to organize numerical data about urban regions. Federal, state, and local government agencies use these geographic and statistical definitions to monitor social change and carry out essential planning functions.

A *metropolitan statistical area* (*MSA*) is a metropolitan area that is not closely associated with other metropolitan areas and typically is surrounded by nonmetropolitan counties. A *primary metropolitan statistical area* (*PMSA*) is defined as a large urbanized county or cluster of economically interdependent counties with a population of at least 100,000 that is part of a metropolitan area with more than 1 million inhabitants. A metropolitan area that contains two or more PMSAs is a *consolidated metropolitan statistical area* (*CMSA*). A CMSA therefore is equivalent to what sociologists often call a "megalopolitan region," such as the Dallas–Fort Worth area or the Los Angeles area.

Central cities are the officially designated largest and most densely populated places in metropolitan areas. There are central cities that are not included in a metropolitan area.

The accompanying chart shows the proportions of the U.S. population living in rural, urban, metropolitan, and nonmetropolitan areas. The organization of data shown in the chart is useful because the curve above the area for each category shows its relative trend in population growth. In order to find out how many millions of people lived in a metropolitan area in 1980, for example, subtract the reading at the bottom of the area for that year from the reading at the top of the area for the same year. For 1980 the line at the bottom of the area falls at about 50 million and the line at the top at about 225 million; thus there were about 175 million residents of metropolitan areas in the United States in that year.

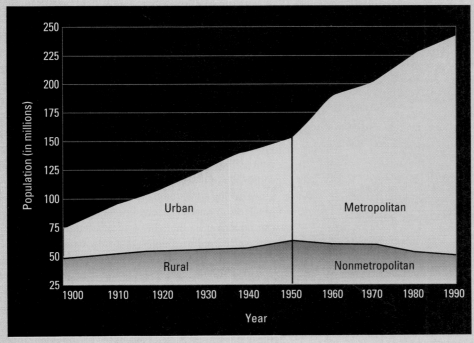

Source: Council on Environmental Quality, Census Bureau.

around a core of office buildings and retail outlets the way industrial cities do. Instead, they were built around temples or other ceremonial buildings (e.g., Notre Dame in Paris). Close by the temple one could find the palaces of the rulers and the courtyards of the royal families. Parade grounds and public shrines made the core of the ancient city a spacious place where the city's population could meet on special occasions. On the outskirts of these ancient cities one found not the rich, as in contemporary cities with well-developed transportation networks, but the poor, who lived in hovels and were often pushed from one location to another according to the whims of those with more wealth and power (Braudel, 1984; Breese, 1966; Sjoberg, 1968). Preindustrial cities are described in more detail in Box 9.4.

A variety of factors limited the size of cities. Among them were farming methods that did not produce enough

Urban sociologists have always looked at the relationship between the planned and unplanned aspects of urban growth and the social groups that represent each aspect. Usually the poor and the immigrants represent unplanned additions to the city, while the rich and the powerful guide the processes of urban planning and organization to suit their interests.

surplus food to feed many city dwellers, the lack of efficient means of transporting goods over long distances, inadequate technology for transporting water in great quantities, and the lack of scientific medicine (which made urban living, as Davis put it, "deadly"). Not until about 1800 did large-scale urbanization become possible.

The speed with which urbanization has changed the size and layout of cities is remarkable. "Before 1850 no society could be described as predominantly urbanized, and by 1900 only one—Great Britain—could be so regarded. Today . . . all industrial nations are highly urbanized, and in the world as a whole the process of urbanization is accelerating rapidly" (Davis, 1968, p. 33). By 1985, 42 percent of the world population lived in urban areas, and by the year 2000 nearly half of the world population is expected to live in urban areas—40 percent of the population in developing countries and 78 percent in developed countries (Census Bureau, 1986). Africa now has the fastest rate of urbanization; and by the turn of the coming century about 70 percent of the population of Latin America will live in urban areas—a rate of urbanization comparable to that of North America and Europe.

As Table 9.3 shows, many metropolitan regions in older advanced nations like the United States (especially Greater New York), Great Britain (Greater London), and Germany (Rhein–Ruhr) reached their peak of growth decades ago and are now growing slowly if at all. In contrast, in many parts of Latin America and Asia metropolitan regions are experiencing explosive growth and attracting vast populations of urban newcomers, many of whom are living as squatters on vacant land. (See the Visual Sociology section of this chapter, which features squatters in Brazil.)

Rapid urbanization occurring throughout the world brings together diverse groups of people in cities that often are not prepared to absorb them. The problems caused by such urbanization are immense. They include housing, educating, and caring for the health of newcomers; preventing gang violence and intergroup hatred; and many other difficult tasks. Moreover, as the world becomes ever more urbanized, populations become increasingly interdependent. Urban populations are supported, for example, by worldwide agricultural production, not just by the produce grown in the surrounding countryside. In the same way, the problems of one major city or one large urbanizing region can no longer be thought of as isolated from the problems of the older, more affluent urbanized regions.

Urban Societies. Urbanization produces *urban societies.* By this we mean not only that cities are the cultural and institutional centers of a society but also that urban life has a pervasive influence on the entire society (Durkheim, 1964/1893; Weber, 1962/1921; Wirth, 1968/1938). Today the United States is spanned by interstate highways that link the nation's rapidly growing urban and suburban places and carry traffic through rural areas at high speeds.

BOX 9.4   GLOBAL SOCIAL CHANGE

Preindustrial Cities Today

The city of Ibadan in Nigeria is a bustling regional capital with a large central business district, a major university, and government buildings. But in the nineteenth century, when what is now Nigeria was conquered and colonized by the British, Ibadan was not considered a city because it lacked the features of European cities. There was no central place to mark the city's administrative and commercial core. Instead, there were dense settlements of Yoruba tribespeople and a complicated pattern of surrounding garden plots. The ancient city was divided into sections according to the clan divisions of the Yoruba people. There were important political and religious institutions, but they had not produced towering structures like those the Europeans were used to. Ibadan was a preindustrial city, but it was not like the ancient European cities, which had formed around a center dominated by a great cathedral or a fortified castle. Ibadan had the population of a great city, but to the ethnocentric colonists it had little else.

Today we understand that Ibadan was a particular type of preindustrial city, one with a dense population but no identifiable center. Preindustrial cities have no central business district. Instead, the city's center is likely to be a cathedral or mosque or a fort or palace (Sjoberg, 1968; Weber, 1962/1921). The rest of the city is divided up into "quarters" or "wards" inhabited by different ethnic and occupational groups. There is little specialization in land use (e.g., no separate areas devoted to factories or businesses or residences). And unlike the upper classes of industrial cities, the elites of the preindustrial city live near the center, with the lower classes inhabiting outlying areas and "outcast" groups living on the fringes.

The large cities of India provide examples of the ecological patterns typical of preindustrial cities. As Gerald Breese (1966) points out, "One of the most noticeable features of large Indian cities is their combination of very high population density in relatively small areas and relatively low population density over other large areas" (p. 56). In addition, many forms of transportation use the same roads and streets: "Animal and vehicular

transportation ranges from the sluggish camel and donkey to the speeding truck. . . . Between these are the tonga cart, pedicab, motorcycle rickshaw, bicycle, oxcart, taxi and private automobile, trucks of various kinds, handcart, bus, and streetcar" (pp. 56–57). Similarly, there is a mixture of land uses within the same area and even on a single site. For example, "It is not uncommon to find manufacturing and sale of the same article combined in one establishment" (p. 59).

It is worth noting that this ecological pattern is not limited to ancient cities or to cities in developing nations. The same characteristics (wealthy citizens living near the center of town, artisans living and working in the same place) could be seen in American cities in the mid-nineteenth century. The modern city began to emerge only after the development of mass transit.

Waterways, forests, hills, and valleys are channeled and cut and bulldozed to make way for expanding settlements. Once considered far from the urban scene, national parks and forests now receive millions of visitors from the metropolitan centers. And in an urban society more and more people, even those living in isolated rural communities, share in the mass culture of that society—the television and radio programs, the movies, the books and magazines, all of which stress themes that appeal to people who are familiar with metropolitan living. In an urban society not everyone lives in the cities, but no one can escape the pervasive influence of urban centers.

The concept of an urban society may become clearer if we look at a society that has not become fully urbanized, such as India. Until the early twentieth century the rate of city growth in India was relatively slow. But beginning in the 1920s the populations of India's cities increased dramatically, and by 1960 seven Indian cities had populations surpassing a million. Yet India has not become an urban society. It remains, in the words of Noel P. Gist (1968), "a land of villagers." Because of persistently high birthrates and declining death rates in the villages, India's rural population is growing almost as fast as its urban population. And although the growth of the cities has affected village life,

TABLE 9.3	Populations of the World's 30 Largest Urbanized Areas, 1950–2000				
RANK IN YEAR 2000	**COUNTRY**	**URBANIZED AREA**	**THOUSANDS OF INHABITANTS**		
			1950	**1975**	**2000**
1	Mexico	Mexico City	3,050	11,610	25,820
2	Japan	Tokyo–Yokohama	6,736	17,668	24,172
3	Brazil	São Paulo	2,760	10,290	23,970
4	India	Calcutta	4,520	8,250	16,530
5	India	Bombay	2,950	7,170	16,000
6	United States	New York–N.E. New Jersey	12,410	15,940	15,780
7	Rep. of Korea	Seoul	1,113	6,950	13,770
8	Brazil	Rio de Janeiro	3,480	8,150	13,260
9	China	Shanghai	10,420	11,590	13,260
10	Indonesia	Jakarta	1,820	5,530	13,250
11	India	Delhi	1,410	4,630	13,240
12	Argentina	Buenos Aires	5,251	9,290	13,180
13	Pakistan	Karachi	1,040	4,030	12,000
14	Iran	Teheran	1,126	4,267	11,329
15	Bangladesh	Dhaka	430	2,350	11,160
16	Egypt	Cairo–Ginza–Imbaba	3,500	6,250	11,130
17	Iraq	Baghdad	579	3,830	11,125
18	Japan	Osaka–Kobe	3,828	8,649	11,109
19	Philippines	Manila	1,570	5,040	11,070
20	United States	Los Angeles–Long Beach	4,070	8,960	10,990
21	Thailand	Bangkok–Thonburi	1,440	4,050	10,710
22	United Kingdom	London	10,369	10,310	10,510
23	USSR	Moscow	4,841	7,600	10,400
24	China	Beijing	6,740	8,910	10,360
25	Germany	Rhein–Ruhr	6,853	9,311	9,151
26	Peru	Lima–Callao	1,050	3,700	9,140
27	France	Paris	5,525	8,620	8,720
28	Nigeria	Lagos	360	2,100	8,340
29	Italy	Milan	3,637	6,150	8,150
30	India	Madras	1,420	3,770	8,150

Note: The urban places listed above are areas of dense contiguous settlement whose boundaries do not necessarily coincide with administrative boundaries; they usually include one or more cities and an urbanized fringe. The list includes all such places projected to contain at least 8 million inhabitants in the year 2000.

Source: Lowry, 1993.

especially through the efforts of city-trained teachers, health officials, administrators, and storekeepers, it has had little effect on the social structure of rural India. Thus, as a whole, Indian society exhibits the extremes of rural isolation and urban dynamism, with all the chaos and poverty that are characteristic of societies undergoing major social change (World Bank, 1992).

Throughout the twentieth century sociologists have devoted considerable study to urbanization and the changes that accompany it. The ways in which the growth of cities and metropolitan regions alters the surface of the planet are part of the sociological study of urbanization. So are questions about how cities change our experience of

community and our relationships with others. Finally, sociologists continue to focus on the changing patterns of inequality and conflict that occur in metropolitan regions. The remainder of this chapter explores these issues in greater detail.

THE URBAN LANDSCAPE

URBAN EXPANSION

The effects of urbanization began to be felt in American society after the Civil War (1861–1865). As the population

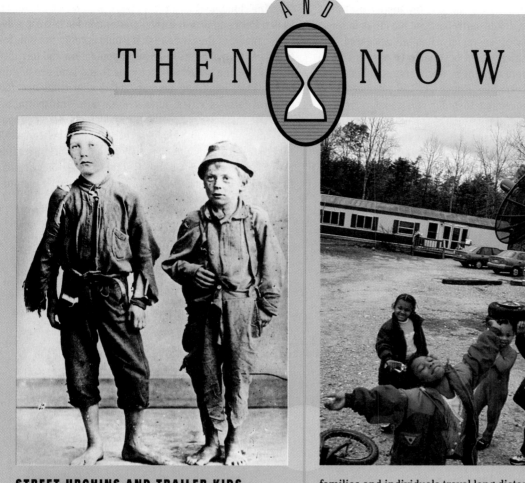

THEN AND NOW

STREET URCHINS AND TRAILER KIDS

Around the turn of the century, as millions of newcomers from throughout the world crowded into U.S. cities in search of opportunity, this rapid social change produced some of the world's most notorious urban slums. Jacob Riis, a photojournalist and amateur sociologist, brought the harsh living conditions in those slums to the attention of the world in his famous photos of "how the other half lives." Children who spent much of their time on the streets and survived by their wits were called "street urchins" (or, as Riis called them, "Street Arabs").

In today's world the central city is no longer viewed as a place to find new opportunities. Mobile families and individuals travel long distances, seeking manufacturing and service jobs outside major city centers. They often find what they hope will be temporary lodging in trailer parks. Poor and lacking health insurance and other forms of social security, residents of trailer parks tend to be stigmatized by those who are more fortunate. They and their children are sometimes called "trailer trash," a term that reveals the deep prejudices that continue to divide Americans, even in a society that is far more affluent than the one described by Riis.

began to push into the West, waves of immigrants from Ireland, Germany, Italy, and many other parts of central and southern Europe streamed into the cities of the East. In the 1840s and 1850s, for example, approximately 1.35 million Irish immigrants arrived in the United States, and in just 12 years, from 1880 to 1892, more than 1.7 million Germans arrived (Bogue, 1985). In other chapters we have more to say about the impact of the great migrations from China and Korea and Latin America, the importation of slaves from Africa, and the large numbers of people of all races and ethnic groups who continue to arrive in U.S. cities. The point here is that for well over a century North American cities have been a preferred destination for people from all over the world; as a result, they have received numerous waves of newcomers since their period of explosive growth in the nineteenth century.

The science of sociology found early supporters in the United States and Canada partly because the cities in those nations were growing so rapidly. It often appeared that North American cities would be unable to absorb all the newcomers who were arriving in such large numbers. Pre-sociological thinkers like Frederick Law Olmsted, the founder of the movement to build parks and recreation areas in cities, and Jacob Riis, an advocate of slum reform, urged the nation's leaders to invest in improving the urban environment, building parks and beaches, and making better housing available to all (Cranz, 1982). As we saw in Chapter 1, these reform efforts were greatly aided by sociologists who conducted empirical research on the social conditions in cities. In the early twentieth century many sociologists lived in cities like Chicago that were characterized by rapid population growth and serious social problems. It seemed logical to use empirical research to construct theories about how cities grow and change in response to major social forces as well as more controlled urban planning.

The founders of the Chicago school of sociology, Robert Park and Ernest Burgess, attempted to develop a dynamic model of the city, one that would account not only for the expansion of cities in terms of population and territory but also for the patterns of settlement and land use within cities. They identified several factors that influence the physical form of cities. Among them are "transportation and communication, tramways and telephones, newspapers and advertising, steel construction and elevators—all things, in fact, which tend to bring about at once a greater mobility and a greater concentration of the urban populations" (Park, 1967/1925a, p. 2). The important role of transportation is described in one of Park's essays:

> The extent to which . . . an increase of population in one part of the city is reflected in every other depends very largely upon the character of the local transportation system. Every extension and multiplication of the means of transportation connecting the periphery of the city with the center tends to bring more people to the central business

FIGURE 9.3 **The Concentric-Zone Model**

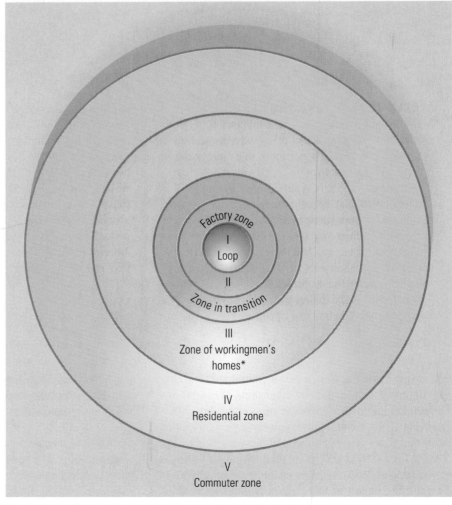

*Workers' homes ("workingmen" was the accepted terminology of the time).
Source: Park & Burgess, 1967/1925.

district, and to bring them there oftener. This increases the congestion at the center; it increases, eventually, the height of office buildings and the values of the land on which those buildings stand. The influence of land values at the business center radiates from that point to every part of the city. (1967/1926, pp. 57–58)

The Concentric-Zone Model. Park and Burgess based their model of urban growth on the concept of *natural areas*—that is, areas in which the population is relatively homogeneous and land is used in similar ways without deliberate planning. In Park's words:

Every great city has its racial colonies, like the Chinatowns of San Francisco and New York, the Little Sicily of Chicago. . . . Most cities have their segregated vice districts . . . their rendezvous for criminals of various sorts. Every large city has its occupational suburbs, like the Stockyards in Chicago, and its residential enclaves, like Brookline in Boston. (1967/1925a, p. 10)

Park and Burgess saw urban expansion as occurring through a series of "invasions" of successive zones or areas surrounding the center of the city. For example, migrants from rural areas and other societies "invaded" areas where housing was cheap. Those areas tended to be close to the places where they worked. In turn, people who could afford better housing and the cost of commuting "invaded" areas farther from the business district, and these became the Brooklines, Gold Coasts, and Greenwich Villages of their respective cities.

Park and Burgess's model, which has come to be known as the *concentric-zone model,* is portrayed in Figure 9.3. (Figure 9.4 applies the model to Chicago.) Because the model was originally based on studies of Chicago, its center is labeled "Loop," the term that is commonly applied to that city's central zone. Surrounding the central zone is a "zone

---

FIGURE 9.4   The Concentric-Zone Model Applied to Chicago

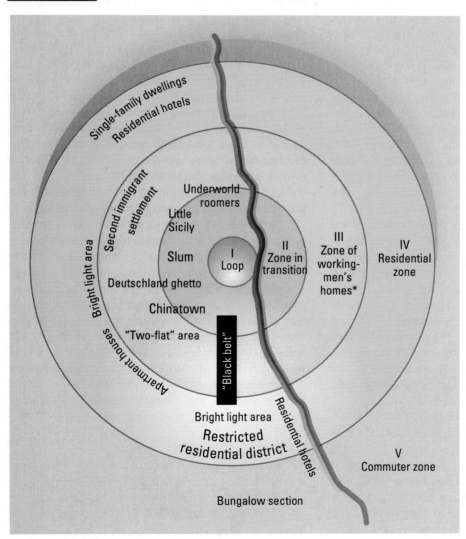

*Workers' homes ("workingmen" was the accepted terminology of the time).

Source: Park & Burgess, 1967/1925.

in transition," an area that is being invaded by business and light manufacturing. The third zone is inhabited by workers who do not want to live in the factory or business district but at the same time need to live reasonably close to where they work. The fourth or residential zone consists of higher-class apartment buildings and single-family homes. And the outermost ring, outside the city limits, is the suburban or commuters' zone; its residents live within a 30- to 60-minute ride of the central business district (Burgess, 1925).

Studies by Park, Burgess, and other Chicago school sociologists showed how new groups of immigrants tended to become concentrated in segregated areas within inner-city zones, where they encountered suspicion, discrimination, and hostility from ethnic groups that had arrived earlier. Over time, however, each group was able to adjust to life in the city and to find a place for itself in the urban economy. Eventually many of the immigrants were assimilated into the institutions of American society and moved to desegregated areas in outer zones; the ghettos they left behind were promptly occupied by new waves of immigrants (Kasarda, 1989).

Note that each zone is continually expanding outward. Thus, Burgess wrote, "If this chart is applied to Chicago, all four of these zones were in its early history included in the circumference of the inner zone, the present business district. The present boundaries of the [zone in transition] were not many years ago those of the zone now inhabited by independent wage-earners" (1925, p. 50). Burgess also pointed out that "neither Chicago nor any other city fits perfectly into this [model]. Complications are introduced by the lake front, the Chicago River, railroad lines, historical factors in the location of industry, the relative degree of the resistance of communities to invasion, etc." (pp. 50–51).

The Park and Burgess model of growth in zones and natural areas of the city can still be used to describe patterns of growth in cities that were built around a central business district and that continue to attract large numbers of immigrants. But this model is biased toward the commercial and industrial cities of North America, which have tended to form around business centers rather than around palaces or cathedrals, as is the case in so many other parts of the world. Moreover, it fails to account for other patterns of urbanization, such as the rise of satellite cities and the rapid urbanization that occurs along commercial transportation corridors.

Satellite Cities. Outside the city of Detroit lies the town of River Rouge, long famous as a center of steel and automobile production. Outside the city of Toronto lies Hamilton, also a smoky manufacturing town where much of Canada's steel is produced. And outside Chicago is Gary, Indiana, another major center of heavy industrial production. Outside New York City there are many other *satellite cities*, some devoted to heavy industries whose needs for space,

rail and water service, and energy make it impossible to locate them in the central business districts.

Other satellite cities are devoted to less environmentally stressful industries. Fort Worth, Texas, for example, is becoming a major center for white-collar industries, such as publishing, that are leaving older central-city locations in search of cheaper space and a well-educated labor force. Still others, like Tysons Corner, Virginia, near Washington, D.C., have grown around large shopping centers and mall complexes. In the second half of the twentieth century the growth of these and other satellite cities has been accelerated by public investment in the interstate and metropolitan highway systems, a point to which we will return shortly in discussing the rise of metropolitan urban systems (Baldassare, 1986; Clay, 1994; Fishman, 1987).

Strip Development. The growth of satellite cities specializing in the production of a particular commodity or product is typical of the period of rapid industrial growth that occurred before World War II. A more current model of urbanization is known as *strip development;* it is shown in schematic form in Figure 9.5. Strip I represents a typical nineteenth- or early twentieth-century farming area bisected by a road and a stream. In time the bridge over the stream and the path along the stream became a road that intersected the original road (Strip II), creating an intersection that stimulated the growth of a village with a mill; families living in the village depended on wages from the mill. As the village grew into a town, population growth and increasing automobile traffic created the need for wider roads and bypass roads, as shown in Strips III and IV. Specialization as an "automobile convenient" strip, with the development of more motels, a drive-in theater, and drive-in businesses, can be seen in Strip V. At this time the residential functions along the strip began to disappear and the area assumed an increasingly commercial character.

Strip VI shows the strip's present stage of development. A spur of the limited-access highway system creates new growth around a cloverleaf (including a new community college situated between the artificial lake and the shopping center). Note that along the original main road are office buildings and a modern industrial park rather than the smaller retail businesses that once defined the town center. Indeed, as the strip has developed and surrounding roads have been enlarged to form part of the metropolitan highway system, the town center itself has largely disappeared (Clay, 1980). The strip development model thus describes the incorporation of smaller communities and towns into a larger metropolitan area.

METROPOLITAN AREAS

Megalopolis. After 1920 new metropolitan areas developed largely as a result of the increasing use of automobiles and the construction of a network of highways covering the entire nation (Flink, 1988). The shift to automobile travel brought former satellite cities within

FIGURE 9.5   **Strip Development**

Source: Clay, 1980.

commuting distance of the major industrial centers, thereby adding to the size of those metropolitan areas. In the South and Southwest, new metropolitan areas developed. In fact, in recent years these have become the fastest growing urban areas in the nation.

Since World War II sociologists have been studying an increasingly important urban phenomenon: the emergence of large multinuclear urban systems. The term **megalopolis** is used to describe these vast complexes, whose total population exceeds 25 million. Jean Gottmann (1978) pointed out that a megalopolis is not "simply an overgrown metropolitan area"; rather, it is a system of cities distributed along "a major axis of traffic and communication" (p. 56). According to Gottmann, there are six megalopolises in the world today: the American Northeastern megalopolis, the Great Lakes megalopolis, the Tokaido megalopolis in Japan, the megalopolis in England (the London area), the megalopolis of northwestern Europe (extending from Am-

sterdam to the Ruhr), and the Urban Constellation in China (centered on Shanghai). Four others are developing rapidly: the Rio de Janeiro–São Paulo complex in Brazil, the Milan–Turin–Genoa triangle in northern Italy, the Valley of Mexico, and the urban swath extending from San Diego to the San Francisco Bay area.

A megalopolis is characterized by an "intertwined web of relationships between a variety of distinct urban centers ... expressed partly in a physical infrastructure consisting of highways, railways, waterways, telephone lines, pipelines, water supply and sewage systems criss-crossing the whole area, and partly in more fluid networks, such as the flows of traffic, the movement of people and goods, the flows of telephone calls [and] of mail" (Gottmann, 1978, p. 57). Despite their interdependence, however, "the sizes and specializations of the various ... components [of a megalopolis] are extremely varied, as demonstrated by the diverse characteristics of the cities, towns, villages,

FIGURE 9.6 The Los Angeles–Anaheim–Riverside Megalopolis

Note: All politcal boundaries are as of January 1, 1980. CMSA, PMSA, and MSA boundaries are as defined on June 30, 1986.

Source: Census Bureau.

suburban and rural areas that form the vast system" (p. 57). Therefore a megalopolis can best be described as a huge social and economic mosaic.

The recent history of Los Angeles provides a good example of the development of a megalopolis (see Figure 9.6). Between 1960 and 1970 the population of Los Angeles increased by more than 2 million, double the growth of Chicago and more than that of New York and San Francisco put together (Smith, 1968). Today the Los Angeles metropolitan area continues to grow, although at a somewhat slower rate. As a result of its extraordinary growth, the region must struggle to control the effects of air pollution from more than 3 million automobiles. It must also struggle to furnish adequate supplies of water for its residents. In a review of conflicts between Angeleno leaders and the residents of smaller towns near water sources, sociologist John Walton (1992) has shown that control over water and other natural resources, especially by powerful groups that dominate the regional real estate markets, is a key to understanding the history not only of the Los Angeles metropolitan region but of the entire desert West.

Decentralization. One effect of the growth of megalopolitan areas is *decentralization*, in which outlying areas become more important at the expense of the central city. This trend is not new. In the 1960s and 1970s large numbers of middle-income city dwellers moved to suburban areas while the poor remained in the central cities. Business and industry also moved to the suburbs, giving rise to widespread speculation that vibrant central cities would become a thing of the past. Recently, however, the central cities of some metropolitan areas—such as New York, Philadelphia, Chicago, and Baltimore—have shown renewed vitality. Far from decaying, they have become major financial and cultural centers serving the needs of huge populations. On the other hand, medium-sized cities like Gary, Indiana, and Paterson, New Jersey, have suffered, because their central business districts have little to offer suburban dwellers in the way of financial services like banking and insurance or cultural attractions like theaters and symphony orchestras (Kasarda, 1988).

An important feature of megalopolitan areas is their diversity. These huge urban regions include many different kinds of communities: ethnic communities in both central cities and suburbs, middle-class "bedroom" suburbs, industrial towns, areas devoted to truck gardening or dairy farming, "second home" communities (e.g., beachfront areas), and so on. Each meets the economic and cultural needs of a specific urban population. Sociologists have devoted considerable study to these urban communities, and we discuss their findings in the next section.

URBAN COMMUNITIES

"The city," wrote Robert Park, is more than a set of "social conveniences—streets, buildings, electric lights, tramways, and telephones, etc.; something more, also, than a mere constellation of . . . courts, hospitals, schools, police, and civil functionaries of various sorts. The city is, rather, a state of mind, a body of customs and traditions. . . . It is a product of nature, and particularly of human nature" (1967/1925a, p. 1).

The connection between the city and human nature has been a recurrent theme in literature throughout history. Many literary images of the city are negative. In the Bible, for example, the cities of Sodom and Gomorrah are symbols of the worst aspects of human nature. The poet Juvenal complained that Rome produced ulcers and insomnia and subjected its residents to burglars and dishonest landlords. American literature also contains many negative images of the city. Thomas Jefferson, for instance, wrote, "I view great American cities as pestilential to the morals, health, and the liberties of man." And Henry David Thoreau escaped from the city to Walden Pond in an effort to "rediscover his soul" (Fischer, 1976).

Social scientists who study cities have devoted a great deal of attention to the tension between "community" and "individualism" as it relates to life in cities. Country dwellers have been thought of as "happily ensconced in warm, humanly rich and supportive social relationships: the family, neighborhood, town," whereas city dwellers are "strangers to all, including themselves. They are lonely, not emotionally touching or being touched by others, and consequently set psychically adrift" (Fischer, 1976, p. 19). On the other hand, country dwellers are sometimes viewed as "stifled by conventionality, repressed by the intrusion and social control of narrow-minded kin, neighbors, and townsmen," whereas city dwellers are "free to develop individual abilities, express personal styles, and satisfy private needs" (p. 20). These views of the city are obviously contradictory, and much research has been devoted to the question of how urban life affects individuals and communities. In this section we look at some of the findings of that research and the theories of urban life that have been proposed on the basis of those findings.

THE DECLINE-OF-COMMUNITY THESIS

Early studies of the nature and effects of urban life were dominated by efforts to evaluate the differences between rural and urban societies. They tended to reach rather gloomy conclusions. We have already noted (Chapter 4) that Ferdinand Tönnies described the process of urbanization as a shift from gemeinschaft (a community based on kinship ties) to gesellschaft (a society based on common

Eastern European sociologists note that cities like Sarajevo were cosmopolitan centers marked by higher levels of ethnic and religious intermarriage than the surrounding areas, which were more homogeneous. They attribute some of the bitterness and hostility of the Bosnian war to antiurban sentiment in the mountain villages and towns.

interests). Émile Durkheim reached a similar conclusion: Small rural communities are held together by ties based on shared ideas and common experiences, whereas urban societies are held together by ties based on the interdependence of people who perform specialized tasks. Both Tönnies and Durkheim believed that urban life weakens kinship ties and produces impersonal social relationships.

In a 1905 essay, "The Metropolis and Mental Life," Georg Simmel focused on the effects of urban life on the minds and personalities of individuals. According to Simmel, cities bombard their residents with sensory stimuli: "Horns blare, signs flash, solicitors tug at coattails, poll-takers telephone, newspaper headlines try to catch the eye, strange-looking and strange-behaving persons distract attention" (quoted in Fischer, 1976, p. 30). The urban dweller is forced to adapt to this profusion of stimuli, which Stanley Milgram (1970) termed *psychic overload*. The usual way of adapting is to become calculating and emotionally distant. Hence the image of the city dweller as aloof, brusque, and impersonal in his or her dealings with others.

This view of the effects of urban life found further expression in the work of Louis Wirth, especially in his essay "Urbanism as a Way of Life" (1968/1938). Wirth began by defining the city as "a relatively large, dense, and permanent settlement of socially heterogeneous individuals" (p. 28). He then attempted to show how these characteristics of cities produce psychological stress and social disorganization. The primary psychological effect of urban life, according to Wirth, is a weakening of the individual's bonds to other people. Without such bonds, the individual must deal with the crises of life alone; often the result is mental illness. In other cases the city dweller, again because of the absence of close ties to friends or kin, lacks the restraints that might prevent him or her from engaging in antisocial behaviors.

Wirth linked social disorganization to the diversity that is characteristic of cities. Unlike rural residents, city dwellers work in one place, live in another, and relax in yet another. They divide their social lives among coworkers, neighbors, friends, and kin. Their jobs, lifestyles, and interests are extremely varied. As a result, no single group, be it the family, the friendship group, or the neighborhood, controls their lives. In Wirth's view, this absence of social control produces anomie or normlessness (see Chapter 7). Urban dwellers frequently do not agree on the norms that should govern their lives, and hence they are likely to either challenge existing norms or ignore them. Consequently, instead of being controlled by the norms of primary groups, the lives of city dwellers are controlled by impersonal agencies like banks and police forces.

One consequence of the impersonality of urban life, some argue, is greater callousness among city dwellers. An often-cited example is the case of Kitty Genovese, discussed in Chapter 6. After that episode, in which a young woman was murdered while 38 residents of nearby apartments who heard her cries did nothing, many commentators called attention to the callous character of city dwellers. Subsequent research on bystander apathy revealed that the presence of many other people tends to diffuse the sense of responsibility. We are less likely to take action if we have reason to believe that someone else will do so (Hunt, 1985; Latané & Darley, 1970). In this sense, the bigger the city and the more one is surrounded by strangers, the more likely it is that such behavior will occur—but this does not mean that city dwellers are alienated from one another when they are among people they know, or that when alone they would not help someone in trouble. The fact that one is likely to feel less responsibility for others when one is surrounded by strangers may be a condition of city life, but it is hardly evidence for the decline-of-community thesis.

THE PERSISTENCE OF URBAN COMMUNITIES

The idea that urbanization leads to the decline of community has been criticized on a number of grounds. Rural life is nowhere near as pleasant as some urban sociologists have assumed it to be; evidence of this is the almost magical attraction that cities often have for rural people. On the other hand, urban social disorganization is not as extensive as the early urban sociologists believed. Many city dwellers maintain stable, intimate relationships with kin, neighbors, and coworkers. Moreover, urban life is not necessarily stressful or anomic.

Subcultural Theory. A more recent view of urban life sees the city as a "mosaic of social worlds" or intimate social groups. Numerous studies have shown that the typical urban dweller does not resemble the isolated, anomic individual portrayed by Simmel and Wirth. In fact, communities of all kinds can be found in cities. Many urban dwellers, for example, are members of ethnic communities who have not become fully assimilated into the melting pot of American society and are unlikely to do so. They may be the children or grandchildren of immigrants who formed ethnic enclaves within large cities in the late nineteenth and early twentieth centuries, or they may be recent immigrants themselves, trying to build a new life in a strange culture.

But group ties among urban dwellers are not based solely on ethnicity. They may be based on kinship, occupation, lifestyle, or similar personal attributes (Fischer, 1976; Hummin, 1990; Suttles, 1972). Thus many cities contain communities of college students, elderly people, homosexuals, artists and musicians, wealthy socialites, and so on. Although the members of any given group do not always live in the same neighborhood, they are in close touch with one another much of the time. Their sense of community is based not so much on place of residence as on the ability to come together by telephone, in special meeting places like churches or synagogues, or even in restaurants and bars (Duneier, 1992; Fischer, 1976; Oldenburg, 1989).

An example of this point of view, known as *subcultural theory,* is Illsoo Kim's (1981) detailed study of the Korean community in New York City. This growing ethnic community has developed since the passage of the Immigration Act of 1965, which eliminated the nationality quotas established earlier in the century. Largely because of population pressure in South Korea (which has led to overcrowded cities and high rates of unemployment), more than 650,000 Koreans have immigrated to the United States since 1970, with more than 100,000 finding new homes in the city of New York.

Like all immigrants, the Koreans have had to create a new way of life. They have had to find new ways of making a living, and they have had to adapt to a new culture. The first problem has been solved mainly by opening small businesses, the second by establishing neighborhoods where the immigrants can maintain their own culture while they and their children learn the values and norms of Western culture. Kim explains the Koreans' inclination to open small businesses (mainly grocery stores) in this passage:

> Old-timers frequently tell newcomers that "running a *jangsa* (commercial business) is the fastest way to get ahead in America." The language barrier partly explains this inclination. . . . This is an insuperable barrier to most Korean immigrants; it deprives them of many opportunities. . . . This fact, combined with differences in both the skills demanded and the system of rewards in the United States, means that occupational status cannot be transferred from the homeland to the new land. A high proportion of Korean immigrants were thus forced to turn to small retail businesses. (1981, pp. 102–103)

Many of the businesses established by Korean immigrants are geared to Korean ethnic tastes and cultural needs. For example, Korean immigrants are often unwilling to change their diet and will buy most of their food from Korean-owned food stores. Other shops import books, gifts, magazines, and other items from South Korea. Numerous Korean travel agencies satisfy the immigrants' strong desire to visit their homeland. But Korean small businesses are not limited to serving the needs of the immigrant population. A growing number cater to all racial and ethnic groups and supply typically American goods and services.

In summing up the situation of Korean immigrants in New York, Kim points out that "until they completely master the American language, education, and culture, Koreans will be forced to rely on one another" (p. 319). For this reason they are likely to maintain their own community within the city for at least two generations. However, in time their commitment to education and a better life will cause them to become more fully assimilated into American society, and their ties to the Korean community will be weakened.

The case of the Koreans echoes that of many other immigrant groups, both past and present, as well as that of

other groups, such as homosexuals and artists. The details may differ somewhat, but the tendency to establish ethnic or cultural enclaves in large cities is universal. In a well-known study titled *The Urban Villagers,* Herbert Gans (1984) described an Italian neighborhood in Boston. This community was a long-established one with many of the characteristics that are typical of ethnic communities everywhere. But at the time that Gans did his research, the neighborhood was being destroyed by an urban renewal project. Its residents were forced to find new homes in other parts of the city, to join new churches, attend new schools, seek out new places to buy food and clothes. For some, the upheaval was so great that it produced depression and anomie (Fried, 1963).

It seems reasonable to conclude that the effects of urban life on communities and individuals are more complex than Durkheim, Simmel, and Wirth suggested. Certainly, social disorganization occurs in cities, but so does social reorganization. Communities that are uprooted by urban renewal eventually may be re-formed in other parts of the city or its suburbs. The new community may be less homogeneous than the old one, but it is a community nonetheless.

The Suburbs. Like city dwellers, suburban dwellers have been said to lack the close attachments that are thought to characterize rural communities. In fact, before the late 1960s most social scientists had a rather dismal view of suburban life. Suburbs had grown rapidly after World War II as large numbers of middle-class Americans

In urban societies, where there are large numbers of people who are strangers to one another, sociologists have noted a propensity to wear identifying "uniforms" that indicate the kind of person one wishes to know and interact with.

left the central cities in search of a less crowded, more pleasant lifestyle. Many suburban dwellers were corporate employees, and in the 1950s and early 1960s they became the subject of a widely held stereotype. The suburbs, it was said, were "breeding a new set of Americans, as mass-produced as the houses they lived in, driven into a never-ending round of group activity ruled by the strictest conformity. Suburbanites were incapable of real friendships; they were bored and lonely, alienated, atomized, and depersonalized" (Gans, 1967, pp. xxvii–xxviii).

In *The Levittowners*, a classic study of a new suburban community in New Jersey, Gans (1967, 1976) challenged this stereotype. He found that the residents of Levittown lost no time in forming attachments to one another. At first they associated only with their neighbors, but before long they formed more extensive associations based on shared interests and concerns. Moreover, far from being bored and isolated, a majority of the Levittowners were satisfied with their lives and felt that Levittown was a good place to live. Gans concluded that "new towns are merely old social structures on new land" (1967, p. vii). In other words, the contrasts between central-city and suburban life are generally exaggerated. Other researchers have reached similar conclusions. They note that as suburban communities age and newcomers buy homes from people whose children are grown, these neighborhoods go through ethnic, racial, and generational changes that are not so different from the patterns occurring inside the cities (Jackson, 1985).

Some comparative research has focused on women born in suburban communities after the 1950s who never lived in other types of communities (Stimson, 1980; Wekerle, 1980). For example, Sylvia Fava (1985) found that younger women born in suburban communities do not think of suburban life as stifling or as limiting their opportunities. They may prefer to live in older, more diverse suburban communities within easy commuting distance of the jobs and nightlife of the central cities, but they normally do not feel that their suburban lifestyle is unsatisfactory. Indeed, as conditions continue to deteriorate in some inner-city communities—with increasing homelessness, exposure to drug markets, and violence—both older and newer suburban areas become more attractive to people seeking to escape the dangers they perceive in urban life.

For the past few decades the phenomenon of "white flight" from older inner-city communities to newer and presumably safer suburban communities has been a subject of concern among urban sociologists and policy makers (Wilson, 1987). Recent data show, however, that African Americans and other minority groups are also fleeing the central cities at an accelerating rate. Demographer William Frey notes that "minority suburbanization took off in the 1980s both as the black middle class came into its own and as more assimilated Latinos and Asians translated their moves up the socioeconomic ladder into a suburban life style" (quoted in De Witt, 1994, p. A1). This outward migra-

TABLE 9.4	Educational Attainment of Residents, Washington, D.C.	
SCHOOLING	**IN THE SUBURBS**	**IN THE CITY**
Only to the	18,896	31,209
eighth grade	5.2%	11.4%
Some high	48,672	66,653
school	12.7%	24.3%
High school	103,799	76,392
graduate only	28.3%	27.8%
Some	112,477	57,341
college	30.7%	20.9%
College	84,815	43,189
graduate	23.1%	15.8%

Source: Data from University of Michigan.

tion threatens to leave central-city communities with even greater concentrations of poor people. In cities with large numbers of immigrants this discouraging trend is countered by increasing racial, ethnic, and class diversity (Huang, 1994), but in other cities the trend toward greater concentration of poor people inside the city and more affluent people in the suburbs is a growing problem. Frey's research in Washington, D.C., shows, for example, that educated, middle-class African Americans are flocking to the suburbs, leaving more concentrated poverty in the communities they leave behind. (See Table 9.4.)

Private Communities. The growth of private communities throughout the United States is another indication of the widespread fear of urban life (Garreau, 1991). Recent data indicate that about 4 million Americans live in private communities where public through-traffic is prohibited. For those who can afford to live there, these heavily patrolled and regulated communities represent a decision to place individual comfort and family safety above more social efforts to create communities. An even larger number of Americans, about 28 million, live in communities represented by private community associations. These include condominiums and cooperatives that require all residents to be members of the association, obey its rules, and pay fees to support its operations. Although they are less restrictive than private communities, these community associations also seek to control public access.

These private and quasi-private communities are the fastest growing types of communities in the United States, and there is some concern about what this growth implies. Supporters of such communities dwell on their safety and their ability to maintain property values. Critics like Gerald Frug, an expert on local government, believe that people are trying to capture the feeling of life in a village without many other qualities of village life. "The village was open to

This "gated community" is an example of a growing trend toward privatization of public space in the interests of security and community prestige.

the public," Frug observes. "The village did not have these kinds of restrictions. The village had poor people, retarded people. Somebody could hand you a leaflet. These private communities are totally devoid of random encounters" (quoted in Egan, 1995, p. A22). Frug and other critics of the trend toward private communities fear that as people choose to live only with others like themselves, "they will become less likely to support schools, parks or roads for everyone else" (p. A22).

CITIES AND SOCIAL CHANGE

In the preceding section we stressed the presence of a wide variety of communities and subcultures within cities. We noted that contemporary social scientists see the city as a place where many different communities coexist and thrive rather than as a place where people are isolated and do not have a feeling of belonging to a particular social group or community. At the same time, however, there is no escap-

ing the fact that various urban communities are often in conflict. For example, ethnic and racial communities may clash in violent confrontations over such issues as the busing of children to achieve school integration. In this section we examine the origins and implications of such conflicts.

Social change in an urban society is likely to be felt most deeply by city dwellers, for it is in the cities that people are most densely congregated. In recent decades this has been the case in North America as manufacturing jobs have been "exported" to Asia and Latin America. As a result of this shift, American cities are undergoing massive social change. "America's major cities are different places today from what they were in the 1960s," concludes John Kasarda (1989, p. 28), one of the nation's foremost urban sociologists. New modes of transportation, new communication technologies such as satellites and computers, and new industrial technologies (e.g., automation and recycling) are transforming our cities from production and distribution centers to administrative, financial, and information centers. "In the process," writes Kasarda, "many blue-collar jobs that once constituted the economic backbone of cities and provided employment opportunities for their poorly educated residents have either vanished or moved." Many of those jobs have been replaced by "knowledge-intensive white-collar jobs with educational requirements that exclude many with substandard education" (1989, p. 28).

INEQUALITY AND CONFLICT

As noted earlier, American cities and metropolitan regions have always attracted streams of migrants and immigrants. Migrants arrive from other parts of the nation—blacks from the rural South, Chicanos from the Southwest. Immigrants come from foreign lands—Haiti, Poland, China, Korea, Italy, and many others. Until the 1970s, except during economic depressions or recessions, the new arrivals had no difficulty finding work in the mills and factories that produced textiles, clothing, steel, rubber, glass, cars, and trucks. And much of their education was gained while working. Formal schooling was not as crucial to job success as it is today.

Today, although there are still many manufacturing jobs, it is much more difficult to make a good living at such a job. Within the cities, where the decline in manufacturing jobs has been greatest, the number of low-status jobs, especially in restaurants and other low-paying services, has increased. So has the number of highly paid jobs in management and the professions, positions that require high levels of education. At the same time, more than 14 million legal immigrants have entered the country since 1970, usually settling in the cities. The result, often, has been fierce competition between immigrants and more established residents.

The net effect of these trends is a growing gap between the "haves" and the "have-nots," especially in large cities (Silk, 1989). The study of *social stratification*—of patterns of inequality and how they produce entire classes of people with differing opportunities to succeed in life—is at the core of sociology and is discussed in detail in later chapters. Certainly the gap between those who enjoy the good things in life and those who spend their lives simply trying to survive is not unique to cities. Small towns and villages also have affluent and poor residents. But the conflicts and social problems associated with social inequality are most visible in the cities. In many poor urban neighborhoods, for example, wealthier city dwellers are buying the buildings in which the poor live, forcing them to move elsewhere. In neighborhoods where this occurs, the shops and stores that once catered to lower-income residents cannot afford the higher rents paid by stores that serve the wealthy newcomers and are forced out of business. This process, whereby poor and dilapidated neighborhoods are renovated by higher-income newcomers while poor residents and merchants are pushed out, is known as *gentrification*.

Status Conflict. In the last section we noted that an urban renewal project had dislocated large numbers of Italian Americans from their Boston neighborhood. Such projects have sometimes been labeled "urban removal" because they remove poor people from decaying neighborhoods and force them to find homes elsewhere. Recently urban renewal has fallen into disfavor and *redevelopment* has become popular. Redevelopment does not involve the destruction of entire neighborhoods, but it may have similar effects. For example, the planned redevelopment of New York City's Times Square by the Disney Corporation and other powerful groups, both public and private, is intended to restore a sleazy area to its former glory as an entertainment center. The goal is to make the area attractive to "decent" people and to eliminate the prostitutes, drug and pornography dealers, and petty criminals that have made Times Square a symbol of vice throughout the world (Kornblum, 1996; Mollenkopf, 1985).

Not everyone agrees that Times Square should be redeveloped. Owners of legal businesses in the area argue that they are being attacked unfairly, and they have fought the redevelopment plan in the courts. This is a typical instance of *status conflict*, in which different groups vie for territory, occupational advantages, and other benefits that will enhance their prestige in the neighborhood or community.

Another example of this type of urban conflict is evident in the research of Elijah Anderson on community and race relations in Philadelphia. Anderson's most recent study examined a neighborhood where there has been a good deal of in-migration by more affluent, predominantly white residents into what was formerly a lower-income, predominantly black neighborhood. Much of the status conflict that occurs in the daily life of this neighborhood is a result of fear of strangers. As Anderson notes:

> People see the streets as a jungle, especially at night, when "all cats are gray" and everyone may seem threatening.

They are then on special alert, carefully monitoring everyone who passes and giving few people the benefit of the doubt. (1990, p. 239)

Anderson found that many residents of the neighborhood are concerned about "wandering homeless people, aggressive beggars, muggers, anonymous black youths, and drug addicts" (p. 238), to name just a few of the categories of people who evoke hostile glances and defensive maneuvers. People who wish to stay in the neighborhood as long-term residents must become streetwise and develop sophisticated ways of judging who is likely to be dangerous to them and who is not. Those who develop the skills that enable them to avoid conflict and increase their security are likely to remain in the neighborhood. Those who do not develop these skills are likely to become discouraged and move to less diverse, less challenging urban communities.

Some urban sociologists see the city as divided into "defended neighborhoods" or territories (Suttles, 1972). This concept was originally developed by Park and Burgess, who viewed such neighborhoods as a type of "natural area" within the city. The defended neighborhood is a territory that a certain group of people consider to be their "turf" or base, which they are willing to defend against "invasion" by outsiders. Neighborhood defense is a common element of urban conflict, although the means used to defend neighborhoods may differ. For example, in wealthy suburban neighborhoods it may take the form of zoning regulations that establish minimum lot sizes of an acre or more. Such regulations effectively defend the neighborhood against invasion by people who cannot afford the large lots or by developers who would like to erect apartment buildings (Perin, 1977). In less affluent neighborhoods, defense is often conducted by neighborhood improvement groups, which sometimes engage in vigilante action when they fear racial "invasion" (Hamilton, 1969). In poor neighborhoods, defense is very often the province of street-corner gangs.

Racial Conflict. Perhaps the most common source of intergroup conflict in American cities has been racial tension. In the belief that the presence of black residents reduces the prestige of a neighborhood and lowers the value of real estate there, whites have resisted efforts by blacks to obtain housing in "their" neighborhoods. This resistance has taken a wide variety of forms, ranging from discrimination by real estate agents to outright violence against black families moving into white neighborhoods. When blacks have succeeded in gaining a foothold in previously all-white neighborhoods, many white families have sold their homes and moved to the suburbs (Massey & Denton, 1993).

For racial and ethnic minorities, the desire to move out of segregated ghettos is based on the need to establish or maintain a residential community while pursuing opportunities to build a better life. This is among the key findings of studies of immigrant groups in South Florida. In looking at the difficulties that Haitian and Cuban refugees encounter in finding jobs in the Miami area, Alejandro Portes and Alex Stepick (1985) found that Cubans could draw upon kin and ethnic networks in Miami neighborhoods in looking for jobs but that the Haitians had no such networks to help them adapt to their new environment.

The riots that took place in 1992 in Los Angeles, Atlanta, and other major U.S. cities were a tragic example of the relationship between social change and racial violence in urban centers. Although the conditions of life had been deteriorating in central-city ghettos throughout the 1980s, it was not until televised bloodshed brought this situation to the attention of the majority of Americans that significant numbers of people began to demand that the federal government take action. But this is by no means a new phenomenon in American social life. As we saw in Chapter 8, conflict between racial and other groups often raises public consciousness and contributes to major social change (Rothenberg, 1992).

RESEARCH FRONTIERS: COPING WITH DISASTERS IN URBAN COMMUNITIES

Riots, epidemics, earthquakes, terrorist bombings, wars, floods, tornadoes, and hurricanes are among the many kinds of disasters that may strike densely populated human settlements. Of course there are important differences in the causes and outcomes of purely social disasters like riots and purely natural ones like the earthquakes in Los Angeles and Kobe described at the beginning of the chapter. But from a sociological vantage point social and natural disasters have a great deal in common. And because we can expect both natural and social disasters to occur with increasing frequency on our urbanizing planet, the study of disasters is a thriving area of sociological theory and research. (See Figure 9.7.)

Recent sociological research on disasters has focused on the longer-term consequences for the victims. On this research frontier the work of sociologist Kai Erikson is particularly noteworthy. Erikson's powerful descriptions of responses to disasters and his development of the sociological theory of trauma are having significant and positive impacts on victims' lives. In a number of precedent-setting cases Erikson has convinced juries and judges that victims have suffered sociological damage, especially in the form of loss of community.

Erikson's recent work on social disasters focuses on the consequences of what he calls "a new species of trouble" that is particularly common in urban industrial societies. The trouble may take the form of toxic spills, nuclear accidents, mercury poisoning, or any of a large number of other disasters attributable to human negligence, greed, or

Contamination and pollution of the earth and water beneath these houses, caused by the criminal dumping of toxic wastes, forced the residents to abandon their homes. Sociologist Kai Erikson has identified such disasters as a "new species of trouble" that has profound consequences for its victims.

FIGURE 9.7

MAPPING SOCIAL CHANGE

This map shows earthquakes of magnitude 4.0 or greater from 1960 to 1989.

4.0 – 7.5 magnitude {
  • 0 – 60 km deep
  • > 60 km deep

> 7.5 magnitude ▲

Urban Locations and Environmental Risk. Millions of people live in highly unstable physical environments where there is a high risk of natural disasters like the recent earthquakes in Los Angeles, California, and Kobe, Japan. This map shows the regions of the earth where earthquake activity is greatest. Along the West Coast of the United States and Latin America, in the Valley of Mexico, in much of Japan, and on the Pacific Rim, where rates of urban growth are among the highest in the world, the risk of devastating earthquakes is an undeniable fact of life. Or is it?

Our knowledge of where and how earthquakes occur has improved considerably in the last 30 years, but the cities in question began growing rapidly long before the risks were well understood. People continue to migrate to these risky environments, often denying that the risks actually apply to them. But denial alone is not an adequate explanation. Social policies that encourage the growth of such cities—through favorable mortgage and insurance terms, for example—also play a significant role. Social policies that require better preparation for earthquakes, better design and construction of buildings and freeways, and advance planning for disaster relief are among the consequences of recent disasters. But the desirable coastal locations of vulnerable cities will result in continued population growth and an increasing need for effective planning to avert disasters.

FAVELAS IN BRAZIL

These photographs by Janice Perlman provide a fascinating glimpse of life in the squatter settlements and shantytowns that typically surround the rapidly growing cities of Latin America, Asia, and Africa. In Rio de Janeiro the shantytowns, or *favelas,* are perched on hillsides above the more affluent commercial and residential core of the city. This pattern is both a feature of Rio's hilly landscape and a consequence of the rising cost of land in the city.

The favelas that Perlman studied were subsequently burned by the authorities, the land fenced off and hidden behind advertising signs to await more lucrative urban development. Many of the inhabitants were relocated to sterile, inadequate row houses, also shown here.

Many Brazilian social scientists and political and business leaders told Perlman that the inhabitants of the favelas were mainly shiftless men who were marginal to the legitimate institutions of Brazilian society. They had "one foot in the countryside and another in the city," or they were too involved in crime or hustling to settle down to regular employment. Yet Perlman's demographic research showed that somewhat more women than men lived in the favelas and that more than 60 percent of the adult residents were married and living in nuclear-family households. More than 80 percent were recent migrants to the city from the countryside.

In her book *The Myth of Marginality* (1976), Perlman shows that the very poverty of the *favelados* made a major contribution to the wealth of those who labeled them as failures. By working "off the books" as servants, unskilled laborers, part-time restaurant workers, and the like, they provided low-cost goods and services to the more secure labor force, thereby helping to keep down the cost of living. Perlman therefore argues for improving life in the favelas by making the land available to their residents rather than wiping them out.

combinations of both. The result is often an abrupt and shattering loss of community.

In one such case, Erikson interviewed the residents of East Swallow Drive in Fort Collins, Colorado. This middle-income neighborhood of private homes with middle-aged or elderly residents was the site of a gasoline spill with devastating consequences. The local service station had been experiencing "inventory losses" over a number of years and had finally replaced three "incontinent" fuel tanks with new ones. Not long afterward, nearby residents began smelling gasoline fumes in their homes. An investigation revealed that there were large pools of gasoline in the ground under the homes along East Swallow Drive. One house near the service station was condemned, and in the months that followed, as Erikson describes it, "waves of concern began to radiate in slow-motion ripples down East Swallow Drive as people began to understand that a plume of petroleum was moving eastward with the sureness of a glacier" (1994a, pp. 99–100).

A group of homeowners brought suit against the companies involved in the spill. As is often the case, however, the companies were able to hire teams of lawyers who could delay the suit for months. Eventually lawyers for the residents asked Erikson to prepare testimony on the sociological damage caused by the spill. He and an assistant conducted observations in the neighborhood and interviewed the residents. Later Erikson shared transcripts of the interviews with the residents and asked them for additional comments. This method, it turned out, had powerful effects. As one resident noted, "I was greatly relieved to see what other people said . . . seeing this report gives me a little reassurance that I wasn't feeling something that other people were not feeling" (quoted in Erikson, 1994a, p. 138).

In his report Erikson argued that the personal distress the residents were experiencing—in the form of anxiety, sleeplessness, anger, and other emotions—was not only a sign of psychological suffering but also a symptom of sociological trauma due to the loss of their attachments to the neighborhood. As one resident said, "Well, we feel that the value of our property has taken a nose dive. It is our only security. We don't feel that it's salable. If we can't sell it, we can't relocate, we can't move, we can't expand or change. We feel that we're sort of stuck" (quoted in Erikson, 1994a, p. 232).

Erikson convinced the court not only that the residents had lost property value in terms of dollars, but also that they had suffered a greater loss in a sociological sense. He noted that they had invested a great deal more than money in their homes:

> It is well understood by social and behavioral scientists who are familiar with accidents of this kind that the loss of a home can be profoundly traumatic. I wrote in my report on the Buffalo Creek flood of 1972 [in West Virginia], for example, that a home in which a person has made a real personal investment "is not simply an expression of one's taste; it is the outer edge of personality, a part of the self itself." (1994a, p. 233)

Similarly, a well-known study of the impact of a tornado in Texas reported that people who had lost their homes felt as if they had lost part of themselves (Moore, 1958). And an equally well-known study of an urban relocation project in Boston's East End was titled simply "Grieving for a Lost Home" (Fried, 1963). In the East Swallow Drive case, the residents benefited from Erikson's sociological insight: Eventually the corporations responsible for the damage had to settle with the residents and pay not only for the damage to their property but for their loss of community as well.

The residents of Los Angeles and Kobe who sustained major losses as a result of an "act of God" also experienced the traumatic loss of community. Erikson and other sociologists who study disasters hope that as a consequence of their research—and their successes in court—there will be more safeguards against negligence and more emphasis on anticipating the risks of natural disasters. In the near term, however, Erikson fears that the balance of power is shifting toward corporations and other powerful actors, to the disadvantage of the victims or potential victims of community disasters.

SUMMARY

THINK ABOUT IT CRITICALLY

The most dire predictions about world population growth state that unless drastic measures are taken to curtail fertility, the world will be so overcrowded by the year 2100 that there will be severe famines, wars, resource depletion, and environmental pollution—in short, a veritable "population bomb." How does knowledge of population processes and the consequences of urbanization help one think critically about this assertion?

Populations change as a consequence of births, deaths, out-migration, and in-migration. The *crude birthrate* is the number of births occurring during a year in a given population divided by the midyear population. The *crude death rate* is the number of deaths occurring during a year divided by the midyear population. The *rate of reproductive change* is the difference between the crude birthrate and the crude death rate for a given population. Since World War II the world population has been increasing at a rate of more than 1.5 percent, which means that by the year 2000 it will have passed 6 billion.

The *demographic transition* is a set of major changes in birth and death rates that has occurred most completely in urban industrial nations in the past 200 years. It takes place in three stages: (1) high birth and death rates, (2) declining death rates, and (3) declining birthrates. These stages are accompanied by changes in the age composition of the population.

Urbanization is closely linked with rapid increases in population, but at the same time the nature of life in cities tends to limit the size of urban families. Cities grow primarily as a result of migration (which is often caused by population increases in rural areas), but new migrants do not find it easy to form families.

The increasing tendency of people throughout the world to live in cities has been referred to as the urban revolution. Not only are increasing proportions of the world's population living in cities, but the cities themselves are larger than ever before. The growth of cities in this century has given rise to the concept of the *metropolitan area,* in which a central city is surrounded by a number of smaller cities and suburbs that are closely related to it both socially and economically.

The growth of cities should be distinguished from *urbanization,* which refers to the proportion of the total population that is concentrated in urban settlements. The end result of urbanization is an "urban society." Not only do cities serve as the cultural and institutional centers of such societies, but urban life has a pervasive influence on the entire society.

Sociologists have devoted a great deal of study to the processes by which cities expand and to patterns of settlement within cities. An early model of urban expansion was the concentric-zone model developed by Park and Burgess. In this model a central business district is surrounded by successive zones or rings devoted to light manufacturing, workers' homes, higher-class apartment buildings and single-family homes, and a commuters' zone. This model is limited to commercial and industrial cities that formed around business centers and does not account for the rise of satellite cities and the rapid urbanization that occurs along commercial transportation corridors. The growth of satellite cities was especially rapid before World War II. A more current model of urbanization is known as strip development and describes the incorporation of smaller communities and towns into a larger metropolitan area.

Metropolitan areas have expanded greatly since the mid-twentieth century, largely as a result of the increasing use of automobiles and the construction of a network of highways covering the entire nation. In some areas this growth has created large multinuclear urban systems that are described by the term *megalopolis.* One effect of the development of such areas is decentralization, in which outlying areas become more important at the expense of the central city.

Social scientists who have studied the effects of urban life have been particularly concerned with the tension between community and individualism as it relates to life in cities. Early studies of urban life tended to conclude that it weakens kinship ties and produces impersonal social relationships. Urban life was also thought to produce "psychic overload" and anomie. More recently these conclusions have been criticized by researchers who have found that many city dwellers maintain stable, intimate relationships with kin, neighbors, and coworkers and that urban life is not necessarily stressful or anomic.

Subcultural theory sees the city as a mosaic of social worlds or intimate social groups. Communities of all kinds can be found in cities. Those communities may be based on ethnicity, kinship, occupation, lifestyle, or similar personal attributes. Suburban dwellers also have been found to be far less bored and isolated than was previously supposed.

Occasionally various communities within cities come into conflict. Such conflict may arise out of different class interests or the conflicting goals of different groups within the city. Some urban sociologists see the city as divided into "defended neighborhoods" or territories whose residents attempt to protect them from "invasion" by outsiders.

CRITICAL RESPONSE

While it is true that population growth is a serious problem for the world today and is likely to remain so well into the future, we know that as societies become urbanized, *educate their people, make birth control available, and develop their economies so that their members can aspire to greater comfort, people are motivated to curtail their fertility so as to enjoy these benefits. The critical question is whether these advances can occur in the less developed regions of the world before the consequences of the population explosion make them impossible.*

GLOSSARY

crude birthrate: the number of births occurring during a year in a given population, divided by the midyear population. (p. 241)

crude death rate: the number of deaths occurring during a year in a given population, divided by the midyear population. (p. 241)

rate of reproductive change: the difference between the crude birthrate and the crude death rate for a given population. (p. 241)

demographic transition: a set of major changes in birth and death rates that has occurred most completely in urban industrial nations in the past 200 years. (p. 242)

urbanization: a process in which an increasing proportion of a total population becomes concentrated in urban settlements. (p. 244)

metropolitan area: a central city surrounded by a number of smaller cities and suburbs that are closely related to it both socially and economically. (p. 246)

megalopolis: a complex of cities distributed along a major axis of traffic and communication, with a total population exceeding 25 million. (p. 255)

WHERE TO FIND IT

BOOKS

Western Times and Water Wars: State, Culture, and Rebellion in California (John Walton; University of California Press, 1992). A seminal work on the relationship of protest movements and collective behavior to metropolitan growth; describes the struggle to control vital natural resources in rapidly growing but arid regions.

Recent Social Trends in the United States, 1960–1990 (Theodore Caplow, Howard M. Bahr, John Modell, & Bruce A. Chadwick; McGill-Queens University Press, 1991). A compilation of statistical tables that document trends in population, urbanization, and other significant aspects of social change, based on data from the U.S. Census Bureau and other government agencies, and from major polling organizations, including the General Social Survey and the Gallup Poll.

The Apple Sliced (Vernon Boggs, Gerald Handel, & Sylvia F. Fava; Bergin and Garvey, 1984). A fascinating collection of sociological studies of New York City by field researchers who know the city well and are able to describe its institutions in vivid terms.

The Social Construction of Communities (Gerald Suttles; University of Chicago Press, 1972). An important theoretical statement; shows how sociology explains phenomena like territoriality and the formation of neighborhoods and communities.

Relations in Public (Erving Goffman; Harper, 1971). Goffman's brilliance in analyzing social interaction is applied to the study of street life in urban environments.

Close-Up: How to Read the American City, 2nd ed. (Grady Clay; University of Chicago Press, 1980). A brilliant, humorous, and extremely well illustrated guide to the physical ecology of American urbanization in the second half of this century.

The Urbanization of the Third World (Joseph Gugler, ed.; Oxford University Press, 1988). A collection of original essays by leading urban researchers, tracing most of the outstanding trends and problems of urbanization in the developing areas of the world.

Below-Replacement Fertility in Industrial Societies (Kingsley Davis, Mitchell S. Bernstam, & Rita Ricardo-Campbell, eds.; Population Council, 1987). A state-of-the-art analysis of how some of the industrialized nations have arrived at slow or no population growth and the consequences of this important change for these nations and the world.

Streetwise: Race, Class, and Change in an Urban Community (Elijah Anderson; University of Chicago Press, 1990). A brilliant and original study of life in two adjacent neighborhoods, one populated primarily by lower-income minority households, the other mixed in terms of class and race but undergoing gentrification. Through detailed ethnographic research the author documents changes in public behavior, norms of sexual conduct, drug use and control, and family life.

JOURNALS

Population and Development Review. Presents international research on population change and the effects of population variables on other aspects of social and economic development. A valuable source of comparative data and studies of population problems in the Third World.

Urban Affairs Quarterly. A leading journal of original research on urban social change.

OTHER SOURCES

Urban Affairs Annual Reviews (Sage Publications). Annual volumes on social change in urban regions, focusing on the impact of technologies and changing economic institutions on urban social classes and city governments.

Demographic Yearbook. Published annually by the United Nations, Department of International Economic and Social Affairs. Presents statistics on population, birth and death rates, marriage and divorce, and economic characteristics.

Global Social Change

One sultry African night, as the people of Blokosso were sleeping, a band of thieves crept into their houses and ransacked them. They stole radios, jewelry, and expensive articles of ceremonial clothing. But as the villagers assessed the damage early the next morning, they mourned a far greater loss. Never before in anyone's memory had a robbery like this occurred in the village. It was not the goods themselves they missed, for these could be replaced. It was the loss of a way of life, a social world, that they lamented. "We loved to sleep outside on the very hot nights," said Mr. Joseph, one of the most respected men in the village— "the women by this palm grove in the soft sand along the lagoon, the men under the lamp a bit. We like to talk and sleep with each other. We are not used to sleeping with our things."

Throughout history theirs had been a village society. Blokosso was one of several fishing villages inhabited by the Ebrié tribe. For as long as they could remember, the Ebrié people had made their living by fishing in the quiet waters of the lagoon, which was protected from the huge ocean swells by a long barrier island. But in recent decades the village had been engulfed by the rapidly growing city of Abidjan, the capital of Ivory Coast and a booming port. More and more of the tribesmen were now working in the city. The women continued to tend their garden plots, but they too were increasingly drawn into the economy of the city and felt an ever-increasing need for spending money, which they earned by renting rooms to migrant workers and selling their extra produce.

Gradually, in the time before the robbery occurred, Blokosso had ceased to be a self-sustaining village with its own economy and tribal culture. Instead, it was becoming a "village enclave," a little island of cultural homogeneity in an urban society. The robbery was a blunt statement to the villagers about how much change had occurred in a short time and how much more was likely to come.

For me, the experience of living in Blokosso at that time (during 1962 and 1963) was as much of a revelation as the robbery was to the villagers.

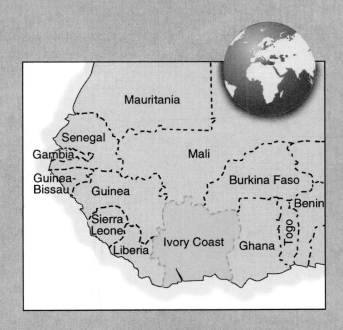

I had been trained as a biologist and was living in Blokosso while teaching physics and chemistry in a junior college. During the day I delighted in opening up to students the secrets of matter and energy. In the evenings, however, the villagers taught me about living in a totally different social world, one that was experiencing even more rapid social change than my own.

Mr. Joseph, my best friend in the village, was a middle-level executive in one of Abidjan's insurance agencies. He commuted across the lagoon in a motorized dugout canoe. During the day his mind was entirely devoted to business. In the evenings he dealt with the problems of a traditional African family. His three wives became more and more jealous of one another as new wealth and their rising expectations led to new opportunities for better health and more leisure and also to new sources of conflict. I watched him and his family deal with the impact of change on their lives. I saw the villagers attempt to invoke their ancestral spirits and to use witchcraft to cope with new phenomena like robberies. The entire colony had become independent from France only 2 years before, and I saw the villagers, now citizens of a new nation called Ivory Coast, becoming interested in politics and current events.

During that time my own interests shifted from the physical to the social sciences. Nothing has ever interested me more than the villagers' questions about what social change has brought to them and what it has caused them to lose. When I began to study sociology, I discovered that such questions are at the core of this young science.

THE NATURE OF SOCIAL CHANGE

Throughout this book we deal with social changes of all kinds. The term **social change** refers to variations over time in the ecological ordering of populations and communities, in patterns of roles and social interactions, in the structure and functioning of institutions, and in the cultures of societies. We have seen that such changes can result from social forces building within societies (**endogenous forces**) as well as from forces for change exerted from the outside (**exogenous forces**).

Ebrié is not a written language. The villagers speak their history to each other and to their children as they gather in the evenings around their home fires. When I was living with them they often told stories about how, in the distant past before the whites came, a tribal village sometimes grew too large. When that happened, severe conflict resulted. Factions formed and fought over land or other resources. Soon there would be a major split: The stronger faction would stay and keep the existing village while the less powerful faction would establish a new village on unused land along the lagoon. This is an example of people adjusting to endogenous change caused by population increase, a very common cause of social change.

The Ebrié also told stories about recent changes in their lives, changes brought on mainly by colonial conquest and, more recently, by their own efforts to create a new nation and maintain its social and economic growth. Colonial rule and rebellion against it are examples of social change produced by exogenous forces, particularly the influence of a powerful conquering society attempting to impose its culture on conquered peoples.

Social change affects people's lives all over the world, sometimes for the better, sometimes for the worse. As I sat under the palm trees with my Ebrié friends, we endlessly debated issues of social change. In many ways our debates were about the difference between change and progress. "Before the white man came," my friends told me, "we had time but no watches. Now we have watches but no time." The village primary school was known in Ebrié as the "paper house" where children struggled to master the three R's in order to be able to earn money, or "white man's paper." But there was also general agreement that many of the technologies introduced by the Europeans were of immense value. Health care innovations that could prevent debilitating diseases like malaria or schistosomiasis were considered a great blessing. Yet the most prestigious Western invention from the villagers' viewpoint was the camera,

This lighthearted sculpture by a traditional African artist shows a missionary or colonial administrator being ferried around in a dugout canoe. Colonial regimes were a major exogenous source of social change.

for with it, they exclaimed, "our children can see their ancestors."

The people of Ivory Coast and other societies that are undergoing rapid social change do not see the future as a matter of becoming Westernized. Rather, they strive to blend their own culture with certain aspects of Western culture. They are aware of a decline in their sense of community and mourn the weakening of their culture, but they actively embrace the aspects of modernity that will permit more of them to lead longer and perhaps more enjoyable lives. For them there is no question of returning to an earlier state. Change is inevitable. They want to help make the change, however, and to do this they understand that they must compete in modern social institutions like schools and businesses while at the same time they attempt to preserve their village life as best they can.

DILEMMAS OF SOCIAL CHANGE

Social change is a dominant theme of this book because it exerts such powerful influences on every aspect of our lives. Macro-level changes in the way the entire society is organized—such as the organization of metropolitan regions around automobile transportation—are relatively rapid. Our grandparents traveled in railroad sleeping cars and never imagined vast shopping malls with acres of automobile parking. Global social change accounts for the decline of whole sectors of the U.S. economy and the rise of new ones. At the middle level of social organization—in

our communities and workplaces—social change can have drastic and immediate impacts. At this writing, for example, there is a trend toward reducing the size and cost of public institutions. Public schools, public hospitals, and governmental agencies are all under attack, and their employees are experiencing the stress of cutbacks and layoffs.

At the micro level, social change also has dramatic impacts. Changing norms of sexuality, for example, may give rise to new and unexpected situations. As gay people realize their need to express their sexuality, they also wish to "come out" and speak frankly about their lifestyle with family members. Issues like abortion, interracial marriage, divorce, and drug abuse create similar conflicts and pressures. When we argue about norms within our intimate circle of family or friends, the result may be even greater confusion. Today no aspect of life seems secure and free from conflict. (More comparative examples of social change at different levels of the social order are presented in Table 10.1.) This raises the question of whether social change is always occurring everywhere, that is, whether social change is universal.

Is Social Change Universal?   It would seem that ever since the industrial revolution about three centuries ago social change has been occurring throughout the world. For thousands of years people had lived in simpler societies that might or might not have been experiencing social change as a consequence of such processes as population growth, factional conflict, war, and disease. But with

TABLE 10.1	Examples of Effects of Social Change		
		TRIBAL SOCIETY (THE EBRIÉ)	**METROPOLITAN SOCIETY (THE UNITED STATES)**
MACRO-LEVEL CHANGES	Population growth	Creates new markets for Ebrié real estate; adds newcomers to villages.	Causes new conflicts and need for social control in increasingly congested regions.
	Globalization: economic and cultural	Gives tribe members jobs at branches of multinational companies; threatens forests and waters if environmental controls are not established.	Encourages manufacturing concerns to move their production overseas; forces people to find more jobs in services and high-tech manufacturing.
MIDDLE-LEVEL CHANGES	Urbanization	Surrounds villages with new neighborhoods and nontribal strangers.	Enmeshes most residents in metropolitan regions, where their community boundaries are blurred and diversity becomes an issue.
	Increased crime	Causes villagers to distrust strangers.	Engenders efforts to control crime and encourages privatization.
MICRO-LEVEL CHANGES	Rising material expectations	Leads village women to rebel against polygyny.	Pushes more women into the labor force, creating the need for child care.
	Changing norms of conduct	Creates a sense of anomie, confusion over expectations.	Increases level of conflict in communities over sexuality, public conduct, and the like.

the advent of industrialization, urbanization, colonial conquest, and global warfare, all the societies of the earth were increasingly brought into what sociologist Immanuel Wallerstein (1974) has called the capitalist world system. Trade and markets, often dominated by the more powerful nations, enmesh all the world's people in a network of relationships and interdependencies that make self-sufficiency and social equilibrium ever more difficult to attain. As we have noted in earlier chapters, perhaps no change in human history has been as far-reaching and universal in its consequences as the transition from an agrarian to an urban, industrial way of life brought about by the industrial revolution. In sum, social change may be more or less rapid in different societies and in different parts of the world, but the forces of global social change are felt everywhere. Thus, at least in our own era, it can be said that social change is universal.

Is Social Change Progress?   Those who promote social change of one kind or another often equate change with progress, but in fact much social change is extremely difficult and disruptive for the people who live through it. "Progress" is defined differently, depending on the values of those who are trying to assess whether a particular change constitutes progress (Harper, 1993). In

some instances social change has positive consequences for many people, and perhaps even for an entire society. Fifty years ago, for example, the United States was a highly segregated society, unable to claim that it was realizing the democratic vision of its founders. Today, after decades of struggle, many aspects of segregation remain, but many of the worst aspects of racism have been reduced or eliminated through protest, compromise, new laws, and other forms of social change. However, for every instance of positive social change, there will be others that people do not agree on or that are seen as negative or too complicated to assess. When factories close and communities lose vital jobs, that is a form of social change that most people in the affected communities do not think of as progress. Yet when the same jobs become available in Mexico, people there rejoice at their good fortune. Similarly, when political leaders persuade local police forces to protect the rights of homosexuals, gay people may feel that progress has been made. Yet in the same communities there will be conservative residents who wish to return to a past in which homosexuals were considered sinners who did not deserve equal rights. On the world scene, the vast majority of people in the former Soviet empire regard the fall of Stalinist communism as progressive social change. But the people of

Bosnia, caught in a bloody conflict that erupted in the power vacuum left by the end of communist rule, are not at all sure that they are witnessing progress.

Can We Control Social Change? The examples of the Bosnian conflict and changing race relations in the United States raise a fundamental question about social change: Is it something we can control intentionally, or is it a result of powerful social forces that are beyond our ability to shape or modify? The answer is that some social change is intentional and some is far beyond our power to control. In a society governed by laws and democratic processes it appears possible to reduce injustice and even to reduce some of the worst forms of inequality. But global forces of social and economic change are extremely difficult to shape even if we can learn to accommodate and adjust to them (Etzkowitz & Glassman, 1991).

Even when we engage in intentional social change, the results are often surprising and unanticipated. Before legislation creating the Social Security and Medicare systems was enacted, the elderly experienced extremely high rates of poverty and untreated illness. These intentional and hotly debated programs changed that situation dramatically. However, it is impossible to control the rapid rise in the number of elderly people who will be covered by these programs in coming decades. This threat to the financial stability of the system may result in a weakening of the scope of Social Security and Medicare coverage in the future.

Can Social Change Be Predicted? Social science has had mixed success in predicting social change. The master trends of our era, such as economic globalization, population growth, urbanization, technological change, and the rising expectations of oppressed people, are well known. Their consequences can be understood and predicted, to a degree. Demographers can predict with reasonable certainty the major population trends that will affect societies over a 20- or 30-year period. Survey researchers can predict the outcomes of election campaigns or referenda on major social issues like immigration or crime. But we have limited ability to predict technological changes or to anticipate the outbreak of wars or the appearance of new social movements. Yet these are some of the most important sources of social change. In fact, one difference between the "pop" sociology books sold in supermarkets and the sociological research conducted at universities is the caution with which the university researchers discuss social change.

Sociological researchers usually make projections based on current trends, with carefully stated assumptions about what will happen if those trends continue into the future. For example, we know that as members of the huge baby boom cohort of the U.S. population grow older and face death, the media will pay more attention to issues involving aging, death, and dying, just as they paid more attention to issues such as day care when the baby boomers

were forming families. But other aspects of social change, especially those due to technological innovations, are far more difficult to predict. We have difficulty predicting their appearance and limited success predicting their consequences.

Consider an example. For decades sociological writers who produce forecasts for popular media have been predicting that computers and telecommunications networks would spell the end of the central city as a place of work and entertainment for masses of people (Naisbitt & Aburdene, 1990; Toffler, 1970). However, research exploring this prediction shows that the new technologies have very mixed consequences for urban downtown areas. In large cities like Los Angeles, Chicago, New York, and Baltimore, there is an unpredicted renaissance of central-city business and entertainment and an explosion of new small businesses, often based on applications of computer and communications technologies. But it is also true that the new communications technologies make it easier for employers in the information industries to distribute work among employees at many different locations. Hence, the future of central cities as employment-generating environments is extremely difficult to predict.

In sum, there are major trends that we can study and use to predict some important aspects of continuing social change, but there are others that are far beyond the power of any social scientist to actually predict. The sudden breakup of the Soviet empire, the outbreak of war in the Balkans, the dramatic changes in U.S. social policies after the conservative sweep of the 1994 congressional elections—none of these events was actually predicted, even though there were some indications that they might occur.

TWO FORCES OF SOCIAL CHANGE

War and modernization are among the most powerful and pervasive forces that produce social change at every level of social life. Of course, as we have noted, social change is caused by many other social forces, especially technological innovation and population growth or mobility—but we will see in this section that war and modernization also stimulate these other forces of change. Many of the most significant technological innovations we have experienced in this century were developed in response to the crisis of war. And many of the greatest movements of people over the planet were first set in motion by the disruptions caused by warfare or modernization (Chirot, 1986, 1994a, 1994b; Janowitz, 1978).

WAR AND CONQUEST
War is among the greatest and certainly the most violent of the forces that produce social change. Ironically, the deadliest forms of warfare are associated with the rise of

modern civilizations. As societies have become more advanced in their command of technology and their social organization, the devastation caused by war has increased. The wars fought by so-called primitive societies were frequently ritual affairs; the combatants often withdrew from the field after a single skirmish. Although not all preindustrial warfare was so ritualistic, relatively few combatants were killed because the technologies for killing were so limited compared with those available today.

In the Middle Ages, often viewed as a warlike time owing to the influence of knights and Crusaders, the rate of fatalities among warriors in battle was about 2 percent. In contrast, in World War I the proportion was 40 percent. Modern warfare is increasingly dangerous not only for the combatants but for civilians as well. In World War I about half of those who died were civilians, but in the Vietnam War the toll rose to more than 75 percent (Galtung, 1985; McNeill, 1982).

Any evaluation of the place of war in social change must consider three broad questions. First, what are the ecological effects of war on human populations? Second, how do wars help shape the consciousness and culture of a people? Third, how does war change the institutions of societies?

The Ecological Impact of War. Casualties and conquest are the major ecological effects of war. People all over the world were shocked by televised scenes of oil fires and polluted coastlines during the 1991 Persian Gulf War, but the most significant ecological impacts of the Gulf War were felt by human populations. Like an epidemic of cholera or bubonic plague, war accounts for extraordinary and rapid declines in population. Pitirim Sorokin (1937) estimated that between A.D. 1100 and 1925 about 35.5 million people died in European wars alone. World War I claimed the lives of about 8.4 million soldiers and about 1.4 million civilians, and in World War II about 17 million military personnel and about 34 million civilians died. It is estimated that the Soviet Union lost about 15 million people during World War II and that in China about 22 million perished. Germany lost 3.7 million, Japan about 2.2 million, and the United States slightly under 300,000 (Beer, 1981).

When millions of soldiers are killed, entire populations are unbalanced for more than a generation. Many women remain single or become widows and either do not have children or raise children alone. The effect may be to reduce population pressure on food and other resources, but at the same time there are labor shortages and economic disarray due to the loss of so many skilled workers.

War also results in large-scale shifts in population and rapid acceleration of economic change. For example, the western parts of the United States and Canada experienced their most rapid growth as a result of mobilization for war during the first half of this century. New dams, new electric power plants, new factories to produce all kinds of goods were built. San Diego, Los Angeles, San Francisco, Portland, Seattle, and Vancouver all experienced massive population growth, as did many inland centers of industry and agriculture. The end of the war saw continued growth in the western states as young families who had come west during the war decided to settle there permanently.

Early in 1941, this was unused land at the tip of Los Angeles Harbor. As a result of full-scale mobilization for World War II production, entire metropolitan regions were transformed into massive industrial production centers like the one shown here.

For the losers in war, the ecological consequences of defeat are usually far more dramatic. Population loss, economic subjugation, the imposition of a foreign language and culture, and forced movement to new towns and industrial areas are common. During more than a century of genocidal wars waged by whites against Native Americans in the nineteenth and early twentieth centuries the consequences for the losers were death, expulsion, and banishment to reservations. For tribal peoples of Africa, invasion, war, and conquest led to colonial rule and rapid social change, often imposed through taxation, labor gangs, military draft, and similar means. In areas of the world that are torn by war today, such as the former states of Yugoslavia (especially Bosnia) and African countries like Rwanda, Burundi, Somalia, and Liberia, war has brought genocidal ethnic conflicts, mass expulsions ("ethnic cleansing"), and years of abject poverty in squalid refugee camps.

The Cultural Impact of War. War changes a society's culture by stamping the memories of chaos and cruelty, heroism and camaraderie on entire generations. Years after a major war its effects on values and norms continue to be felt (Schuman & Scott, 1989). One need only think of the impact of the American Civil War on the former Confederate states, an impact that remains strong today and can be seen in Civil War memorials, rebel yells, the conduct of interracial relations, and North–South animosities. Recent sociological research shows that even for generations that did not experience war firsthand, the memory or threat of warfare is perceived as extremely important. Table 10.2 shows that people will cite specific wars first among "national events or changes that seem especially important to you"—even if they themselves were not alive during the wars they mention.

The impact of a major war can also be seen in the damage done to the minds and bodies of the survivors. In addition to the thousands who have been maimed and mutilated, thousands more suffer from post-traumatic stress disorder, in which the shock of war continues to haunt the victim; others experience survivor guilt, the feeling of shame that many survivors feel because they escaped the fate of their comrades. These effects, which occur at the micro level of interpersonal relations, have been described by the Italian social observer Primo Levi, who was imprisoned at Auschwitz and liberated by Russian soldiers. When the soldiers encountered the piles of dead and the groans of the dying, Levi reports, they felt shame: "They did not greet us, nor smile; they seemed oppressed. . . . It was the shame which the just man experiences when confronted by a crime committed by another, and he feels remorse because of its existence" (1989, p. 72).

This kind of shame and guilt pervades a culture that has been torn by war. People feel that those who died were the best, the most valorous of society's members. Levi describes the shame he felt at the deaths of Chaim, a watchmaker who tried to teach him how to survive in the camp, and Szabo, a tall, silent Hungarian peasant who needed more food than others yet never failed to help his weaker companions. He tells of his guilt over the fact that Robert, a professor at the Sorbonne, died even though he "spread courage and trust all around him," and that Baruch, a longshoreman from Livorno, died on the first day because he hit back when the guards beat him. "These, and innumerable others, died not despite their valor but because of it" (p. 83).

At the macro level, wars change entire cultures by increasing contacts between different cultures. In the case of

			AGE			
EVENT/CHANGE	**18–29**	**30–39**	**40–49**	**50–59**	**60–69**	**70 PLUS**
World War II (265)	14	16	24	29	30	23
Vietnam (144)	18	18	13	2	4	1
Space exploration (93)	8	6	8	10	6	8
Kennedy assassination (62)	3	8	10	3	1	1
Civil rights (77)	7	7	5	7	6	3
Nuclear war, threat of (55)	6	5	6	4	2	3
Communication/transportation (46)	1	4	4	5	3	9
Depression (43)	3	3	2	5	7	13
Computers (23)	2	1	2	3	2	0
Terrorism (43)	4	2	0	1	1	0
Moral decline (28)	2	2	2	2	4	1
Women's rights (20)	1	2	3	0	2	1
Other event/change (357)	30	26	22	29	33	37
	100	100	100	100	100	100
	(289)	(312)	(200)	(167)	(165)	(110)

TABLE 10.2   U.S. Respondents' Rank Ordering of Important Events as They Perceive Them

Source: Schuman & Scott, 1989.

During World War II, American GIs brought their culture to places throughout the world where they lived and fought. Here the orchestra of the First Cavalry Division takes time out for a jam session on Los Negros Island.

modern nations like Japan, Italy, Germany, and Korea, all of which have experienced military occupation by foreign powers, the cultural consequences include the acculturation of new norms and behaviors. For example, baseball was introduced to Japan by U.S. occupation troops after World War II and is now that nation's most popular spectator sport. Indeed, the influence of North American culture, conveyed through movies, sports, consumer goods, and language, spread rapidly throughout Southeast Asia as a result of World War II and its lingering political consequences.

War's Impact on Social Institutions.   The structure of a society, especially its major social institutions, may be drastically changed by war and preparation for war. The mobilization of large numbers of people and the marshaling of new technologies for military purposes have a centralizing effect on social institutions. In the United States, for example, the growth of large research universities in the 1960s was accelerated by huge investments in applied science and technology after the Soviet Union became the first nation to launch a space satellite. Universities that were capable of developing new science programs grew rapidly, and their administrations gained greater power. The power and influence of the national government has also grown, often at the expense of local governmental institutions, as a consequence of the two world wars and the arms race. Providing for national defense is extremely expensive and requires that the central government be granted increased taxing powers.

The French sociologist Raymond Aron (1955) has called the twentieth century "the century of total war" because of the capacity of warfare to shape the destiny of entire regions and because of the unprecedented power of nuclear and other weapons. Aron's phrase also captures the transforming power of modern war, its ability to alter societies. In the United States, for example, there is no doubt that the mobilization necessary to fight two world wars, major regional wars in Korea and Vietnam, and innumerable smaller skirmishes in Africa, Latin America, and Asia contributed to the controversial growth of the federal government during this century. The impetus for creating many of the institutions of the welfare state, such as Aid to Families with Dependent Children, was the need to care for war widows and their children. And the massive growth of the federal budget deficit is attributable in large measure to the expenditure of billions of dollars on military institutions since midcentury (Galbraith, 1995).

Elsewhere in the world, the dominance of military institutions and the fragility of legal and governmental institutions produce "garrison states" in which economic growth and the rule of law are subordinated to the needs of the military (Lasswell, 1941). The end of the cold war has led to political instability in middle Europe and in many areas once dominated by the former Soviet Union, but it has also caused unprecedented economic and social changes in Western Europe. Political instability in many regions of the world is used to justify continued military spending; in the United States, military spending still exceeds $250 billion annually even while other public spending is being drastically reduced. Environmentalists and other opponents of high levels of military expenditures argue that individuals cannot comprehend the magnitude of military spending unless it is presented in terms of trade-offs indicating what alternative social choices would cost. Table 10.3 presents some examples of such trade-offs.

MODERNIZATION

A second major source of social change is the set of trends that are collectively known as **modernization.** This term encompasses all the changes that societies and individuals experience as a result of industrialization, urbanization, and the development of nation-states. These processes occurred during a period of two or more centuries in the Western nations and Japan, but they are taking place at a far more rapid rate in the former colonial societies that are today's new nations.

The term *modernization* should be used cautiously, in its sociological sense rather than as a value judgment about different societies. It does not mean that we can judge life in modern societies as better or more satisfactory

or more humane than life was for people in societies like the one the Ebrié once knew. As noted earlier, modern societies have developed the capacity to cause more destruction and human suffering than any simpler society could possibly have caused. And we have seen in other chapters that many of the advantages enjoyed by the most modern nations have come at a high cost to simpler, less modern societies.

The concept of modernization does not assume that change is irreversible. For example, the rise of nation-states throughout the world during the past few centuries does not imply the end of loyalties based on a sense of "peoplehood" that conflict with the sense of shared citizenship in a nation (see Chapter 4). The bloodshed in the former Yugoslavia and in many places on the African continent, or in the former Soviet Union, bears heartrending witness to the strength of feelings about peoplehood as opposed to loyalty to the modern nation-state with its laws and governments.

Nevertheless, the term *modernization* summarizes most of the major changes, for better or worse, that societies throughout the world are experiencing, albeit at differing rates and with varying amounts of social disruption.

TABLE 10.3	Trade-Offs Between Military and Social or Environmental Priorities	
MILITARY PRIORITY	**COST**	**SOCIAL/ENVIRONMENTAL PRIORITY**
Trident II submarine and F-18 jet fighter programs	$100,000,000,000	Estimated cost of cleaning up the 10,000 worst hazardous waste dumps in the United States
Stealth bomber program	$68,000,000,000	Two thirds of estimated costs to meet U.S. clean water goals by the year 2000
2 weeks of world military expenditure	$30,000,000,000	Annual cost of the proposed UN Water and Sanitation Decade
3 days of global military spending	$6,500,000,000	Cost to fund Tropical Forest Action Plan over 5 years
Development cost for Midgetman ICBM	$6,000,000,000	Annual cost to cut sulfur dioxide emissions by 8–12 million tons/year in the United States to combat acid rain
2 days of global military spending	$4,800,000,000	Annual cost of proposed UN Action Plan to halt Third World desertification, over 20 years
10 days of European Economic Community military spending	$2,000,000,000	Annual cost to clean up hazardous waste sites in 10 European Economic Community countries by the year 2000
1 Trident submarine	$1,400,000,000	Global 5-year child immunization program against 6 deadly diseases, preventing 1 million deaths a year
2 months of Ethiopian military spending	$50,000,000	Annual cost of proposed U.N. Anti-Desertification Plan for Ethiopia
1 nuclear weapon test	$12,000,000	Cost for installation of 80,000 hand pumps to give Third World villages access to safe water
1-hour operating cost, B-1B bomber	$21,000	Cost of community-based maternal health care in 10 African villages for 10 years

Source: Adapted from Renner, 1989.

THEN AND NOW

TWO IMAGES OF THE WARRIOR

When the Plains Indians and the U.S. Cavalry fought bloody battles during the period of westward expansion in the nineteenth century, warfare was brutal and deadly, especially for the less well-equipped Indian warriors. But as deadly as it was, war was not nearly as devastating for noncombatant populations as it is today. A century ago warfare required guns and bayonets, cannons, and a great deal of organization and logistical support, but it did not involve sophisticated technologies like those represented by the modern fighter or bomber plane. As combat has become less a matter of brute force and more dependent on brains and technology, the possibility that well-trained women can compete as warriors has become a reality. This is a change in the conduct of war that would have been inconceivable to General Custer or Sitting Bull.

Neil Smelser (1966) associates modernization with the following set of changes:

1. *In the realm of technology,* a developing society is changing from simple and traditionalized techniques toward the application of scientific knowledge.

2. *In agriculture,* the developing society evolves from subsistence farming toward the commercial production of agricultural goods. This means specialization in cash crops, purchase of nonagricultural products in the market, and often agricultural wage labor.

3. *In industry,* the developing society undergoes a transition from the use of human and animal power toward industrialization proper, or men working for wages at power-driven machines, which produce commodities marketed outside the community of production.

4. *In ecological arrangements,* the developing society moves from the farm and village toward urban concentrations. (pp. 110–111; emphasis added)

These processes can take place simultaneously, but this is not always the case. Many societies mechanize their agriculture and begin to produce cash crops for foreign markets before their cities and urban forms of employment have begun to grow rapidly. This was the case, for example, in Sri Lanka (formerly Ceylon), Indonesia, and many of the newer African nations.

Smelser and others who study modernization have shown that "technical, economic, and ecological changes ramify through the whole social and cultural fabric" (1966, p. 111). In the political sphere of life, we see the authority systems of the village giving way to domination by the institutions of nation-states. In the area of education, as societies attempt to produce workers who can meet the needs of new industries, new educational institutions are established. In the area of religion, there is a decrease in the strength of organized religions. Families change as traditional extended families adapt to new economic institutions that demand greater mobility.

Patterns of inequality in societies also change. Older patterns of gender inequality are modified (and often replaced by new forms of inequality) as women are in greater demand to fill positions in new economic institutions. And the emergence of a new class, the wage workers, increases the power of the common people, usually adding to their determination to become better educated and to participate more fully in political life. None of these changes is inevitable or irreversible; workers, for example, may see their unions "busted" in times of recession or economic change. But in the long run all of these trends are likely to appear in a modernizing society.

Modernity, Technology, and "Cultural Lag."

The central part that technology plays in modern societies has led some sociologists to view it as a basic principle of social change. The classic statement of this view is that of William Fielding Ogburn (1942). Ogburn hypothesized that inventions affect the size of populations, which in turn influences the course of history. (For example, overpopulation often leads to wars and migrations.) Some inventions affect population directly: Improvements in sanitation, the development of cures for fatal illnesses, and more effective contraceptive techniques are examples. But inventions can also have indirect effects on population. For example, techniques that improve crop yields or permit long-term storage of food surpluses make it possible to support a larger population with a given amount of farm land. And improvements in military technology (e.g., the use of horses in warfare, the invention of gunpowder, and the development of the armored tank) have had dramatic effects on the conduct of war and hence on population size.

Ogburn also proposed the theory known as **cultural lag.** In his words, "A cultural lag occurs when one of two parts of culture which are correlated changes before or in greater degree than the other part does, thereby causing less adjustment between the two parts than existed previously" (1957, p. 167). This theory is most often applied to the adaptation of social institutions to changing technologies. For example, the industrial revolution gave birth to many kinds of machines, often with moving parts that made them dangerous to use. The rates of injury and death resulting from industrial accidents climbed rapidly in the decades following the introduction of the new machines to the United States around 1870. Such accidents spelled disaster for workers and their families, since it was hard to prove that the employer was responsible for the accident. It was not until around 1910 that the concepts of employer liability and workers' compensation were adopted, a lag of about 40 years.

One problem with the cultural lag theory is that it fails to account for the effects of social power. For example,

This Mexican woman is a descendant of the ancient Maya. In her village, Amatenango del Valle, the women make pottery for export to nearby towns and cities. Her child stands a far better chance of growing up to adulthood as a result of modern public health and sanitation practices.

workers who sought compensation for the costs of industrial accidents did not have nearly as much power as the owners of the machines. When this power imbalance changed as a result of the labor movement, it became possible to enact legislation that would protect the workers.

The Postmodernist Critique.   For more than two centuries the forces of modernity have been changing societies throughout the world. In fact, all species of life on the earth are affected by these broad-ranging changes in the way humans exist. It is not surprising, then, that the forces of modernity also stimulate a wide variety of countertrends and reactions. The desire for gender and racial equality that accompanies modernity is countered by antifeminist and racial supremacy movements. The increasing influence of scientific thought is countered by revivals of fundamentalist religious beliefs and opposition to scientific education. The demand by some Christian conservative groups that public schools teach an anti-Darwinian view of creation, sometimes called "creation science," is an example of this trend in the United States.

Many other social movements are direct attacks on modernity itself or on specific aspects of modern thought.

According to theories of post-modernity, styles of dress and grooming and preferences for particular lifestyles and tastes in music will become ever more diverse. At the same time, there will be less and less consensus on what the norms of society should be.

One of those aspects is *rationality*, which Max Weber viewed as a central principle of modernity (see Chapter 6). When applied to economic and governmental affairs, rationality fosters the development of bureaucracies, which, at least in principle, apply rational codes and regulations to the conduct of their affairs. The modern emphasis on rationality in scientific thought has been accompanied by an increase in *secularism*—separation of church and state, abolishment of state religions, and protection of free speech (including agnosticism and atheism). However, many critics point out that along with the bounty provided by scientific rationality have come the destructiveness of the nuclear age and the erosion of religious and ethical values.

In recent decades the critique of modernity in the older developed nations has given rise to a diffuse school of thought known as *postmodernism* (Foucault, 1973, 1984; Lash, 1992). Postmodernism can be defined as a critique of modern societies and cultures. It argues that science, rationality, and all the "isms" of the modern world—capitalism, socialism, behaviorism, to name only a few—deprive human lives of spirituality, mystery, myth, and diversity of expression. Modern economic institutions transform popular forms of music and art into mass-produced products. Postmodernist critics also believe that the major institutions of modern societies, including markets, laboratories, clinics, the military, and other bureaucratically controlled administrations, have become instruments of social control by powerful elites (Harper, 1993). According to postmodernist theories (which in some ways resemble New Age ideas), this control is weakening as people feel increasingly estranged from modern institutions and turn to new expressions of fantasy, myth, sexuality, and styles of dress and architecture. In health care, for example, disillusionment with some aspects of modern medicine leads people to try a wide range of alternatives, such as folk healing, holistic medical practices, and remedies that have not been scientifically tested (Deierlein, 1994).

Postmodernism remains influential as a critique of modernity and an explanation for the proliferation of often zany styles and behaviors in today's world. It is especially popular in academic circles, but aside from stimulating the development of some new cultural products (e.g., the movie *Smoke*) it has not had any perceptible influence on modern corporations or other bureaucracies. The postmodernist critique is an important reminder that modernization has many negative effects, but it has not stimulated social movements that seriously challenge the growing influence of modern social institutions such as global corporations. The same cannot be said for other antimodernist cultural movements, such as fundamentalism, as we will see shortly.

Modernization in the Developing Nations.
Social scientists often use the term *Third World* to refer to nations that have won independence from colonial domi-

nance in the decades since World War II. If the "first world" is that of the capitalist nation-states and the "second world" that of the former communist nations, the Third World nations are those that are not aligned with either of these "worlds" but are united in their need to survive in an environment dominated by more politically or economically powerful nations.

But the term *Third World* can be misleading, since in the past 30 years many of these nations have made strides toward modernity. Moreover, trends in global social and economic change have produced impoverished areas—sometimes called the "fourth world"—in affluent nations where illegal immigrants or stigmatized minorities work under conditions similar to those found elsewhere in the Third World (Sassen, 1991). For this reason, we prefer to use the term *developing nations* or *modernizing nations*. A **developing nation** is one that is undergoing a set of transformations whose effect is to increase the productivity of its people, their health, their literacy, and their ability to participate in political decision making. These transformations occur at different rates in different nations. Such differences are evident when we compare nations like Mexico and Brazil, which are industrializing rapidly, with nations like Chad and Mali in the interior of Africa, which are hav-

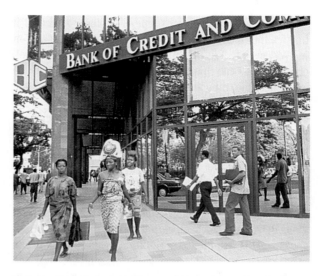

This photo of modern Abidjan could have been taken in the capital city of almost any African nation. The contrast between modern and traditional ways of life and the overwhelming influence of Western economic institutions, such as banks, are visible everywhere.

ing far more trouble achieving the hallmarks of modernization (see Table 10. 4).

TABLE 10.4	Indicators of Social Change in Selected Nations									
	BOLIVIA	**CHILE**	**CUBA**	**EGYPT**	**EL SALVADOR**	**INDIA**	**MEXICO**	**PAKISTAN**	**TURKEY**	**UNITED STATES**
Percentage of population living in urban areas	57.7	85.3	72.8	43.9	50.0	25.7	71.3	32.0	59.0	75.6
Percentage of population literate	77.5	93.4	96.0	48.4	73.0	52.1	85.9	35.0	79.2	95.5
Daily per capita caloric intake	2,013	2,484	3,129	3,310	2,152	2,229	3,062	2,280	3,196	3,642
Daily newspaper circulation per 1,000 population	55	63	124	62	48	21	142	6	71	243
Energy consumption per capita (coal equivalent, in kilograms)	—	1,305	1,152	704	—	350	1,891	299	1,045	10,737
Military expenditure as percentage of GDP	2.4	3.4	4.2	6.0	2.9	2.7	0.4	6.1	5.4	4.9
Percentage of population under age 15	41.2	30.6	23.3	38.7	43.0	36.0	29.6	46.3	35.0	21.9
Life expectancy at birth (years), male	60.3	68.5	73.9	65.0	63.0	60.4	65.6	59.3	69.0	72.3
Life expectancy at birth (years), female	65.3	75.6	77.6	69.3	68.0	61.2	73.4	60.7	73.0	79.0

Source: Data from *Britannica Book of the Year,* 1995; *Statistical Abstract,* 1995.

The theory of modernization as we have described it implies that modernization will occur in a similar fashion in every society. But the differing experiences of the developing nations call this view into question. Not only do we often see the industrialization of agriculture (i.e., the growth of huge mechanized farms) without the rise of industrial cities, or the growth of cities without a decline in the strength of organized religions or the emergence of modern educational institutions, but we also see the rise of antimodernist social movements in some of these nations (Germani, 1973). Events in the Islamic world are a case in point. In Algeria, Pakistan, Iran, Saudi Arabia, Libya, the Sudan, and other Islamic nations, a fundamentalist religious movement has been gaining strength in the past two decades. This resurgence of traditional Islamic beliefs and practices denies that modernization must be accompanied by the rejection of religious faith, by the separation of religion and government, or by more democratic political participation. These and other aspects of the Western version of modernity are being strongly challenged by the Islamic fundamentalist movement.

Studies of these antimodernist movements are being conducted throughout the world. For example, in her studies of Algerian women confronting the antimodernist movement sweeping through the Arab nations, the Algerian American sociologist Marnia Lazreg (1994) has found that these movements are misnamed. In reality, she concludes, they are actually radical attempts to seize political power in which the movement's leaders use the religious fervor of the masses to achieve their goal.

The rise of antimodernist movements is not limited to the Islamic nations. Similar movements can be seen in the United States. Conservative groups plead for a return to more traditional values, and some radical groups advocate a return to self-sufficient communities that would engage in farming on a small scale. The effects of such movements on a society's institutions show that modernization does not necessarily follow a single direction or imply a single set of changes (e.g., the decline of religious faith, the rise of science, or the growth of industrial cities).

Another challenge to this view of modernization is posed by the fact that the world's resources of raw materials, water, and energy are far less plentiful than they once were. Today there are serious doubts about whether those resources are adequate to permit the poor nations to become developed to anywhere near the extent that the Western nations have, or whether the rich nations can continue to grow as they have in the past.

Modernization and Dependency. Some sociologists argue that the development of the more advanced modern nations actually impedes development in the newer nations, or at least channels it in directions that are not always beneficial. In a general statement of this theory, André Gunder Frank (1966) questions the idea that the less developed societies are merely at an earlier stage of modernization than the advanced nations. He cites the development of one-crop economies in many parts of Latin America as evidence of how social forces in the developed nations actually transform the tropical countryside. According to Frank, when peasants give up subsistence agriculture and trading in local markets because their land has been absorbed into huge banana or coffee plantations, the result is a form of underdevelopment that did not exist before, one in which the peasantry is transformed into a class of landless rural laborers.

Immanuel Wallerstein (1974) has proposed a more general theory that he calls *world system theory*. In this theory he divides the world into core states, semiperipheral areas, and peripheral areas. The **core states** include the United States, England, France, Russia, Germany, and Japan—which are the most technologically advanced nations and which dominate the banking and financial functions of the world economy. The **semiperipheral areas** are places like Spain and Portugal, the oil-producing nations of the Middle East, and Brazil and Mexico. In these areas industry and financial institutions are developed to some extent, but they remain dependent on capital and technology provided by the core states. The **peripheral areas** include much of Africa, Asia, and Latin America. They supply basic resources and labor power to the core states and the semiperipheral areas. This world system, Wallerstein asserts, is based on various forms of economic domination and does not require political repression as well.

Wallerstein's theory has the drawback of suggesting that the so-called core states do not include any areas of production that may resemble the peripheral, dependent regions more than they do the fully modernized nations. There is evidence that even the most modern nations contain such regions. For example, in a study of sharecropping in California, Miriam Wells (1984) showed that large California berry growers have been dividing their land into small plots and renting them to low-income farm laborers. Wells contends that the growers have adopted this strategy as a means of avoiding the higher costs of unionized farm labor. "The sharecropper is responsible for maintaining the plots, for harvesting and packing the fruit, and for hiring and paying whatever labor is necessary to accomplish these tasks" (p. 17). In return, the sharecropper receives from 50 to 55 percent of the proceeds minus the costs of handling, loading, hauling, and marketing the crop. Wells points out that modernization theory views sharecropping as an obsolete form of production, yet it can reappear even in the most advanced societies under certain conditions, such as lack of machinery for harvesting. Once again, therefore, we see that modernization is not a unilinear process with inevitable outcomes for every society or nation. People in all societies, including our own, experience social change in an infinite number of ways, as we will see in the next section.

SOCIAL CHANGE IN EVERYDAY LIFE

People often experience social change as highly problematic, and they often blame themselves for not coping with it more effectively. But as we saw in Chapter 1, the sociological imagination requires that we ask how our own troubles are related to larger social forces. And we have seen that modernity brings with it many contradictions. In seeking new opportunities in education, leisure pursuits, intimate relationships, and political participation, we also create new problems for ourselves. Thus, according to social theorist Ralf Dahrendorf (1981), "anomie has become an element of the lives of many and notably of those who are still on the way to becoming full members of their societies" (p. 42). The Ebrié felt such anomie when their peaceful habit of sleeping outside their houses was shattered by a robbery. But in many parts of the world the experience of anomie is even stronger and has stimulated some creative responses, as can be seen in Box 10.1.

BOX 10.1   GLOBAL SOCIAL CHANGE

Singing Out Against Anomie

Bruce Springsteen sings about the feelings of loss that people experience when their factories are torn down. The murdered singer Selena captured the hearts of millions by singing popular Tejano songs that described her people's trials in coping with new social and economic conditions along the rapidly industrializing Texas-Mexico border. And now Susan Aglukark, a popular Eskimo singer from the frozen shores of Hudson Bay, has become the first of her people ever to sign a major recording contract. EMI Music Canada has signed her to produce more of her haunting songs about the struggle of aboriginal people in the Eskimo-controlled region of Nunavut, which extends well above the Arctic Circle in the Northwest Territories.

Aglukark's Inuit or Eskimo name is Uuliniq, which means "scarred from burns." Although she is not literally scarred—the name is purely symbolic—the same symbolic name could easily be applied to all of Canada's 35,000 Eskimo people. Like people living at the edges of industrialization and urbanization throughout the world, they have experienced severe disruptions in their traditional way of life. They can no longer maintain their existence as a hunting-and-gathering people, not only because of depleted supplies of game but also owing to the far-reaching effects of changing lifestyles and technologies. For example, their need for gasoline to power generators and snowmobiles and for televisions and prepared foods like coffee and sugar makes it impossible for them to maintain their traditional culture.

As a result of these social changes, many of Aglukark's people are experiencing anomie or normlessness. Caught between the modern and the traditional, not knowing how to find work or where to go for advice, they often turn to alcohol and drugs, become angry and abusive, or even commit suicide. Aglukark's music has elements of rock and country gospel, but the words may deal with subjects such as a girlhood friend who has taken her own life. She hopes that her songs will help young people everywhere deal with the feelings that lead them to despair and sometimes to suicide. Since this is a particular problem in aboriginal communities, she is concerned with showing her people that "life is the most beautiful thing."

Susan Aglukark is proud to be identified with the newly formed Eskimo region of Nunavut. She notes that the effort to cope with change has challenged her people for many generations. "The trouble was in the past, it was forced on us. At least now we may have some control over our future" (quoted in Farnsworth, 1994, p. A4).

THE
PERSONAL CHALLENGE
Social Change and "Designer Death"

A key feature of social change is that it tends to make choices available that people in traditional societies never dreamed of. Cosmetic surgery allows one to straighten out a nose or lift a sagging jowl. Pension plans and Social Security allow people to embark on new activities like photography or ballroom dancing at an age when their parents would more likely have been rocking quietly on the porch. Sexuality, political beliefs, styles of dress, and tastes in entertainment all present more choices and possibilities than ever before. In fact, the array of choices can become confusing and controversial as traditional norms are challenged by new possibilities.

Death provides an example of how changing norms and new choices may affect your life. Will you choose interment or cremation? If you opt for cremation, will your ashes be scattered or will they be buried under a headstone? For the past 30 years sociologists have been charting the growing diversity of death rituals and the decreasing uniformity of the norms governing this final rite of passage (Blumer, 1968; Pine, 1975). But just because norms are no longer uniform and there are more choices does not mean that people are happy about the situation. Freedom is often accompanied by controversy, and families may fight bitterly over whether to carry out the wishes of departed loved ones that deviate from their own expectations about death.

When evolving norms include the option of actually *choosing* to die, controversy arises over one of the most central social norms of all: In the major religions of the Judeo-Christian world, the commandment "Thou shalt not kill" is generally interpreted as applying to suicide as well as homicide. Yet the timing and method of one's own death are increasingly subject to personal choice. To recognize this trend is not to condone suicide or euthanasia; there is a great deal of moral debate over these issues. Nevertheless, more and more people in advanced societies like the United States and Canada are being forced to make hard choices about their own deaths. For instance, because medical technologies make it possible to prolong life even after the individual no longer feels alive or would wish to continue living, many people are choosing to make their wishes known through living wills that instruct medical personnel not to use resuscitation procedures in cases of terminal illness (Barry, 1994; Cantor, 1993).

The most controversial choice of all is the choice to terminate one's life voluntarily. This area of medical ethics has been brought forcefully to our attention by Dr. Jack Kevorkian, the notorious "death doctor" whose "assisted suicides" make front-page news. Is Kevorkian a villain challenging long-established tradition and religious practice, or a courageous pioneer pointing to a future in which one will be free to choose one's own time and method of death? How we answer this question will depend on our own values and on the strength of the norms in our families and communities.

From a sociological viewpoint, Kevorkian's grim example and all the other new choices we face in dealing with death represent yet another set of norms that are being challenged, for better or worse, in the rapidly changing modern world. The sociologist's role is to chart these changes and try to understand how people are coping with the confusion and the possibilities they present.

Like most social theorists, Dahrendorf does not believe that we can or should attempt to reverse the course of modernization. Instead, he suggests, we need "flexible institutions, capable of adjustment without disruption" (p. 163). We are far from achieving such flexibility, however. When we look at the range of problems we encounter in our daily lives, we can readily see how much more change is needed. To appreciate this point more fully, it will be helpful to review some of the dilemmas of modern life that result from rapid social change. These and related topics will be discussed in more detail in later chapters.

GENDER ROLES AND THE FAMILY

Clearly, one of the most significant social changes in Western societies in the past quarter century has been the changing definition of women's roles. The entry of women into the labor force is only one indicator of this aspect of social change. Today almost 70 percent of all married women with children are at work in offices, factories, and other workplaces, compared with only about 4 percent in 1890 (*Statistical Abstract,* 1995). But it should be noted that there have always been subgroups in the population, especially African Americans and immigrants, for whom women's wages were necessary to the family's survival. And among women who "kept house" toward the turn of the century, some 20 percent took in lodgers and earned cash in this fashion (Aldous, 1982; Modell & Hareven, 1973).

For both women and men, these changes often produce feelings of guilt and stress. One writer on the subject (Fallows, 1985) urged young mothers to reject career goals so that they could raise their children themselves. On the basis of observations of day care centers, she had concluded that day care is a poorly developed institution that cannot substitute for maternal care. Arguments of this nature are common. But other studies show that high-quality day care does not impede a child's development. Moreover, advocates of gender equality question the assumption that child rearing should remain the primary role of women. This assumption has the effect of depriving women of opportunities to contribute their skills and talents to society. If day care is inadequate, a more practical response would be to improve it through public funding, education of child care workers, and the like, rather than forcing women to return to their traditional role as homemakers (Bergmann & Hartmann, 1995; Browne Miller, 1990; England, 1986).

These arguments call attention to the need for more research on the future of families and other intimate groups in which children are reared. Some sociologists attempt to show how day care can be improved. Others conduct research on how people actually cope with changes in the household division of labor. Are we moving toward a "symmetrical society" in which men and women share equally in household and occupational pursuits? If so, the evidence suggests that we still have a long way to go. In an analysis of data from 555 couples, Carmi Schooler, Joanne Miller, and their associates (1985) found that typically the husband's sphere of household work "tends to be limited to household repairs, whereas wives are responsible for and actually do a vastly wider range of the household tasks" (p. 112).

Research on time use conducted by John Robinson confirms these findings. Robinson's analysis of detailed diaries of how men and women use their time each day shows that, on the average, women spend about thirty hours a week on child care, housework, and family care whereas men spend less than ten hours a week on such activities. While men often assume other responsibilities for the family, including putting in extra time at work, the data show that they are not yet close to sharing equally in family chores (Robinson, 1988). Women who have young children and work full time are the most harried segment of the population; they have only an average of thirty-one hours a week of free time, as opposed to thirty-six hours a week for women who stay home with their children.

Another major issue related to changes in the family is whether welfare recipients should be required to work at paid jobs in order to remain eligible for welfare benefits. This question also involves the matter of day care, since single parents must have adequate care for their children while they gain the skills and experience needed to enter the labor force. Are we willing, as a society, to invest in new social-welfare institutions like day care? The answer awaits further debate and political conflict. So too does the question of what, if anything, we can do about problems like teenage pregnancy, sexually transmitted diseases, or high rates of divorce. Changes in values give us more choices, more opportunities to realize our potential as individuals, but at what cost to society (Bellah et al., 1985)?

RACE RELATIONS IN A POST-INDUSTRIAL SOCIETY

Another significant area of social change is race relations. When we look at the bitter racial strife occurring in Rwanda or Bosnia, we often congratulate ourselves on the progress our society has made toward racial and ethnic equality. Racial discrimination in the United States, which until fairly recently was supported by laws in many parts of the nation and by informal norms elsewhere, has decreased a great deal as a result of the civil rights movement of the 1960s. Since that stormy decade, blacks have made gains in all of our society's major institutions. Voting rights, greater access to education and jobs, achievement in sports, and full civil rights for blacks are often taken for granted. Yet as the 1992 Los Angeles riots clearly demonstrated, much needs to be done to address racial inequality. In the words of philosopher and sociologist Cornel West,

> The verdict that sparked the incidents in Los Angeles was perceived to be wrong by the vast majority of Americans. But whites have often failed to acknowledge the widespread

mistreatment of black people, especially black men, by law-enforcement agencies, which helped ignite the spark. The Rodney King verdict was merely the occasion for deep-seated rage to come to the surface. This rage is fed by the "silent" depression ravaging the country—in which real weekly wages of all American workers since 1973 declined nearly 20 percent, while at the same time wealth has been upwardly distributed.

The exodus of stable industrial jobs from urban centers to cheaper labor markets here and abroad, housing policies that have created "chocolate cities and vanilla suburbs," white fear of black crime and the urban influx of poor Spanish-speaking and Asian immigrants—all have helped erode the tax-base of American cities just as the federal government has cut its supports and programs. The result is unemployment, hunger, homelessness, and sickness for millions. (1992, p. 24)

In the chapters that follow we delve far more deeply into the causes and consequences of inequalities of income, race, gender, and age, as well as their importance for social change. It is worth noting here, however, that West's critical observations signal some of the ways in which inequalities of wealth and opportunity overlap with inequalities of race and tend to exacerbate the problem of race relations in American society.

Changes in the economic structure of society supply the main explanation for the growing divergence between the haves and the have-nots. Manufacturing jobs and many kinds of blue-collar service jobs are becoming far less numerous, while the number of jobs in white-collar service industries like finance, insurance, and banking is growing rapidly. Higher levels of production of high-technology items like computers have not yet made up for the loss of jobs in heavy industries like steel, autos, glass, and rubber.

Blacks and Hispanics are more severely affected by these changes because they have long depended on heavy industry as a source of jobs.

ENVIRONMENTAL POLITICS AND POLICIES

A third area in which social change touches the individual is public policy. *Public policies* are laws and administrative regulations that are formulated by governments to control, regulate, or guide behavior. What public policies are likely to emerge as the United States is transformed into a postindustrial society and as other regions of the world industrialize? Clearly one area of policy that will gain in urgency involves measures to safeguard the earth's environment. The contemporary exploration of space, applying the most advanced technologies, has allowed us to see the planet as a whole, which in turn has stimulated the development of environmental thinking and efforts to develop policies that will reduce problems such as global warming. However, to the extent that environmental policies impinge on people's livelihoods and on their reproductive behavior, these policies are bound to be extremely controversial and difficult to formulate (Perutz, 1992).

Environmental issues like the exhaustion of food resources, the spread of deserts, the destruction of forests by acid rain, and the denuding of large tracts of land for fuelwood are fast gaining a high place on the agenda of world politics. Figure 10.1 shows that population growth in excess of food-producing capacity is occurring in the Middle East and many parts of Africa; that fuelwood is scarce in India, Africa, and eastern Brazil; and that deserts are expanding on all the continents. Victims of "food insecurity" (people who lack sufficient food for normal health and physical activity) now total more than 100 million (Brown et al., 1989).

Earthrise, Christmas Eve, 1968. The crew members of Apollo 8 were the first humans to observe and photograph the earth rising above the moon's horizon. As one of them later wrote, "In a world where it was commonplace to say there was nothing new under the sun, here it came—the world, our world, in all its beauty and glory, as we had never before glimpsed it. A vision of unimaginable sweetness" (quoted in Monk, 1989, p. 51). This photograph has become a symbol of our ability to perceive the earth in its totality and our responsibility to care for it more wisely.

FIGURE 10.1 Worldwide Patterns of Environmental Stress

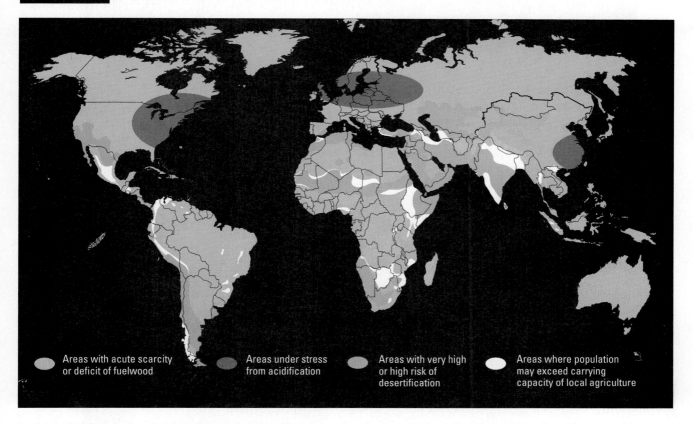

Areas with acute scarcity
or deficit of fuelwood

Areas under stress
from acidification

Areas with very high
or high risk of
desertification

Areas where population
may exceed carrying
capacity of local agriculture

Land degradation results from a variety of human activities. Shown are regions threatened by desertification, overharvesting of firewood, acid rain, and stress induced by efforts to feed more people than the land is actually able to support.
Source: Clark, 1989.

What are the political implications of these physical and social conditions? Gro Harlem Brundtland, chair of the World Commission on Environment and Development, answers that "to secure our common future, we need a new international ethic based on the realization that the issues with which we wrestle are globally interconnected." The only way different nations can pursue their own self-interest, she adds, is for the United Nations or a similar institution in which environmental policy is made. And that policy cannot "insult the poor and tell them that they must remain in poverty to 'protect the environment'" (1989, p. 190). Clearly, the wealthy nations must make equal sacrifices to achieve a stable environment.

As the worldwide environmental crisis worsens, citizens of the United States and Canada will increasingly be faced with the need to regulate their economies and to end practices that contribute to pollution. This will be a costly and politically wrenching process, as evidenced by the difficulties encountered in developing policies for solid-waste disposal or the abatement of acid rain. A divided society, in which many people wish to be responsive to the environmental crisis but many others do not wish to think about it, is certain to produce conflict for years to come—unless a crisis such as flooding due to global warming creates such an obvious threat that unity of purpose is achieved

overnight (see Figure 10.2). Thus we face a dilemma brought on by great changes in the environment coupled with slower changes in the ability of political institutions to deal with them. This situation points to the need to look more closely at the models that sociologists use in assessing social change and predicting its course. (See Box 10.2.)

MODELS OF CHANGE

"We are such stuff as dreams are made on, and our little life is rounded with a sleep." These words from Shakespeare's *The Tempest* capture one of the basic difficulties of studying social change. In one short lifetime we catch glimpses of our ability to create a better world, but we can never realize all our ambitions, nor can we know what will become of our achievements or the problems we leave to later generations. We may see the return of Selective Service (the draft) if the nation goes to war; prices may shoot up again as inflation rates rise; long lines may form at gasoline pumps during a new oil shortage; or we may be faced with new medical problems like AIDS or dengue fever that affect the lives of large numbers of people. To cope with these changes, we may join new social movements and attempt to build new institutions or work to improve

FIGURE 10.2

MAPPING SOCIAL CHANGE

Deltas in Distress. In 1995 the threat of global warming gained a more prominent place in worldwide environmental and social consciousness. Reports issued by the National Academy of Sciences and by international scientific agencies confirmed that there is clear evidence world temperatures are rising. This could be the underlying cause of such phenomena as the heat wave that claimed more than 700 lives in Chicago and produced droughts elsewhere in the United States. But in coming years warming will be felt most directly through rising sea levels.

U.S. scientists now predict an average increase in sea level of 20 inches by the year 2100. If this trend is not reversed through stricter controls over energy consumption and the release of carbon dioxide into the atmosphere, the higher sea levels will have serious effects in heavily populated lowlands and river deltas throughout the world.

The global map shows where major deltas are located. The inset shows the so-called low countries at the mouth of the Rhine in Europe. The photo shows the effects of floods in this densely populated area during the 1990s.

Mississippi River
United States

Paraná River
Argentina

Rhine River
Netherlands

Rhone River
France

Niger River
Nigeria

Po River
Italy

Nile River
Egypt

Indus River
Pakistan

Narnada and
Tapti Rivers
India

Cauvery
River
India

Krishna and
Godavari Rivers
India

Red River
Vietnam

Yellow River
China

Yangtze
River
China

Pearl River
China

Mekong River
Vietnam

Irrawaddy River
Myanmar

Ganges-Brahmaputra River
Bangladesh

Mahanadi River
India

Source: S. P. Leatherman, University of Maryland.

BOX 10.2 GLOBAL SOCIAL CHANGE

The Challenge of Political Stability

Chinua Achebe, one of Africa's most highly respected writers and social commentators, is deeply upset but hardly surprised at the failure of political processes in his homeland. In the spring of 1993 his fellow Nigerians, citizens of the largest democracy (or potential democracy) in sub-Saharan Africa, went to the polls to elect a civilian government. But the election did not produce the desired results. Instead, political instability has worsened, just as it has in many other ethnically diverse and politically volatile regions of the world. Through Achebe's writings we can gain some insight into how political corruption and instability create severe obstacles to positive social change.

For years Nigeria has been a military dictatorship headed by General Ibrahim Babangida. Achebe, now in exile in the United States, has written scathing criticisms of the military regime and its failure to schedule democratic elections as promised. When the elections were finally held and one candidate emerged as the clear victor, the general and his followers annulled the election and called for a new vote. But first they closed all opposition newspapers and television stations. As Achebe observes:

> Nigeria's plight shows that having an abundance of talented and educated people and material wealth will not insure national prosperity when that wealth lies at the disposal of a corrupt leadership. What Nigerians of all classes and religious and ethnic loyalties must do is overcome their differences enough to defeat the dictator. (Achebe, 1993, p. A13)

What can intellectuals—be they social scientists, writers, poets, artists, or lawyers—do to sway their fellow citizens in a time of political crisis? On the surface the answer seems to be precious little. Yet ideals and aspirations can be powerful forces. No government can rule very long if its citizens do not believe its rule is legitimate. By challenging the regime of the dictator, Achebe is calling on his fellow Nigerians to withdraw their consent to be governed. "The only sane path," he warns, "is for Nigerians of all ethnic groups, religious persuasions, classes, and professions to tell him to get out—fast."

Note that twice in his appeal to his fellow citizens Achebe has tried to bridge the divides of ethnicity, religion, and social class. In Nigeria as in the former Soviet Union, Czechoslovakia, and Yugoslavia, and in many other multiethnic, multinational states, dictators and demagogues like General Babangida capitalize on the hostility that citizens from different backgrounds feel toward each other.

In the heady period of post–World War II anticolonial movements, when Africans in Nigeria, Ghana, Senegal, and scores of other colonial territories were fighting against their European rulers, it did not seem impossible to build a political community that could transcend tribal and religious loyalties (Apter, 1980; Wallerstein, 1974). It also seemed that in many other parts of the world—for example, French-speaking Quebec—the strength of ethnic and religious conflicts would diminish in favor of a sense of shared peoplehood. But one of the most difficult lessons of recent years has been the realization that far-reaching social changes like mass education, industrialization and urbanization, global war, and global trade do not eliminate these older loyalties. For social commentators like Chinua Achebe, therefore, how to transcend older animosities and intergroup fears in the interests of democratic participation and positive social change is the central sociological question of our time.

---

the ones we already have. We may also record our desire for a better society in cultural products of all kinds—in poetry and plays and novels, in film and music, and perhaps in social-scientific studies. Yet we know that social change will continue after we are gone, and we wonder whether it is possible to foresee what will happen to our society and civilization in the distant future.

Sociologists have often attempted to develop models of social change that span many generations and predict the future of whole societies or civilizations. Of course, none of these theories can be tested using data from actual experience. As Robert Nisbet has observed, "None of us has ever seen a civilization die, and it is unimaginable, short of cosmic disaster or thermonuclear holocaust, that anyone ever will" (1969, p. 3). Instead, he continues,

We see migrations and wars, dynasties toppled, governments overthrown, economic systems made affluent or poor; revolutions in power, privilege, and wealth. We see human beings born, mating, child-rearing, working, worshipping, playing, educating, writing, philosophizing, governing. We see generation succeeding generation, each new one accepting, modifying, rejecting in different proportions the works of preceding generations. We see, depending upon our moral or esthetic disposition, good and evil, greatness and meanness, tragedy, comedy, and bathos, nobility and baseness, success and failure. (p. 3)

Nisbet's point is that we can trace trends in all of these areas, but it is extremely difficult to develop theories that can explain them all and, more important, predict the decline of existing societies and civilizations or the rise of new ones. Even when we believe we are witnessing the birth of a new society out of the chaos of revolution or war, it takes many generations to distinguish what is truly new, in terms of culture and social structure, from what has been carried over from the past. Despite these difficulties, models of change that seek to predict the future of entire societies or civilizations can be helpful. They allow us at least to compare new ideas about social change with those that have been in use for many decades. In this section, therefore, we review the most significant models of large-scale social change that have been proposed by sociologists in the past two centuries.

EVOLUTIONARY MODELS

Many of the founders of sociology were strongly influenced by evolutionary views of social change even before Darwin's theory seemed to offer an analogy between biological and social evolution (Nisbet, 1969). The main components of the nineteenth-century evolutionary model are as follows:

1. *Social change is natural and constant.* Social order exists even while change occurs; social change, on the other hand, is the means of attaining higher levels of social order.

2. *Social evolution has a direction.* Societies become increasingly complex. Émile Durkheim, for example, viewed societies as evolving from simpler forms based on similar segments like villages into more complex forms based on division of labor and the resultant interdependence among ever-larger numbers of people.

3. *Social evolution is continuous.* Change occurs as a result of social forces acting within a society, even without exogenous influences like colonialism. This happens through a steady series of stages. Many, but not all, evolutionary theories interpret social change as progress toward better conditions of life.

4. *Change is necessary and proceeds from uniform causes.* Because social change occurs naturally, continuously, and from within, it must be necessary. In other words, whether or not we want change, it will occur because of the logic of social evolution. And social evolution will be similar in all societies because all societies are similar in their ways of dealing with the dilemmas of human existence.

Two assumptions implicit in the nineteenth-century model of social evolution have been strongly criticized by twentieth-century social scientists. The first is that all of the world's societies would eventually resemble those of Western Europe in their institutions and even in their cultural values and ideologies. The second is that social evolution represents progress.

Modern evolutionary theorists refer to earlier models as *unilinear* because they predict that all societies will in-

evitably come to resemble Western societies. A less ethnocentric version of evolutionary theory is found in *multilinear* models of social change. These models do not assume that large-scale change in a society represents progress, and they attempt to account for the values that are lost as well as for those that are gained.

Multilinear models also emphasize that one must study each society separately in order to discover the evolutionary stages that are unique to a particular society as well as those that have been experienced by other societies (Lenski & Lenski, 1982; Sahlins & Servide, 1960; Steward, 1955). Thus societies like Ivory Coast, where the Ebrié live, have not developed much heavy industry and may never do so. On the other hand, Ivory Coast has a relatively advanced agricultural base that provides the surpluses needed for modernization to take place in other areas of social life.

Multilinear models can be useful in accounting for the erratic course of modernization in the Islamic world, or in helping the Ebrié in their attempts to understand what aspects of their village culture might remain viable even as their tribe becomes incorporated into a modern African state. But such models do not tell us why societies like Great Britain have declined from the heights of imperial power or why the ancient civilizations of Egypt and Rome flourished, declined, and are now known primarily through courses in ancient history and classics. An alternative viewpoint is found in cyclical theories of social change, which attempt to explain such phenomena by placing the possibility of decline at the same level as that of growth and "progress."

CYCLICAL THEORIES

In 1918, when Europe had been devastated by World War I, Oswald Spengler, a German schoolteacher turned historian, published a controversial book titled *The Decline of the West.* Spengler's gloomy thesis was that all societies pass through stages that are roughly equivalent to the life stages of human beings: infancy, youth, adulthood, and old age. The West, he argued, had passed through its maturity in the eighteenth century and was now experiencing a long period of decline. This process was inevitable and irreversible. There was nothing anyone could do to change its course.

A similar but more positive "rise and fall" theory of social change was developed by the British historian Arnold Toynbee (1972). In his "challenge and response" model, Toynbee suggested that all societies grow and decline as they respond to the challenges posed by their physical and social environments. For example, England needed to solve basic ecological problems, such as the fact that it is a small island nation with a limited supply of farmland. It responded by emphasizing foreign trade and using its superior naval power to protect its trade routes. When its naval power declined, it had to find new ways of meeting its challenges or face further decline. Thus for Toynbee the rise and fall of a society is accounted for by continual innovation in response to changes in its environment. However, although this theory is quite convincing as an explanation of history, it says little about what any particular society may expect in the way of challenges in the future.

Pitirim Sorokin (1937), a Russian immigrant who greatly influenced American social theory in the early twentieth century, also developed a cyclical theory of social change. His theory attempted to account for why a society or civilization might change in a particular way. All societies, he wrote, are continually experiencing social change, and such change originates in their cultures. This is because cultures are not unified but are marked by opposing sets of values, norms, and lifestyles. At one extreme of a society's cultural system is its "ideational culture," so named because it stresses spiritual values, hard work, self-denial, and a strong moral code. At the other extreme is its "sensate culture." This set of cultural traits encourages sensory experiences, self-expression, and gratification of individual desires. Neither of these extremes can produce a stable society. Ideational culture results in benefits that are enjoyed by pleasure seekers in later generations, and the society will decline until this trend is reversed and ideational traits are emphasized once again. At some point in its history a society may combine these two cultural tendencies. Then, according to Sorokin, it has reached its "idealistic point." But such a golden age is not likely to last forever.

CONFLICT MODELS

Cyclical theories of social change, with their cycles of rise and fall and their brief golden ages, may seem to confirm the common notion that history repeats itself. This notion is erroneous, however. Societies may experience similar events, such as wars or revolutions, at different times in their history, but the actual populations and issues involved are never exactly the same. More important, cyclical theories fail to deal with changes in social institutions or class structures. This is where conflict models of social change are most useful. They argue that conflict among groups with different amounts of power produces social change, which leads to a new system of social stratification, which in turn leads to further conflict and further change.

"The history of all hitherto existing societies," wrote Karl Marx and Friedrich Engels in *The Communist Manifesto* (1969/1848), "is the history of class struggles." As we will see in the next chapter, social classes are defined by how people make their living or gain their wealth. Marx argued that struggles between classes (e.g., workers vs. managers and company owners) are the source of social change in every period of history. In any society the main conflicting classes will be the exploiters and the exploited: those who control the means of production and those whose labor power is necessary to make those means of production actually produce. The exploited workers could become a revolutionary class—that is, one that could bring about an entirely new social order. But this can occur only when changes in the means of production—new technologies

like the factory system, for example—make older classes obsolete.

We know that revolutionary class conflict has not occurred in many capitalist societies, nor did the former communist societies of Eastern Europe or the Soviet Union succeed in eliminating worker exploitation. Yet as we look around the world at the struggles between the haves and the have-nots, the rulers and the ruled, the rich nations and the poorer nations, we cannot help but apply Marxian categories and test Marx's theory of social change over and over again.

Some modern conflict theorists depart from the Marxian view of social change, finding conflict among many different kinds of groups and in every social institution. For Ralf Dahrendorf (1959), this conflict produces social change at all times, but the change is not always revolutionary. We cannot change our laws, our bureaucracies, or even our families, for example, without first experiencing conflicts among various group and individual interests. (An example of such a conflict is the half-humorous, half-serious debate that occurred in 1992 between Vice President Dan Quayle and television character Murphy Brown over what is meant by "family values.") In most cases, however, it is only when the deprivation experienced by whole classes or status groups is extreme that conflict is likely to be violent and to produce the unrest that could end in revolutionary social change.

FUNCTIONALIST MODELS

From a functionalist perspective, social change occurs as a result of population growth, changes in technology, social inequality, and efforts by different groups to meet their needs in a world of scarce resources. There is no prediction of rise and fall or unilinear changes like those we find in early evolutionary theory or even in classical Marxian theory. Instead, the functionalist model sees change as occurring on so many fronts that it seems incredible that society can exist at all.

One of the dominant figures in functionalist social theory, Talcott Parsons (1960), developed a *homeostatic* model of society. As change occurs, said Parsons, a society's institutions attempt to restore it to something approaching equilibrium. Conflict is minimized through the emergence of legitimate governing institutions; decisions are made about who governs and with what form and degree of authority. Adjustments are also made in economic institutions: New occupational roles develop; old roles decline; wages and status rankings such as occupational prestige explain who gets what rewards. Cultural institutions, schools, the arts, the media, and religious institutions maintain the shared values that support our feeling that our government is legitimate, that a certain amount of inequality is required to maintain individual initiative, and that opportunities are distributed as well as can be expected.

Parsons and other functionalist theorists do not contend that efforts to adapt to change, to create an integrated,

well-functioning social system, always work. The integrated functioning of social institutions can be disrupted,
sometimes quite severely, when some institutions experience rapid change while others are slow to adapt. Technological innovations in health care, for instance, make
possible longer lives for some individuals at great expense,
but other economic and political institutions have been
slow to develop norms for distributing these costly benefits
among the members of society and finding ways of paying
for them. (All the models and theories of social change that
have been discussed are summarized in the study chart
below.)

APPLYING MODELS OF CHANGE

The last two models we described—the conflict and functionalist models—clearly reflect two of the theoretical perspectives that are among the basic conceptual tools of
sociology. They are most useful at the global or macro level
of analysis. But they can also be used, along with the interactionist perspective, to explain social change at the micro
and middle levels of social analysis. We can best illustrate
this point with a closing example.

How can we apply the basic sociological perspectives
to understand what is happening to the Ebrié as they become part of a bustling West African city? Starting from an
ecological viewpoint, we must ask how the Ebrié are managing to make the transition from rural to urban life. We
see them becoming more dependent on a worldwide economy. Changes in the value of their nation's currency, for example, affect them now just as much as the failure of a yam
crop might have in an earlier time. The interactionist perspective helps us listen as they speak about how these
changes affect them. It lets us see how they are adapting to
a life led largely among strangers. Functionalism helps us
understand how some of their tribal institutions can survive in a modern society. We see new roles emerging, and
at the same time we see old ones declining in the face of
new values like those regarding the place of women in society. Finally, the conflict perspective tells us that a good part
of the answer to how much of Ebrié culture will persist and
how much will be lost depends on the extent to which the
Ebrié themselves resist assimilation into the national culture. Their struggle to maintain their language, their forms
of worship, and their world view will continue, even if it
produces some conflict among themselves.

STUDY CHART Models of Change

MODEL	DESCRIPTION
Evolutionary	
Unilinear	Social change is natural and constant, has a direction, and is continuous. Change is necessary and proceeds from uniform causes.
Multilinear	Large-scale change in a society does not represent progress. Each society must be studied separately to discover the evolutionary stages unique to it.
Cyclical	
Oswald Spengler	All societies pass through stages like the life stages of humans, and eventually decline.
Arnold Toynbee	Societies grow and decline as they respond to the challenges posed by their physical and social environments.
Pitirim Sorokin	Social change originates in a society's culture, which alternates between "ideational" and "sensate."
Conflict	
Karl Marx	Social change results from conflict between social classes, which are defined by how people make their living or gain their wealth.
Ralf Dahrendorf	Social change results from conflicts among many different kinds of groups and in every social institution.
Functionalist	
Talcott Parsons	As change occurs, a society's institutions attempt to restore equilibrium.

RESEARCH FRONTIERS: THE GLOBAL INFORMATION REVOLUTION

Almost everyone associates social change with changes in technology. People born only two decades ago will do the same when they talk about all the changes brought about by computer and telecommunications technologies. Compact discs, camcorders, cable television, digital audio, high-definition video, fiber optics, microcomputers, faster computer chips, and many other innovations have burst upon the scene in the past few years. These technologies will produce immense social changes in coming decades. Sociologists are already at work trying to understand the speed at which the new technologies will diffuse through the population and the consequences they will have for our lives (Pea & Sheingold, 1987). However, sociologists are less concerned with the inventions themselves than with their social uses and the norms and organizations that govern their use (or nonuse or misuse). The new telecommunications technologies provide an example.

Imagine your home only a few years from now. Your living room has an entertainment center connected to the local fiber-optic phone system. You can make video movie selections on your computer screen. Your equipment will record the material (for a modest fee), and you can watch it at your convenience. The same is true for audio selections. Do you want to audition the latest sensations on the music scene? No need to go shopping in a crowded mall. Just order your selection through the computer; it will be automatically recorded on your digital audio recorder (for another fee) and you will have it in your own collection. Those collections are stored in computer memory—no messy little boxes or records to bother with. The entire history of music—video, movies, text, and voice recordings—is available to you over the computer-phone circuitry. Name your pleasure: R & B, country, disco, soul, heavy metal, classic rock, jazz, fusion, pop. Then just dial up a catalog and order the sounds you like (for a modest fee, billed to your credit account; of course, you must have an account).

Health care is just as advanced as entertainment. There's a personal health center in your bathroom. Insert your wrist and it measures your pulse and blood pressure. Insert a finger and it painlessly takes readings of your blood count, blood sugar, cholesterol, and other vital signs. Your lung functioning, muscle tone, brain waves, and heart function can also be measured. All these data are sent to your doctor's mainframe computer, where your medical records are kept. You can have the equivalent of a visit to

the doctor's office every day if you wish (a modest fee is charged for each set of data entered).

Most of these innovations already exist. The technology is available. But then why are the systems not in place? Why are we not experiencing these changes more quickly? The answers to these questions are sociological, not technological.

Ithiel de Sola Pool (1977), the world's most renowned telecommunications researcher until his death in 1987, pointed out that although technologies may be available, society may not be prepared to accept them. There are risks for anyone who is an early adopter of a new technology. The company that chooses to sell a particular invention, for example, bets that one type of equipment will win out over others. Many will make the wrong choice and lose vast amounts of money, as occurred in the case of videodisc versus videotape. Indeed, many of the mega-mergers that have dominated the headlines recently involve major information corporations attempting to hedge their bets. By combining companies with the technological capacity to disseminate information and cultural products (e.g., Turner Broadcasting) with owners of the cultural products themselves (e.g., Time Warner, with its magazines, movies, and movie archives), they hope to diffuse the risks of innovation.

Perhaps the slow pace of adoption of these technologies is reasonable. How well do we understand their social consequences? Will everyone need a credit account to enjoy the benefits of browsing the World Wide Web on the Internet? What about the poor? A central hypothesis of sociologists who are critical of the way technological innovations are spreading is that inequalities in access to computers, modems, and the Internet will further widen the gap between the rich and the poor, not only in the United States but throughout the world. Not only are computers that can access the Internet diffusing more slowly through low-income communities than through more affluent ones, but the information technologies themselves allow companies to "export" jobs to areas of the world where wages are lower—thereby increasing the difficulty of finding secure, better-paying jobs in the United States (Forester, 1988).

Many others dispute this hypothesis, including House Speaker Newt Gingrich, a fervent admirer of the new telecommunications technologies. The Speaker has publicly recommended that laptops with modems be made available to all U.S. schoolchildren, a recognition of the fact that computers and access to information networks are hallmarks of educational innovation. But at this writing Congress has made no effort to consider such proposals.

The Road to Calvary, by Simone Martini, about 1340. Panel, 10" x 6".

ART AND SOCIAL CHANGE

Artists are witnesses to social change just as sociologists are, but they use different forms of expression and different media in assessing the consequences of change. The artist's statement is more emotional and aesthetic, whereas the sociologist strives for greater objectivity and more general conclusions. But each attempts to capture the most significant qualities of changing social worlds. In looking at this series of paintings, we can use the sociological eye to see how artists over the centuries have depicted moments of social upheaval and change.

These paintings span a period of six centuries, from 1340 to 1962, although the majority are from our own century. Each conveys an artist's impression of a time of great social change. People's daily lives are being severely disrupted, for better or worse, by great social movements or far-reaching changes in the fate of entire social classes. There is a dynamism in these paintings; the people they portray are being swept up in the great events of their time.

Simone Martini's depiction of the road to Calvary portrays a scene in which Christ, the Virgin and saints, and the Roman soldiers and commoners all are caught up in a chaotic and violent event. The artist sets the scene against

The Executions of the Third of May, by Francisco de Goya, 1808. Oil on canvas, 8′ 8¾″ x 11′ 3⅞″.

299

the backdrop of a fortified town, suggesting the strains in the medieval social order of Europe that were occurring as a result of the accelerating renaissance in art, science, and commerce. The Renaissance threatened the long-standing dominance of the church and the feudal state. Thus the painting makes a strong connection between the changes that occurred in Jesus's time and those that were occurring in Europe during the fourteenth century.

Revolutions, civil wars, and invasions of the weak by the powerful are often either consequences or causes of lasting social change. It is no wonder, then, that scenes of war are so often portrayed in paintings. Francisco de Goya's painting of an execution is a fierce rendering of the brutality of the Napoleonic conquest of Spain. Firing squad executions like these took place in Madrid after the weak Spanish monarchy had refused to resist the invasion. But it is not necessary to know the details of this moment in history. Goya's painting gains its timeless beauty and horror from the way the artist portrays the behavior of individuals under extreme conditions. The soldiers' faces are hidden. The soldiers are presented as automatons following orders rather than as humans. The dying civilians, in contrast, are all too human in their reactions. Some stare defiantly at their executioners while others cower with their faces covered.

More than a century later another Spanish painter, using an entirely different graphic style and different symbols, captured the terror of war waged against a defenseless population. In one of his greatest paintings, Pablo Picasso captured the agony and confusion that the citizens of Guernica, a little farming town, must have felt as German bombers flattened their homes and barns during the Spanish Civil War. And in yet another artistic style, the Mexican muralist Diego Rivera combined the artistic traditions of Mexican folk art and Italian Renaissance frescos to symbolize the liberation of the peon from the landowning class, whose property is shown in flames in the background.

Guernica, by Pablo Picasso, 1937. Oil, 11'6" x 25'8".

The Liberation of the Peon, by Diego Rivera, 1931. Fresco, 74″ x 95″.

Bal au Moulin de la Galette, by Pierre-Auguste Renoir, 1876. Oil on canvas, 51½" x 69".

In Pierre-Auguste Renoir's painting of a gala scene in a nineteenth-century Parisian cafe, in Reginald Marsh's view of Depression-era Chicago, and in Ben Shahn's stark rendering of life and death in a mining family, we see other modern artists offering insights into their times and the cultures of their societies. The shimmering quality of Renoir's style conveys a vivid impression of France at a time when the rapidly growing bourgeoisie was enjoying new freedoms and new opportunities to enjoy the finer things in life. Women, for example, felt freer to appear in public and interact as equals with men. Marsh, on the other hand, gives us a glimpse into the seedy lives of men without families, set adrift to haunt the skid rows of American cities as a consequence of rapid industrialization and the "boom and bust" cycle of American business. And finally, in *Miners' Wives* Shahn depicts the suffering of women in a poor mining community. Their grief is made more vivid by the distance between the doorway of their home and the mine and its owners, who appear in the background.

Do not let these brief comments prevent you from using your own sociological eye to explore the values and relationships represented in these selected paintings. One of the goals of this book is to help you develop the ability to "read" the meanings and symbols contained in a wide variety of human scenes, whether they are the works of artists or the events of your own life.

Tattoo and Haircut, by Reginald Marsh, 1932.
Tempera on masonite, 46½" x 48".

Miners' Wives, by Ben
Shahn, 1948. Egg tempera
on board, 48" x 36".

303

SUMMARY

THINK ABOUT IT CRITICALLY

How many times have you heard someone begin a sentence by saying, "Young people today don't know how . . ." or "This city [or town] is nothing like it was when . . ." or "If things keep going the way they are, the family as we know it will . . ."? You can predict that most of the sentences will be negative. The past often seems better than the present. As you review this chapter on social change, think critically about these common complaints.

Social change refers to variations over time in the ecological ordering of populations and communities, in patterns of roles and social interactions, in the structure and functioning of institutions, and in the cultures of societies. Such changes can result from forces building within societies *(endogenous forces)* as well as from forces exerted from the outside *(exogenous forces)*. Changes at the micro, middle, and macro levels of social life usually are interrelated.

No social change in human history has been as far-reaching and universal in its consequences as the transition to an urban, industrial way of life. However, not all people who are experiencing such changes think of them as progress. Nor can all forms of social change be controlled, although some changes are intentional. Similarly, while social scientists can understand and predict the master trends of their era, they have limited ability to anticipate major forms of change such as wars, social movements, or technological changes.

One of the major forces that produce social change is war. The primary ecological effects of war are casualties and conquest. War also results in large-scale shifts in population and rapid acceleration of economic change. It can affect a society's culture in a variety of ways, and it may drastically change the structure of a society, especially its major social institutions.

A second major source of social change is *modernization*—the changes that have taken place in societies throughout the world as a result of industrialization, urbanization, and the development of nation-states. These changes include a shift from simple techniques toward the application of scientific knowledge; an evolution from subsistence farming toward the commercial production of agricultural goods; a transition from the use of human and animal power toward the use of power-driven machines; and a movement from the farm and village toward urban concentrations. These processes may or may not take place simultaneously.

Some sociologists view technology as a basic principle of social change. They recognize, however, that social institutions are often slow to adapt to changing technologies. This recognition forms the basis of the theory known as *cultural lag*. Postmodernist critics argue that technology and rationality deprive human lives of spirituality; they also believe that major institutions of modern societies have become instruments of social control by powerful elites.

The so-called Third World nations are those that have won independence from colonial dominance in the decades since World War II. Such nations are also called *developing nations* or modernizing nations. They are undergoing a set of transformations whose effect is to increase the productivity of their people, their health, their literacy, and their ability to participate in political decision making. Wallerstein's world system theory divides the world into *core states, semiperipheral areas,* and *peripheral areas.*

People often experience social change as highly problematic. In pursuing new opportunities in education, leisure activities, intimate relationships, and political participation, they may find themselves without a clear set of norms to guide their lives and hence may experience anomie. The entry of large numbers of women into the labor force, for example, has upset the traditional norms of family life. Similarly, the civil rights movement has greatly reduced racial discrimination in the United States, but for a large proportion of the black population these gains have been offset by changes in the structure of the economy. A third area in which social change touches the individual is public policy, which may involve trade-offs between conflicting goals such as eliminating poverty and protecting the environment.

Sociologists have often attempted to develop models of social change that can be used to predict the future of whole societies or civilizations. Many of the founders of sociology favored an evolutionary model in which social change is seen as natural and constant; all societies inevitably become increasingly complex through a steady series of stages. Modern evolutionary theorists refer to such models as unilinear because they predict that all societies will undergo the same process of change. Multilinear models emphasize that one must study each society separately to discover the evolutionary stages that are unique to a particular society.

A variety of theories have taken a cyclical view of social change, in which civilizations rise and fall, respond to a series of challenges, or alternate between two opposing sets of cultural values. Conflict theorists argue that conflict among groups with different amounts of power produces social change, which leads to a new system of social stratification, which in turn leads to further conflict and further change. From a functionalist perspective, social change occurs as a result of population growth, changes in technology, social inequality, and efforts by different groups to meet their needs in a world of scarce resources. The latter two perspectives can be applied to change at the micro and middle levels of social life as well as to macro level changes.

CRITICAL RESPONSE

A sociological imagination, developed through mastery of the concepts, theories, and trends that sociologists study, leads to a better understanding of the complaints people make about contemporary society. We understand, for example, that as people grow older they remember their youth fondly, even when the conditions of life then may not have been better than they are now. And although the complaints we hear are often well grounded in fact, the sociologist demands greater empirical proof than can be found in one person's views or feelings. We also know that social change does not necessarily make us happier, even if we can better understand the causes and consequences of the conditions in which we live.

GLOSSARY

social change: variations over time in the ecological ordering of populations and communities, in patterns of roles and social interactions, in the structure and functioning of institutions, and in the cultures of societies. (p. 274)

endogenous force: pressure for social change that builds within a society. (p. 274)

exogenous force: pressure for social change that is exerted from outside a society. (p. 274)

modernization: a term used to describe the changes experienced by societies and individuals as a result of industrialization, urbanization, and the development of nation-states. (p. 281)

cultural lag: the time required for social institutions to adapt to a major technological change. (p. 283)

developing nation: a nation that is undergoing a set of transformations whose effect is to increase the productivity of its people, their health, their literacy, and their ability to participate in political decision making. (p. 285)

core state: a technologically advanced nation that has a dominant position in the world economy. (p. 286)

semiperipheral area: a state or region in which industry and financial institutions are developed to some extent but that remains dependent on capital and technology provided by other states. (p. 286)

peripheral area: a region that supplies basic resources and labor power to more advanced states. (p. 286)

WHERE TO FIND IT

BOOKS
How Societies Change (Daniel Chirot; Pine Forge Press, 1994). A review of theories of change by one of the leading sociologists of social change; reflects on the many meanings of the failure of Soviet-style regimes.

Exploring Social Change, 2nd ed. (Charles L. Harper; Prentice-Hall, 1993). A comprehensive text on social change with critical chapters on modernization, postmodernism, development, and world systems theory.

The Wretched of the Earth (Frantz Fanon; Grove Press, 1968). A classic and burning analysis of the psychology of colonial peoples and their yearning for independence even in the face of violence and bloodshed.

Social Change and History (Robert A. Nisbet; Oxford University Press, 1969). A gracefully written history of ideas of social change.

Technology, the Economy, and Society: The American Experience (Joel Colton & Stuart Bruchey, eds.; Columbia University Press, 1987). A collection of eleven articles assessing the role of technology in transforming everything from agriculture, industry, and the structure of corporations to politics, law, the military, education, and religion.

JOURNALS
Politics and Society. A critical journal devoted to studies of social change and theories of social change.

Economic Development and Cultural Change. A journal of economic and sociological writing about the interrelationships between culture and economics, and their influence on social change in developing nations.

World Development Report. Published annually by the World Bank. A valuable source of comparative data on social and economic development for all the world's nations and territories.

OTHER SOURCES
Statistical Yearbook. Published annually by the United Nations, Department of International Economic and Social Affairs. Presents general socioeconomic statistics.

PART 3

Social
Divisions

An American who was born in this half of the twentieth century has lived through events that have dramatically changed the fortunes of many groups in the U.S. population. The economic growth and prosperity of the 1950s brought the promise of relative affluence for all, or almost all, Americans. Blue-collar workers and their families were encouraged to buy houses and cars, to take trips on the new interstate highway system, to send their children to college. Blacks and other minority groups won major advances in civil rights and economic security. Women, too, increasingly rejected their status of cultural and economic inferiority. We will see in this part of the book, however, that these and other victories are incomplete. Social divisions remain, even though in some instances they are becoming less severe.

The next five chapters look in more detail at social inequality,

particularly in American society. Chapter 11 shows how the members of a society are sorted into social layers or strata and how a society's stratification system changes as its economic and political structure changes. Chapter 12 deals with inequalities of social class. After a discussion of how inequalities are defined and measured, the chapter moves on to an analysis of how social inequalities due to lack of wealth, education, prestige, and other rewards affect people's chances of achieving success and "the good life." Chapter 13 examines how present patterns of racial and ethnic inequality have evolved from historical patterns of intergroup hostility, conflict, and cooperation. In Chapters 14 and 15 we will see how the roles a culture defines as appropriate for women and men of different ages are related to patterns of inequality in that society.

Stratification and Social Mobility

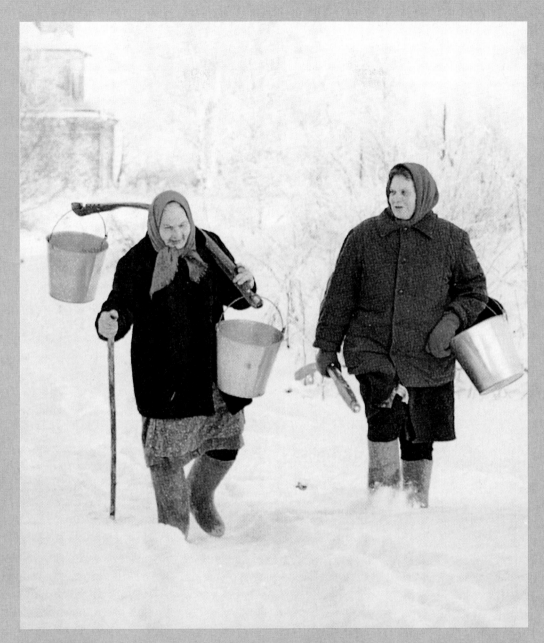

Serge Schmemann, a foreign correspondent, recently visited the Russian village of Koltsovo, the home of his ancestors. Here is one of the reports he sent back from the snowbound agricultural village:

KOLTSOVO, Russia — So far the radical changes in Moscow have brought little more than added confusion and debt to the Suvorov Collective Farm. But the frozen soil has not exhausted its powers: In one hut, a villager celebrates the first publication of his verse.

It is the heart of winter, and from the road Koltsovo looks at rest. Wisps of wood smoke curl from loghouses haphazardly scattered on the white hillsides, calves bellow from a warm and pungent barn, and even the rusting equipment seems less desolate now, half-buried in the snow.

But the peace is only snow-deep. In his small office, Vladimir Sukhorukov, chairman of the *kholkoz*, or collective farm, angrily ticks off the ingredients of what he describes as "an unbearable situation." The "price liberalization" in force since the New Year has increased prices for the farm's milk six times and for its meat eight times. But costs have soared far beyond that, and the Government is taking 28 percent in value-added tax. . . .

"There will be no profit at all this year, that I can tell you now," Mr. Sukhorukov said somberly. (Schmemann, 1992a, p. A1)

Other residents of the village are equally somber in their views of the present and future. One elderly man, a dedicated communist all his life, had for many years run a school for orphans of World War II. Now retired, he is still committed to improving life in the village and on the collective farm. As Schmemann reported:

[He] deplores not so much the loss of the old ideology or brotherhood—he had little use for the current Communist Party bosses known as the partocracy—but the loss of that measure of order and security he worked so hard after the war to restore. "We have no democracy, no authority," he said. "It's pure anarchy, complete disintegration. Russia has fallen apart into petty principalities. The community partocracy at least had levers of control. Now they issue decrees and nothing happens." (Schmemann, 1992a, p. A1)

The villager is referring to the fact that prices for bread and other essentials now fluctuate wildly and can be higher in one village than in another. Under communism the theory was that each commodity had its own price, independent of supply, and that reselling goods for a profit was "speculation" and "private commerce," both of which were crimes against society. Now, suddenly, such activities are being praised and the middleman is not a criminal

speculator but a *kommersant* who is said to be helping to build the new Russia. Naturally many people are deeply confused. "Don't ask me to sell," cries the retired youth worker. "I'd die of shame. I have a conscience still."

Elsewhere in the village Aleksandra Trunin has transformed an old school into a village museum. She wants the young people of the village to know more about the history of their area before the communist revolution, and she wants also to show the changes, positive and negative, caused by the revolution. Under the Stalinist dictatorship such ambitions could land one in a Siberian *gulag* or prison camp. Now efforts to recapture the past are flourishing all over the former Soviet Union.

Trunin's son is happy despite all the confusion. He has just had some

of his poems published by one of the nation's top literary magazines. In the young man's poems and the villagers' other activities there is a promise that the future will be brighter. Some investors are talking about putting up funds to modernize the collective farm in return for all its output. "There was talk of fashioning a genuine collective farm, with defined shares for participants" (Schmemann, 1992a, p. A6). Farmers could own their own land and also share in the collective farm and its equipment, which would make it unnecessary for everyone to own an expensive tractor. Gradually, often painfully, more realistic combinations of capitalism and socialism are being put into practice in communities throughout Russia.

THE MEANING OF STRATIFICATION

A century from now historians may conclude that from a sociological viewpoint the twenty-first century actually began in the years from 1989 to 1992. The breakup of the Soviet empire, the end of the cold war, the unification of Germany, and the eruption of ethnic and national conflicts long suppressed by the Soviet system—all of these events occurred during a span of only 4 years. Schmemann's report from a small Russian agricultural town symbolizes the momentous social changes that are occurring in the largest nation on earth. Under communism, from 1917 to 1992, the Russian people saw a great many improvements in their lives, and their once backward, autocratic society was transformed into an industrial giant. But the dream of ending the inequalities that produced extremes of poverty and unimaginable wealth never came about. Studies by Soviet sociologists continually showed that there were various levels of wealth, even extreme poverty, under communism. The official communist view was that these disparities were being eliminated, yet citizens knew that in fact the Communist party had subverted the dream of equality. They called the party members the "partocracy" or *nomenklatura* and whispered about how they had usurped power and were a new "ruling class."

Now many Russians and citizens of other former Soviet republics fear that the old communists will join with the new capitalists to form a larger class of rich and powerful people and that the dream of equality will fade still further. In North America it is often said that the Soviet experience proves the futility and wrongheadedness of trying to achieve such a dream. Yet we will see in this chapter that while inequalities of income, wealth, or prestige may be inevitable in all societies, the dream of greater equality accounts for much positive social change.

Numerous social-scientific studies have demonstrated that all human societies produce some form of inequality (Bendix & Lipset, 1966; Fallers, 1977; Harris, 1980; Murdock, 1949). In the simplest societies this inequality may be due to the fact that one family's fields produce more than another's do, that one family has accumulated a greater herd than others have, or that one family has produced a larger number of brave warriors and thus has received more esteem from the other families in the tribe. But as societies become more and more complex, encompassing ever-larger populations and more elaborate divisions of labor, these simple forms of inequality give way to more clearly defined systems for distributing rewards among members of the society. And those systems result in the classification of families and other social groups into rather well-defined layers, or *strata.* In each society the various strata are defined by how much wealth people have, the kinds of work they do, whom they marry, and many other aspects of life.

In this chapter we will see how inequality in societies results in systems of social stratification. **Social stratification** is a society's system for ranking people hierarchically (i.e., from high to low) according to various attributes such as income, wealth, power, prestige, age, sex, ethnicity, and religion. In this chapter we will deal primarily with stratification by wealth, power, and prestige.

CASTE, CLASS, AND SOCIAL MOBILITY

In every society people are grouped into different categories according to how they earn their living. This produces an imaginary set of horizontal social layers, or strata, that are more or less closed to entry by people from outside any given layer. Societies that maintain rigid boundaries between social strata are said to have **closed** stratification systems; societies in which the boundaries are easily crossed are said to be **open** societies.

In open societies it is possible for some individuals and their families, and even entire communities, to move from one stratum to another; such movement is termed **social mobility.** A couple whose parents were unskilled workers may become educated, learn advanced job skills, and be able to afford a private house instead of renting a modest apartment as their parents did. Such a couple is said to experience **upward mobility.** If they have enough wealth to make their parents comfortable and to help other family members, the entire family may enjoy upward social mobility. If everyone with the same education and skills and the same occupation experiences greater prosperity and prestige, the entire occupational community is said to be upwardly mobile. But in an open society fortunes can also decline. People with advanced skills—in engineering or higher education, for example—may find that there are too many of them around. They may not be able to afford the kind of housing, medical care, education for their children, and other benefits that they have come to expect. When this occurs they are said to experience **downward mobility.**

The best examples of closed societies are found in caste societies. **Castes** are social strata into which people are born and in which they remain for life. Membership in a caste is an **ascribed status** (a status acquired at birth) rather than an **achieved status** (one based on the efforts of the individual). Members of a particular caste cannot hope to leave that caste. Slaves and plantation owners

THEN AND NOW

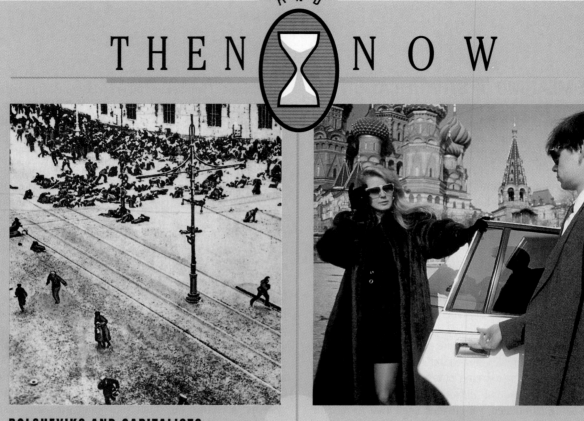

BOLSHEVIKS AND CAPITALISTS

Much of the social thought and ideology of the twentieth century has been shaped by the Russian Revolution. The Bolsheviks, shown here storming the Winter Palace, put an end to the reign of the Russian czars and kindled hopes for a classless society not only among their own followers but among impoverished and politically repressed people throughout the world. However, the theories and ideals of socialism, when put into practice by dictatorial leaders like Lenin and Stalin, soon became corrupted. Although many impoverished Russians benefited from the revolution, the classless society never emerged. Instead, a new Soviet class system emerged, with the Communist party elite at the top. Today, as Russia transforms itself into a capitalist nation, the old party elite and the newly rich class of entrepreneurs are combining to form a powerful new class at the top of Russian society. Other classes—especially blue-collar workers who were protected under Soviet socialism—are experiencing downward mobility, at least during the painful transition to a new social order.

formed a caste society in the United States before the Civil War. The slaves were captives; runaway slaves were pursued and returned to their masters. Their children were born into slavery. Plantation owners, on the other hand, had amassed great wealth, especially in the form of land, and this wealth was passed on to their children. On occasion a plantation family might lose its wealth, or another

family might acquire a plantation and the wealth and prestige that went with it, but this form of social mobility was rather infrequent and did not alter the caste nature of the plantation system.

Today much of modern India remains influenced by caste-based inequalities. (See Box 11.1.) South Africa, on the other hand, is an example of a society that is moving

BOX 11.1 USING THE SOCIOLOGICAL IMAGINATION

The Caste System in India[1]

His name was Natwar Singh, and he was the very image of what you could and could not achieve if you were well-born in Chirora. Natwar . . . was a Thakur, the principal landlord caste in central Uttar Pradesh, and he owned 35 *bighas,* or 17½ acres—a very big farm by local standards. The average farmer owned about 2 acres. After much prodding, he agreed that his annual profit might go as high as $1,500.

Natwar was a passionate adherent of the tenet that physical labor is beneath the dignity of a Thakur, a belief that idled a good many people in the village. I once asked him what he did with himself all day long. He was stumped. Finally, his friend Tripathy, the village merry-andrew, said, "Checking."

Always at the periphery of Natwar's large, cheerful entourage was a character named Guria. He was gloomy and taciturn, with rudely chopped hair and dark, moony eyes. Always he wore the shapeless, grimy pale shirt and baggy white pajamas common throughout northern India.

Guria was a member of one of the "backward" castes, a term used in contrast to the "forward" castes, the Brahmins and Thakurs. He was a Mallah, meaning fisherman—this because his father had been a fisherman, though Guria himself had turned to farming.

Practically everything in the village turned on caste, but not quite in the way I had expected. I had assumed, for example, that the Scheduled Caste[2] farmers were denied sharecropping work out of age-old prejudice, but it turned out to be something far more modern. Landowners, according to Indrapal Singh, were "afraid that the cultivators will claim the farmer's land, and since the Government always comes down on the side of the Scheduled Castes, they may get it." It hadn't happened yet, Indrapal conceded, but you never know.

In Uttar Pradesh, I was told, almost 45 percent of government jobs are reserved for these minorities, and there are preferential loans and scholarships set aside for them. In a magnificent display of ire, Natwar Singh even composed an entire English sentence for me: "All facilities Scheduled Caste, no facilities other caste."

"But what about the Scheduled Caste families in Chirora?" I objected. "They're miserably poor."

"You're right," said Tripathy with a grin. "But they used to be poorer."

The old caste harmony, based on an unquestioned tyranny, is giving way to a modest level of rivalry. The Scheduled Castes have made a tiny bid for power; the upper castes, so accustomed to unquestioned authority, are wildly overreacting. Caste relations have come to resemble class relations as the ritual element of caste has begun to dwindle. Elsewhere in India, especially in areas where powerful landlords exercise feudal control over entire villages, the competition between the landless and the land-owning class has led to riots and horrible violence. In Chirora, where—more typically—no one owns more than 20 acres, it's just raised the temperature a few degrees.

Perhaps one can gauge the power of new ideas by the impression they have made on Chirora. No one, for example, was embarrassed at the degraded status of their wives and daughters. India's extremely tentative feminist

movement had made no inroads at all. Women, especially married women, were invisible. They stayed behind brick walls in their darkened homes, kneading dough, chopping vegetables, nursing fires, spoiling babies. At times as I walked down a dusty lane, I could see clusters of women circling their saris over their heads, alarmed lest a stranger see them and even look them in the eye. The rule of purdah, which Hindu India inherited from its Muslim occupiers, was complete in Chirora.

Certain women did not qualify for modesty, and thus could be seen outside the home—unmarried girls, widows, and Scheduled Caste women, who had to work with men in the fields. An unmarried girl is an insignificant thing, a pair of hands and a mouth, if also a giggle. A villager with three boys and two girls will answer, "Three," when asked how many children he has. Nowadays many of the girls graduate from eighth grade at the local school, but with few exceptions they don't go any further. And once a girl marries at 14 or 15 her life is fixed; her future is her mother's past.

[1]Source: Traub, 1984. Copyright © 1984 by The New York Times Company. Reprinted by permission.
[2]Formerly known as Untouchables but now called "Scheduled Castes" because they are scheduled to receive affirmative-action benefits.

away from a rigid caste system. Under apartheid, blacks in South Africa were a racially defined caste that was kept at the bottommost rungs of the stratification order by violent repression and laws mandating racial segregation. Although this situation has been changing since the remarkable transition to majority African rule, the extreme poverty of the black population indicates that most aspects of the caste system are far from ended.

During the Persian Gulf War in 1991 many Americans discovered that Kuwait and other nations of the Middle East have strong ruling castes. In Kuwait the ruling caste is composed mainly of members of a single large, immensely wealthy family—the Al-Sabahs—many of whom live on the Italian and French rivieras for much of the year. The Al-Sabahs rule Kuwait as a closed leadership caste, and after the Gulf War they were careful to reimpose their rule and forestall any democratic movement that could challenge their authority.

Classes, like castes, are social strata, but they are based primarily on economic criteria such as occupation, income, and wealth. England is famous for its social classes and for the extent to which social class defines how people are thought of and how they think of themselves. George Orwell, the author of *Animal Farm* and *1984,* also wrote about the English class system earlier in this century, when he lived among the homeless and the migrant workers at the very bottom of the class system, and among miners whose lives were sacrificed to the dangers and diseases of the coal mines. In the following passage, he described how class affected his own life:

> All my notions—notions of good or evil, of pleasant and unpleasant, of funny and serious, of ugly and beautiful are essentially *middle class* notions; my taste in books and food and clothes, my sense of honour, my table manners, my turns of speech, my accent, even the characteristic movements of my body, are the products of a special kind of upbringing and a special niche half way up the social hierarchy. (quoted in Campbell, 1984)

Classes are generally open to entry by newcomers, at least to some extent, and in modern societies there tends to be a good deal of mobility between classes. Moreover, the classes of modern societies are not homogeneous—their members do not all share the same social rank. There are variations in people's material well-being and in how much prestige they are accorded by others. Within any given class, these variations produce groups, known as **status groups,** that are defined by how much honor or prestige they receive from the society in general.

The concept of status groups is illustrated by "high society." The nobility of England is one of the world's most prestigious status groups, despite the well-publicized marital troubles of the royal family. In the United States, people

with names like Rockefeller, du Pont, Lowell, Roosevelt, Harriman, and many others, who are of Western European Protestant descent, often have more prestige than people with just as much wealth who are of Italian or Jewish or African American descent. In cities throughout the United States these very rich and prestigious families, who form a status group as defined by wealth and reputation, also tend to form groups that interact among themselves and play significant roles in their communities. The society pages of metropolitan newspapers devote most of their gossip to the philanthropic activities and private affairs of these families. Yet most of the old wealthy families in North America came from quite modest origins, as revealed by the underlying meanings of their names. Rockefeller, for example, means "a dweller in rye fields"; du Pont, "one who lives near the bridge"; Harriman, "a manservant"; Roosevelt, "one living near a rose field." Moreover, people with prestigious family names typically enjoy fortunes gained from activities that were once considered too lowly to permit entry into polite society. Thus the Fords were looked down on by high society because their fortune was linked to "smelly gasoline"; the Whitneys, whose fortune at the turn of the century spread over five states and 36,000 acres of palatial homes, were looked down on by older millionaire families because their funds were derived from five-cent trolley fares rather than from railroad freight charges. In sum, both money and family prestige—gained by living expensively and engaging in public philanthropy—are required for entry into the highest levels of upper-class society (Amory, 1960; Domhoff, 1983).

LIFE CHANCES

Rankings from high to low are only one aspect of social stratification. The way people live (often referred to as their *lifestyle*), the work they do, the quality of their food and housing, the education they can provide for their children, and the way they use their leisure time all are shaped by their place in the stratification system.

The way people are grouped with respect to access to scarce resources determines their **life chances**—that is, the opportunities they will have or be denied throughout life: the kind of education and health care they will receive, the occupations that will be open to them, how they will spend their retirement years—even where they will be buried. The place in a society's stratification system into which a person is born (be it a comfortable home with access to good schools, doctors, and places to relax or a home that suffers from the grinding stress of poverty) has an enormous impact on what he or she does and becomes throughout life. A poor child may overcome poverty and succeed, but the experience of struggling out of poverty will leave a permanent mark on his or her personality. And most people who are born poor will not attain affluence and leisure even in the most open society. (See Box 11.2.)

BOX 11.2 GLOBAL SOCIAL CHANGE

Inequality and Health

Differences in income and wealth can sometimes mean the difference between life and death. In some developing nations health conditions are changing for the better as public health measures such as improved water supply and sewage systems take effect. Nevertheless, the correlation between poverty and death remains extremely high in many nations, and in the United States it has increased in recent years. These trends are so important that social scientists and international planning experts often use health statistics as a barometer of how well a nation is doing in improving the gap between the haves and the have-nots in its population.

Two indicators—infant mortality and life expectancy—are used as primary measures of positive social change. Nations that are investing their growing wealth in their populations should have decreasing rates of child mortality and increasing life expectancy. Chart A shows that high infant mortality rates persist in the poor

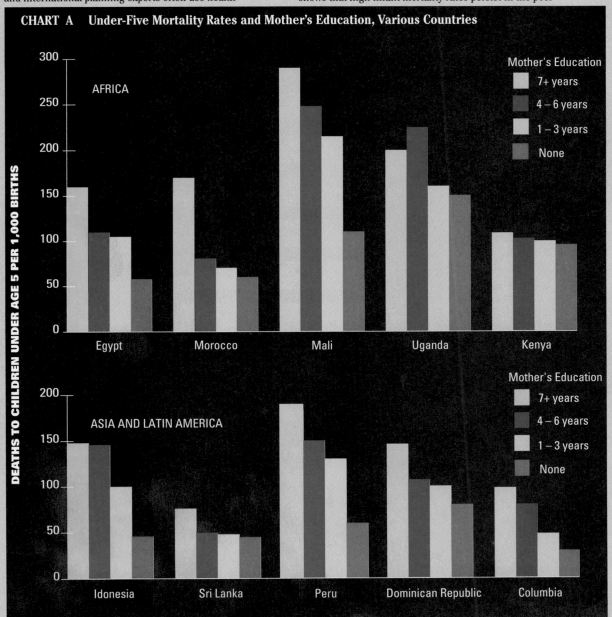

CHART A   Under-Five Mortality Rates and Mother's Education, Various Countries

Source: Rutstein, 1991.

(Continued)

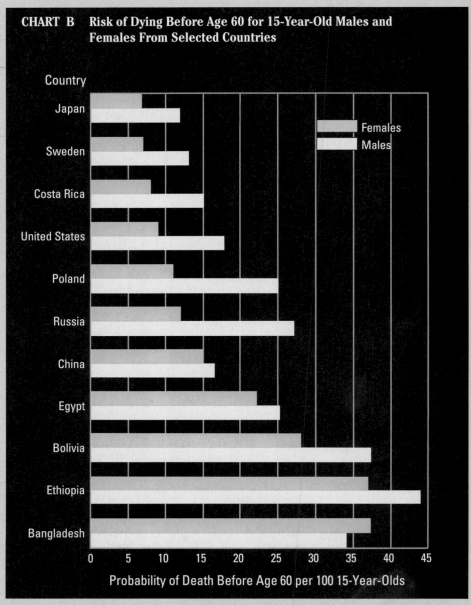

CHART B   Risk of Dying Before Age 60 for 15-Year-Old Males and Females From Selected Countries

Probability of Death Before Age 60 per 100 15-Year-Olds

Source: Feachem et al., 1993.

STRATIFICATION AND THE MEANS OF EXISTENCE

The principal forces that produce stratification are related to the ways in which people earn their living. In the nonindustrial world the majority of the people are small farmers or peasants. When they look up from their toil in the fields, they see members of higher social strata—the landlords, the moneylenders, the military chiefs, the religious leaders. These groups control the peasants' means of existence: the land and the resources needed to make it produce. Even when farmers or peasants are citizens of a modern nation-

nations of Africa, Asia, and Latin America, but that the better-educated (and more affluent) populations in those areas have lower rates of child death than the less-educated (poorer) populations. Since far more people in these nations are poor, their overall infant mortality rates are among the highest in the world. Chart B compares mortality rates for developed and less-developed nations, and also indicates how much greater risk males face (compared with females) of dying before age 60.

Throughout the world income is the single most important factor in determining survival. At the extreme of poverty, in Africa, with annual per capita income of US$800, life expectancy is 52 years. At the other end of the income spectrum, in the United States, with annual per capita income of US$20,000, average life expectancy is 75 years. There are, however, low-income regions that have invested in the health and safety of their populations (e.g., some states of India), and there are affluent regions that still rank relatively low on measures of health and survival (Mosley & Cowley, 1991; Sen, 1993).

In impoverished nations like Ethiopia and Bangladesh, the primary causes of death before old age are diseases such as amoebic dysentery (severe diarrheal diseases), which result from contaminated water supplies and poor sewage systems. In more affluent nations, the rate of death before age 60 increases for adolescents and young adults, especially males, owing to the greater risks they take in their leisure activities (dangerous sports, drug use, etc.) and the higher rates of interpersonal violence in some of these nations (especially the United States).

Recent studies of health and inequality in the United States have shown that over the past three decades the health and mortality gap between the rich and the poor has widened considerably. From 1960 to the mid-1980s the degree of inequality in mortality rates more than doubled. Racial inequality compounds this difference, as can be seen in recent statistics on class, race, and death (Chart C). Medicaid, the federal insurance program that serves more than 30 million people in the United States, has significantly improved the life expectancy of poor people, but poor diet, poor environmental conditions, high risk of contracting contagious diseases (especially new strains of tuberculosis), and high rates of interpersonal violence have helped to widen the mortality gap. Because similar trends have been occurring in affluent nations of Europe, where universal health insurance is the norm, medical sociologists warn that better insurance systems for the United States

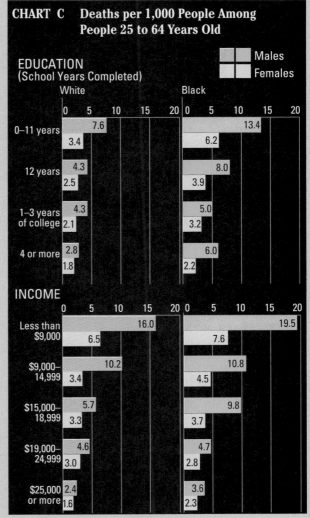

CHART C   Deaths per 1,000 People Among People 25 to 64 Years Old

Source: National Center for Health Statistics, 1986.

will not automatically narrow the gap in the absence of improvements in eating and smoking habits and other lifestyle changes among the poor (Pear, 1993).

state with the right to vote and to receive education, health care, and other benefits, when harvests are poor the landowners still take their full share while the peasants must make do with less. The system of stratification that determines their fate depends on how much the land can yield. In contrast, in the stratification systems of industrial societies, whether capitalist or socialist, most people are urban wage workers whose fates are determined by the managers of public or private firms. If the firms are no longer productive or consumers no longer desire their products, urban workers may lose their jobs and suffer economic hardship.

FIGURE 11.1 Percent of Work Force Engaged in Agriculture, Various Countries

UNITED STATES	3%
CANADA	4%
RUSSIA	14%
INDIA	66%
CHINA	69%
FRANCE	6%
JAPAN	7%
NIGERIA	54%
VENEZUELA	16%

Source: Lye, 1995; Reddy, 1994.

BOX 11.3 GLOBAL SOCIAL CHANGE

Sweetness and Power

Sugar, tobacco, tea, coffee, cocoa, pepper—these and other substances derived from plants that thrive in tropical climates were once unknown in the colder regions of the earth. Of them all, sugar has had perhaps the greatest influence. Sugar can be combined with cocoa to produce chocolate, fermented to produce rum, refined and sold in its pure form, or baked in candy and confections of all kinds. An exotic crop known mainly to European royalty in the fifteenth century, sugar had become an addiction of the masses by the eighteenth century. The craving for sugar and rum stimulated the growth of slavery in the New World and the transformation of entire Caribbean islands into sugar plantations (Mintz, 1985).

Most people do not realize that even today the production of sugar requires extremely dangerous and debilitating labor. This is especially true in Florida, where soft soils prohibit mechanized harvesting of the cane. Let a Jamaican sugar harvester who was brought to Florida as a contract worker continue the description:

In America, we work the roughest way to make a living. Coming over, they ask if you're willing to work seven days a week, willing to wash your own clothes, willing to eat poor, willing to obey, work in all style of weather, eat rice seven days. . . .

A lot of accident happen in the cane. When you working, your hand is sweaty, maybe the bill [cane knife] slip and fly up, maybe take your hand or your foot. Maybe take your partner. . . . Your hand become like part of a machine. Look at my palm, the bill rest here—it make a channel for its shape. When you go home, that one hand you have been cutting with you can't use. It's no good for anything else; you got to use the other one until it heal. . . .

We got to watch dangerous things . . . snake, bobcat, ants climbing up your pants leg to sting you, the cane stalk strike you in the eye, pierce your eardrum. Sometime to make money we got to eat no lunch, we got no time for it, sick and still working. . . . You got to be wise and understand yourself and be quiet, otherwise they send you home. It is very disappointing, the way we are treated. We are slaves. They pay us money, but really they buy us. (quoted in Wilkinson, 1989, pp. 56–57)

Investigations of working conditions for contract labor in Florida and other cane-producing areas of the United States have spurred sporadic efforts to improve conditions on the plantations. But little has changed. In fact, the officials of the cane-producing companies make free use of arbitrary firings and deportations, and they prefer foreign workers who can be easily controlled and summarily dismissed and sent home. A section of a report published by the Florida Fruit and Vegetable Growers Association, "Why Foreign Workers Are More Productive," explains how raw power maintains the flow of sugar:

The "unique and awesome form of management power" that sugar cane growers exert over their foreign workers provides a supermotivated workforce. As a Vice President of U.S. Sugar once said, "If I had a remedy comparable to breaching"—that is, firing and deporting—"an unsatisfactory worker which I could apply to the American worker, they'd work harder too." (quoted in Wilkinson, 1989, p. 64)

The stratification systems of the United States and Canada, where less than one twentieth of the population works the land, are most relevant to understanding people's life chances in modern industrial societies. But to understand the conditions of life for most of the world's population we must study inequalities in rural villages, where well over two thirds of the earth's people till the soil and fish the rivers and oceans. (See Figure 11.1.)

STRATIFICATION IN RURAL VILLAGES

In India and China more than 1.2 billion people spend their lives coaxing an existence from the soil. Millions of other rural villagers squeeze a modest livelihood from the land in Central and South America, Africa, and Southeast Asia. Social divisions in these villages are based largely on land ownership and agrarian labor. Yet even in rural villages inequalities of wealth and power are increasingly affected by world markets for agricultural goods and services, as shown in Box 11.3.

In peasant societies the farm family, which typically works a small plot of land, is the basic and most common productive group. Such families can be found in the villages of modern India. The Indian village reveals some important dimensions of stratification in Third World societies. For example, women are assigned to hard work in the fields and at the same time are expected to perform almost

all of the household duties. This is true even in families that are well off. Men from the higher castes may be innovators, but women of all castes and male members of the "backward" castes do most of the productive work (Myrdal, 1965; Redfield, 1947).

In China before the communist revolution of the late 1940s and early 1950s, a feudal system of stratification organized the lives of peasants and gentry alike. Among the peasants there were four broad strata (Tawney, 1966/1932). The rich peasants (analogous to Natwar Singh in Box 11.1) had enough land to meet their basic needs and to produce a surplus that could be converted into cash at local markets. They usually had one or more draft animals, and they often hired less fortunate villagers to help in their fields. The "middle peasants" were the second stratum of Chinese village life. They had a small plot of land, barely adequate shelter, and enough food and fuel to get through the winter. A small surplus in good years allowed them to own their own houses and even to have a few animals to provide meat on feast days. Only a very few of these "luxuries" were available to the third stratum, the poor peasants, and virtually none were to be had by the fourth and worst off, the tenants and hired laborers. Most Chinese peasants were in this impoverished stratum.

At the top of the stratification system of prerevolutionary China (i.e., above the rich peasants) were the gentry, the class of landowners whose holdings were large enough to allow them to live in relative comfort and freedom from labor.

> What made the lives of the gentry so enviable to the working peasants was the security they enjoyed from hunger and cold. They at least had a roof over their heads. They had warm clothes to wear. They had some silk finery for feast days, wedding celebrations, and funerals. . . . The true landlords among them did no manual labor either in the field or in the home. Hired laborers or tenants tilled the fields. Servant girls and domestic slaves cooked the meals, sewed, washed, and swept up. (Hinton, 1966, p. 37)

As the foregoing examples from contemporary India and prerevolutionary China show, in rural villages the facts of daily life are determined largely by one's place in the local system of agricultural production. The poor peasant family, with little or no land, hovers on the edge of economic disaster. Work is endless for adults and children alike. Meals are meager; shelter is skimpy; there is not much time for play. Among the gentry, who have large land holdings and hired help to ease the burdens of work, there are "the finer things of life": education, ample food and shelter, music and games to pass the time. Of course, wealth brings additional responsibilities. Participation in village or regional politics takes time away from pleasure, at least for some. So does charity work. But the power that comes with such activities provides opportunities to amass still more wealth. Thus it is that, with few exceptions, the poor remain poor while the rich and powerful usually become richer and more powerful. And between the rich and the poor there are other strata—the middle peasants, the middle castes with skills to sell—whose members look longingly at the pleasures of the rich and console themselves with the fact that at least they are not as unfortunate as the humble poor in the strata below them.

How does this scheme of social stratification compare with that found in industrial societies? We will see that there is more mobility in industrial societies but that, just as in rural societies, to be born into the lower strata is to be disadvantaged compared with people who are born into higher strata.

STRATIFICATION IN INDUSTRIAL SOCIETIES

The industrial revolution profoundly altered the stratification systems of rural societies. The mechanization of agriculture greatly decreased the number of people needed to work on the land, thereby largely eliminating the classes of peasants and farm laborers in some societies. This dimension of social change is often called **structural mobility:** An entire class is eliminated as a result of changes in the means of existence. As noted in Chapter 4, the industrial revolution transformed the United States from a nation in which almost 90 percent of the people worked in farming and related occupations into one in which less than 10 per-

cent did so. Similar changes took place in England and most of the European nations and are now taking place in many other parts of the world.

But structural mobility did not end with the industrial revolution. Today automation, foreign competition, and technological advances are creating new patterns of structural mobility. Older smokestack industries like steel and rubber have been steadily losing factories and jobs; newer industries based on information and communication technologies have been creating plants and jobs, but the people who have become "superfluous" as a result of the closing of their plants are not always willing to move to the new jobs, nor are they often trained to meet the demands of such jobs. Thus structural mobility often leads to demands for social policies like job training programs and unemployment insurance.

A second major change brought on by the industrial revolution was a tremendous increase in **spatial mobility** (or geographic mobility). This term refers to the movement of individuals, families, and larger groups from one location or community to another. The increase in spatial mobility resulted from the declining importance of the rural village and the increase in the importance of city-centered institutions like markets, corporations, and governments. Increasingly one's place of work became separate from one's place of residence; people's allegiance to local communities was weakened by their need to move, both within the city and to other parts of the nation; and as a result social strata began to span entire nations. Working-class people created similar communities everywhere, as did the middle classes and the rich (Dahrendorf, 1959; Janowitz, 1978).

Despite these immense changes, our relationship to the means of existence is still the main factor determining our position in our society's stratification system. We continue to define ourselves to one another first and foremost in terms of how we make a living: "I am a professor; she is a doctor; he is a steelworker." Once we have dealt with the essentials of our existence—essentials that say a great deal about the nature and the quality of our daily lives—we go on to talk about the things we like to do with our lives after work or after educating ourselves for future work.

STRATIFICATION AND CULTURE

Why do people accept their "place" in a stratification system, especially when they are at or near the bottom? One answer is that they have no choice; they lack not only wealth and opportunities but also the power to change their situation. But lack of power does not prevent people from rebelling against inequality. Many also believe that their inferior place in the system is justified by their own failures or by the accident of their birth. If people who have good

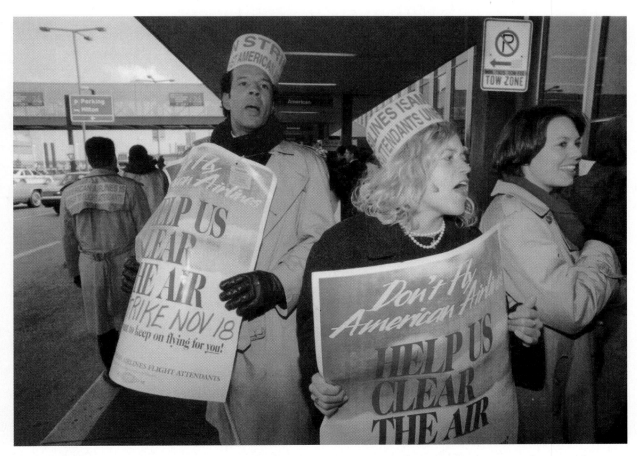

These members of the Airline Flight Attendants Union, AFL–CIO, are trying to maintain the unity of their strike by preventing other workers from crossing the picket line. Labor unions like this one are organized to represent the social-class interest of workers.

cause to rebel do not do so and instead support the existing stratification system, those who do wish to rebel may feel that their efforts will be fruitless.

Another reason people accept their place in a stratification system is that the system itself is part of their culture. Through socialization we learn the cultural norms that justify our society's system of stratification. The rich learn how to act like rich people; the poor learn how to survive, and in so doing they tacitly accept being poor. Women and men learn to accept the places assigned to them, and so do the young and the old. Yet despite the powerful influence of socialization, at times large numbers of people rebel against their cultural conditioning. To understand their reasons for doing so, we need to examine the cultural foundations of stratification systems.

THE ROLE OF IDEOLOGY

You will recall from Chapter 3 that an ideology is a system of ideas and norms that all the members of a society are expected to believe in and act on without question. The retired orphanage director we met at the beginning of the chapter still adhered to the communist ideology, which labeled speculation and profit making as forms of exploitation that would lead to greater class inequality. But in post–cold war Russia the ideology of capitalism is being used to justify competition and profit making. That ideology obviously conflicts with the former ideology of a classless society free of exploitation.

Unlike workers in the former Soviet Union, American workers have been taught that employment in private firms and the pursuit of individual gain are commendable. The ideology of American capitalism teaches that workers are free to sell their labor as individuals to the highest bidder. If they do not like the pay or conditions of their work, they are free to find a better situation. Yet often American workers find it in their interest not to act as individuals but to unite in trade unions and seek to bargain collectively— sometimes sacrificing wages or even their jobs in a strike—until their goals are met. Thus conflicting ideals and values are evident in this nation as well.

Every society appears to have ideologies that justify stratification and are used to socialize new generations to believe that existing patterns of inequality are legitimate. In the United States, for example, people love to hear versions of the "rags-to-riches" theme as embodied in the stories of Horatio Alger. After the Civil War, Alger wrote numerous books based on this theme. In his first novel, *Ragged Dick,* the central character is a poor but honest boy

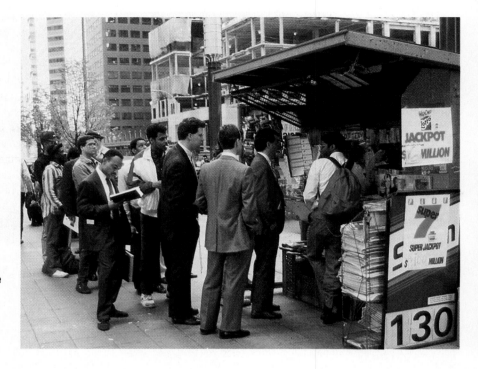

Throughout the world, governments have bowed to demands
to allow gambling and the
"rags-to-riches" dream it
embodies. Rather than continue
to fight a losing battle, they have
tried to use its popularity for
public benefit—for example,
using revenues from lottery
tickets to provide funds for education.

who comes to the city looking for work. As he walks the
streets he sees a runaway carriage; he leaps onto the
horses and stops them. In the carriage is a beautiful young
woman who turns out to have a rich father. The father
takes Dick into his business, where he proves his great motivation and becomes highly successful.

The people of prerevolutionary China were also guided
by ideology; they believed in the teachings of Confucius
(551–479 B.C.), which emphasized the need to accept one's
place in a well-ordered, highly stratified society (McNeill,
1963). Similarly, the castes of Hindu India are supported by
religious ideology. The *Rig-Veda* taught that Hindu society
was, by divine will, divided into four castes, of which the
Brahmins were the highest because they were responsible
for religious ceremonies and sacrifices (Majundar, 1951;
McNeill, 1963). Over time, other castes with other tasks
were added to the system as the division of labor progressed and new occupations developed. Still another powerful ideology had its origins in Europe before the spread of
Christianity. Tribal peoples in what is now France and Germany associated their kings with gods, and that association
became stronger in the feudal era (Dodgson, 1987).

Religious teachings often serve as the ideologies of
civilizations, explaining and justifying the stratification
systems associated with them. But this relationship has
not held in every historical period or for every religious
movement. Originally, for example, the teachings of Jesus
opposed the stratification systems of both the Roman Empire and the Jewish people. Jesus preached a gospel of love
and claimed that "The last shall be first" and "It is easier
for a camel to pass through the eye of a needle than for a
rich man to enter heaven." He showed sympathy for prosti-

tutes and outcasts such as moneylenders. No wonder his
teachings appealed to the poor and downtrodden and enraged the wealthy and powerful. But over many centuries
Christ's teachings were incorporated into church doctrine
and organization, and by the Middle Ages Christianity was
the ideology underlying the stratification system of kings,
lords, merchants, and peasants. The vicars of the church
upheld that system by affirming its legitimacy in corona-
tions and royal weddings. They also presided over the execution of heretics who challenged the system, which was
viewed as divinely ordained.

In our own era the civil rights movement in the United
States, the movement to end apartheid in South Africa, the
struggle of the Northern Irish Catholics for independence
from Britain, and other social movements often invoke the
ideology of radical Christianity. "We Shall Overcome," the
theme song of the civil rights movement, was borrowed
from the African American Baptist spiritual, "I Shall Overcome," and transformed into a moving song of hope and
protest with religious overtones.

STRATIFICATION AT THE MICRO LEVEL

These relationships between religious ideologies and the
stratification systems of civilizations are macro-level examples of how culture maintains stratification systems from
one generation to the next. But we can also see the connection between culture and stratification in the micro-level
interactions of daily life. The way we dress—whether we
wear expensive designer clothes, off-the-rack apparel, or
secondhand clothing from the Salvation Army—says a
great deal about our place in the stratification system. So
does the way we speak, as anyone knows who has been told

to get rid of a southern or Brooklyn accent in order to "get ahead." Our efforts to possess and display **status symbols**—material objects or behaviors that convey prestige—are encouraged by the billion-dollar advertising industry. Many other examples could be given, but here we will concentrate on two sets of norms that reinforce stratification at the micro level: the norms of *deference* and *demeanor* (Goldhamer & Shils, 1939).

Deference. By deference we mean the "appreciation an individual shows of another to that other" (Goffman, 1958, pp. 488–489). In popular speech the word *deference* is often used to indicate how one person should behave in the presence of another who is of higher status. Formulas for showing deference differ greatly within different subcultures. Among teenage gang members, for example, there are ways of showing deference through greeting rituals. Not performing those rituals properly may cause a gang member to feel "dissed" (disrespected), which can lead to violence. (Recall the discussion of "face work" in Chapter 5.) These formulas for showing deference illustrate how our society's stratification system is experienced in everyday life. In the United States, for example, we learn to address judges as "Your Honor" and feel embarrassed for the plaintiff who begins a sentence with "Excuse me, Judge." In most European countries, with their histories of more rigid stratification, people who want to show deference go further and address the judge as "Your Excellence."

But deference is not a one-way process. Erving Goffman pointed out that the act of paying deference to someone in a higher status frequently obligates that other person to pay some form of deference in return: "High priests all over the world seem obliged to respond to offerings [of deference] with an equivalent of 'Bless you, my son' " (Goffman, 1958, p. 489). The point here is that deference is often symmetrical, in that both participants defer according to their place in the stratification system. Through deferent behavior and the appropriate response, both parties affirm their acceptance of the stratification system itself. Intuitively we all know this. When we are stopped by a police officer we may become deferential, using the most polite forms of address ("Yes, sir," "No, sir," and the like) in order to avoid embarrassment. The officer, in turn, may attempt to find out our place in the stratification system and use the appropriate forms of address in speaking to us.

Demeanor. Our **demeanor** is the way we present ourselves—our body language, dress, speech, and manners. It conveys to others how much deference or respect we believe is due us. Here again the interaction can be symmetrical. The professor must make the first move toward informality in relations with students, for instance, but among professors of equal rank there is far more symmetry. The move toward informal demeanor, such as the use of first names, can be initiated by whoever feels most comfortable in his or her status. On the other hand, asymmetry in the use of names can be used to reinforce stratification, as in an office where the secretaries are addressed by their first names but address their supervisor by his or her last name plus a title such as Mr., Dr., or Professor.

Stratification and Social Interactions. These largely taken-for-granted aspects of how we carry out or "construct" social stratification in our social interactions can have far-reaching effects. Maya Angelou, Richard Wright, and other African American writers describe vividly

In this display of deference, then Prime Minister Margaret Thatcher makes her famous "deep curtsy" to Queen Elizabeth II.

the extreme shuffling and obsequious deference demanded of their parents in the era of segregation. Even to lift one's eyes to admire a white woman could cause trouble for a black man in the Jim Crow regions of the United States. And as we saw in Chapter 7, failure to carry out the rules of demeanor—to twitch, to have a runny nose, to encroach on another person's space—can cause a person to be labeled deviant and to be cast out of the "acceptable" strata of society.

Deference, demeanor, and other ways in which we behave according to the micro-level norms of stratification further reinforce our sense of the correctness of those norms. Thus in times of rebellion against a society's stratification system those norms are explicitly rejected. During the 1960s, for example, students from wealthy families often wore jeans and tie-dyed shirts in social situations that would normally call for suits or dresses. Long hair and beards, refusal to wear a bra, and other symbolic acts in violation of generally accepted norms of demeanor were intended to communicate rejection of the society's stratification system.

POWER, AUTHORITY, AND STRATIFICATION

When the macro dimensions of social stratification change, the changes may be reflected in the behavior of people at

This engraving from prerevolutionary France depicts the bourgeoisie, or Third Estate, as a woman being forced to support the burden of the clergy and the nobility, the dominant "estates" before the revolution.

the micro level, and those changes, in turn, accelerate change throughout the entire society. Thus, for example, the civil rights and women's movements of recent decades have altered the norms of demeanor for blacks and women. Blacks insist on being referred to as blacks or African Americans if their ancestors were of African origin, rather than as Negroes. Women refuse to be called "girls" by men and especially by their supervisors, although some women continue to use the term among themselves. These may seem to be trivial matters, but when people demand respect in everyday interactions, they are also demonstrating their determination to create social change at a more macro level—in other words, to bring about a realignment of social power.

Max Weber defined **power** as "the probability that one actor within a social relationship will be in a position to carry out his own will despite resistance" (1947, p. 152). This is a very general definition; it applies equally to a mugger with a gun and to an executive vice president ordering a secretary to get coffee for a visitor. But there is a big difference between the types of power used in these examples. In the first, illegitimate power is asserted through physical coercion. In the second, the secretary may not want to obey the vice president's orders yet recognizes that they are legitimate; that is, such orders are understood by everyone in the company to be within the vice president's power. This kind of power is called **authority.**

Even when power has been translated into authority, there remains the question of how authority originates and is maintained. This is a basic question in the study of stratification. As we saw earlier, the fact that people in lower strata accept their place in society requires that we examine not only the processes of socialization but also how power and authority are used to maintain existing relations among castes or classes.

A brief review of the causes of the French Revolution of 1789 provides a case study in the relationship between power and authority on the one hand and stratification on the other: Why did the French people accept the rule of absolute monarchs for so long before they finally ended that rule in a bloody revolution? In answering this question we can apply all the aspects of stratification discussed so far. We will begin with the feudal stratification system.

The major strata of French society, called *estates,* were the nobility, the clergy, the peasantry, and the bourgeoisie (merchants, shopkeepers, and artisans). Each estate had its own institutions and culture, causing its members to feel that they were part of a unified community with its own norms and values. The estates were linked together by the time-honored norms of feudalism: vassalage and fealty. A *vassal* was someone who received a grant of land from a lord. In return he swore *fealty,* an oath of service and loyalty, to that lord. The lord, in turn, swore fealty to a more powerful lord, until one reached the highest level of society, the king. (The feudal stratification system is described in detail in Box 11.4.) In such a well-ordered and legitimate

BOX 11.4 USING THE SOCIOLOGICAL IMAGINATION

Feudal Relationships

Imagine a peasant in a feudal society whose daughter wishes to marry a young man from another village. She cannot do so without the permission of the lord of the manor, who controls the destiny of everyone dwelling on his land. The peasant must wait for the day when the lord holds court, settling disputes and hearing petitions. Finally the day arrives. The peasant waits nervously until the reeve signals him to come forward. He approaches timidly, his wife following close behind. With the utmost humility he bows, pressing the knuckles of both hands against his forehead, while his wife makes the deepest possible curtsy. He makes his request as briefly as possible and silently awaits the lord's reply.

Feudalism is a form of social organization that has appeared throughout the world as societies have experienced the so-called agrarian revolution. It took somewhat different forms in China, Africa, Japan, and Europe, but it has always been characterized by a fundamental principle: the subordination of one person to another. As social historian Marc Bloch (1964) wrote, the essence of feudalism is "to be the 'man' of another man.... The Count was the 'man' of the king, as the serf was the 'man' of his manorial lord" (p. 145). In this system, known as *vassalage,* it was understood that women shared the loyalties of their male masters.

The swearing of *homage* signified and cemented the relationship of vassalage. In Bloch's words:

Imagine two men face to face; one wishing to serve, the other willing or anxious to be served. The former puts his hands together and places them, thus joined, between the hands of the other man—a plain symbol of submission, the significance of which was sometimes further emphasized by a kneeling posture. At the same time, the person proffering his hands utters a few words—a very short declaration—by which he acknowledges himself to be the "man" of the person facing him. The chief and subordinate kiss each other on the mouth, symbolizing accord and friendship. Such were the gestures—very simple ones, eminently fitted to make an impression on minds so sensitive to visible things—which served to cement one of the strongest bonds known in the feudal era. (1964, pp. 145–146)

The basic relationship of feudalism, signified in the act of homage, is shown in the diagram. In essence, the vassal exchanges independence for protection, but this relationship can also entail more material exchanges: The lord can give his vassal a manor with the associated land and villagers, and the vassal can provide wealth and soldiers when the lord requires them.

Sociologists study feudalism and its relationships not only because some institutions derived from feudalism still exist today but also because the exchange of independence for protection continues to appear in modern social institutions. For example, organized crime "families" often resemble feudal systems, as do many political party organizations and some business corporations. As people in modern societies fight for greater equality in economic and legal institutions, they often demand an end to what they describe as "paternalistic, feudal relations" in those institutions.

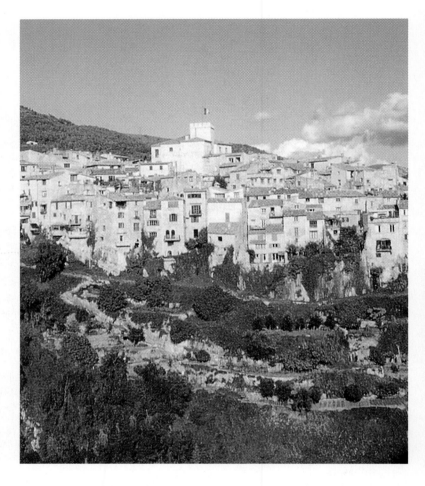

Although feudalism is no longer dominant, its former strength is reflected in the villages of southern France that date from that era. In those villages, perched amid the foothills of the Maritime Alps, the houses of commoners were clustered around a large chateau that dominated not only the village but also the surrounding agricultural fields.

system, where were the seeds of revolution? The answer lies in how power, authority, and changing modes of production combined to shake the foundations of feudal France.

In any system of stratification there are likely to be conflicts. Those conflicts may be caused by the ambitions of a particular leader or group, but sometimes the characteristics of the system, and especially of the way its powerful members try to cope with change, give rise to conflict. Both types of conflict existed in prerevolutionary France. In order to compete with the other major European powers, the king had to raise armies and send fleets abroad, both of which cost huge sums of money and required thousands of men. But the vow of fealty extended only from the king to the highest level of the nobility. The nobles, in turn, were responsible for seeing that their vassals provided more money and men. This system placed severe constraints on the king, who could not easily make direct demands on all his subjects. The king was dependent on the nobles and, through them, on the lesser lords. In return, the lesser lords often demanded more power, thereby challenging the king's authority. In order to reduce the power of the lords, the king went to the clergy and the bourgeoisie for assistance.

As the cities grew and the trading and manufacturing capacities of the bourgeoisie expanded, the king was increasingly successful at drawing on the wealth of the bourgeoisie and undermining the power of the feudal lords. The court flourished; in fact, it seemed that the king's power had become absolute. But beneath the pomp and display of the court the feudal stratification system was in ruins. The weakened nobility could no longer hold the fealty of the peasants. Throughout the countryside the peasants groaned under the heavy debts imposed by their feudal masters, and they began to question the right of the nobility to tax them.

Meanwhile, in the cities and towns the rapidly growing bourgeoisie, along with the new social stratum of urban workers, clearly understood that the king's power derived from their productive activities. They felt that they were not adequately rewarded for their support. At the same time, another new stratum, the intellectuals—people who had been educated outside the church and the court—was creating a new ideology and promoting it through new institutions like the press. This new ideology—"liberty, equality, fraternity"—helped spur revolutionary social movements, but the underlying cause of the revolution was a drastic change in the stratification system, in which the new middle class of wealthy business owners (the bourgeoisie) eventually challenged the ancient aristocracy.

In our own era, revolutions, social upheavals, and the wars often associated with them continue to occur in response to extremes of social stratification. In the early 1990s, for example, peasants in the impoverished province of Chiapas, Mexico, staged an uprising that shook the political and economic institutions of Mexican society. The Chiapas peasants and their rebel leaders continue to press for reforms in the regional economy and government.

STRATIFICATION IN THE MODERN ERA

We saw in the preceding section that under the leadership of the bourgeoisie a new social order known as capitalism largely destroyed the feudal system. Capitalism is a form of economic organization based on private ownership and control of the means of production (land, machines, buildings, etc.). Whereas under feudalism land was viewed as belonging to a family as a matter of birthright, under capitalism land can be bought and sold like any other commodity. And whereas feudal labor systems were based on institutions like serfdom, in which peasants were bound to a particular lord, in capitalist systems workers are free to sell their labor to the highest bidder and to endure unemployment when work is unavailable. Capitalism is also an ideology based on the value of individual rights; the ideology of feudalism, in contrast, stressed the reciprocal obligations of different strata of society.

In descriptions by Karl Marx and other observers of nineteenth-century society, capitalism seemed almost to explode onto the world scene. Capitalism made possible the dramatic change in production methods that we call the industrial revolution, which transformed England and Europe from a world of towns and villages, courts and cathedrals to a world centered on markets, factories, and crowded cities. A few places where the physical structures of feudalism remain, such as Mont-St.-Michel in France or Dubrovnik in Croatia, continue to illustrate the contrast between the old order and the new.

The industrial revolution began in England and other parts of Europe in the late seventeenth century. Today it is still occurring in other parts of the world, including China, India, and Africa. The former colonial outposts of England, France, and Germany are only now undergoing the transformation from rural agrarian societies to urban industrial states in which an ever-decreasing portion of the population is engaged in farming. Although not all of these industrializing societies have capitalist economies, they all are developing a class of managers, entrepreneurs, and political power brokers who resemble the bourgeoisie of early capitalism.

THE GREAT TRANSFORMATION

It is not enough, however, to describe the industrial revolution in terms of the spread of industrial technology and urban settlement. Technological innovations like the steam engine, the railroad, the mechanization of the textile industry, and new processes for making steel and mining coal were accompanied by equally important innovations in social institutions.

In the words of sociologist and historian Karl Polanyi (1944), the industrial revolution was a "Great Transformation." For the first time in human history, the market became the dominant institution of society. By *market* we do not refer only to the places where villagers sold produce or traded handicrafts. Rather, the market created by the industrial revolution was a social network that gradually extended over the entire world and linked buyers and sellers in a system that governed the distribution of goods of every imaginable type, services of all kinds, human labor power, and new forms of energy like coal and fuel oil.

Among other key elements of the Great Transformation were these:

- Goods, land, and labor were transformed into commodities whose value could be calculated and translated into a specific amount of gold or its equivalent—that is, *money* (Marx, 1962/1867; Schumpeter, 1950; Weber, 1958/1922).

- Relationships that had been based on ascribed statuses were replaced with relationships based on *contracts.* A producer hired laborers, for example, rather than relying on kinship obligations or village loyalties to supply workers (Polanyi, 1944; Smith, 1910/1776).

- The business firm or *corporation* replaced the family, the manor, and the guild as the dominant economic institution (Weber, 1958/1922).

- Rural people, displaced from the land, began selling their labor for *wages* in factories and commercial firms in the cities (Davis, 1955).

- In the new industrial order, demands for *full political rights* and *equality of opportunity,* which originated with the bourgeoisie, slowly spread to the new class of wage workers, to the poor, and to women, especially in societies in which revolutions created more open stratification systems (Bendix, 1969; de Tocqueville, 1980/1835; Mannheim, 1941).

The last point deserves further comment. The demand for full political rights originated with the bourgeoisie, which was to become the capitalist class in industrial societies—the owners of the factories, heavy equipment, and other means of producing wealth. To enhance their ability to do business and make profits, members of the bourgeoisie were interested in removing various feudal barriers to economic activity. They therefore called for an end to feudal restrictions on the sale of land, greater freedom for workers to move from one employer to another, the elimination of aristocratic privileges like the right to charge tolls for the use of roads and waterways that happened to cross a lord's property, and an end to voting rights based solely on aristocratic birth. These demands for economic and political rights then spread to the new class of wage workers and to other groups in society. Although the bourgeoisie originally sought rights for itself, it had to form alliances with workers and professionals in order to topple the feudal aristocracy. (Note that these demands originally applied only to men. As we will see in Chapter 14, similar movements for equal participation by women have taken many more generations to develop and gain influence.)

CLASS CONSCIOUSNESS AND CLASS CONFLICT

The Great Transformation had a profound impact on the stratification systems of modern societies. It produced new and powerful social classes and thereby changed the way people thought about their life chances and the legitimacy of their society's institutions. As Marx wrote in the last chapter of *Capital,* "The owners merely of labor-power, owners of capital, and landowners, whose respective sources of income are wages, profit, and ground rent . . . constitute the three big classes of modern society based upon the capitalist mode of production" (1962/1867, pp. 862–863). Here as elsewhere Marx defined classes in terms of the "modes of production" that are characteristic of a society in a given historical period. The workers, by far the largest class in modern societies, must sell their labor to a capitalist or landowner in return for wages. The capitalists and landowners are far less numerous than the workers, but because they own and control the means of production, they command more of everything of value than the workers do.

Of course, Marx recognized that in societies that had not yet undergone the Great Transformation there were classes that were very different from those of capitalist societies. The peasants of Russia, the slaves of America, and the exploited Indians of Latin America were "precapitalist" classes. Marx predicted that these strata would eventually be transformed into what he termed the *proletariat,* workers who did not own the means of production and had to survive by selling their labor.

Marx believed that the class of wage workers created by capitalism would inevitably rise up against the capitalist class and create a classless socialist society. As noted earlier, this prediction was proved wrong: Proletarian revolutions never occurred in the most industrialized nations. Yet Marx's description of how members of the working class become conscious of their situation as a class remains an important subject in the study of stratification.

Sources of Class Conflict. "The history of all hitherto existing societies is the history of class struggles,"

wrote Marx and his collaborator Friedrich Engels in *The Communist Manifesto* (1969/1848, p. 11). In the modern era "society as a whole is more and more splitting up into two great hostile camps, into two great classes directly facing each other, bourgeoisie and proletariat" (p. 11). Why did Marx and other observers of the capitalist system believe that conflict between the bourgeoisie and the proletariat was inevitable? The answer can be found by taking a closer look at Marx's analysis of the evolution of capitalism.

To begin with, Marx observed the misery of industrial workers (many of whom were children) in the smoky factories of industrial England. He saw that however wretched the workers were, there would always be what he called a "reserve army" of unemployed people who were willing to work for lower wages than those who already had jobs. He noticed that the capitalists (and the intellectuals they paid to argue in their defense) always blamed the workers themselves for the miserable conditions in which they were forced to exist. If they were hungry, the capitalists claimed, it was because they did not work hard enough or because they spent their pay on too much alcohol or because they could not curb their sexual passions and bore too many children. Thus the capitalists refused to accept blame for the misery of the working class under capitalism.

Marx also argued that business competition would eliminate less successful firms and result in monopolies, which would control prices and wages and thereby contribute still more to the impoverishment of the workers. Moreover, the capitalists had the power to determine who ran the government and who controlled the police and the army. If the workers were to rebel, the armed forces and police would intervene as agents of the capitalists. Through these means the workers and the unemployed would be forced to remain a huge, helpless population that could be manipulated by the capitalists. Over time, according to Marx and his followers, these masses of people would become increasingly conscious of their plight and would unite in a revolution that would destroy the power of the capitalists and their allies.

But why would workers become more conscious of their situation as a class, rather than merely remaining miserable in their impoverished families and communities? This problem of class consciousness became a central issue in Marxian thought. The study of changing patterns of class consciousness remains a major subject in sociology to this day.

Objective and Subjective Classes. In thinking about how a social class might be able to take collective action, revolutionary or otherwise, Marx distinguished between *objective* and *subjective* classes. All capitalist societies, according to Marx, have **objective classes**—social classes that an observer can identify by simply looking at people's visible, specific relationships to the means of production in their society. The workers, for example, are easily identified as an objective class that does not own the means of production and sells its labor power in return for wages. The capitalists are the objective class that owns the means of production—the machines and property and railroads—and buys the labor power of the working class.

These facts would be visible to an observer equipped with an understanding of what makes a social class, but they might not always be evident to the members of those classes themselves. Thus Marx identified **subjective class** as the extent to which the people in a given stratum of society actually perceive their situation as a class. For example, if the workers in the chicken processing industry in the American South are not aware that their low wages and miserable working conditions are similar to the conditions faced by millions of workers in other industries elsewhere in the world, and if they do not understand that they can improve their fortunes only by taking some of the power of another class (the capitalists), they are not yet a subjective class. Without this awareness of their situation, the workers are said to lack **class consciousness.** And without class consciousness they cannot form the political associations that will allow them to fight effectively against the capitalists.

In an often quoted passage, Marx described the peasants of France as an objective class because of their shared experience as agriculturalists with small landholdings, but he was doubtful about their ability to form a subjective class:

> A small holding, a peasant and his family; alongside them another small holding, another peasant and another family. A few score of these make up a village, and a few score of villagers make up a Department. In this way, the great mass of the French nation is formed by simple addition of homologous magnitudes, much as potatoes in a sack form a sack of potatoes. . . . In so far as there is merely a local interconnection among these small holding peasants, and the identity of their interests begets no community, no national bond and no political organization among them, they do not form a class. (1963/1869, p. 124)

The working class, Marx believed, would be different from the peasantry because its members would become conscious of their shared interests as a class.

The Classless Society. Marx and other observers of early capitalism believed that the growing conflict between the working class or proletariat and the capitalist class or bourgeoisie would produce revolutions. In those revolutions the proletariat and its allies would depose the bourgeoisie and establish a new social order known as socialism. Under socialism the key institutions of capitalism—private ownership of the means of production, the market as the dominant economic institution, and the nation-state controlled by the bourgeoisie—would be abolished. The new society would be classless because the economic institutions that produced classes would have been eliminated and all the members of society would collectively own the means of production.

Koltsovo and thousands of other Russian villages are now dealing with the many problems created by their nation's efforts to realize the Marxian dream of a classless society. But elsewhere in the world, in societies that did not experience the abuses and rigidity of Soviet communism, the Marxian view of class struggle remains one of the powerful forces giving rise to social movements to reduce inequality.

SOCIAL MOBILITY IN MODERN SOCIETIES: THE WEBERIAN VIEW

Max Weber took issue with Marx's view of social stratification and devoted much of his career to refuting it. Marx had defined social class in economic terms; classes are based on people's relationship to the means of production. Weber challenged this definition of social class. People are stratified, Weber reasoned, not only by how they earn their living but also by how much honor or prestige they receive from others and how much power they command. A person could be a poor European aristocrat whose lands had been taken away during a revolution, yet his prestige could be such that he would be invited to the homes of wealthy families seeking to use his social status to raise their own. Another person could have little money compared with the wealthy capitalists, and little prestige compared with the European aristocracy, yet could command immense power. The late Mayor Richard J. Daley of Chicago was such a person. He was born into a working-class Irish American family, and although he was rather well off he was not rich. Yet his positions as mayor and chairman of the Cook County Democratic party organization made him a powerful man. Indeed, Mayor Daley's fame as a politician who led a powerful urban party organization but did not enrich himself in doing so helped his son continue the family tradition of political leadership: In 1989 Richard M. Daley was elected mayor of Chicago.

For Weber and many other sociologists, therefore, wealth or economic position is only one of at least three dimensions of stratification that need to be considered in defining social class. Prestige (or social status) and power are the others. We need to think of modern stratification systems as ranking people on all of these dimensions. A high ranking in terms of wealth does not always guarantee a high ranking in terms of prestige or power, although they often go together.

Other challenges to Marx's view of stratification focus on social mobility in industrial societies. Contrary to Marx's prediction, modern societies have not become polarized into two great classes, the rich and the poor. Instead, there is a large middle class of people who are neither industrial workers nor capitalists (Wright, 1989), and there is considerable social mobility, or movement from one class to another. (See the study chart on page 330.)

STUDY CHART Types of Social Mobility

TYPE	DESCRIPTION	EXAMPLE
Structural	Entire occupations emerge and grow rapidly while others decline because of technological or other major changes.	Workers in high-tech industries (e.g., computers); farmers.
Individual or Family Intergenerational	Children experience mobility in either direction in comparison with their parents.	Upward—father a blue-collar worker, son a lawyer; daughter a professor, mother a factory worker. Downward—parents professionals, children waiters and aspiring actors.
Intragenerational	A person experiences an upward or downward shift in economic and social status.	A steelworker become a janitor, earning less; his wife goes to work to help make ends meet.

Measuring Social Mobility.   Social mobility can be measured either within or between generations. These two kinds of mobility are termed *intragenerational* and *intergenerational* mobility. **Intragenerational mobility** refers to one's chances of rising to or falling from one social class to another within one's own lifetime. **Intergenerational mobility** is usually measured by comparing the social-class position of children with that of their parents. If there is a great deal of stability from one generation to the next, one can conclude that the stratification system is relatively rigid.

Table 11.1 is taken from an influential comparative study of intergenerational mobility among males in the United States, Germany, France, and Sweden at midcentury, when massive changes were taking place in the economic structures of these societies. The table shows that aside from the movement away from farming in Germany and the United States, the shift from manual to nonmanual occupations was similar in all four societies. In each society most men had achieved the same social-class position that their fathers had. However, some 35 percent of the American and French respondents, 27 percent of the German respondents, and 59 percent of the Swedish respondents whose fathers were manual workers had been able to rise into the middle class of nonmanual workers. By this relatively crude measure, about one third to one half of the younger generation had achieved upward social mobility.

Clearly, the lines of social class in capitalist societies are far from rigid.

Downward Mobility.   Unfortunately, not all mobility is upward. Downward mobility involves loss of economic and social standing. It is a problem for families and individuals at all levels of the class structure in the United States and elsewhere. In its broadest sense, downward mobility can be defined as "losing one's place in society" (Newman, 1988, p. 7). In fact, the term encompasses many different kinds of experiences. The married woman who works part-time and then is divorced, loses the family house, and must move with her children to a small apartment and work full-time is experiencing downward mobility. The couple who have been living with the wife's mother in public housing and are forced out during a check of official rosters and must seek refuge in a homeless shelter also experience downward mobility. The affluent young couple living in a downtown condominium experience downward mobility when he loses his job at a brokerage firm and she must go on maternity leave while he is looking for a new job. Often entire groups of people experience downward mobility, as happened to U.S. citizens of Japanese descent when their property was confiscated during World War II, and to people of Indian descent when they were expelled from Kenya and Uganda in the 1970s.

The General Social Survey, conducted annually by the National Opinion Research Center (NORC), charts changes in people's opinions about their prospects for mobility in either direction, using questions like these:

> Compared to your parents when they were the age you are now, do you think your own standard of living now is much better, somewhat better, about the same, somewhat worse, or much worse than theirs was?

> When your children are at the age you are now, do you think their standard of living will be much better, somewhat better, about the same, somewhat worse, or much worse than yours is now? (NORC, 1994, p. 199)

Fear of downward mobility weighs heavily on the minds of many Americans. A central feature of the American dream is that our standard of living, and that of our children, will continue to improve. But that vision is challenged by the realities of global competition and the "export" of jobs to lower-wage regions of the world (Block, 1990; Harrison, Tilly, & Bluestone, 1986). Indeed, the findings of the General

Social Survey show that more respondents claim to have experienced an improvement in their standard of living compared to their parents than believe their children will also enjoy such mobility. These results are presented in Figure 11.2. We will see in later chapters that this doubt about future opportunities for one's children is an extremely powerful force in contemporary politics.

THEORIES OF STRATIFICATION

"The first lesson of modern sociology," wrote C. Wright Mills in his study of white-collar workers, "is that the individual cannot understand his own experience or gauge his own fate without locating himself within the trends of his epoch and the life-chances of all the individuals of his social layer" (1951, p. xx). We have examined the concepts of stratification and life chances and have seen that they are related to the way people gain their existence in different

TABLE 11.1 Social Mobility in Four Western Populations

RESPONDENT'S OCCUPATION	FATHER'S OCCUPATION		
	NONMANUAL	MANUAL	FARM
France			
Nonmanual	73%	35%	16%
Manual	18	55	13
Farm	9	10	71
N	(1,109)	(625)	(1,289)
Germany			
Nonmanual	58%	27%	19%
Manual	38	68	28
Farm	4	5	54
N	(579)	(406)	(321)
United States			
Nonmanual	71%	35%	23%
Manual	25	61	39
Farm	4	4	38
N	(319)	(430)	(404)
Sweden			
Nonmanual	67%	59%	44%
Manual	32	39	44
Farm	1	2	12
N	(57)	(101)	(73)

N = number of respondents.

Intergenerational mobility tables compare people's occupations with those of their parents. Here sons (the respondents) are compared with their fathers. In the United States, for example, 71 percent of sons in nonmanual occupations had fathers who did nonmanual work. The diagonal cells in the tables represent stability, or no intergenerational mobility. Thus, in France, 73 percent of the respondents in nonmanual occupations had fathers who also did nonmanual work; 55 percent of those in manual occupations had fathers who did manual work; and 71 percent of sons who were farmers had fathers who also were farmers.

Source: Adapted from Lipset & Zetterberg, 1966.

FIGURE 11.2 Perceptions of Mobility Opportunities (Respondent's Own and Children's)

Source: NORC, 1994.

societies. But what about the origins of "social layering" or stratification? That subject will be discussed in the next chapter with specific reference to the social-class system of the United States and other nations. In this section we examine some of the basic theories of social stratification. Each of the major sociological perspectives continues to generate important insights into how stratification and inequality emerge and operate in different societies.

CONFLICT THEORIES

As mentioned earlier, Marx's theory of stratification asserts that capitalist societies are divided into two opposing classes, wage workers and capitalists, and that conflict between these two classes will eventually lead to revolutions that will establish classless socialist societies. However, Marx's prediction was not borne out in any society that attempted to implement his ideas on a large scale. Deny it as they might, all of those societies developed well-defined systems of social stratification (Djilas, 1982; Parkin, 1971; Szelenyi, 1983). Each had an elite of high party officials; an upper stratum of higher professionals, scientists, managers of economic enterprises, local party officials, and high police officials; a middle level of well-educated technical workers and lower professionals; a proletariat of industrial and clerical workers and military personnel; and a bottom layer of people who were disabled, criminals, or political outcasts.

No persuasive evidence shows that class conflict is heightening the division between workers and owners of capital in capitalist societies. Conflict does exist, but the industrial working class is shrinking and the new occupational groups do not always share the concerns of the industrial workers. Moreover, reforms of capitalist institutions have greatly improved the workers' situation, thereby reducing the likelihood that the revolution predicted by Marx will occur.

Modern conflict theorists agree with Marx's claim that class conflict is a primary cause of social change, but they frequently debate both the nature of the class structure and the forms taken by class conflict. Thus Erik Olin Wright (1979, 1989) notes that Marxian theorists agree that workers who are directly engaged in the production of goods are part of the working class. However, he makes the following observation:

> There is no such agreement about any other category of wage-earners. Some Marxists have argued that only productive manual workers should be considered part of the proletariat. Others have argued that the working class includes low-level, routinized white-collar workers as well. Still others have argued that virtually all wage-laborers should be considered part of the working class. (1979, p. 31)

This disagreement stems, of course, from the fact that there is far greater diversity within all the classes of modern societies than Marx or his contemporaries imagined there would be. In addition to the bourgeoisie (the owners of large amounts of capital) and the petit bourgeoisie (the owners of small firms and stores), there is a constantly growing professional class, a class of top managers and engineers, another class of lower-level managers, and a class of employees with special skills (e.g., computer specialists, nurses and other medical personnel, and operating engineers). Perhaps many of these people should think of themselves as part of the working class, but they normally do not because they are earning enough to enable them to live in middle-class communities.

Some conflict theorists focus on other aspects of social stratification besides class conflict. Melvin Tumin (1967), for example, pointed out that stratification systems "limit the possibility of discovery of the full range of talent available in a society"; that they create unfavorable self-images that further limit the expression of people's creative potential; and that they "function to encourage hostility, suspicion, and distrust among the various segments of a society" (p. 58). Problems like wasted talent and poor self-image are among what Richard Sennett and Jonathan Cobb (1972) term "the hidden injuries of class," meaning the ways in which a childhood of poverty or economic insecurity can leave its mark on people even after they have risen out of the lower classes. In the next chapter we look more specifically at social stratification in the United States and examine its consequences in human terms.

THE FUNCTIONALIST VIEW

The functionalist view of stratification was originally stated by Talcott Parsons (1937, 1940) and Kingsley Davis and Wilbert Moore (1945). This theory holds that social classes emerge because an unequal distribution of rewards is essential in complex societies. Such societies need to reward talented people and channel them into roles that require advanced training, personal sacrifice, and extreme stress. Thus the unequal distribution of rewards, which allows some people to accumulate wealth and deprives others of that chance, is necessary if the society is to match the most talented individuals with the most challenging positions.

Research by sociologists in the former Soviet Union often provided support for the functionalist idea that extreme "leveling" deprives people of the motivation to achieve more than a minimum of skills. On the basis of extensive surveys of workers in Russia and other former Soviet republics, sociologist Tatyana Zaslavskaya (cited in Aganbegyan, 1989) argues that unless there are incentives in the form of high wages and other advantages (such as better housing in areas where good housing is in short supply), engineers and scientists will resent their situation and will not work hard. In the United States the same arguments are used to justify higher salaries for doctors, lawyers, and other professionals. Too much equality, it is said, reduces the incentive to master difficult skills, and as a result the entire society may suffer from a lack of professional expertise.

Critics of the functionalist view of inequality and stratification point to many situations in which people in positions of power or leadership receive what appear to be excessive benefits. In the early 1990s, during the most prolonged economic recession the United States had experienced since the Great Depression of the 1930s, the multimillion-dollar salaries of many corporate executives were frequently criticized in business magazines and news analyses. For example, Roberto Goizueta, chief executive officer of the Coca-Cola Company, was criticized for taking home more than $10 million in salary and bonuses. Many other executives were earning equally high salaries even when their companies were not doing as well as they might in international competition. With the annual pay of top Japanese executives often running five to ten times less than that of their American counterparts, it became difficult for the American corporate elite to argue that these enormous rates of executive compensation are "functional."

From the point of view of those who are critical of social inequality, the large sums paid to a few people seem wrong, especially when so many others are struggling just to survive. Indeed, the heads of large corporations in the United States often earn more than fifty times as much as the average employee of those corporations. Is such great disparity "functional" when it produces enormous gaps between the very rich and the working classes? Functionalist theory claims that it is, for in a capitalist system of free enterprise top executives will seek the firms that are most willing to reward them for their talents. Those firms will benefit, and so will their workers.

THE INTERACTIONIST PERSPECTIVE

Conflict theory explains stratification primarily in economic terms. So does functionalist theory. Both trace the existence of certain classes to the central position of occupation, income, and wealth in modern life. But neither goes very far toward explaining the prestige stratification that occurs *within* social classes. Among the very rich in America, for example, people who have stables on their property tend to look down on people with somewhat smaller lots on which there is only a swimming pool. And rich families who own sailing yachts look down on equally rich people who own expensive but noisy power boats. The point is that within economic classes people form status groups whose prestige or honor is measured not according to what they produce or how much wealth they own but according to what they buy and what they communicate about themselves through their purchases. Designer jeans and BMW cars are symbols of membership in the youthful upper class. Four-wheel-drive vehicles equipped with gun racks and fishing rods are symbols of the rugged and successful middle- or working-class male. Armani suits are symbols of urbane professionalism; tweed suits and silk blouses are

VISUAL SOCIOLOGY

EXTREME POVERTY

Sebastiao Salgado is one of the foremost photographers of social conditions in the world today. A former social scientist, he has won virtually every major international prize in photography. He spends long periods living with the people he photographs. "Salgado photographs from the inside," claims the Uruguayan writer Eduardo Galeano. "He remained in the Sahel desert for fifteen months when he went there to photograph hunger. He traveled in Latin America for seven years to garner a handful of photographs" (Salgado, 1990, p. 11).

The photos included in this sample of Salgado's "concerned photography" document the agony of extreme poverty. They were taken during the mid- to late 1980s and were first exhibited in the United States in 1991 and 1992.

The Sierra Pelada gold mine. (Brazil, 1986.)

Overall view of the Sierra Pelada gold mine, where more than 50,000 workers were employed. (Brazil, 1986.)

The men are covered with shiny mud. The soil in this mine is rich with iron. (Brazil, 1986.)

Children's ward in the Korem refugee camp. (Ethiopia, 1984.)

Tens of thousands of refugees from the great drought in Brazil's northeast gather near cities. Often the only way to survive is to fight with the vultures for the spoiled food in garbage dumps. (Fortaleza, Brazil, 1983.)

The great pit shown in some of these photos is a gold mine in the province of Paras, Brazil, where more than 50,000 mud-covered men carry heavy bags of dirt up slippery ladders in the hope that now and then one of the bags will yield a nugget of gold.

These haunting photographs capture two very different poverty-producing conditions. The plight of the miners is a result of the exploitation of cheap human labor in a jungle gold rush. The photos of starvation in the Sahel document the conditions of severe drought compounded by extreme political anarchy. Thousands of people have died in Ethiopia, Mali, Somalia, and other drought-stricken areas—not because food was unavailable but because violence and war kept supplies from those without guns and power.

Salgado succeeds in overcoming the "compassion fatigue" that many people in affluent nations experience when confronted with scenes of extreme poverty. He does this by spending so much time with his subjects that his photographs transcend their suffering and capture their dignity and indomitable spirit.

Able-bodied men have left for town looking for work and food. They leave behind them their families and the "drought widows." Here people are walking on what used to be Lake Faguibine. (Mail, 1985.)

signs that a woman is a member of the "country club set." All of these symbols of prestige and group membership change as groups with less prestige mimic them, spurring a search for new and less "common" signs of belonging (Dowd, 1985).

Our tendency to divide ourselves up into social categories and then assert claims of greater prestige for one group or another is of major significance in our lives. The interactionist perspective on stratification therefore may not be very useful in explaining the emergence of economic classes, but it is essential to understanding the behaviors of the status groups that form within a given class. Those behaviors, in turn, often define or reinforce or challenge class divisions. The stratification system, in this view, is not a fixed system but is created over and over again through the everyday behaviors of millions of people.

RESEARCH FRONTIERS: STRATIFICATION AND THE WORLD ECONOMIC SYSTEM

As economic globalization continues to link together cultures and societies all over the world, the study of stratification becomes an especially lively frontier of sociological research. Today it is no longer possible to think of a society's stratification system separately from those of other societies around the world. More than ever before, the life chances of people in the United States and other highly developed nations are influenced by changes in the structure of industrial employment and the worldwide distribution of jobs. The rapidly growing dependence of the developed nations on markets in Third World nations—together with the shift of manufacturing jobs to those newer nations—is creating enormous social upheavals, particularly for industrial workers in the United States.

The increase in blue-collar manufacturing work in the Third World has been accompanied by an increase in unemployment in regions of the United States that have long been dominated by smokestack industries. Thus the number of American steelworkers engaged in the actual production of steel has declined from more than 600,000 in 1970 to about 270,000 today. Similar declines have occurred in rubber manufacture, coal mining, glass production, and automobile assembly, as these industries have closed many of their plants and raced to increase productivity through automation. After all, robots may be expensive at the outset, but unlike humans they do not have social-class positions to maintain—they do not have to "keep up with the Joneses"—and therefore will not be demanding higher pay in the future. Nor do robots call in sick or demand vacations.

Harvard sociologist Daniel Bell has been studying these trends since the 1960s. He believes that the United States and other advanced societies are becoming "post-industrial" societies. Blue-collar workers are a decreasing segment of the labor force, while professional and technical workers continue to increase in importance (see Figure 11.3). In Bell's view, the employment gap left by automation and the shift of industrial jobs to the Third World will be offset by the steady increase in jobs in the service sector. But Bell foresees more than just the expansion of lower-status service occupations:

> A post-industrial society is based on services. Hence, it is a game between persons. What counts is not raw muscle power, or energy, but information. The central person is the professional, for he is equipped, by his education and training, to provide the kinds of skills which are increasingly demanded in the post-industrial society. If an industrial society is defined by the quantity of goods as marking a standard of living, the post-industrial society is measured by the services and amenities—health, education, recreation, and the arts—which are now deemed desirable and possible for everyone. (1973, p. 127)

Bell's optimistic predictions are challenged by social scientists who think the transition to a post-industrial society will involve hardships for millions of people and lead to more, not less, inequality. Their research indicates that "mature" industrial societies will not soon solve the problems of loss of skilled jobs, chronic unemployment, and discrimination brought on by these changes in the world's division of labor (Block, 1990; Esping-Anderson, 1985; Hopkins & Wallerstein, 1980; Portes & Walton, 1981). These critics contend that the jobs now being "exported" to Third World countries like South Korea, Taiwan, the Philippines, and Brazil are near the bottom of the blue-collar prestige ladder. Automation will prevent foreign workers who perform these tasks from ever rising into the higher-paid ranks of the blue-collar labor force. And in developed countries like the United States, Japan, and Australia, the already large population at the bottom of the stratification ladder is likely to grow still larger.

In the United States, for example, research by William J. Wilson (1978, 1987) shows that in the past the mobility of blacks and others depended on employment in the unionized blue-collar sector of an expanding industrial economy. But as such jobs disappear they tend to be replaced with jobs that require far more education and training or with jobs in low-paying occupations in which there is a good deal of employee turnover and little opportunity for upward mobility. Those who are early dropouts from the highly competitive race for quality education are likely to end up in the lowest-paying service jobs or in the welfare-dependent lower class.

The continued search for evidence to support or disprove this thesis and to evaluate policies that address the problem of growth in poverty and welfare dependency is an

| FIGURE 11.3 | Percentages of Goods-Producing and Service-Producing Jobs: United States, 1920–2000 |

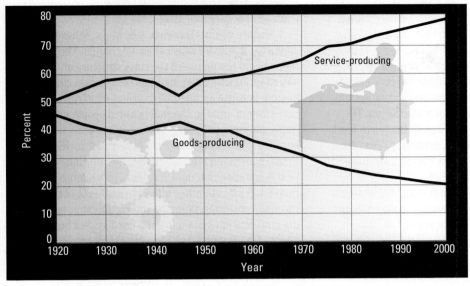

Source: Data from Census Bureau.

important challenge to modern sociology and is discussed further in the next chapter. Will it be possible to develop effective training programs for school dropouts and workers whose factories have been closed? What will be the long-term impact of chronic unemployment of unskilled minority workers? Judging from past experience, the prospects are not bright. In his award-winning analysis of poverty in the United States, Wilson (1987) argues that we need to develop new industrial strategies to bring better jobs to thousands of displaced or redundant workers. Yet he admits that such strategies are unlikely to emerge in the near future.

SUMMARY

THINK ABOUT IT CRITICALLY

People will often say something like "We know from the mistakes of Soviet communism that attempts to level the stratification system are doomed to failure. The ways in which we rank people are inherited from the past; they have evolved over time and are unlikely to change." Many people believe that those who are in the highest strata, who have the most wealth and power, deserve to be there. If they were asked to share their wealth and power, they would lose the incentive to innovate and lead. Keep this idea in mind as you review the material discussed in the chapter.

Social stratification refers to a society's system for ranking people hierarchically according to various attributes such as wealth, power, and prestige. Societies in which there are rigid boundaries between social strata are said to be *closed,* whereas those in which the boundaries are easily crossed are said to be *open.* Movement from one stratum to another is known as *social mobility.*

Most closed stratification systems are characterized by *castes,* or social strata into which people are born and in which they remain for life. Membership in a caste is an *ascribed status* (a status acquired at birth), as opposed to an *achieved status* (one based on the efforts of the individual).

Open societies are characterized by *classes,* which are social strata based primarily on economic criteria. The classes of modern societies are not homogeneous; within any given class there are different groups defined by how much honor or prestige they receive from the society in general. Such groups are sometimes referred to as *status groups.* The way people are grouped with respect to their access to scarce resources determines their *life chances—* the opportunities they will have or be denied throughout life.

The principal forces leading to social stratification are created by the means of existence in a given society. Hence, for small farmers or peasants (the majority of the world's population) social strata are based on land ownership and agrarian labor, with the members of the lowest strata doing the hardest work and those at the top of the stratification system living in relative comfort. Modern industrial societies are characterized by *structural mobility* (the elimination of entire classes as a result of changes in the means of existence) and *spatial mobility* (the movement of individuals and groups from one location to another).

People accept their place in a stratification system because the system itself is part of their society's culture. The facets of culture that justify the stratification system are learned through the processes of socialization. The system is often justified by an ideology. At the micro level, the norms of everyday interactions, especially *deference* and *demeanor,* serve to reinforce the society's stratification system.

Changes in stratification systems may have as much to do with realignments of social power as with economic or cultural changes. *Power* has been defined as "the probability that one actor within a social relationship will be in a position to carry out his own will despite resistance." Legitimate power is called *authority* and is a major factor in maintaining existing relationships among castes or classes.

The rise of industrial capitalism had far-reaching effects on stratification systems. According to Karl Marx, capitalism divided societies into classes based on ownership of the means of production. The largest of these classes, the workers, must sell their labor to capitalists or landowners in return for wages. In time, Marx predicted, the workers would become conscious of their shared interests as a class and would rebel against the capitalist class. The outcome of the revolution would be a classless society.

Marx defined social class in economic terms. Max Weber took issue with this definition and pointed out that people are stratified not only by wealth but also by how much honor or prestige they receive from others and how much power they command. Marx's view of stratification is also challenged by studies of social mobility in industrial societies, which have shown that there is considerable movement between classes.

Modern conflict theorists, like Marx, believe that class conflict is a primary cause of social change. They disagree, however, on the nature of the class structure of capitalist societies. Functionalist theorists believe that classes emerge because an unequal distribution of rewards is necessary in order to channel talented people into important roles in society. This view has been criticized because it fails to account for the fact that social rewards in one generation tend to improve the life chances of the next generation; nor does it explain why talented people from lower-class families often are unable to obtain highly rewarded positions. From the interactionist perspective, the stratification system is not a fixed system but, rather, one that is created out of everyday behaviors.

CRITICAL RESPONSE

The dream of a classless society did become a nightmare under Soviet communism. Those in charge of the state bureaucracies and the Communist party made themselves into a dictatorial class. On the collective farms the lack of incentives based on profit impeded the production of food. But many forms of inequality that had been common under the feudal system of the czars were diminished. In any case, the Soviet communist experience is not always relevant to the situation in the United States and other capitalist nations. There the great inequalities between the incomes of top corporate executives and the average worker can be a problem. And one can criticize the wide gap between the rich and the poor in the United States without adopting a policy of total leveling or embracing the theory of the classless society.

GLOSSARY

social stratification: a society's system for ranking people hierarchically according to such attributes as wealth, power, and prestige. (p. 311)

closed stratification system: a stratification system in which there are rigid boundaries between social strata. (p. 311)

open stratification system: a stratification system in which the boundaries between social strata are easily crossed. (p. 311)

social mobility: movement by an individual or group from one social stratum to another. (p. 311)

upward mobility: movement by an individual or group to a higher social stratum. (p. 311)

downward mobility: movement by an individual or group to a lower social stratum. (p. 311)

caste: a social stratum into which people are born and in which they remain for life. (p. 311)

ascribed status: a position or rank that is assigned to an individual at birth and cannot be changed. (p. 311)

achieved status: a position or rank that is earned through the efforts of the individual. (p. 311) class: a social stratum that is defined primarily by economic criteria such as occupation, income, and wealth. (p. 314)

status group: a category of people within a social class, defined by how much honor or prestige they receive from the society in general. (p. 314)

life chances: the opportunities an individual will have or be denied throughout life as a result of his or her social-class position. (p. 314)

structural mobility: movement of an individual or group from one social stratum to another caused by the elimination of an entire class as a result of changes in the means of existence. (p. 320)

spatial mobility: movement of an individual or group from one location or community to another. (p. 320)

status symbols: material objects or behaviors that indicate social status or prestige. (p. 323)

deference: the respect and esteem shown to an individual. (p. 323)

demeanor: the ways in which individuals present themselves to others through body language, dress, speech, and manners. (p. 323)

power: the ability to control the behavior of others, even against their will. (p. 324)

authority: power that is considered legitimate both by those who exercise it and by those who are affected by it. (p. 324)

objective class: in Marxian theory, a social class that has a visible, specific relationship to the means of production. (p. 328)

subjective class: in Marxian theory, the way members of a given social class perceive their situation as a class. (p. 328)

class consciousness: a group's shared subjective awareness of its objective situation as a class. (p. 329)

intragenerational mobility: a change in the social class of an individual within his or her own lifetime. (p. 330)

intergenerational mobility: a change in the social class of family members from one generation to the next. (p. 330)

WHERE TO FIND IT

BOOKS

Bringing Class Back in Contemporary and Historical Perspectives (Scott C. McNall, Rhonda F. Levine, & Rick Fantasia, eds.; Westview Press, 1991). A collection of essays dealing with theories and empirical studies of stratification in comparative and historical perspective.

The Structures of Everyday Life: Civilization and Capitalism, 15th–18th Century (vol. 1), *The Wheels of Commerce* (vol. 2), *The Perspective of the World* (vol. 3) (Fernand Braudel; Harper, 1981). A work of historical and sociological scholarship that is only beginning to influence the social sciences. The great French social historian shows in marvelous detail how social stratification has been largely explained by the way people earn their daily bread.

The Modern World System (Immanuel Wallerstein; Academic Press, 1974). A sociologist's account of the transformations in social structure and inequality that were brought about by the emergence of two capitalist institutions: the market and the firm.

The Communist Manifesto (Karl Marx & Friedrich Engels; Penguin, 1969/1848). Marx and Engels's classic description of the role of class conflict in history, with a lucid analysis of the consequences of the rise of industrial capitalism and the inevitability of a proletarian revolution. Eclipsed by events in the modern world, *The Communist Manifesto* continues to inspire readers who are critical of human exploitation and imperialism.

The American Perception of Class (Reeve Vanneman & Lynn Weber Cannon; Temple University Press, 1987). Emphasizes the extent to which there is class consciousness even in periods that are relatively lacking in class conflict, and shows how the perception of one's class membership is directly related to one's actual place in the structure of inequality.

The Debate on Classes (Erik Olin Wright; Verso, 1989). An excellent review of theories of social class in the United States and elsewhere by one of the nation's foremost researchers on social class.

OTHER SOURCES

The Europa Yearbook: A World Summary (Europa Publishers). An annual reference work that provides much detailed information on political, economic, and commercial institutions throughout the world.

Inequalities of Social Class

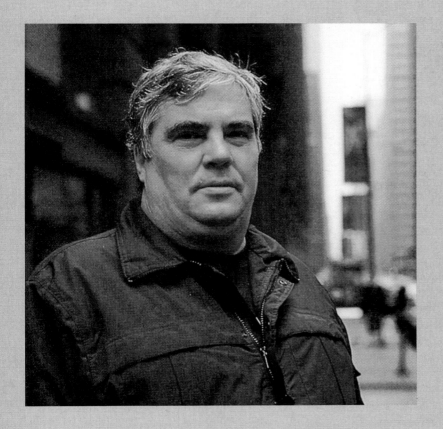

"What I always wonder," he says with a slight shrug, "is how the young people are going to find a way to get ahead now that the mills are gone." Ed Sadlowski is standing in the economically depressed streets of South Chicago, the neighborhood where he was born, where he raised his five children, and where most of them are now living and raising their own children.

"You know, Bill," he continues as we walk slowly past the deserted mill gates, "the United States makes as much steel as we did back when these plants had thousands of workers in them. It's just that we make it so much more efficiently. The productivity of the individual workers is so much greater because of the new technologies, computer control of machines, robotization, and all the rest. So the old system of mass employment in industries like steel is never going to return. The industrial proletariat that Marx wrote about is gone, at least in this country, but not elsewhere in the world where industry is newer."

Edward Sadlowski is among the nation's leading experts in industrial history and the sociology of labor-management relations. We met many years ago when I was working in a local steel mill while gathering material for a book about this famous industrial community. Sadlowski's grandfather came to Chicago as an immigrant from Poland, drawn like millions of others by the chance to use his strong back and hands in the search for a new and better life in America. His father worked in the mills too. He was one of the union's early organizers. From an early age Ed was taught that the unions in steel and railroads and mining were responsible for bringing workers a fairer share of the profits of their industries. To do so they had to constantly struggle against the mill owners, who often seemed ready to kill them rather than relinquish their control or share the wealth.

When Sadlowski was 18 he too entered the mills, but he was able to join an apprenticeship program in which he learned a skilled trade as a machinist. He immediately became active in the union and was elected to represent his workmates as their grievance officer. This meant that he was a shop floor lawyer who assisted workers when they were disciplined or fired. Their union contract afforded the workers a common pay scale and scheduled increases in their hourly wages, as well as health and other benefits that they had not had before the unions gained legal recognition in the 1930s. Overtime pay and the right to a semblance of due process in disciplinary matters were also among the union's achievements.

Eventually Sadlowski was elected president of the union at U.S. Steel's South Works, Chicago's largest steel mill until it was torn down in the late 1980s. Later in his career he ran unsuccessfully for president of the U.S. and Canadian steelworkers' union, but for his entire working life he has remained a staunch union supporter.

As we walk past acre after acre of abandoned railroad tracks and ore docks on the shore of Lake Michigan, Sadlowski wonders about the social groups that came to Chicago more recently to seek employment in the mills, especially the African Americans and Mexicans. It's clear from conditions in their communities that they are suffering the consequences of a long-term economic slump. The traditional industrial routes to the American dream of upward mobility are no longer as readily available as they were in earlier decades, he comments: "Too many people are looking for too few good jobs—you know, the kind that pay a decent wage you can raise a family on, and that pay for adequate health care."

DIMENSIONS OF SOCIAL INEQUALITY IN AMERICA

The Sadlowskis and other families in South Chicago are struggling to adapt to a set of social changes that are global in scope. People in different parts of the world are experiencing these changes in differing ways. South of the U.S. border, for example, parents in hundreds of communities miss their children, who have migrated to manufacturing towns along the border. And in the industrial centers of North America people mourn the loss of jobs to countries or regions where labor costs are lower. These changes are forcing many people to go back to school and gain new skills and credentials so that they can be more competitive in changing labor markets. Union members in manufacturing industries are being forced to end strikes and go back to work to avoid losing their jobs to "replacement workers." But these are only some of the realities of life in a stratified and rapidly changing industrial society. The U.S. economy also generates immense wealth and a growing number of jobs. The society boasts an enormous middle class, many of whose members are far more affluent than their parents and grandparents ever dreamed of becoming. Thus social mobility and class conflict, the subjects of this chapter, remain important aspects of life in the United States and

elsewhere in the world. No wonder they are central issues in contemporary sociology.

In the United States inequalities of class and status have worsened in the past decade (Krugman, 1992, 1995; Wolff, 1995). In the nation's poorest communities—in urban ghettos and on Indian reservations and in the hill country of the South—many people doubt whether the conditions of poverty and depression in which they live can ever be improved. Sociologists are currently debating the possibility that there is a permanent underclass of people who are out of the labor force, trapped in a cycle of poverty and welfare dependency that makes it almost impossible for them to experience any upward mobility. At the same time, sociological research has shown that the rich are doing better than ever and that the gap between the haves and the have-nots is widening. In different regions of the nation the details of social inequality differ, but the basic patterns of wealth and prestige and power are the same (Gans, 1995; Wilson, 1987).

This chapter further develops many of the terms and concepts defined in the preceding chapter and applies them to the study of inequality and stratification in the United States. First we discuss the ways in which sociologists measure inequality and their changing views of how inequalities result in the formation of social classes. Then we examine social classes and life chances in the United

For the upper classes, food becomes a symbol of status; its cost and the artistry of its presentation assume an importance well beyond mere nutrition.

FIGURE 12.1 Annual Individual Income, 1947–1993, by Income Quintiles

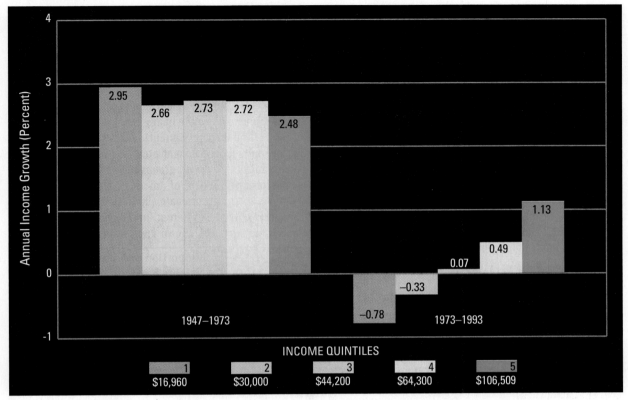

Source: Data from Census Bureau.

Note: Dollar figures are for 1992 and indicate the upper limit of each quintile except the richest. In the richest quintile, incomes can be so high (in the millions, in some cases) that the Census Bureau uses a lower figure: the lower limit of the top 5 percent.

States today and analyze the influence of social-class position on opportunities for upward mobility. We will see that there is nothing static about social inequality in the United States; changes in the class structure of North America are occurring even as this chapter is being written.

MEASURES OF SOCIAL INEQUALITY

The basic and most readily available measures of inequality in any society are income, wealth, occupational prestige, and educational attainment. Of these measures, income is the one that is most often used to give an initial view of social-class inequality. A common method of comparing incomes in a large population like that of the United States is to divide the population into fifths, or *quintiles,* on the basis of personal or household income. The researcher starts at the lowest level of reported income and continues upward until one fifth of the population has been accounted for. This establishes the upper and lower income boundaries for that quintile. The same procedure is used to identify each of the other four quintiles; the average income for each quintile can then be compared with the average incomes for the other four quintiles.

By comparing the average incomes of quintiles at different points in time, social scientists and policy makers can see how changes in income over time are distributed among different strata of the population. For example, a comparison of incomes in the periods from 1947 to 1973 and from 1973 to 1993 reveals a dramatic shift in income distribution (see Figure 12.1). The years from the end of World War II to the early 1970s are often referred to as the golden age of American social mobility. As indicated in the figure, the incomes of all the quintiles were increasing at roughly the same rate. The incomes of the richest fifth of the population were increasing by 2.48 percent per year, while those of the poorest fifth were increasing at a somewhat faster rate—2.95 percent per year. The situation today is drastically different. The incomes of people in the bottom quintile have been *decreasing* at a rate of 0.78 percent per year. Only people in the top quintile have experienced income increases comparable to those of the "golden years."

The actual distribution of income in the population is even more unequal than indicated in the figure. In 1973, for example, the 5 percent of American households with the most income earned 16.6 percent of all the nation's income. By 1993, that affluent 5 percent took home 20 percent of all income (Census Bureau, 1995). Critics point out that these figures do not include medical and other noncash benefits received by many poorer Americans. They also note that these are pretax figures; taxes have the effect of reducing income disparities. There is some merit to these criticisms. Nevertheless, when public benefits and the effects of taxes are accounted for, the proportional results shown in Figure 12.1 still hold (Gramlich, Kasten, & Sammartino, 1993).

The distribution of wealth in the United States is even more skewed than the distribution of income. Only about 6 percent of American households have a net worth of $250,000 or more, whereas more than 25 percent have a net worth of less than $5,000. Recent studies show that the United States has replaced Great Britain as the Western industrial nation with the largest gap between rich and poor (Wolff, 1995). Figure 12.2 shows that the percentage of total private wealth owned by the richest 1 percent of the U.S. population is rising quickly while the opposite is true in Great Britain, which, unlike the United States, has never been thought of as an egalitarian society.

Figure 12.3 shows how net worth is distributed among some of the most significant aspects of household wealth. The richest 10 percent of families own homes valued at about 35 percent of the total worth of American homes. The same 10 percent, however, own almost 80 percent of other

real estate, more than 90 percent of securities (stocks and bonds), and about 60 percent of the money in bank accounts (Nasar, 1992). Remember, too, that inequality expressed in dollars of income or possession of property and stocks translates into large differences in what people can spend on health care, shelter, clothing, education, books, movies, trips to parks and museums, vacations, and other necessities and comforts.

The distribution of educational attainment and occupational prestige is more nearly equal than the distribution of wealth and income. **Educational attainment,** or number of years of school completed, has become more equal among major population groups in the United States. The educational attainment of America's black population, for example, has risen dramatically in the past 25 years, and today it is not much different from that of whites. Hispanic Americans have also shown great improvement in educa-

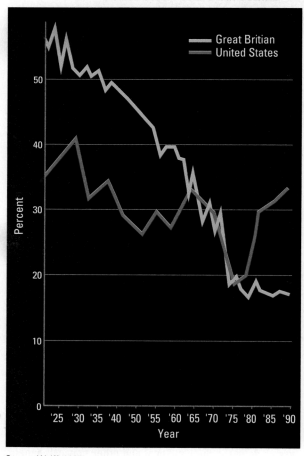

FIGURE 12.2 Percent of Private Wealth* Owned by Richest 1 Percent of Population, United States and Great Britain

Source: Wolff, 1995.

*All non-government-owned stocks, bonds, housing, vehicles, real estate, and other assets—minus mortgages, consumer loans, and other debts.

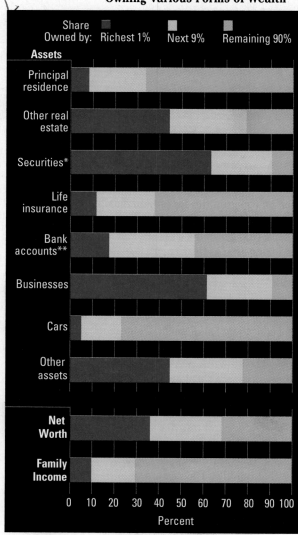

FIGURE 12.3 Proportion of American Families Owning Various Forms of Wealth

Source: Federal Reserve.

*Includes stocks, bonds, and trusts.
**Includes all deposits in checking, savings, and other accounts.

FIGURE 12.4 Educational Attainment, by Race and Ethnicity, United States (persons age 25 and over)

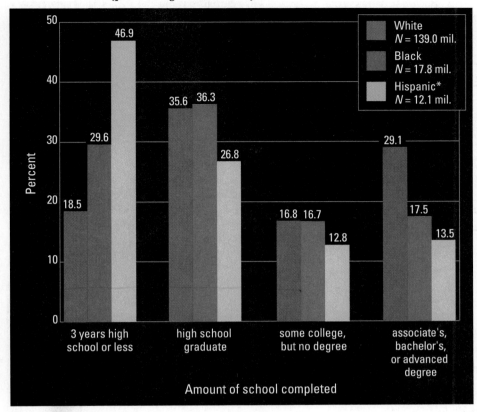

Source: *Statistical Abstract,* 1994.

*Hispanic can be of any race.

tional attainment, but they continue to lag behind blacks and whites, as can be seen in Figure 12.4.

In a rapidly changing economy like that of the United States, educated people are in increasing demand and education thus becomes a more common route to upward mobility. Improvements in **educational achievement—in** basic reading, writing, and computational skills—are increasingly vital to individual careers. For the entire society, improvements in educational achievement represent improvements in the nation's "human capital," the wealth-producing capacity of its people (Harbison, 1973). But educational attainment and educational achievement are not always correlated. When students are moved through the school system without meeting certain minimum achievement criteria, attainment figures mask significant gaps in achievement. As a result, large segments of the population are unable to achieve nearly as much as they might, either for themselves or for their society.

Another aspect of social inequality, **occupational prestige,** is measured using surveys of how people throughout a society rate different jobs. Such surveys find that the prestige people attach to an occupation is heavily influenced by the education required for the job or the authority it offers its holder, as well as by income (Blau & Duncan 1967; Bose & Rossi, 1983; Hodge, Siegel, & Rossi,

1964). Thus many occupations that do not pay extremely high salaries are highly rated nonetheless. Table 12.1 shows how selected occupations are ranked according to their prestige.

These measures of wealth, income, education, and occupational prestige indicate that not all Americans share equally in "the good life." But what are the larger consequences of these patterns of inequality, both for individuals and for society? Do they combine to form an identifiable system of social-class stratification in the United States? In the rest of this chapter we explore these questions, but before doing so it is helpful to look at how views of inequality have changed over the past century and a half, as the United States has been transformed from an agrarian society to an urban industrial society and, finally, to a post-industrial society.

CHANGING VIEWS OF SOCIAL INEQUALITY

The dominant view of American society before the industrial revolution was the Jeffersonian view, which envisioned a society in which the majority of families lived on their own farms or ran small commercial or manufacturing enterprises (Lipset, 1979; Shi, 1985; Stone & Mennell, 1980). This view emphasized the value of economic self-sufficiency through hard work—a value that has persisted

TABLE 12.1	Prestige Scores of Selected Occupations		
OCCUPATION	**PRESTIGE**	**OCCUPATION**	**PRESTIGE**
Physician	95.8	Private secretary	60.9
Mayor	92.2	Floor supervisor in a hospital	60.3
Lawyer	90.1	Supervisor of telephone operators	60.3
College professor	90.1	Plumber	58.7
Architect	88.8	Police officer	58.3
City superintendent of schools	87.8	Manager of a supermarket	57.1
Owner of a factory employing 2,000 people	81.7	Car dealer	57.1
Stockbroker	81.7	Practical nurse	56.4
Advertising executive	80.8	Dental assistant	54.8
Electrical engineer	79.5	Warehouse supervisor	54.2
Building construction contractor	78.9	Assembly-line supervisor in a manufacturing plant	53.8
Chiropractor	75.3	Carpenter	53.5
Registered nurse	75.0	Locomotive engineer	52.9
Sociologist	74.7	Stenographer	52.6
Accountant	71.2	Office secretary	51.3
High school teacher	70.2	Inspector in a manufacturing plant	51.3
Manager of a factory employing 2,000 people	69.2	Housewife	51.0
Office manager	68.3	Bookkeeper	50.0
Administrative assistant	67.8	Florist	49.7
Grade school teacher	65.4	Tool machinist	48.4
Power house engineer	64.5	Welder	46.8
Hotel manager	64.1	Wholesale salesperson	46.2
Circulation director of a newspaper	63.5	Telephone operator	46.2
Social worker	63.2	Auto mechanic	44.9
Hospital lab technician	63.1	Typist	44.9
Artist	62.8	Typesetter	42.6
Electrician	62.5	Postal clerk	42.3
Insurance agent	62.5		

(Continued)

to the present time. Yet even in Jefferson's time the pattern of agrarian and small-town independence was not universal. In the early nineteenth century American society was already developing a rather complex and diverse set of stratification systems. In New England and the Middle Atlantic states, the Jeffersonian ideal of rural farmers and town-dwelling tradesmen, all with similar degrees of power and prestige, was reflected in reality. But in the larger cities a landless wage-earning class was emerging, as was a class of factory owners, bankers, and entrepreneurs. Throughout most of the southern states, in contrast, the major classes were the plantation owners and their families and staffs, the town merchants and tradesmen, and the marginal "poor white" farmers; in addition to these classes there was a caste: the slaves.

Native Americans were not included in any of these stratification systems. By the 1830s they were already a *pariah group*—excluded from the stratification system and considered too different or inferior to be eligible for citi-

zenship. As a consequence of their pariah status in many parts of the nation, together with the settlers' desire to inhabit their lands, most Native Americans were steadily pushed west of the Mississippi.

The Impact of the Depression. A century later, in the mid-1930s, a quite different view of inequality had emerged. In the midst of the most severe economic and social depression in world history, President Franklin D. Roosevelt claimed that "one third of the nation [was] ill-housed, ill-clad, and ill-nourished." Faced with mass poverty and unemployment, with able-bodied workers selling apples on street corners, the grandparents of many of today's college students questioned the reality of the American dream. Many observers saw heightened conflict between workers and the owners of capital. To many intellectuals it seemed that the dire predictions of Karl Marx were coming true and that only a communist revolution could save millions of people from starvation. Largely as a result of the Depression and fear of social disorder,

TABLE 12.1

OCCUPATION	PRESTIGE	OCCUPATION	PRESTIGE
Beautician	42.1	Fruit harvester, working for own family	26.0
Piano tuner	41.0	Blacksmith	26.0
Landscape gardener	40.5	Housekeeper	25.3
Truck driver	40.1	Flour miller	25.0
House painter	39.7	Stock clerk	24.4
Hairdresser	39.4	Coal miner	24.0
Pastry chef in a restaurant	39.4	Boardinghouse keeper	23.7
Butcher in a shop	38.8	Warehouse clerk	22.4
Washing machine repairman	38.8	Waitress/waiter	22.1
Automobile refinisher	36.9	Short-order cook	21.5
Someone who sells shoes in a store	35.9	Baby-sitter	18.3
Cashier	35.6	Rubber mixer	18.1
File clerk	34.0	Feed grinder	17.8
Dress cutter	33.3	Garbage collector	16.3
Cattledriver, working for own family	33.0	Box packer	15.1
Cotton farmer	32.4	Laundry worker	14.7
Metal-container maker	31.1	Househusband	14.5
Hospital aide	29.5	Salad maker in a hotel	13.8
Fireman in a boiler room	29.2	Janitor	12.5
Floor finisher	28.8	Yarn washer	11.8
Assembly-line worker	28.3	Maid (F)/household day worker (M)	11.5
Book binder	28.2	Bellhop	10.6
Textile machine operator	27.9	Hotel chambermaid (F)/hotel bedmaker (M)	10.3
Electric-wire winder	27.6	Carhop	8.3
Vegetable grader	27.4	Person living on welfare	8.2
Delivery truck driver	26.9	Parking lot attendant	8.0
Shirt maker in a manufacturing plant	26.6	Rag picker	4.6
Person who repairs shoes	26.0		

Source: Adapted from Bose & Rossi, 1983.

legislators in the United States passed reform measures like the Social Security Act to alleviate the worst effects of poverty.

Muncie, Indiana, made famous by Helen and Robert Lynd in their study *Middletown* (1929), provided numerous examples of the gap in income and lifestyle between the working class and the owners or managers of capital. In the decades since 1880, industrialization had transformed Muncie from an agricultural trade center with 6,000 inhabitants into a bustling city of more than 36,000. According to the Lynds (1937), Muncie's businessmen "lived in a culture built around competition, the private acquisition of property, and the necessity for eternal vigilance in holding on to what one has" (p. 25). Below them was a middle class of managers, teachers, and clergymen who believed in the right of the business class to control wealth and power. In contrast, "across the railroad tracks from this world of businessmen [was] the other world of wage earners—constituting a majority of the city's population" (p. 25).

As a result of the Depression, there was more hostility between economic classes in Muncie in the late 1930s than there had been when the Lynds had first studied Muncie's class system a few years before the Depression. The workers and their families were far less likely to feel that the business class had a right to its wealth, and they were increasingly drawn to social movements, especially the labor movement, that challenged the power of the business class. The business class itself was far less unified because the managers of the large corporations moving into the city did not feel obligated to join the clubs and churches of the established elite. The Lynds' study is described in more detail in Box 12.1.

Yankee City and the Black Metropolis.   In the mid-twentieth century a number of studies of inequality in American communities refined our knowledge of how income and prestige combine to produce stratification in modern communities. The research of William Lloyd Warner on social class in a New England town and Drake

BOX 12.1 **USING THE SOCIOLOGICAL IMAGINATION**

Social Classes in Middletown: 1925–1985

Muncie, Indiana, or "Middletown," is the most famous community in American sociology. In 1924 and 1925, and again in 1935, Helen and Robert Lynd studied this small midwestern industrial city. They selected Muncie because it "was not extraordinary in any way and so could be taken as a good specimen of American culture, at least of its midwestern variant" (Caplow et al., 1983, p. 3). Their books, *Middletown* (1929) and *Middletown in Transition* (1937), were "the first to describe the total culture of an American community with scientific detachment. They were also the first to replicate a community study in order to trace the velocity and direction of social change" (Caplow et al., 1983, p. vii).

When the Lynds first studied Middletown, they became convinced that social-class divisions, especially those between the working class and the owners of local firms, were reaching a state of crisis. When they returned during the Great Depression, they continued to find evidence that the business class dominated the city's social institutions. In one famous passage, a local factory worker described the influence of the "X family": "If I'm out of work I go to the X plant; if I need money I go to the X bank, and if they don't like me I don't get it; my children go to the X college; when I get sick I go to the X hospital" (Lynd & Lynd, 1937, p. 74).

The X family (actually the Ball family) owned the large glass works in Middletown. The Ball brothers had built a fortune in glass jar making and then had expanded into real estate, railways, banking, and retail stores. They worked so hard that they had little time to enjoy the pleasures their wealth could obtain. But their children appeared to be creating a distinctive upper class with exclusive country clubs, farms where their horses could be maintained, and private planes.

In the late 1970s Theodore Caplow, Howard Bahr, Bruce Chadwick, and their collaborators returned to Middletown to see how the community had changed over more than 40 years. They found that the city's stratification system had changed a great deal since the Depression. The population had increased from about 40,000 to more than 80,000. This size increase brought new patterns of mobility:

> The local dominance of a handful of rich families that looked so threatening in 1935 quietly faded away during the decades of prosperity that followed World War II. Hundreds of fortunes were made in the old ways and new—building subdivisions and shopping centers; trading in real estate; selling insurance, advertising, farm machinery, building materials, fuel

oil, trucks and automobiles, furniture. . . . Middletown's new rich . . . lived much less ostentatiously than their industrial predecessors, and much of their money was spent away from Middletown (for yachts in Florida, condominiums in Colorado, boarding schools for their children, and luxury tours to everywhere for themselves). . . . The handful of families whose wealth antedated World War II adopted the same style. The imitation castles of the X, Y, and Z families were torn down or converted for institutional uses. (1983, p. 12)

The distinctive upper class that the Lynds saw emerging in Middletown in the 1930s had vanished by the 1970s:

> Meanwhile, at the lower end of the socioeconomic scale, life-styles were becoming more homogeneous. The residential building boom that began after World War II continued, year after year, to submerge the flat, rich farmlands at the edge of town under curved subdivision streets bordered by neat subdivision houses with various exteriors but nearly identical interiors. They all had central heating, indoor plumbing, telephones, automatic stoves, refrigerators, and washing machines. (pp. 12–13)

By the 1970s the factory workers of Middletown were much better off than they had been in 1935. They enjoyed job security, health insurance, and paid vacations, and their average incomes were higher than those of many white-collar workers. These changes had come about largely as a result of the activities of labor unions, which had been excluded from Middletown's factories in 1935 but were accepted soon afterward (Caplow et al., 1983). But in the 1980s the tide turned again, and Middletown, like many other industrial cities, began losing manufacturing jobs and gaining more low-paying service jobs.

Today the community of Middletown is far less self-contained than it was in the early decades of the twentieth century. It is subject to the influence of outside forces such as the shift of manufacturing jobs to other regions and even to other countries. Members of all social classes are more dependent on impersonal institutions such as corporations, national labor unions, and international markets. As a result, the old upper class has less influence, and the class structure is less cohesive and much less clear-cut than it was in the 1930s.

and Cayton's classic study of the caste system in an urban ghetto are important examples because they describe class relations more clearly than earlier studies did.

Warner's study was conducted in the seaside town of Newburyport, Massachusetts. Once famous for its whaling fleet and Yankee sea captains, Newburyport had become a small city with 17,000 inhabitants. It had a number of textile and shoe factories and had managed to hang on to quite a few of its Yankee families, descendants of the hardy seafarers of the nineteenth century. For this reason, Warner dubbed the community "Yankee City."

Here is how Warner began his description of the class structure of Yankee City:

> Studies of communities in New England clearly
> demonstrate the presence of a well-defined social-class
> system. At the top is an aristocracy of birth and wealth. This
> is the so-called "old family" class. The people of Yankee City
> say the families who belong to it have been in the
> community for a long time—for at least three generations
> and preferably many generations more than three. "Old
> family" means not only old to the community but old to the
> class. (1949, p. 12)

The new families of Yankee City's upper class, who possessed wealth but had not gained "old family" status, "came up through the new industries—shoes, textiles, silverware—and finance" (p. 12). Below this upper class, people in Yankee City identified an upper-middle class of highly respectable people who "may be property owners, such as storekeepers, or highly educated professionals, but they do not have the wealth or family status to be included in the upper class" (p. 13).

Below these classes Warner's respondents identified three "common man" levels. These made up the lower-middle class, which was composed primarily of clerks, skilled tradesmen, other white-collar workers, and some skilled manual workers. Directly below this class, and most difficult for the respondents to separate from those above and below it, was the "upper-lower class," or the people Yankee City residents identified as "poor but honest workers, who more often than not are only semi-skilled or unskilled" (p. 14).

In Yankee City the lowest class, which Warner called the "lower-lower class," was described as the "low-down Yankees [and immigrants] who live in the clam flats" and have a bad reputation among the classes above them. "They are thought to be improvident and unwilling or unable to save money . . . and therefore often dependent on the philanthropy of the private or public agency and on poor relief" (p. 14).

The six "prestige classes" that Warner identified on the basis of the Yankee City interviews are listed in Table 12.2, along with the percentage of the city's population in each class and the proportion of income spent on necessities by members of each class. It is interesting that Warner's terms, such as *upper-middle class* and *lower-middle class,* have become part of our everyday vocabulary.

At about the same time that Warner was conducting his study, other social scientists were attempting to describe stratification in larger, more complex communities. Among those efforts was the first full-scale study of Chicago's African American community. It was carried out by St. Clair Drake and Horace Cayton in the 1940s and published under the title *Black Metropolis.*

Studies of inequality in southern communities had already documented the existence of a racially based caste system in the South (Dollard, 1937). But did this racial caste system also operate in northern cities like Chicago? At the time of Drake and Cayton's study, Chicago's black population was almost entirely concentrated in a single urban ghetto. A **ghetto** is a section of a city that is segregated either racially or culturally (e.g., by race, religion, or ethnicity). Large numbers of blacks worked outside the ghetto, but even those who could afford housing elsewhere were excluded from other neighborhoods by long-established patterns of residential segregation. In addition, despite the integration of workers in industrial occupations, especially steel and meatpacking, Drake and Cayton

TABLE 12.2	Prestige Classes in "Yankee City" and Proportion of Income Spent on Necessities of Life, 1941*	
PRESTIGE CLASS	**PERCENT OF TOTAL POPULATION**	**PERCENT SPENT ON NECESSITIES**
Upper-upper	1.4	33
Lower-upper	1.6	35
Upper-middle	10.2	51
Lower-middle	28.1	59
Upper-lower	32.6	66
Lower-lower	25.2	75

*"Necessities of life" include food, shelter, and clothing.

(1970/1945) showed that Chicago's blacks were barred from more comfortable, better-paying jobs in other fields. They called this pattern of occupational segregation, in which blacks could rise only so far, the *job ceiling*. In their view the job ceiling, together with the segregation of blacks in the ghetto, constituted a northern form of the racial caste system (see Figure 12.5). Many of the persistent racial inequalities in contemporary U.S. society have their origins in this urban job ceiling and the ways in which blacks and other people of color adapted to this form of stratification earlier in the century. We return to this subject in the next chapter.

Social Classes in Post-Industrial Society. In the decades since these studies were conducted, stratification in the United States has been strongly affected by technological and social changes. As we saw in Chapter 10, the study of these changes, which are thought to be producing a "post-industrial" society, is a lively area of sociological theory and research. The black workers whose struggles for dignity and economic security are described in *Black Metropolis,* the auto workers whom the Lynds encountered in Middletown, the members of Ed Sadlowski's family who worked in the steel mills—all were part of an earlier form of industrial society in which masses of workers were employed in large-scale manufacturing enterprises. By the 1990s, however, service workers were equal in number to workers in manufacturing (Bell, 1973; Fuchs, 1968). In 1990, three quarters of all workers were engaged in providing services rather than producing goods of any kind (*Statistical Abstract,* 1990). According to Daniel Bell (1973), this change represents a "revolution taking place in the structure of occupations and, to the extent that occupation determines other modes of behavior . . . it is a revolution in the class structure of society as well" (pp. 125–126). Bell and other sociologists believe that we now live in a post-industrial society in which what counts is not "raw muscle power" but scientific, technical, and financial information. The dominant person in this new order of society is the professional, who is equipped by education and training to supply the skills and information that are in most demand.

Although Marx argued that social-class divisions in industrial societies would become sharper and that class conflict would become more bitter, many American sociologists find evidence to the contrary. Their research shows that changes in the structure of the American economy, and especially in the types of jobs it produces, have resulted in a blurring of class lines and an easing of class conflict between industrial workers and the owners and managers of the means of production. More people work in offices, fewer in factories. More people live in metropolitan suburbs, fewer in industrial communities surrounding large factories. The union electrician or plumber wears a work shirt but maintains a home in a suburb with neighbors who work in offices. The computer operator wears a white shirt and has graduate training in computer science but may re-

ceive an hourly wage. The social-class membership of these employees and many others appears to be more than a simple matter of worker versus owner. Some sociologists argue, therefore, that the various dimensions of stratification—educational attainment, occupational prestige, income, wealth, and family status—overlap in complicated ways that make it difficult for people to form well-defined ideas about social-class membership (Hodge & Treiman, 1968; Nisbet, 1970). Moreover, such factors as race, ethnicity (national origin), religion, and lifestyle crisscross economic class divisions and further blur what may once have been clearly defined class boundaries (Jackman & Jackman, 1983; Polsby, 1980).

However, other sociologists are convinced that inequalities in income, wealth, and family status still produce clear social-class divisions in the American population. Although it is true that industrial workers make up a declining proportion of the labor force, they are still a large segment of the population, as are the poor below them. And these populations continue to demand social-welfare policies like unemployment insurance and medical benefits, in keeping with their interests as less-advantaged classes. Members of the more affluent middle and upper classes also recognize the interests that they share; they may demand such benefits as tax reductions or aid to college students (NORC, 1994; Szymanski & Goertzel, 1979; Wright et al., 1982). Thus some sociologists contend that the American public does recognize class divisions and that class inequalities do play an important role in determining life chances. Although this debate continues, the empirical evidence shows that people in the United States have a good idea of the social class to which they belong.

CLASS AWARENESS IN AMERICA TODAY

As mentioned in the preceding chapter, Marx reasoned that social class has both subjective and objective dimensions. In his view, objective social class depends on a person's relationship to the means of production (whether the person owns capital or land, sells his or her labor power, engages in a profession, etc.). Subjective social class is determined by how a person thinks about his or her membership in a social class. In Marx's view, many people who objectively are members of the working class because they sell their labor power and do not own capital in fact identify with the concerns of the owners of capital because they help run the businesses that employ them; in other words, they think of themselves as members of a higher class (subjective class) but their occupation places them in a lower class (objective class).

Research on class awareness distinguishes between these two views of social class. The *subjective method* of measuring social-class membership uses interviews in which respondents give their opinions about their class rankings. This method of assigning people to classes is based on personal opinions. The *objective method* uses in-

| FIGURE 12.5 | The Job Ceiling in Government and Private Industry Prior to the Civil Rights Movement |

Source: *Black Metropolis*, © 1945 by St. Clair Drake and Horace R. Cayton; renewed 1973 by Susan C. Woodson. Reproduced by permission of Harcourt Brace.

dicators of rank such as occupational prestige (see Table 12.1), place of residence and type of home, level of education, and income, which are combined to form a composite index. These measures are not affected by the respondents' opinions. Researchers have found high correlations between the data generated by both methods (Hollingshead,

1949; Kahl, 1965). However, there is a tendency for people who work in blue-collar occupations, and therefore are in the working class by objective measures, to identify themselves as members of the middle class (Vanneman & Cannon, 1987).

Sociologists often use opinion surveys when they are studying subjective perceptions of class membership, but they use the objective method when they are interested in the effects of class membership on other aspects of a person's life, such as political views or access to health care.

In one of the best studies of subjective social class in the United States, sociologists Mary and Robert Jackman (1983) asked a random sample of Americans the following question: "People talk about social classes such as the poor, the working class, the middle class, the upper-middle class, and the upper class. Which of these classes would you say you belong to?" From Table 12.3 it is clear that very few people had trouble assigning themselves to a social class. The largest proportion, 43.3 percent, thought of themselves as members of the middle class. Blacks and Hispanics were less likely than whites to assign themselves to the middle class and more likely to place themselves in the working class.

When the National Opinion Research Center measures subjective social class, it uses somewhat different terms, which produce important differences in the way people respond. Instead of the term *poor*, the NORC uses *lower class*. Over the last 20 years the NORC's General Social Survey has found that an average of about 5 percent of Americans perceive themselves as being in the lower class (NORC, 1994). In contrast, the Jackmans found that a higher proportion of respondents perceive themselves as poor. This difference probably occurs because the term *lower class* has a negative connotation for many people.

Despite the problems of terminology just described, the Jackmans concluded that "at their basis, classes take shape in the public awareness as clusters of people with similar socioeconomic standing" (1983, p. 217). The term *socioeconomic standing* (usually referred to as **socioeconomic status** or **SES**) requires further definition. When people think of social-class divisions in American society, they first assign various occupations to broad class ranks. When there is confusion about how an occupation is ranked, people tend to think of other aspects of social class, such as family prestige, education, and earned income. And as they think about these factors they tend to reach a consensus about what social class they belong to and what classes others should be assigned to.

But that consensus is by no means perfect. Some blue-collar occupations—for example, many skilled trades, such as plumber and electrician—are relatively well paid; in fact, they are better paid than many office jobs. This leads people to classify the holders of such jobs as members of the middle class, while at the same time they may assign holders of jobs in offices and stores to the working class. Remember also that the distinction between the lower-middle and upper-middle classes was the most difficult one for Warner's respondents in Yankee City and the other communities he studied.

In addition to this ambiguity in how people distinguish among social classes, there is the problem of how classes are perceived in rural, as opposed to urban, areas.

TABLE 12.3		Distribution of Responses to Class-Identification Question (for total sample, by race and sex)								
	POOR	**WORKING**	**MIDDLE**	**UPPER-MIDDLE**	**UPPER**	**OTHER***	**NO SOCIAL CLASSES**	**DON'T KNOW**	**NOT ASCERTAINED**	**TOTAL *N***
Total Sample	7.6%	36.6%	43.3%	8.2%	1.0%	1.3%	0.5%	1.5%	0.2%	1,914
Whites	4.8	35.8	46.4	9.0	1.0	1.1	0.5	1.3	0.2	1,648
Blacks	27.7	41.5	22.1	1.5	1.5	2.6	0.5	2.6	0.0	195
Other**	14.1	39.1	32.8	7.8	0.0	1.6	0.0	3.1	1.6	64
Men	5.4	41.4	40.5	8.5	1.1	1.4	0.9	0.5	0.4	802
Women	9.2	33.1	45.2	8.0	0.9	1.2	0.2	2.2	0.1	1,112

*This category includes identification with two classes (for example, "poor and working," "working and middle") and irrelevant responses.

**This category includes Asians, Hispanics, and Native Americans but excludes seven cases for whom data were missing.

Note: The Jackmans argued that the best way to ask people how they perceive themselves in a class-stratification hierarchy is to give them information about how others define class and allow them to refuse to categorize themselves and even to deny that classes exist at all. Other studies have shown that when people are asked simply, "What social class do you belong to?" the answer "Don't know" can attain response rates of almost 20 percent, and denials that there are classes account for almost 14 percent. But when questions are asked in the form preferred by the Jackmans, sociologists find denial rates of only about 1 percent and "Don't know" response rates of only about 2 percent.

Source: Jackman & Jackman, 1983.

THEN AND NOW

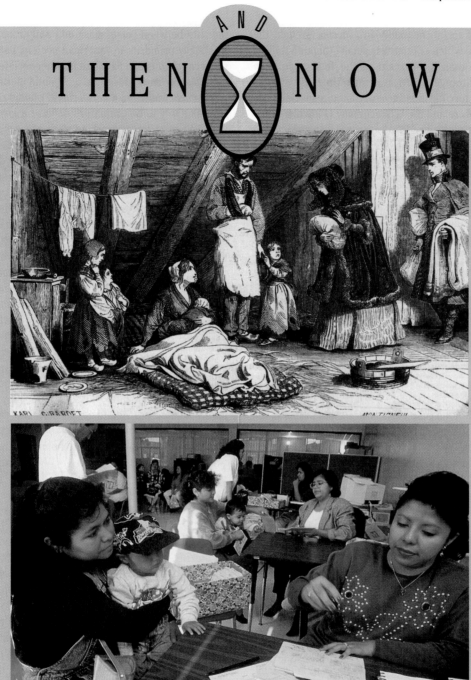

FROM FOOD BASKETS TO FOOD STAMPS

The late nineteenth-century drawing and the modern photograph shown here represent two quite different approaches to aiding the poor. The drawing depicts a well-off family bringing a basket of food to the poor. This form of individual charity, which the rich often thought of as their responsibility and obligation, frequently engendered hostility rather than gratitude. The modern welfare system replaces the individual gift with "entitlements"—that is, payments and other services to poor people who qualify for them. But the modern system is inadequate to provide a dignified quality of life. And as we see in the antiwelfare sentiment prevailing in the United States in the mid-1990s, the notion of entitlement to welfare is an easy political target, since many middle- and working-class voters are persuaded that the welfare system unfairly takes money from them to sustain "undeserving" poor people.

Most studies of social inequality in America exclude the farm population, which is relatively small—about 6 million people, or less than 2.4 percent of the total population (Smiley, 1992; Strange, 1988). But since the early years of the nation's history farmers have occupied a special place in American culture and the U.S. economy (Vidich & Bensman, 1960). The problems faced by farmers in a society that is steadily eliminating family farms have caused them to develop a strong class identity despite differences in their actual wealth. Hence, in the next section, which describes America's major social classes, we will include farmers and people living in rural areas dominated by agriculture, forestry, and mining.

SOCIAL CLASS AND LIFE CHANCES IN THE UNITED STATES

People all over the world make social-class distinctions. There are rich and poor, professionals and skilled tradespeople, farmers and shopkeepers in all nations. But the relative size of different classes, and how social class affects people's lives, vary greatly from one nation to another. As Table 12.4 shows, there are wide differences in the distribution of wealth and social class. The United States is the world's richest nation in terms of gross domestic product per capita. The poorest 20 percent of U.S. citizens have more income than the richest 20 percent in nations like India, Egypt, and the Philippines. The rich in the United States, on the other hand, have more than 10 times the annual income of the poorest 20 percent (a point to which we return shortly). Some nations listed in the table (e.g., Hungary and Poland) have smaller income gaps between their rich and poor citizens, while others, such as Brazil, have very wide gaps (Townsend, 1993). The gap between the incomes of the rich and the poor in a society is a good indicator of the potential for resentment of the haves by the have-nots.

The differences revealed in the table suggest that the meanings of wealth and poverty depend on the particular society we are looking at. Rich people in many industrialized nations may have less annual income than rich people in the United States, but some of the disparity may be offset by differences in critical variables such as life expectancy, which are not reflected in simple income data. For example, on average people in the United States spend twice as much of their income for health care than people in Japan, but life expectancy in Japan is 3 years longer than in the United States. Thus people in the United States, including the rich, may have more income yet have less time in which to enjoy their good fortune (Spector, 1994).

Numerous social-scientific studies have shown that one's social class tells a great deal about how one will behave and the kind of life one is likely to have. In the rest of this section we present some typical examples of the rela-tionship between social class and daily life. These examples apply primarily to American society, but many of the same conditions can be found in other societies as well.

Class and Health. A child born into a rich upper-class family or a comfortable middle-class family is far less likely to be premature or have a low birth weight than one born into a working-class or poor family. And a baby born into a family in which the parents are working at steady jobs is far less likely to be born with a drug addiction or AIDS or fetal alcohol syndrome than a child born to parents who are unemployed and homeless.

Among adults, a salaried member of the upper class who directs the activities of other employees is less likely to be exposed to toxic chemicals or to experience occupational stress and peptic ulcers than wage workers at their machines and computer terminals. Those workers, in turn, are more likely to have adequate health insurance and medical care than the working poor—dishwashers, migrant laborers, temporary help, low-paid workers, and others whose wages for full-time work do not elevate them above the poverty level (Ellwood, 1988). The working poor are the largest category of poor Americans, and like those who lack steady jobs they often depend on local emergency rooms for medical care and report that they have neither family doctors nor health insurance. The same poor and working-class population is also more likely to smoke, consume alcohol, and be exposed to homicide and accidents—while receiving less police protection—than members of the classes above them.

Education. Children of upper-class families are more likely to be educated in private schools than children from the middle or working classes. Sociologists have shown that education in elite private schools is a means of socializing the rich. As we saw in Chapter 5, Cookson and Persell's (1985) study of socialization in elite American prep schools found that "preppies" develop close ties to their classmates, ties that often last throughout life and become part of a network they can draw upon as they rise to positions of power and wealth. The segregation of upper-class adolescents in prep schools also serves the purpose of limiting dating and marriage opportunities to members of the same class.

Although middle-class parents are more likely than rich parents to send their children to public schools, they tend to select suburban communities where the schools are known to produce successful college applicants. The public schools that serve the middle classes spend more per pupil than the schools attended by working-class and poor children, and they offer a wider array of special services in such areas as music, sports, and extracurricular activities. Children in the middle and upper classes also tend to have parents who insist that they perform well in school and who can help them with their schoolwork. Moreover, children from working-class and poor families are more likely to drop out of school than children from upper-class families.

TABLE 12.4	Average Annual Income per Person, Richest 20 Percent, Poorest 20 Percent, and Percent in Poverty, Various Countries			
	REAL GDP PER PERSON (PPP $)[1] (1988)	RICHEST 20%[2]	POOREST 20%	PERCENT POPULATION BELOW POVERTY LINE[3]
U.S.	19,850	41,565	4,662	(13)
Canada	17,680	35,454	5,027	(15)
Sweden	14,940	27,419	5,944	—
Germany	14,620	28,200	4,943	(10)
Hong Kong	14,010	32,934	3,783	—
Japan	13,650	25,618	5,944	—
France	13,590	27,586	4,271	(16)
UK	13,060	25,806	3,789	(18)
Italy	13,000	26,780	4,441	(15)
Spain	8,250	16,603	2,858	(19)
Ireland	7,020	—	2,817	(19)
Hungary	5,920	9,599	3,225	—
Korea	5,680	—	1,893	16
Venezuela	5,650	14,308	1,329	—
Mexico	5,320	16,300	1,360	—
Malaysia	5,070	12,953	1,154	27
Yugoslavia	4,860	10,407	1,482	—
Brazil	4,620	14,469	554	—
Syria	4,460	—	1,301	—
Argentina	4,360	—	1,553	—
WORLD	4,340	—	—	—
Costa Rica	4,320	11,789	714	—
Poland	4,190	7,366	2,029	—
Colombia	3,810	10,100	762	—
Panama	3,790	10,500	715	25
Thailand	3,280	10,600	1,050	30
Peru	3,080	7,200	616	—
Jamaica	2,630	6,472	700	80
Botswana	2,510	7,420	314	51
Guatemala	2,430	6,682	637	71
Morocco	2,380	4,692	1,168	37
Phillipines	2,170	5,141	588	58
Sri Lanka	2,120	5,954	510	—
Egypt	1,930	4,900	819	23
Indonesia	1,820	3,763	803	39
Pakistan	1,790	4,078	695	30
Cote d'Ivoire	1,430	3,768	355	28
Kenya	1,010	—	191	44
Ghana	970	2,159	315	44
India	870	1,802	353	48
Bangladesh	720	1,336	373	86

Notes:

1. Instead of using exchange rates to compare cross-national living standards, this table uses a common "international dollar" calculated according to a scale of purchasing power in each nation.

2. Measures of income distribution are taken from one of the years between 1979 and 1989, depending not only on their availability but also, in the case of the richer countries, on the selection in fact made by the international agencies.

3. The "poverty line" is defined here as "that income level below which a minimum nutritionally adequate diet plus nonessential requirements are not affordable." Figures in parentheses illustrate results from the latest national surveys in rich countries, based on measures linked directly or indirectly to subsistence.

Source: Townsend, 1993.

Politics.   The poor and members of the working class are more likely to vote for Democratic party candidates, whereas upper- and middle-class voters are more likely to choose Republican candidates. Throughout the industrialized world, voters with less wealth, prestige, and power tend to vote for candidates who promise to reduce inequalities, while voters with higher socioeconomic status tend to choose candidates who support the status quo. Thus in their studies of social-class identification the Jackmans found that 48.5 percent of poor respondents and 43 percent of respondents who assign themselves to the working class believe the federal government should be doing more to achieve full employment and job guarantees, as opposed to only 24 percent of upper-middle-class respondents. They also found that about 48 percent of working-class respondents believe that "some difference" in levels of income (though less than currently exists) is desirable to sustain people's motives to achieve, whereas almost 50 percent of upper-middle-class respondents feel that a "great difference" is desirable. Members of all classes tend to agree that whatever differences there are ought to be based on individual achievement rather than on advantages inherited at birth. Members of the working class and the poor, however, are more likely than members of other classes to vote for candidates who propose measures that would increase equality of opportunity.

Photographer Barbara Norfleet was studying the lifestyles of the very wealthy in the United States when she caught this patrician gentleman stepping off his yacht on a summer day in Massachusetts.

Many other examples could be presented to illustrate the influence of social class on individuals in American society. But social-class divisions also affect the society as a whole. Let us turn, therefore, to the macro-level consequences of social class.

THE UPPER CLASSES

Only 1 percent of the respondents in the Jackmans' study identified themselves as members of the upper class. Warner and his colleagues estimated the size of the upper class at less than 3 percent of the population. For the past 10 years the General Social Survey has found that approximately 4 percent of Americans classify themselves as members of the upper class (NORC, 1994). As we saw at the beginning of the chapter, the richest members of the upper class, about 1 percent of the total population, control almost 40 percent of all personal wealth in the United States.

One of the most controversial issues of the 1992 presidential election campaign was Bill Clinton's proposal to increase taxes on the wealthiest households, those earning over $200,000 a year. Since those households had gained a disproportionate share of income and wealth during the previous 12 years, Clinton argued that they should bear a larger share of the burden of funding government and reducing the national debt. His opponents argued that "soaking the rich" would reduce their ability to invest in business enterprises. In 1994 the Republicans succeeded in persuading voters that big government was the cause of limited income growth and that tax cuts and shrinking public payments were part of the solution. These arguments continue to focus attention on the privileges of the upper class and on the fairness of the tax system.

Sociologists regard the upper class as divided roughly into two subgroups: the richest and most prestigious families, who constitute the elite or "high society" and tend to be white Anglo-Saxon Protestants, and the "newly rich" families, who may be extremely wealthy but have not attained sufficient prestige to be included in the communities and associations of high society. Earlier in this century, families whose wealth came from railroads and banking looked down on "upstarts" like Rockefeller and Ford, whose money came from oil and automobiles. More recently, the great manufacturing families—the du Ponts (chemicals), the Rockefellers (oil), the Carnegies and Mellons (steel and coal)—have questioned the upper-class status of families like the Kennedys, whose wealth originally came from merchandising and whose Irish descent marked them off from the rich Protestant families.

Members of the upper class tend to create special places in which to live and relax. They often maintain apartments in exclusive city neighborhoods as well as country estates in secluded communities. They send their children to the most expensive private schools and universities, maintain memberships in the most exclusive social clubs, and fly throughout the world to leisure resorts frequented by members of their own class.

A question that sociologists continually debate is whether the upper class in America is also the society's ruling class. Some, like C. Wright Mills and William Domhoff, argue that the upper class not only holds a controlling share of wealth and prestige, which it can pass along to its children, but also maintains a virtual monopoly over power in the United States. A ruling class, Domhoff states, "is socially cohesive, has its basis in the large corporations and banks, plays a major role in shaping the social and political climate, and dominates the federal government through a variety of organizations and methods" (1983, p. 1). Mills (1956) attempted to show that this ruling class produces a *power elite* composed of its most politically active members plus high-level employees in the government and the military. The power elite, in other words, is the leadership arm of the ruling class.

Other sociologists and political scientists contend that there is no single, cohesive ruling class with an identifiable power elite that carries out its bidding. This is known as the *pluralist* concept (Keller, 1963; Parsons, 1965; Polsby, 1980). These researchers agree that there is a readily identifiable upper class in American society. However, its power is not exerted in a unified fashion because there are competing centers of wealth and power within the upper class; moreover, its members' viewpoints on social policy are often opposed to one another. (We return to the debate between the power elite and pluralist theories in Chapter 20.)

THE MIDDLE CLASSES

Unlike the upper classes, in which family status establishes who is included in the highest stratum and who is not, the middle class includes far more varied combinations of wealth and prestige. This makes it more difficult to establish precise boundaries between the upper-middle, middle, and lower-middle classes. Thus 8.2 percent of the Jackmans' respondents assigned themselves to the upper-middle class while 43.3 percent felt that they belonged in the middle class. These estimates vary in other surveys, an indication that people have no firm dividing line in mind when they ask themselves whether they are in the upper-middle class or the middle class.

One group of Americans who usually identify themselves as members of the middle class are highly educated professionals. Most often they have attended graduate schools and built successful careers as engineers, lawyers, doctors, dentists, stockbrokers, or corporate managers. But their comfortable incomes, often well above $100,000 a year, may also be derived from family-owned businesses. Members of this class typically live in the suburbs. They join expensive country clubs, are active in community affairs, and spend a good deal of time transporting their children to "enriching" activities.

Another segment of the middle class is composed of people whose income is derived from small businesses, especially stores and community-oriented enterprises (in contrast with large corporations that have offices at many locations). Often referred to as the *petit bourgeoisie* or independent small-business owners, the members of this class may be found among the leaders of local chambers of commerce and other business associations that advocate local economic growth. Erik Olin Wright and his colleagues (1982) found that of the 9 percent of Americans who employ other workers, the majority are members of the petit bourgeoisie and employ fewer than 10 people.

The American concept of the middle class is based far more on patterns of consumption and the American dream of shared affluence than on the kinds of economic realities that Marx used to describe social classes. Americans have always believed that they could achieve individual affluence and become part of a great middle class. Thus in subjective terms the middle class is the largest single class in American society, but in cultural terms it is highly diverse because so many different lifestyles are represented within it.

The dominant image of the middle class from the end of World War II until the mid-1970s was of a suburban population living in relatively new private homes. The culture of the suburban middle class was thought to be shaped by the experience of frequent changes of residence and long-distance commuting, together with status symbols like "the ranch house with its two car garage, lawn and barbecue, and the nearby church and shopping center" (Schwartz, 1976, p. 327). The suburban middle class was said to be oriented toward family life and suspicious of the offbeat (Fava, 1956; Riesman, 1957; Seeley, Sim, & Loosley, 1955). However, empirical research by a number of sociologists, including Bennett Berger (1961), Herbert Gans (1967, 1976), and M. P. Baumgartner (1988), has shown that suburban communities are far from homogeneous, that many people who think of themselves as members of the working class can be found in them, and that there is no easily identified middle-class suburban culture.

Another change in the nature of the middle class has to do with education. In the 1950s and 1960s a college diploma was often viewed as a passport to the American middle-class way of life. But we will see later that, although education remains the primary route to upward mobility for people without inherited wealth, the college diploma has lost some of its power to open the door to middle-class prestige.

The most general points that sociologists can make about the middle class are that its members tend to be employed in nonmanual occupations and that they usually have to work hard to afford the material things that are more easily acquired by the upper-middle class. Identification with the middle class is likely to be highest among teachers, middle- and lower-level office managers and clerical employees, government bureaucrats, and workers in the uniformed services.

Effects of Economic Insecurity. Political candidates attempt to win the support of the middle class because they recognize that large numbers of voters think of themselves as members of that class, rather than as rich or poor. But as we have seen, the idea of an all-inclusive American middle class is more a myth than a reality for increasing numbers of working Americans. Between the extremes of poverty and wealth are, instead of a unified middle class, two increasingly distinct groups that think of themselves as middle class but face far different life chances and economic realities.

In the more secure segment of the middle class are highly skilled, highly educated professionals and managerial women and men who are doing rather well, although they increasingly experience income stagnation and must find ways to supplement their incomes. But below this segment there is a larger stratum of less skilled and less educated people who are experiencing ever-greater economic insecurity due to stagnant incomes and declining living standards. Appealing to this growing insecure middle-class stratum is a central goal of political leaders.

Politics aside, it is doubtful that the problems of the middle class can be solved through social policy. Recent figures released by the Department of Labor show that people in the middle income quintile are now spending almost half their incomes on three basic necessities of life: housing (approximately 32 percent), utilities (approximately 8 percent), and health care (approximately 7 percent). A generation ago these expenditures accounted for only one third of a typical middle-class income. (Spending on food has remained fairly constant.) Also, during the period from 1975 to 1995 the average price of a house rose by nearly 330 percent while the consumer price index increased by 220 percent. As a result, fewer young people can afford to buy a private home, perhaps the central symbol of membership in the American middle class (Cassidy, 1995). These indicators point to some of the most far-reaching aspects of social change in our nation and others like it, and in later chapters we will have many reasons to examine their consequences for adults and children in all social classes.

THE WORKING CLASS

The Jackman survey found that 36.6 percent of Americans identify themselves as part of the working class, and the General Social Survey estimates its proportion at slightly more than 40 percent of the population (NORC, 1994). This is the class that is undergoing the most rapid and difficult changes in America today. Changing production technologies and the spread of industrialization throughout the world have resulted in plant shutdowns in the United States and a shrinking number of stable, benefits-paying jobs for members of this class.

The most important characteristic of the working class is employment in skilled, semiskilled, or unskilled manual occupations. Another distinguishing feature of this class is union membership; in fact, labor unions refer to their members as "working people." However, the proportion of workers who are union members is declining. In the mid-1970s approximately 23 percent of the American labor force

These hotel workers, proudly showing off the luxurious accommodations they help maintain, are part of the working class. In fact, far more people are now employed in restaurants and hotels than in metal, automobile, and textile production combined.

belonged to labor unions. Today that proportion has declined to less than 16 percent, largely as a result of the decline in factory employment. One result of this trend is that many workers have less protection against arbitrary changes in their working conditions and earnings. Another is that the wages of working people are decreasing—especially in semiskilled and unskilled blue-collar jobs. This controversial issue has been thoroughly documented in the research of Richard Freeman (1994), who has shown that the decreases in union membership and hourly wages account for as much as half of the increase in income inequality referred to in Figure 12.1.

There are two major divisions within the American working class. The first is often known as the industrial working class and consists of blue-collar workers who work in large manufacturing industries and are members of industrial unions. The United Automobile Workers, the United Steelworkers, the International Ladies' Garment Workers' Union, the United Mine Workers, and the International Brotherhood of Teamsters are examples of such unions (Aronowitz & DiFazio, 1994; Blauner, 1964; Burawoy, 1980; Kornblum, 1974). The second major division of the American working class is composed of workers employed in skilled crafts, especially in the construction trades (Halle, 1984; LeMasters, 1975).

Sociologists have found that the industrial working class is more conscious of its class identity and more prone to believe that its fortunes as a class depend on its ability to win in labor-management conflicts. Members of the skilled trades, by contrast, are more likely to be uncertain about their class identity or to think of themselves as members of the middle class. For both segments of the working class, financial worries are a routine fact of life (Halle, 1984). The situation of women in this class is especially problematic, since they are often the first to suffer the effects of layoffs and plant closings (Rosen, 1987), an issue that is discussed further in Chapter 14.

There is more racial and ethnic diversity in the working class than in other classes. White workers in the working class are far more likely to work alongside black and Hispanic workers, for example, than are white members of other classes. This situation often brings workers of different races and ethnic backgrounds into competition when jobs are in short supply or an industry is shrinking as a result of automation. The animosity produced by such competition is due largely to the fear of losing one's job and skidding downward into the ranks of the poor.

THE POOR

Studies of subjective class membership usually underestimate the poor population because many people in this class think of themselves as working people who are underpaid or "down on their luck." Thus in the Jackmans' survey only 7.6 percent of the respondents identified with the poor as a social class, a far smaller proportion than is indicated by official statistics, which show that 14.5 percent of Americans—36.9 million people—are living in poverty (*Statistical Abstract*, 1994). As shown in Figure 12.6, minority group members, children, and people with limited education are disproportionately represented in this social class.

Social scientists often point out that poverty is not an absolute concept. A family of four in the United States with an annual income of $14,335 is poor by official standards, yet compared with equivalent families in India or Africa it is doing quite well. The U.S. family probably has permanent shelter, even if it is in a slum or a run-down neighborhood. It probably receives some form of government income supplement, if only in the form of food stamps and federal medical insurance (Medicaid). The poor family in Africa or India, by contrast, may be living without permanent shelter, forced to beg and sift through scraps to obtain enough food to survive. Although there are poor families and individuals in the United States who exist under similar conditions, most of the U.S. poor are not yet in immediate danger of starvation.

Does this mean that the poor in the United States are better off? In absolute terms (that is, in comparison with the poor in very poor nations), they are not deprived of the necessities of life. In relative terms (that is, in comparison with the more affluent majority in the United States), they are severely deprived. This distinction between absolute and relative deprivation is important in explaining how people feel about being poor. It is no comfort to a child in a poor family in the United States whose parents cannot afford fancy sneakers or a color TV that there are people starving in Africa. In short, people feel poor in comparison with others around them who have more.

In the United States official poverty measures have always taken into consideration the fact that poverty should be measured in relation to the condition of others who have more of the "essentials" of life. Box 12.2 describes how the poverty threshold is defined.

One of the chief causes of poverty is that people who are working full-time are not being paid wages that give them enough income to raise them above the poverty line. In a study of the working poor, David Ellwood found that among two-parent families who were poor, 44 percent had at least one member who was working full-time. Low wages, Ellwood states, are a major cause of poverty:

> Work does not always guarantee a route out of poverty. A full-time minimum-wage job (which pays $4.25 per hour) does not even come close to supporting a family of three at the poverty line. Even one full-time job and one half-time job at the minimum wage will not bring a family of four up to the poverty line.[1] (1988, p. 88)

---

[1] Forty hours a week at a wage of $4.25 an hour earns $170; this amount multiplied by 52 yields an annual income of $8,840.

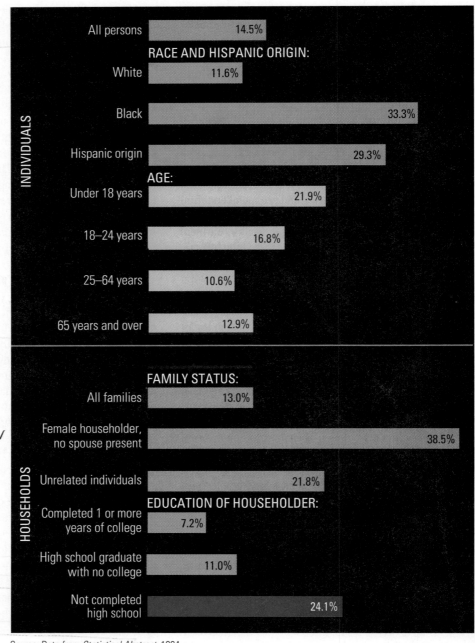

| FIGURE 12.6 | Percent of Individuals and Households Below Poverty Level: Selected Characteristics, 1992 |

INDIVIDUALS

All persons — 14.5%

RACE AND HISPANIC ORIGIN:
White — 11.6%
Black — 33.3%
Hispanic origin — 29.3%

AGE:
Under 18 years — 21.9%
18–24 years — 16.8%
25–64 years — 10.6%
65 years and over — 12.9%

HOUSEHOLDS

FAMILY STATUS:
All families — 13.0%
Female householder, no spouse present — 38.5%
Unrelated individuals — 21.8%

EDUCATION OF HOUSEHOLDER:
Completed 1 or more years of college — 7.2%
High school graduate with no college — 11.0%
Not completed high school — 24.1%

Source: Data from *Statistical Abstract*, 1994.

Since so many of the jobs created during the economic expansion of the 1980s were low-wage jobs, rates of employment and poverty have risen simultaneously.

Another reason for the increase in poverty is the increase in the number of single-parent, female-headed families. The breakup of marriages or long-term relationships leaves women alone with the responsibility for raising small children and earning the income to do so. Such families often become poor because it is more difficult for a woman to support a family alone than it is for a man. As we will see in Chapter 16, one result of this trend toward the "feminization" of poverty is that a rising proportion of the nation's children are growing up in poor female-headed families and are deprived of the advantages enjoyed by children from more affluent homes.

A common stereotype of the poor in the United States is that they are heavily concentrated in inner-city minority ghettos. Ellwood's study of poverty shows this notion to be

BOX 12.2 SOCIOLOGICAL METHODS

Measuring Poverty in the United States

The official method for measuring poverty in the United States was established in the mid-1960s by Social Security Administration statistician Mollie Orshansky. Orshansky rejected the practice of choosing an arbitrary level of income, such as $3,000 a year (a figure that was commonly selected at the time), to calculate how many Americans were poor. Instead, she argued, one should calculate simple but nutritionally adequate food budgets for families of different sizes. She assumed that food accounts for about one third of total family expenditures, basing this assumption on a food consumption survey done in 1955 (Orshansky, 1965). By this reasoning, "any family whose income was less than three times the cost of the minimum food budgets of the Department of Agriculture was classified as poor" (Ruggles, 1992).

This measure is still used today with minor changes, such as multiplying by 4 instead of 3 on the basis of data showing that food accounts for close to one fourth of average family income. The measure is also adjusted for inflation. The calculations allow government agencies, especially the Social Security Administration and the Department of Agriculture, to establish poverty thresholds for households of different sizes; the official poverty threshold for a family of four in 1993 was $14,763. (Thresholds are somewhat lower for farm families because they can grow some of their own food.) Note that the official thresholds do not include noncash forms of income like food stamps and Medicaid.

Patricia Ruggles, one of the nation's leading experts on the measurement of poverty, claims that current poverty thresholds, based on the Orshansky formula corrected for inflation, underestimate the number of people living in poverty in the United States. Today, she argues, the average family spends only one sixth of its annual income on food. This means that the cost of a family's basic "market basket" should be multiplied by 6 rather than by 4 to establish a poverty threshold. Ruggles also observes that it is necessary to continually recalculate the basic food requirements of an average family because as new foods come to the market, there are changes in the public's definitions of what is required for an adequate diet. According to Ruggles's revised formula, the poverty threshold for a family of four would be about $23,000 instead of approximately $14,000. This would place almost 27 percent of the U.S. population below the poverty threshold.

Ruggles realizes that her estimates are higher than those most politicians and policy makers would care to accept. She believes that relative measures that include items in the "market basket" that people consider essential are subject to criticism by policy makers who wish to minimize the official poverty rate. "Not all needs or desires are generally considered equal in judging whether or not some should be counted as poor," she notes. "The need to eat regularly and to have someplace warm and dry to sleep is widely recognized; the need to own a particular brand of sneakers or jeans, while deeply felt by many teenagers, is rarely considered of equal importance by policy makers" (Ruggles, 1990, p. 9).

Ruggles's updated estimates modify the original Orshansky calculations to account for the lower share of an average family's budget spent on food. Her calculations do not actually consider such items as decent clothing and sneakers. Were they to do so, her estimates of the proportion of the population living in poverty would be even higher than the estimates given here.

false, as can be seen in Figure 12.7. The poor in large central cities account for approximately 19 percent of the total poor population, with only about 7 percent concentrated in high-poverty neighborhoods. Fully 29 percent of the poor reside in rural and small-town communities, and 19 percent live in the affluent suburbs of large cities. In short, the poor live everywhere and are not concentrated in a single type of community.

One reason for this pattern is that the poor are an extremely diverse population. A large portion of the poor are aged people living on fixed incomes (Social Security or very modest savings or pensions). Other categories of poor people include marginally employed rural workers and part-time miners in communities from Appalachia to Alaska; migrant farm workers in agricultural areas throughout the United States; chronically unemployed manual workers in the industrial cities; disabled workers and their families;

and people who have been displaced by catastrophes like hurricanes, drought, or arson. For all of these groups, poverty brings enormous problems of insecurity and instability. Many poor people do not even know where they will be living next month or next year. This problem is especially acute for farm families who have been driven from their land. (See Figure 12.8.)

FARMERS AND FARM FAMILIES

In analyzing the situation of the poor in America, it is helpful to look at what is occurring in rural areas, where a large proportion of the poor live. Although many rural communities are experiencing renewed economic growth as factories relocate to areas where the costs of energy, space, training, and wages are lower, in communities based on agricultural production poverty rates continue to increase. A survey of 1,700 American farmers (Robbins, 1985) indi-

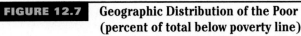

The percentages in this chart have changed somewhat since Ellwood conducted his study, but the basic distribution remains the same (the percentages do not add up to 100 because of rounding).

Source: Ellwood, 1988.

FIGURE 12.7 Geographic Distribution of the Poor (percent of total below poverty line)

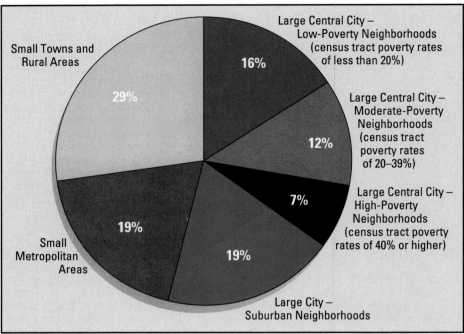

Small Towns and Rural Areas — 29%

Small Metropolitan Areas — 19%

Large Central City – Low-Poverty Neighborhoods (census tract poverty rates of less than 20%) — 16%

Large Central City – Moderate-Poverty Neighborhoods (census tract poverty rates of 20–39%) — 12%

Large Central City – High-Poverty Neighborhoods (census tract poverty rates of 40% or higher) — 7%

Large City – Suburban Neighborhoods — 19%

cated that approximately 36 percent owed more than 40 percent of their assets (land and equipment, livestock, and crops in the ground) to lending institutions. Within this category of heavily indebted farmers, 15 percent (or more than 5 percent of all farmers) owed 70 percent or more of their total assets. The consequences of these debt pressures can be seen in the changing demographics of farm families. Figure 12.9 on page 364 shows that the proportion of young farmers is decreasing while that of farmers over age 65 is increasing; overall, the number of farmers is decreasing steadily each year.

This situation repeats a condition that has been part of American social life for more than a century as the nation has been transformed from a rural to an urban society. Although the dream of owning a family farm, or keeping one in the family, has always been an important part of American culture, the rising cost of farm technology, together with the need for ever larger amounts of land to make farms profitable, has steadily pushed farm families off the land. Very large farms devoted to the production of a narrow range of crops and farm products now dominate North American agriculture. In the United States, more than half of total farm production comes from only about 4 percent of the nation's farms. In consequence, more farmers are employed by large agribusiness operations, and each decade a smaller percentage own family farms (Strange, 1988).

Larger farms are typically owned by corporations that may also can, freeze, package, or otherwise prepare the crop for sale in supermarkets. These agribusinesses may be highly efficient producers, but they have some negative social consequences for rural counties. Studies by rural sociologists have shown that communities dominated by large farms are characterized by a declining population, a decreasing number of local businesses and civic associations, and an increase in poverty. One study done for the U.S. Congress in 200 of the richest agricultural counties in the United States found that the more farm size increases, the more the poverty rate in the county also increases as people are displaced from the land and must search for marginal employment (Goldschmidt, 1978; MacCannell, n.d.; Office of Technology Assessment, 1986).

As a social class, farmers still take pride in the fact that the United States has the highest level of agricultural production in the world, but this does little to alleviate their difficulties. Moreover, as a class American farmers are continually at the mercy of a fickle world economy, a condition that they will increasingly share with the farmers on the private collective farms of Russia described in Chapter 11.

One method farmers have traditionally used to hold on to the land they love is for some family members to find work in a nearby town while others continue to work the land. In fact, about half of all farmers farm part-time and work at wage-paying jobs full-time. An increasing number

FIGURE 12.8

M A P P I N G   S O C I A L   C H A N G E

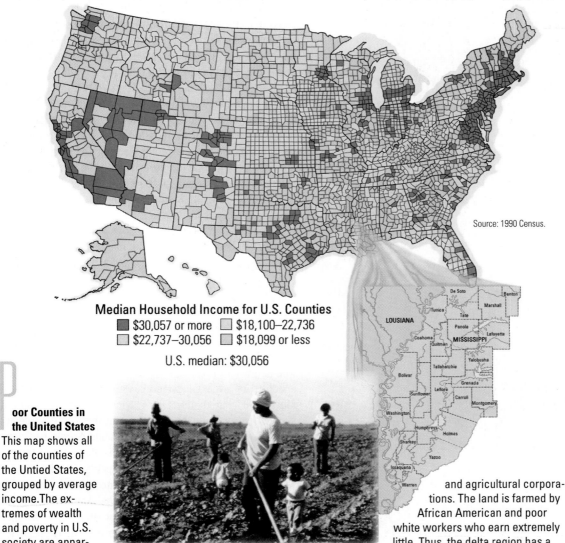

Source: 1990 Census.

Median Household Income for U.S. Counties

- ■ $30,057 or more
- ☐ $22,737–30,056
- ☐ $18,100–22,736
- ☐ $18,099 or less

U.S. median: $30,056

Poor Counties in the United States

This map shows all of the counties of the Untied States, grouped by average income. The extremes of wealth and poverty in U.S. society are apparent. Or are they?

Actually, such a map is more useful in revealing areas of poverty outside central cities than within them. This is because impoverished inner-city communities usually are only a portion of a densely urban county that may also include affluent and middle-class communities. Their incomes raise the average so that the pockets of inner-city poverty do not appear on the map.

This map still reveals a great deal about the places where poor people live. For example, along the Mississippi river, especially in Arkansas and Mississippi, we see groups of counties whose residents' average income is in the lowest range. The same is true in parts of the arid Southwest. Why are there such high concentrations of poor residents in these counties?

The Mississippi delta region has rich agricultural land, but most of it is owned by a few white families and agricultural corporations. The land is farmed by African American and poor white workers who earn extremely little. Thus, the delta region has a pattern of agrarian stratification that results in high rates of poverty. In the impoverished counties of the Southwest, the land often contains mineral and water resources that are controlled by a small number of wealthy individuals and corporations; Chicanos, Native Americans, and poor whites do not share in the wealth created by these resources, and the counties in which they live have low average incomes.

The isolated poor counties of the mountain states in the West often suffer from a newer form of poverty. In these areas economic growth is due to tourism, second-home developments, skiing, and other pursuits of the affluent upper and upper-middle classes. Farms, small-town businesses, and the trailer parks where the resort workers live may be located in a nearby valley, which may be part of a separate county with a lower average income.

FIGURE 12.9 Number of Farmers, by Age, 1984–1990

Source: Bureau of Labor Statistics.

of women in farm families work full- or part-time in rural factories. Many also work at home producing knitwear and other apparel on a piecework basis or performing electronic data processing via computer networks. Still others have service jobs.

The strategy of trying to maintain the household's economic position by adding more wage earners is increasingly common in other social classes as well. This is a trend with far-reaching implications, not only for the way Americans think about social class but for all of the society's institutions. For farmers, however, the numbers are discouraging. As an economic class they are diminishing steadily, especially as young people leave farming for other occupations.

MORE EQUALITY?

A large proportion of the world's people are extremely poor. India, China, Bangladesh, the Philippines, Malaysia, most of sub-Saharan Africa, the mountain regions of Latin America, and many other parts of the world are inhabited by large numbers of people with drastically limited incomes and only the most rudimentary health care, education, and other resources. If poverty continues to increase in those areas and the hopes of impoverished millions for a better life are frustrated, it will become increasingly difficult to maintain peace, achieve slower population growth, and prevent massive environmental damage.

Poverty is reduced through better health care, more schools, more food and shelter, and more jobs, all of which require economic and social development. The experience of the more affluent nations indicates that such development is likely to produce larger working and middle classes and reduce the rate of poverty. But the persistence of poverty and near-poverty in the United States and other industrialized nations shows how difficult it is to promote greater equality elsewhere in the world.

The presence of millions of poor people in a country as affluent as the United States is a major public-policy issue as well as a subject of extensive social research. However, policy debates on this issue are often clouded by problems of definition. Most Americans will say that they believe in equality, citing the claim of the nation's founders that "all men are created equal." But when pressed to define equality they may stumble over the difference between **equality of opportunity** (equal opportunity to achieve material well-being and prestige) and **equality of result** (actual equality in levels of material well-being and prestige). Americans may believe that opportunities to succeed should be distributed equally and that the rules that determine who succeeds and who fails should be fair. But their commitment to the ideal of equality falters in the face of their belief that hard work and competence should be rewarded and laziness and incompetence punished (Jencks et al., 1972). Thus many Americans believe that poverty is proof of personal failure. They do not stop to ask whether poor Americans have ever been given equality of opportunity, nor do they stop to notice how hard many poor people work (Liebow, 1967).

Sociologists who study inequality in modern societies usually ask how equality of opportunity can be increased and the gaps between the haves and the have-nots decreased. Yet they are also highly aware of how difficult it is to narrow that gap in the United States or any other society. For, as sociologist Herbert Gans (1985, 1995) observes somewhat ironically, poverty is so persistent that one can well ask whether it might have some positive functions. He describes a number of "positive" functions of poverty:

- The existence of poverty ensures that society's dirty work will be done. . . . Society can fill these jobs by paying higher wages than for "clean" work, or it can force people who have no other choice to do the dirty work.

- Because the poor are required to work at low wages, they subsidize a variety of economic activities that benefit the affluent. For example, domestics subsidize the upper middle and upper classes, making life easier for their employers.

- Poverty creates jobs for a number of occupations and professions that serve or "service" the poor, or protect the rest of society from them. . . . Penology would be minuscule without the poor, as would the police.

- The poor can be identified and punished as alleged or real deviants in order to uphold the legitimacy of conventional norms. (1985, pp. 155–161)

These and other hidden functions of poverty, Gans argues, are far outweighed by its dysfunctions—suffering, violence, and waste of human and material resources. And they could be eliminated by "functional alternatives" such as higher pay for doing dirty work, or by the intentional redistribution of income. He believes welfare payments and tax credits for the poor should be increased so that they can qualify for the housing and other subsidies available to better-off Americans (Gans, 1995).

The role the government should play in alleviating poverty is a major issue in American society today. It is frequently asserted, both in government and in the social sciences, that government has no business engaging in large-scale redistribution of income in the interests of the lower classes. This viewpoint, which is represented in the writings of conservative social scientists like Milton Friedman (1962), George Gilder (1982), and Charles Murray (1984, 1988), as well as in current social policies, agrees that public funds must be spent to provide the poor with a "safety net" of programs to prevent suffering, but it also holds that programs to redistribute wealth infringe on individual freedom and the right of private property.

For much of this century, from the 1930s to the early 1980s, the dominant policies regarding inequalities of social class were based on a more liberal political philosophy. The policies that established the Social Security system, unemployment insurance, Aid to Families with Dependent Children, Medicare and Medicaid, disability insurance—in short, the social safety net itself—depended for funding on taxation and were based in part on the idea that the rich should pay proportionately more for these programs through a system of graduated taxation. In the past two decades, however, the concept of tax equity (taxation according to one's means) has been subjected to much criticism.

INEQUALITY AND MOBILITY

"More equality" means more opportunities for upward mobility. Consider two children, one born to a laborer and a homemaker, neither of whom completed high school, and the other born to parents who are both highly educated businesspeople. If (assuming equal intelligence, motivation, etc.) both children have the same probability of attaining wealth, power, and prestige, we could argue that equality of opportunity exists. It is evident, however, that full equality of opportunity does not exist in any known so-

ciety. On the other hand, although the laborer's child has a greater chance of becoming poor and powerless, some children from humble origins will become well educated and have successful careers and may even gain powerful positions in society—that is, they may experience upward mobility.

In the preceding chapter we noted that there is substantial upward mobility in the United States. But Americans have traditionally hoped for more. They have long cherished the idea of going from rags to riches, the dream that a person of poor or very modest origins and upbringing could achieve great success through his or her own efforts. This highly symbolic form of upward mobility, in which a person rises during his or her own lifetime from low family status to membership in the professional or managerial elite, is known as **long-distance upward mobility.**

In a classic study carried out by Peter Blau and Otis Dudley Duncan (1967) with the help of the Current Population Survey, 20,700 respondents representing approximately 45 million men between the ages of 20 and 64 were asked a series of questions about their occupations and those of their parents. The responses provided social scientists with the most reliable estimates of social mobility available up to that time. The data confirmed that overall mobility in the United States had not changed much since the end of World War II. But a new and significant finding of the Blau and Duncan study concerned long-distance mobility. The data revealed that "nearly 10 percent of manual sons achieve elite status [high-prestige occupations] in the United States, a higher proportion than in any other country. . . . In respect to mobility from the middle class into the elite, however, the ratio . . . though high, is not outstanding" (p. 436). The researchers concluded that "it is the underprivileged class of manual sons that has exceptional chances for mobility into the elite of this country" (p. 435). Subsequent studies have replicated the Blau and Duncan research (Hauser & Featherman, 1977; Tyree & Treas, 1974).

These findings seem to confirm the popular notion that America is a land of opportunity. Hard work and diligent application to studies are rewarded. But the relatively high rates of long-distance mobility by children of manual workers are misleading. Only about 10 percent of all occupations are in the "elite" category, and therefore the proportion of all workers who achieve long-distance mobility is extremely small. Yet the fact that some individuals can "pull themselves up by their own bootstraps" helps maintain the myth that long-distance mobility is possible for everyone.

As we saw in Chapter 11, people may experience downward as well as upward mobility. Every year many thousands of people face hard times. They lose their jobs; disasters wreck their homes and lives; illnesses sharply curtail their income and exhaust their savings; divorce deprives them of income and security. In her study of downwardly mobile middle-class women and men, Katherine S.

THE PERSONAL CHALLENGE

Social Change and the Minimum Wage Debate

Do you think the minimum wage should be raised? Do you think employers should be required to pay $5.15 per hour instead of the current $4.25, as many members of Congress and state legislatures believe? Or do you agree with those who fear that an increase in the minimum wage would decrease employers' ability to compete and reduce job opportunities for entry-level workers?

Many people in the United States and Canada begin their working lives at minimum wage jobs, often in short-order restaurants or food stores. If they work 35 hours a week for $4.25 an hour, their take-home pay is less than $150. A raise of $0.90 an hour would increase their weekly checks by approximately 20%, a significant increase. This is why so many people who earn low hourly wages want to see an increase in the minimum wage. People who own businesses and employ low-wage workers have a different perspective. They typically do not want to see payroll expenses rise, nor do they like the idea of government telling them how much to pay employees. They often argue that the market—that is, the supply and demand for low-skilled labor—should dictate what they pay.

Do employers owe it to the communities in which they operate to pay their workers something

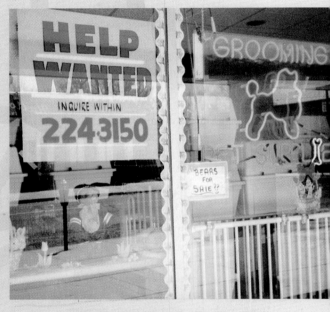

Neighborhood businesses often hire young people at or near the minimum wage. Those who favor raising the minimum wage point out that businesses will still need workers even if the wage is increased.

close to a wage they can live on? Or should they be free to let the market determine wages? Your position in this debate will most likely stem from your own experiences and those of your family members, and those experiences have a lot to do with social class.

Newman (1988) found that most men and women who lose good white-collar jobs spend months searching for new jobs and often must accept jobs that pay less and offer less prestige than the ones they lost. This is especially true for people over the age of 40.

According to Newman, downward mobility "is a hidden dimension of our society's experience because it simply does not fit our cultural universe." We are rich in symbols that celebrate success, such as lavish balls and weddings, but we are poor in myths or ceremonies to help people caught in the grip of downward mobility "make the transi-

tion from a higher to a lower status" (1988, p. 9). Moreover, American society has not developed adequate institutions for coping with downward mobility and its effects on individuals and families. Programs for disaster relief and community reconstruction, job retraining, day care, and the like need to be made more effective.

EDUCATION AND MOBILITY

For people who are downwardly mobile as well as those who are just entering the labor force, education is the primary route to individual success and upward mobility. In recent decades, as opportunities in the manufacturing sector of the economy have declined, educational attainment has become an ever more important route to a better career. Hundreds of thousands of displaced workers are being urged to move into other careers through retraining programs or by returning to school. But sociologists have ample evidence that although educational attainment is the most important single route to occupational success, the benefits of education are highly influenced by the society's class system.

In a review of data on educational attainment and social mobility, Christopher Jencks and his colleagues (1972) reported the following:

> Roughly half the children born into the upper-middle class will end up with what we might call upper-middle-class educational credentials, i.e., with more schooling than 80 percent of their age-mates. Likewise, about half the children born into the lower class will end up with what we might call lower-class credentials, i.e., less schooling than 80 percent of their age-mates. Upper-middle-class children will average 4 years more schooling than lower-class children. (p. 138)

No one is surprised when sociologists find that children from advantaged homes do better in school than those from homes in which the parents are less well educated and less able to help their children with schoolwork, and that children from advantaged backgrounds usually obtain more formal schooling than disadvantaged children—as well as "extras" like tutoring and SAT-preparation courses. But how important is family background compared with other social and individual variables? People often contend that individual intelligence is at least as important as family background in explaining educational attainment. Others assert that the quality of the schools children attend is the key variable.

Jencks and other sociologists have found that most of the differences in educational attainment can be explained by the pressure placed on children by upper-middle-class parents (Jencks et al., 1972; Sewall, Haller, & Ohlendorf, 1970). And they have reached the surprising conclusion that intelligence, as measured by early-childhood IQ scores, does not explain nearly as much of the difference in educational attainment as is often thought: "If we compare the most genetically advantaged fifth of the population to the least genetically advantaged fifth, and hold everything else constant [e.g., class, race, sex, and school quality], their educational attainments will probably differ by about two years" (Jencks et al., 1972, p. 145).

What happens, apparently, is that many children with high levels of innate intelligence do not do as well as they might because pressures and models in the home are lacking; conversely, less intelligent children who come from advantaged homes in which they are pressured to excel overcome their innate deficits and do well enough to go on to college. We encountered this idea in Chapter 5, where we noted that the specific environment in which a person is raised can have a tremendous effect on the extent to which that person is able to fulfill his or her genetic potential.

The effects of social class do not end with formal education. People from upper-middle-class families whose educational attainment is below average still tend to find better jobs than people from lower social-class backgrounds. Upper-class families often help their children find jobs in companies that they own or control. They can also use their networks of influential friends and associates for this purpose. And they socialize their children to behave in ways that are favored by employers. These advantages lend further support to the claim that family background has as great an influence on social mobility as educational attainment.

SOCIAL MOBILITY AND THE TWO-PAYCHECK FAMILY

Another area in which large-scale social change has affected the possibility of upward mobility pertains to the position of women in American society. For most of American history it was taken for granted that "a woman's place is in the home" (Hayghe, 1982). A married woman was expected to be in charge of the household, and her husband was supposed to "bring home the bacon"; women's work in the home was not considered equivalent to men's work. At the turn of the century, therefore, only 4.6 percent of married women were in the labor force.

Women's participation in the labor force increased slowly in the first half of the twentieth century, but in the 1960s a number of factors combined to produce a rush of women into jobs outside the home. Those factors included changing ideas about women's needs and abilities, an increase in the proportion of relatively well-educated young adults in the population, and the beginning of a period of rapid inflation, which eroded men's ability to earn enough to maintain their family's economic position. During the 1970s and 1980s millions of women entered the labor force. Today, as a result, 60.6 percent of all married women in the United States are in the labor force (*Statistical Abstract*, 1995).

The implications of this trend are far-reaching. The trend helps explain the rise of social movements calling for more day care services, increased enforcement of occupational safety rules, and comparable pay for work that is of comparable worth. But sociologists are also interested in the impact of women's labor force participation on larger patterns of social stratification and inequality.

The data in Table 12.5 show that in 1993 the median income of dual-earner families was about $21,000 higher than that of families in which only the husband was an earner. This added income may make it easier for such families to pay their bills. But the table also shows that much of the apparent difference disappears when we control for the effects of inflation. Between 1970 and 1993 real household income did not increase by very much. Thus, even dual-earner families are having trouble achieving the

TABLE 12.5	Median Income, by Type of Family, 1970–1993 (in current and constant 1993 dollars)			
CURRENT DOLLARS	**1970**	**1980**	**1985**	**1993**
Married-couple families	$10,516	$23,141	$31,100	$43,005
Wife in paid labor force	12,276	26,879	36,431	51,204
Wife not in paid labor force	9,304	18,972	24,556	30,218
Male householder, no wife present	9,012	17,519	22,622	26,467
Female householder, no husband present	5,093	10,408	13,660	17,443
CONSTANT 1993 DOLLARS				
Married-couple families	35,724	39,449	40,551	43,005
Wife in paid labor force	41,703	45,822	47,502	51,204
Wife not in paid labor force	31,607	32,342	32,019	30,218
Male householder, no wife present	30,615	29,865	29,497	26,467
Female householder, no husband present	17,301	17,743	17,811	17,443

Source: *Statistical Abstract*, 1995.

American dream of well-being for all. The addition of a second paycheck does not add enough to the family's income to raise the household to another social class. It usually serves to maintain its existing economic position and perhaps add a few extras to its quality of life. In more difficult times, when one earner loses a job, the "second" job often becomes the household's primary means of survival.

RESEARCH FRONTIERS: WINNERS AND LOSERS IN THE NEW STRATIFICATION

Cultural and economic changes in the United States are rapidly altering the society's stratification system, and the changes are producing distinct sets of winners and losers. People at the bottom of the class system are experiencing a decline in their already precarious standard of living, while wealthy people are continuing to enjoy substantial gains in wealth, income, and overall standard of living. People in the middle classes are under pressure to make ends meet as they pursue their version of the American dream. These broad patterns of change are producing changes in the stratification of American society that are a subject of active sociological research. One area of study is the so-called "winner-take-all society." Another is the issue of whether economic and social changes are producing a permanent "underclass" of people trapped in poverty.

The Winner-Take-All Society. The dream of achieving fame and fortune is a central theme in American culture. But for every star basketball player like those portrayed in the film *Hoop Dreams* there are thousands of aspiring but totally unknown athletes and an even larger number of athletes whose moment of glory is long past. In the nation's cultural centers, thousands of would-be actors, script writers, and disk jockeys wait on tables and feed copier machines. In business, there are "stars" among the chief executive officers who receive astronomical salaries, but as the number of large corporations shrinks through mergers and acquisitions, their numbers decrease as well. Sociologists and economists who study the implications of high-stakes competition in the business and entertainment worlds warn that the media attention and huge bonuses earned by "stars" sustain the hope of stardom for millions of people who have little chance of becoming celebrities or making a fortune. In fact, the winner-take-all society may actually decrease the range of opportunities open to most people (Frank, 1995). For example, regional theater, local television, and small orchestras are finding it increasingly difficult to compete with national television broadcasts, and as a result there are fewer opportunities for young actors and musicians.

The dashed hopes of thousands of actors whose chance never came, and of thousands of high school and college athletes who were never drafted for professional teams, could produce a dangerous increase in disappointed, disaffected people whose youth has been lost in the pursuit of stardom. A unique feature of American society, however, is the variety and scope of opportunities for lifelong individual development. The community college system, for example, is especially well adapted to allow people to change course, to retrain and reeducate themselves. Along with other educational opportunities, they serve as an important counterinfluence to the effects of the winner-take-all culture.

An Emerging Underclass? Many sociologists and political leaders believe that there is a class of Americans who are not only poor but actually trapped in poverty by de facto segregation, lack of education and skills, lack of power to change such institutions as schools and the labor market, and lack of the personality traits needed for success in an increasingly technological society. The name given to this population is the _underclass_ (Auletta, 1982; Glasgow, 1981; Myrdal, 1970). But is there really such a class? And if there is, how can we recognize it, and what can be done to reduce its numbers?

Debates about what constitutes an underclass extend back into history. In his classic survey of poverty during the industrial revolution, _London Labour and the London Poor_, Harry Mayhew (1968/1861–1862) identified a large non-working class that he could divide into three distinct groups: those with physical impairments, those with "intellectual defects" (e.g., the insane and the retarded), and those with "moral defects." In his account of the United States in the 1830s, Alexis de Tocqueville described a dangerous "rabble" of nonworking poor who inhabited and endangered the cities. And Karl Marx referred to the lowest class of capitalist society, the lumpenproletariat, as the "dangerous class."

The so-called underclass of contemporary societies is said to consist of people who have grown up in a world of chronic poverty, especially in central-city ghettos and other areas with extremely high rates of welfare recipiency. According to William J. Wilson (1987, 1989), the existence of this "truly disadvantaged" class is due to a "structural cleavage" that separates ghetto residents from other members of society. Ghetto residents are cut off not only spatially (i.e., by segregation) but also in terms of economic opportunities; they cannot find jobs with decent pay and benefits. This situation, in turn, is a result of "the continuous industrial restructuring of American capitalism" (1989, p. 183).

Wilson argues that we do not need to use the term _underclass_ in describing people who have lived in poverty and without work for most of their lives. The term, he feels, is often used in discussions of black poverty and can easily become a pejorative label. Instead of _underclass_ he uses the term _ghetto poor_. Whatever term is used, Wilson believes that persistent inner-city poverty is a result of structural change, a view that is shared by most social scientists (Raymond, 1991). Conservative critics argue, however, that there is an underclass and that it is a product of chronic welfare recipiency—that there is, in fact, a "welfare subculture" that perpetuates poverty. For sociologists, this translates into an empirical question: Who are the welfare poor, and how probable is it that once they go on welfare they will become dependent on it?

In a creative study of the issue of welfare dependency, David Ellwood (1988) describes a "natural environment" for testing whether welfare payments encourage poor single women to have children (see Figure 12.10). Proponents of the theory of the underclass argue that by providing payments to poor women with children the welfare system

---

FIGURE 12.10 **Percentage of Children Not Living With Two Parents, by Benefit Levels for AFDC and Food Stamps, 1980**

Source: Ellwood, 1988.

BEYOND CARING

The public assistance system in the United States is undergoing major changes. The right or "entitlement" of women with children under age 18 to receive federal Aid to Families with Dependent Children is ending, to be replaced by a variety of state systems subsidized by federal funds. Underlying the changes is the assumption that poor people need incentives and opportunities to work rather than to receive welfare payments.

Similar trends are occurring elsewhere in the industrialized world. In Great Britain, for example, men as well as women are eligible for government payments when they are disabled or unable to find work. But as in the United States, people who are on welfare—or, as the British term it, "on the dole"—are stigmatized. Arguments about whether welfare is depriving them of their desire to work are just as frequent in Great Britain as in the United States. And like the United States, Great Britain must adjust to the economic dislocations caused by the rapid loss of manufacturing industries and the resulting shortage of jobs that pay enough to support a family. In consequence, millions of people spend long hours each week waiting in overcrowded, dingy social security offices.

Photographer Paul Graham (1986) visited hundreds of social security offices throughout England to capture the mood of hopelessness engendered by the experience of being on the dole. His photos of depressing waiting rooms and the people in them are meant to raise questions about whether such conditions must always exist. Although the larger issue in welfare debates is how to produce jobs that will replace welfare payments, Graham's photos address the issue of stigmatization of welfare recipients. "Make no mistake," he comments, "monies could be found to redecorate, shorten queues with simplified procedures and additional staff, but a decision has obviously been reached that this is an acceptable state of affairs, and certainly not an area worthy of serious consideration. So what if people had to queue all day? If they were elderly or unemployed then surely they've nothing better to do anyway."

encourages them to have more children, which then swell the size of the poor, welfare-dependent population. Ellwood reasoned that since welfare benefits vary greatly among the states, there ought to be more single-parent families in the states where benefits were highest. But there were not, as one can see by examining Figure 12.10. Mississippi, which at the time paid less than $350 per month to a family of three, has a higher percentage of dependent children than California. The data in the chart show that there is no clear association between the level of welfare benefits in a state and the percentage of children not living in two-parent families.

Ellwood's research nonetheless confirms that a significant proportion of the poor—at least 10 million Ameri-

cans—are part of a large and perhaps growing population of people trapped in chronic unemployment and welfare recipiency. This population is characterized by lack of education, segregation in areas with high rates of poverty, and dependence on various forms of welfare. The danger revealed in this and other research on poverty is that the high rates of teenage pregnancy and dropping out of school found among the poor, especially the minority poor, will contribute to the continued growth of the poor population and perhaps, in time, to a true underclass. It is for this reason that strategies to help people on welfare gain skills and find jobs are popular among policy makers, regardless of their political ideology.

SUMMARY

THINK ABOUT IT CRITICALLY

We often hear people say that the United States does not have a class system like that of England or other European nations. In the United States a child born into a poor family can get an education in the public schools, and if he or she is willing to work hard, the sky is the limit. Yet all around us we see extremes of wealth and poverty. So what explains the idea that there is no class system in the United States?

The basic measures of inequality in any society are income, wealth, *occupational prestige*, and *educational attainment.* In American society the distribution of educational attainment and occupational prestige is more nearly equal than the distribution of wealth and income.

Sociological views of inequality in America have changed as the nation has been transformed from an agrarian society to an urban industrial society and then to a post-industrial society. The Jeffersonian view of America envisioned a society in which the majority of families lived on their own farms or ran small commercial or manufacturing enterprises. However, this view did not apply to the larger cities, the southern states, or Native Americans. During the Great Depression, the effects of industrialization tended to increase hostility between workers and the owners of businesses. In the mid-twentieth century, several important studies of inequality in American communities revealed the existence of a complex social-class system as well as a racial caste system.

The shift from an economy based on manufacturing to one based on services has resulted in a blurring of class lines and an easing of class conflict between industrial workers and the owners and managers of the means of production. Nevertheless, some sociologists argue that Americans continue to recognize social-class divisions. When people are asked what social class they belong to, the largest proportion say that they are members of the middle class. They base their class assignments on *socioeconomic status,* which is derived primarily from occupation but also takes into account family status, education, and earned income.

Social-class position has important consequences for the daily life of individuals and households. Members of the upper classes tend to have better health and more adequate health care than people in the lower classes. They are also likely to receive more and better education. In politics, the poor and members of the working class generally support the Democratic party while those in the middle and upper classes support the Republican party.

The upper class is estimated at less than 3 percent of the U.S. population. The richest among them control 40 percent of all personal wealth in the United States. This class may be divided into the wealthiest and most prestigious families, who make up the elite or "high society," and families that have acquired their money more recently. Sociologists continually debate whether the upper class in America is also the society's ruling class.

Members of the upper-middle class tend to be highly educated professionals. The middle class, the largest single class in American society, is culturally extremely diverse. In the past it was thought to be associated with a family-oriented, conservative, suburban lifestyle, but recent studies have shown that there is no easily identified middle-class suburban culture.

The working class, which accounts for at least one third of the U.S. population, is undergoing rapid and difficult changes as production technologies change and industrialization spreads throughout the world. Members of this class are employed in skilled, semiskilled, or unskilled manual occupations, and many are union members. The American working class can be divided into industrial workers and those employed in skilled crafts. There is more racial and ethnic diversity in the working class than in other classes.

Estimates of the proportion of the population living in poverty vary widely, depending on the standard used to define poverty. According to official statistics, 14.5 percent of Americans are living in poverty. A significant proportion of the poor have jobs that do not pay enough to support their families. Another large percentage of poor families are single-parent families headed by women. Other categories of poor people include aged people living on fixed incomes, marginally employed rural workers and part-time miners, chronically unemployed manual workers, and disabled workers and their families. Another group of people in danger of becoming poor are farmers.

Policy debates on the issue of poverty are often clouded by problems of definition. Although many Americans believe in *equality of opportunity,* they are less committed to the ideal of *equality of result.* Most sociologists agree that it is impossible to achieve a completely egalitarian society; instead, they concentrate on how much present levels of inequality can and should be reduced.

Research on *long-distance upward mobility* has revealed relatively high rates of mobility into elite occupations by children of fathers in manual trades. Although this suggests that such mobility is possible for everyone, in reality only a very small number of people are able to achieve this dramatic form of upward mobility.

In recent decades educational attainment has become an ever more important route to a better career. Yet the benefits of education are highly influenced by social class.

It has been shown that family background is the most important variable in the extent to which children succeed in school and the amount of education they eventually receive—more important than individual intelligence or the quality of the schools children attend. Another trend that has affected the possibility of social mobility in the United States is the large-scale participation of women in the labor force. It appears, however, that the addition of a second paycheck does not add enough to the family's income to raise the household to another social class.

CRITICAL RESPONSE

It is true that we believe our social-class system to be less rigid than those of other nations. Indeed, the American dream insists on every American's right to success through hard work. But the facts of class inequality are more complex than the myths. We do have a class system that includes extremes of wealth and poverty. Many people experience social mobility, but it is also true that the class one is born into has a significant effect on one's life chances from birth to death.

GLOSSARY

educational attainment: the number of years of school an individual has completed. (p. 344)

educational achievement: mastery of basic reading, writing, and computational skills. (p. 345)

occupational prestige: the honor or prestige attributed to specific occupations by adults in a society. (p. 345)

ghetto: a section of a city that is segregated either racially or culturally. (p. 349)

socioeconomic status (SES): a broad social-class ranking based on occupational status, family prestige, educational attainment, and earned income. (p. 352)

equality of opportunity: equal opportunity to achieve desired levels of material well-being and prestige. (p. 364)

equality of result: equality in the actual outcomes of people's attempts to improve their material well-being and prestige. (p. 364)

long-distance upward mobility: a form of upward mobility in which a person rises during his or her own lifetime from low family status to membership in a professional or managerial elite. (p. 365)

WHERE TO FIND IT

BOOKS

The American Class Structure: A New Synthesis
(Dennis Gilbert & Joseph A. Kahl; Dorsey Press, 1982). A valuable summary of American sociological writing about class, with good reviews of the work of Warner, the Lynds, Mills, and many others, together with clear explanations of modern studies in stratification and mobility.

Class in Twentieth-Century American Sociology: An Analysis of Theories and Measurement Strategies
(Michael D. Grimes; Praeger, 1991). A comprehensive review of the way social class has been studied in American sociology, with emphasis on why recent decades have brought renewed emphasis on the presence of classes and class conflict, in opposition to the functionalist theories and studies that were prevalent before the 1970s.

The War Against the Poor (Herbert Gans; Basic Books, 1995). A timely and thorough review of antipoverty policies and debates by one of the world's foremost experts on the subject.

JOURNALS

Monthly Review. A monthly journal of critical social-scientific writing and research on class and inequality. Most articles are Marxian in orientation.

The Public Interest. A valuable interdisciplinary social science journal with highly readable articles on issues of class, race, poverty, and social policy, with special emphasis on policy debates.

Focus. The official publication of the Institute on Poverty of the University of Wisconsin. An invaluable source for current sociological and economic research on poverty and social policy (welfare reform, family policies, early education, and much more).

OTHER SOURCES

Current Population Reports. Published monthly by the Bureau of the Census, U.S. Department of Commerce. Presents data on income and employment patterns for American households.

Handbook of Economic Statistics. Published annually by the U.S. Department of Labor. Compares economic statistics for the communist nations, the Common Market, the United States, and selected other nations, permitting measures of relative inequality and stratification.

Handbook of Labor Statistics. A compilation of statistical data published annually by the U.S. Department of Labor. Presents material on labor conditions and labor-force characteristics for the United States and selected foreign countries.

CHAPTER 13

Inequalities of Race and Ethnicity

"So many people think the civil rights movement began in the 1960s with all that praying and singing and marching. But let me tell you, down here in Mississippi we were in a movement for civil rights long before all that began. I think for many of us in Meridian it began in the 1930s, when we sent the men to see President Roosevelt to ask for the government commodities."

The speaker is Polly Heidelberg, a founder of the civil rights movement in Meridian, Mississippi.

Among the events that have burned themselves into her memory are the murders of three civil rights workers—James Chaney, Michael Schwerner, and Andrew Goodman—who worked together in Mississippi during the "Freedom Summer" of 1964. Chaney was an African American resident of Meridian; Schwerner and Goodman were volunteers from northern colleges. And Polly Heidelberg was one of the last people the young men saw before they set out for the little village of

Philadelphia, Mississippi, where they were murdered and hastily buried in an earthen dam.

"Miz" Heidelberg, as she is known in Meridian, was a neighbor of Chaney's, and she feels responsible for "bringing him into the movement." She knew all three men, and even now when she thinks of them her eyes cloud over and she prays for their souls. In this interview, however, she is reminiscing about the origins of the civil rights movement, which began much earlier. "Our folk down here in Mississippi were starving during the thirties," she says. "It wasn't only us blacks, mind you, but we were hit particularly bad. And toward the later years of the Depression, when it began to get a bit better for the whites, we were still sunk in a great misery. There were people who just didn't have enough to eat, and we had done about as much sharing as we could do. I said to my husband, who was in the Brotherhood [of Sleeping Car Porters], 'Listen, you better get up to Washington with the others and tell President Roosevelt that we need food down here. We need some carloads of government food, you know, the commodities, or we are going to have a lot of children die soon.'

"Well, they did go to Washington and they did talk to the President, and sure enough we did begin to get some of the emergency commodities here in Meridian and in other towns in the Black Belt. Now that was when the singing and the real organizing began. People can't sing and get themselves together on empty bellies."

As she speaks, Heidelberg and I are sitting in a white-owned coffee shop in a white neighborhood of Meridian. One of her granddaughters, a child of about 4, has finished eating and is playing quietly on the floor. I am scribbling Heidelberg's words on a notepad while attempting to eat an ample southern breakfast. An interview with Polly Heidelberg is fun. She often slips riddles into her speech to gently tease the listener. She is also a deeply religious and patriotic person, and her speech is filled with allusions to God and country.

Heidelberg tells me about the movement to integrate the armed forces during the war, about the bitterness of racial strife during the 1950s, and about the exhausting, exhilarating years of the 1960s. There is no end to the movement as she sees it. Civil rights was only one aspect of the struggle for true equality of opportunity. Now there must be more progress toward economic equality.

We have finished our breakfast and the child is becoming restless. Heidelberg asks me, "Do you know the hymn that goes, 'The great trees are bending/The Good Lord is sending/His people up to higher ground'? What do you think 'higher ground' is?" Stammering a bit, I begin saying something about loftier values, greater spirituality . . . "Sure, you could think about it that way," she interrupts, "but to me 'higher ground' is right where we are now. It's you and me and the child having breakfast in this coffee shop here in Meridian, Mississippi."

THE MEANING OF RACE AND ETHNICITY

Why is it that so many African Americans like Polly Heidelberg have had to struggle out of poverty—and still feel that their people have a long way to go? How can we explain prejudice and racial discrimination, and how can we measure their effects on individuals and social institutions? Many social scientists focus their research on why some groups in a society have been subordinated and the consequences of that subordination for them and their children. The effects of various forms of subordination, such as slavery, expulsion, and discrimination, on a society's patterns of inequality are at the center of the study of race and ethnicity, not only in the United States but throughout the world.

The United States is not unique in the extent to which inequality and hostility among its ethnic and racial groups result in severe social problems. In Canada, conflict between Anglo and French Canadians in Quebec periodically threatens national unity. In Germany there have been severe riots as native-born Germans have pressed for limits on the nation's acceptance of refugees from Eastern European nations that were formerly dominated by the Soviet Union. In what used to be Yugoslavia, hostility among Croats, Serbs, and Bosnians has produced the bloodiest ethnic war in recent history. In the former Soviet Union there is great fear that ethnic nationalism unleashed by the demise of the communist dictatorship will produce even more terrible wars than the one in Bosnia because there are nuclear arms in the former Soviet republics.

Given its importance throughout the world, it is no wonder that the study of racial and ethnic relations has always been a major subfield of sociology. Most societies include minority groups, people who are defined as different according to the majority's perceptions of racial or cultural differences. And in many societies, as the ironic song from the musical *South Pacific* goes, "You've got to be taught to be afraid/of people whose eyes are differently made/or people whose skin is a different shade./You've got to be carefully taught." Sociologists try to get at the origins of these fears and groundless distinctions that categorize people as different and influence their life chances, often in dramatic ways.

In this chapter we first look at how race and ethnicity lead to the formation of groups that have a sense of themselves as different from the dominant group. In the second section of the chapter we analyze patterns of inequality and intergroup relations, particularly in American society. This is followed by a presentation of social-scientific theories that seek to explain the phenomena of intergroup conflict and accommodation. Rather than discussing each of the major racial and ethnic groups in American society in turn, throughout the chapter we present examples from the experience of blacks, Hispanic Americans, Native Americans, and other ethnic groups that have played an important part in American history.

RACE: A SOCIAL CONCEPT

Of the millions of species of animals on earth, ours, *Homo sapiens,* is the most widespread. For the past 10 millennia we have been spreading northward and southward and across the oceans to every corner of the globe. But we have not done so as a single people; rather, throughout our history we have been divided into innumerable societies, each of which maintains its own culture, thinks of itself as "we," and looks upon all others as "they." Through all those millennia of warfare, migration, and population growth, we have been colliding and competing and learning to cooperate. The realization that we are one great people despite our immense diversity has been slow to evolve. We persist in creating arbitrary divisions based on physical differences that are summed up in the term *race.*

In biology, **race** refers to an inbreeding population that develops distinctive physical characteristics that are hereditary. Such a population therefore has a shared genetic heritage (Coon, 1962; Marks, 1994). But the choice of which physical characteristics to use in classifying people into races is arbitrary. Skin color, hair form, blood type, and facial features such as nose shape and eyefolds have been used by biologists in such efforts. In fact, however, there is a great deal of overlap among the so-called races in the distribution of these traits. Human groups have exchanged their genes through mating to such an extent that any attempt to identify "pure" races is bound to be fruitless (Alland, 1973; Dobzhansky, 1962; Gould, 1981).

Yet doesn't common sense tell us that there are different races? Can't we see that there is a Negro, or "black," race of people with dark skin, tightly curled hair, and broad facial features; a Caucasian, or "white," race of people with pale skin and ample body hair; and a Mongoloid, or "Oriental," race of people with yellowish or reddish skin and deep eyefolds that give their eyes a slanted look? Of course these races exist. But they are not a set of distinct populations based on biological differences. The definitions of race used in different societies emerged from the interaction of various populations over long periods of human history. The specific physical characteristics that we use to assign people to different races are arbitrary and meaningless—people from the Indian subcontinent tend to have dark skin and straight hair; Africans from Ethiopia have dark skin and narrow facial features; American blacks have skin colors ranging from extremely dark to extremely light; and whites have facial features and hair forms that include

those of all the other supposed races. There is no scientifically valid typology of human races; what counts is what people in a society define as meaningful.

In short, race is a social concept that varies from one society to another, depending on how the people of that society feel about the importance of certain physical differences among human beings. In reality, as Edward O. Wilson (1979) has written, human beings are "one great breeding system through which the genes flow and mix in each generation. Because of that flux, mankind viewed over many generations shares a single human nature within which relatively minor hereditary influences recycle through ever-changing patterns, between the sexes and across families and entire populations" (p. 52).

RACISM

Throughout human history, many individuals and groups have rejected the idea of a single human nature. Tragic mistakes and incalculable suffering have been caused by the application of erroneous ideas about race and racial purity. They are among the most extreme consequences of the attitude known as racism.

Racism is an ideology based on the belief that an observable, supposedly inherited trait, such as skin color, is a mark of inferiority that justifies discriminatory treatment of people with that trait. In their classic text on racial and cultural minorities, Simpson and Yinger (1953) highlighted several beliefs that are at the heart of racism. The most common of these is the "doctrine of biologically superior and inferior races" (p. 55). Before World War I, for example, many of the foremost social thinkers in the Western world firmly believed that whites were genetically superior to blacks in intelligence. However, when the U.S. Army administered an IQ test to its recruits, the results showed that performance on such tests was linked to social-class background rather than to race. And when investigators controlled for differences in social class among the test takers, the racial differences in IQ disappeared (Kleinberg, 1935).

Since that time there have been other attempts to demonstrate innate differences in intelligence among people of different races. The most recent of these efforts is Herrnstein and Murray's controversial study, *The Bell Curve* (1994), which we discussed in Chapter 5. This study argues that because scores on intelligence tests are distributed along a "normal" bell curve, there will necessarily be a large number of people whose scores fall well below the mean and who are not capable of performing well in situations requiring reasoning ability or other academic skills. Because the bell curves for African Americans and whites are different, with that of blacks peaking at a somewhat lower mean score, the authors argue that group differences in IQ establish biological limits on ability. This conclusion, in turn, leads them to argue that programs intended to correct differences in educational opportunities, such as Head Start, are doomed to failure.

THEN AND NOW

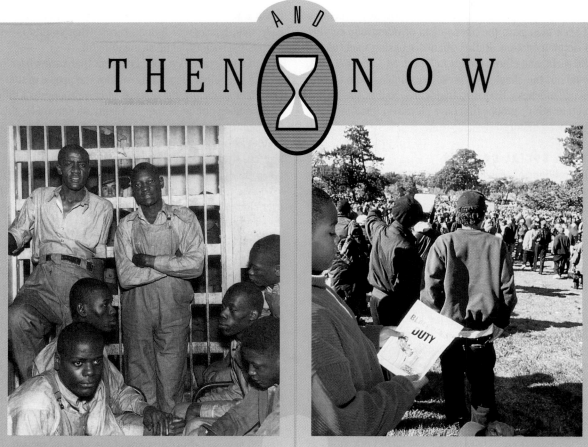

FROM THE SCOTTSBORO BOYS TO THE MILLION MAN MARCH

In 1995 a march by hundreds of thousands of African American men captured the fleeting attention of the national audience. Most of the marchers were descendants of men and women who had been slaves in the American South or on the rum and sugar islands of the Caribbean. In a peaceful and thoughtful demonstration, they marched on Washington, D.C., to signal their desire for constructive social change. They dedicated themselves to return home and work with the women of their communities to address problems of fatherlessness, drug abuse, poverty, and crime. The media made much of the political capital gained from the march by black leaders such as Louis Farrakhan, but the dominant emotions of the day were surely those of the masses of black men who shared a moment of solidarity in the spotlight of national attention.

If the march signaled the amount of hard work lying ahead, it also symbolized how much has already been accomplished. In the first half of this century the lives of black men and women were regulated by the harsh norms of Jim Crow. Thousands of black men were lynched by white mobs for daring to challenge the rules of white supremacy that relegated them to distinctly inferior status, insisting that they turn their eyes away from white women and address white men as "Mister."

In 1931 nine young black men were accused of raping two white prostitutes on a freight train in Alabama. The Scottsboro Boys, as they came to be known, were imprisoned and accused of black-on-white rape, a potentially capital offense. Their case focused world attention on the disparities between the American ideals of democracy and equality and the realities of racial oppression. The Scottsboro Boys were eventually acquitted after two decades of legal struggles. Their case was a major chapter in the mobilization of African American communities to fight racism and white supremacy. Many of the older participants in the Million Man March learned their first lessons about the need for unity and political action through the example of the Scottsboro case.

Critics of these conclusions argue that studies like *The Bell Curve* merely dredge up old academic justifications for the status quo of racial and class inequality (Gould, 1995). There is a great deal of evidence that IQ tests are biased against members of minority groups and that something as complex and elusive as intelligence cannot be summarized by a single score on a test. As we saw in Chapter 12, the history of efforts to address inequalities in education shows that when they have access to quality educational programs, minority students quickly begin to achieve at the same levels as white students. (See Figure 12.4.)

The notions that members of different races have different personalities, that there are identifiable "racial cultures," and that ethical standards differ from one race to another are among the other racist doctrines that have been debunked by social-scientific studies over the past 50 years. But even though these doctrines have been discredited, we will see shortly that they continue to play a major role in intergroup relations in many nations. Racist beliefs in the innate inferiority of populations that are erroneously thought of as separate races remain one of the major social problems of the modern world. And this tendency to denigrate socially defined racial groups extends to members of particular ethnic groups as well.

ETHNIC GROUPS AND MINORITIES

Ethnic groups are populations that have a sense of group identity based on a distinctive cultural pattern and, usually, shared ancestry, whether actual or assumed. Ethnic groups often have a sense of "peoplehood" that is maintained within a larger society (Davis, 1978; Kornblum, 1974). Their members usually have migrated to a new nation or been conquered by an invading population. In the United States and Canada, a large proportion of the population consists of people who either immigrated themselves or are descended from people who immigrated to the New World or were brought there as slaves. If one traces history back far enough, it appears that everyone living in the Western Hemisphere can trace his or her origins to other continents. Even the Native Americans are believed to have crossed the Bering Strait as migrant peoples between 14,000 and 20,000 years ago.

European conquests of the Americas in the sixteenth and seventeenth centuries resulted in people of Iberian (Spanish and Portuguese) origins becoming the dominant population group in Central and South America. People of English, German, Dutch, and French origins became the dominant population groups throughout much of North America. By the late 1770s almost 80 percent of the population of the 13 American colonies had been born in England or Ireland or were the children of people who had come from those countries. A century later, owing to the influence of slavery and large-scale immigration, the populations of the United States and Canada were far more diverse in terms of national origins, but people from England were still dominant.

According to sociological definitions of the term *dominance,* a dominant group is not necessarily numerically larger than other population groups in a nation. More important in establishing dominance is control or ownership of wealth (farms, banks, manufacturing concerns, and private property of all kinds) and political power—especially control of political institutions like legislatures, courts, the military, and the police. Thus by the beginning of this century white Anglo-Saxon males (or WASPs, as they are sometimes called) had established dominance over U.S. society even though they no longer constituted a clear majority of the population.

Between 1820 and 1960 approximately 42 million people immigrated to the United States. Since 1960 an average of at least 300,000 immigrants have arrived each year, with the number increasing to more than 500,000 in the past few years. Since its earliest history the United States has had one of the most liberal immigration policies of any nation on earth, a situation that is in part a consequence of the fact that many of its inhabitants can trace their origins to other countries. And except in the case of the Native Americans, who were expelled from their ancestral lands and forced to resettle on reservations, no area of the nation is seen as the ancestral homeland of a particular people. Unlike many nations, the United States is a multiethnic society where notions of "blood" (descent) do not coincide with claims to ancestral land. In the United States, therefore, there are no separatist movements that claim territory and threaten national unity. There are, however, severe inequalities that affect particular populations, especially Native Americans, African Americans, Latinos, and Appalachian whites. Many of these inequalities date back to major periods of settlement and ethnic group formation, which are summarized in Box 13.1. (See also Figure 13.1.)

Immigrant groups that are distinct because of racial features or culture (language, religion, dress, etc.) are often treated badly in the new society and hence develop the consciousness of being a minority group. Louis Wirth (1945), a pioneer in the study of racial and ethnic relations, defined a **minority group** as a set of "people who, because of their physical or cultural characteristics, are singled out from the others in the society in which they live for differential and unequal treatment, and who therefore regard themselves as objects of collective discrimination" (p. 347). The existence of a minority group in a society, Wirth explained, "implies the existence of a corresponding dominant group with a higher social status and greater privileges. Minority status carries with it exclusion from full participation in the life of the society" (p. 347).

In the United States the term *minority* often suggests "people of color," meaning African Americans, American Indians, Mexicans (many of whom have the darker coloring

BOX 13.1 GLOBAL SOCIAL CHANGE

Periods of Migration and Settlement in the United States

In 1790, when the republic was formed, the vast majority of U.S. citizens and resident foreigners (77 percent) had come from Great Britain and the counties that are now included in Northern Ireland. People from Germany (7.4 percent), Ireland (4.4 percent), the Netherlands (3.3 percent), France (2 percent), Mexico (1 percent), and other countries were present in the population, but with the exception of the Irish they were also white Protestants. Blacks—involuntary immigrants—and their children actually accounted for 19 percent of the total population, but neither they nor Native Americans were citizens.

1820–1885: The "Old" Northwest European and Asian Migration

By about 1830 the mass migration of different groups into the new nation was under way. The largest flows of immigrants came from Ireland and Germany, with well over a million people from each of these countries coming to the United States to escape political or economic troubles. Smaller waves of immigrants originated in the northern European nations of Sweden, Norway, and Denmark.

Although people from northern Europe made up the most important immigrant groups, far exceeding the continuing influx from Great Britain, 1885 marked the beginning of a flow of immigrants from China that continued at high rates for the next 30 years. Chinese immigrants settled primarily in the West and contributed immensely to the development of the western states, although they met with sporadic and often violent hostility.

1885–1940: The "Intermediate" Migration From Southern and Eastern Europe and the Beginning of Heavy Immigration From Mexico

From 1880 to 1900 the flow of immigrants from Italy, Poland, Russia, the Baltic states, and southern Europe (Serbs, Croats, Slovenes, Romanians, Bulgarians, Greeks, etc.) exceeded the flow of people from older immigrant groups by about four to one. In 1907 alone more than 250,000 Italians and 338,000 Poles and other central Europeans were admitted through New York's Ellis Island. Many of these immigrants were Jewish, Roman Catholic, or Orthodox Christian. The newcomers' tendency to live in neighborhoods known as "Little Italy" or "Little Poland" convinced more established Americans that the immigrants would never learn English or become fully American. The mass arrival of physically distinctive groups such as Mexicans and Japanese during this period also aroused fear and hostility among those who disliked the newcomers.

During World War I thousands of impoverished black southerners were attracted to the cities of the North and the Midwest. This began a trend that would continue throughout the century whenever wars or economic booms made it possible for blacks to overcome discrimination and get factory jobs.

1921–1959: Immigration by Quota and Refugee Status

Agitation against the "new" immigrants and demands for "Oriental exclusion" led Congress to establish a quota system that drastically altered the flow of newcomers into the nation after 1920. At first the quotas were fixed at 3 percent of the number of people from each country who had been counted as U.S. residents in the 1910 census. But because that formula still allowed large numbers of "new" immigrants to enter the nation, in 1924 the law was changed so that quotas would be based on the national origins of the foreign-born population as of the 1890 census. This biased the quota system in favor of northern Europeans; in fact, Asians were explicitly excluded.

World War II and the cold war produced millions of homeless and stateless refugees, especially from Germany, Poland, and the Soviet Union. Almost half a million of these displaced persons arrived in the United States between 1948 and 1950; another 2 million came between 1950 and 1957. Their arrival swelled the populations of ethnic enclaves in America's industrial cities.

1960 to the Present: Worldwide Immigration

In the 1960s national quotas were replaced with a system based on preference for skilled workers and professionals, regardless of country of origin, as well as refugees and people with families already in the United States. Gradually Congress has increased the number of immigrants who may enter the country legally—from 280,000 in 1980 to more than 450,000 in 1992. Today the United States is once again the foremost immigrant-receiving nation in the world. The largest streams of immigrants are from Mexico, other Central American and Caribbean nations, Asia (especially Korea, China, India, and Pakistan), and South America. Untold numbers of undocumented, or illegal, immigrants also arrive each year—especially from Mexico, Canada, and the Dominican Republic—but studies show that a high proportion of these newcomers eventually become legal residents or return to their country of origin (Bogue, 1985; Portes & Rumbaut, 1990).

---

of Amerindian ancestry), and Asians. But the term can also be applied to people with lighter skin coloring. In Great Britain, for example, the Irish were a conquered people who were subjected to economic and social discrimination by the English. It is not surprising, therefore, that when the Irish began immigrating to the United States in the nineteenth century they were treated as an inferior minority by

Americans of English ancestry. This attitude was especially prevalent in cities like Boston and New York, to which the Irish came in large numbers.

It should also be noted that the term *minority* does not always imply that the population is numerically inferior to the dominant group. There are counties in some states in the South, and entire cities in the North, in which African

FIGURE 13.1 Major Sources of Immigration to the United States

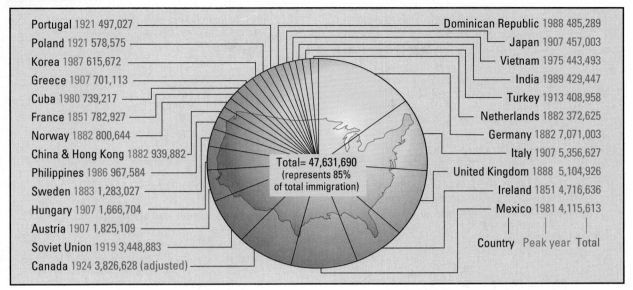

Portugal 1921 497,027
Poland 1921 578,575
Korea 1987 615,672
Greece 1907 701,113
Cuba 1980 739,217
France 1851 782,927
Norway 1882 800,644
China & Hong Kong 1882 939,882
Philippines 1986 967,584
Sweden 1883 1,283,027
Hungary 1907 1,666,704
Austria 1907 1,825,109
Soviet Union 1919 3,448,883
Canada 1924 3,826,628 (adjusted)

Dominican Republic 1988 485,289
Japan 1907 457,003
Vietnam 1975 443,493
India 1989 429,447
Turkey 1913 408,958
Netherlands 1882 372,625
Germany 1882 7,071,003
Italy 1907 5,356,627
United Kingdom 1888 5,104,926
Ireland 1851 4,716,636
Mexico 1981 4,115,613

Country   Peak year   Total

Total= 47,631,690
(represents 85%
of total immigration)

Source: Data from U.S. Immigration and Naturalization Service.   *Note:* Statistics are based on the last country of residence.

Americans constitute a numerical majority yet cannot be considered the dominant group because they lack the power, wealth, and prestige enjoyed by the white population.

Ethnic and Cultural Minority Groups. Ethnic groups often form in cities or metropolitan regions for reasons of choice as well as necessity. In fact, very often the identity of a group is defined through the experience of coping with life in the new society as well as through the group's desire to hold on to its language, food, and other cultural ways (Handlin, 1992; Rodriguez, 1992). In one of the first and best studies of ethnic group formation, W. I. Thomas (1971/1921) described how in the early decades of this century Italian immigrants settled in small neighborhoods in Manhattan where they could live with people who had emigrated from the same region and spoke the same dialect of Italian. At first these immigrants identified themselves as Calabrians or Sicilians or Piedmontese, the way they had before leaving those regions. Thomas found that they identified with their home regions rather than with the nation of Italy. In New York, however, they could speak to each other and appreciate each other's food, and they had reason to join together to compete with other ethnic groups for jobs and homes. They were also called Italians by people outside their neighborhoods. Gradually, therefore, they began to think of themselves as Italians or Italian Americans, but this identity was forged out of their experience in the United States and did not mean the same thing as being an Italian in Italy.

Most ethnic populations have had similar experiences that caused them to develop a group consciousness and create organizations to represent their interests. Homosexuals and other populations that are defined in terms of their behavior and cultural traits may become organized into cultural minority groups, but they differ from true ethnic groups because they do not trace their ancestry to another society.

Today sociologists are interested in knowing whether a similar process of ethnic group formation is occurring in regions where there are large Spanish-speaking populations. They seek to discover whether Mexicans, Puerto Ricans, Colombians, and Dominicans are beginning to think of themselves as Latinos in cities where they are all present in large numbers, or whether their allegiance to their nationality of origin will prevent them from taking on the more inclusive Latino identity. Researchers are asking similar questions about whether a new Asian ethnicity will be forged out of the experience of various Asian immigrant groups, especially the Koreans and Chinese, in American cities (Moore & Pachon, 1985; Portes & Rumbaut, 1990). (See Box 13.2.)

WHEN WORLDS COLLIDE: PATTERNS OF INTERGROUP RELATIONS

Throughout history, when different racial and ethnic groups have met and mixed, the most usual outcome has been violence and warfare. In fact, the desire for peaceful and cooperative relations among diverse peoples has emerged relatively recently. In this section we explore a continuum of relations between dominant and minority groups that extends from complete intolerance to complete tolerance, as shown in the study chart on page 385. At one extreme is extermination or genocide; at the other is assimilation.

BOX 13.2 SOCIOLOGICAL METHODS

Racial Categories and the Census

At this writing a battle is raging in Congress and governmental agencies over the question of how the U.S. census should measure race and ethnicity. At issue is whether a "Multiracial" category should be created on census and other forms, such as school registration forms, in which data on race and ethnicity are collected.

Advocates of the "Multiracial" category cite a number of statistics to support their position. The present question allows people to answer "Other" if they do not consider themselves black, white, American Indian, or Asian or Pacific Islander. In the 1990 census about 10 million people placed themselves in the "Other" category. In addition, other census data and surveys show that there are an estimated 1.2 million interracial marriages in the United States today, compared to about 310,000 in 1970. Children born to interracial couples often have difficulty classifying themselves in one of the standard racial categories. Increasingly, therefore, people of mixed-race heritage call for a new category that reflects their social reality (Della Piana, 1995).

On the other side of the issue are some black activists and social scientists, who argue that the inclusion of a "Multiracial" category is a political ploy whose purpose is to reduce the official count of minorities in the population so that statistics on racial inequality would improve and arguments for policies such as affirmative action would be less convincing. They point out that people of mixed race are considered not to be white. As Samuel L. Myers, Jr., writes:

> It matters not whether I have $\frac{1}{32}$ Cherokee "blood," $\frac{19}{32}$ black "blood" and who knows how much Irish, French, Spanish, Cuban and perhaps German (note the name "Myers") blood. What matters is that I am black. My mother and father are black. My sisters and my daughter are black. And regardless of who my daughter eventually marries, her children will also be black. And as black people in America, we are deemed less able, less deserving, and less equal than whites. What matters is race. (1995, p. 14)

Demographer Reynolds Farley points out that the issue is an important one and should be addressed. After all, the census is mandated by the Constitution as a means of determining the voting representation of the states in Congress; census data are used to create voting districts. To avoid the common practice of drawing district boundaries so as to exclude or underrepresent a given group, the government must have accurate data on the racial and ethnic composition of the population. Farley notes that it is probably impossible to develop a set of categories that will settle all the arguments and account for all the possible mixtures of race and ethnicity. Yet he offers one possibility:

> If there is any consensus emerging it is that, for purposes of federal policy, persons may be members of only one major group and that almost all persons may

---

PROPOSED QUESTION
Question to Simultaneously Obtain Race
and Hispanic Identity

What is this person's primary identity?

Fill in only one circle and write appropriate term:

○ WHITE
Write ethnicity or origin, such as English, German, Czech, or Irish: _____

○ BLACK OR AFRICAN AMERICAN
Write ethnicity or origin, such as Jamaican, Nigerian, Ibo, or Ethiopian: _____

○ HISPANIC OR LATINO
Write ethnicity or origin, such as Mexican, Cuban, Puerto Rican, or Argentinian: _____

○ ASIAN OR PACIFIC ISLANDER
Write ethnicity or origin, such as Filipino, Chinese, Thai, or Japanese: _____

○ NATIVE AMERICAN
Write ethnicity or origin, such as Cherokee, Navajo, Eskimo, Aleut, or Hawaiian: _____

---

reasonably be classified into one of the following five groups:

- Whites not Spanish in origin
- Blacks or African-Americans not Spanish in origin
- Hispanic or Latino
- Asian or Pacific Islander not Spanish in origin
- Native American not Spanish in origin (1995, p. 15)

Farley supports the testing of a single census question to determine racial and ethnic identity, one that recognizes the difficulty of identifying racial and ethnic categories and attempts to allow the respondent to do so with relative ease. The text of the proposed question is presented in the accompanying chart. It would require people to classify themselves in one of the five major groups but would also allow them to provide information that could be used to classify them as people of mixed racial and ethnic heritage.

Will such a question be included in the preliminary tests for eventual use in the census in the year 2000? That is difficult to predict because of the current conflict over the role of the census and whether it should include any questions at all about race and ethnicity. No doubt the census will continue to collect such information, but the wrangling over the issue at the highest levels of government is an indication of how politically and emotionally charged these sociological questions can be.

STUDY CHART   A Continuum of Intergroup Relations

TOLERANCE → INTOLERANCE

Genocide	Expulsion	Slavery	Segregation	Assimilation
The intentional extermination of a population, defined as a "race" or a "people."	The forcible removal of a population from a territory claimed by another population.	Ownership of one population by another, which can buy and sell members of the enslaved population and controls every aspect of their lives.	Ecological and institutional separation of races or ethnic groups.	The process by which a minority group blends into the majority population and eventually disappears as a distinct people within the larger society.

GENOCIDE

In a study of a New Guinea tribe, the Siane, anthropologist Richard Salisbury (1962) found that the members of this isolated highland tribe believed that anyone from another tribe wanted to kill them. Therefore, the Siane felt that they must kill any member of another tribe they might encounter. (Fortunately, they excluded the anthropologist from this norm.) We often think of such behavior as primitive, savage, or barbarous. Yet barbarities on a far greater scale have been carried out by supposedly advanced societies. The most extreme of these is **genocide**, the intentional extermination of a population, defined as a "race" or a "people," by a more dominant population.

There have been numerous instances of genocide in recent history. Those incidents have been characterized by a degree of severity and a level of efficiency unknown to earlier civilizations. Consider the following:

- The Native American populations of North, Central, and South America were decimated by European explorers and settlers between the sixteenth and twentieth centuries. Millions of Native Americans were killed in one-sided wars, intentional starvation, forced marches, and executions. The population of Native Americans in North America was reduced from more than 4 million in the eighteenth century to less than 600,000 in the early twentieth century (Thornton, 1987).

- When England, France, Germany, Portugal, and the Netherlands were engaged in fierce competition for colonial dominance of Africa during the nineteenth and early twentieth centuries, millions of native people were exterminated. The introduction of the Gatling machine gun made it possible for small numbers of troops to slaughter thousands of tribal warriors.

- Six million Jews, 400,000 gypsies, and about 2 million Russian civilians were killed by the Nazis during World War II; thousands of Pakistanis and Indians were slaughtered after the partition of India in 1947; and thousands of Tamils living in Sri Lanka were exterminated by Sinhalese in the 1980s. "Ethnic cleansing" by Serbian troops in the former Yugoslav republic of Bosnia and Herzegovina, where entire Muslim-Bosnian villages have been wiped out, is a recent example of genocidal action. (See Box 13.3.)

Mass executions and other forms of genocide are almost always justified by the belief that the people who are being slaughtered are less than human and in fact are dangerous parasites. Thus the British and Dutch slaughtered members of African tribes like the Hottentots in the belief that they were a lower form of life, a nuisance species unfit even for enslavement. The Nazis rationalized the extermination of Jews and gypsies by the same twisted reasoning.

BOX 13.3 GLOBAL SOCIAL CHANGE

The Tragedy of Rwanda: Some Lessons for Ethnic Relations

To horrified audiences watching on international television, the ethnic massacres that took place in Rwanda in 1994 seemed to be the ultimate nightmare. Children and pregnant women were hacked to death with machetes. Schoolteachers were hunted down by illiterate mobs. Entire villages were decimated. Now hundreds of thousands of refugees are living in squalid camps on the nation's borders, and crops are rotting in the fields outside looted villages.

There are important lessons to be learned from the tragedy of Rwanda. According to one writer on the subject, "Many outside observers, especially in the early days of the slaughter, have tended to dismiss what has happened in Rwanda as African mayhem-as-usual. They saw the Hutu-Tutsi conflict as little more than a savage tribal freak show" (Block, 1994, p. 3). But those who watched with a more sociological eye understand that the causes of the slaughter are complex and by no means limited to Africa.

The slaughter of Hutus by Tutsi soldiers in 1994 was preceded by an even larger slaughter of Tutsis by Hutu militia and soldiers in 1991. Almost all informed observers concur that most of those who did the killing on either side did so not because they personally hated those whom they killed but because they were told to do so by their leaders. In fact, there was a history of cooperation and intermarriage among the Hutus and Tutsis. In many villages there was a tradition of sharing among members of the two tribal groups. With wise leadership and emphasis on the rule of law, the bloodshed could have been prevented.

Among Tutsi and Hutu leaders, the animosities that led to the recent massacres are based to a large extent on Rwanda's colonial history. Colonialism came to Rwanda early in the century in the form of Belgian conquest and

rule. Before that time, the Tutsis were a pastoral people. The Hutus, who are related to the Bantu-speaking people of central and southern Africa, had developed a complex feudal kingdom. European explorers and colonizers refused to believe "that the Bantu peoples of Central Africa could have developed relatively sophisticated kingdoms such as existed in precolonial Rwanda. So the Europeans explained these 'anomalies' by inventing a race of 'African Aryans,' the Hamites, who supposedly migrated from northeastern Africa, bringing civilization to the 'savages' further south" (Block, 1994, p. 6).

Today this theory is universally dismissed, but during the colonial era it was used by Europeans to rationalize actions that favored the Tutsis over the Hutus. Over the course of colonial rule, the animosity between the two tribal groups grew more severe and became part of the thinking of both Tutsi and Hutu leaders. Today leaders and intellectuals on both sides accuse each other of being inferior and back their claims with "theories" that they teach to children and uneducated adults. These theories of racial superiority spread rapidly among illiterate members of both tribes, but they have their origins among the affluent and educated elite.

At this writing, it is not at all clear what can be done to close the rifts that have torn Rwanda apart. One lesson of the disaster, however, is that although intergroup hatreds may be widespread among the mass of people in a society, they may be forgotten over time as intermarriage and economic and social cooperation heal old wounds. But if political and intellectual leaders continue to benefit from intergroup hatreds and use their influence to maintain old stereotypes and grievances, there is little hope for ethnic harmony.

EXPULSION

In many societies, extended conflicts between racial or ethnic groups have ended in **expulsion,** the forcible removal of one population from territory claimed by the other. Thus on the earliest map of almost every major American city there appears a double line drawn at the edges where the streets end. This is the Indian Boundary Line, and it symbolizes the expulsion of Native Americans from lands that were taken from them in order to create a city in which they would be strangers.

Expulsion was the usual fate of North America's native peoples, who also experienced massacres, deadly forced marches, and other genocidal attacks. These actions were rationalized, in part, by the nineteenth-century doctrine of "manifest destiny," which asserted the inevitability of the westward expansion of Europeans across the territories of the Southwest and West (Davis, 1995). As white settlement expanded westward, Native Americans were continually ex-

pelled from their tribal lands. After the 1848 gold rush and the rapid settlement of the West Coast, the pressure of white settlement pushed the Indian tribes into the high plains of the West and Southwest. Between 1865 and the 1890 massacre of Sioux Indians at Wounded Knee, South Dakota, the remaining free tribes in the West were forced to settle on reservations. In the process the Indians lost more than their ancestral lands. As the famous Sioux chief Black Elk put it, "A people's dream died" (quoted in Brown, 1970, p. 419).

The forced settlement of Native Americans on reservations is only one example of expulsion. Asian immigrants in the American West also suffered as a result of intermittent attempts at expulsion referred to as the Oriental exclusion movement. In an effort to prevent the large-scale importation of Chinese laborers into California and other states, Congress passed the Chinese Exclusion Act of 1882, which excluded Chinese laborers from entry into the

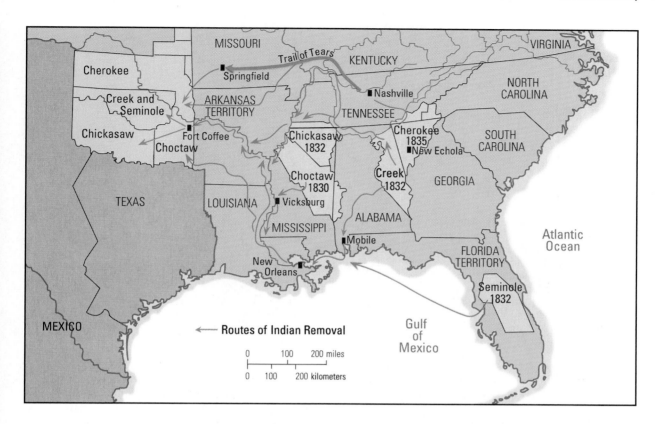

Routes of Indian Removal

United States for 10 years. But this legislation did little to relieve the hostility between whites and Asians. Riots directed against Chinese workers were common throughout the West during this period, and Chinese immigrants were actually expelled from a number of towns. In 1895, for example, a mob killed 28 Chinese immigrants in Rock Springs, Wyoming, and expelled the remaining Chinese population from the area (Lai, 1980).

The most severe example of expulsion directed against Asians in the United States occurred in 1942 after the Japanese attack on Pearl Harbor and the American entry into World War II. On orders from the U.S. government, more than 110,000 West Coast Japanese, 64 percent of whom were U.S. citizens, were ordered to leave their homes and their businesses and were transported to temporary assembly centers (Kitano, 1980). They were then

The Cherokee "Trail of Tears": In the winter of 1838–1839 the Cherokee were forcibly removed from their homeland in Georgia and compelled to travel 400 miles to what is now northeastern Oklahoma. The removal was a disaster, as nearly 25 percent of the tribe's members died of disease and exposure.

As the property of their masters, slaves could be punished in whatever way their owners and overseers saw fit, as this scene from a Caribbean plantation illustrates. Sociologist Orlando Patterson showed that the slaves' rate of natural increase (that is, their birthrate) varied inversely with the severity of their treatment.

assigned to detention camps in remote areas of California, Arizona, Idaho, Colorado, Utah, and Arkansas. When the United States Supreme Court declared unconstitutional the incarceration of an entire ethnic group without a hearing or formal charges (*Endo* v. *United States,* 1944), the Japanese were released, but by then many had lost their homes and all their possessions. In 1989 Congress finally voted to pay modest reparations to the families of Japanese Americans who had been imprisoned during the war.

SLAVERY

Somewhat farther along the continuum between genocide and assimilation is slavery. **Slavery** is the ownership of a population, defined by racial or ethnic or political criteria, by another population that not only can buy and sell members of the enslaved population but also has complete control over their lives. Slavery has been called "the peculiar institution" because, ironically, it has existed in some of the world's greatest civilizations. The socioeconomic systems of ancient Greece and Rome, for example, were based on the labor of slaves. And the great trading cities of late medieval Europe, such as Venice, Genoa, and Florence, developed plantation systems in their Mediterranean colonies that were based on slave labor. In fact, the foremost student of slave systems, Orlando Patterson, makes the following comment:

> There is nothing notably peculiar about the institution of slavery. It has existed from before the dawn of human history right down to the twentieth century, in the most primitive of human societies and in the most civilized. . . . Probably there is no group of people whose ancestors were not at one time slaves or slaveholders. (1982, p. vii)

Figure 13.2 indicates the magnitude of the transatlantic slave trade; the widths of the arrows represent the relative size of each portion of that terrible traffic in humanity. The arrows do not show, however, that for the Americas to acquire 11 million slaves who survived the voyage on the slave ships and the violence and diseases of the New World, approximately 24 million Africans had to be captured and enslaved (Fyfe, 1976; Patterson, 1982, 1991). It is evident from Figure 13.2 that the United States imported a proportionately small number of slaves. However, although somewhat less than 10 percent of all slaves were sold in the United States, by 1825 almost 30 percent of the black population in the Western Hemisphere was living in the United States (Patterson, 1982). This was due to the high rate of natural increase among the American slaves. In Brazil, by contrast, the proportion of slave imports was relatively high, but there was also a high mortality rate among the slaves owing to disease and frequent slave revolts.

At the time of the first U.S. census in 1790, there were 757,000 blacks counted in the overall population. By the outbreak of the Civil War, the number had increased to 4.4 million, of whom all but about 10 percent were slaves. In the southern states that fought in the war, one third of white families owned slaves, the average being nine "chattels" per owner (Farley & Allen, 1987). (The term *chattels* refers to living beings that are considered property, including slaves and, in some cultures, women.)

It can be inferred from the great increase in the U.S. slave population that slaveholders in the United States treated their slaves less badly than did slaveholders in other parts of the Western Hemisphere. This does not

FIGURE 13.2 **The Transatlantic Slave Trade**

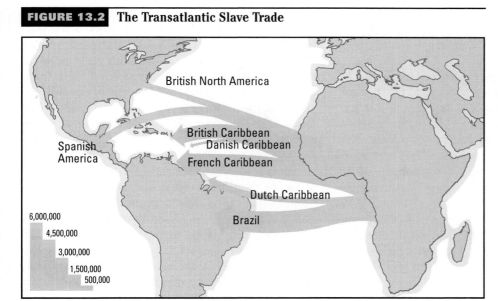

British North America

Spanish America

British Caribbean
Danish Caribbean
French Caribbean

Dutch Caribbean

Brazil

6,000,000
4,500,000
3,000,000
1,500,000
500,000

From the end of the sixteenth century to the early decades of the nineteenth, approximately 11 to 12 million Africans were imported to the New World (Patterson, 1982). The map shows that the largest numbers of slaves were sent to the European colonies in the Caribbean and to Brazil.

Source: Curtin, 1969.

mean, however, that the American slaves did not bitterly resent their condition and struggle against it. Patterson points out that the slave has always striven, against all odds, "for some measure of regularity and predictability in his social life. . . . Because he was considered degraded, he was all the more infused with the yearning for dignity" (1982, p. 337). Patterson concludes that one of the chief ironies of slavery throughout history has been that "without [it] there would have been no freedmen" (p. 342). In other words, the very idea of freedom developed in large part from the longing of slaves to be free.

SEGREGATION

Although African American slaves gained their freedom during the Civil War and became citizens of the United States, this did not mean that they became fully integrated into American society. A long period of segregation followed. **Segregation** is the ecological and institutional separation of races or ethnic groups. The segregation of racially or ethnically distinct peoples within a society may be voluntary, resulting from the desire of a people to live separately and maintain its own culture and institutions. The Amish, the Hutterites, and the Hasidic Jews are examples of groups that voluntarily segregate themselves. But segregation is often involuntary, resulting from laws or other norms that force one people to be separate from others. Involuntary separation may be either **de jure**—created by laws that prohibit certain peoples from interacting with others or place limits on such interactions—or **de facto**—created by unwritten norms that result in segregation, just as if it were "in fact" legally required.

South Africa recently experienced a stunning reversal of its system of de jure segregation. Known as *apartheid*,

South Africa's racial laws insisted that blacks, whites, and "coloreds" (people of mixed ancestry) remain separate. Intermarriage and integrated schools and communities were forbidden. In 1991, after years of struggle and violence, the white-dominated government agreed to repeal the apartheid laws. A constitutional convention—at which all segments of the population were represented—created a democratic regime in which all citizens' votes count equally. The African majority, led by Nelson Mandela and the African National Congress, assumed power in a relatively peaceful transition. Nevertheless, whites continue to

ZIMBABWE

NAMIBIA   BOTSWANA   MOZAMBIQUE

Wes-Rand
Johannesburg

SWAZILAND
LESOTHO

Alexander Bay   Durban

ATLANTIC OCEAN   SOUTH AFRICA   INDIAN OCEAN

East London
Cape Town   Port Elizabeth

hold most of the nation's wealth, while the majority of South African blacks are trapped in dire poverty and illiteracy, just as the former slaves were in the United States after the Civil War.

In the United States, legally sanctioned segregation no longer exists, but this has been true only in recent years. Before the civil rights movement of the 1960s, de jure segregation was common, especially in the southern states. The system that enforced segregation was supported by **Jim Crow** laws in many southern states. This term refers to laws that enforced or condoned segregation, barred blacks from the polls, and the like. (Jim Crow was a nineteenth-century white minstrel who performed in blackface and thereby reinforced black stereotypes.) This system was in effect for about a hundred years, from just after the Civil War until the early 1970s. During that period the so-called color line was applied throughout the United States to limit the places where blacks could live, where they could work and what kinds of jobs they could hold, where they could go to school, and under what conditions they could vote.

At first the color line was an unwritten set of norms that barred or restricted black participation in many social institutions. By the turn of the century, however, segregation had become officially sanctioned through legislation and court rulings. This official segregation was rationalized by the "separate but equal" doctrine set forth by the Supreme Court in *Plessy* v. *Ferguson* (1896). Under this doctrine, separate facilities for people of different races were legal as long as they were of equal quality. In addition, de facto segregation and the existence of a "job ceiling" based on race served to keep blacks in subordinate jobs and segregated ghettos, as we saw in Chapter 12 in the case of Chicago's "black metropolis."

Only after years of struggle by opponents of de jure segregation did the U.S. Supreme Court finally decide, in the landmark case of *Brown* v. *Board of Education, Topeka* (1954), that "separate but equal" was inherently unequal. The *Brown* ruling put an end to legally sanctioned segregation of schools, hospitals, public accommodations, and the like. But it took frequent, often violent demonstrations and the mobilization of thousands of citizens in support of civil rights to achieve passage of the Civil Rights Act of 1964. That act mandated an end to segregation in private accommodations, made discrimination in the sale of housing illegal, and initiated a major attack on the job ceiling through the strategy known as affirmative action. Despite these judicial and legislative victories, however, de facto segregation remains a fact of life in the United States, especially in large cities (Massey & Denton, 1993).

Ecological studies of racial segregation show that despite some improvements in the past 20 years, residential segregation persists in almost all U.S. cities. Table 13.1 is based on a measure known as the *segregation index*. It shows "the minimum percentage of nonwhites who would have to change the block on which they live in order to produce an unsegregated distribution—one in which the percentage of nonwhites living on each block is the same throughout the city (0 on the index)" (Taeuber & Taeuber, 1965, p. 30). A value of 100 on the index would mean that all nonwhite people live on segregated blocks—that is, the city is 100 percent segregated. In 1970, for example, 81.2 percent of the nonwhite population in Boston would have had to move to another block to produce an unsegregated distribution of whites and nonwhites. By 1990 that proportion had declined to 68.2 percent, clearly an improvement.

Despite such improvements in many metropolitan regions, the table shows that most cities, especially in the North, continue to be highly segregated. Although segregation in some regions has fallen below the 70 percent level, high segregation indexes remain a fact of American life. Urban ecologists point out that most changes in segregation patterns are due to the movement of blacks into newer suburban communities and older white neighborhoods in the cities (Jaynes & Williams, 1989; Massey & Denton, 1993). (See also Figure 13.3.)

Other problems of inequality follow from these persistent patterns of racial segregation. It is extremely difficult, for example, to have integrated schools, especially in the primary grades, when children live in segregated neighborhoods. And it is difficult to establish tolerance and understanding among racial and ethnic groups whose members have grown up in segregated neighborhoods and schools.

ASSIMILATION

One of the factors that led to segregation was the fear of racial intermarriage, since the ideology of white supremacy held that intermarriage would weaken the white race. As late as 1950, 30 states had laws prohibiting such marriages, and even after racist sentiments began to diminish in the 1950s, 19 states (17 of them in the South) maintained such laws until the Supreme Court declared them unconstitutional in 1967 (Holt, 1980).

Intermarriage between distinct racial and ethnic groups is an important indicator of **assimilation,** the pattern of intergroup relations in which a minority group is forced or encouraged or voluntarily seeks to blend into the majority population and eventually disappears as a distinct people within the larger society. (We saw in Chapter 3 that assimilation refers to the process by which a culturally distinct group adopts the language, values, and norms of a larger society. Here we are using the term in a broader sense, to include social as well as cultural blending.) Needless to say, it makes a great deal of difference whether an ethnic or racial group has been the victim of forced assimilation or has been allowed to absorb the majority culture at its own pace. Many Latin American societies offer examples of peaceful, long-term assimilation of various racial and ethnic groups. For example, as a result of generations of intermarriage, Brazilians distinguish among many shades of skin color and other physical features rather than relying on crude black–white distinctions (Fernandes, 1968).

In the United States, assimilation has had a more troubled history. In an influential treatise on this subject, Milton Gordon (1964) identified three "ideological tendencies" that have affected the treatment of minority groups at various times. These ideologies specify how ethnic or racial groups should change (or resist change) as they seek acceptance in the institutions and culture of American society. They can be summarized as follows:

1. *Anglo-conformity*—the demand that culturally distinct groups give up their own cultures and adopt the norms and values of the dominant Anglo-Saxon culture

2. *The melting pot*—the theory that there would be a biological merging of ethnic and racial groups, resulting in a "new indigenous American type"

3. *Cultural pluralism*—the belief that culturally distinct groups can retain their communities and much of their culture even though they participate in the institutions of the larger society

Because these ideological tendencies have played an important role in intergroup relations in the United States, we will examine them in some detail.

Anglo-Conformity. The demand for Anglo-conformity rests on the belief that the persistence of ethnic cultures, ethnic and racial communities, and foreign languages in an English-speaking society should be aggressively

TABLE 13.1	Trends in Black-White Segregation in 20 Metropolitan Areas With Largest Black Populations, 1970–1990		
METROPOLITAN AREA	1970	1980	1990
Northern Areas			
Boston	81.2	77.6	68.2
Chicago	91.9	87.8	85.8
Cleveland	90.8	87.5	85.1
Detroit	88.4	86.7	87.6
Kansas City	87.4	78.9	72.6
Los Angeles–			
Long Beach	91.0	81.1	73.1
Milwaukee	90.5	83.9	82.8
New York	81.0	82.0	82.2
Philadelphia	79.5	78.8	77.2
St. Louis	84.7	81.3	77.0
San Francisco–			
Oakland	80.1	71.7	66.8
Northern			
Average	84.5	80.1	77.8
Southern Areas			
Atlanta	82.1	78.5	67.8
Baltimore	81.9	74.7	71.4
Birmingham	37.8	40.8	71.7
Dallas–			
Fort Worth	86.9	77.1	63.1
Houston	78.1	69.5	66.8
Memphis	75.9	71.6	69.3
New Orleans	73.1	68.3	50.3
Washington, D.C.	81.1	70.1	66.1
Southern			
Average	75.5	68.3	66.5

Source: Adapted from Massey & Denton, 1993.

FIGURE 13.3

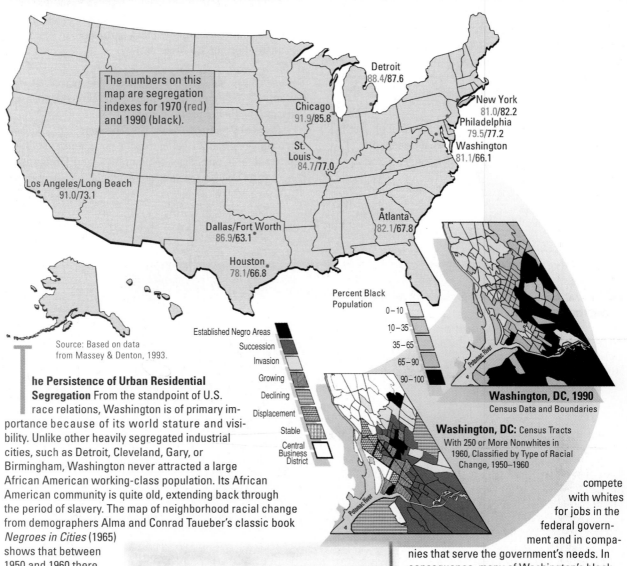

MAPPING SOCIAL CHANGE

The numbers on this map are segregation indexes for 1970 (red) and 1990 (black).

Detroit
88.4/87.6

New York
81.0/82.2

Philadelphia
79.5/77.2

Washington
81.1/66.1

Chicago
91.9/85.8

St. Louis
84.7/77.0

Los Angeles/Long Beach
91.0/73.1

Dallas/Fort Worth
86.9/63.1

Atlanta
82.1/67.8

Houston
78.1/66.8

Source: Based on data from Massey & Denton, 1993.

Established Negro Areas
Succession
Invasion
Growing
Declining
Displacement
Stable
Central Business District

Percent Black Population
0 – 10
10 – 35
35 – 65
65 – 90
90 – 100

Washington, DC, 1990
Census Data and Boundaries

Washington, DC: Census Tracts With 250 or More Nonwhites in 1960, Classified by Type of Racial Change, 1950–1960

he Persistence of Urban Residential Segregation From the standpoint of U.S. race relations, Washington is of primary importance because of its world stature and visibility. Unlike other heavily segregated industrial cities, such as Detroit, Cleveland, Gary, or Birmingham, Washington never attracted a large African American working-class population. Its African American community is quite old, extending back through the period of slavery. The map of neighborhood racial change from demographers Alma and Conrad Taueber's classic book *Negroes in Cities* (1965) shows that between 1950 and 1960 there were areas along the Potomac River, such as the well-known community of Georgetown, where the African American population was being displaced by whites. The census tract analysis shows that in the same period there were large areas, especially in the eastern portion of the city, where blacks were replacing whites and racial segregation was increasing.

The African American population in Washington grew rapidly during the middle decades of the century, when the combination of federal antidiscrimination policies and the expansion of government agencies made it possible for African Americans to compete with whites for jobs in the federal government and in companies that serve the government's needs. In consequence, many of Washington's black neighborhoods are economically secure, but they are nonetheless segregated. The city also has some quite poor African American neighborhoods where high levels of addiction, violence, and homelessness are a persistent problem.

Other neighborhoods are undergoing a process of renewal and racial integration. Young white families and business owners, along with members of new immigrant groups, are mingling with their black neighbors. If these changes accelerate, coming census surveys may find that segregation has diminished. But as the 1990 census tract map shows, the separation of the races in residential neighborhoods is still a dominant social fact in the nation's capital.

discouraged. The catchword of this ideology is *Americanization,* the idea that immigrants and their children must become "100 percent American" by losing all traces of their "foreign" accents, abandoning their ethnic cultures, and marrying nonethnic Americans. This demand is reflected in the movement to make English the official language of the United States, along with opposition to bilingual education. In some cases discrimination against members of certain ethnic groups is rationalized by the statement that they are not yet fully American.

The Melting Pot. In an 1893 paper, a young historian named Frederick Jackson Turner challenged the notion that American culture and institutions had been formed by the nation's original Anglo-Saxon settlers. Turner's essay argued that the major influences on American culture were the experiences of the diverse array of people who met and mixed on the western frontier. Turner held that "in the crucible of the frontier the immigrants were Americanized, liberated, and fused into a mixed race" (1920/1893, pp. 22–23).

Turner's "crucible" became widely known as the "melting pot," a term taken from a play by Israel Zangwell about a Russian immigrant. David, the play's hero, makes the following declaration:

> America is God's crucible, the great Melting Pot where all the races of Europe are melting and re-forming! Here you stand, good folk . . . in your fifty groups, with your fifty languages and histories, and your fifty blood hatreds and

rivalries. . . . Germans and Frenchmen, Irishmen and Englishmen, Jews and Russians—into the Crucible with you all! God is making the American. (1909, p. 37)

The melting-pot view of assimilation attracted many scholars, artists, and social commentators, but sociologists were not convinced that it was an accurate view of what actually happens to ethnic groups in American society. Their research showed that certain ethnic groups have not been fully assimilated, either through intermarriage or through integration into the nation's major institutions. Instead, there remain distinct patterns of **ethnic stratification;** that is, different groups are valued differently depending on how closely they conform to Anglo-Saxon standards of appearance, behavior, and values. People of Scandinavian or northern European descent, for example, are more readily accepted into the top levels of corporate management than people of Mediterranean descent, who in turn are more readily accepted than black, Hispanic, and Asian minorities.

In an early empirical study of assimilation, Ruby Jo Reeves Kennedy (1944) analyzed rates of ethnic intermarriage in New Haven, Connecticut. She found that intergroup marriages increased in frequency between 1870 and 1940 but that while there was a growing tendency for people to marry outside their *ethnic* group, there remained a very strong tendency for people not to marry outside their own *religious* group. From this finding Kennedy developed the hypothesis of the "triple melting pot," the idea that assimilation occurs first among groups that share the same

The young black woman shown in this 1888 engraving from *Harper's Weekly* titled "Their Pride" is about to go away to a teacher-training college. All newcomers to urban America, be they blacks from the rural South or immigrants from European countries, have recognized that education is the best route to upward social mobility.

religion and later among groups with different religions. More recently, in *Beyond the Melting Pot,* Nathan Glazer and Daniel Patrick Moynihan (1970) also concluded that ethnic and racial assimilation is far from inevitable. Ethnicity does not disappear as a result of assimilation; ethnic subcultures are continually being created and changed. Thus *Beyond the Melting Pot* pointed to the emergence and significance of cultural pluralism in American life.

Cultural Pluralism. As new waves of immigrants from all over the world have streamed into the United States—Jews fleeing religious intolerance in Russia, Italians and Poles fleeing economic depression in their communities, Central and Latin Americans fleeing dictatorships and poverty, refugees from Asian countries torn by conflict—all have tended to join other members of their nationality group who settled in the United States in earlier decades. Although the influx of new immigrants has led to conflicts between older and newer residents of some communities, in many cases it has resulted in new growth in those communities—in new ethnic businesses such as restaurants and grocery stores, and new social institutions such as churches and social clubs. It has also reinforced pride in ethnic identity as expressed in language and other aspects of ethnic subcultures. This infusion of new energy into ethnic communities confirms Glazer and Moynihan's thesis that the emergence of cultural pluralism is a significant aspect of life in American society.

The recognition that ethnic groups maintain their own communities and subcultures even while some of their members are assimilated into the larger society gave support to the concept of cultural pluralism. A **pluralistic society** is one in which different ethnic and racial groups are able to maintain their own cultures and lifestyles even as they gain equality in the institutions of the larger society. Michael Waltzer's (1980) comparative research on pluralism in the United States and other societies has shown that although white ethnic groups like the Italians, Jews, and Scandinavians may have the option of maintaining their own subcultures and still be accepted in the larger society, blacks and other racial minorities frequently experience attacks on their subcultures (e.g., opposition to bilingual education or African studies courses) and, at the same time, are discriminated against in social institutions. Waltzer concludes that "racism is the great barrier to a fully developed pluralism" (p. 787). In his study of Latinos in the United States, Earl Shorris (1992) essentially agrees with Waltzer. He finds that despite intense pressure to assimilate, many people from Spanish-speaking nations continue to speak their native language and are using their growing influence in some parts of the country to promote bilingualism. Shorris also notes, however, that Latinos are embracing their own version of the American dream and are not advancing separatist claims.

The problems of pluralism are illustrated by the case of the French-speaking Quebecois minority in Canada. The Quebecois account for almost 28 percent of the Canadian population and are the majority in the province of Quebec. This leads to a situation in which a group with its own culture and language seeks protection against pressure to assimilate into the dominant culture, and yet demands equal access to the society's political, economic, and cultural institutions. The resulting tensions and hardships have led to the demand that Canada become a bilingual nation, with English and French given equal status. Although the Canadian government has taken firm steps to ensure that French is Quebec's first language, the memory of past discrimination has given rise to a social movement calling for the creation of an independent French-speaking nation. This movement is especially strong in small towns and rural areas whose entire population is French-speaking. This population strongly backed the separation referendum held in Quebec in 1995. However, the referendum was defeated by an extremely narrow margin, largely owing to voters in the more multicultural districts of Montreal, Quebec's largest and most diverse city.

As this example shows, a truly pluralistic society is very difficult to achieve. The various ethnic and racial subgroups within a society often feel a strong sense of cultural identity, which they wish to preserve. They also demand equal access to the society's institutions: access to better schools, opportunities to obtain jobs in every field, opportunities to hold important positions—in short, a fair share of the wealth and power available in the society. These desires sometimes conflict, with the result that some groups may be tempted to "go it alone"—that is, form their own cultural and political institutions (their own businesses, newspapers and other media, labor unions, etc.)—or else give up their ethnic identity in order to gain greater access to the society's major institutions.

CULTURE AND INTERGROUP RELATIONS

Why do ethnic stratification and inequality persist in societies that are becoming increasingly pluralistic, like those of the United States and Canada? Sociologists have proposed a variety of theories to explain racial and ethnic inequality. Before we explore them, however, we need to understand the cultural basis of ethnic diversity and intergroup hostility—that is, the underlying values and attitudes that shape people's consciousness of other groups and, hence, their behavior toward members of those groups. Chief among these are the tendency to view members of other groups in terms of stereotypes and to use those stereotypes to justify differential attitudes (prejudice) and behaviors (discrimination) toward such individuals.

STEREOTYPES

People often express the opinion that specific traits of members of certain groups are responsible for their disadvantaged situation. Thus in South Africa it was common for whites to assert that blacks were not ready for full citizenship because "they remain childlike and simple." In the United States, the fact that Hispanics are more likely to be found in low-paying jobs is explained by the assertion that "they don't want to learn English." And the fact that black unemployment rates are generally twice as high as white unemployment rates is explained by the statement that "they don't want to work; they like sports and music, but not hard work, especially in school." These explanations are **stereotypes,** inflexible images of a racial or cultural group that are held without regard to whether they are true.

Sociologist William Helmreich (1982) conducted a study of widely held stereotypes regarding America's major ethnic and racial groups. He found that "every single stereotype discussed turns out to have a reason, or reasons" (p. 242). Those reasons usually stem from earlier patterns of intergroup relations. For example, jokes about stupid Poles stem from a period in the nineteenth century when uneducated Polish peasants immigrated to the United States. The idea that blacks are good at music or sports also has some basis, not because blacks are naturally superior in those areas but because when blacks were barred from other avenues to upward mobility they were able to succeed in entertainment and sports; as a result, many young blacks have developed their musical and athletic talents more fully than whites have. But even though stereotypes usually have some basis, they never take account of all the facts about a group. As the famous social commentator Walter Lippmann once quipped, "All Indians walk in single file, at least the one I saw did."

PREJUDICE AND DISCRIMINATION

The fact that many people hold stereotypical ideas about other groups may be an indication that they are ignorant or prejudiced, but it does not imply that they will actually discriminate against people whom they perceive as different. In a classic study of prejudice, social psychologist Richard LaPiere (1934) traveled throughout the United States with a Chinese couple, stopping at about 250 restaurants and hotels. Only one of the establishments refused them service. Six months later LaPiere wrote to each establishment and requested reservations for a Chinese couple. More than 90 percent of the managers responded that they had a policy of "nonacceptance of Orientals." This field experiment was replicated for blacks in 1952, with very similar results (Kutner, Wilkins, & Yarrow, 1952; Shibutani & Kwan, 1965).

The purpose of such experiments is to demonstrate the difference between prejudice and discrimination. **Prejudice** is an attitude that prejudges a person, either positively or negatively, on the basis of real or imagined characteristics (stereotypes) of a group to which that person belongs. **Discrimination,** on the other hand, refers to actual unfair treatment of people on the basis of their group membership.

The distinction between attitude and behavior is important. Prejudice is an attitude; discrimination is a behavior. As Robert Merton (1948) pointed out, there are people who are prejudiced and who discriminate against members of particular groups. There are also people who are not prejudiced but who discriminate because it is expected of them. With these distinctions in mind, Merton constructed the typology shown in Figure 13.4.

Merton's typology is valuable because it points to the variety of attitudes and behaviors that exist in multicultural and multiracial societies. However, it fails to account for situations in which certain groups are discriminated against regardless of the attitudes and behaviors of individuals. This form of discrimination is part of the "culture" of a social institution; it is practiced by people who are simply conforming to the norms of that institution and hence is known as institutional discrimination.

FIGURE 13.4   **Merton's Typology of Prejudice and Discrimination**

		PREJUDICE	
		Yes	No
DISCRIMINATION	Yes	TRUE BIGOT: does not believe in the American creed and acts accordingly	WEAK LIBERAL: not prejudiced, yet afraid to go against the bigoted crowd
	No	CAUTIOUS BIGOT: does not believe in the American creed but is afraid to discriminate	STRONG LIBERAL: not prejudiced and refuses to discriminate

Source: Adapted from pp. 99–126 of *Discrimination and National Welfare,* edited by R. M. MacIver. Copyright © 1948 by the Institute for Religious and Social Studies. Reprinted by permission of Harper & Row Publishers, Inc.

THE PERSONAL CHALLENGE

Social Change and Racism

Detective Mark Fuhrman's admitted racism in the trial of O. J. Simpson, the trial of three men for the racially motivated shotgun killing of African American men in Texas, "ethnic cleansing" in Bosnia, religious and ethnic strife in India . . . where will it strike next? Will it ever end? Perhaps more to the point, what can we as individuals do in the face of the seemingly overwhelming racial and ethnic divisions in our society and the world? One answer is that we can try not to tolerate racism and bigotry and not fail to speak out when confronted by these forms of ignorance and hatred. This goes as much for the victims of these behaviors as it does for those who witness them.

An example of a person who refused to accept racism is Earl G. Graves, Jr., a senior executive at *Black Enterprise* magazine. Graves was mistakenly detained and frisked by detectives on a railroad platform in New York City's Grand Central Terminal. The detectives were seeking an alleged perpetrator who was reported to be African American, 5 feet 10 inches tall, with a moustache, and carrying a concealed weapon. Graves is an African American but is 6 feet 4 inches tall and has no moustache. Mortified at having been victimized in front of fellow commuters with whom he rides every day, Graves sued the railroad, which was forced to publish the accompanying apology in local newspapers.

What can we as individuals do when we witness hostility directed against people just because they are different? We may find it difficult to confront racism or ethnic prejudice in people who are our peers and with whom we must interact on a daily basis. Often we look away and pretend to "go along," hiding our feelings of shame and confusion. Another strategy is to confront the problem head-on, as Graves did. It may take courage, but we can tell someone that their behavior is racist or prejudiced. Of course, this could result in the loss of a friend, but perhaps that is not the end of the world. We can befriend others who are not hampered by racism or ethnic bigotry.

It can also help to try to understand the origins of prejudice in people we know and love. Try to see how their attitudes have been affected by social changes such as new forms of competition with recently arrived ethnic or racial groups, or appeals to fear and prejudice by political leaders who stand to benefit from divisions among working people. You won't get very far by giving sociological lectures to those close to you, but by applying your sociological imagination you may come up with some strategies for changing their minds—or at least giving them an opportunity to see things a bit differently.

Metro-North wants its riders and Mr. Graves's neighbors and fellow commuters to know that Mr. Graves was not the subject its detectives were looking for and that Metro-North detectives were wrong in making the decision to detain and pat down Mr. Graves.

Metro-North deeply regrets this most unfortunate and insensitive incident, and seeks by this notice to apologize publicly to Mr. Graves and his family.

Metro-North wants to assure its ridership that it is committed to taking the steps necessary to reduce the risk of future such incidents and to assure that all of its riders are treated with respect and sensitivity, without regard to their race, color or national origin.

Donald Nelson

Donald N. Nelson
President

METRO-NORTH COMMUTER RAILROAD COMPANY

At its simplest, **institutional discrimination** is the systematic exclusion of people from equal access to and participation in a particular institution because of their race, religion, or ethnicity. But over time this intentional exclusion leads to another type of discrimination, which has been described as "the interaction of the various spheres of social life to maintain an overall pattern of oppression" (Blauner, 1972, p. 185). This form of institutional discrimination can be quite complex.

The conditions that led to the riot that broke out in South Central Los Angeles in 1992 after the acquittal of the police officers who beat a black motorist, Rodney King, conform very well to what sociologists have observed in similar communities where blacks or other minority groups are trapped in a self-perpetuating set of circumstances due largely to historical patterns of discrimination (Blauner, 1972, 1989). Blocked educational opportunities result in low skill levels, which together with job discrimination limit the incomes of minority group members. Low income and residential discrimination force them to become concentrated in ghettos. The ghettos never receive adequate public services such as transportation, thus making the search for work even more difficult. In those neighborhoods, also, the schools do not stimulate achievement, thereby repeating the pattern in the next generation. The young often grow up bitter and angry and may form violent gangs that engage in vandalism and other activities that the outside world sees as antisocial. At the same time, the police patrol ghettos to the point of harassment, with the result that young blacks are more likely to be arrested—and to be denied jobs because of their arrest records. Recent research shows that dark-skinned African American males with a criminal record have a jobless rate of 54 percent, compared with 41.7 percent for light-skinned African American males and 25 percent for white males with similar records (Johnson & Farrell, 1995). When these conditions are combined with a precipitating event such as the savage beating of a black person and the acquittal of the police officers responsible for the beating, the results often take the form of violence like that which erupted in South Central Los Angeles.

All of the institutions involved—employers, local governments, schools, real estate agencies, agencies of social control—may claim that they apply consistent standards in making their decisions: They hire the most qualified applicants; they sell to the highest bidder; they apply the law evenhandedly; in short, they do not discriminate. Yet in adhering to its institutional norms each perpetuates a situation that was created by past discrimination.

ETHNIC AND RACIAL NATIONALISM

The conditions that contributed to the Los Angeles riot are an example of the pervasive and discouraging effects of institutional discrimination. In the face of such discrimination, racial and ethnic groups frequently organize their members into movements to oppose social inequality. Those social movements often appeal to ethnic or racial nationalism—that is, to the "we feeling" or sense of peoplehood shared by the members of a particular group.

Ethnic (or racial) nationalism is the belief that one's ethnic group constitutes a distinct people whose culture is and should be separate from that of the larger society. Feelings of nationalism among America's ethnic and racial groups have often been strongly affected by nationalist movements outside the United States. American Jews, for example, were deeply influenced by Zionism, a movement that arose in the late nineteenth century with the goal of creating a Jewish homeland in the holy land of Palestine (now Israel). Similarly, Irish Americans have been influenced by the struggle of the Catholic minority in Northern Ireland to gain independence from England. Often nationalist movements produce a new or renewed ideology of pluralism that replaces the goal of complete assimilation into the larger society. We can see this very clearly among African Americans.

In his famous study *An American Dilemma* (1944), the Swedish social scientist Gunnar Myrdal noted that African Americans were in fact "exaggerated Americans." Myrdal believed that blacks had assimilated American values and norms more than any other ethnic or racial group and that they had no distinctive subculture of their own. This theme was repeated in the influential work of E. Franklin Frazier (1957), the leading black sociologist of his generation. Frazier, like Myrdal, believed that African Americans had no distinctive culture. They had the same religions, language, and values as white Americans, and the folkways they had developed (e.g., musical forms like jazz and the blues) had become part of mainstream American culture.

Events of the late 1950s and the 1960s drastically changed these views of black cultural assimilation. Along with the civil rights movement of the 1960s came a wave of nationalism. Black intellectuals and community leaders began calling not merely for integration but for cultural pluralism. Leaders like Stokely Carmichael, of the Student Nonviolent Coordinating Committee (SNCC), and Malcolm X, the charismatic Black Muslim leader, preached that "black is beautiful" and that African Americans should drop the term *Negro* in favor of *black*. In Carmichael's words, "They oppress us because we are black and we are going to use that blackness. . . . Don't be ashamed of your color" (quoted in Bracey, Meier, & Rudwick, 1970, p. 471). In recent years many black Americans have gone further and adopted the term *African American* in order to emphasize their common heritage and to deemphasize the racial character of their shared background.

People in the United States are not alone in struggling with issues of nationalism. Now that the cold war between the former Soviet Union and the United States has ended, ethnic and religious nationalism is the primary threat to peace throughout the world. Although North America is

Racial violence and rioting invariably disrupt neighborhoods, often for long periods. During the 1919 Chicago race riots, many African Americans were evicted from homes in integrated working-class neighborhoods and forced back into the ghetto. During the 1992 Los Angeles riots, so many stores and businesses were burned that people like this mother and child felt severe disorientation long after the rioting had ended.

relatively free of the extreme nationalism that results in bloodshed, at various times in North American history ethnic or racial nationalism has strained the social fabric. Entire populations, such as African Americans, Puerto Ricans, or French Canadians, have yearned to become entirely separate from the larger culture and society.

At other times nationalism has been a creative social force, welding a racial or ethnic group into a more politically conscious community able to struggle more effectively for its rights. As the Native American sociologist Russell Thornton notes, there are some highly positive aspects of nationalism or, in the case of Native Americans, tribalism:

> Research shows that American Indians make considerable efforts to reaffirm tribalism in urban areas by living in Indian neighborhoods, by maintaining contacts with reservation areas and extended families, and by creating urban American Indian Centers. Frequent results are a new tribalism for urban American Indians and, sometimes, "bicultural" individuals, that is, American Indians who live successfully in Indian and non-Indian worlds. (1987, p. 239)

A key to Indian survival, Thornton concludes, is the ability to maintain an Indian identity while interacting with non-Indians in an urban environment. The same point is often made by Hispanic and African American sociologists. One difficulty in maintaining a bicultural existence is that it requires assertion of the minority group's values, its ways of expression, its history, and its demands for greater equality. Frequently the demand for greater equality is expressed in terms of the need for affirmative action.

AFFIRMATIVE ACTION

What separates relatively peaceful multiethnic and multiracial nations from those in which racial, ethnic, or religious hatreds result in war and massacres? One important answer is the rule of law. When minority populations believe that their rights can be protected by government and laws, when they feel that their past grievances will be corrected in time, they will lend their support to the government and laws of their nation. However, in too many countries—even in the United States at times—minorities do not hold these beliefs. It is for this reason that the quest for racial and ethnic equality is a persistent issue in national affairs (Hacker, 1995).

Our society's foremost governmental and economic institutions are besieged with demands for *affirmative ac-*

tion—that is, policies designed to correct persistent racial and ethnic inequalities in promotion, hiring, and access to other opportunities. Even more forceful in many parts of the country are the demands to do away with affirmative action policies. Conservatives bitterly oppose affirmative action (Glazer, 1975; Sowell, 1972), whereas liberals feel that such policies are necessary if our society is to undo the effects of past discrimination (Ezorsky, 1991; Horowitz, 1979).

At present the conservative view is in the ascendance. Congress has done away with preferential treatment for minority-owned firms in awarding small government contracts. In California steps have been taken to eliminate affirmative action policies in the state's universities and colleges. It is likely that efforts to eliminate affirmative action will continue and will be increasingly successful. But it is also true, as Martin Kilson points out, that affirmative action has been essential to the advancement of African Americans and, increasingly, Latinos in job markets that were formerly out of bounds to minorities. In 1970, for example, "barely 2 percent of the officers in the armed forces were black; twenty years later, thanks (partly) to affirmative action, 12 percent of officers were African Americans" (Kilson, 1995, p. 470).

We saw earlier that the Supreme Court struck down the doctrine that "separate but equal" facilities and institutions did not violate the constitutional rights of African Americans. It did so largely because social-scientific evidence showed that separate institutions are inherently unequal. Similar arguments have been advanced in affirmative action cases that have reached the Court. If a fire department in a city whose inhabitants are 30 percent black and Hispanic has no firefighters from those minority groups, it can be demonstrated that there is a pattern of discrimination that can be changed only if the department is required to hire a certain number of minority applicants—a quota—within a designated time. However, members of the majority may then feel that they are victims of "reverse discrimination," in which they are being penalized for the wrongs of earlier generations. Thus, difficult choices remain: Should employers mix or replace hiring decisions based on experience and merit with decisions based on race and ethnicity? In essence, the courts have said that they must. Opposition to affirmative action is increasing, however, and at this writing it is not clear whether the courts will continue to rule in favor of affirmative action policies.

It should be noted that affirmative action applies to women as well as to racial and ethnic minorities (Epstein, 1995). The effects of institutional discrimination against women are explored in the next chapter.

THEORIES OF RACIAL AND ETHNIC INEQUALITY

For large numbers of people a dominant aspect of life in American society is racial or ethnic inequality and, often, hostility. How can we explain the persistence of these patterns of hostility and inequality? The first thought that comes to mind is that many people are prejudiced against anyone who is different from them in appearance or behavior. This may seem to explain phenomena like segregation and discrimination, but it fails to explain the variety of possible reactions to different groups. Social-psychological

Abby Abinanti, a Yurok Indian, has worked as a lawyer in private practice and public interest law. "In 1970 when I was graduating from college," she comments, "the Bureau of Indian Affairs announced a scholarship program. At that time nationally, only a handful of Indian people had become lawyers, and many of them were not 'Indian' identified in their work. The importance of lawyers to my community was emphasized to me by the older women. They understood our increasing need to look to the courts to protect our rights against encroachment . . . and to enforce promises given at an earlier time."

theories that focus on prejudice against members of out-groups find the origins of racism and ethnic inequality in individual psychological processes, but there are also more sociological theories that view prejudice as a symptom of other aspects of intergroup relations.

SOCIAL-PSYCHOLOGICAL THEORIES

The best-known social-psychological theories of ethnic and racial inequality are the frustration-aggression, projection, and authoritarian personality theories. All of these see the origins of prejudice in individual psychological orientations toward members of out-groups, but they differ in important ways.

Frustration-Aggression. The frustration-agression hypothesis, which is associated with the research of John Dollard, Neil Miller, and Leonard Doob (1939), holds that the origin of prejudice is a buildup of frustration. When that frustration cannot be vented on the real cause, the individual feels a "free-floating" hostility that may be taken out on a convenient target, or scapegoat. For example, in the case of workers in eastern Germany who have lost jobs in antiquated factories as a result of unification with western Germany, with its far more modern industries, a convenient scapegoat may be found in gypsies, Turks, or even Jews, all groups that have historically been accused of causing negative conditions for native-born Germans. To justify the hostility directed at the out-group, the prejudiced individual often grasps at additional reasons (usually stereotypes) for hating the "others," such as "Gypsies steal children"; "Jews are usurers"; or "Turks will work for almost nothing."

Projection. The concept of projection is also used to explain hostility toward particular ethnic and racial groups. **Projection** is the process whereby we attribute to other people behaviors and feelings that we are unwilling to accept in ourselves. John Dollard (1937) and Margaret Halsey (1946) applied the concept of projection to white attitudes toward black sexuality. Observers had noted that southern whites frequently claimed that black males are characterized by an uncontrollable and even vicious sexuality. The theory of projection explains this claim as resulting from the white males' attraction to black females, an attraction that was forbidden by strong norms against interracial sexual contact. Thus the white male projected his own forbidden sexuality onto blacks and developed an attitude that excused his own sexual involvement with black women.

The Authoritarian Personality. The frustration-aggression and projection explanations of prejudice are quite general in that anyone can develop pent-up frustrations that will engender hostility under certain conditions, and anyone can project undesirable traits onto others. A more specific explanation of prejudice is the theory of the authoritarian personality, which emerged from attempts to discover whether there is a particular type of person who is likely to display prejudice.

In 1950 a group of social scientists led by Theodor Adorno published an influential study titled *The Authoritarian Personality.* Their research had found consistent correlations between prejudice against Jews and other minorities and a set of traits that characterized what they called the authoritarian personality. Authoritarian individuals, they found, were punished frequently as children. Consequently, such individuals feel an intense anger that they fail to examine (Pettigrew, 1980). They submit completely to people in positions of authority, greatly fear self-analysis or introspection, and have a strong tendency to blame their troubles on people or groups that they see as inferior to themselves. Unfortunately for Jews, blacks, and other minorities that have been subordinated in the past, the anger and hostility of the authoritarian personality is often directed against them.

INTERACTIONIST THEORIES

Not far removed from these social-psychological theories of intergroup hostility are theories derived from the interactionist perspective in sociology. But instead of locating the origins of intergroup conflict in individual psychological tendencies, interactionists tend to look at how hostility or sympathy toward other groups, or solidarity within a group, is produced through the norms of interaction and the definitions of the situation that evolve within and between groups. A few examples will serve to illustrate how the interactionist perspective is applied.

From his analyses of interaction in different groups, Georg Simmel concluded that groups often find it convenient to think of nonmembers or outsiders as somehow inferior to members of the group. But why does this familiar in-group—out-group distinction develop? Simmel explained it as arising out of the intensity of interactions within the group, which leads its members to feel that other groups are less important. Once they have identified another group as inferior, it is not a great leap to think of its members as enemies, especially because doing so increases their sense of solidarity (Coser, 1966; Simmel, 1904).

Conflict and hostility between racial or ethnic groups can be overcome by creating situations that require the groups to cooperate to achieve a common goal. Such situations occasionally occur—for example, when people from different ethnic and racial backgrounds compete in sports or when they work side by side in school and in industry. Unfortunately, the integration and friendship found in such settings are not sufficient to overcome the more deep-seated prejudices and fears of many racist individuals. As film director Spike Lee observes, racists place all black people in one of two categories: "entertainers and niggers." By this he means that people with racist sentiments tend to exclude famous entertainers and sports figures from their negative feelings about blacks as a group, thereby accentuating their failure to see all blacks as individual human beings.

FUNCTIONALIST THEORIES

The difficulty of reducing racism and discrimination through interaction leads to the question of whether racial and ethnic inequalities persist because they function to the advantage of certain groups. One answer was provided by the functionalist theorist Talcott Parsons (1968), who wrote that "the primary historic origin of the modern color problem lies in the relation of Europeans to African slavery" (p. 366). Parsons was not denying that racism is produced through interactions. Rather, he was pointing out that the specific form taken by those interactions—oppression, subordination, domination of blacks by whites—is directly related to the perceived need of white colonialists and traders to use blacks for their own purposes. The whites could abduct, enslave, and sell Africans because their societies had developed technologies (e.g., oceangoing ships and navigational instruments) and institutions (e.g., markets and trading corporations) that made them immensely more powerful than the Africans.

From the functionalist perspective, inequalities among ethnic or racial groups exist because they have served important functions for particular societies. Thus in South Africa it was functional for the white government to insist on maintaining apartheid because to do otherwise would mean that whites would become a minority group in a black-dominated society. But as world opinion continued to condemn the white regime and blacks continued to build group solidarity and challenge that regime, it became less and less "functional" for the white government to insist on complete apartheid. Indeed, some have speculated that the nation's white rulers released Nelson Mandela and took steps to legalize the formerly banned African National Congress as a way of showing the world that they were willing to begin negotiations toward some form of shared power. Their move incurred the wrath of many South African whites, who feared the consequences of majority black rule under a new constitution. Similarly, the Israeli government's negotiations with the Palestine Liberation Organization enraged many Jewish settlers living in areas that would be placed under the control of Palestinians. This rage resulted in the shocking assassination of Israeli prime minister Yitzhak Rabin in November 1995 as peace negotiations were under way.

In both Israel and South Africa it appears that the status quo of intergroup relations had become dysfunctional. Change had to come either through peaceful negotiations or through bloodshed. The processes whereby power is redistributed and new social relations develop are often best understood with the help of conflict theories.

CONFLICT THEORIES

Conflict theories do a better job than functionalist theories of explaining why groups with less power and privilege, like the South African blacks or the Palestinians in the Middle East, do not accept their place in the status quo. Conflict theories try to explain why these groups often mobilize to change existing intergroup relations (Blauner, 1989). Conflict changes societies, as we see clearly in the case of South Africa, where many years of conflict waged by the disenfranchised blacks led to the creation of a new constitution and majority black rule. But conflict can also destroy societies and nations, as we see all too clearly in the war-torn nations of the former Yugoslavia, where a long history of ethnic conflict has prevented the achievement of a stable, well-functioning society.

Conflict theories trace the origins of racial and ethnic inequality to the conflict between classes in capitalist societies. Marx believed, for example, that American wage earners were unlikely to become highly class conscious because ethnic and racial divisions continually set them against one another and the resulting strife could be manipulated by the capitalist class. Thus in American history we see many examples of black and Mexican workers being brought in as strikebreakers by the owners of mines and mills, especially during the 1920s and 1930s. Strikebreakers from different racial and ethnic groups often absorbed the wrath of workers, anger that might otherwise have been directed at the dominant class. To forge class loyalties despite the divisions created by racial and ethnic differences, Marx believed, it would be necessary for workers to see that they were being manipulated by such strategies.

Internal Colonialism. Conflict perspectives on racial inequality also include the theory of **internal colonialism**. According to this theory, many minority groups, especially racial minorities, are essentially colonial peoples within the larger society. Four conditions mark this situation:

1. The "colonial" people did not enter the society voluntarily.

2. The culture of the "colonial" people has been destroyed or transformed into a version of the dominant culture that is considered inferior.

3. The "colonial" population is controlled by the dominant population.

4. Members of the "colonial" people are victims of racism; that is, they are seen as inferior in biological terms and are oppressed both socially and psychologically (Blauner, 1969; Davidson, 1973; Hechter, 1974). This is why African Americans, Native Americans, and Jewish Americans react with such anger to suggestions that they may be different from other populations on measures of intelligence or any other biological trait. They have seen such notions used to rationalize slavery or genocide and hence are not disposed to let them pass as harmless speculation or "value-free" science.

Although these characteristics describe colonial peoples everywhere, the theory of internal colonialism asserts that they also apply to subordinated ethnic and racial groups in societies like England, the United States, Canada, and the nations of the former Soviet Union. Michael Hechter (1974) extended the theory to show that societies that have created colonial or "ghettoized" populations within their boundaries also develop a "cultural division of labor" in which the subordinated group is expected to perform types of work that are considered too demeaning to be done by members of the dominant population. The South African institution of *Baaskop* was (and in some parts of the nation still is) an example of this phenomenon. It is a set of norms specifying that lower-status, physically exhausting work is appropriate for blacks and higher-status work is appropriate for whites, and that whites should never accept "black" work nor allow themselves to be subordinate to blacks.

ECOLOGICAL THEORIES

Are the segregated ghetto communities of black and Hispanic Americans a product of internal colonialism? The answer to this question depends on whether the residents of those communities are able to achieve upward mobility. According to ecological theories of intergroup relations, such mobility should occur naturally in the course of a group's adaptation to the culture and institutions of the larger society. The eventual outcome should be the existence of racially and ethnically integrated communities.

Ecological theories explore the processes by which conflict between racial or ethnic groups develops and is resolved. Along these lines, Robert Park (1914) devised a cyclical model to describe intergroup relations in modern cities. That model consisted of the following stages:

1. *Invasion:* One or more distinct groups begin to move into the territory of an established population.

2. *Resistance:* The established group attempts to defend its territory and institutions against newcomers.

3. *Competition:* Unless the newcomers are driven out, the two populations begin to compete for space and for access to social institutions (housing, jobs, schooling, recreational facilities, etc.); this extends to competition for prestige in the community and power in local governmental institutions.

4. *Accommodation and Cooperation:* Eventually the two groups develop relatively stable patterns of interaction. For example, they arrive at understandings about segregated and shared territories (Suttles, 1967).

5. *Assimilation:* As accommodation and cooperation replace competition and conflict, the groups gradually merge, first in secondary groups and later through cultural assimilation and intermarriage. They become one people. A new group arrives, and the cycle begins again.

Of course, this is an abstract model. It represents what Park and other human ecologists believe are the likely stages in intergroup relations. The Korean American sociologist Ilsoo Kim (1981) found that Korean merchants in

As a result of their unsuccessful resistance to the European invasion, Native Americans were segregated on reservations, many of which lacked adequate resources to permit them to share in the American Dream.

BOX 13.4 USING THE SOCIOLOGICAL IMAGINATION

The Case of Eskimo Starvation

During the 1950s a severe famine struck thousands of Inuit Eskimos in the frozen barrens of northern Canada. Untold numbers died of starvation. Many more survived the famine but became dependent on the government dole. What do intergroup relations have to do with this situation?

Ecological theory demands that we look first at the material basis of Eskimo life and the people's relationship to the land they inhabit. Centuries of conflict between Eskimos and Indians had forced the Inuit to the far north. There they had become "the people of the deer." They were hunters and gatherers who lived by following herds of caribou, on which they were totally dependent. A seemingly endless supply of deer meat and hides for clothing and tents was the basis of the Eskimos' adaptation to the hardships of life in the Arctic. But interracial contact was to drastically change this situation.

With the coming of white settlers to the more temperate portions of Canada and to the United States, the demand for furs rose. White and silver fox furs were especially valued by the settlers. Well before the end of the nineteenth century the Eskimos were in contact with white traders, who exchanged trinkets for furs and soon exchanged rifles for even more furs. Large numbers of caribou were slaughtered to be used as bait for fox trapping. The "people of the deer" became the "people of the fox" (Mowat, 1975). But this meant that the Eskimos were no longer a people apart. They had become dependent on the world demand for furs. When that demand shifted because of the changing tastes of fur wearers, the Eskimos' way of life was destroyed.

Faced with starvation, the Inuit trekked for hundreds of miles to seek help from white traders, soldiers, and missionaries at trading posts and army communications bases. There they were given grudging handouts, often insufficient to maintain life. The government's policy was to avoid creating dependence, to encourage the native people to live in their traditional ways even though this was no longer possible. The result was widespread famine and, for the survivors, dependence on the dole. Not until the Eskimos themselves began to demand entry into the economic and political institutions of the white-dominated society did assimilation and pluralism become possible.

New York City met resistance both from white merchants and from black residents of ghetto communities when they purchased stores in those communities, but eventually they have reached an accommodation with those groups. This finding tends to support Park's model, although the extent to which assimilation will occur remains an open question. On the other hand, critics point out that there is not always a steady progression from one of these stages to the next. Moreover, as Box 13.4 shows, accommodation, cooperation, and assimilation do not occur in every case. The ecological model fails to explain why and how groups compete for power and under what conditions they eventually come to cooperate. Nevertheless, the model presents a general picture of the stages that culturally distinct groups often (but by no means always) go through over time.

A PIECE OF THE PIE

Up to this point we have explored the patterns of intergroup relations, the cultural basis of those patterns, and some of the theories that have been proposed to explain them. But we have not discussed how groups actually win, or fail to win, a fair share of a society's valued statuses and other rewards—that is, a piece of the social pie. In particular, the persistence of racial inequality in the United States requires more attention. This is a complex problem that is a source of continuing controversy.

How can we explain the fact that so many social problems in the United States today are associated with race? As William Julius Wilson (1984) has stated, "Urban crime, drug addiction, out-of-wedlock births, female-headed families, and welfare dependency have risen dramatically in the last several years and the rates reflect a sharply uneven distribution by race" (p. 75). Wilson and others doubt that racial prejudice and discrimination adequately account for the severity of these problems, for the period since the early 1970s has seen more antidiscrimination efforts than any other period in American history. The answers are to be found, Wilson argues, in how older patterns of racism and discrimination affect the present situation.

In an important study of this issue, sociologist Stanley Lieberson (1980) asked why the European immigrants who arrived in American cities in the late nineteenth and early twentieth centuries have fared so much better, on the whole, than blacks. Sociologist Marta Tienda asks similar questions about people of Latino ancestry (Tienda & Singer, 1995; Tienda & Wilson, 1992). All three agree that the problem of lagging black mobility is a complex one. For African Americans, the situation can be summarized as follows:

1. African Americans have experienced far more prejudice and discrimination than any immigrant group, partly because they are more easily identified by their physical characteristics. As a result of the

Marta Tienda, a leading scholar of poverty among Latino Americans, chose this research area in part because she herself came from a Mexican American family of modest means.

legacy of slavery, which labeled blacks as inferior, they have been excluded from full participation in American social institutions far longer than any other group.

2. Black families have higher rates of family breakup than white families. The problems of the black family are not part of the legacy of slavery, however. As Herbert Gutman (1976) has shown, slavery did not destroy black families to the extent that earlier scholars believed it did. Nor did the migration of blacks to the North during industrialization. A comprehensive review of the status of black Americans (Jaynes & Williams, 1989) notes that "there was no significant increase in male-absent households even after the massive migration to the urban North." Until the 1960s three quarters of black households with children under age 18 included both husband and wife. "The dramatic change came only later, and in 1986, 49 percent of black families with children under age 18 were headed by women" (Jaynes & Williams, 1989, p. 528). The report reasons that if black two-parent families remained the norm through slavery, the Great Depression, migration, urban disorganization, and ghettoization, then it appears unlikely that there is a single cause for the dramatic decline in two-parent families during the last two decades.

3. Structural changes in the American economy—first the shift from work on farms to work in factories and then the shift away from factory work to high-technology and service occupations—have

continually placed blacks at a disadvantage. No sooner had they begun to establish themselves as workers in these economic sectors than they began to suffer the consequences of structural changes in addition to job discrimination.

Recent research by social scientists points to the decrease in manufacturing jobs and the increase in service-sector jobs as contributing to the sharp decline in the fortunes of black males. (Black females also suffer, but they are more readily recruited into clerical employment.) Throughout the second half of this century, the unemployment rate for black males has been twice that for white males. This is as true in the 1990s as it was in the 1970s, but the situation is even worse for black men who do not have high school diplomas. Their unemployment rate is more than three times higher than that for white males (Oliver & Shapiro, 1990). A great deal of research shows that difficulty in securing adequate employment contributes to the problems young couples experience in forming lasting relationships (Danziger & Gottschalk, 1993; Garfinkel & McLanahan, 1986).

It is significant that among Hispanic groups in the United States, Puerto Ricans have experienced northward migration and problems of discrimination that are very similar to those experienced by African Americans in northern cities. Still a dependent territory of the United States, since World War II Puerto Rico has sent hundreds of thousands of working people to cities like New York, Philadelphia, and Chicago, which have been rapidly losing manufacturing jobs. The status of Puerto Ricans in the population is very similar to that of blacks. There is a growing Puerto Rican middle class and an even more rapidly growing number of Puerto Ricans among the poor. This situation is due largely to changes in the types of jobs available to unskilled blacks and Puerto Ricans (Sandefur & Tienda, 1988).

It is worth noting that social mobility is more available to blacks today than it was before the civil rights movement. Today there are millions of middle-class African Americans, and the earnings of black males who have completed college are about 85 to 90 percent of those of whites with comparable education. But although the black middle class is growing, the majority of black workers remain dependent on manual work in industry or lower-level service jobs—types of jobs that are in decreasing supply and in which unemployment is common. Another important segment of black workers, male and female, are employed in the public sector. Drastic cuts in public budgets in the 1990s are driving their earnings down as well. Chronic unemployment is associated with family breakup, alcohol and drug addiction, and depression. These social problems, in turn, severely hamper the ability of individuals to learn the attitudes and skills they need for entry into available jobs (Oliver & Shapiro, 1990; Wilson, 1987).

Nor is the life of middle-class blacks free from the continuing consequences of racism and prejudice. In interviews with a sample of middle-class black Americans in 16 cities, sociologist Joe R. Feagin found that "they reported hundreds of instances of blatant and subtle bias in restaurants, stores, housing, workplaces, and on the street" (1991, p. A44). And for the past few years, as the U.S. economy's ability to create good jobs has declined, the number of crimes against minority individuals of all social classes has continued to increase (Feagin, 1991).

RESEARCH FRONTIERS: THE GROWING HISPANIC PRESENCE IN NORTH AMERICA

In 1994 California voters approved Proposition 187, which denies public education, public medical services (except emergency services), and social services to undocumented immigrants and requires doctors, teachers, social service providers, and police officers to report suspected undocumented aliens to the Immigration and Naturalization Service. The debates over the referendum were a clear indication of how deeply divided and confused Americans are about the increasing diversity of the nation's population, especially in states that attract large numbers of immigrants. While many people see Proposition 187 as cruel

and discriminatory, many others are concerned about the rapid growth of immigrant populations, especially the growing Hispanic presence in places like Southern California (Tamayo, 1995).

Sociological research is extremely valuable in providing a less emotional, more factual background to debates over immigration policy. Research on the ecological and historical characteristics of Spanish-speaking people in the United States shows that by far the largest portion of this population consists of immigrants from Mexico; they account for about two thirds of the total. U.S. citizens from Puerto Rico constitute another 15 percent. Political refugees from Central America—especially El Salvador, Guatemala, and Cuba—as well as from many nations of South America add further to the diversity of the Spanish-speaking population of North America (Sandefur & Tienda, 1988; Shorris, 1992).

As can be seen in Table 13.2 on page 408, the influx of Spanish-speaking people into the United States began long ago in the case of Mexicans; they were living in parts of the Southwest and California before those regions were incorporated into the United States. In contrast, Cubans and Puerto Ricans began entering the country relatively recently. Like the Mexicans, the Puerto Ricans come mainly in search of low-wage jobs; they differ from the Mexicans in that they are U.S. citizens and can move freely between their island territory and the mainland. Many gravitate to large cities like New York and Chicago. The Cuban immigration is quite different; its origins lie in the Cuban revolution of the late 1950s, and hence it consists largely of middle-class refugees.

The historical facts about each of these groups contribute to the problems experienced by the Hispanic population in attempting to become a more cohesive political force in American society. In the future even greater cohesion will be required to counter claims that they are illegal or that they pose a threat because of their growing numbers. Leaders of these groups often call for a "Latino" cultural and political identity that would unite the various Hispanic groups. But the emergence of a common Latino identity remains problematic, partly because of the geographic separation of the various Hispanic ethnic groups. Mexicans are heavily concentrated in the Southwest and California, Puerto Ricans in the Northeast, Cubans in Miami and elsewhere in Florida. In each of these areas there may be some members of the other groups, but usually not enough to form a real coalition. As a result, when leaders of the various groups seek support for programs such as bilingual education, they have difficulty speaking with one voice and proposing a unified set of policies.

The outlook for cultural and political unity for Hispanic Americans is further complicated by the prevalence of poverty among these groups. As noted earlier, Cuban immigrants tend to come from middle-class backgrounds, so their major settlements do not include high proportions of

MAYA LIN: A STRONG, CLEAR VISION

When she was only 20 and still an undergraduate architecture student at Yale University, Maya Lin had an astounding experience. Her design for a monument to commemorate the 58,156 Americans killed in the Vietnam War was chosen out of more than 1,500 entries in an international competition. Earlier in the semester she had submitted the design as a project in her architecture course, but the professor had not liked the concept very much. However, Lin had a strong vision of how the polished black granite monument would offer people a chance to reflect on the meaning of the war and remember those who died in it. She believed in her work.

After spending many weeks revising a one-page statement describing the intent of her design, Lin submitted the drawings to the competition's jury, never expecting to win. The rest is history. The Vietnam Veterans Memorial has become the most popular and moving piece of commemorative sculpture in the nation. "I knew people would have a personal experience as they searched for the names of

those they knew," Lin (1995) explains, "but I never expected that they would leave things there. That was a surprise to me."

Although the monument commemorates the Vietnam War and does not directly address racism or ethnic conflict, Lin had to deal with a fair amount of racial abuse as the monument was being constructed. Mingled with the praise were letters that said, among other hateful things, that "a gook should not have been chosen to design a Vietnam War memorial." Even at the dedication, which Lin attended with her family, there were racial slights that wounded her deeply. But the popularity of the monument, and the way it brings together Americans of all races to contemplate death and heroism, more than compensate for the hurt. And the universal appeal of her vision has resulted in other commissions. One of them, the Civil Rights Memorial in Montgomery, Alabama, has special meaning for Lin as a person of Japanese American ancestry.

Commissioned in 1988 by the Southern Poverty Law Center, an influential civil rights organization, the Civil Rights Memorial is another example of Lin's genius. Like the Vietnam Veterans Memorial, it draws the viewer into a personal meditation. Water from a deep pool on the monument's upper level "spills down in even sheets across the face of the wall, on which is a gold-leafed inscription of Martin Luther King's inspiring statement that the fight will continue (in the words of the Bible) 'until justice rolls down like waters and righteousness like a mighty stream.' An elliptical table, on which are engraved the landmark events in the civil rights era from 1955 to 1968, including the names of forty people who died in the struggle, glistens with a film of water from above. People walk slowly around the monument reading the engraved text, and as they do so many feel compelled to run their fingers across the wet surface in an 'act of communion' " (Stein, 1994, p. 70).

TABLE 13.2	American Indian, Black, Hispanic, and White Populations, 1492–1990 (in thousands)					
YEAR	AMERICAN INDIAN	BLACK	MEXICAN	PUERTO RICAN	CUBAN	WHITE
1492	5,000	0	0	0	0	0
1790	700	800	20	0	0	3,000
1860	400	4,400	28	0	0	27,000
1900	237	8,800	103*	0	11	67,000
1950	357	15,000	1,342*	301	33	135,000
1960	524	18,900	1,725*	893	125	159,000
1970	793	22,600	4,532	1,392	561	178,000
1980	1,364	26,495	8,740	2,014	803	188,372
1990	1,878	29,986	13,496	2,728	1,044	199,686

*These population figures refer to individuals born in Mexico or with parents born in Mexico.

Source: Sandefur & Tienda, 1988; *Statistical Abstract,* 1995.

poor households. The same cannot be said, however, for Mexicans and Puerto Ricans. Because so many members of these groups work in agriculture and related industries, Mexicans tend to be disproportionately represented among the poor. The situation of Puerto Ricans is more complex. Unlike most other Hispanic groups in the U.S. population, Puerto Ricans have experienced a decline in economic well-being and an increase in poverty. Marta Tienda, one of the nation's foremost authorities on minority poverty, explains that during the past decade "poverty rates soared for Puerto Rican families while they declined for black families" (Tienda & Jensen, 1988, p. 51). This change, she finds, is due largely to the greater success of black women in the labor market and the relative decline in employment of Puerto Rican women in the past 25 years. For a variety of reasons, Puerto Rican women have been unable to enter the white-collar labor force in large numbers. Segregated in industrial jobs that do not require high levels of education, Puerto Rican women (as well as men) have suffered dis-

proportionately from the general decline in industrial employment.

Hispanic groups whose populations will increase in coming years will encounter a vastly changed labor market. The number of jobs that require higher education and specialized training will grow, while the number of jobs that do not require a high school diploma (and hence are attractive to immigrants for whom English is a second language) will decrease steadily. This situation affects all minority groups with high proportions of less-educated and unskilled members, but it is especially significant for Hispanic groups because they constitute the largest population of newcomers. As Hispanic communities confront the effects of fears like those that produced Proposition 187 in California, they will have to mobilize to increase their participation in all institutions of American life. They are already voting in increasing numbers, a vital step toward more equal political and economic representation in the larger society.

THINK ABOUT IT CRITICALLY

In the aftermath of the O. J. Simpson trial many Americans expressed dismay about the prospects for diminishing racism and racial tensions in the United States. The spectacle of a racist detective perjuring himself, the joyful celebration of Simpson's acquittal in black neighborhoods where the trial was seen as evidence of the persecution of black men—these and other racially charged aspects of the trial and its outcome seemed to demonstrate how wide the racial chasm has become. What are your views on this issue? Does reading this chapter cause you to question any of your earlier opinions about the future of race relations in the United States?

In biology, the term *race* refers to an inbreeding population that develops distinctive physical characteristics that are hereditary. However, the choice of which physical characteristics to consider in classifying people into races is arbitrary. And human groups have exchanged their genes through mating to such an extent that it is impossible to identify "pure" races.

The social concept of race has emerged from the interactions of various populations over long periods of human history. It varies from one society to another, depending on how the people of that society feel about the importance of certain physical differences among human beings. *Racism* is an ideology based on the belief that an observable, supposedly inherited trait is a mark of inferiority that justifies discriminatory treatment of people with that trait.

Ethnic groups are populations that have a sense of group identity based on a distinctive cultural pattern and shared ancestry. They usually have a sense of "peoplehood" that is maintained within a larger society. Ethnic and racial populations are often treated as *minority groups*—people who, because of their physical or cultural characteristics, are singled out from others in the society for differential and unequal treatment.

Intergroup relations can be placed on a continuum ranging from intolerance to tolerance, or from genocide through assimilation. *Genocide* is the intentional extermination of one population, defined as a "race" or a "people," by a more dominant population. It is almost always rationalized by the belief that the people who are being slaughtered are less than human.

Expulsion is the forcible removal of one population from territory claimed by another population. It has taken a variety of forms in American history, including the expulsion of Native Americans from their ancestral lands, the Oriental exclusion movement of the nineteenth century, and the detention of Japanese Americans during World War II.

Slavery is the ownership of a population, defined by racial or ethnic or political criteria, by another population that has complete control over the enslaved population. Slavery has been called "the peculiar institution" because it has existed in some of the world's greatest civilizations, including the United States.

Although African American slaves gained their freedom during the Civil War, a long period of segregation followed. *Segregation* is the ecological and institutional separation of races or ethnic groups. It may be either voluntary or involuntary. Involuntary segregation may be either *de jure* (created by laws that prohibit certain groups from interacting with others) or *de facto* (created by unwritten norms).

Assimilation is the pattern of intergroup relations in which a minority group is forced or encouraged or voluntarily seeks to blend into the majority population and eventually disappears as a distinct people within the larger society. In the United States, three different views of assimilation have prevailed since the early nineteenth century. They are Anglo-conformity, the demand that culturally distinct groups give up their own cultures and adopt the dominant Anglo-Saxon culture; the melting pot, the theory that there would be a social and biological merging of ethnic and racial groups; and cultural pluralism, the belief that culturally distinct groups can retain their communities and much of their culture and still be integrated into American society.

Stereotypes are inflexible images of a racial or cultural group that are held without regard to whether they are true. They are often associated with *prejudice,* an attitude that prejudges a person, either positively or negatively, on the basis of characteristics of a group to which that person belongs. *Discrimination* refers to actual behavior that treats people unfairly on the basis of their group membership; *institutional discrimination* is the systematic exclusion of people from equal participation in a particular social institution because of their race, religion, or ethnicity. Social movements whose purpose is to oppose institutional discrimination are often supported by *ethnic nationalism,* the belief that one's ethnic group constitutes a distinct people whose culture is and should be separate from that of the larger society. Policies designed to correct persistent racial and ethnic inequalities in promotion, hiring, and access to other opportunities are referred to as affirmative action.

Social-psychological theories of ethnic and racial inequality argue that a society's patterns of discrimination stem from individual psychological orientations toward members of out-groups. Interactionist explanations go beyond the individual level to see how hostility or sympathy toward other groups is produced by the norms of interaction that evolve within and between groups. The functionalist perspective generally seeks patterns of social integration that help maintain stability in a society. Conflict theories trace the origins of racial and ethnic inequality to the conflict between classes in capitalist societies. The conflict perspective includes the theory of *internal colonialism,* which holds that many minority groups are essentially colonial peoples within the larger society. Finally, ecological theories of race relations explore the processes by which conflict between racial or ethnic groups develops and is resolved.

The persistence of racial inequality in the United States is a source of continuing controversy. This complex problem is a result of a number of factors besides racial prejudice and discrimination. Other factors are high rates of family breakup and the effects of structural changes in the American economy. Although social mobility is more available to blacks today than it was before the civil rights movement, the majority of blacks are in insecure working-class jobs or unemployed.

CRITICAL RESPONSE

Efforts to reduce racial and ethnic divisions in a society never progress smoothly toward an ideal final condition. There are always major setbacks and episodes of misunderstanding, hatred, and violence. But the chapter offers many examples of more constructive solutions to racial and ethnic conflict. Through conflict can come accommodation and cooperation. Through the rule of law can come an end to bloodshed and violence. The Simpson trial and its aftermath may have been a dark moment in U.S. race relations, but there are many examples in the civil rights movement, and even in the conduct of everyday life, that offer hope for greater racial harmony in the future.

GLOSSARY

race: an inbreeding population that develops distinctive physical characteristics that are hereditary. (p. 379)

racism: an ideology based on the belief that an observable, supposedly inherited trait is a mark of inferiority that justifies discriminatory treatment of people with that trait. (p. 379)

ethnic group: a population that has a sense of group identity based on shared ancestry and distinctive cultural patterns. (p. 381)

minority group: a population that, because of its members' physical or cultural characteristics, is singled out from others in the society for differential and unequal treatment. (p. 381)

genocide: the intentional extermination of one population by a more dominant population. (p. 385)

expulsion: the forcible removal of one population from a territory claimed by another population. (p. 386)

slavery: the ownership of one racial, ethnic, or politically determined group by another group that has complete control over the enslaved group. (p. 388)

segregation: the ecological and institutional separation of races or ethnic groups. (p. 388)

de jure segregation: segregation created by formal legal sanctions that prohibit certain groups from interacting with others or place limits on such interactions. (p. 388)

de facto segregation: segregation created and maintained by unwritten norms. (p. 388)

Jim Crow: the system of formal and informal segregation that existed in the United States from the late 1860s to the early 1970s. (p. 390)

assimilation: a pattern of intergroup relations in which a minority group is absorbed into the majority population and eventually disappears as a distinct group. (p. 390)

ethnic stratification: the ranking of ethnic groups in a social hierarchy on the basis of each group's similarity to the dominant group. (p. 393)

pluralistic society: a society in which different ethnic and racial groups are able to maintain their own cultures and lifestyles while gaining equality in the institutions of the larger society. (p. 394)

stereotype: an inflexible image of the members of a particular group that is held without regard to whether it is true. (p. 395)

prejudice: an attitude that prejudges a person on the basis of a real or imagined characteristic of a group to which that person belongs. (p. 395)

discrimination: behavior that treats people unfairly on the basis of their group membership. (p. 395)

institutional discrimination: the systematic exclusion of people from equal participation in a particular institution because of their group membership. (p. 397)

ethnic (or racial) nationalism: the belief that one's own ethnic group constitutes a distinct people whose culture is and should be separate from that of the larger society. (p. 397)

scapegoat: a convenient target for hostility. (p. 400)

projection: the psychological process whereby we attribute to other people behaviors and attitudes that we are unwilling to accept in ourselves. (p. 400)

internal colonialism: a theory of racial and ethnic inequality that suggests that some minorities are essentially colonial peoples within the larger society. (p. 401)

WHERE TO FIND IT

BOOKS

Threatened People, Threatened Borders: World Migration and U.S. Policy (Michael S. Teitlebaum & Myron Weiner; Norton, 1995). A review of world patterns of population movement and U.S. policy responses to the growing demand for entry into North America, by a panel of renowned experts on migration and immigration.

The Declining Significance of Race: Blacks and Changing American Institutions, 2nd ed. (William Julius Wilson; University of Chicago Press, 1980). A well-documented study of how changing economic conditions in the United States have altered the fortunes of black Americans.

Race Relations (Harry H. I. Kitano; Prentice-Hall, 1980). An excellent text on race relations, especially in the United States.

Drylongso: A Self Portrait of Black America (John Langston Gwaltney; Vintage Books, 1981). A detailed portrait of black American culture as expressed in interviews; a complex view of a stable and rich consciousness.

American Apartheid: Segregation and the Making of the Underclass (Douglas S. Massey & Nancy A. Denton; Harvard University Press, 1993). An up-to-date review of the continuing persistence of residential segregation in American cities.

Ethnic America: A History (Thomas Sowell; Basic Books, 1981). A comparative treatise on the success and contributions of the major nationality groups that have made the United States their home.

A Common Destiny: Blacks and American Society (Gerald David Jaynes & Robin M. Williams, Jr., eds.; National Academy Press, 1989). A volume covering most aspects of racial inequality and racial progress in the United States. Widely regarded as the most important recent summary of the status of black Americans, it was compiled by a distinguished group of social scientists convened by the National Academy of Sciences and including most of the nation's foremost students of American racial inequality.

Latinos: A Biography of the People (Earl Shorris; Norton, 1992). A beautifully written and thoughtful book describing Spanish-speaking peoples' search for cultural unity in the face of historical, socioeconomic, and racial diversity.

U.S. Race Relations in the 1980's and 1990's: Challenges and Alternatives (Gail S. Thomas, ed.; Hemisphere, 1990). Covers the recent rise in racism, racially motivated incidents, and race-hatred groups, as well as efforts to address issues of education, poverty, and other problems that disproportionately affect racial minorities. Argues that improvement in race relations will be difficult in the years ahead and will require a far greater national commitment than exists at present.

OTHER SOURCES

Harvard Encyclopedia of American Ethnic Groups. A valuable collection of essays about ethnic and racial relations in American society. Covers almost every imaginable group in the United States and offers summary essays on such sociologically relevant subjects as slavery, assimilation, ethnic accommodation, and conflict.

Inequalities of Gender

For most people the word safari conjures up images of wild animals—lions, elephants, and rhinos roaming the savannahs. I wanted to go and experience all that Kenya had to offer and yet there was something more that tugged at me. I felt a calling from deep within me to go to East Africa, to go and see the beginnings of all humankind.

The writer is sociologist Carol Chenault of Calhoun Community College in Decatur, Alabama. She and her husband, Ellis Chenault, traveled to Kenya to observe the way of life of the Maasai people. "I am confident," she says, "that the teaching of culture in college sociology classes for 15 years is a major source of my interest in the Maasai." For her and for the students with whom she now shares her experiences, this sociological voyage was an eye-opening one.

What I observed was an extremely independent people whose entire lives revolve around the care and herding of their cattle. They truly believe that all of the cattle on earth are their gift from God (Engai). One Maasai warrior asked me if I had any cows. When I told him no, he said, "Good, because we would come get them if you did."

For Chenault, some of the most challenging aspects of life among the Maasai centered on the differences between the roles of men and women. "The Maasai culture has a very traditional division of labor between men and women," she writes.

Women are nurturing, loving mothers who spend a great deal of their time hugging, holding, and kissing their children. However, care of the children is a responsibility that is also shared with the fathers. Early childhood has few responsibilities; time is spent learning the ways of the adults, the language skills and play. The girls gradually begin to learn the tasks of the women such as care of the animals, making clothing, food preparation, and doing beadwork. Girls are initiated into womanhood through circumcision; however, their attitude toward this is not one of fearful anticipation and bravery. The young women see this as a time when they have to give up their freedom for a strict married life. No longer will they be free to choose their lovers as they once did. Circumcision occurs in the mother's house and does not require the public demonstration of courage and bravery that is required of the males in their circumcision rituals. An elderly Maasai woman told me that it is unclean not to be circumcised.

Maasai girls are betrothed during infancy, or in some cases before they are born. A young couple may be approached and asked if their firstborn is a girl, then may she become the wife of their son. The wedding ceremony is a simple one in which the bride's head is shaved and then adorned with bands of beadwork. Her clothing at the wedding is very colorful in that it is all new and dyed with the familiar red ochre. Both the bride and groom are washed with milk at the time of the wedding. (Chenault, 1996, pp. 1–3)

413

Carol Chenault's observations of the Maasai are an example of the sociological imagination at work. Before judging or discussing her own opinions, she seeks to understand what is being done and said in terms of the Maasai culture itself. But does the sociologist's dispassionate understanding of cultural practices like arranged marriages and female circumcision imply acceptance of these controversial forms of gender inequality? Hardly! As a professional sociologist who teaches in the United States, Chenault knows full well that many women in her own culture feel oppressed and exploited, just as do many impoverished rural and urban women in Kenya. Among Chenault's students are many women and men who are attempting to confront the sources of gender inequality at work and in the home.

GENDER AND INEQUALITY

Many women in the nations of Asia and Africa are confronting the cultural norms that keep them in subservient positions and prevent them from asserting their own choices about their futures. The Maasai are unusual in the contemporary world. They are pastoralists who are relatively isolated from the powerful social forces that are rapidly changing other tribes in Kenya and elsewhere in Africa. In consequence, the Maasai insist on the necessity of continuing to adhere to the norms of their own tribal culture. For the sociologist, the example of the Maasai is extremely useful because it challenges assumptions about gender and society.

As observant sociologists like Carol Chenault travel to other cultures, they invariably recognize that despite cultural differences, the differences in the life chances of men and women remain one of the major dimensions of inequality in human societies. This chapter therefore begins by presenting some of the key patterns of gender inequality in the United States and throughout the world. It then examines the social and biological concepts of gender and sex that are essential to understanding the inequalities people experience as a consequence of their gender or sexual orientation. Gender stratification and gender roles are also discussed.

Throughout the world people in different cultures tend to justify patterns of inequality; therefore, the chapter will also explore these cultural norms and ideologies, especially as they are manifested in industrial societies. The next two sections explore the women's movement and the situation of women in the workplace, where some of the most exciting and difficult changes in patterns of gender inequality are occurring today. The final section highlights women in the developing world, truly a frontier of sociological research and thought in our time.

PATTERNS OF GENDER INEQUALITY

Gender inequality and the effects on women of social and economic development are central themes of global social science. The United Nations International Conference on Population and Development, held in Cairo in 1994, concluded that "the empowerment of women and improvement of their status are important ends in themselves and are essential for the achievement of sustainable development" (United Nations, 1995b). Some graphic examples of how gender inequality differs in the developed and less-developed regions of the world are presented in Table 14.1 and Figure 14.1.

Table 14.1 shows that in the United States there is a continuing gap in income between men and women in the same occupations. We will see later in the chapter that even as increasing numbers of women join the labor force and compete for jobs and careers in ways that were almost unheard of earlier in this century, men still tend to move into the higher-paying jobs in each occupation. Figure 14.1 shows quite dramatically that in the less-developed regions women shoulder a far greater number of domestic burdens than men do. Much of the difference may seem to be due to the fact that women take primary responsibility for bearing and nurturing children (see Box 14.1). And one might argue that in a developed country like the United States, the differences in men's and women's incomes could be

TABLE 14.1	Median Weekly Earnings of Full-Time Wage and Salary Workers, 1994		
OCCUPATION		**MEN**	**WOMEN**
Managerial and professional		$803	$592
Technical, sales, and administrative support		548	376
Service		350	257
Precision production		515	370
Operators, fabricators, and laborers		406	293
Farming, forestry, and fishing		290	234

Source: *Statistical Abstract*, 1995.

FIGURE 14.1 A Woman's Day or a Man's Day?

Which would you prefer if you could choose? The Swedish International Development Agency outlined a typical day for a man and a woman in a family that grows both cash crops and its own food supply, in its journal *Striking a Balance*. The family lives "somewhere in Africa."

The woman's day does not change if she is pregnant. There is little time to spare to visit a medical center for regular prenatal care.

A WOMAN'S DAY	A MAN'S DAY
rises first	
kindles the fire	
breast-feeds the baby	
fixes breakfast/eats	rises when breakfast is ready
washes and dresses children	eats
walks 1 km to fetch water	
walks 1 km home	walks 1 km to field
gives the livestock food and water	
washes cooking utensils, etc.	works in the field
walks 1 km to fetch water	
walks 1 km home	
washes clothing	walks 1 km home
breast-feeds the baby	
walks 1 km to field with food for husband	
walks 1 km back home	eats when wife arrives with food
walks 1 km to her field	
weeds field	works in the field
breast-feeds the baby	
gathers firewood on the way home	
walks 1 km home	walks 1 km home
pounds maize	rests
walks 1 km to fetch water	
walks 1 km home	
kindles the fire	
prepares meal/eats	eats
breast-feeds the baby	walks to village to visit other men
puts house in order	goes to bed
goes to bed last	

Source: Sadik, 1995.

Hard Choices

"I remember saying out loud that, if I had been a boy, I would want to go to law school. . . . But I didn't really think at all about the future and a career. I sort of assumed that I would one day get married and have children" (Gerson, 1985, p. 58). The speaker, a law student with no children, is talking to sociologist Kathleen Gerson about how her family created a "baseline" of expectations regarding her future. Another woman, who experienced a similar baseline in her family, explains that under some conditions it is possible for the baseline to change. "My brother's marriage was a very stormy one," she reports. "When he was married, it was my eighth birthday, and there was lots of anger, emotions, screaming, drinking, irregular hours, bad communication. I had a very split image [of marriage], but from about twelve on, I was very aware that life was not calico curtains and picking out silver patterns" (pp. 62–63).

For many women, Gerson found, a stable home and family did not necessarily create a desire to lead the same kind of life themselves. Some women from such homes wanted both a career and their own family. A biologist and mother of three says, "I wanted to be a medical doctor from age nine or ten. I also wanted to be a nurse or a scientist." When asked whether she wanted marriage and children, she responds, "I wanted that too. I wanted everything. I did expect to have everything" (pp. 64–65).

These excerpts are from Gerson's book *Hard Choices: How Women Decide About Work, Career, and Motherhood*, which describes the choices and decisions made by a cohort of women who came of age (i.e., college or work age) during the 1970s. These women, Gerson explains, are part of a "subtle revolution." The most salient aspect of that revolution is the rapid rise in the percentage of women in the labor force in recent decades, from less than 40 percent in 1960 to about 60 percent in 1990 (see chart). For many women, however, the result is childlessness. Choices between career and childbearing are not usually either-or propositions, but they often require delay of childbearing or significant career sacrifices for both men and women.

In her interviews Gerson found that no matter how a woman was raised, "the adult life course is neither a predetermined outcome of childhood experiences, nor a series of predictable, orderly steps from one stage to the next" (p. 122). For example, many women who as teenagers expected to pursue occupational careers found that the inequalities and hassles of the work world made child rearing more attractive. A secretary who opted for a second child explains:

Labor Force Participation of Women With Children

As more women over 20 have a job or are looking for one...

...more mothers join the work force as their children get older

14 to 17
17.2%

Under 3
23.4%

6 to 13
40.7%

3 to 5
18.7%

Age of children of women in the workplace

Source: Data from Bureau of Labor Statistics.

I had intended to quit work when I got pregnant with Jenny, to wait until Jenny was in school, and then go back to work. But when I went back, I wanted to go back as other than a secretary. I thought, would I like to be an electrician, a fireman? What is there in the world that I want to spend the rest of my life at? Then it came to me that I really enjoy what I'm doing now more than anything else I've done or anything that I could think of doing. So I decided to have another baby. (pp. 111–112)

Gerson also found many women whose life course veered toward work rather than home. Often the twists and turns in their lives were unplanned and, hence, accompanied by a great deal of confusion and stress. Although the men in their lives shared their dilemmas and frustrations, Gerson's research shows that women continue to bear a disproportionate share of the burden imposed by these hard choices.

attributed to the fact that so many women take time out from work and careers to bear and raise children. These familiar (and flawed) arguments raise further questions about biological versus social causes of gender inequality, which, in turn, may create confusion about the differences between sex and gender and the role of sexuality and sexual orientation in defining an individual's life chances. Before exploring the contours of gender inequality further, therefore, we turn to a discussion of the basic concepts of sex and gender.

SEX VERSUS GENDER

Masculine and *feminine* are among the most confusing words used both in everyday speech and in the social sciences. The confusion stems largely from the fact that our ideas of what is male and female in human individuals are based on overlapping influences from biology and culture. As in all such situations, it is difficult to sort out the relative contributions of each source of influence. But the underlying concepts are not hard to grasp: One's sex is primarily a biological quality, while one's gender is formed largely (but not entirely) by the cultural forces we experience through socialization from infancy on (Connell, 1995).

Sex refers to the biological differences between males and females, including the primary sex characteristics that are present at birth (i.e., the presence of specific male or female genitalia) and the secondary sex characteristics that develop later (facial and body hair, voice quality, and so on). Note that these biological qualities differ considerably among individuals, so that the differences between the sexes are not always as marked as the male–female distinction suggests. Moreover, some people are born as **hermaphrodites;** their primary sexual organs have features of both male and female organs, making it difficult to categorize the person as male or female. Hermaphrodism is uncommon, but it occurs in societies throughout the world.

Another ambiguous sexual category consists of the many thousands of people who feel very strongly that the sexual organs they were born with do not conform to their deep-seated sense of what their sex should be. These **transsexuals** sometimes undergo a course of endocrine hormonal treatments to change their secondary sex characteristics and may eventually have irreversible sex change operations. Most such operations are performed to change the individual from a male to a female.

One of the most famous transsexuals in the contemporary world is the writer Jan Morris. As a male, James Morris reported on an expedition to Mount Everest and engaged in many activities that are associated with masculinity. But as Morris explains it, "I was born with the wrong body, being feminine by gender but male by sex, and I could achieve completeness only when the one was adjusted to the other" (quoted in Money & Tucker, 1975, p. 31). In making this distinction, Morris is calling attention to the difference between her biologically determined sex and her socially and emotionally influenced gender.

Gender refers to the culturally defined ways of acting as a male or a female that become part of an individual's personal sense of self. The vast majority of people develop a "gut-level" sense of themselves as male or female, boy or girl, early in life; however, as we will see shortly, some people's gender identities are more ambiguous. It is not entirely clear exactly how a person's gender identity is formed, but much of the research done to date suggests that the assignment of a gender at birth has a strong influence during the early years of life. In other words, children's feelings of being a boy or a girl are defined more by how they they are treated by their parents than by their actual biological sex characteristics (Stockard & Johnson, 1992).

GENDER SOCIALIZATION AND GENDER SEPARATION

In Chapter 5 we introduced the concept of gender socialization and discussed its powerful influence on how men and women develop as members of society. We showed, for example, that the values of beauty and youth, especially as they are applied to women by the media, have a powerful and often negative influence on how women feel about their bodies and about themselves (Wolf, 1991). Current research on gender inequality is focusing increasing attention on these issues, not only for women but for men as well. According to many comparative studies and international population reports, a central problem of gender socialization throughout the world is that the traditional separation of men and women in socializing agencies leads to the failure of men to recognize their responsibilities as sexual partners and fathers later in life. As a recent United Nations report states:

> It is clear that women cannot adequately protect their sexual and reproductive health in the context of power imbalances with their male partners. . . . Men must be involved because they share the responsibility of reproductive health, and both men and women do not understand their own and each other's bodies. (Sadik, 1995, p. 23)

In the United States, a major theme in social-scientific research is the way gender socialization in the family and particularly in schools tends to separate males and females into different social worlds with their own forms of activity and language. The theory that boys and girls are socialized to perform in more or less separate worlds receives a great deal of support in the sociological literature (Fine, 1987; Gilligan, 1982; Lever, 1978; Tannen, 1990). However, we will see shortly that the "separate worlds" thesis also has many limitations (Thorne, 1993).

A broad version of the gender separation theory as experienced in urban industrial societies is that children absorb ideas about their gender identities from their parents and the media. By the time they are preschoolers they have strong ideas about what types of dress are appropriate. Boys especially are mortified if they are caught wearing something they feel is inappropriate for their gender. But children's expressions of gender identity are also shaped through interactions in play groups throughout many years of schooling. From their separate, gender-segregated interactions with peers in school, it is argued, boys and girls develop different values, different ways of bonding with each other, different types of conflict and ways of resolving conflict. In many ways they develop separate cultures with their own norms, values, and languages. These differences are thought to persist through life and to exert a lasting influence on how the individual fares in the job market (Kanter, 1977).

In their insightful observation of preadolescent boys' interactions on Little League baseball teams, sociologist Gary Allen Fine and popular writer Stephen King were struck by the depth of male bonding that occurs as the boys undergo the pressure of competition and support each other through their successes and failures on the playing field (Fine, 1987; King, 1994). Fine notes that adult males often want their sons to join teams so that they can "teach their preadolescent boys to see the world from their perspective," which includes teaching what the men consider core values as these emerge in sports competition. However, "whereas adults focus on hustle, teamwork, sportsmanship, and winning and losing"—as desirable moral behaviors developed through team sports—"the preadolescent transforms these concerns" (Fine, 1987, p. 78). The team members respect the adults' teachings, but they are more concerned with their self-presentation, which includes some of the adult values and some of those that are part of the preadolescent moral code—learning to be tough or fearful under the appropriate conditions; learning to control aggressions, fears, tears; not being a "rat" (telling on others); and hustling in order to help the team win games. The boys engage in a great deal of sexual talk, much of which expresses their ambiguity about relationships with girls, in which their desire to have sexual experiences is offset by their fears of embarrassment and loss of male friends. The boys' banter with each other also expresses their fear of not being masculine enough. Although they have little or no experience with homosexuality, they use words like *faggot* or *gay* to tease each other or denigrate other boys.

Sociologists who study gender and socialization often point out that the strong same-sex bonds formed by boys in preadolescence and during their teen years may prove invaluable in the corporate world. In their research on life in American corporations, Rosabeth Moss Kanter and her associates find that sports analogies and language are commonplace. The male business leader typically thinks of those he works with as members of a team, and as a result of his early socialization experiences he is more comfortable with male team members than with females (Kanter & Stein, 1980).

Studies of girls' play groups note that although boys and girls are increasingly likely to play some games together, the separation of the genders in playgrounds and schoolyards remains a norm (Sutton-Smith & Rosenberg, 1961; Whiting & Edwards, 1988). These studies confirm that girls' games are likely to involve small groups, rather than large ones with more complex structures and hierar-

chies of status. They are interrupted not by arguments over rules or specific plays but by emotional issues, feelings of being slighted, or other hurts—which the girls repair in private conversations rather than in public protests to umpires or other adults. In addition, girls tend to engage in turn-taking games that emphasize cooperation, while boys more often engage in competitive team sports in which they become extremely concerned with establishing hierarchies of skill and success (e.g., batting averages, won–lost records) (Lever, 1976, 1978).

Of course, from their parents and playmates children learn many other social distinctions besides gender. Barrie Thorne, who observed children's peer interactions in two primary schools, makes this observation:

> In the lunchrooms and on the playgrounds of the two schools, African-American kids and kids whose main language was Spanish occasionally separated themselves into smaller, ethnically homogeneous groups.... I found that students generally separate first by gender and then, if at all, by race or ethnicity. (1993, p. 33)

PROBLEMS WITH THE GENDER SEPARATION THEORY

How fully are men and women socialized into separate social worlds with separate cultures? As mentioned earlier, there is a great deal of popular and social-scientific writing in support of this thesis. The immense success of Deborah Tannen's analysis of men's and women's spoken communication in her popular book *You Just Don't Understand: Women and Men in Conversation* suggests that men and women do feel separate and different in their everyday lives. But recent research on gender differences is quite critical of the idea of separate gender cultures (Thorne, 1993).

While there is an undeniable tendency for boys and girls to be socialized in gender-segregated peer groups, they are also raised together in families and often spend a great deal of time together. Boys and girls are increasingly participating in the same types of activities in their schools and communities. In some communities these changes are controversial, but in many others teachers, parents, and administrators seek to avoid the worst effects of gender separation (Meier, 1995). Girls' and women's team sports, for example, are undergoing rapid and steady growth. And as they review the literature on separate gender cultures, or conduct new research, students of gender often find that the previous emphasis on gender separateness was based on what they refer to as "the Big Man bias"—the tendency to observe only the activities of the most powerful and socially successful individuals. More isolated, less successful children are less likely to be subjects of research, yet their experiences are very important since they do not adhere strictly to the norms of gender separation (see Box 14.2 on pages 420–421). Finally, as Thorne (1993) argues, generalizations about "girls' culture" are based primarily on research with upper-class white girls, while the experiences of girls from other class, race, and ethnic backgrounds tend to be neglected.

GENDER AND SEXUALITY

Sexuality refers to the manner in which a person engages in the intimate behaviors connected with genital stimulation, orgasm, and procreation. Like most areas of human behavior, sexuality is profoundly influenced by cultural norms and social institutions like the family and the school, as well as by social structures like the class system of a society. Sociologists and historians believe that there have been major changes in sexuality as a result of changes in the economy, politics, and the family. Over the past 300 years, for example, the meaning and place of sexuality in American life have changed: from a family-centered system for ensuring reproduction and social stability during the colonial period; to a romantic and intimate sexuality in nineteenth-century marriage, with many underlying conflicts; to a commercialized sexuality in the modern period, when sexual relations are expected to provide personal identity and individual happiness apart from reproduction (D'Emilio & Freedman, 1988).

While these changes are important and controversial, they hardly begin to exhaust the range of sexual norms in cultures throughout the world. Polygyny, which is illegal (bigamy) in North America and Europe, is condoned throughout much of the Islamic world. Marriage between adult men and preadolsecent girls is practiced in some Asian cultures but would be be considered a form of child abuse in the West. Women bare their breasts on the beaches of Europe but may be issued summonses for the same behavior on the beaches of North America. On American television screens women and men expose their bodies in a fashion that is horrifying to people in many parts of Asia. Catholic priests and nuns are expected to remain celibate, while Protestant ministers are encouraged to have families, as are Jewish rabbis. With all these contrasting cultural norms governing sexuality, can it be said that there are any universal sexual norms?

Universal cultural norms exerting social control over sexuality include the *incest taboo, marriage,* and *heterosexuality,* but even these norms include variations and differing degrees of sanction. As noted in Chapter 3, the incest taboo is known in every existing and historical society and serves to protect the integrity of the family. Incest norms prohibit sexual intimacy between brothers and sisters and between parents and children, and usually specify what other family relatives are excluded. However, the specific relatives involved vary in different cultures; for example, sex between first cousins is permissible in some societies and strictly taboo in others.

Every society also has marriage norms that specify the relationships within which sexual intimacy is condoned. Marriage norms protect the institution of the family, confer legitimacy on children, and specify parental rights and obligations. But while marriage norms are found in all cultures, there are vast differences in how they operate. In addition to variations having to do with polygyny, there are some important variations with regard to the strength of sanctions on adultery (sexual intimacy outside marriage). The majority of cultures prohibit adultery, but the sanctions vary widely. Former French President François Mitterand, who died early in 1996, specified in his funeral instructions that both his wife and his mistress were to be present at his funeral. Although adultery is not openly condoned in France, it is far less strongly sanctioned than in the United States, where evidence that a presidential candidate may have had an affair can terminate a candidacy (Stockard & Johnson, 1992).

Heterosexuality refers to sexual orientation toward the opposite sex, in contrast to **homosexuality,** or sexual orientation toward the same sex, and **bisexuality,** or sexual orientation toward either sex. Heterosexuality is a norm in every society, but it too is subject to wide variations. Norms of heterosexuality function to ensure that there is genital sexual intercourse between men and women in the interest of population replacement and growth. The Shakers of colonial North America were an example of a society that attempted to curtail or eliminate heterosexuality in favor of celibacy in the interest of religious piety. Because Shaker society could continue only through recruitment of new members, it eventually declined and essentially disappeared.

While heterosexuality is practiced in some form in all societies, about one third of them actively ban homosexual practices, while many other societies tolerate them in some form (Murdock, 1983). Historically, the best-known examples of heterosexual societies that condoned some forms of homosexuality and bisexuality were ancient Greece, Confucian China, and Hawaii before it was colonialized by Europeans (Connell, 1995). In most Western cultures the norm of heterosexuality is quite strong, but older taboos against homosexualty and bisexuality are changing as well.

Homosexuality and Bisexuality. The intensity of debate over homosexuality in the United States is an indication, on the one hand, of how controversial the behavior remains and, on the other, of the growing, if grudging, acceptance of alternatives to traditional norms of heterosexuality. In the mid-twentieth century homosexuality was a taboo subject. Homosexual men and women remained secretive or "in the closet" about their true sexual feelings. Today there is at least one homosexual member of Congress and many other openly homosexual elected officials and public figures. At the same time, fear and loathing of homosexuals—gay men and lesbian women—is a major social problem that continues to cause immense human suffering.

Estimates of the rate of incidence of homosexuality—that is, the proportion or number of women and men in a

BOX 14.2　SOCIOLOGICAL METHODS

Problems in Research on Peer Socialization

Gary Alan Fine charted the friendship choices among the 11- and 12-year-old players on the Little League teams he observed for his study *With the Boys: Little League Baseball and Preadolsecent Culture.* A typical result is the sociogram depicted in the accompanying chart. Note that the arrows in the diagram can be either one-way or reciprocal, depending on whether the choices are one-way or mutual. Clearly, on this team there was a "ruling clique" consisting of Justin, Harry, and Whit, each of whom also chose each other and who were extremely likely to be chosen by the other boys, even when the three leaders did not reciprocate.

It should come as no surprise that these three "sociometric stars" were the best ballplayers on the team. They were also most admired for their toughness and masculinity. The most popular, Justin, was extremely fair with his teammates but was especially aggressive, prone to call opposing players "faggots" and to use racial epithets. Fine notes that not all the teams had this particular clique structure and that emphasis on the activities of the elite boys on teams and in peer groups tends to neglect the experiences of the larger number of boys who are not the stars. He also found that Justin had the closest contact with girls, who also looked up to him as a leader, and was able to avoid the jibes of his male peers about this because of his sports ability and leadership.

In her studies of what she calls "gender play," Barrie Thorne is quite critical of research that focuses on central figures like Justin because they tend to become models from which generalizations are made. "Assertions about gender differences in actual behavior refer, at best," she argues, "to *average* differences between girls and boys, or between groups of girls and groups of boys" (1993, p. 103). She cites studies of boys' and girls' play groups that conclude, from observations of the most dominant boys or most popular girls in the study, that boys are more likely to enjoy "rough and tumble" play. In fact, if one looks at data for the less dominant boys, it appears that the gender differences on this issue are not wide at all. While this bias is one that Fine tries to avoid, Thorne points out that it occurs in numerous other studies:

> The literature on "the boys' world" suffers from a "Big Man bias" akin to the skew found in anthropological research that equates male elites with men in general. In many observational studies of children in preschools and early elementary school, large, bonded groups of boys who are physically assertive, engage in "tough talk," and actively devalue girls anchor descriptions of "the boys' world" and themes of masculinity. Other kinds of boys may be mentioned, but not as the core of the gender story. (p. 98)

While "being tough" and "being nice" may be core values that distinguish boys' and girls' peer groups, Thorne can point to many instances in her field observations in which girls act tough and even beat up the boys. The more one builds racial, ethnic, and class diversity into the sample of children under observation, the more the gender behaviors overlap and the less rigid the gender borders appear in the data from the study.

population who are sexually attracted to people of the same sex—raise a number of social-scientific and political problems. In his pathbreaking and courageous studies of male and female sexual behavior, Alfred Kinsey interviewed thousands of Americans about their sexual preferences and behavior. Kinsey described sexuality as a continuum extending from exclusive heterosexuality to equal attraction for the same and the opposite sex (bisexuality) to exclusive homosexuality. By his estimates, about 4 percent of men and 2 percent of women were exclusively homosexual, while far more, perhaps as many as one third of men and about 12 percent of women, said that they had had a homosexual experience leading to orgasm at least once in their lives (Kinsey, Pomeroy, & Martin, 1948, 1953). Subsequent reinterpretations of Kinsey's data led social scientists to estimate that 10 percent of the population was homosexual or had strong homosexual tendencies. This estimate became a commonly cited statistic in the politics of the gay rights movement. However, the most recent major study of sexuality in the United States, conducted by the National Opinion Research Center, finds this estimate to be too high. For instance, in the NORC sample about 4 percent of men and about 1.4 percent of women said that they are exclusively

homosexual, but only about 10 percent of men (not the 30% to 35% cited by Kinsey) admitted to having had prior homosexual experiences even if they did not claim to be homosexual in their daily lives (see Figure 14.2). Data from the NORC study also indicate that there are wide differences among men and between men and women in how sexual pleasure is defined and derived (see Table 14.2) (Laumann et al., 1994).

Given the anxiety that many people feel about discussing their sexual orientation and behavior, however, there are some who feel that the NORC study may underestimate the incidence of homosexuality in the population (Gould, 1995). It should also be noted that the ambitious study would have included a far larger sample and somewhat greater scientific accuracy if the federal funds that had been scheduled for its budget had not been withdrawn by conservative members of Congress opposed to research on sexuality.

Only about 0.8 percent of men and 0.9 percent of women in the NORC sample ($n = 3,432$) said that they were bisexual. But when they were asked more indirectly whether they were sexually attracted to both sexes, the proportions who said yes increased to 4.1 percent of women

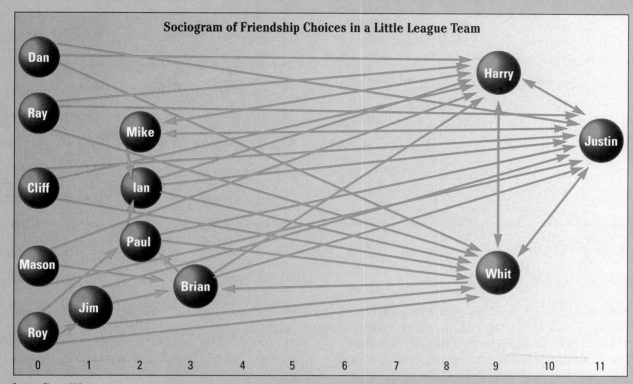

Sociogram of Friendship Choices in a Little League Team

Source: Fine, 1987.

and 3.9 percent of men. Martin S. Weinberg observes that many people "would say that the person who feels the sexual attraction to both sexes but never acts on it is not bisexual, but in my definition they are" (quoted in Gabriel, 1995b, p. A12). The findings of his recent study of bisexuality refute the common assumption that bisexuality is a stage leading to eventual homosexual orientation. His sample included women and men who had come to their bisexuality from both heterosexual and homosexual orientations and for whom bisexuality appeared to be a stable lifestyle.

Many homosexuals, along with an increasing number of biologists and social scientists, believe that homosexuality will be shown to have genetic origins (Tobach & Rosoff, 1994; Wilson, 1979). In accounts of their earliest sexual feelings homosexual men, and to a lesser degree lesbian women, recount their experiences of sexual attraction to members of the same sex. These experiences convince many gay people that their sexual orientation is not merely a "lifestyle choice," as critics often claim. However, as yet there is insufficient evidence from genetic studies to resolve this issue (Kemper, 1990).

Homophobia.   Most of the young boys in Barrie Thorne's study of gender play used negative images of

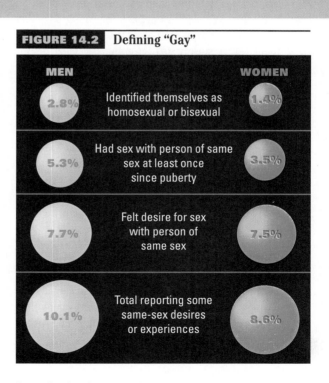

FIGURE 14.2   Defining "Gay"

MEN		WOMEN
2.8%	Identified themselves as homosexual or bisexual	1.4%
5.3%	Had sex with person of same sex at least once since puberty	3.5%
7.7%	Felt desire for sex with person of same sex	7.5%
10.1%	Total reporting some same-sex desires or experiences	8.6%

Source: Data from Laumann et al., 1994.

TABLE 14.2	The Appeal of Various Sexual Practices (percentages of respondents)							
	APPEALING TO MEN AGES 18–44				APPEALING TO WOMEN AGES 18–44			
	VERY	SOMEWHAT	NOT REALLY	NOT AT ALL	VERY	SOMEWHAT	NOT REALLY	NOT AT ALL
Vaginal intercourse	83%	12%	1%	4%	78%	18%	1%	3%
Watching partner undress	50	43	3	4	30	51	11	9
Receiving oral sex	50	33	5	12	33	35	11	21
Giving oral sex	37	39	9	15	19	38	15	28
Active anal intercourse	5	9	13	73	—	—	—	—
Passive anal intercourse	3	8	15	75	1	4	9	87
Group sex	14	32	20	33	1	8	14	78
Same-sex partner	4	2	5	89	3	3	9	85
Sex with a stranger	5	29	25	42	1	9	11	80
Forcing someone to do something sexual	0	2	14	84	0	2	7	91
Being forced to do something sexual	0	3	13	84	0	2	6	92

Source: Laumann et al., 1994.

homosexuals well before they ever encountered a gay person. Fear of homosexuals and same-sex attraction is known as *homophobia*. Although it is quite common in the United States, its causes are not entirely clear. Most social-scientific (as opposed to religious or ideological) explanations of homophobia hinge on an analysis of the problems of masculinity and the male role in Western societies.

Identification with the male gender and the ability to take male roles, as these are defined for young boys and later for men, are two different aspects of what it means to "be a man." Every society has its notions of what distinguishes men from women and seeks to teach boys and girls how to perform the roles assigned to their gender. In Western societies the male role is often depicted in movies, on television, and in advertising as distinct from that of the female and imbued with more strength, power, and rationality—a subject to which we return later in the chapter. Because as children they lack the power and strength they admire in images of masculinity, young boys typically become concerned about being seen as lacking in masculinity and the ability to take on male roles. Thus their vocabulary is rich with terms of abuse for anyone they believe to be lacking in masculinity: wimp, nerd, turkey, sissy, lily liver, yellowbelly, candy ass, ladyfinger, cream puff, motherfucker, mother's boy, dweeb, geek, and so on (Connell, 1995). As they grow older, a small but socially significant proportion of boys may become violently homophobic and go out of their way to abuse males whom they consider effeminate or "queer."

Girls may also develop homophobic attitudes early in life, often through identification with their male siblings, but homophobia among females often occurs during the teenage years. Female socialization stesses the ability to attract men, to appear feminine, and anxiety over these aspects of the female role may lead young women to reject other women whom they do not regard as feminine enough.

These early patterns can have lasting consequences. Throughout their lives the early habit of avoiding emotions for fear of seeming effeminate tends to make men in the United States and other Western societies wary of expressing their feelings and of admitting vulnerability: "Men are thus denied an important part of their . . . well-being when they cannot touch and cannot express their tender feelings for other men. Needless to say, gay men are damaged by the negative implications of homophobia" (Blumenfeld, 1992, p. 37). And of course homophobia causes untold suffering for gay men and women (Richmond-Abbott, 1992).

Fundamentalist religious beliefs are another important source of negative attitudes and strong disapproval of homosexuality, including vehement homophobia. For example, 77 percent of fundamentalist Baptists disagreed or strongly disagreed with the statement, "Even if homosexuality is wrong, the civil rights of gays should be protected." They believe that homosexuality is immoral and inimical to the propagation of the species. In the United States it is common for prominent fundamentalist Christian leaders to state that AIDS is God's punishment for the homosexual lifestyle (Ammerman, 1990). Despite the vehemence of such religiously motivated attacks, gay men and women in smaller towns and communities with fundamentalist congregations are increasingly choosing to assert their right to live as they choose as long as they do not violate the rights of others (Miller, 1989).

Controversies over male and female roles, homosexuality, norms of sexual conduct, and the origins of sexual orientation all point to the extent to which these central areas of social life are subject to change and reactions to change. In the study of gender inequalities, the origins and patterns of change in the condition of women and the continuing inequalities between the sexes are a central focus, to which we now turn.

GENDER STRATIFICATION

After class and race, the most important dimensions of inequality in modern societies are gender and age. As stated earlier, gender refers to a set of culturally conditioned traits associated with maleness or femaleness. There are two sexes, male and female; these are biologically determined ascribed statuses. There are also two genders, masculine and feminine; these are socially constructed ways of being a man or a woman. **Gender roles** are the sets of behaviors considered appropriate for individuals of a particular gender. Controversies over whether women in the armed forces can serve in combat or whether men with children ought to be eligible for family leave from work are examples of issues arising out of the definition of gender roles.

All human societies are stratified by gender, meaning that males and females are channeled into specific statuses and roles. "Be a man"; "She's a real lady"—with these familiar expressions we let each other know that our behavior is or is not conforming to the role expectations associated with our particular gender. When women's roles are thought to require male direction, as is the case in many households and organizations, the unequal treatment of men and women is directly related to gender roles. The roles assigned to men and women are accorded differing amounts of income, power, or prestige, and these patterns of inequality contribute to the society's system of stratification.

GENDER ROLES: A CULTURAL PHENOMENON

Until quite recently it was assumed that there were two spheres of life, one for women and the other for men:

> Church, school and family—these chief agents of a child's socialization—worked together to transmit the notion that boys should grow up to be the doers, thinkers, and movers in the world at large. Girls, on the other hand, were expected to grow up to be wives and mothers. Any involvement in the world outside the home would be indirect rather than direct. (Scanzoni & Scanzoni, 1976, pp. 18–19)

Out of this gender-based division of labor, which defined the activities that were appropriate for men and women,

grew the notion of differences in men's and women's abilities and personalities. These differences were thought to be natural—an outgrowth of biological and psychological differences between males and females (Epstein, 1985). Behaviors that did not fit these patterns were viewed as deviant and in some cases as requiring severe punishment.

In the twentieth century, evidence from the social sciences has called into question the assumption that there are innate biological or psychological reasons for the different roles and temperaments of men and women. Margaret Mead's (1950) famous research in New Guinea directly challenged this assumption. Mead was one of the first social scientists to gather evidence to show that gender-specific behavior is learned rather than innate. In her study of gender roles in three tribes, Mead found that different tribes had different ways of defining male and female behavior. In one tribe, the Mundugumor, men and women were equally aggressive and warlike, traits that Westerners usually associate only with men. In a second tribe, the Tchambuli, the men spent their time gossiping about women and worrying about their hairdos, while the women shaved their heads and made rude jokes among themselves. In the third tribe, the Arapesh, both men and women behaved in sympathetic, cooperative ways and spent a great deal of time worrying about how the children were getting along, all behaviors that Westerners traditionally associate with women.

Mead's research has been criticized in that she may have been actively looking for gender-role patterns that differed from those that Westerners usually associate with males and females. Nevertheless, her study was highly significant, since it began a line of inquiry that established that gender roles are not innate. Nor are gender roles wholly determined by a society's relationship to its environment. Although hunting-and-gathering societies sent men out to hunt while women cared for the home, in early agrarian societies there was a less rigid division of labor. In early horticultural societies women had more power than they did in hunting-and-gathering societies or in later feudal societies. Women maintained the grain supply and knew the lore of cultivation, and they were priestesses who could communicate with the harvest and fertility gods (Adler, 1979; Balandier, 1971/1890). Table 14.3 illustrates the sexual division of labor in 224 preliterate societies. It shows that as societies evolve from hunting and gathering to agrarian production, the division of labor by sex becomes more varied, although women tend to specialize in household tasks and men in tasks that take them outside the home (d'Andrade, 1966).

The lesson of this cross-cultural research is that gender roles are heavily influenced by culture. Although the relationship of earlier societies to their natural environment often required that women tend the hearth and home while men went out to hunt for big game, women were also hunting for small game around the encampment and

TABLE 14.3　Cross-Cultural Data from 224 Societies on Subsistence Activities and Division of Labor by Sex

	NUMBER OF SOCIETIES IN WHICH ACTIVITY IS PERFORMED BY				
ACTIVITY	MEN ALWAYS	MEN USUALLY	EITHER SEX	WOMEN USUALLY	WOMEN ALWAYS
Pursuit of sea mammals	34	1	0	0	0
Hunting	166	13	0	0	0
Trapping small animals	128	13	4	1	2
Herding	38	8	4	0	5
Fishing	98	34	19	3	4
Clearing land for agriculture	73	22	17	5	13
Dairy operations	17	4	3	1	13
Preparing and planting soil	31	23	33	20	37
Erecting and dismantling shelter	14	2	5	6	22
Tending fowl and small animals	21	4	8	1	39
Tending and harvesting crops	10	15	35	39	44
Gathering shellfish	9	4	8	7	25
Making and tending fires	18	6	25	22	62
Bearing burdens	12	6	35	20	57
Preparing drinks and narcotics	20	1	13	8	57
Gathering fruits, berries, nuts	12	3	15	13	63
Gathering fuel	22	1	10	19	89
Preservation of meat and fish	8	2	10	14	74
Gathering herbs, roots, seeds	8	1	11	7	74
Cooking	5	1	9	28	158
Carrying water	7	0	5	7	119
Grinding grain	2	4	5	13	114

Source: d'Andrade (1966). Reprinted from *The Development of Sex Differences*, edited by Eleanor E. Maccoby, with the permission of the publishers, Stanford University Press. © 1966 by the Board of Trustees of the Leland Stanford Junior University.

experimenting with new seeds and agricultural techniques. The division of labor by gender was never fixed; it could always be adapted to new conditions. In industrial societies, as the greater strength of males becomes less important as a result of advances in technology, it makes less sense to maintain the earlier divisions of labor. Indeed, modern societies have demanded more involvement of women in a broader range of tasks. Women are now competing with men as military and police officers, engineers, scientists, judges, political leaders, and the like; they may be found in many roles that were assumed to be unsuitable for women earlier in this century.

Table 14.4 shows that women have increased their share of employment in many occupational groups that were formerly male "turf." The proportions of female exec-

utives and managers have increased dramatically, as have those of technicians and professionals. But older barriers and assumptions continue to stand in the way of equal access to male-dominated occupations such as precision production. Conversely, women continue to be disproportionately represented in "pink-collar" occupational sectors such as clerical and administrative support and domestic service (Bianchi & Spain, 1986).

HISTORICAL PATTERNS OF GENDER STRATIFICATION

In preindustrial societies gender often plays a greater role in social stratification than wealth and power. Fewer members of such societies are wealthy or powerful than is true

THEN *AND* NOW

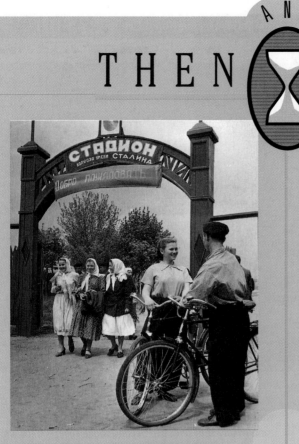

COSMOPOLITAN
МАЙ 1994

Секс или
шоколад?
**Всему
свое
время!**

Не позволяй
зависти
заслонить
тебе жизнь

ТЕСТ:
Хорошо
ли вы знаете
друг друга?

Тридцатилетние,
независимые,
уверенные
в себе...
**Нужен ли
им муж?**

Также в номере:

Ирина
Хакамада

Владимир
Пресняков

Красота по
абонементу

Международная
мода в Москве

Cosmopolitan в России!
Журнал с международной славой
- впервые в русском издании

FROM BABUSHKA TO "COSMO GIRL"

Who would have predicted that the international
magazine publishing success story of the decade
would be Russia's *Cosmo?* With the end of the Soviet
empire, Russia and its former satellites have become
one of the world's marketing hot spots. Under the
stern control of Stalinist communist leaders, the
Russian people longed for access to some of the
consumer goods produced in the West. Women were
especially oppressed under Soviet communism
despite that system's claims to have ended gender
stratification. A few Soviet women were known to the
world as graceful figure skaters or gymnasts, but the
dominant image of the Soviet woman was as a toiler
in the field, a sullen factory hand, or a swaddled street
sweeper in a lumpy gray overcoat and babushka. More
educated and accomplished women also spoke openly
about how unromantic and cloddish they felt their
men to be (Gray, 1990). But none of this explains why
the Russian version of *Cosmopolitan* would be a
runaway hit.

Cosmo's publisher, Anne Marie Van Gaal, had
started the *Moscow Times,* a wildly successful English-
language newspaper. Observing the success of
Cosmopolitan in the United States, Van Gaal realized
that a magazine containing explicit articles about how
to be romantic and glamorous, with a generous
element of the beauty ideal and much appeal to
women's fantasy lives, could be successful with the
rising Russian middle and upper classes, just as it had
been first in the United States and then in many other
nations with increasing numbers of educated young
women. She was right: *Cosmo*'s sales now exceed half
a million per issue.

---

in modern societies, but all are male or female. Cross-
cultural research has provided some insight into the development of gender-based stratification in such societies.
Among the main findings of that research are the following:

- Preindustrial societies are usually rigidly
  sex-segregated. Males and females tend to pass
  through life in cohesive peer groups. Even after
  marriage, women and men tend to spend more time

TABLE 14.4	Percentage of Women in Major Occupational Groups, 1970–1994	
MAJOR OCCUPATIONAL GROUP	**1970**	**1994**
Executive, administrative, and managerial	18.5%	43.0%
Professional specialty	44.3	52.8
Technicians and related support	34.4	52.0
Sales occupations	41.3	49.1
Administrative support, including clerical	73.2	78.9
Private household	96.3	96.3
Protective service	6.6	16.7
Other service	61.2	64.3
Farming, forestry, fishing	9.1	19.3
Precision production, craft, and repair	7.3	9.3
Machine operators, assemblers, and inspectors	39.7	38.1
Transportation and material-moving occupations	4.1	9.4
Handlers, equipment cleaners, helpers, and laborers	17.4	18.1
Total	38.0	46.0

Sources: Data from Bianchi and Spain, 1986; and *Statistical Abstract*, 1995.

with their same-sex peers than they do with their spouses.

- As societies increase in size and complexity, women usually become subordinated to men. There have been few if any societies in which women as a group controlled the distribution of wealth or the exercise of power (Harris, 1980; Leacock, 1978).

Larger, more complex societies also exhibit distinct patterns of gender-role stratification, but these are more likely to be part of a multidimensional system of stratification in which class, race, ethnicity, gender, and age are intertwined.

The origins of gender inequality in most modern societies can be traced to their feudal periods. Most industrial societies developed out of feudal societies, either as a result of revolutions (in Europe) or through changes brought about by colonialism (in North and South America, Asia, and parts of Africa). Although they are no longer as easily justified, many of the norms that specify separate spheres of activity for males and females, as well as the subordination of women to men, were carried over into modern societies.

In some feudal societies these norms were far more repressive than those found in modern societies; in others, the subordination of women was disguised as reverence or worship. In European feudal societies, for example, the norms of chivalry and courtly love seemed to elevate women to an exalted status, but in reality they reinforced practices that kept women in undervalued roles. They gave rise to a set of norms that specified that women do not initiate sexual activity, do not engage in warfare or politics but wait for men to resolve conflicts, and do not compete with men in any sphere of life beyond those reserved for women.

The situation of Guinevere in the tales of King Arthur aptly illustrates this point (de Rougemont, 1983; Elias, 1978/1939). Courtly love applied only to women of the nobility. It specified that a woman must be chaste—either a virgin or entirely faithful to her husband at all times. Like Guinevere, she could be worshipped from afar by a noble knight (Lancelot), but she could not be touched or even spoken to without the consent of her male guardian (King Arthur). Figuratively she was set upon a pedestal. In reality, however, she was imprisoned—kept forever separate from the knightly suitor who worshipped her from a distance and engaged in chivalrous acts in her name. Adultery and the subordination of women were common in the lower orders of feudal society, but the women of the nobility were more likely to be constrained by the norms of chastity.

As feudal societies developed and changed, the norms of courtly love were extended to the new middle classes, and in greatly modified forms they still exist today. They can be seen, for example, in the traditions of courtship that persist in Spanish-speaking nations, in which a man serenades a woman (or hires someone to do it on his behalf) and the woman is never without a chaperone. It should be noted that courtly (or romantic) love eventually elevated the status of women from that of property to that of significant other, a change that had far-reaching implications for the position and influence of women in the family. At the same time, in many Western cultures norms derived from medieval notions of courtly love continue to justify the notion that there are "good women," whom one reveres and protects, and "bad women," who are available for sexual exploitation. This denial of normal female sexuality and the assertion of the male's sexual needs is associated with a host of psychological and social problems, including the conflict that some women feel about their sexuality and the inability of some men to relate to their wives as sexual partners.

GENDER INEQUALITY IN INDUSTRIAL SOCIETIES

In modern industrial societies age and gender interact to shape people's views of what role behavior is appropriate at any given time. Before puberty, boys and girls in the United States tend to associate in sex-segregated peer groups. Be-

cause they model their behavior on what they see in the home and on television, girls spend more of their time playing at domestic roles than boys do; boys meanwhile play at team sports more than girls do. These patterns are changing at different rates in different social classes, but they remain generally accepted norms of behavior. And they have important consequences: Women are more likely to be socialized into the "feminine" roles of mother, teacher, secretary, and so on, while men are more likely to be socialized into roles that are considered "masculine," such as those of corporate manager or military leader. It is expected that men will concern themselves with earning and investing while women occupy themselves with human relationships (Baron & Bielby, 1980; Chodorow, 1978; Rossi, 1980).

Childhood socialization explains some of the inequalities and differences between the roles of men and women, but we also need to recognize the impact of social structures. In the United States, for example, it was assumed

This medieval illustration depicts the values of chivalry in action. Notice the women standing on the battlements, aloof from the fray. Their lot is to watch the combat and hope that their hero will not be skewered by his opponent.

until fairly recently that boys and girls needed to be segregated in their games. Boys were thought to be much stronger and rougher than girls, and girls were thought to need protection from unfair competition with boys. This widespread belief translated into school rules that did not permit coeducational sports. Those rules, in turn, reinforced the more general belief that girls' roles needed to be segregated from those of boys. Such patterns have significant long-term effects. As sociologist Cynthia Epstein points out, human beings have an immense capacity "to be guided, manipulated, and coerced into assuming social roles, demonstrating behavior, and expressing thoughts that conform to socially accepted values" (1988, p. 240). Through such means, gender roles become so deeply ingrained in many people's consciousness that they feel threatened when women assert their similarities with men and demand equal opportunity and equal treatment in social institutions.

In their adult years men enjoy more wealth, prestige, and leisure than women do. Working women earn less than men do, and they are frequently channeled into the less prestigious strata of large organizations. Even as executives they are often shunted into middle-level positions in which they must do the bidding of men in more powerful positions. Similar patterns are found in all advanced industrial nations.

THE GENDER POVERTY RATIO

Earlier in the chapter we showed that women earn less than men in the same occupations (Table 14.1). Coupled with existing patterns of gender inequality, these income disparities mean that women are more likely to be living at or below the poverty line. The U.S. Census shows that about 16 percent of women and about 12 percent of men are officially classified as poor. "The ratio of women to men's poverty—the gender poverty ratio—was 1.30 in 1991 [following the last major census], which means that women are 30 percent more likely to be poor than men" (Casper, McLanahan, & Garfinkel, 1994, p. 594). To compare this gender poverty gap to that in other industrial nations, sociologists use an international study of income and poverty known as the Luxembourg Income Study. That study classified people as poor if they "live in a household whose disposable income (after taxes and government cash transfers) is less than 50 percent of the median disposable income for all households in that country" (Casper, McLanahan, & Garfinkel, 1994, p. 595). This definition (with adjustments for differing household size) is based on a relative measure rather than the absolute income standard used to determine the official "poverty line" in the United States. It allows investigators "to examine differences in poverty between men and women in different countries relative to the common standard of living in those countries" (p. 596).

Some findings of this international comparison are presented in Figures 14.3 and 14.4. While the figures show that the United States lags behind other industrial nations in reducing the gender poverty gap, an analysis of the findings reveals that the causes of these differences are quite varied. Disparities in employment, with women concen-

FIGURE 14.3 **Poverty Rates of Women and Men (percentages)**

Women   Men

United States: 18.2 / 12.9
Canada: 12.9 / 10.1
Australia: 12.7 / 9.5
Italy: 10.5 / 10.3
United Kingdom: 10.1 / 8.5
Sweden: 8.6 / 9.6
West Germany: 6.7 / 5.2
Netherlands: 4.9 / 4.8

Source: Casper, McLanahan, & Garfinkel, 1994.

trated in lower-paying jobs, is a major factor in explaining the situation in the United States, but some nations do not have high rates of female labor force participation. In those nations—Italy, for example—female poverty is reduced by the tendency for women to marry men who can support them, and to remain married. In still other nations social policies play an important role. In "social democratic" nations like Sweden there is less gender integration in occupations than in the United States. Single women with young children are not obliged to work but are given generous subsidies through income support, child care, education, and other policies (Kammerman & Kahn, 1993). As a result, rates of female poverty are low.

In sum, comparative research indicates that gender inequality and female poverty rates are very much related to the specific workings of other social institutions—particularly those of the economy and government—and that they can be reduced when the society has the resources and will to do so.

Another example of the relationship between economic institutions and gender inequality can be seen in the research of Mary Brinton (1989) on gender stratification in Japan. Brinton found that although educated young men and women enter large firms at approximately the same rate, by age 45 to 49 women's participation in those firms is approximately three fifths that of men, while their participation in small firms is one and a half times that of

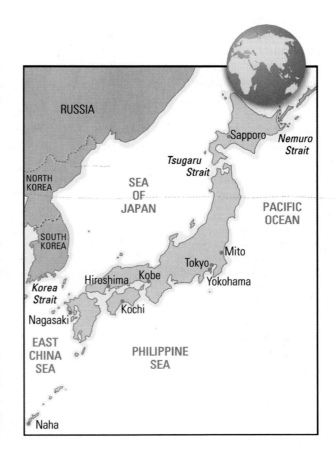

FIGURE 14.4 Ratio of Women's to Men's Poverty Rates

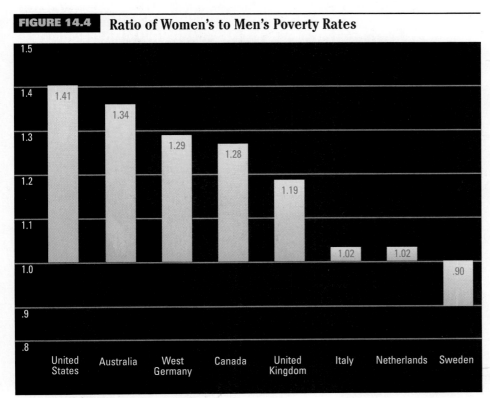

Source: Casper, McLanahan, & Garfinkel, 1994.

men. These differences are significant because in Japan it is the large firms that provide the best wages, benefits, and job security, whereas in small firms careers are more uncertain. "It is clear," Brinton observes, "that women are not moving up career ladders in the internal labor markets of large firms" (1989, p. 552).

SEXISM

Gender stratification is reflected in attitudes that reinforce the subordinated status of women. The term **sexism** is used to refer to an ideology that justifies prejudice or dis-

crimination based on sex. It results in the channeling of women into statuses considered appropriate for women and their exclusion from statuses considered appropriate for men. Sexist attitudes also tend to "objectify" women, meaning that they treat women as objects for adornment or sex rather than as individuals worthy of a full measure of respect and equal treatment in social institutions. This can be seen in the case of beautiful women. Such women receive special treatment from both men and women, but their beauty is a mixed blessing. The beautiful woman is often viewed as nothing more than an object for admira-

This photo from the 1950s shows the degree of explicit sexism in the airlines industry at the time. We have not found an equivalent photo for male flight crews. Although female airline employees still must conform to dress codes, they have formed unions and have won more stable careers and greater job security.

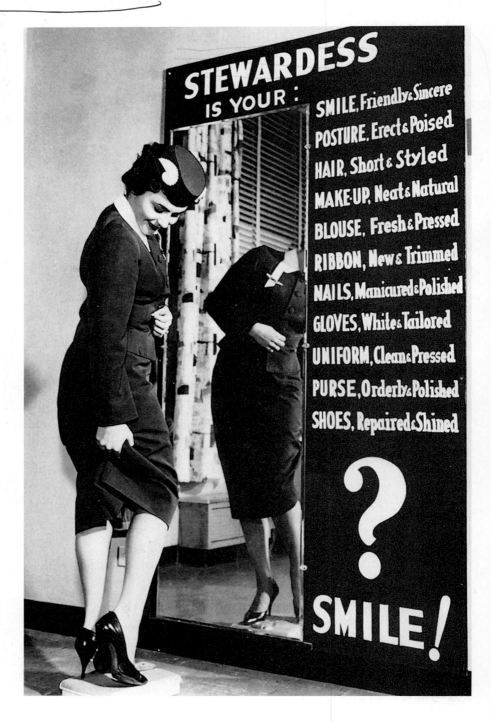

who part of the country?

Men are often compelled by gender norms to behave in stereotypically "masculine" ways in public.

tion. Being a woman is a master status (see Chapter 4) in that gender tends to outweigh the person's achieved statuses. This is even more painfully true for beautiful women. Someone like Marilyn Monroe is thought of only in terms of her beauty; the person beneath the surface is ignored.

The objectification of women can be seen in the beauty contest, which came into being in the United States in the summer of 1921 when the first Costume and Beauty Show was held at a bathing beach on the Potomac River. There the women wore tunic bathing suits and hats, but later that year a similar contest was held at Atlantic City, New Jersey, that eventually developed into the Miss America Pageant. In that contest women wore one-piece bathing suits that showed their calves and thighs and created a sensation in the tabloid newspapers. These contests and the publicity they generated made beauty a way for women to gain celebrity and wealth, but they also reflected the dominant male view that the most extraordinary women are those with the most stunning faces and the shapeliest figures (Allen, 1931). Women have been struggling against this view throughout the modern era, a struggle that has frequently been opposed not only by men but also by women who feel threatened by changes in their traditional statuses.

Sexism is also expressed in violence against women. Two million American women are severely beaten in their homes every year, and 20 percent of visits by women to hospital emergency rooms are caused by battering. (Thousands of men are battered by their wives each year as well,

but they are far outnumbered by women victims.) In popular American culture, especially movies and television, violence against women is not condoned, but it is presented as a form of thrilling entertainment. Films like *Nightmare on Elm Street* and *Looking for Mr. Goodbar* suggest that the brightest and most independent women are most likely to be victimized. Examples like these hardly exhaust the overt types of sexism that exist in employment and other aspects of social life in the United States, but they are aspects of American culture that too often go unnoticed. Despite advances in women's rights and changes in women's access to careers, sexism remains commonplace in many areas of American life (Benokraitis & Feagin, 1986; Connell, 1995).

THE WOMEN'S MOVEMENT

In the 1950s, the women's movement was dormant. In the late nineteenth and early twentieth centuries women had organized social movements to gain full citizenship rights and greater control over reproduction (e.g., through family planning and birth control). In the United States they were known as suffragettes because they campaigned vigorously for woman suffrage—the right of women to vote. But in 1920, after the Nineteenth Amendment to the Constitution extended suffrage to women, the movement faded.

The victory of the suffragettes did not change the patterns of gender stratification, however. For example, in

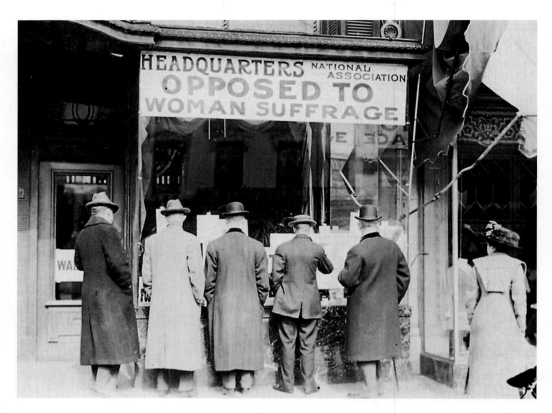

Early in the twentieth century, women in the suffrage movement were fighting for the right to vote. Their movement often met with organized resistance from men.

their famous studies of Middletown, Helen and Robert Lynd (1929, 1937) found that women who had worked their way into good factory jobs and professional occupations were severely set back during the Great Depression. Like blacks and members of other minority groups, women were the last to be hired and the first to be fired when times were bad. And although women were hired as factory workers in unprecedented numbers during World War II, they often faced discrimination and harassment and were usually "bumped off" their jobs by returning GIs after the war (Archibald, 1947). Nor did this situation change greatly when women began entering the professions and the corporate world in the 1950s. Women still tended to be limited to roles that were either subordinate to those of men or part of an entirely separate sphere of "women's work."

In her review of the origins of the modern women's movement, Jo Freeman (1973) wrote that even in the mid-1960s the resurgence of the women's movement "caught most social observers by surprise." After all, women were widely believed to have come a long way toward equality with men. Their average educational level was rising steadily and they were gaining access to the better professions and even to positions in the top ranks of corporate management. Freeman suggested that the movement developed out of an existing network of women's organizations that made many women aware of the inequality still prevailing in American society and encouraged them to organize to demand equal rights. Influential writing by women activists, such as Betty Friedan's *The Feminine Mystique* (1963), and studies of gender inequality by social scientists like Alice Rossi (1964) and Jessie Bernard (1964), played a major part in this growing awareness.

Meanwhile another, less formal network of women was developing. Women who were experiencing sexism within other social movements—the antiwar movement, the civil rights movement, the environmental protection movement, and the labor movement—began to form small "consciousness-raising" groups (Morgan, 1970). By questioning traditional assumptions and providing emotional and material support, these groups attempted to develop a sense of "sisterhood." Their members formed a loosely connected network of small groups that could mobilize resources and develop into a larger and better-organized movement.

The women's movement achieved significant victories during the 1960s and 1970s. In 1963 Congress passed "equal pay for equal work" legislation, and Title VII of the 1964 Civil Rights Act prohibited discrimination against women. In the 1970s the federal Equal Employment Opportunity Commission began to enforce laws barring gender-based discrimination in employment. Lawsuits filed under the Civil Rights Act and other federal laws forced many employers to pay more attention to women's demands for equality in pay and promotion and an end to sexual harassment on the job. Research shows that men very slowly began to accept roles that had previously been considered "women's work" (Rosen, 1987), and at work they were more likely to have women as supervisors than was true only a decade earlier. Throughout American society the attitudes of both men and women were becoming more favorable toward a more equal allocation of political and economic roles (Yankelovich, 1981).

Despite these changes, gender equality is far from complete. Studies of the sharing of household tasks reveal that women continue to do more such tasks than men do (Hochschild, 1989). And as we have seen, women in the same occupational categories as men continue to earn substantially less, even for the same type of work. This persistent pattern of wage inequality, together with the tendency for women to be segregated in such occupations as secretary, bank teller, and primary school teacher, has led activists in the women's movement to call for new policies designed to reduce inequality (National Academy of Sciences, 1986). Increasingly they have pressed for "comparable worth"—that is, for increases in the salaries paid in traditionally female occupations to levels comparable to those paid in similar, but traditionally male, occupations. And the controversy over sexual harassment generated by Anita Hill's testimony at the Supreme Court nomination hearings of Judge Clarence Thomas exposed a deep vein of emotion and a sense of injustice among American women. The feeling that sexual harassment and unequal treatment persist helps to account for the tendency of women to vote for candidates who support such issues as family leave, better enforcement of child support laws, measures to protect spouses and children from abuse, and adequate child care.

WOMEN AT WORK

In the industrial nations of North America, Europe, and Oceania, the increasing proportion of women who are in the labor force as paid employees is one of the most important aspects of social change in those societies. At midcentury, 34 percent of U.S. women were in the labor force, but that proportion has increased steadily since then; in the 1990s, almost 70 percent of women considered themselves to be employees, either at work or looking for work (*Statistical Abstract*, 1995).

In fact, women assumed an important economic role well before industrialization created a sharp distinction between work in the paid labor force and work at home or in the fields. When the United States was an agrarian society, women planted and harvested crops, including extensive household gardens, and were also expected to take responsibility for housework and child rearing, both of which were highly labor intensive in the pre-electricity era. And since women have higher life expectancies than men, widows routinely ran farms or businesses after their husbands

died, and many middle-class women gained additional income by taking in lodgers and selling handicrafts or other products of their labor. With the industrial revolution came growing demand for factory workers. Although male workers were often preferred, thousands of women and children also swelled the ranks of the new industrial working class. A recent Census Bureau study showed that many of the working women were immigrants or poor single women from rural backgrounds. Large numbers of African American women were also working for wages in fields and factories and as domestic servants (Richmond-Abbott, 1992).

World War II marked a significant turning point in women's labor force participation. Although returning servicemen "bumped" women (and minority men) from jobs in factories and offices, there were thousands of war widows and single women who had to continue earning wages whether they wanted to or not. As a result, although in the 1950s women's labor force participation was still far lower than it is today, in fact female employment was increasing at a far faster rate than male employment.

At the same time, the 1950s were a time of relative economic prosperity. The middle classes were expanding, and a suburban home became a central feature of the American dream. Popular culture, including the powerful new medium of television, emphasized the ideal norms of the middle-class nuclear family in which the mother was a homemaker and the father worked in the labor force. This "feminine mystique" asserted that women would find fulfillment as wives and mothers. In reality, thousands of women were entering the labor force in a trend that would continue throughout the second half of the century (Epstein, 1988).

Whether they worked outside the home because they wanted to or because necessity forced them to do so, women in the labor force encountered problems of gender segregation and discrimination. In a survey of 150,000 working women conducted during the mid-1980s by the National Commission on Working Women, the most frequently cited problems were low wages, differentials in fringe benefits, dead-end jobs with little opportunity for training or advancement, sexual harassment on the job, lack of child care or difficulty obtaining it, stress over multiple roles, and lack of leisure time (Richmond-Abbott, 1992).

An enduring problem for women in the labor force is segregation into what are known as "pink-collar ghettos." Secretarial and clerical work especially remain heavily gender segregated, but child care, nursing, and dental assistants also remain largely female occupations despite some increases in the proportions of males in these fields in recent decades. Largely as a result of antidiscrimination laws and women's efforts to break into occupations that previously were more or less closed to them, women have made considerable gains in some areas. Occupations like bus driver, psychologist, and others show significant gains in female employment, but clerical occupations remain a

THE PERSONAL CHALLENGE
Social Change and the Workplace

Are you prepared to deal with changing gender relations in the workplace? Here is a diagnostic quiz:

Question: A boss has been interviewing potential assistants and has narrowed the field to three candidates, all of whom have fine educations, excellent computer skills (a must in his business), and glowing recommendations from previous bosses. Which candidate does he choose?

Answer: The one with the biggest t--s.

This joke has made the rounds in the personnel departments of U.S. companies for a number of years. It is an ironic commentary on prevailing practices in many businesses. Jokes like this one are merely one aspect of efforts to confront sexual harassment and abuse of power in the workplace. The resignation of Senator Robert Packwood of Oregon after multiple charges of sexual harassment and the resignation, also after charges of sexual harassment, of one of the highest executives in the W. R. Grace Corporation—to mention only two recent and well-publicized cases—are having a significant effect on the economic and political institutions of American society.

Many men are confused and angered by accusations of sexual harassment for behavior that they consider normal flirtation. These feelings have produced a tangible backlash against the goals of gender equality in some regions of the country and in some industries, such as construction. But it is clear that norms concerning gender relations at work are changing. Behavior that once could be passed off as innocent flirtation can easily be viewed as sexual harassment. What are the implications of these normative changes for individuals entering the world of work?

What women at work are demanding is that they be treated as people whose abilities are measured by their contribution to the common effort rather than by aspects of their sex. This means that references to their physical attributes are out of place and unwelcome. So are suggestive comments, hints,

winks, or more aggressive advances. It also means that both men and women need to be more sensitive to the nuances of language. If women at work choose to refer to each other as "the girls," that is their choice—but if men, especially men in superior positions, do so, the term can be taken to emphasize differences in status. Men need to avoid referring to women as girls unless they are quite certain of the situation. In some parts of the country the terms *girls* and *boys* are used more casually in referring to women and men—but in the world of work, where companies do business in different regions and the ability to get along with others is a key to success, sensitivity to these issues takes on greater importance.

For their part, women need to be firm about where they stand on these matters. When they shrug off suggestive comments without making a diplomatic but firm response, they may be sending a tacit message of approval. In cases of clear harassment the behavior needs to be challenged or it is likely to worsen. In addition, women need to avoid making sexually suggestive comments about men.

Doesn't this hamper the normal easy banter among men and women? It may, but it may also place it on a more equal footing of affection and respect. You may feel that this is just another form of "politically correct" behavior being imposed by disgruntled political activists—that depends on your political views and personal experiences. From a sociological viewpoint, however, the issue is that norms are changing, and the changes will require changes in individual behavior. Those who deny the changes—in particular, men who continue to use their power in organizations for sexual advantage—will face increasingly negative sanctions, as many are learning to their shame. The easy exchange between men and women at work can continue; personal relations, including romantic ones that extend beyond work, can continue; but they need to be based on mutual consent, not on the exploitation of power and position (Henriques, 1995).

pink-collar ghetto: Clerical work employs one in five working women, a figure that has not changed since the 1950s (Roberts, 1995). (See Table 14.5.)

Even when women successfully enter a formerly male-dominated field, their wages are often lower even though they do the same work and have the same length of service. Among psychologists, for example, the median income for men was $31,000 in 1990 while that of women was $22,000. For psychologists under age 35 the men's median was $19,000 while that of women was $17,000. According to sociologists and activists in the movement for pay equity, these differences reflect a more general trend: As women hold an increasing proportion of the jobs in an occupation, its average pay decreases, as does its status. This is particularly true of fields in which the proportion of minority women is increasing (Wright & Jacobs, 1994).

Throughout the world new occupations are emerging in professional and technical fields, and as women achieve greater educational parity with men the comparative statistics show that they are sharing these positions quite equally with men. Figure 14.5 shows that this is the case in Latin America, the Caribbean, and the economically developed regions of the world, but that in much of Asia and Africa, where women still lag in education, there are wide disparities.

In administrative and managerial positions the situation is far less favorable for women. Competition for these desirable positions is much more intense and is often based not only on education but on access to social networks and political power. Since women are far less likely than men to have such access, their entry into the managerial ranks is stymied. An exception is found in the island nations of the Caribbean, where women have had access to education and training in business schools longer than in many other regions. Caribbean women often accumulate money and power through their own business activities, which enable them to become owners, managers, and administrators at a greater rate than is true in the more affluent regions of the world.

THE SECOND SHIFT

Sociologist Arlie Hochschild (1989) coined the term *the second shift* to describe the extra time working women spend doing household chores after working at a job outside the home. This term emphasizes the expectation that women who work will also perform the bulk of domestic and child care work. This is an example of the persistence of **patriarchy,** the dominance of men over women. Although women often attempt to influence their male partners to share household chores that were formerly considered "women's work," the men continue to resist despite slow changes—especially in two-career families in which both partners are highly educated. These topics are discussed further in Chapter 16.

TABLE 14.5	Proportion of Jobs in Certain Occupations Filled by Women, 1970–1990	
OCCUPATION	1970	1990
Bartender	27%	57%
Chemist	17	29
Doctor	11	22
Economist	14	44
Farmer	7	17
Industrial engineer	3	27
Lawyer, judge	6	27
Librarian	84	85
Nurse	91	94
Police detective	5	13
Psychologist	43	59
Public official	24	59
Secretary	98	98
Teacher	74	74

Source: Program for Applied Research, Queens College.

Some sociologists have proposed that as women gained greater parity with men in occupations, the disparities between men and women's roles would begin to diminish and gender roles in the household would become more symmetrical (Bernard, 1982; Willmott & Young, 1971). But as Hochschild (1989) and others report, this remains a speculative hypothesis despite the exceptions one might cite here and there. On the average, data on time budgets show that working women in the United States have at least 10 hours a week less leisure time than their husbands or partners because they shoulder far more of the domestic responsibilities. The same disparities do not exist in all industrial nations. France and Holland, for example, incorporate gender equality into national social policies. These nations provide excellent universal child care, family leave, and longer vacations than do lagging nations like the United States, and these policies ease the burdens of dual-earner families in coping with the demands of work and family life (Kammerman & Kahn, 1981).

In the developing areas of the world, many of the conditions that women face are similar to those in the industrial nations. This is particularly true in the urban centers of Asia, Africa, and Latin America. As sociologist Carol Chenault learned in observing the Maasai people, however, women in the Third World face many other issues and situations, including illiteracy, lack of power in the face of strong traditions of patriarchy, and severe threats to their reproductive health. These issues constitute an important frontier of sociological research on gender and inequality.

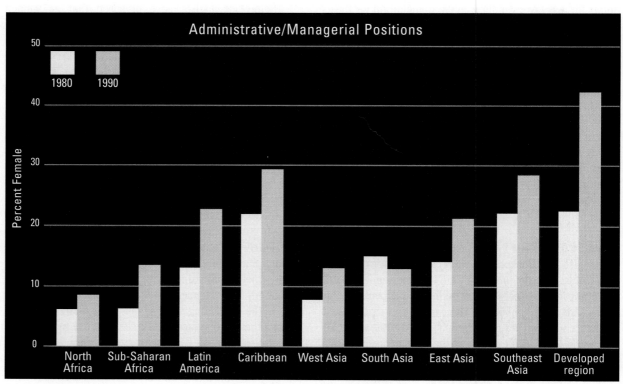

FIGURE 14.5 | **Improvement in Women's Share in Selected Occupations**

Source: Sadik, 1995.

RESEARCH FRONTIERS: WOMEN IN THE DEVELOPING WORLD

Social scientists estimate that more than 80 million women in various parts of the world have undergone what is known as female circumcision. At most world population and development conferences this is a subject of hot debate along with contraception and other reproductive issues. So although there are many gender issues on the frontier of sociological research, the controversy over female genital mutilation is highly instructive, for it highlights the problems of patriarchy, illiteracy, powerlessness, and threats to their health faced by so many Third World women, whether they are exposed to this practice or not.

Female genital mutilation is common in about 40 nations, especially in East and West Africa and on the Arabian peninsula—but worldwide migrations have brought the practice to Europe and North America as well. Public health officials and critics note that female circumcision differs dramatically from male circumcision, which entails removal of skin only. Female circumcision, they argue, is actually the removal of all or part of a female genital organ, the clitoris, and as such constitutes mutilation. In cultures where it is practiced, it is justified by the patriarchal argument that it diminishes sexual desire and therefore "protects" the woman from temptation and infidelity. Among the Maasai, for example, a woman who is not circumcised is considered unmarriageable. But the operation is performed with crude instruments and usually without anesthesia or antibiotics. It can result in death from infection, shock, and psychological trauma (Fathalla, 1992).

The International Conference on Population and Development, held in Cairo in 1994, was the first such gathering to debate the practice and to call for its eradication on the ground that it violates basic human rights and constitutes a lifelong risk to women's health. A number of African nations, including Ghana and Ivory Coast, have passed laws forbidding the practice, and many others are debating such measures at this writing. But as the proceedings of the Cairo conference note, traditions are deeply rooted. To eradicate female circumcision, more national and community education programs need to be created (Sadik, 1995).

Recommendations to ban a deeply rooted cultural practice like this one stimulate much debate at international gatherings of social scientists and policy makers. Some participants take an extremely relativistic position, insisting that the practices of a culture must be understood from that culture's point of view and should not be subject to Western assumptions and values. But a far larger number of voices are raised in criticism of the Western legalistic approach, which calls for prohibitions and bans. According to this line of thought, while prohibitions based

Today much research and policy making in developing nations emphasizes the problems of women and girls, who until recently were often neglected in favor of large-scale infrastructure projects such as dams, irrigation, and road-building.

on theories of human rights are desirable, they will have little effect unless they are accompanied by social action, especially action that promotes social and economic development (Murti, Guio, & Dreze, 1995). In this regard, as we have noted, female genital mutilation is only one of many severe threats to women's equality and human rights. Reproductive diseases, death during childbirth, AIDS, and other sexually transmitted diseases claim the lives of millions of women each year. They are indicators of the low status and condition of women in poor regions of the world, and their cost to their societies and the world is immense. So rather than merely attacking the symptoms of women's underdevelopment, world gatherings like the Cairo conference are working to reach a consensus around action programs based on the concept of women's empowerment.

The conference proceedings stated that "power to make decisions within the family is the basis for the power of decision in other areas. Empowerment begins with winning equality, autonomy and respect for women within the household" (Sadik, 1995, p. 19). The powerlessness of women in the Third World is rooted in failure to value women for anything other than their reproductive role. The empowerment approach insists that "social and economic development cannot be secured in a sustainable way without the full participation of women" (United Nations, 1995a, p. 1). Figures 14.6, 14.7, and 14.8 present data on literacy, use of contraceptives, and women's share of political representation. These were all used at the Cairo conference in discussions of women's empowerment and development. The participants agreed overwhelmingly that in the poor and underdeveloped regions of the world there must be more investment in basic education and literacy for women so that they can participate in decisions in the family and in the larger community. With more education would come greater control over reproductive behavior and improved reproductive health. And eventually, with more education and local empowerment would come increased participation in national political institutions.

FIGURE 14.6   **Growth in Female Literacy Levels**

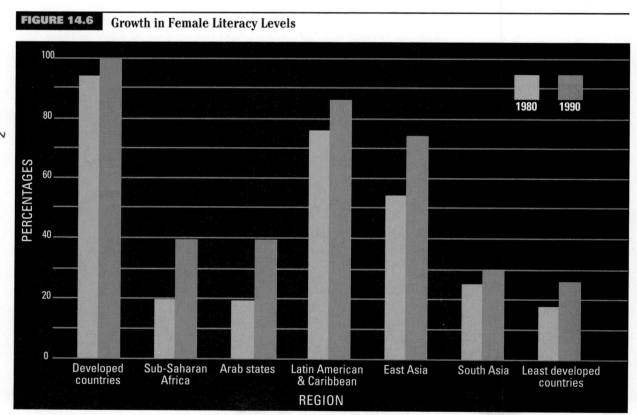

Source: Sadik, 1995.

FIGURE 14.7   Average Percentage of Couples Using Contraception

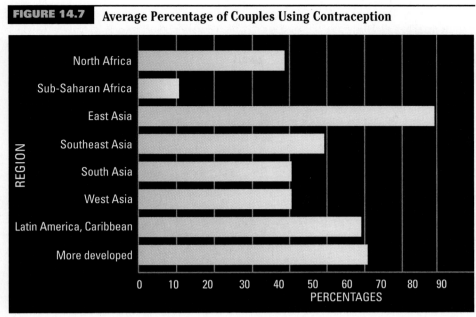

Source: Sadik, 1995.

FIGURE 14.8   Women's Share of National Legislatures in Selected Countries

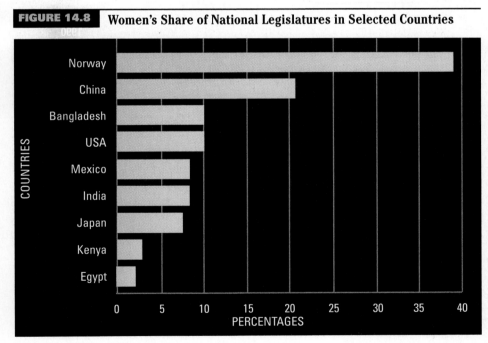

Source: United Nations, 1995.

GENDER ROLES AMONG THE MAASAI

When sociologist Carol Chenault and her photographer husband, Ellis, spent time with the Maasai people in 1995, they sometimes felt as if they had wandered back in time to the biblical era. For, as Carol Chenault explains, the Maasai are true pastoralists:

> The people are Nilotic, migrating from the Nile regions of North Africa into the Great Rift Valley of Kenya and Tanzania. Myth has it that they lived in a deep crater where life was plagued with drought, famine, and discouragement. The only ray of hope for them was to follow the birds that kept bringing green grass and twigs. Scouts went up and over the steep escarpment and found green, fertile valleys with rivers and streams, and this is where they made their home. The language they speak is Maa; hence the term *Maasai,* meaning Maa-speaking people. The only transmission of the language is through the spoken word; their language is not written.

As we saw at the beginning of the chapter, gender role distinctions are very marked among the Maasai. But unlike Western industrial societies (where women are expected to spend more time on personal adornment), among the Maasai attention to beauty is a preoccupation of both males and females.

> Even the smallest of children are dressed with necklaces and anklets. Ear piercing is done during childhood, well before circumcision. A slit is cut in the earlobe and a green stick is placed in it. Over time this is replaced with successively larger [sticks] until the opening is large enough to be decorated with an earring and leather-beaded strands.

Chenault notes that despite their relative lack of acculturation to Western ways, she saw a Maasai man wearing a 35mm plastic film canister as an ear adornment, a vivid reminder of the spread of Western culture.

The Maasai were extremely open and willing to share their culture with the visiting sociologist. "They are a proud people," Chenault concludes, "committed to passing their culture on to their future generations. I think this is the quality that I admire most about them."

440

These photos provide some clues about social status and gender roles among the Maasai. The elderly woman with close-cropped hair wears a limited number of personal adornments. Like most elderly women in traditional societies, she seems to feel no need to impress the viewer with her physical appearance. Not so for the woman with the elaborate headpiece and gorgeous array of necklaces. She is dressed in the fashion of the Maasai warrior herdsmen, but only the women wear these headpieces. In another photo the same woman, the wife of a prominent warrior, is shown with her children. The Maasai women bear children almost as long as they are physically capable of doing so.

The man with a shawl over his shoulders looking quizzically into the camera was one of a group who conducted their own "interview" with the sociologists. They thought it was terrible that the American sociologist was no longer having babies. The women also asked whether the American women were circumcised. "When we told them we were not, they clapped their hands down at their sides, indicating their disapproval."

The Maasai man playing the flute also makes sandals out of old tires. These are called "thousand milers" because the Maasai walk endlessly and need tough, cheap footwear. Making musical instruments and footgear are examples of tasks that are specifically "men's work" among the Maasai. The man wearing the distinctive headdress and smiling at the sociologist is a professional guide. He has a high school education and moves easily between Westerners and Maasai. With one foot in the traditional world and another in the tourist industry, his role allows the Maasai people to remain culturally distinct while benefiting from their contact with interested visitors.

SUMMARY

THINK ABOUT IT CRITICALLY

Here is a stanza from a poem, "The Princess," by the English poet Alfred, Lord Tennyson:

> *Men for the field and women for the hearth,*
> *Man for the sword and for the needle she,*
> *Man with the head and women with the heart,*
> *Man to command and woman to obey,*
> *All else confusion.*

What reactions do you have to this poem on the basis of your reading of this chapter?

Sex refers to the biological differences between males and females, including the primary sex characteristics that are present at birth and the secondary sex characteristics that develop later. Some people are born as *hermaphrodites;* their primary sexual organs have features of both male and female organs, making it difficult to categorize the person as male or female. Another ambiguous sexual category consists of *transsexuals,* who feel very strongly that the sexual organs they were born with do not conform to their deep-seated sense of what their sex should be.

Gender refers to the culturally defined ways of acting as a male or a female that become part of an individual's personal sense of self. Gender socialization in the family and in schools tends to separate males and females into different social worlds with their own forms of activity and language. However, boys and girls are increasingly participating in the same types of activities in their schools and communities, and many teachers, parents, and administrators seek to avoid the worst effects of gender separation.

Sexuality refers to the manner in which a person engages in the intimate behaviors connected with genital stimulation, orgasm, and procreation. It is profoundly influenced by cultural norms and social institutions like the family and the school, as well as by social structures like the class system of a society. Universal cultural norms exerting social control over sexuality include the incest taboo, marriage, and heterosexuality, but even these norms include variations and differing degrees of sanction.

Heterosexuality refers to sexual orientation toward the opposite sex, in contrast to *homosexuality,* or sexual orientation toward the same sex, and *bisexuality,* or sexual orientation toward either sex. Norms of heterosexuality function to ensure that there is genital sexual intercourse between men and women in the interest of population replacement and growth. Fear of homosexuals and same-sex attraction is known as homophobia.

All human societies are stratified by gender, meaning that males and females are channeled into specific

statuses and roles. Until quite recently it was assumed that there were two separate spheres of life for men and women. Out of this gender-based division of labor grew the notion of differences in men's and women's abilities and personalities. These differences were thought to be based on biological and psychological differences between males and females. In the twentieth century, however, evidence from the social sciences has established that *gender roles* are not innate but are strongly influenced by culture.

Preindustrial societies are usually rigidly sex-segregated. As societies increase in size and complexity, women usually become subordinated to men. The origins of gender inequality in most modern societies can be traced to their feudal periods. In Europe, for example, the norms of courtly love specified that women do not engage in warfare or politics or compete with men in any sphere of life beyond those reserved for women.

In modern industrial societies boys and girls are socialized into "masculine" and "feminine" roles. In their adult years men enjoy more wealth, prestige, and leisure than women do. Gender stratification in modern societies is reflected in attitudes that reinforce the subordinate status of women. *Sexism* refers to an ideology that justifies prejudice or discrimination based on sex.

The modern women's movement arose in the mid-1960s out of an already existing network of women's organizations, together with a less-formal network of women in consciousness-raising groups. The movement won significant victories during the 1960s and 1970s and began to change the way men and women think about gender roles.

The most frequently cited problems of women in the workplace are low wages, differentials in fringe benefits, dead-end jobs, sexual harassment, lack of child care, stress over multiple roles, and lack of leisure time. Another problem is the segregation of women into the pink-collar ghettos of secretarial and clerical work. Women who work outside the home are also expected to perform the bulk of domestic and child care work. This "second shift" is an example of the persistence of *patriarchy,* the dominance of men over women.

CRITICAL RESPONSE

The Tennyson poem expresses one version of a traditional, male-dominated view of gender norms in Western societies. Yet in many traditional societies women do heavy work in the fields as well as tend the hearth, so this is not an especially accurate view of traditional gender roles. From a contemporary perspective, we can agree that changing gender roles leads to some confusion and conflict, but is this an adequate reason to insist on an older set of gender norms that produced stark inequalities between men and women? In fact, this chapter shows that social changes during this and previous centuries have made it increasingly difficult to support the traditional gender roles described in the poem.

GLOSSARY

sex   the biological differences between males and females, including the primary sex characteristics that are present at birth (i.e., the presence of specific male or female genitalia) and the secondary sex characteristics that develop later (facial and body hair, voice quality, etc.). (p. 417)

hermaphrodite: a person whose primary sexual organs have features of both male and female organs, making it difficult to categorize the individual as male or female. (p. 417)

transsexuals: people who feel very strongly that the sexual organs they were born with do not conform to their deep-seated sense of what their sex should be. (p. 417)

gender: the culturally defined ways of acting as a male or a female that become part of an individual's personal sense of self. (p. 417)

sexuality: the manner in which a person engages in the intimate behaviors connected with genital stimulation, orgasm, and procreation. (p. 419)

heterosexuality: sexual orientation toward the opposite sex. (p. 419)

homosexuality: sexual orientation toward the same sex. (p. 419)

bisexuality: sexual orientation toward either sex. (p. 419)

gender role: a set of behaviors considered appropriate for an individual of a particular gender. (p. 423)

sexism: an ideology that justifies prejudice and discrimination based on sex. (p. 430)

patriarchy: the dominance of men over women. (p. 435)

WHERE TO FIND IT

BOOKS
Manhood in America: A Cultural History (Michael S. Kimmel; Free Press, 1996). A sociological analysis of changing norms of masculinity and ideas of manhood in North America.

Women and Children First: Environment, Poverty, and Sustainable Development (Filomena Cioma Steady; Schenkman Books, 1993). A recent review of international issues of gender, inequality, and development.

Women in Law, 2nd ed. (Cynthia Fuchs Epstein; University of Illinois Press, 1993). A fine empirical study of the structural and cultural barriers women face in the legal profession.

Science and Gender: A Critique of Biology and Its Theories on Women (Ruth Bleier; Pergamon, 1984). A critical review of the controversial literature on gender and biology.

Gender Advertisements (Erving Goffman; Harvard University Press, 1979). A subtle treatment of the

symbolism of gender and its use in everyday life, with excellent examples of visual material used as sociological data.

Gender, Family, and Economy: The Triple Overlap (Rae Lesser Blumberg, ed.; Sage Publications, 1991). A collection of original essays based on recent research on gender stratification. Includes some excellent material on sharing, and lack of sharing, of household chores among heterosexual couples, and valuable historical material on the stratification of minority women in the United States and elsewhere.

JOURNALS
Signs. A quarterly journal published by the University of Chicago Press that presents new research and theory in gender studies and feminist social science.

Gender & Society. The official publication of Sociologists for Women in Society.

CHAPTER 15

Inequalities of Youth and Age

Heard in the halls of Bronx Community College: "Check it out, Karen. This paycheck has $45 taken out for Social Security. I won't see that money until I'm like 60. What am I gonna want to do then? Who needs the money then?"

Later that week the TV news shows featured a French woman sipping a glass of red wine. She was celebrating her 121st birthday. She laughed and joked with the reporters and photographers gathered in recognition of the fact that she had become the oldest documented person on earth.

The modest French widow made the celebrated comedian George Burns seem like a mere kid. In 1996 Burns was only 100. But despite his growing frailty, the venerable Burns could take satisfaction from knowing that he was perhaps the most famous and beloved centenarian in the United States. In a nation where faces are most likely to be recognized when young and beautiful, Burns was a trendsetter. Meanwhile, the Delany sisters' autobiography, *Having Our Say*, celebrated almost a century of African American sisterhood. Shortly after their story became a hit show on Broadway, the younger of the two authors, who wrote their first and only book in their nineties, passed away at the age of 96.

These and many other examples point to a master trend of our time: People in affluent industrial nations are living longer. They can be productive far longer than people in previous epochs of human history could have imagined. A young adult like the student quoted earlier may think that a 65-year-old man or woman is too old to enjoy life. But in fact age 65 may be just the beginning of a highly productive stage of life.

FIGURE 15.1 Population Pyramids for Three Advanced Industrial Nations

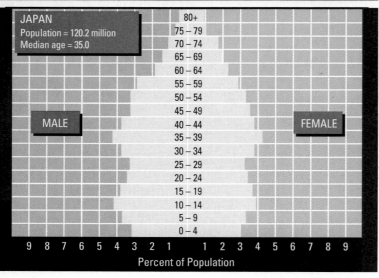

Source: Data from United Nations, 1992.

SOURCES OF AGE STRATIFICATION

In many societies age determines a great deal about the opportunities open to a person and what kind of life that person leads. Only a little over half a century ago, for example, becoming old in the United States almost automatically meant becoming poor. Today children are the most impoverished and vulnerable population group in many nations, including the United States. This chapter examines how age stratification—the roles assigned to young people, adults, and the elderly—contributes to inequality. From a discussion of the life course and age structure of societies, the chapter proceeds to a closer examination of the situation of young people. The remainder of the chapter is devoted to the growing sociological subfield known as **gerontology,** the study of aging and the elderly in this and other societies.

THE LIFE COURSE—SOCIETY'S AGE STRUCTURE

All societies divide the human life span into "seasons of life" (Hagestad & Neugarten, 1985; Zerubavel, 1986). This is done through cultural norms that define periods of life, such as adulthood and old age, and channel people into **age grades**—sets of statuses and roles based on age. These systems of age grades "create predictable, socially recognized turning points that provide roadmaps for human lives" (Hagestad & Neugarten, 1985, p. 35). Graduations, communions, weddings, retirements, and funerals are among the ceremonies that are used to mark these turning points.

Age strata are rough divisions of people into layers according to age-related social roles. We speak of infants, preschoolers, primary-school children, teenagers, young adults, and so on; these categories form a series of younger-to-older layers, or strata, in the population. People in different age strata command different amounts of scarce resources like wealth, power, and prestige (Riley, Foner, & Waring, 1988). Numerous laws establish inequalities between youth and adults; they include laws governing the rights to vote, to purchase alcoholic beverages, to incur debt, and the like. In theory, a person who lacks the rights of adult citizenship will be protected by adults, who are responsible for providing him or her with adequate food, shelter, and education (and are presumed to have the resources to do so). In practice, however, hundreds of thousands of children and teenagers do not receive the care that is intended to offset their unequal status under the law.

Social scientists often refer to the **life course,** which may be defined as a "pathway along an age-differentiated, socially created sequence of transitions" (Hagestad & Neugarten, 1985, p. 36; see also Cain, 1964; Clausen, 1968; Elder, 1981). The cultural norms that specify the life course and its important transitions create what is thought of as "the normal predictable life cycle" (Neugarten, 1969, p. 121). We expect that we will go to school, find a job, get married, have children, and so on at certain times in our lives, and we consider it somewhat abnormal not to follow this pattern. Social scientists often refer to ceremonies that mark the transition from one phase of life to another as **rites of passage** (Van Gennep, 1960/1908). The confirmation, the bar mitzvah, the graduation, and the retirement party are examples of rites of passage in modern societies.

In the United States and other Western cultures, the life course is constructed from categories like childhood, adolescence, young adulthood, adulthood, mature adulthood, and old age. But our definitions of these categories lack the stability and uniformity of the age grades found in many traditional societies. For example, the French historian Philippe Ariès (1962) showed that in Western civilization the concept of childhood as a phase of life with distinct characteristics and needs did not develop until the late seventeenth century. Before that time children were treated as small adults. They were expected to perform chores and to conform to adult norms to the extent possible. When they reached puberty they were usually married, often to spouses to whom they had been promised in infancy.

Norms regarding gender are closely linked to the life course established by a society. Thus Ariès's study of the emergence of childhood revealed that ideas about the appropriate forms of play and education for boys, and indeed the very concept of boyhood, developed at least a century before the concept of girlhood emerged. In eighteenth-century European societies boyhood was conceived of as a time when male children could play among themselves and receive education in the skills they would need as adults. Girls, in contrast, were treated as miniature women who were expected to work alongside their mothers and sisters.

COHORTS AND AGE STRUCTURES

When we think about age, we tend to think in terms of **age cohorts,** or people of about the same age who are passing through the life course together (Bogue, 1969). We measure our own successes and failures against the standards and experiences of our own cohorts—our schoolmates, our workmates, our senior circle—as we pass through life.

Demographers use the cohort concept in studying how populations change. If we divide populations into 5-year cohorts, grouped vertically from age 0 to 100+ and divided into male and female, we can form a *population pyramid,* a useful way of looking at the influence of age on a society. Figure 15.1 shows population pyramids for three advanced industrial nations; Figure 15.2 presents population pyramids for three Third World nations. Note that high birthrates expand the base of the typical Third World pyramid and that high rates of infant mortality cause the base to decrease rather dramatically within the first 10 or 15 years. High mortality rates in later cohorts bring the pyramid to a sharp point. In the advanced nations, by contrast,

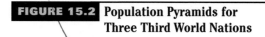

FIGURE 15.2 Population Pyramids for Three Third World Nations

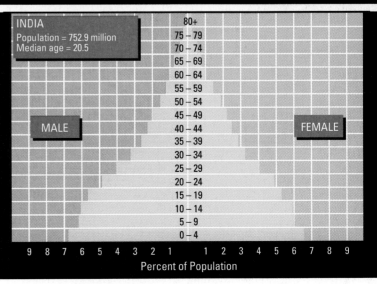

Source: Data from United Nations, 1992.

FIGURE 15.3 **Impact of the Baby Boom on the U.S. Population, 1950–2020**

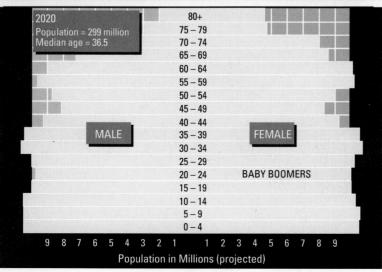

Sources: Data from Census Bureau, 1985, and United Nations, 1992.

the birthrate is far lower and much more constant. There are bulges in the pyramid for particular cohorts, but for the most part the cohorts pass in regular fashion through the stages of life.

The Baby Boom. When a population experiences marked fluctuations in fertility, there are bulges in its population pyramid that have important effects. Perhaps nowhere in the world has this phenomenon been better studied than in the United States. The "baby boom" cohorts, which were produced by rapid increases in the birthrate from about 1945 through the early 1960s, have profoundly influenced American society and will continue to do so for the next three decades.

Throughout Europe and North America the baby boom generations did not have nearly as many children as their parents had. A mean family size of 2.1 children per couple is required for a population to remain constant over time (rapid growth requires a mean number of children closer to 3.0 per family). But since the 1970s the mean number of children per family in industrial societies has been about 1.85 (and much lower in nations like Japan and Germany); as a result, the baby boom has been followed by a relative shortage of children known as the "baby bust" (Keyfitz, 1986). One way to visualize the impact of the baby boom and baby bust is to compare the population pyramids in Figure 15.3.

As these cohorts mature, they make new demands on the society's institutions. During the 1960s and 1970s, for example, when the baby boom cohorts passed through their college years, the nation's universities and colleges expanded; the slogan of the day was "Never trust anyone over 30." Now the baby boom cohorts are moving into the dominant age groups of the population. Bill and Hillary Clinton, Tipper and Al Gore, and many of Clinton's appointees are in these cohorts. Their succession to national leadership in 1992 represents a transfer of power from the generation of George Bush, the generation that fought in World War II and is now in its late sixties and early seventies, to the generation that experienced the Vietnam War and the social movements of the 1960s.

The Baby Boom Echo. Sometimes referred to as the "baby boomlet" or the "baby boom echo," the children of parents who were part of the original baby boom are themselves an important demographic phenomenon. Note in Figure 15.4 that in the late 1980s the number of births exceeded 4 million per year, a threshold reached over a longer period during the original baby boom, which extended from the 1940s to the 1960s. Like any "bulge" in a society's age structure, the wave of children born during the 1980s and early 1990s promises to have significant effects on social institutions like schools and businesses.

Figure 15.5 shows that a sizable proportion of the "second wave" or "boomlet" children are members of minority groups. This trend, combined with high rates of immigration, will increase the proportion of minority children

FIGURE 15.4 Number of Births Each Year:
United States, 1920–1993
(in millions)

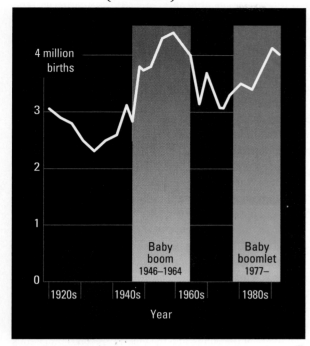

Source: Data from Census Bureau.

FIGURE 15.5 Racial and Ethnic Composition of
the Baby Boom and Boomlet
Generations

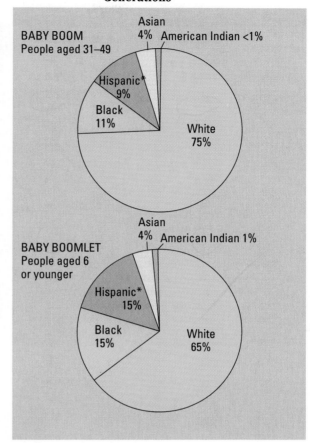

Note: Because of rounding, figures do not add to 100%.

*Hispanic people can be of any race.

Source: Data from Census Bureau.

moving through the nation's schools and colleges in coming decades. Between 1988 and 1993, for example, kindergarten enrollments rose by 7.2 percent and preschool enrollments by 14 percent, both trends that presage increasing enrollments in many school districts. This demographic effect, in turn, increases debate over the investment of public funds in schools versus other uses, such as medical care for the poor and elderly (Gabriel, 1995a).

A Graying Population.   As the parents of these children, the baby boom cohorts, move into middle age, the problems of their own parents, the aged, also take on increasing importance. Table 15.1 shows that the proportion of elderly people in the American population is increasing steadily. This increase—often referred to as the "graying" of America—will result in greater concern about the needs of the elderly and will augment the influence of the aged on American culture and social institutions.

Demographers and biologists disagree over estimates of how many very elderly people there will be in the U. S. population during the next century. Most Census Bureau demographers estimate that the population over age 85 will increase from about 3.3 million persons (mainly women) in 1990 to about 18.7 million in the year 2080. But demographers working with the U. S. Institute of Aging argue that there may be no biological limits on life expectancy. With advances in medicine and better prevention of disease, more people may live into their nineties. If that happens

there could be as many as 70 million people over age 85 in the U. S. population late in the next century, a change that would have enormous effects on all aspects of social life (Kolata, 1992).

LIFE EXPECTANCY

At age 65 and beyond, more than 50 percent of North American women are widowed, whereas only 13.6 percent of men have lost their wives. This is because the life expectancy of females is at least 7 years longer than that of males. (By **life expectancy** we mean the average number of years a member of a given population can expect to live beyond his or her present age.) Typically, men die before their wives do. And they tend to marry younger women, making widows the single largest category in the elderly population.

In the future, if male and female roles become more similar and women experience the stresses and risks that are thought to cause earlier death in men, the gap between

TABLE 15.1	Projected Proportions of Population in Various Age Categories: United States, 1980–2080		

PERCENT OF POPULATION BY AGE*

YEAR	UNDER 18 YEARS	18–64 YEARS	65+ YEARS
1980	28.0%	60.7%	11.3%
1985	26.3	61.7	12.0
1990	25.8	61.5	12.7
1995	25.9	61.1	13.1
2000	25.1	61.8	13.0
2010	22.9	63.3	13.8
2020	22.3	60.4	17.3
2030	21.6	57.2	21.2
2050	21.0	57.3	21.8
2080	20.3	56.2	23.5

*Totals may not add to 100% because of rounding.

Source: Reprinted with permission of The Free Press, a Division of Macmillan, Inc., from *The Population of the United States: Historical Trends and Projections,* by Donald J. Bogue. Copyright © 1985 by The Free Press.

the life expectancies of the sexes may narrow. Research on sex differences in the causes of death indicates that women may be less vulnerable to death for genetic reasons, but it is extremely difficult to prove this scientifically. The research of Lois M. Verbrugge (1985) on health trends among males and females indicates that the lifestyles of men and women in the United States have become similar; in particular, women's lives are more like men's. This change has unfortunate implications for women's health and longevity. For example, women are now smoking almost as much as men. Smoking among men declined from 50.2 percent in 1965 to 28.7 percent in 1990, but the rate for women decreased only slightly, from 31.9 percent to 25.5 percent (*Statistical Abstract,* 1992). Among older smokers, men were twice as likely to quit as women. It is no surprise that lung cancer now almost equals breast cancer as a leading cause of death for women.

Age and Dependency. The college student quoted at the beginning of the chapter may have sounded somewhat naive about the potential of elderly people, but he was voicing a common complaint. People in the working adult cohorts—that is, those between the ages of 18 and 64 (although many continue to work well after age 64 and may start before age 18)—contribute disproportionately to the well-being of the young and the elderly. Of course, societies

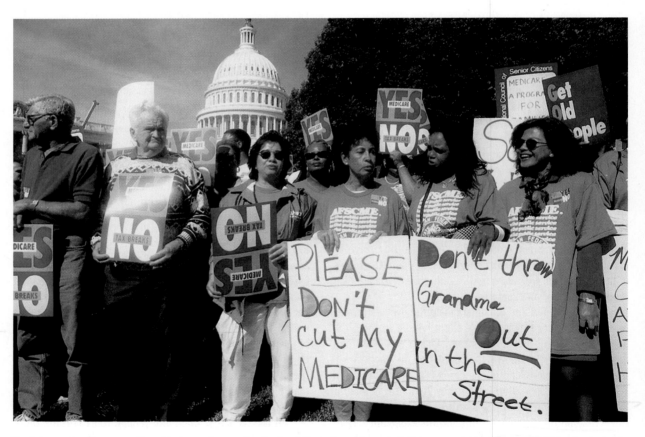

Social movements among the elderly are increasing in strength as the older population grows in numbers. Older Americans have taken a very active interest in recent efforts to reform the nation's health care system.

THEN AND NOW

THE DREAM OF SOCIAL SECURITY

Before the passage of the Social Security Act in 1935, the average working-class individual or couple could expect to live in a state of poverty or near-poverty in old age. Elderly people often were highly dependent on their adult children, who themselves had to struggle to make ends meet. The emergence of pensions and legislation to protect workers' pension rights, along with the passage of federal Social Security legislation, made life easier for millions of elderly women and men. It also opened up possibilities for independent living in senior citizen communities in the sunbelt regions of the United States.

The image of elderly Americans socializing in a hot tub is a reminder of how the migration of retired people to the South and West has dramatically changed the social landscape, especially in states like Florida, Arizona, and California. The decision to leave communities where they have raised their families is only one of the many choices that elderly people may make during this important stage in their lives. Throughout the life course, people may choose among an increasing diversity of lifestyles.

justify this pattern of dependency by recognizing that adults are merely doing in their turn what was done for them as children or will be done for them when they are among the frail elderly. Institutions of modern societies, such as public education and Social Security, ensure that a share of wealth passes to the dependent cohorts.

When there are very large numbers of children in a society, as is the case in the developing nations, or increasing numbers of elderly people, as is the case in the older nations of Western Europe and North America, working adults may shoulder an increased burden. Table 15.1 shows, for example, that children being born now will be adults in the early decades of the next century. If population projections are accurate, working adults will constitute a decreasing proportion of the total population and larger proportions of young people and the elderly will be dependent on their productivity. Will this burden be too great? It may, but on the other hand improvements in productivity and changes in social policy, such as improved health care policies, may actually ease the burden compared with that of contemporary adults. (See Box 15.1.)

AGE STRATIFICATION AND INEQUALITY

In urban industrial societies there are distinct patterns of stratification in which age defines the roles one plays and the rewards one can expect. We speak of the "age of majority"—the age at which a person crosses the legal boundary between childhood and adulthood. In fact, this age is not always clearly defined. A person can vote at age 18 but cannot legally consume alcohol until age 21. In addition to the age of majority, there are other distinct ages that mark the passage toward the full rights of adulthood. At age 18 one can join the armed forces without parental permission. At age 16 in many states one is no longer obliged by law to attend school, even though parents still share responsibility for the behavior of the school dropout. Teenagers can drive at age 16 in many U. S. counties, but their parents remain responsible, through insurance systems, for their actions and can be held liable for the consequences. We also make clear distinctions between children in the primary grades and teenagers in high school, and in most homes a child's passage through these age grades is accompanied by various privileges and responsibilities. So although the passage to full adult status may be somewhat vague, it is clear that to be young is to be less equal.

Later in life, as people become elderly, they may yield some of their autonomy to their grown children—either willingly through trusts and wills, or unwillingly as they are committed to nursing homes because their care has become too great a burden for their children. Thus it is at the early and late extremes of youth and age that the relationship between age and inequalities of power and material resources are most evident.

There are also age-based inequalities that may affect the life chances of nonelderly adults. As corporations downsize—that is, lay off employees in order to increase profit margins—higher-paid people in their fifties may find that their jobs are combined with other work and offered to younger, less well-paid replacements. Mature adult status and years of accumulated seniority in the corporation may be of no avail. Once on the job market, these former employees—still in their productive adult years and well below the normal age of retirement—may find that they are less likely to be hired than younger workers; often they must reduce their expectations and experience downward mobility (Newman, 1988).

As these examples show, age influences life chances in important ways and can help produce the patterns of inequality we often take for granted, especially among the young and the old. But from a comparative perspective these effects of age stratification are not as strong as they are in smaller-scale, more traditional agrarian or pastoral societies. For example, among the Maasai, whom we met in the preceding chapter, there are fixed age grades for males and females that strictly define an individual's roles and opportunities throughout life. Children and adolescents have no individual status in Maasai society. It is not until their passage through circumcision and other rituals during puberty that they achieve status as autonomous individuals.

Initiation into adult status occurs for a group of Maasai of roughly similar age, who then constitute an age grade. There are four age grades in the Maasai system, each covering about 15 years and involving a mandatory set of activities, especially for males. Young initiates engage in military activity. Young elders are married adults with family and economic responsibilities. Elders have political decision-making power, and senior elders have religious ritual power. Each of these age grades has a name in the Maasai language, and passage into it is marked by rituals that convey differing degrees of authority and responsibility (Bernardi, 1985). Other smaller-scale societies throughout the world organize age grades according to their own cultural norms, but most, like the Maasai, invest the different age grades with distinct degrees of power and control over the society's wealth.

Throughout the world the forces of social change unleashed by colonialism, industrialization, urbanization, and population growth have tended to disrupt the formal age grade systems of smaller, more isolated societies. Often the loss of their ways of dealing with the passage from one age to another has been among the more disorienting aspects of social change for people in those societies. The passage into old age is a good example. In most small-scale tribal and peasant societies the elderly are revered as guardians of moral values, rituals, and religious beliefs. In urban in-

BOX 15.1 GLOBAL SOCIAL CHANGE

Effects of Changes in Life Expectancy

As life expectancy increases throughout the world, the number of aged people also increases, often with unanticipated consequences. In the developing nations, larger numbers of older people add to the burdens of dependency and population pressure. In more affluent nations, changes in life expectancy may be experienced quite differently by men and women.

The typical population pyramid for a developing nation has a sharply pointed apex. This means that relatively few men or women live to an advanced age. But as medical advances and improved sanitation result in greater life expectancy, there are more elderly people in rural villages and farming communities. At the same time, able-bodied younger men and women are attracted to the towns and cities. Increasing numbers of children and aged people are left in the countryside, where they are dependent on the labor of a dwindling number of rural workers. As a result of these changes, elderly people in rapidly industrializing nations often feel neglected. Where formerly they were revered for their knowledge of tradition and ritual, they are now frequently seen as a burden.

In affluent nations recent studies by sociologists and demographers have found that the fortunes of older people are affected as much by gender as by age. Women of advanced age, especially those over age 85, are three times more likely than older men to be living in poverty. "A major cause of impoverishment among older women is widowhood," notes Richard Suzman, director of demographic studies for the Institute on Aging (quoted in Barringer, 1992, p. A1). Although in the United States men live an average of 6.5 years less than women, men who live a decade or more beyond retirement age are far less likely than women of the same age to require financial and medical assistance. One of the main reasons for this difference is that elderly women are likely to have outlived their pension benefits or not to have had an adequate pension in the first place. Men who live into their eighties tend to have had less debilitating illnesses earlier in life and to have had higher than average earnings, so they enjoy relatively good pensions and retirement benefits. In addition, men tend to die suddenly from short-term fatal diseases; women are more likely to develop chronic, long-term illnesses, which can involve high medical costs.

Similar trends can be seen in the nations of Western Europe as the proportion of people over age 80 in their populations increases. The problems posed by large numbers of frail elderly people in those societies are largely accommodated by superior systems of social security and medical care. In the United States, more than 3 million people over age 85 were counted in the 1990 census, and

State Population Age 65 and Older

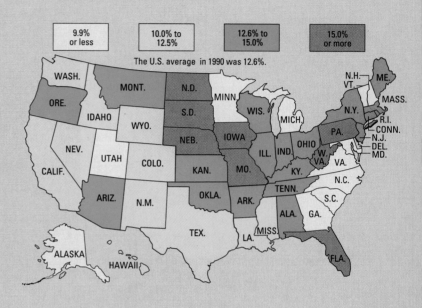

Source: Data from Census Bureau.

this figure is expected to increase by at least another million by the end of the century. It is likely that this increase will spur efforts to provide better systems for meeting the needs of the very elderly.

An additional problem is the uneven distribution of elderly persons in societies in which the proportion of older people is growing. In the United States large numbers of people live in specialized retirement communities. However, as the accompanying map shows, the farming states of the Midwest, especially the Dakotas, Iowa, Nebraska, and Missouri, have among the highest proportions of elderly persons—a pattern similar to that found in less developed, more agrarian nations. The map suggests what the census data also indicate: As increases in the proportion of elderly persons in the population occur, the effects will be experienced most heavily in regions where there have been high rates of rural–urban migration of younger people, leaving behind high proportions of dependent elderly persons of often limited means.

dustrial societies, in contrast, they are typically treated as dependents with little status and few rights. The situation of children is similar. In traditional societies children have

well-defined roles. The young girls are typically helpers while the boys are expected to play games that teach them the skills they will need as adult males. But all this changes

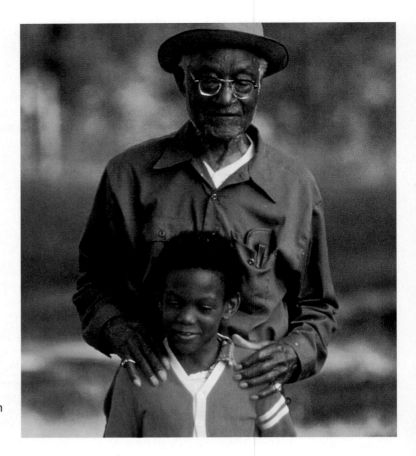

Given the opportunity, elderly men and women can have a profound influence on the lives of children in their families and neighborhoods.

in urban industrial societies. In those societies the status of children is extremely fluid and subject to many conflicting ideas and rapid changes in norms (Ariès, 1962).

THE CHALLENGE OF YOUTH

In *The Challenge of Youth* Erik Erikson (1965) makes the following observation:

> Youth shares with other groups, such as women and old people, the fact that the role assigned to it by nature has been elaborated by cultures as a set of differences from some standard human being, the norm, of course, being usually the normal adult male. The group is then judged on the basis of what it is not and never will be, or is not quite yet, or is not any more. (p. vii)

Kenneth Keniston (1965), another expert on the problems of growing up in modern societies, points out that the challenges young people face are further complicated by such rapid and far-reaching changes that they are often bewildered about such questions as what careers to pursue, what standards to apply to personal relationships, how much to devote to oneself and how much to the community and the society. Many young people have parents or other adults in their lives who can help them solve these dilemmas, but many others do not. As we saw in Chapter 7, they may react to the problems and failures of those around them (e.g., alcoholism or divorce) by with-

drawing into a world of anomic, alienated youth that explicitly rejects the values of the larger society, sometimes through gang violence.

In this regard, one of the most fascinating unanswered questions in the social sciences is why some children growing up under extremely adverse social conditions appear to be resilient, to be able to succeed in school and in other social settings, while so many others are set back and defeated by the same adverse conditions (Conger, Ge, & Elder, 1994; Garmezy, 1993; Williams & Kornblum, 1994). On a broader sociological level, however, Keniston and others note that changing norms of childhood and youth, on the one hand, and the decreasing well-being of young people in industrial nations, on the other, strongly influence the fortunes of youth everywhere.

Variations in the Value Placed on Children. Social definitions of childhood—what we expect of children, how we value the child and treat the child—differ immensely throughout the industrial world as well as between modern and traditional societies. In her study of the changing meanings of childhood, sociologist Viviana Selizer shows that in the United States there occurred a "profound transformation in the economic and sentimental value of children—fourteen years of age or younger—between the 1870s and the 1930s" (1985, p. 3). During that period child labor laws ended a common practice, at least among poorer families, of requiring children to work for wages. Earlier in the nineteenth century the incomes of the middle classes had risen enough so that they could keep their young ones out of the labor force; by the 1930s this became the norm for all classes.

As a result of this transformation, Selizer points out, children became economically "worthless" but emotionally "priceless," and this is true today as well. We think of our children as priceless beings to be nurtured, protected, socialized, and gradually introduced to the world of work and careers—not forced into that world abruptly after a very brief period of innocent childhood, as was the case in the early years of industrialization. Studies of children's responsibilities in the home find that people justify giving their children chores to do on the grounds that doing so builds character, discipline, responsibility, and so on, not because it contributes to the economic well-being of the family. In fact, in many middle-class homes the allowance system operates in lieu of any form of wages; the allowance is seen as a form of token money that the child has a right to receive but must also learn to spend responsibly.

But Selizer also shows that this transformation in the value placed on children was surrounded by a great deal of social conflict as the institutions of the larger society, especially courts and schools, were given the responsibility for enforcing new norms about child protection. Debates over definitions of childhood and the proper roles of children continue today. For example, the home schooling movement has arisen among people who reject the values of the public schools and wish to maintain the absolute authority of parents over their children by educating them in the home.

More important than these conflicts are the class contradictions inherent in the value placed on childhood. Many families are not able to give their children the array of goods and opportunities that are available to children in more affluent families. The worst situations of material deprivation experienced by children and young people, along with their parents, are often hidden from view in racial and ethnic ghettos and class-segregated communities "across the tracks" or in isolated trailer parks (Kozol, 1995). Overall trends in child welfare show that there is a growing gap between "priceless" children and children who bear a heavy burden of poverty and deprivation.

Indicators of Youth and Well-Being. There is a growing consensus among social scientists on the need for a quantitative measure of well-being among youth. In recent years, as ideological debates over social problems like teenage fertility have become more rancorous, this need has become even more pressing (Zill, 1995). Toward this end, a group of eminent sociologists has been working to create a set of data books titled *Kids Count*. These data books provide an invaluable and up-to-date array of indicators of trends in child well-being in the United States. They are available for use by local officials, scholars, and those who work with the youth of their communities.

Although in many communities the large majority of children are healthy and well cared for, the *Kids Count* data indicate that increasing numbers of young people are experiencing poverty and near-poverty conditions. Senator Daniel Patrick Moynihan of New York, himself a skilled social scientist, comments: "As we approach the end of the twentieth century, a child in America is almost twice as likely to be poor as an adult. This is a condition that has never before existed in our history" (1988, p. 5).

Table 15.2 presents some indicators of well-being among youth. Measures of children in poverty, rates of violent death, infant mortality, teenagers not in school, and births to single teenagers are among the most important ways of looking at the proportion of children and young people whose well-being is questionable and whose daily lives are fraught with risk of further trouble. Perhaps the most controversial of these indicators are those dealing with births to teenagers. In the United States and other urban industrial societies there is a great deal of debate about increasing rates of teenage childbearing. But the facts show that, contrary to what many people believe, rates of births to teenagers decreased from 1960 through 1980, when they began increasing again but never reached the same levels as those prevailing at the end of the 1950s (see Figure 15.6). But by separating out births to teenagers aged 15–17 and 18–19, one sees that births to older teenagers have been decreasing since 1960, while births to younger teenagers shot up during the 1960s and, although they are not nearly as high now, have not returned to earlier levels.

The data on births outside marriage are most revealing. The most significant change is not so much the overall

TABLE 15.2	Indicators of the Well-Being of U. S. Children		
INDICATOR		**1985**	**1991**
Percentage of low–birth weight babies		6.8	7.1
Infant mortality rate (per 1,000 live births)		10.6	8.9
Child death rate, ages 1–14 (per 100,000 children)		33.8	30.7
Percentage of all births that are to single teens		7.5	9.0
Juvenile violent crime arrest rate, ages 10–17 (per 100,000 youths)		305	457
Percentage of teens not in school and not in labor force, ages 16–19		5.3	5.0
Teen violent death rate, ages 15–19 (per 100,000 teens)		62.8	71.1
Percentage of children in poverty		20.8	20.0
Percentage of children in single-parent families		22.7	25.1

Source: *Focus*, Spring 1995, p. 15.

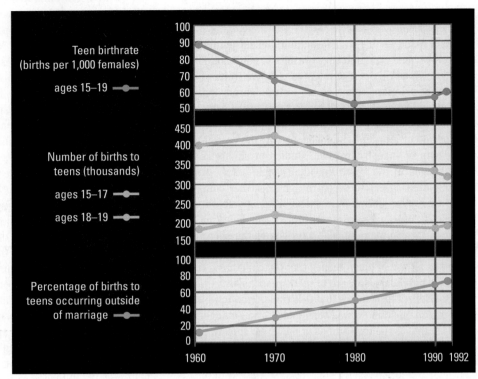

FIGURE 15.6 Births to Teenage Mothers in the United States, 1960–1992

Teen birthrate
(births per 1,000 females)

ages 15–19

Number of births to
teens (thousands)

ages 15–17

ages 18–19

Percentage of births to
teens occurring outside
of marriage

Source: Data from *Focus,* Spring 1995, p. 27.

rate of fertility among teenage women as the rate of marriage among teenagers, which has declined drastically. This fact is at the center of debates over "family values." While there is no question that children have a better chance of avoiding poverty if there are two parents present in the household, it is also true that separation and divorce are among the leading causes of poverty for young mothers and children. In consequence, efforts to influence and oblige young fathers, whether married or not, to take responsibility for their children are an important social policy trend in American communities and throughout the world (United Nations, 1995c).

It should be noted that some of the indicators presented in Table 15.2, such as the rate of violent death among teenagers, have actually improved in the past year or two. Others, however, such as the percentage of low–birth weight babies, have worsened. These indicators are sensitive to changes in society (declining use of crack-cocaine, efforts to reduce truancy, dropout prevention programs, etc.). The low–birth weight indicator is especially sensitive to changes in the economic situation of low-income households.

Throughout the world the infant mortality rate is considered the single most important indicator of the relative well-being of a nation's people (see Chapter 21). It measures the extent and efficacy of a nation's investment in the health of its people. The infant mortality rate in the United States—8.0 per 1,000 live births—ranks among the world's best, but it is higher than those in Japan (4.3), the Netherlands (5.9), or Australia (6.1), while it is much lower than that in Russia (19.0) and far lower than those in relatively impoverished nations like India (56.0) (Population Reference Bureau, 1995). Thus the United States, one of the world's most affluent nations, actually ranks on the lower end of the scale of infant mortality among the developed nations with which it is often compared. Much of the difference is due to the large number of underweight babies born in the United States.

The infant mortality rate for African Americans in the United States (18.0 in 1990) is more than twice the rate for whites (7.6). Much of this disparity is due to the high percentage of babies with low birth weights among members of minority groups, especially those in poverty. Birth weights below 5.5 pounds are a cause of infant death and are also associated with higher rates of illness in later years as well as a higher incidence of neurological and developmental handicaps and poor academic performance (Partin & Palloni, 1995). Figure 15.7 shows that the incidence of low–birth weight babies among African Americans declined from more than 14 percent in 1970 to a little over 12 percent in the mid-1980s, but began climbing again after 1984.

In explaining these trends, sociologists Melissa Partin and Alberto Palloni (1995) point out that while poverty is always associated with low birth weight, a woman's access to prenatal care in her community combined with her decision not to have an abortion are important factors. As more poor minority women choose not to have abortions and find it more difficult to obtain adequate care during pregnancy, the risk of low birth weight increases. Neither side in the abortion debate wishes to see more abortions among poor women. The central implication of these findings is that the rate of low–birth weight babies would be reduced by improved access to health care for young mothers and more education about the need to decrease behaviors such as smoking during pregnancy.

AGE AND INEQUALITY

At the turn of the century the largest segment of the U. S. population living in poverty or near-poverty conditions was the elderly (Preston, 1984). This was also true throughout much of Europe. Until the development of modern systems of employee pensions, Social Security, and basic health insurance (both private insurance systems and public systems like Medicare), people over age 60 were highly likely to be poor. Although poor and working-class elderly people without substantial wealth or savings might receive assistance from adult children and other family members, even those relatively fortunate individuals often felt deep resentment about having worked all their lives only to end up powerless and dependent (Atchley, 1991).

The Social Security Act of 1935 established federal old-age pensions based on employee and employer contributions (Social Security) as well as unemployment insurance and other antipoverty programs. The results of these programs, and the Medicare system instituted in 1965, have been dramatic. Rates of poverty among the elderly, which were close to 40 percent in the early decades of this century, declined to about 28 percent in the early 1960s and then to about 14 percent after Medicare had gone into effect. At present about 12 percent of people age 65 and over in the United States live at or below the poverty line, compared to about 14 percent of the population as a whole.

Among elderly members of minority groups, however, the situation is not nearly so positive. Twenty-eight percent of African Americans and 21.4 percent of Hispanics over age 65 are living in poverty (*Statistical Abstract,* 1995). These differences are often due to the fact that elderly people who previously worked at lower-paying jobs, which contributed little or nothing to private pension plans, may be forced to live almost exclusively on their federal Social Security payments, which by themselves are not enough to raise them above the official poverty line. And elderly blacks and Hispanics are especially likely to have had jobs that did not provide pensions.

As more people join the ranks of the elderly, concern about their economic situation becomes an ever more powerful theme in American life. Many Americans in their early sixties are subject to mandatory retirement. Once

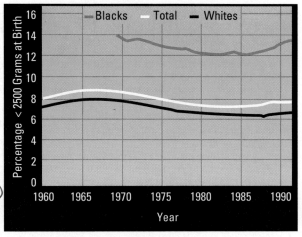

FIGURE 15.7 **Percentage of Low–Birth Weight Babies, by Race, 1960–1990**

Source: Partin & Palloni, 1995.

they are forced into retirement, they are limited in what they can earn without experiencing cuts in their Social Security payments and decreases in Medicare support. Matilda White Riley, a leading authority on the sociology of aging, asserts that there is a growing gap between the number of skilled and energetic elderly people in the population and the availability of "meaningful opportunities in work, family, and leisure" (Riley, Kahn, & Foner, 1994). We return to this theme shortly.

Age and Disability. As life expectancies have increased throughout the world, so have the numbers of people with major disabilities that seriously impair their ability to function effectively in their daily lives. In the United States the average life expectancy for people age 60 is 19 years for women and 15 years for men. On the average, women who live that many years after their sixtieth birthday can expect to experience major disabilities for 5 of those years (4 years for men). In Germany, another affluent industrial nation, life expectancies for women and men over age 60 are 22 years and 18 years, respectively, and the chances of experiencing major disabilities are the same as those in the United States. In Egypt, a developing nation, the comparable figures are 13 years of life expectancy for women after age 60 and 12 years for men, but because of less advanced health care the average Egyptian woman can expect to experience 6 years of disability (4 years for men) (Haber & Dowd, 1994). People who live longer do not automatically suffer major disabilities. As they age and become more frail, however, the experience of living with disability inevitably affects higher proportions of women because of their greater life expectancy. (See Box 15.2.)

The problems of health and disability among the elderly are compounded by inequalities of socioeconomic status. The more affluent and educated people are as they enter their sixties, the healthier they tend to be. In their

BOX 15.2   USING THE SOCIOLOGICAL IMAGINATION

Staying Involved to Stay Healthy

Recent social–scientific evidence confirms what many elderly people already know: To age well, it helps to pursue an active life. The data also disprove the worrisome idea that as increasing numbers of frail and disabled elderly people are kept alive through medical science, there will be an accumulation of older people living in pain or with crippling disabilities.

The accompanying chart is taken from a major new study by the National Long Term Care Surveys. It shows that if 1982 disability rates had held steady through 1995, there would have been an increase of almost 40 percent in the number of disabled people over age 85. Instead, because of better lifestyles and improved health care, the increase in the proportion of disabled elderly persons was only 10 percent, while for those age 85 and over it was slightly less than 30 percent.

The graphs also show that the total number of people in all the age categories, and especially in the eldest one, grew far more rapidly than did the proportion of disabled elderly people (Kolata, 1996).

The new data also show that education plays a highly significant part in explaining the lower rates of disability and disabling diseases among the elderly. Demographer Samuel Preston has calculated that "in 1980 more than 40 percent of Americans from 85 to 89 had fewer than 8 years of schooling. But by the year 2015, that figure will have dropped to 10 percent or to 15 percent" (quoted in Kolata, 1996, p. C3). Researchers agree that the effects of education on health in old age demand further study. It seems certain, however, that education helps people understand how to

take better care of themselves, may lead to higher incomes (and thus to better health care), and may allow people to remain mentally active throughout life (Brody, 1996).

Gerontological research at Pennsylvania State University indicates that self-education as well as formal education is important in maintaining cognitive activity. People who read, travel, take courses, and otherwise continue to develop their minds are able to maintain intellectual functioning longer than people who become "couch potatoes." Intellectual activity leads, in turn, to greater attention to personal health, social activities, and moderate physical exertion. Recent research shows that social involvement, mental stimulation, and the presence of social support are important to a healthy and relatively vigorous advanced old age. Social support—the presence of family and friends in one's daily life—is highly correlated with physical and mental health among the elderly.

The new studies might seem to suggest that if an elderly person becomes ill and disabled or loses his or her mental abilities, it is a result of poor health habits and lack of education. However, a study of Alzheimer's disease among Catholic nuns shows that the propensity to develop this mentally debilitating and fatal disease is independent of education and that signs of the disease may appear very early in some individuals. Among people who do not have genetic predispositions toward certain diseases and did not experience highly stressful work and family lives when they were younger, continued mental development and social activity may be the keys to a robust old age (Brody, 1996).

Robert Frost, shown here in his advanced years, was far more than a poet of rural America. Among other things, he advocated the need for people to remain passionate participants in the world around them throughout their lives.

Living Longer and Better

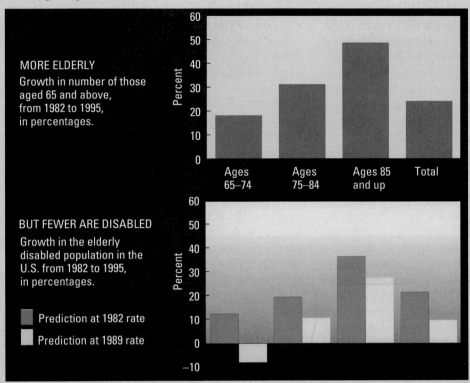

MORE ELDERLY
Growth in number of those aged 65 and above, from 1982 to 1995, in percentages.

BUT FEWER ARE DISABLED
Growth in the elderly disabled population in the U.S. from 1982 to 1995, in percentages.

Prediction at 1982 rate
Prediction at 1989 rate

Source: Dr. Kenneth G. Manton, Duke University.

last years, however, the effects of socioeconomic status diminish (House et al., 1994). People who have worked for decades in factories tending machines, often in polluted and stressful conditions, are more likely to have health problems and to have difficulty obtaining regular medical care than people who have worked in more physically and emotionally favorable conditions. Data on aging and health also show, however, that people from poor and working-class backgrounds are more likely to engage in **psychosocial risk behaviors** like smoking and heavy drinking (90 or more drinks a month). They also tend to experience a higher than average number of **lifetime negative experiences** (e.g., the death of a child or spouse, divorce, physical assault), which cause long-term stress. Even when risk behaviors and sources of chronic stress are considered, however, quantitative studies show a strong positive relationship between higher socioeconomic status and better health in elderly people (House et al., 1994).

Loss of Social Functions with Age. As people age, they experience more medical problems and dis-

abilities—but does this mean that they must inevitably withdraw from social life? Can anyone deny the biological facts of aging and death? Isn't it only natural for the elderly to perform less important roles as their physical capacities diminish? The answer, of course, is that it is not obvious at all. The increasing participation of elderly widows in securities investment clubs throughout the nation is a good example of how elderly people may perform socially important roles even as their physical strength diminishes. It is not uncommon for members of these clubs to impress far younger stockbrokers with their skill as players in the volatile securities market.

Sexual behavior among the elderly is another area in which popular notions about the influence of biology on age roles have been disproved. In the late nineteenth century and well into the twentieth it was widely believed that people lose their sexual desire and potency after middle age. In fact, however, a number of studies have shown that the image of the elderly as lacking sexual desire and the ability to enjoy sex is an ageist stereotype. For example,

Eric Pfeiffer, Adrian Verwoerdt, and Glenn Davis (1972) gathered data from several samples of elderly people—including individuals as old as 94—that showed conclusively that although sexual interest and activity tended to decline with age, sex remained an important aspect of the subjects' lives. The researchers also found, however, that elderly men are more interested in sex than women of the same age. The explanations for this difference are cultural rather than biological. Elderly men are in short supply. They tend to be married to women with whom they have had a long-standing relationship that includes an active sex life. If they are not married, they are in such great demand that they have less difficulty than women of the same age in finding a sexually compatible partner (Kornblum & Julian, 1995; Greeley, Michael, & Smith, 1990; Pfeiffer, Verwoerdt, & Davis, 1972).

Aging and Structural Lag. As noted earlier, social scientists who study the situation of the elderly increasingly recognize that longer life spans need to be accompanied by new concepts of social roles in more advanced years. The well-known gerontologists Matilda White Riley and John W. Riley, Jr., believe there is a growing mismatch between the strengths and capacities of older people and their roles in society. As people live longer, they often find themselves living alone with few constructive roles that demand their time and attention. Neglect of the elderly further reduces their mental and physical strength. The Rileys believe that "increasing numbers of competent older people and diminishing role opportunities cannot long coexist" (1989, p. 28). In their view, there is an urgent need for many small-scale programs that create work and volunteer opportunities in which older people can use their skills and feel needed (Riley, Kahn, & Foner, 1994).

Shifts in age statuses can have dysfunctional effects for society as well. A research project of the Carnegie Foundation attempted to assess the impact of an aging society (i.e., one in which the median age is increasing) on social roles. For example, whose responsibility is it to pay for long-term care of the elderly? A family may have to pay $40,000 a year or more to provide nursing home care for a disabled elderly mother or father. Should the sons and daughters take on this responsibility? Most of us would say yes, if we are able to do so. The Carnegie study found, however, that an increasing proportion of people say, in effect, "No sir, that's a public responsibility, let them go on Medicaid." But in that case we would force the elderly to sell all their assets in order to qualify for government aid, since Medicaid is available only to people who have exhausted their own funds before applying to the government for assistance (Pifer & Bronte, 1986).

The question of responsibility for caring for the frail elderly is a controversial policy issue. The conservative position is that family members or close relatives should be required to pay for such care until funds are no longer available. The liberal position is that individuals should not have to be dependent on possibly reluctant family members; moreover, the high costs of long-term care for the elderly are an especially heavy burden for households with low incomes. The elderly themselves, who form a major segment of the U.S. voting population, are increasingly concerned about threats to their economic and social security, especially as represented by efforts to reduce the extent of health coverage under the Medicare system. They also are increasingly sensitive to any slights or discriminatory behavior based on their age.

Ageism. The attitude known as **ageism** is similar to sexism (see Chapter 14). The term refers to an ideology that justifies prejudice or discrimination based on age. Ageism limits people's lives in many ways, both subtle and direct. It may label the young as incapable of learning. It labels the elderly as mentally incapable or asexual or too frail to get around. But people of all ages increasingly reject these notions. In their everyday lives in families and communities, for example, older people continually struggle against the debilitating effects of ageism. "Just because I need help crossing the street doesn't mean I don't know where I'm going," an elderly woman said to community researcher Jennie Keith (1982, p. 198).

Gerontologist Robert Butler observes that "ageism allows the younger generation to see older people as different from themselves; thus they subtly cease to identify with their elders as human beings" (1989, p. 139). Butler, a physician and social scientist, has found that as the proportion of older people in a society increases (as is occurring in the United States and Europe), the prevalence of ageism also increases. The younger generations, he notes, tend to fear that the older, increasingly frail and dependent generations will deprive them of opportunities for advancement. This fear is expressed in demands for reduced spending on Medicare and other programs that assist the elderly, as well as in the belief that the elderly are affluent and do not need social supports. (See Box 15.3.)

SOCIAL MOVEMENTS AMONG THE ELDERLY

Although they have been less far-reaching than the women's movement, social movements among the elderly—led by organizations like the Gray Panthers and the American Association of Retired Persons—have had a significant impact on American society. And as the population continues to age, we can expect to see more evidence of the growing power of the elderly. Consider, for instance, how changes in the consciousness of elderly people themselves are altering the way sociologists formulate questions about old age.

Until the social movements of the 1960s prompted the elderly to form movements to oppose ageism and fight for their rights as citizens, the most popular social-scientific

BOX 15.3 USING THE SOCIOLOGICAL IMAGINATION

Confronting Ageism

In 1900 there were 3.1 million people over age 65 in the United States; in 1990 there were more than 30 million. An increasing proportion of this age group consists of people over age 85, often termed the "oldest old." These individuals now constitute about 10 percent of the over-65 population. Projections by the Census Bureau indicate that by the middle of the next century this group may account for almost 22 percent of people over age 65 in the United States.

A major demographic trend like this one produces many types of social change. For example, the increasing number of frail elderly persons raises new questions about how best to care for people at the end of their lives. The presence of elderly persons who may have outlived their children and other relatives raises additional questions about the responsibility of societies and communities to care for isolated elderly individuals.

The growing presence of people over 65 can be expected to lead to efforts to confront ageism in its many forms. Ageism can occur in organizations and institutions, as when corporations insist on mandatory retirement at a certain age even though the employees affected may be perfectly capable and even more skilled than their younger replacements. Ageism can also occur in interpersonal interactions—for example, when elderly people are teased or abused because they do not move quickly enough or because they do not conform to the cultural ideal of youthful beauty. Ageism can take extremely vicious forms, or it can be a more insidious daily experience of devaluation.

Elder abuse. Often known as "granny bashing," abuse of elderly persons takes a variety of forms. In addition to direct violence, elder abuse may include withholding food, stealing savings and Social Security payments, and engaging in verbal abuse and threats. Although there are no reliable statistics on these phenomena, incidents of violence against elderly persons are being reported to authorities with increasing frequency. As the numbers of elderly people increase, so will incidents of elder abuse, especially in the absence of improved systems of family support and alternative living arrangements for older people.

Stereotyping of the elderly. Another form of ageism that can be corrected through greater sociological knowledge about aging is the tendency to view all old people as frail, dependent, incapable, and asexual. But as this proportion of the population increases, older people will be found doing many things that are viewed as inappropriate for their age. A woman in her eighties recently set the age record for solo sailing across the Atlantic. Just before reaching the age of 100, George Burns dedicated a book "to his past five doctors."

Just as other groups in the population reject labels that deprive them of their individuality and self-esteem, elderly people reject ageist labels that relegate them to dependent, unequal status. There will of course be large numbers of dependent older people, but there will also be large numbers of vigorous people of advanced age who need and demand encouragement and support in maintaining their vitality and in continuing to live life to its fullest. Younger people who can apply their sociological imagination to these issues will be highly valued (Kornblum & Julian, 1995).

---

view of aging was *disengagement theory.* Numerous empirical studies had shown that old people gradually disengage from involvement in the lives of younger people and from economic and political roles that require responsibility and leadership. In a well-known study of aging people in Kansas City, Elaine Cumming and William Henry (1971) presented evidence that as people grow older, they often gradually withdraw from their earlier roles, and that this process is a mutual one rather than a result of rejection or discrimination by younger people. From a functionalist viewpoint, disengagement is a positive process both for society as a whole (because it opens up roles for younger people) and for the elderly themselves (because it frees them from stressful roles in their waning years).

The trouble with disengagement theory is that, on the one hand, it appears to excuse policy makers' lack of interest in the elderly and, on the other hand, it is only a partial explanation of what occurs in the social lives of elderly people. An alternative view of the elderly is that they need to be reengaged in new activities. Known as *activity theory,* this view states that the elderly suffer a sense of loneliness and loss when they give up their former roles. They need activities that will serve as outlets for their creativity and energy (Palmore, 1981).

Theories of aging are not simply abstract ideas that are taught in schools and universities. The disengagement and activity theories lead to different approaches that often impose definitions of appropriate behavior on people who do not wish to conform to those definitions. Today gerontologists tend to reject both theories. They see older people demanding opportunities to lead their lives in a variety of ways based on individual habits and preferences developed earlier in life. Elderly people themselves express doubt that activity alone results in successful adjustment to aging or happiness in old age. For example, in her study of a French retirement community, Jennie Keith (1982) made this observation:

> The residents . . . seem to offer support to the gerontologists who have tried to mediate the extreme positions,

disengagement vs. activity, by introducing the idea of styles
of aging.... Some people are happy when they are very
active, others are happy when they are relatively inactive.
From this point of view, life-long patterns of social
participation explain the kinds and levels of activity that are
satisfying to different individuals. (p. 59)

In sum, for the elderly as well as for women, there is a
growing tendency among social scientists to emphasize individual needs and capabilities. The social movements for
gender and age equality also advance the needs of individuals, but in a collective manner, by asserting the needs of entire populations and rejecting preconceived notions of what
is best for all women, all youth, all men, or all the elderly.

THE HOSPICE MOVEMENT

As the large baby boom generation moves through the adult
years and approaches middle age, their parents enter the
ranks of the elderly. This demographic change has led to increased concern about the quality of life of the elderly and
about death and the dying process. The questions of how
best to prepare to die and whether one can have a "good
death" might have seemed strange to Americans of an earlier time, when so many people died as a result of sudden,
acute illnesses like pneumonia or tragic accidents in mines
and mills. Today, however, about 75 percent of deaths occur
among people over age 65, often after a prolonged illness.

People who are dying often experience a period between life and death known as the living–dying interval
(Kübler-Ross, 1989). For many dying people and their loved
ones, this is a time of extreme importance. During this
time there may be reconciliations, clarifications, expressions of love and understanding, and, under the best circumstances, a sense of closure and repose for the dying
person. But most people die in hospitals. Nurses, doctors,
and orderlies may intrude on these emotional scenes to
minister to the patient. The hospital is dedicated to pro-
longing life, even in a dying patient. As the Rileys express
it: "The hospital is geared for treatment and cure, it functions according to standards of efficiency and bureaucratic
rules, its environment is sterile and unwelcoming to those
who would visit patients *in extremis*" (1989, p. 27).

In recent decades, first in Great Britain and later in
the United States, a social movement has emerged that is
known as the hospice movement. The term *hospice* refers
to a place, a set of services, or both; increasingly it refers
to a service that can be brought into the dying person's home.
The purpose of the hospice is to make the patient as comfortable as possible so that all concerned can use the
living–dying interval effectively and humanely. In a hospice
the patient and his or her surrounding social group are
viewed as the relevant social unit. Medical personnel and
other professionals, such as social workers, are available to
help everyone involved.

Although it is still true that many people die in hospitals, hospice care is available in most parts of the United
States and is an increasingly popular alternative to hospital
death. This change is a result of modifications in the insurance laws, which now allow Medicare reimbursements for
home hospice care. Since 1983, when these rule changes
were made in response to pressure from the hospice movement, the number of people who choose to die at home has
more than doubled, and it continues to increase despite the
additional sacrifices that home hospice care requires from
loved ones (Belkin, 1992; Kearl, 1989).

Dying is never an easy experience, and the hospice
movement cannot make it so. Nevertheless, the hospice
movement is providing opportunities for new definitions of
the last social role in the life course—the dying role—as
well as the roles of those who will remain behind to continue their own life course.

RESEARCH FRONTIERS: POPULATION AGING AND STEWARDSHIP

The baby boom generation is not the only identifiable cohort of people passing through the life course in the United
States and other urban industrial nations. The parents of
the baby boomers, people who lived through the Depression
and World War II, are now in their declining years, but they
continue to exert a powerful influence on society. Similarly,
the children of the baby boomers, now passing through
their school years, constitute a population segment that is
having its own particular experiences and struggles in a society with rapidly changing career prospects.

Just as social scientists study the changing roles of
aging people as individuals, they also study the phenomenon of *population aging*. This term can refer to the changing age structure of a population, as represented, for
example, in a society's population pyramids (such as Figures 15.1 and 15.2 at the beginning of the chapter). It can
also refer to the influence of specific age cohorts as they
pass through the life course (Davis & Combs, 1950; Riley,
Foner, & Waring, 1988). The long-term trend in industrial
societies toward greater life expectancies and lower fertility creates an aging population. The passage of large or socially important cohorts through a population produces its
own social effects, but these are less well understood. The
study of the influence of aging cohorts thus is an active
frontier of sociological research (Elder, 1974; Elder &
Pavalko, 1990).

Recent studies of aging and community participation
are a good example of research on the effects of population
aging. The Americans who experienced the Depression and
World War II were deeply involved in community affairs, the
arts, and charitable activities. These social involvements

are sometimes referred to as *stewardship,* meaning the set of norms that specify what people ought to do to help build their communities and their society. Many institutions of communities and cities, such as sports teams, colleges, museums, orchestras, and libraries, depend on the voluntary stewardship activity and charitable contributions of individuals. If different major cohorts passing through a population differ in their involvement in such activities, the effects on society can be significant.

The Depression and World War II cohorts seem to have lived in a time of unusual social solidarity in which the idea of individual actions on behalf of society was extremely popular. This experience marked their behavior in many ways as they grew older. Their children, many of whom are in the baby boom generation, inherited some of this stewardship ethic, but recent research indicates that stewardship norms and behaviors are diminishing in younger age cohorts (Miller, 1996).

In 1995 an African American woman who had spent her entire life working as a domestic and a laundress bequeathed $200,000 to a Mississippi university. She believed in higher education and wanted to do something to help. At about the same time, an elderly widow in New York City, who also had been poor for much of her life, donated $2 million to a university in her city because she wanted to promote the study of science, especially by women. These are just two examples of the many thousands of philanthropic activities engaged in by members of this unusual generation. Later generations do not show the same readiness to pursue stewardship activities. The average household donation to philanthropies of any kind dropped by 11 percent between 1987 and 1993.

It is not entirely clear why more recent generations are less prone to engage in stewardship activities and private charitable acts. We do know, however, that unless this situation changes, many communities and public cultural institutions will experience difficult times. Robert Putnam of Harvard, who studies these trends and their political ramifications, places the blame largely on television. He claims that television causes people to stay home more and to be less involved in community affairs.

Research by sociologist Robert Wuthnow (1994) documents an increase in participation in community groups by younger adults, suggesting a possible shift in the present situation as these participants grow older and seek to help others. However, participation in self-help groups or religious study meetings does not necessarily imply a return to norms of stewardship in these younger age cohorts. It seems that the experiences of forming labor unions to deal with the effects of economic recession, of joining the military to fight fascism in Europe, and of helping to rebuild the war-torn nations of the world had a deep and lasting impact on the generation of people now entering their frail years. Research on this aspect of population aging suggests that U.S. society is going to miss this extraordinary generation, not only as individual mothers, fathers, and grandparents, but as a population segment that contributed disproportionately to the public good.

VISUAL SOCIOLOGY

AFTER 90

Imogen Cunningham's life spanned this century, and she spent it making loving photographic portraits of people in the cities where she lived. Born in Scranton, Pennsylvania, at the end of the nineteenth century, she learned photography in its early days, when camera equipment was extremely cumbersome and unpredictable. With the encouragement of her artistic and thoughtful father, shown here in a photo she took when he was well into his nineties, Cunningham built her own darkroom and learned every aspect of the fledgling art of photographic portraiture.

In her adult years Cunningham lived and worked mainly in Seattle and San Francisco, but her career gave her opportunities to take photographs of people all over the world. During the period before World War II she was one of the most celebrated photographers working for the innovative magazine *Vanity Fair.* The subjects of her portraits range from world-famous artists and scientists to unknown but singular characters such as the tattooed woman who spent her life in the carnival.

Self-portrait.

This woman had been at the carnival all her life, but I found her in the hospital. It looks like lace, doesn't it?

At the end of her life Cunningham became interested in a sociological question: What ideas and activities occupy the minds of very old people? The photos shown here are a representative sample from a collection of stirring portraits she made of people who were, as she put it, "alive and kicking." She photographed many people in their nineties, like Old Norton in his shack and the nursing home resident feeling forgotten and forlorn, for whom the main challenge of life was merely to live through each day. She also photographed people who, like Cunningham herself (shown here in a self-portrait), had the good fortune to have a passion for work and activity and felt little concern about their physical deterioration because they were absorbed in their creative efforts.

464

Cunningham died at the age of 93, just as the volume containing these photographs was about to be published. Although she missed the chance to celebrate the appearance of her book about the very old, she herself lived long enough to have the pleasure (denied to many artists) of seeing her work honored during her lifetime. Even from the few photos presented here we can readily see that her work captures the mystery of the human spirit and demonstrates that extreme age does not extinguish the love of life.

My father at 90.

Old Norton lives by himself in his shack.

She said to me, "When you come here nobody knows where you are."

She is a distinguished radiobiologist who asked me to photograph her. I wasn't taking on commissions anymore, but I did it because she didn't care if she looked old and she didn't hate her face.

SUMMARY

THINK ABOUT IT CRITICALLY

Some young people feel that forced saving, in the form of Social Security and similar programs, is senseless because by the time one is over age 65 much of what makes life attractive and pleasurable is already over. Now that you have read this chapter, how would you respond to this notion?

In many societies age determines a great deal about the opportunities open to a person and what kind of life that person leads. The study of aging and the elderly is termed *gerontology.*

All societies channel people into *age grades,* or sets of statuses and roles based on age. The transitions among these age grades create a *life course* and are often marked by ceremonies known as *rites of passage.*

Age cohorts are people of about the same age who are passing through life's stages together. The baby boom cohorts, which were produced by rapid increases in the birthrate from about 1945 through the early 1960s, have profoundly influenced American society. A sizable proportion of the children of the baby boom generation, the "baby boom echo," are members of minority groups.

By *life expectancy* we mean the average number of years a member of a given population can expect to live beyond his or her present age. As life expectancy in a population increases, the proportion of the population that is dependent on the adult cohorts also increases.

In urban industrial societies there are distinct patterns of stratification in which age defines the roles one plays and the rewards one can expect. The forces of social change unleashed by colonialism, industrialization, urbanization, and population growth have tended to disrupt the formal age grade systems of smaller, more isolated societies.

Social definitions of childhood differ immensely throughout the industrial world as well as between modern and traditional societies. As a result of increasing incomes and the passage of child labor laws, children became economically "worthless" but emotionally "priceless." However, there is a growing gap between "priceless" children and children who bear a heavy burden of poverty and deprivation.

At the turn of the century the largest segment of the U. S. population living in poverty or near-poverty conditions was the elderly. As a result of programs such as Social Security and Medicare, rates of poverty among the elderly have decreased dramatically. However, the situation is not nearly so positive for elderly members of minority groups.

As people age, they experience more medical problems and disabilities, but this does not mean that they must inevitably withdraw from social life. Social scientists who study the situation of the elderly point out that longer life spans need to be accompanied by new concepts of social roles in more advanced years.

Ageism is an ideology that justifies prejudice or discrimination based on age. As the proportion of older people in a society increases, as is occurring in the United States and Europe, the prevalence of ageism also increases.

As the population as a whole has aged, the impact of the elderly on American society has increased. This is changing the way sociologists view old age. Before the 1970s the most popular social-scientific view of aging was disengagement theory, the belief that as people grow older they gradually disengage from their earlier roles. An alternative view of the elderly, known as activity theory, states that the elderly need activities that will serve as outlets for their creativity and energy. Today gerontologists tend to reject both of these theories, seeing older people demanding opportunities to lead their lives in a variety of ways based on individual habits and preferences.

The growing proportion of elderly people in the population has led to increased concern about the quality of life of the elderly and about death and the dying process. One outcome of this concern is the hospice movement, which attempts to provide dying people and their loved ones with a comfortable, dignified alternative to hospital death.

CRITICAL RESPONSE

Young people are not the only ones who denigrate the aged. Some adults are also guilty of ageism—for example, when they assert that older people can no longer enjoy life. Sociological data show, however, that ever larger proportions of the elderly are fully capable of leading active and productive lives. Young people may think that they will no longer enjoy life when they are old, but the research shows that they are mistaken. As more people live longer, there is no reason for society not to invest in resources to ensure that every person will have a decent lifestyle in old age.

GLOSSARY

gerontology: the study of aging and older people. (p. 446)

age grade: a set of statuses and roles based on age. (p. 446)

life course: a pathway along an age-differentiated, socially created sequence of transitions. (p. 446)

rite of passage: a ceremony marking the transition to a new stage of a culturally defined life course. (p. 447)

age cohort: a set of people of about the same age who are passing through the life course together. (p. 447)

life expectancy: the average number of years a member of a given population can expect to live. (p. 449)

psychosocial risk behaviors: behaviors that are detrimental to health, such as smoking and heavy drinking. (p. 459)

lifetime negative experiences: experiences that cause long-term stress, such as the death of a child or spouse. (p. 459)

ageism: an ideology that justifies prejudice and discrimination based on age. (p. 460)

WHERE TO FIND IT

BOOKS

Age and Structural Lag (Matilda White Riley, Robert L. Kahn, & Anne Foner; Wiley, 1994). A comprehensive collection of articles covering many recent research initiatives. Dr. Riley is one of the world's foremost authorities on the demography of aging and the comparative situation of elderly people throughout the world.

Pricing the Priceless Child: The Changing Social Value of Children (Viviana Selizer; Free Press, 1985). An extremely innovative sociological and historical analysis of changing norms of childhood in the United States and other Western nations. Develops a thesis about the changing value placed on childhood as the economy and society change.

The Coming of Age (Simone de Beauvoir; Warner, 1973). A classic statement by one of this century's most influential thinkers about the combined effects of gender and age on human development and society.

Number Our Days (Barbara Myerhoff; Simon & Schuster, 1978). A haunting study of how elderly people struggle to survive and die with dignity. The setting is a senior citizen center in Venice Beach, California, and the people are elderly Jewish immigrants and refugees from Europe.

OTHER SOURCES

Kids Count Data Book. A timely and scientifically accurate source of comparative demographic data on the situation of children in the United States and elsewhere.

Age in America: Trends and Projections. A chartbook that analyzes demographic and socioeconomic trends affecting the United States and its elderly population.

Handbook of Aging and the Social Sciences. A valuable source of interdisciplinary research and policy studies dealing with the condition of the aged in the United States and other Western societies.

PART 4

Social Institutions

Change is occurring all the time in every major institution of society: The family must adapt to high rates of divorce and remarriage; markets are continually introducing new products and new methods of production; governments must constantly adjust to pressures from opposing interest groups . . . the list could be made much longer. The processes of institutional change are endless and often complex, but increasingly they can be understood and even predicted through the application of sociological concepts and research.

In this set of chapters the concepts and perspectives discussed earlier in the book will be applied to an analysis of several major social institutions. Chapter 16 explores the changing nature of the family, and especially research on the ways in which family statuses

and roles are changing and the social forces that seem to account for these changes. The other chapters in Part 4 explore other institutions—proceeding from an analysis of how each is typically organized to a discussion of how it is changing. Chapters 17 and 18 discuss three major cultural institutions—religion, education, and the media—whose role is to transmit and reinforce a society's most cherished values. Chapter 19 deals with the roles and statuses that generate jobs and income. Chapter 20 shows how political institutions determine "who gets what, when, and how." It also deals with the grave difficulties facing nations attempting to institute the rule of law. Finally, in Chapter 21 the institutions of science and technology are analyzed, with special attention to their role in health care and environmental issues.

CHAPTER 16

The Family

Dinner was over and four women stayed at the table to talk. The topic of conversation bounded around and, as often happened, came to rest on the subject of homelessness.

"I'm not homeless," protested Abigail. "I'm familyless."

That simple assertion bore eloquent witness to the important and complex connection between family relationships and homelessness. Homeless women had not always been homeless and familyless women had not always been familyless. Like everyone else, they were born into families or family-like networks of human relationships. On the street and in the shelters, one meets many homeless women who had been kept afloat by family members, until, for one reason or another, the family had to let go. For most women, living with relatives or receiving significant financial or other support from them was the last stage in their descent into homelessness.

Family relationships ranged from no family or no contact at all to regular and intense contacts. At the low end were some of the older women who had been familyless a long time and were more or less accepting of this condition. For them, family was not an issue, one way or the other; at best, it was simply something other women talked about a lot. Phyllis, for example, was 72 and had never married. Her only brother had been killed in World War II and her mother died in 1965. Since 1955, Phyllis had lived alone. If she had more distant relatives, they were not a part of her remembered life, and Phyllis was never heard to associate having no family with homelessness.

Maude, at 61, said she had no family, no, no family at all. She hadn't had a family in 40 years, not since she disowned the family she was born into. "You're my family," she said, making a circle with her arms to embrace everyone in the day shelter. "All you people here, you're my family. My family is whoever I happen to be with, if they're congenial." (Liebow, 1995, pp. 82–83)

The foregoing paragraphs were written by Elliot Liebow and are based on years of participant observation of homeless people, mainly women, in various shelters and food kitchens in the Washington, D.C., metropolitan area. This important study is a "companion" volume to *Tally's Corner* (1967), Liebow's classic account of street-corner men in Washington. The excerpt presented here sheds light on the difficulty of maintaining family relationships among women who are, for one reason or another, at the bottom of society's class system. As Liebow observes, "Homeless women are mainly from working-class and lower-class families that can no longer support them or from families whose members can no longer live together as husband and wife or parent and child. The weakest one (wife, mother, daughter) gets pushed out" (p. 112).

Liebow adds that many homeless women fight to maintain their family relationships, often against impossible odds. "Many of them attempt to function as mothers-at-a-distance and sometimes wives as well, working for the day when they can close the gap" (p. 11). This fierce desire to maintain family relationships, even under the most difficult social conditions, is a powerful reminder of how important the family is to many people, even if many others take their family relationships for granted.

THE NATURE OF FAMILIES

We continually hear warnings of the "death of the family" in modern societies. As early as 1934, sociologists like William Fielding Ogburn were writing about the decline of the family. "Prior to modern times," according to Ogburn, "the power and prestige of the family was due to . . . functions it performed. . . . The dilemma of the modern family is caused by the loss of many of these functions in recent times" (Ogburn & Nimkoff, 1934, p. 139). More recent commentators have pointed to the so-called sexual revolution as a threat to this basic social institution. Others insist that even in the face of trends toward single parenthood, cohabitation without marriage, divorce and remarriage, and smaller family size, the family is "here to stay" (Goode, 1971; National Commission on America's Urban Families, 1993).

In this chapter we will see that there are so many variations in family form even within a single society that it has become increasingly difficult to speak of "the family" as a single set of statuses, roles, and norms. For example, among the homeless women to whom Elliot Liebow devoted the last years of his career there were families with a mother, father, and children, all of whom lived in different shelters or foster care situations yet dreamed of being able to find an affordable home so that they could live together. And there were others, like Maude, whose "family" was composed of those around her with whom she felt congenial. Nevertheless, it remains true that in all known societies almost everyone is socialized within a network of family rights and obligations known as *family role relations* (Goode, 1964). In the first section of this chapter, therefore, we examine the family as an institution and show how family role relations have changed in the twentieth century. In the second section we look at issues of family formation, especially mate selection, marriage, divorce, and remarriage. The final section focuses on how the basic sociological perspectives explain changes in family roles and functions and in the interactions between parents and children.

THE FAMILY AS AN INSTITUTION

There is a big difference between a particular family and the family as a social institution. Your family, for example, has a particular structure of statuses (mother, father, sister, brother, grandmother, etc.), depending on who and where its members are. Your immediate family is also part of an extended kinship system (aunts, uncles, cousins, grandparents, etc.) that also varies according to how many branches you and your immediate family actually keep track of. The family as a social institution, however, comprises a set of statuses, roles, norms, and values devoted to achieving important social goals. Those goals include the social control of reproduction, the socialization of new generations, and the "social placement" of children in the institutions of the larger society (colleges, business firms, and so forth).

These are not the only goals that the family is expected to fulfill. In many societies, especially tribal or peasant societies, the family performs almost all the functions necessary to meet the basic needs of its members. Those needs are listed in Figure 16.1, which compares less differentiated gemeinschaft or village-type societies with more differentiated gesellschaft societies like that of the United States. It shows that most of the functions that were traditionally performed by the family are now performed either partly or wholly by other social institutions that are specially adapted to performing those functions.

Figure 16.1 only begins to illustrate the institutional complexity of modern societies. Not only are there many more separate institutions in modern societies, but basic social functions are often divided among several institu-

tions. Thus the institutions that meet protective and social-control needs include governments at all levels, the military, the judiciary, and the police. Replacement needs are met by the family through mating and reproduction. In addition to the family, religious institutions, education, and other cultural institutions meet the need to socialize new generations.

The family's ability to meet the goals society expects it to meet is often complicated by rapid social change. For example, many families in industrial communities throughout the United States were quite good at preparing their children for blue-collar manufacturing jobs, but as those jobs have been eliminated owing to automation and the globalization of the economy, it is no longer clear how families can equip their offspring to compete in the new job market.

When there are major changes in other institutions in a society, such as economic institutions, families must adapt to those changes. Similarly, when the family changes, other institutions will be affected. As an example, consider the impact of the "sexual revolution" that began in the 1920s. During that decade, often called the Roaring Twenties, young adults began to upset the moral code that had

FIGURE 16.1 Institutional Differentiation

SOCIAL FUNCTION	TYPE OF SOCIETY	
	Less Differentiated (gemeinschaft)	More Differentiated (gesellschaft)
Communication among members: first through language alone and then through specialized institutions devoted to communication	Family, kin networks	Mass media
Production of goods and services: from the basic items required for survival to items designed to satisfy new, more diverse needs created by increasing affluence	Family groups	Economic institutions
Distribution of goods and services: within societies at first, and later with the rise of trade and markets, between societies as well	Extended family, local markets	Markets, transportation institutions
Protection and defense: including protection from the elements and predators and extending to defense against human enemies	Family, village, tribe	Armed forces, police, insurance agencies, health care institutions
Replacement of members: both the biological replacement of the deceased and the socialization of newcomers to the society	Family	Family, schools, religious institutions
Control of members: to ensure that the society's institutions continue to function and that conflict is reduced or eliminated	Family	Family, religious institutions, government in all forms

Source: Adapted from Lenski & Lenski, 1982.

regulated the behavior of couples for generations, at least among people who considered themselves "respectable." According to this traditional set of norms, women were the guardians of morality. Men were more likely to give in to sexual desire, "but girls of respectable families were supposed to have no such temptations" (Allen, 1931, p. 74). After World War I, however, "respectable" young women began to reject the so-called double standard, by which they had to adhere to a different and more restrictive moral code than that applied to men. They began smoking cigarettes, wearing short skirts, and drinking bootleg gin in automobiles or at "petting parties." These changes in the behavior of couples produced far-reaching changes in other institutions. Women demanded more education and more opportunities to earn income. This in turn led to demands for new institutions such as coeducational colleges and integrated workplaces, as well as greater access by women to existing institutions such as medicine, law, and science. These changes in women's expectations and behavior, along with the increasing educational and occupational mobility of men after the world wars, contributed immensely to changes in traditional family roles—especially the weakening of the role of the father as the central and most powerful authority figure in the family. The consequences of these fundamental changes in family roles are still felt today.

Changes in the institutions in one area of social life can place tremendous pressure on those in other sectors. This is especially true in the case of the family, as will be evident throughout this chapter. But before we examine the ways in which families have changed in this century, it is necessary to define some terms that are frequently used in discussing the family.

DEFINING THE FAMILY

The family is a central institution in all human societies, although it may take many different forms. A **family** is a group of people related by blood, marriage, or adoption. Blood relations are often called *consanguineous attachments* (from the Latin *sanguis,* meaning "blood"). Relations

These photos show a conventional nuclear family, with father, mother, and two children, and an extended family, with three generations of family members, including aunts, uncles, and cousins. Although these may once have been the most common forms of traditional and modern family structures, we have seen that the number of single-parent families, and of families that share custody of children after divorce, is increasing.

between adult persons living together according to the norms of marriage or other intimate relationships are called *conjugal relations*. The role relations among people who consider themselves to be related in these ways are termed **kinship.**

The familiar kinship terms—*father, mother, brother, sister, grandfather, grandmother, uncle, aunt, niece, nephew, cousin*—refer to specific sets of role relations that may vary greatly from one culture to another. In many African societies, for example, "mother's brother" is someone to whom the male child becomes closer than he does to his father and from whom he receives more of his day-to-day socialization than he may from his father. It must be noted that biological or "blood" ties are not necessarily stronger than ties of adoption. Adopted children are usually loved with the same intensity as children raised by their biological parents. And many family units in the United States and other societies include "fictive kin"—people who are so close to members of the family that they are considered kin despite the absence of blood ties (Liebow, 1967; Stack, 1974). Finally, neither blood ties nor marriage nor adoption adequately describes the increasingly common relationship between unmarried people who consider themselves a couple or a family.

The smallest units of family structure are usually called **nuclear families.** This term is usually used to refer to a wife and husband and their children, if any. Nowadays one frequently hears the phrase "the traditional nuclear family" used to refer to a married mother and father and their children living together. But as we will see throughout this chapter, there is no longer a "typical" nuclear family structure. Increasingly, therefore, sociologists use the term *nuclear family* to refer to two or more people related by consanguineous or conjugal ties or by adoption who share a household; it does not require that both husband and wife be present in the household or that there be any specific set of role relations among the members of the household (Laslett & Wachter, 1978).

The nuclear family in which a person is born and socialized is termed the **family of orientation.** The nuclear family a person forms through marriage or cohabitation is known as the **family of procreation.** The relationship between the two is shown in Figure 16.2.

Kinship terms are often confusing because families, especially large ones, can be rather complex social structures. It may help to devote a little time to working through Figure 16.2. "Ego" is the person who is taken as the point of reference. You can readily see that Ego has both a family of

---

FIGURE 16.2 **Nuclear and Extended Family Relationships**

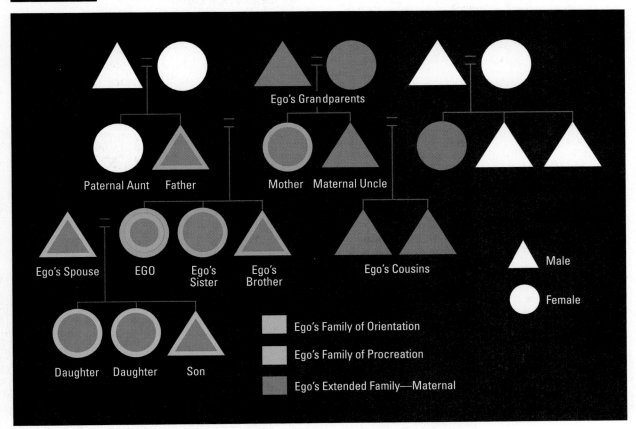

This diagram shows the family relationships of a hypothetical individual, Ego. Ego was born and socialized into what sociologists call the family of orientation. Ego formed a family of procreation through marriage or cohabitation.

orientation and a family of procreation. So does Ego's spouse. Ego's parents become the in-laws of the spouse, and the spouse's parents are Ego's in-laws. But like the vast majority of people, Ego also has an **extended family** that includes all the nuclear families of Ego's blood relatives—that is, all of Ego's uncles, aunts, cousins, and grandparents. Ego's spouse also has an extended family, which is not indicated in the figure, nor is it defined as part of Ego's extended family. But relationships with the spouse's extended family are likely to occupy plenty of Ego's time. Indeed, as the figure shows, the marriage bond brings together far more than two individuals. Most married couples have extensive networks of kin to which they must relate in many, varied ways throughout life.

VARIATIONS IN FAMILY STRUCTURE

For the past several years sociologists have been demonstrating that the traditional household consisting of two parents and their children is no longer the typical American family. In the 1940s there were about eight times as many households headed by a married couple as there were households headed by unrelated individuals. By 1980 there were only about two and a half times as many. While the majority of children in the United States still live with a married mother and father who are the child's biological parents, that arrangement is becoming less common. This fact is illustrated in Figure 16.3, which shows that as of the 1990 census only 57.7 percent of children were living with

both their biological parents. (Figure 16.4 also presents data on children's living arrangements.)

This trend points to a growing diversity of family types, including far more people living alone and far more women raising children alone. There are also more households composed of unrelated single people who live together not just because they are friends but because only by doing so can they afford to live away from their families of orientation. Thus, when they discuss family norms and roles, sociologists must be careful not to represent the traditional nuclear family, or even the married couple, as typical. As an institution, the contemporary family comprises a far greater array of household types than ever before.

Sociologists are divided on the meaning and implications of these facts. For some, the trend toward greater diversity of family forms means that the family as an institution is adapting to change (Skolnick, 1991; Stacey, 1990). For others, the decline of the family composed of two married parents living with their biological children poses a serious threat to the well-being of children (Popenoe, 1994). We will return to this debate over the meaning of changes in family form and function, but first we consider additional aspects of the ways in which families have changed during this century.

THE CHANGING FAMILY

In his pioneering study of changes in the family, William J. Goode (1963) argued that the structure of family units

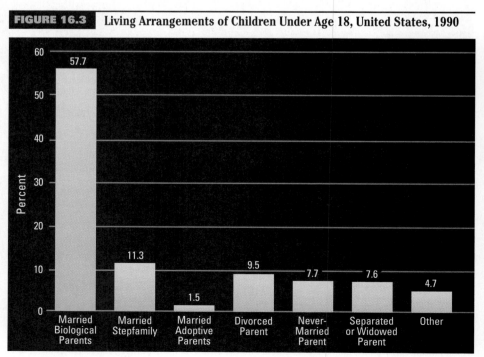

FIGURE 16.3 **Living Arrangements of Children Under Age 18, United States, 1990**

Source: Data from Census Bureau.

FIGURE 16.4 Living Arrangements of Children Under Age 18, United States, 1970–1990

Source: Data from Census Bureau.

becomes simpler as societies undergo industrialization. Goode was not the first social scientist to make this observation; however, his study was the first to be based on extensive historical and comparative data. After reviewing changes in family structure in Europe and North America during the preceding 75 years, Goode concluded that the smaller family unit composed of a married couple and their children (i.e., the conjugal family) was increasingly dominant in industrial societies. For Goode, the change from the larger extended family to the smaller and more geographically mobile nuclear family was part of an even larger worldwide revolution in which people demand greater control over the conditions that shape their lives.

From the standpoint of the family, this "revolution" translates into demands for freedom to select one's mate, to decide where to live after marriage, to decide whether to have children and how many to have, and even whether to terminate the marital relationship. Such choices were often impossible in earlier family systems in which marriages were arranged, the married couple was expected to live within a larger extended family, and couples were expected to have numerous children.

According to Goode, the driving forces behind the large-scale changes in family structure in this century were economic and technological. The more families had to adapt to an economy in which income was earned outside the family, the more the family had to be mobile and flexible. Families must be willing to move from one place to another in search of employment. Geographic mobility, in turn, meant that children would not be able to maintain households in which their parents could live; extended families consisting of three generations under one roof would become a thing of the past. And because children no longer worked in the home or on the farm, they became less important in economic terms than they had been in earlier epochs; families therefore had fewer children.

In the three decades since Goode's study appeared, there has been a wealth of new research that has further developed the idea of a transition from extended to nuclear family systems as a result of industrialization (Huber & Spitz, 1988; Osmond, 1985). In addition, recent studies show that as the range of choices regarding family structure increases, there is also more controversy over "family values" (May, 1995). In consequence, more recent studies often focus on historical studies of families and social change, international comparisons, and distinguishing between ideal and actual family patterns.

Studies of Family History. Studies of family form and patterns of family interaction over time have found a good deal of evidence that challenges the conclusions of Goode's research. For example, demographer Peter Laslett (1972) found that in some parts of England the emergence of the nuclear family seems to have preceded industrialization by many decades. When people migrated to new agricultural regions, they often left behind extended kin groups and became more dependent on the smaller nuclear family group. Laslett and other researchers have found that modern technologies like the telephone and the automobile enable members of smaller family units, who formerly might have lost touch with their extended families, to maintain their kinship ties (May, 1995).

Similarly, in her research on industrialization in the mill towns of Massachusetts, Tamara Hareven (1978) found evidence that extended families often sent family

THEN AND NOW

UPROOTED FAMILIES AND THE GENERATION GAP

Immigration and migration are often experienced by entire families. An enduring theme of the immigration experience is the difference in outlook between immigrant parents and children born in the United States. A good deal of the conflict that occurs in immigrant or migrant families stems from this difference between the generations. The parents may cling to the language and styles of dress and behavior, as well as friends and associates, that represent "the old country," while the children are more fully

assimilated into the new society and impatient with their parents for trying to interest them in the cultural ways of the society they left behind. A century or more ago, these issues were prevalent among Irish, Polish, Jewish, German, and Chinese immigrants. Today they frequently arise in Caribbean, African, and Asian immigrant families. At the same time, however, many young people from immigrant backgrounds enjoy carrying on the traditions of their parents' generation. This can be seen in the quinceañera, an elaborate fifteenth birthday celebration that marks the coming of age of a Mexican American girl.

members whom the land could not support, especially young women, to the towns. There they might marry and form urban families, but often they returned home and married into farm families. In most cases the urban workers managed to maintain close ties with their rural kin, especially through letters and visits to friends.

In the case of the black family, research by social historian Herbert Gutman (1976) on the effects of slavery and industrialization has shown that slaves often formed extended families that included strong nuclear units. During the Reconstruction period after the Civil War, many families that had been torn apart by slavery were reunited. Toward the end of the nineteenth century, however, migration caused by the industrialization of agriculture in the South

and the demand for unskilled labor in large northern cities created instability in many black families, a pattern that would become prevalent in later decades of the twentieth century. In sum, therefore, the theory that industrialization creates the nuclear family as the dominant family form, with predictable patterns of family interaction, is no longer widely accepted in the social sciences.

International Comparisons.   If one studies who lives in households (i.e., who lives together and eats together more or less regularly), the traditional or "Dick and Jane" family (Mom, Dad, Dick, Jane, and their dog Spot) appears to be the most prevalent family form. However, if one also considers patterns of interaction with others, the family unit might include, say, a grandmother living in a nearby apartment with an unmarried aunt, as well as a divorced uncle in a nearby community. This approach is illustrated in a recent volume titled *Families in Focus* (Bruce, Lloyd, & Leonard, 1995), which compares patterns of family structure in several industrial societies. Some findings from this study are presented in Figure 16.5. They reveal that most industrial societies (with the notable exception of Japan) have experienced rapid changes in the strength of norms regarding divorce and out-of-wedlock fertility. The researchers make the following observation:

> The idea that the family is a stable and cohesive unit in which father serves as economic provider and mother serves as emotional care giver is a myth. The reality is that trends like unwed motherhood, rising divorce rates, smaller households, and the feminization of poverty are not unique to America, but are occurring worldwide. (Judith Bruce, quoted in Lewin, 1995, p. A5)

Other international research comparing family structure and interaction in industrial societies finds a wide range of possible household patterns (Lee & Haas, 1993;

Lenero-Otero, 1977). For example, although families may not live with three generations under one roof, they may live in nuclear family units in close proximity to one another, a pattern that continues to sustain large extended families. Technologies like the telephone and jet travel allow family members to see one another fairly frequently when they are separated by geographic distance. And when divorce breaks apart a nuclear family and the parents remarry, the reconstituted family may be embedded in a larger set of extended family relations that may occupy even more of its members' time. None of these patterns was predicted in the theories of Goode and others who studied the revolution in family structure.

Ideal Versus Actual Family Patterns.   When politicians and government officials talk about "preserving family values," they often have in mind the traditional two-parent nuclear family. To many people this remains the ideal family form. In reality, however, such families are less prevalent today than they were in earlier decades. Increasing numbers of families are headed by a single parent, usually the mother but sometimes the father. Moreover, two-parent families may actually be *reconstituted*—that is,

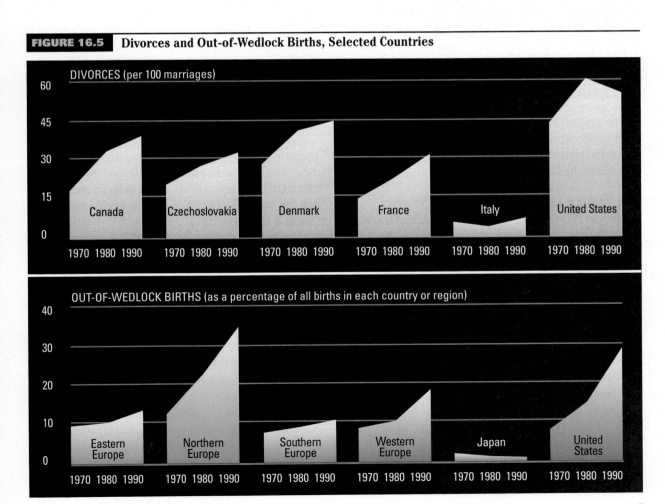

FIGURE 16.5   Divorces and Out-of-Wedlock Births, Selected Countries

Source: Data from *Population Council.*

created by remarriage after divorce or the death of a spouse. Thus what appears to be a conventional nuclear family is really a far more complicated family form with extended ties among parents and siblings in different nuclear families.

Among lower-income people these patterns are especially prevalent—so much so that some researchers have concluded that families without fathers are a direct consequence of poverty. Although they tend to share the same norms of family life as other members of society, poor people bear added burdens that make it difficult, if not impossible, for them to actually meet those norms. In particular, men in such families may not be able to provide their expected share of family income and hence may become demoralized and unable to maintain family relationships. This is especially true when teenagers father children before they are adequately prepared to take economic responsibility for them. Thus in poor families the father often is not a central figure, and female-headed families are the dominant family form (Furstenberg & Cherlin, 1991; Osmond, 1985).

Contemporary social-scientific research on family structure and interaction increasingly focuses on issues like those just described. At the same time, there is growing recognition that the actual form the family takes may vary greatly at different stages of the life course. In his research on homeless women, for example, Elliot Liebow (1995) observed that as they grow older, women who have lived lives marked by poverty and abuse are often left without real families and must create surrogate family relationships in caregiving institutions. And as the proportion of elderly people in the population increases, more families must decide whether to care for an aging parent at home. Let us therefore take a closer look at how families change throughout the family life cycle.

THE FAMILY LIFE CYCLE

Sociologist Paul Glick, an innovator in the field of family demography and ecology, developed the concept of the *family life cycle,* the idea that families pass through a sequence of five stages:

1. Family formation: first marriage
2. Start of childbearing: birth of first child
3. End of childbearing: birth of last child
4. "Empty nest": marriage of last child
5. "Family dissolution": death of one spouse (Glick & Parke, 1965)

These are typical stages in the life cycle of conventional families. Although there are other stages that could be identified within each of these—such as retirement (the years between the time of retirement and the death of one spouse) or the "baby" stage (during which the couple is rearing preschool-age children)—the ones that Glick listed are most useful for comparative purposes.

As the "typical" family structure becomes ever more difficult to identify owing to changes in family norms, the stages of family development also vary. In fact, the stages of the family life cycle have become increasingly useful as indicators of change rather than as stages that all or most families can be expected to experience. The Census Bureau estimates, for example, that there are at least 3.6 million heterosexual couples in the United States who are cohabiting. This number represents a sevenfold increase since 1970, when an estimated 500,000 cohabiting couples were counted (*Statistical Abstract,* 1995). (Note also that the census figures include only heterosexual couples and therefore vastly underestimate the total number of cohabiting couples.) Although the majority of cohabiting couples will eventually marry, many others will break up or continue to live together without marrying. A study based on data from the 1990 U.S. census concluded that 55 percent of white women and 42 percent of black women in their first cohabiting union eventually marry their male partner (Condon, 1991).

When sociologists look at the median age at which people experience the various stages of the family life cycle, significant trends emerge. Consider age at first marriage. In 1890 the median age of Americans at first marriage was 26.1 years for men and 22 years for women; in the 1950s and 1960s it reached the historic lows of 22.8 and 20.3. Then it began rising again slowly, until by 1990 it was 26.3 for men and 24.1 for women (see Figure 16.6). Age at first marriage tends to be somewhat higher for males than for females and is associated with educational attainment; more highly educated people are more likely to delay marriage. There is also a tendency for members of minority groups to marry later owing to the proportionately lower income levels of these populations. People with lower incomes tend to delay marriage or not to marry because they lack the material means to sustain a marital relationship (Sweet & Bumpass, 1987).

As it passes through the family life cycle, every family experiences changes in its system of role relations. In analyzing these changes, social scientists often modify Glick's stages so as to focus more sharply on interactions within the family. An example is the set of developmental stages shown in Figure 16.7. There are major emotional challenges at each of these stages. For example, families with adolescent children must adapt to the children's growing independence. This may involve going through a stage of negotiation over such issues as money, cars, and dating. But researchers who study family life note that parents are often confused about how to interact with their adolescent children. They may assume that it is normal for adolescents to leave the family circle and to become enmeshed in their own peer groups, which often get into trouble. However, as Carol Gilligan (1987) has pointed out, adolescents also want the continuing guidance and involvement of adults.

Earlier research by Erik Erikson (1975) and Bruno Bettelheim (1962) also found that placing too much em-

FIGURE 16.6   **Estimated Median Age at First Marriage, United States, 1890–1990**

Source: Data from Census Bureau.

phasis on adolescence as a time of "normal" separation from the family can be a form of social cop-out in which adults fail to provide meaningful goals and activities for adolescents. Many social scientists feel that adolescence is a time for building interdependence as well as independence. By this they mean that adolescents need to become involved in prosocial interactions such as assistance in caring for elderly or younger family members, or involvement in community agencies or social movements (Coles, 1986; Gottman, 1983).

Social changes that create shortages of jobs for young people—especially declines in less skilled manufacturing jobs and increases in low-wage service-sector jobs—have a major impact on the transition from dependence to independence for many young adults in the United States and elsewhere in the world. The Population Reference Bureau reports that "compared with the 1970s, more young adults (ages 18 to 24) are living at home with their parents. . . . Over half (54 percent) of all 18–24 year olds lived with their parents in 1991" (Ahlburg & De Vita, 1992, p. 9). Shortages in low-rent housing and continuing difficulties in finding work will oblige many young adults to live with their family of orientation, a situation that often frustrates family members' expectations about "normal" movement through the

life course (Elder, Modell, & Parke, 1992; Rossi & Rossi, 1990).

In later stages of family life the parents must be willing to watch their grown children take on the challenges of family formation while they themselves worry about maintaining their marital roles or caring for their own parents. The latter issue is taking on increasing importance in aging societies like the United States. And since women are still expected to be more nurturing and emotionally caring than men, it often falls to women to worry about the question of "where can Mom live?" (Hochschild, 1989). According to Elaine Brody, a leading researcher on this issue, "It's going to be primarily women for a long time. Women can go to work as much as they want, but they still see nurturing as their job." Moreover, "with many more very old people, and fewer children per family, almost every woman is going to have to take care of an aging parent or parent-in-law" (quoted in Lewin, 1989, p. A1).

As if these stages were not stressful enough, consider the complications resulting from divorce, remarriage, and the combining of children of different marriages in a new family. It is increasingly common, for example, for teenagers and young adults to have parents who are dating and marrying, and for children to have four parental figures in

---

FIGURE 16.7   Stages of the Family Life Cycle

STAGE	EMOTIONAL PROCESS	REQUIRED CHANGES IN FAMILY STATUS
1. Between families: The unattached young adult	Accepting parent–offspring separation	a. Differentiation of self in relation to family of origin b. Development of intimate peer relationships c. Establishment of self in work
2. The joining of families through marriage: The newly married couple	Commitment to new system	a. Formation of marital system b. Realignment of relationships with extended families and friends to include spouse
3. The family with young children	Accepting new generation of members into the system	a. Adjusting marital system to make space for children b. Taking on parenting roles c. Realignment of relationships with extended family to include parenting and grandparenting roles
4. The family with adolescents	Increasing flexibility of family boundaries to include children's independence	a. Shifting of parent–child relationships to permit adolescents to move in and out of system b. Refocus on midlife marital and career issues c. Beginning shift toward concerns for older generation
5. Launching children and moving on	Accepting a multitude of exits from and entries into the family system	a. Renegotiation of marital system as a dyad b. Development of adult-to-adult relationships between grown children and their parents c. Realignment of relationships to include in-laws and grandchildren d. Dealing with disabilities and death of parents (grandparents)
6. The family in later life	Accepting the shifting of generational roles	a. Maintaining own and/or couple functioning and interests in face of physiological decline; exploration of new familial and social role options b. Support for a more central role for middle generation c. Making room in the system for the wisdom and experience of the elderly; supporting the older generation without overfunctioning for them d. Dealing with loss of spouse, siblings, and other peers, and preparation for own death; experiencing life review and integration

Source: Adapted from McGoldrick & Carter, 1982.

their lives instead of two. We therefore turn to a discussion of role relations in reconstituted families.

PARENTING, STEPPARENTING, AND SOCIAL CHANGE

It has never been easy to be a parent at any stage of the family life cycle. Keeping a family intact and raising children who are confident and capable and will become loving, capable parents themselves is a domestic miracle. For better or (sometimes) worse, most people learn to be parents by following the examples set by their own parents when they were children. Much as we may swear that when our turn comes we will improve on the way our parents performed their roles, we often find ourselves acting toward our children much as our parents acted toward us. In fact, many parents seek help from family counselors because they are shocked to find themselves doing and saying the same things to their children that their parents did to them (Scarf, 1995).

Many other adults and children will experience major reorganizations of their families as parents divorce and remarry. When stepfamilies are formed, family members must adapt to new role relations as stepchildren and stepparents, often while maintaining many of their obligations in the original family. Sharon L. Hanna, an expert on stepfamilies, notes that there are more than 20.6 million stepparents in the United States; it is estimated that by the year 2000 almost 50 percent of all Americans will be part of a stepfamily (Hanna, 1994).

"Stepfamilies," sociologists Frank Furstenberg and Andrew Cherlin point out, "are a curious example of an organizational merger; they join two family cultures into a single household" (1991, p. 83). While this joining of family cultures also occurs in first marriages, in those marriages the couple usually has time to work out differences before children are born. In the case of stepfamilies, the task of working out a mutually acceptable concept of the family may be more stressful than the partners anticipated.

Sociologists point out that positive relationships in any family do not just happen but are worked on consciously through much learning and discussion. These efforts are particularly necessary in stepfamilies (Hanna, 1994). Some studies of stepfamilies show that new stepparents often conceive of themselves as "healers," people who can use the force of love to form strong bonds of attachment between two sets of children. Very often, however, the children cling to the fantasy that their original parents will get back together, and the stepparents' efforts may meet with frustration. Stepparents who manage to reorganize the family successfully tend to be diplomatic and sensitive and to avoid competing with biological parents. They gain the support of their spouses and wait for opportunities to gain the acceptance of their stepchildren (Papernow, 1988).

However, resolving the complexity and ambiguity of roles in reorganized families is no simple matter. Many factors come into play when a new family is formed. For example, Furstenberg and Cherlin point out that legal norms "reinforce the second-class status of stepparents" as nonbiological partners (1991, p. 80). A biological father is held responsible for child support even if he has never lived with the child, while a stepfather incurs no financial responsibility for a child even if he has lived with that child for many years. "The only legal recourse for stepparents who want to claim rights and responsibilities is to adopt their stepchildren, an act that seems to symbolize a deeper and more permanent tie, more like a biological relationship" (Furstenberg & Cherlin, 1991, p. 80).

Members of all kinds of families experience particular stress in times of economic hardship or when other social changes influence the family. Stress and change in the larger society may cause parents to feel unable to perform their roles as providers of material and emotional support. Earlier in this century, for example, the combination of frequent severe recessions, high rates of industrial accidents, and lack of adequate health care had a significant impact on families. Fathers were often forced to leave their families in search of work; infection often claimed the lives of mothers during childbirth. Demographers estimate that at the beginning of the century, when divorce rates were still extremely low, almost 25 percent of all children lost at least one parent through death before reaching the age of 15 (Uhlenberg, 1980).

By midcentury, improvements in health care had reduced this proportion to 5 percent, but divorce rates had increased to 11 percent, and another 6 percent of children were born to unmarried parents. Thus even in the 1950s—the most stable decade for families and children—demographers estimate that 22 percent of children were being raised in families that had only one parent as a result of death, separation, divorce, or single parenthood (Bumpass & Sweet, 1989). Even this relative stability lasted only a decade. By the end of the 1950s divorce rates had begun their precipitous rise, and so had rates of births to unmarried parents. By 1990 about 25 percent of all births occurred out of wedlock (Furstenberg & Cherlin, 1991).

When individuals fail to maintain their marital commitments or do not marry despite pregnancy, the results are cause for concern in any society. The difficulties faced by children in "intact" families as well as in troubled ones raise the age-old questions of how people decide whom to marry and what makes marriages last. In the next section, therefore, we examine the sociology of mate selection and marriage.

DYNAMICS OF MATE SELECTION AND MARRIAGE

"In the animal kingdom, mating involves only the two partners. For mankind, it is the joining of two enormously complex systems" (McGoldrick & Carter, 1982, p. 179). We may think of mate selection and marriage as matters that affect only the partners themselves, but in reality the concerns of parents and other family members are never very far from either person's consciousness. And as we will see shortly, the values of each partner's extended family often have a significant impact on the mate-selection process.

MARRIAGE AS EXCHANGE

People in Western cultures like to think that interpersonal attraction and love are the primary factors in explaining why a couple forms a "serious" relationship and eventually marries. But while attraction and love are clearly important factors in many marriages, social scientists point out that in all cultures the process of mate selection is carried out according to basic rules of bargaining and exchange (Becker, 1973; Goode, 1964; Levitan & Belous, 1981). Sociologists and economists who study mate selection and marriage from this exchange perspective ask who controls the marriage contract, what values each family is attempting to maximize in the contract, and how the exchange process is shaped by the society's stratification system.

Among the upper classes of China and Japan before the twentieth century, marriage transactions were controlled by the male elders of the community—with the older women often making the real decisions behind the scenes. In many societies in the Middle East, Asia, and preindustrial Europe, the man's family negotiated a "bride price" with the woman's family. This price usually consisted of valuable goods like jewelry and clothes, but in some cultures it took the form of land and cattle. Throughout much of Hindu India, in contrast, an upper-class bride's family paid a "groom price" to the man's family.

Although such norms appear to be weakening throughout the world, arranged marriages remain the customary pattern of mate selection in many societies. The following account describes factors that are often considered in arranging a marriage in modern India:

> Every Sunday one can peruse the wedding ads in the classifieds. Many people still arrange an alliance in the traditional manner—through family and friend connections. Caste is becoming less important a factor in the selection of a spouse. Replacing caste are income and type of job. The educational level of the bride-to-be is also a consideration, an asset always worth mentioning in the ad. A faculty member at a college for girls has estimated that 80–90 percent of the students there will enter an arranged marriage upon receiving the B.A. Perhaps 10 percent will continue their studies. In this way, educating a daughter is parental investment toward securing an attractive, prosperous groom. (Smith, 1989)

In all of these transactions the families base their bargaining on considerations of family prestige within the community, the wealth of the two families and their ability to afford or command a given price, the beauty of the bride and the attractiveness of the groom, and so on. Different cultures may evaluate these qualities differently, but in each case the parties involved think of the coming marriage as an exchange between the two families (Goode, 1964). But do not get the idea that only selfish motives are involved in such marriages. Both families are also committing themselves to a long-standing relationship because they are exchanging their most precious products, their beloved young people. Naturally, they want the best for their children (as this is defined in their culture), and they also want a climate of mutual respect and cooperation in their future interfamily relationships.

NORMS OF MATE SELECTION
Endogamy/Exogamy.
All cultures have norms that specify whether a person brought up in that culture may marry within or outside the cultural group. Marriage within the group is termed **endogamy;** marriage outside the group and its culture is termed **exogamy.** In the United States, ethnic and religious groups normally put pressure on their members to remain endogamous—that is, to choose mates from their own group. These rules tend to be especially strong for women. Among Orthodox Jews, for example, an infant is considered to have been born into the religion only if the mother is Jewish; children of mixed marriages in which the mother was not born a Jew are not considered Jewish. This conflict between Orthodox and Reform Jews over the status of children born to non-Jewish mothers—even when the mothers have converted to Judaism and the children have been raised as Jews from birth—is an example of conflict over endogamy/exogamy norms. Many African tribes have developed norms of exogamy that encourage young men to find brides in specific villages outside the village of their birth. As we saw in Box 4.1, such marriage systems tend to promote strong bonds of kinship among villages and serve to strengthen the social cohesion of the tribe while breaking down the animosity that sometimes arises between villages within a tribe.

Homogamy.
Another norm of mate selection is **homogamy,** the tendency to marry a person from a similar social background. The parents of a young woman from a wealthy family, for example, attempt to increase the chances that she will associate with young men of the same or higher social-class standing. She is encouraged to date boys from "good" families. After graduating from high school she will be sent to an elite college or university, where the pool of eligible men is likely to include many who share her social-class background. She may surprise her parents, however, and fall in love with someone whose social-class, religious, or ethnic background is considerably different from hers. But when this happens she will invariably have based her choice on other values that are considered important in the dating and marriage market—values like outstanding talent, good looks, popularity, or sense of humor. She will argue that these values outweigh social class, especially if it seems apparent that the young man will gain upward mobility through his career. Often the couple will marry and not worry about his lower social-class background. On the other hand, "the untalented, homely, poor man may aspire to a bride with highly desirable qualities, but he cannot offer enough to induce either her or her family to choose him, for they can find a groom with more highly valued qualities" (Goode, 1964, p. 33).

Homogamy in mate selection generally serves to maintain the separateness of religious groups. Because the Census Bureau does not collect systematic data on religious preferences, it is extremely difficult to obtain accurate data on religious intermarriage. Yet sociologists and religious leaders agree that although parents continue to encourage their children to marry within their religion, there is a trend away from religious homogamy, particularly among Protestants and Catholics (Scanzoni & Scanzoni, 1976). This trend may affect rates of divorce and separation. Recent research shows that families that maintain an active religious life tend to have lower divorce rates than those that do not participate in religious worship together (National Commission on America's Urban Families, 1993). Similarly, a study by Howard Weinberg (1994) found that shared religion has the strongest effect on the likelihood that couples will be able to overcome a period of separation and achieve a successful reconciliation.

The norm of homogamy also applies to interracial marriage. Before 1967, when the United States Supreme Court struck them down as unconstitutional, many states had laws prohibiting such marriages. After that decision, marriages between blacks and whites began to increase rapidly, although they remain a very small proportion of all marriages. In 1960 there were about 51,000 black-white couples; by 1994 that number had risen to 296,000, an almost sixfold increase. Intermarriage of Hispanic and non-Hispanic whites also increased during the same period, from about half a million marriages in 1960 to almost 1.3 million in 1994 (*Statistical Abstract,* 1995). Both of these trends are signs that more people are choosing to marry across racial and ethnic lines, but since the vast majority of marriages are within racial categories, it is clear that the norm of racial homogamy remains strong in the United States.

ROMANTIC LOVE

Although exchange criteria and homogamy continue to play a significant role in mate selection, for the past century romantic attraction and love have been growing in importance in North American and other Western cultures. Indeed, the conflict between romantic love and the parental requirement of homogamy is one of the great themes of Western civilization. "Let me not to the marriage of true minds/Admit impediments," wrote Shakespeare in a famous sonnet. The "star-crossed lovers" from feuding families in *Romeo and Juliet*—like the lovers who have forsaken family fortunes to be together in innumerable stories and plays written since Shakespeare's time—attest to the strong value we place on romantic love as an aspect of intimate relationships between men and women.

In his review of worldwide marriage and family patterns, William J. Goode (1964) found that compared with the mate-selection systems of other cultures, that of the United States "has given love greater prominence. Here, as in all Western societies to some lesser degree, the child is socialized to fall in love" (p. 39). Yet although it may be taken for granted now that people will form couples on the basis of romantic attachment, important changes in the structure of Western societies had to occur before love as we know it could become such an important value in our lives. In particular, changes in economic institutions as a result of industrialization required workers with more education and greater maturity. These changes, in turn, lengthened the period of socialization, especially in educational institutions. This made it possible for single men and women to remain unattached long enough to gain the emotional maturity they needed if they were to experience love and make more independent decisions in selecting their mates.

However familiar it may seem to us, love remains a mysterious aspect of human relationships. We do not know very much—from a verifiable, scientific standpoint—about this complex emotional state. We do not know fully what it means to "fall in love" or what couples can do to make their love last. But two promising avenues of research on this subject can be found in Winch's theory of *complementarity* and Blau's theory of *emotional reciprocity*.

Complementary Needs and Mutual Attraction. Robert F. Winch's (1958) theory of complementary needs, based on work by the psychologist Henry A. Murray, holds that people who fall in love tend to be alike in social characteristics such as family prestige, education, and income but different in their psychological needs. Thus, according to Winch, an outgoing person often falls in love with a quiet, shy person. The one gains an appreciative audience, the other an entertaining spokesperson. A person who needs direction is attracted to one who needs to exercise authority; one who is nurturant is attracted to one who needs nurturance; and so on.

Winch and others have found evidence to support this theory, but there are some problems with this research. It is difficult to measure personal needs and the extent to which they are satisfied. Moreover, people also show a variety of patterns in their choices of mates. Some people, in fact, seem to be attracted to each other because of their similarities in looks and behavior rather than because of their differences.

Attraction and Emotional Reciprocity. Blau's (1964) theory of emotional reciprocity as a source of love is based on his general theory that relationships usually flourish when people feel satisfied with the exchanges between them. When people feel that they are loved, they are more likely to give love in return. When they feel that they love too much or are not loved enough, they will eventually come to feel exploited or trapped and will seek to end the relationship. In research on 231 dating couples, Zick Rubin (1980) found that among those who felt this equality of love, 77 percent were still together 2 years later, but only 45 percent of the unequally involved couples were still seeing each other. As Blau explained it, "Only when two lovers' affection for and commitment to one another expand at roughly the same pace do they mutually tend to reinforce their love" (quoted in Rubin, 1980, p. 284).

Blau's exchange approach confirms some popular notions about love—particularly the ideas that we can love someone who loves us and that inequalities in love can lead to separation. And yet we still know little about the complexities of this emotion and how it translates into the formation of the most basic of all social groups, the married couple. This is ironic, because books, movies, and popular songs probably pay more attention to love than to just about any other subject.

Francesca M. Cancian (1987), a leading researcher on love in a changing society, notes that when men and women place a high value on individuality the price may be "a weakening of close relationships." As people spend time enhancing their own lives they may become more self-centered and feel less responsible for providing love and nurturance. Cancian's research on loving relations among couples of all kinds has convinced her that people are increasingly seeking a form of love that "combines enduring love with self-development." She regards this kind of relationship as based on interdependencies in which each member of the couple attempts to assist the other in realizing his or her individual potential and at the same time seeks to strengthen the bond between them. But she finds that in order to foster

BOX 16.1 USING THE SOCIOLOGICAL IMAGINATION

Love of a Lifetime?

It takes a lot of imagination to sustain love. Insight into both oneself and one's mate is vital, but so is a sociological imagination. It is not hard to know how social conditions affect a person's feelings in the long and short term, but it is surprising how few people develop the capacity to see the world the way those close to them see it. When caught up in the early passion of love this may not be a problem. But as a relationship develops, people need as much imagination and understanding as possible. An awareness of the various dimensions of intimate love may help.

Social psychologists who study love in married and unmarried couples are finding new evidence that confirms what many people have long known intuitively: It is in fact quite difficult for couples to maintain the level of passion they experienced in the early stages of their marriage. "People don't know what they are in for when they fall in love," asserts Yale's Robert Sternberg. "The divorce rate is so high, not because people make foolish choices, but because they are drawn together for reasons that matter less as time goes on" (quoted in Goleman, 1985b, p. C1).

Sternberg believes that love has three components: intimacy, passion, and commitment. Intimacy is a shared sense that the couple can reveal their innermost feelings to each other even as those feelings change. Passion is largely a matter of physical attraction and sexuality. Commitment is a shared sense that each member of the couple is permanently devoted to the other. Research shows that the fullest love demands all three of these qualities but that over a long relationship passion is the first to fade; intimacy develops slowly and steadily as a result of shared experiences and values; and commitment develops more gradually still (see chart).

In the early stages of a love relationship, the couple may become so caught up in their passion that they do not help each other develop as autonomous individuals. This can produce serious problems in later stages of the relationship. At the same time, commitment alone cannot substitute for the other two qualities of love. "You have to work constantly at rejuvenating a relationship," Sternberg explains. "You can't just count on its being OK, or it will tend toward a hollow commitment, devoid of passion and intimacy. People need to put the kind of energy into it that they put into their children or career" (quoted in Goleman, 1985b, p. C5).

Studies by Sternberg and many others find that children who have been deprived of parental love, especially by the parent of the opposite sex, often have trouble developing commitment and sharing intimacy. Often they avoid feeling vulnerable and dependent on another person by avoiding strong emotional ties altogether.

a loving interdependent relationship couples often need to sacrifice a certain amount of independence and career advancement—not a simple matter in a culture that places a high value on individual achievement.

The nature of loving relationships is likely to be a subject of highly creative sociological research in coming years. Since the capacity to love and be loved depends on individual characteristics as well as on social conditions, much of the research in this area will be done by social psychologists. An example is presented in Box 16.1.

MARRIAGE AND DIVORCE

More than any other ritual signifying a major change in status, a wedding is a joyous occasion. Two people are legally and symbolically joined before their kin and friends. It is expected that their honeymoon will be pleasant and that they will live happily ever after. But about 20 percent of first marriages end in annulment or divorce within 3 years (Bogue, 1985; Furstenberg & Cherlin, 1991). Of course, di-

vorce can occur at any time in the family life cycle, but the early years of family formation are the most difficult for the couple because each partner experiences new stresses that arise from the need to adjust to a complex set of new relationships. As Monica McGoldrick and Elizabeth A. Carter (1982) point out, "Marriage requires that a couple renegotiate a myriad of personal issues that they have previously defined for themselves or that were defined by their parents, from when to sleep, have sex, or fight, to how to celebrate holidays and where and how to live, work, and spend vacations" (p. 178). For people who were married before, these negotiations can involve former spouses and shared children, resulting in added stress for the new couple.

In the United States and other Western societies, the rate of divorce rose sharply after World War II, accelerated even more dramatically during the 1960s and 1970s, and has decreased only slightly since then. These statistics often lead sociologists to proclaim that there is an "epidemic" of divorce in the United States. But demographer Donald Bogue has concluded that "the divorce epidemic is

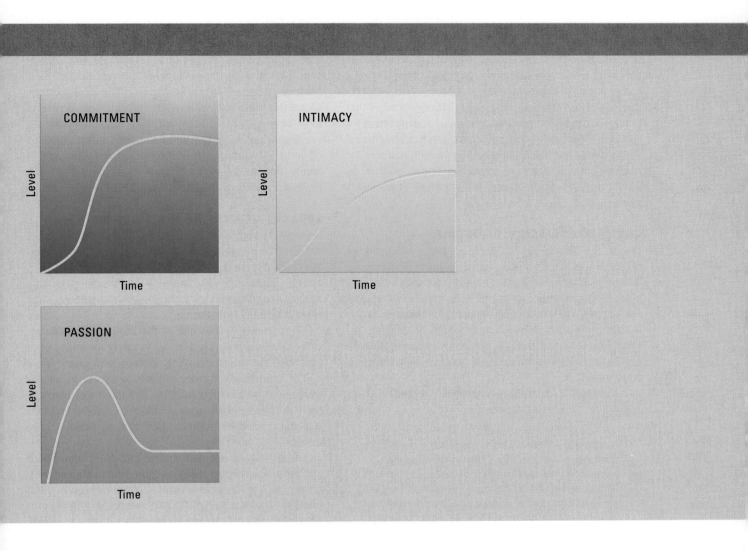

not being created by today's younger generation. It has been created by today's population aged thirty or more, who married in the 1960s and before" (1985, p. 190). This generation was noted for its search for self-realization, often at the expense of intimate family relationships. It is not yet clear whether subsequent generations, who appear to be somewhat more pragmatic, will continue this trend. If they do, we can expect high divorce rates to continue.

Most states in the United States now have some form of no-fault divorce that reduces the stigma of divorce by making moral issues like infidelity less relevant than issues of child custody and division of property. While the growing acceptance of divorce helps account for why divorce rates are so much higher in the United States than in other nations with highly educated populations, Americans today also place a higher value on successful marriage than their parents may have. This means that they often divorce in the expectation of forming another, more satisfying and mutually sustaining relationship (Ahlburg & De Vita, 1992).

Trial Marriage. In the 1980s it was widely believed that the practice of "trial marriage," or cohabitation before marriage, would result in greater marital stability: Couples who lived together before marriage would gain greater mutual understanding and a realistic view of marital commitment, and this would result in a lower divorce rate among such couples after they actually married. However, by the 1990s it had become evident that these expectations were unfounded; in fact, the divorce rate among couples who had lived together before marriage was actually higher than the rate for couples who had not done so. Within 10 years of the wedding, 38 percent of those who had lived together before marriage had divorced, compared to 27 percent of those who had married without cohabiting beforehand.

On the basis of an analysis of data from a federal government survey of more than 13,000 individuals, Larry Bumpass and James Sweet (cited in Barringer, 1989) concluded that couples who cohabit before marriage are generally more willing to accept divorce as a solution to marital problems. They also found that such couples are less likely to be subject to family pressure to continue a marriage that is unhappy or unsatisfactory. In addition, cohabitation has become a predictable part of the family life cycle, not only before marriage but in the interval between divorce and remarriage. Once again, these changes in families mean that family life has become ever more variable and uncertain for children. Thus while some advocate a return to traditional family norms and values, others urge greater tolerance for a variety of family types and accommodation to their needs. This conflict is most evident in discussions of same-sex relationships.

GAY AND LESBIAN RELATIONSHIPS

In 1995 the Disney Corporation, long viewed as a defender of traditional family values, shocked many conservative Americans by announcing that it would provide spousal benefits (health insurance, pension rights, etc.) for its employees who were part of a same-sex relationship or marriage. In taking this action, Disney was simply acknowledging that norms are changing and it is becoming less acceptable for companies to impose their definitions of the family on their employees.

Margaret L. Andersen, a noted expert on issues of sex and gender, makes this observation:

> Sociological and popular understanding of gay and lesbian relationships has been greatly distorted by the false presumption that only heterosexual relationships are normal ways of expressing sexual intimacy and love. We live in a culture that tends to categorize people into polar opposites: men and women, Black and white, gay and straight. (1993, p. 57)

However, an unknown but significant number of people do not conform to conventional heterosexual behaviors. They may have felt a preference for intimacy with members of the same sex very early in life without knowing how to identify their feelings. Often they went through long periods of confusion and self-doubt before learning to understand and accept their homosexuality.

Our culture makes homosexual love into a form of deviance. Homosexuals, in consequence, are victims of homophobia of all descriptions (from individual acts of insensitivity or aggression to antigay legislation), which places additional burdens on homosexual relationships (Meyer, 1990). Because homosexual couples are not welcome or do not feel comfortable in many social situations, they often feel a need to keep their relationship secret. This deprives homosexual men and women of the social approval that heterosexual couples enjoy—and take for granted—in their peer and work relations.

In large measure owing to the stigma attached to homosexual relationships, there are no accurate census counts of homosexual families, nor is there much research

about life in gay and lesbian households. The research that has been done, however, shows that fewer children live in male homosexual families than in female homosexual ones, mainly because women tend to win custody of their children in divorce cases. Recent research on gay fathers shows that compared with heterosexual fathers they tend to be better at setting limits on their children's behavior, are somewhat more nurturing, and place more emphasis on verbal communication with their children—features of family life that are often the province of the mother in a heterosexual family (Bigner & Bozett, 1989).

SOURCES OF MARITAL INSTABILITY

Because it generally causes a great deal of emotional stress and pain for everyone involved, to say nothing of its financial costs, divorce is a subject of intense study by social scientists. Space does not permit a full treatment of this subject here, but we can discuss some of the major variables associated with divorce.

Age at marriage is one of the leading factors in divorce. It seems that it is best not to marry too young or to wait too long before marrying. Women who marry while still in their teens are twice as likely to divorce as women who tie the knot in their twenties. But those who marry in their thirties are half again as likely to divorce as those who marry in their twenties. How can we explain these differences?

In a study of age and marital instability, Alan Booth and John N. Edwards (1985) examined data obtained from a national sample of more than 1,700 couples. Among the younger couples, a pattern that the authors identified as inadequate role performance—especially not being attuned to the other partner's sexual needs and not being comfortable with the role of husband or wife—seemed to explain much of the instability in their relationships. Among those who married at an older age, another pattern appeared. These couples were more likely to engage in bitter disputes over the division of labor within the family—that is, over the definition of gender roles. Women who marry at older ages, for example, are more likely to demand that both partners share equally in the housework.

It appears that earlier in this century, when women were more likely to assume the role of homemaker, marriages had a higher probability of lasting. The demand by women for sharing of household roles—what sociologists often call the demand for a "symmetrical family" in which partners share equally in the roles of provider and homemaker—creates new opportunities for both men and women, but it also places more stress on the family in its early stages (Brody, 1992; Pearson & Hendrix, 1979; Weir & Weir, 1976; Willmott & Young, 1971). Symmetrical families are not necessarily more dissatisfied with their marriages than nonsymmetrical families, nor do they necessarily encounter more marital problems. It appears, however, that the greater ability of both partners to be economically inde-

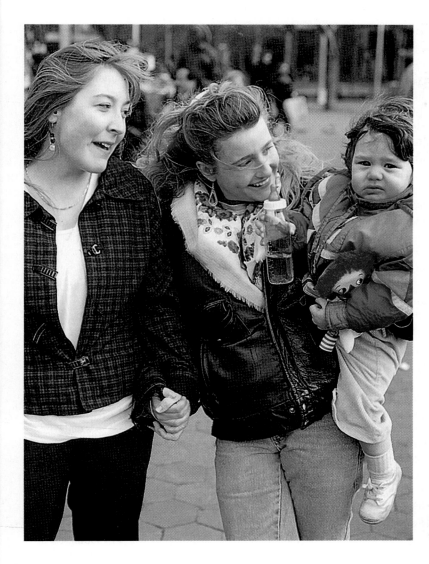

This couple and their young child are part of an increasing trend toward family formation among gay and lesbian couples.

pendent may allow them to consider divorce sooner than would a couple in which the wife is not in the labor force.

Even when a couple is doing well economically, researchers find that the husband's role in the couple's problem-solving efforts is a key predictor of whether or not the couple will divorce. Couples in which the husband "stonewalls," withdraws from arguments, and fails to make an effort to work things out are more likely to divorce (Brody, 1992).

A number of other factors have also been found to be correlated with marital instability and divorce. They include the following:

- The couple met "on the rebound" (i.e., after one or both partners had experienced a great loss or hurt) and the new relationship may be flawed as a result.

- One of the partners wants to live far away from his or her family of orientation, suggesting that feelings of hostility toward family members may complicate the relationship.

- The spouses' family backgrounds are markedly different in terms of race, religion, education, or social class, which may result in differences in values that can cause conflict between the spouses.

- The couple is dependent on one of the extended families for income, shelter, or emotional support.

- The couple married after an acquaintanceship of less than 6 months or after an engagement of more than 3 years.

- Marital patterns in either spouse's extended family were unstable.

- The wife became pregnant before or within the first year of marriage (McGoldrick & Carter, 1982, based on a survey of research by Becker, 1977; Bumpass & Sweet, 1972; and Goodrich, Ryder, & Rausch, 1968).

These correlates of marital instability do not, of course, necessarily mean that marriages that occur under these conditions are doomed to break up. They merely suggest that on the basis of statistical probabilities such marriages have a higher chance of ending in divorce.

THE IMPACT OF DIVORCE

At midcentury it was still considered almost impossible for a divorced man to run for the presidency. Ronald Reagan was the first President who had previously been divorced. Senators Robert Dole and Phil Gramm, candidates in the 1996 presidential election, had each been divorced. Divorce has become much more prevalent than it was earlier in the century. Nevertheless, it remains a significant event in people's lives—as significant as marriage itself. But unlike a wedding, a divorce is not a happy event. Although some divorces turn out well for both partners, the majority do not.

Research on divorce has shown that many of the most disruptive consequences are due to its economic impact. Women suffer an average decline of about 30 percent in their income in the year following separation, while men experience a 15 percent increase. In fact, the majority of women who apply for various forms of public support do so because they have recently experienced a drastic decline in income due to divorce, separation, or abandonment. In addition, almost 40 percent of divorced mothers (and the children in their custody) move within the first year after divorce, and another 20 percent move after a year, a rate far higher than that for married couples (Furstenberg & Cherlin, 1991; McLanahan, 1984). And as if the breakup of their families were not stressful enough, many children also experience the loss of friends and familiar neighborhoods.

Beyond the material effects of divorce, there are the longer-term effects on family roles and the feelings of family members. In an important longitudinal study, Wallerstein and Blakeslee (1989) tracked 60 families with a total of 131 children for a period of 10 to 15 years after divorce. Both parents and children were interviewed at regular intervals. The data from those interviews show that the turmoil and stress of divorce may continue for a year or more. Many divorced adults continue to feel angry, humiliated, and rejected as much as 18 months later, and the children of divorced parents tend to exhibit a variety of psychological problems. Moreover, both men and women have a diminished capacity for parenting after divorce. They spend less time with their children, provide less discipline, and are less sensitive to their needs. Even a decade after the divorce, the parents may be chronically disorganized and unable to meet the challenges of parenting. Instead, they come to depend on their children to help them cope with the demands of their own lives, thereby producing an "overburdened child"—one who, in addition to handling the normal stresses of childhood, also must help his or her parent ward off depression (Wallerstein & Blakeslee, 1989).

There is a silver lining to the dark cloud of divorce, however. Since so many adults who are now marrying for the first time come from families that have experienced divorce, they are likely to take more time in selecting their mates in an effort to make sure that their choice is best for both partners; in addition, they try to become economically secure before marrying, thereby eliminating a major source of stress in a new marriage (Blumstein & Schwartz, 1983). If this is true, the recent modest downturn in the divorce rate may be expected to continue in the future. In any case, the data on the effects of divorce on adults and children suggest that societies need to do more to ease the stress experienced by young families—for example, by providing more day care facilities, establishing more flexible work schedules, and offering opportunities for family leave so that they can care for family members in times of need.

PERSPECTIVES ON THE FAMILY

High divorce rates do not indicate that the family is about to disappear as an institution in modern societies. Even though many marriages end in divorce and increasing numbers of young adults postpone marriage or decide not to marry at all, the large majority do marry, and the majority of those who divorce will eventually remarry. Far from disappearing, the family is adapting to new social values and to changes in other institutions, especially economic ones. In this section we review some current research on family roles and relationships from the standpoint of the three basic sociological perspectives.

THE INTERACTIONIST PERSPECTIVE

Interactions within the family cover a wide range of emotions and may take very different forms in different families. Families laugh and play together, work together, argue and bicker, and so on. All of these aspects of family interaction are important, but frequently it is the arguing and bickering that drives family members apart. Studies of family interaction therefore often focus on the sources of tension and conflict within the family.

Problems of family interaction can stem from a variety of sources. Often problems arise in connection with critical life stages or events, such as the loss of a job or the time when adolescent children begin to assert their independence in ways that threaten established family roles and arrangements. And conflicts often occur because of the particular ways in which the family's experiences are shaped by larger social structures. In the armed forces, for example, families often experience severe stress because of frequent moves from one base to another (Shaw, 1979). In many cases such moves draw family members closer together, but in other cases family interactions are marked by tension because children resent their inability to maintain stable friendships.

The context within which family life occurs can affect family interactions in other ways as well. At the lower levels of a society's stratification system, for example, money (or the lack of it) is often a source of conflict between parents or between parents and children. But the rich are by no means immune to problems of family interaction. Because they do not have to be concerned about the need to earn a living as adults and because their parents can satisfy any desires they may have, the children of the very rich often develop a sadness that resembles anomie (Wixen, 1979). Their lack of clear goals, which sometimes expresses itself in a compulsion to make extravagant purchases, may give rise to conflict between them and their parents.

In order to study these situations, either to help a family resolve its problems or to understand the nature of family conflict more thoroughly, the social scientist must interact with and observe the family, either at home, in a lab, or in a therapy setting (Minuchin, 1974; Satir, 1972; Whitchurch & Constantine, 1993). In the following example two family therapists, Augustus Napier and Carl Whitaker (1980), describe a family in which the parents are deeply troubled by the behavior of their 17-year-old daughter, the oldest of their three children. The father is a prominent attorney, the mother a college-educated woman who has devoted herself to homemaking. The parents' definition of the situation that has brought them into therapy is that they are worried about their daughter. She disobeys, is delinquent, and is depressed enough to make them fear that she might commit suicide. The mother and daughter fight bitterly, but usually the mother retreats. The father often attempts to defend the daughter, but eventually he sides with the mother.

After a few sessions Napier and Whitaker begin to challenge the parents' assumption that it is the daughter who is "the problem." They guess that her depression, anger, and delinquent behavior are symptoms of larger problems in the family. After some gentle probing they identify a triangle of family conflict in which "two parents are emotionally estranged from each other and in their terrible aloneness they overinvolve their children in their emotional distress" (p. 83). The children blame themselves for their parents' problems and develop a low sense of self-worth. The therapists help the couple face the issues that divide them and that motivate their children to offer themselves as scapegoats or intermediaries who divert attention from the parents' basic problems.

Families like the one just described need to resolve a contradiction inherent in the institution of the family: the need to maintain the *individuality* of each member while providing love and support for him or her within a set of *interdependent* relationships. Many families never succeed in developing ways of encouraging each member to realize his or her full potential within the context of family life. And research shows that the core problem is usually the failure of the adult couple, even in intact families, to understand and develop their own relationship. Such a couple may become what John F. Cuber and Peggy B. Haroff (1980) term

"conflict-habituated" or "devitalized." Couples of the first type have evolved ways of expressing their hostility toward each other through elaborate patterns of conflict that persist over many years. In contrast, the devitalized or "empty-shell" marriage may have begun with love and shared interests, but the partners have not grown as a couple and have drifted apart emotionally. Each has the habit of being with the other, a habit that may be strongly supported by the norms of a particular ethnic or religious community. Neither partner is satisfied by the relationship, but neither feels that he or she can do anything to change the situation. Thus the conflicts that might have produced change are reduced to indifference.

Today social scientists who study family interaction must deal with family structures that are more complex than the traditional nuclear family. Divorce and remarriage create many situations in which children have numerous sets of parental figures—parents and stepparents, grandparents and surrogate grandparents, and so on. These changes in family form result in new patterns of family interaction. For example, in a study of 2,000 children conducted over a 5-year period, sociologist Frank Furstenberg found that 52 percent of children raised by their mothers do not see their fathers at all, not only because the fathers are absent by choice but because the opportunities for visits decrease as parents remarry or move away (cited in Aspaklaria, 1985). This produces situations in which parents strive to maintain long-distance relationships with their children and occasionally have brief, intense visits with them. Although this specific type of relationship may not be the most desirable, it appears that if parents and children can express love and affection even when the parents are divorced, the children's ability to feel good about themselves and to love others in their turn may not be impaired.

THE CONFLICT PERSPECTIVE

The conflict perspective on families and family interactions assumes that "social conflict is a basic element of human social life." Conflict exists "within all types of social interaction, and at all levels of social organization. This is as true of the family as it is of any other type of social entity" (Farrington & Chertok, 1993, p. 368). From this perspective one can observe actual family interactions (the micro level) and ask why conflict occurs, what the issues are, and how they are resolved. At a more macro level, one can ask how conditions of inequality and class conflict influence actual families or the laws and policies governing the family as a central institution in society.

Family researchers Jeffrey L. Edleson and Ngoh Tiong Tan (1993) describe two cases of family conflict (specifically, spouse abuse) that highlight the conflict approach to understanding families. Their research compares Chinese and North American families that have experienced incidents of abuse of wives by their husbands.

Spouse Abuse in a Chinese Family. Mrs. Lee is referred to a social worker after seeking aid at a police station when she was struck in the face by her husband. In Chinese and other Asian cultures, the wife is expected to leave her family of orientation to take up residence with her husband and his extended family. Mrs. Lee's husband's family is dominated by her mother-in-law, a powerful widow who treats Mrs. Lee as the person with the lowest status in the family. Mrs. Lee wishes her mother-in-law would be less autocratic and complains about her dictatorial behavior to her own parents and to her husband. Her husband, on the other hand, believes his wife should conform to the ancient norms of Chinese family life and obey his mother. He and his mother consider Mrs. Lee a "traitor" because she has appealed to authorities outside the family.

The police and social workers are representatives of the larger society, which seeks to help families avoid violence. But they cannot simply impose a new form of power on this complex extended family. Instead, they apply conflict theory to the situation. The social worker convenes a meeting of the family to which Mrs. Lee's older brother is also invited. Together the group works out a detailed understanding of the roles of all the family members. The social worker explains that Mrs. Lee is not seeking to challenge her mother-in-law. In fact, however, the social worker has demonstrated to the extended family that Mrs. Lee has a support network and resources outside the family—a new notion for a traditional Chinese family. No doubt there will be further conflict, but power relations within the family have been subtly altered as a result of this intervention.

A North American Family Copes With Violence. Susan was a regular victim of her husband Bob's violent anger. The beatings began on their honeymoon and ended 20 years later when he struck her with a baseball bat, almost killing her. During those years their children suffered emotionally from the violence they witnessed and the unhappiness their mother experienced. But Susan loved Bob and struggled to make the marriage work. Now the couple are in court because after the last assault Bob was arrested. He faces a jail sentence, and Susan has abandoned hope of making the marriage work. She understands that she must make a new life for herself. She is seeking opportunities to do so but knows that she also needs protection from possible future assaults.

Unlike Mr. and Mrs. Lee, neither Bob nor Susan lives near or in an extended-family network. Many Americans do not live in close contact with relatives; on the average, "extended families do not figure as prominently in the lives of Caucasian Americans as they do in other subcultures and in many Asian societies" (Edleson & Tan, 1993, p. 384). Bob and Susan had left their extended families in search of economic opportunity. Susan now has nowhere to turn for help except the police and social-welfare agencies. This "social safety net" will act to protect her so that she and her children can live in peace. Susan will also rely on these

agencies to enforce Bob's responsibilities toward his children.

Susan needs the help of outside agencies to gain relief from the deadly conflict that has destroyed her family. Yet these very agencies came into being as a result of conflict in the larger society. They emerged after decades of protests and demands by women and social activists for ways to protect innocent family members from their abusers. But as we learn almost daily from reports of incidents of spouse and child abuse, it is never easy to ensure that the agencies society has created will intervene effectively. Even if they have the necessary resources, there is no guarantee that they will always act wisely to balance the conflicting values of individual rights and preservation of the family.

"Family Values" and Class Conflict. At this writing, citizens of the United States are engaged in a major public debate over issues related to the family, including homosexual marriage, freedom to obtain abortions, enforcement of child support and child abuse laws, and a host of other controversies that have a direct bearing on the family as an institution in society. The federal budget battle of the mid-1990s is also an arena of conflict over family policies, for it centers on the social safety net of welfare agencies, payments to families with dependent children, and many other spending categories that transfer money from more affluent families and individuals to those with fewer resources and, often, great need.

Figure 16.8 shows that there are approximately 7.7 million families in the United States living at or below the official poverty line, and 10.2 million living at or below 125 percent of the poverty line. Figure 16.9 reveals that poverty affects a far greater proportion of black and Hispanic families than white families, even though the majority of poor families are white. Box 16.2 presents additional information on family poverty. (See also Box 12.2, which discusses how poverty in families is measured.)

Sociologists who study poverty argue that most families are poor for the obvious reason that they do not earn or receive enough income. But critics of liberal social-welfare policies argue that self-destructive behaviors of family members themselves, such as dropping out of school, drug use, and out-of-wedlock childbearing, are causes of poverty. Social-welfare policies that are too generous or take the form of entitlements that do not have to be earned are said to encourage behaviors that cause poverty.

Social scientists who study class conflict and poverty policies, notably Herbert Gans (1995), Christopher Jencks (1993), and Michael Katz (1983), point out that earlier in this century a large proportion of impoverished families were composed of elderly couples who did not have Social Security or Medicaid, two programs that have drastically reduced poverty among elderly Americans. Yet at the time that these policies were being debated, many members of the upper classes opposed them, viewing them as undemo-

FIGURE 16.8 Number of Families in Poverty,
United States, 1987–1991
(including value of all benefits)

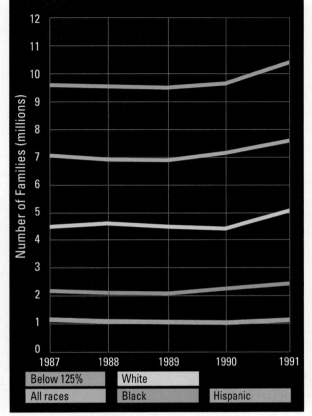

Source: Data from *Statistical Abstract,* 1993.

FIGURE 16.9 Percent of Families in Poverty,
United States, 1987–1991
(including value of all benefits)

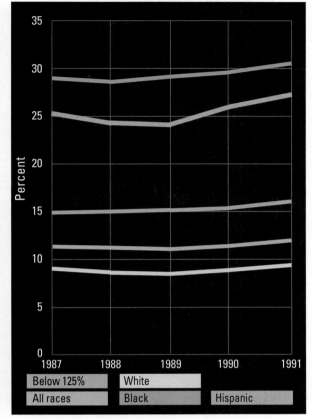

Source: Data from *Statistical Abstract,* 1993.

cratic transfers of wealth to less deserving members of society. The situation today is similar, as members of the upper classes oppose adequate funding for day care and other policies that can help move adult family members from dependence on public support to employment at decent jobs.

FUNCTIONALIST VIEWS OF THE FAMILY

From a functionalist perspective, the family evolves in both form and function in response to changes in the larger social environment. As societies undergo such major changes as industrialization and urbanization, the family must adapt to the effects of those changes. Functionalist theorists like Talcott Parsons and William Goode have called attention to the loss of family functions that occurs as other social institutions like schools, corporations, and social-welfare agencies perform functions that were previously reserved for the family. We have discussed numerous examples of this trend in earlier chapters—the tendency of families to have fewer children as the demand for agricultural labor decreased, the changing composition of households as people were required to seek work away from their

families of orientation, the increasing number of dual-income households, and so on. The functionalist explanation of these changes is that as the division of labor becomes more complex and as new, more specialized institutions arise, the family too must become a more specialized institution. Thus modern families no longer perform certain functions that used to be within their domain, but they do play an increasingly vital part in early-childhood socialization, in the emotional lives of their members, and in preparing older children for adult roles in the economic institutions of industrial societies (Parsons & Bales, 1955).

A good example of empirical studies of how family functioning adapts to social change is research on the effects of child care on infant development. Figure 16.10 on page 496 shows that the percentage of women aged 18 to 44 who are in the labor force after having a child in the last year has risen from slightly more than 30 percent in 1976 to over 50 percent in 1990. The figure also shows that there is a wide array of child care arrangements, with day care centers less common than care by a nonrelative in another home. An often cited study (Belsky, 1988; see also Belsky & Steinberg, 1991) offered some evidence that infants who

BOX 16.2 SOCIOLOGICAL METHODS

Interpreting Statistics on Family Poverty

The number and characteristics of families in poverty in the United States are subjects of controversy. How one defines family poverty has a major bearing on the number of families identified as poor. The way one interprets statistics on families living in poverty influences the way one explains the causes and consequences of family poverty. Social scientists and policy makers can consult the same

statistics and produce widely differing explanations. The accompanying charts illustrate these points.

Chart A shows that in 1959 there were 8,320,000 families in poverty, meaning that total family income was below the official poverty line (based on number of family members and income, but not counting the value of other benefits such as food stamps). That number accounted for

CHART A Families Below Poverty Level, United States, 1959–1991

Source: Data from *Statistical Abstract,* 1993.

are given over to a nonparent early in life may suffer developmental problems. This finding has been widely challenged. More recent research using more sophisticated methods shows that with quality care there are no discernible disadvantages for children of working mothers. Of course, the larger issue is how to provide quality care while parents are away working (Eckholm, 1992).

Researchers who approach the issue of child care from a functionalist perspective ask how societies cope with the dilemma faced by families in which both parents work out-

side the home. In an influential study, Kammerman and Kahn (1981) found that advanced industrial societies are struggling with the question: "Can adults manage productive roles in the labor force at the same time as they fulfill productive roles within the family—at home?" (p. 2). Many European nations answered this question by developing policies to assist working parents, including the development of high-quality child and infant care services (e.g., universal day care and school meal programs), paid parental leave, and family allowances that ease the finan-

18.5 percent of all families. By 1973 the figure had declined to 4.8 million, or 8.8 percent of all families—a historic low. Family poverty began to rise again in the early 1980s; by 1986, 10.9 percent of families fell below the official poverty line.

Some policy makers and social scientists argued that these trends were misleading because they did not take into account the value of food stamps, Medicaid, school lunches, and other benefits received by families. These sources of "income" were factored into the calculations, but the new figures did not differ significantly from the earlier ones. Even when the value of federal and state benefits was factored in, the results showed that 10.7 percent of families were poor.

A report titled *Families First,* issued by a task force convened by the Bush administration, included Chart B on single-mother families in poverty. The chart shows that poverty among single-mother families rose precipitously during the 1960s and 1970s, leveled off during the 1980s, and began rising again at the end of the decade. Taken by itself, this chart could make a casual observer think that poverty in families has risen dramatically since the 1960s and that the increase must be a result of single parenthood. The implication is that families are poor because there is only one breadwinner present. An alternative interpretation is that poor people have trouble forming families or keeping them together. When they become poor because of unemployment, their number increases.

Economic conditions can produce drastic changes in the number of families with incomes below the official poverty line. From 1989 to 1991, for example, there was a severe recession in the U.S. economy. Hundreds of thousands of women and men lost their jobs. During this period 254,000 black families, 231,000 Hispanic families, and 551,000 white families joined the millions already in poverty. If we consider all families earning or receiving benefits that fall below 125 percent of the poverty level (meaning another 25 percent of income above the official poverty line), we see that slightly more than 10 million U.S. families (30 percent) are poor by this standard. (See Figure 16.8.)

It is also true that when adolescents have children out of wedlock, these families are extremely likely to have

CHART B   **Single-Mother Families as a Percent of All Poor Families, United States, 1960–1990**

Source: Data from Census Bureau.

incomes that fall below the official poverty line. Thus in 1991, of the 7,712,000 families in poverty, 937,000 (35.5 percent) were headed by a householder who was between 15 and 24 years old. Not all of these families were composed of a single adolescent or young adult mother and her children, but at least three quarters were of that type.

One can conclude from these statistics that the number of families in poverty is very large in absolute terms but remains a small proportion of all families. Poverty in families increases as a result of changes in patterns of employment and unemployment, but it has also been increasing as a consequence of more out-of-wedlock births and a higher rate of family breakup.

cial burden on families with several children. In the United States, however, there is a great deal of debate about whether such policies are appropriate functions of government or whether they lead to higher taxes, forcing more mothers into the labor force (Pittman, 1993).

In a related study, sociologist Arlie Hochschild (1989) asked how adult family members adjust to what she calls the "second shift." Earlier in this century, housework and child care were viewed as primarily the mother's duty even if she worked outside the home. Today, many working par-

ents cooperate and share domestic roles and responsibilities. But it is often difficult to achieve such cooperation. Hochschild found that "most egalitarian women—those with strong feelings about sharing—did one of two things. They married men who planned to share at home or they actively tried to change their husband's understanding of his role at home" (p. 193). Many of the women Hochschild interviewed were like Adrian Sherman, who "took the risky step of telling her husband 'It's share the second shift or it's divorce.' She staged a 'sharing showdown' and won"

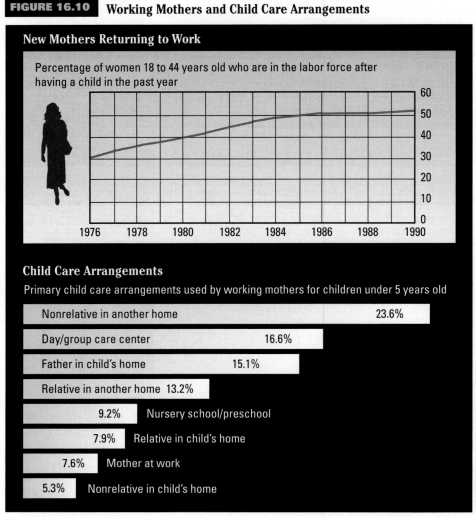

FIGURE 16.10   Working Mothers and Child Care Arrangements

New Mothers Returning to Work

Percentage of women 18 to 44 years old who are in the labor force after having a child in the past year

(Graph showing an increasing line from about 30 in 1976 to over 50 in 1990, with y-axis values 0, 10, 20, 30, 40, 50, 60 and x-axis years 1976, 1978, 1980, 1982, 1984, 1986, 1988, 1990)

Child Care Arrangements

Primary child care arrangements used by working mothers for children under 5 years old

Arrangement	Percentage
Nonrelative in another home	23.6%
Day/group care center	16.6%
Father in child's home	15.1%
Relative in another home	13.2%
Nursery school/preschool	9.2%
Relative in child's home	7.9%
Mother at work	7.6%
Nonrelative in child's home	5.3%

Source: Data from Census Bureau.

(p. 193). Other women do not go so far as to stage a showdown. They may make incremental efforts to change their husbands' attitudes. Still others discuss the issue with their husbands, but the process is not an easy one. More than half of the working women Hochschild interviewed had tried in one way or another to change domestic roles. As Hochschild notes, "If women lived in a culture that presumed active fatherhood, they wouldn't need to devise personal strategies to bring it about" (p. 193).

In sum, research from all the major sociological perspectives supports the view that the family is a resilient institution; it adapts to changing economic conditions and changing values. But the strength of the family as an institution does not mean the divorce rate will decrease rapidly or families that experience severe stress due to unemployment, ill health, and the like will have an easier time remaining intact. Indeed, few of the challenges we face in our lives are greater than that of selecting a mate and making family decisions. Thus social scientists who do research on the family will continue to find that there is a need for the

information they provide. Those who work on macrosocial questions—issues of government policy regarding welfare or retirement or home financing, for example—will continue to study the impact of social policies on families. And those who delve into the microsocial world of family interaction will continue to ask how changes in norms and values affect the roles we play in families. As Napier observes:

> Every family is a miniature society, a social order with its own rules, structure, leadership, language, style of living. . . . The hidden rules, the subtle nuances of language, the private rituals and dances that define every family as a unique microculture may not be easy for an outsider to perceive at first glance, but they are there. (Napier & Whitaker, 1980, p. 78)

RESEARCH FRONTIERS: THE BLACK FAMILY

At this writing, the United States and many other Western nations are engaged in vigorous debates about the role of public funding for poor families. In the United States this debate is complicated by the fact that poverty rates are higher for black and other minority families than for white families even though in absolute terms there are many more poor white families. Adding to the confusion is the controversy over "family values." In the case of the black family, the central issue is whether high rates of poverty, crime, and school failure in low-income, segregated black communities are a *cause* or a *consequence* of the large number of black single-parent families.

This issue is not a new one. Earlier in this century the eminent African American sociologist E. Franklin Frazier argued in *The Negro Family in the United States* (1939) that the violence of the Middle Passage, in which Africans were captured, shipped in chains, and sold into slavery, had wiped out their previous family ties. Frazier believed that as a result of that experience, the only enduring family form among blacks was the bond between mother and child. He urged black Americans to emulate the white middle-class family. In 1965 his views were endorsed by the famous Moynihan Report, which attributed the higher rates of social problems found in poor black communities to inadequate family functioning and the "tangle of pathology" that results from fatherlessness.

Critics of this theory argue that it neglects the effects of both past and present discrimination, which have been particularly severe for black men in America. The extreme difficulty experienced by black men in gaining the economic security necessary to sustain a family, it is argued, becomes a formidable obstacle to marriage (Sweet & Bumpass, 1987). Focusing on the problems of the black family suggests that there is something wrong with poor black people rather than with the larger society (Miller, 1993).

Demographer Valerie Kincade Oppenheimer (1994) notes that the number of men between the ages of 20 and 35 who are not in the labor force has been rising since the 1950s and has accelerated since 1970. This trend is particularly evident among black men, especially those with no college education. In 1960 approximately 26 percent of this group were not in school or in the labor force; by 1990 that figure had risen to more than 50 percent. (The comparable figures for white men are 11 percent and 23 percent, respectively.) One consequence of this trend has been a marked increase in delay of marriage and rates of nonmarriage. Oppenheimer observes that among black women "there seems little doubt that, in addition to greater delays in marriage, the proportion who will never marry has been rising significantly and is historically unprecedented. It is unclear whether this represents a rejection of marriage or is indicative of the difficulties blacks have been experiencing in making a satisfactory marriage" (p. 306).

Most sociologists agree that the rapid rise in black female-headed families is due primarily to the difficulties faced by young black men with limited education when seeking jobs. Harriet P. McAdoo, a specialist in the study of

disadvantaged women and children, makes the following point:

> The tradition used to be that if a woman got pregnant, they were expected to get married, if not forced to get married, to supply income and a name for the child. But if the man has no job, there's no impetus for them to get married. Her parents would have three people to support instead of just two. The boy would become an additional burden on the family. Parents feel: "Why should I force her to marry him? He'll be a drain." (quoted in Cummings, 1983, p. 56)

Other sociologists believe that the problem is multidimensional. As family sociologist Bonnie Thornton Dill points out, "Poverty, unemployment, welfare programs that penalize families: these things explain a major portion of the variance between blacks and whites in the number of female-headed households, not all of it." She notes that changes in the nature of urban poverty that increasingly isolate poor people from quality education and employment opportunities also deprive them of the opportunity to marry. "Teen-age pregnancy among blacks has not increased so much," Dill concludes, "but the rate of marriage among teen-agers has dropped and the number of children born to married couples has dropped. These things are related to perceptions of opportunity" (quoted in Suro, 1992, p. A12).

Even though the data show that the phenomena of teenage pregnancy, female-headed families, and children being raised in poverty are related to social class rather than to race, the fact that more blacks than whites are found in the lower income levels of society means that these problems are proportionally more serious for blacks. In the words of sociologist Joyce Ladner (1973), "Life in the black community has been conditioned by poverty, discrimination, and institutional subordination" (p. 425). Under these conditions, she concludes, the black family has shown surprising resilience. Although within a given black family there may be households headed by single women, the extended family often provides substantial support for its less fortunate members.

Clearly, there is a need to find ways of helping teenagers of all racial and ethnic groups avoid becoming parents before they are economically ready to do so. This also applies to low-income Hispanic and Native American families, and especially to Mexican and Puerto Rican families that, like low-income black families, tend to be segregated in impoverished inner-city communities where jobs are scarce (Sandefur & Tienda, 1988). The policy of requiring single mothers to work rather than go on welfare may act as a deterrent to teenage pregnancy, but it will not prevent poor teenagers from being exposed to a culture that tells them that sex is fun and that parenthood is a route to adulthood. Black and Latino leaders therefore are urging organizations in their communities to provide guidance and support for poor teenagers.

VISUAL SOCIOLOGY

AN EXTENDED FAMILY

The members of the Ivanovich family shown in these photos are gypsies of the Boyash tribe. Only a few of the family's 73 members are shown here. A remarkable fact about this gypsy family is that in the midst of poverty and a transient lifestyle, a highly cohesive extended family thrives from one generation to the next (Kornblum, 1975). All of the family's members—from Alexandre and Marie, the patriarch and matriarch, to the youngest children—live in a single settlement, although of course there are nuclear families within the extended family. The man in the handsome couple shown outside their wagon is the son of Marie and Alexandre Ivanovich. The man training the monkey has married into the family. His name is Cortez, and he is a Boyash whose family had traveled in Spain, which is how he acquired his Spanish name.

During many centuries of wandering through more sedentary societies, the gypsies have become an urban people. They thrive in towns and cities, yet they are constantly moving from one urban base to another. In the case of the Ivanovich family, their occupation keeps them on the road; because the family earns much of its income by training animals for circuses and street shows, they must do a great deal of traveling to buy animals or trade them. Yet wherever they move they keep the extended family together, and with it the gypsy language and culture.

498

Before the age of radio and television, traveling carnivals and circuses often featured trained bears. But today such shows are dying out, as they cannot compete with the thrills offered by television and the movies. And the younger members of the Ivanovich family are more interested in learning how to repair autos and trucks than in training animals. Only Marie and Alexandre are fully versed in the ancient lore of bear training. Cortez may take over in time, but even so no one is sure who will follow him.

Despite these changes, there is still a demand for the folk entertainment provided by the Boyash gypsies and other carnival people. In this age of electronic entertainment, they are a curious throwback to an age of minstrels and bear tamers. And so they draw crowds in the streets of Paris, where these pictures were taken. The trickle of coins from the crowds enables the Ivanovich family to stay together and to socialize new generations into gypsy life in the midst of one of the world's most modern and cosmopolitan cities.

SUMMARY

THINK ABOUT IT CRITICALLY

During the 1994 congressional election campaigns, family policies and "family values" were used as wedge issues to create divisions in the electorate. These issues were raised by some candidates to suggest that people in single-parent or gay families are deviant or otherwise threatening to the nation's values. From what you have learned in this chapter, can you describe the voters this appeal to "family values" might attract and the voters it would repel?

In all known societies almost everyone is socialized within a network of family rights and obligations that are known as family role relations. In simple societies the family performs a large number of other functions as well, but in modern societies most of the functions that were traditionally performed by the family are performed partly or entirely by other social institutions.

A *family* is a group of people related by blood, marriage, or adoption, and the role relations among family members are known as *kinship* relations. The smallest unit of family structure is the *nuclear family,* consisting of two or more people related by consanguineous ties or by adoption who share a household. The nuclear family in which a person is born and socialized is the *family of orientation,* and the nuclear family a person forms through marriage or cohabitation is the *family of procreation.* An *extended family* includes an individual's nuclear family plus all the nuclear families of his or her blood relatives.

The traditional household consisting of two parents and their children is no longer the typical American family. Since the 1940s there has been a dramatic increase in female-headed single-parent families and in nonfamily households, as well as in the numbers of women and men living alone and in the numbers of unmarried same-sex couples.

Studies of changes in family structure have shown that family units become simpler as societies undergo industrialization. Economic and technological changes require the family to adapt to an economy in which income is earned outside the family; this means that families must become smaller, more mobile, and more flexible. More recent research has found that nuclear families have not entirely replaced extended families, although extended families do not always live under one roof. Modern technologies like the telephone and the automobile enable members of smaller family units to maintain kinship ties with their extended families.

The typical stages of the family life cycle are family formation, start of childbearing, end of childbearing, "empty nest," and family dissolution (i.e., the death of one spouse). As it passes through this cycle, every family experiences changes in its system of role relations. These changes present major emotional challenges, which are often complicated by divorce, remarriage, and the combining of children of different marriages in stepfamilies.

In all cultures the process of mate selection is carried out according to basic rules of bargaining and exchange. In many societies the customary pattern of mate selection is the arranged marriage, in which the families of the bride and groom negotiate the marriage contract. All cultures also have norms that specify whether a person brought up in that culture may marry within or outside the cultural group. Marriage within the group is termed *endogamy;* marriage outside the group is termed *exogamy.* In societies in which marriages are based on attraction and love, individuals tend to marry people similar to themselves in social background, a tendency that is referred to as *homogamy.* Homogamy generally serves to maintain the separateness of religious and racial groups.

Compared with the mate selection systems of other cultures, that of the United States gives love greater prominence. Yet from a scientific standpoint little is known about this complex emotional state. It appears that people who fall in love tend to be alike in social characteristics but different in their psychological needs; however, this is not always the case. There is also considerable evidence that love relationships are more lasting when the partners' affection for each other is roughly equal.

In the United States and other Western societies, the rate of divorce has risen sharply since World War II. In the 1980s it was widely believed that the practice of cohabitation before marriage would result in greater marital stability, but in fact the divorce rate among couples who had lived together before marriage was higher than the rate for couples who had not done so.

Age at marriage has been found to be one of the leading factors in divorce. Marriages that take place when the woman is in her teens or in her thirties are much more likely to end in divorce than marriages that take place when the woman is in her twenties. Among other factors that have been found to be correlated with divorce are marked differences in the family backgrounds of the spouses, dependence on either spouse's extended family, patterns of marital instability in either spouse's extended family, and early pregnancy. Studies of the impact of divorce have found that the turmoil and distress of divorce may continue for a year or more. Both men and women have a diminished capacity for parenting after divorce and may come to depend on their children to help them cope with the demands of their own lives.

The structural context within which family life occurs can affect family interactions in a variety of ways. Problems may arise in connection with the demands placed on the family by institutions of the larger society, or as a result of its position in the society's stratification system. A basic contradiction inherent in the institution of the family is the need to maintain the individuality of each member while providing love and support for him or her within a set of interdependent relationships.

From a conflict perspective, changes in the family as an institution cannot occur without conflict both within the family and between the family and other institutions. Such conflict is illustrated by public debates over family policies and "family values."

Functionalist theorists have called attention to the loss of family functions that occurs as other social institutions assume functions that were previously reserved for the family. At the same time, they note that modern families play a vital part in early-childhood socialization, in the emotional lives of their members, and in preparing older children for adult roles.

CRITICAL RESPONSE

The data on changes in the structure of American families clearly show that there is no longer a typical family form. By singling out families that differ from the traditional two-parent, undivorced family, proponents of "family values" seek to win over voters who are concerned about these changes. At the same time, however, they risk alienating those who are in nontraditional families and households.

GLOSSARY

family: a group of people related by blood, marriage, or adoption. (p. 474)

kinship: the role relations among people who consider themselves to be related by blood, marriage, or adoption. (p. 475)

nuclear family: two or more people related by blood, marriage, or adoption who share a household. (p. 475)

family of orientation: the nuclear family in which a person is born and raised. (p. 475)

family of procreation: the nuclear family a person forms through marriage or cohabitation. (p. 475)

extended family: an individual's nuclear family plus the nuclear families of his or her blood relatives. (p. 476)

endogamy: a norm specifying that a person brought up in a particular culture may marry within the cultural group. (p. 484)

exogamy: a norm specifying that a person brought up in a particular culture may marry outside the cultural group. (p. 484)

homogamy: the tendency to marry a person who is similar to oneself in social background. (p. 484)

WHERE TO FIND IT

BOOKS

How Americans Use Time (John P. Robinson; Praeger, 1977). An excellent source of comparative data on how much time men and women spend on various activities in their families and households.

Divided Families: What Happens to Children When Parents Part (Frank F. Furstenberg, Jr., & Andrew J. Cherlin; Harvard University Press, 1991). An assessment of the impact of divorce on the emotional, educational, and economic lives of children who experience the divorce of their parents.

The Reconstruction of Family Policy (Elaine A. Anderson & Richard C. Hula, eds.; Greenwood Press, 1991). A series of original essays on the problems of developing family policies, with special emphasis on conflicting interests of parents, children, and society. Includes good material on latchkey children and after-school care, welfare policies, and problems of the elderly in families.

World Revolution and Family Patterns (William J. Goode; Free Press, 1970). A useful source of information on how the institution of the family has changed with revolutions in the productive organization and technologies of societies.

The Family Crucible (Augustus Y. Napier & Carl Whitaker; Bantam, 1980). An introduction to the dynamics of family interaction and family therapy.

JOURNALS

Journal of Marriage and the Family. Published quarterly by the National Council on Family Relations, Minneapolis, Minnesota. The best journal on family research in the United States.

Sex Roles: A Journal of Research. A monthly journal published by Plenum Press.

OTHER SOURCES

Current Population Reports. A series of special reports on household composition, marriage and divorce, and labor force participation; available in the census section of your library or from the nearest office of the U.S. Department of Labor or U.S. Publications Office. These reports present detailed demographic and economic data and include comparisons with earlier years.

Vital Statistics of the United States, Vol. III: Marriage and Divorce. An annual compilation that presents a complete count of marriages and divorces in the preceding year. Data are broken down by age, race, previous marital status, and other characteristics.

CHAPTER 17

Religion

It was not yet 8:00 A.M. that rainy Tuesday morning, but the dozens of Baptists who were staying in the suburban La Quinta motel outside of Dallas had already begun to make their way toward the center of town. . . . In all the history of Southern Baptist Conventions, barely more than 22,000 people had ever come to one of these annual meetings. But when registration had closed the night before, more than 35,000 had already signed in for this one.

The writer is sociologist Nancy Tatom Ammerman, who describes the historic convention in her book *Baptist Battles* (1990). Hers is a story of deeply felt division and debate in one of the most influential religious denominations in the United States. The key issue at the convention was whether the Baptist fundamentalists, whose strength was increasing rapidly, would wrest control of the denomination's affairs from its moderate and liberal leaders. But Ammerman was not merely a sociological observer at these dramatic proceedings. She grew up in the deeply religious social world of

Southern Baptists and attended a small Baptist college; her husband attended the Southern Baptist Seminary. The denomination's leaders and activists, she tells us, "are important people in my life, and I have shared with them in the griefs of these years. Many of the people about whom I care most deeply have been a part of the ministry of the Southern Baptist Convention."

In the 1980s the Southern Baptists became embroiled in conflicts between fundamentalist and more moderate leaders. Ammerman used her sociological training and her extensive personal knowledge of Baptist congregations to try to understand the causes and consequences of these divisions. She conducted hundreds of interviews with church members and sent thousands of questionnaires to Baptist leaders throughout the nation. Many people spoke to her with deep feeling about their religious convictions. One convention

participant, for example, explained why he had chosen a fundamentalist congregation in these words:

> I sort of had been wondering why I couldn't find a church that was more evangelical, teaching the Word the way it should be, not the Social Gospel, a church where people were being saved, being taught to live the Christian life. . . . The church I'm going to now has a dynamic pastor, and the church is growing at a phenomenal rate. The people there have a sweet spirit and have dedication to the Lord—they're interested in doing His work and not ashamed that they are evangelical type Christians. (quoted in Ammerman, 1990, p. 118)

A moderate church leader told her that Baptists stand for "religious liberty. That's very important. Fundamentalists play that down, and that's where the rubber hits the road" (quoted in Ammerman, 1990, p. 119).

Deeply split over how to cope with issues of modernity and social change, the Southern Baptists eventually rejected more moderate versions of their faith and chose a fundamentalist leadership. Through the years of turmoil Ammerman struggled to remain objective and not favor one side over the other. In her attempt to be evenhanded she imposed rules on herself. "Most basically, the questions I would ask about this conflict would be informed by sociological theory, not by any desire to prove one side right or wrong" (p. xii).

RELIGION IN SOCIETY

Religion, one of the oldest human institutions, is also among the most changeable and complex. On the one hand, religion expresses our deepest yearnings for spiritual enlightenment and understanding; on the other, conflicts over religious beliefs and practices have given rise to persecution, wars, and much human suffering, as can be seen, for example, in the violence between Muslim and Serbian Orthodox Christians in war-torn Bosnia. Compared to that tragic conflict the dispute among Southern Baptists is mild, but extremely important nonetheless. Little wonder, therefore, that the founders of sociology—including Émile Durkheim, Karl Marx, and Max Weber—all wrote extensively about the power of religion and the great changes religion has undergone as societies have evolved.

DEFINING RELIGION

Religion is not easy to define. One could begin with a definition that has a concept of God as its core, but many religions do not have a clear concept of God. One could define religion in terms of the emotions of spirituality, oneness with nature, awe, mystery, and many other feelings, but that would not be a very helpful definition because emotions are extremely difficult to capture in words. Taking another tack, one might think in terms of organized religion—churches, congregations, ministers, rabbis, and so on—but clearly the organizational aspect of religion is just one of its many dimensions. It is frustrating to have to work so hard to define something that seems so commonplace, yet without a good working definition of religion it is impossible to compare different religions or refer to particular aspects of religion.

We can approach a working definition of religion by saying that **religion** is any set of coherent answers to the dilemmas of human existence that makes the world meaningful. From this point of view, religion is how human beings express their feelings about such ultimate concerns as sickness or death or the meaning of human life. Almost all religions involve their adherents in a system of beliefs and practices that express devotion to the supernatural and foster deep feelings of spirituality. In this sense, we say that religion functions to meet the spiritual needs of individuals.

But religion has also been defined in terms of its social function: It is a system of beliefs and rituals that serves to bind people together through shared worship, thereby creating a social group. **Rituals** are formal patterns of activity that express symbolically a set of shared meanings; in the case of religious rituals such as baptism or commu-

504

Throughout most of human history, until the past century or two, religion dominated all cultural life, as it still does in many societies. This photo shows Muslim worshipers praying outdoors in Mecca, Saudi Arabia, the most sacred site of the Islamic faith.

nion, the shared meanings are sacred. The term **sacred** refers to phenomena that are regarded as extraordinary, transcendent, and outside the everyday course of events—that is, supernatural. That which is sacred may be represented by a wide variety of symbols, such as a god or set of gods; a holy person such as the Buddha; various revered writings like the Bible, the Torah, or the Koran; holy objects such as the cross or the star of David; holy cities like Jerusalem or Mecca; and much else. The term **profane** refers to all phenomena that are not sacred.

RELIGION AS AN INSTITUTION

Religion is a major social institution because it carries out important social functions and encompasses a great variety of organizations (e.g., churches, congregations, charities), each with its own statuses and roles (e.g., ministers, priests, rabbis, parishioners, fund-raisers) and specific sets of norms and values (e.g., the Ten Commandments, the Golden Rule, the Koranic rules). As an institution, religion carries out the function of helping people express their feelings of spirituality and faith. Religion is often said to be a cultural institution because it guides a society's mental life, especially its ideas about morality, goodness, and evil. Of course, religion is not alone in performing these functions, but it remains a powerful source of moral precepts.

Religion also serves to confer legitimacy on a society's norms and values. Families seek the "blessing of holy matrimony" in wedding ceremonies. Baptisms, bar mitzvahs, confirmations, and other religious ceremonies mark the passage of children through their developmental stages and are occasions for statements about proper behavior

and good conduct. Swearing on a Bible is common in courtrooms and on other occasions when norms of truth and fairness are being enforced. The political institutions of society also frequently look to religion for legitimation. The monarchs of eighteenth-century Europe invoked the will of God in their activities and sometimes claimed to rule by "divine right." The Pledge of Allegiance includes the phrase "under God" to reinforce the feeling that the destiny and unity of the nation and the values of liberty and justice are human efforts to carry out an even higher purpose.

Our society insists on separation of the influence of religion from the laws of government. There is always controversy, however, over how much legitimacy religions can confer on political behavior. Fundamentalist Muslims may deny women rights that would be thought routine in our own culture (such as the right to drive a car); in the United States, Christian fundamentalists may claim that God does not favor political candidates who support abortion or homosexual rights. But these claims that religion legitimates particular norms and that God does not condone their transgression by political leaders usually clash with more secular interpretations of the society's norms. Thus debates over the role of religion in the political process can become extremely controversial.

THE POWER OF FAITH

Until comparatively recent times religion dominated the cultural life of human societies. Activities that are now performed by other cultural institutions, particularly education, art, and the media, used to be the province of religious leaders and organizations. In hunting-and-gathering bands and in many tribal societies, the holy person, or shaman, was also the teacher and communicator of the society's beliefs and values. In early agrarian societies the priesthood was a powerful force; only the priests were literate and, hence, able to interpret and preserve the society's sacred texts, which represented the culture's most strongly held values and norms. For example, in ancient Egypt, where the pharaoh was worshipped as a god, his organization of regional and local priests controlled the entire society.

Today religion continues to play an important part in the lives of people throughout the world even though the influence of organized religions is diminishing in many societies. In the United States, for example, the Gallup Poll routinely asks Americans whether they believe in God. In 1944, 96 percent of the population said they were believers; in the 1990s the proportion of believers remains over 90 percent (NORC, 1994; Piazza & Glock, 1979). The strength of religious attitudes and the influence of some religions can also be seen in the conflict over abortion, which plays such a prominent role in American politics, and in the controversies generated by Christian fundamentalists who believe in the literal interpretation of the Bible and may therefore deny the validity of evolutionary theory. Outside the United States, the Islamic world is torn by religious strife between liberals and fundamentalists, and Lebanon and Northern Ireland remain deeply divided owing largely to conflict between Protestants and Catholics or between Christians and Muslims.

At the same time that religion is a source of division and conflict, it can also be a force for healing social problems and moving masses of people toward greater insight into their common humanity. This occurs at the micro level of interaction, for example, in groups like Alcoholics Anonymous, in which spirituality is an essential part of the recovery program. At the macro level, the power of faith can be seen in impoverished rural and urban communities throughout Latin America. In those communities Catholic church leaders, parish priests, and lay parishioners have embraced the ideals of a "social gospel" that seeks the liberation of believers from poverty and oppression. These "base Christian communities," as they are often called, have become a powerful force in the movement for social justice and other far-reaching changes in their societies (Tabb, 1986).

Secularization and Its Limits.   Despite the great power of spirituality, since medieval times the traditional dominance of religion in many spheres of life has

These two pictures of cathedrals provide a graphic illustration of secularization. In the medieval town, the cathedral dominated the landscape; it was the highest, and symbolically the most important, building. In the modern city, even the great cathedral is dwarfed by the greater scale and importance of the commercial buildings that surround it.

been greatly reduced. The process by which this has occurred is termed **secularization.** This process, according to Robert A. Nisbet (1970), "results in . . . respect for values of utility rather than of sacredness alone, control of the environment rather than passive submission to it, and, in some ways most importantly, concern with man's present welfare on this earth rather than his supposed immortal relation to the gods" (p. 388). Secularization usually accompanies the increasing differentiation of cultural institutions—that is, the separation of other institutions from religion. In Europe in the Middle Ages, for example, there were no schools separate from the church. The state, too, was thought of as encompassed by the church or at least as legitimated by the official state religion and church organization. Laws and courts were guided by religious doctrine, and clerical law could often be as important as civil law—indeed, to be tried as a heretic often meant torture and death. Churches engaged in large-scale economic activity, owned much land and property, and often mounted their own armed forces.

The Renaissance, the Enlightenment, and the revolutions of the eighteenth and nineteenth centuries all speeded the process of differentiation in which schools, science, laws, courts, and other institutions gained independence from religious control. However, this process has not occurred at the same rate throughout the world. For example, the removal of education from the control of religious institutions has occurred more slowly in some societies than in others. In Eastern Europe all education was controlled by the state until very recently. In most Western European and American countries there are religious schools, but these are separate from and overshadowed by the state-run educational system (van den Berghe, 1975).

Another example of the increasing differentiation of religion from other institutions is the diminished importance of religion in the arts. Pierre van den Berghe (1975) made the following observation:

> Traditionally, much of music, painting, sculpture, and architecture was devoted to the glorification of God (or his representative, the king). The medieval cathedrals soared loftily from [a] sea of puny houses. . . . In Manhattan, it is St. Patrick's Cathedral that is dwarfed in a forest of skyscrapers. Bach was a church organist; Leonard Bernstein . . . a jet-set entrepreneur. Van Eyck . . . painted chaste madonnas: Renoir . . . luscious nudes. (p. 213)

Box 17.1 describes a form of artistic expression that has not become secularized, although it is admired in secular societies.

The emergence of new cultural institutions and the weakening of the influence of religion does not result in complete secularization. People who are free to determine their own religious beliefs and practices may attend church less often or not at all, but total secularization does not occur (Stark & Bainbridge, 1980). Moreover, in almost every society that has experienced secularization one can find examples of religious revival. Indeed, modern communication technologies, especially television, have contributed immensely to the revival of interest in religion, as witnessed by the popularity of "televangelists" like Oral Roberts and Pat Robertson.

VARIETIES OF RELIGIOUS BELIEF

Religious sentiments and behavior persist even in highly secularized societies like the United States. As sociologist Robert Wuthnow (1988) points out,

> The assumption that religion in modern societies would gradually diminish in importance or else become less capable of influencing public life was once widely accepted. That assumption has now become a matter of dispute. . . . Modern religion is resilient and yet subject to cultural influences; it does not merely survive or decline, but adapts to its environment in complex ways. (p. 474)

Many of the adaptations that religions make to social change become evident when one examines the varieties of religious belief in the world today, and especially when one studies the major world religions.

MAJOR WORLD RELIGIONS

In a 1913 essay Max Weber commented that "by 'world religions' we understand the five religions or religiously determined systems of life-regulation which have known how to gather multitudes of confessors around them" (1958/1913, p. 267). Among these Weber included, in addition to Christianity, "the Confucian, Hinduist, Buddhist, and Islamic religious ethics." He added that despite its small population of adherents, Judaism should also be considered a world religion because of its influence on Christianity and Islam as well as on Western ethics and values even outside the religious sphere of life.

In discussing religion sociologists often refer to the "Islamic world" of the Middle East, the "Roman Catholic world" of Latin America and southern Europe, the "Hindu world" of the Indian subcontinent, and the "Buddhist world" of the Far East. The United States, northern Europe, and Australia are among the societies in which Protestantism is strongest. There are also, of course, the nations of Eastern Europe and the former Soviet Union, where until recently communism as a civil religion was the only legitimate belief system (although millions of people resisted the state's efforts to eradicate traditional religious faiths) (Robertson, 1985).

BOX 17.1 GLOBAL SOCIAL CHANGE

The Huichol Artist

The conquest of what is now Latin America by Spain and Portugal in the seventeenth century also established the Catholic church as the dominant religious institution in that part of the world. Missionary priests enlisted the help of Indians to build churches, missions, and schools as bases from which they would work diligently "to destroy or incorporate religious practices with which the Indians had met their religious needs, relieved their anxieties, and established a moral order" (Stinchcombe, 1968, p. 116). One result of these efforts was that the artistic expressions that represented the Indians' conception of the universe were replaced with expressions of Christian symbolism.

But in remote valleys the ancient cultures still survive. The Huichol Indians, for example, live on communal land in an extremely isolated part of Mexico's Sierra Madre Occidental. There they create pictures by laying brightly colored yarns on boards covered with beeswax. Each picture represents an aspect of the ancient religious beliefs of the Central American Indians. All of the symbolic and sacred figures on each board are ablaze with color.

In 1985 an art gallery in New York City showed a selection of works by the Huichol artist José Benítez Sánchez. Sophisticated New Yorkers who had read reviews of Sánchez's work crowded the small gallery and marveled at his pictures. At other times the gallery might exhibit more secular art: the "hard-edge" art of the school known as neorealism (or pop art), which uses the imagery of advertising, or abstract-expressionist art, which explores shape, form, and color without using objects or symbols. These forms of art differ dramatically from the work of Indian artists like Sánchez or the art of African woodcarvers or Asian calligraphers. In the Indian and African societies art is not differentiated from religion; it is a form of religious expression, and from the viewpoint of the artist the work has less meaning when it decorates the home of a well-off couple in a Western capital than it does when it is

placed in the home of kin who can appreciate its symbolic meaning.

To fully understand the art of the Huichol artists, one must first try to understand their spiritual or religious world view. When Sánchez explains the symbolism of his art, for example, he begins with the Huichols' perception of their relationship to nature: "Everything is sacrificed on our behalf: the Corn gives us its daughters, Deer its young, the Sun its arrows, and the Sea its plumed-serpent daughters, the rain-filled clouds" (quoted in Negrin, 1985–1986, p. 11). The Huichol are brought up to understand these relationships between humans and nature, and therefore they can feel the spiritual power of the works of Indian artists like Sánchez. People in more secular societies are less able to appreciate this aspect of Huichol art, though they may be impressed by its bold designs and vivid colors.

Figure 17.1 shows the distribution of the world's major religions. Note that in many parts of the world, particularly in Asia and Africa, large numbers of people practice other religions. Many are indigenous peoples whose religious practices may be influenced by the major world religions but continue to be based on beliefs and ways of worship that are unique to that culture. For example, in her sociological portrait of Mama Lola, a Haitian priestess, Karen McCarthy Brown notes that many Haitians practice voodoo, which is derived from African religious beliefs. Some of Mama Lola's followers may worship in Catholic churches yet continue to practice the traditional rituals of voodoo as well (Brown, 1991, 1992).

CLASSIFICATION OF RELIGIOUS BELIEFS

The religions practiced throughout the world today vary from belief in magic and supernatural spirits to compli-

cated ideas of God and saints, as well as secular religions in which there is faith but not God. With such a wide range of religious beliefs and practices to consider, it is useful to classify them in a systematic way. One often-used system classifies religions according to their central belief. In this scheme the multiplicity of religious forms is reduced to a more manageable list consisting of five major types: simple supernaturalism, animism, theism, abstract ideals, and civil religion. (See the study chart on page 511.) In this section we describe each type briefly. Be warned, though, that not all religions fit neatly into these basic categories.

Simple Supernaturalism. In less complex and rather isolated societies, people may believe in a great force or spirit, but they may not have a well-defined concept of God or a set of rituals involving God. Studies by anthropologists have found that some isolated peoples—for example, South Pacific island cultures and Eskimo tribes—

believe strongly in the power of a supernatural force but do not attempt to embody that force in a visualized conception of God. In this form of religion, called **simple supernaturalism,** there is no discontinuity between the world of the senses and the supernatural; all natural phenomena are part of a single force. Consider these remarks by an Inuit Eskimo:

> When I was small I knew a man who came from the polar bears. He had a low voice and was big. That man knew when he was a cub and his bear mother was bringing him to the land from the ocean. He remembered it. (quoted in Steltzer, 1982, p. 111)

Animism. More common among hunting-and-gathering societies is a form of religion termed **animism,** in which all forms of life and all aspects of the earth are inhabited by gods or supernatural powers. Most of the indigenous peoples of the Western Hemisphere were animists, and so were many of the tribal peoples of Africa before the European conquests. Europeans almost invariably branded American Indians "heathens and barbarians" because, among other things, the Indians believed that "people journeyed into supernatural realms and returned, animals conversed with each other and humans, and the spirits of rocks and trees had to be placated" (Jennings, 1975, p. 48). The same can be said of European attitudes toward African religions. Determined to subjugate nature and make the earth yield more wealth for new populations, the Europeans could not appreciate the meanings of animism for people who lived more closely in touch with nature.

Yet if one takes some time to read about the perceptions of animistic religions, it becomes clear that they contain

FIGURE 17.1   Estimated Religious Membership, by Continent (in millions)

NORTHERN AMERICA (282)

Roman Catholic	98 (35%)
Protestant	97 (34%)
Other Christian	46 (16%)
Jewish	7 (2%)
(All other)	34 (12%)

LATIN AMERICA (475)

Roman Catholic	412 (87%)
Other Christian	31 (6%)
(All other)	32 (7%)

EUROPE (502)

Roman Catholic	260 (52%)
Protestant	73 (15%)
Other Christian	76 (15%)
(All other)	92 (18%)

AFRICA (703)

Muslim	285 (41%)
Christian	341 (49%)
Tribal Religionist	70 (10%)
(All other)	7 (1%)

THE WORLD (5,576)

Christian	1,870 (34%)
Muslim	1,014 (18%)
Hindu	751 (13%)
Buddhist	334 (6%)
(All other)	1,606 (29%)

EURASIA (295)

Orthodox Christian	96 (32%)
Other Christian	16 (5%)
Muslim	43 (15%)
Jewish	2 (—)
(All other)	138 (47%)

ASIA (3,292)

Hindu	747 (23%)
Muslim	668 (20%)
Buddhist	332 (10%)
Christian	300 (9%)
(All other)	1,244 (38%)

OCEANIA (28)

Christian	23 (82%)
(All other)	5 (18%)

Percentages may not add up to 100 percent because of rounding.
— = less than 1 percent.

Source: Data from *Britannica Book of the Year,* 1994.

Among the Quechua-speaking Indian peoples of the Andes, Christianity and older religious practices often coexist. Shown here is a ritual in which guinea pigs, believed to possess magical powers, are sacrificed for the well-being of the community.

STUDY CHART Forms of Religion

FORM	DESCRIPTION	EXAMPLE
Simple Supernaturalism	A form of religion in which there is no discontinuity between the world of the senses and the supernatural; all natural phenomena are part of a single force	Some Inuit Eskimo cultures
Animism	A form of religion in which all forms of life and all aspects of the earth are inhabited by gods or supernatural powers	Native American cultures; some African tribal cultures
Theism	A form of religion in which gods are conceived of as separate from humans and from other living things on the earth, although the gods are in some way responsible for the creation of humans and for their fate	
Polytheism	A form of theism in which there are numerous gods, all of whom occupy themselves with some aspect of the universe and of human life	The pantheon of gods of the ancient Greeks and Romans
Monotheism	A form of theism that is centered on belief in a single all-powerful God who determines human fate and can be addressed through prayer	Christianity, Islam, Judaism
Abstract Ideals	A form of religion that is centered on an abstract ideal of spirituality and human behavior	Buddhism, Confucianism
Civil Religion	A collection of beliefs, and rituals for communicating those beliefs, that exists outside religious institutions	Marxism-Leninism; some versions of humanism

much wisdom for our beleaguered planet. In one beautifully written account, an Oglala Sioux medicine man, Black Elk, speaks "the story of all life that is holy and is good to tell, and of us two-leggeds sharing in it with the four-leggeds and the wings of the air and all green things; for these are children of one mother and their father is one Spirit" (Neihardt, 1959/1932, p. 1). Black Elk's prayer continues:

Grandfather, Great Spirit, lean close to the earth that you may hear the voice I send. You towards where the sun goes down, behold me; thunder Beings, behold me! You where the White Giant lives in power, behold me! You where the sun shines continually, whence come the day-break star and the day, behold me! You in the depths of the heavens, an eagle of power, behold! And you, Mother Earth, the only Mother, you who have shown mercy to your children! (p. 5)

Traces of animism can also be seen in the religious beliefs of the ancient Egyptians, Greeks, and Romans. The Greeks, for example, spoke of naiads inhabiting rivers and springs, and of dryads inhabiting forests. These varieties of nymphs were believed to be part of the natural environment in which they dwelled, but sometimes they took on semihuman qualities. They thus bridged the gap between a quasi-animistic religion and the more familiar theistic systems that evolved in Greece and Rome.

Theism. Religions whose central belief is **theism** usually conceive of gods as separate from humans and from other living things on the earth—although these gods are in some way responsible for the creation of humans and for their fate. Many ancient religions were **polytheistic,** meaning that they included numerous gods, all of whom occupied themselves with some aspect of the universe and of human life. In the religion of the ancient Greeks, warfare was the concern of Ares; music, healing, and prophecy were the domain of Apollo; his sister Artemis was concerned with hunting; Poseidon was the god of seafaring; Athena was the goddess of handicrafts and intellectual pursuits; and so on. A similar division of concerns and attributes could be found among the gods of the Romans and, later, among the gods of the Celtic tribes of Gaul and Britain.

The ancient Hebrews were among the first of the world's peoples to evolve a **monotheistic** religion—one centered on belief in a single all-powerful God who determines human fate and can be addressed through prayer. This belief is expressed in the central creed of the Jews: "Hear O Israel, the Lord our God, the Lord is One." Jewish monotheism, based on the central idea of a covenant between God and the Jewish people (as represented in the written laws of the Ten Commandments, for example), helped stimulate the codification of religious law and ritual, so that the Jews became known as "the people of the book." As they traveled and settled throughout the Middle East, the Jews were able to take their religion with them and hold on to the purity of their beliefs and practices (Johnson, 1987; Smith, 1952).

Christianity and Islam are also monotheistic religions. The Roman Catholic version of Christianity envisions God as embodied in a Holy Trinity consisting of God the Father, Christ the Son, and the Holy Spirit of God, which has the ability to inspire the human spirit. The fundamental beliefs of Islam are similar in many respects to those of Judaism and Christianity. Islam is a monotheistic religion centering on the worship of one God, Allah, according to the teachings of the Koran as given by Allah to Mohammed, the great prophet of the Muslim faith. In his early preachings, Mohammed appears to have believed that the followers of Jesus and the believers in Judaism would recognize him as God's messenger and realize that Allah was the same as the God they worshipped. The fundamental aim of Islam is to serve God as he demands to be served in the Koran.

Another basically monotheistic religion, Hinduism, is difficult to categorize. On the one hand, it incorporates the strong idea of an all-powerful God who is everywhere yet is "unsearchable"; on the other hand, it conceives of a God who can be represented variously as the Creator (Brahma), the Preserver (Vishnu), and the Destroyer (Shiva). Each of these personifications takes a number of forms in Hindu ritual and art. Of all the great world religions, Hinduism teaches most forcefully that all religions are roughly equal "paths to the same summit."

Abstract Ideals. In China, Japan, and other societies of the Far East, religions predominate that are centered not on devotion to a god or gods but on an abstract ideal of spirituality and human behavior. The central belief of Buddhism, perhaps the most important of these religions, is embodied in these thoughts of Siddhārtha Gautama, The Buddha:

Life is a Journey
Death is a return to the Earth
The universe is like an inn
The passing years are like dust

Like all of the world's great religions, Buddhism has many branches. The ideal that unifies them all, however, is the teaching that worship is not a matter of prayer to God but a quest for the experience of godliness within oneself through meditation and awareness.

Another important religion based on abstract ideals is Confucianism, which is derived from the teachings of the philosopher Confucius (551–479 B.C.). The sayings of Confucius are still revered throughout much of the Far East, especially among the Chinese, although the formal study of Confucius's thought has been banned since the communist revolution of the early 1950s. The central belief of Confucianism is that one must learn and practice the wisdom of the ancients. "He that is really good," Confucius taught, "can never be unhappy. He that is really wise can never be perplexed. He that is really brave can never be afraid" (quoted in McNeill, 1963, p. 231).

In Confucianism the central goal of the individual is to become a good ruler or a good and loyal follower and thus to carry out the *tao* of his or her position. *Tao* is an untranslatable word that refers to the practice of virtues that make a person excellent at his or her discipline. As is evident even in this brief description, Confucianism is a set of ideals and sayings that tend toward conservatism and acceptance of the status quo, although the wise ruler should be able to improve society for those in lesser positions. Little wonder that under communism this ancient and highly popular set of moral principles and teachings was banned in favor of what sociologists call a civil religion.

Civil Religion. In recent years some social scientists, notably Robert Bellah (1970), have expanded the definition of religion to include so-called **civil religions.** These are collections of beliefs, and rituals for communicating those beliefs, that exist outside religious institutions. Often, as in the former Soviet communist societies, they are attached to the institutions of the state. Marxism-Leninism can be thought of as a civil religion, symbolized by the reverence once paid to Lenin's tomb. Central to communism as a civil religion is the idea that private property is evil while property held in common by all members of the society (be it the work group, the community, or the entire nation) is good. The struggle against private property results in the creation of the socialist personality, which values all human lives and devalues excessive emphasis on individual success, especially success measured by the accumulation of property. Although the communist regimes of the Soviet Union and Eastern Europe have fallen, there are millions of people in those nations and in China who were socialized to believe in these principles.

In the United States, certain aspects of patriotic feeling are sometimes said to amount to a civil religion: reverence for the flag, the Constitution, the Declaration of Independence, and other symbols of America is cited as an example. Thus most major public events, be they commencements, political rallies, or Super Bowl games, begin with civil-religious rituals like the singing of the national anthem or the recitation of the Pledge of Allegiance, in which a nonsectarian God is invoked to protect the nation's unity ("One nation under God").

Although there is no doubt that Lenin's image and the American flag may be viewed as sacred in some contexts, neither communism nor American patriotism can compete with the major world religions in the power of their central ideals and their spirituality. In consequence, sociologists tend to concentrate on religions in the traditional sense—that is, on the enactment of rituals that represent the place of sacred beliefs in human life. In the remainder of this chapter we discuss the structure of religious institutions and the processes by which new ones arise.

RELIGION AND SOCIAL CHANGE

Now that the nations behind the former "iron curtain" are enjoying new freedoms, the role of religion in bringing about social change is an important aspect of life in those societies. Indeed, in many parts of the world, religion is one of the primary forces opposing or supporting change. However, it is not always a simple matter to predict whether religion will encourage change or hinder it. In Israel, for example, highly orthodox Jews, though they account for a small minority of the electorate, hold the votes necessary to keep the ruling party in power. The orthodox political parties favor continued settlement on the West Bank of the Jordan River and oppose the creation of a Palestinian state near Israel's borders.

In the United States, the Catholic church plays an active role in seeking social change. The church strongly opposes women's right to obtain abortions legally. Instead, it supports a return to the traditional view of abortion as a crime, which is based on the belief that humans must submit to the will of God and not use their technological skills to achieve power over life and death. In this instance, therefore, although the church is promoting social change, the change represents a return to an earlier moral standard. Throughout much of Latin America, in contrast, the Catholic church is fighting in support of the masses of urban and rural poor who seek social justice and equitable economic development. In Brazil, for example, the typical Catholic priest or nun favors the political left, which seeks a more egalitarian distribution of wealth and income and is highly critical of the rich.

We could add many other examples of the role played by religion and religious organizations in social change. But in attempting to generalize about the relationship between religion and social change it is useful to return briefly to classic sociological theories. The pioneering European sociologists, particularly Karl Marx and Max Weber, noted the prominent role of religion in social change. But they wondered whether the influence of religious faith is a determining force in social change, or whether religious sentiments and the activities of religious organizations are an outgrowth of changes in more basic economic and political institutions.

Marx, as we have seen, believed that economic institutions are fundamental to all societies and that they are the source of social change. In his view, religion and other cultural institutions are shaped by economic and political institutions; they are a "superstructure" that simply reflects the values of those institutions—of markets, firms, the government, the military, and so on. The function of cultural institutions, especially religion, is to instill in the masses the values of the dominant class. In this sense they can be said to shape the consciousness of a people, but they do so in such a way as to justify existing patterns of economic exploitation and the existing class structure. Religion, in Marx's words, is "the opium of the people" because it eases suffering through prayer and ritual and deludes the masses into accepting their situation as divinely ordained rather than organizing to change the social system.

For Weber, on the other hand, religion can be the cause of major social change rather than the outcome or reflection of changes in other institutions. Weber set forth this thesis in one of his most famous works, *The Protestant Ethic and the Spirit of Capitalism* (1974/1904). Noting that the rise of Protestantism in Europe had coincided with the emergence of capitalism, Weber hypothesized that the Protestant Reformation had brought about a significant change in cultural values and that this was responsible for the more successful development of capitalist economic systems in Protestant regions. As Weber explained it, Protestantism instilled in its followers certain values that were conducive to business enterprise, resulting in the accumulation of wealth. Because the early Protestants believed that wealth was not supposed to be spent on luxuries or "the pleasures of the flesh," the only alternative was to invest it in new or existing business enterprises—in other words, to contribute to the rapid economic growth characteristic of capitalist systems (Brown, 1965). This view was reinforced by the belief—also part of the Protestant ethic—that a person who worked hard was likely to be among those predestined for salvation.

Some have questioned the validity of Weber's thesis regarding Protestantism and early capitalism, but there can be no doubt that religious institutions are capable of assuming a major role in shaping modern societies. Throughout the Islamic world there are currents of orthodoxy and reform that threaten to cause both civil and international wars. And as noted earlier, in many Latin American communities the Catholic church leads the movement for large-scale social change. So Marx was wrong in his claim that religion functions largely to maintain the existing values of more basic social institutions. On the contrary, religion can often lead to new ways of organizing societies—to new political and economic institutions as well as whole new lifestyles.

The Marxian view of religion is still relevant to those who are critical of the influence of religious institutions. These critics assert that religion, along with other cultural institutions such as education, serves to reaffirm and perpetuate inequalities of wealth, prestige, and power. When the poor are encouraged to pray for a better life, for example, they are further oppressed by a religion that prevents them from realizing that they need to marshal their own power to challenge the status quo. Thus there is still some question as to whether (and how much) religious institutions change society in any fundamental way.

To make informed judgments about this and related issues, we need to have a better understanding of the nature of religious organizations and how they function in modern societies. In the next section, therefore, we describe the main types of religious organizations. We then focus on trends in religious belief and practice in the United States.

STRUCTURE AND CHANGE IN MODERN RELIGIONS

Religion today is a highly structured institution, with numerous statuses and roles within a variety of organizations as well as many kinds of smaller, less bureaucratic groups. This was not always so. The religions of tribal peoples were not highly institutionalized; that is, there were no separate organizations like churches or interfaith councils or youth fellowships. It is true that the occupational status of holy person or priest might exist. Thus most Native American peoples had spiritual leaders who specialized in the rituals and symbols through which the members of the tribe could address the Great Spirit and the sacred spirits of their ancestors. But even in societies that had spiritual leaders or priests, religious practice was intertwined with tribal and family life: There was no concept of the church as a separate institution specializing in religious rituals.

Religion as a fully differentiated institution developed in agrarian societies, and it was in such societies that formal religious organizations first appeared. As we saw in Chapter 4, agrarian societies produce enough surplus food to support a class of priests and other specialists in religious rituals. In those less complex societies religion was incorporated into village and family life; it had not yet be-

come differentiated into a recognized, separate institution with its own statuses and roles (Parsons, 1966). Over time, however, the development of religious institutions resulted in a wide variety of organizations devoted to religious practice. Today those organizations include the church, the sect, and the denomination.

FORMS OF RELIGIOUS ORGANIZATION

Churches and Sects.   A **church** may be defined as a religious organization that has strong ties to the larger society. Often in its history it has enjoyed the loyalty of most of the society's members; indeed, it may have been linked with the state itself (Weber, 1963/1922). An example is the Church of England, or Anglican church. A **sect,** by contrast, is an organization that rejects the religious beliefs or practices of established churches. Whereas the church distributes the benefits of religious participation to anyone who enters the sanctuary and stays to follow the service, the sect limits the benefits of membership (i.e., salvation, fellowship, common prayer) to those who qualify on narrower grounds of membership and belief (McGuire, 1987; Weber, 1963/1922).

Sects require strong commitment on the part of their members and usually are formed when a small group of church members splits off to form a rival organization. The sect may not completely reject the beliefs and rituals of the church from which it arose, but it changes them enough to be considered a separate organization. Most "storefront churches" are actually sects that have developed their own particular interpretations of religious ritual.

An important difference between churches and sects is that churches draw their adherents from a large social environment—that is, from a large pool of possible members—whereas the size of the population from which a sect draws its members tends to be small (Stark & Bainbridge, 1979). Also, churches make relatively limited demands on their members while sects make heavy claims on their members' time, money, and emotional commitment. As Robert Wuthnow (1988) writes, "Churches attempt to regulate or fulfill a few of the activities or needs of large numbers of people; sects attempt to regulate or fulfill many of the activities or needs of small numbers of people" (p. 495).

Denominations.   A third type of religious organization is the **denomination.** Unlike a sect, a denomination is on good terms with the religious institution from which it developed, but it must compete with other denominations for members. An example of a denomination is the United Methodist Church, a Protestant denomination that must compete for members with other Protestant denominations such as Presbyterians, Episcopalians, and Baptists. Denominations sometimes evolve from sects. This occurs when the sect is successful in recruiting new members and grows in both size and organizational complexity. Sociologists who study religion have found that the bureaucratic growth of a sect and its increasing influence over nonreli-

T H E N AND N O W

CHANGING COMMUNITIES, CHANGING CONGREGATIONS

When the United States was a predominantly rural nation, people usually walked to their house of worship, where they met their neighbors for prayer and sociability. In fact, the tradition of walking to a house of worship remains strong in some religions, notably Orthodox Judaism, in which driving or being driven on the Sabbath is forbidden and walking to synagogue is required. In the rural United States early in this century, Christians like those shown here often walked to church or rode in wagons over relatively short distances. It was important to get to church on Sunday because there were few other ways to hear the gospel and socialize with one's neighbors.

Today, despite the availability of televised services, the practice of going to church and participating in services remains widespread. But as rural villages and towns have given way to metropolitan regions with immense central cities and sprawling suburbs, churches have had to adapt to these changes. Superchurches are an example of such an adaptation. Often located conveniently near the main highways in a metropolitan region, these immense churches draw their congregations from a territory that is far too wide to be considered a single neighborhood. In fact, these churches offer an array of spiritual and social services and actually serve as catalysts for the formation of groups of "neighbors" whose attachments are a result of participation in church activities (e.g., membership in the choir or a singles group or a Bible study group). The superchurch thus provides a means of escaping from the anonymity and estrangement many people feel in modern metropolitan regions.

gious matters in the community is associated with a decline in the fervor with which the sect pursues its spiritual ideals and a decrease in its efforts to remain faithful to the claims that originally made it so different. This aspect of religious change is an active area of research (Niebuhr, 1929; Pope, 1942; Troeltsch, 1931; Welch, 1979).

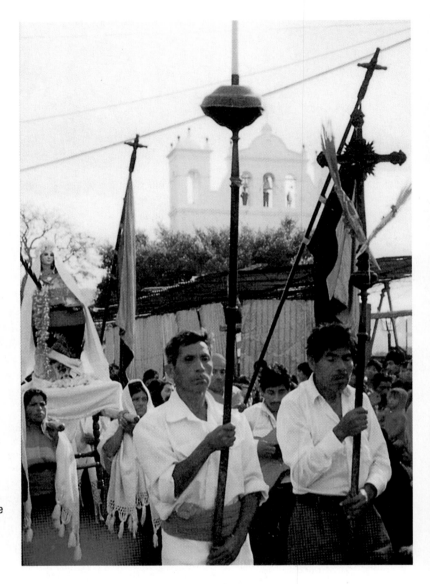

This photograph of a religious festival in the province of Chiapas in Mexico clearly shows the social organization of the village church. The male officials of the church (visible in the background) march with banners and candles while the women bear the saint through the village.

Cults. Still another type of religious body, the **cult**, differs in significant ways from the organizations just described. Cults are usually entirely new religions whose members hold beliefs and engage in rituals that differ from those of existing religions. Some cults have developed out of existing religions. This occurred in the case of early Christianity, which began as a cult of Jews who believed that Jesus of Nazareth was the Messiah and who practiced rituals that were often quite different from those of Judaism. Cults may also be developed by people who were not previously involved in a church or sect, such as those who become active in pagan cults such as those based on ancient forms of witchcraft (Adler, 1979). Most major religions began as seemingly insignificant cults, but new cults are formed every day throughout the world, and very few of them last long enough to become recognized religions. The Mormons, who began as a cult in 1830 with six members,

grew into a large religious organization with more than 60,000 members by 1850 and today is one of the fastest growing Christian churches in the world (Finke & Stark, 1992).

In a recent study of trends in church, sect, and cult membership, sociologists Roger Finke and Rodney Stark find that, contrary to common assumptions, the rate at which cults are formed is no higher today than it was in earlier historical periods. Moreover, compared to some of the earlier cults, contemporary cults often have less success in gaining members:

No cult movement of the sixties or early seventies seems ever to have attracted more than a few thousand American members, and most of even the well-publicized groups counted their true membership in the hundreds, not the thousands. For example, after more than thirty years of missionizing, it is estimated that there have never been more than 5,000 followers of the Unification Church (the Moonies) in the United States, and some of them are from abroad (Finke & Stark, 1992, p. 241; also see Melton, 1989).

In a similar example, Barry Kosmin and his colleagues (1991) estimate, on the basis of the largest sample survey of religious beliefs ever conducted in the United States ($n = 113,000$), that actual membership in the Church of Scientology very likely does not exceed 45,000, despite the cult's claims that its domestic membership is more than 450,000. On the basis of findings like these, Finke and Stark conclude that cults have always interested some relatively small proportion of U.S. citizens and still do. Despite sensational media accounts of the activities of cults like the Branch Davidians, the rate of cult formation in the United States has not increased appreciably in recent decades, nor are cults more successful in gaining members than they were before.

One reason cults and sects do not always grow in numbers or influence is that established religions often absorb them through the process known as *co-optation.* This term is not limited to religious institutions; we encountered it in Chapter 8 in connection with social movements. It refers to any process whereby an organization deals with potentially threatening individuals or groups by incorporating them into its own organizational structure (Selznick, 1966). Over the centuries the Roman Catholic church has been particularly successful at co-opting regional Catholic sects by including their leaders in the panoply of lesser saints, thereby allowing people to worship a holy person of their own culture while remaining true to the world church.

RELIGIOUS INTERACTION AND CHANGE

Sects and cults are a major source of change in religious organizations. People who are not satisfied with more established churches and denominations, or are otherwise alienated from society, often form or join a cult or sect (Nelson, 1984; Smelser, 1984). One of the most convincing explanations of the emergence of sects was suggested by H. Richard Niebuhr (1929), borrowing from Max Weber's (1922) pioneering analysis of churches and sects. According to Weber, churches tend to justify the presence of inequality and stratification because they must appeal to people of all classes. Sects, on the other hand, may be led by charismatic individuals who appeal to people who have felt the sting of inequality. Niebuhr agreed with Weber that class conflict was a primary cause of sect formation. But he observed that as a sect becomes more successful and better organized, it becomes more like a church and begins to justify existing systems of stratification. This creates the conditions in which new sects may emerge.

Another motivation for the formation of sects or cults is dissatisfaction with the interactions that occur in more established organizations. In church rituals, for example, prayer is often led by a priest or other religious professional and is relatively restrained, whereas in sects and cults communication between God and the individual is more direct and typically allows the individual to express deep emotions. The different styles of interaction in different types of religious organizations can be illustrated by the contrast between the hierarchy of statuses and roles that characterizes the Catholic church (with its pope, cardinals, bishops, priests, and other well-defined statuses) and the seemingly greater equality and looser structure of a cult like Krishna Consciousness or the Unification Church.

Often people who are attracted to cults are influenced by a charismatic leader who inspires them to new and very personal achievements, such as ecstatic experiences, a sense of salvation, or a release from physical or psychological suffering. Some become cult members simply because they are lonely; others are born to cult members and are socialized into the cult.

Some but by no means all cults are extremely authoritarian and punitive. Their leaders may demand that members cut themselves off entirely from family and friends and sacrifice everything for the sake of the cult. The leaders may also insist that they themselves are above the moral teachings to which their followers must adhere. Under these conditions of isolation and submission to a dominant authority, cult members may be driven to incredible extremes of behavior—even mass suicide, as occurred in the case of Jim Jones's People's Temple (Hall, 1987). However, not all cults are so dangerous or so easily condemned, and there is an ongoing conflict between norms that protect the right of individuals to belong to cults and efforts to protect people from the harm that can occur when cult leaders place themselves above morality and the law.

G. K. Nelson (1984) draws on the free and expressive nature of cults in describing how new religious movements are born. Such movements, he writes, "may be seen as the result of religious innovation . . . [which] involves the discovery of new methods by which spiritual needs may be satisfied" (p. 317). According to Nelson, a new cult or movement arises when a "religious innovator" attracts a number of followers. This is particularly likely to occur when traditional religions are failing to meet the needs of their members or when a society is undergoing rapid secularization. Yet it appears that secularization never eliminates people's desire for religious expression. Indeed, some studies of recruitment into cults show that their members often received a high-quality secular education and a nonreligious upbringing (Stark & Bainbridge, 1985). Such people might be expected to have the most secular views regarding human existence. The fact that they join cults is evidence that secularization itself can lead to religious innovation.

Many of the functions of religion as a fundamental cultural institution—meeting the spiritual needs of individuals, binding together the members of social groups, and

BOX 17.2 USING THE SOCIOLOGICAL IMAGINATION

The Black Church in America

The respected black sociologist E. Franklin Frazier was a firm believer in the principles of the Chicago school of ecological research and an astute student of race relations. He specialized in two of the most basic social institutions—the family and the church—as they affected and were affected by the situation of black Americans.

Frazier's (1966) study of the history of the black church in America emphasized the role of religion in the social organization of blacks ever since they were imported from Africa to the New World to be sold as slaves. Few aspects of the slaves' African culture were able to survive the experience of abduction and slavery, but one of those that did was dancing, which Frazier refers to as the most elemental form of religious expression. Although the slaves were encouraged to dance, the religious beliefs expressed in their dances were not permitted to flourish in America.

With the coming of Baptist and Methodist missionaries, the slaves found a form of religion in which they could express their most intense feelings. The religious services in which they participated served to bind them together into close-knit groups, replacing the bonds of kinship and tribal membership they had lost when they were sold into slavery. However, the freed slaves resented the subordinate status of blacks in the white-dominated churches. They left those churches and established all-black churches.

Out of these black churches, Frazier noted, other forms of black organizational activity emerged. The churches began to play an important role in the organization of the black community in such areas as economic cooperation and the building of educational institutions. The church also became the center of political life for black Americans, the arena in which they learned how to compete for power and position.

The large-scale urbanization of blacks that began in World War I transformed the black church. In particular, the church became more secular, placing less emphasis on salvation and turning its attention to the serious problems of blacks in the here and now. Changes in the class structure of the black community have also been reflected in the black church, with many middle-class blacks shifting to the Presbyterian, Episcopalian, and Congregational churches. A countertrend may be seen in the emergence of "storefront churches" (i.e., sects) that satisfy the spiritual needs of those who prefer a more intimate and expressive form of worship. And some blacks have joined so-called holiness cults that seek to return to an earlier form of expressive Christianity.

At the same time, blacks have become more fully integrated into American society. This has naturally affected the organization of black communities and the black church. Today the church is no longer the dominant institution for blacks that it once was. Nevertheless, as Frazier pointed out, the black church has left its imprint on most aspects of black life. And it is clear that the black church (including the Black Muslims and other Islamic sects) provides much of the leadership and many of the rank-and-file supporters of movements for political and economic justice among minority groups in the United States.

Internationally acclaimed singer Aretha Franklin attributes her success to the vitality of the black church in the United States, which sustains an immense market for gospel songs and records.

sometimes engendering social change—are illustrated by the history of the black church in America, summarized in Box 17.2.

TRENDS IN RELIGION IN THE UNITED STATES

In studying religion in the United States, sociologists are unable to use census data because the Census Bureau does not collect data on religious affiliation. However, some statistics are available from smaller sample surveys such as those conducted by the National Opinion Research Center (NORC). The available data indicate that more than half of Americans over age 18 identify themselves as Protestant, about one quarter are Roman Catholic, and about 2 percent identify themselves as Jewish. All other religions combined account for about 7 percent of the population. The remaining 9 percent say that they have no religious affiliation; they constitute the third-largest category of religious preference in the United States (Bogue, 1985; NORC, 1994). (See Figure 17.2.)

The religious preferences of Americans have been changing slowly but steadily over the last two generations. The Protestant majority has gradually declined, owing partly to upward mobility and the tendency of more affluent and educated people to be less active in religious institutions. Meanwhile the proportion of the population who identify themselves as Catholics has been growing, primarily as a result of the large numbers of Hispanic immigrants who have entered the United States in recent years. Also, since the mid-1960s there has been an increase in the percentage of people who express no religious preference. Thus it is possible that by the turn of the century less than half of all Americans will be Protestant (NORC, 1994; Roozen, 1985).

Membership in a religious organization is quite different from identification with a religious faith, and this is reflected in statistics on Christian church membership in the United States. Because data on membership are obtained from the organizations themselves, there are significant differences in who is included. (Some churches, for example, count all baptized infants, whereas others count only people above a certain age who are enrolled as members.) Figure 17.3 illustrates the geographic distribution of reported church membership in the United States. As can readily be seen, different regions of the country are quite different with respect to the church membership of the majority of their residents. Protestants outnumber members of all other religions in the South, for example, and in the West and Southwest the Roman Catholic church is dominant. There are also significant differences in church membership by size of place: Protestants are most likely to

live in rural places, small cities, and suburbs of smaller cities, while native-born Catholics are found in medium-sized cities and suburbs of larger cities. Much of the rapid growth of Catholic congregations in the United States is accounted for by immigrants to major cities like Miami, Los Angeles, and New York (Niebuhr, 1995). Jews, who originally migrated to the nation's largest cities, are most numerous in major metropolitan regions like New York, Los Angeles, Chicago, and Miami (Bogue, 1985).

UNOFFICIAL RELIGION
Religion in the United States is increasingly voluntaristic. People are less likely to practice a religion simply because their parents did so. They are more likely than ever to join a religious group that appeals to their desire for membership in a community of like-minded peers and that upholds their particular moral standards (Roof, 1985). People in the United States and Canada are also more likely to engage in what sociologists term *unofficial religion*—a set of beliefs and practices that are "not accepted, recognized, or controlled by official religious groups" (McGuire, 1987, p. 89). Sometimes called folk or popular religion because it is practiced by ordinary people rather than by religious professionals in formal organizations, unofficial religion takes many forms. It is engaged in by people who purchase religious books and magazines, follow religious programs on

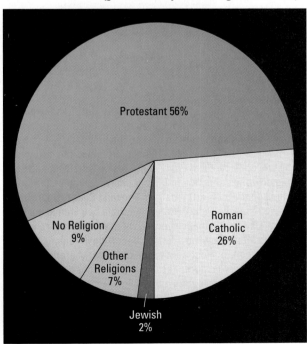

FIGURE 17.2 Percentage Distribution of Religious Preference in the United States (persons 18 years of age and older)

Source: Data from *Statistical Abstract,* 1995.

FIGURE 17.3

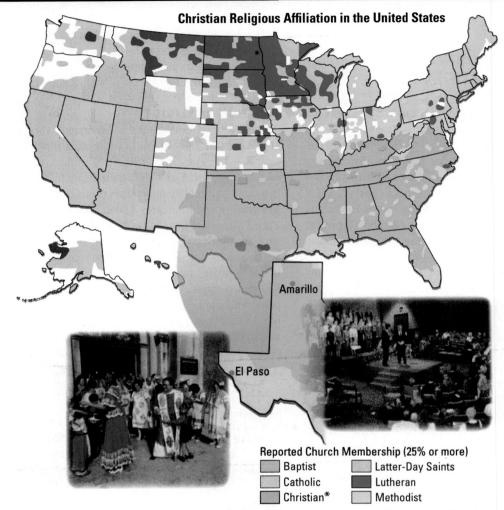

MAPPING SOCIAL CHANGE

Christian Religious Affiliation in the United States

Amarillo

El Paso

Reported Church Membership (25% or more)

Baptist	Latter-Day Saints
Catholic	Lutheran
Christian*	Methodist

* Includes Christian Church (Disciples of Christ), Christian Churches/Churches of Christ, and Churches of Christ. Blank areas indicate counties where no group has 25 percent or more of the adherents in that county.
Source: *Churches and Church Membership in the United States: 1980*, by Bernard Quinn et al. Copyright © 1982 by the National Council of Churches of Christ in the U.S.A.

Religious Pluralism in the "Bible Belt."** The wide swath of states in the South and Southwest where Baptist church congregations predominate is often known as the "Bible belt." This term refers to the strong religious convictions of many of the region's residents and to the powerful influence of Baptist churches in thousands of small communities. On the map showing Christian religious affiliation in the United States, the Bible belt stands out quite clearly. But maps showing the distribution of religious beliefs often mask the changes occurring in regions that appear more homogeneous than they are. Migration, urbanization, and differences in the growth of specific religious groups can lead to more religious pluralism (or less, depending on the region) even though a map shows a static distribution.

When we look closely at communities in west Texas, at the western end of the area of heavy Baptist church membership, we find higher levels of Catholic church membership. This is due in large part to the growing presence of Latino residents, especially people of Mexican and Chicano backgrounds. Wherever there are changing patterns of church membership (represented here by photos of Baptist and Catholic congregations in this region), there is also likely to be more interfaith communication and more freqent discussion of the need for religious tolerance.

Similar evidence of pluralism can be found in other regions of the United States. In the heavily Catholic Northeast, for example, the map of Christian congregations does not indicate non-Christian, particularly Jewish, congregations, which are concentrated in the larger cities of this region. Catholic-Jewish interfaith dialogues are strongest in these urban centers. So while ecological maps like this one are useful, they only begin to suggest the important sociological facts that will be revealed by further research.

television, make religious pilgrimages, or practice astrology, faith healing, transcendental meditation, occult arts, and the like—and who may belong to organized churches at the same time. Contrary to older sociological theories that viewed these practices as holdovers from rural folk cultures, research has shown that urban societies continually produce their own versions of popular religion (Fischer, 1974, 1987).

RELIGIOSITY

Neither church membership figures nor self-reports of religious identification are accurate indicators of the aspect of religious behavior known as **religiosity.** This term refers to the depth of a person's religious feelings and how those feelings are translated into religious behavior. Responses to questions about whether one believes in God and how strongly, whether one believes in a life after death, whether one's religious beliefs provide guidance in making major decisions, and the frequency of one's church or temple attendance all can be used to measure religiosity.

When sociologists study religiosity as opposed to church membership, some important results emerge. For example, Rodney Stark and William S. Bainbridge (1985) found that about 62 percent of Americans are church members. But church membership varies rather sharply by region. The southwestern states have the highest rate of membership—about 65 percent of adults. Other regions have rates ranging between 53 and 62 percent, but the Pacific states have by far the lowest proportion of adult church members, only 36 percent. Quite different results are obtained on measures of religiosity: About 90 percent of Americans believe in the existence of God, and 86 percent express certainty in a life after death. Adults in the Pacific states do not differ very much on these measures from those in other regions. These figures highlight the difference between church membership and religiosity. The lower rates of church membership on the West Coast are correlated with the greater spatial mobility and lower median age of the populations of those states. People who

move frequently tend to sever their attachments not only to churches but to all organizations in the community. Yet people who do not belong to organized churches can nevertheless hold deeply cherished religious beliefs.

Data on church attendance do not support the notion that the United States is becoming an increasingly secular society. In fact, as can be seen in Table 17.1, for some major religions church attendance has been increasing since 1950 (Hout & Greeley, 1987). There are no clear patterns in rates of church attendance between 1939 and 1984. Although Catholics have the highest weekly attendance rates and Jews the lowest, those rates can change considerably from one year to the next, for reasons that are not fully understood. Nevertheless, it is clear that the data do not bear out the secularization hypothesis. It should also be noted that increases in immigration during the 1980s and 1990s are significantly increasing the diversity of religious practice in the United States. Muslims, Hindus, Buddhists, and others are well represented among the new immigrants.

RELIGIOUS PLURALISM

Differences in the distribution of religious belief are important because they show how religion helps account for cultural differences among populations within a society. Thus we use the expression "Bible Belt" to refer to the most strongly Protestant areas of the nation—the South and Midwest. The large Catholic populations in some cities make them quite different in cultural terms from the Protestant-dominated suburbs. And the large Jewish populations in New York and Miami are reflected in the cultural life of those cities—in joint Hanukkah/Christmas celebrations in offices and schools, for example, and the incorporation of Jewish holidays into the school calendar.

The United States is an example of a society in which the state protects religious pluralism. The First Amendment to the Constitution guarantees freedom of religion, which in turn allows different religions to exist and to compete for adherents if they wish to do so. Religious pluralism is also protected in most European nations today, although

TABLE 17.1	Percent of Adults Attending Services Last Week, by Religion and Year, United States, 1939–1990				
			RELIGION		
YEAR	**PROTESTANT**	**CATHOLIC**	**JEWISH**	**OTHER**	**NONE**
1939	40	64	12	—	1
1969	39	64	8	18	0
1979	40	53	19	40	5
1990	47	50	30*	31*	6*

*Small sample size accounts for large fluctuations in these percentages.

Sources: Hout & Greeley, 1987; NORC, 1992.

THE PERSONAL CHALLENGE
Social Change and Religious Pluralism

As societies become more culturally diverse as a result of global migrations, there is an increase in the occurrence of behaviors that seem to violate widely held norms and values. Debates and conflicts over such behaviors become more and more frequent. In France, where the Islamic population has been greatly augmented by recent immigration, there have been numerous conflicts over Muslim women wearing veils and head scarves to school or work. In California, Sikh students have been banned from wearing *kirpans,* sheathed blades worn next to the skin that are considered sacred. The state of Oregon refused to pay unemployment benefits to a Native American who was fired for using peyote, a drug used in tribal religious rituals. A Florida law banning the ritual sacrifice of chickens by practitioners of Santeria, a religion with African roots, was overturned by the Supreme Court.

A recent case in St. Paul, Minnesota, shows what can happen when religious practices run counter to local customs or laws. A veiled Muslim woman shopping in a downtown mall was detained by police for concealing her identity "by means of a robe, mask or other disguise." When she refused to take off the veil, she was taken to a room where the police forced her to remove it. The incident outraged Muslims throughout the nation; to them, it was a violation of religious freedom. The woman later commented, "Why is it that people can walk around half naked and nobody will say anything? I choose to cover up and people have a problem with it" (quoted in Pesce, 1994).

Incidents like this are not uncommon in communities that are growing more diverse. The wave of arson directed against African American churches in many regions of the United States is another indication that cultural diversity is difficult for some people to tolerate. The burning of black churches is a strong symbolic act against norms of religious and cultural tolerance and diversity. The recent attacks are reminiscent of similar incidents during the civil rights era. In this regard, Ralph Reed, director of the Christian Coalition, acknowledges that "there was a time in our nation's history when the white evangelical church was not only on the sidelines, but on the wrong side of the most central struggle for social justice in this century." Reed also asserts that his organization must "work to make racial conciliation a major priority" if it is to be "a morally resonant voice" in addressing other social issues (quoted in Herbert, 1996, p. A27).

As immigrant groups move from major metropolitan centers to smaller cities and towns, they are likely to encounter incidents of hostility. If the number of such incidents continues to increase, citizens will be forced to choose among several alternatives. Should they try to discourage immigrants and the diversity they bring? Should they try to help one another understand and accommodate people who are different? Should they insist that the newcomers conform to their norms, or should they welcome new customs and beliefs? These are not abstract issues. What choices will you make in response to the pluralist challenge?

before the Protestant Reformation of the sixteenth century many European states made Roman Catholicism the official state religion and attempted to force all their citizens to convert to Catholicism. And in the early 1990s the religious diversity and tolerance of the former Yugoslavia dissolved into a genocidal religious and nationalist war.

In societies in which religious pluralism is protected, one usually can observe the continual formation of new religious organizations. New religious groups tend to arise either out of schisms within existing organizations or as a result of the teaching of charismatic leaders who attract people to new religious movements. But religious pluralism, whether it originates in immigration or through the formation of new cults and sects, presents many personal questions and challenges for people who have difficulty living with diversity. One consequence of this problem can be seen in the rise of fundamentalism in the United States and elsewhere.

FUNDAMENTALISM

Religious *fundamentalists* are believers (and their leaders) who are devoted to the strict observance of ritual and doctrine. They hold deep convictions about right and wrong in matters of faith and lifestyle, with little tolerance for differences in belief and practice, and they are fiercely opposed to astrology, magic, unorthodox conceptions of religion, and any form of civil religion. In all the world religions there are fundamentalist movements or divisions between liberal and conservative approaches to religious norms that guide daily life. Box 17.3 describes how Islamic nations vary along some important comparative dimensions, particularly norms concerning the behavior of women. In the United States, fundamentalist believers may be found in every major religion, but fundamentalism is especially strong among some Protestant churches and sects.

Historically, the influence of religious fundamentalism on the culture and politics of American life reached its height in 1919, when the Eighteenth Amendment to the U.S. Constitution prohibited the manufacture, sale, or transportation (and hence the consumption) of "intoxicating liquors," regardless of whether one supported the fundamentalist view of alcohol consumption. The repeal of Prohibition represented a defeat for religious fundamentalism in American culture and politics.

Another famous episode involving fundamentalism was the so-called "monkey trial" of 1925, in which John T. Scopes, a biology teacher in Tennessee, was charged with teaching the then forbidden theory of evolution, which many religious fundamentalists oppose because it contradicts the account of creation presented in the Bible. The prominent lecturer and religious fundamentalist (and former presidential candidate) William Jennings Bryan prosecuted the controversial case, which received worldwide attention. Despite a strong defense by Scopes's lawyer,

BOX 17.3 **GLOBAL SOCIAL CHANGE**

Women in Islam

More than 1 billion people adhere to the Islamic faith. Most of them live in the Arab states of the Middle East and North Africa, but Muslims may be found in growing numbers in every corner of the globe.

Relations between the Islamic world and Western societies are colored by a great deal of misinformation and bias. An example from the social sciences is the theory that social changes do not affect the Islamic world in the same way that they do, or did, affect the Western nations. In particular, it is argued that because of the subordinate status of women in the Islamic religion, the movements for gender equality, limiting of family size, and greater equality in politics that have brought about such dramatic change in the West will not occur in the Islamic world (Caldwell & Caldwell, 1988). This hypothesis attributes the slow pace of demographic change in many Islamic nations to orthodox Islam's traditional values, such as polygyny, which permits men to father many children with as many as four wives. The tradition of female submission in orthodox Islam is also said to account for the persistence of gender inequalities in those nations. Islamic sociologists point out, however, that there are significant differences among the various Islamic societies and that some have long-standing norms supporting birth control and education for women.

When we examine empirical data about the Islamic nations, many ironies become apparent. There are nations where traditional Islamic norms are quite powerful and women cannot hope for educational or occupational equality with men, and there are others where these differences are diminishing rapidly. For example, in Saudi Arabia patriarchal norms are in effect and the subordination of women is strictly enforced. Women are not allowed to drive, yet that nation is the world's foremost producer of petroleum. As shown in the accompanying table, in Saudi Arabia only 65 percent of girls of primary school age are enrolled in school, among the lowest rates in the Arab world. Extremely poor, peripheral Islamic nations like Somalia (with only 13 percent female primary school attendance) are even less advanced, but in these nations it is usually the challenge of day-to-day survival rather than religious orthodoxy that prevents children from attending school. In Iraq, on the other hand, orthodoxy is less powerful and women's average level of education is among the highest in the Islamic world.

Many other differences among the Arab nations in the heart of the Islamic world show up clearly in the table. (Note that Iran is not included in this list because, although it is an Islamic nation, its culture is Persian, not Arab.) There are major differences among these nations in basic social and demographic indicators. All have high fertility rates, but in more urbanized Arab nations like Kuwait, where education for women is more easily available and polygyny is waning, rates of fertility and child mortality are closer to those of other more developed nations. In more agrarian societies like Egypt, which also tend to have larger populations, fertility remains extremely high, as does child mortality. Sociologists from these societies find, however, that Islamic teachings themselves do not account for these disparities so much as economic conditions such as poverty and concentration of the population in rural villages and farms (Obermeyer, 1992).

Demographic and Socioeconomic Indicators in Arab Countries

	POPULATION (MILLIONS) (1)	GROSS NATIONAL PRODUCT PER CAPITA (US$, 1989) (2)	PERCENT URBAN (3)	PERCENT OF AGE GROUP ENROLLED IN PRIMARY SCHOOL* MALE (4)	FEMALE (5)	TOTAL FERTILITY RATE 1985–1990 (6)	INFANT MORTALITY RATE 1985–1990 (7)	LIFE EXPECTANCY 1985–1990 (YEARS) MALE (8)	FEMALE (9)
Algeria	24.9	2,230	51.7	105	87	5.4	74	63	65
Bahrain	0.5	6,340	82.9	111	110	4.1	16	69	73
Egypt	52.4	640	46.7	100	79	4.5	65	58	60
Iraq	18.9	—	71.3	105	91	6.4	69	63	65
Jordan	4.0	1,640	68.0	98	99	6.2	44	64	68
Kuwait	2.0	16,150	95.6	95	92	3.9	18	71	75
Lebanon	2.7	—	83.7	105	95	3.8	48	63	67
Libya	4.5	5,310	70.2	128	119	6.9	82	59	63
Mauritania	2.0	500	46.8	61	42	6.5	127	44	48
Morocco	25.1	880	48.0	85	56	4.8	82	59	63
Oman	1.5	5,220	10.6	103	92	7.2	40	62	66
Qatar	0.4	15,500	89.4	121	121	5.6	31	67	72
Saudi Arabia	14.1	6,020	77.3	78	65	7.2	71	62	65
Somalia	7.5	170	36.4	26	13	6.6	132	43	47
Sudan	25.2	480	22.0	59	41	6.4	108	49	51
Syria	12.5	980	50.4	115	104	6.8	48	63	67
Tunisia	8.1	1,260	54.3	126	107	4.1	52	65	66
United Arab Emirates	1.6	18,430	77.8	98	100	4.8	26	69	73
Yemen, YAR (North)	9.2	640	25.0	141	40	8.0	120	50	50
Yemen, PDRY (South)	2.5	430	43.3	96	35	6.7	120	49	52

*Enrollment ratios are expressed as a percent of the total population of primary-school age. For countries with universal primary education, the gross enrollment ratio may exceed 100 percent because some pupils are above or below the official primary-school age.

Source: Obermeyer, 1992.

Clarence Darrow, Scopes was convicted and fined $100. (Although courts later reversed the conviction on a technicality, it would be more than 30 years before the Tennessee legislature repealed the law that prohibited teaching evolution theory in state-supported schools.) Despite the conviction, the Scopes trial is seen as a turning point for the intellectual opponents of fundamentalism. Although fundamentalism continued to pose a challenge to mainline Baptist, Methodist, and Presbyterian denominations, after the Scopes trial it lost influence—until recently—as a religious ideology (Simpson, 1983).

Nancy Tatom Ammerman, whose research we described at the beginning of the chapter, views issues of pluralism and social change as central to understanding the split between fundamentalist and moderate Southern Baptists. She writes:

> The disruption against which fundamentalists struggle is often labeled "modernity." Whatever else that label may mean, the "modern" world is one in which change is a fact of life, in which people of multiple cultures live side by side, and in which religious rules have been largely relegated to a private sphere of influence. (1990, p. 150)

To assess differences among Baptists in the way they view social change and diversity, Ammerman surveyed hundreds of Baptist leaders in congregations throughout the United States. Her survey sample ($n = 944$) included men who were pastors and church deacons and women who were presidents of their local Baptist women's organizations. After examining their responses to key questions about their beliefs, Ammerman developed categories (or "theological parties") with labels corresponding to the terms respondents often used to describe themselves (e.g.,

fundamentalist, conservative, moderate). She also developed a scale for measuring individuals' degree of opposition to modernity. The questions on which the scale is based and the method of scoring responses are discussed in Box 17.4. Table 17.2 shows that "among those who disapprove of pluralism, fundamentalists outnumber moderates nearly ten to one" (Ammerman, 1990, p. 151). But the data in the table and in Box 17.4 also show that Baptists classified as "conservative," whose views fall somewhere between those of the fundamentalists and moderates, are the most numerous category and are quite divided in their views of pluralism.

When she examined how respondents felt about modernity in relation to such variables as education, occupation, and rural versus urban residence, Ammerman found some surprising results. Although people often think of individuals who hold strong fundamentalist beliefs and reject modernity as uneducated people living in remote farming hamlets, and of individuals who approve of modernity as educated middle-class urban dwellers, Ammerman's results challenge this conventional wisdom:

> Those among Southern Baptists who were the most skeptical of change, choice, and diversity were blue collar workers, those with middle incomes, people who had moved from farm to city, and those who had been to college, but did not have a degree. And combinations were important: people who had moved from farm to city *and* had some college or people with middle income *and* blue collar households, for instance. These were people who knew exactly what the modern world was all about, and they were less enthusiastic about embracing it than were any other Southern Baptists. And the less enthusiasm they had for modern attitudes, the more likely they were to adopt fundamentalist beliefs and identity. (1990, p. 155)

TABLE 17.2	Percent in Different Theological Parties, by Responses to Pluralism			
THEOLOGICAL PARTY	**STRONG APPROVAL OF PLURALISM**	**MODERATE APPROVAL OF PLURALISM**	**DISAPPROVAL OF PLURALISM**	**TOTAL**
Self-Identified Moderate	21%	5%	3%	9%
Moderate Conservative	16	8	3	9
Conservative	38	55	43	48
Fundamentalist Conservative	18	24	27	23
Self-Identified Fundamentalist	8	9	23	11
Total	101%	101%	99%	100%
(Number of Cases)	(256)	(500)	(187)	(944)

NOTE: Difference statistically significant at $p < .001$. Some percentages do not total 100 due to rounding.

Source: Ammerman, 1990.

BOX 17.4   SOCIOLOGICAL METHODS

Scales and Composite Scores

Sociologists who are analyzing questionnaire responses often create *scales* in order to arrive at a composite score for a particular variable. Nancy Tatom Ammerman created scales to measure the strength of a person's fundamentalist beliefs and opposition to modernity. (See the accompanying tables.) A *scale* is a set of statements that fit together conceptually in that they deal with aspects or examples of the same attitude or behavior. For each statement, the respondent may be asked to choose among responses ranging, for instance, from 1 ("Strongly disagree") to 5 ("Strongly agree"), with "Unsure" in the middle. The statements in a particular scale (e.g., fundamentalist beliefs) are scattered throughout the questionnaire to avoid *response set,* the tendency to answer all such items similarly without giving them much thought; response set is a frequent problem when similar items are grouped together. To ensure that the statements in a scale actually measure the behavior or attitude the researcher is studying, great

care must be taken in their selection and wording.

Once the questionnaires have been completed and the data entered into a computer, the researcher can arrive at a simple composite score by adding up the scores on all the items in a scale. Then the researcher can either use each respondent's composite score as a continuous variable or establish cutoff points that will create categories for analysis, as Ammerman did. In her measurement of opposition to modernity, for example (see table), Ammerman decided that those who agreed or strongly agreed with all the items (i.e., whose scores ranged from 5 to 9) could be classified as "strongly agreeing with pluralism." Those who agreed with most of the items but not all of them (i.e., scored from 10 to 14) were classified as showing "moderate approval." Those who scored 15 or above—in other words, those who disagreed as often as they agreed—were classified as "disapproving."

Fundamentalist Beliefs

ITEMS	SCORING
The Scriptures are the inerrant Word of God, accurate in every detail.	Strongly agree = 5
God recorded in the Bible everything He wants us to know.	Strongly agree = 5
The Genesis creation stories are there more to tell us about God's involvement than to give us a precise "how and when."	Strongly disagree = 5
The Bible clearly teaches a premillennial view of history and the future.	Strongly agree = 5
It is important that Christians avoid worldly practices such as drinking and dancing.	Strongly agree = 5

DISTRIBUTION

RANGE	PERCENT
5–10	5
11–15	14
16–20	47
21–25	34

Opposition to Modernity

ITEMS	SCORING
I like living in a community with lots of different kinds of people.	Very untrue = 5
Public schools are needed to teach children to get along with lots of different kinds of people.	Strongly disagree = 5
I sometimes learn about God from friends in other faiths.	Very untrue = 5
One of the most important things children can learn is how to deal creatively with change.	Strongly disagree = 5
Children today need to be exposed to a variety of educational and cultural offerings so they can make informed choices.	Strongly disagree = 5

DISTRIBUTION

RANGE	PERCENT
5–9	29
10–14	52
15–19	17
20–25	2

Eventually, Ammerman believes, these differences in out-look may lead to an irremediable schism in which moder-ates may form a new Baptist denomination.

Sociologists of religion tend to view the rise of funda-mentalist religious movements such as that occurring among Southern Baptists as part of a larger effort by people in modern societies to make moral and spiritual sense of their lives. Clearly, religion continues to play an important role in the contemporary world. This fact is reflected in the remarks of Robert Bellah, a well-known commentator on American culture. For several centuries, he writes, Ameri-cans "have been embarked on a great effort to increase our freedom, wealth, and power. For over a hundred years, a large part of the American people, the middle class, has imagined that the virtual meaning of life lies in the acqui-sition of ever-increasing status, income, and authority, from which genuine freedom is supposed to come" (Bellah et al., 1985, p. 284). Yet many Americans seem uneasy about their lives despite their material comfort. They seem to yearn for spiritual values without necessarily wanting to return to traditional religious practices. They adhere to the values of individualism, but at the same time they long for the stronger sense of community and commitment that one finds in religious congregations. Bellah predicts that Amer-icans will continue to seek self-actualization as individuals, but that increasingly they will express their desire for com-munity attachments and higher values, either in traditional religions or in civil-religious practice. Research on the challenges faced by the Catholic church in the United States and elsewhere in the world also suggests that reli-gious beliefs and practices can lean in many moral and po-litical directions.

RESEARCH FRONTIERS: SOCIAL CHANGE AND THE CATHOLIC CHURCH

It is a striking fact that throughout the world one finds deeply devout individuals involved in movements for social change. Religious workers were killed in El Salvador be-cause they advocated greater democracy and equality. In Poland the Catholic church was a leader in the movement to democratize that nation. American bishops speak out against poverty and inequality in the United States. The civil rights movement has tended to be led by clergymen and bases many of its appeals on biblical principles of jus-tice and equity. Yet on the other hand we could cite many examples of religious intolerance and an apparently high correlation between devotion to religious faith and resis-tance to social change.

Support for and resistance to social change are rela-tive ideas—relative, that is, to the position of their advo-cates. If one supports a woman's right to choose whether to have an abortion or not, the social change in question is

tolerance for abortion rights (which does not necessarily mean that one favors abortion). If one is opposed to abor-tion rights, the change one seeks is a return to a situation in which abortion is illegal. As noted earlier in the chapter, by opposing abortion rights the Catholic church stands for social change in a conservative direction.

In religious life the same institution can stand for con-servative social change in one place and for more radical change in another. For example, the conservative Episco-palian (Anglican) church in Northern Ireland supports the continuation of British colonial rule there, while the Epis-copalian church in the United States supports liberal causes such as abortion rights and environmental action. The relationship between the Catholic church and social change is even more complex. In the United States the church is accused by some of its own leaders of having too conservative a view of social change. In Brazil, by contrast, the church is accused of being too liberal. How can a single institution be perceived so differently in two societies?

Part of the answer is that a church that is so large and embraces so many separate organizations can never be free from internal politics. Many Catholic theologians agree with Father Richard P. McBrien of Notre Dame Uni-versity that "since his election in 1978, Pope John Paul II has been determinedly appointing a certain type of cleric to important archdioceses and dioceses all around the world" (1990, p. A17). According to McBrien and others, these bishops and cardinals tend to be "uncritically loyal to the Pope" and "rigidly authoritarian and solitary" in their lead-ership style. They are unlikely to take their parishioners' views into account when they differ from those of the pope and his curial associates. For their part, high church offi-cials argue that their function is to keep the church on the right track in defending the sanctity of life while seeking constructive social change where possible. Hence, on many social issues—abortion rights, the rights of homosexuals, treatment of AIDS patients, ordination of women, economic reform—the leadership of the Catholic church (though not always its rank-and-file adherents) tends to act as a conser-vative force in the United States and other industrial nations.

The opposite is true in Brazil and other Latin Ameri-can nations, where the Catholic church is identified with movements for radical social reforms. In Brazil, theologian Leonardo Boff and bishop Dom Helder Camara have devel-oped and taught the idea that spiritual salvation is not pos-sible without action to liberate the oppressed. Religion itself could help transform the miserable conditions of the peasantry and the Indians and the impoverished working people (Adriance, 1986; McGuire, 1987). This view has come to be known as "liberation theology."

As liberation theology took hold during the 1960s and 1970s, church leaders began to develop what they called "the preferential option for the poor." Recognizing that the so-called miracle of Brazilian economic growth had not

The pope, shown here mingling with a crowd of devout followers, often takes a conservative position on social issues like abortion and women's roles. In many parts of Latin America, however, the Catholic church is an important force for social change, and its leaders play an important part in the struggle against severe economic inequality.

helped most of the nation's poor people, they proposed to correct this situation even at the expense of the spiritual needs of the affluent. Church leaders and lay activists organized thousands of small groups known as Communidades Eclesial de Base, or CEBs. These 30- to 40-person groups were the building blocks of a powerful social movement to bring both spiritual comfort and economic uplift to the nation's poor masses. Never a very popular strategy in Rome, the CEBs seem nevertheless to have had a real impact in moving Brazil's elite classes toward the realization that if

they did not do more to distribute the benefits of economic development they might be swept out of power in the next elections.

At this writing it is not clear what the future holds either for liberation theology or for the liberal-conservative dispute among Catholics in the United States. It is clear, however, that like all the major religions of the world, Catholicism will continue to face the challenges of social change.

FORMS OF RELIGIOUS EXPRESSION

This series of photos reminds us that despite outward differences in religious expression, all religions stimulate a deeply felt spiritual experience in their members. But religious emotions are usually experienced by groups of worshipers who follow the same set of rituals, rituals that have a great deal to do with the quality of the individual's religious experience. For example, in the group of African tribespeople who are dancing and chanting, each member of the community feels transported outside his or her normal consciousness into a realm of ecstasy brought on by the frenzy of the ritual. In the photos of Muslim worshipers at a mosque and of women participating in a Catholic festival in Central America, we see that some sacred rituals are more restrained.

Religious emotions may be deeply felt, and the individual may sometimes feel transported outside his or her normal self, but much of the power of the religious experience comes from being with others of the same faith in a sacred building—a mosque, a synagogue, a church. Outside such places one is in the secular world, but it is nevertheless possible for a person to carry the spirituality of his or her religious faith into everyday life. And we can see in the photos of the street prayer group and the evangelical revival meeting that even in highly secular societies some people seek the greater intensity offered by sect rituals.

These photos may also be viewed in terms of what they tell us about the social organization of religious expression. Notice, for example, the patterns of gender segregation that appear in many of the photos. For instance, in the Islamic religion, men and women worship in separate places. Roman Catholic rituals are often integrated in terms of gender, but there are local variations of the standard rituals in which women and men are separated. In the Episcopal church, both men and women can serve at the altar, but this is a relatively recent development that has resulted from increased demands by women for equal access to church leadership. The modern Protestant sects also display a good deal of gender equality, but as we see in the revival meeting photo, particular rituals often attract more women than men.

SUMMARY

THINK ABOUT IT CRITICALLY

Religions are often criticized for supporting the status quo. In legitimating moral codes by associating them with God's approval, religions would seem to oppose ideas that foster dissent, reform, or other types of social change. But is this always a consequence of religious devotion?

Religion is among the oldest and most changeable and complex of human social institutions. It has been defined as any set of coherent answers to the dilemmas of human existence that makes the world meaningful. It has also been defined as a system of beliefs and rituals that serves to bind people together into a social group. *Rituals* are formal patterns of activity that express a set of shared meanings; in the case of religious rituals, the shared meanings are *sacred,* pertaining to phenomena that are regarded as extraordinary, transcendent, and outside the everyday course of events.

Until comparatively recent times religion dominated the cultural life of human societies. Since medieval times, however, the traditional dominance of religion over other institutions has been reduced by a process termed *secularization.* This process is never complete; religion continues to play an important role in the contemporary world.

In simpler and rather isolated societies, people may believe in a great force or spirit, but they do not have a well-defined concept of God or a set of rituals involving God. This form of religion is called *simple supernaturalism.* More common among hunting-and-gathering societies is *animism,* in which all forms of life and all aspects of the earth are inhabited by gods or supernatural powers. *Theism,* in contrast, comprises belief systems that conceive of a god or gods as separate from humans and from other living things on the earth. Many ancient religions were *polytheistic,* meaning that they included numerous gods. The ancient Hebrews were among the first of the world's peoples to evolve a *monotheistic* religion, one centered on belief in a single all-powerful God.

In China, Japan, and other societies of the Far East, religions predominate that are centered not on devotion to a god or gods but on an abstract ideal of spirituality and human behavior. In addition, some social scientists have expanded the definition of religion to include *civil religions,* or collections of beliefs and rituals that exist outside religious institutions.

A major controversy in the study of religious institutions has to do with the role they play in social change. Karl Marx believed that cultural institutions like religion are shaped by economic and political institutions, and they function to instill in the masses the values of the dominant class. Max Weber, on the other hand, argued that religion can cause major social change by instilling certain

values in the members of a society, in turn causing changes in other institutions.

Religion today is a highly structured institution, with numerous statuses and roles within a variety of organizations as well as many kinds of smaller, less bureaucratic groups. The main types of religious organizations are the church, the sect, and the denomination. A *church* is a religious organization that has strong ties to the larger society and has at one time or another enjoyed the loyalty of most of the society's members. A *sect* rejects the religious beliefs or practices of an established church and usually is formed when a group of church members splits off to form a rival organization. A third type of religious organization is the *denomination,* which is on good terms with the religious institution from which it developed but must compete with other denominations for members.

A *cult* is an entirely new religion. Along with sects, cults are a major source of change in religious organizations. People who are not satisfied with more established churches and denominations may form or join a cult or sect. New religious movements arise when a "religious innovator" attracts a number of followers. This is particularly likely when traditional religions fail to meet the needs of their members or when a society is undergoing rapid secularization.

Membership in a religious organization is quite different from identification with a religious faith, and this is reflected in trends in religion in the United States. Among those trends are a growing tendency to practice unofficial or "folk" religion and an emphasis on religiosity as opposed to church membership. *Religiosity* refers to the depth of a person's religious feelings and how those feelings are translated into religious behavior. Studies of religiosity find high percentages of Americans believing in the existence of God and in a life after death.

In societies characterized by religious pluralism, one usually can observe the continual formation of new religious organizations.

Religious fundamentalists are believers devoted to the strict observance of ritual and doctrine and lack tolerance for differences in belief and practice. In the United States fundamentalism experienced a resurgence during the 1980s, encouraged by conservative social movements.

CRITICAL RESPONSE

It is true that some religions oppose social change, but it is also true that others promote it. In fact, religions are often on the front line of social change. In the case of the base Christian communities in Latin America, religion is challenging the status quo of inequality between rich and poor, landowners and landless. In the United States, on the other hand, fundamentalist Protestant movements seek to revive older practices such as prayer in public schools. These are social changes as well, and they are actively promoted by particular religious organizations.

GLOSSARY

religion: any set of coherent answers to the dilemmas of human existence that makes the world meaningful; a system of beliefs and rituals that serves to bind people together into a social group. (p. 504)

ritual: a formal pattern of activity that expresses symbolically a set of shared meanings. (p. 504)

sacred: a term used to describe phenomena that are regarded as extraordinary, transcendent, and outside the everyday course of events. (p. 505)

profane: a term used to describe phenomena that are not considered sacred. (p. 505)

secularization: a process in which the dominance of religion over other institutions is reduced. (p. 507)

simple supernaturalism: a form of religion in which people may believe in a great force or spirit but do not have a well-defined concept of God or a set of rituals involving God. (p. 509)

animism: a form of religion in which all forms of life and all aspects of the earth are inhabited by gods or supernatural powers. (p. 509)

theism: a belief system that conceives of a god or gods as separate from humans and from other living things on the earth. (p. 511)

polytheistic: a term used to describe a theistic belief system that includes numerous gods. (p. 511)

monotheistic: a term used to describe a theistic belief system centered on belief in a single all-powerful God. (p. 512)

civil religion: a collection of beliefs and rituals that exist outside religious institutions. (p. 512)

church: a religious organization that has strong ties to the larger society. (p. 514)

sect: a religious organization that rejects the beliefs and practices of existing churches; usually formed when a group leaves the church to form a rival organization. (p. 514)

denomination: a religious organization that is on good terms with the institution from which it developed but must compete with other denominations for members. (p. 514)

cult: a new religion. (p. 516)

religiosity: the depth of a person's religious feelings. (p. 521)

WHERE TO FIND IT

BOOKS

One God: Peoples of the Book (Edith S. Engel & Henry W. Engel, eds.; Pilgrim Press, 1990). An introduction to the major monotheistic religions with a message of peace, commonality, and openness.

"The Sociology of Religion" (Robert Wuthnow; in Neil Smelser, ed., *Handbook of Sociology;* Sage Publications, 1988). An extremely useful review of current trends in the sociology of religion by one of the field's leading scholars. Includes an excellent bibliography of classic and recent sociological research on religion.

Base Communities and Social Change in Brazil (W. E. Hewitt; University of Nebraska Press, 1991). A fine case study of the influential Catholic ecclesiastical base communities movement in Latin America, based primarily on research in São Paulo, Brazil. A good example of empirical research on religion and social change at the community level.

Religion and Religiosity in America (Jeffrey K. Hadden & Theodore E. Long; Crossroad, 1983). Contains many good empirical papers on religions and religious beliefs.

Radical Departures: Desperate Detours to Growing Up (Saul V. Levine; Harcourt Brace, 1984). A highly readable empirical study of why some middle-class young people join cults.

Religion: The Social Context, 3rd ed. (Meredith B. McGuire; Wadsworth, 1992). A comprehensive text on the sociology of religion with excellent material on religion and social change.

JOURNALS

Journal for the Scientific Study of Religion. Available in most college and university libraries; publishes recent research on religious practices, religiosity, and changes in religious institutions.

OTHER SOURCES

The Encyclopedia of American Religions, 4th ed. (Gale Research). Contains useful descriptions of religions in America; covers beliefs, organization, distribution in the population, and other aspects.

CHAPTER 18

Education and Communications Media

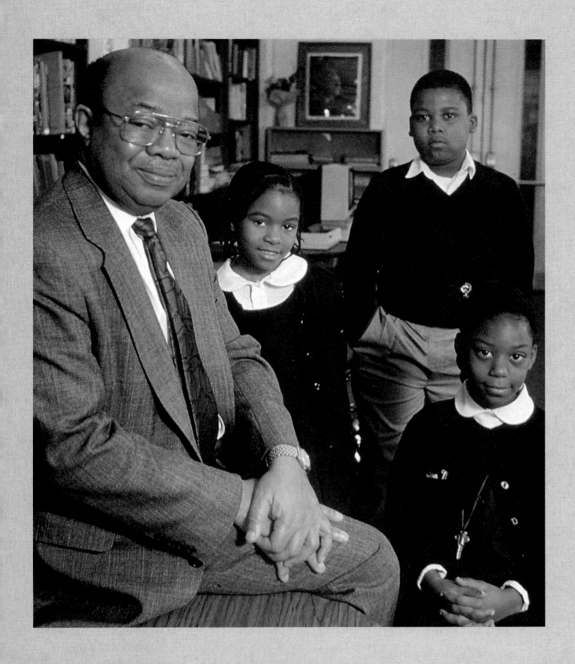

Schoolchildren in Prince George's County, Maryland, are taking part in a historic educational experiment. So are their parents, their teachers, and their principals. In Chicago, Miami, New York, and many other school districts throughout the United States, serious efforts at educational reform are under way, but nowhere are their goals quite as ambitious as those of the Prince George's County school district. In that county, one of the nation's largest and most rapidly growing, efforts at educational

reform have brought about a dramatic improvement in the county's most troubled schools.

James P. Comer, a child psychiatrist and educational philosopher, inspires and guides the Prince George's County program. In fact, everyone involved refers to the program as the Comer School Development Program. But Comer first came to national prominence as an educational pioneer in the ghetto schools of New Haven, Connecticut, where he applied his ideas of school

management and planning teams to "turn around" that city's most failure-scarred primary schools.

Comer traces his educational innovations to his experiences as an African American child in East Chicago, Indiana: "My three friends with whom I started elementary school—one died at an early age from alcoholism; one spent most of his life in jail; and one has been in and out of mental institutions all of his life. I was the only one to survive whole." Comer's father, a steelworker, and his mother, a domestic, played an active role in their sons' education:

> [They] came to school if there was a problem, and knew how to make sure that people were sensitive and concerned about us. What I've tried to do here in New Haven [and later in Prince George's County] is to shape the system, the school, so that it becomes the advocate and support for the kid, and a believer in the kid in the same way that my parents were. (quoted in Schorr, 1988, p. 232)

Comer's research and experience convinced him that children from neighborhoods that are undergoing severe strain—owing to poverty, racism, unemployment, violence, drug addiction, and related social problems—enter school with major deficits. They are often "underdeveloped in their social, emotional, linguistic, and cognitive growth." As a result, they often withdraw, act up, and do not learn. Of course, not all such students have these problems. Those who do, however, are labeled "slow learners" or "behavior problems" and consequently fall even further behind their classmates. Comer's solution appears very simple on the surface: Change the "climate of demoralized schools by paying much more attention to child development and to basic management of the school" (quoted in Schorr, 1988, p. 233).

Of course, the process of changing school climates and management is much more difficult than this simple formula suggests. The Comer model of institutional change calls for the formation of a School Planning and Management Team in each school; the team is directed by the principal and has from 12 to 14 members, including teachers, aides, and parents. A second team is made up of helping professionals—the school psychologist, social workers, special education teachers, and counselors; it acts as an advisory group. The purpose of the teams is to ally the parents with the school so that, in Comer's words, "you reduce the dissonance between home and school and you give the kid a long-term supporter for education at home" (quoted in Schorr, 1988, p. 233; see also Comer, 1980, 1984, 1985, 1987).

EDUCATION FOR A CHANGING WORLD

Efforts to change the goals and methods of education are not new. One of the most famous trials in history took place in ancient Greece when Socrates was accused of corrupting the morals of Athenian youth with his innovative ideas and educational methods. Today, the fact that educational reforms like those proposed by James Comer are receiving so much hopeful attention is evidence of the importance of education in modern societies. There is great concern with the need to improve education in order to train new generations of workers. We will see at many points in this chapter that there is a widespread desire to reform schools without significantly increasing school funding. However, although critics of the public schools abound, there is little consensus about how to achieve better student performance (Mulkey, 1993).

Education may be defined as the process by which a society transmits knowledge, values, norms, and ideologies and in so doing prepares young people for adult roles and adults for new roles; in other words, it transmits the society's culture to the next generation. Education thus is a form of socialization that is carried out by institutions outside the family, such as schools, colleges, preschools, and adult education centers. Each of these is an educational institution because it encompasses a set of statuses and roles designed to carry out specific educational functions—it is devoted to transmitting a specific body of knowledge, values, and norms of behavior. A particular school or college may be referred to as an *institution* in everyday language, but in sociological terms it is an *organization* that exemplifies an educational institution. Thus, El Centro College in Dallas is an organization that exemplifies the institution of higher education. The high school you attended was also an organization, but its curriculum and norms of conduct were those of the institution known as secondary education.

Educational institutions have a huge effect on communities in the United States and other modern societies. Upwardly mobile couples often base their choice of a place to live on the quality of the public schools in the neighborhood. Every neighborhood has at least an elementary school, and every large city has one or more high schools and at least one community college or four-year college. Cities usually also have a variety of school administrations—public and private—and some owe their existence, growth, and development to the presence of a college or university (Ballantine, 1993).

THE NATURE OF SCHOOLS

Educational institutions affect not only the surroundings but also the daily lives of millions of Americans: children and their parents, college and university students, teachers and professors. Hence, education is a major focus of social-scientific research. To the sociologist, the most common educational institution, the school, is a specialized structure with a special function: preparing children for active participation in adult activities (Katz, 1964). Schools are sometimes compared with total institutions (see Chapter 5), in which a large group of involuntary "clients" is serviced by a smaller group of staff members (Boocock, 1980). The staffs of such institutions tend to emphasize the maintenance of order and control, and this often leads to the development of elaborate sets of rules and monitoring systems. This comparison cannot be taken too literally (schools are not prisons, although some of their "inmates" may think of them as such), but the typical school does tend to be characterized by a clearly defined authority system and set of rules. In fact, sociologists often cite schools as examples of bureaucratic organizations (Mulkey, 1993; Parelius & Parelius, 1987).

A more interactionist viewpoint sees the school as a set of behaviors; that is, the central feature of the school is not its bureaucratic structure but the kinds of interactions and patterns of socialization that occur in schools. In the words of Frederick Bates and Virginia Murray (1975), the basic feature of schools is "the behavior of a large number of actors organized into groups that are joined together by an authority structure, and by a network of relationships through which information, resources, and partially finished projects flow from one group to another" (p. 26). In other words, "school-related behavior (e.g., doing homework or grading papers) is part of the school as a social system, whether or not it takes place in the school building" (Boocock, 1980, p. 129). So, too, is the involvement of parents in schools and in the school careers of their children. Students with parents who feel comfortable dealing with teachers, who understand what activities to encourage their children to join, who know where and how to challenge and when to defer to the principal's authority—such children, according to interactionists, have a significant advantage over others.

Conflict theorists, by contrast, view education in modern societies as serving to justify and maintain the status quo (Aronowitz & Giroux, 1985; Bowles & Gintis, 1977). For example, on the basis of his field research on secondary school students in a working-class community, the British sociologist Paul Willis (1983) concluded that "education

This photo of Tibetan refugee children in a classroom in northern India illustrates the similarity of classroom organization in many parts of the world.

was not about equality, but inequality. . . . Education's main purpose . . . could be achieved only by preparing most kids for an unequal future, and by insuring their personal underdevelopment" (p. 110). The group of boys from low-income homes whom Willis observed thought of themselves as "the lads" and delighted in making fun of higher achievers, whom they called "earholes." But in many different ways the "lads" indicated that they believed their teachers were pushing them into low-prestige futures. Willis interpreted the hostility and alienation of these students as a way of resisting the social forces channeling them into working-class careers.

As we will see shortly, this critical perspective challenges the more popular view that education is the main route to social mobility and that it can offset inequalities in family background (Bell, 1973). When sociologists analyze the impact of educational institutions on society, they generally conclude that the benefits of education are unequally distributed and tend to reproduce the existing stratification system (Fullan, 1993; Jencks et al., 1972).

WHO GOES TO SCHOOL?

The idea that all children should be educated is a product of the American and French revolutions of the late eighteenth century. In the European monarchies the suggestion that the children of peasants and workers should be educated would have been considered laughable. In those societies children went to work with adults at an early age, and adolescence was not recognized as a distinct stage of development. Formal schooling, generally reserved for the children of the elite, typically lasted 3 or 4 years, after which the young person entered a profession.

Even after the creation of republics in France and the United States and the beginning of a movement for universal education, the development of a comprehensive system of schools took many generations. In the early history of the United States, the children of slaves, Native Americans, the poor, and many immigrant groups, as well as almost all female children, were excluded from educational institutions. The norm of segregated education for racial minorities persisted into the twentieth century and was not overturned until 1954 in the Supreme Court's famous ruling in *Brown* v. *Board of Education of Topeka*. Even after that decision it took years of civil rights activism to ensure that African Americans could attend public schools with whites. Thus, although the idea of universal education in a democracy arose early, it took many generations of conflict and struggle to transform it into a strong social norm (Ariès, 1962; Cremin, 1980).

The idea of mass education based on the model created in the United States and other Western nations has spread throughout the world. Mass education differs from elite education, which is designed to prepare a small number of privileged individuals (generally sons of upper-class families) to run the institutions of society (the military, the clergy, the law, etc.). Mass education focuses instead on the socialization of all young people for membership in the society (Trow, 1966). It is seen as a way for young people to become citizens of a modern nation-state. Mass education establishes an increasingly standardized curriculum and tries to link mastery of that curriculum with personal and national development (Benavot et al., 1991; Meyer, Ramirez, & Soysal, 1992).

Figure 18.1 indicates that by 1980 all the nations of the world had adopted the basic model of a mass educational system (although many had not extended educational opportunities to the majority of young citizens). Note the sharp upsurge in the 1950s. This was the decade when large numbers of colonial nations in Africa and Asia became independent. Commitment to a mass educational system became a hallmark of modernity for these and other new nations. It was also a time when agencies like the World Bank, UNESCO (United Nations Educational, Social, and Cultural Organization), and the U.S. Agency for International Development began to actively encourage and provide financial support for mass educational institutions.

An extension of mass education in the United States was the expansion of public institutions of postsecondary education (and the parallel expansion of private colleges and universities, often with federal aid and research funding). This expansion was fueled by the post–World War II baby boom and the massive increase in the college-age population in the 1960s. During those years there was a parallel boom in employment for elementary school teachers and then for high school teachers and college professors. But after the boom came the bust: The birthrate fell sharply beginning in the late 1950s, and by the mid-1970s college enrollments also began to decline. These changes had dramatic effects on primary schools, but at the college level they were partially offset by an unprecedented countertrend: the immense increase in the number of older students seeking higher education. Today large numbers of adults are returning to college. Unlike the typical student of earlier years, they are in the labor force, are married and living with their spouses, are going to school part-time, and are seeking skills and knowledge to enhance their careers (Bogue, 1985; Mulkey, 1993).

The return of so many adults to educational institutions has led many social scientists to describe a future in which education will be a lifelong process in which people of all ages will move in and out of educational institutions (Parelius & Parelius, 1987; Reich, 1992a). Nevertheless, the most rapidly growing area of education is preschool programs, an important trend that is discussed later in the chapter.

SCHOOLS AND ADOLESCENT SOCIETY

A key feature of education is the fact that schools structure the lives of children and adolescents. This is particularly true at the high school level. A famous study of the effect of

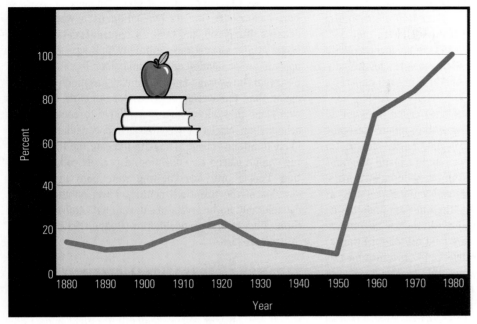

FIGURE 18.1 Percentage of Nations Developing Systems of Mass Education, by Decade

Source: Adapted from Meyer, Ramirez, & Soysal, 1992.

schools on adolescents and youth, *The Adolescent Society,* was published by James Coleman in 1961. Its main point was that schools help create a social world for adolescents that is separate from adult society. According to Coleman, this is an almost inevitable result of the growing complexity of industrial societies, in which, as we saw earlier, functions that were formerly performed by the family are increasingly shifted to other institutions, especially educational institutions. Yet schools cannot provide the same kind of support and individual attention that the family can. As a result, according to Coleman, the student is pushed into associations primarily with others of the same age. These small groups of agemates come to "constitute a small society, one that has most of its important interaction within itself, and maintains only a few threads of connection with the outside adult society" (1961, p. 3).

Coleman's research was not unique. Other social scientists have analyzed what has come to be known as the "youth culture" in terms of changes in the structure of American society. Briefly, what has happened is that the rising level of expectations regarding educational attainment has placed more and more demands on the student, resulting in "an almost compulsive independence, a touchiness with respect to any adult expectations and demands; [together with] an equally compulsive conformity and loyalty to the peer group, with very literal observation of group norms and intolerance of deviance" (Boocock, 1980, p. 213).

The risk for society in the development of isolated adolescent cultures is that teenagers will fail to learn how they can become involved in shaping their own society. Great

cultural gaps between youth and their parents are often a signal that the older generation has not offered young people enough opportunities to work with adults for constructive social change (Gilligan, 1987; Moscos, 1988).

EDUCATION AND CITIZENSHIP

Another important aspect of education in the United States is the relationship between education and citizenship. Throughout its history this nation has emphasized public education as a means of transmitting democratic values, creating equality of opportunity, and preparing new generations of citizens to function in society. In addition, the schools have been expected to help shape society itself. During the 1950s, for example, efforts to combat racial segregation focused on the schools. Later, when the Soviet Union launched the first orbiting satellite, American schools and colleges came under intense pressure and were offered many incentives to improve their science and mathematics programs so that the nation would not fall behind the Soviet Union in scientific and technological capabilities.

Education is often viewed as a tool for solving social problems, especially social inequality. The schools, it is thought, can transform young people from vastly different backgrounds into competent, upwardly mobile adults. Yet these goals seem almost impossible to attain (Cahill, 1992). In recent years, in fact, public education has been at the center of numerous controversies arising from the gap between the ideal and the reality. Part of the problem is that different groups in society have different expectations. Some feel that students need better preparation for careers in a technologically advanced society; others believe children should be taught basic job-related skills; still others believe education should not only prepare children to compete in society but also help them maintain their cultural identity (and, in the case of Hispanic children, their language). On the other hand, policy makers concerned with education emphasize the need to increase the level of student achievement and to involve parents in their children's education (Wilson, 1993).

Some reformers and critics have called attention to the need to link formal schooling with programs designed to address social problems. Sociologist Charles Moscos, for example, is a leader in the movement to expand programs like the Peace Corps, VISTA, and Outward Bound into a system of voluntary national service. National service, as Moscos defines it, would entail "the full-time undertaking of public duties by young people—whether as citizen soldiers or civilian servers—who are paid subsistence wages" and serve for at least a year (1988, p. 1). In return for this period of service, the volunteers would receive assistance in paying for college or other educational expenses.

Advocates of national service and school-to-work programs believe that education does not have to be confined to formal schooling. In devising strategies to provide opportunities for young people to serve their society, they emphasize the educational value of citizenship experiences gained outside the classroom. Early in his administration President Clinton, a believer in national service, implemented a modest program known as Americorps. Americorps is a volunteer community service program targeted at young people who normally would not apply to existing volunteer programs like the Peace Corps. At this writing, however, the future of Americorps is extremely uncertain.

ATTAINMENT, ACHIEVEMENT, AND EQUALITY

While some educational reformers focus on the need to expand learning opportunities through nonschool service experiences, by far the majority of scholars and administrators seek improvements in educational institutions themselves. Their efforts often focus on *educational attainment,* or the number of years of schooling that students receive, and *educational achievement,* or the amount of learning that actually takes place. Both aspects of education are closely linked to economic inequality and social mobility.

EDUCATIONAL ATTAINMENT

In any discussion of education as a major social institution, the concept of **educational attainment** (number of years of school completed) holds a central place. Educational attainment is correlated with income, occupation, prestige, attitudes and opinions, and much else. It is essential, therefore, for social scientists to understand the impact of recent trends in school enrollment on the educational at-

tainment of the population as a whole and of various subgroups of the population.

Table 18.1 shows the median number of years of school completed by the population as a whole in the decades since 1940, and Table 18.2 presents data on educational attainment by race, ethnicity, and sex. Both tables apply to the population aged 25 and older. It is immediately clear that the average American today has much more education than the average American of the early 1940s. It is also clear that whites are more likely to complete high school than blacks or Hispanics, and considerably more likely to attend college. The data indicate the increasingly high value placed on education, especially college education. People over age 75, who were born in the early decades of the twentieth century, have, on the average, considerably lower levels of educational attainment than their children and grandchildren (Bogue, 1985; *Statistical Abstract,* 1995).

BARRIERS TO EDUCATIONAL ATTAINMENT

Tracking and Inequality. The rise of mass education gave the middle and lower classes greater opportunities for upward social mobility through educational attainment. But as early as the 1920s many schools began to use "tracking" systems in which higher-achieving students were placed in accelerated classes while others were shunted into vocational and other types of less challenging classes. Today tracking remains a major problem in public schools. Parents of "gifted" children seek educational challenges for their sons and daughters and do not want them to be held back by slower learners. However, tracking systems can make average students feel less valued, and there is a danger that gifted but alienated students will be labeled as nonachievers.

Figure 18.2 (see page 542) is based on a national study of more than 14,000 eighth grade students in public schools. It shows quite clearly that white and Asian students are far more likely than black and Hispanic students to be tracked into high-ability groups, and that students from high socioeconomic backgrounds are also far more

TABLE 18.1	Median Years of School Completed
YEAR	**MEDIAN YEARS OF SCHOOL COMPLETED**
1990	12.7
1980	12.5
1970	12.2
1960	10.6
1950	9.3
1940	8.6

Source: Data from Census Bureau.

TABLE 18.2	Educational Attainment, by Race, Ethnicity, and Sex: 1947–1994											
	PERCENT HIGH SCHOOL GRADUATE						PERCENT COLLEGE GRADUATE					
	WHITE		BLACK		HISPANIC		WHITE		BLACK		HISPANIC	
YEAR	M	F	M	F	M	F	M	F	M	F	M	F
1994	82%	82%	72%	74%	53%	53%	26%	20%	13%	13%	10%	9%
1991	80	80	67	67	51	51	25	19	11	12	10	9
1987	77	77	63	64	52	50	25	17	11	10	10	8
1980	71	70	51	51	46	44	22	14	8	8	10	6
1970	57	58	32	35	NA	NA	15	9	5	4	NA	NA
1962	47	50	23	26	NA	NA	12	7	4	4	NA	NA
1947	33	37	13	15	NA	NA	7	5	2	3	NA	NA

NA = Data not available

Sources: Census Bureau, 1988, 1992; *Statistical Abstract*, 1995.

likely to be tracked into such groups. (Ability grouping is synonymous with tracking.) Some social scientists argue that these differences are a result of ability differences among racial and class groups; others assert that they are a consequence of race and class bias (Murray, 1993; Oakes, 1985). Since there are far more Hispanic and black students in the lower socioeconomic classes, there is little question that social factors outweigh biological ones in explaining these results. In any case, tracking separates children and is increasingly viewed as leading to educational inequalities. A current trend in educational practice, therefore, is to institute detracking programs and to provide highly gifted students with additional challenges through cooperative education (in which they have opportunities to teach others) and through after-school programs (Mansnerus, 1992).

Dropping Out. The educational attainment of various subgroups of the population is virtually identical up to the age of 13 (Jencks et al., 1972). The picture begins to change in the early secondary school years, however. Until quite recently the dropout rate for black and Hispanic students in high school was almost twice the rate for white students. In 1970, 10.8 percent of white students dropped out without finishing high school, while among black students the proportion was 22.2 percent. By 1993, the situation had improved remarkably as a result of strenuous efforts by students, parents, and teachers across the United States. In that year 8.8 percent of white students and 11.2 percent of black students dropped out (*Statistical Abstract,* 1995). Table 18.3 (see page 543) shows that high school graduation rates (the opposite of dropout rates) vary among the states, with the highest in Alaska at 86.6 percent and the lowest in Mississippi at 64.3 percent.

The main reason for dropping out of school is poor academic performance, but there are other reasons as well. Students often drop out because of the demands of work and family roles; many are married, or unmarried and preg-

nant, and/or working at regular jobs. Whatever the reason, the effects of dropping out can be serious. Dropouts have less chance of joining the labor force than high school graduates; whatever jobs they find tend to be low-paying ones. From 1974 to 1992 the income advantage from completing college increased for all individuals, regardless of gender or minority status. But black–white differentials are found at each level of attainment. White college graduates, for example, earned 23 percent more in 1992 than black college graduates of the same age (National Center for Educational Statistics, 1995).

Degree Inflation. The trend toward increasingly higher levels of educational attainment has had an unexpected effect known as "degree inflation." Employers have always paid attention to the educational credentials of potential employees, but today they require much more education than in the past. For example, in earlier decades of this century a person could get a teaching job with a high school diploma; now a bachelor's and often a master's degree is usually required. The same is true of social work. And secretaries, who formerly could get by without a high school diploma, now are often required to have at least some college education and, in some cases, a college degree.

Degree inflation is discouraging to some students and prevents them from continuing their education. It also adds to the expense of education (both directly and indirectly in terms of lost income), and hence prevents less advantaged students from undertaking advanced studies. Degree inflation also increases the amount of time that must be devoted to formal education. It therefore raises questions about the meaning of educational achievement—that is, the value of the time spent attaining educational credentials.

EDUCATIONAL ACHIEVEMENT

Differences in levels of educational attainment are viewed as a sign that public education is not meeting the expectations of society in terms of the quantity of education

FIGURE 18.2   Ability Grouping ("Tracking") in U.S. Public Schools

BY RACE AND ETHNICITY

High ability   Middle ability   Low ability   Mixed

Eighth-grade English classes

Asian White Hispanic Black American Indian

Eighth-grade math classes

Asian White Hispanic Black American Indian

BY SOCIOECONOMIC STATUS

Top Socioeconomic Quarter

39% High ability
8% Mixed
14% Low
39% Middle

Bottom Quarter

36% Middle
13% High ability
14% Mixed
37% Low

*Some of the classes in the survey were heterogeneous groupings, as shown for each ethnic and racial group in the chart.

Source: Adapted from Mansnerus, 1992.

provided to citizens. There is also controversy over the quality of education, or educational achievement as reflected in scores on standardized tests like the Scholastic Aptitude Test (SAT). **Educational achievement** refers to how much the student actually learns, measured by mastery of reading, writing, and mathematical skills. It is widely believed that the average level of educational achievement has declined drastically in the past two decades. In a 1983 report titled *A Nation at Risk,* the National Commission on Excellence in

Education pointed to the decline in the average test scores of high school students since the mid-1960s and stated that the schools have failed to maintain high educational standards. In recent years standardized scores in math have risen somewhat, but verbal scores (reading and vocabulary) have not (Murray, 1993). Many observers attribute the decline in test scores to a variety of social conditions such as too much television viewing and changing values related to family life.

TABLE 18.3	High School Graduation Rates, by State (persons age 25 and over)
STATE	**PERCENT**
Alabama	66.9
Alaska	86.6
Arizona	78.7
Arkansas	66.3
California	76.2
Colorado	84.4
Connecticut	79.2
Delaware	77.5
Dist. of Columbia	73.1
Florida	74.4
Georgia	70.9
Hawaii	80.1
Idaho	79.9
Illinois	76.2
Indiana	75.6
Iowa	80.1
Kansas	81.3
Kentucky	64.6
Louisiana	68.3
Maine	78.8
Maryland	78.4
Massachusetts	80.0
Michigan	76.8
Minnesota	82.4
Mississippi	64.3
Missouri	73.9
Montana	81.0
Nebraska	81.8
Nevada	78.8
New Hampshire	82.2
New Jersey	76.7
New Mexico	75.1
New York	74.8
North Carolina	70.0
North Dakota	76.7
Ohio	75.7
Oklahoma	74.6
Oregon	81.5
Pennsylvania	74.7
Rhode Island	72.0
South Carolina	68.3
South Dakota	77.1
Tennessee	67.1
Texas	72.1
Utah	85.1
Vermont	80.8
Virginia	75.2
Washington	83.8
West Virginia	66.0
Wisconsin	78.6
Wyoming	83.0

Source: Adapted from *Statistical Abstract,* 1995.

Critics of excessive reliance on standard tests might agree with prominent educational reformer Ted Sizer, who points out that "none of the major tests used in American elementary and secondary education correlates well with long-term success or failure. SAT scores, for example, suggest likely grades in the freshman year at college; they do not predict much thereafter" (1995, p. 58). For better or worse, however, the SAT and other standard tests continue to be used as primary measures of individual and school performance.

Another problem related to educational achievement is the high rate of "functional incompetency" among Americans. A large number of people are unable to read, write, keep a family budget, and the like (see Figure 18.3).

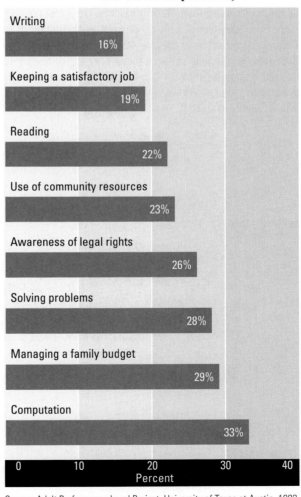

FIGURE 18.3 Functional Incompetency Among Americans (percentage of all adults who are incompetent in)

Source: Adult Performance Level Project, University of Texas at Austin, 1982.

Note: Most studies of literacy are based on a single indicator and hence do not provide as broad a view of the many forms of functional incompetency as the one represented here. There are no indications from more recent studies that these figures have changed significantly.

Although more and more people are obtaining a college education, many others are being left behind, particularly members of the lower social classes, people for whom English is a second language, and people with learning disabilities. As increasing amounts of education are required for better jobs, this cleavage between educational haves and have-nots becomes an ever more dangerous trend. (See Box 18.1.)

Recent research on school achievement offers even more disturbing evidence of deficiencies in the educational achievement of U.S. students, beginning at an early age. Tests of achievement by thousands of schoolchildren in comparable U.S. and Asian cities—Minneapolis, Chicago, Sendai (Japan), Beijing (China), and Taipei (Taiwan)—reveal that the mathematics scores of American first-graders were lower than those of Asian first-graders. In some American schools first-graders' scores were similar to those of Asian students, but by the fifth grade all the American students had fallen far behind. In computation, for example, only 2.2 percent of children in Beijing scored as low as the mean score for U.S. fifth-graders. On a test consisting of word problems, only 10 percent of fifth-graders in Beijing scored as low as the average U.S. student. Gaps also appeared in reading skills, although vast differences in written languages make it somewhat difficult to compare achievement in those skills (H. W. Stevenson, 1992; Tobin, Wu, & Davidson, 1989).

Americans are likely to suggest that these differences occur because citizens of Asian nations value education more than Americans do and that in Asian schools children are placed under great stress, learn by rote and drill, and spend long hours in school. The researchers found that only the first of these explanations is correct. It is true that Asian parents value education more than American parents do, but it is not true that Asian schoolchildren experience more stress, do more rote learning, and spend more time at their desks. In fact, the opposite is true: Asian children experience less stress and anxiety than American children, enjoy school more, and have far more opportunities for recreation and breaks from classroom work despite their longer school day. The frequency of recreation breaks appears to help them pay more attention to their classroom work than is typical of children in U.S. schools.

Close observation of teaching in the different schools revealed that Asian teachers tend to use work that the students do at their desks (seatwork) as an opportunity to pay attention to individual students. Teachers in U.S. schools are less likely to circulate through the class and comment on individual students' efforts.

Finally, Figure 18.4 shows important differences in the way parents perceive schooling in Asia and the United States. Mothers in the United States tend to be far more positive than Asian mothers about their children's schoolwork at all grade levels. They are also more likely to believe that the school is doing an excellent job in educating their children. American parents tend to believe far more in the effects of innate ability and less in the value of effort in school than Asian parents do. This difference is especially important because it seems to lead U.S. parents to more readily accept their children's performance in school and to demand less of them. Parents' belief in innate ability also appears to make them far less critical of the schools than they might otherwise be (H. W. Stevenson, 1992).

This research has many practical implications for social change in the schools. It is apparent, for example, that simply lengthening the school day in the United States would not have the desired results. Indeed, it might well have negative results without far greater provision for time when children can play and socialize with their peers as they do in Asian schools.

EDUCATION AND SOCIAL MOBILITY

Studies by educational sociologists have consistently found a high correlation between social class and educational attainment and achievement, so much so that major efforts to address inequalities in educational opportunities were undertaken during the 1960s and 1970s. Nevertheless, there is evidence that the promise of equal education for all remains far from being fulfilled. Educational institutions

BOX 18.1 GLOBAL SOCIAL CHANGE

Literacy in a Changing World

There is a strong correlation between illiteracy and poverty throughout the world (see map). The poor nations of the Sahel, such as Mali, Chad, Niger, Ethiopia, and the Sudan, suffer from some of the highest rates of illiteracy in the world. High rates of illiteracy are also evident in much of South Asia, especially on the Indian subcontinent. On the other hand, illiteracy rates are quite low in poor nations like Mexico and Cuba, where the ideology of social development places strong emphasis on educating the mass of citizens to the fullest extent possible.

Sociological theories of modernization stress the need for populations to become literate so that their members will be better-informed voters, more highly skilled workers, more careful parents, and generally better able to realize their human potential. Literacy, it is argued, significantly increases a society's human capital. Reductions in the level of ignorance yield improvements in every aspect of a nation's social and civic life.

This line of argument is clearly supported by the correlation between poverty and illiteracy in India (see chart). Overall, the chart shows that as illiteracy decreases, the amount of money a household is able to spend each month increases. The chart also shows that illiteracy and the poverty associated with it are much more prevalent among women than among men, with rural women showing the highest rates of illiteracy and poverty (about 90 percent illiterate in the high-poverty category). That men are far more likely than women to become literate in India is a reflection of the immense gap in prestige between the sexes in that society; men are considered far more worthy of education than women.

Recent research on the effects of literacy on vital measures of social change such as reduced fertility clearly show the importance of educating women. Data from research conducted in Thailand and other Southeast Asian nations suggest that until women gain access to at least minimal educational opportunities fertility rates in those nations will remain high. This research confirms the hypothesis that "demographic change is unlikely if the movement towards mass schooling is confined largely to males" (London, 1992, p. 306).

These relationships among gender, illiteracy, and social indicators like poverty and fertility offer a warning that investments in literacy alone are necessary but not sufficient to accelerate social change in a population. Investments in literacy must be accompanied by strategies to reach the most impoverished and discriminated-against segments of the population (such as rural women in many societies). Such stratagems, in turn, are difficult to develop in a society in which the powerful may fear their effects. In nations where poor rural women are offered more education, for example, the women often begin to demand greater equality. It takes farsighted leadership to actively promote such strategies.

Another consequence of increasing literacy and education in poor societies is that some of the "best and brightest" are attracted by opportunities in richer societies.

Poverty and Illiteracy in India

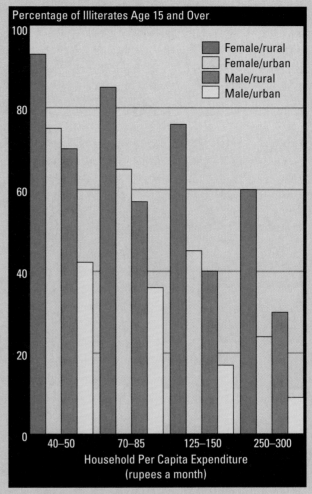

Source: Data from third quinquennial survey on employment and unemployment, Ministry of Planning, New Delhi, India.

This phenomenon is known as the "brain drain" and is a significant problem for developing nations (Alam, 1988; Cortes, 1980). Relatively well-educated people, often with professional training, are an important source of migration from Third World nations to the wealthier nations of North America and Western Europe. Indeed, immigration policies in North America actively encourage immigration by well-trained individuals and establish quotas that discourage less educated persons from seeking entry.

In order to address the problems created by the brain drain phenomenon, the poorer nations have developed policies requiring that people trained at public expense (e.g., through scholarships and training programs) must serve in their own nation until it has recouped its investment in their education. Such policies are not popular with educated people in those nations, especially if they are aware of more attractive opportunities outside their own society. But if the full benefits of literacy and education are to be applied to national development, such policies are necessary.

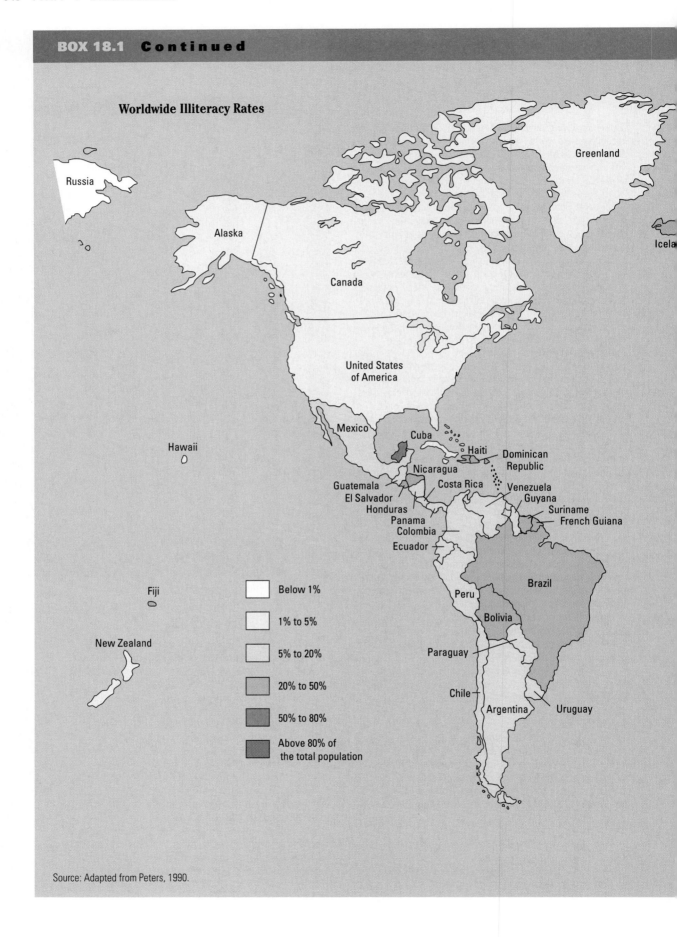

BOX 18.1 Continued

Worldwide Illiteracy Rates

Russia

Greenland

Icela

Alaska

Canada

United States
of America

Hawaii

Mexico

Cuba

Haiti

Dominican
Republic

Nicaragua

Guatemala

Costa Rica

Venezuela

El Salvador

Guyana

Honduras

Suriname

Panama

French Guiana

Colombia

Ecuador

Fiji

Brazil

Peru

Bolivia

New Zealand

Paraguay

Chile

Argentina

Uruguay

Below 1%

1% to 5%

5% to 20%

20% to 50%

50% to 80%

Above 80% of
the total population

Source: Adapted from Peters, 1990.

1 Czech Republic
2 Slovakia
3 Austria
4 Hungary
5 Estonia
6 Latvia
7 Bosnia and Herzegovina
8 Yugoslavia

9 Macedonia
10 Bulgaria
11 Lithuania
12 Moldova
13 Belarus
14 Syria
15 Jordan
16 Israel

FIGURE 18.4 Parents' Satisfaction With Academic Performance of Students and Schools in Selected U.S. and Asian Cities

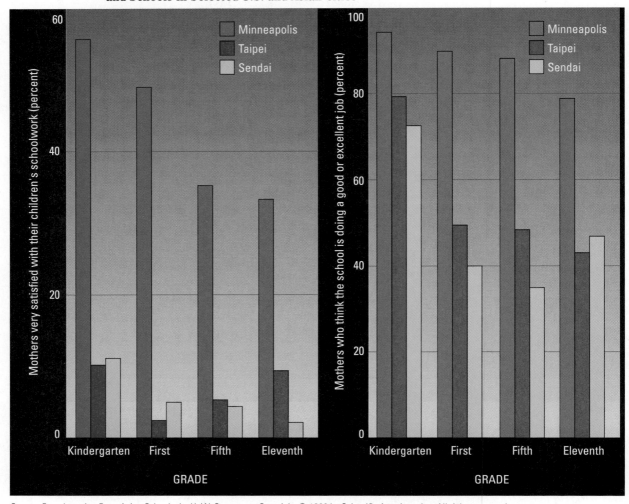

have been subjected to considerable criticism by observers who believe that they hinder, rather than enhance, social mobility (Fullan, 1993). Christopher Jencks (1972), for example, argued that schools serve primarily to reproduce the existing stratification system. He asserted that "schools serve primarily as selection and certification agencies, whose job is to measure and label people, and only secondarily as socialization agencies, whose job is to change people" (p. 135).

Jencks noted that the main criterion for granting a diploma or degree (i.e., certification) is usually the amount of time spent in school, not the skills learned. "Imagine," he wrote, "what would happen to high school enrollment if states allowed anyone, regardless of age, to take a high school equivalency examination. Most capable students would probably leave high school by the time they were 16"

(1972, pp. 135–136). In their study of the relationship between educational certification and inequality, Jencks and his researchers assumed that "the value of any given credential depends solely on how long it takes to acquire" (p. 136). And the chief factor that keeps some students in school and college longer than others, according to Jencks, is family background—in other words, social class. Members of the upper classes often regard college as an important transition to high-status occupations and therefore encourage their children to finish high school and attend college.

Inequality in the Classroom. In his book *The Urban School: A Factory for Failure* (1973), Ray C. Rist went even further, bluntly stating that "the system of public education in the United States is specifically designed to aid in the perpetuation of the social and economic inequalities found within the society" (p. 2)—despite the widespread belief that education increases social mobility. He went on to state:

> Schooling has basically served to instill the values of an expanding industrial society and to fit the aspirations and motivations of individuals to the labor market at approximately the same level as that of their parents. Thus it is that some children find themselves slotted toward becoming workers and others toward becoming the managers of those workers. (1973, p. 2)

These highly influential studies of educational inequality inspired many additional studies that have attempted to discover the actual processes through which education reproduces patterns of inequality rather than correcting them. In one example of such research, Jay MacLeod (1987) studied teenagers in a poor community who came from the same housing projects and attended the same high school. The members of one group, the Hallway Hangers, were predominantly white. They often cut classes, misbehaved in the classes they did attend, and used drugs. The members of the other group, the Brothers, were largely black but came from the same neighborhood and the same social class as the Hallway Hangers. In contrast to the Hallway Hangers, the Brothers tended to study hard, attend classes, and behave well in class. They accepted the idea that achievement in school would lead to success in the outside world, an idea the Hallway Hangers rejected.

These findings show that the economic aspects of social class are insufficient to explain success and failure in school. One must also understand the social influences that shape the actual experiences of individual students. The Brothers, it turns out, came primarily from black families who believed in equality of educational opportunity. Most of the Hallway Hangers came from families that did not value education or believe their children had much of a chance to succeed through education. The Brothers' parents were strict with their sons and punished school failure. The parents of the Hallway Hangers gave their sons much more leeway and paid far less attention to what they were doing (or not doing) in school. Of course, these differences are specific to these particular groups. One could find situations in which the outcomes are quite different. The point here is that working-class and poor children do not automatically inherit their lower-class position through the failure of education to reach them or through their own failure to accept the value of education. The influence of specific family and school environments is of great importance (MacLeod, 1987; Mehan, 1992).

Other firsthand observations of educational settings shed light on the importance of culture in explaining how inequalities persist despite educational opportunity. For example, studies in schools where there are significant numbers of students who do not hear English spoken at home show that problems with learning are not caused by language differences alone. They may also result from different styles of expression and interaction in the non-English culture. Studies have shown, for example, that white middle-class teachers often use questions rather than the direct demands that students may be used to at home— "Don't you want to try to work on your math?" instead of "Now sit down and work on your math" (Cazden, 1988; Delgado-Gaiton, 1987). And some groups, such as Native Americans, may not respond well to the competitive environment of the typical classroom but do far better in a class where cooperative work and sociability are valued (Philips, 1982).

Important as these cultural issues may be in explaining school achievement, economic class may be even more significant. It remains true that students from poor families are likely to attend schools with far fewer resources, less favorable student–teacher ratios, and more staff turnover than the schools attended by middle- and upper-class students (Karabel & Halsey, 1988). These class differences are also striking at the level of higher education.

Inequality in Higher Education. Inequality in higher education is primarily a matter of access—that is, ability to pay. Ability to pay is unequally distributed among various groups in society, and as a result students from poor, working-class, and lower-middle-class families, as well as members of racial minority groups, are most likely to rely on public colleges and universities. Social-scientific evidence indicates that such inequalities are alleviated by federal aid to students from families with low or moderate income. It is likely that without Pell grants, work-study funds, and student loan programs the proportion of students from such families would be far lower than it currently is. Even with such aid, the proportion of low-income students in colleges and universities is lower than that of students from high-income families.

Sandra Baum (1987) examined the educational careers of 2,000 students who were high school seniors in 1980. She found that college attendance rates were higher for students from high-income families than for students from low-income families (60 percent versus 46 percent). However, achievement in school seemed to account for an even larger difference. Students who scored high on achievement tests but came from low-income families had far higher rates of college attendance than low-scoring students from affluent homes. Thus achievement in the primary school grades seems to be at least as important as family income in explaining a student's success in higher education—but remember that in the lower grades students from more affluent homes tend to achieve more than students from less advantaged homes.

Baum and other researchers have also found that low-income students tend to be concentrated in two-year colleges and that students in such colleges are much more likely to drop out before completing a degree than students who enter four-year colleges. On the basis of findings like these, most educational researchers agree that without college assistance for needy students, differences in educational attainment and achievement would be much greater. And since public higher-education institutions remain the primary route to college degrees for low-income students, increased support for such institutions also tends to diminish inequality in access to higher education (Baum, 1987; Hansen & Stampen, 1987; U.S. Department of Education, 1994).

EDUCATION FOR EQUALITY

The question of whether and in what ways education leads to social mobility remains open. Some social scientists view education as an investment like any other: The amount invested is reflected in the future payoff. This is known as *human capital theory*. In this view, differences in payoffs (jobs and social position) are justified by differences in investment (hard work in school and investment in a college education). However, critics of the educational system point out that the resources required to make such "investments" are not equally available to all members of society.

The question of whether the society as a whole, or only its more affluent members, will invest in its "human capital" through such means as preschool programs and student loans is a major public-policy issue. This is especially true as technological advances coupled with degree inflation increase the demand for educated people (Bell, 1973; Reich, 1992a). Empirical evidence of the effectiveness of such investments may be seen in the results of an innovative study conducted by the High/Scope Educational Research Foundation (Berrueta-Clement et al., 1984).

The subject of the study was a preschool program at the Perry Elementary School, located in a low-income black neighborhood of Ypsilanti, Michigan, a small industrial city on the outskirts of Detroit. The researchers randomly selected 123 three-year-old boys and girls and assigned them either to the preschool group or to another group that would not go to the preschool program. The latter children, like the majority of children at that time, would not be enrolled in school for another 2 years.

About twice a year for the next 20 years the researchers traced the experiences of the experimental (preschool) and control (no-preschool) groups. The data in Table 18.4 show that there were important differences between the two groups as a consequence of the preschool experience. Members of the preschool group achieved more in school, found better jobs, had fewer arrests, and had fewer illegitimate children; in short, they experienced more success and fewer problems than members of the control group. These findings confirm what other, less well-known studies had shown. For example, studies by Benjamin Bloom (1976) and by Piaget and Inhelder (1969) had indicated that as much as 50 percent of variance in intellectual development takes place before the age of 4.

The most significant contribution of studies like the High/Scope research is their documentation of the actual improvements that a good preschool program can produce in disadvantaged children. The High/Scope study was also able to translate its findings into dollar figures. A year in the Perry program cost about $1,350 per child. The researchers showed that the "total social benefit" from the program (measured by higher tax revenues, lower welfare payments, and lower crime costs) was equivalent to $6,866 per person.

This research became a classic in the social-scientific study of education because it demonstrated the undeniable benefits of preschool education to society. It also appeared

TABLE 18.4	Major Findings at Age 19 in the Perry Preschool Study		
CATEGORY	NUMBER RESPONDING*	PRESCHOOL GROUP	NO-PRESCHOOL GROUP
Employed	121	59%	32%
High school graduation (or its equivalent)	121	67%	49%
College or vocational training	121	38%	21%
Ever detained or arrested	121	31%	51%
Females only: teen pregnancies, per 100**	49	64	117
Functional competence (APL Survey: possible score 40)	109	24.6	21.8
% of years in special education	112	16%	28%

*Total N = 123
**Includes all pregnancies

Source: Data from Berrueta-Clement et al., 1984.

during a period when funding for public preschool programs was in danger of being drastically reduced. The findings of the High/Scope study gave congressional advocates of preschool education the evidence they needed to justify continued federal funding. In many instances, however, social scientists know what needs to be done to improve educational achievement and increase equality of educational opportunity but are frustrated by the resistance to change that is inherent in large-scale bureaucratic systems such as the public school systems of many states and municipalities.

THE STRUCTURE OF EDUCATIONAL INSTITUTIONS

A significant barrier to educational reform is the bureaucratic nature of school systems. We noted earlier that sociologists view the school as a specialized structure with a special socializing function and that it is also a good example of a bureaucratic organization. As any student knows, there is a clearly defined status hierarchy in most schools. At the top of the hierarchy in primary and secondary schools is the principal, followed by the assistant principal and/or administrative assistants, the counselors, the teachers, and the students. Although the principal holds the highest position in the system, his or her influence on students usually is indirect. The teacher, on the other hand, is in daily command of the classroom and therefore has the greatest impact on the students. In this section we discuss several aspects of the structure of educational institutions and attempts to change those institutions.

SCHOOLS AS BUREAUCRACIES

As the size and complexity of the American educational system have increased, so has the tendency of educational institutions to become bureaucratized (Parelius & Parelius, 1987). The one-room schoolhouse is a thing of the past; today's schools have large administrative staffs and numerous specialists such as guidance counselors and special education teachers. Teachers themselves specialize in particular subject areas or grade levels. Schools are also characterized by a hierarchy of authority. The number of levels in the hierarchy varies, depending on the nature of the school system. In large cities, for example, there may be as many as seven levels between the superintendent and school personnel, making it difficult for the superintendent to control the way policies are carried out. Similarly, in any given school it may be difficult for the principal to determine what actually happens in the classroom.

The reforms sought by educational leaders like James Comer are being implemented in schools throughout the United States. Large cities like Chicago and New York are instituting more opportunities for parents to get involved in school issues and seeking to reduce the size of schools so that teachers, students, and administrators feel that they are part of a "learning community" in which they all know one another and are concerned with one another's well-being—conditions that may not be possible in larger schools, where bureaucratic rules and regulations often seem to take precedence over personal relations (Lee & Smith, 1993; Meier, 1994).

In many school districts, however, the pace of reform is slowed by bitter disagreements about how to fund the schools in an era of reduced public spending. There are also controversies over issues such as sex education, tolerance for homosexual students, distribution of condoms to prevent AIDS and teenage pregnancy, and school prayer. These can divide communities and prevent structural changes like the move toward smaller schools and more local responsibility for educational decisions (Fernandez, 1992; Rose, 1995).

The Classroom.   In most modern school systems the primary school student is in the charge of one teacher, who instructs in almost all subjects. But as the student advances through the educational structure, the primary school model (which evolved from the one-room school with a single teacher) is replaced by a "departmental" structure in which the student encounters a number of specialized teachers. The latter structure is derived largely from that of the nineteenth-century English boarding school. But these two basic structures are frequently modified by alternative approaches like the "open" primary school classroom, in which students are grouped according to their level of achievement in certain basic skills and work in these skill groups at their own pace. The various groups in the open classroom are given small group or individual instruction by one or more teachers rather than being expected to progress at the same pace in every subject.

Open classrooms have not been found to produce consistent improvements in student performance, but they have improved the school attendance rates of students from working-class and minority backgrounds. Students in open classrooms tend to express greater satisfaction with school and more commitment to classwork. The less stratified authority structure of the open classroom and the greater amount of cooperation that occurs in such settings may help students enjoy school more and, in the long run, cause them to have a more positive attitude toward learning.

The Teacher's Role.   Given the undeniable importance of classroom experience, sociologists have done a considerable amount of research on what goes on in the classroom. Often they start from the premise that, along with the influence of peers, students' experiences in the classroom are of central importance to their later development. One study (Pedersen & Faucher, 1978) examined the impact of a single first grade teacher on her students' subsequent adult status (see Box 18.2). The surprising results of this study have important implications. It is evident that good

BOX 18.2 SOCIOLOGICAL METHODS

Tracing the Influence of a Remarkable Teacher

In an unusual study of teacher–student interaction, Eigil Pedersen and Therese Annette Faucher (1978) demonstrated the persisting value of an outstanding primary school teacher. The study is unusual because the social scientists were actually looking for a general pattern of low teacher expectations. Instead, they found an exception that demonstrated the powerful effects an exceptional teacher can have on students. In scientific research, an unexpected result that leads to a new insight is known as *serendipity*.

Pedersen and Faucher began their study of IQ and achievement patterns among disadvantaged children at a school that was marked by high rates of failure. A high percentage of the school's graduates failed in their first year of high school and dropped out. The researchers attempted to explain these failure rates in terms of the concept of the "self-fulfilling prophecy," the idea that if teachers expect students to do poorly, the students are likely to perform accordingly. But if the negative prophecy seems to work in many instances, can we find evidence that a *positive* self-fulfilling prophecy—the belief that students can perform well—will also work? This is what makes Pederson and Faucher's study so interesting.

As they examined the IQ scores of pupils in the school's first grade classes, the researchers found a clear association between changes in a pupil's IQ and the pupil's family background, first grade teacher, and self-concept. Further examination of the school's records revealed a startling fact: The IQs of pupils in one particular teacher's first grade class were significantly more likely to increase in subsequent years than the IQs of pupils in first grade classes taught by other teachers. And pupils who had been members of that class were more than twice as likely to achieve high status as adults as pupils who had been members of other first grade classes (see table).

What was so special about Miss A, as the outstanding teacher was labeled? First, she was still remembered by her students when they were interviewed 25 years after they had been in her class. More than three quarters of those students rated her as very good or excellent as a teacher. "It did not matter what background or abilities the beginning pupil had; there was no way that the pupil was not going to read by the end of grade one." Miss A left her pupils with a "profound impression of the importance of schooling, and how one should stick to it" and "gave extra hours to the children who were slow learners." In nonacademic matters, too, Miss A was unusual:

> When children forgot their lunches, she would give them some of her own, and she invariably stayed after hours to help children. Not only did her pupils

remember her, but she apparently could remember each former pupil by name even after an interval of 20 years. She adjusted to new math and reading methods, but her success was summarized by a former colleague this way: "How did she teach? With a lot of love!" (pp. 19–20)

In summing up their findings, Pedersen and Faucher stated that their data "suggest that an effective first-grade teacher can influence social mobility" (p. 29). Their findings differ from those of Coleman (1976) and Jencks (1972), who believe that there is little correlation between school experiences and adult status. Pedersen and Faucher agree that further research on the relationship between teacher effects and adult status is needed. However, "In the meantime, teachers . . . should not accept too readily the frequent assertion that their efforts make no long-term difference to the future success of their pupils" (p. 30). As debates continue over how much difference good teaching can make and as governments and school systems wonder whether they should do more to reward good teaching, the results of this study bear careful review.

Adult Status, by First Grade Teacher

ADULT STATUS	FIRST GRADE TEACHER			
	MISS A	MISS B	MISS C	OTHER
High	64%	31%	10%	39%
Medium	36	38	45	22
Low	0	31	45	39
Total	100%	100%	100%	100%
(N)	(14)	(16)	(11)	(18)
Mean adult status	7.0	4.8	4.3	4.6

Note: (N) = Number of students who could be located and interviewed 25 years later.

"Adult status" was determined from interviews that included questions on occupational status and work history, highest grade completed, rent paid and number of rooms, and related indicators of social position.

Source: Eigil Pedersen & Therese Annette Faucher, "A New Perspective on the Effects of First-Grade Teachers on Children's Subsequent Adult Status," *Harvard Educational Review*, 1978, 48:1, 1–31. Copyright © 1978 by the President and Fellows of Harvard College. All rights reserved.

teachers can make a big difference in children's lives, a fact that gives increased urgency to the need to improve the quality of primary school teaching. The reforms carried out by ed-

ucational leaders like James Comer suggest that when good teaching is combined with high levels of parental involvement the results can be even more dramatic.

Because the role of the teacher is to change the learner in some way, the teacher–student relationship is an important part of education. Sociologists have pointed out that this relationship is asymmetrical or unbalanced, with the teacher being in a position of authority and the student having little choice but to passively absorb the information provided by the teacher. In other words, in conventional classrooms there is little opportunity for the student to become actively involved in the learning process. On the other hand, students often develop strategies for undercutting the teacher's authority: mentally withdrawing, interrupting, and the like (Csikszentmihalyi, Larson, & Prescott, 1977; Holt, 1965, 1967; Meier, 1994; Rose, 1995). Much current research assumes that students and teachers influence each other instead of assuming that the influence is always in a single direction.

CHANGING THE SYSTEM: DESEGREGATION

The bureaucratic organization of school systems makes them highly resistant to change. The basic classroom unit has remained essentially unchanged since the days of the one-room school, as has the structure in which one teacher is in charge of a roomful of students. Some efforts have been made to apply technological advances, especially closed-circuit television and computerized teaching techniques, to improve instruction in public schools. Although these efforts have had some positive results, including better instructional materials and a greater variety of courses, some teachers oppose such innovations out of fear that they will undermine their authority.

Despite the difficulties encountered in changing educational institutions, there are some areas in which they have been forced to change. Perhaps the most significant change in educational institutions in the past quarter century was desegregation. Efforts to desegregate public schools began in 1954 with the Supreme Court's ruling in *Brown* v. *Board of Education of Topeka,* when the Court held that segregation had a negative effect on black students even if their school facilities were "separate but equal" to those of white students. In the first few years after this landmark decision, most of the states in which schools had been legally segregated instituted desegregation programs. However, in some states, particularly in the Deep South, desegregation orders were resisted, and by 1967 only 26 percent of the nation's school districts were desegregated (Rist, 1979).

Further progress toward desegregated schools was made after the passage of the Civil Rights Act of 1964 and the Elementary and Secondary Education Act of 1965; by 1973, de jure (legally sanctioned) segregation had been almost entirely eliminated. However, de facto (in-practice) segregation remained common in many parts of the nation. This pattern was created by two factors: school districts' traditional policy of requiring students to attend schools in their own neighborhoods, and "white flight," the tendency of whites to move to the suburbs in order to take advantage of suburban housing opportunities and, in some cases, to avoid sending their children to central city schools with large percentages of black students. On the basis of an extensive study of the impact of desegregation programs, Coleman (1976) concluded that "policies of school desegregation which focus wholly on within-district segregation . . . are increasing, rather than reducing or reversing, the tendency for our large metropolitan areas to consist of black central cities and white suburbs" (p. 12).

Coleman's findings had a significant influence on the policy debates that took place throughout the 1970s and 1980s over what could be done to increase racial equality in public education, especially the issue of whether schoolchildren should be bused across city lines. Educational policy makers are now seeking ways of promoting racial integration, not only by means of busing plans but also through changes in school curriculums and instructional methods.

When education critic Jonathan Kozol visited public schools in central cities and suburban communities, he was shocked by the stark evidence of continuing racial and class segregation he found:

> What startled me most was the remarkable degree of racial segregation that persisted almost everywhere. . . . Moreover, in most cities, influential people that I met showed little inclination to address this matter and were sometimes even puzzled when I brought it up. Many people seemed to view the segregation issue as "a past injustice" that had been sufficiently addressed. . . . I was given the distinct impression that my inquiries about this matter were not welcome. (1991, pp. 2–3)

The children Kozol interviewed understood quite well the way class and racial segregation affected their own educational opportunities. Samantha, an eighth-grader in the impoverished schools of East St. Louis, Illinois, described to Kozol the great differences in resources between the schools she attended and those in the nearby white suburbs—lack of adequate texts, no computers, fewer after-school programs, and the like. Her mother had tried to get her into one of the better schools but had been told that she had to stay "in her jurisdiction." "Is it a matter of race?" Kozol asked Samantha. He notes that in answering him the girl chose her words slowly and with great care. "Well, the two things, race and money, go so close together what's the difference? I live here, they live there, and they don't want me in their school" (pp. 30–31). Clearly, the process of racial integration still has a long way to go. Along with other educational issues, it is likely to occupy a central place on the national policy agenda for the foreseeable future.

THE COMMUNICATIONS MEDIA

If education is the process by which a society transmits knowledge, values, norms, and ideologies, as discussed in the first part of this chapter, it is easy to see how education and information go hand in hand. In the remainder of the chapter, therefore, we turn to another major institution of modern societies: the communications media, or *mass media*. The decade of the 1990s began with a stirring lesson on the importance of communications media in the modern world. Throughout the world people were riveted to their television sets as they learned about the overthrow of a tyrant in Romania. For several weeks they had watched as one after another of the communist states of Eastern Europe faltered and toppled—first Poland, then Hungary, then Czechoslovakia, then East Germany. But the situation in Romania was far more violent—and much more public. In that nation, in fact, television played a dominant role in the revolution that put an end to communist rule.

Shortly before the uprising the Romanian dictator, Nicolae Ceausescu, had ordered security forces to massacre citizens who had participated in a demonstration in the provincial capital of Timisoara. The shootings were ordered over a closed-circuit television network. Following the massacre Ceausescu called for a "spontaneous demonstration" by his supporters in the main square of the capital, Bucharest; the demonstration would be televised and broadcast throughout the nation. However, by giving this order he in effect organized the demonstration that would lead to his downfall.

Students at the University of Bucharest were on their first day of winter vacation when they heard the news of the Timisoara massacre. Many went to the main square, where the university is located. There they encountered the offi-cial demonstration in support of the dictator. When Ceausescu tried to defend the killings he had ordered, the students hissed and booed. The dictator reacted with a stunned look and paused in his speech. After a few minutes the television broadcast was stopped. For the first time, viewers throughout the nation became aware not only that a massacre had taken place but also that the dictator who had ordered it was vulnerable himself. In the following days demonstrations against Ceausescu evolved into a full-scale revolution. The revolutionary forces occupied the national television studios, and the world watched the downfall of a notorious tyrant via satellite transmission.

The media institutions in the United States are arguably the most active and powerful of any in the world, both because of their diversity and revenue and because they reach a larger proportion of homes than their counterparts anywhere else in the world. Thus events like the trial of O. J. Simpson and the bombing of the federal office building in Oklahoma City take on national significance in part because people throughout the nation can share in the immediate experience of the situation. It is not surprising, then, that television and other media play an immense role in U.S. politics. To take just one example, in 1992 a vast number of new voters, especially women, came to the polls vowing to avenge what they saw as the unfair treatment of Anita Hill in televised Senate hearings the previous year.

We could give many other examples of the overwhelming power of television in American life, but we will see in this chapter that the media play a significant role in many other societies as well. In many parts of the world the media are strictly controlled and are viewed as institutions for maintaining stability and legitimacy. In others the media are more independent and often promote social change.

MEDIA INSTITUTIONS IN MODERN SOCIETIES

Communications media are institutions that specialize in communicating information, images, and values about ourselves, our communities, and our society. Typical media institutions in modern societies are the print media (newspapers and magazines), movies, radio, and television. In the United States the messages communicated by the media can be political or nonpolitical, religious or secular, educational or purely entertaining, but in every case they use symbols to tell us something about ourselves and our environment.

Many social scientists have been deeply impressed by the media's ability to incorporate people into a society's national life and bring about changes in their traditional values. The media are run by professional communicators, people who are skilled in producing and transmitting news

THEN AND NOW

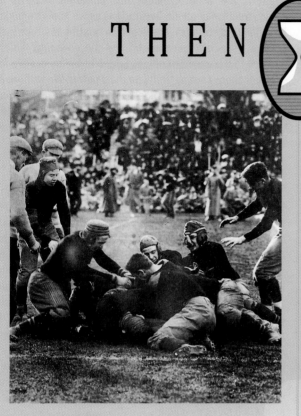

PIGSKIN MANIA

Football emerged in more or less its present form in the 1890s as a popular sport among wealthy young men at elite eastern universities like Yale and Harvard. In North America, football has become not only a sport but a generator of enormous revenues and a cultural form that many people almost feel they could not live without. The growth in popularity of the sport was intimately associated with the powerful influence of the mass media (see Box 18.3), which can broadcast games to ever-larger audiences. But the growth of media institutions, in turn, is dependent on the revenues made possible by the huge audiences attracted to major games. Thus there is a symbiotic relationship between television and the educational institutions that can afford to support football teams (Kriegel, 1993; Lawton, 1984).

More than 50 million fans attend one or more football games in a given year, and no one attending a college or university in the United States needs to be told that football games are central events in the life of many campuses. In fact, for many men and an increasing number of women football has come to resemble a civil religion. There are fans whose lives become subordinated to the rituals of preparation for the Saturday game. Legendary coaches like Alabama's Bear Bryant or Penn State's Joe Paterno assume a status that is well below that of a god but far above that of an ordinary mortal (Wilson, 1987). The rivalries that emerge between regional powerhouse teams and are played out each year become material for local legends. Many will admit to having prayed for a successful third-down conversion.

The metaphors inherent in football—success, hard work, strength, speed, organization, strategy—all make the sport a study in cultural ritual that mirrors the values of the larger society in which it has flourished (Brokaw, 1993). These cultural qualities of the game also make it extremely popular to television viewers and enable broadcasters to make large payments to the universities; these, in turn, help support other, less profitable sports. The popularity of football also enhances the university's prestige and its ability to compete for students and faculty.

and other communications. These skills can be used to enhance the ability of national leaders to influence and persuade the masses. For this reason, the media are always under pressure to communicate the information and values that people in power want to have communicated.

The influence of the media is a source of continual controversy as different groups strive for greater control over media communications. In many societies the media are subject to strict censorship. The very idea of news and entertainment institutions that are free from censorship by political or religious institutions is a relatively recent development. But even in societies like the United States, which pride themselves on laws that protect the freedom of the press and other media, we can find numerous examples of conflict between norms that establish media freedom and norms that are designed to control the media. During the Persian Gulf War of 1991, military officials formed a pool of reporters who were taken through preapproved sites. Media coverage of the war was tightly controlled. On the domestic front, a reporter was sentenced to prison for refusing to divulge his sources of information regarding an organized crime figure. His appeal, which was not considered by the Supreme Court, claimed that the law guaranteed his right to maintain the confidentiality of his informants. We could add many other examples. The point is that the freedom of the press and the other media and their existence as separate institutions can never be taken for granted.

In the remainder of this section we look at some typical patterns of media consumption in the United States and at how the media influence individual behavior. We then examine the issue of media differentiation: What is the basic structure of media institutions as we know them, and how has that structure developed in relation to other institutions, especially government and the economy? Finally, we turn to the question of how powerful the media are and whether there are any limits on their power. We will see evidence of the immense influence of the media in American political life, together with other evidence suggesting that the media's ability to determine people's behavior is far from absolute.

PATTERNS OF MEDIA CONSUMPTION

"Everyone agrees," wrote Harold Wilensky (1964) in an influential paper, "that abundance everywhere brings a rise in mass communications, through radio, television, and press; the development of mass education and the concomitant spread of literacy; and finally, mass entertainment on a grand scale" (p. 173). But he and other sociologists also believe that the media have produced a mass culture in which an increasing number of people have similar cultural tastes and political values, which are shaped by the media. At the middle and lower levels of the stratification system, according to this view, people form an increasingly homogeneous mass with similar thoughts and feelings. However, those thoughts and feelings are not anchored in spiritual and moral values; they are fluid and can be easily manipulated by those who control media organizations.

But what are the facts? As usual, the first responsibility of the sociologist when faced with claims like these is to

TABLE 18.5	**Media Consumption by American Adults, 1975–1994**			
THE PRESS	**1975**	**1985**	**1990**	**1994**
Read every day	66.9%	53.6%	52.5%	49.5%
Once a week	8.5	22.2	22.1	23.0
Less than once a week	5.4	6.6	10.7	10.0
Never	4.3	5.8	4.9	4.0
RADIO (HRS./DAY)	**1975**	**1985**	**1990**	**1994**
None	1.0%	0.0%	0.7%	NA
1–4 hours	77.0	75.5	74.7	NA
5 or more hours	22.0	24.1	25.3	NA
TELEVISION (HRS./DAY)	**1975**	**1985**	**1990**	**1994**
None	3.4%	4.5%	3.1%	4.0%
1–4 hours	78.1	79.0	80.6	83.0
5 or more hours	18.3	16.7	16.2	14.0

Note: Total number of respondents in the samples varies between 1,380 and 1,520. Percentages may not add up to 100 percent owing to small number of "Don't know" answers and because of rounding.

Source: Data from National Opinion Research Center (NORC).

try to support or refute them with empirical facts. This effort begins with measures of how much time people actually spend as consumers of different kinds of media communications. For example, survey data show that most Americans have their television sets turned on for as much as 4 hours per day. To understand what such numbers signify, it is necessary to compare television viewing with the use of other media and to see how patterns of media consumption change over time. Data from National Opinion Research Center (NORC) polls are presented in Table 18.5. They indicate that there has been a decrease in newspaper reading, yet at the same time they show that for large numbers of American adults the daily paper remains an important source of news, information, and entertainment. The data also show that contrary to what many people think, television did not make radio obsolete. In fact, radio competes well with television for people's attention, especially at work and in cars, where television generally is not available. Still, television ranks far above all other media in surveys of how people use their leisure time.

The data in Table 18.5 also suggest that there have been small but potentially significant decreases in television watching. Remember that in large populations even small percentage changes can mean large changes in absolute numbers. In fact, the major networks and communications corporations are worried about this trend, for it could mean huge losses of advertising revenue if it continues. In sum, the data do not lend much support to the mass culture theory. They show that people consume a great deal of media communication, but their tastes are diverse, and they continue to read as well as to watch and listen. As a result, they are not really homogeneous in their tastes, and the decrease in television viewing time suggests that they are not unduly influenced by media communications.

TELEVISION AND VIOLENCE

Does watching a lot of television lead people to commit violent acts? Few questions about the media have generated as much research and debate as this one (Reiss & Roth, 1993). A 1995 CBS/New York Times opinion poll indicates that parents believe the portrayal of violence in the popular media, especially television, is a cause of violence among adolescents. Some of the key results of this survey are presented in Figure 18.5. The television shows most often mentioned as forbidden to children were MTV's *Beavis and Butt-Head* and Fox's *Mighty Morphin Power Rangers.* However, it has proven far more difficult to establish an actual behavioral link between media consumption and violence than the results of opinion polls would suggest. Indeed, this question is a good test of the media's power to influence behavior, as opposed to attitudes and opinions.

Each hour of prime-time television programming presents an average of five acts of violence. Various studies have examined the connection between televised violence and violent behavior, especially in children and teenagers.

FIGURE 18.5   Attitudes About the Effects of Televised Violence on Behavior (percent of U.S. adults)

How much do portrayals of violence in popular culture contribute to whether teenagers are violent?

A lot — 56
Some — 26
Little — 5
None — 11

Have you ever forbidden your child from seeing or listening to a particular (television program, movie, or musical recording) because you objected to its content?

TV PROGRAM
Yes — 84
No — 16

MOVIE
Yes — 64
No — 36

MUSICAL RECORDING
Yes — 42
No — 57

What do you think is most to blame for teenage violence? The top five causes cited by all adults:

Television — 21
Lack of supervision — 13
Parents, unspecified — 8
Breakdown of family — 8
Drugs — 7

Source: Kolbert, 1995.

Many of these studies have found a causal relationship between the viewing of violence on television and later aggressive behavior, but some have concluded that such a relationship cannot be demonstrated (e.g., Kaplan & Singer, 1976; Milavsky, 1977). In 1982, however, the National Institute of Mental Health reported that "there is now 'overwhelming' scientific evidence that 'excessive' violence on television leads directly to aggression and violent behavior among teen-agers" (Reinhold, 1982).

There have been so many individual studies of television watching and aggression that researchers have recently turned to a technique known as *meta-analysis,* which involves the statistical analysis of numerous studies in an attempt to discover what common patterns they may reveal. Such analyses indicate that very frequent exposure to aggression on television leads to aggression in children and adults. The explanations for this finding are still being debated. The most common explanation is that television violence produces a form of "social learning"—that is, televised violence provides models showing the viewer how to act violently and also provides an approved social context for this learning: television watching in the home (Paik, 1990). Of course, not all viewers are equally likely to be affected by what they see on television. Eli Rubinstein (1981) studied the effects of televised violence on emotionally disturbed children. He found that the children's behaviors were related to what they saw on television: They imitated aggressive behavior and pretended to be characters in their favorite programs.

It is obvious that not every viewer of televised violence is tempted to act out that violence. It is equally clear that there is some not-yet-determined relationship between televised violence and aggressive behavior in some individuals. The relationship appears to depend at least in part on the viewer's emotional condition. Contending that the research findings are inconclusive, the major television networks have resisted efforts to regulate the content of their programming, although the first hour of prime time, from 8:00 to 9:00 P.M., has been labeled the "family hour" and is limited to programs deemed appropriate for family viewing.

DIFFERENTIATION OF MEDIA INSTITUTIONS

In describing the development of media institutions, a good place to begin is Robert Park's (1967/1925) essay on the development of the newspaper, which was one of the first communication institutions to become differentiated from other institutions. Pointing out that "the power of the press may be roughly measured by the number of people who read it" (p. 80), Park emphasized the role of urbanization in increasing the size of the reading public: "Reading, which was a luxury in the country, has become a necessity in the city" (p. 81). The growth of newspapers thus is closely linked to the growth of cities.

The earliest newspapers, Park observed, were newsletters whose purpose was to keep their readers informed of the latest gossip, whether of the court or of the village. As the number of people to be gossiped about increased, cov-

Although they are extremely popular, especially among young male television viewers, the Mighty Morphin Power Rangers have been criticized by opponents of violent television programming. The critics believe that exposing children to violence, even when it is highly stylized, may create patterns of imitation that increase the level of violence in children's behavior.

erage began to be limited to the most prominent individuals among them. When the paper could no longer cover every incident that would interest its readers, it had to choose the ones that were in some way romantic or symbolic and treat them as human interest stories. Thus the newspaper became "an impersonal account of manners and life" (p. 84).

As time went by, different kinds of newspapers developed. There were politically oriented papers whose purpose was to report on the doings of government. Such papers tended to come under the control of a particular party, and eventually some rebelled. The rebels—the so-called independent press—included *The New York Times,* which attacked and eventually overthrew the political machine run by Boss Tweed. Over time there also developed a variety of newspapers known as the *yellow press.* The goal of such papers, according to Park, was "to write the news in such a way that it would appeal to the fundamental passions. The formula was: love and romance for the women; sport and politics for the men" (p. 95). Newspapers of this type attracted many more readers than the party papers or the independent press, thereby extending the "newspaper habit" to the mass public.

The outcome of this process of differentiation was what is now known as the press, a cultural institution that is also a business. Newspaper publishers are interested in making a profit by offering news and features that will interest the greatest possible number of readers. However, the press continually struggles to remain independent from other institutions. The freedom of the press is never fully guaranteed. To cite just one example, the outspoken columnist Sidney Schanberg was forced to resign from his position at *The New York Times* after some of his statements provoked an angry outcry from landlords and real estate financiers. (The story of Schanberg's partnership with a Cambodian journalist is told in the film *The Year of Living Dangerously.*)

Today the dominant communications institutions in the United States are the electronic media: broadcasting corporations like CBS, NBC, ABC, and Turner Broadcasting, which own television and radio stations of their own and have affiliated local stations throughout the nation. Their growth has been based primarily on the effectiveness of these media as vehicles for advertising, which is their main source of revenue. Can they be depended on to broadcast news that is free from the influence of the advertisers that support them and, by extension, the owners and managers of large corporations? This too is an area of much social-scientific research. In what is still one of the best studies of this subject, Herbert J. Gans (1979) conducted observations and interviews at many of the nation's major newspapers, news magazines, and television networks. He reached the following conclusion:

> Since national news is produced commercially, one might imagine that story selectors are under constant pressure to choose news which will attract the most profitable audience. In practice, however, they are not. In the news media I studied, as in most others, editorial and business departments operate independently of each other. Business departments would like to influence editorial decisions in order to increase audience size and attract advertisers, but they can only make proposals. (p. 214)

Recent research on the media and its coverage of controversial social issues would seem to dispute Gans's conclusion. Todd Gitlin (1992) finds evidence that the commercial interests of advertisers do influence what stories get told in the media. A notable example is the inverse correlation between the amount of money a magazine receives for tobacco advertisements and the likelihood that it will publish information about the dire consequences of smoking—the more tobacco ad revenue a magazine receives, the less often such stories appear in it. An even more sensational example is the scandal that erupted in 1995 over the decision by *60 Minutes,* one of television's most respected "magazine" news shows, not to broadcast an interview with a former Philip Morris executive because of possible legal consequences (the executive had signed an agreement not to discuss his knowledge of the industry with the media even after retiring). Thus the issue of how powerful and objective the media are remains an open field of research.

MEDIA POWER AND ITS LIMITS

A familiar expression in modern societies is "information is power." And because the media control such a large and diverse flow of information, they have immense power. Questions about the power of the media become especially urgent when one imagines what could happen if control of the media fell into the hands of groups that oppose democratic institutions. In such a case, could the persuasive power of the media be used to destroy individual and political freedom?

George Orwell addressed this issue in his famous book *1984,* which portrays a society in which everyone is constantly watched on two-way television. Not only the actions but also the thoughts of each member of the society are monitored in this way by a powerful central government. Originally published in 1949, *1984* presents a terrifying vision of the potential power of the media when used by a dictator to control the thoughts and behavior of the population. But it is not merely an imaginative fantasy. It is based on the efforts of totalitarian regimes, especially those of Hitler and Stalin, to control the media and use them to control the masses.

In contemporary societies where totalitarian regimes try to control the minds of citizens (e.g., Romania before the revolution of 1989–1990) or in which oppressive regimes attempt to suppress democratic movements (e.g., China), total control over the media is a major goal of the state. In the United States, as noted earlier, media institutions are protected against undue political influence and are governed by professional norms regarding the gathering and broadcasting of information. There is also an increasingly wide range of channels to choose among. However, even in the United States and other democratic societies in which freedom of the press is guaranteed, there are still many problems related to access to the media and their power to attract large audiences. For example, as we will see in Chapter 20, the media exert a powerful influence over the conduct of American politics.

On the other hand, in a democratic society television and other media can be a two-edged sword, conferring power on those in the spotlight but also subjecting them to sometimes embarrassing public scrutiny. Richard Nixon, Jimmy Swaggart, O. J. Simpson, and Jim and Tammy Bakker are only a few public figures who have risen, and fallen, in front of a national television audience. The public has a stake, therefore, in determining whether the media are adequately and evenhandedly investigating the actions of the powerful and the famous.

Technological Limits. When media institutions are well differentiated from political and other institutions, it is actually quite difficult for powerful individuals or groups to manipulate mass audiences. This becomes even more true as changing technologies give people more opportunities to choose the types of messages they receive via the media. Cable television offers the potential for much greater diversity in program content: Viewers can watch everything from public affairs to pornography. Videocassette equipment also makes possible a wider range of choices. So although it is entirely likely that the size of the television audiences for special events like the Super Bowl will continue to increase (see Box 18.3), the audience of media consumers is becoming ever more diverse and fickle and, hence, ever more difficult to reach as a mass audience. Even in societies like China, in which the media are agencies of the state and may broadcast only material that has been approved by political leaders, new technologies like VCRs promise to make it more difficult to control the flow of information.

Social Limits. Another limit on the power of the media is the nature of communication itself. Researchers have not found a direct link between persuasive messages and actual behavior. People do not change their cultural values and norms just because the media tell them to. Instead, investigators have identified a **two-step flow of communication:** The messages communicated by the media are evaluated by certain respected individuals, who in turn influence the attitudes and behavior of others (Katz, 1966). Such individuals function as **opinion leaders** in matters ranging from voting to the purchase of paper towels, which is one reason advertisements so often portray a knowledgeable person praising a product to eager, if ignorant, listeners. The role of influential individuals in the process is a reminder that communication via the media has not replaced oral, interpersonal communication, nor is it likely to.

Another example of social limits on television's power to shape individual behavior comes from recent research on people's actual behavior while the television set is on. Comparative research in societies throughout the world suggests that television is an extremely powerful medium

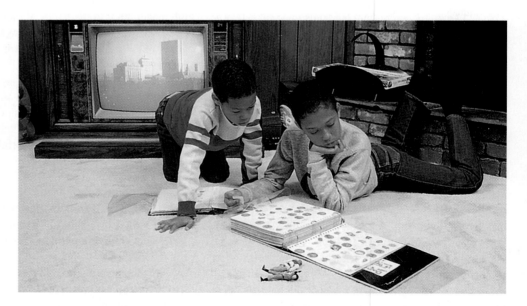

Studies that report on the number of hours Americans watch television can be misleading because people are often involved in other activities while the television is on and are not actually watching it. It is also true, however, that the constant presence of television may distract attention from family activities or schoolwork.

BOX 18.3 USING THE SOCIOLOGICAL IMAGINATION

The National Hookup

It happens every January. After a long season of grueling competition, the two surviving professional football teams face each other in the Super Bowl. The day is now called Super Bowl Sunday. More than 100 million people from coast to coast will watch the game on television. Each minute of advertising time will cost over $2 million, and America's most successful corporations and their advertising agencies will bid against one another for the time. Truly we have in the Super Bowl an occasion when mass interest in a national sports event creates an audience that crosses all lines of class, race, ethnicity, and religion.

But this level of national attention to one game—and the profits it generates for the team owners, the players, and many others—was not possible before the technology of television made it possible to broadcast events simultaneously across the continent. Television gave football the national hookup it needed to become a billion-dollar industry. At the same time, football and other professional sports created the media's largest audiences and influenced the scheduling of television time.

In this example two social institutions are intimately connected. Sports is a social institution that is structured in different ways throughout the society. In communities, the most common sports organizations are Little Leagues and school teams. At some large colleges, sports are structured in ways that will generate revenues that can be used to support the college's entire athletic program. The bigger and more competitive a college's football program is, the more it depends on television revenues as well as ticket sales, and the more heavily recruited its players are. Finally, the biggest, fastest, and most talented players are drafted into the business of professional football, which is intimately linked with the nation's most pervasive media institution, television.

Sociologists who conduct research on sports and the media point out that in many societies sports are not conducted as a business that depends on television and advertising. For example, in her study of soccer (the most popular team sport in the world) Janet Lever (1983) found that players may have professional careers but that their teams are not organized as businesses. In Brazil, as in many other nations, sports are engaged in by social clubs in cities and towns. The clubs pay their players, and the clubs with the largest dues-paying membership get the best players. Volunteer directors are elected by councilmen, who in turn are elected by all the shareholders of a club. To qualify as a club director, a man must be a shareholder; making large donations to the club also helps.

Soccer in Brazil thus may not be as profitable or as "national" as football in America, but Lever has shown that it also creates a "national hookup." In fact, soccer stars like the famed Pélé are national heroes, as can be seen in the following description:

> [Returning from the Mexican World Cup] the team flew to Rio de Janeiro, where they were greeted by close to 2 million ecstatic people waiting in the rain. The secretary of tourism coordinated a special Carnival parade of samba schools. . . . The major clubs from the major cities had contributed players to the winning team. Animosities were suspended for a time of alliance. In a land where communication is problematic, the team's contribution to national unity was of great value. (Lever, 1983, pp. 68–69)

The essential similarity between sports in nations like Brazil and those in which professional sports are a major business is that at the national level, where audiences for championship games are drawn from homes throughout the society, it is television that has enhanced the appeal of sports and given it such a central place in people's identification with their city and their nation.

for reaching masses of people and involving them in shows that raise important issues of morality—serials and story shows are popular wherever they appear. However, the fact that the television set is turned on for several hours each day does not necessarily mean that people are actually absorbed in watching the shows. Many people have become used to television as an accompaniment to their daily activities, but they do not necessarily always watch it or allow themselves to be influenced by it (Lull, 1988). On the other hand, the media convey a great deal of information about our cultural environment and cannot help but affect how we perceive that environment. The extent to which they shape our perceptions is a subject of ongoing research and debate.

RESEARCH FRONTIERS: COMPUTERS, EDUCATION, AND INEQUALITY

At this writing there are proposals to extend fiber-optic data transmission lines to every school and classroom in the United States. Such a vast undertaking, costing approximately $12 billion, would allow schools to share in the benefits of the computer and telecommunications revolution. It would enable students to access the most sophisticated images and materials available on the Internet and allow them to engage in real-time communications across the nation and throughout the world. But would it make a difference in educational quality? On this subject there is a

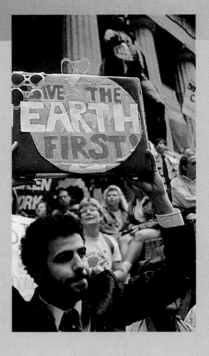

STUDENTS AND SOCIAL CHANGE

The common theme running through all of these photos is that high school and university students can often be found at the core of movements for social change. In our own society some observers complain that students are complacent and do not become involved enough in the issues of the day. But this is the age group that swells the ranks of the environmental movement, as can be seen in the Earth First demonstration. And students and other college-age youth were the most active segment of the U.S. population demanding sanctions against South Africa for its policy of apartheid. To be sure, young people are not alone in these movements, but they are among the most active participants.

Throughout the world, wherever there are demonstrations for social change, large numbers of young people are likely to be in the forefront—with the news media nearby, scrambling to cover the story. People around the world were thrilled by the photos of students and others breaking through the wall between East and West Berlin in 1989. The global audience watched in amazement as the movement for democracy and political freedom spread into China and focused on the massive sit-in in Tiananmen Square. But their hopes were dashed as young lives were taken when the army moved in. The photo of the violence in Tiananmen Square also captures the limits of student protest, its vulnerability to armed repression.

In *The Communist Manifesto,* one of the documents that inspired the Chinese Communist Revolution, Marx wrote, "Workers of the world, unite; you have nothing to lose but your chains." Should he have written, "Students of the world, unite"? Was Marx missing a great force for social change by not considering student movements? These photos remind us that student protest may be a necessary but insufficient force in bringing about large-scale social change. The students in China directed attention to that nation's desire for greater democracy, but without the support of more urban workers and rural peasants there was not quite enough mass sentiment to swing the army over to the cause of freedom, and the movement failed. Without the students nothing might have happened, but their efforts alone were not enough.

great deal of debate and not nearly enough empirical fact (Kling & Iacono, 1991; Scully, 1991). Before becoming enmeshed in the theoretical debates, however, consider a specific example of how the new technologies are being applied in classrooms.

The seventh-graders sit two by two in front of computer monitors, solving problems in basic arithmetic and simple algebra. Time flies as they watch *The Voyage of the Mimi,* an interactive computer program that looks much like an advanced arcade game with real adventure situations presented in full color and sound. But the action stops as the children on the spaceship *Mimi* use some basic math to figure out how to get themselves out of a jam or plot a new course. They must solve the problem before they can go on. If they need help, they can call up an instructional program keyed to the problem they are trying to solve.

Schools throughout the United States and Canada are experimenting with programs like *The Voyage of the Mimi.* Such programs require access to sophisticated computer equipment, of course, but many schools have already invested in such equipment. And this is only the beginning. Much more software and hardware are being designed for the educational market. In fact, the technology to revolutionize the classroom has existed for more than 15 years (Becker, 1984; de Sola Pool, 1983). Already many schools send children into classrooms with a microcomputer at each desk. The National Science Foundation and many state economic development agencies are promoting the spread of educational computer networks for interactive learning. CD-ROM players and Pentium computers allow students to call up text and photos and do research on any subject without leaving their desks. Typing is no longer taught in the well-equipped junior or senior high school; the course is called keyboarding and encompasses old-fashioned typing and modern word processing. And many more innovations are on the way.

These new technologies pose some major challenges, however. Among the social issues associated with educational technologies are the problem of learning and equity and the problem of diffusion.

Let us assume that we are dealing only with computer-based systems that have been demonstrated to aid learning (this in itself is a major assumption requiring further research). This means that some rather expensive systems are available to aid and accelerate learning. Which children will have access to those systems? More to the point, how will children in ghetto schools with limited budgets or children in remote rural locations or on Indian reservations gain access to them? The issue of equal access to new educational technologies is an example of the broader issue of equity in funding the nation's public schools, referred to in the chapter. There is clearly a danger that the new educational technologies—even those already available in your local computer store—will further widen the gap between the haves and the have-nots in American society (Martinez & Mead, 1988).

The problem of diffusion is also a classic social dilemma; as we saw in Chapter 10, it applies to any new technology. *Diffusion* refers to the spread of a behavior or trait through a population. If we wish a technology to diffuse quickly, we hope that there won't be much conflict about which technology is best (as there was in the case of videodisc versus videotape) and that the early adopters will be happy with the innovation and will spread the word to other potential adopters. But new technology is expensive. It may be worthwhile to wait and see what others are doing. Let them make the mistakes and waste their money. Such a policy can delay the formation of a market that can support production of the new technology and reduce its price. This is where applied research and policy come in. Social scientists, in cooperation with innovative school districts, can test new systems and accelerate their diffusion.

At this writing, however, perhaps the thorniest issue related to educational technology is equity and the potential for the technology to widen the gap between wealthy schools and poor ones. Private schools promise to involve all their students in the new technologies, but this will be far more difficult for poor public school systems, especially those of the inner cities (Kozol, 1991).

SUMMARY

THINK ABOUT IT CRITICALLY

Education is one of the few institutions in contemporary industrial societies that can give young people opportunities for social mobility. But we see so often that children from lower-class families receive less in the way of educational opportunity than those from upper-class families. Does this not contradict the promise of mobility through education?

Education is the process by which a society transmits knowledge, values, norms, and ideologies and in so doing prepares young people for adult roles and adults for new roles. It is accomplished by specific institutions outside the family, especially schools and colleges.

Schools are often cited as examples of bureaucratic organizations, since they tend to be characterized by a clearly defined authority system and set of rules. A more interactionist viewpoint sees the school as a distinctive set of interactions and patterns of socialization. Conflict theorists view schools as institutions whose purpose is to maintain social-class divisions and reproduce the society's existing stratification system.

The post–World War II baby boom caused a bulge in elementary school enrollments beginning in 1952 and an expansion of the college-age population in the 1960s. These trends were reversed in the 1960s and 1970s, but at the same time more and more adults have sought additional education.

A key feature of education is the fact that schools structure the lives of children and adolescents. They help create a social world for adolescents that is separate from adult society. Another important aspect of education in the United States is the relationship between education and citizenship. Education is also viewed as a tool for solving social problems, especially social inequality.

Educational attainment refers to the number of years of school a person has completed. It is correlated with income, occupation, prestige, and attitudes and opinions. The average American today has much more education than the average American of the early 1940s. One effect of higher levels of educational attainment is "degree inflation," in which employers require more education of potential employees.

Educational achievement refers to how much the student actually learns, measured by mastery of reading, writing, and mathematical skills. The steady decline in mean SAT scores in the 1970s and 1980s has been viewed as a sign that average levels of educational achievement have declined. Cross-cultural research has shown that these deficiencies are apparent from an early age. American parents are more likely than Asian parents to be satisfied with their children's schoolwork and to believe that the schools are doing a good job; they therefore are

less likely to be critical of the schools or to demand more of their children.

Educational institutions have been criticized by observers who believe that they hinder, rather than enhance, social mobility. Schools have been accused of serving as "selection and certification agencies" and thereby legitimizing inequality. Higher levels of educational attainment provide the credentials required for better jobs, and students who are able to obtain those credentials usually come from the middle and upper classes. A factor that has been shown to affect students' school careers is teacher expectations regarding students, which are affected by the teacher's knowledge of the student's family background.

Inequality in higher education is primarily a matter of access—that is, ability to pay. Students from poor, working-class, and lower-middle-class families, as well as members of racial minority groups, are most likely to rely on public colleges and universities. Most educational researchers agree that without college assistance for needy students, differences in educational attainment and achievement would be much greater.

The American educational system is highly bureaucratized, a fact that acts as a major barrier to educational change. Nevertheless, when they have been required to change—as in the case of desegregation—schools have often proved to be very adaptable.

Communications media are institutions that specialize in communicating information, images, and values about a society and its members. The media are run by professional communicators who are skilled in producing and transmitting news and other communications. In some societies the media are subject to strict censorship, and even in societies in which the freedom of the press and other media is protected, that freedom is often threatened by attempts to control the nature of the information communicated by the media.

Some sociologists have criticized the media for producing a "mass culture" in which an increasing number of people have similar cultural traits and values and can be easily manipulated by those who control media institutions. However, data on media consumption do not support the mass culture theory. They show that listeners and viewers are not homogeneous in their tastes and are not unduly influenced by the media. Other research has shown that there is a complex relationship between the viewing of violent acts on television and subsequent aggressive behavior in some subgroups of the population.

The differentiation of the communications media from other institutions is illustrated by the development of newspapers. Over time "the press" became an independent cultural institution that is also a business whose goal is to make a profit. The same can be said of the electronic media, the dominant communications media today.

Because the media in modern societies control such a large and diverse flow of information, they have immense power. In the United States, they exert a powerful influence over the conduct of politics. Political candidates without large budgets to spend on media advertising cannot compete effectively in election campaigns, and presidents and other powerful leaders must be able to perform well on television. On the other hand, changing technologies have given media consumers a wider range of choices, thereby limiting the power of the media to influence mass audiences.

CRITICAL RESPONSE

Inequalities in the resources of schools, measured by such variables as class size, dedication and experience of teachers, and availability of special programs, do help perpetuate existing patterns of inequality rather than increasing social mobility. But this does not mean that educational reforms cannot correct these inequalities. Educational institutions can change. They can do a better job for children in need of more educational opportunities. But such change occurs through the difficult and often frustrating political process, making it likely that reforms will be slow in coming.

GLOSSARY

education: the process by which a society transmits knowledge, values, norms, and ideologies and in so doing prepares young people for adult roles and adults for new roles. (p. 536)

educational attainment: the number of years of school an individual has completed. (p. 540)

educational achievement: how much the student actually learns, measured by mastery of reading, writing, and mathematical skills. (p. 542)

communications media: institutions that specialize in communicating information, images, and values about ourselves, our communities, and our society. (p. 554)

two-step flow of communication: the process in which messages communicated by the media are evaluated by certain respected individuals, who in turn influence the attitudes and behavior of others. (p. 560)

opinion leader: an individual who consistently influences the attitudes and behavior of others. (p. 560)

WHERE TO FIND IT

BOOKS

The Power of Their Ideas: Lessons for America From a Small School in Harlem (Deborah Meier; Beacon, 1995). The portrait of a model school that has played a seminal role in the current school reform movement, by one of the most innovative educators in the world today.

Savage Inequalities: Children in America's Schools (Jonathan Kozol; Crown, 1991). A chilling view of the persistent inequalities of race and social class that bar children and teachers in the nation's urban public schools from achieving educational success.

Culture as History: The Transformation of American Society in the Twentieth Century (Warren I. Sussman; Pantheon, 1984). A brilliant social history dealing with the transformation of American culture in this century. Contains excellent material on the role of fairs, communications, fashions, and much more.

The Sociology of Education, 3rd ed. (Jeanne H. Ballantine; Prentice Hall, 1993). A comprehensive text in the sociology of education, with many additional bibliographic sources.

The TV Establishment: Programming for Power and Profit (Gaye Tuchman, ed.; Prentice-Hall, 1974). A collection of critical essays about American television.

Deciding What's News (Herbert Gans; Pantheon, 1979). The best sociological study of how the news we see on television is processed by the media institutions.

JOURNALS

Social Problems. A sociological journal devoted to research and policy analysis related to major social problems. Publishes good articles on family research.

Sociology of Education. A quarterly journal published by the American Sociological Association. Presents recent research on education and human social development.

Variety. The weekly magazine of the entertainment business. Offers fascinating insights into the power of media institutions.

CHAPTER 19

Economic Institutions

CHAPTER OUTLINE

E. L. Winthrop, an American businessman from a major city north of the Rio Grande, was on a vacation trip to Mexico. While there he traveled to a remote and rather quaint village somewhere in the province of Oaxaca. While wandering through the dusty streets of that little pueblo, which had neither electricity nor running water, he came upon an Indian man squatting on the earthen-floored porch of his palm hut. The Indian was weaving baskets.

These were not ordinary baskets. Winthrop had never seen such colors and such fine detail as the Indian was weaving into the little containers, using only natural fibers and dyes from the nearby jungle. Winthrop immediately decided that he must buy one no matter what the price.

When Winthrop learned that the Indian was selling his wares for only 50 centavos, perhaps a tenth of what he had expected to pay, Winthrop could not help thinking that here was a fine opportunity to start a thriving business. They would make ideal containers for gift candy; he could sell them at home for three or four times the price. And even counting shipping costs and other expenses, both Winthrop and the Indian would surely make out very well.

"I've got big business for you, my friend," he announced to the surprised Indian. "Do you think you can make me one thousand of those little baskets?"

Winthrop imagined that the Indian would enlist the help of his family and kin in the project, and at the prices he could pay they all stood to gain tremendously.

That might be true enough, the Indian admitted, but who then would look after the corn and beans and goats? Yes, the Indian could see that he and his kin would have plenty of money to buy these things as well as many other items that they did not yet possess, but, he explained, "Of the corn that others may or may not grow, I cannot be sure to feast upon."

Not easily discouraged, Winthrop proceeded to show the Indian how wealthy he and his entire village could become even if they continued to sell the baskets for only 50 centavos. The Indian seemed interested, which spurred Winthrop on to more detailed descriptions of the basket assembly line they could begin together in the dusty little town. But after it was all explained, the Indian was still unmoved. The thousands of pesos that could be earned in this way were more than he could reckon with, since he had always used the few pesos from his basket selling only to supplement the modest needs of his family. There was another reason, too:

> Besides, señor, there's still another thing which perhaps you don't know. You see, my good lordy and caballero, I've to make these canastitas my own way and with my song in them and with bits of my soul woven into them. If I were to make them in great numbers there would no longer be my soul in each, or my songs. Each would look like the other with no difference whatever and such a thing would slowly eat up my heart. Each has to be another song which I hear in the morning when the sun rises and when the birds begin to chirp and the butterflies come and sit down on my baskets so that I may see a new beauty, because, you see, the butterflies like my baskets and the pretty colors on them, that's why they come and sit down, and I can make my canastitas after them. And now, señor jefecito, if you will kindly excuse me, I have wasted much time already, although it was a pleasure and a great honor to hear the talk of such a distinguished caballero like you. But I'm afraid I've to attend to my work now, for day after tomorrow is market day in town and I got to take my baskets there. Thank you, señor, for your visit. Adios. (Traven, 1966, p. 72)

SOCIOLOGY AND ECONOMICS

The foregoing episode is not simply a failure to communicate, nor is it merely an example of ethnocentrism. It goes to the heart of the difference between the subsistence economy of a folk society and the market economy of an industrial society. Winthrop's world is one in which economic institutions like markets and corporations guide his thoughts and actions even when he is on vacation. The Indian's actions and thoughts are also influenced by social institutions, but they are less likely to be economic institutions. Chief among them are the family and the male peer group or *cofradía.* Thus the story of Winthrop's attempt to form a basket assembly line catches the essence of what Max Weber meant when he observed that as societies grow in size, complexity, and rationality there is less enchantment in human life. The Indian could never imagine himself as a captain of industry, the manager of a work force of Indians who would buy their corn in a store with a portion of their wages. But neither could Winthrop appreciate the full meaning of the Indian's refusal and the metaphor of his song.

In this chapter we turn to an analysis of the major economic institutions of modern industrial societies. As we do so, it will be well to keep in mind examples from nonindustrial societies like that of the basket weaver in order to appreciate the enormous impact of economic and social change in the past two centuries. Such examples will also show that there is not just one path toward economic modernization, or only one blueprint for how the economic institutions of a modern society should work.

In any society economic institutions specialize in the production of goods and services. How we survive in modern societies depends on whether we have jobs and income, on the nature of markets, on the public policies that involve governments in economic affairs, on worker–management relations, and so on. Thus it is little wonder that sociologists have dedicated much research to these questions. But if that is true, what distinguishes sociology from economics? In our review of the sociology of economic institutions we begin by distinguishing between these two social-scientific fields.

The well-known economist Paul Samuelson has defined *economics* as "the study of how people and society end up choosing, with or without the use of money, to employ scarce productive resources that could have alternative uses—to produce various commodities and distribute them for consumption, now or in the future, among various persons and groups in society" (1980, p. 2). Sociologists are also concerned with how individuals and societies

570

make choices involving scarce resources like time, talent, and money. But sociologists do not assume that scarcity or supply and demand are the only reasons for making such choices. Sociologists are deeply concerned with showing how the norms of different cultures affect economic choices. For example, we cannot assume that people with equal amounts of money or talent are free to choose the same values or activities. We often find that women who might have chosen to pursue careers in business management have been channeled into such occupations as teaching or social work. Until quite recently, American culture defined the latter occupations as appropriate for women, whereas managerial roles were viewed as appropriate for men. Women therefore did not have the same choices open to them even when they had equal amounts of scarce resources like talent.

It would not be accurate to stress only the differences between sociology and economics, however. Increasingly there are sociologists (and economists) who use the central theory of economics to study all situations in which people choose to allocate scarce resources to satisfy competing ends (Coleman, 1986; Hechter, 1983). By "central theory" we mean the central proposition of economics: *People will attempt to maximize their pleasure or profit in any situation and will also try to minimize their loss or pain.* Applying this idea to nonbusiness situations, the Nobel Prize–winning economist and sociologist Gary S. Becker has conducted research on racial discrimination, marriage, and household choices. In this research he applies an economic "rational choice" approach to the study of the behavior of people in groups and organizations that do not produce goods or services. Becker points out that even the choice of a mate or the decision to have a child can be looked upon as an economic decision because people who make these decisions intuitively calculate the "price" of their actions in terms of opportunities gained or lost. Having a child means giving up other scarce resources, such as free time or income that could be used in other ways. And we saw in Chapter 16 how intuitive calculations enter into the choice of a marriage partner.

Following the lead of rational-choice theorists like Becker, sociologist Michael Hechter (1987) has studied the larger social consequences of the individual propensity to maximize pleasure and avoid pain. He concludes, among other things, that the larger the number of individuals in an organization, the more the organization will be required to invest in inspectors, managers, security personnel, and the like in order to control its members' propensity to "do their own thing." The same point was made over a century ago by Karl Marx: "All combined labour on a large scale requires . . . a directing authority. . . . A single violin player is his own conductor, an orchestra requires a separate one" (1962/1867, pp. 330–331).

Although it is tempting to apply principles of rational choice or exchange theory to noneconomic institutions like the family and the church, in this chapter we focus specifically on behavior in economic institutions such as businesses and markets and on the social implications of changes in these institutions. We will see that sociologists are continually comparing the ways in which such institutions are organized in different societies. The comparative study of how these differences relate to other features of a society's culture and social structure are very much a part of the sociological perspective on economic institutions.

Sociologists who study economic institutions are also interested in how markets for goods and services change as people learn to use new technologies and to divide up their labor in increasingly specialized ways. They also look at how competition for profits may lead to illegal activities and cause governments to try to regulate economic institutions. In addition, sociologists attempt to show how the labor market is organized and how professions develop. Thus markets and the division of labor, the interactions between government and economic institutions, and the nature of jobs and professions are the major subjects of sociological research on economic institutions. In the rest of this chapter we discuss each of these subjects in turn.

MARKETS AND THE DIVISION OF LABOR

A hallmark of an industrial society is the production of commodities and services to be exchanged in markets. In London, Hong Kong, New York, and other major cities throughout the world there are markets for gold, national currencies, stocks and bonds, and commodities ranging from pork bellies to concentrated frozen orange juice. However, not all societies have economies dominated by industry and markets. Subsistence economies, where people live in small villages like that of the Mexican basket weaver, do not have highly developed markets. In such economies people seek to produce enough food and other materials to enable them to meet their own needs, raise their children, and maintain their cultural traditions. The basic unit of production is the family, rather than the business firm as is the case in a capitalist economy. But there are few, if any, purely subsistence economies in the world today. Most subsistence economies must engage in some trade in international markets to obtain goods such as medicine or tools. These markets are dominated by the larger firms and entrepreneurs of the global capitalist economy, as we saw in the case of the basket weaver and Mr. Winthrop.

Socialist economies like Cuba or China also buy and sell products in international markets. Within their societies, however, they usually try to limit the influence of markets. Prices for essential goods, especially foodstuffs, are not entirely subject to the laws of supply and demand;

THEN ⧖ NOW
AND

Spring and Summer 1927

1889

1939

1969

AT&T

Courtesy AT&T Archives

SYMBOLS OF CORPORATE AMERICA

When Sears, Roebuck and Company announced in 1993 that it was discontinuing its mail-order catalog, a chapter of American economic history came to an end. For generations the Sears catalog had been a mainstay of American merchandising. At the turn of the century Americans discovered the wonders of their expanding industrial society by leafing through the Sears catalog. Every conceivable product or fashion was available at a reasonable cost. The beauty of the Sears catalog was that one could order goods by mail, to be delivered at the local post office. The tools and other goods offered

often they are prevented by law from rising too high or falling too low. Many types of goods and services, including firms themselves, cannot be sold to private buyers because they are said to belong to all the people of the society. We will return to the conceptual differences among these types of economies later in the chapter. For now, remember that few contemporary societies conform to one or another of the basic economic types. Most nations encompass capital-

ist markets, subsistence economies, and elements of socialism as well. Nevertheless, the market is an increasingly dominant economic institution throughout the world.

THE NATURE OF MARKETS

Markets are economic institutions that regulate exchange behavior. In a market, different values or prices are established for particular goods and services, values that vary ac-

The RCA Home Theatre. Now with SRS sound.

It will pin your ears back. It will send goose bumps down your spine. The SRS (•)° Sound Retrieval System on the RCA Home Theatre will envelop you. It will surround you. It will lift you out of your seat and put you in the show. It will do all this with no extra speakers, wires, or magic wands. Just the click of a button. Stop by your local RCA dealer for a demonstration of the big sound and big picture of the RCA Home Theatre. Sounds good, doesn't it? **Changing Entertainment. Again.** **RCA**

through the catalog helped American farmers and rural people become far more productive than ever before. And when people moved from the farm to the city, they often turned to Sears stores for products that were familiar and moderately priced.

As retailing changed, following ever more specialized trends and marketing strategies, the giant Sears corporation could not adapt quickly enough and its profits fell drastically. By discontinuing its catalog, Sears hoped to become "leaner and meaner" in order to compete with Wal-Mart and other more aggressive competitors. Sears is not the first, nor will it be the last, American corporation to succumb to relentless competition or fail to adapt to changing times. The history of American business is a story of continual replacement of formerly successful firms by more innovative or simply more fortunate competitors.

Corporate symbols, logos, trademarks, and advertising signs are a rich mine of historical evidence of changes in American business. Like photographs, they are visual images that illustrate social facts and social change. They can tell us much about the way companies have presented themselves to the public over the years. For example, earlier advertising, such as the 1927 Sears catalog cover, was more likely to include people (almost always

middle-class whites) than modern ads, which emphasize design symbols like the AT&T logo.

The desire of businesses to incorporate nonverbal associations into their symbols can be seen in the evolution of the AT&T symbol to its current version suggesting a worldwide communication system. But sometimes an older symbol has become so familiar and even beloved that a wise management will revive it, as in the case of Nipper, the RCA dog, who was brought back to life in 1984 for his hundredth birthday.

cording to changing levels of supply and demand and are usually expressed in terms of a common measure of exchange, or currency. A market is not the same thing as a marketplace. As an economic institution, a market governs exchanges of particular goods and services throughout a society. This is what we mean when we speak of the "housing market," for example. A marketplace, on the other hand, is an actual location where buyers and sellers make

exchanges. Buyers and sellers of jewelry, for instance, like to be able to gather in a single place to examine the goods to be exchanged. The same is true for many other goods, such as clothing and automobiles.

Market transactions are governed by agreements or contracts in which a seller agrees to supply a particular item and a buyer agrees to pay for it. Exchanges based on contracts are a significant factor in the development of

BOX 19.1 **USING THE SOCIOLOGICAL IMAGINATION**

Markets in a Subsistence Economy

In precolonial times the Tiv, a small West African tribal society, were a good example of a *subsistence economy,* one in which producers try to meet the needs of their immediate and extended families and do not produce goods or services for export beyond the family, village, or tribe. Among the Tiv the land was divided up into garden plots on which each family grew its own food. When the harvest was completed, the remaining vegetation was slashed and burned. The ashes served to fertilize the soil, but sometimes a plot was allowed to lie fallow for a few seasons. This meant that there was always a lot of discussion about which plots were to be used by which families in any given season. Never was a garden plot bought or sold—the idea that land could be bought and sold was not part of Tiv culture. The land belonged to the tribe as a whole. Individual families were granted the right to use the land, but there was no such thing as private property in the form of land that could be bought and sold.

Nor were the products of the land thought to be the property of the grower. Food was distributed according to need, and a person who accepted food was expected to return the gift at some future time. Only a few goods, mainly items of dress worn on ceremonial occasions, were traded for currency—in this case, short brass bars. The Tiv also accepted brass bars from foreign traders in exchange for carvings or woven cloths. But they would have laughed at the idea of trading the bars for food. They would have shared their food with strangers without any expectation of payment.

The conquest of Tivland by the British in the early twentieth century brought immense changes to this nonmarket society. The British colonial administrators were shocked when they observed Tiv weddings, in which it appeared to them that young women were being traded for ceremonial goods. In reality, these exchanges were not market transactions; the items that were given in exchange for a bride were a symbol of respect for the bride's family.

The British also noted that the Tiv seemed always to be at war, either with neighboring tribes or among themselves. To them this was a further sign that they needed to "civilize" the Tiv; in fact, however, the warfare was an outcome of the colonial system of taxation. Each tribal chief was required to pay a certain sum, either in British currency or in a commodity such as pigs. Because the Tiv had no currency and had to struggle to produce the required commodities, they were forced to cultivate more land. Their conflicts with neighboring clans or tribes were caused by the need to acquire more land. Thus the wars that the British observed were an almost immediate result of their own policies.

When the British succeeded in ending the warfare that had broken out among the Tiv, the only remaining source

modern societies. As the social theorist Niklas Luhmann (1982) observes, the use of contracts "makes 'impersonal' relations possible: It neutralizes the relevance of the other roles of the participants" (p. 199), such as kinship and other personal relationships, that govern exchanges in nonmarket situations. In contractual relations, for example, the fact that people are friends or kin does not, in principle, change the terms of their agreement and the need to repay debts.

Among hunting-and-gathering peoples and in relatively isolated agrarian societies before this century, markets in the modern sense of the term did not exist. Think of the Mexican Indian basket weaver who could not imagine

buying corn and other foods. He was used to growing foodstuffs himself and exchanging them with members of his extended family. The idea of buying them with currency was foreign to him. In social-scientific terms, a society cannot be said to have a fully developed market economy if many of the commodities it produces are not exchanged for a common currency at prices determined by supply and demand.

The spread of markets into nonmarket societies has been accelerated by political conquest and colonialism as well as by the desire among tribal and peasant peoples to obtain the goods produced by industrial societies. To illustrate this point and to show what happens as a smaller-scale soci-

In this idealized depiction of British colonial rule in Africa, white administrators confer in the foreground while happy natives work in the background. In reality, the "blessings" of colonialism were extremely mixed. As we see in the case of the Tiv, the experience of becoming part of the world market system made it difficult to maintain a small-scale society and culture.

of cash to pay the taxes was wage labor on the colonial plantations. The Tiv therefore sent their sons and daughters to work for the British, and on their own land they began to grow crops that they could sell. Before long they were part of the British market economy, selling their crops and labor for cash with which they could buy manufactured goods. Eventually, like many other small tribal societies, they were engulfed by the larger market system of the more powerful European nations (Bohannon & Bohannon, 1953, 1962).

ety becomes integrated into world markets, consider the case of the Tiv, a tribal society living in what is now Nigeria. The story of the Tiv is told in Box 19.1.

MARKETS AND THE WORLD ECONOMIC SYSTEM

In the late fifteenth and early sixteenth centuries, according to sociologist Immanuel Wallerstein (1974), "there came into existence what we may call a European world-economy. . . . It was not an empire yet it was as spacious as a grand empire and shared some features with it. But it was different, and new. It was a kind of social system the world had not really known before." The new system was based on economic relationships, not on political empires; in fact, it encompassed "empires, city-states, and the emerging 'nation-states' " (p. 15).

Great empires had been a feature of the world scene for at least 5,000 years before the dawn of the modern era. But the empires of China, India, Africa, the Mediterranean, and the Middle East were primarily political rather than economic systems. Wallerstein argues that because the great empires dominated vast areas inhabited by peoples that lacked military and political power, they were able to establish a flow of economic resources from the outlying regions to the imperial centers. The means used were taxation, tribute (payments for protection by the imperial army), and trade policies in which the outlying societies were forced to produce certain goods for the imperial merchants.

But this system—exemplified most clearly in the case of the Roman empire—required a huge military and civil bureaucracy, which absorbed much of the imperial profit. Local rebellions and wars continually increased the expense of maintaining imperial rule. Political empires thus can be viewed as a primitive means of economic domination. "It is the social achievement of the modern world," Wallerstein comments, "to have invented the technology that makes it possible to increase the flow of the surplus from the lower strata to the upper strata, from the periphery to the center, from the majority to the minority" (p. 16) without the need for military conquest.

What technologies made the new world system possible? They were not limited to tools of trade, such as the compass or the oceangoing sailing vessel, or to tools of domination like the Gatling machine gun. They also included organizational techniques for bringing land, labor, and local currencies into the larger market economy: ways of enclosing and dividing up land in order to charge rent for its use; financial and accounting systems that led to the creation of new economic institutions like banks; and many others. We discuss the role of science and technology in social change more thoroughly in Chapter 21, but it is important to note here that the term **technology** refers not only to tools but also to the procedures and forms of social organization that increase human productive capacity (Polanyi, 1944).

Although the European colonial powers (and the United States) often used political and military force to bring isolated societies into their markets, in this century they allowed their former colonies to gain independence yet still maintained economic control over them. This occurred because the economies of the colonial societies had become dependent on the technologies and markets controlled by the Western powers. Today former colonies are developing independent economic systems, but their ability to compete effectively in world markets is limited by the increasing power of **multinational corporations,** or *multinationals.* These are economic enterprises that have headquarters in one country and conduct business activities in one or more other countries (Barnet, 1980). (See Box 19.2.)

Multinationals are not a new phenomenon. Trading firms like the Hudson's Bay Company and the Dutch East India Company were chartered by major colonial powers and granted monopolies over the right to trade with native populations for furs, spices, metals, gems, and other valued commodities. Thus exploitation of the resources of colonial territories has been directed by multinational corporations for over two centuries. Modern multinationals do not generally have monopolies granted by the state, yet these powerful firms, based primarily in the United States, Europe, and Japan, are transforming the world economy by "export-

ing" manufacturing jobs from nations in which workers earn high wages to nations in which they earn far less. This process, which is particularly evident in the shoe, garment, electronics, textile, and automobile industries, has accelerated the growth of industrial working classes in the former colonies while greatly reducing the number of industrial jobs in the developed nations.

Changes in worldwide production patterns challenge Wallerstein's thesis that there is a world economic order dominated by the former colonial powers. In particular, industrial nations like the United States and Japan are increasingly losing manufacturing jobs while newly industrializing nations like Brazil and Korea are gaining them. But as Box 19.3 shows, the economic survival of millions of rural workers continues to be heavily influenced by changing markets in the highly developed nations.

ECONOMICS AND THE STATE

The earliest social scientists were deeply interested in understanding the full importance of modern economic institutions. In fact, since the eighteenth century almost all attempts to understand large-scale social change have dealt with the question of how economic institutions operate. But the age-old effort to understand economic institutions has not been merely an academic exercise. The fate of societies throughout the world has been and continues to be strongly influenced by theories about how economic institutions operate, or fail to do so, in nation-states with different types of political institutions. The major economic ideologies thus are also political ideologies, and economics is often called *political economics.* In this section we review three economic ideologies—mercantilism, capitalism, and socialism—and some variations of them. (See the study chart on page 580.)

POLITICAL-ECONOMIC IDEOLOGIES

Mercantilism. The economic philosophy known as mercantilism, which was prevalent in the sixteenth and seventeenth centuries, held that a nation's wealth could be measured by the amount of gold or other precious metals held by the royal court. The best economic system, therefore, was one that increased the nation's exports and thereby increased the court's holdings of gold.

The mercantilist theory had important consequences for economic institutions. For example, the guilds, or associations of tradespeople, that had arisen in medieval times were protected by the monarch, to whom they paid tribute. The guilds controlled their members and determined what they produced. In this way they were able to produce goods cheaply, and those goods were better able to compete in world markets, thereby increasing exports and bringing in more wealth for the court. But the workers were not free to

BOX 19.2   GLOBAL SOCIAL CHANGE

Two Faces of U.S. Corporations Overseas

The recent news stories shown here, which appeared in *The New York Times,* graphically illustrate two contrasting and extremely common situations created by the globalization of business activity. As U.S. corporations move their manufacturing operations overseas in order to benefit from cheaper labor and capture new markets, their presence is greeted with a combination of enthusiasm and criticism. This is true not only of American firms but of those from all the nations involved in the expansion of manufacturing and trade throughout the less developed world. In the case of American firms rushing to do business in Vietnam, however, there is a special irony. The billboard shown in the photo is located outside the main airport of Ho Chi Minh City (formerly Saigon)—but far from being seen as a sign of renewed American imperialism, it is a welcome indication that the United States is pouring vital capital into a former enemy nation.

Although social critics in the developing nations fear the growing influence of global capital, represented by major U.S. and other firms, most leaders welcome the flow of dollars regardless of political ideology. In 1995 direct investment by U.S. corporations to fund economic activities in other nations amounted to more than $74 billion, almost double the amount invested in 1994. Throughout the world there is fierce competition "for American capital, to finance factories, public works, telecommunications, technology transfers and jobs" (Myerson, 1995, p. 1). But the article about U.S.-owned smelting plants in Peru exemplifies the darker side of the rapid industrial growth that occurs when global firms establish plants in developing nations.

Southern Peru Copper's smelting plant in the city of Ilo emits 2,000 tons of noxious sulfur dioxide into the air each day. The pollution created by these emissions regularly forces drivers to use headlights in the middle of the afternoon. Families whose members work in the plant suffer from extremely high rates of respiratory illness. Brown sludge from the plant pollutes the nearby ocean shores. Ilo's mayor, Ernesto Herrera Becerra, says that emissions from the smelter have destroyed a large portion of the agricultural and fishing resources in the area. He adds: "This situation would not be allowed to exist in the United States" (quoted in Sims, 1995, p. D1). But plant officials note that their activities do not violate any local environmental or labor laws. For their part, the mayor and others point out that Peru had to have extremely liberal laws governing pollution, as well as lax enforcement of safety standards, in order to attract global firms in the first place.

The New York Times
Week in Review

Sunday, December 17, 1995

Section **4**

Yankee Come Back

American Money Makes the Whole World Sing

The Vietnamese, among others, are happy to have former imperialists' investment, which is visible on the road to the Ho Chi Minh City airport.

Business Day
The New York Times

In Peru, a Fight for Fresh Air
U.S.-Owned Smelter Makes Residents Ill and Angry

The Southern Peru Copper's smelter in Ilo, Peru, spews 2,000 tons of sulfur dioxide into the air daily, casting a heavy fog that forces motorists to use headlights during the day. The company denies the plant has caused health problems.

By CALVIN SIMS

ILO, Peru — Every night before she goes to bed, Anna Gilapa gets down on her knees and stuffs cloth in the cracks around her doors and windows to protect her family from the acrid smoke released by the nearby smelter of the Southern Peru Copper Corporation.

Mrs. Gilapa fears for the health of her 1-year-old son, Brian, who suffers from severe respiratory problems and often coughs up thick mucous. And for that, she and other residents of this bleak coastal town 580 miles south of

BOX 19.3 GLOBAL SOCIAL CHANGE

Addictive Substances and World Markets

In 1983, when sociologist Edmundo Morales returned to his birthplace in northern Peru to conduct research on land reform, he found that the peasants of the Andes villages had become dependent on the worldwide traffic in cocaine. Their efforts to gain cooperative ownership of the land they farmed had faded. Instead, most of the able-bodied men in the villages were busy packing for the long trip down the eastern face of the Andes. Most of them would work for months in coca-processing laboratories hidden in the jungle. Some would earn cash income by selling food, especially pork and beef, to the managers of the cocaine factories. The worldwide demand for cocaine had changed their lives.

Morales was dismayed to see so much urgently needed food being shipped from the impoverished highlands to the jungles. He felt that the enormous growth of the cocaine market had led his people down a false path. They were gaining cash income, perhaps, but in the bargain they were becoming increasingly addicted to cocaine and were neglecting the need for more basic economic progress in their own villages (Morales, 1986, 1989).

Morales was able to use his knowledge of the culture and his training as a sociologist to identify the connections between the plight of the Andean peasants and the world market for addictive substances. He knew that cocaine was simply another in a long line of substances for which huge markets had emerged in the richer nations, with drastic results for the less-developed world. Foremost among those substances was sugar. In the thirteenth century, sugar was a luxury available only to royalty. But as its use as a source of energy and as a basis for alcoholic beverages—especially rum—became more widespread, the demand for sugar production became one of the main causes of European expansion into the tropical regions of the world. Moreover, sugar production required that huge amounts of land be devoted to growing sugar cane, and many cane cutters were needed to harvest the crop. Thus along with the expansion of sugar production went slavery, first in parts of North Africa and the Azores and later in the Caribbean islands and Latin America (Bennett, 1954; Mintz, 1985). And sugar was only the beginning. The cultivation of wheat, tea, and coffee, the extraction of iron, tin, gold, silver, and copper, and the widespread cutting of primeval forests were all spurred by the emergence of mass markets in the developed nations of the West. Andean coca for cocaine and Indochinese poppies for heroin were latecomers in a series of crops that had changed the earth and all its peoples.

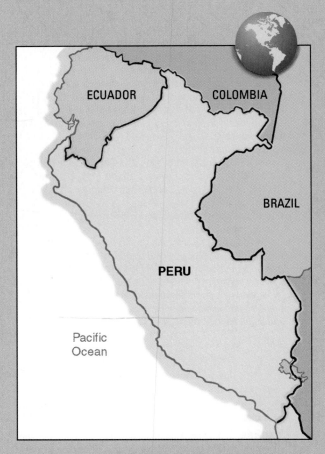

Some scholars argue that economic development in the world's commercial capitals actually produced *underdevelopment*—dependency and poverty and overpopulation—in huge parts of Africa, Asia, and Latin America. But Morales questions the notion of "development of underdevelopment." He believes that despite their tendency to become addicted to cocaine, the villagers of northern Peru are becoming more sophisticated in their market dealings and their understanding of politics. When they turn their attention once again to land reform, as eventually they must, their experiences in recent years will have made them less culturally isolated and more politically effective.

---

seek the best jobs and wages available. Rather, the guilds required them to work at assigned tasks for assigned wages, and the guildmasters fixed the price of work (wages), entry into jobs, and all working conditions. Land in mercantilist systems was not subject to market norms either. As in feudalism, land was thought of not as a commod-

ity that can be bought and sold—that is, a commodity subject to the market forces of supply and demand—but as a hereditary right derived from feudal grants.

Laissez-Faire Capitalism. The ideology of **laissez-faire capitalism** attacked the mercantilist view that the wealth of nations could be measured in gold and

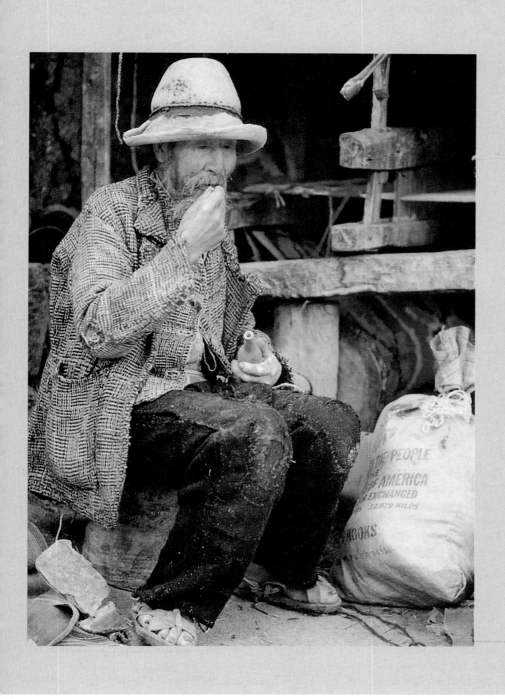

that the state should dominate trade and production in order to amass more wealth. The laissez-faire economists believed that a society's real wealth could be measured only by its capacity to produce goods and services—that is, by its resources of land, labor, and machinery. And those resources, including land itself, could best be regulated by

free trade in world markets (Halevy, 1955; Smith, 1910/1776).

The ideology of laissez-faire capitalism also sought to free workers from the restrictions that had been imposed by the feudal system and maintained under mercantilism. Thus it is no coincidence that the first statement of modern

STUDY CHART Political-Economic Ideologies

IDEOLOGY	DESCRIPTION	EXAMPLE
Mercantilism	An economic philosophy based on the belief that the wealth of a nation can be measured by its holdings of gold or other precious metals and that the state should control trade	European nations under feudalism
Laissez-Faire Capitalism	An economic philosophy based on the belief that the wealth of a nation can be measured by its capacity to produce goods and services and that these can be maximized by free trade	England at the time of the industrial revolution
Socialism	An economic philosophy based on the concept of public ownership of property and sharing of profits, together with the belief that economic decisions should be controlled by the workers	The Soviet Union before 1989; China and Cuba today
Democratic Socialism	An economic philosophy based on the belief that private property may exist at the same time that large corporations are owned by the state and run for the benefit of all citizens	Holland and the Scandinavian nations
Welfare Capitalism	An economic philosophy in which markets determine what goods will be produced and how, but the government regulates economic competition	The United States

economic principles, Adam Smith's *The Wealth of Nations,* was published in 1776. Revolution was in the air—not only political revolution but the industrial revolution as well. And some of the most revolutionary ideas came from the pens of people like Adam Smith, Jeremy Bentham, and John Stuart Mill, who understood the potential for social change contained in the new capitalist institutions of private property and free markets.

Private property (as opposed to communal ownership such as existed among the Tiv), is not merely the possession of objects but a set of rights and obligations that specify what their owner can and cannot do with them. The laissez-faire economists believed that the owners of property should be free to do almost anything they liked with their property in order to gain profit. Indeed, the quest for profit would provide the best incentive to produce new and cheaper products. This, in turn, required free markets in which producers would compete to provide better products at lower prices.

These economic institutions are familiar to us today, but the founders of laissez-faire capitalism had to struggle to win acceptance for them. No wonder they thought of themselves as radicals. In fact, their economic and political beliefs were so opposed to the rule of monarchs and to feudal institutions like guilds that they could readily be seen as revolutionary. They believed that the state should leave economic institutions alone (which is what *laissez faire* means). In their view, there is a natural economic order, a system of private property and competitive enterprise that functions best when individuals are free to pursue their own interests through free trade and unregulated production. As Smith put it, "Every individual . . . intends only his own gain, and he is in this, as in many other cases, led by an invisible hand to promote an end which was no part of his intention" (quoted in Halevy, 1955, p. 90). One of the most famous images in the history of the social sciences, Smith's "invisible hand" refers to the pervasive influence of the forces of supply and demand operating in markets for goods and services. Laissez-faire economists believe that in the long run these forces will improve the lives of people everywhere.

Socialism. As an economic and political philosophy, **socialism** began as an attack on the concepts of private property and personal profit. These aspects of capitalism, socialists believed, should be replaced by public ownership of property and sharing of profits. As we have noted in earlier chapters, this attack on capitalism was motivated largely by horror at the atrocious living conditions caused by the industrial revolution. The early socialists (Robert Owen in England and Henri de Saint-Simon in France) thought of economics as the "dismal science" because it seemed to excuse a system in which a few people were made rich at the expense of the masses of workers. They detested the laissez-faire economists' defense of low wages and wondered how workers could benefit from the industrial revolution instead of becoming "wage slaves." They proposed the creation of smaller-scale, more self-sufficient communities that would produce modern goods but would do so within a cooperative framework.

Later in the eighteenth century, Karl Marx viewed these ideas as utopian dreams. He taught that the socialist state must be controlled by the working class, led by their own trade unions and political parties, which would do away with markets, wage labor, land rent, and private ownership of the means of production. These aspects of capitalism would be replaced by socialist economic institutions in which the workers themselves would determine what should be produced and how it should be distributed.

Marx never completed his blueprint of how an actual socialist society might function. That chore was left to the political and intellectual leaders of the communist revolutions—Lenin, Leon Trotsky, Rosa Luxemburg—and, finally, to authoritarian leaders like Joseph Stalin, Mao Zedong, and Fidel Castro. They believed that all markets and all private industry must be eliminated and replaced by state-controlled economic planning, collective farms, and worker control over industrial decision making. Unless capitalist economic institutions were completely rooted out, they believed, small-scale production and market dealings would give rise to a new bourgeois class.

In the socialist system as it evolved under the communist regimes of the Soviet Union and China, centralized planning agencies and the single legal party, the Communists, would have the authority to set goals and organize the activities of the worker collectives, or soviets. Party members and state planners would also devise wage plans that would balance the need to reward skilled workers against the need to prevent the huge income inequalities found in capitalist societies. In Soviet-style societies markets were not permitted to regulate demand and supply; this vital economic function was supposedly performed by government agencies. Societies that are managed in this fashion are said to have *command economies*. The state commands economic institutions to supply a specific amount (a quota) of each product and to sell it at a particular price. (Note that not all command economies are dominated by communist parties. Germany under the Nazis and Italy under the fascists were also command economies.)

With the collapse of the Soviet political empire, the economies of Russia and the other nations of the former Soviet Union (as well as its satellites in Eastern Europe) are attempting a transition to capitalist economic institutions. It has become evident that command economies provided these nations with overdeveloped industrial infrastructures and limited capability to compete in world markets for goods and services. Indeed, it has been said that the command economic system of the former Soviet Union gave it "the most impressive nineteenth century industrial infrastructure in the world, 75 years too late" (Ryan, 1992, p. 22).

The Soviet system was notorious for the inefficiency of its economic planning and industrial production. Under the command system factory managers must continually hoard supplies, or raid supplies destined for similar factories in other regions, in order to meet their production quotas. Or they must trade favors with other factory managers to obtain supplies, a system that creates a hidden level of exchange based on bribes and favoritism. And because there

These children worked in a Rhode Island textile mill in the 1890s. Children were preferred as workers in this industry because it was believed that their nimble fingers helped maintain the pace of production.

are no free markets, goods that are desired by the public often are not available simply because the planners have not ordered them. In fact, in the Soviet-style economies there were always clandestine markets that operated outside the control of the authorities and supplied goods and services to those with the means to pay for them. These underground markets thereby increased inequality in those societies and generated greater public disillusionment with command economies and one-party communist rule.

The massive social upheavals of 1989–1990 brought an end to the communist command economic system, but they also initiated a period of great economic and social uncertainty in the former Soviet-dominated nations. At present, efforts to privatize their economies and use market forces to regulate the supply of goods and services, including labor, have begun to produce economic growth in those nations, but these rapid changes have also produced new forms of insecurity that have caused many people to wish for the relative stability and security of the communist past (Bohlen, 1993; Prybyla, 1990; Woo, 1994). In 1995 elections in Russia and Poland, many people voted for former Communist party officials who wish to slow down the conversion to a capitalist economy.

Democratic Socialism. A far less radical version of socialism than that attempted in the Soviet bloc is known as **democratic socialism.** This economic philosophy is practiced in the Scandinavian nations, especially Sweden, Denmark, and Norway, as well as in Holland and to a lesser extent in Germany, France, and Italy. It holds that the institution of private property must continue to exist because people want it to, and that competitive markets are needed because they are efficient ways of regulating production and distribution. But large corporations should be owned by the nation or, if they are in private hands, required to be run for the benefit of all citizens, not just for the benefit of their stockholders. In addition, economic decisions should be made democratically.

Democratic socialists look to societies like Sweden and Holland for examples of their economic philosophy in practice (Harrington, 1973). In Sweden, workers can invest their pension benefits in their firm and thereby gain a controlling interest in it. This process is intended to result in socialist ownership of major economic organizations.

In the United States there is a long history of conflicted relations between workers and owners of capital. Cooperative systems in which authority and even ownership are shared are developing, but more slowly than in the social democracies of Europe. Social scientists who study the U.S. economy note that in recent years there has been a reaction among owners of capital against the principles of democratic socialism, especially those that stress cooperation between labor and management and the right of workers to organize unions and engage in collective bargaining (Freeman, 1993). Employers have also shown diminished commitment to welfare capitalism, the political-economic model that until recently has had a great deal of influence in the noncommunist modern economies (Harrison, 1990).

Welfare Capitalism. Emerging to some extent as a response to the challenge posed by the Russian Revolution (which called attention to many of the excesses of uncontrolled or laissez-faire capitalism), **welfare capitalism** represented a new way of looking at relationships between governmental and economic institutions. Welfare capitalism affirms the role of markets in determining what goods and services will be produced and how, but it also affirms the role of government in regulating economic competition (e.g., by attempting to prevent the control of markets by one or a few firms).

Welfare capitalism also stresses the role that governments have always played in building the roads, bridges, canals, ports, and other facilities that make trade and industry possible. Expanding on this role, the theory of welfare capitalism asserts that the state should also invest in the society's human resources—that is, in the education of new generations and the provision of a minimum level of health care. Welfare capitalism also guarantees the right of workers to form unions in order to reach collective agreements with the owners and managers of firms regarding wages and working conditions. It creates social-welfare institutions like Social Security and unemployment insurance. And in order to stimulate production and build confidence in times of economic depression, welfare capitalism asserts that governments must borrow funds to finance large-scale public works projects like the construction of the American interstate highway system during the 1950s.

The theory of welfare capitalism is associated with the writings of John Maynard Keynes, Joan Robinson, John Kenneth Galbraith, and James Tobin, all of whom contributed to the revision of laissez-faire economic theory. Welfare capitalism dominated American economic policy from World War II until the 1970s, when a succession of economic crises—inflation, energy shortages, and unemployment—turned the thoughts of many Americans once again toward laissez-faire capitalism. Today, however, the increasingly evident gap between the haves and the have-nots in American society has given rise to renewed interest in enhancing the institutions of the welfare state—unemployment insurance, health insurance, low-income housing, public education, and others. At the same time, fear of governmental control over people's lives, and its costs in the form of higher taxes, is generating a revolt against the "welfare state" in many segments of the population in the United States and other industrial nations. This trend has resulted in conservative electoral victories and unprecedented reductions in social spending. What is not clear is whether the public's desire for relative security from economic stress will outweigh the desire for lower taxes and reductions in the scope of government bureaucracies.

POLITICAL ECONOMICS IN PRACTICE: AFTER THE COLD WAR

The cold war lasted from about 1949 to 1989. It cost the United States, the Soviet Union, and the nations of Europe untold billions of dollars. It also fostered not-so-cold wars in Korea, Vietnam, Afghanistan, and Central America. At the beginning of the 1990s this long-drawn-out political conflict between the superpowers ended. The fall of dictatorships in Hungary, Romania, Czechoslovakia, Poland, and East Germany; the tearing down of the wall separating East and West Berlin; the passage of laws permitting individual ownership of businesses and property in the former Soviet Union—these and related changes have already had a major impact throughout the world. However, their full effect remains to be felt, especially as political instability and fear of economic insecurity (e.g., unemployment) challenge the ability of political and economic reformers in the former communist nations (Tripolskaya-Mitlyng, 1994).

The end of the cold war raises some important issues for the study of economic institutions. How will the transition from command economies to entrepreneurial market economies unfold in socialist nations? What are the implications for economic institutions in the United States? Will there be a new social contract, and if so, how will it change the conditions of life in post-industrial society? In the rest of this section we take a closer look at these issues.

From Commissars to Entrepreneurs. As the cumbersome and inefficient bureaucracies of state planning are stripped of their power, the commissar (planning bureaucrat) is replaced by the entrepreneur (Ash, 1989). In early 1990 the Soviet Union passed legislation allowing citizens to own the means of production (the terms *private property* and *capital* were avoided). New businesses soon appeared throughout the nation. But it is not so easy to transform command economies into market economies. There have been many incidents of conflict between state planners and the owners or managers of the new business cooperatives. Meanwhile, the black market has continued to flourish as officials attempt to formulate economic policy.

In Hungary and the Czech Republic there have been efforts to distribute coupons that can be used to purchase shares in newly privatized industries, since under the former socialist regimes those industries were, at least in principle, owned by the citizens. Such plans have had limited success, partly because many of the industries offered for sale were not adequately modernized. Often entrepreneurs prefer to buy modern machines and start new, entirely private businesses. Meanwhile large-scale industries like railroads and electricity limp along under public ownership, with limited capital for modernization (Burawoy, 1994).

The closing of noncompetitive factories, layoffs of unneeded workers in factories that remain open, uncertainty about the status of government-issued currency, and confusion over economic policy make a difficult situation worse.

In Russia and other former socialist "republics" there has been an increase in underground, untaxed business activities. Already weakened by dissension, the government must find ways to regulate and tax the goods and services traded in this huge black market. In fact, the black market must be merged into the overall market economy. At this writing these problems are seriously hampering the progress of economic transformation.

As Figure 19.1 shows, the new emphasis on private initiative has increased the number of private farms and

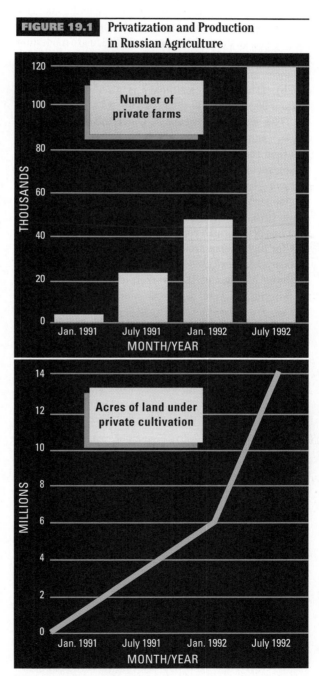

FIGURE 19.1 Privatization and Production in Russian Agriculture

the amount of land under private cultivation. But collective farms, formed under the old Soviet system, still account for the vast majority of farms and must transform themselves not into small family farms but into modern, highly efficient agribusinesses. Farm production is lagging because of the difficulty of modernizing other sectors of the economy, such as the production of fertilizers, and especially because of problems in coordinating the shipment of goods over the vast Russian territory.

These problems are made even worse by the collapse of the political system, which has enabled organized criminal gangs known as the *mafiya* (not related to the Mafia) to flourish. Without the rule of law established by a legitimate system of government, it is extremely difficult to modernize an economy and prevent severe abuses of power through violence and terror (Handelman, 1993; Schmemann, 1992b). (The role of legitimacy is discussed further in Chapter 20.)

The United States: A Post-Industrial Society? Although many people in the United States see the failure of socialism in the Soviet bloc as a victory for capitalism, sociologists and poll takers have called attention to a growing sense of unease about the U.S. economy. As demographer Valerie Kincade Oppenheimer observes, "Since about 1970, the average real earnings position of young men has deteriorated considerably. This has been true not only for high school dropouts but also for high school and college graduates" (1994, p. 331). (See Figure 19.2.) The declining incomes of U.S. workers over the past quarter

century have contributed to the growth in dual-earner households.

The disparity between the incomes of people with professional and technologically sophisticated jobs and those of people with less intellectually demanding jobs is likely to increase as economic growth centers on computers, telecommunications, and biological technologies. Jobs that require lower levels of education and training may be more onerous, but the number of people who can perform them is relatively large. The basic economic laws of supply and demand therefore drive up the wages of highly educated workers while those of less-educated workers are driven downward.

In an influential study, *The Coming of Post Industrial Society,* sociologist Daniel Bell (1973) reviewed changes in American economic institutions indicating that we are undergoing a transition from an industrial to a post-industrial society. A post-industrial society "emphasizes the centrality of theoretical knowledge as the axis around which new technology, economic growth, and the stratification of society will be organized" (p. 116). As societies undergo the transition to post-industrial economic institutions, an "intellectual technology" based on information arises alongside machine technology. Industrial production does not disappear, but it becomes less important. New industries devoted to providing knowledge and information become the primary sources of economic growth (Block, 1990; Montagna, 1977; Piore & Sabel, 1984).

Changes in the distribution of jobs in the goods-producing and service-producing sectors of the American economy clearly show the growing importance of services, especially those employing professional and technical workers. For Bell, this change is inevitable. Industries decline, but new ones appear. At the turn of the century, for example, more than 70 percent of Americans were employed in agriculture and related occupations. Now this figure is below 3 percent. Similar transformations are taking place in manufacturing today, and they can be made less painful if the society is willing to invest in education and the retraining of workers in declining industries like mining, steel production, or manufacturing for military purposes (Heilbroner, 1990).

Other social scientists view these changes less optimistically. Some note that declines in industrial production have pushed thousands of skilled workers into lower-paying jobs in the service sector—for example, in the fast-food industry or as janitors or security guards—which helps explain the decline in average wages shown in Figure 19.2 (Aronowitz, 1984; Fallows, 1985; Harrison, Tilly, & Bluestone, 1986). Others are concerned that the gains made by blacks and women in access to better-paying industrial jobs since World War II are being erased. William Julius Wilson (1978) has commented that "access to the means of production is increasingly based on educational criteria . . . and thus threatens to solidify the position of the black underclass" (p. 151).

FIGURE 19.2 Median Earnings for Men Age 25–34 According to Education Level, United States (in constant dollars)

Source: Data from Economic Policy Institute and Joint Economic Committee.

Automation in the banking industry, represented here by automated teller machines, is making it possible to eliminate thousands of jobs in that industry.

European sociologists have criticized the theory of post-industrial society on even broader grounds, saying that it tends to promote belief in the inevitability of an increasingly impoverished working class with even more reason to demand a more equal distribution of wealth (Touraine, 1971). In the United States, the theory of post-industrial society has been criticized on the ground that even though manufacturing accounts for a declining share of the labor force, the society still depends on manufactured goods of all kinds. Critics argue that the United States cannot relinquish its manufacturing base simply because a theory says it is outmoded (Cohen & Zysman, 1987).

A Changing Social Contract? Conversion from a wartime to a peacetime economy, together with the massive changes brought about by economic globalization, technological advances, and the growth of service industries, is increasing the pressure on employers to keep their costs down in order to be competitive. This results, as we have seen, in declining real wages and widening economic inequalities. In the social democracies of Europe, especially Scandinavia, the impact of these changes is eased by

social-welfare policies. In the United States, the welfare state and its "safety net" of economic and social policies (Medicare, the minimum wage, unemployment insurance, etc.) are considered important by those who need to be protected from the harshest consequences of sudden economic change. Others, however, attack them as wasteful and costly government intervention in the economy.

The 1994 congressional elections brought in a conservative leadership committed to a "contract with America" that promised to balance the federal budget, reduce the size of government, and cut taxes. These and related measures are consistent with laissez-faire principles that argue against government intervention in the economy and insist that individual choices about how to spend income and wealth should be protected to the extent possible. But these are controversial issues. As can be seen in Figure 19.3, there is a deep division between those who believe government should reduce income inequality and those who oppose taxation or other policies that reduce the wage and income gap. (See also Box 19.4 on pages 588–589.)

Note that the percentages in Figure 19.3 represent the responses of people who felt strongly, one way or the other,

FIGURE 19.3 Trends in Opinion on the Question "Should Government Reduce Income Inequality?" (United States, 1972–1994)

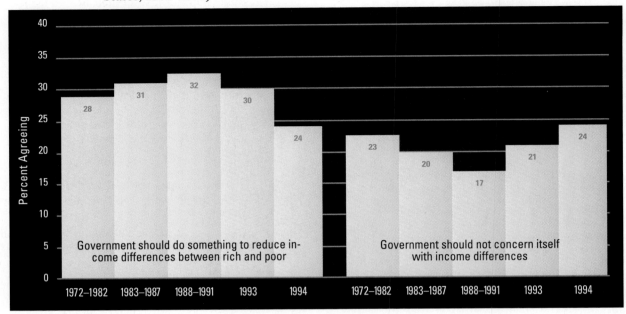

Source: NORC, 1994.

about the issue of taxation to achieve greater income equality. Those whose responses were more neutral are not represented. Yet these are the people in the "middle of the road" whose shifting allegiances and opinions will make all the difference in coming years.

As Figure 19.3 shows quite clearly, there has been considerable change in Americans' opinions about the desirability of government intervention to achieve greater equality. In 1994 the public was rather evenly divided on the issue, whereas for the previous quarter century or more the majority had favored taxation for this purpose. Note, however, how volatile opinions on this issue can be. In the period from 1988 to 1991, during a rather severe economic recession, 32 percent of respondents strongly favored taxation to reduce inequality; that proportion fell to only 24 percent in the relatively better economic climate of 1994. It appears that the conservative attack on the welfare state has persuaded large numbers of Americans to oppose taxation for the purpose of reducing inequality, but it remains to be seen how stable this trend will be as the gap between rich and poor widens.

In his analysis of post-industrial society, Daniel Bell (1973) assumed that the "social contract" in the United States and other advanced nations would be maintained. In return for hard work, saving, and efforts to improve their skills, citizens could expect modest increases in their living standards, adequate health care, protection from crime, decent public education for their children, and protection of their rights. However, the Reagan administration of the 1980s and the conservative Congress of the mid-1990s have challenged the assumption that government would provide these benefits if they were not provided by the economy itself. This alteration in the basic social contract that has guided social policy for the past half century will have far-reaching consequences (Blau, 1993; Buchanan, 1991; Davey, 1995).

WORKERS, MANAGERS, AND CORPORATIONS

When American business managers and sociologists compare the U.S. economy with others, they most often choose Japan as the standard. In the early 1990s the Japanese economy experienced a severe downturn from which it is still recovering; American managers also realized that Japan was excluding the products of other nations. However, despite these indications that Japan was as vulnerable as other capitalist economies, U.S. businesses continued to regard Japanese firms as their chief competitors (McCord, 1991). This is hardly surprising. Japanese firms not only produce steel and automobiles and other industrial products more cheaply and often better than U.S. manufacturers do, but also compete aggressively in world markets for products like computer components and office machines, important symbols of the post-industrial age. A major factor in Japan's phenomenal success is the attitudes of its workers and managers. Therefore it is useful to look at how work is typically organized in Japan and in the United States.

Japanese Factories. In the typical Japanese factory the workers bargain collectively with managers over wages and working conditions, just as they do in unionized factories in the United States. And in both societies workers expect similar pay and other benefits. However, in the Western nations workers and managers are viewed as natural adversaries. Whatever rights workers and their unions possess are gained at the cost of "continuous inch-by-inch pressure against dogged managerial resistance" (Dore, 1973, p. 115; also see Shimada, 1993). In Japan, by contrast, the typical worker in a large corporation like Sony feels that he or she "belongs to the company" as opposed to merely working for the company (Dore, 1982, 1990). During the years following Japan's defeat in World War II, the Japanese developed new forms of labor–management cooperation based on the idea that workers and management have a shared interest in what is good for the company as a whole. Wage inequalities between workers and managers were decreased; time clocks and separate cafeterias were eliminated; and most important, a system of "lifetime commitment" or permanent tenure for workers who entered the plant at a young age was established in large corporations (McCord, 1991; Samuels, 1991). Because they know they are in the corporation for life, the workers are committed to the corporation's goals. And because of their commitment to the company, they devote their full energy to improving their productivity, much of which comes through high-quality work.

Not all Japanese workers enjoy the advantages of permanent tenure, however. An increasing amount of work in Japanese firms is "outsourced" to smaller factories in which only a few of the workers have tenure. Even within the large firms, a decreasing proportion of employees are guaranteed jobs with the firm. Lifetime employment, for which the Japanese economy is famous, covers only about 35 percent of the labor force. Younger men and women thus form a secondary class of less advantaged, and perhaps less loyal, employees. Forty percent of Japanese workers are women, and about 25 percent of them (some 5 million women) are designated as part-time workers even though they work up to 48 hours a week for an average of $2.40 per hour and few benefits. (Japan has no law requiring equal pay for equal work.) Thus, although Japanese workers are said to be more productive than workers in the United States or Europe, a large part of this productivity stems from the fact that they work far longer hours for lower pay. As the level of affluence in Japan increases, sociologists are finding evidence that, as in other nations, workers are demanding more leisure time and benefits (Dore, 1990; Kamata, 1982; Samuels, 1991).

U.S. Industry. In the United States, workers appear to be far less committed to the goals of the company, a point that was illustrated in a study of a modern oil refinery by David Halle (1984). Halle reported that 52 percent of the workers declined opportunities for promotion to top positions in their work crews because they did not want to exercise authority. He continued:

> Nor do they wish to take responsibility for production—they do not want to be concerned about whether the chemical reactions are occurring in the right way. They prefer to take a detached attitude to their jobs, treating work as an intrusion into their social life both inside and outside the plant. They will do their jobs, but they also enjoy the various social activities that go on in the workplace. (p. 155)

These attitudes were held by a minority of the workers Halle studied, but their numbers may be greater than one would expect in a Japanese firm, in which the organization's goals appear to be more widely shared by managers and workers. Other evidence shows that many American workers want to produce high-quality products but feel an organizational and cultural gap separating them from managers even when they share the same goals (Edwards, 1979; HHS, 1973). Recent trends in hours of work show that more Americans are working longer hours than ever, demonstrating that management rather than motivation remains the challenge for U.S. business (Schor, 1992).

WORKER ALIENATION

Many sociologists use the concept of alienation to explain the gap between workers and managers. Karl Marx first applied the term to the situation of workers under early capitalism. The worker in a factory performed only a fraction of the work that went into a product and therefore could feel little sense of ownership of the final product. And because the worker typically could not control the work process very much, he or she came to feel like a mere cog in a giant machine, a feeling that produced a sense of not being able to control one's own actions on the job (Fromm, 1961; Marx, 1961/1844). Today the term **alienation** is often used to describe the feeling of being powerless to control one's own destiny (Blauner, 1964; Seeman, 1959). At work, people may feel alienated because their labor is divided up into activities that are meaningless to them. Robert Blauner (1964), for example, found that workers who perform highly repetitive tasks on an assembly line are more alienated than workers in groups whose tasks involve teamwork.

In a study of organizational techniques that have been used successfully in Japan, Ezra Vogel (1979) pointed out that Japanese firms tend to avoid worker alienation by strengthening the role of the small group:

> The essential building block of a company is not a man with a particular role assignment and his secretary and assistants. The essential building block of the organization is the section. . . . The lowly section, within its sphere, does not await executive orders but takes the initiative. . . . For

BOX 19.4   SOCIOLOGICAL METHODS

How the NORC Asks Americans About Policies to Reduce Inequality

Much of the data about how people in the United States view social issues comes from the General Social Survey (GSS) conducted by the National Opinion Research Center (NORC) at the University of Chicago. One of the most prestigious opinion surveys in the nation, the GSS is a random sample survey that has been conducted annually since 1972. It therefore allows social scientists to track changes in opinion over time.

The question about government intervention to reduce income inequality is an example of a question for which the GSS provides longitudinal data. Note that Figure 19.3 presents data from the two ends of the scale, but not from the middle, in order to compare changes in the distribution of liberal and conservative opinions on this critical issue. The actual data, shown here in a table from the 1994 *NORC Codebook,* include other categories of responses along with hundreds of nonapplicable responses from people who were not asked this particular question in a given year.

Note that this question emphasizes actions that "the government in Washington ought" to take. In a sense,

Some people think that the government in Washington ought to reduce the income differences between the rich and the poor, perhaps by raising the taxes of wealthy families or by giving income assistance to the poor. Others think that the government should not concern itself with reducing this income difference between the rich and the poor.*

Here is a card with a scale from 1 to 7. Think of a score of 1 as meaning that the government ought to reduce the income differences between rich and poor, and a score of 7 as meaning that the government should not concern itself with reducing income differences. What score between 1 and 7 comes closest to the way you feel?
(CIRCLE ONE)

GOVERNMENT SHOULD DO SOMETHING TO REDUCE INCOME DIFFERENCES BETWEEN RICH AND POOR.

GOVERNMENT SHOULD NOT CONCERN ITSELF WITH INCOME DIFFERENCES.

1   2   3   4   5   6   7

this system to work effectively leading section personnel need to know and to identify with company purposes to a higher degree than persons in an American firm. They achieve this through long experience and years of discussion with others at all levels. (pp. 143–145)

The irony of this finding and others like it is that even before World War II American and European industrial soci-

ologists had demonstrated the benefits of team approaches to work (McCord, 1991). The famous studies by Elton Mayo, discussed in Chapter 2, were designed to find out how workers at any level of an organization could be made to feel less alienation and a greater sense of ownership of their jobs. This research demonstrated the importance of primary-group relationships at work. But the function of the manager is to motivate employees to work more effi-

RESPONSE**		YEAR				
		1972–1982	1983–1987	1988–1991	1993	1994
Government should	1	392	1,237	764	184	289
	2	218	605	460	122	183
	3	368	977	709	201	322
	4	447	1,135	793	187	420
	5	261	719	440	130	292
	6	163	431	278	81	167
Government should not	7	321	784	402	130	303
Don't know	8	51	98	91	18	27
No answer	9	8	22	11	4	8
Not applicable	BK	11,397	1,534	1,959	549	981

Source: From 1994 NORC Codebook.

*This is the exact wording of the question as presented to respondents.
**The denominators used in calculating the percentages presented in Figure 19.3 are the totals of the responses in which an opinion was expressed (1–7). The figures in the "Don't know," "No answer," and "Not applicable" categories are not included.

therefore, it combines two issues: whether income inequality is a problem that should be addressed, and what policies should be used to address it—that is, whether government ought to raise taxes on the wealthy and/or provide assistance to people with limited incomes. No doubt many people respond to this question on the conservative side of the scale not because they feel comfortable with the existing income distribution but because they do not want government to have the dominant role in dealing with this or any other major social issue. To identify the independent effects of these different attitudes, the investigator would ask additional questions about income inequality and would cross-classify the responses to those questions with the responses to the question about government intervention.

ciently and at higher levels, a goal that is not easily achieved.

INDIVIDUALS AND CORPORATIONS
One possible source of worker alienation is the increasing power of the corporation relative to the individual. In the United States and other industrialized societies, the corporation has gained ever greater dominance over other economic institutions. Although they may have been established by entrepreneurs like Andrew Carnegie or John D. Rockefeller, who took great risks to build personal empires, modern corporations are bureaucratic organizations whose executive leadership may, at least in principle, be replaced. Sociologists like James S. Coleman (1982) point out that the idea of the *corporate actor* was essential to the development of the modern corporation. "As economic enterprise

FIGURE 19.4   Growth in Number of Corporations in the United States, 1916–1968

Source: "Distribution of Economic Resources in the United States," an unpublished paper prepared for *Actions of Individuals and Groups as Indicators of Power Distribution,* a project sponsored by the National Science Foundation. National Opinion Research Center, Chicago, 1974.

FIGURE 19.5   Participation of Persons and Corporate Actors in Court Cases: New York State Court of Appeals, 1853–1973

Source: "A Study of the Relative Participation of Persons and Corporate Actors in Court Cases," an unpublished paper prepared for *Actions of Individuals and Groups as Indicators of Power Distribution,* a project sponsored by the National Science Foundation. National Opinion Research Center, Chicago, 1974.

outgrew the family," Coleman writes, "it became useful for several persons to join together to carry out the enterprise. They were able to do this only if they were protected [as individuals] from the liabilities that the joint enterprise might incur" (p. 8). This was accomplished by the creation of a new class of fictional "persons"—corporations—that could incur debts and liabilities on their own account. The liability of any individual member of the corporation was limited to the amount that he or she had invested in it.

The emergence of the concept of the corporate actor had far-reaching effects. By the beginning of our own century, the importance of corporate actors (most of which are bureaucratic organizations) had begun to outweigh the importance of individuals in most of the institutional sectors of society. These trends are illustrated in Figures 19.4 and 19.5, which show the dramatic rise in the number of corporations over the past half century and the changing balance in the participation of individuals versus corporate actors in cases heard in the New York State Court of Appeals. "What these changes suggest," Coleman concluded, "is a structural change in society over the past hundred years in which corporate actors play an increasing role and natural persons play a decreasing role" (1982, p. 15).

A further effect of the dominance of corporate actors is that the individual is at a disadvantage in dealings with these entities. Today, corporate actors generally have access to much more information, derived from surveys, advertising, credit ratings, and the like. In conflicts that reach the courts, although the corporate actor and the individual are equal parties in the eyes of the law, in fact the corporate actor usually has the upper hand as it is backed up by numerous specialists, whereas the individual, even with the best legal aid, usually can draw on only limited resources.

Social movements like the labor movement and the consumer and environmental protection movements attempt to reduce the asymmetry or imbalance in these relationships (for example, they seek to regulate corporations by making them reveal information). Countermovements try to restore the rights of corporate actors (as in the movement to deregulate business and industry). Such movements are one consequence of the imbalance between the individual and the corporate actor. Another consequence may be an increase in the number of deviant acts directed against corporations of all kinds. People may cheat or steal from corporate actors—for example, they may take out their frustrations by destroying public telephones, scrawling graffiti on mass transit facilities, or illegally tapping into cable television boxes—without feeling nearly as guilty as they might if their actions were directed against individuals. Sociological perspectives on work and workers can offer some leads to further progress in dealing with such problems in the future.

SOCIOLOGICAL PERSPECTIVES ON THE WORKPLACE

Industrial sociology is concerned with the social organization of work and the types of interactions that occur in the workplace. Like sociologists in other fields, industrial sociologists use the functionalist, conflict, and interactionist perspectives in their research. The results of that research have been used to support various approaches to labor–management relations.

Human Relations in Industry: A Functionalist Perspective. The *human relations* perspective on management is associated with the research of Elton Mayo and his colleagues at Western Electric's Hawthorne plant and in aircraft and metal production plants. Their goal was to use experimental methods and observation of workers and managers on the job in an attempt to understand how the factory's formal organization and goals are affected by patterns of informal organization within the workplace. This was in sharp contrast with earlier approaches to labor–management relations, especially the *scientific management* approach developed early in this century by Frederick W. Taylor.

Scientific management, or Taylorism, as it is often called, was one of the earliest attempts to apply objective standards to management practices. After rising through the ranks from laborer to chief engineer in a large steel company, Taylor turned his attention to the study of worker productivity. He noticed that workers tend to adhere to informal norms that require them to limit their output. For example, he found that the rate of production in a machine shop was only about one third of what might normally be expected. Taylor decided to use the authority of management to speed up the workers. He fired stubborn men, hired "green hands" who did not know the norms of the experienced workers, and experimented with ways of breaking down the labor of each worker into its components. Every job, he claimed, could be scientifically studied to determine how it could be performed most efficiently. Such "time and motion studies," combined with piecework payment systems that induced workers to produce more because they were paid for each unit produced above a set number, became the hallmarks of scientific management (Miller & Form, 1964). Taylor's principles were quickly incorporated into the managerial practices of American businesses, but they were often resisted by workers and their unions (Braverman, 1974).

Mayo's experiments were intended to determine what conditions would foster the highest rates of worker productivity. His observations convinced him that increased productivity could be obtained by emphasizing teamwork among workers and managers, rather than through pay incentives or changes in such variables as lighting, temperature, and rest periods (Bendix, 1974). We saw in Chapter 2 that Mayo's research showed that the attention given to the workers was what mattered, not the various experimental conditions. But Mayo drew another, more important conclusion from the Hawthorne experiments:

> The major experimental change was introduced when those in charge sought to hold the situation humanly steady . . . by getting the cooperation of the workers. What actually happened was that six individuals became a team and the team gave itself wholeheartedly and spontaneously to cooperating in the experiment. (Mayo, 1945, pp. 72–73)

Although Mayo's research focused on the interactions between workers and managers, the human relations approach that grew out of that research can be said to represent the functionalist perspective on the workplace because it stresses the function of managerial efforts in increasing worker productivity. The functionalist perspective is also illustrated by William F. Whyte's classic study of the restaurant industry, which we encountered in Chapter 4. In a small restaurant, the organization's structure is simple. "There is little division of labor. The owner and employees serve together as cooks, countermen, and dishwashers." But when the restaurant expands, a number of supervisory and production occupations are added to its role structure. According to Whyte, this magnifies old problems and gives rise to new ones:

> In a large and busy restaurant a waitress may take orders from fifty to one hundred customers a day (and perhaps several times at each meal) in addition to the orders (much less frequent) she receives from her supervisor. When we add to this the problem of adjusting to service pantry workers, bartenders, and perhaps checkers, we can readily see the possibilities of emotional tension—and, in our study, we did see a number of girls break down and cry under the strain. (1949, p. 304)

Whyte discovered that tension and stress could be reduced, and customers served more happily, if the restaurant was organized in such a way that lower-status employees were not required to give orders directly to higher-status ones. For example, waiters and waitresses should not give orders directly to cooks but should place their orders with a pantry worker or use a system of written orders. By changing the organization of statuses and roles in the restaurant (and, thus, the way they functioned as a social system) it would be possible to increase work satisfaction and output.

Conflict at Work. The human relations approach seeks to improve cooperation between workers and managers in order to achieve the organization's goals. Industrial sociologists who take a conflict perspective feel that this approach automatically condones the goals of managers and fails to consider more basic causes of worker–management conflict such as class conflict. This results in continual "fine-tuning" of organizational structures rather than in more thorough reforms.

In a study of a midwestern metal products factory, Michael Burawoy (1980) found that even after changes were made on the basis of the human relations approach, the workers continued to limit their output. The workers called this "making out" and saw it as a way of maximizing two conflicting values: their pay and their enjoyment of social relations at work. But instead of wondering why the workers refused to produce more, Burawoy asked why they worked as hard as they did. He concluded that the workers were actually playing into the hands of the managers and owners because neither they nor the unions ever questioned management's authority to control basic production decisions. The norms of the shop-floor culture, of which "making out" is an example, caused the workers to feel that they were resisting the managers' control. As a result, they did not feel a need to engage in more direct challenges to the capitalist system itself.

Conflict-oriented industrial sociologists also study how class and status relations outside the workplace influence shop-floor cultures. For example, in an analysis of work relations in a large midwestern steel mill, William Kornblum (1974) described how ethnic and racial conflicts among whites, blacks, and Chicanos are carried into the plant itself. These conflicts diminish as the steelworkers work together in teams over periods of many years, but the basic class differences that divide workers from managers remain and are institutionalized in the norms of union–management bargaining.

A fundamental problem for conflict sociologists is that class conflict must be shown to exist; it cannot be assumed to exist simply because Marxian theory defines workers and business owners as opposing classes. In fact, there is considerable evidence that despite their misfortunes workers do not view their interests as automatically opposed to those of owners and managers. As workers and supervisory personnel lost their jobs in the severe recession of the early 1990s, they often expressed discontent with the nation's leadership and with company managers. Generally, however, the anguish of the unemployed tends to be turned inward, taking the form of depression rather than militant class consciousness. Class consciousness may be popularized in the lyrics of a Bruce Springsteen song—"They're closing down the textile mill across the railroad track/Foreman says these jobs are going boys/and they ain't coming back to your hometown"—but it has not produced much overt class conflict or new social movements (Bensman & Lynch, 1987).

On the other hand, continuing changes in the American economy during the 1990s may result in demands for new social policies. This trend is especially evident in calls for new approaches to health insurance. As *Fortune* 500 companies like GE, Boeing, Sears, IBM, and General Motors drastically cut their work forces, growing numbers of workers are losing jobs that provide health and pension benefits. As can be seen in Figure 19.6, the American economy is successful in creating new jobs (the labor force grew from 89.8 million employees in 1979 to 108.4 million in 1992), but many of those jobs pay lower wages and provide fewer benefits than the jobs that were lost (Harrison, 1990; Uchitelle, 1993). These changes suggest that feelings of anger and concern among working people will continue to increase and may result in new social movements or revivals of old ones like the labor movement (Fantasia, 1988).

Professions: An Interactionist Perspective. Factory workers and other low-status employees are not the only subjects of research by sociologists who study work and employment. Because they are a growing segment of modern economic institutions, professionals have also been studied extensively. A **profession** is an occupation with "a body of knowledge and a developed intellectual technique . . . transmitted by a formal educational process and testing procedures. A code of professional ethics governs each profession and regulates relations with colleagues, clients, and the public [and] most professions are licensed by the state" (Montagna, 1977, p. 197). This definition could be applied to a variety of occupations. For example, doctors and attorneys have long been considered professionals, but what about nurses and stockbrokers? Sociologists have addressed this question in their research on the "professionalization" of occupations—that is, on the way different occupations attempt to achieve the status of professions.

According to Everett C. Hughes (1959), a profession is a set of role relationships between "experts" and "clients," in which the professional is an expert who offers knowledge and judgments to clients. Often the professional must assume the burden of the client's "guilty knowledge": The lawyer must keep secret the client's transgressions, and the physician must hide any knowledge of the sexual behavior or drug use of famous and not-so-famous patients. Professions thus "rest on some bargain about receiving, guarding, and giving out communications" (Hughes, 1959, p. 449; also see Abbott, 1988, 1993).

Interactionist sociologists pay special attention to the role relationships that develop in various professions. They are particularly interested in the processes of *professional socialization*—learning the profession's formal and informal norms. For example, in a well-known study of professional socialization in medical schools, Howard Becker and his colleagues (1961) found that in the later years of their training medical students' attention is devoted more and more to learning the informal norms of medical practice. The formal science they learn in class is supplemented by the practical knowledge of the working doctor, and the student's skill at interacting with higher-status colleagues becomes extremely important to achieving the status of a

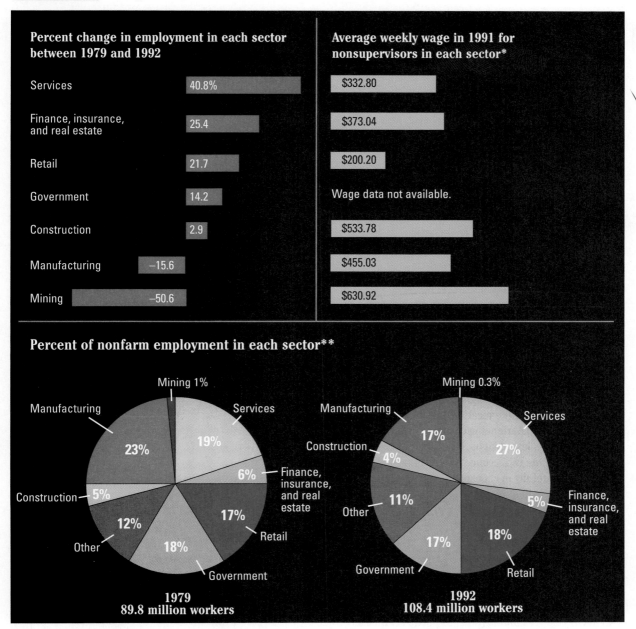

FIGURE 19.6 Changes in the U.S. Job Market Between 1979 and 1992

Percent change in employment in each sector between 1979 and 1992

Sector	Percent change
Services	40.8%
Finance, insurance, and real estate	25.4
Retail	21.7
Government	14.2
Construction	2.9
Manufacturing	−15.6
Mining	−50.6

Average weekly wage in 1991 for nonsupervisors in each sector*

Wage
$332.80
$373.04
$200.20
Wage data not available.
$533.78
$455.03
$630.92

Percent of nonfarm employment in each sector**

1979 — 89.8 million workers
- Mining 1%
- Services 19%
- Finance, insurance, and real estate 6%
- Retail 17%
- Government 18%
- Other 12%
- Construction 5%
- Manufacturing 23%

1992 — 108.4 million workers
- Mining 0.3%
- Services 27%
- Finance, insurance, and real estate 5%
- Retail 18%
- Government 17%
- Other 11%
- Construction 4%
- Manufacturing 17%

Source: Data from Bureau of Labor Statistics.

*Latest available.
**Because of rounding, percentages do not add to 100.

professional physician. In a more recent study on the same subject, Charles Bosk (1979) showed that resident surgeons in a teaching hospital are forgiven if they make mistakes that the older surgeons believe to be "normal" aspects of the learning process, but not when their mistakes are repeated or are thought to be due to carelessness. The point of these and similar studies is that role performance is learned through interaction. Role expectations vary from one profession to another, as do the ways in

which these expectations are experienced by members of the profession (Abbott, 1988).

Our discussion of professions can serve as a reminder of a basic characteristic of economic institutions, one that we noted early in the chapter: Economic institutions are concerned with allocating scarce resources to satisfy competing ends. Thus, just as the guilds of feudal societies controlled access to skilled trades in medieval times, professional associations like the American Medical

THE
PERSONAL CHALLENGE
Social Change and the Choice of an Employer

As you think about how economic conditions will affect your future in the job market, there are a number of lessons to take notice of. First, and perhaps most obvious, is the realization that it is impossible to overestimate the importance of the investments you and your family make in your education and training. The longer a person stays away from higher education and postgraduate training in favor of "temporary" work situations, the more difficult it is to find the time and financial resources to return. People who drop out of high school or college are at a double disadvantage. Not only will they earn significantly less than people who complete their education, but they face a greater likelihood of experiencing economic insecurity.

Another, less obvious, lesson is that because of changes in the U.S. economy in recent years you need to think carefully in choosing an employer. If you join a company with more than 100 employees, you will improve the odds of receiving adequate pension and medical benefits (see chart). If you choose to work for a government agency or one that relies on public funds, you will probably receive better benefits, but you also risk the possibility that budget reductions will lead to job insecurity. Finally, whatever your opinion of unions, you will be better off in an industry that recognizes unions, such as public utilities or transportation manufacturing, than in one that does not, such as textiles or wholesale and retail trade. At this writing, the average amount spent on employees by employers in the United States is $14,807 per year; in textiles it is about $8,000, while in public utilities it is more than $20,000. The heavily unionized transportation manufacturing sector (including automobile manufacturing) pays more than $3,500 per year per employee in medical benefits, while the far less unionized wholesale and retail trade sector pays about $2,300 (Uchitelle, 1995).

In coming years, as employees realize that vital benefits are higher in some industries than in others, there will likely be a resurgence of labor unrest and efforts to form unions. If you choose an industry with relative labor peace, in which union benefits are the rule rather than the exception, the data indicate that you will also be gaining a great deal of economic security.

Percentage of Companies Offering Various Benefits, by Size of Company

Source: U.S. Chamber of Commerce employee benefits surveys (average employer contribution); Employee Benefits Research Institute Databook on Employee Benefits, 3rd edition (benefits by size of company).

VISUAL SOCIOLOGY

THE CHANGING LANDSCAPE OF LABOR

Michael Jacobson-Hardy's photographs contrast the work environment in traditional, basic industries such as paper mills, foundries, textile mills, and shipyards with that in newer, high-technology industries such as computer manufacturing and aircraft production. In addition to examining the physical environment in which industrial production occurs, his images give visibility and voice to the workers themselves—the men and women whose lives and livelihoods have been affected most directly by the social and economic transformations now under way. The photographer explains his approach as follows:

> In 1989 I decided to seek out the effects of capitalism on workers and to record their stories through photography. The division of labor in a factory mirrors society as a whole. I sought out the impact of class oppression on different ethnic, racial, and gender groups. I became enamored with creating dignified portraits of entry-level workers. Images of the rich and famous are plentiful. It is the factory worker who needs visibility and a voice. One worker I met told me, "I've been working in this factory for forty years and nobody's ever asked to take my picture." (1995, p. 43)

"When I started in the paper industry, it was still . . . a trade. You had to fight to get to be a machine tender . . . It would take you sometimes 15 or 20 years to get to that position . . . you had to wait. You had to grow into your job."

"It's a very dirty job [extracting oil from metal shavings]. When you walk downstairs, it's a . . . big cloudy mist of oil. Sometimes you come home and you're oil from head to toe."

"When the mills shut down some workers never even bothered to return to pick up their pay. . . . We just lost track of them . . . What people got, if they were old enough, wouldn't be enough money to last for a week. . . . They had the worse pension plans you ever saw in your life. It wouldn't amount to a pot of beans."

The photos shown here are part of an exhibition titled "The Changing Landscape of Labor: Workers and Workplace." Although the focus of the exhibition is New England, the issues addressed are relevant to the United States as a whole, as can be seen in the accompanying comments by workers.

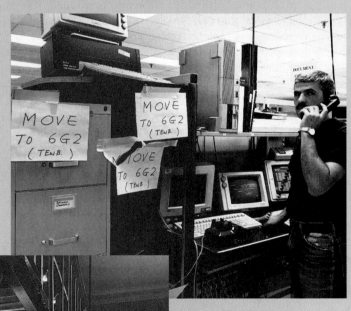

"The plan is to do away with manufacturing. A lot of good people have been laid off. Both of my parents once worked here and lost their jobs. We can't compete. I like it here. I like the people I work with. Three and a half years ago we had about 32,000 employees—now, there are about 6,000. Every 3 or 4 months, more people get laid off. It's a slow process."

"I'm tired. I want to quit. . . . I have to work until I'm 65. Maybe I'll never make it."

Association attempt to control access to the professions. Efforts by nation-states to regulate markets and trade, and efforts by managers to increase the productivity of workers, are all concerned with achieving the most advantageous use of scarce resources. This fundamental fact is at the heart of the sociological study of economic institutions.

RESEARCH FRONTIERS: GLOBAL CHANGE AND ADAPTING ECONOMIES

Social forces on a global scale are changing the fortunes of people in rich and poor nations alike. These changes also challenge the predictive ability of sociological and economic theories, especially because technological changes like those brought on by computers and telecommunications-based information systems are occurring so rapidly (Slater, Schutz, & Dorr, 1993). Automation of factories reduces the number of jobs on assembly lines; biological engineering promises to bring about new ways of producing foodstuffs and possibly to eliminate centuries-old agricultural practices; globalization of production allows multinational firms to quickly move their operations from one country to another in search of cheaper labor or lower production costs.

These and other massive changes in economic institutions are matched by equally challenging demographic changes. As birthrates in the richer societies plunge, they continue to rise in many of the poorer nations, with ominous results. Overpopulation in the poor nations con-

tributes to the denuding of forests and the depletion of already thin topsoils. In the rich nations the unchecked consumption of energy produces environmental stresses such as acid rain and, possibly, atmospheric warming (see Chapter 21 for further discussion of these issues). And the imbalances in population growth and regional wealth produce waves of immigration as people from the impoverished nations desperately seek ways to enter the richer ones (Kennedy, 1993).

In the United States the globalization of manufacturing and the far-reaching effects of technological change have been accompanied by declines in employment security and benefits for many workers, as well as by increases in the numbers of dual- or multiple-earner households. Despite these efforts to adapt, people in the United States and other advanced industrial nations are experiencing declining real wages. Since consumers in these nations continue to desire the goods and services they see advertised, one consequence of these trends is an increase in consumer debt (see Figure 19.7). Note the huge increase from 1975, when average consumer debt per household was less than $500, to 1995, when average credit card debt was estimated at more than $3,000. This is an ominous trend not only for the United States but also for the Third World nations where many of the goods consumed in the United States are produced.

Economic activity in the advanced economies continues to stimulate rapid growth in the developing nations, but that growth is not evenly distributed (Slater, Schutz, & Dorr, 1993). Sociological theories of economic development argue that regions with some political stability will experience greater economic growth than those with unstable regimes and higher levels of political strife. To some degree the facts bear this out. South Korea, which has achieved political stability despite authoritarian rule, has experienced an economic boom, while Ghana and Nigeria, once considered promising economies, are stagnating at best. In 1960 South Korea had the same per capita gross national product (GNP) as Ghana (US$230). Today South Korea's per capita GNP is US$5,000, but Ghana's has not improved. Political strife does not explain all the differences among regions, however. In India, overpopulation and related problems, rather than severe political instability, prevent per capita GNP from rising above US$340.

To a large extent, regional differences in global economic growth are a result of the rapid industrialization occurring in some East Asian nations, notably Korea, Singapore, and Taiwan. In 1965 the industrializing economies of East Asia accounted for only 1.5 percent of the world's exports of manufactured goods; by 1986 they accounted for 8.5 percent.

Within the wealthier nations, change will continue to create uncertainty and insecurity. Training and retraining programs will proliferate, but it is not clear whether such programs can actually produce new jobs (Kuttner, 1993; Reich, 1992b). Efforts to create large regional markets in

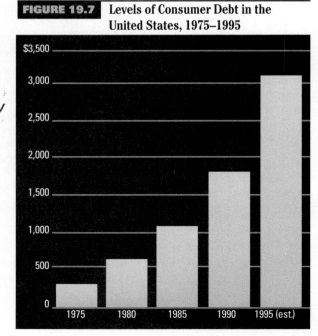

FIGURE 19.7 Levels of Consumer Debt in the United States, 1975–1995

Source: Hansell, 1995.

Note: Includes only credit card debt.

One consequence of the globalization of manufacturing production is an accelerated pace of automation in the advanced industrial societies.

Europe (through the European Community) and North America (through the North American Free Trade Agreement) may be successful in stimulating economic growth in the participating nations, but there are many indications that continuing competition among the participants will limit the growth of regional economies (Bell, 1993).

The computer revolution has yet to make itself felt as fully in all sectors of the economy as it has in manufacturing, in which applications of computer control have speeded the development of robot machines to replace human workers. But the Nobel Prize–winning economist Wassily W. Leontief believes that in coming years computers will have the effect of slowing the rate of growth of many service occupations, especially in clerical fields.

Moreover, where manufacturing concerns are relocating to developing nations, they are often installing modern plants with automated production lines. This results in the creation of few better-paying jobs, with those employees who are hired usually working at unskilled jobs (Rifkin, 1995).

All of these economic and social trends combine to produce a great deal of volatility in patterns of employment and rates of economic growth. Still, it appears certain that economic globalization will continue to accelerate, new markets for goods and services will continue to be developed, and those who have succeeded in investing in their own education and professional training will be in the best position to adapt and thrive.

SUMMARY

THINK ABOUT IT CRITICALLY

In the 1980s the leading U.S. economists believed that efforts by government to improve economic performance were counterproductive. Leave the economy alone and it will do far better than if one attempts to shape its outcomes. How would a sociologist view this issue?

Economics is the study of how individuals and societies choose to employ scarce resources to produce various commodities and distribute them among various groups in the society. Sociologists are also concerned with how individuals and societies make such choices, but much of their research focuses on how cultural norms affect those choices. The main subjects of sociological research in this area are markets and the division of labor, the interactions between government and economic institutions, and the nature of jobs and professions.

A hallmark of an industrial society is the production of commodities and services to be exchanged in markets. A *market* is an economic institution that regulates exchange behavior. In a market, different values are established for particular goods and services; those values are usually expressed in terms of a common measure of exchange, or currency. Market transactions are governed by agreements, or contracts, in which a seller agrees to supply a particular item and a buyer agrees to pay for it. The spread of markets throughout the world began in the late fifteenth century as a result of the development of new *technologies* that facilitated trade. Today world markets are dominated by *multinational corporations,* economic enterprises that have headquarters in one country and conduct business activities in one or more other countries.

The fate of societies throughout the world has been strongly influenced by the economic ideologies of mercantilism, capitalism, and socialism. *Mercantilism* held that the wealth of a nation could be measured by its holdings of gold, so the best economic system was one that increased the nation's exports and thereby increased its holdings of gold. *Laissez-faire capitalism,* on the other hand, argued that a society's wealth could be measured only by its capacity to produce goods and services—that is, its resources of land, labor, and machinery. The major institutions of capitalism are private property and free markets.

Socialism arose out of the belief that private property and personal profit should be replaced by public ownership of property and sharing of profits. According to Marx, the socialist state would be controlled by the workers, who would determine what should be produced and how it should be distributed. Soviet-style socialist societies were characterized until recently by command economies, in which the state commands economic institutions to supply a specific amount of each product and to sell it at a particular price. *Democratic socialism* holds that private property must continue to exist but that large corporations should be owned by the nation or, if they are in private hands, required to be run for the benefit of all citizens.

In *welfare capitalism,* markets determine what goods and services will be produced and how, but the government regulates economic competition. Welfare capitalism also asserts that the state should invest in the society's human resources through policies promoting education, health care, and social welfare.

The end of the cold war has raised the question of how the transition from command economies to entrepreneurial market economies will be carried out in the former socialist nations. Those nations are groping toward social democratic economic systems, but in the meantime they retain elements of the older command system and the unregulated black market. In the United States, the transition from an economy based on the production of goods to one based on the provision of services has resulted in the displacement of thousands of skilled workers into lower-paying jobs in the service sector. These trends appear to signal a change in the basic "social contract" in which individuals who work hard can expect increases in their living standards.

American workers feel an organizational and cultural gap separating them from managers even when they share the same goals. Many sociologists use the concept of *alienation* to explain this gap. This term refers to the feeling of being powerless to control one's own destiny. At work, people may feel alienated because their labor is divided up into activities that are meaningless to them.

In the United States and other industrialized societies, the corporation has gained ever-greater dominance over other economic institutions. Corporations are "fictional persons" that can incur debts and liabilities on their own account. In this century the importance of corporations has come to outweigh that of individuals in most of the institutional sectors of society, and the individual is often at a disadvantage in dealings with corporations.

The scientific management approach to labor–management relations attempted to increase productivity by determining how each job could be performed most efficiently and by using piecework payment systems to induce workers to produce more. Efforts to determine what conditions would result in the highest rates of worker productivity led to the recognition that cooperation between workers and managers is an important ingredient in worker satisfaction and output. This gave rise to the human relations approach to management, which seeks to improve cooperation between workers and managers.

Conflict theorists feel that the human relations approach fails to consider the basic causes of worker–management conflict. They study how social class and status both at work and outside the workplace influence relations between workers and managers. Interactionist theorists have devoted considerable study to professionalization, or the way in which occupations attempt to gain the status of *professions,* and to the processes of professional socialization (i.e., learning the formal and informal norms of the profession).

CRITICAL RESPONSE

The world's economies are changing extremely rapidly. Sociological views of economic institutions indicate that the laissez-faire approach favored by economists has some serious drawbacks. Primary among these is the fact that people seem to need help from government in coping with economic change. Also, there is a tendency for market dealings, when left alone, to produce a wider gap between the haves and the have-nots. This is why most economies in the world today are "mixed" in that laissez-faire principles are combined with practices that promote social welfare.

GLOSSARY

market: an economic institution that regulates exchange behavior through the establishment of different values for particular goods and services. (p. 572)

technology: tools, procedures, and forms of social organization that increase human productive capacity. (p. 576)

multinational corporation: an economic enterprise that has headquarters in one country and conducts business activities in one or more other countries. (p. 576)

mercantilism: an economic philosophy based on the belief that the wealth of a nation can be measured by its holdings of gold or other precious metals and that the state should control trade. (p. 576)

laissez-faire capitalism: an economic philosophy based on the belief that the wealth of a nation can be measured by its capacity to produce goods and services (i.e., its resources of land, labor, and machinery) and that these can be maximized by free trade. (p. 578)

socialism: an economic philosophy based on the concept of public ownership of property and sharing of profits, together with the belief that economic decisions should be controlled by the workers. (p. 580)

democratic socialism: an economic philosophy based on the belief that private property may exist at the same time that large corporations are owned by the state and run for the benefit of all citizens. (p. 582)

welfare capitalism: an economic philosophy in which markets determine what goods will be produced and how, but the government regulates economic competition. (p. 582)

alienation: the feeling of being powerless to control one's own destiny; a worker's feeling of powerlessness owing to inability to control the work process. (p. 587)

profession: an occupation with a body of knowledge and a developed intellectual technique that are transmitted by a formal educational process and testing procedures. (p. 592)

WHERE TO FIND IT

BOOKS

Capitalism, Socialism, and Democracy (Joseph A. Schumpeter; Harper, 1950). A classic description of capitalist and socialist economic institutions and the political consequences of the ways in which they operate.

Lean and Mean: The Changing Landscape of Corporate Power in the Age of Flexibility (Bennett Harrison; Basic Books, 1994). An analysis of the origins of corporate "downsizing" in a global economy and its consequences for stratification.

The Winner-Take-All Society (Robert H. Frank & Philip J. Cook; Free Press, 1995). An influential analysis of the

U.S. economy that shows that as more Americans compete for fewer and bigger prizes, income inequality and economic waste are the consequences.

Out to Work (Alice Kessler Harris; Oxford University Press, 1982). A history of wage-earning women in the United States with much insight into the impact of changing economic institutions on women and their careers.

Capitalism and Freedom (Milton Friedman; University of Chicago Press, 1962). A lucid statement of the laissez-faire perspective on economic and governmental institutions.

Industrial Sociology (Delbert C. Miller & William H. Form; Harper, 1964). A classic text in the field of economic sociology, with particular emphasis on labor and industry. Contains an excellent discussion of the research of Mayo and others in the human relations school.

Post Industrial Possibilities: A Critique of Economic Discourse (Fred Block; University of California Press, 1990). A sociologist skilled in economic and sociological analysis illuminates the quandaries and possibilities of post-industrial society.

JOURNALS

Monthly Labor Review. Published by the U.S. Department of Labor; an excellent source of data on employment and unemployment, plant closings and openings, and other economic trends. Also contains analytical articles that interpret major economic trends and changes in the labor market.

The Labor Relations Reporter. A valuable tool for anyone interested in research on labor–management issues. Consult bound volumes for weekly news and trend analysis and longer articles on important economic events, which are cited in the weekly summaries. Usually available in law, business, or other specialized libraries.

OTHER SOURCES

Current Population Reports: Economic Characteristics of Households in the United States. A quarterly report published by the Bureau of the Census. Presents monthly averages of household income and participation in cash and noncash transfer programs.

Handbook of Economic Statistics. Published annually by the Central Intelligence Agency. Compares economic statistics for communist, OECD, and selected other countries.

Handbook of Labor Statistics. Published annually by the Bureau of Labor Statistics. A compilation of statistical data on labor conditions and labor force characteristics in the United States and selected foreign countries.

Employment and Earnings. Published by the Bureau of Labor Statistics. A monthly report that presents current statistics on U.S. employment, unemployment, hours worked, and earnings.

CHAPTER 20

Politics and Political Institutions

This girl is holding the flag of Estonia. With the new freedoms in the Baltics and other regions formerly under Soviet rule comes the need to create a sense of national identity among new generations of citizens.

Much to his dismay, political sociologist Bogdan Denitch has become deeply involved in the politics of the former nation of Yugoslavia. An American citizen who received his doctorate in sociology from Columbia University and now teaches at Queens College in New York City, Denitch is a Serbian by birth. In 1992, after the fall of the communist government of Yugoslavia, he and some of his compatriots formed a political party dedicated to creating more democratic institutions in the former communist state.

Although Denitch is an American, Yugoslavian law permitted dual citizenship. He therefore was eligible to seek political office in Croatia, where he owns a home. In 1992 he and other social democrats ran for parliamentary seats just as war was breaking out between Croatia and Serbia. Faced with threats of violence

from opposing parties, they nevertheless continued their campaign. Denitch did not win a seat in parliament, but neither was the election a fair test of the voters' preferences. Intimidation and violence marked the contest from the beginning.

In this multiethnic, religiously diverse region, no group—Serbian–Eastern Orthodox, Bosnian–Muslim, or Croatian–Catholic—feels that it can trust the majority to protect the interests of the minority. This fear leads to the desire to live in a territory with a homogeneous population, and in a climate of war and social breakdown this desire for "ethnic purity" produces ghastly episodes of violence, including mass rape, shelling of defenseless civilian neighborhoods, forced expulsions ("ethnic cleansing"), concentration

camps, and destruction of priceless historical sites.

When asked why the United States and other North Atlantic Treaty Organization (NATO) nations should risk the lives of their soldiers to enforce a peace settlement in the former Yugoslavia, Denitch argues that the warring sides need a year or more of peace before they can begin to live together on their own. He believes that the bloodshed in the region indicates "the danger of a politics of identity rather than a politics of universal values and norms. This tragedy has to teach us that human rights are more important than the national sovereignty of a given cultural group" (B. Denitch, personal communication, January 1996). Denitch knows that ethnic and cultural identity is of vital interest to people who have suffered the horrors of slavery or genocide or bombing—but the pain of these past injuries must not, he believes, lead to emphasis on separate futures rather than an effort to build a society in which people can live together under a democratic regime.

For Denitch and other political sociologists, the problem of how a society establishes the rule of law and the protection of minorities—as in the Bill of Rights and other key amendments to the United States Constitution—is the central issue of our time. Denitch was attracted to political sociology through his participation in social movements during the 1940s. As a machinist in factories in California and New York he became a civil rights activist and labor leader before returning to school to obtain his degree in sociology. It pains him, therefore, that few of his students care about the Constitution and the difficulty of bringing about lawful social change without bloodshed (Denitch, 1990, 1992).

THE NATURE OF POLITICS AND POLITICAL INSTITUTIONS

"Politics," Max Weber liked to tell his students, "is the slow boring of hard boards." By this he meant that political change is almost never achieved easily. Creating new political institutions or changing old ones, even just changing the leadership of existing institutions, usually requires years of effort. There will be endless meetings, ideological debates, fund-raising, negotiations, and campaigning. At times, however, especially during times of revolutionary social change, the pace of political change is fast and furious.

We are living through a period of severe crisis and dramatic change in world politics. It is not at all clear that the democratic nation-state, the rule of law, and guarantees of the rights of minorities can be established in many parts of the world (Meštrović, 1991). In the view of many political sociologists, the twentieth century is ending with the world in a state of political unrest and nationalistic conflict much like that which existed at the end of the last century (J. Abu-Lugod, personal communication, January 1996). This uncertainty in world and national politics makes the comparative study of political institutions—established by the pioneering political sociologist Barrington Moore (1968)— a major growth area in sociology.

The fall of the Berlin Wall in 1989 symbolized the beginning of a new era in world politics. The cold war between the former Soviet Union and the Western capitalist democracies had dominated the politics of many parts of the world for more than 40 years. Although many nations, including the United States, still feel the effects of the arms race that accompanied the competition between the superpowers, with the end of the cold war has come an end to the nuclear "balance of terror" and the suppression of political expression within the former Soviet empire. Nationality groups in the former Soviet republics are asserting their desire for independence or, at least, for protection of their rights within a multiethnic state.

The fall of authoritarian communist parties in regions like the former Yugoslavia means that there is often no central authority to restrain populations who yearn to form their own independent nation or who covet the lands of their neighbors. Political sociologists like Bogdan Denitch are studying ways to stop the bloody consequences of these ethnic conflicts. The situation is not encouraging, however. The political upheavals in Eastern Europe, Africa, and India, the struggle to transform South Africa into a truly democratic state, the potential for disunion in Canada, and the rise of violently antigovernment hate groups in the United States—all these changes and others promise to make the comparative study of politics a central area of social-scientific research for years to come.

We can gain much insight into what the nationality groups in Eastern Europe, the blacks in South Africa, and others who are trying to bring about political change are experiencing by looking more carefully at politics and political institutions and the place they occupy in national life. This section of the chapter reviews some of the essential concepts of politics, with special emphasis on power, authority, and legitimacy. The second section discusses the political ecology of states and territories. The third section examines the political institutions that are most typical of modern nations and the major theories that have been proposed to explain why they operate as they do as well as how they change or resist change. The fourth section discusses the difficulty of establishing the rule of law, and the final section looks at the role of the military in the political life of contemporary nations.

POLITICS, POWER, AND AUTHORITY

In any society, Harold Lasswell (1936) argued, politics determines "who gets what, when, and how." Different societies develop their own political institutions, but everywhere the basis of politics is competition for power. **Power** is the ability to control the behavior of others, even against their will. To be powerful is to be able to have your way even when others resist (Mills, 1959). The criminal's power may come through a gun and the threat of injury— but many people wield power over others without any threat of violence, merely through the agreement of the governed. We call such power *authority*. **Authority** is institutionalized power—power whose exercise is governed by the norms and statuses of organizations. Those norms and statuses specify who can have authority, how much authority is attached to different statuses, and the conditions under which that authority can be exercised.

Political institutions are sets of norms and statuses that specialize in the exercise of power and authority. The complex set of political institutions—judicial, executive, and legislative—that operate throughout a society form the **state** (see Figure 20.1). This chapter will concentrate primarily on these explicitly political institutions, but keep in mind that in modern societies many institutions that are active in politics are not part of the state. Labor unions, for example, are economic institutions because they represent their members in bargaining with business owners and managers, but they play an active role in politics when they support particular political candidates or when they lobby for government-funded benefits for workers and their families.

When we look at the way in which conflicts over scarce resources like wealth, power, and prestige occur, we are looking at politics. From this perspective there can be a politics of the family, in which its members vie for attention, respect, use of the family car, money, and other resources. There can be a politics of the school, in which teachers compete for benefits such as smaller class size or better students. And of course the politics of government at all levels of society determines how the society's resources are allocated among various groups or classes. This view of politics, which looks at competition for power and at conflict over the use of power in a variety of settings, was reflected in the works of Karl Marx and Max Weber, two pioneering sociologists who devoted much of their work to the analysis of politics and change in political institutions. According to Marx, the way power is distributed in a society's institutions is a feature of its system of stratification. People and groups that have power in economic institutions, for example, are most likely to have power in political institutions as well (Washburn, 1982). However, much research in political sociology is devoted to the analysis of competition for power in political parties and electoral campaigns (Janowitz, 1968). A central problem of political sociology is whether the electoral process can sustain legitimate authority in a society in which power and wealth are stratified.

LEGITIMACY AND AUTHORITY

A basic dilemma that every political institution must solve is how to exercise legitimate authority—that is, how to govern with the consent and goodwill of the governed. "You can't sit on bayonets," goes an old political expression. This is a way of saying that although a state can exercise its power through the use of police force or coercion, eventually this will not be sufficient to govern a society. When the Soviet Union abandoned the use of force to control its satellite states in Eastern Europe, the governments of those nations (Romania, Czechoslovakia, East Germany) were soon toppled by popular revolts. The communist parties in those nations had governed for too long without the consent of the governed—that is, without legitimacy.

But why do people consent to be governed without the use of force? For political sociologists since Weber's time, the answer to this question begins with the concept of legitimacy. As defined by political sociologist Seymour Martin Lipset (1981), **legitimacy** is the capacity of a society "to engender and maintain the belief that the existing political institutions are the most appropriate for the society" (p. 64). In other words, legitimacy results from citizens' belief in the norms that specify how power is to be exercised in their society. Even if they disagree with some aspects of their political institutions or dislike their current leaders, they still hold to an underlying belief in their political system.

Traditional, Charismatic, and Legal Authority. Weber (1947) recognized that shared beliefs about legitimate authority may differ widely in different groups or societies. These differences result in three basic types of authority—traditional, charismatic, and legal—that have important effects on the way societies cope with social change. (See the study chart on page 606.)

In tribal and feudal societies, Weber observed, **traditional authority** prevails. The rulers usually attain authority through heredity, by succeeding to power within a ruling family or clan. Traditional authority is legitimated by the

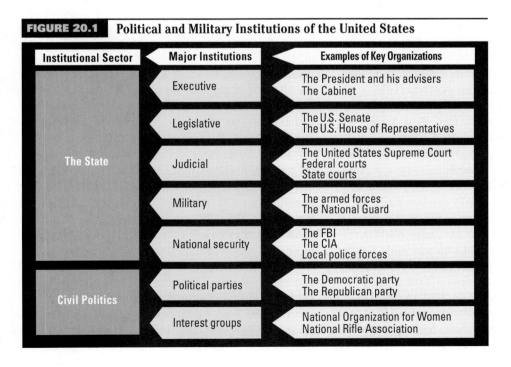

FIGURE 20.1 Political and Military Institutions of the United States

Institutional Sector	Major Institutions	Examples of Key Organizations
The State	Executive	The President and his advisers The Cabinet
	Legislative	The U.S. Senate The U.S. House of Representatives
	Judicial	The United States Supreme Court Federal courts State courts
	Military	The armed forces The National Guard
	National security	The FBI The CIA Local police forces
Civil Politics	Political parties	The Democratic party The Republican party
	Interest groups	National Organization for Women National Rifle Association

TYPE	DEFINITION	EXAMPLE
Traditional Authority	Authority that is hereditary and is legitimated by traditional values, particularly people's idea of the sacred	Tribal chiefs; absolute monarchs
Charismatic Authority	Authority that comes to an individual through a personal calling, often claimed to be inspired by supernatural powers, and is legitimated by people's belief that the leader does indeed have God-given powers	Joan of Arc; Mahatma Gandhi
Legal Authority	Authority that is legitimated by people's belief in the supremacy of the law; obedience is owed not to a person but to a set of impersonal principles	Presidents; prime ministers

STUDY CHART   Weber's Three Types of Authority

people's idea of the sacred, and traditional leaders are thought to derive their authority from God. The absolute monarchs of Europe, for example, were believed to rule by "divine right."

Traditional leaders usually embrace all the traditional values of the people they rule. This gives immense scope to their authority but makes it difficult for them and their systems of government to adapt to social changes that challenge those values. Thus the absolute monarchs of Europe had difficulty adapting their methods of governing to the growing power of new social classes like the proletariat and the bourgeoisie. The traditional chiefs of African societies today find it difficult to retain their authority as people in those societies gain more education and wealth and abandon their traditional village and agrarian way of life.

Charismatic authority, Weber's second type, finds its legitimation in people's belief that their leader has God-given powers to lead them in new directions. A charismatic leader, such as Jesus or Joan of Arc, comes to power not through hereditary succession but through a personal calling, often claimed to be inspired by supernatural powers. The charismatic leader usually develops a new social movement that challenges older traditions. Charismatic leaders may appear in all areas of life, "as prophets in religion, demagogues in politics, and heroes in battle. Charismatic authority generally functions as a revolutionary force, rejecting the traditional values and rebelling against the established order" (Blau & Scott, 1962, pp. 30–31).

Charismatic authority tends to bring about important social changes but is usually unstable because it depends on the influence of a single leader. Moreover, as noted in Chapter 8, charisma tends to become institutionalized as

the charismatic leader's followers attempt to build the values and norms of their movement into an organization with a structure of statuses and roles and its own traditions. This process occurred in the early history of Christianity as the disciples built organizations that embodied the spirit and teaching of Christ.

Weber's third type of authority, **legal authority,** is legitimated by people's belief in the supremacy of the law. This type of authority "assumes the existence of a formally established body of social norms designed to organize conduct for the rational pursuit of specified goals. In such a system obedience is owed not to a person—whether a traditional chief or a charismatic leader—but to a set of impersonal principles" (Blau & Scott, 1962, p. 31). The constitutions of governments establish legal forms of authority. All formal organizations, not only modern nation-states but also factories, schools, military regiments, and so on, have legal forms of authority.

Ideally, legal forms of authority adhere to the principle of "government of laws, not of individuals." We may be loyal to a leader, but that leader, in turn, must adhere to the laws or regulations that establish the rights and obligations of the leader's office. In practice, individual leaders often abuse their office by using their authority for private gain, as we have seen in cases of government corruption ranging from Watergate to the savings and loan scandal. But legal systems and the rule of law cannot long maintain their legitimacy if official wrongdoing is not punished.

Of Weber's three basic types, legal systems of authority are the most adaptable to social change. In legal systems, when the governed and their leaders face a crisis they can modify the laws to adapt to new conditions. This

Lincoln at Gettysburg

The documents that establish the legal authority of the government of the United States, particularly the Declaration of Independence and the Constitution, are often said to be "living documents." By this we mean that their meaning is not forever fixed, either in our laws or in our minds. We constantly interpret and reinterpret their meaning in light of our changing experience as a people and as a nation. What did the founders of the American nation mean by such ringing words as "All Men are created equal" or the rights to "Life, Liberty, and the Pursuit of Happiness"? Do these lofty phrases imply, for example, that we must strive to undo the consequences of past wrongs, such as slavery and colonial domination, through contemporary policies like affirmative action? To what extent are we responsible for trying to achieve "liberty and justice for all"?

In every era of American history there have been controversies over these questions. But at no time did debate over justice and law so threaten the nation's future as during the Civil War. That war was one of the bloodiest and most fratricidal in history. At the Battle of Gettysburg (July 1–3, 1863) alone there were more than 50,000 casualties. This battle was the turning point of the war, but the bloodshed and destruction continued for many more months. When President Abraham Lincoln agreed to dedicate the military cemetery at Gettysburg, therefore, he did so in the conviction that his role as President required him to interpret the meaning of the soldiers' sacrifice and of the war itself.

Political historian Gary Wills (1992) notes that in his Gettysburg Address (November 19, 1863) Lincoln did not condemn the Constitution as a document that legitimated slavery. Instead, through his interpretive words he "altered the document from within, by appeal from its letter to the spirit" (p. 38). Lincoln told the vast throng gathered to mourn the war dead that the nation was "conceived in Liberty, and dedicated to the proposition that all men are created equal." This opening line drew applause from the mourners, as did other lines in the brief but moving speech. But the almost revolutionary implications of the speech did not please all listeners then, nor do they please all Americans now. The *Chicago Times*'s review of the Gettysburg Address reminded readers that the dead officers and soldiers had given their lives to uphold the U.S. Constitution and the Union it created. "How dare [Lincoln], then standing on their graves, misstate the cause for which they died, and libel the statesmen who founded the government? They were men possessing too much self respect to declare that negroes were their equals, or were entitled to equal privileges" (from Wills, 1992, p. 39).

Time has vindicated Lincoln's broad interpretation of the Declaration and the Constitution. "For most people now," Wills concludes, "the Declaration means what Lincoln told us it means, as a way of correcting the Constitution itself without overthrowing it" (1992, p. 147). Although there are many people who argue for a stricter interpretation of the Constitution, one that does not necessarily grant equality to all and insists on the rights of states to set their own policies on questions of civil rights, the revolution in thought that Lincoln created with the Gettysburg Address holds sway over the American spirit. In Wills's words:

> The proponents of states' rights may have arguments, but they have lost their force, in courts as well as in the popular mind. By accepting the Gettysburg Address, its concept of a single people dedicated to a proposition, we have been changed. Because of it, we live in a different America. (p. 147)

does not always occur easily or without political conflict, however, especially when momentous changes are under way, as described in Box 20.1.

Political Culture. Because the stability of political institutions depends so directly on the beliefs of citizens, we can readily see that political institutions are supported by cultural norms, values, and symbols like the Statue of Liberty. These are commonly referred to as the society's *political culture*. When we look at other societies, it is clear that their political cultures differ quite markedly from ours. Americans justify a political system based on competitive elections by invoking the values of citizen participation in politics and equality of political opportunity. Chinese Communist party leaders justify their single-party political system by downplaying the value of citizen participation in politics and asserting the need for firm leaders and a centralized state that will hold the society together

The Lincoln Memorial is a shrine not only to a great president but also to the essential values of American political culture. It evokes feelings of reverence for the ideas of national unity and the rule of law.

and reduce inequalities. Since there is widespread skepticism about the ability of most people to participate in the political process, political sociologists believe that it will be difficult to promote democracy and the rule of law in many parts of the world (Meštrović, 1991; Moore, 1968; Smith, 1976).

Nationalism.   Perhaps the strongest and most dangerous political force in the world today is nationalism. **Nationalism** is the belief of a people that they have the right and the duty to constitute themselves as a nation-state. Religion, language, and a history of immigration or oppression are among the shared experiences that can cause a people to feel that they ought to have their own state. The situation of the French-speaking population of Quebec is a good example. Their language sets the Quebecois apart from English-speaking Canadians. So does their history of discrimination in English-dominated workplaces. In 1995 the people of Quebec narrowly defeated a separatist referendum, but it is still possible that nationalist sentiments in Quebec may result in the formation of a new nation on the North American continent.

In the case of Quebec, where political institutions and the rule of law are well-established, such a change would not necessarily be traumatic. But elsewhere in the world the rise of ethnic hostility and nationalism threaten to produce chaos. As Secretary of State Warren Christopher noted in a recent statement before the House Foreign Relations Committee, "If we don't find some way that the different ethnic groups can live together in a country, how many countries will we have? We'll have 5,000 countries rather than the one hundred plus we have now" (quoted in Blinder & Crossette, 1993, p. A1). While the numbers may be exaggerated, few political sociologists doubt that new nations will be created as a consequence of nationalist conflicts in coming years.

Crises of Legitimacy.   Societies occasionally undergo political upheavals like those that are occurring at this writing in Nigeria, Liberia, the former Yugoslavia, and

This American GI is part of the multinational peacekeeping force in the war-torn mountains of Bosnia. The hope is that the troops will be able to separate the Bosnian and Serbian enemies long enough for the passions of nationalism to cool.

the former Soviet Union. When these periods of unrest and instability involve enough of the citizens to such a degree that they challenge the legitimacy of the nation's political institutions, sociologists call the situation a *crisis of legitimacy.* For example, the Declaration of Independence was written during a crisis in which the American colonists challenged the legitimacy of British rule. In modern South Africa, where the black majority now rules with the cooperation and participation of the white minority, it still remains to be seen whether political legitimacy can be maintained in the face of extremes of wealth and poverty.

In sum, as we scan the globe today, it is evident that the world's political ecology includes many states that are extremely stable and many others in which political instability threatens to develop into a crisis of legitimacy.

THE POLITICAL ECOLOGY OF STATES AND TERRITORIES

The term *political ecology* refers to the distribution of populations among territories and to the kinds of political institutions that operate within those territories. Everyone in the United States, for example, lives simultaneously in a nation, a state, a county, and a municipality. The political ecology of any modern society can be represented by a map of political territories or jurisdictions, each with its own institutions with specific authority to tax and spend or to enforce laws or maintain public welfare.

The most important political territory in world affairs is the **nation-state.** We noted in Chapter 4 that nation-states claim a legitimate monopoly over the use of force within their borders. By this we mean that within a nation-state's borders, only organizations designated by the state (i.e., the government) may use force. But if the citizens believe that their government is legitimate, why is force necessary at all? The answer is that even when citizens believe their government to be legitimate, force (or, more often, the threat of force) may be needed to maintain order and ensure compliance with the law. For example, citizens may agree in principle that some of their income should be taken by the state through taxes to cover its expenses, but some individuals may attempt to avoid paying taxes. In fact, it is estimated that the U.S. government loses well over $65 billion in tax revenues annually because of various kinds of tax evasion (Goleman, 1988b). The state may use the threat of imprisonment to enforce compliance with tax laws, but it cannot catch all tax evaders. One of the main reasons even more income does not go untaxed is

This photo shows the first peaceful transfer of power and legitimate authority in Haiti's modern history. President Jean-Bertrand Aristide embraces the new president, René Preval, at the latter's inauguration early in 1996.

that most citizens believe the government has the legitimate right to collect taxes.

In many parts of the world bribery and corruption among public officials are commonplace. When elites do not observe the rule of law, it is difficult to convince less powerful and less wealthy citizens to do so. Conflicts arising from this issue take the form of scandals such as the Watergate break-in, which led to the resignation of President Richard Nixon, or the sexual harassment charges that eventually resulted in the resignation of Senator Robert Packwood. The point is that those charged with enforcing the laws should be beyond reproach. Otherwise the legitimacy of government and the laws is diminished in the minds of citizens—and in their behavior.

People who feel that the state uses its power in an illegitimate manner are not allowed to form private armies to resist the state. They may challenge the legitimacy of a particular law in the courts, where rational arguments and interpretations of law replace violent conflict. Nevertheless, all the institutions of the state, including the courts, are ultimately based on the state's monopoly over the use of force (Goode, 1972). In societies in which the state is weak or in which its legitimacy is denied by particular groups, it is common to find bandits, guerrilla armies, or terrorist groups.

STATES AND BORDERS

The borders that mark off one nation-state from another do not always correspond to what people believe the rightful boundaries of their societies to be. In the United States and Canada we are accustomed to thinking of American or Canadian society as existing within the borders of those two nation-states. In fact, the U.S.–Canadian border is the longest peaceful and uncontested national boundary in the world. In the Middle East and Africa, however, the territories claimed by nation-states and societies do not overlap nearly so well. A good example is the case of Israel and the Palestinians.

For at least 5,000 years the territory that is now Israel has been fought over by a succession of societies and states. The creation of the state of Israel in 1948 was a victory for the Zionist movement, which had sought a homeland for Jews who did not feel welcome or safe in other societies. But the creation of a Jewish state in the area known as Palestine simultaneously deprived many Palestinians of their territory. The Palestinians thus became a society without a homeland, and many of its members were dispersed to refugee settlements in Jordan and elsewhere, much as the Jews had been dispersed when they were expelled from the same region centuries earlier.

Many other examples of conflict over the borders of societies and states can be found in Africa. In the eighteenth and nineteenth centuries, when several European nations established colonies in Africa, many tribal societies found their territory divided into English and French or German colonies. In other cases different societies were combined within a single colony. Thus in Nigeria the Ibo, the Yoruba, and the Hausa (among many others), each a separate society with its own territory and culture, were combined into a single colony. The struggle for independence from colonial rule united these peoples, but after Nigeria gained its independence in the early 1960s, jealousy and competition again divided them and weakened the Nigerian state. When oil was discovered in Iboland, the Ibo attempted to establish a separate nation and the result was a civil war. The Ibo were defeated and Nigeria's boundaries remained intact, but thousands of people lost their lives.

World Government? In 1945, at the end of the most devastating war the world had ever experienced, the United Nations was founded in an effort to reduce the frequency and severity of conflicts among states. The UN, which celebrated its fiftieth annniversary in 1995, has gradually become recognized by almost all the nations in the world. Yet for many reasons, including competition among nations for power and influence, the UN has not been very effective as an international peacekeeping organization. Nevertheless, it remains the only world forum and meeting place of nations. The very fact that it continues to exist offers some hope that we may someday develop a system of world citizenship. In the meantime we will continue to live within a political ecology in which each nation defends and controls its own borders (Goodrich, 1974; Wainhouse, 1973).

CITIZENSHIP AND POLITICAL PARTICIPATION

If you travel abroad, you must obtain a passport. The passport serves as official proof of citizenship; without it you would not be allowed to return to the nation of which you are a citizen. The international system of passports, visas, and border checks is how nation-states control the movement of people across their borders. Migration from less affluent to more affluent nations is held in check by these techniques. Within many nations, also, citizens must carry passports or identity cards as proof of citizenship. But citizenship is far more than a technique for controlling the movement of populations; it is a central feature of political life in modern societies (Janowitz, 1978; Shils, 1962).

Rights of Citizenship. The term **citizenship** refers to the status of membership in a nation-state. Like all statuses, citzenship is associated with a specific set of rights and obligations (Bendix, 1969; Weber, 1968). As political sociologist Reinhard Bendix put it, "A core element of nation-building is the codification of the rights and duties of all adults who are classified as citizens" (1969, p. 89). In other words, the roles of citizens in the society's political life must be made clear to all.

In feudal societies most of the members of the society did not participate in political life. The needs of various groups in the population were represented, if at all, by the edicts of powerful landholders, generals, and clergymen. In

These new citizens at a swearing-in ceremony have had to demonstrate knowledge of basic English and awareness of the rights and responsibilities of United States citizens.

modern nation-states as a result of major social movements this form of representation has been replaced by a form based on citizen participation, in which representatives elected by the citizens are entitled to vote on important public issues. But as societies adopted the principle of citizen participation, conflicts arose over the question of who would be included among a society's citizens. This is illustrated by the violent struggle over citizenship and political participation for blacks in South Africa, led by Nelson Mandela and the African National Congress, that finally resulted in a new constitution and majority rule.

The rights of citizenship include much more than the right to vote. T. H. Marshall (1964) defined those rights as follows:

- *Civil rights* such as "liberty of person, freedom of speech, thought and faith, the right to own property and to conclude valid contracts, and the right to justice."
- *Political rights* such as the right to vote and the right of access to public office.
- *Social rights* ranging from "the right to a modicum of economic welfare and security to the right to share to the full in the social heritage and to live the life of a civilized being according to the standards prevailing in the society" (pp. 71–72).

This list does not necessarily imply that these rights actually exist in a given society or that they are shared equally by all of the society's citizens. In the United States, for example, before 1920 women were considered citizens but were denied the right to vote.

Participation in Local Politics.   The question of who is entitled to full participation in politics is a key issue at the local level as well as at the national level. At the national level, participation is vital to a group's position in society, as can be seen in the struggles by women and blacks to win the right to vote. But in the cities and towns and communities in which daily life is lived, the same guarantee of full participation plays a role in social mobility. W. E. B. Du Bois's study, *The Philadelphia Negro,* which we discussed in Chapter 1, includes this poignant petition by black community leaders to the city's mayor:

> We are here to state to your excellency that the colored citizens of Philadelphia are penetrated with feelings of inexpressible grief at the manner in which they have thus far been overlooked and ignored by the Republican party in this city. . . . We are therefore here, sir, to earnestly beseech of you as a faithful Republican and our worthy chief executive, to use your potent influence as well as the good offices of your municipal government, if not inconsistent with the public weal, to procure for the colored people of this city a share at least, of the public work and the recognition which they now ask for and feel to be justly due to them. (1967/1899, p. 374)

At the turn of the century Philadelphia, like most American cities, was dominated by the leaders of the local Republican party organization, who were among the town's richest and most powerful citizens. Immigrant workers and the poor were effectively excluded from political participation. The party that represented their interests, the

TABLE 20.1	Party of Mayors in Cities of Over 100,000 Population, Selected Years, 1929–1942									
	1929		**1932**		**1935**		**1938**		**1942**	
	N	%	*N*	%	*N*	%	*N*	%	*N*	%
Republican	45	48.9	21	22.8	17	18.4	14	15.2	16	17.4
Democratic	48	30.4	43	46.7	45	48.9	42	45.7	41	44.5
Third	2	2.2	1	1.1	4	4.4	3	3.3	2	2.2
Nonpartisan and city manager	14	15.2	23	25.0	23	25.0	33	35.8	30	32.6
No information	3	3.3	4	4.4	3	3.3	0	0.0	3	3.3
Total	92	100.0	92	100.0	92	100.0	92	100.0	92	100.0

Source: From *Socialism and the Cities*, by Bruce Stave, Kennikat Press 1985. Reprinted by permission of Associated Faculty Press.

Democratic party, was unable to gain power in the city. But the Great Depression drastically altered this pattern. Fearing that the misery created by the Depression would lead to unrest among the lower classes that could result in social disorder and even revolution, upper- and middle-class Americans began to look more favorably on the Democrats'

TABLE 20.2	New Nations Established Since 1943				
YEAR	**DATE**	**NATION**	**YEAR**	**DATE**	**NATION**
1943	Nov. 22	Lebanon	1960	Aug. 7	Côte d'Ivoire
1944	Jan. 1	Syria		Aug. 11	Chad
	June 17	Iceland		Aug. 13	Central African Republic
1946	Mar. 22	Jordan		Aug. 15	Congo
	July 4	Philippines		Aug. 16	Cyprus
1947	Aug. 14	Pakistan		Aug. 17	Gabon
	Aug. 15	India		Aug. 20	Senegal
1948	Jan. 4	Burma		Sept. 22	Mali
	Feb. 4	Sri Lanka		Oct. 1	Nigeria
	May 15	Israel		Nov. 28	Mauritania
	Aug. 15	Korea, South	1961	Apr. 27	Sierra Leone
	Sept. 9	Korea, North		June 19	Kuwait
1949	Mar. 8	Vietnam		Dec. 9	Tanzania
	July 19	Laos	1962	Jan. 1	Western Samoa
	Nov. 8	Cambodia		July 1	Burundi
	Dec. 28	Indonesia		July 1	Rwanda
1951	Dec. 24	Libya	1962	July 5	Algeria
1956	Jan. 1	Sudan		Aug. 6	Jamaica
	Mar. 2	Morocco		Aug. 31	Trinidad and Tobago
	Mar. 20	Tunisia		Oct. 9	Uganda
1957	Mar. 6	Ghana	1963	Dec. 12	Kenya
	Aug. 31	Malaysia	1964	July 6	Malawi
1958	Oct. 2	Guinea		Sept. 21	Malta
1960	Jan. 1	Cameroon		Oct. 24	Zambia
	Apr. 27	Togo	1965	Feb. 18	Gambia, The
	June 27	Madagascar		July 26	Maldives
	June 30	Zaire		Aug. 9	Singapore
	July 1	Somalia	1966	May 26	Guyana
	Aug. 1	Benin		Sept. 30	Botswana
	Aug. 3	Niger		Oct. 4	Lesotho
	Aug. 5	Burkina Faso		Nov. 30	Barbados

call for the creation of new social-welfare institutions. Such institutions would ease the plight of the poor and the unemployed without fundamentally changing capitalist economic institutions. At the same time, the poor and the working class began to exercise the right to vote in increasing numbers. The result was the political turnabout that brought the Democratic candidate, Franklin D. Roosevelt, to the presidency in 1932. As Table 20.1 shows, there was an equally marked turnabout in the political leadership of American cities.

In 1994 the Republican party gained a sweeping victory that gave it control of the House of Representatives, largely because of its new strength in suburban and small-town communities. Both major parties, however, are faced with declines in political participation. Clearly, the problem of making political participation meaningful to more citizens will continue to be a subject of sociological research in coming years (Katznelson, 1981; Putnam, 1995).

POLITICAL INSTITUTIONS IN MODERN SOCIETIES

The central problem of contemporary politics, according to Seymour Martin Lipset, is this: "How can a society incorporate continuous conflict among its members and social groups and yet maintain social cohesion and legitimacy of state authority?" (1979, p. 108). This question has taken on particular urgency since World War II, when the colonial empires of Europe crumbled in the face of nationalistic movements and dozens of new nations were created (see Table 20.2). Writing in 1963, Edward Shils wondered how modern political institutions could emerge in societies in which most of the citizens lived in traditional communities. "All the founders of the new states," he commented, "face the problems of establishing an effective government and staffing it" (p. 3). Moreover, they faced the problems of creating "a rationally conducted administration, a cadre of

(continued)

YEAR	DATE	NATION	YEAR	DATE	NATION
1968	Jan. 31	Nauru	1981	Sept. 21	Belize
	Mar. 12	Mauritius		Nov. 1	Antigua and Barbuda
	Sept. 6	Swaziland	1983	Sept. 19	Saint Kitts and Nevis
	Oct. 12	Equatorial Guinea	1984	Jan. 1	Brunei
1970	June 4	Tonga	1986	Oct. 21	Marshall Islands
	Oct. 10	Fiji		Nov. 3	Micronesia, Federated States of
1971	Aug. 14	Bahrain	1990	Mar. 21	Namibia
	Sept. 3	Qatar		May 22	Yemen
	Dec. 2	United Arab Emirates	1991	April 9	Georgia
1972	Apr. 4	Bangladesh		June 25	Slovenia
1973	July 10	Bahamas, The		Aug. 24	Russia
1974	Feb. 7	Grenada		Aug. 25	Belarus
	Sept. 10	Guinea-Bissau		Aug. 27	Moldova
1975	June 25	Mozambique		Aug. 30	Azerbaijan
	July 5	Cape Verde		Aug. 31	Kyrgyzstan
	July 12	São Tomé and Principe		Aug. 31	Uzbekistan
	Sept. 16	Papua New Guinea		Sept. 6	Estonia
	Nov. 11	Angola		Sept. 6	Latvia
	Nov. 25	Suriname		Sept. 6	Lithuania
	Dec. 31	Comoros		Sept. 9	Tajikistan
1976	June 28	Seychelles		Oct. 27	Turkmenistan
1977	June 27	Djibouti		Nov. 20	Macedonia
1978	July 7	Solomon Islands		Dec. 1	Ukraine
	Oct. 1	Tuvalu		Dec. 16	Kazakhstan
	Nov. 3	Dominica	1992	April	Bosnia and Herzegovina
1979	Feb. 22	Saint Lucia		Apr. 11	Serbia and Montenegro
	July 12	Kiribati		June	Croatia
	Oct. 27	Saint Vincent and the Grenadines	1993	Jan. 1	Czech Republic
1980	Apr. 18	Zimbabwe		Jan. 1	Slovakia
	July 30	Vanuatu			

Source: Reddy, 1994.

leaders grouped in the public form of a party system . . . and a machinery of public order" (p. 3). Because these are some of the many political institutions one expects to find in any modern state, it is helpful to examine in greater detail their structure and the problems associated with their development.

A Rational Administration.   Modern nations are governed by elected and appointed officials whose authority is defined by laws. To the extent possible, they are expected to use their authority for the good of all citizens rather than for their own benefit or for that of particular groups. They are forbidden to use their authority in illegitimate ways—that is, in ways that violate the rights of the citizens.

Modern political institutions usually specify some form of separation of powers. The authors of the United States Constitution, for example, were careful to create a system of checks and balances among the nation's legislative, executive, and judicial institutions so that abuses of authority by one could be remedied by the others. Thus when agents of the Nixon campaign organization were caught breaking into the Democratic party headquarters during the 1972 presidential election campaign and the President and some of his advisers were found to have covered up their role in this and other illegal activities, the impeachment proceedings carried out by the legislative and judicial branches of the government led to the President's resignation.

In many other nations abuses of state authority are far more common. The power of rulers is unchecked by other political institutions, and although citizens may question the legitimacy of their rule, they are powerless to prevent the rulers' use of coercion in violation of their rights. Such states are often ruled by **demagogues,** or leaders who use personal charisma and political symbols to manipulate public opinion. Demagogues appeal to the fears of citizens and essentially trick them into giving up their rights of political participation. Hitler's ability to sway the suffering German masses made him the outstanding example of demagoguery in this century.

A Party System.   Organizations of people who join together in order to gain legitimate control of state authority—that is, of the government—are **political parties.** Parties may be based on ideologies, or they may simply represent competing groups with the same basic values. Many American political sociologists assert that nations must make certain that other political parties are able to compete with the ruling party (Janowitz, 1968; Lipset, 1981; Oberschall, 1973). Failure to protect the existence of an opposition party or parties leads to **oligarchy**—rule by a few people who seek to stay in office indefinitely rather than for limited terms of office.

Parties that seek legitimate power and accept the rule of other legitimate parties form a "loyal opposition" that monitors the actions of the ruling party, prevents official corruption, and sustains the hopes of people whose needs are not adequately met by the ruling party. Revolutionary political parties, it should be noted, do not view the state as legitimate. They therefore do not agree to seek authority through legitimate procedures like elections. For this rea-

WHO STOLE THE PEOPLE'S MONEY? — DO TELL. N.Y.TIMES.   'TWAS HIM.

This drawing by the great American political cartoonist Thomas Nast was one of a series that helped destroy the corrupt political machine headed by William Marcy "Boss" Tweed in the 1870s—but not before Tweed and his cronies had defrauded the people of New York City of over $30 million.

son they tend to be banned by most governments. On the other hand, many modern nations, including the United States, have banned or repressed nonrevolutionary communist parties, largely because of their opposition to private property and their sympathy for the communist-dominated regime of the former Soviet Union.

Institutions for Maintaining Order. We have seen that states control the use of force within their borders. They also seek to protect their territories against attacks by other states. For these purposes most states maintain police forces and armies. But sometimes the state's leaders have difficulty controlling these institutions, and quite often military factions seize power in what is called a *coup d'état* (or simply *coup*).

A coup usually results in the establishment of an oligarchy in which the state is ruled by a small elite that includes powerful members of the military. The Latin American *junta* is a special type of oligarchy in which military generals rule, usually with the consent of the most powerful members of the nation's nonmilitary elite. Their rule is commonly opposed by members of the intellectual professions, especially journalists, professors, writers, and artists. The dissent expressed by these individuals often leads to censorship and further repression of nonmilitary political institutions.

Regimes that accept no limits to their power and seek to exert their rule at all levels of society, including the neighborhood and the family, are known as **totalitarian regimes;** Nazi Germany and the Soviet Union under Stalin are examples. Such regimes cannot exercise total power without the cooperation of the military. It would be incorrect, however, to attribute the existence of oligarchies and totalitarian regimes to the power of the military alone. On many occasions military leaders have led coups that deposed the state's existing rulers and then turned over state power to nonmilitary institutions.

Nevertheless, in modern societies military institutions have become extremely powerful. Even before the end of World War II Harold Lasswell (1941) warned that nations might be moving toward a system of "garrison states—a world in which the specialists in violence are the most powerful group in society" (p. 457). This theme was echoed by Dwight D. Eisenhower, one of the nation's celebrated soldier-Presidents. As he was leaving office, Eisenhower warned that the worldwide arms buildup, together with the increasing sophistication of modern weapons, was producing an "industrial-military complex." By this he meant that the military and suppliers of military equipment were gaining undue influence over other institutions of the state. (We discuss military institutions more fully in the final section of the chapter.)

DEMOCRATIC POLITICAL SYSTEMS

In contrast to oligarchies and totalitarian regimes, democratic societies offer all of their citizens the right to participate in public decision making. Broadly defined,

democracy means rule by the nation's citizens (the Greek *demos,* from which *democracy* is derived, means "people"). In practice, democratic political institutions can take many different forms as long as the following conditions are met:

1. The political culture legitimizes the democratic system and its institutions.
2. One set of political leaders holds office.
3. One or more sets of leaders who do not hold office act as a legitimate opposition (Lipset, 1981).

The two most familiar forms of democratic political rule are the British and American systems. In the British *parliamentary* system, elections are held in which the party that wins a majority of the seats in the legislature "forms a government," meaning that the leader of the party becomes the head of the government and appoints other party members to major offices. Once formed, the government generally serves for a specified length of time. If no party gains a majority of the legislative seats, a coalition may be formed in which smaller parties with only a few seats can bargain for positions in the government. Such a system encourages the formation of smaller parties.

In the American *representative* system, political parties attempt to win elections at the local, state, and national levels of government. In this system the President is elected directly, and the party whose candidate is elected President need not have a majority of the seats in the legislature. Success therefore depends on the election of candidates to national office. In the United States two political parties, the Republicans and the Democrats, have developed the resources and support necessary to achieve this. It is difficult for smaller parties to gain power at the national level because voters do not believe they have much chance of electing national leaders, and even if they do win a few legislative seats they will not be asked to form coalitions, as they would in a parliamentary system.

One-Party Systems. Suppose that a nation has only one political party. Does this mean that it is undemocratic? Not in principle. A one-party state or region can be democratic as long as the citizens are free to form other parties, as long as the party's leaders can be replaced through democratic processes, and as long as the leaders do not violate the rights of citizens. But how likely are these conditions to be met if there are no opposing parties? The evidence suggests that the odds are against democracy in one-party states and regions. For example, David Apter's (1980) study of one-party rule in Ghana showed that a charismatic leader, Kwame Nkrumah, used his power as party leader to perpetuate his own rule. When opposition groups attempted to pursue legitimate political ends, their leaders were imprisoned and Nkrumah dissolved the supreme court. Nkrumah was eventually deposed by a military coup—the fate of many leaders who assume dictatorial power through one-party rule (Zolberg, 1974).

Studies of local politics in the United States have also shown that in cities or counties in which the majority of voters traditionally vote for candidates of only one party an oligarchical political system may develop. Such systems have been dubbed "machines." Usually headed by a dominant party leader or "boss," the machine trades favors and **patronage**—jobs and economic benefits of various kinds—for votes and political influence. Mayor Richard J. Daley of Chicago was considered America's strongest party boss until his death in 1976. His rule over the Cook County Democratic party machine enabled him to control thousands of patronage jobs, to stifle opponents, and to influence the Democratic party's presidential nominations. After his death there was widespread speculation that the Cook County machine would decline, but in a study of Chicago politics Thomas Guterbock (1980) found that the party machine continues to operate (with many exceptions) at the community level under the leadership of a ward or district boss. Indeed, Richard M. Daley, son of the former party boss, won his second term as Chicago's mayor in 1995 largely through the continuing influence of the Democratic party machine. To a large extent, however, urban party machines like the one in Chicago are a carryover from America's political past. Social-welfare legislation enacted since the 1930s has decreased people's need for the favors offered by local politicians, and decreasing party identification by voters has weakened local party organizations.

PERSPECTIVES ON POLITICAL INSTITUTIONS

Our description of democratic political institutions leaves open the question we posed earlier: "How can a society incorporate continuous conflict among its members and social groups and yet maintain social cohesion and legitimacy of state authority?" (Lipset, 1979, p. 108). One answer to this question is that a society can resolve conflicts through democratic processes. But this leads us to ask what conditions allow democratic institutions to form and, once formed, what ensures that they actually function to reduce the inequalities that engender conflict. The broadest test of democratic institutions is not whether they are embodied in formal organizations like legislatures and courts but whether they are able to address the problems of inequality and injustice in a society.

There are at least three schools of sociological thought regarding these questions. The first, derived from the functionalist perspective, asserts that democratic political institutions can develop and operate only when certain "structural prerequisites," such as a large middle class, exist in a society. The second school of thought, often referred to as the **power elite model,** is based on the conflict perspective. It is highly critical of the functionalist view,

supporting its criticism with evidence of the ways in which so-called democratic political institutions actually operate to favor the affluent. A third position, known as the **pluralist model,** asserts that the existence of ruling elites does not mean that a society is undemocratic, as long as there are divisions within the elite and new groups are able to seek power and bargain for policies that favor their interests.

STRUCTURAL PREREQUISITES OF DEMOCRACY AND THE RULE OF LAW

Seymour Martin Lipset (1981, 1994) argues that democratic political institutions are relatively rare because if they are to exist and function well, the society must have attained a high level of economic and cultural development. To prove his theory, Lipset surveyed data on elections, civil rights, freedom of the press, and party systems in 48 nation-states, and subsequently in many other countries (Lipset, 1994). He found that the presence of these institutions was correlated with a nation's level of economic development, its degree of urbanization, the literacy of its citizens, and the degree to which its culture values equality and tolerates dissent. Table 20.3 and Box 20.2 present these findings in more detail.

In this cross-cultural research and in his research on democracy in the United States, Lipset attempted to show that the growth of a large middle class is essential to democracy. The middle-class population tends to be highly literate and, hence, able to make decisions about complex political and social issues. Moreover, middle-class citizens feel that they have a stake in their society and its political institutions. Accordingly, they often support policies that would reduce the class and status cleavages—the distinctions between the haves and the have-nots—that produce social conflict.

Sociologists who study voting behavior tend to support Lipset's thesis that the stability of democratic institutions rests on structural features that diminish conflict in a society. But their research has revealed something less than complete stability. Morris Janowitz (1978) made this observation:

> Since 1952, there has been an increase in the magnitude of shifts in voting patterns from one national election to the next. . . . Increasingly important segments of the electorate are prepared to change their preference for president and also to engage in ticket splitting [voting for candidates of different parties]. (p. 102)

These shifts in voting behavior may represent new alignments of voters that could lead to major changes in the nation's public policies. The important point, however, is that these realignments, while they influence which parties and political leaders gain or lose power, do not affect the process of democratic competition itself.

THE POWER ELITE MODEL

However important elections are to the functioning of democratic institutions, there are strong arguments against the

TABLE 20.3 A Comparison of European and Latin American Democracies and Dictatorships, by Wealth, Industrialization, Education, and Urbanization

A. INDICES OF WEALTH

	PER CAPITA INCOME IN $	THOUSANDS OF PERSONS PER DOCTOR	PERSONS PER MOTOR VEHICLE	TELEPHONES PER 1,000 PERSONS	RADIOS PER 1,000 PERSONS	NEWSPAPER COPIES PER 1,000 PERSONS
European and English-speaking stable democracies	685	0.86	17	205	350	341
European and English-speaking unstable democracies and dictatorships	305	1.4	143	58	160	167
Latin American democracies and unstable dictatorships	171	2.1	99	25	85	102
Latin American stable dictatorships	119	4.4	274	10	43	43

B. INDICES OF INDUSTRIALIZATION

	PERCENTAGE OF MALES IN AGRICULTURE	PER CAPITA ENERGY CONSUMED
European stable democracies	21	3.6
European dictatorships	41	1.4
Latin American democracies	52	0.6
Latin American stable dictatorships	67	0.25

C. INDICES OF EDUCATION

	PERCENTAGE LITERATE	PRIMARY EDUCATION ENROLLMENT PER 1,000 PERSONS	POST-PRIMARY ENROLLMENT PER 1,000 PERSONS	HIGHER EDUCATION ENROLLMENT PER 1,000 PERSONS
European stable democracies	96	134	44	4.2
European dictatorships	85	121	22	3.5
Latin American democracies	74	101	13	2.0
Latin American dictatorships	46	72	8	1.3

D. INDICES OF URBANIZATION

	PERCENT IN CITIES OVER 20,000	PERCENT IN CITIES OVER 100,000	PERCENT IN METROPOLITAN AREAS
European stable democracies	43	28	38
European dictatorships	24	16	23
Latin American democracies	28	22	26
Latin American stable dictatorships	17	12	15

Source: *Political Man: The Social Bases of Politics,* by Seymour Martin Lipset (Baltimore: Johns Hopkins University Press, 1981, expanded and updated edition). Reprinted by permission of the author.

Diagramming Social Change

The accompanying chart is an example of how a diagram can effectively communicate ideas about the directions and influences of social change. This diagram presents the social structures from which democratic political institutions arise (listed on the left) and some possible further consequences of the emergence of those political institutions (on the right).

The arrows in the diagram indicate either conditions that contribute to democracy or possible consequences of the emergence of democratic institutions. As in most social-scientific analysis, the author, political scientist Seymour Martin Lipset, is careful not to make direct assertions about causality. He does not state, for example, that an open class system (measured by upward and downward social mobility) inevitably leads to the emergence of democratic regimes. Instead, social mobility and the other aspects of social structure listed on the left are "necessary but not sufficient" preconditions for the emergence of democracy. That is, they must exist to some degree in a society, but they are not sufficient to "cause" democracy. For that to happen, other conditions must also be present, such as the leadership of people who can sacrifice their desire for personal power in the interest of creating democratic political institutions. George Washington, for example, is revered as a pioneer of democracy, because when he had the chance to become a monarch he chose to relinquish personal power and lead the newly independent colonies toward the creation of a constitutional monarchy.

Note that the arrows on the right side of the diagram suggest that democratic rule is associated with the emergence of social phenomena that run counter to democracy. Bureaucracy, for example, is a common consequence of democratic regimes. Laws passed by democratic processes tend to spawn administrations designed to deliver services, provide protection, enforce regulations, and much more. These bureaucracies, in turn, may stifle democracy by replacing the will of the majority with rules, regulations, and procedures. Note, however, that these excesses can be corrected by the actions of democratic institutions (e.g., further legislation). The arrows merely indicate that democratic rule has certain counter-democratic consequences.

In an expansion of the comparative research on which this diagram is based, Lipset makes the following comment:

> Not long ago, the overwhelming majority of the members of the United Nations had authoritarian systems. As of the end of 1993, over half, 107 out of 186 countries, have competitive elections and various guarantees of political and individual rights—that is, more than twice the number two decades earlier in 1970. (1994, p. 1)

But Lipset, a veteran of many decades of close observation of democratic rule in nations throughout the world, is quite cautious about predicting a trend toward the emergence of democratic regimes. Too many nations, like Nigeria and Russia, have turned toward more authoritarian rule after promising attempts to develop democratic political institutions. Above all, Lipset warns:

> [If nations] can take the high road to economic development they can keep their political houses in order. The opposite is true as well. Governments that defy the elementary laws of supply and demand will fail to develop and will not institutionalize genuinely democratic systems. (1994, p. 1)

idea that they significantly affect the way a society is governed. Some social scientists find, for example, that political decisions are controlled by an elite of rich and powerful individuals. This "power elite" tolerates the formal organizations and procedures of democracy (elections, legislatures, courts, etc.) because it essentially owns them and can make sure that they act in its interests no matter what the outcome of elections may be. C. Wright Mills, the chief proponent of this point of view, has described the power elite as follows:

> The power elite is composed of men whose positions enable them to transcend the ordinary environments of ordinary men and women. They are in positions to make decisions having major consequences. . . . They are in command of the major hierarchies and organizations of modern society. They rule the big corporations. They run the machinery of the state. . . . They direct the military establishment. They occupy the strategic command posts of the social structure. . . .
>
> The power elite are not solitary rulers. . . . Immediately below the elite are the professional politicians of the middle levels of power, in the Congress and in the pressure groups, as well as among the new and old upper classes of town and city and regions. Mingling with them in curious ways . . . are those professional celebrities who live by being continually displayed. (1956, p. 4)

When it was first published, Mills's *The Power Elite* created a stir among sociologists. Mills challenged the assumption that societies that have democratic political institutions are in fact democratic. He asserted instead that

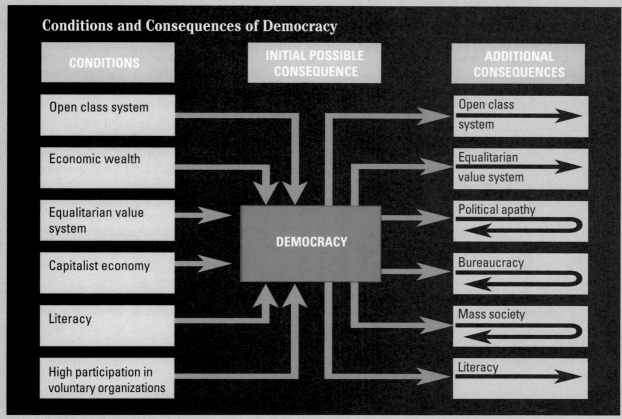

Conditions and Consequences of Democracy

Source: From *Political Man: The Social Bases of Politics,* by Seymour Martin Lipset (Baltimore: Johns Hopkins University Press, 1981, expanded and updated edition). Reprinted by permission of the author.

party politics and elections are little more than rituals. Power is exercised by a ruling elite of immensely powerful military, business, and political leaders that can put its members into positions of authority whenever it wishes to do so. Mills's claim was significant for another reason as well: Although Mills appreciated Marx's views on the role of class conflict in social change, he did not believe that the working class could win power without joining forces with the middle class. He therefore attempted to demonstrate the existence of a ruling elite to an educated public, which would then, he hoped, be able to see through the rituals of political life and make changes through legitimate means.

Other sociologists have questioned the power elite thesis on methodological grounds. For example, Talcott Parsons (1960) noted that the power elite was supposed to

act behind the scenes rather than publicly. Therefore its actions could not be observed, and the power elite thesis could not be either proved or disproved. The power elite thesis therefore was not scientifically sound, according to Parsons.

Numerous adherents of the power elite thesis have attempted to show that a ruling elite does indeed exist and that its activities can be observed. One of the best known of these researchers is Floyd Hunter (1953), whose classic studies of Atlanta's "community power structure" attempted to show that no more than 40 powerful men were considered to have the ability to make decisions on important issues facing the city and its people. Most of these men were conservative, cost-conscious business leaders. The Hunter study stimulated many attempts to find similar power structures in other cities and in the nation as a whole (Domhoff, 1978, 1983). But although the term *power structure* has found its way into the language of politics, these studies have been strongly criticized for basing their conclusions on what people say about who has power rather than on observations of what people with power actually do (Walton, 1970).

THE PLURALIST MODEL

The power elite thesis has not gone unchallenged. In another famous study of politics—this one in New Haven, Connecticut—Robert Dahl (1961) found that different individuals played key roles in different types of decisions. No single group was responsible for all of the decisions that might affect the city's future. No power elite ruled the city, Dahl argued. Instead, there were a number of elites that interacted in various ways on decisions that affected them. In situations in which the interests of numerous groups were involved, a plurality of decision makers engaged in a process of coalition building and bargaining.

The pluralist model calls attention to the activities of interest groups at all levels of society. Interest groups are not political parties; they are specialized organizations that attempt to influence elected and appointed officials on specific issues. These attempts range from lobbying—the process whereby interest groups seek to persuade legislators to vote in their favor on particular bills—to making contributions to parties and candidates who will support their goals. Trade unions seeking legislation that would limit imports, organizations for the handicapped seeking regulations that would give them access to public buildings, and ethnic groups seeking to influence U.S. policy toward their country of origin are among the many kinds of interest groups that are active in the United States today.

In recent decades, as the number of organized interest groups has grown, so has the complexity of the bargaining that takes place between them and the officials they want to influence. Social scientists who study politics from the pluralist perspective frequently wonder whether the activities of these groups threaten the ability of elected officials to govern effectively. Thus a study of a federal economic development project in Oakland, California, found that the personnel in the agency responsible for such projects had to learn to deal with supporting and opposing interest group leaders and elected officials throughout the life of the project. It took 6 years of constant negotiation on many unanticipated issues—affirmative action in employment, environmental concerns, design specifications—before a firm could win a contract to build an airplane hangar (Pressman & Wildavsky, 1984).

POLITICS AND SOCIAL INTERACTION

From the interactionist perspective, political institutions, like all others, are "socially constructed" in the course of human interaction. They do not simply come into being as structures of norms, statuses, and roles and then continue to function without change. Instead, they are continually being shaped and reshaped through interaction. This view closely parallels the popular notion that democratic political institutions must be continually challenged if they are to live up to their ideals. Otherwise they will become oligarchies that rule for the benefit of small cliques rather than for the mass of citizens.

The question of how social interaction affects a society's political institutions was a central concern of the leading philosophers of ancient Greece. In his *Politics,* for example, Aristotle "held that humans were made for life in society just as bees were made for life in the hive" (Bernard, 1973, p. 30). Because humans are "political animals," Aristotle believed, their constant discussions of political issues and their ability to form coalitions allow them to arrive at a consensus regarding what a good society is and how it should be governed. Unfortunately, he concluded, existing political systems were flawed. The divisions and gaps in interaction created by wealth prevented consensus and gave rise to conflict. Moreover, people in occupations like farming did not have enough time to examine all the sides of an issue and work toward agreement with their fellow citizens. In a good society, therefore, all the citizens must be free to devote their full attention to political affairs. (In practice, Greek democracy required an economy based on the labor of slaves.)

Nearly 2,000 years later the Italian political adviser Niccolò Machiavelli (1469–1527) again took up the relationship between human interaction and political institutions. Machiavelli believed that political institutions had to be based on the recognition that all human beings are capable of evil as well as good. In his *Discourses* he made this observation:

> All those who have written upon civil institutions demonstrate . . . that whosoever desires to found a state and give it laws, must start by assuming that all men are bad and ever ready to display their vicious nature, whenever they may find an occasion for it. (1950/1513, Vol. 1, p. 3)

Some people, he admitted, are merciful, faithful, humane, and sincere, but even though there are virtuous people in every society, political leaders must anticipate the worst possible behavior. In his most famous work, *The Prince,* Machiavelli suggested that the wise ruler or prince would be a master of astuteness—the ability to "read" the intentions of allies and opponents in the tiniest of gestures and reactions—and would also have mastered the skills of diplomacy. He used the following comparison to make this point:

> A prince . . . must imitate the fox and the lion, for the lion cannot protect himself from the traps, and the fox cannot defend himself from wolves. One must therefore be a fox to recognize traps, and a lion to frighten wolves. Those that wish to be only lions do not understand this. (1950/1513, Vol. 1, p. 66)

In the five centuries since they were originally formulated, these ideas have had a powerful influence on political thinkers. The authors of the U.S. Constitution, for example, attempted to avoid situations in which "foxes" or "lions" could take advantage of the weaknesses of others. They anticipated the more self-serving aspects of political interaction rather than simply assuming that a new society would bring about cooperation among citizens: "If men were angels, no government would be necessary" (*The Federalist,* No. 51). It is for this reason, as we noted earlier in the chapter, that they planned a government in which each of the major branches would be able to check any abuse of power by the other branches.

Political Interaction in the "Democratic Experiment." In the 1830s Alexis de Tocqueville, a young French aristocrat, visited the world's first experiment in national democracy. Although the United States was by no means a true democracy since it condoned slavery, indentured servants, and war against Native Americans, European social thinkers took a keen interest in the model of citizen rule through democratic institutions that was being established in the new nation. Tocqueville was stunned by the "tumult" of American political interactions, which "must be seen in order to be understood." In America, he wrote, political activity was in evidence everywhere:

> A confused clamor is heard on every side; and a thousand simultaneous voices demand the immediate satisfaction of their social wants. Everything is in motion around you; here, the people of one quarter of a town are met to decide upon the building of a church; there, the election of a representative is going on; a little further, the delegates of a district are traveling in a hurry to the town in order to consult upon some local improvements; or, in another place, the labourers of a village quit their plows to deliberate upon the project of a road or a public school. (1980/1835, p. 78)

Tocqueville expressed surprise at the fact that although they were denied the vote, in the United States "even the women frequently attend public meetings, and listen to political harangues as recreation after their household labours" (p. 79). In fact, the culture of America was so suffused with political issues that he believed Americans could not converse except to discuss issues. The typical American, he observed, "speaks to you as if he were addressing a meeting" (p. 79).

Tocqueville was concerned that democratic societies might encourage the rise of demagogues who could manipulate the masses. But his observations persuaded him that the immense number of competing groups in the American political system would prevent this from happening. And although he worried about the possibility of political conflict tearing the young nation apart, he became convinced that Americans' love of liberty and belief in the legitimacy of their political institutions would carry them through any crisis that might arise.

Political Communication Today. For those out of power as well as those in power, political communication and the ability to gain the attention of the mass media are major concerns. Sociologist Todd Gitlin (1980) reminds us how important this aspect of politics was to the student radicals who challenged U.S. policies in Vietnam in the 1960s and 1970s. They were only one among many social movements of that period that discovered the great power of television in a society with mass publics (see Chapter 8). Through skillful use of television coverage of staged confrontations, sit-ins, and demonstrations, it was possible for a relatively small group of activists to mobilize larger numbers of supporters. The labor movement had used similar tactics in earlier decades, but by the 1960s it had become easier to communicate to mass audiences and sway public opinion—at least in a society in which the press, including the television news, is relatively free from governmental interference.

In a world in which the techniques of communication are increasingly sophisticated, it becomes ever more important to analyze political communications and to read between the lines of political rhetoric. Often political jargon masks deeds that leaders would rather not admit to. George Orwell, a master of political commentary, made this point in his essay "Politics and the English Language," part of which is presented in Box 20.3.

MILITARY INSTITUTIONS

The problem of civilian control of the military remains the most important issue in many of the world's nation-states. At this writing, for example, Haiti is celebrating the first peaceful transition of leadership in its history. This transition, in which President Jean-Bertrand Aristide voluntarily gave up power by agreeing not to run for reelection, came after the United States and other nations assisted in overthrowing Haiti's military rulers, who had seized power in an illegal coup. Haiti is not an isolated example of the problem of social control over the military. Throughout the world the problem of how to maintain the allegiance of the military often looms as the largest threat to democracy and to the legitimacy of governments. These situations raise a major question in political sociology: How can states control their military institutions? Answers are to be found in knowledge about the nature of the modern military as a social institution as well as in the political culture of different nations.

A key question about military institutions in all societies, and especially in democracies, is how the military can be made to submit to the guidance of civilian political institutions. A democratic society cannot remain democratic for very long if the military usurps the authority granted to it by the civilian institutions of the nation-state. This is a

BOX 20.3 USING THE SOCIOLOGICAL IMAGINATION

Politics and the English Language

George Orwell, the author of *Animal Farm* and *1984*, addressed the abuse of language for political purposes in his essay "Politics and the English Language":

Political speech and writing are largely the defense of the indefensible. Things like the continuance of British rule in India, the Russian purges and deportations, the dropping of the atom bombs on Japan, can indeed be defended, but only by arguments which are too brutal for most people to face, and which do not square with the professed aims of political parties. Thus political language has to consist largely of euphemism, question-begging, and sheer cloudy vagueness. Defenseless villages are bombarded from the air, the inhabitants driven out into the countryside, the cattle machine-gunned, the huts set on fire with incendiary bullets: this is called *pacification.* Millions of peasants are robbed of their farms and sent trudging along the roads with no more than they can carry: this is called *transfer of population* or *rectification of frontiers.* People are imprisoned for years without trial, or shot in the back of the neck or sent to die of scurvy in Arctic lumber camps: this is called *elimination of unreliable elements.* Such phraseology is needed if one wants to name things without calling up mental pictures of them. Consider for instance some comfortable English professor defending Russian totalitarianism. He cannot say outright, "I believe in killing off your opponents when you can get good results by doing so." Probably, therefore, he will say something like this:

While freely conceding that the Soviet regime exhibits certain features which the humanitarian may be inclined to deplore, we must, I think, agree that a certain curtailment of the right to political opposition is an unavoidable concomitant of transitional periods, and that the rigours which the Russian people have been called upon to undergo have been amply justified in the sphere of concrete achievement. (p. 136)

If Orwell sounds highly pessimistic about the conduct of politics, remember that he was writing in a time of even greater political cruelty and chaos than our own. In his lifetime he had seen nations with the most advanced constitutions commit the most brutal acts of war and repression. The point of his essay is that to be politically objective, to seek the true meanings of political acts and the consequences of political beliefs, we must "start at the verbal end":

The great enemy of clear language is insincerity. When there is a gap between one's real and one's declared aims, one turns as it were instinctively to long words and exhausted idioms, like a cuttlefish squirting out ink. . . . If you simplify your English . . . when you make a stupid remark its stupidity will be obvious, even to yourself. Political language . . . is designed to make lies sound truthful and murder respectable, and to give an appearance of solidity to pure wind. One cannot change this all in a moment, but one can at least change one's own habits, and from time to time one can even, if one jeers loudly enough, send some worn-out and useless phrase . . . into the dustbin where it belongs. (p. 140)

common occurrence—taking the form of coups led by military "strongmen"—in nations in which the military is not adequately controlled by other institutions.

The problem of civilian control of the military was recognized by Alexis de Tocqueville, who noted that in aristocratic nations the military could be controlled by the government because the military leaders were aristocrats and therefore were part of the court. "The officer is noble, the soldier is a serf," Tocqueville observed. "The one is naturally called upon to command, the other to obey" (1980/1835, p. 128). Tocqueville formed the hypothesis that greater equality would make a nation less likely to go to war, since its citizens would have more to lose in wars and more power to prevent them. Yet he also feared the ambitions of military leaders in democratic nations. "In democratic armies," he wrote, "all the soldiers may become officers, which . . . immeasurably extends the bounds of military ambition" (p. 129).

Morris Janowitz (1960) responded to Tocqueville's concerns in his analysis of the history of military institutions in democratic nations. He argued that the military has often played a crucial role in establishing and protecting democratic institutions. In the Greek city-states and the Roman republic, as well as the democracies that emerged from the revolutions of the late eighteenth century, citizens were obligated to serve in the armed forces. The military institution could function only through the enlistment of "citizen soldiers." Because the citizen soldier was committed to democratic institutions and was serving because such service was a requirement of citizenship, the military would be unlikely to take over the functions of democratic political institutions. Soldiers would presumably place the values of their society above the demands of the military.

When Janowitz reviewed the impact of new methods of warfare on the military, he concluded that because of the

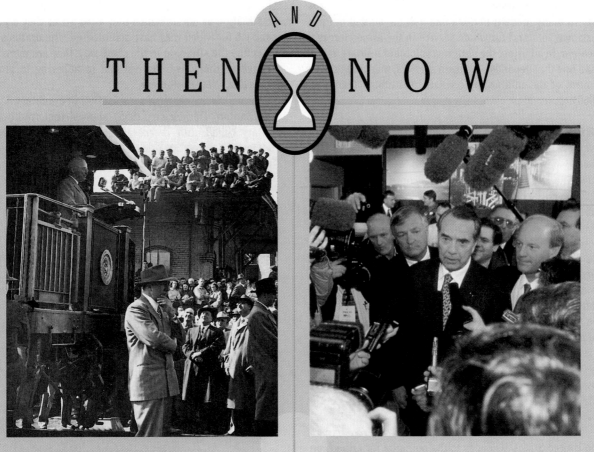

THEN AND NOW

TELEVISION RESHAPES THE CAMPAIGN TRAIL

In 1948 Harry Truman campaigned across the United States, making speeches from a special car at the back of a train. This was one of the last "whistle stop" campaigns in American presidential politics. The older style of campaign, in which the candidate attempted to meet as many voters as possible, was accompanied by a great deal of "back room" politics—the candidate met with local political leaders, who bargained for favors in return for bringing out their supporters on election day. These dealings, of course, were not visible to the people who gathered at the "whistle stops."

Today the power of television brings the candidate and the campaign message into the homes of millions of voters, diminishing the importance of town-by-town campaigning. But television demands camera skills that many politicians do not necessarily possess. Television has also vastly increased the importance of fundraising to pay the high costs of television advertising. The influence of local political party leaders has declined, but "back room" politics and the influence of wealthy and powerful contributors have yet to disappear.

increasing sophistication of military technology, the military in many modern nations had become staffed by "professional soldiers" for whom service in the armed forces is a career. In addition, the shift to a volunteer military, rather than one that depends on citizen soldiers, may threaten the control of the military by civilian institutions (Janowitz, 1960).

THE ECONOMIC ROLE OF THE MILITARY

Even in the United States, where the threat of military coups is not considered great, the military has so much influence on the economy that social control of the military becomes difficult. The function of the military is, of course, the defense of the nation-state. However, in the United States the military also serves an important economic function as a producer of jobs and revenue. The economies of states like Alaska, Connecticut, Maryland, California, and Virginia became highly dependent on the wealth gained from defense contracts during the decades of the cold war and the arms race. In addition, the private companies that vie for military contracts became a major source of employment, often providing some of the most highly paid and secure jobs in their regions. Throughout the United States the influence of the military "pork barrel"—federal spending on defense contracts and the resulting employment—often makes it difficult for legislators to support cuts in military budgets and programs.

The growth of military production in different parts of the United States also adds to the potential for armed conflict elsewhere in the world. Faced with declining domestic sales, U.S. arms makers seek to supply advanced weapons to buyers in other nations. Indeed, weapons account for a significant portion of U.S. exports.

MILITARY SOCIALIZATION

Social control of the military is partially explained by the professional socialization of military personnel. This point was vividly illustrated by Tom Wolfe in *The Right Stuff* (1980). "There were many pilots in their thirties," Wolfe wrote, "who to the consternation of their wives, children, mothers, fathers, and employers, volunteered to go active in the reserves and fly in combat in the Korean War." This was in vivid contrast to the attitude of the foot soldiers in that war, whose morale during some periods of the prolonged conflict "was so bad it actually reached the point where officers were prodding men forward with gun barrels and bayonets" (p. 32).

This contrast between the "fighter jocks," socialized to want to prove they had "the right stuff" and thus win promotion to higher ranks, and the far more cautious draftees and recruits on the ground, raises a series of questions: What motivates a person to face death in war? Is it desire for glory and advancement? Is it fear of punishment? Is it the pressure of collective action? From an interactionist perspective, this contrast results from the ways in which people are socialized in military institutions, coupled with

their definitions of the situation. The fighter jocks define the situation as one in which they *must* act as they do—it is the job for which they have volunteered. The draftees do not define the situation in the same way; they are more interested in their own survival and in adhering to group norms like "Never volunteer."

In his classic study of socialization in a military academy, Sanford Dornbusch (1955) showed that traditional military socialization processes are designed to develop a high level of motivation and commitment to the institution. Those processes include the following:

- *Suppression of previous statuses.* Through haircuts, uniforms, and the like, the recruit is deprived of visible clues to his or her previous social status.
- *Learning of new norms and rules.* At the official level, the recruit is taught obedience to the rules of the military; through informal socialization, he or she is taught the culture of the military institution.
- *Development of solidarity.* Both informal socialization and harsh discipline build solidarity and lasting friendships among recruits; they learn to depend on one another.
- *The bureaucratic spirit.* The recruit is taught unquestioning acceptance of tradition and custom; orders are taken and given from morning to night.

The controversy that greeted President Bill Clinton's order that the military cease discriminating against homosexuals is an indication of the sensitivity that surrounds issues of military socialization. Gay men and women have been serving in the armed forces for decades but have had to deny their sexual preferences in military exams and screening procedures. Objections to openly admitting homosexuals into the military centered on the possibility that gay sexuality would be a divisive influence and a detriment to fighting morale. Gay activists in and outside the military answered that there is no reason why the norms of military conduct would not apply to openly gay soldiers just as they always have to gay and nongay military personnel.

Despite his personal opposition to the president's order, General Colin L. Powell, then chairman of the Joint Chiefs of Staff, stated that "we know that there will be changes and . . . you and the Commander in Chief [the President] can always count on us for faithful support and execution of your decisions" (quoted in Schmitt, 1993, p. A1). General Powell was referring not only to the issue of acceptance of homosexuals in the military but also to the issue of cuts in military budgets. His statement is indicative of the control the constitutional rule of law provides over the powerful institution of the military.

SOCIAL CHANGE AND MILITARY INSTITUTIONS

Like all major social institutions, the military has undergone many changes, some of which can be seen in the

As minorities in the U.S. Army's officer training program, women face special hardships. This makes them doubly proud of their achievements, as can be seen in this West Point graduation scene.

transformation of American military institutions in the past two centuries. In the era of the citizen soldier, people expected to be called into service only in emergency situations and to be trained by a small cadre of professional officers. Today, in contrast, the permanent armed forces have more than 1.8 million uniformed members, and the annual military budget amounts to more than $230 billion (Schmitt, 1993).

Today the requirements of highly technological forms of warfare and the need to maintain a complex set of military organizations throughout the world have changed our concept of a military career. The military as a modern social institution requires professionally trained officers who commit themselves to spending much of their working lives in the military. Thus, as the military has evolved, so has its need to recruit and train career officers in specialized military academies.

Over time, the institutions that train professional soldiers have had to adapt to certain changes. For example, as the larger society has accepted the demand for gender equality and women have gained access to occupations that were previously reserved for men, the military has had to redefine its historical perception that women soldiers are better equipped for desk duty than for service in combat. Although to date few women have fought in ground warfare, women in the military are now being trained for combat roles. The idea of women engaging in combat remains controversial, however, as is illustrated by the conflict that arose when a female military officer was suspected of having fought in Panama in 1989.

ELECTIONS

Few political institutions are more important than free, contested elections. But how difficult it is to protect this vital institution! We need only think of the Philippines, where for more than 20 years, until the victory of Corazón Aquino in 1986, the regime led by Ferdinand Marcos was able to manipulate elections in order to control state power. Nor is the right of citizens to participate in elections ever fully guaranteed; rather, it must be protected by laws and by the vigilance of an educated citizenry.

Images of our own political campaigns and elections serve to remind us that the right to vote has had to be won by certain groups in the course of American history. Here we see women and blacks voting for the first time after long struggles to win this fundamental right of citizenship.

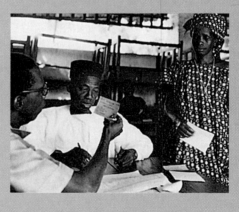

The existence of elections is not in itself a measure of democracy. There must also be a contest, and it must make a difference who wins. In China, national elections are considered important events, and most people vote. But these elections are usually mere rituals in which citizens are expected to vote for a single slate of candidates and thus affirm their support of the government. Access to state authority is not changed by the election itself.

Wherever there are single-party states, elections are usually either uncontested or rigged. Latin American states are often characterized by such elections, in which citizens are eager to vote yet have little hope that the outcome will change their lives. Even so, the existence of elections holds out the promise that a time may come when an election will be free from coercion and the outcome will make a difference in how the state is governed. But for this to happen there must be other institutions too, such as an independent legal system that protects the rights of citizens who support opposition candidates. And the elections themselves must be protected so that ballots are secret and are counted fairly. Although these conditions are extremely difficult to establish, we have seen time and again that given an opportunity, people will press for a free, competitive electoral system.

At least in the United States, the military tends to be rather responsive to civilian demands. Yet cuts in military budgets as a result of the end of the cold war will offer the U.S. military one of its greatest challenges since the end of World War II: how to remain an effective fighting force, adapted to new forms of conflict (e.g., antiterrorism, small wars, and peacekeeping interventions) while it is scaled down in an era of increasing demand for reductions in military spending.

RESEARCH FRONTIERS: TRENDS IN POLITICAL PARTICIPATION

Results from the annual Gallup survey of American college students reveal that a record low of 28.8 percent believe it is important to stay informed about political events (Gallup, 1996). This is a disturbing statistic because it helps explain why so few American citizens are exercising their right to vote in key elections. What theories do sociologists propose to explain Americans' disaffection with politics?

Veteran political analyst E. J. Dionne, Jr., asserts in his book, *Why Americans Hate Politics* (1991), that the constant political warfare between liberals and conservatives has discouraged many Americans from participating in politics. "Americans believe in social concern and self-reliance," Dionne observes. "They want to match rights and obligations; they think public moral standards should exist but are skeptical of too much meddling in the private affairs of others" (p. 14). But the standoff between liberals and conservatives that developed during the late 1980s caused a governmental "gridlock" that impeded progress on vital fronts like health care, welfare reform, and economic policy. Many Americans became disillusioned with the political process, and voter turnout declined.

According to Dionne, the liberals went off course "because so many voters in the middle stopped believing that government programs were operating in their interests. Indeed, they stopped believing that government could work at all." The conservatives, for their part, paid homage to the values of family, stability, and hard work that the liberals seemed to neglect. However, Dionne notes that the reality was quite different from the ideal:

> By allowing the standard of living of so many Americans in the middle to deteriorate, partly through regressive tax politics, the Reagan and Bush administrations and the culture they promoted have sent exactly the opposite message. For the last decade we have given honor of place not to those who labored daily for wages and salaries or who built businesses through long-term, painstaking effort, but to those who reached instant wealth, instant fame, and instant luxury.

Faced with these unappealing alternatives, "the American electorate has uneasily split the difference, looking to Republicans to set broad policy in the White House and to Democrats in Congress for protection against Republican excess" (p. 345).

Suppose Dionne had written his book after the 1994 congressional elections. He might have concluded that his thesis about "splitting the difference" continues to hold, but with a new configuration. President Clinton's 1992 election victory seemed to promise an end to the impasse between Republicans and Democrats, but the Democrats' control of government was to be short-lived. The Republican sweep of the 1994 congressional elections gave the party strong majorities in the Senate and the House of Representatives. As a result, during the second half of the Clinton administration the impasse between Republicans and Democrats resumed, with increasing rancor and conflict over the federal budget and the closure of the government for weeks at a time in 1995 and 1996.

Social scientists note that it is difficult to view the stunning Republican takeover of Congress in 1994 as a fundamental shift in U.S. politics because so few citizens actually voted (Mollenkopf, 1995). Only about one third of eligible voters went to the polls in this momentous election. In this context, the recent Gallup Poll results are not surprising even if they are alarming.

As we saw earlier in the chapter, the legitimacy of democratic political institutions depends on citizen participation. If voters are alienated from political institutions and do not believe government acts in their interests, the consequences can be devastating. Political alienation results in apathy and the feeling that no political action matters (Putnam, 1995). It results in resentment of government and a weakening of the rule of law. Catastrophic violence like the Oklahoma City bombing may be a symptom of a growing crisis in political legitimacy.

Another aspect of the trend toward political alienation is the decline in membership in political parties, as indicated by the number of people who do not affiliate with either political party. Clearly, there will have to be a renewal of interest in political participation among young people, but at this writing it is not clear what can be done to reverse the trend toward alienation and apathy. Studies of political participation therefore will remain an active frontier of sociological research in coming years.

SUMMARY

THINK ABOUT IT CRITICALLY

Does politics make a difference? Many people think that politics is a sham. The powerless are always exploited and the powerful come out ahead. Therefore it is not worth the trouble to vote or to participate in other ways.

Politics determines "who gets what, when, and how." The basis of politics is competition for *power,* or the ability to control the behavior of others, even against their will. *Authority* is institutionalized power, or power whose exercise is governed by the norms and statuses of organizations. Sets of norms and statuses that specialize in the exercise of power and authority are *political institutions,* and the set of political institutions that operate in a particular society forms the *state.*

Although a state can exercise its power through the use of force, eventually this will not be enough to govern a society. When people consent to be governed without the use of force, the state is said to be legitimate. *Legitimacy* is a society's ability to engender and maintain the belief that the existing political institutions are the most appropriate for that society. It is the basis of a society's political culture—the cultural norms, values, and symbols that support and justify its political institutions. According to Max Weber, the political cultures of different societies give rise to three different types of authority: *traditional, charismatic,* and *legal.* Perhaps the strongest and most dangerous political force in the world today is *nationalism,* the belief of a people that they have the right and the duty to constitute themselves as a nation-state.

The most important political territory in world affairs is the *nation-state,* the largest territory within which a society's political institutions can operate without having to face challenges to their sovereignty. The borders that mark off one nation-state from others do not always correspond to what people believe to be the rightful boundaries of their societies. Conflicts over the borders of states and societies have been a fact of political life throughout human history.

Citizenship is the status of membership in a nation-state. The rights of citizenship include civil rights (e.g., freedom of speech, thought, and faith), political rights (e.g., the right to vote), and social rights (e.g., the right to a certain level of economic welfare and security). The question of who is entitled to full participation in politics is a key issue at the local level as well as at the national level.

Modern nations are governed by elected and appointed officials whose authority is defined by laws. In order to prevent abuses of authority, modern political institutions usually specify some form of separation of powers in which abuses by one institution can be remedied by others. *Political parties* are organizations of people who join together in order to gain legitimate control of state authority. Parties that accept the rule of other legitimate parties form a "loyal opposition" that monitors the actions of the ruling party and prevents the emergence of *oligarchy,* or rule by a few people who stay in office indefinitely. Regimes that accept no limits to their power and seek to exert their rule at all levels of society are known as *totalitarian regimes.*

Democracy means rule by the nation's citizens: Citizens have the right to participate in public decision making, and those who govern do so with the explicit consent of the governed. In the British parliamentary system, elections are held in which the party that wins a majority of the seats in the legislature "forms a government": The leader of the party becomes the head of government and appoints other party members to major offices. In the American representative system, the party whose candidate is elected President need not have a majority of the seats in the legislature. In nations or regions in which a single party is dominant, oligarchical political systems are more likely to develop.

Functionalist theorists assert that certain "structural prerequisites" must exist in a society for democratic political institutions to develop and operate. Among these are high levels of economic development, urbanization, and literacy, as well as a culture that tolerates dissent. The *power elite model* holds that the presence of democratic institutions does not mean that a society is democratic; political decisions are actually controlled by an elite of rich and powerful individuals. This view is challenged by the *pluralist model,* which holds that political decisions are influenced by a variety of *interest groups* through a process of coalition building and bargaining.

Many political thinkers have been concerned with the relationship between social interaction and political institutions. Among the most influential was Machiavelli, who argued that political institutions must be based on the recognition that human beings are capable of evil as well as good. This recognition played a major part in the planning of the government of the United States, in which each branch of the government is able to check abuses of power by the other branches.

In modern nation-states political communication is a major concern for those out of power as well as those in power. Analyzing political communications and reading between the lines of political rhetoric is very important. This is particularly true in societies characterized by mass publics and sophisticated communication techniques.

A major question in political sociology is how states can control their military institutions. A society cannot remain democratic very long if the military usurps the authority granted to it by civilian institutions. One factor that contributes to this problem is the fact that the military is staffed by professional soldiers for whom service in the armed forces is a career. Another factor is the immense influence of the military on the economy. On the other hand, military socialization instills norms and values that may contribute to social control of the military.

CRITICAL RESPONSE

This criticism of politics is not without some basis. It is true that people without power tend not to gain very much, no matter who wins an election. But there is another way of looking at the issue. Politics is a long-term struggle for victories that are never complete. Is the health care system improving? Is there any improvement in the welfare system, in public education, in environmental protection? The answers to such questions suggest that politics makes some difference after all.

GLOSSARY

power: the ability to control the behavior of others, even against their will. (p. 604)

authority: power whose exercise is governed by the norms and statuses of organizations. (p. 604)

political institution: a set of norms and statuses pertaining to the exercise of power and authority. (p. 604)

state: the set of political institutions operating in a particular society. (p. 604)

legitimacy: the ability of a society to engender and maintain the belief that the existing political institutions are the most appropriate for that society. (p. 605)

traditional authority: authority that is hereditary and is legitimated by traditional values, particularly people's idea of the sacred. (p. 605)

charismatic authority: authority that comes to an individual through a personal calling, often claimed to be inspired by supernatural powers, and is legitimated by people's belief that the leader does indeed have God-given powers. (p. 606)

legal authority: authority that is legitimated by people's belief in the supremacy of the law; obedience is owed not to a person but to a set of impersonal principles. (p. 606)

nationalism: the belief of a people that they have the right and the duty to constitute themselves as a nation-state. (p. 608)

nation-state: the largest territory within which a society's political institutions can operate without having to face challenges to their sovereignty. (p. 609)

citizenship: the status of membership in a nation-state. (p. 610)

demagogue: a leader who uses personal charisma and political symbols to manipulate public opinion. (p. 614)

political party: an organization of people who join together to gain legitimate control of state authority. (p. 614)

oligarchy: rule by a few people who stay in office indefinitely rather than for limited terms. (p. 614)

totalitarian regime: a regime that accepts no limits to its power and seeks to exert its rule at all levels of society. (p. 615)

democracy: a political system in which all citizens have the right to participate in public decision making. (p. 615)

patronage: jobs and economic benefits that party leaders can exchange for votes and political influence. (p. 616)

power elite model: a theory stating that political decisions are controlled by an elite of rich and powerful individuals even in societies with democratic political institutions. (p. 616)

pluralist model: a theory stating that no single group controls political decisions; instead, a plurality of interest groups influence those decisions through a process of coalition building and bargaining. (p. 616)

interest group: an organization that attempts to influence elected and appointed officials regarding a specific issue or set of issues. (p. 620)

lobbying: the process whereby interest groups seek to persuade legislators to vote in their favor on particular bills. (p. 620)

BOOKS

"Politics as a Vocation," in *From Max Weber* (Hans Gerth & C. W. Mills, eds.; Oxford University Press, 1946). A fascinating sociological statement about what it takes to live the life of a professional politician and what kinds of people and professions are best suited to that life.

Politics: Who Gets What, When and How (Harold Lasswell; McGraw-Hill, 1936). Another classic treatment of the meaning of politics and political life. Contains some exceptional insights into political interaction and the personalities of politicians.

Political Behavior of the American Electorate, 8th ed. (William Flanigan & Nancy H. Zingale; Congressional Record Press, 1994). A thorough analysis of changing patterns of election turnout and voting among Americans.

Politics Against Markets (Gosta Esping-Anderson; Princeton University Press, 1985). Describes the politics of welfare states and the emergence of social-democratic institutions that place limits on the capitalist economies of the Scandinavian nations.

Political Man (Seymour Martin Lipset; Johns Hopkins University Press, 1981). A revision of a classic of political sociology. Traces the rise of democratic political institutions to other changes in a nation's stratification system and economic institutions.

Continental Divide: The Values and Institutions of the United States and Canada (Seymour Martin Lipset; Canadian-American Committee, 1989). Lipset is the dean of American political sociologists. In this empirical study comparing the United States and Canada, he shows why Canada has had more success in adapting its political institutions to address social problems.

Shooting an Elephant and Other Essays (George Orwell; Harcourt Brace Jovanovich, 1950). A collection of Orwell's essays; includes "Politics and the English Language" and his writing on colonialism and class politics.

JOURNALS

Political Science Quarterly. A leading journal in the field of political science. Publishes good articles on voting behavior and change in political institutions.

Public Opinion Quarterly. A journal of public opinion studies. Often presents recent research on how Americans and other publics view recent political and economic events.

OTHER SOURCES

World Almanac and Book of Facts. Published annually by Funk & Wagnalls, Mahwah, NJ.

America Votes. Published biennially by the Elections Research Center, Washington, DC. Presents data on both federal and state elections.

Statistics of the Presidential and Congressional Election. Official statistics on federal elections, collected by the clerk of the House and published annually.

CHAPTER 21

Science, Technology, and Medicine

In January 1996 Jeff Getty walked out of the San Francisco hospital where he had been under treatment for AIDS. It took some seconds for his eyes to adjust to the glare of a score of television spotlights, accompanied by dozens of press photographers and journalists. They were there because Getty was the first person to receive an innovative and risky bone marrow transplant to fight the destruction of his body's immune system by the AIDS virus. What made the bone marrow transplant especially noteworthy was that the transplanted tissue came from a baboon. Not only was the medical procedure experimental, but the fact that the donor was not a human being made its success highly problematic. Doctors used every available technique to prevent Getty's body from rejecting the transplant, and for a few days it was not clear what the results would be.

As he gathered strength after the operation, Getty also regained his courage and sense of humor. On leaving the hospital he quipped to reporters that he felt great and had not yet felt an intense craving for bananas.

Xenotransplants, as the cross-species operation is called, are widely hailed as a possible triumph of medical technology (Altman, 1996). But this episode also highlights a central problem of new medical technologies. As they are developed, and especially in their early phases, they are extremely costly—but if they can save lives they are much sought after. How to allocate these scarce but potentially lifesaving scientific and technological innovations is one of the key social issues in health care today.

Michael Donaldson, another AIDS patient, has had a very different experience in his battle against the disease. The new system of managed health care in his state obliged him to join a health maintenance organization (HMO) if he wanted his medical insurance to cover the cost of his treatment. But the HMO had only limited experience with AIDS patients. Its rules required that Donaldson first see a general practice doctor rather than an AIDS specialist, no matter what his symptoms were. This resulted in long delays in obtaining needed treatment, as he was first prescribed drugs that were less effective than those that would have been prescribed by a doctor with more direct experience with AIDS patients.

Many HMOs were originally set up to provide medical services to healthy populations. Often they have not modified their practices to accommodate patients with chronic and deadly diseases like AIDS. Cost is also a major factor. The average annual allocation per healthy patient in an HMO is less than $2,000, but the cost of treatment for a patient in advanced stages of AIDS can exceed $50,000, and many HMOs do not have the funds to deal with these costs (Rosenthal, 1996).

From a broader sociological viewpoint, the challenge AIDS presents to HMOs is about coping with social change. The AIDS epidemic has stimulated a host of new medical technologies, many of them quite expensive, whose application requires highly paid experts. But the social systems that organize and deliver health care—the HMOs in this case—need to modify their organizations and funding systems to make the new technologies available in a fair manner. Dramatic innovations like xenotransplants continually create major challenges for the social organizations that develop and disseminate them; even less dramatic technologies, such as those required to treat patients like Donaldson, raise a great many sociological issues, as we will see in this chapter.

THE NATURE OF SCIENCE AND TECHNOLOGY

Just as the atom bomb did for previous generations, the AIDS epidemic has revealed some of the problems of science and technology to a broad public. On the one hand, there have been new developments in treatment, such as new drugs and innovative methods of diagnosis. On the other hand, the public's faith in the ability of science to solve major social problems has been shaken as medical researchers have been unable to develop a vaccine or otherwise prevent the disease's lethal course. Social approaches to prevention, such as "safe sex" campaigns, have become key strategies while an anxious world continues to hope for scientific breakthroughs.

Our optimism about science and technology is frustrated not only by the AIDS virus but by many other consequences of technological change. Depletion of the ozone layer in the atmosphere, air and water pollution, controversies over disposal of radioactive wastes, global warming, unemployment due to technological change—these and many other problems result from our dependence on modern technologies and the scientific research that develops them. But if technologies are a source of negative change and global problems, they are also the basis of much of our material well-being. For better and, too often, for worse, science and technology are among the most powerful forces for social change in our world. In this chapter, therefore, we explore the ways in which science and technologies develop and are controlled and how they can be used to meet the challenges of our future existence on the earth.

Science is a major institutional sector of modern societies: A hallmark of the modern social order is the conduct of scientific research in universities and other research organizations. And as we saw in Chapter 19, the control of information, especially scientific and technical information, is a source of prestige and power in post-industrial societies. The study of science and technology is therefore an increasingly important sociological specialty.

Science is, essentially, knowledge. (The Latin word *scientia*, from which *science* is derived, means "knowledge.") But science is a particular kind of knowledge, knowledge that has been obtained through the scientific method (see Chapter 2)—that is, as a result of the process of developing and testing hypotheses. Even so, science encompasses an extremely diverse array of subjects—"from subatomic reactions to mental processes; from mathematical laws of thermodynamics to the economics of race relations; from the births and deaths of stars to the migration of birds; from the study of ultramicroscopic viruses to that of extragalactic nebulas; from the rise and dissolution of cultures and crystals to the rise and dissolution of atoms and universes" (*Encyclopaedia Britannica,* 1967, Vol. 20, p. 7). These diverse topics are grouped together under the label "Science" because they all involve systematic and repeated observations.

Science is customarily divided into "pure" and "applied" branches. *Pure science* is scientific investigation that is devoted exclusively to the pursuit of knowledge for its own sake, with no immediate concern for using that knowledge to solve practical problems. For example, for more than 30 years Barbara McClintock did genetics research on corn plants, which had no immediate application to agricultural technology but eventually was recognized as having applications in molecular biology. *Applied science,* in contrast, is the application of known scientific principles to a practical problem; the outcome in many cases is new technologies. And those technologies can have a tremendous impact on the quality of human life.

We saw in Chapter 3 that **technology** is an aspect of culture. It can be defined as the use of tools and knowledge to manipulate the physical environment in order to achieve desired practical goals. Although modern technologies are often based on scientific discoveries, technology is much older than science; it has its roots in the tool-making and fire-building skills of the earliest human groups. People have always needed to find better ways of doing things or ways of making their lives more comfortable. Technological innovations have met those needs for thousands of years. In fact, technological change proceeded without the benefit of scientific knowledge for the bulk of human history. Science as we know it today is a relatively recent development. Although its origins may be traced to the mathematicians and philosophers of the ancient world, its emergence as a separate sphere of knowledge, with its own norms and values, dates from the late sixteenth century. From that time on, science "mathematicized and mechanized nature, tested and experimented on nature, pushed and pressed far beyond what nature spontaneously had ever revealed; and . . . not only mastered, but also learned to transform, nature" (Cohen, 1982, p. 62).

Accelerated by the discoveries of modern science, technology rapidly expanded the human capacity to live in and exploit different habitats. Indeed, in the past two centuries it has changed the face of the earth (Gutkind, 1956). Airports, skyscrapers, housing developments, oil refineries, superhighways, the Panama Canal, the rocket launching pad at Cape Canaveral are all products of technology that have transformed the surroundings in which human be-

BOX 21.1   USING THE SOCIOLOGICAL IMAGINATION

The Gaia Hypothesis

The late Lewis Thomas, a writer and research physician and former chancellor of Memorial Sloan-Kettering Cancer Center, provided these speculations about the relationship between human beings and the earth:

> The notion that life on Earth resembles, in detail, the sort of coherent, connected life we attribute to an organism is now something more than a notion. Thanks in large part to the studies begun in the 1970s by James Lovelock, Lynn Margulis, and their associates, we now know that planetary life, the "biosphere," regulates itself.
>
> It maintains in precision the salinity and acid-base balance of its oceans, holds constant over millions of years the exactly equilibrated components of its atmosphere with the levels of oxygen and carbon dioxide at just the optimal levels for respiration and photosynthesis. It lives off the sun, taking in the energy it requires for its life and reflecting away the rest into the unfillable sink of space. This is the "Gaia hypothesis," the new idea that the Earth itself is alive.
>
> The one biological function the Earth does not yet perform to qualify for the formal definition of an organism is reproduction. But wait around, and keep an eye on it. In real life, this may turn out to be what it started to do twenty years ago [on the occasion of the first moon walk].
>
> Given enough time, and given our long survival as working parts of the great creature (a chancy assumption for the moment), the Earth may be entering the first stages of replication, scattering seeds of itself, perhaps in the form of microorganisms similar to those dominating the planet's own first life for the first two billion years of its Precambrian period. Atmospheres similar to ours may emerge over planets or moons now uninhabitable somewhere in our solar system, and then, with enough time and luck, out in the galaxy, even beyond.
>
> So the first moon walk brought forth two new possibilities of viewing ourselves and our home. First, the Gaia idea of a living Earth, not at all the mystical notion that it would have seemed a few years back (but still carrying the same idea of "oneness" that has long preoccupied the mystics among us), is now becoming the most practical, down-to-earth thought ever thought. And second is the idea of the Earth reproducing itself, and the possible role we might be playing, consciously or unconsciously, in the huge process.
>
> Finally, as something to think about, there is the strangest of all paradoxes: the notion that an organism so immense and complex, with so many interconnected and communicating central nervous systems at work, from crickets and fireflies to philosophers, should be itself mindless. I cannot believe it. (1989, p. 25)

ings live and work. It is this interrelationship between science and technology that is responsible for the breathtaking speed of technological change in our century. (Box 21.1 introduces the Gaia hypothesis, the idea that humans and their cultures and technologies are also part of the living earth and must act accordingly.)

The benefits of technological change are not always distributed equally. Quite often, in fact, technologies allow people in wealthier nations to produce substances that formerly could be obtained only from the poor nations. For example, sugar beets grown in Europe and the United States are replacing the sugar cane produced in tropical nations as a source of sugar. At the same time, new technologies designed to increase crop yields—the fertilizers and pesticides that created the so-called "green revolution" in parts of Asia—appear to be adding excessive amounts of pollution to the environment, thereby creating huge costs for future generations. These problems of technology and industrial side effects have led many social scientists and environmental activists to call for **sustainable development,** or development that does not damage the environment or create new environmental burdens (World Commission on Environment and Development, cited in Keyfitz, 1991). Sustainable development leads to economic and social growth without compromising the ability of future generations to meet their needs.

Because technology has had such an enormous impact on modern life, we devote a large portion of this chapter to the ways in which new technologies arise, how they affect social life, and how they lead to social change. As an especially revealing example of how technological change can shape the values and institutions of a society, we will examine the evolution and social impact of medical technology. But first we need to explore the nature of scientific institutions, since they generate the knowledge on which much technological change is based.

These two photos, one of an ancient irrigation system in Iran (c. A.D. 900) and one of the Grand Coulee Dam on the Colorado River, show the impact of human technology on the earth's surface. Today, there are few parts of the globe that do not bear the traces and scars of human technology.

SCIENTIFIC INSTITUTIONS: THE SOCIOLOGICAL VIEW

THE SOCIOLOGY OF SCIENCE

Sociologists who study scientific institutions generally follow one of two basic approaches, described as *interactionist* and *institutional* (Ben-David, 1984). Those who use the interactionist approach observe how scientists interact among themselves—for example, how they divide and coordinate work in laboratories and how they approach scientific problems. Those who use the institutional approach study the role of the scientist in different countries, the structure of scientific organizations, and the culture of scientific institutions (i.e., the norms and values of science). This distinction is not total, however; there is a great deal of overlap between the two approaches.

The Interactionist Approach. Studies using the interactionist approach have focused on the scientific community—that is, on "the network of communication and social relationships between scientists working in given fields or in all fields" (Ben-David, 1984, p. 3). The questions asked by sociologists who take this approach pertain to how scientists go about the daily work of research and why scientific "revolutions" sometimes occur. In a well-known study titled *The Structure of Scientific Revolutions,* Thomas Kuhn (1962) explored the nature of the scientific community. He found that the rules of the scientific method are not adequate to describe what scientists do. Rather than spending their time testing and refuting existing hypotheses in order to establish new, more valid ones, they often take it for granted that existing theories are valid and use them in their efforts to solve specific problems. In other words, the researcher uses existing theories and methods as a **paradigm,** or model, to guide future research.

This view of the scientific community (or, rather, communities of specialized researchers) implies that science is insulated from the rest of society. Scientists are guided by the tradition of research in their field, which is passed along from one generation of scientists to the next. The problems they choose to solve are determined by that tradition, as are the methods they use in trying to solve them. This process continues, according to Kuhn, until the paradigm is no longer useful—that is, until enough members of the scientific community believe a particular set of observations can no longer be explained by existing theories and procedures. Then the community becomes more open to outside influences. Its members explore a variety of ideas not directly related to the dominant paradigm in their field, ideas that in some cases lead to a scientific revolution. When this occurs, the old paradigm is set aside in favor of a new one that will henceforth guide the work of the members of a particular scientific community. Some of the most famous scientific revolutions have occurred in physics— for example, in the shift from Newtonian physics to Einstein's theory of relativity and quantum theory and most recently in the discovery of the existence of subatomic particles.

The Institutional Approach. The institutional approach to the study of science does not contradict the interactionist view. Instead, it asks why science develops differently in different societies, and with what consequences. In this approach, certain conditions encourage the development of scientific institutions. Those conditions include the recognition of empirical research as a legitimate way of gaining new knowledge. In addition, science must be independent from other fields, such as theology or philosophy. Under such conditions separate institutions devoted to scientific research, such as graduate schools and

institutes of technology, can develop. This has been the case in the United States, where the introduction of graduate training in the sciences, together with research related to professional training (as occurs, for example, in medical schools) led to the establishment of fully equipped research institutes at major colleges and universities. One effect of the presence of such institutes is a large proportion of Americans among the winners of Nobel Prizes in the sciences (see Table 21.1).

The institutionalization of science in the United States has had dramatic and far-reaching effects: "In agriculture, education, sociology, and eventually in nuclear research the universities pioneered research on a scale that far exceeded the needs of training students and was, from the very outset, an operation distinct from teaching" (Ben-David, 1984, p. 146). Attempts have been made to establish similar research organizations in Europe, but these were hampered by the rigid structure of European universities. European universities have a closed system of professorships that cannot accommodate scientists who want to conduct research. A number of specialized research institutes have been established outside the universities, but none is as extensive or as influential as the research institutes associated with American universities.

In the 1950s, during the cold war, there was widespread recognition that the United States needed to improve its scientific research capacity. As a result, government and universities began cooperating even more closely than they had before. As Daniel Bell (1973) has pointed out, the rush to invest in scientific research had some important consequences:

> [It produced] the expansion of the universities as research institutions, the creation of large scientific laboratories at universities supported by government (the jet propulsion lab at Cal Tech, the Argonne atomic lab at the University of

TABLE 21.1	Nationality of Nobel Prize Winners in the Sciences, 1901–1993						
	1901–1915	1916–1930	1931–1945	1946–1960	1961–1975	1976–1990	1991–1993
United States	3	3	14	38	41	63	8
United Kingdom	7	8	11	14	20	9	—
Germany	15	12	11	4	8	7	2
France	10	3	2	—	5	2	2
Russia	2	—	—	4	3	1	—
Japan	—	—	—	1	2	1	—
Other Countries	15	15	11	13	13	15	2

Note: This table shows changes in the quality of science in various nations, as measured by an international standard—the Nobel Prize. Wealthier nations that direct more funds to scientific institutions (such as the United States) account for a large proportion of Nobel Prize winners. Although the size of a nation's population is also important, some wealthy nations with large populations (such as Japan) are not significantly increasing their share of Nobel Prizes, largely because they are not investing in the scientific institutions that conduct basic research.

Source: Data from *Statistical Abstract,* 1995.

Chicago, MITRE and Lincoln Lab at MIT, the Riverside electronics lab at Columbia, and the like), [and] the growth of "consortiums" such as the Brookhaven lab on Long Island managed by a half-dozen universities. After these have come the large government health-research centers such as those at the National Institutes of Health, the major National Science Foundation–supported laboratories, the creation of a vast number of nonprofit research "think tanks" such as Rand, the Institute of Defense Analysis, the Aerospace Corporation, and so on. (p. 248)

One consequence of this unplanned growth of scientific organizations in universities, government, the military, and the private sector, Bell concludes, is that it became impossible to create a single set of policies for the support of science. The various organizations must compete for resources and are vulnerable to changing national needs as well as new demands for scientific knowledge by business and industry. This adds to the complexity and competitiveness of scientific institutions.

These aspects of scientific institutions may also explain their continuing differentiation in the United States and other Western nations. For example, the departmental structure of American colleges and universities has been shown to encourage the growth of new disciplines (Ben-David, 1984). Interdisciplinary programs and new fields of study can be sponsored by existing departments until they can compete for support as independent disciplines. An example is the development of statistics as a separate field of study. Originally a branch of mathematics, statistics has been studied and taught by mathematicians and physicists in Europe and Great Britain since the seventeenth century. In the United States, however, departments of biology, education, psychology, economics, and other fields (e.g., demography) developed specialties in statistics. Eventually separate departments of statistics were established.

In sum, since its origins in the independent and often secretive experiments of philosophers and clerics, scientific research has become institutionalized in complex organizations. Yet we will see at many points in this chapter that the process of differentiation in which science becomes an institution separate from others is never complete. The work of scientists must be paid for, and the more their research is "pure" (in that it has no apparent uses that generate profits), the more it must be supported by other institutions like government or industry. This dependence of science on other institutions continually subjects scientists to pressure to make their work relevant to the needs of business or the military. Conflict between scientists and their sponsors thus has been a feature of science since its origins. To understand that conflict more fully, we will take a more detailed look at the norms of scientific institutions.

THE NORMS OF SCIENCE

We saw in Chapter 3 that every social institution develops norms that specify how its special functions are to be car-

ried out. This is readily illustrated by the institutions of science. The function of those institutions is to extend knowledge by means of a specific set of procedures (i.e., the scientific method). The norms of science are derived from that function (Merton, 1973).

Universalism.   One of the basic norms of scientific institutions is *universalism,* which holds that the truth of scientific knowledge must be determined by the impersonal criteria of the scientific method, not by criteria related to race, nationality, religion, social class, or political ideology. This would seem to be self-evident until one remembers that international rivalries have been part of the history of science since the Renaissance. And consider the case of the Russian geneticist Trofim D. Lysenko, who, on the basis of some extremely unscientific research on plant genetics during the Stalinist era, claimed that acquired characteristics of plants could be inherited by the next generation (Bell, 1973). This claim seemed to offer hope for improvement of the Soviet Union's faltering agricultural production. It also fit well with Soviet ideology, which held that better human beings could be created through adherence to the ideals of the revolution. To Stalin and his advisers, science seemed to have proved the value of the Soviet culture and social system. Lysenko was granted a virtual dictatorship over biological research in the Soviet Union, and hundreds of geneticists lost their jobs (Joravsky, 1971; Medvedev, 1971). Lysenko was deposed during the Khrushchev era, but the damage done to Soviet agriculture and biological research in the name of ideology lasted many years longer.

Common Ownership.   Another norm of science is *common ownership of scientific findings.* Those findings are a result of collaboration and hence are not the property of any individual, although in some cases they may bear the name of the person who first published them, as in "Darwin's theory of evolution" or "Einstein's theory of relativity." One outcome of this norm is frequent conflicts over scientific priority—that is, over who was the first to discover or publish a particular item of scientific knowledge. Thus there may be disagreements over who discovered the differential calculus—Newton or Leibniz—but there are no limitations on the use of that calculus. A further consequence of the norm of common ownership is the norm of *publication*—the requirement of full and open communication of scientific findings in journals accessible to all. Secrecy is out of place in science.

However, because scientific research is so often conducted in the interests of national defense or under the sponsorship of private firms that hope to profit from applications of the findings, the norms of common ownership and publication are often suspended. Such situations have led to innumerable conflicts in scientific circles. An outstanding example is the case of J. Robert Oppenheimer, one of the leaders in the development of the atomic bomb during World War II. Although Oppenheimer's sympathy for certain radical causes was well known, he was given a full security clearance both during and after the war, when he continued his pioneering research on the applications of nuclear physics. But when he publicly stated his support of international sharing of findings in nuclear physics—and opposed the development of a thermonuclear or hydrogen bomb—his opponents brought up the old charge that he was a subversive and could not be trusted with scientific secrets. In 1953 President Dwight D. Eisenhower ruled that Oppenheimer was to be denied access to secret scientific information, which meant that he would also be denied access to the laboratories where the most important research in nuclear physics was being conducted (Lakoff, 1970; Rieff, 1969).

Disinterestedness. A further norm of scientific institutions is *disinterestedness.* The scientist does not allow the desire for personal gain to influence the reporting and evaluation of results; fraud and irresponsible claims are outlawed. In fact, more than most other activities, scientific research is subject to the scrutiny of others. This is part of the nature of that research, which involves the search for results that can be verified; in other words, science is, in a sense, self-policing. The norm of disinterestedness does not imply that scientists cannot hope to profit from their findings, and there are many instances in which scientists have held lucrative patents for their discoveries. But it does imply that related norms of scientific research, such as unbiased observation and thoroughness in reporting findings, must take precedence over any selfish motives.

Sociologists are concerned that the pressure on scientists to make discoveries that will earn large sums of money will damage the credibility of scientific institutions. The trend toward partnerships between private corporations and scientific institutions may also put pressure on scientists to violate scientific norms. The Monsanto Chemical Corporation, for example, gave $23.5 million to Washington University for biological research and a West German pharmaceutical company invested $40 million in research at Harvard Medical School. Dorothy Nelkin, one of the nation's leading experts on scientific policy, warns that when businesses form alliances with universities to conduct research in such areas as biological technologies, the scientists involved must keep their findings secret until patents have been applied for. Nelkin concludes that such secrecy "violates the social nature of science, the idea that science is shared, that it's a cumulative activity" (quoted in Broad, 1988, p. C1).

Similarly, when chemists at universities in Utah and Great Britain announced in 1989 that their collaboration had achieved "cold fusion," the production of energy through the fusion of hydrogen atoms at low temperatures (a reaction that scientists believe requires extremely high temperatures), it appeared that a new era of low-cost energy might be on the horizon. But other scientists were highly skeptical. The so-called discoveries had not been published in scientific journals prior to their announcement to the press—a violation of the norm of publication.

The cold fusion apparatus was also kept secret for a time so that the scientists and their universities could apply for patents and enlist the support of major corporations for further research. These actions made scientists suspicious. Before too long the results were found to be incorrect, an outcome perhaps of too much hope for profit and not enough careful measurement (Wilford, 1989).

The norms we have just described are well-established aspects of modern science, which is increasingly differentiated from other institutions, particularly religion and the state. But science was not always viewed as a legitimate institution or a respectable occupation. In fact, early in its history science was often regarded as a dangerous activity with the potential to threaten the existing social order. This can be seen quite clearly in the repression of Galileo by the Inquisition, described in Box 21.2.

TECHNOLOGY IN MODERN SOCIETIES

We noted earlier that a significant aspect of modern science is its contribution to the rapid pace of technological change. The technologies produced by scientific research are applied to all aspects of human life and hence are a major force in shaping and changing other institutions in addition to scientific institutions themselves. An example is the impact of technological change on the institutions of mass communication. As we saw in Chapter 18, the advent of radio and then television dramatically changed the ways in which social and cultural values are transmitted to various groups in society. We will note other examples of the impact of technology in the following pages. But first it is necessary to enlarge our understanding of what is meant by the term *technology.*

DIMENSIONS OF TECHNOLOGY

In Chapter 19 we pointed out that there is more to technology than tools and skills, that ways of organizing work are also part of technology. Technology has three dimensions, which may be summarized as follows:

1. Technological tools, instruments, machines, gadgets, which are used in accomplishing a variety of tasks. These material objects are best referred to as *apparatus,* the physical devices of technical performance

2. The body of technical skills, procedures, routines— all *activities* or behaviors that employ a purposive, step-by-step, rational method of doing things

3. The *organizational networks* associated with activities and apparatus (Winner, 1977, pp. 11–12)

The last of these dimensions may be clarified by an example. Organizational networks are sets of statuses and roles.

BOX 21.2 USING THE SOCIOLOGICAL IMAGINATION

Galileo and the Inquisition

The first person to use a telescope to study the skies was Galileo Galilei, an Italian mathematician who lived from 1564 to 1642. His observations convinced him that the earth revolved around the sun. Up to that time it had been taken for granted that the earth was the center of the universe, and this belief was strongly entrenched in the doctrines of the Catholic church. Galileo's views were so radical that he was tried by the Inquisition, ordered to deny what he knew to be the truth, and forced to spend the last 8 years of his life under house arrest.

Galileo's fate illustrates a principle we have mentioned at numerous points in this book: As societies become more complex, the process termed *differentiation* removes various functions from existing institutions and creates new institutions to perform them. Galileo was tried by the Inquisition because in his time science had not yet become differentiated from philosophy and religion. A scientist must on no account discover anything that contradicted the doctrines of the church.

In his play *Galileo,* Bertolt Brecht paints a vivid picture of the constraints placed on Galileo by the situation of science in his day: An assistant has delivered a gift from the Court of Naples—a model of the sky according to the wise men of ancient Greece—and has asked him to explain it. "You see the fixed ball in the middle?" says Galileo. "That's the earth. For two thousand years man has chosen to believe that the sun and all the host of stars revolve about him. Well. The Pope, the cardinals, the princes, the scholars, captains, merchants, housewives, have pictured themselves squatting in the middle of an affair like that." Galileo goes on to predict that before long people "will be learning that the earth rolls round the sun, and that their mothers, the captains, the scholars, the princes, and the Pope are rolling with it."

The assistant is not convinced, but he admits that he has mentioned Galileo's ideas to his mother, Galileo's housekeeper. The housekeeper says to Galileo, "Last night my son tried to tell me that the earth goes round the sun. You'll soon have him saying that two times two is five." Later Galileo says to the assistant, "Andrea, I wouldn't talk about our ideas outside." "Why not?" asks Andrea. "Certain of the authorities won't like it," replies Galileo. His statement is confirmed by a friend: "How can people in power leave a man at large who tells the truth, even if it be the truth about the distant stars?"

Today scientists are studying subatomic particles called quarks. They have proposed that dinosaurs had feathers rather than scales, and they have suggested that the universe began with a big bang and that stars eventually become black holes. They have discovered the process by which the continents were formed and the structure of human genes. In none of these cases have the findings been challenged by "the authorities," religious or otherwise. Rather, they have been judged by the standards of scientific investigation, one of the functions of the institution we call science.

But the process of differentiation is never complete. In recent years the ancient tension between science and religion has taken a new turn: The scientific theory of evolution has been challenged by fundamentalist religious groups because it contradicts statements made in the Bible. These groups have put pressure on publishers to delete discussions of evolution from school and college textbooks, or at least to mention "creation science" as well as evolution. Although their efforts have had only limited success, they have not been ignored.

All technologies establish or modify such networks. Thus the automobile owner is part of a network that includes dealers, mechanics, parts suppliers, insurers, licensing agents, and junkyard owners. Our great-great-grandparents were probably part of a network of horse dealers, harness makers, buggy suppliers, and blacksmiths, a network that has been largely eliminated by the advent of motorized vehicles.

Technological change can occur in any or all of the dimensions just listed. The most far-reaching changes involve all three, especially the third. For example, the industrial revolution completely changed the organization of economic institutions and also had significant effects on other institutions, such as the family. Likewise, the internal combustion engine, which made possible the development of the automobile, has completely transformed the ecology of North America (Flink, 1975, 1988). On the other hand, some technological changes are limited to modifications in the apparatus or technical skills needed for a particular task (the surgical stapler is an example) and do not affect large numbers of people or have major social impacts.

Not only do technological changes affect various groups and institutions within a society, and sometimes transform a society, but technology itself is affected by the social conditions prevailing at any given time. The acceptance of a particular technological innovation may depend on prior changes in other aspects of a society. Thus television might not have had as great an impact if it had been invented in the nineteenth century, when working people had far less leisure time than they do today. Other innovations have failed to gain acceptance because they appeared too soon. An example is the Sony Corporation's unsuccessful attempt to introduce tape recorders in Japan in 1950. Japanese consumers did not perceive a need or use for them, and they went unsold. Much the same thing is happening today in the case of home computers. Once the thrill of computer games wears off, the computer often stands idle because the average household has no other uses for it. In consequence, the home computer industry is hoping that by selling computers equipped with modems, which enable users to browse the World Wide Web and interact in electronic communities on the Internet, they will maintain consumer interest in the new information technologies (Rheingold, 1993; Sanger, 1984).

TECHNOLOGICAL DUALISM

It should be noted that the effects of new technologies are not always positive. The phrase *technological dualism* is sometimes used to refer to the fact that technological changes often have both positive and negative effects. The introduction of diesel locomotives, for example, greatly increased the efficiency of railroad operations, but it also led to the decline and eventual abandonment of railroad towns whose economies were based on the servicing of steam locomotives (Cottrell, 1951). Another example is the automation of industrial production. Automation has greatly

improved manufacturing processes in many industries. It has increased the safety of certain production tasks and led to improved product quality in many cases. But it has also replaced thousands of manual workers with machines, and significant numbers of those workers find themselves unemployed and lacking the skills required by the high-tech occupations of post-industrial society (see Box 21.3).

Some observers go so far as to say that technology is a danger to the modern world. They feel that it has become an autonomous force, that it is out of control. This is a recurrent theme in movies and science fiction—HAL, the computer that takes over the ship in *2001: A Space Odyssey,* is a good example. But it is also claimed that technology is increasingly independent from human control in the real world. Events like the accident at the Three Mile Island nuclear power plant in 1979; the toxic gas leak that killed more than 2,000 people in Bhopal, India, in 1984; and the disaster at the Chernobyl nuclear power plant in the Soviet Union in 1986 seem to indicate that human beings cannot control the technologies they have created.

Sociologists who have studied this issue point out that the problem is not one of humans being dominated by machines but, rather, one of depending on technology to meet a wide and growing range of human needs. The Three Mile Island power plant provided electricity for thousands of homes and businesses; the Bhopal facility produced a pesticide that made possible larger harvests of much-needed grain. The result of our dependence on the benefits of complex technologies is an increasingly complex set of organizations and procedures for putting those technologies to work. This requires more human effort and skill, and the chances of error and breakdown are greater. The point is

This spectacular display of nature's power is a reminder of the precarious existence of humans on earth. Thunderstorms, tornadoes, and hurricanes destroy billions of dollars' worth of property and disrupt untold numbers of lives every year.

BOX 21.3 GLOBAL SOCIAL CHANGE

Worker Responses to High Technology

The rapid growth of employment in industrial regions like California's "Silicon Valley," Route 128 outside Boston, and the "Silicon Prairie" in the Dallas–Fort Worth area, as well as in hundreds of industrial parks throughout the United States, is viewed as one of the benefits of investment in high-technology industries. The term *high technology* is associated with computers, advanced electronics, genetic engineering, and other frontiers of technological change, but it is rarely well defined. And without a clear definition of this term it is almost impossible to assess its impact on society.

As the term is used by academics, policy makers, and journalists, high technology refers to at least one of the following features of technology:

- An extensive degree of technological sophistication embodied in a product
- A rapid rate of employment growth associated with an innovative product
- A large research and development effort associated with production (Markson & Bloch, 1985)

One implication of this definition is that it includes job-creating processes like research and development as well as technologies like computers, which also have created new growth in employment. Yet the employment-producing features of high technology can be problematic. Many high technologies, such as robotics and computer-aided design, are intended to reduce employment by substituting the work of machines guided by computers for human production of all kinds. Early machine technologies

tended to replace human labor power, but high technology tends to reduce the need for human brain power. Employment in occupations like drafting and industrial drawing in engineering and architecture, for example, is threatened by the accelerating use of computer design and graphics programs (Shaiken, 1985).

During the industrial revolution in England, workers sometimes rioted and wrecked the machinery that was replacing their labor. Such violence against machines was termed *Luddism* after an English stocking maker, Ned Ludlam, who smashed his employer's knitting frame with a sledgehammer and thereby touched off the famous Luddite riots of 1811 and 1812 (Hobsbawm, 1975, Rudé, 1964). Outbursts of collective behavior directed against automation have been relatively rare, however. Instead, workers have generally accepted their fate and looked for other sources of employment.

Nevertheless, the effects of high technology are so threatening to so many workers that unions have taken a number of initiatives designed to alleviate those effects. An example occurred at Britain's Lucas Aerospace, a maker of landing gear and electronic equipment, in the mid-1970s. Automation had reduced the Lucas work force from 18,000 to 13,000. At that point the employees and their union leaders conducted an ambitious study that showed that highly skilled workers were losing their jobs at the same time that many of the society's needs remained unmet. The study suggested hundreds of ways in which the company could employ its skilled work force to meet these needs and still earn profits. Although the plan was rejected, it has served as a model for other worker strategies.

not that technology is out of control but that often there is a lag between the introduction of new technologies and the development of adequate controls over the application of those technologies.

One of the main issues that concerns social scientists in this regard is why such lags occur. Consider the problem known as wind shear. In recent years numerous major plane crashes have been caused by sudden downdrafts associated with severe thunderstorms on the approaches to airport runways. These downdrafts literally slam large aircraft to the ground. Industry and government officials have known about the wind shear problem since at least 1975, when an Eastern Airlines jet crashed at New York's Kennedy Airport under such conditions. But not until a similar crash occurred in New Orleans in 1984 were airports ordered to install instruments that could predict such conditions. Why the delay? Some sociologists have argued that the pressure on corporations to show a profit causes them to neglect spending on safety measures. Others, tak-

ing a more functionalist view, tend to explain such lags in terms of the time required for organizations to recognize the causes of the problem and develop new statuses and roles to cope with them (Perrow, 1984).

TECHNOLOGY AND SOCIAL CHANGE

Among catalysts of social change, technological innovation ranks extremely high, along with major social forces such as population growth, war, epidemics, and rising expectations for better lives. Technological change can also bring about large-scale social change quite rapidly, often well within an individual lifespan. One need only think of the impact of television on life in society. This powerful communications medium, introduced in the United States on a mass basis in the 1950s, has significantly altered the way people receive information about their society and the world, how they behave as consumers, how they engage in politics, and how they use their leisure time. The production of new cultural products (ads, sitcoms, new shows, etc.) accounts for thousands of jobs and billions of dollars of revenue.

In Chapter 10 we discussed William Fielding Ogburn's theory of **cultural lag,** the classic sociological treatment of how societies adjust to technological change and the problems that can result. One example of cultural lag can be seen in the case of cable and satellite television. The actual technological change occurred rapidly, with the result that many new broadcasting channels became available. But the social development of new material for those channels requires further investment, creativity, and organization.

Thus there is a lag between the immediate effects of technological change and the social adjustments necessary to make effective use of the new technology.

A problem with the cultural lag theory is that it often fails to account for the effects of social power. For example, AIDS activists and public health officials would like to see condoms advertised on television. They argue that people who are already suffering from AIDS, as well as people who might be exposed to AIDS and other sexually transmitted diseases, need as much information as possible about safe sex. Condom companies want to advertise on television, as

Here is a vivid example of the risks and unintended effects of technology. This bizarre accident, which occurred in France early in this century, proved to some skeptics that humans could not control the power of their technology. As technology advances, the risks generally increase in proportion to the benefits.

is common in other nations, especially in Europe. However, television stations generally do not accept condom ads because they are worried about the reaction of individuals and organizations that oppose public discussion of sex and birth control. The power to block advertising of condoms on television is an example of a cultural lag that will not necessarily be overcome, because it stems from a deep and unresolved cultural conflict in American society. Other cultural lags resulting from technological change may be more amenable to intentional efforts to address them, as can be seen in the case of air pollution.

The lags described by Ogburn can be at least partially reduced by the process of **technology assessment,** or efforts to anticipate the consequences of particular technologies for individuals and for society as a whole. For instance, the massive plan to reduce air pollution in the Los Angeles basin requires careful assessment. According to the National Environmental Policy Act of 1972 and related state laws, any major action by a public agency that affects the environment must be assessed for its impact on the environment and on the citizens involved. Laws that require technology assessment—especially those that require corporations to abide by the findings of such assessments—tend to increase the power of citizens in communities affected by technological change. They are therefore a source both of conflict and of movements for social reform.

In the Los Angeles case, a number of small, inadequately funded environmental organizations were able to force the California Environmental Policy Administration to fund the plan to reduce air pollution (Weisman, 1989).

Theories that view technological innovations as a source of social change must also recognize that technological changes do not occur at an even pace. Some analysts, such as economist N. D. Kondratieff, believe that technological innovation follows a cyclical pattern. They have shown that the growth of particular industries produces a "long boom," a period of economic expansion and prosperity that lasts about 25 years and is followed by a period of decline and depression of about the same duration or slightly longer (Schilling, 1991). This pattern is illustrated in Table 21.2, which shows the cycles of industrial development in Britain since the late 1700s.

It may be that the new technologies of computers and automation will begin another long boom or wave of economic growth in the next decade, as many people in advanced industrial societies hope. But it is clear that in the late 1970s the previous long boom, stimulated in part by the availability of cheap energy, was over. A new long economic boom therefore may depend on continued new developments in computers, telecommunications, and biotechnologies, and especially on new breakthroughs in energy technologies.

THE QUEST FOR ENERGY

Throughout human history a central aspect of technological change has been the quest for new sources of energy to meet the needs of growing populations. That quest has given rise to a succession of energy technologies, each more sophisticated than the last. Animal power gave way to steam-driven machinery, which in turn was replaced by the internal combustion engine. Reliance on oil and its derivatives, especially gasoline, encouraged the growth of powerful energy corporations, which often lobby government agencies for assistance in developing new technologies like nuclear energy. And today the technologically advanced nations are attempting to control the fusion reaction, in which hydrogen atoms are fused into helium, thereby producing an enormous release of energy. The implications of this energy technology, if it can be achieved, are staggering. Fusion promises to bring about a major revolution in human existence. It could make possible the colonization and exploration of space, the rapid development of the less-developed nations, the elimination of energy technologies based on oil and coal (which pollute the environment), and much else. But the effort to develop fusion power is also indicative of a fundamental crisis in modern life: the dwindling supply of finite energy resources.

The problem of oil depletion is only the most recent in a series of energy crises that began with the depletion of the supply of game animals by hunting in Paleolithic times. The shortage of meat created conditions that spurred the

TABLE 21.2	Long Booms and Associated Industries	
DATES	**INDUSTRY**	
1790–1815	Cotton	Mechanization of spinning
1848–1873	Textiles	Mechanization of spinning and weaving
	Engineering	Production by machine of textile machinery, steam engines, and locomotives
1896–1921	Engineering	Batch production; semiautomatic machinery; marine engineering; automobiles
	Electrical	
	Chemical	Rise of science-based industries
	Steel	Bulk production
1945–1974	Automobiles	
	Mechanical and electrical consumer durables	Assembly-line mass production
	Petrochemicals	Continuous-flow process production

Source: From CSE Microelectronics Group, 1980. Reprinted with permission from CSE Books, London.

THEN AND NOW

LOS ANGELES: THE PROMISE OF AIR POLLUTION CONTROL

About 1 in 20 residents of the United States live in the Los Angeles region, and this proportion is likely to increase somewhat in the coming decade. Within the Los Angeles basin there are about 14 million people "who speak 85 languages, partition themselves into 168 separate cities, drive nearly 100 milliion vehicle-miles *per day,* and live in a state that consumes more gasoline than anywhere save the rest of the United States and all of Russia" (Weisman, 1989, p. 16). The area constitutes the sixth largest economy in the world, and it is estimated that by the year 2010 it will be home to 18 million people, an increase of about 4 million from the 1990 figure and equal to the combined populations of Chicago and Detroit.

Thirty-five years ago the level of pollution in the Los Angeles basin, measured by the amount of ozone present, exceeded minimum federal health standards on four out of every five days. Today, after two decades of emission controls on vehicles, factories, and private residences, that standard is exceeded on fewer than two out of five days. But the clear skies over Los Angeles are not necessarily a permanent feature of the region's environment. There are still many days of smog and pollution, and environmental scientists warn that efforts to scale back pollution regulations could reverse the gains made in recent years.

Even with the progress due to environmental laws and regulations, air pollution in the Los Angeles region is still rated as the worst in the United States. Indeed, of the 10 cities with the highest levels of air pollution, 9 are in automobile-dependent California. The people of Los Angeles are now investing in a new mass transit system, which, along with continued antipollution regulations, may contribute to clearer skies over the city of angels (Ayres, 1995).

development of agriculture. Later, in the waning years of the Roman empire, a shortage of labor power to grind flour encouraged the use of water power. The industrial revolution had its origins in the depletion of the supply of wood during the Renaissance. Coal was plentiful, and experiments with its use as an energy source led to the development of new techniques for producing energy—and new machinery and processes for manufacturing goods. Today, as supplies of oil and coal diminish, the search for new energy sources continues (Hardy, 1973; Lovins, 1991).

It would seem from what we have said so far that the quest for energy is a positive force that results in new, sometimes revolutionary technologies that greatly improve the quality of human life. Many people believe that societies can meet their growing energy needs by continually investing in more sophisticated technologies. This approach has led to the development of huge nuclear power plants to replace oil-fueled generators, and it is widely hoped that investment in fusion, an even more complex technology, will eliminate the dangers posed by nuclear power.

This view is subject to considerable criticism, however. Amory Lovins (1977), for example, distinguishes between "hard" and "soft" energy paths. The former "relies on rapid expansion of centralized high technologies to increase supplies of energy, especially in the form of electricity." The latter "combines a prompt and serious commitment to efficient use of energy [and] rapid development of renewable energy sources" (p. 25). Present and proposed energy policies favor the "hard" path, which involves intensive use of available coal, oil, and natural gas plus heavy investment in nuclear power. These are *capital-intensive* technologies because they rely heavily on sophisticated equipment (capital) rather than labor power.

"Soft" energy technologies depend on renewable sources like sun and wind and tend to be *labor-intensive* in that larger numbers of people are needed to produce a given amount of energy. They are more diverse than "hard" energy technologies and are more directly matched to energy needs. (Solar energy, for example, can be used to heat water without first being converted into electricity.) But the major difference between the two paths, according to Lovins, is that whereas the soft path depends on "pluralistic consumer choice in deploying a myriad of small devices and refinements, the hard path depends on difficult, large-scale projects [e.g., nuclear power plants and fusion reactors] requiring a major social commitment under centralized management" (1977, p. 54). Such projects are characterized by a "remote and . . . uncontrollable technology run by a faraway, bureaucratized, technical elite who have probably never heard of you" (p. 55).

Whether or not one accepts Lovins's thesis, the trend toward greater use of nuclear power to generate electricity has become a major social and political issue (Lovins, 1993). We saw evidence of this in Chapter 8 in the case of

Three Mile Island. Underlying the conflict over the safety of nuclear power plants is the issue of control. In the ancient world those who controlled the irrigation systems were the ruling elite; in the United States the "robber barons" of the late nineteenth century often gained both wealth and political influence from their control of oil and coal supplies. Thus much of the opposition to nuclear power plants stems from the recognition that control over energy supplies is a key source of economic and political power.

TECHNOLOGY IN EVERYDAY LIFE

In a review of research on the impact of new technologies on the daily lives of Americans, Claude S. Fischer (1985) found that such research has not kept pace with technological innovation. Even revolutionary innovations like the invention of the automobile and the telephone remain poorly understood. Conflicting claims abound. For example, in 1937 Helen and Robert Lynd were told by residents of Middletown that automobile use seemed to be decreasing church attendance and generating conflict within the family. But other studies suggested that the automobile was increasing church attendance, especially among more isolated people who found it easier to get to church on Sunday (Flink, 1980–1981).

Given such gaps in our understanding of the impact of technology on social life, Fischer argued that sociologists should avoid assuming that the effects of innovations are experienced by everyone in more or less the same way. Instead, he and others (e.g., de Sola Pool, 1977; Westrum, 1983) believe that technologies should be thought of as facilitators of human action rather than as forces that dictate what we do. Often, for example, our uses of technologies do not conform with what their innovators believed possible or desirable. A case in point is the growing incidence of computer crimes and the use of home antenna dishes to tap into satellite video transmissions.

The place of technology in modern societies is a subject of continuing controversy. Key issues include not only the impact of technology on daily life but also the need to control the development and uses of technological innovations so that they benefit all sectors of society. The complex interactions between technology and other aspects of the social order can be seen in the case of medical technology.

MEDICAL TECHNOLOGY

Throughout most of human history, limitations on food production, together with lack of medical knowledge, have placed limits on the size of populations. Dreadful diseases like the bubonic plague have actually reduced populations. In England the plague, known as the Black Death, was responsible for a drastic drop in the population in 1348 and for the lack of population growth in the seventeenth cen-

FIGURE 21.1 Long-Term Population Trends in England and Wales, 1000–1800

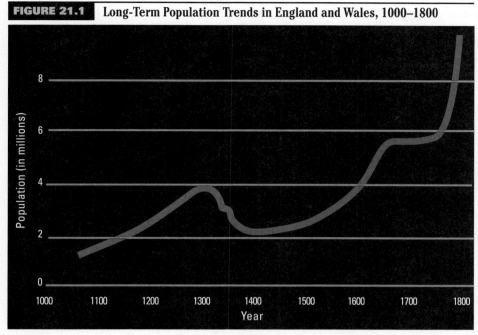

Source: Reprinted with permission from Wrigley's *Population and History,* 1969. Copyright © McGraw-Hill Book Company.

tury (see Figure 21.1). In 1625 alone, 35,417 residents of London died of the plague. Smallpox and dysentery have had similar, though less dramatic, effects (Wrigley, 1969).

Until relatively recently physicians were powerless either to check the progress of disease or to prolong life. In fact, they often did more harm than good—their remedies were more harmful than the illnesses they were intended to cure. As Lewis Thomas (1979) has stated:

> Bleeding, purging, cupping, the administration of infusions of every known plant, solutions of every known metal, every conceivable diet including total fasting, most of these based on the weirdest imaginings about the cause of the disease, concocted out of nothing but thin air—this was the heritage of medicine up until a little over a century ago. (p. 133)

Thomas's point is that before the nineteenth century, when scientists finally began to understand the nature of disease, physicians based their treatments on folklore and superstition. In fact, with few exceptions the practice of healing, like many other aspects of science, was closely linked to religion. In ancient Greece people who suffered from chronic illnesses and physical impairments would journey to the temple of Asclepius, the god of healing, in search of a cure. In medieval times pilgrims flocked to the cathedral at Lourdes in France (as many still do today) in the belief that they would thereby be cured of blindness, paralysis, or leprosy. Not until Louis Pasteur, Robert Koch, and other researchers developed the germ theory of disease did medicine become fully differentiated from religion.

Their discoveries, together with progress in internal medicine, pathology, the use of anesthesia, and surgical techniques, led to the twentieth-century concept of medicine as a scientific discipline (Cockerham, 1992).

During the nineteenth century scientific research resulted in the discovery of the causes of many diseases, but at first this progress led physicians to do less for their patients rather than more: They began to allow the body's natural healing processes to work and ceased to engage in damaging procedures like bloodletting. At the same time, they made major strides toward improving public health practices. They learned about hygiene, sterilization, and other basic principles of public health, especially the need to separate drinking water from waste water. These innovations, which occurred before the development of more sophisticated drugs and medical technologies, contributed to a demographic revolution that is still under way in some parts of the world. Suddenly rates of infant mortality decreased dramatically, births began to outnumber deaths, and life expectancy increased. As we saw in Chapter 9, this change resulted not from the highly sophisticated techniques of modern medicine but largely from the application of simple sanitation techniques and sterilization procedures (McKinlay & McKinlay, 1977). In fact, these simple technologies have had such a marked effect on infant survival that the rate of infant mortality in a society is often used as a quick measure of its social and economic development (see Figure 21.2).

In sum, as medical science progressed toward greater understanding of the nature of disease and its prevention,

FIGURE 21.2 Infant Mortality Rates for Selected Countries

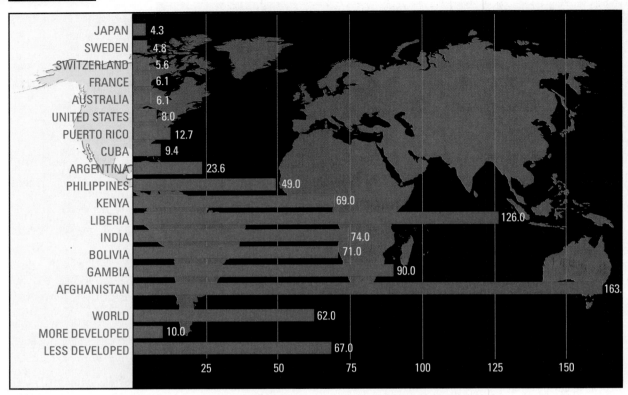

Note: The infant mortality rate is the annual number of deaths of infants under 1 year of age per 1,000 live births in a given year.

Source: Data from Population Reference Bureau, 1995.

new public health and maternal care practices contributed to rapid population growth. In the second half of the nineteenth century, such discoveries as antiseptics and anesthesia made possible other life-prolonging medical treatments. In analyzing the effects of these technologies, sociologists ask how people in different social classes gain access to them and how they can be more equitably distributed among the members of a society. The ways in which medical technologies have been institutionalized in hospitals and the medical profession are a central focus of sociological research on these questions.

THE HOSPITAL: FROM POORHOUSE TO HEALING INSTITUTION

In the twentieth century the nature of medicine has changed dramatically as scientific investigation has expanded our knowledge of the causes and cures of disease. That knowledge has led to the development of a vast array of technologies for the prevention and cure of many known illnesses, as well as the long-term care of terminally ill patients. Because the more complex of these technologies are applied in a hospital setting, it is worthwhile to consider the development of the hospital as the major social institution for the delivery of health care.

Historically, hospitals evolved through several stages, beginning as religious centers and eventually developing into centers of medical technology (Cockerham, 1992). The first hospitals were associated with the rise of Christianity; they were community centers for the care of the sick and the poor, providing not only limited medical care but also food, shelter, and prayer. During the Renaissance, hospitals were removed from the jurisdiction of the church and became public facilities. Because they offered food and shelter to the poor regardless of their health, they soon became crowded with invalids, the aged, orphans, and the mentally ill. The third phase in the development of hospitals began in the seventeenth century, when physicians gained influence over the care of patients in hospitals. Gradually the nonmedical tasks of hospitals disappeared and the hospital took on its present role as an institution for medical care and research.

The modern hospital began to emerge at the end of the nineteenth century as a result of the development of the science of medicine. Especially important were advances in bacteriology and increased knowledge of human physiology, along with the use of ether as an anesthetic. Because the new medical technologies were more complex and often more expensive than earlier forms of treatment, they were centralized in hospitals so that many physicians could use them. Physicians also began to refer patients of all social classes to hospitals, and those patients paid for the services provided to them there.

In the United States the number of hospitals grew rapidly in the twentieth century—from a few hundred at the turn of the century to more than 6,500 in the 1990s. Today hospitals play an important role in the control of medical practice and access to medical care. For example, doctors who want to practice in a particular hospital must be accepted by the hospital's medical board. Patients who want high-quality care in private hospitals must be able to pay the fees charged by those hospitals or have the necessary insurance coverage. And hospitals have a monopoly on advanced medical technologies, a fact that has had a major impact on the American health care system.

HYPERTROPHY IN HEALTH CARE?

Today the technologies available for the diagnosis and treatment of serious illnesses are often described as "miracles of modern medicine." The MRI scanner, for example, allows hospital technicians to observe a patient's internal organs without the use of X rays; renal dialysis is used to prevent patients from dying of kidney failure; open-heart surgery is practically a routine operation, with the patient kept alive during the process by an external heart-lung machine; other surgical procedures involve the use of laser beams and fiber optics to perform delicate operations. All of these technologies require the use of extremely expensive equipment and highly trained personnel.

The development of increasingly sophisticated and costly medical technologies, together with the practice of requiring patients (or their insurance companies) to pay for hospital services, has led to a crisis in American medical care. The high and continually rising cost of medical care has become a major public issue, as has the fact that some groups in the population are unable to obtain adequate care. Some critics claim that the American health care system is suffering from *hypertrophy,* by which they mean that it has expanded to a size and complexity at which it has become dysfunctional. In their view, excessive emphasis on technological progress has created a situation in which the needs of the patient are subordinated to those of the providers of health care.

According to Paul Starr (1982), the problems of the American health care system stem from the way in which medical institutions evolved. As medical knowledge increased and technological advances were made, physicians developed narrow specialties and hospitals invested in specialized equipment. The physicians referred their patients to the hospitals for sophisticated medical testing and treatment. At the same time, the institution of health insurance emerged in response to demands for a more equitable distribution of health care. Insurance companies or the government began to pay for the services provided by hospitals. Physicians and hospitals became highly interdependent, so much so that they began to "assert their long-run collective interests over their short-run individual interests" (Starr, 1982, p. 230). Their collective interests involve continued investment in complex technologies,

This painting by Jan Beerblock (1739–1806) depicts the sick wards in Sint-Janshospital in Bruges, Belgium, a bleak forerunner of modern hospital organization.

with the result that medical care is becoming more and more expensive. The rising cost of medical care makes it more difficult for the poor, the elderly, and other groups to afford high-quality care and heroic life-preserving measures. In the closing years of the twentieth century, efforts to make health care less costly while preserving the insurance systems that provide medical coverage for the majority of Americans are proving to be one of the most controversial and rancorous issues in U.S. political life.

MEDICAL SOCIOLOGY

Starr's study of the evolution of health care institutions is an example of *medical sociology*. This relatively new field of study has emerged in response to the development of medicine as a major institution of modern societies. Many sociologists are employed by health care institutions, and some medical schools have established faculty positions for sociologists. These trends are further evidence of the increasing role of sociology in assessing the effects of technological change on other aspects of society.

Medical sociologists use all of the major perspectives we have discussed in this book. Starr's study shows how conflict over access to medical care influences public policies in the United States. William Goode's (1957, 1960) research on how the structure of the medical profession influences the practice of medicine draws on the functionalist perspective, and a number of interactionist studies have dealt with the role behavior of physicians and patients. Marcia Millman (1976), for example, found that many doctors are willing to point out colleagues' errors in small group discussions but will not do so at official meetings because of "a recognition of common interests."

In recent years medical sociologists have faced a new and serious challenge: helping society cope with the ethical issues that arise as it becomes increasingly possible to prolong human life by artificial means. Procedures such as heart transplants are extremely expensive and cannot possibly be made available to all patients who need them. Are they to be limited to those who can pay for them? If not, how should the patients who will benefit from such procedures be chosen? Medical sociologists are frequently asked to conduct research that will affect decisions of this nature—a form of technology assessment.

Another issue that has arisen as a result of advances in medical technology is what exactly constitutes death. Should a person whose brain has stopped functioning be considered dead even if other life functions can be maintained by artificial means? Do patients have a "right to die"—that is, to request that life-sustaining equipment be disconnected if the brain has ceased to function? These are extremely difficult questions, and health care institutions, whose function is to strive to maintain life whatever the cost, are ill equipped to deal with them. Critics charge that medical technologies simply prolong the dying process, but courts and legislatures have been reluctant to accept the

notion of a right to die—a good example of what Ogburn meant by the phrase *cultural lag*.

THE IMPACT OF TECHNOLOGY

TECHNOLOGICAL SYSTEMS

The case of medical technology illustrates once again that technology can be both a blessing and a curse. In recent decades we have become increasingly aware that the problems of human life cannot always be solved by technological means. The "technological fix" can have adverse consequences. In the case of medical technology, vital ethical issues must be addressed. Other technologies, such as nuclear power and chemical plants, can directly threaten human life. As Charles Perrow (1984) wrote, "Human-made catastrophes appear to have increased with industrialization as we built devices that could crash, sink, burn, or explode" (p. 11). Perrow also pointed out that the increasing complexity of modern technology has led to a new kind of catastrophe: the failure of whole systems (i.e., activities and organizational networks as well as apparatus)—for example, the Three Mile Island accident or the *Challenger* disaster.

The enormous risks associated with complex technologies have led many observers to call for more thorough assessment of the potential impact of new technologies before they are put into operation. According to Perrow, it is important to study technological systems in their entirety rather than focusing on individual components of those systems. For example, in the case of Three Mile Island, the accident was not a simple matter of a faulty valve but the consequence of a combination of factors—an overworked maintenance staff, equipment failures, ineffective safety precautions, inadequate training, and the unwillingness of scientists and bureaucrats to admit that they might be mistaken. Similar conditions led to the explosion of the *Challenger* space shuttle in 1986. Once again we are reminded that technology consists not just of apparatus that can malfunction but also of knowledge and skills that may be deficient and of organizational networks that occasionally break down.

ENVIRONMENTAL STRESS

New technologies often cause new forms of pollution and environmental stress. *Pollution* may be defined as the addition to the environment of agents that are potentially damaging to the welfare of humans or other organisms (Ehrlich, Ehrlich, & Holdren, 1977). *Environmental stress* is a more general term that refers to the effects of society on the natural environment. Pollution is the most common form of environmental stress, but it is not the only one.

One example of environmental stress resulting from technology is the surprising finding that winter fish kills in Wisconsin lakes were caused by snowmobiles. Heavy snowmobile use on a lake compacts the snow, thereby reducing the amount of sunlight filtering through the ice and thus interfering with photosynthesis by aquatic plants. As the plant life dies, its decomposition further reduces the amount of oxygen in the water. The fish then die of asphyxiation.

The fish–plant–oxygen relationship is a natural ecological system. The snowmobile is a technological innovation whose potential uses are highly varied. The production, marketing, and use of snowmobiles are elements of a social system. It is this social system that is responsible for the environmental stress resulting from snowmobile use. The land available for snowmobiling is increasingly scarce in an urban society like the United States. Frozen lakes near urban centers thus seem ideal for this purpose, but snowmobiles cause environmental stress in the form of fish kills and thereby create the need for new social controls over the uses of this technology.

Often the need for such controls does not become apparent until a great deal of damage has been done. Nor is it ever entirely clear that new social controls or new technologies can solve the problem at hand. In a recent study of comparative environmental risks, for example, sociologist Kai T. Erikson (1994b) examined the vast area of Nevada where the U.S. government carried out its nuclear bomb testing and where it now plans to bury large quantities of high-level nuclear wastes. These wastes can remain extremely dangerous for thousands of years. Erikson points out that scientists can assess the geological risks of storing nuclear waste deep underground but have much less experience in assessing the social risks. As seen in the Visual Sociology section of this chapter, symbols for danger that are familiar to us could easily be as undecipherable to our descendants in 10,000 years as the writing on many ancient tombs is to us today.

Studies of the impact and social control of technologies are an active frontier of sociological research. The Environmental Sociology section of the American Sociological Association routinely publishes research reports that assess the polluting and environmentally stressful impacts of technology. Many such studies have shown that the people who bear the heaviest burden of pollution are most often those who are least able to escape its effects. The poor, minorities, and workers and their families in industrial regions are exposed to higher levels of air, water, and solid-waste pollution than more affluent people are (Erikson, 1994a). But these studies have also shown that the effects of pollution frequently either are not perceived or are denied by the people who feel them most. For example, a random sample survey on perceptions of pollution in two highly polluted mining and lumbering towns in central Canada (Boldt, Frideres, & Stephens, 1978) found that "half of the total number of respondents interviewed either did not perceive a pollution problem at all, or else regarded it as being of very little importance" (p. 159). The study also found that even among those who did perceive the ef-

fects of pollution in the air and water and on the landscape, a huge majority (83–89 percent) were "not prepared to do anything about it" (p. 161).

This is not a surprising finding. People whose livelihoods depend on polluting industries generally learn to tolerate and even ignore the pollution associated with those industries. In fact, when environmental activists protest against the polluting effects of mines and smelters, they often find that their most vocal opponents are those who are most negatively affected by the pollution. In the past 20 years, however, there has been a significant change in attitudes, especially on the part of trade union leaders in polluting industries; such leaders are more likely to press for pollution controls than they were in the past.

RESEARCH FRONTIERS: ENVIRONMENTAL CHANGE AND VIOLENT CONFLICT

Within the next 50 years the world's population is expected to increase to more than 9 billion, almost double its present size. Ecologists and social scientists also expect significant declines in some of the earth's most vital resources. And there is growing evidence that high rates of population growth and environmental stress in the less developed regions of the world are causing higher levels of violent conflict. Depletion of fertile soils and arable land, the spread of deserts, and the exhaustion and burning of tropical forests produce the conditions for severe conflict among people who are directly affected by these environmental changes. This is a hypothesis of the Project on Environmental Change and Acute Conflict undertaken by the University of Toronto and the American Academy of Arts and Sciences (Homer-Dixon, Boutwell, & Rathjens, 1993; Leonard, 1989).

Scarcities of renewable resources contribute to violence without always appearing to do so. The media may cover a brutal riot or a local war in a far-off part of the world without understanding the environmental origins of the conflict. However, the Toronto project has examined hundreds of episodes of intergroup violence around the world and has found that resource issues figure prominently in the explanations of those conflicts. Depletion of resources, population growth, and concentration of resources in the hands of a few members of society, subjecting the rest to extreme deprivation (as occurred in Somalia when warlords gained control over food supplies), are the three major dimensions of environmental change that produce conditions that can lead to severe violence.

In Bangladesh and the adjoining provinces of India, for example, depletion of resources, population shifts, and concentration of resources are the primary factors

12001 A.D. ARE YOU LISTENING?
CAN YOU UNDERSTAND?

As sociologist Kai Erikson learned in his study of new forms of risk and danger, the disposal of dangerous radioactive wastes poses a staggering variety of technical and social dilemmas. From a sociological standpoint, however, few are as challenging as that of how to communicate with people in a future civilization that might have nothing in common with our own.

Radioactive waste products are dangerous for thousands of years. Even if buried in caverns deep below the desert, it will be necessary to post warnings in case, for whatever reason, people penetrate the barriers and come near the dangerous materials. Conventional symbols or signs, such as "Danger, Radioactive Wastes—Do Not Enter" might suffice if we could assume that the intruders read English. But can we make that assumption?

Archaeologists can often interpret the purpose of ancient monuments like the Sphinx, although they may not be entirely sure of their interpretations. For example, they cannot always decipher hieroglyphics like those shown here, found in ancient Assyria. How to communicate in a universal fashion with people who do not know our language and culture is the subject of a recent study by the Sandia National Laboratories. The photos and diagrams shown here illustrate some of the possible warnings that could be posted near the materials buried at Yucca Mountain, Nevada, the most likely site for the deposition of nuclear wastes in the United States.

The Sandia researchers doubt that the well-known symbol for radiation will stand the test of time. They believe that if we are to communicate with people from a future civilization, we must find more universal symbols. For example, some ancient monuments used masks that might evoke dread, like these from Medinet el Fayyum, Egypt. Perhaps warnings using such universal symbols of fright would work. Another proposed solution involves using dangerous shapes such as the "landscape of thorns" to warn away the curious without relying on language. Still another noncultural, nonlinguistic means of communication is the "black hole" design that evokes fear.

explaining an increased level of violence and conflict. United Nations demographers predict that the population of Bangladesh, currently 120 million, will reach 235 million by the year 2025. Population densities in this impoverished and frequently flooded nation at the mouth of the Ganges River average 785 persons per square kilometer, compared with 284 per kilometer in the neighboring Indian state of Assam. For this reason, over the past 40 years millions of Bengalis have migrated into Assam, where the standard of living is higher. But this migration has disrupted the lives of people in Assam. Those with the richest farm land fear that they will lose it to the migrating Bengalis, and politicians fear the influence of Bengali voters. In 1983 these fears resulted in a massacre of nearly 1,700 Bengalis in Assam, and the tensions between the two peoples have mounted ever since (Homer-Dixon et al., 1993). Other examples of such conflicts abound throughout India, Asia, and Africa, threatening the prospects for world peace.

These relationships are portrayed in schematic form in Figure 21.3. The diamonds indicate possible outcomes of increased scarcities of renewable resources. It is not at all certain, however, that these outcomes are inevitable given the possibility of greater international cooperation. More important, it is not clear whether the poor nations will be able to control their rates of population growth and depletion of resources. By focusing on the preservation of renewable resources, conserving topsoils, combating erosion, conserving forests, developing new water resources, and taking many other similar steps, both rich and poor nations can ensure a brighter future for generations yet unborn. These intentional social changes are possible, given new technologies of birth control and conservation, but it remains to be seen whether the world's nations can develop the moral and political consensus needed to pursue these ends.

FIGURE 21.3 Some Sources and Consequences of Renewable Resource Scarcity

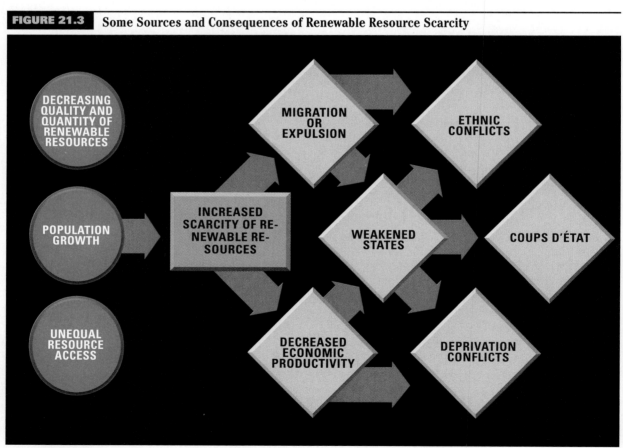

Source: Homer-Dixon et al., 1993.

SUMMARY

THINK ABOUT IT CRITICALLY

Many people believe that the world's environmental and population problems can be solved, in time, through scientific and technological "breakthroughs." In this view, there is no need to control population growth or the appetites of the affluent classes or the steadily increasing consumption of water and fossil fuels. Science will make discoveries that will replace the losses and repair the damage. Is this a realistic appraisal?

A hallmark of the modern social order is the conduct of scientific research in universities and other research organizations. *Science* is knowledge obtained as a result of the process of developing and testing hypotheses. Pure science is scientific investigation devoted to the pursuit of knowledge for its own sake. Applied science is the application of known scientific principles to a practical problem.

Technology involves the use of tools and knowledge to manipulate the physical environment to achieve desired practical goals. Technology is much older than science, but the discoveries of modern science are creating new technologies at a rapid rate and have greatly expanded the human capacity to live in and exploit different habitats. Negative effects of technological change have led to calls for *sustainable development*, or development that does not damage the environment or create new environmental burdens.

The interactionist approach to the study of scientific institutions focuses on the scientific community or communities, the network of communication and social relationships among scientists. A well-known study based on this perspective found that in many cases scientific researchers do not test and refute existing theories but, rather, assume that they are valid and use them as a *paradigm* for future research. This view of the scientific community implies that science is insulated from the rest of society and that the problems scientists choose to solve are determined by the tradition of research in their field.

The institutional approach to the study of science asks why science develops differently in different societies. In this view, certain conditions encourage the development of scientific institutions. They include recognition of empirical research as a legitimate way of acquiring new knowledge. In addition, science must be independent from other fields. However, scientific institutions are never entirely separate from other institutions because scientific research is often supported by government or industry, a situation that puts pressure on scientists to meet the practical needs of those institutions.

One of the most basic norms of scientific institutions is universalism, which holds that the truth of scientific knowledge must be determined by the impersonal criteria of the scientific method. Another norm of science is the common ownership of scientific findings (although such findings sometimes bear the name of the person who first published them). A third norm of scientific institutions is disinterestedness, meaning that scientists do not allow the desire for personal gain to influence the reporting and evaluation of results.

The technologies produced by scientific research are a major force in shaping and changing other institutions. The basic dimensions of technology are physical devices or apparatus, the activities associated with their use, and the organizational networks within which those activities are carried out. The fact that technological changes often have both positive and negative effects is sometimes referred to as technological dualism.

Sociologists recognize that social institutions are often slow to adapt to changing technologies. This recognition forms the basis of the theory known as *cultural lag.* The time required for social institutions to adapt to technological change can be reduced by the process of *technology assessment,* or efforts to anticipate the consequences of particular technologies for individuals and for society as a whole.

The complex interactions between technology and other aspects of the social order are illustrated by the case of medical technology. Until relatively recently, physicians were powerless either to check the progress of disease or to prolong life. Scientific research led to the discovery of the causes of many diseases during the nineteenth century, but in the twentieth century a vast array of technologies have been developed both for the prevention and cure of illnesses and for the long-term care of terminally ill patients.

The technologies used in the diagnosis and treatment of serious illnesses require extremely expensive equipment and highly trained personnel. This has caused health care to become very expensive, and as a result some groups in the population are unable to obtain adequate care. Some critics claim that extreme emphasis on technological progress has created a situation in which the needs of the patient are subordinated to those of the providers of health care. In recent years medical sociologists have been faced with the challenge of helping society cope with the ethical issues that arise as it becomes increasingly possible to prolong human life by artificial means.

The increasing complexity of modern technology has led to a new kind of catastrophe: the failure of whole systems. The enormous risks associated with complex technologies have led many observers to call for a more thorough assessment of the potential impact of new technologies before they are put into operation. This is especially important from the standpoint of protection of the environment.

CRITICAL RESPONSE

The belief that science and technology will solve all our environmental and social problems is often known as *"techno-fix thinking." Unfortunately, many of the most severe environmental problems are themselves caused by technologies such as supertankers, chlorofluorocarbons, and pesticides. Often more developed nations use science and technology to enrich their populations at the expense of the poorer areas of the world. For this reason, many social scientists no longer view science and technology as synonymous with progress.*

GLOSSARY

science: knowledge obtained as a result of the process of developing and testing hypotheses. (p. 634)

technology: the use of tools and knowledge to manipulate the physical environment in order to achieve desired practical goals. (p. 634)

sustainable development: development that does not damage the environment or create new environmental burdens. (p. 635)

paradigm: a model comprising existing theories and methods; a general way of seeing the world that dictates what kind of scientific work should be done and what kinds of theory are acceptable. (p. 637)

cultural lag: the time required for social institutions to adapt to a major technological change. (p. 643)

technology assessment: efforts to anticipate the consequences of particular technologies for individuals and for society as a whole. (p. 644)

BOOKS

Autonomous Technology (Langdon Winner; MIT Press, 1977). A fine review of the control-of-technology debate.

The Social Transformation of American Medicine (Paul Starr; Basic Books, 1982). A sociological history that shows why American medical institutions have become increasingly cumbersome and costly.

The Jobless Future: Sci Tech and the Dogma of Work (Stanley Aronowitz & William DiFazio; University of Minnesota Press, 1994). A critical reading of the changes brought about by technology and automation and their impact on the prospects for work in the next century.

The Sociology of Science (Robert K. Merton; University of Chicago Press, 1973). An original work by one of the founders of the sociology of science. Extremely useful for concepts and theoretical frameworks.

False Prophets (Alexander Kohn; Basil Blackwell, 1986). A study of dishonesty in the natural sciences and medicine that includes a separate chapter on Lysenko. Raises the question of how widespread scientific fraud may be.

The Healing Experience: Readings on the Social Context of Health Care (William Kornblum & Carolyn D. Smith, eds.; Prentice Hall, 1994). An anthology that explores medical and health-related problems from the perspectives of well-known health care providers and medical sociology researchers.

Rivers of Empire: Water, Aridity, and the Growth of the American West (Donald Worster; Pantheon, 1985). A study of the large-scale earth and water projects that were required before the American West could be developed into the social and industrial giant it is today. By the author of *Nature's Economy,* the best available history of American ecological ideas.

JOURNALS

Scientific American. A well-known monthly magazine that usually includes at least one important article dealing with the impact of new technologies on society.

Bulletin of the Atomic Scientists. A renowned and respected journal, founded by a coalition of physicists and social scientists, that focuses on the control of nuclear energy and weapons.

Journal of Health and Social Behavior. A quarterly journal that presents sociological research on problems of human health and illness. Also features articles on change in social institutions and organizations as a consequence of new technologies.

OTHER SOURCES

Resources, Environment and Population: Present Knowledge and Future Options (Kingsley Davis & Mikhail S. Bernstam, eds.; Population Council, 1991). A special edition of *Population and Development Review* containing invaluable reviews of issues like sustainable development, energy development, world population forecasts, pollution, and climate.

APPENDIX

CAREERS IN SOCIOLOGY

What could be more stimulating than to spend a lifetime learning and teaching about human society? But can one really make a living as a sociologist? And what use is a sociology major if one does not go on to do graduate work in sociology?

In attempting to answer these questions, it is helpful to distinguish between careers in sociology itself and applications of sociology in other fields. In North America most sociologists with graduate degrees teach and conduct research in colleges and universities. This has been true since the early decades of this century, but there is a growing trend toward the application of sociology in many fields outside academia. More than 25 percent of sociologists now work for nonacademic employers (Lyson & Squires, 1993; Manderscheid & Greenwald, 1983). But sociological training does not have to lead to a sociological career. It can be valuable preparation for careers in a wide variety of other professions, including law, business, education, architecture, medicine, social work, politics, and public administration. Whatever the specific occupation, the emphasis will be on understanding human behavior and relationships in different kinds of social settings.

For most careers in sociology, a graduate degree is necessary—a Ph.D. in the case of academic sociology, and an M.A. or Ph.D. for most jobs in applied fields. However, a B.A. in sociology can often be of value in occupations outside of sociology. In addition, at any educational level a sociologist is likely to specialize in a particular area, such as the family, education, health, environmental issues, sex roles, the military, or law enforcement.

The majority of sociologists earn more than $40,000 a year. As in many professions, men tend to earn more than women. The American Sociological Association continues to promote equality of opportunity for women and minorities; a recent survey of sociologists found that about 70 percent of the women thought their opportunities for promotion and advancement were either very good or pretty good (Lyson & Squires, 1993). The association has also established a minority scholarship program and continually seeks to improve the representation of minority groups in sociology.

Academic Careers

Colleges and universities may place differing amounts of emphasis on teaching and on conducting research. At major universities, professors of sociology are expeced to devote a significant portion of their time to original research and writing for publication, while at smaller colleges there is more emphasis on teaching. This is not to say that sociologists in smaller institutions do not do research, just that more importance is attached to their teaching.

A professor of sociology at a large university must have a Ph.D. He or she may teach four or five courses a year, including advanced seminars for graduate students. But research and writing are likely to play a greater role in his or her career development. Research projects may be financed by grants from federal or other research agencies, and graduate students may be hired as research assistants using funds from the grant. The professor then can use the project as a means of teaching at the graduate level, while concentrating on publishing scholarly articles and, sometimes, books. The latter are an important element in the university's decision regarding tenure, or guaranteed employment, which is generally made during the individual's fifth or sixth year on the faculty.

A sociology instructor in a community college may have an M.A., although many of these institutions now require a Ph.D. He or she typically does a great deal of teaching—perhaps five courses a semester. Although this teaching load becomes less demanding as courses are repeated, the instructor must continually seek out up-to-date materials and be alert to innovations in teaching techniques. In addition to preparing for courses, he or she is expected to serve on academic and research committees, meet with individual students, and keep abreast of new developments in sociology and related fields.

Another important consideration is that sociologists at colleges and universities not only teach sociology to graduate and undergraduate sociology majors, but also teach students in other disciplines such as law, education, medicine, social work, and nursing. Almost eight out of ten practicing sociologists are teaching in universities, colleges, and high schools.

Careers in Applied Sociology

Opportunities for sociologists in government, business, and not-for-profit organizations are extremely varied and can be categorized in a number of ways. One approach (Rossi & Whyte, 1983) is to divide applied sociology into three main branches: applied social research, social engineering, and clinical sociology. *Applied social research* is similar in many ways to the basic research conducted at universities, except that it is conducted in order to obtain empirically based knowledge of applied issues. It may take the form of descriptive studies such as victimization surveys, analytical research such as studies of voter preferences, or evaluation research—that is, systematic attempts to estimate the potential effects of a proposed social program or a new approach to management in a business firm. *Social engineering* goes a step further and attempts to use sociological knowledge to design social policies or institutions with a specific purpose. An example is the federally funded preschool program known as Head Start. *Clinical sociology* refers to the use of sociological knowledge in providing assistance to individuals and organizations. A clinical sociologist might, for example, work with a large corporation to find ways of improving employee morale.

To get an idea of the variety of job opportunities in applied sociology, consider the following examples (American Sociological Association, 1995):

Research Director in a Health Center
Sociologists employed by a state-supported health science center teach future physicians, nurses, and other health care professionals about the sociological aspects of health care. Among other

things, they provide data about the population groups served by the center and the distribution of disease and health care needs in those groups.

Staff Researcher in a Federal Agency

Many sociologists are employed in varied positions by federal agencies. An example is a staff member of a program that administers grants to researchers at universities throughout the country. This involves discussing research plans with applicants and monitoring grants that have been awarded.

Member of the Planning Staff in a State Department of Transportation

Opportunities for sociologists in state agencies are also varied. An example is performing long-range forecasting for the transportation department, which entails projecting population shifts in major urban and suburban areas. The sociologist must keep informed about relevant research and prepare frequent reports and analyses based on recent studies.

Staff Administrator in a Public Assistance Agency

In local government, a sociologist might serve as program coordinator for a city social-service department. This job would include processing reports and legal forms as well as direct contact with clients of the agency—particularly individuals who are poor, disabled, aged, or members of minority groups. In addition, it would involve helping clients solve personal problems by referring them to other public and private agencies that provide assistance of various kinds.

Staff Member of a Research Institute

A sociologist employed by a private research institute might help carry out studies of specific problems at the request of government agencies, businesses, or political organizations. This could involve developing new research projects (including writing grant proposals) as well as supervising existing ones.

Careers in Other Fields

People with sociological training often work in other occupations that use their training, even if they are not specifically referred to as sociologists. For example, a personnel manager in a small manufacturing firm would be considered a business executive rather than a sociologist. But training in industrial sociology and social psychology can be immensely valuable in carrying out the responsibilities of a personnel manager—for instance, in setting strategies and programs for hiring, training, supervising, and promoting employees. Many businesses and other organizations have come to recognize that sociological training is worthwhile for administrators and executives.

Kenneth Donow, a senior adviser to the Public Service Satellite Consortium in Washington, D.C., is an example of a sociologist who has made a successful transition from an academic career to a career in business. Although his training was geared toward a university position, Donow's interest in communications and information policy steered him toward the business world. He was hired by a consulting firm to analyze the worldwide semiconductor industry. It soon became clear to him that business analysis involves the study of formal organizations and social networks, something for which sociologists are ideally suited. He was able to convince other business clients to incorporate sociological approaches into their operations and notes that today "sociological

practice has become fully integrated into the largest U.S. corporations" (1990, p. 6). Donow believes that people with sociological training will be increasingly sought by American businesses during the next few decades.

There are many other areas in which sociological training is viewed as appropriate preparation for employment. A publication of the American Sociological Association (1995) lists the following positions among those that can be obtained with an undergraduate degree in sociology: interviewer, research assistant, recreation worker, group worker, teacher (if certified), administrative assistant, probation and parole worker, career counselor, community planner, editorial assistant, social worker (not certified), and statistical assistant. A graduate degree can also be useful outside of sociology. For example, if you seek a career in a particular industry or field—such as transportation—participating in original research in that field as part of a graduate degree program can provide a means of entering the field with the help of individuals who notice and respect your work.

Employment Prospects for the 1990s and Beyond

The directors of the American Sociological Association believe that "the future appears bright for sociology. The next century may be the most exciting and critical period in the field's history." The Association anticipates a surge in the hiring of younger sociologists as professors, research personnel, and administrators with sociological backgrounds who were part of the baby boom generation retire from the work force. Moreover, "internationalization of both higher education and the profession of sociology will also lead to new opportunities inside academia and in applied settings" (American Sociological Association, 1995, p. 22).

A decade ago (Huber, 1984), a study of the specific types of jobs held by recipients of M.A. and Ph.D. degrees in sociology found that close to half the M.A.'s and one third of the Ph.D.'s were employed by government agencies. About one third of the Ph.D.'s were employed by not-for-profit organizations, as were about one fourth of the M.A.'s. About a fifth of each group were employed in the private sector. These patterns hold true today as well, but with some significant changes. More sociologists are working in the private sector—especially in advertising, telecommunications, computers and software development, and personnel—and somewhat fewer are working in the public sector.

Not-for-profit foundations and companies continue to look to people with sociological training. In this era of corporate downsizing and reductions in funding for public institutions, people with diverse training in sociological methods and theories often find that they have the flexibility required in today's employment market. The American Sociological Association notes that "solid training in sociology at the undergraduate or graduate levels forms a foundation for flexible career development. The better your training and the more skills you have acquired, the better you will be able to take advantage of new opportunities" (1995, p. 22).

Preparing for a Career in Sociology

A bachelor's degree in sociology provides excellent preparation for either graduate study or employment. However, few employers look specifically for sociology B.A.'s in preference to other liberal arts degrees. To enhance the value of a B.A. in sociology relative to degrees in other fields, it is advisable to emphasize courses in research methods and statistics.

A graduate degree is necessary to become a practicing sociologist. It is required for any career in academic sociology and for most careers in applied sociology. An M.A. or M.S. is sufficient for teaching in high schools or two-year colleges, or for employment in public agencies and private firms. A Ph.D. is usually necessary for teaching and research in universities and for high-level positions in research institutes, private industry, and government agencies.

The Ph.D. generally requires 4 or 5 years of study, often including the completion of an M.A. In many graduate schools, work is available as part of the learning experience; the graduate student may be employed as a teaching assistant (TA) or research assistant (RA). A TA typically grades exams, meets with students who need extra help, and leads discussion sections. As noted earlier, RAs are generally hired by faculty members who have received grants for specific research projects.

Most graduate degree programs begin with courses on basic theoretical issues, research methods, and statistics. After a year of such courses the student may take an examination and perhaps be awarded the Master's degree. Subsequently the emphasis shifts from course work to actual research. In this phase the student is exposed to a wide variety of research methods, including computer skills, in-depth interviewing, participant observation, and use of census materials, questionnaires, and surveys. This is followed by a set of Ph.D. examinations, which may be written or oral, and then by the writing of a dissertation. The dissertation must be an original piece of scholarship. Usually it entails submitting a formal proposal to a committee of faculty advisers, who also preside over the student's oral defense of the dissertation when it is completed.

More than 130 universities in the United States offer a Ph.D. in sociology, and most of them also offer an M.A. or M.S. More than 150 other schools offer only an M.A. Some graduate programs in sociology are designed specifically to prepare students for nonacademic careers in business or government. They may, for example, substitute internships in agency offices for the traditional TA or RA experience.

Applicants to graduate sociology programs do not have to have an undergraduate major in sociology, but the requirements of graduate departments differ considerably in such areas as foreign language skills and statistics courses. Many departments require applicants to take the Graduate Record Examination (GRE) and have scores available by the beginning of the calendar year. This is particularly important for financial aid decisions. Letters of recommendation can greatly influence the decisions of graduate admissions committees.

The reputation of the institution from which an individual receives a graduate degree can have a significant effect on career opportunities. In addition, graduate departments differ in the quality of their programs in various specialties, such as criminology, demography, the study of the family, and so on. The prospective degree candidate should pay careful attention to the department's reputation in specific areas as well as the reputation of the college or university itself. And, of course, it is a good idea to apply to several graduate programs.

To aid students in choosing a graduate program in sociology, the American Sociological Association issues an annual publication titled *Guide to Graduate Departments of Sociology.* This guide contains information about more than 200 degree programs in the United States and Canada—including degrees awarded, names and specialties of faculty members, special programs, tuition and fees, availability of fellowships and assistantships, deadlines for applications, and how to obtain further information and application forms. The guide is available in college libraries or can be ordered from the American Sociological Association, 1722 N Street N.W., Washington, D.C. 20036.

References

American Sociological Association. (1995). *Careers in sociology.* Washington, DC: American Sociological Association.

Donow, K. R. (1990, April). On the transition from the academy to a career in business. *Footnotes* (American Sociological Association), p. 6.

Huber, B. J. (1984). *Career possibilities for sociology graduates.* Washington, DC: American Sociological Association.

Lyson, T. A., & Squires, G. D. (1993, February). The "lost generation" of sociologists. *Footnotes* (American Sociological Association), pp. 4–5.

Manderscheid, R. W., & Greenwald, M. (1983). Trends in employment of sociologists. In H. E. Freeman, R. R. Dynes, P. H. Rossi, & W. F. Whyte (Eds.), *Applied sociology.* San Francisco: Jossey-Bass.

Rossi, P. H., & Whyte, W. F. (1983). The applied side of sociology. In H. E. Freeman, R. R. Dynes, P. H. Rossi, and W. F. Whyte (Eds.), *Applied sociology.* San Francisco: Jossey-Bass.

GLOSSARY

accommodation the process by which a smaller, less powerful society is able to preserve the major features of its culture even after prolonged contact with a larger, stronger culture.

acculturation the process by which the members of a civilization incorporate norms and values from other cultures into their own.

achieved status a position or rank that is earned through the efforts of the individual.

age cohort a set of people of about the same age who are passing through the life course together.

age grade a set of statuses and roles based on age.

ageism an ideology that justifies prejudice and discrimination based on age.

agencies of socialization the groups of people, along with the interactions that occur within those groups, that influence a person's social development.

agents of socialization individuals who socialize others.

alienation the feeling of being powerless to control one's own destiny; a worker's feeling of powerlessness owing to inability to control the work process.

animism a form of religion in which all forms of life and all aspects of the earth are inhabited by gods or supernatural powers.

anomie a state of normlessness.

anticipatory socialization socialization that prepares an individual for a role that he or she is likely to assume later in life.

ascribed status a position or rank that is assigned to an individual at birth and cannot be changed.

assimilation a pattern of intergroup relations in which a minority group is absorbed into the majority population and eventually disappears as a distinct group; the process by which culturally distinct groups in a larger civilization adopt the norms, values, and language of the host civilization and are able to gain equal statuses in its groups and institutions.

authority power that is considered legitimate both by those who exercise it and by those who are affected by it, and whose exercise is governed by the norms and statuses of organizations.

behaviorism a theory stating that all behavior is learned and that this learning occurs through the process known as conditioning.

bisexuality sexual orientation toward either sex.

bureaucracy a formal organization characterized by a clearly defined hierarchy with a commitment to rules, efficiency, and impersonality.

capitalism a system for organizing the production of goods and services that is based on markets, private property, and the business firm or company.

caste a social stratum into which people are born and in which they remain for life.

charisma a special quality or "gift" that motivates people to follow a particular leader.

charismatic authority authority that comes to an individual through a personal calling, often claimed to be inspired by supernatural powers, and is legitimated by people's belief that the leader does indeed have God-given powers.

church a religious organization that has strong ties to the larger society.

citizenship the status of membership in a nation-state.

civilization a cultural complex formed by the identical major cultural features of a number of societies.

civil religion a collection of beliefs and rituals that exist outside religious institutions.

civil society the sphere of nongovernmental, nonbusiness social activity carried out by voluntary associations, congregations, and the like.

class a social stratum that is defined primarily by economic criteria such as occupation, income, and wealth.

class consciousness a group's shared subjective awareness of its objective situation as a class.

closed question a question that requires the respondent to choose among a predetermined set of answers.

closed society a society in which social mobility does not exist.

closed stratification system a stratification system in which there are rigid boundaries between social strata.

collective behavior nonroutine behavior that is engaged in by large numbers of people responding to a common stimulus.

communications media institutions that specialize in communicating information, images, and values about ourselves, our communities, and our society.

community a set of primary and secondary groups in which the individual carries out important life functions.

conditioning the shaping of behavior through reward and punishment.

confidentiality the promise that the information provided to a researcher by a respondent will not appear in any way that can be traced to that respondent.

conflict theory a sociological perspective that emphasizes the role of conflict and power in society.

control group in an experiment, the subjects who do not experience a change in the independent variable.

controlled experiment an experimental situation in which the researcher manipulates an independent variable in order to observe and measure changes in a dependent variable.

core state a technologically advanced nation that has a dominant position in the world economy.

correlation a specific relationship between two variables.

counterculture a subculture that challenges the accepted norms and values of the larger society and establishes an alternative lifestyle.

crime an act or omission of an act that is prohibited by law.

crowd a large number of people who are gathered together in close proximity to one another.

crude birthrate the number of births occurring during a year in a given population, divided by the midyear population.

crude death rate the number of deaths occurring during a year in a given population, divided by the midyear population.

cult a new religion.

cultural evolution the process by which successful cultural adaptations are passed down from one generation to the next.

cultural lag the time required for social institutions to adapt to a major technological change.

cultural relativity the recognition that all cultures develop their own ways of dealing with the specific demands of their environments.

culture all the modes of thought, behavior, and production that

are handed down from one generation to the next by means of communicative interaction rather than by genetic transmission.

de facto segregation segregation created and maintained by unwritten norms.

de jure segregation segregation created by formal legal sanctions that prohibit certain groups from interacting with others or place limits on such interactions.

deference the respect and esteem shown to an individual.

demagogue a leader who uses personal charisma and political symbols to manipulate public opinion.

demeanor the ways in which individuals present themselves to others through body language, dress, speech, and manners.

democracy a political system in which all citizens have the right to participate in public decision making.

democratic socialism an economic philosophy based on the belief that private property may exist at the same time that large corporations are owned by the state and run for the benefit of all citizens.

demographic transition a set of major changes in birth and death rates that has occurred most completely in urban industrial nations in the past 200 years.

denomination a religious organization that is on good terms with the institution from which it developed but must compete with other denominations for members.

dependent variable the variable a hypothesis seeks to explain.

developing nation a nation that is undergoing a set of transformations whose effect is to increase the productivity of its people, their health, their literacy, and their ability to participate in political decision making.

deviance behavior that violates the norms of a particular society.

differential association a theory that explains deviance as a learned behavior determined by the extent of a person's association with individuals who engage in such behavior.

differentiation the processes whereby sets of social activities performed by one social institution are divided among different institutions.

discrimination behavior that treats people unfairly on the basis of their group membership.

downward mobility movement by an individual or group to a lower social stratum.

dramaturgical approach an approach to research on interaction in groups that is based on the recognition that much social interaction depends on the desire to impress those who may be watching.

dyad a group consisting of two people.

education the process by which a society transmits knowledge, values, norms, and ideologies and in so doing prepares young people for adult roles and adults for new roles.

educational achievement how much the student actually learns, measured by mastery of reading, writing, and mathematical skills.

educational attainment the number of years of school an individual has completed.

ego according to Freud, the part of the human personality that is the individual's conception of himself or herself in relation to others.

endogamy a norm specifying that a person brought up in a particular culture may marry within the cultural group.

endogenous force pressure for social change that builds within a society.

equality of opportunity equal opportunity to achieve desired levels of material well-being and prestige.

equality of result equality in the actual outcomes of people's attempts to improve their material well-being and prestige.

ethnic group a population that has a sense of group identity based on shared ancestry and distinctive cultural patterns.

ethnic (or racial) nationalism the belief that one's own ethnic group constitutes a distinct people whose culture is and should be separate from that of the larger society.

ethnic stratification the ranking of ethnic groups in a social hierarchy on the basis of each group's similarity to the dominant group.

ethnocentrism the tendency to judge other cultures as inferior to one's own.

ethnomethodology the study of the underlying rules of behavior that guide group interaction.

exogamy a norm specifying that a person brought up in a particular culture may marry outside the cultural group.

exogenous force pressure for social change that is exerted from outside a society.

experimental group in an experiment, the subjects who are exposed to a change in the independent variable.

expulsion the forcible removal of one population from a territory claimed by another population.

extended family an individual's nuclear family plus the nuclear families of his or her blood relatives.

family a group of people related by blood, marriage, or adoption.

family of orientation the nuclear family in which a person is born and raised.

family of procreation the nuclear family a person forms through marriage or cohabitation.

feral child a child reared outside human society.

field experiment an experimental situation in which the researcher observes and studies subjects in their natural setting.

folkways weakly sanctioned norms.

formal organization a group that has an explicit, often written, set of norms, statuses, and roles that specify each member's relationships to the others and the conditions under which those relationships hold.

frequency distribution a classification of data that describes how many observations fall within each category of a variable.

functionalism a sociological perspective that focuses on the ways in which a complex pattern of social structures and arrangements contributes to social order.

gemeinschaft a term used to refer to the close, personal relationships of small groups and communities.

gender the culturally defined ways of acting as a male or a female that become part of an individual's personal sense of self.

gender role a set of behaviors considered appropriate for an individual of a particular gender.

gender socialization the ways in which we learn our gender identity and develop according to cultural norms of masculinity and femininity.

generalized other a person's internalized conception of the expectations and attitudes held by society.

genocide the intentional extermination of one population by a more dominant population.

gerontology the study of aging and older people.

gesellschaft a term used to refer to the well-organized but impersonal relationships among the members of modern societies.

ghetto a section of a city that is segregated either racially or culturally.

group any collection of people who interact with one another on the basis of shared expectations regarding one another's behavior.

Hawthorne effect the unintended effect that results from the attention given to subjects in an experimental situation.

hermaphrodite a person whose primary sexual organs have features of both male and female organs, making it difficult to categorize the individual as male or female.

heterosexuality sexual orientation toward the opposite sex.

homogamy the tendency to marry a person who is similar to oneself in social background.

homosexuality sexual orientation toward the same sex.

horticultural society a society whose primary means of subsistence is raising crops, which it plants and cultivates, often developing an extensive system for watering the crops.

human ecology a sociological perspective that emphasizes the relationships among social order, social disorganization, and the distribution of populations in time and space.

hypothesis a statement that specifies a relationship between two or more variables that can be tested through empirical observation.

id according to Freud, the part of the human personality from which all innate drives arise.

ideas ways of thinking that organize human consciousness.

identification the social process whereby an individual chooses role models and attempts to imitate their behavior.

ideologies systems of values and norms that the members of a society are expected to believe in and act on without question.

impression management the strategies one uses to "set a stage" for one's own purposes.

in-group a social group to which an individual has a feeling of allegiance; usually, but not always, a primary group.

independent variable a variable the researcher believes causes a change in another variable (i.e., the dependent variable).

informal organization a group whose norms and statuses are generally agreed upon but are not set down in writing.

informed consent the right of respondents to be informed of the purpose for which the information they supply will be used and to judge the degree of personal risk involved in answering questions, even when an assurance of confidentiality has been given.

institution a more or less stable structure of statuses and roles devoted to meeting the basic needs of people in a society.

institutional discrimination the systematic exclusion of people from equal participation in a particular institution because of their group membership.

interactionism a sociological perspective that views social order and social change as resulting from all the repeated interactions among individuals and groups.

interest group an organization that attempts to influence elected and appointed officials regarding a specific issue or set of issues.

intergenerational mobility a change in the social class of family members from one generation to the next.

internal colonialism a theory of racial and ethnic inequality that suggests that some minorities are essentially colonial peoples within the larger society.

intragenerational mobility a change in the social class of an individual within his or her own lifetime.

Jim Crow the system of formal and informal segregation that existed in the United States from the late 1860s to the early 1970s.

kinship the role relations among people who consider themselves to be related by blood, marriage, or adoption.

labeling a theory that explains deviance as a societal reaction that brands or labels as deviant people who engage in certain behaviors.

laissez-faire capitalism an economic philosophy based on the belief that the wealth of a nation can be measured by its capacity to produce goods and services (i.e., its resources of land, labor, and machinery) and that these can be maximized by free trade.

laws norms that are written by specialists, collected in codes or manuals of behavior, and interpreted and applied by other specialists.

legal authority authority that is legitimated by people's belief in the supremacy of the law; obedience is owed not to a person but to a set of impersonal principles.

legitimacy the ability of a society to engender and maintain the belief that the existing political institutions are the most appropriate for that society.

life chances the opportunities an individual will have or be denied throughout life as a result of his or her social-class position.

life course a pathway along an age-differentiated, socially created sequence of transitions.

life expectancy the average number of years a member of a given population can expect to live.

lifetime negative experiences experiences that cause long-term stress, such as the death of a child or spouse.

linguistic-relativity hypothesis the belief that language determines the possibilities for thought and action in any culture.

lobbying the process whereby interest groups seek to persuade legislators to vote in their favor on particular bills.

long-distance upward mobility a form of upward mobility in which a person rises during his or her own lifetime from low family status to membership in a professional or managerial elite.

macro-level sociology an approach to the study of society that focuses on the major structures and institutions of society.

market an economic institution that regulates exchange behavior through the establishment of different values for particular goods and services.

mass a large number of people who are all oriented toward a set of shared symbols or social objects.

mass public a large population of potential spectators or participants who engage in collective behavior.

master status a status that takes precedence over all of an individual's other statuses.

material culture patterns of possessing and using the products of culture.

megalopolis a complex of cities distributed along a major axis of traffic and communication, with a total population exceeding 25 million.

mercantilism an economic philosophy based on the belief that the wealth of a nation can be measured by its holdings of gold or other precious metals and that the state should control trade.

metropolitan area a central city surrounded by a number of smaller cities and suburbs that are closely related to it both socially and economically.

micro-level sociology an approach to the study of society that focuses on patterns of social interaction at the individual level.

middle-level sociology an approach to the study of society that focuses on relationships between social structures and the individual.

minority group a population that, because of its members' physical or cultural characteristics, is singled out from others in the society for differential and unequal treatment.

modernization a term used to describe the changes experienced by societies and individuals as a result of industrialization, urbanization, and the development of nation-states.

monotheistic a term used to describe a theistic belief system centered on belief in a single all-powerful God.

mores strongly sanctioned norms.

multinational corporation an economic enterprise that has headquarters in one country and conducts business activities in one or more other countries.

nationalism the belief of a people that they have the right and the duty to constitute themselves as a nation-state.

nation-state the largest territory within which a society's political institutions can operate without having to face challenges to their sovereignty.

natural selection the relative success of organisms with specific genetic mutations in reproducing new generations with the new trait.

nonterritorial community a network of relationships formed around shared goals.

normative order the array of norms that permit a society to achieve relatively peaceful social control.

norms specific rules of behavior.

nuclear family two or more people related by blood, marriage, or adoption who share a household.

objective class in Marxian theory, a social class that has a visible, specific relationship to the means of production.

occupational prestige the honor or prestige attributed to specific occupations by adults in a society.

oligarchy rule by a few people who stay in office indefinitely rather than for limited terms.

open question a question that does not require the respondent to choose from a predetermined set of answers. Instead, the respondent may answer in his or her own words.

open society a society in which social mobility is possible for everyone.

open stratification system a stratification system in which the boundaries between social strata are easily crossed.

opinion leader an individual who consistently influences the attitudes and behavior of others.

out-group any social group to which an individual does not have a feeling of allegiance; may be in competition or conflict with the in-group.

paradigm a model comprising existing theories and methods; a general way of seeing the world that dictates what kind of scientific work should be done and what kinds of theory are acceptable.

participant observation a form of observation in which the researcher participates to some degree in the lives of the people being observed.

pastoral society a society whose primary means of subsistence is herding animals and moving with them over a wide expanse of grazing land.

patriarchy the dominance of men over women.

patronage jobs and economic benefits that party leaders can exchange for votes and political influence.

peer group an interacting group of people of about the same age that has a significant influence on the norms and values of its members.

percent analysis a mathematical operation that transforms an absolute number into a proportion as a part of 100.

peripheral area a region that supplies basic resources and labor power to more advanced states.

plea bargaining a process in which a person charged with a crime agrees to plead guilty to a lesser charge.

pluralist model a theory stating that no single group controls political decisions; instead, a plurality of interest groups influence those decisions through a process of coalition building and bargaining.

pluralistic society a society in which different ethnic and racial groups are able to maintain their own cultures and lifestyles while gaining equality in the institutions of the larger society.

political institution a set of norms and statuses pertaining to the exercise of power and authority.

political party an organization of people who join together to gain legitimate control of state authority.

political revolution a set of changes in the political structures and leadership of a society.

polytheistic a term used to describe a theistic belief system that includes numerous gods.

power the ability to control the behavior of others, even against their will.

power elite model a theory stating that political decisions are controlled by an elite of rich and powerful individuals even in societies with democratic political institutions.

prejudice an attitude that prejudges a person on the basis of a real or imagined characteristic of a group to which that person belongs.

primary deviance an act that results in the labeling of the offender as deviant.

primary group a small group characterized by intimate, face-to-face associations.

privacy the right of a respondent to define when and on what terms his or her actions may be revealed to the general public.

profane a term used to describe phenomena that are not considered sacred.

profession an occupation with a body of knowledge and a developed intellectual technique that are transmitted by a formal educational process and testing procedures.

projection the psychological process whereby we attribute to other people behaviors and attitudes that we are unwilling to accept in ourselves.

psychosocial risk behaviors behaviors that are detrimental to health, such as smoking and heavy drinking.

public opinion the values and attitudes held by mass publics.

race an inbreeding population that develops distinctive physical characteristics that are hereditary.

racism an ideology based on the belief that an observable, supposedly inherited trait is a mark of inferiority that justifies discriminatory treatment of people with that trait.

rate of reproductive change the difference between the crude birthrate and the crude death rate for a given population.

recidivist a criminal who is returned to prison after having served at least one term there.

reference group a group that an individual uses as a frame of reference for self-evaluation and attitude formation.

relative deprivation deprivation as determined by comparison with others rather than by some objective measure.

religion any set of coherent answers to the dilemmas of human existence that makes the world meaningful; a system of beliefs and rituals that serves to bind people together into a social group.

religiosity the depth of a person's religious feelings.

resocialization intense, deliberate socialization designed to change major beliefs and behaviors.

rite of passage a ceremony marking the transition to a new stage of a culturally defined life course.

ritual a formal pattern of activity that expresses symbolically a set of shared meanings.

role the way a society defines how an individual is to behave in a particular status.

role conflict conflict that occurs when in order to perform one role well a person must violate the expectations associated with another role.

role expectations a society's expectations about how a role should be performed, together with the individual's perceptions of what is required in performing that role.

role strain conflict that occurs when the expectations associated with a single role are contradictory.

role taking trying to look at social situations from the standpoint of another person from whom one seeks a response.

sacred a term used to describe phenomena that are regarded as extraordinary, transcendent, and outside the everyday course of events.

sample a set of respondents selected from a specific population.

sample survey a survey administered to a selection of respondents drawn from a specific population.

sanctions rewards and punishments for abiding by or violating norms.

scapegoat a convenient target for hostility.

science knowledge obtained as a result of the process of developing and testing hypotheses.

scientific method the process by which theories and explanations are constructed through repeated observation and careful description.

secondary deviance behavior that is engaged in as a reaction to the experience of being labeled as deviant.

secondary group a social group whose members have a shared goal or purpose but are not bound together by strong emotional ties.

sect a religious organization that rejects the beliefs and practices of existing churches; usually formed when a group leaves the church to form a rival organization.

secularization a process in which the dominance of religion over other institutions is reduced.

segregation the ecological and institutional separation of races or ethnic groups.

semiperipheral area a state or region in which industry and financial institutions are developed to some extent but that remains dependent on capital and technology provided by other states.

sex the biological differences between males and females, including the primary sex characteristics that are present at birth (i.e., the presence of specific male or female genitalia) and the secondary sex characteristics that develop later (facial and body hair, voice quality, etc.).

sexism an ideology that justifies prejudice and discrimination based on sex.

sexuality the manner in which a person engages in the intimate behaviors connected with genital stimulation, orgasm, and procreation.

significant other any person who is important to an individual.

simple supernaturalism a form of religion in which people may believe in a great force or spirit but do not have a well-defined concept of God or a set of rituals involving God.

slavery the ownership of one racial, ethnic, or politically determined group by another group that has complete control over the enslaved group.

social category a collection of individuals who are grouped together because they share a trait deemed by the observer to be socially relevant.

social change variations over time in the ecological ordering of populations and communities, in patterns of roles and social interactions, in the structure and functioning of institutions, and in the cultures of societies.

social conditions the realities of the life we create together as social beings.

social control the set of rules and understandings that control the behavior of individuals and groups in a particular culture.

social Darwinism the notion that people who are more successful at adapting to the environment in which they find themselves are more likely to survive and to have children who will also be successful.

social group a set of two or more individuals who share a sense of common identity and belonging and who interact on a regular basis.

social mobility movement by an individual or group from one social stratum to another.

social movement organized collective behavior aimed at changing or reforming social institutions or the social order itself.

social revolution a complete transformation of the social order, including the institutions of government and the system of stratification.

social stratification a society's system for ranking people hierarchically according to such attributes as wealth, power, and prestige; the process whereby the members of a society are sorted into different statuses.

social structure the recurring patterns of behavior that create relationships among individuals and groups within a society.

socialism an economic philosophy based on the concept of public ownership of property and sharing of profits, together with the belief that economic decisions should be controlled by the workers.

socialization the processes whereby we learn to behave according to the norms of our culture.

society a population that is organized in a cooperative manner to carry out the major functions of life.

sociobiology the hypothesis that all human behavior is determined by genetic factors.

socioeconomic status (SES) a broad social-class ranking based on occupational status, family prestige, educational attainment, and earned income.

sociological imagination according to C. Wright Mills, the ability to see how social conditions affect our lives.

sociology the scientific study of human societies and human behavior in the groups that make up a society.

spatial mobility movement of an individual or group from one location or community to another.

state the set of political institutions operating in a particular society.

status a socially defined position in a group.

status group a category of people within a social class, defined by how much honor or prestige they receive from the society in general.

status symbols material objects or behaviors that indicate social status or prestige.

stereotype an inflexible image of the members of a particular group that is held without regard to whether it is true.

stigma an attribute or quality of an individual that is deeply discrediting.

structural mobility movement of an individual or group from one social stratum to another caused by the elimination of an entire class as a result of changes in the means of existence.

subculture a group of people who hold many of the values and norms of the larger culture but also hold certain beliefs, values, or norms that set them apart from that culture.

subjective class in Marxian theory, the way members of a given social class perceive their situation as a class.

superego according to Freud, the part of the human personality that internalizes the moral codes of adults.

sustainable development development that does not damage the environment or create new environmental burdens.

technologies the products and the norms for using them that are found in a given culture.

technology tools, procedures, and forms of social organization that increase human productive capacity; the use of tools and knowledge to manipulate the physical environment in order to achieve desired practical goals.

technology assessment efforts to anticipate the consequences of particular technologies for individuals and for society as a whole.

territorial community a population that functions within a particular geographic area.

theism a belief system that conceives of a god or gods as separate from humans and from other living things on the earth.

theoretical perspective a set of interrelated theories that offer explanations for important aspects of social behavior.

theory a set of interrelated concepts that seeks to explain the causes of an observable phenomenon.

total institution a setting in which people undergoing resocialization are isolated from the larger society under the control of a specialized staff.

totalitarian regime a regime that accepts no limits to its power and seeks to exert its rule at all levels of society.

traditional authority authority that is hereditary and is legitimated by traditional values, particularly people's idea of the sacred.

transsexuals people who feel very strongly that the sexual organs they were born with do not conform to their deep-seated sense of what their sex should be.

triad a group consisting of three people.

two-step flow of communication the process in which messages communicated by the media are evaluated by certain respected individuals, who in turn influence the attitudes and behavior of others.

unobtrusive measures observational techniques that measure behavior but intrude as little as possible into actual social settings.

upward mobility movement by an individual or group to a higher social stratum.

urbanization a process in which an increasing proportion of a total population becomes concentrated in urban settlements.

values the ideas that support or justify norms.

variable a characteristic of an individual, group, or society that can vary from one case to another.

voluntary association a formal organization whose members pursue shared interests and arrive at decisions through some sort of democratic process.

welfare capitalism an economic philosophy in which markets determine what goods will be produced and how, but the government regulates economic competition.

REFERENCES

Abbott, A. (1993). The sociology of work and occupations. *Annual Review of Sociology, 19,* 187–209.

Abbott, A. D. (1988). *The system of professions: An essay on the division of expert labor.* Chicago: University of Chicago Press.

Achebe, C. (1993, July 27). The high price of patience. *New York Times,* p. A13.

Addams, J. (1895). *Hull House maps and papers.* New York: Crowell.

Adler, M. (1979). *Drawing down the moon: Witches, druids, goddess-worshippers, and other pagans in America today.* Boston: Beacon.

Adorno, T. (1950). *The authoritarian personality.* New York: Harper.

Adriance, M. (1986). Opting for the poor: A social-historical analysis of the changing Brazilian Catholic church. *Sociological Analysis, 46,* 131–146.

Aganbegyan, A. (1989). *Perestroika 1989.* New York: Scribner.

Ahlburg, D. A., & De Vita, C. J. (1992, August). New realities of the American family. *Population Bulletin* (Population Reference Bureau).

Alam, M. (1988). *Studies on brain drain.* Monticello, IL: Vance Bibliographies.

Aldous, J. (1982). From dual-earner to dual-career families and back again. In J. Aldous (Ed.), *Two paychecks: Life in dual-career families.* Newbury Park, CA: Sage Publications.

Alland, A. (1973). *Human diversity.* Garden City, NY: Doubleday.

Allen, F. L. (1931). *Only yesterday: An informal history of the 1920s.* New York: Harper.

Altman, D. (1987). *AIDS in the mind of America.* Garden City, NY: Doubleday.

Altman, L. K. (1996, January 9). Cross-species transplants raise concerns. *New York Times,* p. C1.

American Assembly (1990). The American Assembly on population growth and the global environment. *Population and Development Review, 16,* 384–386.

Ammerman, N. T. (1990). *Baptist battles: Social change and religious conflict in the Southern Baptist Convention.* New Brunswick, NJ: Rutgers University Press.

Amory, C. (1960). *Who killed society?* New York: Harper.

Andersen, M. L. (1993). *Thinking about women: Sociological perspectives on sex and gender* (3rd ed.). New York: Macmillan.

Anderson, E. (1990). *Street wise: Race, class, and change in an urban community.* Chicago: University of Chicago Press.

Apter, D. (1980). *Ghana in transition* (Rev. ed.). Princeton, NJ: Princeton University Press.

Archibald, K. (1947). *Wartime shipyard.* Berkeley: University of California Press.

Ariès, P. (1962). *Centuries of childhood.* New York: Vintage Books.

Aron, R. (1955). *The century of total war.* Boston: Beacon.

Aronowitz, S. (1984). *Working class hero.* New York: Schocken.

Aronowitz, S., & DiFazio, W. (1994). *The jobless future: Sci-tech and the dogma of work.* Minneapolis: University of Minnesota Press.

Aronowitz, S., & Giroux, H. A. (1985). *Education under siege.* South Hadley, MA: Bergin and Garvey.

Asch, S. E. (1966). Effects of group pressure upon the modification and distortion of judgments. In H. Proshansky & B. Seidenberg (Eds.), *Basic studies in social psychology.* Fort Worth, TX: Holt, Rinehart and Winston.

Ash, T. G. (1989). *The uses of adversity.* New York: Random House.

Aspaklaria, S. (1985, September 12). A divorced father, a child, and a summer visit together. *New York Times,* p. C1.

Atchley, R. C. (1991). *Social forces and aging: An introduction to social gerontology.* Belmont, CA: Wadsworth.

Auletta, K. (1982). *The underclass.* New York: Random House.

Austin, G. A. (1978). *Perspectives on the history of psychoactive substance abuse.* Rockville, MD: National Institute on Drug Abuse.

Ayres, B. D., Jr. (1995, November 3). California smog cloud is cleaning up its act. *New York Times,* p. A14.

Backer, B. (1982). *Death and dying: Individuals and institutions.* New York: Wiley.

Bakke, E. W. (1933). *The unemployed man.* London: Nisbet.

Balandier, A. (1971/1890). *The delight makers.* Orlando: Harcourt Brace Jovanovich.

Balbus, I. (1978). Commodity form and legal form: An essay on the relative autonomy of the law. In C. E. Reasons & R. M. Rich (Eds.), *Sociology of law: A conflict perspective.* Toronto: Butterworths.

Balch, E. G. (1910). *Our Slavic fellow citizens.* New York: Charities Publication Committee.

Baldassare, M. (1986). *Trouble in paradise: The suburban transformation in America.* New York: Columbia University Press.

Bales, R. F., & Slater, P. E. (1955). Role differentiation in small decision-making groups. In T. Parsons & R. F. Bales (Eds.), *Family, socialization, and interaction process.* New York: Free Press.

Ballantine, J. H. (1993). *The sociology of education: A systematic analysis* (3rd ed.) Englewood Cliffs, NJ: Prentice-Hall.

Baltzell, E. D. (1958). *Philadelphia gentlemen: The making of a national upper class.* Chicago: Quadrangle.

Bane, M. J. (1992, February). *Report to the Mayor's Commission on Homelessness, New York City.* New York: Mayor's Task Force on the Homeless.

Bane, M. J., & Ellwood, D. (1983). *The dynamics of dependence: The routes to self sufficiency.* Report to the U.S. Department of Health and Human Services. Washington, DC: U.S. Government Printing Office.

Barnet, R. J. (1980). *The lean years.* New York: Simon & Schuster.

Baron, J. N., & Bielby, W. T. (1980). Bringing the firms back in: Stratification, segmentation and the organization of work. *American Sociological Review, 45,* 737–765.

Barringer, F. (1989, June 9). Divorce data stir doubt on trial marriage. *New York Times,* pp. A1, A28.

Barringer, F. (1992, November 10). Prospects for the elderly differ widely by sex. *New York Times*, pp. A1, A21.

Barry, R. L. (1994). *Breaking the thread of life: On rational suicide.* New Brunswick, NJ: Transaction.

Bashi, V. (1991). Mentoring of at-risk students. *Focus* (University of Wisconsin, Institute for Research on Poverty), *13,* 26–32.

Bassuk, E. L. (1984, July). The homelessness problem. *Scientific American,* 40–45.

Bates, F. L., & Murray, V. K. (1975). The school as a behavior system. *Journal of Research and Development in Education, 2,* 23–33.

Baum, S. (1987). *Financial aid to low-income college students: Its history and prospects.* (Institute for Research on Poverty Discussion Paper No. 846–87). Madison: University of Wisconsin.

Baumgartner, M. P. (1988). *The moral order of a suburb.* New York: Oxford University Press.

Bayer, R. (1988). *Private acts, social consequences: AIDS and the politics of public health.* New York: Free Press.

Bayer, R. (1991). The great drug policy debate. *Millbank Quarterly, 69,* 341–364.

Becker, G. S. (1973). A theory of marriage. In T. W. Schultz (Ed.), *Economics of the family: Marriage, children, and human capital.* Chicago: University of Chicago Press.

Becker, G. S. (1977). The economics of marital instability. *Journal of Political Economy, 84,* 1141–1187.

Becker, H. J. (1984, June). *School uses of microcomputers.* Baltimore: Johns Hopkins University, Center for Social Organization of Schools.

Becker, H. S. (1961). *Boys in white: Student culture in medical school.* Chicago: University of Chicago Press.

Becker, H. S. (1963). *The outsiders: Studies in the sociology of deviance.* New York: Free Press.

Beer, F. A. (1981). *Peace against war: The ecology of international violence.* San Francisco: Freeman.

Beijer, G. J. (1969). Modern patterns of international migratory movement. In J. A. Jackson (Ed.), *Migration.* Cambridge, England: Cambridge University Press.

Belkin, L. (1992, March 2). Choosing to die at home: Dignity has its burdens. *New York Times,* pp. A1, B4.

Bell, D. (1962). Crime as an American way of life. In D. Bell, *The end of ideology.* New York: Free Press.

Bell, D. (1973). *The coming of post industrial society: A venture in social forecasting.* New York: Basic Books.

Bell, D. (1993, Winter). Beyond the European currency crisis. *Dissent,* pp. 50–54.

Bellah, R. N. (1970). *Beyond belief.* New York: Harper.

Bellah, R. N., Madison, R., Sullivan, W. M., Swidler, A., & Tipton, S. M. (1985). *Habits of the heart: Individualism and commitment in American life.* Berkeley: University of California Press.

Belsky, J. (1988). The "effects" of infant day care reconsidered. *Early Childhood Research Quarterly, 3,* 235–272.

Belsky, J., & Steinberg, L. D. (1991). *Infancy, childhood & adolescence: Development in context.* New York: McGraw-Hill.

Ben-David, J. (1984). *The scientist's role in society: A comparative study.* Chicago: University of Chicago Press.

Benavot, A., et al. (1991). Knowledge for the masses: World models and national curricula, 1920–1986. *American Sociological Review, 56,* 85–91.

Bendix, R. (1969). *Nation-building and citizenship.* Garden City, NY: Doubleday.

Bendix, R. (1974). *Work and authority in industry.* Berkeley: University of California Press.

Bendix, R., & Lipset, S. M. (1966). *Class, status, and power: Social stratification in comparative perspective* (2nd ed.). New York: Free Press.

Bennett, M. K. (1954). *The world's food.* New York: Harper.

Benokraitis, N. V., & Feagin, J. R. (1986). *Modern sexism: Blatant, subtle, and covert discrimination.* Englewood Cliffs, NJ: Prentice-Hall.

Bensman, D., & Lynch, R. (1987). *Rusted dreams: Hard times in a steel community.* New York: McGraw-Hill.

Bentham, J. (1789). *An introduction to the principles of morals and legislation.* London: T. Payne.

Bentham, J. (1864). *Theory of legislation.* London: Trubner.

Berger, B. (1961). The myth of suburbia. *Journal of Social Issues, 17,* 38–48.

Berger, G. (1968). *Working class suburb: A study of auto workers in suburbia.* Berkeley: University of California Press.

Bergmann, B. R., & Hartmann, H. (1995, May 1). A program to help working parents. *The Nation,* pp. 592ff.

Bernard, J. (1964). *Academic women.* University Park: Pennsylvania State University Press.

Bernard, J. (1973). *The sociology of community.* Glenview, IL: Scott, Foresman.

Bernard, J. (1982). *The future of marriage* (2nd ed.). New Haven, CT: Yale University Press.

Bernardi, B. (1985). *Age class systems: Social institutions and politics based on age.* Cambridge, England: Cambridge University Press.

Bernstein, R. (1988, August 30). Sociology branches out but is left in splinters. *New York Times,* p. A14.

Berrueta-Clement, J. R., Schweinhart, L. J., Barnett, W. S., Epstein, A. S., & Weikart, D. P. (1984). *Changed lives: The effects of the Perry preschool program on youths through age 19.* Ypsilanti, MI: High/Scope Press.

Berry, B. (1978). Latent structure of urban systems: Research methods and findings. In L. S. Bourne & J. W. Simmons (Eds.), *Systems of cities: Readings on structure, growth, and policy.* New York: Oxford University Press.

Bettelheim, B. (1962, Winter). The problem of generations. *Daedalus,* pp. 68–96.

Bianchi, S. M., & Spain, D. (1986). *American women in transition.* New York: Russell Sage.

Bierstedt, R. (1963). *The social order.* New York: McGraw-Hill.

Bigner, J. J., & Bozett, F. W. (1989). Parenting by gay fathers. *Marriage and Family Review, 14,* 155–175.

Birdwhistell, R. (1970). *Kinesics and context: Essays on body motion and communication.* Philadelphia: University of Pennsylvania Press.

Black, D. (Ed.). (1984). *Toward a general theory of social control.* Orlando: Academic Press.

Blau, J. R. (1993). *Social contracts and economic markets.* New York: Plenum Press.

Blau, P. (1964). *Exchange and power in social life.* New York: Wiley.

Blau, P., & Duncan, O. D. (1967). *The American occupational structure.* New York: Wiley.

Blau, P. M., & Scott, R. W. (1962). *Formal organizations: A comparative approach.* San Francisco: Chandler.

Blauner, R. (1964). *Alienation and freedom.* Chicago: University of Chicago Press.

Blauner, R. (1969). Internal colonialism and ghetto revolt. *Social Problems, 16,* 393–408.

Blauner, R. (1972). *Racial oppression in America.* New York: Harper.

Blauner, R. (Ed.). (1989). *Black lives, white lives: Three decades of race relations in the United States.* Berkeley: University of California Press.

Blinder, D., & Crossette, B. (1993, February 7). As ethnic wars multiply, U.S. strives for a policy. *New York Times,* p. A1.

Bloch, M. (1964). *Feudal society* (Vol. 1). Chicago: University of Chicago Press.

Block, F. (1990). *Post industrial possibilities: A critique of economic discourse.* Berkeley: University of California Press.

Block, R. (1994). The tragedy of Rwanda. *New York Review of Books, 41,* 3–8.

Bloom, B. S. (1976). *Human characteristics and school learning.* New York: McGraw-Hill.

Blumenfeld, W. J. (Ed.). (1992). *Homophobia.* Boston: Beacon.

Blumer, H. (1968). America's changing rituals of death. In M. Truzzi, *Sociology and everyday life.* Englewood Cliffs, NJ: Prentice Hall.

Blumer, H. (1969a). Elementary collective groupings. In A. M. Lee (Ed.), *Principles of sociology* (3rd ed.). New York: Barnes & Noble.

Blumer, H. (1969b). *Symbolic interactionism.* Englewood Cliffs, NJ: Prentice-Hall.

Blumer, H. (1978). Elementary collective behavior. In L. E. Genevie (Ed.), *Collective behavior and social movements.* Itasca, IL: Peacock.

Blumstein, P., & Schwartz, P. (1983). *American couples: Money, work, sex.* New York: Morrow.

Boggs, V. W., & Meyersohn, R. (1988). The profile of a Bronx salsero: Salsa's still alive! *Journal of Popular Music and Society, 11,* 7–14.

Bogue, D. J. (1969). *Principles of demography.* New York: Wiley.

Bogue, D. J. (1985). *The population of the United States: Historical trends and future projections.* New York: Free Press.

Bohannon, L., & Bohannon, P. (1953). *The Tiv of central Nigeria.* London: International African Institute.

Bohannon, L., & Bohannon, P. (1962). *Markets in Africa.* Evanston, IL: Northwestern University Press.

Bohlen, C. (1993, November 13). Russians discover capitalism's harsher realities. *New York Times,* p. 3.

Boldt, E. D., Frideres, J. S., & Stephens, J. J. (1978). Perception of pollution and willingness to act. In W. R. Burch (Ed.), *Readings in ecology, energy, and human society.* New York: Harper.

Bonner, R. (1994, August 25). Hutu and Tutsi mill the rice and set an example. *New York Times,* p. A1.

Bonnett, A. W. (1981). *Institutional adaptation of West Indian immigrants to America.* Lanham, MD: University Press of America.

Boocock, S. S. (1980). *Sociology of education: An introduction* (2nd ed.). Boston: Houghton Mifflin.

Booth, A., & Edwards, J. N. (1985, February). Age at marriage and marital instability. *Journal of Marriage and the Family,* pp. 67–75.

Bose, C. E., & Rossi, P. H. (1983). Gender and jobs. *American Sociological Review, 48,* 316–330.

Bosk, C. (1979). *Forgive and remember: Managing medical failure.* Chicago: University of Chicago Press.

Bott, E. (1977). Urban families: Conjugal roles and social networks. In S. Leinhardt (Ed.), *Social networks: A developing paradigm.* Orlando: Academic Press.

Bottomore, T. (Ed.). (1973). *Karl Marx.* Englewood Cliffs, NJ: Prentice-Hall.

Bowles, S., & Gintis, H. (1977). *Schooling in capitalist America.* New York: Basic Books.

Bracey, J. H., Meier, A., & Rudwick, E. (1970). *Black nationalism in America.* Indianapolis: Bobbs-Merrill.

Braidwood, R. S. (1967). *Prehistoric man* (7th ed.). Glenview, IL: Morrow.

Brake, M. (1980). *The sociology of youth cultures and youth subcultures.* London: Routledge and Kegan Paul.

Braudel, F. (1976/1949). *The Mediterranean and the Mediterranean world in the age of Philip II.* New York: Harper.

Braudel, F. (1981). *The structures of everyday life: Vol. 1. Civilizations and capitalism: 15th–18th century.* New York: Harper.

Braudel, F. (1984). *The perspective of the world: Vol. 3. Civilizations and capitalism: 15th–18th century.* New York: Harper.

Braverman, H. (1974). *Labor and monopoly capital.* New York: Monthly Review Press.

Breese, G. (1966). *Urbanization in newly developing countries.* Englewood Cliffs, NJ: Prentice-Hall.

Brimelow, P. (1995). *Alien nation: Common sense about America's immigration disaster.* New York: Random House.

Brinton, M. (1989). Gender stratification in contemporary urban Japan. *American Sociological Review, 54,* 549–565.

Broad, W. J. (1988, May 24). As science moves into commerce, openness is lost. *New York Times,* pp. C1, C6.

Brody, D. (1960). *Steelworkers in America: The non-union era.* Cambridge, MA: Harvard University Press.

Brody, J. (1992, August 11). To predict divorce, ask 125 questions. *New York Times,* pp. C1, C9.

Brody, J. E. (1996, February 28). Good habits outweigh genes as key to a healthy old age. *New York Times,* p. C9.

Brokaw, T. (1994, January 2). Learning lessons for life in football. *New York Times,* sec. 8, p. 11.

Bronfenbrenner, U. (1981). Children and families. *Society, 18,* 38–41.

Brown, C. (1966). *Manchild in the Promised Land.* New York: Macmillan.

Brown, D. (1970). *Bury my heart at Wounded Knee.* New York: Washington Square Press.

Brown, K. M. (1991). *Mama Lola: A Vodou priestess in Brooklyn.* Berkeley: University of California Press.

Brown, K. M. (1992, April 15). Writing about "the other." *Chronicle of Higher Education,* p. A56.

Brown, L. R., Durning, A., Flavin, C., Heise, L., Jacobson, J., Postel, S., Renner, M., Shea, C. P., & Starke, L. (1989). *State of the world 1989: A Worldwatch Institute report on progress toward a sustainable society.* New York: Norton.

Brown, L. R., Wolf, E., Starke, L., Chandler, W. U., Flavin, C., & Postel, S. (1984). *State of the world 1984: A Worldwatch Institute report on progress toward a sustainable society.* New York: Norton.

Brown, R. (1965). *Social psychology.* New York: Free Press.

Browne, M. W. (1987, September 1). Relics of Carthage show brutality amid the good life. *New York Times,* pp. C1, C10.

Browne Miller, A. (1990). *The day care dilemma: Critical concerns for American families.* New York: Plenum Press.

Bruce, J., Lloyd, C. B., & Leonard, A. (1995). *Families in focus.* New York: Population Council.

Buchanan, J. M. (1991). *The economics and the ethics of constitutional order.* Ann Arbor: University of Michigan Press.

Bumpass, L., & Sweet, J. (1972). Differentials in marital instability: (1970). *American Sociological Review, 37,* 754–766.

Bumpass, L. L., & Sweet, J. A. (1989). Children's experience in single-parent families: Implications of cohabitation and marital transitions. *Family Planning Perspectives, 21,* 256–260.

Burawoy, M. (1980). *Manufacturing consent.* Chicago: University of Chicago Press.

Burawoy, M. (1994). Why coupon socialism never stood a chance in Russia: The political conditions of economic transition. *Politics & Society, 22,* 585–594.

Burgess, E. W. (1925). The growth of the city: An introduction to a research project. In R. E. Park & E. W. Burgess, (Eds.), *The city.* Chicago: University of Chicago Press.

Burstein, R. (1991). Legal mobilization as a social movement tactic: The struggle for equal employment opportunity. *American Journal of Sociology, 96,* 1201–1225.

Buruma, I. (1984). *Behind the mask: On sexual demons, sacred mothers, transvestites, gangsters, drifters and other Japanese cultural heroes.* New York: Pantheon.

Bury, J. B. (1932). *The idea of progress: An inquiry into its origin and growth.* New York: Dover.

Butler, R. (1989). Dispelling ageism: The cross-cutting intervention. *Annals of the American Academy of Political and Social Science, 503,* 138–148.

Butterfield, F. (1992a, July 19). Are American jails becoming shelters from the storm? *New York Times,* p. E4.

Butterfield, F. (1992b, January 13). Studies find a family link to criminality. *New York Times,* pp. A1, A16.

Cahill, S. E. (1992). The sociology of childhood at and in an uncertain age. *Contemporary Sociology, 21,* 669–672.

Cain, L. D. (1964). Life course and social structure. In R. F. Faris (Ed.), *Handbook of modern sociology.* Chicago: Rand McNally.

Caldwell, J., & Caldwell, P. (1988). Women's position and child mortality and morbidity in LDCs. In *Conference on women's position and demographic change in the course of development.* Liege: IUSSP.

Cameron, W. B. (1966). *Modern social movements: A sociological outline.* New York: Random House.

Campbell, B. (1984). *Wigan Pier revisited: Poverty and politics in the eighties.* London: Virago Press.

Cancian, F. (1987). *Love in America: Gender and self development.* New York: Cambridge University Press.

Cantor, N. L. (1993). *Advance directives and the pursuit of death with dignity.* Bloomington: Indiana University Press.

Cantril, H., with Gaudet, H., & Herzog, J. (1982/1940). *The invasion from Mars.* Princeton, NJ: Princeton University Press.

Caplan, A. L. (1978). *The sociobiology debate: Readings on ethical and scientific issues.* New York: Harper.

Caplow, T. (1969). *Two against one: Coalition in triads.* Englewood Cliffs, NJ: Prentice-Hall.

Caplow, T., Bahr, H. M., Chadwick, B. A., Hill, R., & Williamson, M. H. (1983). *Middletown families: Fifty years of change and continuity.* New York: Bantam.

Caplow, T., Bahr, H. M., Modell, J., & Chadwick, B. A. (1991). *Recent social trends in the United States 1960–1990.* Montreal: McGill-Queen's University Press.

Carter, L. J. (1975). *The Florida experience.* Baltimore: Johns Hopkins University Press.

Casper, L. M., McLanahan, S. S., & Garfinkel, I. (1994). The gender–poverty gap: What can we learn from other countries? *American Sociological Review, 59,* 594–605.

Cassidy, J. (1995, October 16). Who killed the middle class? *New Yorker,* pp. 113–124.

Caudill, H. M. (1976). *The watches of the night.* Boston: Little, Brown.

Cazden, C. B. (1988). *Classroom discourse.* New York: Heinemann.

Census Bureau, U.S. Department of Commerce. (1986, October). *World Population Profile: 1985.* Washington, DC: U.S. Government Printing Office.

Chambliss, W. J. (1973, December). The Saints and the Roughnecks. *Society,* pp. 23–31.

Chenault, C. (1996). *Maasai.* Unpublished manuscript, Calhoun Community College, Decatur, AL.

Cherlin, A. J. (1981). *Marriage, divorce, remarriage.* Cambridge, MA: Harvard University Press.

Chernin, K. (1981). *The obsession: Reflections on the tyranny of slenderness.* New York: Harper.

Chirot, D. (1986). *Social change in the modern era.* San Diego, CA: Harcourt Brace Jovanovich.

Chirot, D. (1994a). *How societies change.* Thousand Oaks, CA: Pine Forge Press.

Chirot, D. (1994b). *Modern tyrants: The power and prevalence of evil in our age.* New York: Free Press.

Chodorow, N. (1978). *The reproduction of mothering: Psychoanalysis and the sociology of gender.* Berkeley: University of California Press.

Chomsky, N. (1965). *Aspects of the theory of syntax.* Cambridge, MA: MIT Press.

Chwast, J. (1965). Value conflicts in law enforcement. *Crime and Delinquency, 2,* 151–161.

Clark, W. C. (1989, September). Managing planet Earth. *Scientific American,* pp. 46–54.

Clarke, L. (1989). *Acceptable risk? Making decisions in a toxic environment.* Berkeley: University of California Press.

Clausen, J. A. (1968). *Socialization and society.* Boston: Little, Brown.

Clay, G. (1980). *Close-up: How to read the American city.* Chicago: University of Chicago Press.

Clay, G. (1994). *Real places: An unconventional guide to America's landscape.* Chicago: University of Chicago Press.

Cloward, R., & Ohlin, L. (1960). *Delinquency and opportunity: A theory of delinquent gangs.* New York: Free Press.

Cochran, M., Larner, M., Riley, D., Gunnarson, L., & Henderson, C. R., Jr. (1990). *Extending families: The social networks of parents and their children.* Cambridge, England: Cambridge University Press.

Cockerham, W. C. (1992). *Medical sociology* (5th ed.). Englewood Cliffs, NJ: Prentice-Hall.

Cohen, N. (1961). *The pursuit of the millennium.* New York: Harper.

Cohen, R. S. (1982). Science and technology in global perspective. *International Social Sciences Journal, 34,* 61–70.

Cohen, S. A., & Zysman, J. (1987). *Manufacturing matters: The myth of the post industrial economy.* New York: Basic Books.

Coleman, J. S. (1961). *The adolescent society.* New York: Free Press.

Coleman, J. S. (1964). Research chronicle: The adolescent society. In P. E. Hammond (Ed.), *Sociologists at work.* Garden City, NY: Doubleday.

Coleman, J. S. (1976). Liberty and equality in school desegregation. *School Policy, 6,* 9–13.

Coleman, J. S. (1982). *The asymmetric society.* Syracuse, NY: Syracuse University Press.

Coleman, J. S. (1986, May). Social theory, social research, and a theory of action. *American Journal of Sociology, 91,* 1309–1335.

Coles, R. (1986). *The moral life of children.* Boston: Atlantic Monthly Press.

Collier, J. (1981). Urban Indians. In H. S. Becker, *Exploring society photographically.* Chicago: University of Chicago Press.

Collins, E. G. C., & Scott, P. (Eds.). (1978). Everyone who makes it has a mentor. *Harvard Business Review, 56,* 89–101.

Comer, J. P. (1980). *School power.* New York: Free Press.

Comer, J. P. (1984). Home-school relationships as they affect the academic success of children. *Education and Urban Society, 16,* 323–327.

Comer, J. P. (1985). *Investing in our children.* New York: Committee for Economic Development.

Comer, J. P. (1987). *Children in need: Investment strategies for the educationally disadvantaged.* New York: Committee for Economic Development.

Comte, A. (1971/1854). The positive philosophy. In M. Truzzi (Ed.), *Sociology: The classic statements.* New York: Random House.

Condon, K. A. (1991). Cohabitation, marriage, marital dissolution, and remarriage, U.S., 1988. *Advance data from vital and health statistics* (No. 194). Hyattsville, MD: National Center for Health Statistics.

Conger, D., Ge, X., & Elder, G. H., Jr. (1994). Economic stress, coercive family process, and developmental problems of adolescence. *Child Development, 65,* 541–561.

Connell, R. W. (1995). *Masculinities.* Berkeley: University of California Press.

Cookson, P. W., & Persell, C. H. (1985). *Preparing for power: America's elite boarding schools.* New York: Basic Books.

Cooley, C. H. (1909). *Social organization: A study of the large mind.* New York: Scribner.

Coon, C. (1962). *The origin of races.* New York: Knopf.

Cortes, C. E. (Ed.). (1980). *The Latin American brain drain.* New York: Arno Press.

Coser, L. A. (1966). *The functions of social conflict.* New York: Free Press.

Cottrell, W. F. (1951). Death by dieselization: A case study in the reaction to technological change. *American Sociological Review, 16,* 358–365.

Cranz, G. (1982). *The politics of park design: A history of urban parks in America.* Cambridge, MA: MIT Press.

Creel, M. W. (1988). *"A peculiar people": Slave religion and community-culture among the Gullahs.* New York: New York University Press.

Cremin, L. A. (1980). *American education: The national experience 1783–1876.* New York: Harper.

Cressey, D. R. (1971/1953). *Other people's money: A study in the social psychology of embezzlement.* Belmont, CA: Wadsworth.

Cronon, W. (1983). *Changes in the land: Indians, colonists, and the ecology of New England.* New York: Hill and Wang.

Crowder, M. (1966). *A short history of Nigeria* (Rev. ed.). New York: Praeger.

Csikszentmihalyi, M., Larson, R., & Prescott, S. (1977). The ecology of adolescent activity and experience. *Journal of Youth and Adolescence, 6,* 281–294.

Cuber, J. F., & Haroff, P. B. (1980). Five types of marriage. In A. Skolnick & J. Skolnick (Eds.), *Family in transition.* Boston: Little, Brown.

Cumming, E., & Henry, W. (1971). *Growing old: The process of disengagement.* New York: Basic Books.

Cummings, J. (1983, November 20). Breakup of black family imperils gains of decades. *New York Times,* p. 56.

Curtin, P. D. (1969). *The Atlantic slave trade.* Madison: University of Wisconsin Press.

Curtiss, S. (1977). *Genie: A psycholinguistic study of a modern-day "wild child."* New York: Academic Press.

Dahl, R. (1961). *Who governs?* New Haven, CT: Yale University Press.

Dahrendorf, R. (1959). *Class and class conflict in industrial society.* Stanford, CA: Stanford University Press.

Dahrendorf, R. (1981). *Life chances.* Chicago: University of Chicago Press/Phoenix.

d'Andrade, R. G. (1966). Sex differences and cultural institutions. In E. E. Maccoby (Ed.), *The development of sex differences.* Stanford, CA: Stanford University Press.

Dankert, C. E., Mann, F. C., & Northrup, H. R. (Eds.). (1965). *Hours of work.* New York: Harper.

Danziger, K. (1971). *Socialization.* Harmondsworth, England: Penguin.

Danziger, S., & Gottschalk, P. (Eds.). (1993). *Uneven tides: Rising inequality in America.* New York: Russell Sage.

Davey, J. D. (1995). *The new social contract: America's journey from welfare state to police state.* Westport, CT: Praeger.

Davidson, D. (1973). The furious passage of the black graduate student. In J. Ladner (Ed.), *The death of white sociology.* New York: Vintage Books.

Davis, F. J. (1978). *Minority-dominant relations: A sociological analysis.* Arlington Heights, IL: AHM.

Davis, K. (1939). Illegitimacy and the social structures. *American Journal of Sociology, 45,* 215–233.

Davis, K. (1947). Final note on a case of extreme isolation. *American Journal of Sociology, 52,* 432–437.

Davis, K. (1955). The origin and growth of urbanization in the world. *American Journal of Sociology, 60,* 429–437.

Davis, K. (1968). The urbanization of the human population. In S. F. Fava (Ed.), *Urbanism in world perspective: A reader.* New York: Crowell.

Davis, K. (1991). Population and resources: Fact and interpretation. In K. Davis and M. S. Bernstam (Eds.), *Resources, environment, population: Present knowledge, future options.* New York: Oxford University Press.

Davis, K., & Combs, J. W., Jr. (Eds.). (1950). *The social and biological challenge of our aging population.* New York: Columbia University Press.

Davis, K., & Moore, W. E. (1945). Some principles of stratification. *American Sociological Review, 10,* 242–249.

Davis, K. C. (1995, September 3). Ethnic cleansing didn't start in Bosnia. *New York Times,* sec. 4, pp. 1, 6.

Davis, N. J. (1975). *Deviance: Perspectives and issues in the field.* Dubuque, IA: Brown.

Deaux, K., & Wrightsman, L. S. (1988). *Social psychology* (5th ed.). Pacific Grove, CA: Brooks/Cole.

Deierlein, K. (1994). Ideology and holistic alternatives. In W. Kornblum & C. D. Smith (Eds.), *The healing experience: Readings on the social context of health care.* Englewood Cliffs, NJ: Prentice-Hall.

Delgado-Gaiton, C. (1987). Traditions and transitions in the learning process of Mexican American children. In G. Spindler & L. Spindler (Eds.), *Interpretive ethnography of education.* Hillsdale, NJ: Erlbaum.

Della Piana, L. (1995). Categories count. *Poverty & Race, 4,* 11–12.

D'Emilio, J., & Freedman, E. B. (1988). *Intimate matters: A history of sexuality in America.* New York: Harper.

Denitch, B. (1990). *The end of the cold war.* Minneapolis: University of Minnesota Press.

Denitch, B. (1992). *After the flood: Politics and democracy in the wake of communism.* Middletown, NY: Wesleyan University Press.

Denno, D. W. (1990). *Biology and violence: From birth to adulthood.* New York: Cambridge University Press.

de Rougemont, D. (1983). *Love in the western world.* Princeton, NJ: Princeton University Press.

de Sola Pool, I. (Ed.). (1977). *The social impact of the telephone.* Cambridge, MA: MIT Press.

de Sola Pool, I. (1983). *Technologies of freedom.* Cambridge, MA: Belknap Press.

de Tocqueville, A. (1955/1856). *The old regime and the French revolution* (S. Gilbert, Trans.). Garden City, NY: Doubleday.

de Tocqueville, A. (1980/1835). *On democracy, revolution, and society* (J. Stone & S. Mennell, Trans.). Chicago: University of Chicago Press.

Dewey, R. (1948). Charles Horton Cooley: Pioneer in psychosociology. In H. F. Barnes (Ed.), *An introduction to the history of sociology.* Chicago: University of Chicago Press.

De Witt, K. (1994, August 15). Wave of suburban growth is being fed by minorities. *New York Times,* pp. A1, B6.

Dionne, E. J., Jr. (1991). *Why Americans hate politics.* New York: Simon & Schuster.

Djilas, M. (1982). *The new class: An analysis of the communist system.* Orlando: Harcourt Brace Jovanovich.

Dobzhansky, T. (1962). *Mankind evolving.* New Haven, CT: Yale University Press.

Dodgson, R. A. (1987). *The European past: Social evolution and spatial order.* London: Macmillan.

Dollard, J. (1937). *Caste and class in a southern town.* New Haven, CT: Yale University Press.

Dollard, J., Miller, N., & Doob, L. (1939). *Frustration and aggression.* New Haven, CT: Yale University Press.

Domhoff, G. W. (1978). *The powers that be.* New York: Random House.

Domhoff, G. W. (1983). *Who rules America now?* New York: Simon & Schuster.

Donow, K. R. (1990, April). On the transition from the academy to a career in business. *Footnotes* (American Sociological Association), p. 6.

Dore, R. (1973). *British factory–Japanese factory: The origins of national diversity in industrial relations.* Berkeley: University of California Press.

Dore, R. (1982). Introduction. In S. Kamata, *Japan in the passing lane: An outsider's account of life in a Japanese auto factory.* New York: Pantheon.

Dore, R. (1990). Support and be supported: Japan's strategies of interdependence. *Government and Opposition, 25,* 438–445.

Dornbusch, S. (1955). The military as an assimilating institution. *Social Forces, 33,* 316–321.

Douglas, J. D., & Rasmussen, P. K. (1977). *The nude beach.* Newbury Park, CA: Sage Publications.

Dowd, M. (1985, November 17). Youth, art, hype: A different bohemia. *New York Times Magazine,* pp. 26ff.

Drake, S. C., & Cayton, H. (1970/1945). *Black metropolis: Vol. 1. A study of Negro life in a northern city* (Rev. ed.). Orlando: Harcourt Brace Jovanovich.

Du Bois, W. E. B. (1967/1899). *The Philadelphia Negro: A social study.* New York: Schocken.

Duneier, M. (1992). *Slim's table: Race, respectability, and masculinity.* Chicago: University of Chicago Press.

Dunlap, R. E., & Scarce, R. (1991). Environmental problems and protection. *Public Opinion Quarterly, 55,* 651–672.

Durkheim, E. (1964/1893). *The division of labor in society* (2nd ed.). New York: Free Press.

Durkheim, E. 1951/1897. *Suicide, a study in sociology.* New York: Free Press.

Eckholm, E. (1985, June 25). Kanzi the chimp: A life in science. *New York Times,* pp. C1, C3.

Eckholm, E. (1992, October 6). Learning if infants are hurt when mothers go to work. *New York Times,* pp. A1, A21.

Edleson, J. I., & Tan, N. T. (1993). Conflict and family violence: The tale of two families. In P. G. Boss, W. J. Doherty, R. LaRossa, W. R. Schumm, & S. K. Steinmetz (Eds.), *Sourcebook of family theories and methods: A contextual approach.* New York: Plenum Press.

Edwards, R. (1979). *Contested terrain: The transformation of the workplace in the twentieth century.* New York: Basic Books.

Egan, T. (1995, September 3). Many seek security in private communities. *New York Times,* pp. A1, A22.

Ehrlich, P. R., Ehrlich, A. H., & Holdren, J. P. (1977). *Ecoscience: Population, resources, environment.* New York: Freeman.

Eibl-Eibesfeldt, I. (1989). *Human ethology.* Hawthorne, NY: Aldine de Gruyter.

Eisley, L. (1961). *Darwin's century.* Garden City, NY: Doubleday Anchor.

Eisley, L. (1970). *The invisible pyramid.* New York: Scribner.

Elder, G. H., Jr. (1974). *The children of the Great Depression.* Chicago: University of Chicago Press.

Elder, G. H. (1981). History and the life course. In D. Berteaux (Ed.), *Biography and society: The life history approach to the social sciences.* Newbury Park, CA: Sage Publications.

Elder, G. H., Jr., & Pavalko, E. K. (1990). World War II and divorce: A life course perspective. *American Journal of Sociology, 95,* 1213–1234.

Elder, G. H., Jr., Modell, J., & Parke, R. D. (Eds.). (1992). *Children in time and place: Intersecting historical and developmental insights.* New York: Cambridge University Press.

Eldridge, C. C. (1978). *Victorian imperialism.* Atlantic Highlands, NJ: Humanities Press.

Elias, N. (1978/1939). The civilizing process. In N. Elias (Ed.), *The development of manners.* New York: Urizen.

Elkin, F., & Handel, G. (1989). *The child and society: The process of socialization* (5th ed.). New York: Random House.

Elkind, D. (1970). *Children and adolescents: Interpretative essays on Jean Piaget.* New York: Oxford University Press.

Ellul, J. (1964). *The technological society.* New York: Vintage Books.

Ellwood, D. (1988). *Poor support: Poverty in the American family.* New York: Basic Books.

Ellwood, D., & Summers, L. H. (1986). Poverty in America: Is welfare the answer or the problem? In S. H. Danziger & D. H. Weinberg (Eds.), *Poverty: What works and what doesn't?* Cambridge, MA: Harvard University Press.

England, P. (1986). *Households, employment, and gender: A social, economic, and demographic view.* New York: Aldine.

Epstein, C. (1995, Fall). Affirmative action. *Dissent,* pp. 463–465.

Epstein, C. F. (1985). Ideal roles and real roles. *Research in Social Stratification and Mobility, 4,* 29–51.

Epstein, C. F. (1988). *Deceptive distinctions: Sex, gender, and the social order.* New Haven, CT: Yale University Press.

Erikson, E. (1963). *Childhood and society.* New York: Norton.

Erikson, E. (Ed.). (1965). *The challenge of youth.* Garden City, NY: Doubleday Anchor.

Erikson, E. (1975). Reflections on the dissent of humanist youth. In E. Erikson (Ed.), *Life history and the historical moment.* New York: Norton.

Erikson, K. T. (1962). Notes on the sociology of deviance. *Social Problems, 9,* 307–314.

Erikson, K. T. (1966). *Wayward puritans: A study in the sociology of deviance.* New York: Wiley.

Erikson, K. T. (1976). *Everything in its path.* New York: Simon & Schuster.

Erikson, K. T. (1994a). *A new species of trouble.* New York: Norton.

Erikson, K. T. (1994b, March 6). Out of sight, out of our minds. *New York Times Magazine,* pp. 34ff.

Esping-Anderson, G. (1985). *Politics against markets.* Princeton, NJ: Princeton University Press.

Etzkowitz, H., & Glassman, R. (1991). *The renaissance of sociological theory: Classical and contemporary.* Itaska, IL: Peacock.

Ezorsky, G. (1991). *Affirmative action.* Ithaca, NY: Cornell University Press.

Fallers, L. (1977). Equality and inequality in human societies. In S. Tax & L. Freeman (Eds.), *Horizons of anthropology.* Hawthorne, NY: Aldine.

Fallows, D. (1985). *A mother's work.* Boston: Houghton Mifflin.

Fantasia, R. (1988). *Cultures of solidarity: Consciousness, action, and contemporary American workers.* Berkeley: University of California Press.

Farley, R. (1995). A single census question to measure race, Spanish-origin and ancestry. *Poverty & Race, 4,* 14–15.

Farley, R., & Allen, W. R. (1987). *The color line and the quality of life in America.* New York: Russell Sage.

Farnsworth, C. H. (1994, August 15). With her songs, Eskimo bares her people's pain. *New York Times,* p. A4.

Farrington, K., & Chertok, E. (1993). Social conflict theories of the family. In P. G. Boss, W. J. Doherty, R. LaRossa, W. R. Schumm, & S. K. Steinmetz, *Sourcebook of family theories and methods: A contextual approach.* New York: Plenum Press.

Fathalla, M. F. (1992). *Reproductive health in the world: Two decades of progress and the challenge ahead.* Discussion note, Expert Group Meeting on Population and Women, Gaborone, Botswana, June 22–26.

Fava, S. (1956). Suburbanism as a way of life. *American Sociological Review, 21,* 34–38.

Fava, S. (1985). Residential preferences in the suburban era: A new look? *Sociological Focus, 18,* 109–117.

FBI. (1995). *Crime in the United States, 1994 (UCR).* Washington, DC: U.S. Department of Justice.

Feachem, R. G. A., et al. (Eds.). (1993). *The health of adults in the developing world.* New York: Oxford University Press.

Feagin, J. R. (1991, November 27). Blacks still face the malevolent reality of white racism. *Chronicle of Higher Education,* p. A44.

Fernandes, F. (1968). The weight of the past. In J. H. Franklin (Ed.), *Color and race.* Boston: Beacon.

Fernandez, J. (1992). *Tales out of school: Joseph Fernandez's crusade to rescue American education.* Boston: Little, Brown.

Fine, G. A. (1987). *With the boys: Little League baseball and preadolescent culture.* Chicago: University of Chicago Press.

Finke, R., & Stark, R. (1992). *The churching of America 1776–1992.* New Brunswick, NJ: Rutgers University Press.

Fischer, C. S. (1974). Astrology and French society: The dialectic of anarchism and modernity. In E. Tiryakian (Ed.), *On the margin of the visible.* New York: Wiley.

Fischer, C. S. (1976, 1987). *The urban experience.* Orlando: Harcourt Brace Jovanovich.

Fischer, C. S. (1982). *To dwell among friends: Personal networks in town and city.* Chicago: University of Chicago Press.

Fischer, C. S. (1985). Studying technology and social life. In M. Castells (Ed.), *High technology, space, and society.* Newbury Park, CA: Sage Publications.

Fishman, R. (1987). *Bourgeois utopias: The rise and fall of suburbia.* New York: Basic Books.

Fiske, M., & Chiriboga, D. A. (1990). *Change and continuity in adult life.* San Francisco: Jossey-Bass.

FitzSimons, R. (1970). *The Charles Dickens show: An account of his public readings 1858–1879.* London: Geoffrey Bles.

Flink, J. J. (1975). *The car culture.* Cambridge, MA: MIT Press.

Flink, J. J. (1980–1981). The car culture revisited: Some comments on the recent historiography of automotive history. *Michigan Quarterly Review, 19–20,* 772–781.

Flink, J. J. (1988). *The automobile age.* Cambridge, MA: MIT Press.

Flores, J. (1988, Fall). Rappin', writin', and breakin': Black and Puerto Rican street culture in New York. In *In search of New York* [Special issue]. *Dissent,* pp. 580–585.

Forester, T. (1988). *High tech society: The story of the high technology revolution.* Cambridge, MA: MIT Press.

Fortin, N., & Ecker, M. (1978). *Social problems at Cape Cod National Seashore.* Unpublished report to U.S. Department of the Interior, National Park Service.

Foster, J. (1990). *Villains: Crime and community in the inner city.* London: Routledge.

Foucault, M. (1973). *Madness and civilization: A history of insanity in the Age of Reason.* New York: Vintage Books.

Foucault, M. (1984). *The Foucault reader.* New York: Pantheon.

Fox, R. (1971). *The imperial animal.* New York: Dell.

Fox, R. (1989). *The search for society: Quest for a biosocial science and morality.* New Brunswick, NJ: Rutgers University Press.

Frank, R. H. (1988). *Passions within reason: The strategic role of the emotions.* New York: Norton.

Frank, R. H., & Cook, P. J. (1995). *The winner-take-all society: How more and more Americans compete for ever fewer and bigger prizes, encouraging economic waste, income inequality, and an impoverished cultural life.* New York: Free Press.

Frazier, E. F. (1939). *The Negro family in the United States.* Chicago: University of Chicago Press.

Frazier, E. F. (1957). *The Negro in the United States* (Rev. ed.). New York: Macmillan.

Frazier, E. F. (1966). *The Negro church in America.* New York: Schocken.

Freeman, J. (1973). The origins of the women's liberation movement. In J. Huber (Ed.), *Changing women in a changing society.* Chicago: University of Chicago Press.

Freeman, R. (1994). *Working under different rules.* New York: Russell Sage.

Freeman, R. B. (1993). How much has de-unionization contributed to the rise in male earnings inequality? In S. Danziger & P. Gottschalk (Eds.), *Uneven tides: Rising inequality in America.* New York: Russell Sage.

Fried, M. (1963). Grieving for a lost home. In L. J. Duhl (Ed.), *The urban condition.* New York: Basic Books.

Friedan, B. (1963). *The feminine mystique.* New York: Dell.

Friedan, B. (1992). Their turn: How men are changing. In M. S. Kimmel & M. A. Messner (Eds.), *Men's lives* (2nd ed.). New York: Macmillan.

Friedlander, D. (1969). Demographic responses and population change. *Demography, 6,* 359–381.

Friedman, M. (1962). *Capitalism and freedom.* Chicago: University of Chicago Press.

Fromm, E. (1961). *Marx's concept of man.* New York: Ungar.

Fuchs, V. (1968). *The service economy.* New York: National Bureau of Economic Research; dist. by Columbia University Press.

Fullan, M. (1993). *Change forces: Probing the depths of educational reform.* New York: Falmer Press.

Furstenberg, F. (1976). *Unplanned parenthood: The social consequences of unplanned childbearing.* New York: Free Press.

Furstenberg, F. F., & Cherlin, A. J. (1991). *Divided families: What happens to children when parents part.* Cambridge, MA: Harvard University Press.

Fyfe, C. (1976). The dynamics of African dispersal. In M. L. Kilson & R. I. Rothberg (Eds.), *The African diaspora.* Cambridge, MA: Harvard University Press.

Gabriel, T. (1995a, February 12). A generation's heritage: After the boom, a boomlet. *New York Times,* pp. 1, 34.

Gabriel, T. (1995b, June 12). A new generation seems ready to give bisexuality a place in the spectrum, *New York Times,* p. A12.

Galbraith, J. K. (1995, September 19). Blame history, not the liberals. *New York Times,* p. A21.

Gallup Organization. (1996). *The Gallup poll, monthly index.* Princeton, NJ: Gallup Organization.

Galtung, J. (1985). War. In A. Kuper & J. Kuper (Eds.), *The social science encyclopedia.* London: Routledge and Kegan Paul.

Gamson, W. A. (1992). *Talking politics.* Cambridge, England: Cambridge University Press.

Gans, H. (1967, 1976). *The Levittowners: Way of life and politics in a new suburban community.* New York: Pantheon.

Gans, H. (1979). *Deciding what's news.* New York: Pantheon.

Gans, H. (1984). *The urban villagers.* New York: Free Press.

Gans, H. (1985). The uses of poverty: The poor pay all. In W. Feigelman (Ed.), *Sociology: Full circle* (4th ed.). Fort Worth, TX: Holt, Rinehart and Winston.

Gans, H. (1995). *The war against the poor.* New York: Basic Books.

Gardner, H. (1983). *Frames of mind: The theory of multiple intelligences.* New York: Basic Books.

Garfinkel, H. (1967). *Studies in ethnomethodology.* Englewood Cliffs, NJ: Prentice-Hall.

Garfinkel, I., & McLanahan, S. S. (1986). *Single mothers and their children: A new American dilemma.* Washington, DC: Urban Institute.

Garmezy, N. (1993). Children in poverty: Resilience despite risk. *Psychiatry, 56,* 127–136.

Garreau, J. (1991). *Edge city: Life on the new frontier.* Garden City, NY: Doubleday Anchor.

Geertz, C. (1973). The growth of culture and the evolution of mind. In C. Geertz, *The interpretation of culture.* New York: Basic Books.

Genevie, L. E. (Ed.). (1978). *Collective behavior and social movements.* Itasca, IL: Peacock.

Geoghegan, T. (1991). *Which side are you on?* New York: Farrar Straus Giroux.

Gerbner, G. (1990). *Violence profile.* Philadelphia: Annenberg School of Communications.

Gerson, K. (1985). *Hard choices: How women decide about work, career, and motherhood.* Berkeley: University of California Press.

Gerth, H., & Mills, C. W. (1958). *From Max Weber: Essays in sociology.* New York: Oxford University Press.

Geschwender, J. A. (1977). *Class, race and worker insurgency.* New York: Cambridge University Press.

Giddens, A. (1984). *The constitution of society.* Berkeley: University of California Press.

Gilder, G. (1982). *Wealth and poverty.* New York: Basic Books.

Gilligan, C. (1982). *In a different voice: Psychological theory and women's development.* Cambridge, MA: Harvard University Press.

Gilligan, C. (1987). Adolescent development reconsidered. In C. E. Irwin, Jr. (Ed.), *New directions for child development:* No. 37, *Adolescent social behavior and health.* San Francisco: Jossey-Bass.

Gist, N. P. (1968). Urbanism in India. In S. F. Fava (Ed.), *Urbanism in world perspective: A reader.* New York: Crowell.

Gitlin, T. (1980). *The whole world is watching: Mass media in the making and unmaking of the new left.* Berkeley: University of California Press.

Gitlin, T. (1992, March–April). Following the money: Where does your advertising dollar go? *The Democratic Left,* pp. 3–5.

Glasgow, D. (1981). *The black underclass: Poverty, unemployment and entrapment of ghetto youth.* New York: Vintage Books.

Glazer, N. (1975). *Affirmative discrimination: Ethnic inequality and public policy.* New York: Basic Books.

Glazer, N., & Moynihan, D. P. (1970). *Beyond the melting pot: The Negroes, Puerto Ricans, Jews, Italians, and Irish of New York City* (2nd rev. ed.). Cambridge, MA: MIT Press.

Glick, P. C., & Parke, R., Jr. (1965). New approaches in studying the life cycle of the family. *Demography, 2,* 187–202.

Glueck, S., & Glueck, E. T. (1950). *Unraveling juvenile delinquency.* New York: Commonwealth Fund.

Goffman, E. (1958). Deference and demeanor. *American Anthropologist, 58,* 488–489.

Goffman, E. (1959). *The presentation of self in everyday life.* Garden City, NY: Doubleday.

Goffman, E. (1961). *Asylums.* Garden City, NY: Doubleday.

Goffman, E. (1963). *Stigma: Notes on the management of spoiled identity.* Englewood Cliffs, NJ: Prentice-Hall.

Goffman, E. (1965). *Interaction ritual: Essays on face-to-face behavior.* Garden City, NY: Doubleday.

Goffman, E. (1972). Territories of the self. In E. Goffman (Ed.), *Relations in public.* New York: Harper.

Goldfarb, W. (1945). Psychological privation in infancy and subsequent adjustment. *American Journal of Orthopsychiatry, 15,* 247–253.

Goldhamer, H., & Shils, E. (1939). Types of power and status. *American Journal of Sociology, 45,* 171–182.

Goldschmidt, W. (1978). *As you sow: Three studies in the social consequences of agribusiness.* Montclair, NJ: Allanheld, Osmun.

Goleman, D. (1985a, March 19). Dislike of own body found common among women. *New York Times,* pp. C1, C5.

Goleman, D. (1985b, September 10). Patterns of love charted in studies. *New York Times,* pp. C1, C5.

Goleman, D. (1988, April 11). The tax cheats: Selfish to the bottom line. *New York Times,* pp. A1, D2.

Goodall, J. V. L. (1968). A preliminary report on expressive movements and communications in Gombe Stream chimpanzees. In P. Jay (Ed.), *Primates: Studies in adaptation and variability.* Fort Worth, TX: Holt, Rinehart and Winston.

Goode, E. (1992). *Collective behavior.* Fort Worth, TX: Harcourt Brace.

Goode, E. (1994). *Deviant behavior* (4th ed.). Englewood Cliffs, NJ: Prentice-Hall.

Goode, W. J. (1957). Community within a community. *American Sociological Review, 22,* 194–200.

Goode, W. J. (1960). Encroachment, charlatanism, and the emerging profession: Psychology, sociology, and medicine. *American Sociological Review, 25,* 902–914.

Goode, W. J. (1963). *World revolution and family patterns.* New York: Free Press.

Goode, W. J. (1964). *The family.* Englewood Cliffs, NJ: Prentice-Hall.

Goode, W. J. (1971, November). World revolution and family patterns. *Journal of Marriage and the Family,* pp. 624–635.

Goode, W. J. (1972). The place of force in human society. *American Sociological Review, 37,* 507–519.

Goodrich, D. W., Ryder, R. G., & Rausch, H. L. (1968). Patterns of newly wed marriage. *Journal of Marriage and the Family, 30,* 383–390.

Goodrich, L. M. (1974). *The United Nations in a changing world.* New York: Columbia University Press.

Gordon, M. (1964). *Assimilation in American life.* New York: Oxford University Press.

Goslin, D. A. (1965). *The school in contemporary society.* Glenview, IL: Scott, Foresman.

Gottman, J. M. (1983). How children become friends. *Society for Research in Child Development Monograph, 48,* 1–86.

Gottmann, J. (1978). Megalopolitan systems around the world. In L. S. Bourne & J. W. Simmons (Eds.), *Systems of cities: Readings on structure, growth, and policy.* New York: Oxford University Press.

Gould, S. J. (1981). *The mismeasure of man.* New York: Norton.

Gould, S. J. (1995, February). Ghosts of bell curves past. *Natural History,* pp. 12–19.

Graham, P. (1986). *Beyond caring.* London: Grey Editions.

Gramlich, E. M., Kasten, R., & Sammartino, F. (1993). Growing inequality in the 1980s: The role of federal taxes and cash transfers. In S. Danziger & P. Gottschalk (Eds.), *Uneven tides: Rising inequality in America.* New York: Russell Sage.

Gramsci, A. (1971). *Selections from prison notebooks.* London: Routledge and Kegan Paul.

Gray, F. D. (1990). *Soviet women: Walking the tightrope.* Garden City, NY: Doubleday.

Greeley, A., Michael, R. T., & Smith, T. (1990). Americans and their sexual partners. *Society, 27,* 36–42.

Grønbjerg, K. A. (1977). *Mass society and the extension of welfare 1960–1970.* Chicago: University of Chicago Press.

Gross, J. (1992, March 29). Collapse of inner-city families creates America's new orphans. *New York Times,* pp. 1, 20.

Gunder Frank, A. (1966). The development of underdevelopment. *Monthly Review, 18,* 3–17.

Gusfield, J. (1966). *Symbolic crusade: Status politics and the American temperance movement.* Urbana: University of Illinois Press.

Gusfield, J. (1981). *The culture of public problems: Drinking, driving and the symbolic order.* Chicago: University of Chicago Press.

Guterbock, T. M. (1980). *Machine politics in transition: Party and community in Chicago.* Chicago: University of Chicago Press.

Gutkind, E. A. (1956). Our world from the air: Conflict and adaptation. In W. L. Thomas (Ed.), *Man's role in changing the face of the earth.* Chicago: University of Chicago Press.

Gutman, H. (1976). *The black family in slavery.* New York: Pantheon.

Haber, L. D., & Dowd, J. E. (1994, January). *A human development agenda for disability: Statistical considerations* (Working Paper for the Statistical Division of the United Nations Secretariat). New York: United Nations.

Hacker, A. (1995, Fall). Affirmative action. *Dissent,* pp. 465–467.

Hagestad, G. O., & Neugarten, B. L. (1985). Age and the life course. In R. H. Binstock & E. Shanas (Eds.), *Handbook of aging and the social sciences* (2nd ed.). New York: Van Nostrand Reinhold.

Halevy, E. (1955). *The growth of philosophic radicalism* (M. Morris, Trans.). Boston: Beacon.

Hall, E. (1959). *The silent language.* Greenwich, CT: Fawcett.

Hall, J. (1987). *Gone from the Promised Land.* New Brunswick, NJ: Transaction Books.

Halle, D. (1984). *America's working man: Work, home and politics among blue-collar property owners.* Chicago: University of Chicago Press.

Halle, D. (1993). *Inside culture: Art and class in the American home.* Chicago: University of Chicago Press.

Halsey, M. (1946). *Color blind.* New York: Simon & Schuster.

Hamilton, C. V. (1969). The politics of race relations. In C. U. Daley (Ed.), *The minority report.* New York: Pantheon.

Handelman, S. (1993, January 24). Inside Russia's gangster economy: Why capitalism and the Mafia mean business. *New York Times,* pp. 12ff.

Handlin, O. (1992). The newcomers. In P. S. Rotherberg (Ed.), *Race, class and gender in the United States.* New York: St. Martin's Press.

Hanna, S. L. (1994). *Person to person: Positive relationships don't just happen.* Englewood Cliffs, NJ: Prentice-Hall.

Hansell, S. (1995, December 28). A shaky house of plastic with no quick fix in sight. *New York Times,* p. D1.

Hansen, W. L., & Stampen, J. O. (1987, April). *Economics and financing of higher education: The tension between quality and equity* (Rev.). Paper presented at the annual meeting of the Association for the Study of Higher Education, San Diego.

Harbison, F. H. (1973). *Human resources as the wealth of nations.* New York: Oxford University Press.

Hardy, A. (1973, October). Man's age-old struggle for power. *Natural History,* pp. 27–34.

Hare, A. P. (1992). *Groups, teams, and social interaction.* Westport, CT: Praeger.

Hare, A. P., Blumberg, H. H., Davis, M. F., & Kent, V. (1994). *Small group research: A handbook.* Norwood, NJ: Ablex.

Hareven, T. K. (1978). *Transitions: The family and the life course in historical perspective.* Orlando: Academic Press.

Harper, C. L. (1993). *Exploring social change* (2nd ed.). Englewood Cliffs, NJ: Prentice-Hall.

Harper, D. A. (1982). *Good company.* Chicago: University of Chicago Press.

Harrington, M. (1973). *Socialism.* New York: Bantam.

Harrington, M. (1987). *The next lift: The history of a future.* New York: Holt.

Harris, M. (1980). *Culture, people, nature: An introduction to general anthropology.* New York: Harper.

Harris, M. (1983). *Cultural anthropology.* New York: Harper.

Harrison, B. (1990). *The great U-turn: Corporate restructuring and the polarizing of America.* New York: Basic Books.

Harrison, B. B., Tilly, C., and Bluestone, B. (1986, March–April). Wage inequality takes a great U-turn. *Challenge,* pp. 26–32.

Hauser, P. M. (1957). The changing population pattern of the modern city. In P. K. Hatt & A. J. Reiss (Eds.), *Cities and society.* New York: Free Press.

Hauser, R. M., & Featherman, D. I. (1977). *The process of stratification.* Orlando: Academic Press.

Hawkins, G. (1976). *The prison: Policy and practice.* Chicago: University of Chicago Press.

Hayghe, H. (1982). Dual earner families: Their economic and demographic characteristics. In J. Aldous (Ed.), *Two paychecks.* Newbury Park, CA: Sage Publications.

Hechter, M. (1974). *Internal colonialism.* Berkeley: University of California Press.

Hechter, M. (1983). *The microfoundations of macrosociology.* Philadelphia: Temple University Press.

Hechter, M. (1987). *Principles of group solidarity.* Berkeley: University of California Press.

Heilbroner, R. (1990, February 15). Seize the day. *New York Review of Books,* pp. 30–31.

Helmreich, W. B. (1982). *The things they say behind your back.* Garden City, NY: Doubleday.

Helvarg, D. (1994). *The war against the greens.* San Francisco: Sierra Club Books.

Henriques, D. B. (1995, March 30). Sexual harassment and a chief executive. *New York Times,* p. D1.

Henry, D. O. (1989). *From foraging to agriculture.* Philadelphia: University of Pennsylvania Press.

Henslin, J., & Briggs, M. (1971). Dramaturgical desexualization: The sociology of the vaginal examination. In J. Henslin (Ed.), *Studies in the sociology of sex.* New York: Appleton-Century-Crofts.

Herbert, B. (1996, June 21). Burning their bridges. *New York Times,* p. A27

Herrnstein, R., & Murray, C. (1994). *The bell curve.* New York: Free Press.

Hewes, G. W. (1954). A conspectus of the world's cultures in 1500 A.D. *University of Colorado Studies,* no. 4, pp. 1–22.

HHS (U.S. Department of Health and Human Services). (1973). *Work in America.* Washington, DC: U.S. Government Printing Office.

Hill, J. (1978). Apes and language. *Annual Review of Anthropology, 7,* 89–112.

Hinton, W. (1966). *Fanshen: A documentary of revolution in a Chinese village.* New York: Vintage Books.

Hirschi, T., & Gottfredson, M. R. (1980). *Understanding crime: Current theory and research.* Newbury Park, CA: Sage Publications.

Hobsbawm, E. (1975). *The age of capital.* New York: Scribner.

Hobsbawm, E. (1981). *Bandits* (Rev. ed.). New York: Pantheon.

Hochschild, A. (1979). Emotion work, feeling rules, and social structure. *American Journal of Sociology, 85,* 551–575.

Hochschild, A. (1983). *The managed heart: Commercialization of human feeling.* Berkeley: University of California Press.

Hochschild, A. (1989). *The second shift: Working parents and the revolution at home.* New York: Viking.

Hodge, R. W., Siegel, P. M., & Rossi, P. H. (1964). Occupational prestige in the United States, 1925–1965. *American Journal of Sociology, 70,* 286–302.

Hodge, R. W., & Treiman, D. J. (1968). Class identification in the United States. *American Journal of Sociology, 73,* 535–547.

Hoffman, L. M. (1989). *The politics of knowledge: Activist movements in medicine and planning.* Albany: State University of New York Press.

Hollingshead, A. (1949). *Elmtown's youth.* New York: Wiley.

Holt, J. (1965). *How children fail.* New York: Dell.

Holt, J. (1967). *How children learn.* New York: Pitman.

Holt, T. C. (1980). Afro-Americans. In *Harvard encyclopedia of American ethnic groups.* Cambridge, MA: Belknap Press.

Holy, L. (1985). Groups. In A. Kuper & J. Kuper (Eds.), *The social science encyclopedia.* London: Routledge and Kegan Paul.

Homans, G. (1950). *The human group.* Orlando: Harcourt Brace Jovanovich.

Homans, G. (1951). The Western Electric researches. In S. D. Hoslett (Ed.), *Human factors in management.* New York: Harper.

Homans, G. (1961). *Social behavior: Its elementary forms.* Orlando: Harcourt Brace Jovanovich.

Homer-Dixon, T. F., Boutwell, J. H., & Rathjens, G. W. (1993, February). Environmental change and violent conflict. *Scientific American,* pp. 38–45.

Hopkins, T. K., & Wallerstein, I. (Eds.). (1980). *Processes of the world-system.* Newbury Park, CA: Sage Publications.

Hopper, R. D. (1950). The revolutionary process: A frame of reference for the study of revolutionary movements. *Social Forces, 25,* 270–279.

Horowitz, M. (1979). The jurisprudence of Brown and the dilemmas of liberalism. *Harvard Civil Rights–Civil Liberties Review, 14,* 599–610.

Horowitz, R. (1985). *Honor and the American dream: Culture and identity in a Chicago neighborhood.* New Brunswick, NJ: Rutgers University Press.

House, J. S., Lepkowski, J. M., Kinny, A. M., Mero, R. P., Kessler, A., & Herzog, R. (1994). The social stratification of aging and health. *Journal of Health and Social Behavior, 35,* 213–234.

Hout, M., & Greeley, A. M. (1987). The center doesn't hold: Church attendance in the United States, 1940–1984. *American Sociological Review, 52,* 325–345.

Howe, I. (1983). *1984 revisited: Totalitarianism in our century.* New York: Harper.

Huang, C. (1994). *Immigration and the underclass.* Unpublished doctoral dissertation, City University of New York Graduate School.

Hubbard, J. (1991). *Shooting back: A photographic view of life by homeless children.* San Francisco: Chronicle Books.

Huber, J., & Spitz, G. (1988). Trends in family sociology. In N. J. Smelser (Ed.), *The handbook of sociology.* Newbury Park, CA: Sage Publications.

Hughes, E. (1945). The dilemmas and contradictions of status. *American Journal of Sociology, 50,* 353–359.

Hughes, E. (1958). *Men and their work.* New York: Free Press.

Hughes, E. (1959). The study of occupations. In R. K. Merton, L. Broom, & L. S. Cottrell, Jr. (Eds.), *Sociology today: Problems and prospects.* New York: Basic Books.

Hummin, D. (1990). *Commonplaces: Community ideology and identity in American cities.* Albany: State University of New York Press.

Humphreys, L. (1970, 1975). *Tearoom trade: Impersonal sex in public places.* Hawthorne, NY: Aldine.

Hunt, M. (1985). *Profiles of social research: The scientific study of human interactions.* New York: Russell Sage.

Hunter, F. (1953). *Community power structure: A study of decision makers.* Chapel Hill: University of North Carolina Press.

Ianni, F. (1972). *A family business: Kinship and social control in organized crime.* London: Routledge.

Iglesia, R. (1990). *Cronistas e historiadores de la conquista de Mexico.* Mexico City: Biblioteca de la Ciudad de Mexico.

Jackman, M. R., & Jackman, R. W. (1983). *Class awareness in the United States.* Berkeley: University of California Press.

Jackson, B. (1972). *In the life: Versions of the criminal experience.* New York: NAL.

Jackson, K. (1985). *The crab grass frontier: The suburbanization of the United States.* New York: Oxford University Press.

Jacobson, J. L. (1992). Improving women's reproductive health. In L. R. Brown (Ed.), *State of the world.* New York: Norton.

Jacobson-Hardy, M. (1995). The changing landscape of labor: Workers and workplace. *Labor's Heritage, 6,* 40–57.

Jahoda, M. (1982). *Employment and unemployment: A social-psychological analysis.* London: Cambridge University Press.

Jahoda, M., Lazarsfeld, P., & Zeisel, H. (1971). *Marienthal: A study of an unemployed community.* Hawthorne, NY: Aldine.

Janowitz, M. (1960). *The professional soldier: A social and political portrait.* New York: Free Press.

Janowitz, M. (1968). Political sociology. In D. Sills (Ed.), *The international encyclopedia of the social sciences.* New York: Free Press.

Janowitz, M. (1978). *The last half century: Societal change and politics in America.* Chicago: University of Chicago Press.

Janowitz, M., & Shils, E. A. (1948). The cohesion and disintegration of the Wehrmacht in World War II. *Public Opinion Quarterly, 12,* 280–315.

Jaynes, G. D., & Williams, R. M., Jr. (1989). *A common destiny: Blacks and American society.* Washington, DC: National Academy Press.

Jencks, C. (1993). *Rethinking social policy: Race, poverty and the underclass.* Cambridge, MA: Harvard University Press.

Jencks, C., Smith, M., Acland, H., Bane, M. J., Cohen, D., Gintis, H., Heyns, B., & Michelson, S. (1972). *Inequality: A reassessment of the effect of family and schooling in America.* New York: Basic Books.

Jennings, F. (1975). *The invasion of America: Indians, colonialism and the cant of conquest.* New York: Norton.

Johansson, S., & Nygren, O. (1991). The missing girls of China. *Population and Development Review, 17,* 35–52.

Johnson, J. H., Jr., & Farrell, W. C., Jr. (1995, July 7). Race still matters. *Chronicle of Higher Education,* p. A48.

Johnson, P. (1987). *A history of the Jews.* New York: Harper.

Jones, E. F., et al. (1986). *Teenage pregnancy in industrialized countries.* New Haven, CT: Yale University Press.

Joravsky, D. (1971). *The Lysenko affair.* Cambridge, MA: Harvard University Press.

Kagay, M. R., & Elder, J. (1992, August 9). Numbers are no problem for pollsters. Words are. *New York Times.* sec. 4, p. 5.

Kahl, J. A. (1965). *The American class structure.* Fort Worth, TX: Holt, Rinehart and Winston.

Kahneman, D., Knetsch, J., & Thaler, R. (1986). Fairness and the assumptions of economics. *Journal of Business, 59,* S285–S300.

Kamata, S. (1982). *Japan in the passing lane: An outsider's account of life in a Japanese auto factory.* New York: Pantheon.

Kammerman, S., & Kahn, A. (1981). *Child care, family benefits, and working parents: A study in comparative policy.* New York: Columbia University Press.

Kammerman, S., & Kahn, A. J. (1993, Fall). What Europe does for single parent families. *The Public Interest,* pp. 70–86.

Kanter, R. M. (1977). *Men and women of the corporation.* New York: Basic Books.

Kanter, R. M., & Stein, B. A. (Eds.). (1980). *Life in organizations: Workplaces as people experience them.* New York: Basic Books.

Kaplan, R. M., & Singer, R. D. (1976). Television violence and viewer aggression: A reexamination of the evidence. *Journal of Social Issues, 32,* 35–70.

Karabel, J., & Halsey, A. H. (Eds.). (1988). *Power and ideology in education.* New York: Oxford University Press.

Kasarda, J. D. (1988). *Metropolis era.* Newbury Park, CA: Sage Publications.

Kasarda, J. D. (1989). Urban industrial transition and the underclass. *Annals of the American Academy of Political and Social Science, 501,* 26–47.

Katz, E. (1957). The two step flow of communication: An up-to-date report on an hypothesis. *Public Opinion Quarterly, 21,* 61–78.

Katz, E. (1966). Communication research and the image of society: Convergence of two traditions. In A. G. Smith (Ed.), *Communication and culture: Readings in the codes of human interaction.* Fort Worth, TX: Holt, Rinehart and Winston.

Katz, F. E. (1964). The school as a complex social organization. *Harvard Educational Review, 34,* 428–455.

Katz, M. (1983). *Poverty and policy in American history.* New York: Academic Press.

Katz, M. B. (1990). *The undeserving poor: From the war on poverty to the war on welfare.* New York: Pantheon.

Katznelson, I. (1981). *City trenches: Urban politics and the patterning of class in the United States.* Chicago: University of Chicago Press.

Kearl, M. (1989). *Endings: A sociology of death and dying.* New York: Oxford University Press.

Keith, J. (1982). *Old people, new lives: Community creation in a retirement residence* (2nd ed.). Chicago: University of Chicago Press.

Keller, S. (1963). *Beyond the ruling class: Strategic elites in modern society.* New York: Random House.

Kempe, H., & Helfer, R. E. (Eds.) (1980). *The battered child* (3rd ed.) Chicago: University of Chicago Press.

Kempe, R., & Kempe, H. (1978). *Child abuse.* Cambridge, MA: Harvard University Press.

Kemper, T. D. (1990). *Social structure and testosterone: Explorations of the socio-bio-social chain.* New Brunswick, NJ: Rutgers University Press.

Keniston, K. (1965). Social change and youth in America. In E. H. Erikson (Ed.), *The challenge of youth.* Garden City, NY: Doubleday Anchor.

Keniston, K. (1977). *All our children.* Orlando: Harcourt Brace Jovanovich.

Kennedy, P. (1993). *Preparing for the twenty first century.* New York: Random House.

Kennedy, R. J. R. (1944). Single or triple melting pot? *American Journal of Sociology, 49,* 331–339.

Kessler, S. J., & McKenna, W. (1978). *Gender: An ethnomethodological approach.* Chicago: University of Chicago Press.

Keyfitz, N. (1986). The population that does not reproduce itself. In K. Davis, M. S. Bernstam, & R. Ricardo-Campbell (Eds.), *Below replacement fertility in industrial societies: Causes, consequences, policies, Population and Development Review, 12* (Suppl.), 139–145.

Keyfitz, N. (1991). Toward a theory of population-development interaction. In K. Davis & M. S. Bernstam (Eds.), *Resources, environment and population: Present knowledge and future options* (special edition of *Population and Development Review*). New York: Population Council.

Kidder, T. (1985). *House.* Boston: Houghton Mifflin.

Killian, L. (1952). Group membership in disaster. *American Journal of Sociology, 57,* 309–314.

Kilson, M. (1995, Fall). Affirmative action. *Dissent,* pp. 469–470.

Kim, I. (1981). *New urban immigrants: The Korean community in New York.* Princeton, NJ: Princeton University Press.

Kimmel, M. S. (1990). *Revolution: A sociological interpretation.* Philadephia: Temple University Press.

King, S. (1994, May). Diamonds are forever. *Life,* p. 26.

Kinsey, A. C., Pomeroy, W. B., & Martin, C. E. (1948). *Sexual behavior in the human male.* Philadelphia: Saunders.

Kinsey, A. C., Pomeroy, W. B., & Martin, C. E. (1953). *Sexual behavior in the human female.* Philadelphia: Saunders.

Kitano, H. H. I. (1980). *Race relations.* Englewood Cliffs, NJ: Prentice-Hall.

Kitsuse, J. I. (1962). Societal reaction to deviant behavior; problems of theory and method. *Social Problems, 9,* 247–257.

Klass, P. (1988, October 30). Wells, Welles and the Martians. *New York Times Book Review,* pp. 1, 48–49.

Kleinberg, O. (1935). *Race differences.* New York: Harper.

Kling, R., & Iacono, S. (1991). Making a "computer revolution." In C. Dunlop & R. Kling (Eds.), *Computerization and controversy: Value conflicts and social choices.* Orlando: Academic Press.

Kohlberg, L., & Gilligan, C. (1971). The adolescent as a philosopher: The discovery of the self in a post-conventional world. *Daedalus, 100,* 1051–1086.

Kolata, G. (1992, November 11). New views on life span alter forecasts on elderly. *New York Times,* p. A1.

Kolata, G. (1996, February 27). New era of robust elderly belies the fears of scientists. *New York Time,* pp. A1, C3.

Kolbert, E. (1995, August 20). Americans despair of popular culture. *New York Times,* sec. 2, pp. 1, 23.

Komarovsky, M. (1946). The voluntary associations of urban dwellers. *American Sociological Review, 11,* 686–698.

Kornblum, W. (1974). *Blue collar community.* Chicago: University of Chicago Press.

Kornblum, W. (1975). Boyash gypsies: Shantytown ethnicity. In F. Rehfisch (Ed.), *Gypsies, tinkers and other travellers.* Orlando: Academic Press.

Kornblum, W., & Julian, J. (1995). *Social problems.* Englewood Cliffs, NJ: Prentice-Hall.

Kornblum, W., & Williams, T. (1996). *West 42nd Street: The bright lights.* Berkeley: University of California Press.

Kornhauser, W. (1952). The Negro union official: A study of sponsorship and control. *American Journal of Sociology, 57,* 443–452.

Kosmin, B. (1991). *Research report: The national survey of religious identification.* New York: Center for Jewish Studies, City University of New York Graduate Center.

Kozol, J. (1991). *Savage inequalities.* New York: Crown.

Kozol, J. (1995). *Amazing grade: The lives of children and the conscience of a nation.* New York: Crown.

Kriegel, L. (1993). From the catbird seat: Football, baseball, and language. *Sewanee Review, 101,* 213–225.

Kroc, R. (1977). *Grinding it out: The making of McDonald's.* Chicago: Henry Regnery.

Kronus, C. L. (1977). Mobilizing voluntary associations into a social movement: The case of environmental quality. *Sociological Quarterly, 18,* 267–283.

Krugman, P. W. (1992). *The sum of diminished expectations: U.S. economic policy in the 1990s.* Cambridge, MA: MIT Press.

Krugman, P. W. (1995, August 21). The wealth gap is real and it's growing. *New York Times,* p. A15.

Kübler-Ross, E. (1989). *Death: The final stage of growth.* Englewood Cliffs, NJ: Prentice-Hall.

Kuhn, T. (1962). *The structure of scientific revolutions.* Chicago: University of Chicago Press.

Kunen, J. S. (1995, July 10). Teaching prisoners a lesson. *New Yorker,* pp. 34–39.

Kutner, B., Wilkins, C., & Yarrow, P. R. (1952). Verbal attitudes and overt behavior involving racial prejudice. *Journal of Abnormal and Social Psychology, 47,* 649–652.

Kuttner, R. (1993, Winter). The corporation in America: How has it changed? Can it be controlled? *Dissent,* pp. 35–49.

Kwamena-Poh, M., Tosh, J., Waller, R., & Tidy, M. (1982). *African history in maps.* Burnt Hill, England: Longman.

Ladner, J. (Ed.). (1973). *The death of white sociology.* New York: Vintage Books.

Lai, H. M. (1980). The Chinese. In S. Thornstrom (Ed.), *Harvard encyclopedia of ethnic groups.* Cambridge, MA: Harvard University Press.

Lakoff, S. (1970, Autumn). Science and conscience. *International Journal,* pp. 754–765.

Land, K. C. (1989). [Review of *Predicting Recidivism Using Survival Models,* by Peter Schmidt and Ann Dryden Witte]. *Contemporary Sociology, 18,* 245–246.

LaPiere, R. (1934). Attitudes vs. actions. *Social Forces, 13,* 230–237.

Lash, S. (1992). *Modernity and identity.* Cambridge, MA: Blackwell.

Laslett, P. (1972). Introduction. In P. Laslett & R. Wall (Eds.), *Household and family in past time.* Cambridge, England: Cambridge University Press.

Laslett, P. (1983). *The world we have lost* (3rd ed.). London: Methuen.

Laslett, P., & Wachter, K. W. (1978). *Statistical studies of historical social structure.* New York: Academic Press.

Lasswell, H. (1936). *Politics: Who gets what, when and how.* New York: McGraw-Hill.

Lasswell, H. D. (1941). The garrison state. *American Journal of Sociology, 46,* 455–468.

Latané, B., & Darley, J. (1970). *The unresponsive bystander: Why doesn't he help?* New York: Meredith.

Laumann, E. O., Gagnon, J. H., Michaels, R. T., & Michaels, S. (1994). *The social organization of sexuality: Sexual practices in the United States.* Chicago: University of Chicago Press.

Lawton, J. (1984). *The all American war game.* Oxford, England: Blackwell.

Lazreg, M. (1994). *The eloquence of silence: Algerian women in question.* New York: Routledge.

Leacock, E. (1978). Women's status in egalitarian society: Implications for social evolution. *Current Anthropology, 19,* 247–275.

LeBon, G. (1947/1896). *The crowd.* London: Ernest Bonn.

Lee, G. R., & Haas, L. (1993). Comparative methods in family research. In P. G. Boss, W. J. Doherty, R. LaRossa, W. R. Schumm, & S. K. Steinmetz (Eds.), *Sourcebook of family theories and methods: A contextual approach.* New York: Plenum Press.

Lee, R. D. (1991). Long-run global population forecasts: A critical appraisal. In K. Davis and M. S. Bernstam (Eds.), *Resources, environment, population: Present knowledge, future options.* New York: Oxford University Press.

Lee, V. E., & Smith, J. B. (1993). Effects of school restructuring on the achievement and engagement of middle-grade students. *Sociology of Education, 66,* 148–163.

Lemann, N. (1992). *The promised land: The great black migration and how it changed America.* New York: Vintage Books.

LeMasters, E. E. (1975). *Blue collar aristocrats.* Madison: University of Wisconsin Press.

Lemert, E. M. (1967). *Human deviance, social problems and social control.* Englewood Cliffs, NJ: Prentice-Hall.

Lenero-Otero, L. (Ed.). (1977). *Beyond the nuclear family model.* Newbury Park, CA: Sage Publications.

Lenski, G., & Lenski, J. (1982). *Human societies* (4th ed.). New York: McGraw-Hill.

Leonard, J. H. (Ed.). (1989). *Environment and the poor: Development strategies for a common agenda.* New Brunswick, NJ: Transaction Books.

Lever, J. (1976). Sex differences in the games children play. *Social Problems, 23,* 478–487.

Lever, J. (1978). Sex differences in the complexity of children's play and games. *American Sociological Review, 43,* 471–483.

Lever, J. (1983). *Soccer madness.* Chicago: University of Chicago Press.

Levi, P. (1989). *The drowned and the saved.* New York: Vintage International.

Levitan, S., & Belous, R. S. (1981). *What's happening to the American family?* Baltimore: Johns Hopkins University Press.

Lewin, T. (1989, November 14). Aging parents: Women's burden grows. *New York Times,* pp. A1, B12.

Lewin, T. (1995, May 30). Family decay global, study says. *New York Times,* p. A5.

Lewis, M., & Fiering, C. (1982). Some American families at dinner. In L. M. Laosa & I. E. Sigel (Eds.), *Families as learning environments for children.* New York: Plenum Press.

Lewontin, R. C. (1977). Biological determinism as a social weapon. In Ann Arbor Science for the People Editorial Collective, *Biology as a social weapon.* Minneapolis: Burgess.

Lewontin, R. C. (1982). *Human diversity.* New York: Scientific American Library.

Lieberson, S. (1980). *A piece of the pie: Blacks and white immigrants since 1880.* Berkeley: University of California Press.

Liebow, E. (1967). *Tally's corner: A study of Negro streetcorner men.* Boston: Little, Brown.

Liebow, E. (1995). *Tell them who I am.* Baltimore: Penguin.

Lin, M. (1995, November 1). Interview by Terri Gross on *Fresh Air,* National Public Radio.

Linton, R. (1936). *The study of man.* New York: Appleton.

Lipset, S. M. (1979). *The first new nation.* New York: Norton.

Lipset, S. M. (1981). *Political man.* Baltimore: Johns Hopkins University Press.

Lipset, S. M. (1994). The social prerequisites of democracy revisited. *American Sociological Review, 59,* 1–22.

Lipset, S. M., & Zetterberg, H. L. (1966). A theory of social mobility. In R. Bendix & S. M. Lipset (Eds.), *Class, status, and power: Social stratification in comparative perspective* (2nd ed.). New York: Free Press.

Lofland, J. F. (1981). Collective behavior: The elementary forms. In N. Rosenberg & R. H. Turner (Eds.), *Social psychology: Sociological perspectives.* New York: Basic Books.

Lombroso, C. (1911). *Crime: Its cause and remedies.* Boston: Little, Brown.

London, B. (1992). School-enrollment rates and trends, gender, and fertility: a cross-national analysis. *Sociology of Education, 65,* 305–318.

Lovins, A. (1977). *Soft energy paths: Toward a durable peace.* Cambridge, MA: Ballinger.

Lovins, A. (1991). Energy, people and industrialization. In K. Davis & M. S. Bernstam (Eds.), *Resources, environment and population: Present knowledge and future options.* New York: Population Council.

Lovins, A. (1993, April 20). Generate "nega-watts," says fossil fuel foe. *New York Times,* pp. C1, C11.

Lowey, I. S. (1990). World urbanization in perspective. In K. Davis & M. S. Bernstam (Eds.), *Resources, environment, and population. Population and Development Review, 15,* (Suppl.), 148–178.

Lowry, E. H. (1993). *Freedom and community: The ethics of interdependence.* Albany: State University of New York Press.

Luce, I. (1964). *Letters from the Peace Corps.* Washington, DC: Robert B. Luce.

Luhmann, N. (1982). *The differentiation of society.* New York: Columbia University Press.

Lull, J. (Ed.). (1988). *World families watch television.* Newbury Park, CA: Sage Publications.

Lurie, A. (1981). *The language of clothes.* New York: Random House.

Lye, K. (1995). *The complete atlas of the world.* Austin, TX: Raintree Steck-Vaughn.

Lynd, R. S., & Lynd, H. M. (1929). *Middletown: A study in American culture.* Orlando: Harcourt Brace Jovanovich.

Lynd, R. S., & Lynd, H. M. (1937). *Middletown in transition: A study in cultural conflicts.* Orlando: Harcourt Brace Jovanovich.

Lyson, T. A., & Squires, G. D. (1993, February). The "lost generation" of sociologists. *Footnotes* (American Sociological Association), pp. 4–5.

MacCannell, D. (n.d.). *Agribusiness and the small community* (Manuscript). University of California, Davis.

Machiavelli, N. (1950/1513). *The prince* and *The discourses.* New York: Modern Library.

Machlis, G., & Tichnell, D. L. (1985). *State of the world's parks: An international assessment.* Boulder, CO: Westview Press.

MacIver, R. M. (Ed.). (1948). *Discrimination and national welfare.* New York: Institute for Religious and Social Studies.

MacLeod, J. (1987, 1995). *Ain't no makin' it: Leveled aspirations in a low-income neighborhood.* Boulder, CO: Westview Press.

Majundar, R. C. (Ed.). (1951). *The history and culture of the Indian people.* London: Allen and Unwin.

Malinowski, B. (1927). *Sex and repression in savage society.* London: Harcourt Brace.

Malson, L. (1972). *Wolf children and the problem of human nature* (E. Fawcett, P. Aryton, & J. White, Trans.). New York: Monthly Review Press.

Malthus, T. (1927–1928/1798). *An essay on population.* New York: Dutton.

Mannheim, K. (1941). *Man and society in an age of reconstruction.* Orlando: Harcourt Brace Jovanovich.

Mansnerus, L. (1992, November 1). Should tracking be derailed? *Education Life, New York Times,* pp. 14–16.

Marks, J. (1994, December). Black, white, other. *Natural History,* pp. 32–35.

Markson, A. R., & Bloch, R. (1985). Defensive cities: Military spending, high technology, and human settlements. In M. Castells (Ed.), *High technology, space, and society.* Newbury Park, CA: Sage Publications.

Marshall, T. H. (1964). *Class, citizenship and social development.* Garden City, NY: Doubleday.

Martinez, M. E., & Mead, N. E. (1988). *Computer competence: The first national assessment.* Princeton, NJ: Educational Testing Service.

Martinson, R. (1972, April 29). Planning for public safety. *New Republic,* pp. 21–23.

Marwell, G., & Ames, R. E. (1985). Experiments on the provision of public goods II: Provision points, stakes, experience, and the free-rider problem. *American Journal of Sociology, 90,* 926–937.

Marx, K. (1961/1844). *Economic and philosophical manuscripts of 1844.* Moscow: Foreign Languages Publishing House.

Marx, K. (1962/1867). *Capital: A critique of political economy.* Moscow: Foreign Languages Publishing House.

Marx, K. (1963/1869). *The eighteenth Brumaire of Louis Bonaparte.* New York: International Publishers.

Marx, K., & Engels, F. (1955). Wage labor and capital. In *Selected works in two volumes.* Moscow: Foreign Languages Publishing House.

Marx, K., & Engels, F. (1969/1848). *The communist manifesto.* New York: Penguin.

Mascie-Taylor, C. G. N. (1990). *Biosocial aspects of social class.* New York: Oxford University Press.

Massey, D. S., & Denton, N. A. (1993). *American apartheid: Segregation and the making of the underclass.* Cambridge, MA: Harvard University Press.

Matras, J. (1973). *Populations and societies.* Englewood Cliffs, NJ: Prentice-Hall.

Matthews, F. H. (1977). *Quest for an American sociology: Robert Park and the Chicago school.* Montreal: McGill-Queens University Press.

Mauss, M. (1966/1925). *The gift.* New York: Free Press.

Mawson, A. R. (1989). [Review of *Homicide,* by Martin Daly and Margo Wilson]. *Contemporary Sociology, 18,* 238–240.

Maxwell, M. (1991). *The sociobiological imagination.* Albany: State University of New York Press.

May, E. T. (1995). *Barren in the promised land: Childless Americans and the pursuit of happiness.* New York: Basic Books.

Mayfield, L. (1984). *Teenage pregnancy.* Unpublished doctoral dissertation, City University of New York.

Mayhew, H. (1968/1861–1862). *London labour and the London poor.* New York: Dover.

Mayo, E. (1945). *The social problems of an industrial civilization.* Boston: Harvard University, Graduate School of Business Administration.

McAdam, D. (1992). Gender as a mediator of the activist experience: The case of Freedom Summer. *American Journal of Sociology, 97,* 1211–1240.

McAdam, D., McCarthy, J. D., & Zald, N. (1988). Social movements. In N. J. Smelser (Ed.), *The handbook of sociology.* Newbury Park, CA: Sage Publications.

McAndrew, M. (1985). Women's magazines in the Soviet Union. In B. Holland (Ed.), *Soviet sisterhood.* Bloomington: Indiana University Press.

McBrien, R. P. (1990, March 12). A papal attack on Vatican II. *New York Times,* p. A17.

McCord, W. (1991). *The dawn of the Pacific century: Implications for three worlds of development.* New Brunswick, NJ: Transaction Books.

McGoldrick, M., & Carter, E. A. (1982). *The family life cycle in normal family processes.* London: Guilford Press.

McGuire, M. B. (1987). *Religion: The social context* (2nd ed.). Belmont, CA: Wadsworth.

McKendrick, N., Brewer, J., & Plump, J. H. (1982). *The birth of a consumer society.* Bloomington: Indiana University Press.

McKinlay, J. B., & McKinlay, S. M. (1977). The questionable contribution of medical measures to the decline of mortality in the United States in the twentieth century. *Health and Society, 53,* 405.

McLanahan, S. S. (1984). Family structure and stress: A longitudinal comparison of two-parent and female-headed families. *Journal of Marriage and the Family,* 347–357.

McNeill, W. (1963). *The rise of the West: A history of the human community.* Chicago: University of Chicago Press.

McNeill, W. H. (1982). *The pursuit of power: Technology, armed force, and society since A.D. 1000.* Chicago: University of Chicago Press.

Mead, G. H. (1934). *Mind, self and society.* Chicago: University of Chicago Press.

Mead, M. (1950). *Sex and temperament in three primitive societies.* New York: NAL Mentor.

Mead, M. (1971). Comment. In J. Tanner & B. Inhelder (Eds.), *Discussions on child development.* New York: International Universities Press.

Medvedev, Z. (1971). *The Medvedev papers.* New York: Macmillan.

Mehan, H. (1992). Understanding inequality in schools: The contribution of interpretative studies. *Sociology of Education, 65,* 1–20.

Meier, D. (1995). *The power of their ideas: Lessons from a small school in Harlem.* Boston: Beacon.

Melton, J. G. (1989). *The encyclopedia of American religions,* (3rd ed.) Detroit: Gale Research.

Merton, R. K. (1938). Social structure and anomie. *American Sociological Review, 3,* 672–682.

Merton, R. K. (1948). Discrimination and the American creed. In R. M. MacIver (Ed.), *Discrimination and national welfare.* New York: Institute for Religious and Social Studies; dist. by Harper.

Merton, R. K. (1968). *Social theory and social structure* (3rd ed.). New York: Free Press.

Merton, R. K. (1973). *The sociology of science: Theoretical and empirical investigations.* Chicago: University of Chicago Press.

Merton, R. K., & Kitt, A. (1950). Contributions to the theory of reference group behavior. In R. K. Merton & P. Lazarsfeld (Eds.), *Continuities in social research.* New York: Free Press.

Městrović, S. G. (1991, September 25). Point of view: Why East Europe's upheavals caught social scientists off guard. *Chronicle of Higher Education,* p. A56.

Meyer, J. (1990). Guess who's coming to dinner this time? A study of gay intimate relationships and the support for those relationships. *Marriage and Family Review, 14,* 59–82.

Meyer, J. W., Ramirez, F. O., & Soysal, Y. N. (1992). World expansion of mass education, 1870–1980. *Sociology of Education, 65,* 128–149.

Milavsky, W. R. (1977, August 19). *TV and aggressive behavior of elementary school boys.* Paper delivered at the meeting of the American Psychological Association, San Francisco.

Milgram, S. (1970). The experience of living in cities. *Science, 167,* 1461–1468.

Milgram, S. (1974). *Obedience to authority: An experimental view.* New York: Harper.

Miller, A. T. (1993). African American families. In M. B. Katz (Ed.), *The "underclass" debate: View from history.* Princeton, NJ: Princeton University Press.

Miller, D. C., & Form, W. H. (1964). *Industrial sociology* (2nd ed.). New York: Harper.

Miller, J. (1996, February 12). Aging audiences point to a grim arts future. *New York Times,* p. A1.

Miller, N. (1989). *In search of gay America: Women and men in a time of change.* New York: Atlantic Monthly Press.

Miller, W. B. (1958). Lower class culture as a generating milieu of gang delinquency. *Journal of Social Issues, 14,* 5–19.

Millman, M. (1976). *The unkindest cut: Life in the backrooms of medicine.* New York: Morrow.

Mills, C. W. (1951). *White collar.* New York: Oxford University Press.

Mills, C. W. (1956). *The power elite.* New York: Oxford University Press.

Mills, C. W. (1959). *The sociological imagination.* New York: Oxford University Press.

Mintz, S. (1985). *Sweetness and power: The place of sugar in modern history.* New York: Viking.

Minuchin, S. (1974). *Families and family therapy.* Cambridge, MA: Harvard University Press.

Modell, J., & Hareven, T. K. (1973). Urbanization and the malleable household: An examination of boarding and lodging in American families. *Journal of Marriage and the Family, 35,* 466–479.

Mollenkopf, J. (1985). *The contested city.* Princeton, NJ: Princeton University Press.

Mollenkopf, J. (1995). What future for federal urban policy? *Urban Affairs Review, 30,* 657–660.

Money, J., & Tucker, P. (1975). *Sexual signatures.* Boston: Little, Brown.

Monk, L. (Ed.). (1989). *Photographs that changed the world.* Garden City, NY: Doubleday.

Monnier, M. (1993). *Mapping it out: Expository cartography for the humanities and social sciences.* Chicago: University of Chicago Press.

Montagna, P. D. (1977). *Occupations and society.* New York: Wiley.

Moore, B. (1968). *The social origins of dictatorship and democracy: Lord and peasant in the making of the modern world.* Boston: Beacon.

Moore, H. E. (1958). *Tornados over Texas.* Austin: University of Texas Press.

Moore, J. W. (1991). *Going down to the barrio: Homeboys and homegirls in change.* Philadelphia: Temple University Press.

Moore, J., & Pachon, H. (1985). *Hispanics in the United States.* Englewood Cliffs, NJ: Prentice-Hall.

Morales, E. (1986). Coca and the cocaine economy and social change in the Andes of Peru. *Economic Development and Cultural Change, 35,* 143–161.

Morales, E. (1989). *Cocaine: White gold rush in Peru.* Tucson: University of Arizona Press.

Morgan, R. (Ed.). (1970). *Sisterhood is powerful: An anthology of writings from the women's liberation movement.* New York: Random House.

Morton, M. (1995). *The tunnel: The architecture of despair.* New Haven, CT: Yale University Press.

Moscos, C. A. (1988). *Call to civic service.* New York: Free Press.

Mosley, W. H., & Cowley, P. (1991, December). *The challenge of world health.* Washington, DC: Population Reference Bureau.

Mowat, F. (1975). *The desperate people* (Rev. ed.). Toronto: Seal Books.

Moynihan, D. P. (1988, Spring). Our poorest citizens. *Focus,* p. 5.

Moynihan, P. (1965). *The Negro family,* an internal report of the Office of Policy Planning and Research, U.S. Department of Labor.

Mulkey, L. M. (1993). *Sociology of education: Theoretical and empirical investigations.* Fort Worth, TX: Harcourt Brace.

Murdock, G. (1949). *Social structure.* New York: Macmillan.

Murdock, G. (1967). *Ethnographic atlas.* Pittsburgh: University of Pittsburgh Press.

Murdock, G. (1983). *Outline of world cultures* (6th ed.). New Haven: Human Relations Area Files.

Murray, C. A. (1988). *In pursuit: of happiness and good government.* New York: Simon & Schuster.

Murray, C. (1984). *Losing ground.* New York: Basic Books.

Murti, M., Guio, A., & Dreze, J. (1995). Mortality, fertility, and gender bias in India. *Population and Development Review, 21,* 745–782.

Myers, S. L., Jr. (1995). The error of the third type. *Poverty & Race, 4,* 13–14.

Myerson, A. R. (1995, December 17). American money makes the whole world sing. *New York Times,* sec. 4, pp. 1, 14.

Myrdal, G. (1944). *An American dilemma.* New York: Harper.

Myrdal, G. (1970). *The challenge of world poverty.* New York: Vintage Books.

Myrdal, J. (1965). *Report from a Chinese village.* New York: Random House.

Nagel, T. (1994, May 12). Freud's permanent revolution. *New York Review of Books,* pp. 34–39.

Naisbitt, J., & Aburdene, P. (1990). *Megatrends 2000.* New York: Morrow.

Napier, A. Y., & Whitaker, C. (1980). *The family crucible.* New York: Bantam.

National Academy of Sciences. (1986). *Women's work, men's work: Sex segregation in the workplace* (B. F. Reskin & H. I. Hartmann, Eds.). Washington, DC: National Academy Press.

National Advisory Commission on Civil Disorders. (1968). *Report.* New York: Bantam.

National Center for Educational Statistics. (1995). *The educational progress of black students.* Washington, DC: U.S. Department of Education.

National Commission on America's Urban Families. (1993). *Families first.* Washington, DC: U. S. Government Printing Office.

Negrin, J. (1985–1986, Winter). The Huichol: A pre-Columbian culture in Mexico today. *The Free Spirit,* pp. 10–11.

Neihardt, J. G. (1959/1932). *Black Elk speaks: Being the life story of a holy man of the Oglala Sioux.* New York: Washington Square Press.

Nelson, G. K. (1984). Cults and new religions: Towards a sociology of religious creativity. *Sociology and Social Research, 68,* 301–325.

Neugarten, B. L. (1969). Continuities and discontinuities of psychological issues into adult life. *Human Development, 12,* 121–130.

Newcomb, T. (1958). Attitude development as a function of reference groups: The Bennington study. In E. Maccoby, T. M. Newcomb, & E. L. Hartley (Eds.), *Readings in social psychology* (3rd ed.). Fort Worth, TX: Holt, Rinehart and Winston.

Newman, K. S. (1988). *Falling from grace.* New York: Free Press.

Niebuhr, G. (1995, October 3). With every wave of newcomers, a church more diverse. *New York Times,* p. B6.

Niebuhr, H. R. (1929). *The social sources of denominationalism.* New York: Meridian.

Ning, P. (1995). *Red in tooth and claw: Twenty six years in communist Chinese prisons.* New York: Grove Press.

Nisbet, R. A. (1969). *Social change and history.* New York: Oxford University Press.

Nisbet, R. A. (1970). *The social bond.* New York: Knopf.

NORC (National Opinion Research Center). *General social survey, cumulative codebook* [Various years]. Chicago: University of Chicago Press.

Nyden, P. (1984). *Steelworkers rank and file.* New York: Praeger.

Oakes, J. (1985). *Keeping track: How schools structure inequality.* New Haven, CT: Yale University Press.

Obermeyer, C. M. (1992). Islam, women, and politics: The demography of Arab countries. *Population and Development Review, 18,* 33–60.

Oberschall, A. (1973). *Social conflict and social movements.* Englewood Cliffs, NJ: Prentice-Hall.

Office of Technology Assessment, U.S. Congress. (1986). *Technology, public policy, and the changing structure of agriculture: Vol. 2. Background papers: Part D. Rural communities.* Washington, DC.

Ogburn, W. F. (1942). Inventions, population and history. In American Council of Learned Societies, *Studies in the history of culture.* Freeport, NY: Books for Libraries Press.

Ogburn, W. F. (1957). Cultural lag as theory. *Sociology and Social Research, 41,* 167–174.

Ogburn, W. F., & Nimkoff, M. F. (1934). *The family.* Boston: Houghton Mifflin.

Oldenburg, R. (1989). *The great good place.* New York: Paragon.

Oliver, M. L., & Shapiro, T. M. (1990). Wealth of a nation: A reassessment of asset inequality in America shows at least one third of households are asset-poor. *American Journal of Economics and Sociology, 49,* 129–150.

Olojede, D. (1995, June 5). Chaos lurks in Nigeria. *Newsday,* pp. A6, A22.

Olson, M. (1965). *The logic of collective action.* Cambridge, MA: Harvard University Press.

O'Neill, J. A., et al. (1984). *An analysis of time on welfare.* Report to the U.S. Department of Health and Human Services. Washington, DC: U.S. Government Printing Office.

Opie, I., & Opie, P. (1969). *Children's games in street and playground.* Oxford, England: Oxford University Press.

Oppenheimer, V. K. (1994). Women's rising employment and the future of the family in industrial societies. *Population and Development Review, 20,* 293–342.

Orshansky, M. (1965, January). Counting the poor: Another look at the poverty profiles. *Social Security Bulletin,* pp. 3–26.

Orwell, G. (1949). *1984.* New York: New American Library.

Orwell, G. (1950). *Shooting an elephant and other essays.* New York: Harcourt Brace Jovanovich.

Osmond, M. W. (1985). Comparative marriage and the family. In B. C. Miller & D. H. Olson (Eds.), *Family studies review yearbook* (Vol. 3). Newbury Park, CA: Sage Publications.

Paik, H. J. (1991). *The effects of television violence on aggressive behavior: A meta-analysis.* Doctoral dissertation, Syracuse University.

Palmore, E. (1981). *Social patterns in normal aging.* Durham, NC: Duke University Press.

Papernow, P. (1988). Stepparent role development: From outsider to intimate. In W. R. Beer (Ed.), *Relative strangers.* Totowa, NJ: Rowman and Littlefield.

Parelius, A. P., & Parelius, R. J. (1987). *The sociology of education* (2nd ed.). Englewood Cliffs, NJ: Prentice-Hall.

Park, R. E. (1914). Racial assimilation in secondary groups. *Publications of the American Sociological Society, 8,* 66–72.

Park, R. E. (1967/1925a). The city: Suggestions for the investigation of human behavior in the urban environment. In R. E. Park & E. W. Burgess (Eds.), *The city.* Chicago: University of Chicago Press.

Park, R. E. (1967/1925b). The natural history of the newspaper. In R. E. Park & E. W. Burgess (Eds.), *The city.* Chicago: University of Chicago Press.

Park, R. E. (1967/1926). The urban community as a spatial pattern and a moral order. In R. H. Turner (Ed.), *Robert E. Park on social control and collective behavior.* Chicago: University of Chicago Press.

Park, R. E., & Burgess, E. W. (1921). *Introduction to the science of sociology* (Rev. ed.). Chicago: University of Chicago Press.

Park, R. E., & Burgess, E. W. (Eds.). (1967/1925). *The city.* Chicago: University of Chicago Press.

Parkin, F. (1971). *Class inequality and political order.* New York: Praeger.

Parry, J. H. (1963). *The age of reconnaissance.* Cleveland: World.

Parsons, T. (1937). *The structure of social action.* New York: McGraw-Hill.

Parsons, T. (1940). An analytic approach to the theory of social stratification. *American Journal of Sociology, 45,* 841–862.

Parsons, T. (1951). *The social system.* New York: Free Press.

Parsons, T. (1960). *Structure and process in modern societies.* New York: Free Press.

Parsons, T. (1965). The concept of political power. In S. M. Lipset & R. Bendix (Eds.), *Class, status, and power* (2nd ed.). New York: Free Press.

Parsons, T. (1966). *Societies: Evolutionary and comparative.* Englewood Cliffs, NJ: Prentice-Hall.

Parsons, T. (1968). The problem of polarization along the axis of color. In J. H. Franklin (Ed.), *Color and race.* Boston: Beacon.

Parsons, T., & Bales, R. F. (1955). *Family, socialization, and interaction process.* New York: Free Press.

Partin, M., & Palloni, A. (1995, Spring). Accounting for the recent increases in low birth weight among African Americans. *Focus,* pp. 33–38.

Patterson, O. (1982). *Slavery and social death.* Cambridge, MA: Harvard University Press.

Patterson, O. (1991). *Freedom, Vol. 1: Freedom in the making of Western culture.* New York: Basic Books.

Pavlov, I. (1927). *Conditioned reflexes: An investigation of the physiological activity of the cerebral cortex* (G. V. Anrep, Trans. & ed.). London: Oxford University Press.

Pea, R. D., & Sheingold, K. (Eds.). (1987). *Mirrors of minds: Patterns of experience in educational computers.* Norwood, NJ: Ablex.

Pear, R. (1993, July 8). Big health gap, tied to income, is found in U.S. *New York Times,* pp. A1, B10.

Pearson, W., & Hendrix, L. (1979). Divorce and the status of women. *Journal of Marriage and the Family, 41,* 375–386.

Pedersen, E., & Faucher, T. A., with Eaton, W. W. (1978). A new perspective on the effects of first-grade teachers on children's subsequent adult status. *Harvard Educational Review, 48,* 1–31.

Perin, C. (1977). *Everything in its place: Social order and land use in America.* Princeton, NJ: Princeton University Press.

Perlman, J. E. (1976). *The myth of marginality: Urban poverty and politics in Rio de Janeiro.* Berkeley: University of California Press.

Perrow, C. (1984). *Normal accidents: Living with high-risk technologies.* New York: Basic Books.

Perutz, M. F. (1992). The fifth freedom. *New York Review of Books, 39,* 5–7.

Pesce, C. (1994, October 5). In Minn., a crime of cover-up. *USA Today,* p. A3.

Peters, A. (1990). *Peters atlas of the world.* New York: Harper-Collins.

Pettigrew, T. F. (1980). Prejudice. In *Harvard encyclopedia of American ethnic groups.* Cambridge, MA: Belknap Press.

Pfeiffer, E., Verwoerdt, A., & Davis, G. (1972). Sexual behavior in middle life. *American Journal of Psychiatry, 128,* 1262–1267.

Philips, S. (1982). *The invisible culture: Communications in classroom and community on the Warmsprings Indian Reservation.* White Plains, NY: Longman.

Piaget, J., & Inhelder, B. (1969). *The psychology of the child.* New York: Basic Books.

Piazza, T., & Glock, C. Y. (1979). Images of God and their social meaning. In R. Wuthnow (Ed.), *The religious dimension: New directions in quantitative research.* Orlando: Academic Press.

Pifer, A., & Bronte, L. (Eds.). (1986, Winter). The aging society. *Daedalus.*

Pine, V. R. (1975). *Caretaker of the dead: The American funeral director.* New York: Irvington.

Piore, M. J., & Sabel, C. F. (1984). *The second industrial divide: Possibilities for prosperity.* New York: Basic Books.

Pittman, J. F. (1993). Functionalism may be down, but it surely is not out. In P. G. Boss, W. J. Doherty, R. LaRossa, W. R. Schumm, & S. K. Steinmetz (Eds.), *Sourcebook of family theories and methods: A contextual approach.* New York: Plenum Press.

Piven, F. F., & Cloward, R. (1971). *Regulating the poor: The functions of public welfare.* New York: Vintage Books.

Piven, F. F., & Cloward, R. (1982). *The new class war: Reagan's attack on the welfare state and its consequences.* New York: Pantheon.

Platt, A. M. (1977). *The child savers* (2nd ed.). Chicago: University of Chicago Press.

Polansky, N. A., Chalmers, M. A., Buttenweiser, E., & Williams, D. P. (1981). *Damaged parents, an anatomy of child neglect.* Chicago: University of Chicago Press.

Polanyi, K. (1944). *The great transformation.* Boston: Beacon.

Polsby, N. (1980). *Community power and political theory* (2nd ed.). New Haven, CT: Yale University Press.

Pope, L. (1942). *Millhands and preachers.* New Haven, CT: Yale University Press.

Popenoe, D. (1994). Family decline and scholarly optimism. *Family Affairs, 6,* 9–10.

Population Reference Bureau. (1995). *1995 world population data sheet.* Washington, DC: U.S. Government Printing Office.

Portes, A., & Rumbaut, R. G. (1990). *Immigrant America: A portrait.* Berkeley: University of California Press.

Portes, A., & Stepick, A. (1985). Unwelcome immigrants. *American Sociological Review, 50,* 493–514.

Portes, A., & Walton, J. (1981). *Labor, class, and the international system.* Orlando: Academic Press.

Pressman, J. L., & Wildavsky, A. (1984). *Implementation* (3rd ed.). Berkeley: University of California Press.

Preston, S. H. (1984). Children and the elderly: Divergent paths for America's dependents. *Demography, 21,* 435–457.

Putnam, R. (1995). Bowling alone: America's declining social capital. *Journal of Democracy, 6,* 65–78.

Quadagno, J. S. (1979). Paradigms in evolutionary theory—Sociobiological models of natural selection. *American Sociological Review, 44,* 100–109.

Queen, S., & Debler, M. M. (1940/1925). *Social pathology.* New York: Crowell.

Quinn, B., Anderson, B., Bradley, M., Goetting, P., & Shriver, P. (1981). *Churches and church membership in the United States 1980: An enumeration by region, state and county based on data reported by 111 church bodies.* Atlanta: Glenmary Research Center.

Quinney, R. (1978). The ideology of law: Notes for a radical alternative to legal oppression. In C. E. Reasons & R. M. Rich (Eds.), *Sociology of law: A conflict perspective.* Toronto: Butterworths.

Quinney, R. (1980). *Class, state, and crime.* White Plains, NY: Longman.

Radelet, M. L., & Bedau, H. A. (1992). *In spite of innocence: Erroneous convictions in capital cases.* Boston: Northeastern University Press.

Rainwater, L., & Yancy, W. (Eds.). (1967). *The Moynihan report and the politics of controversy.* Cambridge, MA: MIT Press.

Rathje, W. L. (1993). Less fat? Aw, baloney. Garbage Project studies indicate misreporting of fatty meat consumption. *Garbage, 5,* 22–23.

Rauschning, H. (1940). *The voice of destruction.* New York: Putnam.

Ravenholt, R. G. (1990). Tobacco's global death march. *Population and Development Review, 16,* 213–240.

Raymond, C. (1991, October 30). Results from a Chicago project lead social scientists to a rethinking of the urban underclass. *Chronicle of Higher Education,* pp. A9, A12.

Reckless, W. C. (1933). *Vice in Chicago.* Chicago: University of Chicago Press.

Reddy, M. A. (Ed.). (1994). *Statistical abstract of the world.* Detroit: Gale Research.

Redfield, R. (1947). The folk society. *American Journal of Sociology, 52,* 293–308.

Reich, R. B. (1992a, Winter). Training a skilled work force. *Dissent,* pp. 42–46.

Reich, R. B. (1992b). *The work of nations: Preparing ourselves for 21st century capitalism.* New York: Knopf.

Reid, S. T. (1993). *Criminal justice.* New York: Macmillan.

Reinhold, R. (1982, May 6). An "overwhelming" violence-TV tie. *New York Times,* p. C27.

Reiss, A. J., Jr., & Roth, J. A. (Eds.). (1993). *Understanding and preventing violence.* Washington, DC: National Academy Press.

Reissman, F. (1984). *The self-help revolution.* New York: Human Sciences Press.

Rheingold, H. (1993). *The virtual community: Homesteading on the electronic frontier.* New York: Harper.

Richards, E. (1989). *The knife and gun club: Scenes from an emergency room.* New York: Atlantic Monthly Press.

Richmond-Abbott, M. (1992). *Masculine and feminine: Gender roles over the life cycle,* (2nd ed.). New York: McGraw-Hill.

Rieff, P. (1969). *On intellectuals: Theoretical studies, case studies.* Garden City, NY: Doubleday.

Riesman, D. (1957). The suburban dislocation. *Annals of the American Academy of Political and Social Science, 314,* 123–146.

Rifkin, J. (1995, May–June). After work: A blueprint for social harmony in a world without jobs. *Utne Reader,* pp. 52–62.

Riis, J. A. (1890). *How the other half lives: Studies among the tenements of New York.* New York: Scribner.

Riley, M. W., Foner, A., & Waring, J. (1988). The sociology of age. In N. E. Smelser (Ed.), *The handbook of sociology.* Newbury Park, CA: Sage Publications.

Riley, M. W., Kahn, R. L., & Foner, A. (1994). *Age and structural lag.* New York: Wiley.

Riley, M. W., & Riley, J. W., Jr. (1989). The lives of older people and changing social roles. *Annals of the American Academy of Political and Social Science, 503,* 14–28.

Rist, R. C. (1973). *The urban school: A factory for failure.* Cambridge, MA: MIT Press.

Rist, R. C. (1979). *Desegregated schools.* Orlando: Academic Press.

Robbins, W. (1985, February 10). Despair wrenches farmers' lives as debts mount and land is lost. *New York Times,* pp. 1, 30.

Roberts, S. (1995, April 27). Women's work: What's new, what isn't. *New York Times,* p. B6.

Robertson, R. (1985). The sacred and the world system. In P. Hammond (Ed.), *The sacred in a secular age.* Berkeley: University of California Press.

Robinson, J. (1988). *The rhythm of everyday life.* Boulder, CO: Westview Press.

Robinson, P. (1994). *Freud and his critics.* Berkeley: University of California Press.

Robinson, W. C. (1963). Urbanization and fertility: The nonwestern experience. *Millbank Memorial Fund Quarterly, 4,* 291–308.

Rock, P. (1985). Symbolic interactionism. In A. Kuper & J. Kuper (Eds.), *The social science encyclopedia.* London: Routledge and Kegan Paul.

Rodriguez, C. E. (1992). The Puerto Rican community in the South Bronx: Contradictory views from within and without. In P. S. Rotherberg (Ed.), *Race, class and gender in the United States.* New York: St. Martin's Press.

Roof, W. C. (1985). *Religion in America today.* Newbury Park, CA: Sage Publications.

Roozen, D. A. (1985). What hath the 1970s wrought? Religion in America. In C. H. Jacquet (Ed.), *Yearbook of American and Canadian churches 1984.* Nashville, TN: Abingdon Press.

Rose, M. (1995). *Possible lives: The promise of public education.* Boston: Houghton Mifflin.

Rosen, E. I. (1987). *Bitter choices: Blue-collar women in and out of work.* Chicago: University of Chicago Press.

Rosenberg, M., & Turner, R. H. (Eds.). (1981). *Social psychology: Sociological perspectives.* New York: Basic Books.

Rosenhan, D. L. (1973). On being sane in insane places. *Science, 179,* 250–258.

Rosenthal, E. (1996, January 15). Managed care has trouble treating AIDS, patients say. *New York Times,* p. A1.

Rosett, A., & Cressey, D. R. (1976). *Justice by consent: Plea bargains in the American courthouse.* Philadelphia: Lippincott.

Rosow, I. (1965). Forms and functions of adult socialization. *Social Forces, 44,* 38–55.

Ross, H. L. (1963). *Perspectives on the social order.* New York: McGraw-Hill.

Rossi, A. (1964). Equality between the sexes: An immodest proposal. In R. J. Lifton (Ed.), *The woman in America.* Boston: Beacon.

Rossi, A. (1977). The biosocial basis of parenting. *Daedalus, 106,* 1–31.

Rossi, A. (1980). Aging and parenthood in the middle years. In P. B. Baltes & O. G. Brim, Jr. (Eds.), *Life-span development and behavior* (Vol. 3). Orlando: Academic Press.

Rossi, A. S., & Rossi, P. H. (1990). *Of human bonding: Parent–child relationships across the life course.* New York: Aldine.

Roszak, T. (1969). *The making of a counterculture.* Garden City, NY: Doubleday.

Rothenberg, P. S. (Ed.). (1992). *Race, class and gender in the United States* (2nd ed.). New York: St. Martin's Press.

Rothenberg, R. (1990, October 5). Surveys proliferate, but answers dwindle. *New York Times,* pp. A1, D4.

Rubin, Z. (1980). The love research. In A. Skolnick & J. H. Skolnick (Eds.), *Family in transition.* Boston: Little, Brown.

Rubington, E., & Weinberg, M. (1987). *Deviance.* New York: Macmillan.

Rubinstein, E. (1981). Effects of television on violent behavior. In J. R. Hays, T. K. Roberts, & K. S. Solway (Eds.), *Violence and the violent individual: Proceedings of the twelfth annual symposium, Texas Research Institute of Mental Sciences.* New York: SP Medical & Scientific Books.

Rudé, G. (1964). *The crowd in history.* New York: Wiley.

Ruggles, P. (1990). *Drawing the line: Alternative poverty measures and their implications for public policy.* Washington, DC: Urban Institute.

Ruggles, P. (1992). Measuring poverty. *Focus* (University of Wisconsin–Madison, Institute for Research on Poverty), *14,* 2.

Rushton, J. P. (1980). *Altruism, socialization and society.* Englewood Cliffs, NJ: Prentice-Hall.

Ruskin, C. (1988). *The quilt: Stories from the NAMES Project.* New York: Pocket Books.

Rutstein, S. O. (1991). *Levels, trends and differentials in infant and child mortality in the less developed countries.* Paper presented at the seminar on Child Survival Interventions: Effectiveness and Efficiency, at the Johns Hopkins University School of Hygiene and Public Health, Baltimore, June 20–22.

Rutter, M. (1974). *The qualities of mothering: Maternal deprivation reassessed.* New York: Jason Aronson.

Ryan, A. (1992). Twenty-first century limited. *New York Review of Books, 39,* 20–24.

Rybczynski, W. (1987). *Home: A short history of an idea.* New York: Penguin.

Rymer, R. (1992a, April 13). A silent childhood. *New Yorker,* pp. 41–53.

Rymer, R. (1992b, April 20). A silent childhood, part II. *New Yorker,* pp. 43–47.

Sadik, N. (1995). Decisions for development: Women, empowerment and reproductive health. In *The state of the world population 1995.* New York: United Nations Population Fund.

Sagarin, E. (1975). *Deviants and deviance: A study of disvalued people and behavior.* New York: Praeger.

Sahlins, M. D. (1960, September). The origin of society. *Scientific American,* pp. 76–87.

Sahlins, M. D. (1976). *The use and abuse of biology: An anthropological critique of sociobiology.* Ann Arbor: University of Michigan Press.

Salgado, S. (1990). *An uncertain grace.* New York: Aperture Foundation.

Salisbury, R. F. (1962). *From stone to steel.* Parkville, Australia: Melbourne University Press.

Samuels, R. J. (1991). Reinventing security: Japan since Meiji. *Daedalus, 120,* 47–68.

Samuelson, P. (1980). *Economics* (11th ed.). New York: McGraw-Hill.

Sanchez-Jankowski, M. S. (1991). *Islands in the street: Gangs and American urban society.* Berkeley: University of California Press.

Sandefur, G. D., & Tienda, M. (Eds.). (1988). *Divided opportunities: Minorities, poverty, and social policy.* New York: Plenum Press.

Sanger, D. E. (1984, June 4). The expected boom in home computers fails to materialize. *New York Times,* p. A1.

Sarvekshana, Journal of the National Sample Survey Organization. (1988). *Report of the third quinquennial survey on employment and unemployment.* New Delhi: Department of Statistics, Ministry of Planning.

Sassen, S. (1991). *Global city.* Princeton, NJ: Princeton University Press.

Sassen, S. (1994). *Cities in a world economy.* Thousand Oaks, CA: Pine Forge Press.

Satir, V. (1972). *Peoplemaking.* Palo Alto, CA: Science and Behavior Books.

Savage-Rumbaugh, S., & Lewin, R. (1995). *Kanzi: The ape at the brink of the human mind.* New York: Wiley.

Scanzoni, L., & Scanzoni, J. (1976). *Men, women and change.* New York: McGraw-Hill.

Scarf, M. (1995). *Intimate worlds: Life inside the family.* New York: Random House.

Schaller, G. B. (1964). *The year of the gorilla.* Chicago: University of Chicago Press.

Schilling, A. G. (1991, March 18). This could be the eve of a false recovery. *Forbes,* pp. 74–75.

Schmemann, S. (1992a, February 17). Fear deep as Russia's snow, but poetry, too. *New York Times,* pp. A1, A6.

Schmemann, S. (1992b, October 6). Free-market ideas grow on Russian farms. *New York Times,* pp. A1, A10.

Schmitt, E. (1993, February 6). The top soldier is torn between 2 loyalties. *New York Times,* p. A1.

Schooler, C., & Miller, J. (1985). Work for the household: Its nature and consequences for husbands and wives. *American Journal of Sociology, 90,* 97–124.

Schor, J. (1992). *The overworked American.* New York: Basic Books.

Schorr, L. B. (1988). *Within our reach: Breaking the cycle of disadvantage.* Garden City, NY: Doubleday.

Schuman, H., & Scott, J. (1989). Generations and collective memories. *American Sociological Review, 54,* 359–381.

Schumpeter, J. A. (1950). *Capitalism, socialism, and democracy* (3rd ed.). New York: Harper.

Schur, E. M. (1971). *Labeling deviant behavior: Its sociological implications.* New York: Harper.

Schur, E. M. (1973). *Radical nonintervention: Rethinking the delinquency problem.* Englewood Cliffs, NJ: Prentice-Hall.

Schur, E. M. (1984). *Labeling women deviant: Gender, stigma, and social control.* New York: Random House.

Schwartz, B. (1976). Images of suburbia: Some revisionist commentary and conclusions. In B. Schwartz (Ed.), *The changing face of the suburbs.* Chicago: University of Chicago Press.

Schwartz, F. (1989, January–February). Management women and the new facts of life. *Harvard Business Review,* pp. 65ff.

Scull, A. T. (1988). Deviance and social control. In N. Smelser (Ed.), *The handbook of sociology.* Newbury Park, CA: Sage Publications.

Scully, J. (1991). The relationship between business and higher education: A perspective on the 21st century. In C. Dunlop & R. Kling (Eds.), *Computerization and controversy: Value conflicts and social choices.* Orlando: Academic Press.

Seeley, J. R., Sim, R. A., & Loosley, E. W. (1955). *Crestwood Heights: A study of the culture of suburban life.* New York: Basic Books.

Seeman, M. (1959). On the meaning of alienation. *American Sociological Review, 24,* 783–791.

Selizer, V. (1985). *Pricing the priceless child: The changing social value of children.* New York: Free Press.

Selznick, P. (1952). *The organizational weapon: A study of Bolshevik strategy and tactics.* New York: McGraw-Hill.

Selznick, P. (1966). *TVA and the grass roots: A study in the sociology of formal organization.* New York: Harper.

Sen, A. (1993, May). The economics of life and death. *Scientific American,* pp. 40–47.

Sennett, R., & Cobb, J. (1972). *The hidden injuries of class.* New York: Random House.

Sewall, W., Haller, A., & Ohlendorf, G. (1970). The educational and early occupational status attainment process: Replication and revision. *American Sociological Review, 35,* 1014–1027.

Shaiken, H. (1985). *Work transformed: Automation and labor in the computer age.* Fort Worth, TX: Holt, Rinehart and Winston.

Shanks, B. (1991). The endangered ranger. *National Parks, 65,* 32–36.

Shaw, C. R. (1929). *Delinquency areas: A study of the geographic distribution of school truants, juvenile delinquents, and adult offenders in Chicago.* Chicago: University of Chicago Press.

Shaw, J. A. (1979). The child in the military community. In J. D. Call, J. D. Noshpitz, R. L. Cohen, & I. N. Berlin (Eds.), *Basic handbook of child psychiatry.* New York: Basic Books.

Shi, D. E. (1985). *The simple life: Plain living and high thinking in American culture.* New York: Oxford University Press.

Shibutani, T., & Kwan, K. M. (1965). *Ethnic stratification.* New York: Macmillan.

Shils, E. (1962). The theory of mass society. *Diogenes, 39,* 45–66.

Shils, E. (1963). On the contemporary study of the new states. In C. Geertz (Ed.), *New societies and old states: The quest for modernity in Asia and Africa.* New York: Free Press.

Shils, E. (1970). Tradition, ecology and institution in the history of sociology. *Daedalus, 99,* 760–825.

Shils, E. (1985). Sociology. In A. Kuper & J. Kuper (Eds.), *The social science encyclopedia.* London: Routledge and Kegan Paul.

Shimada, H. (1993). Recession and change in labour practices in Japan. *International Labour Review, 132,* 159–160.

Shorris, E. (1992). *Latinos: A biography of the people.* New York: Norton.

Shotland, R. L. (1985). When bystanders just stand by. *Psychology Today, 19,* 50–55.

Silberman, C. (1980). *Criminal violence, criminal justice.* New York: Random House.

Silk, L. (1989, May 12). Rich and poor: The gap widens. *New York Times,* p. D2.

Simmel, G. (1904). The sociology of conflict. *American Journal of Sociology, 9,* 490ff.

Simmons, J. L. (1985). The nature of deviant subcultures. In E. Rubington & M. S. Weinberg (Eds.), *Deviance: The interactionist perspective.* New York: Macmillan.

Simpson, C. E., & Yinger, J. M. (1953). *Racial and cultural minorities: An analysis of prejudice and discrimination.* New York: Harper.

Simpson, J. H. (1983). Moral issues and status politics. In R. C. Liebman & R. Wuthnow (Eds.), *The new Christian right: Mobilization and legitimation.* Hawthorne, NY: Aldine.

Sims, C. (1995, December 12). In Peru, a fight for fresh air. *New York Times,* pp. D1, D4.

Siwolop, S. (1995, August 27). Have I got a business opportunity for you. *New York Times,* pp. D1, D8.

Sizer, T. (1995, January 8). What's wrong with standard tests. *Education Life, New York Times,* p. 58.

Sjoberg, G. (1968). The preindustrial city. In S. Fava (Ed.), *Urbanism in world perspective: A reader.* New York: Crowell.

Skinner, B. F. (1976). *Walden two.* New York: Macmillan.

Skocpol, T. (1979). *States and social revolutions.* New York: Cambridge University Press.

Skolnick, A. S. (1991). *Embattled paradise: The American family in an age of uncertainty.* New York: Basic Books.

Slater, R. O., Schutz, B. M., & Dorr, S. R. (Eds.) (1993). *Global transformation and the Third World.* Boulder, CO: L. Rienner.

Smelser, N. J. (1962). *Theory of collective behavior.* New York: Free Press.

Smelser, N. J. (1966). The modernization of social relations. In M. Weiner (Ed.), *Modernization.* New York: Basic Books.

Smelser, N. J. (1984). *Sociology.* Englewood Cliffs, NJ: Prentice-Hall.

Smigel, E. O. (1964). *The Wall Street lawyer: Professional organizational man.* New York: Free Press.

Smiley, J. (1992). *A thousand acres.* New York: Ballantine.

Smith, A. (1910/1776). *The wealth of nations.* London: University Paperbacks.

Smith, C. D. (1994). *The absentee American: Repatriates' perspectives on America and its place in the contemporary world.* Bayside, NY: Aletheia.

Smith, D. (1989). *Promises* (Letter from Madurai). Oberlin, OH: Oberlin Shansi Memorial Association.

Smith, H. (1952). *The religions of man.* New York: Mentor.

Smith, J. D., & Franklin, S. D. (1974, May). Concentration of personal wealth, 1922–1969. *American Economic Review: Papers and Proceedings, 64,* 162–167.

Smith, R. A. (1968). Los Angeles, prototype of supercity. In S. F. Fava (Ed.), *Urbanism in world perspective: A reader.* New York: Crowell.

Snipp, C. M. (1991). *American Indians: The first of this land.* New York: Russell Sage.

Snow, D. A., & Benford, R. D. (1992). Master frames and cycles of protest. In A. D. Morris & C. M. Mueller, (Eds.), *Frontiers in social movement theory.* New Haven, CT: Yale University Press.

Sorenson, A. B., Weinert, F. E., & Sherrod, L. R. (Eds.). (1986). *Human development and the life course: Multidisciplinary perspectives.* Hillsdale, NJ: Erlbaum.

Sorokin, P. (1937). *Social and cultural dynamics: Vol. 3. Fluctuation of social relationships, war, and revolution.* New York: American Book.

Sowell, T. (1972). *Black education: Myths and tragedies.* New York: McKay.

Spector, P. (1994, September 24). Failure by the numbers: Life span, health and wealth. *New York Times,* p. A19.

Spencer, H. (1874). *The study of sociology.* New York: Appleton.

Spengler, O. (1965/1918). *The decline of the West.* New York: Modern Library.

Spitz, R. A. (1945). Hospitalism: An inquiry into the genesis of psychiatric conditions in early childhood. In A. Freud (Ed.), *The psychoanalytic study of the child.* New York: International Universities Press.

Stacey, J. (1990). *Brave new families: Stories of domestic upheaval in late twentieth century America.* New York: Basic Books.

Stack, C. (1974). *All our kin.* New York: Harper.

Stark, R., & Bainbridge, W. S. (1979). Of churches, sects, and cults: Preliminary concepts for a theory of religious movements. *Journal for the Scientific Study of Religion, 18,* 117–133.

Stark, R., & Bainbridge, W. S. (1980). Toward a theory of religion: Religious commitment. *Journal for the Scientific Study of Religion, 19,* 114–128.

Stark, R., & Bainbridge, W. S. (1985). *The future of religion: Secularization, revival and cult formation.* Berkeley: University of California Press.

Starr, P. (1982). *The social transformation of American medicine.* New York: Basic Books.

Statistical abstract of the United States [Various years]. Washington, DC: U.S. Bureau of the Census.

Stave, B. M. (Ed.). (1985). *Socialism and the cities.* Port Washington, NY: Kennikat Press.

Steelworkers Research Project. (1985). *Chicago steelworkers: The cost of unemployment.* Chicago: Hull House.

Stein, J. (1994, December). Space and place. *Art in America*, pp. 66–71.

Steltzer, U. (1982). *Inuit: The north in transition.* Chicago: University of Chicago Press.

Stevens, W. K. (1986, December 16). Prehistoric society: A new picture emerges. *New York Times,* pp. C1, C15.

Stevens, W. K. (1988, December 20). Life in the Stone Age: New findings point to complex societies. *New York Times,* pp. C1, C15.

Stevenson, H. W. (1992, December). Learning from Asian schools. *Scientific American,* pp. 70–76.

Stevenson, R. W. (1992, July). U.S. judge orders $7.5 million award to whistleblower. *New York Times,* pp. 1, 12.

Stewart, G. R. (1968). *Names in the land.* Boston: Houghton Mifflin.

Stimson, C. (1980). Women and the American city. *Signs, 5* (Suppl.).

Stinchcombe, A. L. (1968). *Constructing social theories.* Orlando: Harcourt Brace Jovanovich.

Stockard, J., & Johnson, M. M. (1992). *Sex and gender in society.* Englewood Cliffs, NJ: Prentice-Hall.

Stone, J., & Mennell, S. (1980). *Alexis de Tocqueville on democracy, revolution, and society.* Chicago: University of Chicago Press.

Stouffer, S. A., Suchman, E. A., DeVinney, L. C., Star, S. A., & Williams, R. A., Jr. (1949) *Studies in social psychology in World War II. Vol. 1. The American soldier: Adjustment during army life.* Princeton, NJ: Princeton University Press.

Strange, M. (1988). *Family farming: A new economic vision.* Lincoln: University of Nebraska Press.

Sudman, S., & Bradburn, N. (1982). *Asking questions: A practical guide to questionnaire design.* San Francisco: Jossey-Bass.

Sudnow, D. (1967). *Passing on: The social organization of dying.* Englewood Cliffs, NJ: Prentice-Hall.

Sumner, W. G. (1940/1907). *Folkways.* Boston: Ginn.

Sumner, W. G. (1963). *Social Darwinism: Selected essays.* Englewood Cliffs, NJ: Prentice-Hall.

Suro, R. (1992, May 26). For women, varied reasons for single motherhood. *New York Times,* p. A12.

Sutherland, E. H. (1940). White collar criminality. *American Sociological Review, 5,* 1–12.

Suttles, G. (1967). *The social order of the slum.* Chicago: University of Chicago Press.

Suttles, G. (1972). *The social construction of communities.* Chicago: University of Chicago Press.

Sutton-Smith, B., & Rosenberg, B. G. (1961). Sixty years of historical change in the game preferences of American children. *Journal of American folklore, 74,* 17–46.

Sweet, J. A., & Bumpass, L. (1987). *American families and households.* New York: Russell Sage.

Szelenyi, I. (1983). *Urban inequalities under state socialism.* New York: Oxford University Press.

Szymanski, A. J., & Goertzel, T. G. (1979). *Sociology: Class, consciousness, and contradictions.* New York: Van Nostrand Reinhold.

Tabb, W. (1986). *Churches in struggle: Liberation theologies and social change.* New York: Monthly Review Press.

Taeuber, K. E., & Taeuber, A. F. (1965). *Negroes in cities.* Hawthorne, NY: Aldine.

Tamayo, B. (1995). Proposition 187: Racism leads to deaths and more poverty. *Poverty & Race, 4,* 16.

Tannen, D. (1990). *You just don't understand: Women and men in conversation.* New York: Morrow.

Tarrow, S. G. (1994). *Power in movement: Social movements, collective action, and politics.* Cambridge, England: Cambridge University Press.

Tawney, R. A. (1966/1932). *Land and labor in China.* Boston: Beacon.

Terrace, H. S. (1979). *Nim.* New York: Knopf.

Thomas, L. (1979). *The medusa and the snail.* New York: Bantam.

Thomas, L. (1989, July 15). Beyond the moon's horizon—Our home. *New York Times,* p. 25.

Thomas, W. I. (1971/1921). *Old world traits transplanted.* Montclair NJ: Patterson Publishers.

Thomas, W. L. (1956). *Man's role in changing the face of the earth.* Chicago: University of Chicago Press.

Thorne, B. (1993). *Gender play: Boys and girls in school.* New Brunswick, NJ: Rutgers University Press.

Thornton, R. (1987). *American Indian holocaust and survival: A population history since 1492.* Norman: University of Oklahoma Press.

Tienda, M., & Jensen, L. (1988). Poverty and minorities: A quarter-century profile of color and socioeconomic disadvantage. In G. D. Sandefur & M. Tienda (Eds.), *Divided opportunities: Minorities, poverty, and social policy.* New York: Plenum Press.

Tienda, M., & Singer, A. (1995). Wage mobility of undocumented workers in the United States. *International Migration Review, 29,* 112–138.

Tienda, M., & Wilson, F. D. (1992). Migration and the earnings of Hispanic men. *American Sociological Review, 57,* 661–678.

Tilly, C. (1993). *European revolutions, 1492–1992.* Oxford, England: Blackwell.

Tobach, E., & Rosoff, B. (Eds.). (1994). *Challenging racism and sexism: Alternatives to genetic explanations.* New York: Feminist Press at the City University of New York.

Tobin, J. J., Wu, D. Y. H., & Davidson, D. H. (1989) *Preschool in three cultures: Japan, China, and the United States.* New Haven, CT: Yale University Press.

Toffler, A. (1970). *Future shock.* New York: Bantam.

Tonnies, F. (1957/1887). *Community and society* (C. P. Loomis, Trans. & Ed.). East Lansing: Michigan State University Press.

Touraine, A. (1971). *The post industrial society: Tomorrow's social history: Classes, conflicts and culture in the programmed society.* New York: Random House.

Townsend, P. (1993). *The international analysis of poverty.* Hertfordshire, England: Harvestor & Wheatsheaf/Simon & Schuster.

Toynbee, A. J. (1972). *A study of history.* New York: Oxford University Press.

Traub, J. (1984, September 9). A village in India: Reluctant progress. *New York Times Magazine,* pp. 106ff.

Traven, B. (1966). Assembly line. In *The night visitor, and other stories.* New York: Hill and Wang.

Trent, J. W., Jr. (1995, July–August). Suffering fools. *The Sciences,* pp. 18–22.

Tripolskaya-Mitlyng, V. (1994). The new new Russians. *Bulletin of the Atomic Scientists, 50,* 18–19.

Troeltsch, E. (1931). *The social teachings of the Christian churches* (O. Wyon, Trans.). New York: Macmillan.

Trow, M. (1966). The second transformation of American secondary education. In R. Bendix & S. M. Lipset (Eds.), *Class, status, and power* (2nd ed.). New York: Free Press.

Truzzi, M. (1971). *Sociology: The classic statements.* New York: McGraw-Hill.

Tumin, M. M. (1967). *Social stratification: The forms and functions of inequality.* Englewood Cliffs, NJ: Prentice-Hall.

Turk, A. T. (1978). Law as a weapon in social conflict. In C. E. Reasons & R. M. Rich (Eds.), *Sociology of law: A conflict perspective.* Toronto: Butterworths.

Turner, F. J. (1920/1893). *The frontier in American history.* Fort Worth, TX: Holt, Rinehart and Winston.

Turner, R. (Ed.). (1967). *Robert E. Park on social control and collective behavior.* Chicago: University of Chicago Press.

Turner, R. H. (1974). The theme of contemporary social movements. In R. E. L. Faris (Ed.), *Handbook of modern sociology.* Chicago: Rand McNally.

Tyree, A., & Treas, J. (1974). The occupational and marital mobility of women. *American Sociological Review, 39,* 293–302.

Uchitelle, L. (1993, May 14). Pay of college graduates is outpaced by inflation. *New York Times,* pp. A1, B12.

Uchitelle, L. (1995, July 16). For employee benefits, it pays to wear the union label. *New York Times,* sec. F, p. 10.

Uhlenberg, P. (1980). Death and the family. *Journal of Family History, 5,* 313–320.

United Nations (1987). *The prospects of world urbanization.* New York: United Nations.

United Nations. (1995a, March). *Adoption of the declaration and programme of action of the World Summit for Social Development.* New York: United Nations.

United Nations, (1995b). *Gender, population & development: The role of the United Nations Population Fund.* New York: United Nations, UNFPA.

United Nations. (1995c, March). *Summary of the programme of action of the International Conference on Population and Development.* New York: United Nations, Department of Public Information.

U.S. Bureau of the Census. (1990). *Census of population: 1990.* Washington, DC: U. S. Bureau of the Census.

U.S. Department of Education. (1994). *High school students ten years after "A Nation at Risk": Findings from the condition of education 1994.* Washington, DC: U.S. Department of Education, Office of Educational Research and Development.

Valentine, B. (1978). *Hustling and other hard work.* New York: Free Press.

van den Berghe, P. L. (1975). *Man in society: A biosocial view.* New York: Elsevier.

van den Berghe, P. L. (1979). *Human family systems: An evolutionary view.* New York: Elsevier.

Van Gennep, A. (1960/1908). *The rites of passage.* Chicago: University of Chicago Press.

Vanneman, R., & Cannon, L. W. (1987). *The American perception of class.* Philadelphia: Temple University Press.

Vass, W. K. (1979). *The Bantu speaking heritage of the United States.* Los Angeles: Center for Afro-American Studies, University of California.

Verbrugge, L. M. (1985). Gender and health: An update on hypotheses and evidence. *Journal of Health and Social Behavior, 26,* 156–182.

Vidich, A., & Bensman, J. (1960). *Small town in mass society.* Garden City, NY: Doubleday.

Vilas, C. M. (1993). The hour of civil society. *NACLA Report on the Americas, 27,* 38–43.

Vining, D. R., Jr. (1985, April). The growth of core regions in the Third World. *Scientific American,* pp. 42–49.

Vogel, E. (1979). *Japan as number one: Lessons for America.* Cambridge, MA: Harvard University Press.

Wainhouse, D. W. (1973). *International peacekeeping at the crossroads: National support—Experience and prospects.* Baltimore: Johns Hopkins University Press.

Wallerstein, I. (1974). *The modern world system: Capitalist agriculture and the origins of the European world-economy in the sixteenth century.* Orlando: Academic Press.

Wallerstein, J., & Blakeslee, S. (1989). *Second chances: Men, women & children a decade after divorce.* New York: Ticknor & Fields.

Walsh, E. J. (1981). Resource mobilization and citizen protest in communities around Three Mile Island. *Social Problems, 29,* 1–21.

Walsh, E. J., & Warland, R. H. (1983). Social movement involvement in the wake of a nuclear accident: Activists and free riders in the TMI area. *American Sociological Review, 48,* 764–780.

Walton, J. (1970). A systematic survey of community power research. In M. Aiken & P. Mott (Eds.), *The structure of community power.* New York: Random House.

Walton, J. (1992). *Western times and water wars: State, culture, and rebellion in California.* Berkeley: University of California Press.

Waltzer, M. (1980). Pluralism. In *Harvard encyclopedia of American ethnic groups.* Cambridge, MA: Belknap Press.

Warner, W. L., & Lunt, P. S. (1941). *The social life of a modern community.* New Haven, CT: Yale University Press.

Warner, W. L., Meeker, M., & Calls, K. (1949). *Social class in America: A manual of procedure for the measurement of social status.* Chicago: Science Research Associates.

Washburn, P. C. (1982). *Political sociology.* Englewood Cliffs, NJ: Prentice-Hall.

Watson, J. B. (1930). *Behaviorism.* New York: Norton.

Weaver, M. A. (1994, September 12). A fugitive from justice. *New Yorker,* pp. 46–60.

Webb, E., Campbell, D. T., Schwarz, R. D., & Sechrest, L. (1966). *Unobtrusive measures: Nonreactive research in the social sciences.* Chicago: Rand McNally.

Weber, Marianne (1975/1926). *Max Weber: A biography* (H. Zohn, Trans. & Ed.). New York: Wiley.

Weber, M. (1922). *Gesammelte aufsatze zur Religionssoziologie.* Tubingen, Germany: Mohr.

Weber, M. (1947). *The theory of social and economic organization* (A. M. Henderson & T. Parsons, Trans.). New York: Free Press.

Weber, M. (1958/1913). World religion. In H. Gerth & C. W. Mills (Trans. & Eds.), *From Max Weber: Essays in sociology.* New York: Oxford University Press.

Weber, M. (1958/1922). Economy and society. In H. Gerth & C. W. Mills (Trans. & Eds.), *From Max Weber: Essays in sociology.* New York: Oxford University Press.

Weber, M. (1962/1921). *The city.* New York: Collier.

Weber, M. (1963/1922). *The sociology of religion* (E. Fischoff, Trans.). Boston: Beacon.

Weber, M. (1968). The concept of citizenship. In S. N. Eisenstadt (Ed.), *Max Weber on charisma and institution building.* Chicago: University of Chicago Press.

Weber, M. (1974/1904). *The Protestant ethic and the spirit of capitalism* (T. Parsons, Trans.). New York: Scribner.

Weinberg, H. (1994). Marital reconciliation in the United States: Which couples are successful? *Journal of Marriage and the Family, 56,* 80–88.

Weir, B. R. J., & Weir, T. (1976). The relationships of wives' employment to husband, wife, and pair satisfaction. *Journal of Marriage and the Family, 2,* 279–287.

Weisman, A. (1989, July 30). L.A. fights for breath. *New York Times Magazine,* pp. 14ff.

Wekerle, G. (Ed.). (1980). *New space for women.* Boulder, CO: Westview Press.

Welch, M. R. (1979). Quantitative approaches to sect classification and the study of sect development. In R. Wuthnow (Ed.), *The religious dimension: New directions in quantitative research.* Orlando: Academic Press.

Wellins, S. (1990). *Children's use of television in England and the United States.* Doctoral dissertation, City University of New York.

Wells, M. J. (1984). The resurgence of sharecropping: Historical anomaly or political strategy? *American Journal of Sociology, 90,* 1–30.

West, C. (1992, February 8). Learning to talk of race. *New York Times Magazine,* pp. 24–25.

Westin, A. (1967). *Privacy and freedom.* New York: Atheneum.

Westrum, R. (1983). *What happened to the old sociology of technology?* Paper presented to the Society for the Sociological Study of Science, Blacksburg, VA.

Whitchurch, G. G., & Constantine, L. L. (1993). Systems theory. In P. G. Boss, W. J. Doherty, R. LaRossa, W. R. Schumm, & S. K. Steinmetz (Eds.), *Sourcebook of family theories and methods: A contextual approach.* New York: Plenum Press.

White, M. J. (1987). *American neighborhoods and residential differentiation.* New York: Russell Sage.

Whiting, B. B., & Edwards, C. P. (1988). *Children of different worlds.* Cambridge, MA: Harvard University Press.

Whorf, B. L. (1961). The relation of habitual thought and behavior to language. In J. B. Carroll (Ed.), *Language, thought, and reality: Selected writings of Benjamin Lee Whorf.* Cambridge, MA: MIT Press.

Whyte, W. F. (1943). *Street corner society.* Chicago: University of Chicago Press.

Whyte, W. F. (1949). The social structure of the restaurant. *American Journal of Sociology, 54,* 302–310.

Whyte, W. F. (1984). *Learning from the field.* Newbury Park, CA: Sage Publications.

Whyte, W. H. (1980). *The social life of small urban spaces.* Washington, DC: Conservation Foundation.

Wilensky, H. (1964). Mass society and mass culture: Interdependence or independence. *American Sociological Review, 29,* 173–193.

Wilford, J. N. (1989, April 24). Fusion furor: Science's human face. *New York Times,* pp. A1, B6.

Wilkinson, A. (1989, July 24). Sugarcane. *New Yorker,* pp. 56ff.

Williams, T. (1989). *The cocaine kids.* Reading, MA: Addison-Wesley.

Williams, T. (1992). Crack house. Reading, MA: Addison-Wesley.

Williams, T., & Kornblum, W. (1994). *The uptown kids: Struggle and hope in the projects.* New York: Putnam.

Willis, P. (1983). Cultural production and theories of reproduction. In L. Barton & S. Walker (Eds.), *Race, class and education.* London: Croom-Helm.

Willmott, P., & Young, M. (1971). *Family and class in a London suburb.* London: New American Library.

Wills, G. (1992). *Lincoln at Gettysburg: The words that remade America.* New York: Simon & Schuster.

Wilson, B. L. (1993). *Mandating academic excellence: High school responses to state curriculum reform.* New York: Teachers College Press.

Wilson, C. R. (1987). The death of Bear Bryant: Myth and ritual in the modern South. *South Atlantic Quarterly, 86,* 282–295.

Wilson, E. O. (1975). *Sociobiology.* Cambridge, MA: Belknap Press.

Wilson, E. O. (1979). *On human nature.* New York: Bantam.

Wilson, J. Q. (1977). *Thinking about crime.* New York: Vintage Books.

Wilson, W. J. (1978). *The declining significance of race: Blacks and changing American institutions.* Chicago: University of Chicago Press.

Wilson, W. J. (1984). The urban underclass. In L. W. Dunbar (Ed.), *The minority report.* New York: Pantheon.

Wilson, W. J. (1987). *The truly disadvantaged: The inner city, the underclass, and public policy.* Chicago: University of Chicago Press.

Wilson, W. J. (1989). The underclass: Issues, perspectives, and public policy. *Annals of the American Academy of Political and Social Science, 501,* 182–192.

Winch, R. F. (1958). *Mate selection.* New York: Harper.

Winner, L. (1977). *Autonomous technology: Technics-out-of-control as a theme in political thought.* Cambridge, MA: MIT Press.

Wirth, L. (1945). The problem of minority groups. In R. Linton (Ed.), *The science of man in the world crisis.* New York: Columbia University Press.

Wirth, L. (1968/1938). Urbanism as a way of life. In S. F. Fava (Ed.), *Urbanism in world perspective: A reader.* New York: Crowell.

Wittfogel, K. (1957). *Oriental despotism: A comparative study of total power.* New Haven, CT: Yale University Press.

Wixen, B. N. (1979). Children of the rich. In J. D. Call, J. D. Noshpitz, R. L. Cohen, & I. N. Berlin (Eds.), *Basic handbook of child psychiatry.* New York: Basic Books.

Wolf, E. R. (1984a, November 4). The perspective of the world. *New York Times Book Review,* pp. 13–14.

Wolf, E. R. (1984b, November 4). Unifying the vision. *New York Times Book Review,* p. 11.

Wolf, N. (1991). *The beauty myth.* New York: Morrow.

Wolfe, T. (1980). *The right stuff.* New York: Bantam.

Wolff, E. N. (1995). *Top heavy: A study of the increasing inequality of wealth in America.* New York: Twentieth Century Fund.

Wolfgang, M. E., & Riedel, M. (1973). Race, judicial discretion, and the death penalty. *Annals of the American Academy of Political and Social Science, 407,* 119–133.

Woo, W. T. (1994). The art of reforming centrally planned economies: Comparing China, Poland, and Russia. *Journal of Comparative Economics, 18,* 276–308.

World Bank (1992). *World tables 1992.* Baltimore: Johns Hopkins University Press.

Wright, E. O. (1989). *The debate on classes.* New York: Verso.

Wright, E. O., Costello, C., Hachen, D., & Sprague, J. (1982). The American class structure. *American Sociological Review, 47,* 702–726.

Wright, R., & Jacobs, J. A. (1994). Male flight from computer work: A new look at occupational resegregation and ghettoization. *American Sociological Review, 59,* 511–536.

Wrigley, E. A. (1969). *Population and history.* New York: McGraw-Hill.

Wrong, D. H. (1961). The oversocialized conception of man in modern sociology. *American Sociological Review, 24,* 772–782.

Wu, H., & Wakeman, C. (1995). *Bitter winds: A memoir of my years in China's gulag.* New York: Wiley.

Wuthnow, R. (1988). Sociology of religion. In N. E. Smelser (Ed.), *The handbook of sociology.* Newbury Park, CA: Sage Publications.

Wuthnow, R. (1994). *Sharing the journey: Support groups and America's new quest for community.* New York: Free Press.

Yankelovich, D. (1981). *New rules: Searching for self-fulfillment in a world turned upside down.* New York: Random House.

Yu, P. (1994). China's experience in population matters: An official statement. *Population and Development Review, 20,* 488–491.

Zangwell, I. (1909). *The melting pot.* New York: Macmillan.

Zeisel, H. (1982). *The limits of law enforcement.* Chicago: University of Chicago Press.

Zerubavel, E. (1986). *Hidden rhythms: Schedules and calendars in social life.* Chicago: University of Chicago Press.

Zill, N. (1995, Spring). Back to the future: Improving child indicators by remembering their origins. *Focus,* pp. 17–24.

Zolberg, A. (1974). *Creating political order.* Chicago: University of Chicago Press.

Zolberg, A. (1981). International migrations in political perspective. In M. M. Kritz, C. B. Keely, & S. M. Tomasi (Eds.), *Global trends in migration: Theory and research on international population movements.* New York: Center for Migration Studies.

CREDITS AND ACKNOWLEDGMENTS

Photo Credits

Chapter 1 © Joel Gordon, 5; Courtesy of William Kornblum, 6; © M. Dwyer / Stock Boston, 8; © Gina Doggett, Paris, 11 (left); Courtesy of Manjula Giri, 11 (right); Culver Pictures, 12; Corbis / Bettmann, 13 (left); Culver Pictures Inc., 13 (right); © UPI / Corbis / Bettmann, 16 (top); Library Company of Philadelphia, 16 (bottom); © Reuters / Corbis / Bettmann, 19; © Marleen Daniels / Gamma Liaison Network, 21; © Mike Greenlar / Black Star, 23; © Vatican Museums, 24 (left); © Douglas Mazonowicz / Monkmeyer, 24 (right); Egyptian Museum, Cairo, 25; National Museum, Tokyo, 26 (top); Museum of Civilization, Hull, Quebec, 26 (bottom); The National Gallery, London, 27; Kunsthistorisches Museum, Vienna, 28; Musee d'Orsay, Paris, 29

Chapter 2 © J. Scott Applewhite / AP / Wide World Photo, 35; © UPI / Corbis / Bettmann, 37 (left); © AP / Wide World Photo, 37 (right); © Margaret Morton / courtesy Lowinsky Gallery, New York, 41; © Dan Miller / The New York Times, 44; Courtesy of William Kornblum, 52 (left); © Margo Smith, 52 (right); © Margo Smith, 53 (top left); © Margo Smith, 53 (bottom left); © Margo Smith, 53 (top right); Courtesy of William Kornblum, 53 (bottom right)

Chapter 3 © Jeffrey Jay Foxx / Foxx Archive, 59; © Chenault Photography Studio, Decatur, Alabama, 60; © David R. Austen / Stock Boston, 62; © Photofest, 63 (left); © Matthew Neal McVay / Stock Boston, 63 (right); © Gaye Hilsenrath / The Picture Cube, 65; Coram Foundation, London / Bridgeman Art Library, 66; Personal property of Margaret Washington, 79; All photos and captions by John Collier, 82; All photos and captions by John Collier, 83; © AP / Wide World Photo, 84 (top); © Photofest, 84 (bottom)

Chapter 4 © Nik Wheeler, 89; © Rick Strange/The Picture Cube, 96 (top); © Owen Franken / Stock Boston, 96 (bottom); © Robert F. Sisson / National Geographic Society, 97; © Patricia J. Wynne, 98; © Gerhard Hinterleitner / Gamma Liaison Network, 99; © John Marshall, 106 (top); © John Marshall, 106 (bottom left); © New York Public Library Picture Collection / New York Public Library, Astor, Lenox & Tilden Foundations, 106 (bottom right); © The Granger Collection, New York, 107 (left); © David J. Sams / Stock Boston, 107 (top right); © Bachmann / Stock Boston, 107 (bottom right); © AP / Wide World Photo, 110; All photos © Eugene Richards, 112; All photos © Eugene Richards, 113

Chapter 5 © Shackman / Monkmeyer Press Photo, 121; © Jeffry W. Myers / Stock Boston, 122; All photos by I. Eibl-Eibesfeldt, HUMAN ETHOLOGY (New York: Aldine de Gruyter). Used by permission, 125; S. Curtiss, *Genie: A Psycholinguistic Study of a Modern Day "Wild Child"* (Academic Press, 1977). Used by permission, 126; © AP / Wide World Photo, 127 (left); © David Pokress / NEWSDAY, 127 (top right); © UPI / Corbis / Bettmann, 127 (bottom right); © Barton Silverman / The New York Times, 131; The New York Public Library, Astor, Lenox & Tilden Founda-

tions, 134; © Chris Heflin / Shooting Back, 142 (left); © Charlene Williams / Shooting Back, 142 (right); © Shawn Nixon / Shooting Back, 143 (top left); © Jim Hubbard / Shooting Back, 143 (right); © Calvin Stewart / Shooting Back, 143 (bottom left)

Chapter 6 © Deborah Copaken / Gamma Liaison Network, 149; © Gregg Hadel / Tony Stone Images, 151; From Frederic M. Thrasher, The Gang: A Study of 1,313 Gangs in Chicago, abridged edition by James F. Short, Jr., 1963. Used by permission of University of Chicago Press, 156 (top); © A. Ramey / Woodfin Camp & Associates, 156 (bottom); © Miro Vintoniv / Stock, Boston, 163; © AP / Wide World Photo, 171; All photos © Ken Heyman, 174; All photos © Ken Heyman, 175

Chapter 7 © Bob Daemmrich / The Image Works, 181; Essex Institute, Salem, Massachusetts, 183; © Brooksfilms Limited, 185; New York City Department of Health, 187; © Rafiqur Rahman / Reuters / Corbis / Bettmann, 188; Stock Montage, Inc., 189 (top left); Corbis / Bettmann, 189 (bottom left); © Patrick Ward / Stock Boston, 189 (top right); © Michael Newman / PhotoEdit, 189 (bottom right); Culver Pictures Inc., 194 (bottom right); © UPI / Corbis / Bettmann, 194 (top right); Culver Pictures Inc., 194 (left); © Alon Reininger / Contact / Woodfin Camp & Associates, 199; © The Granger Collection, New York, 202 (top); © Ted Mathias / AP / Wide World Photo, 202 (bottom); © Donna Binder / Impact Visuals, 204; All photos © Douglas Harper, 206; All photos © Douglas Harper, 207

Chapter 8 © McGlynn / The Image Works, 213; Chicago Historical Society, 215 (top); © Robert E. Clark / Los Angeles News Service, 215 (bottom); © W. Campbell / Sygma, 217; © Popperfoto / Archive Photos, 223; Culver Pictures Inc., 225; © Barry Thumma / AP / Wide World Photo, 227; © Juan Carlos Rojas / Impact Visuals, 228; New York Public Library Picture Collection / New York Public Library, Astor, Lenox & Tilden Foundations, 232; All photos © Matt Herron 1987, 234; All photos © Matt Herron 1987, 235

Chapter 9 © Reuters / Corbis / Bettmann, 239; © Alon Reininger / Woodfin Camp & Associates, 245; © David L. Brown / The Picture Cube, 246; © Peter Menzel / Stock Boston, 248; © In Stock / Photo Researchers, 249; Corbis / Bettmann, 251 (left); © Kirk Condyles / Impact Visuals, 251 (right); © R. Richards / Gamma Liaison, 257; © J. B. Diederich / Contact Press Images, 260 (bottom left); © Freda Leinwand, 260 (bottom right); © Dennis Stock / Magnum, 260 (top); © A. Ramey / Stock Boston, 262; © Kirk Condyles / Impact Visuals, 264; © Jean Wentworth / The Picture Cube, 265; All photos © Janice Perlman, 266; All photos © Janice Perlman, 267

Chapter 10 © Betty Press / Woodfin Camp & Associates, 273; © F. Willett, 275; Corbis / Bettmann, 278; Corbis / Bettmann, 280; © The Granger Collection, New York, 282 (top); © Jon Anderson / Sygma, 282 (bottom); All photos courtesy of Susan Kornblum, 283; © Michael Grecco / Stock Boston, 284; © Betty Press / Woodfin Camp & Associates, 285; © Brian Willer / NYT Pictures, 287;

Literary Acknowledgments

Chapter 1

19 Figure 1.1 Calorie Consumption Chart, from *Peters Atlas of the World* by Arnold Peters. Copyright © 1990 by Akademische Drunk- und Verlagsanstalt. Reprinted by permission of HarperCollins Publishers, Inc.

Chapter 2

51 Figure 2.4 Percentage of White Collar Workers in San Antonio (map), from *American Neighborhoods and Residential Differentiation* by Michael White, © 1987. Reprinted with permission of Russell Sage Foundation.

Chapter 3

69 Box 3.2 Adult per Capita Consumption of Manufactured Cigarettes, reprinted and modified with the permission of the Population Council, from R. T. Ravenholt, "Tobacco's Global Death March," *Population and Development Review* 16, no. 2 (June 1990): 226–7.

76 Figure 3.2 The British Empire in 1901 (map), from *Victorian Imperialism* by C. C. Eldridge, © 1987 Hodder and Stoughton Limited, England. Reprinted by permission.

80 Figure 3.3 Annual Divorce Rates, United States, from *Marriage, Divorce, Remarriage* by Andrew J. Cherlin. Copyright © 1981, 1992 by the President and Fellows of Harvard College. Reprinted by permission of Harvard University Press.

81 Figure 3.4 Premarital Sex With Eventual Spouse, adapted from *The Social Organization of Sexuality: Sexual Practices in the United States* by E. O. Laumann, et al., copyright © 1994. Reprinted by permission of the University of Chicago Press.

Chapter 4

92 Box 4.1 Kinship Diagram, from "The Origin of Society" by Marshall D. Sahlins. Copyright © September 1960 by Scientific American, Inc. All rights reserved.

100 Figure 4.3 Agriculture Origins (map), from *The Rise of the West: A History of the Human Community* by W. McNeill, copyright © 1963. Reprinted by permission of the University of Chicago Press.

111 Figure 4.6 Composition of Immigrant Flows to Six Metropolitan Destinations, adapted from *Immigrant America: A Portrait* by A. Portes and R. G. Rumgaut, copyright © 1990. Reprinted by permission of the Regents of the University of California, University of California Press.

114 Figure 4.7 Principal Destinations of the Eight Largest Immigrant Groups, adapted from *Immigrant America: A Porttrait* by A. Portes and R. G. Rumgaut, copyright © 1990. Reprinted by permission of the Regents of the Univeristy of California, University of California Press.

Chapter 5

129 (top) Box 5.1 Defining the Cognitive Classes, reprinted with the permission of The Free Press, a division of Simon & Schuster from *The Bell Curve: Intelligence and Class Structure in American Life* by Richard J. Herrnstein and Charles Murray. Copyright © 1994 by Richard J. Herrnstein and Charles Murray.

129 (bottom) Box 5.1 White Poverty by Cognitive Class, reprinted with the permission of The Free Press, a division of Simon & Schuster from *The Bell Curve: Intelligence and Class Structure in American Life* by Richard J. Herrnstein and Charles Murray. Copyright © 1994 by Richard J. Herrnstein and Charles Murray.

131 Box 5.2 Beehive Soccer, from *The New York Times,* July 24, 1984. Copyright 1984 by The New York Times Company. Reprinted by permission.

135 Box 5.3 U.S. Children Living in Households not Headed by a Parent, reprinted with permission of the Annie E. Casey Foundation and the Center for the Study of Social Policy.

136 Figure 5.1 Pregnancies per 1000 Women by Single Year Age, from *Teenage Pregnancies in Industrialized Nations* by E. F. Jones, et al. Published by Yale University Press. Copyright © 1986 by the Alan Guttmacher Institute. Reprinted by permission.

136 Figure 5.2 Abortions per 1000 Women, from *Teenage Pregnancy in Industrialized Nations* by E. F. Jones, et al. Published by Yale University Press. Copyright © 1986 by the Alan Guttmacher Institute. Reprinted by permission.

138 Box 5.4 The 3-Year-Old Child's Social Network, from "Some American Families at Dinner" in L. M. Laosa and I. E. Sigel (eds.) *Families as Learning Environments for Children,* by M. Lewis and C. Feiring, copyright © 1982. Reprinted by permission of Plenum Publishing Corporation.

Chapter 6

158 Table 6.1 The Most Socially Prestigious American Boarding Schools, from *Philadelphia Gentlemen: The Making of a National Upper Class* by E. D. Baltzell, copyright © 1958 by Quadrangle. Reprinted by permission of the author.

165 Table 6.2 Aggregate Matrix for 18 Sessions of 6-Man Groups, adapted from *Social Behavior: Its Elementary Forms, Revised Edition* by George C. Homans, copyright © 1974 by Harcourt Brace & Company, reproduced by permission of the publisher.

169 Figure 6.3 Mean Maximum Shocks in Four Variants of Milgram's Experiment, from *Obedience to Authority* by Stanley Milgram. Copyright © 1974 by Stanley Milgram. Reprinted by permission of HarperCollins Publishers, Inc.

170 Table 6.3 Maximum Shock Administered in Four Variants of Milgram's Experiment, from *Obedience to Authority* by Stanley Milgram. Copyright © 1974 by Stanley Milgram. Reprinted by permission of HarperCollins Publishers, Inc.

173 Table 6.4 Estimates of Various Types of Groups, reprinted with the permission of The Free Press, a division of Simon & Schuster from *Sharing the Journey: Support Groups and America's New Quest for Community* by Robert Wuthnow. Copyright © 1994 by Robert Wuthnow.

176 Table 6.5 Membership in Small Groups, reprinted with the permission of The Free Press, a division of Simon & Schuster from *Sharing the Journey: Support Groups and America's New Quest for Community* by Robert Wuthnow. Copyright © 1994 by Robert Wuthnow.

176 Table 6.6 Meeting the Need for Community, reprinted with the permission of The Free Press, a division of Simon & Schuster from *Sharing the Journey: Support Groups and America's New Quest for Community* by Robert Wuthnow. Copyright © 1994 by Robert Wuthnow.

Chapter 7

201 Box 7.3 Homicide Rates, Selected Countries, from *Understanding and Preventing Violence,* National Academy Press, 1993. Reprinted by permission.

203 Figure 7.6 Homicide Rates in States With and Without Death Penalty, from *The Limits of Law Enforcement* by H. Zeisel, copyright © 1982. Reprinted by permission of the University of Chicago Press.

Chapter 8

218 Figure 8.1 Lofland's Typology of Spontaneous Collective Behaviors, from *Social Perspectives,* edited by Morris Rosenberg and Ralph Turner. Copyright © 1981 by The American Sociological Association. Reprinted by permission of the publisher and author.

Chapter 9

241 Table 9.2 Relationship of Population Growth per Year and per Century, reprinted with the permission of Worldwatch Institute, Washington, DC.

242 Figure 9.1 The Demographic Transition: Sweden, 1691–1963 by Judah Matras, from *Introduction to Population: A Sociological Approach,* © 1977. Adapted by permission of Prentice Hall, Upper Saddle River, NJ.

244 Figure 9.2 Crude Birth and Death Rates: Singapore, 1930–1988, from *Resources, Environment, and Population: Present Knowledge, Future Options,* edited by Davis and Bernstam, copyright © 1991, Oxford University Press.

250 Table 9.3 Population of the 30 Largest Urbanized Areas: World, 1950–2000, from *Freedom and Community: The Ethics of Interdependence* by E. H. Lowry, copyright © 1993.

252 Figure 9.3 The Concentric-Zone Model, 1967 and 1925, from "The Natural History of the Newspaper" by R. E. Park and E. W. Burgess in *The City.* Reprinted by permission of the University of Chicago Press.

253 Figure 9.4 The Concentric-Zone Model Applied to Chicago, 1967 and 1925, from "The Natural History of the Newspaper" by R. E. Park and E. W. Burgess in *The City.* Reprinted by permission of the University of Chicago Press.

255 Figure 9.5 Strip Development, from *Close-Up: How to Read the American City,* by G. Clay, copyright © 1980. Reprinted by permission of the University of Chicago Press.

261 Table 9.4 Educational Attainment, Washington DC, by William Frey, University of Michigan. Reprinted by permission of the author.

Chapter 10

279 Table 10.2 U.S. Respondent's Rank Ordering of Important Events as They Perceive Them, by Howard Schuman and Jacqueline Scott, from *The American Sociological Review,* Vol. 54, pp. 359–381. Copyright © 1989 by The American Sociological Association. Reprinted by permission of the publisher and the authors.

281 Table 10.3 Trade-Offs Between Military and Social or Environmental Priorities, Renner, 1989, "Enhancing Global Security," from *State of the World 1989: A Worldwatch Institute Report on Progress Toward a Sustainable Society* by Lester R. Brown, et al. eds., Copyright © 1989 by Worldwatch Institute. Reprinted by permission of W. W. Norton & Company, Inc.

291 Figure 10.1 Worldwide Patterns of Enviromental Stress, from Managing Planet Earth by William C. Clark. Copyright © September 1989 by Scientific American, Inc. All rights reserved.

292 Figure 10.2 Deltas in Distress (map), from "Scientists Say the Earth's Warming Could Set Off Widespread Disruptions," by S. P. Leatherman, University of Maryland, in *The New York Times,* September 18, 1995. Copyright © 1995 by The New York Times Company. Reprinted by permission.

Chapter 11

313 Box 11.1 The Caste System in India, from "A Village in India: Reluctant Progress" by J. Traub in *The New York Times,* September 9, 1984. Copyright © 1984 by The New York Times Company. Reprinted by permission.

331 Table 11.1 Social Mobility in Four Western Populations, adapted from "The Theory of Social Mobility" by S. M. Lipset and H. L. Zetterberg originally published in *Transactions of the Third World Congress of Sociology,* vol. 2, 1956, pp. 155–177.

Chapter 12

344 Figure 12.2 Share of All Private Wealth Owned by the Richest 1 Percent of the Population, from *Top Heavy: A Study of the Increasing Inequality of Wealth in America* by E. N. Wolff, copyright © 1995. Reprinted with permission from The Twentieth Century Fund, New York.

346 Table 12.1 Prestige Scores of Selected Occupations, by C. E. Bose and P. H. Rossi, adapted from *The American Sociological Re-*

view, Vol. 48, pp. 316–330. Copyright © 1983 by The American Sociological Association. Reprinted by permission of the authors.

349 Table 12.2 Prestige Classes in "Yankee City" and Proportion of Income Spent on Necessities of Life, from *The Social Life of a Modern Community* by W. Lloyd Warner and Paul S. Lunt, copyright © 1941. Reprinted by permission of Yale University Press.

351 Figure 12.5 The Job Ceiling in Government and Private Industry Prior to the Civil Rights Movement, adapted from *Black Metropolis: A Study of Negro Life in a Northern City,* copyright 1945 by St. Clair Drake and Horace R. Cayton and renewed 1973 by St. Clair Drake and Susan Woodson, reprinted by permission of Harcourt Brace & Company.

352 Table 12.3 Distribution of Responses to Class-Identification Question, from *Class Awareness in the United States* by M. R. Jackman and R. W. Jackman, copyright © 1983. Reprinted by permission of the Regents of the University of California, University of California Press.

362 Figure 12.7 Geographical Distribution of the Poor, adapted from *Poor Support: Poverty in the American Family* by David T. Ellwood. Copyright © 1988 by Basic Books, Inc. Reprinted by permission of HarperCollins Publishers, Inc.

369 Figure 12.10 Percentage of All Children Not Living with Two Parents, adapted from *Poor Support: Poverty in the American Family* by David T. Ellwood. Copyright © 1988 by Basic Books, Inc. Reprinted by permission of HarperCollins Publishers, Inc.

Chapter 13

391 Table 13.1 Trends in Black-White Segregation in Twenty Metropolitan Areas With Largest Black Populations, from *American Apartheid* by D. S. Massey and N. A. Denton. Copyright © 1993 by the President and Fellows of Harvard College. Reprinted by permission of Harvard University Press.

389 Figure 13.2 The Transatlantic Slave Trade, from *The Atlantic Slave Trade: A Census* by Philip D. Curtin, copyright 1969. (Madison: The University of Wisconsin Press.) Reprinted by permission of The University of Wisconsin Press.

395 Figure 13.4 Merton's Typology of Prejudice and Discrimination, adapted from *Discrimination and National Welfare* by Robert M. MacIver. Copyright 1949 by the Institute for Religious and Social Studies. Reprinted by permission of HarperCollins Publishers, Inc.

384 Box 13.2 Proposed Question: Question to Simultaneously Obtain Race and Hispanic Identity, from "A Single Census Question to Measure Race, Spanish-Origin and Ancestry" by R. Farley, copyright © 1995. Reprinted by permission of *Poverty & Race,* newsletter of the Poverty & Race Research Action Council, Washington, DC.

396 Personal Challenge Apology from Metro-North Commuter Railroad Company, public notice in *The New York Times,* May 10, 1995. Reprinted by permission of Metro-North Commuter Railroad Company.

413 Excerpt The Maasai Culture, written by Carol Chenault, Calhoun Community College, Decatur, AL. Reprinted by permission of the author.

Chapter 14

415 Figure 14.1 A Woman's Day or a Man's Day?, from *The State of the World Population Report,* 1995 by N. Sadik. Reprinted by permission of United Nations Population Fund, State of World Population, 1995.

421 Figure 14.2 Defining "Gay," from *The Social Organization of Sexuality: Sexual Practices in the United States,* by E. O. Laumann, et al., copyright © 1994. Reprinted by permission of The University of Chicago Press.

421 Box 14.2 Sociogram of Friendship Choices in a Little League Team, from *With the Boys: Little League Baseball and Preadolescent Culture* by G. A. Fine, copyright © 1987. Reprinted by permission of The University of Chicago Press.

422 Table 14.2 The Appeal of Various Sexual Practices, from *The Social Organization of Sexuality: Sexual Practices in the United States,* by E. O. Laumann, et al., copyright © 1994. Reprinted by permission of The University of Chicago Press.

425 Table 14.3 Cross-Cultural Data From 224 Societies on Subsistence, reprinted from *The Development of Sex Differences,* edited by Eleanor E. Maccoby with the permission of the publishers, Stanford University Press. Copyright © 1966 by the Board of Trustees of the Leland Stanford Junior University.

428 Figure 14.3 Poverty Rates of Women and Men, in "The Gender-Poverty Gap: What Can We Learn From Other Countries?" by Casper, et al., from *The American Sociological Review,* Vol. 59, pp. 594–605. Copyright © 1994 by The American Sociological Association. Reprinted by permission of the publisher and authors.

429 Figure 14.4 Ratio of Women's to Men's Poverty Rates, in "The Gender-Poverty Gap: What Can We Learn From Other Countries?" by Casper, et al., from *The American Sociological Review,* Vol. 59, pp. 594–605. Copyright © 1994 by The American Sociological Association. Reprinted by permission of the publisher and authors.

435 Table 14.5 Proportion of Jobs in Certain Occupations Filled by Women, from the Program for Applied Research, Queens College, Flushing NY.

436 Figure 14.5 Improvement in Women's Share in Selected Occupations, from *The State of the World Population Report, 1995* by N. Sadik. Reprinted by permission of United Nations Population Fund, State of World Population, 1995.

438 Figure 14.6 Growth in Female Literacy Levels, from *The State of the World Population Report, 1995* by N. Sadik. Reprinted by permission of United Nations Population Fund, State of World Population, 1995.

439 Figure 14.7 Average Percentage of Couples Using Contraception, from *The State of the World Population Report, 1995* by

N. Sadik. Reprinted by permission of United Nations Population Fund, State of World Population, 1995.

Chapter 15

450 Table 15.1 Projected Proportions of Population in Various Age Categories: United States, 1980–2080, reprinted with the permission of The Free Press, a division of Simon & Schuster from *The Population of the United States: Historical Trends and Projections* by Donald J. Bogue. Copyright © 1985 by The Free Press.

455 Table 15.2 Indicators of the Well-Being of U.S. Children, from *Focus* (newsletter of The Institute for Research on Poverty, University of Wisconsin-Madison) Spring, 1995, p. 15. Reprinted by permission.

456 Figure 15.6 Births to Teenage Mothers in the United States, 1960–1992, from *Focus* (newsletter of The Institute for Research on Poverty, University of Wisconsin-Madison) Spring, 1995, p. 27. Reprinted by permission.   .

457 Figure 15.7 Percentage of Low-Birth Weight Babies by Race, 1960–1990, by Partin and Palloni, from *Focus* (newsletter of The Institute for Research on Poverty, University of Wisconsin-Madison) Spring, 1995, p. 33–38. Reprinted by permission.

Chapter 16

473 Figure 16.1 Institutional Differentiation, adapted from *Human Societies,* 4e, by G. Lenski and J. Lenski, copyright © 1982. Reprinted by permission of The McGraw-Hill Companies.

482 Figure 16.7 Stages of the Family Life Cycle, from *The Family Life Cycle in Normal Family Processes,* by M. McGoldrick and E. A. Carter, copyright © 1982. Reprinted by permission of The Guilford Press.

Chapter 17

520 Figure 17.3 Christian Religious Affiliation in the United States, from *Churches and Church Membership in the United States: 1980* by Bernard Quinn, et al., copyright © 1982. Reprinted by permission of the National Council of Churches of Christ in the U.S.A.

525 Table 17.3 Demographic and Socioeconomic Indicators in Arab Countries, reprinted with the permission of the Population Council, by Carla Makhlouf Obermeyer, from "Islam, Women, and Politics: The Demography of Arab Countries," *Population and Development Review* 18, no. 1 (March 1992): 36.

526 Table 17.2 Percent in Different Theological Parties by Responses to Pluralism, from *Baptist Battles: Social Change and Religious Conflict in the Southern Baptist Convention* by Nancy Tatom Ammerman. Copyright © 1990 by Nancy Tatom Ammerman. Reprinted by permission of Rutgers University Press.

Chapter 18

542 Figure 18.2 Ability Grouping ("Tracking") in U.S. Public Schools, from "Should Tracking Be Derailed?" by L. Mansnerus in *The New York Times,* November 1, 1992. Copyright © 1992 by The New York Times Company. Reprinted by permission.

543 Figure 18.3 Functional Incompetency Among Americans, from the Adult Performance Level Project, University of Texas at Austin, 1982.

545 Box 18.1 Poverty and Illiteracy in India, by Sarvekshana, from *Journal of the National Sample Survey Organization,* 1988, Department of Statistics, New Delhi, India. Public domain.

548 Figure 18.4 Parents' Satisfaction With Academic Performance of Students, adapted from "Learning From Asian Schools" by Harold W. Stevenson, December 1992. Copyright © 1992 by Scientific American, Inc. All rights reserved.

550 Table 18.4 Major Findings at Age 19 in the Perry Preschool Study from *Changed Lives: Effects of the Perry Preschool Program on Youths Through Age 19,* by J.R. Berrueta-Clement, et al., copyright © 1984. Reprinted by permission of High/Scope Press, Ypsilanti, MI.

552 Box 18.2 Adult Status by First-Grade Teacher, from "A New Perspective on the Effects of First-Grade Teachers on Children's Subsequent Adult Status," by Pedersen, et al., *Harvard Educational Review,* 48:1, pp. 1–31. Copyright © 1978 by the President and Fellows of Harvard College. All rights reserved.

557 Figure 18.5 Attitudes About the Effects of Televised Violence on Behavior, by E. Kolbert, from *The New York Times,* August 20, 1995. Copyright © 1995 by The New York Times Company. Reprinted by permission.

Chapter 19

583 Figure 19.1 Privatization and Production in Russian Agriculture, from "Free-Market Ideas Grow on Russian Farms," by Schmemann, in *The New York Times,* October 6, 1992. Copyright 1992 by The New York Times Company. Reprinted by permission.

586 Figure 19.3 Trends in Opinion on the Question "Should Government Reduce Income Inequality?" from National Opinion Research Center, 1994. Public domain.

590 Figure 19.4 Growth in Number of Corporations in the United States, 1916–1968, from an unpublished paper prepared for *Actions of Individuals and Groups as Indicators of Power Distribution,* a project sponsored by the National Science Foundation, National Opinion Research Center. Public domain.

590 Figure 19.5 Participation of Persons and Corporate Actors in Court Cases, from "A Study of the Relative Participation of Persons and Corporate Actors in Court Cases," in an unpublished paper prepared for *Actions of Individuals and Groups as Indicators of Power Distribution,* a project sponsored by the National Science Foundation, National Opinion Research Center. Public domain.

598 Figure 19.7 Levels of Consumer Debt in the United States, 1975–1995, from "A Shaky House of Plastic with No Quick Fix in Sight" by S. Hansell, in *The New York Times,* December 28, 1995.

Chapter 20

Chapter 21

NAME INDEX

SUBJECT INDEX

car confirmula
131 35748 US3

1-800 831-2847
AVIS